Microsoft® Office

Access 2003

Revised Edition

COMPREHENSIVE

ROBERT T. GRAUER
UNIVERSITY OF MIAMI

MARYANN BARBER
UNIVERSITY OF MIAMI

PEARSON

Prentice Hall

Upper Saddle River,
New Jersey 07458

Library of Congress Cataloging-in-Publication Data

Grauer, Robert T.
   Microsoft Office Access 2003 revised comprehensive / Robert T. Grauer, Maryann Barber.
      p. cm.
   Includes index.
   ISBN 0-13-187741-0 (alk. paper)
   1. Database management. 2. Microsoft Access. I. Barber, Maryann M. II. Title.
QA76.9.D3G71959 2005
005.75'65—dc22   2005012933

Executive Acquisitions Editor: Melissa Sabella
VP/ Publisher: Natalie E. Anderson
Product Development Manager: Eileen Bien Calabro
Senior Project Manager, Editorial: Eileen Clark
Editorial Assistants: Brian Hoehl, Alana Meyers, and Sandy Bernales
Media Project Manager: Cathleen Profitko
Marketing Manager: Sarah Davis
Marketing Assistant: Lisa Taylor
Managing Editor: Lydia Castillo
Project Manager, Production: Lynne Breitfeller
Production Editor: Greg Hubit
Associate Director, Manufacturing: Vincent Scelta
Manufacturing Buyer: Lynne Breitfeller
Design Manager: Maria Lange
Interior Design: Michael J. Fruhbeis
Cover Design: Michael J. Fruhbeis
Cover Printer: Phoenix Color
Composition and Project Management: Techbooks/GTS
Printer/Binder: Banta Menasha

Microsoft and the Microsoft Office Specialist logo are trademarks or registered trade-marks of Microsoft Corporation in the United States and/or other countries. Prentice Hall is independent from Microsoft Corporation, and not affiliated with Microsoft in any manner. This publication may be used in assisting students to prepare for a Microsoft Office Specialist Exam. Neither Microsoft Corporation, its designated review companies, nor Prentice Hall warrants that use of this publication will ensure passing the relevant Exam.

Use of the Microsoft Office Specialist Approved Courseware Logo on this product signifies that it has been independently reviewed and approved in complying with the following standards:
Acceptable coverage of all content related to the Specialist level Microsoft Office Exams entitled "Access 2003" and sufficient performance-based exercises that relate closely to all required content based on sampling of text.

10 9 8 7 6 5 4 3
ISBN 0-13-187741-0

To Marion —
my wife, my lover, and my best friend

Robert Grauer

To Frank and Jessica —
I love you

Maryann Barber

What does this logo mean?

It means this courseware has been approved by the Microsoft® Office Specialist Program to be among the finest available for learning **Microsoft Access 2003**. It also means that upon completion of this courseware, you may be prepared to take an exam for Microsoft Office Specialist qualification.

What is a Microsoft Office Specialist?

A Microsoft Office Specialist is an individual who has passed exams for certifying his or her skills in one or more of the Microsoft Office desktop applications such as Microsoft Word, Microsoft Excel, Microsoft PowerPoint, Microsoft Outlook, Microsoft Access, or Microsoft Project. The Microsoft Office Specialist Program typically offers certification exams at the "Specialist" and "Expert" skill levels.[*] The Microsoft Office Specialist Program is the only program approved by Microsoft for testing proficiency in Microsoft Office desktop applications and Microsoft Project. This testing program can be a valuable asset in any job search or career advancement.

More Information:

To learn more about becoming a Microsoft Office Specialist, visit
www.microsoft.com/officespecialist

To learn about other Microsoft Office Specialist approved courseware from Pearson Education visit www.prenhall.com

---

[*]The availability of Microsoft Office Specialist certification exams varies by application, application version, and language. Visit www.microsoft.com/officespecialist for exam availability.

Microsoft, the Microsoft Office Logo, PowerPoint, and Outlook are trademarks or registered trademarks of Microsoft Corporation in the United States and/or other countries, and the Microsoft Office Specialist Logo is used under license from owner.

Contents

Preface xi

MICROSOFT® OFFICE ACCESS 2003

one

Introduction to Access: What Is a Database? 1

Objectives	1	HANDS-ON EXERCISE 2:	
Case Study: The South Vancouver Preschool	1	FILTERS AND SORTING	21
The College Bookstore	2	Looking Ahead: A Relational Database	27
Introduction to Microsoft Access	3	HANDS-ON EXERCISE 3:	
The Database Window	3	A LOOK AHEAD	29
Tables	4		
Forms, Queries, and Reports	5	Summary	36
HANDS-ON EXERCISE 1:		Key Terms	36
INTRODUCTION TO ACCESS	7	Multiple Choice	37
Filters and Sorting	19	Practice with Access	39
		Mini Cases	48

two

Tables and Forms: Design, Properties, Views, and Wizards 49

Objectives	49	HANDS-ON EXERCISE 2:	
Case Study: Debbie's Fine Fashions	49	CREATING A FORM	70
A Student Database	50	A More Sophisticated Form	78
Include the Necessary Data	51	HANDS-ON EXERCISE 3:	
Store Data in Its Smallest Parts	51	A MORE SOPHISTICATED FORM	79
Avoid Calculated Fields	52		
Creating a Table	53	Summary	88
Primary Key	53	Key Terms	88
Views	54	Multiple Choice	89
Properties	55	Practice with Access	91
HANDS-ON EXERCISE 1:		Mini Cases	104
CREATING A TABLE	56		
Forms	65		
Properties	66		
AutoForms and the Form Wizard	68		
Modifying a Form	68		

three

Information from the Database: Reports and Queries   105

Objectives	105	Access Functions and Calculated Controls	130
Case Study: The Garden Club	105	Grouping Records	131
Data versus Information	106	HANDS-ON EXERCISE 3:	
Reports	106	GROUPING RECORDS	133
Anatomy of a Report	108	Crosstab Queries	143
The Report Wizard	108	Action Queries	143
Apply What You Know	108	HANDS-ON EXERCISE 4:	
Bound, Unbound, and		CROSSTAB AND ACTION QUERIES	144
Calculated Controls	110		
HANDS-ON EXERCISE 1:		Summary	152
THE REPORT WIZARD	111	Key Terms	152
Introduction to Queries	118	Multiple Choice	153
Query Design View	120	Practice with Access	155
Selection Criteria	121	Mini Cases	165
HANDS-ON EXERCISE 2:			
CREATING A SELECT QUERY	123		

four

Proficiency: Relational Databases, Pivot Charts, and the Switchboard   167

Objectives	167	The User Interface	193
Case Study: The Disc Jockey	167	The Switchboard Manager	195
The Investment Database	168	Other Access Utilities	195
Multiple-table Queries	169	HANDS-ON EXERCISE 3:	
Maintaining the Database	170	THE SWITCHBOARD MANAGER	196
The Import Spreadsheet Wizard	171		
HANDS-ON EXERCISE 1:		Summary	203
IMPORTING DATA FROM EXCEL	172	Key Terms	203
Total Queries	180	Multiple Choice	204
Microsoft Graph	180	Practice with Access	206
Pivot Tables and Pivot Charts	183	Mini Cases	215
HANDS-ON EXERCISE 2:			
TOTAL QUERIES, CHARTS, AND PIVOT TABLES	185		

five

One-to-many Relationships: Subforms and Multiple-table Queries   217

Objectives	217	HANDS-ON EXERCISE 3:	
Case Study: The Residential Colleges	217	QUERIES AND REPORTS	241
A Database for Consumer Loans	218	Expanding the Database	248
The AutoNumber Field Type	221	Multiple Subforms	250
Referential Integrity	221	HANDS-ON EXERCISE 4:	
Implementation in Access	221	LINKED SUBFORMS	251
HANDS-ON EXERCISE 1:			
ONE-TO-MANY RELATIONSHIPS	223	Summary	258
Subforms	228	Key Terms	258
The Form Wizard	230	Multiple Choice	259
HANDS-ON EXERCISE 2:		Practice with Access	261
CREATING A SUBFORM	231	Mini Cases	271
Multiple-table queries	239		

six

Many-to-many Relationships: A More Complex System   273

Objectives	273	HANDS-ON EXERCISE 3:	
Case Study: At Your Service	273	ADVANCED QUERIES	297
The Computer Super Store	274	Expanding the Database	305
The AutoNumber Field Type	277	The Sales Commission Query	307
The Relationships Window	277	HANDS-ON EXERCISE 4:	
HANDS-ON EXERCISE 1:		EXPANDING THE DATABASE	309
RELATIONSHIPS AND			
REFERENTIAL INTEGRITY	279	Summary	317
Subforms, Queries, and AutoLookup	284	Key Terms	317
HANDS-ON EXERCISE 2:		Multiple Choice	318
SUBFORMS AND MULTIPLE-TABLE QUERIES	286	Practice with Access	320
Parameter Queries	293	Mini Cases	331
Total Queries	293		
Learning by Doing	296		

seven

Building Applications: Macros and a Multilevel Switchboard 333

Objectives	333
Case Study: The Movie Studio	333
A Recreational Sports League	334
The Switchboard Manager	337
The Linked Tables Manager	337
HANDS-ON EXERCISE 1:	
THE SWITCHBOARD MANAGER	339
Introduction to Macros	348
The Macro Window	348
The AutoExec Macro	349
Debugging	349
Application Development	350

HANDS-ON EXERCISE 2:	
MACROS AND PROTOTYPING	352
The Player Draft	359
Macro Groups	360
HANDS-ON EXERCISE 3:	
THE PLAYER DRAFT	361
Summary	371
Key Terms	371
Multiple Choice	372
Practice with Access	374
Mini Cases	385

eight

Creating More Powerful Applications: Introduction to VBA 387

Objectives	387
Case Study: Return to the Auction	387
Introduction to VBA	388
A Better Student Form	389
Modules and Procedures	391
HANDS-ON EXERCISE 1:	
CREATING A COMBO BOX AND	
ASSOCIATED VBA PROCEDURE	393
Facilitating Data Entry	401
HANDS-ON EXERCISE 2:	
FACILITATING DATA ENTRY	403
Error Trapping	411

HANDS-ON EXERCISE 3:	
ERROR TRAPPING	413
Data Validation	420
HANDS-ON EXERCISE 4:	
DATA VALIDATION	421
Summary	428
Key Terms	428
Multiple Choice	429
Practice with Access and VBA	431
Mini Cases	439

nine

Design and Implementation: A Capstone Chapter   441

Objectives   441
Case Study: The SD Coffee Company   441
The Development Cycle   442
   From Output to Input   442
   Database Design   444
HANDS-ON EXERCISE 1:
   DATABASE DESIGN   446
Detailed Design   452
   AutoNumber and Field Type   452
   Referential Integrity and Required Fields   452
HANDS-ON EXERCISE 2:
   THE DETAILED DESIGN   454
The Visual Design—Version 1.0   460
   The Templates   460
HANDS-ON EXERCISE 3:
   THE VISUAL DESIGN   462
A Basic Form and Report   470
HANDS-ON EXERCISE 4:
   A BASIC FORM AND REPORT   472
Prototyping—"Complete the System"   478
   Macros—A Quick Review   478

HANDS-ON EXERCISE 5:
   PROTOTYPING—COMPLETE THE SYSTEM   480
Add the Reports   486
HANDS-ON EXERCISE 6:
   ADD THE REPORTS   488
The Orders Form   494
HANDS-ON EXERCISE 7:
   THE ORDERS FORM   496
Security Issues   504
HANDS-ON EXERCISE 8:
   SUBMISSION TO THE CLIENT   506

Summary   511
Key Terms   511
Multiple Choice   512
Practice with Access   514
The Group Project   524

Appendix A: The Design of a
   Relational Database   525
Appendix B: Toolbars   541
Appendix C: Mail Merge   549
Appendix D: Using XML   559

GETTING STARTED WITH **VBA**

Getting Started with VBA: Extending Microsoft® Office 2003   577

Objectives	577	Debugging	606
Case Study:On-the-Job Training	577	HANDS-ON EXERCISE 3:	
Introduction to VBA	578	LOOPS AND DEBUGGING	608
The MsgBox Statement	579	Putting VBA to Work (Microsoft Excel)	617
The InputBox Function	580	HANDS-ON EXERCISE 4:	
Declaring Variables	581	EVENT-DRIVEN PROGRAMMING	
The VBA Editor	582	(MICROSOFT EXCEL)	619
HANDS-ON EXERCISE 1:		Putting VBA to Work (Microsoft Access)	628
INTRODUCTION TO VBA	583	HANDS-ON EXERCISE 5:	
If . . . Then . . . Else Statement	592	EVENT-DRIVEN PROGRAMMING	
Case Statement	594	(MICROSOFT ACCESS)	630
Custom Toolbars	595	Summary	638
HANDS-ON EXERCISE 2:		Key Terms	638
DECISION MAKING	596	Multiple Choice	639
For . . . Next Statement	604		
Do Loops	605		

MICROSOFT® **WINDOWS® XP**

Getting Started with Microsoft® Windows® XP   641

Objectives	641	HANDS-ON EXERCISE 3:	
Case Study: Unforeseen Circumstances	641	WINDOWS EXPLORER	672
Welcome to Windows XP	642	Increasing Productivity	681
The Desktop	643	The Control Panel	681
Moving and Sizing a Window	643	Shortcuts	682
Anatomy of a Window	646	The Search Companion	683
Pull-down Menus	647	HANDS-ON EXERCISE 4:	
Dialog Boxes	648	INCREASING PRODUCTIVITY	684
Help and Support Center	649	Fun with Windows XP	692
HANDS-ON EXERCISE 1:		Windows Media Player	692
WELCOME TO WINDOWS XP	650	Digital Photography	693
Files and Folders	658	Windows Messenger	694
The Exploring Office Practice Files	660	HANDS-ON EXERCISE 5:	
Connecting to the Internet	660	FUN WITH WINDOWS XP	695
HANDS-ON EXERCISE 2:		Summary	704
DOWNLOAD THE PRACTICE FILES	661	Key Terms	704
Windows Explorer	669	Multiple Choice	705
Personal Folders	669	Practice with Windows XP	707
Moving and Copying a File	671	Mini Cases	712
Deleting a File	671		
Backup	671		

INDEX	713

Preface

Continuing a tradition of excellence, Prentice Hall is proud to announce the new *Exploring Microsoft Office 2003* series by Robert T. Grauer and Maryann Barber. The hands-on approach and conceptual framework of this comprehensive series helps students master all aspects of the Microsoft Office 2003 software, while providing the background necessary to transfer and use these skills in their personal and professional lives.

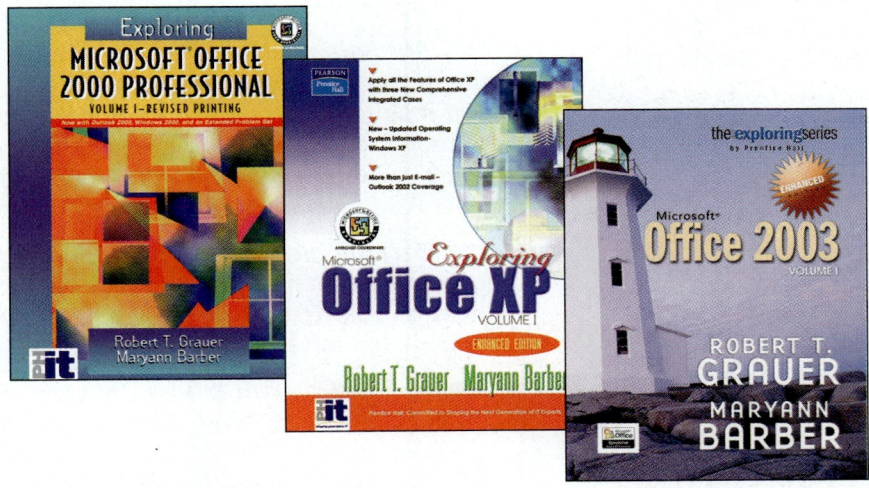

The entire series has been revised to include the new features found in the Office 2003 Suite, which contains Word 2003, Excel 2003, Access 2003, PowerPoint 2003, Publisher 2003, FrontPage 2003, and Outlook 2003.

In addition, this edition includes fully revised end-of-chapter material that provides an extensive review of concepts and techniques discussed in the chapter. Each chapter now begins with an *introductory case study* to provide an effective overview of what the reader will be able to accomplish, with additional *mini cases* at the end of each chapter for practice and review. The conceptual content within each chapter has been modified as appropriate and numerous end-of-chapter exercises have been added.

The new *visual design* introduces the concept of *perfect pages*, whereby every step in every hands-on exercise, as well as every end-of-chapter exercise, begins at the top of its own page and has its own screen shot. This clean design allows for easy navigation throughout the text.

Continuing the success of the website provided for previous editions of this series, Exploring Office 2003 offers expanded resources that include online, interactive study guides, data file downloads, technology updates, additional case studies and exercises, and other helpful information. Start out at **www.prenhall.com/grauer** to explore these resources!

Organization of the Exploring Office 2003 Series

The new Exploring Microsoft Office 2003 series includes five combined Office 2003 texts from which to choose:

- **Volume I** is Microsoft Office Specialist certified in each of the core applications in the Office suite (Word, Excel, Access, and PowerPoint). Five additional modules (*Essential Computing Concepts, Getting Started with Windows XP, The Internet and the World Wide Web, Getting Started with Outlook,* and *Integrated Case Studies*) are also included. **Volume I Enhanced Edition** adds 18 new chapter-opening case studies, two new integrated case studies, 30 additional end-of-chapter problems, and 20 new mini cases to the existing Volume I.

- **Volume II** picks up where Volume I leaves off, covering the advanced topics for the individual applications. A *Getting Started with VBA* module has been added.

- The **Plus Edition** extends the coverage of Access and Excel to six and seven chapters, respectively (as opposed to four chapters each in Volume I). It also maintains the same level of coverage for PowerPoint and Word as in Volume I so that both applications are Microsoft Office Specialist certified. The Plus Edition includes a new module on XML but does not contain the Essential Computing Concepts or Internet modules.

- The **Brief Microsoft Office 2003** edition provides less coverage of the core applications than Volume I (a total of 10 chapters as opposed to 18). It also includes the *Getting Started with Windows XP* and *Getting Started with Outlook* modules.

- **Getting Started with Office 2003** contains the first chapter from each application (Word, Excel, Access, and PowerPoint), plus three additional modules: *Getting Started with Windows XP, The Internet and the World Wide Web*, and *Essential Computing Concepts*.

Individual texts for Word 2003, Excel 2003, Access 2003, and PowerPoint 2003 provide complete coverage of the application and are Microsoft Office Specialist certified. For shorter courses, we have created brief versions of the Exploring texts that give students a four-chapter introduction to each application. Each of these volumes is Microsoft Office Specialist certified at the Specialist level.

This series has been approved by Microsoft to be used in preparation for Microsoft Office Specialist exams.

The Microsoft Office Specialist program is globally recognized as the standard for demonstrating desktop skills with the Microsoft Office suite of business productivity applications (Microsoft Word, Microsoft Excel, Microsoft PowerPoint, Microsoft Access, and Microsoft Outlook). With a Microsoft Office Specialist certification, thousands of people have demonstrated increased productivity and have proved their ability to utilize the advanced functionality of these Microsoft applications.

By encouraging individuals to develop advanced skills with Microsoft's leading business desktop software, the Microsoft Office Specialist program helps fill the demand for qualified, knowledgeable people in the modern workplace. At the same time, Microsoft Office Specialist helps satisfy an organization's need for a qualitative assessment of employee skills.

Instructor and Student Resources

The **Instructor's CD** that accompanies the Exploring Office series contains:

- Student data files
- Solutions to all exercises and problems
- PowerPoint lectures
- Instructor's manuals in Word format that enable the instructor to annotate portions of the instructor manuals for distribution to the class
- Instructors may also use our *test creation software,* TestGen and QuizMaster. TestGen is a test generator program that lets you view and easily edit test-bank questions, create tests, and print in a variety of formats suitable to your teaching situation. Exams can be easily uploaded into WebCT, BlackBoard, and CourseCompass. QuizMaster allows students to take the tests created with TestGen on a local area network.

Prentice Hall's Companion Website at www.prenhall.com/grauer offers expanded IT resources and downloadable supplements. This site also includes an online study guide for students containing true/false and multiple choice questions and practice projects.

WebCT www.prenhall.com/webct

Gold level customer support available exclusively to adopters of Prentice Hall courses is provided free-of-charge upon adoption and provides you with priority assistance, training discounts, and dedicated technical support.

Blackboard www.prenhall.com/blackboard

Prentice Hall's abundant online content, combined with Blackboard's popular tools and interface, result in robust Web-based courses that are easy to implement, manage, and use—taking your courses to new heights in student interaction and learning.

CourseCompass www.coursecompass.com

CourseCompass is a dynamic, interactive online course management tool powered by Blackboard. This exciting product allows you to teach with marketing-leading Pearson Education content in an easy-to-use, customizable format.

Training and Assessment www2.phgenit.com/support

Prentice Hall offers Performance Based Training and Assessment in one product, Train&Assess IT. The Training component offers computer-based training that a student can use to preview, learn, and review Microsoft Office application skills. Web or CD-ROM delivered, Train IT offers interactive multimedia, computer-based training to augment classroom learning. Built-in prescriptive testing suggests a study path based not only on student test results but also on the specific textbook chosen for the course.

The Assessment component offers computer-based testing that shares the same user interface as Train IT and is used to evaluate a student's knowledge about specific topics in Word, Excel, Access, PowerPoint, Windows, Outlook, and the Internet. It does this in a task-oriented, performance-based environment to demonstrate proficiency as well as comprehension on the topics by the students. More extensive than the testing in Train IT, Assess IT offers more administrative features for the instructor and additional questions for the student.

Assess IT also allows professors to test students out of a course, place students in appropriate courses, and evaluate skill sets.

New! Each chapter now begins with an introductory case study to provide an effective overview of what students will accomplish by completing the chapter.

1

Getting Started with Microsoft® Windows® XP

OBJECTIVES

After reading this chapter you will:

1. Describe the Windows desktop.
2. Use the Help and Support Center to obtain information.
3. Describe the My Computer and My Documents folders.
4. Differentiate between a program file and a data file.
5. Download a file from the Exploring Office Web site.
6. Copy and/or move a file from one folder to another.
7. Delete a file, and then recover it from the Recycle Bin.
8. Create and arrange shortcuts on the desktop.
9. Use the Search Companion.
10. Use the My Pictures and My Music folders.
11. Use Windows Messenger for instant messaging.

hands-on exercises

1. WELCOME TO WINDOWS XP
   Input: None
   Output: None

2. DOWNLOAD PRACTICE FILES
   Input: Data files from the Web
   Output: Welcome to Windows XP (a Word document)

3. WINDOWS EXPLORER
   Input: Data files from exercise 2
   Output: Screen Capture within a Word document

4. INCREASING PRODUCTIVITY
   Input: Data files from exercise 3
   Output: None

5. FUN WITH WINDOWS XP
   Input: None
   Output: None

CASE STUDY
UNFORESEEN CIRCUMSTANCES

Steve and his wife Shelly have poured their life savings into the dream of owning their own business, a "nanny" service agency. They have spent the last two years building their business and have created a sophisticated database with numerous entries for both families and nannies. The database is the key to their operation. Now that it is up and running, Steve and Shelly are finally at a point where they could hire someone to manage the operation on a part-time basis so that they could take some time off together.

Unfortunately, their process for selecting a person they could trust with their business was not as thorough as it should have been. Nancy, their new employee, assured them that all was well, and the couple left for an extended weekend. The place was in shambles on their return. Nancy could not handle the responsibility, and when Steve gave her two weeks' notice, neither he nor his wife thought that the unimaginable would happen. On her last day in the office Nancy "lost" all of the names in the database—the data was completely gone!

Nancy claimed that a "virus" knocked out the database, but after spending nearly $1,500 with a computer consultant, Steve was told that it had been cleverly deleted from the hard drive and could not be recovered. Of course, the consultant asked Steve and Shelly about their backup strategy, which they sheepishly admitted did not exist. They had never experienced any problems in the past, and simply assumed that their data was safe. Fortunately, they do have hard copy of the data in the form of various reports that were printed throughout the time they were in business. They have no choice but to manually reenter the data. ■

Your assignment is to read the chapter, paying special attention to the information on file management. Think about how Steve and Shelly could have avoided the disaster if a backup strategy had been in place, then summarize your thoughts in a brief note to your instructor. Describe the elements of a basic backup strategy. Give several other examples of unforeseen circumstances that can cause data to be lost.

New! A listing of the input and output files for each hands-on exercise within the chapter. Students will stay on track with what is to be accomplished.

PERFECT PAGES

1   Welcome to Windows XP

Objective	To log on to Windows XP and customize the desktop; to open the My Computer folder; to move and size a window; to format a floppy disk and access the Help and Support Center. Use Figure 7 as a guide.

Step 1:   **Log On to Windows XP**

■ Turn on the computer and all of the peripheral devices. The floppy drive should be empty prior to starting your machine.

■ Windows XP will load automatically, and you should see a login screen similar to Figure 7a. (It does not matter which version of Windows XP you are using.) The number and names of the potential users and their associated icons will be different on your system.

■ Click the icon for the user account you want to access. You may be prompted for a password, depending on the security options in effect.

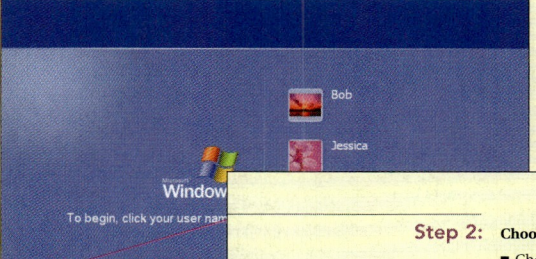

Click icon for user account to be accessed

(a) Log On to Windows XP (step 1)

FIGURE 7   Hands-on Exercise 1

USER ACCOUNTS

The available user names are cr... Windows XP, but you can add or d... click Control Panel, switch to the Ca... the desired task, such as creating... then supply the necessary informati... user accounts in a school setting.

Each step in the hands-on exercises begins at the top of the page to ensure that students can easily navigate through the text.

Step 2:   **Choose the Theme and Start Menu**

■ Check with your instructor to see if you are able to modify the desktop and other settings at your school or university. If your network administrator has disabled these commands, skip this step and go to step 3.

■ Point to a blank area on the desktop, click the **right mouse button** to display a context-sensitive menu, then click the **Properties command** to open the Display Properties dialog box. Click the **Themes tab** and select the **Windows XP theme** if it is not already selected. Click **OK**.

■ We prefer to work without any wallpaper (background picture) on the desktop. **Right click** the desktop, click **Properties**, then click the **Desktop tab** in the Display Properties dialog box. Click **None** as shown in Figure 7b, then click **OK**. The background disappears.

■ The Start menu is modified independently of the theme. **Right click** a blank area of the taskbar, click the **Properties command** to display the Taskbar and Start Menu Properties dialog box, then click the **Start Menu tab**.

■ Click the **Start Menu option button**. Click **OK**.

Click Desktop tab

Click right mouse button to display shortcut menu

Click None

Right click blank area on taskbar

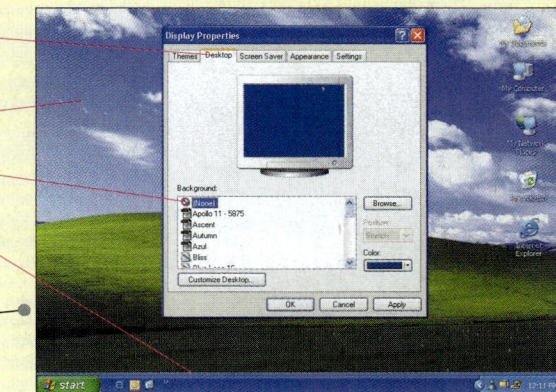

(b) Choose the Theme and Start Menu (step 2)

FIGURE 7   Hands-on Exercise 1 *(continued)*

IMPLEMENT A SCREEN SAVER

A screen saver is a delightful way to personalize your computer and a good way to practice with basic commands in Windows XP. Right click a blank area of the desktop, click the Properties command to open the Display Properties dialog box, then click the Screen Saver tab. Click the down arrow in the Screen Saver list box, choose the desired screen saver, then set the option to wait an appropriate amount of time before the screen saver appears. Click OK to accept the settings and close the dialog box.

New! Larger screen shots with clear callouts.

Boxed tips provide students with additional information.

MINI CASES AND PRACTICE EXERCISES

MINI CASES

Mail Merge

A mail merge takes the tedium out of sending form letters, as it creates the same letter many times, changing the name, address, and other information as appropriate from letter to letter. The form letter is created in a word processor (e.g., Microsoft Word), but the data file may be taken from an Excel workbook or an Access table or query. Use the *Our Students* database that you have worked with throughout the chapter as the basis for two different form letters that are to be sent to two different groups of students. The first letter is to congratulate students on the Dean's list (GPA of 3.50 or higher). The second letter is a warning to students on academic probation (GPA of less than 2.00).

We have created the form letters for you as the Word documents *Chapter 3 Mini Case Study—Probation Letter* and *Chapter 3 Mini Case Study—Dean's List*, with both documents stored in the Exploring Access folder. Open the Access database and create the required queries, then select each query individually, pull down the Tools menu, click Office Links, and click the command to Merge it with Microsoft Word. Word provides step-by-step assistance, and you should be able to complete the mail merge without difficulty. Print the first form letter for each query to show your instructor that you have completed the assignment.

Oh Canada

If you ask the average Canadian how many states there are in the United States, you are very likely to get the correct answer. If you reverse the question and ask the average American about Canadian provinces, the response is far less accurate. This assignment enables you to learn about our neighbor to the North. Open the *Chapter 3 Mini Case Study—Oh Canada* database in the Exploring Access folder. You will find a single table with four fields—the name of the province or territory, the estimated population for 2002 (in thousands), the area in square kilometers, and an indication of whether the data pertains to a province or territory.

Your assignment is to create a report that parallels the Population Density report in the United States database that was described in practice exercise 2. Your first task will be to create a query to compute the population density, after which you can create a report based on that query. The report should be grouped by province or territory, with population and area totals for each group, the average population density for each group, as well as statistics for Canada as a whole.

The Oh Canada data[...]
the statistics that appear[...]
asked to copy to the rep[...]
so that it contains your[...]
for your instructor.

Compacting ver[...]

An Access database bec[...]
reports and forms) are m[...]
pact a database to reduc[...]
base with multiple obje[...]
the Windows Explorer t[...]
Access, open the datab[...]
compact the database, t[...]
compress a compacted[...]
further reduce the requi[...]
of the compressed datab[...]
Try compacting and co[...]
these techniques. Be su[...]
loaded) more quickly. (N[...]
to a colleague because C[...]

New!

We've added mini cases at the end of each chapter for expanded practice and review.

New!

Each project in the end-of-chapter material begins at the top of a page—now students can easily see where their assignments begin and end.

PRACTICE WITH ACCESS

1. **The Oscars:** The Academy Awards®, also known as the Oscars®, are given out each year to honor the best efforts in motion pictures for the previous year. We enjoy the movies and we have created a database that contains the Oscar winners in the major categories. Your first task is to update the table in our database to include any additional awards since the publication of our text. Proceed as follows:

   a. Open the *Chapter 1 Practice 1* database in the Exploring Access folder. Click the Forms button and open the Award Winners form shown in Figure 1.9. Maximize the form. Use the navigation bar at the bottom of the form to go to the last record to determine the last year in our table.

   b. Skip this step if the database is current; otherwise, click the hyperlink in the Award Winners form to go to the Oscars site and determine the winners for the years since we published our text. Use the existing form to enter the winners for the six major awards (best picture, best actor and actress, best director, and best supporting actor and actress) into the Award Winners table.

   c. The form should display the most recent year for which data is available. Click the selection area at the left of the form to select this record. Pull down the File menu, click the Print command, then click the option button to print the selected record. Click OK. (You can also click the Print button on the form to print only the current record.) Close the form.

   d. Return to the Database window, click the Tables button and open the Award Winners table. Adjust the column widths (if necessary) so that you see all of the information for each field in each column. Pull down the File menu, click the Page Setup command, and change to landscape printing with one-half-inch margins all around. Use the Print Preview button to see how the table will appear prior to actually printing the table. Unless you change to a font that is too small to read, the data for one year will not fit on one page. Do not print the table. Close the Print Preview window, then close the table.

   e. Return to the Database window. Click the Reports button. Open the Major Winners by Year report and print the first page. (All of the data for a given year appears on the same page.) Close the report.

   f. Add a cover sheet, then submit the form and report to your instructor.

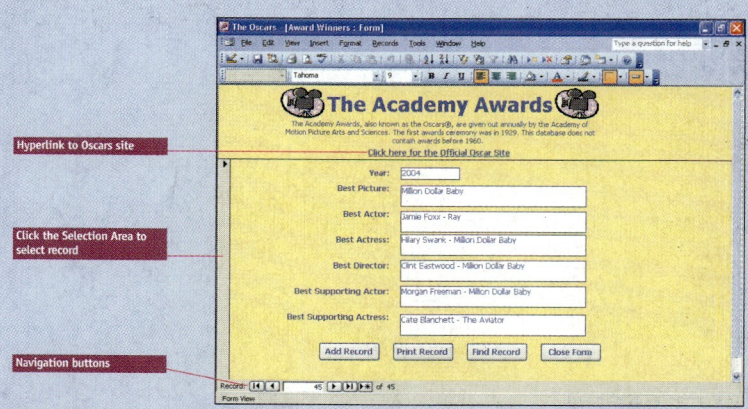

FIGURE 1.9 The Oscars (exercise 1)

NEW! DESIGN AND IMPLEMENTATION

New!

This capstone chapter reviews material from previous chapters as it takes the student through the development cycle.

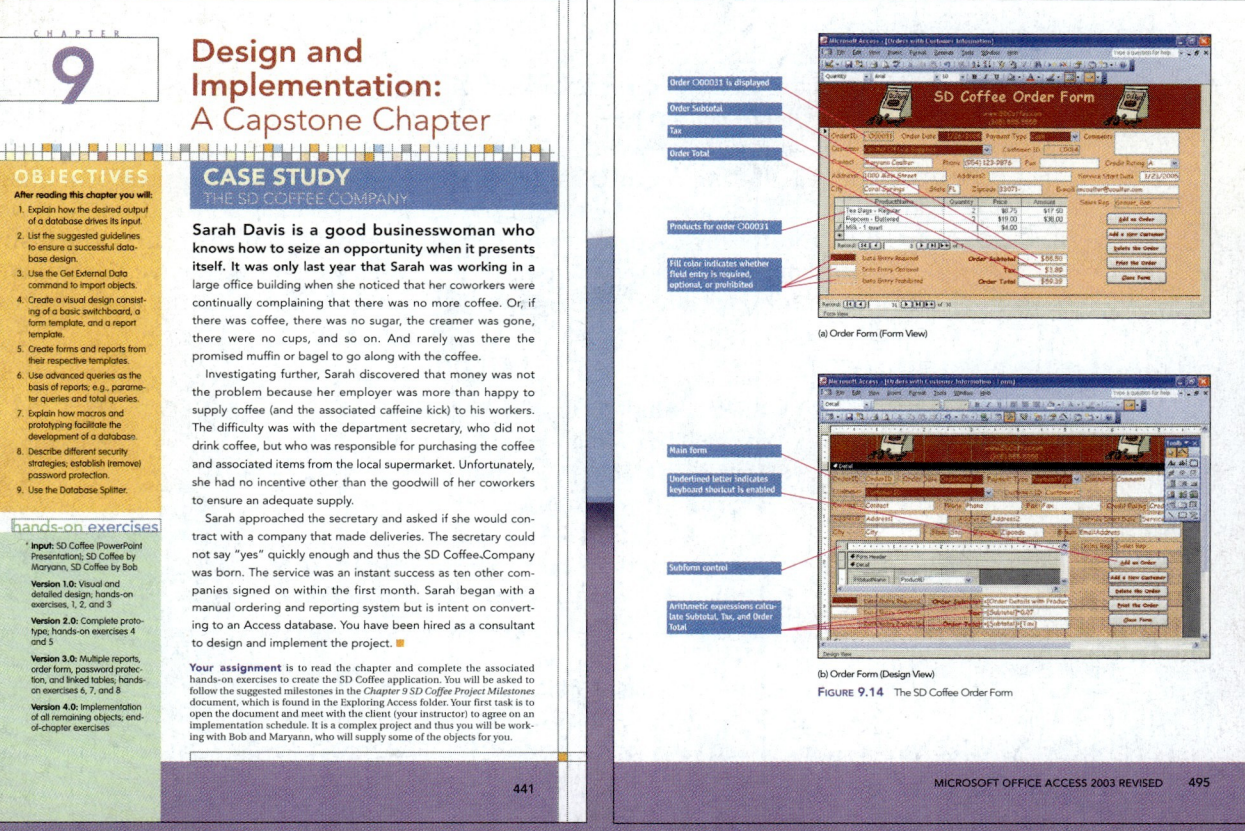

FIGURE 9.14 The SD Coffee Order Form

(a) Order Form (Form View)

(b) Order Form (Design View)

CHAPTER

9

Design and Implementation:
A Capstone Chapter

OBJECTIVES

After reading this chapter you will:

1. Explain how the desired output of a database drives its input.
2. List the suggested guidelines to ensure a successful database design.
3. Use the Get External Data command to import objects.
4. Create a visual design consisting of a basic switchboard, a form template, and a report template.
5. Create forms and reports from their respective templates.
6. Use advanced queries as the basis of reports; e.g. parameter queries and total queries.
7. Explain how macros and prototyping facilitate the development of a database.
8. Describe different security strategies; establish (remove) password protection.
9. Use the Database Splitter.

hands-on exercises

- **Input:** SD Coffee (PowerPoint Presentation); SD Coffee by Maryann, SD Coffee by Bob
- **Version 1.0:** Visual and detailed design; hands-on exercises, 1, 2, and 3
- **Version 2.0:** Complete prototype; hands-on exercises 4 and 5
- **Version 3.0:** Multiple reports, order form, password protection, and linked tables; hands-on exercises 6, 7, and 8
- **Version 4.0:** Implementation of all remaining objects; end-of-chapter exercises

CASE STUDY
THE SD COFFEE COMPANY

Sarah Davis is a good businesswoman who knows how to seize an opportunity when it presents itself. It was only last year that Sarah was working in a large office building when she noticed that her coworkers were continually complaining that there was no more coffee. Or, if there was coffee, there was no sugar, the creamer was gone, there were no cups, and so on. And rarely was there the promised muffin or bagel to go along with the coffee.

Investigating further, Sarah discovered that money was not the problem because her employer was more than happy to supply coffee (and the associated caffeine kick) to his workers. The difficulty was with the department secretary, who did not drink coffee, but who was responsible for purchasing the coffee and associated items from the local supermarket. Unfortunately, she had no incentive other than the goodwill of her coworkers to ensure an adequate supply.

Sarah approached the secretary and asked if she would contract with a company that made deliveries. The secretary could not say "yes" quickly enough and thus the SD Coffee.Company was born. The service was an instant success as ten other companies signed on within the first month. Sarah began with a manual ordering and reporting system but is intent on converting to an Access database. You have been hired as a consultant to design and implement the project. ◼

Your assignment is to read the chapter and complete the associated hands-on exercises to create the SD Coffee application. You will be asked to follow the suggested milestones in the *Chapter 9 SD Coffee Project Milestones* document, which is found in the Exploring Access folder. Your first task is to open the document and meet with the client (your instructor) to agree on an implementation schedule. It is a complex project and thus you will be working with Bob and Maryann, who will supply some of the objects for you.

441

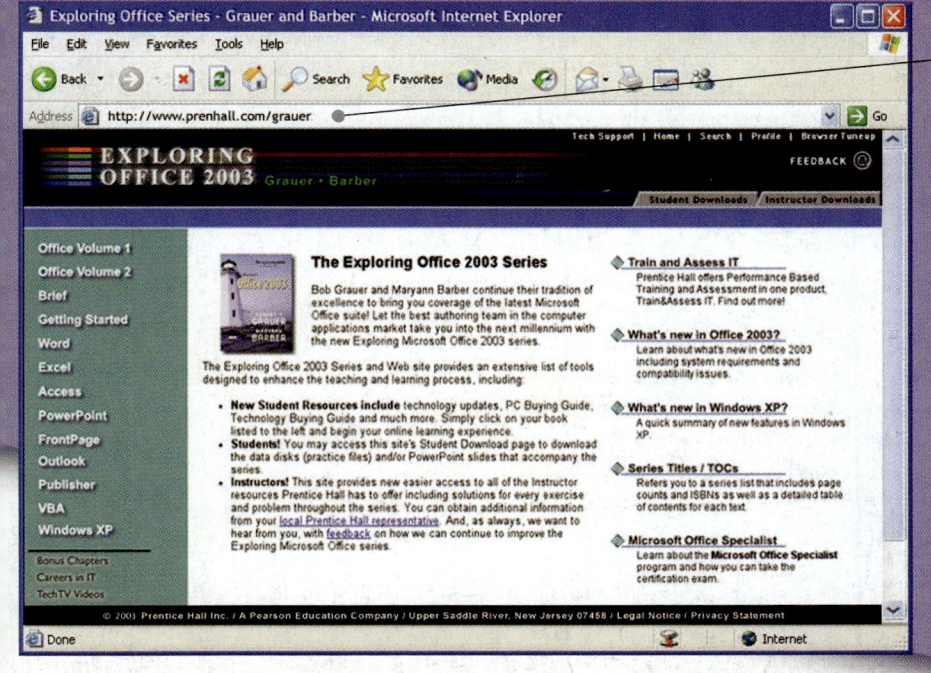

Companion Web site

New!

Updated and enhanced Companion Web site. Find everything you need— student practice files, PowerPoint lectures, online study guides, and instructor support (solutions)!

www.prenhall.com/grauer

Acknowledgments

We want to thank the many individuals who have helped to bring this project to fruition. Melissa Sabella and Jodi McPherson, our editors at Prentice Hall, have provided new leadership in extending the series to Office 2003. Cathi Profitko did an absolutely incredible job on our Web site. Shelly Martin was the creative force behind the chapter-opening case studies. Sarah Davis and Emily Knight coordinated the marketing and continue to inspire us with suggestions for improving the series. Greg Hubit has been masterful as the external production editor for every book in the series from its inception. Eileen Clark coordinated the myriad details of production and the certification process. Lynne Breitfeller was the project manager and manufacturing buyer. Jessica Street created the Instructor Resources CD. Lori Brice was the project manager at Techbooks/GTS and in charge of composition. Chuck Cox did his usual fine work as copyeditor. Cindy Stevens, Tom McKenzie, and Michael Olmstead wrote the instructor manuals. Michael Fruhbeis developed the innovative and attractive design. We also want to acknowledge our reviewers who, through their comments and constructive criticism, greatly improved the series.

Richard Albright, Goldey-Beacom College
Lynne Band, Middlesex Community College
Don Belle, Central Piedmont Community College
Richard Blamer, John Carroll University
Stuart P. Brian, Holy Family College
Carl M. Briggs, Indiana University School of Business
Kimberly Chambers, Scottsdale Community College
Jill Chapnick, Florida International University
Alok Charturvedi, Purdue University
Barbara Cierny, William Rainey Harper College
Jerry Chin, Southwest Missouri State University
Dean Combellick, Scottsdale Community College
Cody Copeland, Johnson County Community College
Larry S. Corman, Fort Lewis College
Janis Cox, Tri-County Technical College
Douglass Cross, Clackamas Community College
Martin Crossland, Southwest Missouri State University
Bill Daley, University of Oregon
Paul E. Daurelle, Western Piedmont Community College
Shawna DePlonty, Sault College of Applied Arts and Technology
Rory J. De Simone, University of Florida
Carolyn DiLeo, Westchester Community College
Judy Dolan, Palomar College
William J. Dorin, Indiana University Northwest
David Douglas, University of Arkansas
Carlotta Eaton, Radford University
Beverly Fite, Amarillo College
Judith M. Fitspatrick, Gulf Coast Community College
James Franck, College of St. Scholastica
Raymond Frost, Central Connecticut State University
Susan Fry, Boise State University

Midge Gerber, Southwestern Oklahoma State University
James Gips, Boston College
Vernon Griffin, Austin Community College
Ranette Halverson, Midwestern State University
Michael Hassett, Fort Hays State University
Barbara Anne Hearn, Community College of Philadelphia
Mike Hearn, Community College of Philadelphia
Wanda D. Heller, Seminole Community College
Fred Hills, McLennan Community College
Bonnie Homan, San Francisco State University
Ernie Ivey, Polk Community College
Dana Johnson, North Dakota State University
Walter Johnson, Community College of Philadelphia
Mike Kelly, Community College of Rhode Island
Jane King, Everett Community College
Rose M. Laird, Northern Virginia Community College
Jackie A. Lamoureux, Albuquerque TVI
David Langley, University of Oregon
John Lesson, University of Central Florida
Maurie Lockley, University of North Carolina at Greensboro
Daniela Marghitu, Auburn University
David B. Meinert, Southwest Missouri State University
Alan Moltz, Naugatuck Valley Technical Community College
Kim Montney, Kellogg Community College
Bill Morse, DeVry Institute of Technology
Kevin Pauli, University of Nebraska
Mary McKenry Percival, University of Miami
Laura McManamon, University of Dayton
Joseph M. Manzo, Lehigh University
Marguerite Nedreberg, Youngstown State University
Joshua L. Mindel, San Francisco State University
James Pepe, Bentley College
Jim Pruitt, Central Washington University
Delores Pusins, Hillsborough Community College
Gale E. Rand, College Misericordia
Judith Rice, Santa Fe Community College
David Rinehard, Lansing Community College
Behrooz Saghafi, Chicago State University
Marilyn Salas, Scottsdale Community College
Herach Safarian, College of the Canyons
John Shepherd, Duquesne University
Barbara Sherman, Buffalo State College
Karl L. Smart, Central Michigan University
Carol Smith, Johnson Community College
Robert Spear, Prince George's Community College
Diane Stark, Phoenix College
Michael Stewardson, San Jacinto College—North
Helen Stoloff, Hudson Valley Community College

... **continued**

Jessica Street, Broward Community College
Joe Teng, Barry University
Margaret Thomas, Ohio University
Mike Thomas, Indiana University School of Business
Suzanne Tomlinson, Iowa State University
Karen Tracey, Central Connecticut State University
Antonio Vargas, El Paso Community College
Sally Visci, Lorain County Community College
William Wagner, Villanova University
David Weiner, University of San Francisco
Connie Wells, Georgia State University
Wallace John Whistance-Smith, Ryerson Polytechnic University
Karen Wisniewski, County College of Morris
Jack Zeller, Kirkwood Community College

A final word of thanks to the unnamed students at the University of Miami who make it all worthwhile. Most of all, thanks to you, our readers, for choosing this book. Please feel free to contact us with any comments and suggestions.

Robert T. Grauer   Maryann Barber
rgrauer@miami.edu   mbarber@miami.edu
www.prenhall.com/grauer

Introduction to Access:
What Is a Database?

OBJECTIVES

After reading this chapter you will:

1. Define the terms field, record, table, and database.

2. Describe the objects in an Access database.

3. Download the practice files (data disk) for use in hands-on exercises.

4. Add, edit, and delete records within a table.

5. Use existing forms and reports.

6. Explain the importance of data validation in maintaining a table.

7. Apply a filter by form or selection.

8. Sort a table on one or more fields.

9. Identify the one-to-many relationships in a database.

10. Explain how changes in one table of a relational database affect the other tables in the database.

hands-on exercises

1. INTRODUCTION TO ACCESS
   Input: Bookstore database
   Output: Bookstore database (modified)

2. FILTERS AND SORTING
   Input: Employee database
   Output: Employee database (modified)

3. A LOOK AHEAD
   Input: Look Ahead database
   Output: Look Ahead database (modified)

CASE STUDY
THE SOUTH VANCOUVER PRESCHOOL

The South Vancouver Preschool was founded fifty years ago, and it has played a prominent role in the community for much of the time since then. The school is known for its strong academic and social programs, as well as its ability to provide financial aid to needy students. The school employs a variety of fund-raising techniques, and it has come to depend on an annual auction to raise money to support special programs throughout the year. The school appeals to the parents of its students as well as the local community to donate items for the auction.

The headmaster, Kris King, is your best friend, and Kris has asked you for help in planning the auction. Kris has asked you to maintain the Access database that was created to track the items donated for auction. The hard work has already been done in that the database already exists. Your task is essentially data entry; that is, you will record the donations as they come in, together with the name, address, and telephone number of the donor. You will then print the various reports in the database for Kris to help her plan for the gala event. The reports include a list of all donations, a list of donors and their guests, and a set of mailing labels for all donors. ■

Your assignment is to read the chapter, paying special attention to each of the hands-on exercises. You will open the *Chapter 1 Case Study— South Vancouver Preschool* database, and examine each of its objects (tables, forms, and reports). You will then use the existing Donors form to enter data about yourself. Enter a gift certificate of your choice (be creative) to be donated, and indicate that two people will be attending— yourself and one guest. Print the completed form containing your data, and then all of the reports that exist within the database. Submit all of the printed information to your instructor. Add a cover sheet to complete the assignment.

Imagine, if you will, that you are the manager of a college bookstore and that you maintain data for every book in the store. Accordingly, you have recorded the specifics of each book (the title, author, publisher, price, and so on) in a manila folder, and have stored the folders in one drawer of a file cabinet.

One of your major responsibilities is to order books at the beginning of each semester, which in turn requires you to contact the various publishers. You have found it convenient, therefore, to create a second set of folders with data about each publisher—such as the publisher's phone number, address, and discount policy. You also found it necessary to create a third set of folders with data about each order—such as when the order was placed, the status of the order, which books were ordered, and how many copies.

Normal business operations will require you to make repeated trips to the filing cabinet to maintain the accuracy of the data and keep it up to date. You will have to create a new folder whenever a new book is received, whenever you contract with a new publisher, or whenever you place a new order. In similar fashion, you will have to modify the data in an existing folder to reflect changes that occur, such as an increase in the price of a book, a change in a publisher's address, or an update in the status of an order. And, lastly, you will need to remove the folder of any book that is no longer carried by the bookstore, or of any publisher with whom you no longer have contact, or of any order that was canceled.

The preceding discussion describes the bookstore of 40 years ago—before the advent of computers and computerized databases. The bookstore manager of today needs the same information as his or her predecessor. Today's manager, however, has the information readily available, at the touch of a key or the click of a mouse, through the miracle of modern technology.

Information systems have their own vocabulary. A *field* is a basic fact (or data element)—such as the name of a book or the telephone number of a publisher. A *record* is a set of fields. A *table* is a set of records. Every record in a table contains the same fields in the same order. A *database* consists of one or more tables. In our example each record in the Books table will contain the identical six fields—ISBN (a unique identifying number for the book), title, author, year of publication, price, and publisher. In similar fashion, every record in the Publishers table will have the same fields for each publisher just as every record in the Orders table has the same fields for each order.

You can think of the file cabinet in the manual system as a database. Each set of folders in the file cabinet corresponds to a table within the database. Thus, the Bookstore database consists of three separate tables—of books, publishers, and orders. Each table, in turn, consists of multiple records, corresponding to the folders in the file cabinet. The Books table, for example, contains a record for every book title in the store. The Publishers table has a record for each publisher, just as the Orders table has a record for each order.

The real power of Access is derived from a database with multiple tables—such as Books, Publishers, and Orders tables within the Bookstore database. For the time being, however, we focus on a simpler database with only one table so that you can learn the basics of Access. After you are comfortable working with a single table, we will show you how to work with multiple tables and relate them to one another.

GARBAGE IN, GARBAGE OUT

The information produced by a system is only as good as the data on which the information is based. In other words, no system, be it manual or electronic, can produce valid output from invalid input. The phenomenon is described by the acronym "GIGO"—garbage in, garbage out.

INTRODUCTION TO MICROSOFT ACCESS

Microsoft Access, the fourth major application in the Microsoft Office suite, is used to create and manage a database such as the one for the college bookstore. Consider now Figure 1.1, which shows how Microsoft Access appears on the desktop. Our discussion assumes a basic familiarity with the Windows operating system and the user interface that is common to all Windows applications. You should recognize, therefore, that the desktop in Figure 1.1 has two open windows—an application window for Microsoft Access and a document (database) window for the database that is currently open. (Microsoft Office Access 2003 uses the Access 2000 file format by default, to maintain compatability with earlier versions of Access.)

Each window has its own title bar and Minimize, Maximize (or Restore), and Close buttons. The title bar in the application window contains the name of the application (Microsoft Access). The title bar in the document (database) window contains the name of the database that is currently open (Bookstore). The application window for Access has been maximized to take up the entire desktop, and hence the Restore button is visible. The database window has not been maximized.

A menu bar appears immediately below the application title bar. A toolbar (similar to those in other Office applications) appears below the menu bar and offers alternative ways to execute common commands.

The Database Window

The ***Database window*** displays the various objects in an Access database. There are seven types of objects—tables, queries, forms, reports, pages, macros, and modules. Every database must contain at least one table, and it may contain any or all (or none) of the other objects. Each object type is accessed through the appropriate button within the Database window. In this chapter we concentrate on tables, but we briefly describe the other types of objects as a preview of what you will learn as you read our book.

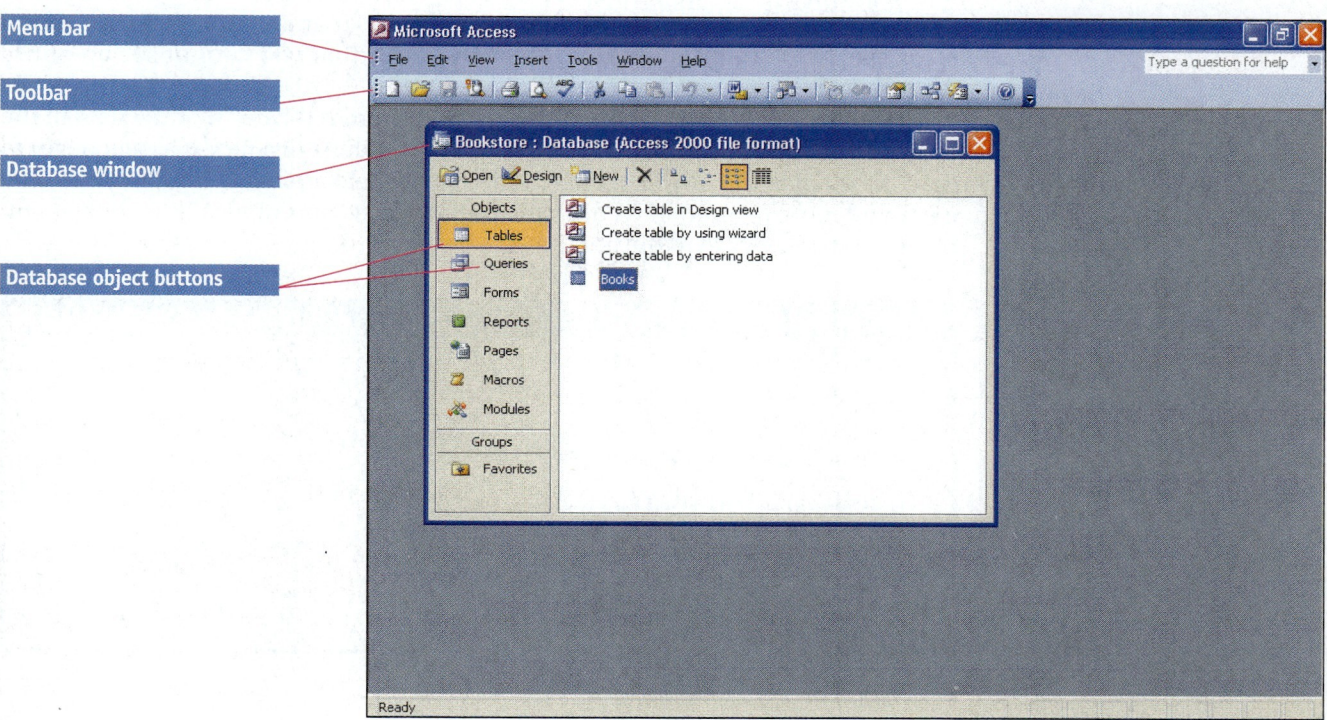

FIGURE 1.1   The Database Window

Tables

A table stores data about a physical entity such as a person, place, or thing, and it is the basic element in any database. A table is made up of records, which in turn are made up of fields. It is similar to an Excel worksheet in appearance, with each record appearing in a separate row. Each field appears in a separate column.

Access provides different ways in which to view a table. The *Datasheet view* is where you add, edit, and delete records of a table, and it is the view on which we concentrate throughout the chapter. The *Design view* is used to create (and/or modify) the table by specifying the fields it will contain and the associated properties for each field. The field type (for example, text or numeric data) and the field length are examples of field properties. (The Design view is covered in detail in Chapter 2, where we show you how to create a table.)

Access also includes two additional views that provide a convenient way to display summary information from a table. The *PivotTable view* is similar in concept to an Excel pivot table and provides a convenient way to summarize data about groups of records. The *PivotChart view* creates a chart from the associated PivotTable view. (These views are discussed further in Chapter 4 and need not concern you at this time.)

Figure 1.2 shows the Datasheet view for the Books table in our bookstore. The first row in the table displays the field names. Each additional row contains a record (the data for a specific book). Each column represents a field (one fact about a book). Every record in the table contains the same fields in the same order: ISBN number, Title, Author, Year, List Price, and Publisher.

The *primary key* is the field (or combination of fields) that makes each record in a table unique. The ISBN is the primary key in the Books table; it ensures that every record in a table is different from every other record, and hence it prevents the occurrence of duplicate records. A primary key is not required but is strongly recommended. (We cannot think of an example where you would not want to use a primary key.) There can be only one primary key per table.

The status bar at the bottom of Figure 1.2 indicates that there are 22 records in the table and that you are positioned on record number 13. You can work on only one record at a time. The vertical scroll bar at the right of the window indicates that there are more records in the table than can be seen at one time. The horizontal scroll bar at the bottom of the window indicates that you cannot see an entire record.

The triangle that appears to the left of the record indicates that the data in the *current record* has been saved. The triangle will change to a pencil as you begin to enter new data, then it will change back to a triangle after you complete the data entry and move to another record, since data is saved automatically as soon as you move from one record to the next.

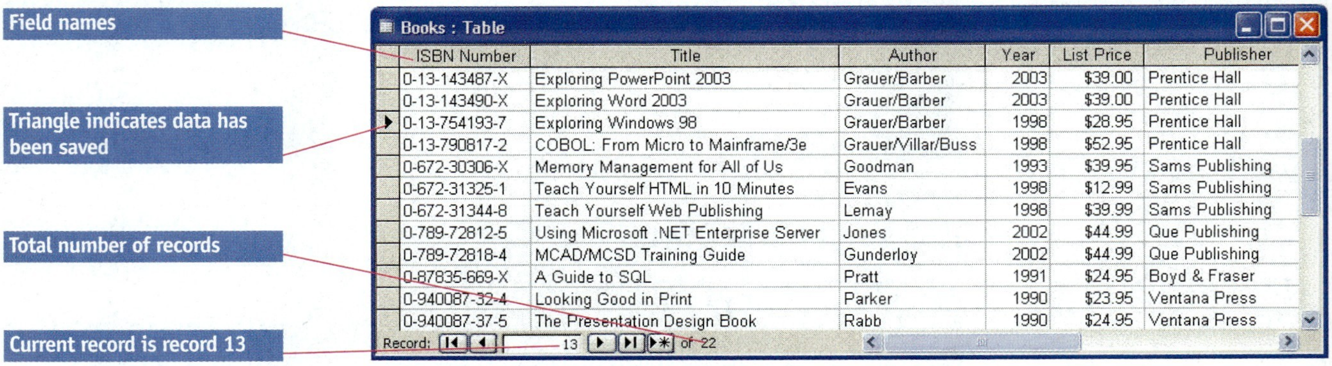

	ISBN Number	Title	Author	Year	List Price	Publisher
	0-13-143487-X	Exploring PowerPoint 2003	Grauer/Barber	2003	$39.00	Prentice Hall
	0-13-143490-X	Exploring Word 2003	Grauer/Barber	2003	$39.00	Prentice Hall
▶	0-13-754193-7	Exploring Windows 98	Grauer/Barber	1998	$28.95	Prentice Hall
	0-13-790817-2	COBOL: From Micro to Mainframe/3e	Grauer/Villar/Buss	1998	$52.95	Prentice Hall
	0-672-30306-X	Memory Management for All of Us	Goodman	1993	$39.95	Sams Publishing
	0-672-31325-1	Teach Yourself HTML in 10 Minutes	Evans	1998	$12.99	Sams Publishing
	0-672-31344-8	Teach Yourself Web Publishing	Lemay	1998	$39.99	Sams Publishing
	0-789-72812-5	Using Microsoft .NET Enterprise Server	Jones	2002	$44.99	Que Publishing
	0-789-72818-4	MCAD/MCSD Training Guide	Gunderloy	2002	$44.99	Que Publishing
	0-87835-669-X	A Guide to SQL	Pratt	1991	$24.95	Boyd & Fraser
	0-940087-32-4	Looking Good in Print	Parker	1990	$23.95	Ventana Press
	0-940087-37-5	The Presentation Design Book	Rabb	1990	$24.95	Ventana Press

Books : Table

Field names

Triangle indicates data has been saved

Total number of records

Current record is record 13

Record: 13 of 22

FIGURE 1.2 An Access Table

Forms, Queries, and Reports

As previously indicated, an Access database contains different types of objects. A table (or set of tables) is at the heart of any database because it contains the actual data. The other objects in a database—such as forms, queries, and reports—are based on an underlying table. Figure 1.3a displays a form based on the Books table that was shown earlier.

A *form* provides a friendlier interface than does a table and it is easier to use when entering or modifying data. Note, for example, the command buttons that appear in the form to add a new record, to find or delete an existing record, to print a record, and to close the form. In short, the form provides access to all of the data maintenance operations that are available through a table. The status bar and navigation buttons at the bottom of the form are similar to those that appear at the bottom of a table.

Figure 1.3b displays a query that lists the books for a particular publisher (Prentice Hall in this example). A *query* provides information based on the data within an underlying table. The Books table, for example, contains records for many publishers, but the query in Figure 1.3b shows only the books that were published by a specific publisher. The results of the query are similar in appearance to the underlying table, except that the query contains selected records and/or selected fields for those records. The query may also list the records in a different sequence from that of the table. (A query can also be used to add new records and/or modify existing records.)

Figure 1.3c displays a *report* that contains the same information as the query in Figure 1.3b. The report, however, provides the information in a more attractive format than the query. Note, too, that a report can be based on either a table or a query. Thus, you could have based the report on the Books table, rather than the query, in which case the report would list every book in the table, as opposed to a limited subset of the records within the table.

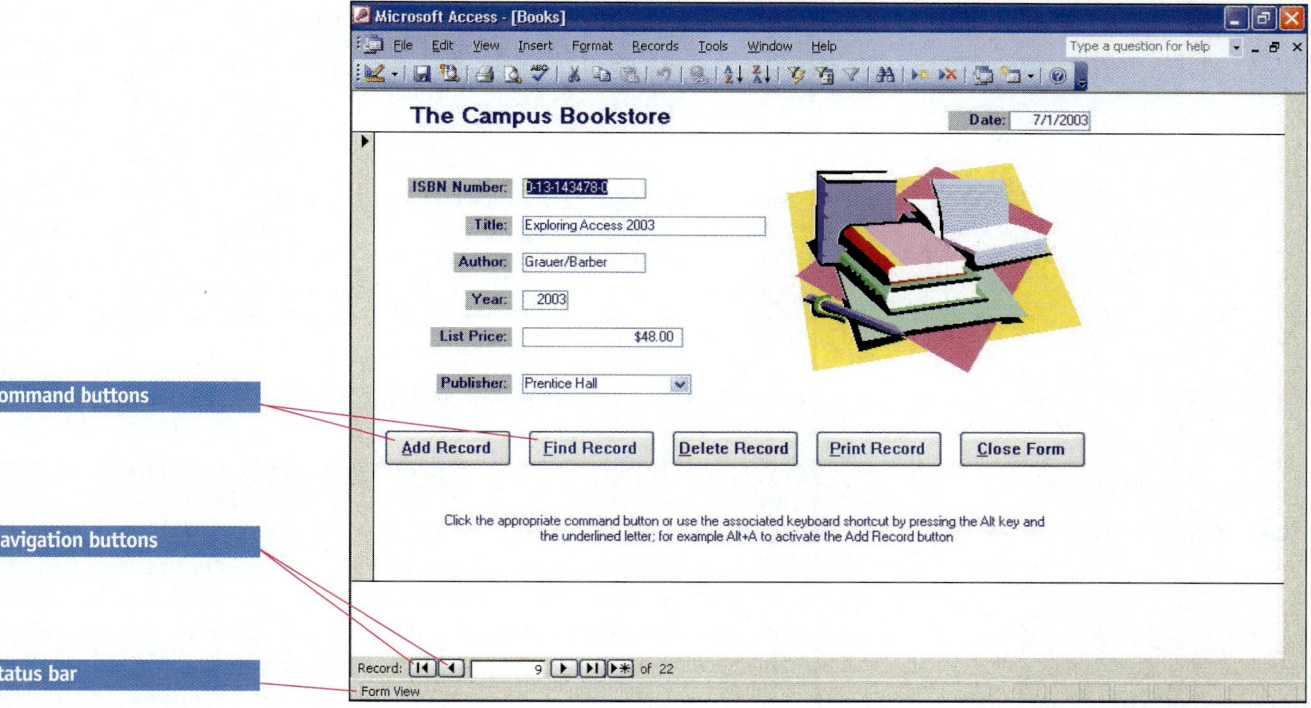

(a) Form

FIGURE 1.3 Forms, Queries, and Reports

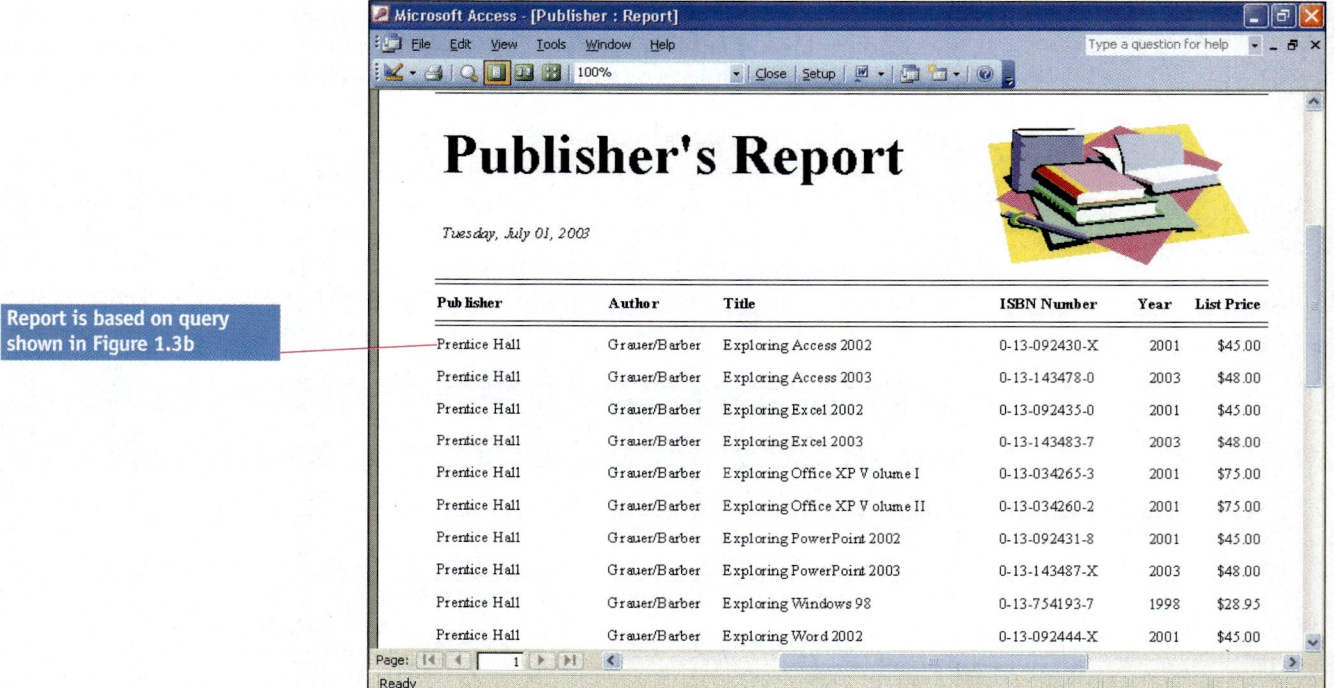

Only books published by Prentice Hall are displayed

(b) Query

Report is based on query shown in Figure 1.3b

(c) Report

FIGURE 1.3 Forms, Queries, and Reports (*continued*)

ONE FILE HOLDS EVERYTHING

All of the objects in an Access database are stored in a single file. The database can be opened from within Windows Explorer by double clicking the file name. It can also be opened from within Access through the Open command in the File menu or by clicking the Open button on the Database toolbar. The individual objects within a database are opened from the Database window.

1   Introduction to Access

Objective   To open an existing Access database; to add, edit, and delete records within a table in that database; to open forms, queries, and reports within an existing database. Use Figure 1.4 as a guide in the exercise.

Step 1:   **Log on to Windows XP**

- Turn on the computer and all of its peripherals. The floppy drive should be empty prior to starting your machine.

- Your system will take a minute or so to get started, after which you should see the desktop in Figure 1.4a. Do not be concerned if the appearance of your desktop is different from ours.

- Click the icon for the user account you want to access. You may be prompted for a password, depending on the security options in effect.

- You should be familiar with basic file management and be able to copy files from one folder to another. If not, you may want to review this material in the "Getting Started with Microsoft Windows" section in the text.

Click icon for your user account

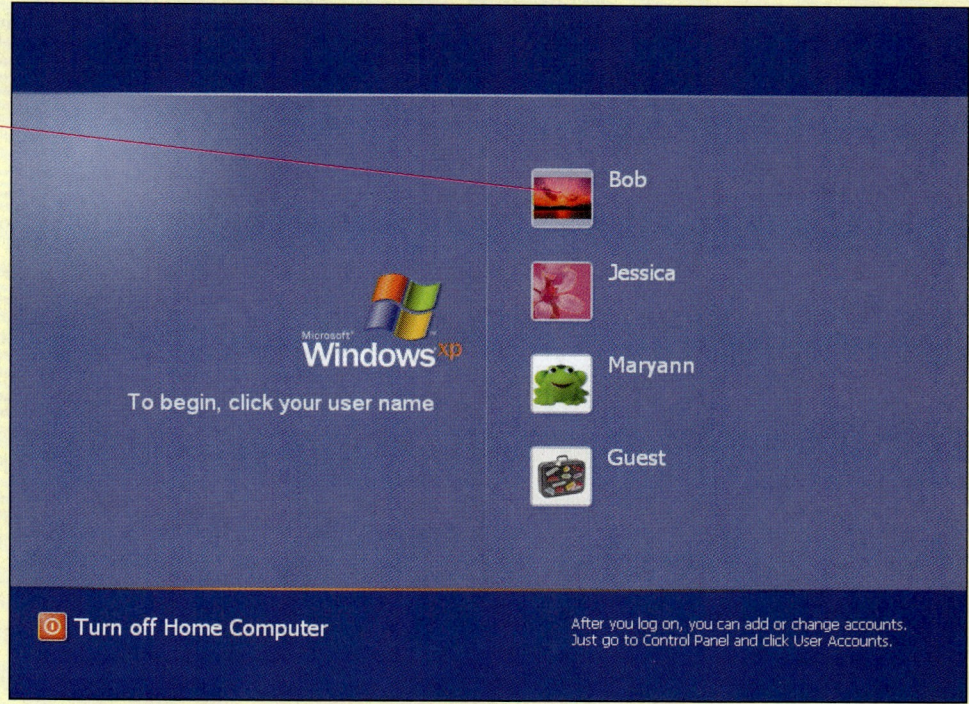

(a) Log onto Windows XP (step 1)

FIGURE 1.4   Hands-on Exercise 1

USER ACCOUNTS

The available user names are created automatically during the installation of Windows XP, but you can add or delete users at any time. Click the Start button, click Control Panel, switch to the Category view, and select User Accounts. Choose the desired task, such as creating a new account or changing an existing account. Do not expect, however, to be able to modify accounts in a school setting.

Step 2: **Obtain the Practice Files**

- Start Internet Explorer, and go to **www.prenhall.com/grauer**. Click the book for **Office 2003**, which takes you to the Office 2003 home page.

- Click the **Student Downloads tab** (near the top of the window) to go to the Student Download page as shown in Figure 1.4b.

- Click the link to download the file for the **Exploring Access 2003 Revised Edition**.

- You will see the File Download box asking what you want to do. Click the **Save button**. The Save As dialog box appears.

- Click the **down arrow** in the Save In list box and select the drive and folder where you want to save the file. Click **Save**.

- Start Windows Explorer, select the drive and folder where you saved the file, then double click the file to follow the onscreen instructions.

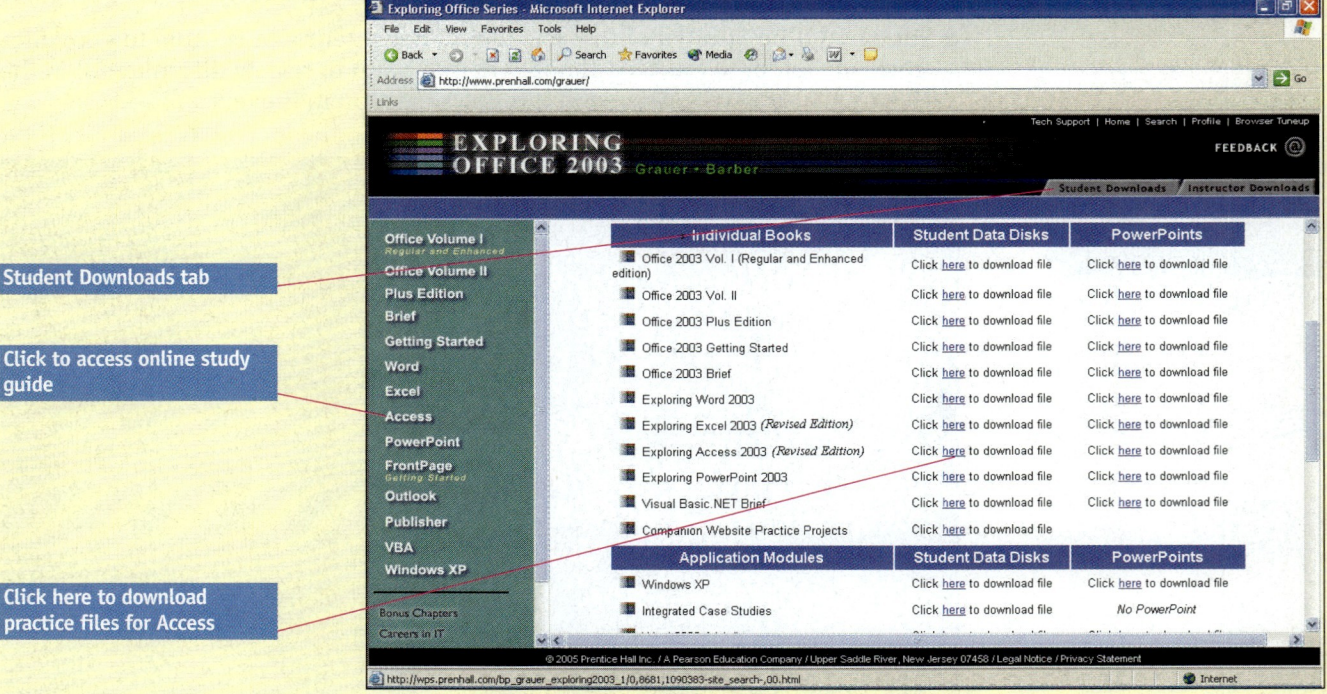

(b) Download the Practice Files (step 2)

FIGURE 1.4 Hands-on Exercise 1 (*continued*)

EXPLORE OUR WEB SITE

The Exploring Office Series Web site offers an online study guide (multiple-choice, true/false, and matching questions) for each individual textbook to help you review the material in each chapter. You can take practice quizzes by yourself and/or e-mail the results to your instructor. These online study guides are available via the tabs in the left navigation bar. You can return to the Student Download page at any time by clicking the tab toward the top of the window and/or you can click the link to Home to return to the home page for the Office 2003 series. And finally, you can click the Feedback button at the top of the screen to send a message directly to Bob Grauer.

Step 3:   **Start Microsoft Access**

- Click the **Start button**, click the **All Programs button**, click **Microsoft Office**, then click **Microsoft Office Access 2003** to start the program.

- Pull down the **File menu** and click the **Open command** to display the Open dialog box in Figure 1.4c. (Do this even if the task pane is open.)

- Click the **down arrow** on the **Views button**, then click **Details** to change to the Details view.

- Click and drag the vertical border between columns to increase (or decrease) the size of a column.

- Click the **drop-down arrow** on the Look In list box. Click the appropriate drive (drive C is recommended rather than drive A) depending on the location of your data. Double click the **Exploring Access folder**.

- Click the down scroll arrow (if needed) to click the **Bookstore database**. Click the **Open command button** to open the database.

- Click the **Open button** within the Security Warning dialog box if you see a warning message saying that the database may contain code to harm your computer. (The message is caused by the programming statements that are behind the command buttons in the various forms within the database.)

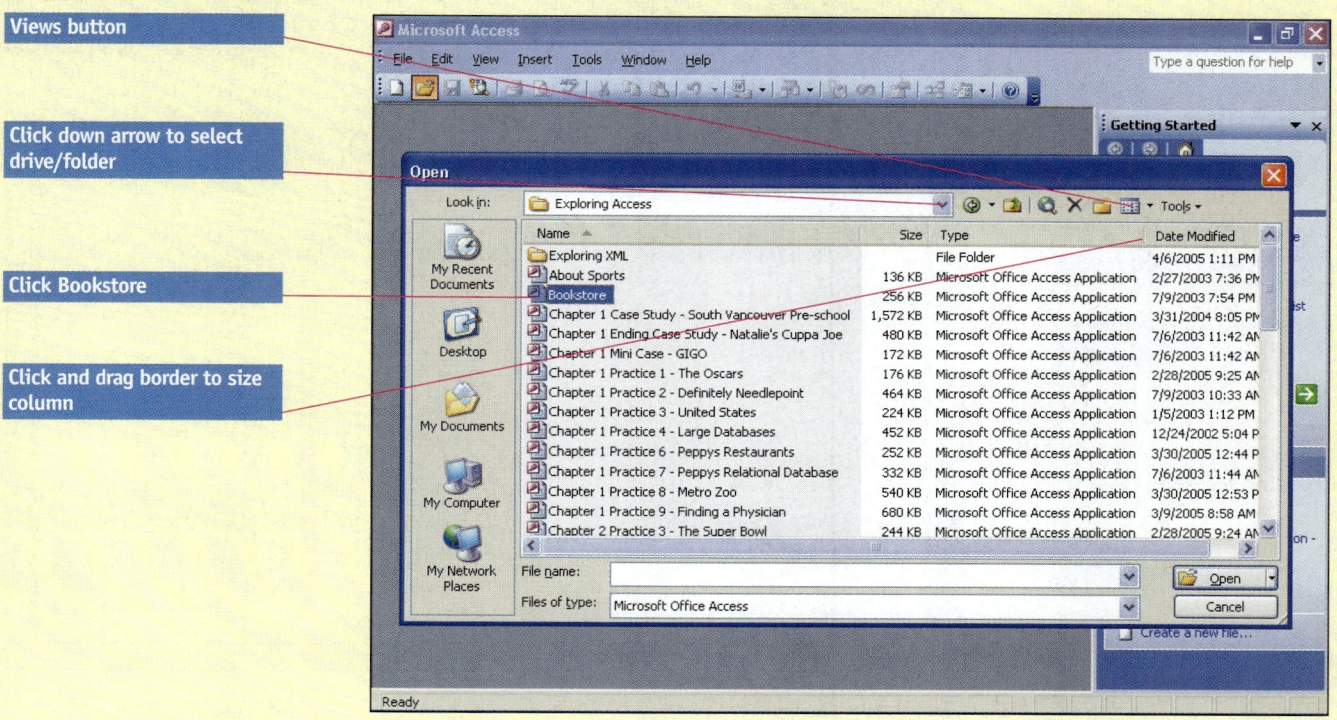

(c) Start Microsoft Access (step 3)

FIGURE 1.4   Hands-on Exercise 1 (*continued*)

FILE FORMATS

Access 2002 (Office XP) introduced a new file format that was continued in Access 2003. Access 2000, however, cannot read the new format, and thus, it is convenient to save files in the Access 2000 format to maintain compatibility with anyone using Microsoft Office 2000. Pull down the Tools menu, click Options, click the Advanced tab, and change the Default File Format to Access 2000.

Step 4: **Open the Books Table**

- If necessary, click the **Maximize button** in the application window so that Access takes the entire desktop.

- You should see the database window for the Bookstore database. Click the **Tables button**. Double click the icon next to Books to open the table as shown in Figure 1.4d.

- Click the **Maximize button** so that the Books table fills the Access window and reduces the clutter on the screen.

- Practice with the navigation buttons above the status bar to move from one record to the next. Click ▶ or ◀ to move forward to the next record or return to the previous record.

- Click |◀ to move to the first record in the table or ▶| to move to the last record in the table.

- Click in any field of the first record. The status indicator at the bottom of the Books table indicates record 1 of 22. The triangle symbol in the record selector column indicates that the record has not changed since it was last saved.

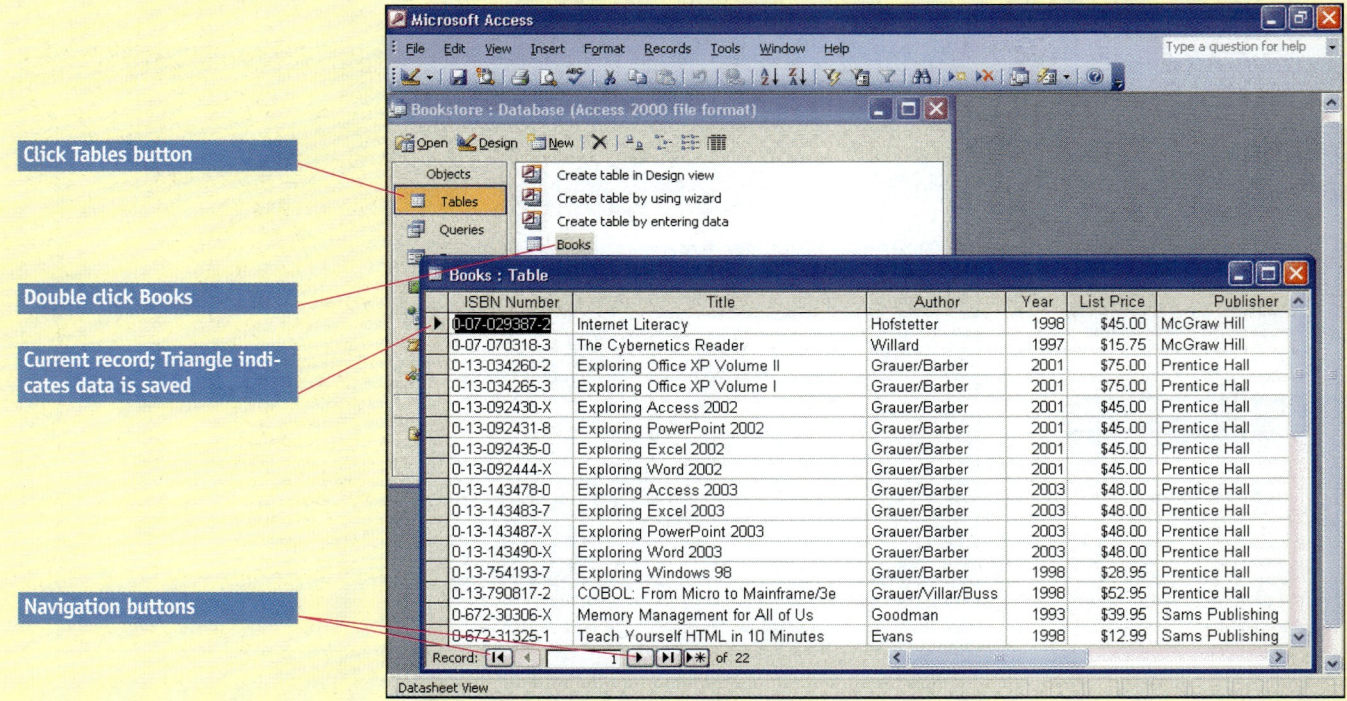

(d) Open the Books Table (step 4)

FIGURE 1.4 Hands-on Exercise 1 (*continued*)

MOVING FROM FIELD TO FIELD

Press the Tab key, the right arrow key, or the Enter key to move to the next field in the current record (or the first field in the next record if you are already in the last field of the current record). Press Shift+Tab or the left arrow key to return to the previous field in the current record (or the last field in the previous record if you are already in the first field of the current record). Press Home or End to move to the first or last field, respectively.

Step 5: Add a New Record

- Pull down the **Insert menu** and click **New Record** (or click the **New Record button** on the Table Datasheet toolbar). The record selector moves to the last record (record 23). The insertion point is positioned in the first field (ISBN Number).

- Enter data for the new book (Exploring Microsoft Office 2003 Volume I) as shown in Figure 1.4e. The record selector changes to a pencil as soon as you enter the first character in the new record.

- Press **Enter** when you have entered the last field for the record. The record has been saved to the database, and the record selector changes to a triangle.

- Add another record. Enter **0-13-143442-X** as the ISBN. The title is **Exploring Microsoft Office 2003 Volume II** by **Grauer/Barber**. The price is **$79.00**. The book was published by **Prentice Hall** in **2003**. Be sure to press **Enter** when you have completed the data entry.

- There are now 24 records in the table.

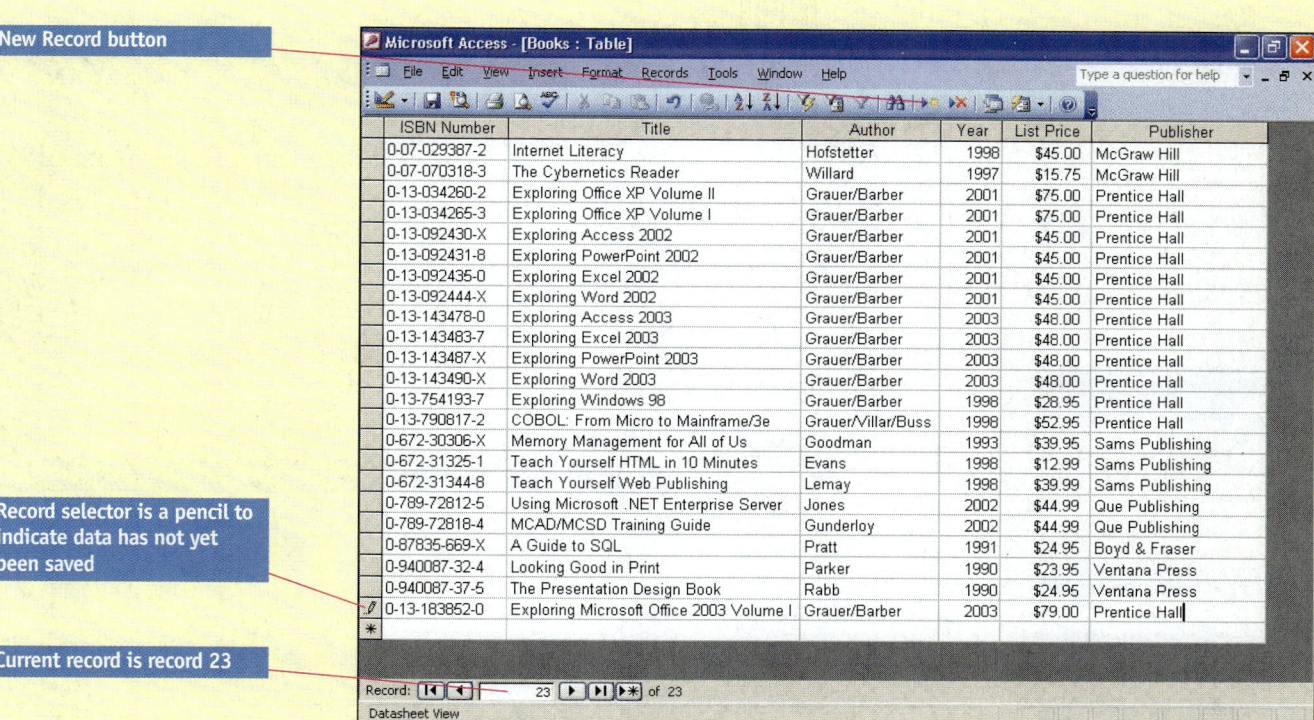

New Record button

Record selector is a pencil to indicate data has not yet been saved

Current record is record 23

(e) Add a New Record (step 5)

FIGURE 1.4   Hands-on Exercise 1 (*continued*)

CREATE YOUR OWN SHORTHAND

Use the AutoCorrect feature that is common to all Office applications to expand abbreviations such as "PH" for Prentice Hall. Pull down the Tools menu, click AutoCorrect Options, type the abbreviation in the Replace text box and the expanded entry in the With text box. Click the Add command button, then click OK to exit the dialog box and return to the document. The next time you type PH (in uppercase) as you enter a record, it will be automatically expanded to Prentice Hall. (This feature may not work in a laboratory setting.)

Step 6: Edit a Record

- Click in the **Title field** for the first record, pull down the **Edit menu**, and click **Find** (or click the **Find button** on the toolbar) to display the dialog box in Figure 1.4f.

- Enter **COBOL** in the Find What text box. Check that the other parameters for the Find command match the dialog box in Figure 1.4f. Be sure that the **Title field** is selected in the Look In list box and **Any Part of Field** is selected in the Match text box.

- Click the **Find Next command button**. Access moves to record 14, the record containing the designated character string, and selects the matching word in the Title field for that record. Click **Cancel** to close the Find dialog box.

- Press the **Tab key** three times to move from the Title field to the Price field (or click directly in the price field). The current price ($52.95) is already selected.

- Type **$58.95**, then press the **down arrow** to move to the next record and save the data. (The changes are saved automatically; i.e., you do not have to click the Save button.)

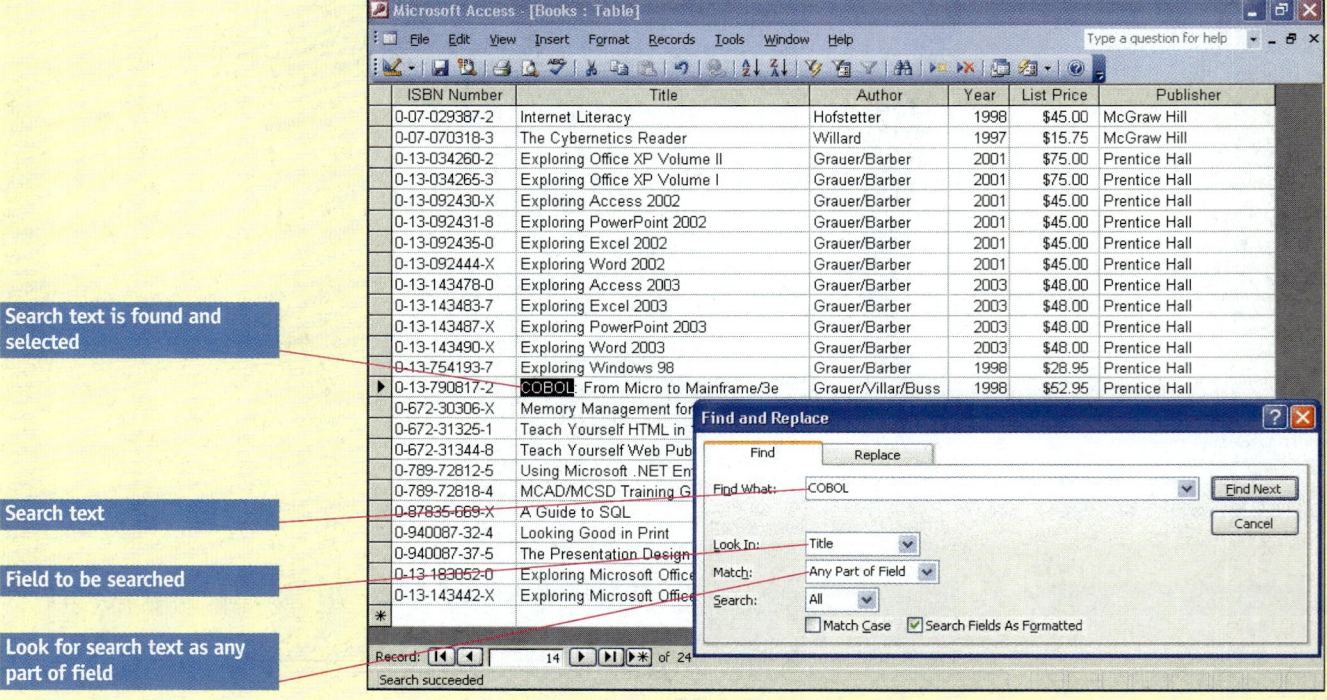

Search text is found and selected

Search text

Field to be searched

Look for search text as any part of field

(f) Edit a Record (step 6)

FIGURE 1.4 Hands-on Exercise 1 (*continued*)

USE WHAT YOU KNOW

The Find command is contained in the Edit menu of every Office application, and it is an ideal way to search for specific records within a table. You have the option to search a single field or the entire record, to match all or part of the selected field(s), to move forward or back in a table, and to specify a case-sensitive search. The Replace command can be used to substitute one value for another. Be careful, however, about using the Replace All option for global replacement because unintended replacements are far too common.

Step 7: Delete a Record

- Use the Find command to search for the book **A Guide to SQL**. (You can click in the Title field, enter "SQL" in the Find What dialog box, then use the same search parameters as in the previous step.)

- The Find command should return the appropriate record, which is *not visible* in Figure 1.4g. (This is because we have deleted the record to display the dialog box in the figure.)

- Pull down the **Edit menu** and click the **Select Record command** to highlight the entire record. You can also click the **record selector column** (the box immediately to the left of the first field) to select the record without having to use a pull-down menu.

- Press the **Del key** (or click the **Delete Record button** on the toolbar) to delete the record. You will see the dialog box in Figure 1.4g indicating that you are about to delete a record and asking you to confirm the deletion. Click **Yes** to delete the record.

- Pull down the **Edit menu**. The Undo command is dim, indicating that you cannot undelete a record. Press **Esc** to continue working.

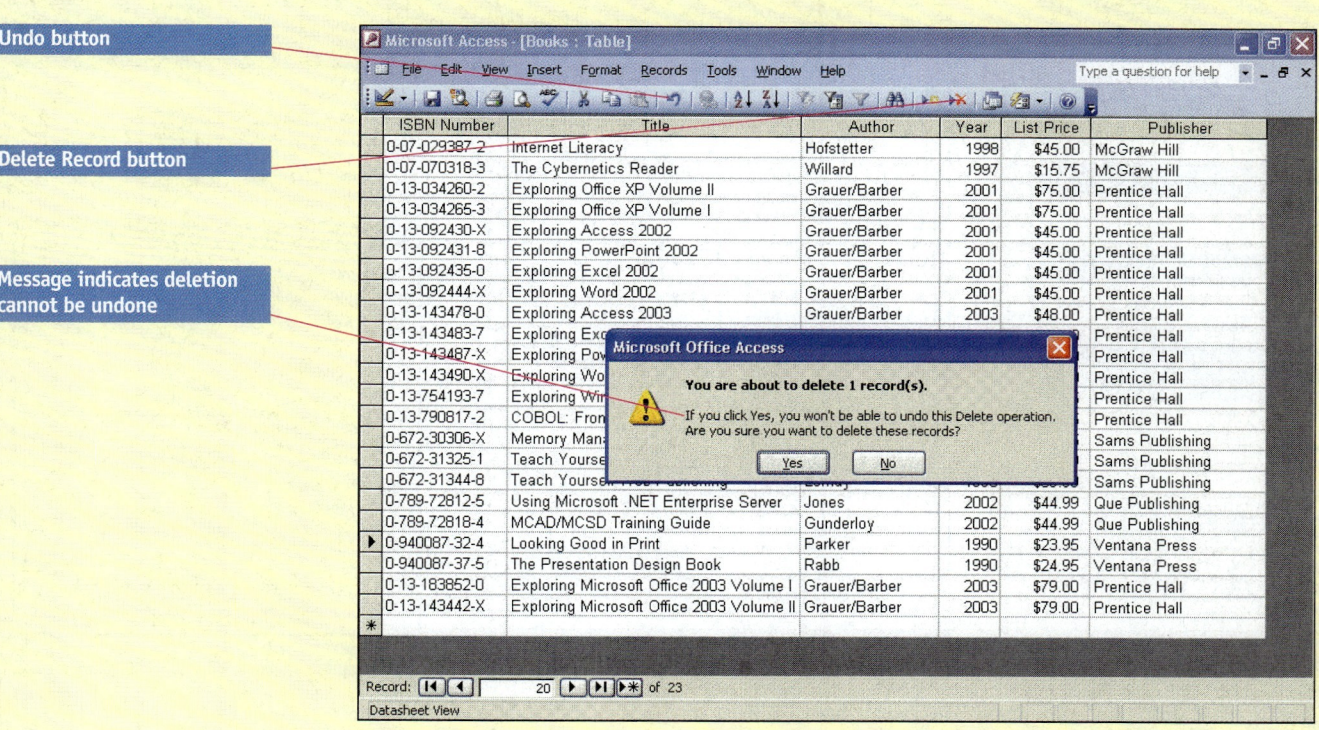

(g) Delete a Record (step 7)

FIGURE 1.4 Hands-on Exercise 1 *(continued)*

THE UNDO COMMAND

The Undo command is common to all Office applications, but it is implemented differently in Access. Word, Excel, and PowerPoint let you undo the last several operations. Access, however, because it saves changes automatically as soon as you move to the next record, lets you undo only the last command that was executed. Even this is limited, because once you delete a record, you cannot undo the deletion; that is, the record is permanently deleted.

Step 8: Print the Table

- Pull down the **File menu** and click the **Print Preview command** to see the table prior to printing. The status bar indicates that you are viewing page 1 (and further, the active scroll buttons indicate that there are additional pages).

- Click the **Setup button** on the Print Preview toolbar to display the Page Setup dialog box as shown in Figure 1.4h.

- Click the **Page tab**. Click the **Landscape option button**. Click **OK** to accept the settings and close the dialog box.

- The table should now fit on one page. (If it still does not fit on one page, click the Setup button on the Print Preview toolbar to display the Page Setup dialog box, click the **Margins tab**, and make the margins smaller.)

- Click the **Print button** to print the table. Alternatively, you can pull down the File menu, click **Print** to display the Print dialog box, click the **All options button**, then click **OK**.

- Click **Close** to close the Print Preview window. Close the table.

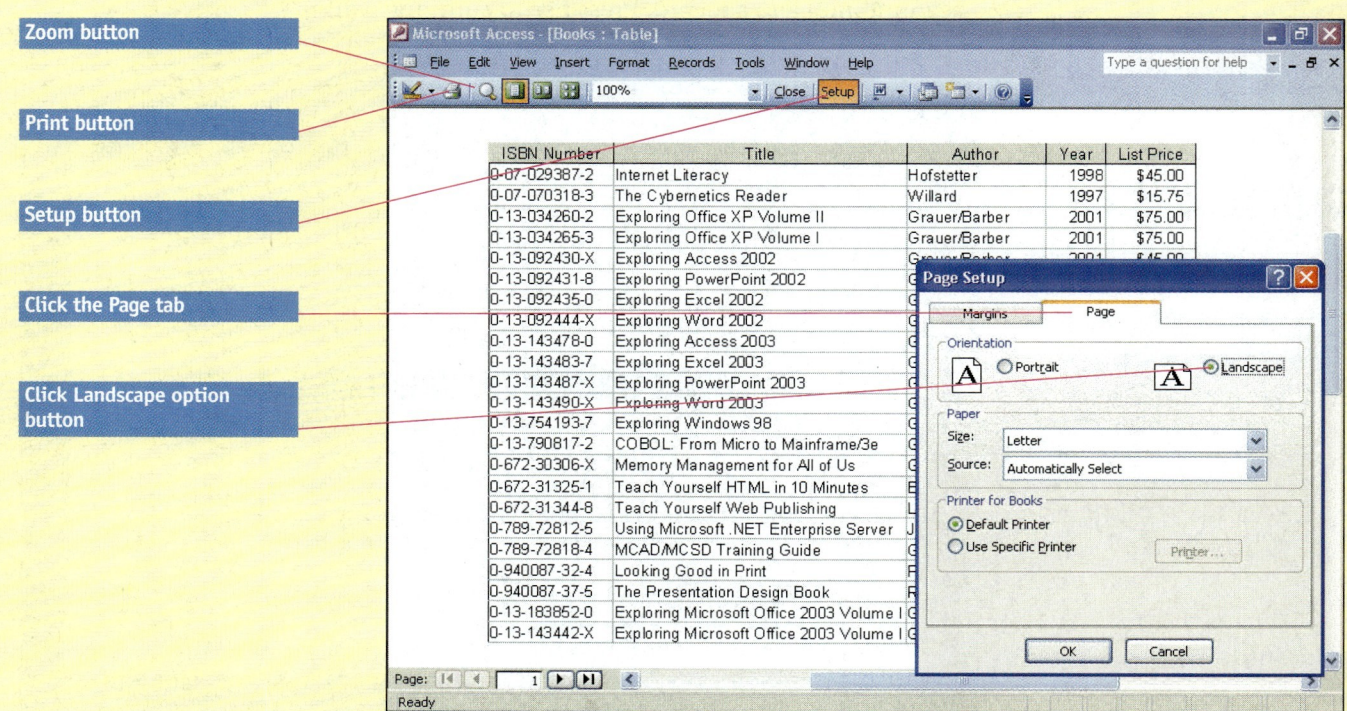

(h) Print the Table (step 8)

FIGURE 1.4 Hands-on Exercise 1 (*continued*)

THE PRINT PREVIEW TOOLBAR

The Print Preview toolbar is displayed automatically when you preview a report prior to printing. Click the Zoom button to toggle back and forth between fitting the entire page in the window and viewing the report at 100% magnification. Click the one, two, and multiple page buttons, to view different portions of the report in reports that extend over multiple pages. Use the Setup button to change the margins and/or orientation. Click the Close button to exit Print Preview.

Step 9: **Open the Books Form**

- Click the **Forms button** in the Database window. Double click the **Books form** to open the form, and if necessary, maximize the form so that it takes the entire window.

- Click the **Add Record command button**, or use the keyboard shortcut, **Alt+A**. (Each command button has a different underlined letter to indicate the keyboard shortcut.)

- Click in the text box for **ISBN number**, then use the **Tab key** to move from field to field as you enter data for the book as shown in Figure 1.4i.

- Enter text in the **Price field** to view the data validation that is built into Access. Click **OK** when you see the error message, then enter the indicated price. Click the **drop-down arrow** on the Publisher's list box to display the available publishers and to select the appropriate one. The use of a combo box ensures that you cannot misspell a publisher's name.

- Click the button to **Print Record** (or press **Alt+P**) to print the form for the record that you just added.

- Close the Books form to return to the Database window.

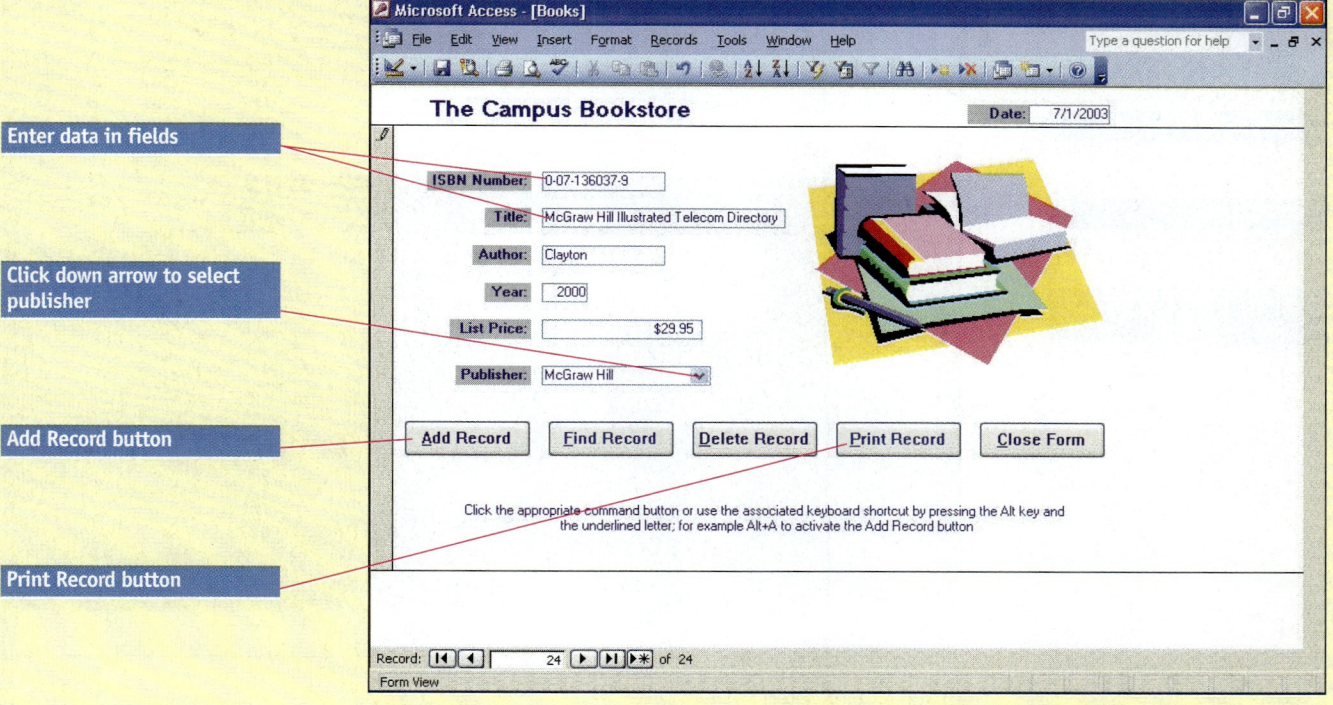

(i) Open the Books Form (step 9)

FIGURE 1.4 Hands-on Exercise 1 (*continued*)

DATA VALIDATION

No system, no matter how sophisticated, can produce valid output from invalid input. Thus, good systems are built to anticipate errors in data entry and to reject those errors prior to saving a record. Access will automatically prevent you from adding records with a duplicate primary key or entering invalid data into a numeric or date field. Other types of validation, such as requiring the author's name, are implemented by the database developer.

Step 10: **Run a Query**

■ Click the **Queries button** in the Database window. Double click the **Publisher query** to run the query. You will see a dialog box asking you to enter the name of a publisher.

■ Type **McGraw Hill** and press **Enter** to see the results of the query, which should contain three books by this publisher. (If you do not see any books, it is because you spelled the publisher incorrectly. Close the query to return to the Database window, then rerun the query.)

■ You can use a query to display information, as was just done, and/or you can modify data in the underlying table. Click in the **Publisher field** for the blank record in the last row (the record selector is an asterisk). Type **McGraw Hill** to begin entering the data for a new record as shown in Figure 1.4j.

■ You can enter data for any publisher within the query, but you must satisfy the requirements for data validation. See what happens if you omit the ISBN number or Author's name, or enter alphabetic data for the year or price. (The missing ISBN is **0-07-561585-1**.)

■ Click the **Close button** to close the query and return to the Database window.

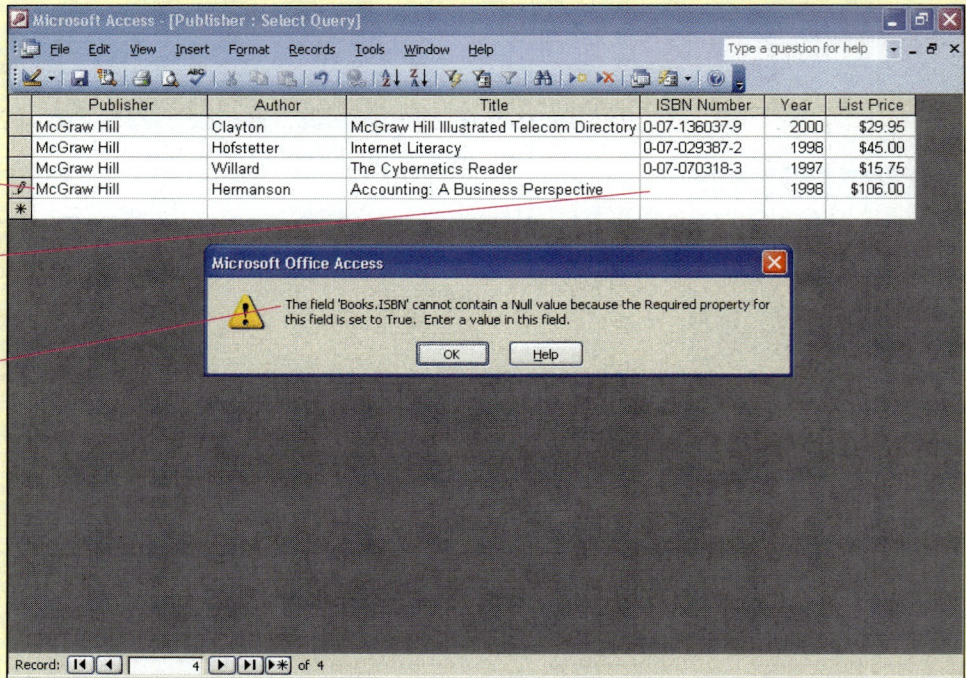

Enter data for a new book

Omit ISBN Number

Message indicates ISBN number is required

(j) Run a Query (step 10)

FIGURE 1.4 Hands-on Exercise 1 (*continued*)

FORMAT A DATASHEET

Format your tables and/or queries to make the results stand out. Click anywhere in a table or query (in Datasheet view), pull down the Format menu, and click the Datasheet command to display the Format Datasheet dialog box. You can change the style of the table to sunken or raised, change the color of the gridlines or suppress them altogether. The Format command also enables you to change the row height or column width and/or to hide columns. See practice exercise 4 at the end of the chapter.

Step 11: Open a Report

- Click the **Reports button** in the Database window to display the available reports. Double click the icon for the **Publisher report**. Type **McGraw Hill** in the Parameter dialog box. Press **Enter**.

- Click the **Maximize button** in the Report Window so that the report takes the entire screen as shown in Figure 1.4k.

- Click the **Zoom button** to toggle to 100% so that you can read the report, which should contain four records.

- Two books were in the original database. One book was entered through a form in step 9. The other book was entered through a query in step 10. All of the books in the report are published by McGraw Hill, which is consistent with the parameter you entered at the beginning of this step.

- Click the **Print button** on the Report toolbar. Click the **Close button** to close the Report window.

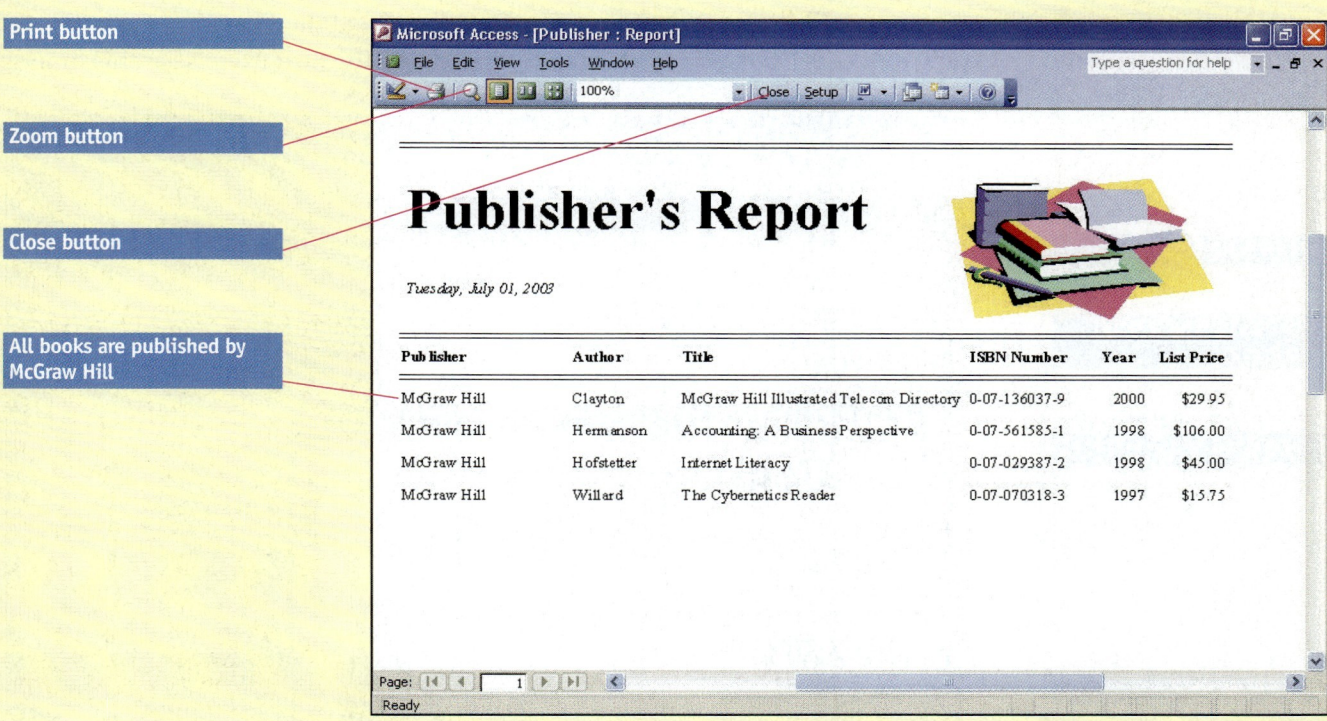

Print button

Zoom button

Close button

All books are published by McGraw Hill

(k) Open a Report (step 11)

FIGURE 1.4 Hands-on Exercise 1 (*continued*)

TIP OF THE DAY

Pull down the Help menu, click the command to Show the Office Assistant, click the Office Assistant when it appears, then click the Options button to display the Office Assistant dialog box. Click the Options tab, check the box to Show the Tip of the Day at Startup, and then click OK. The next time you start Access, you will be greeted by the Assistant, who will offer you the tip of the day. (You can display a Tip of the Day for the other Office applications in similar fashion.)

Step 12: Help with Access

- There are several different ways to request help, but in any event, the best time to obtain help is when you don't need any. Try any of the following:
  - ❑ Pull down the **Help menu** and click the command to **Show the Office Assistant**. Click the **Assistant**, then enter the question, "**What is a table?**" in the Assistant's balloon and click **Search**, or
  - ❑ Type the question directly in the **Ask a Question list box** in the upper right of the Access window and press **Enter**, or
  - ❑ Pull down the **Help menu**, click **Microsoft Access Help** to display the task pane, enter the question in the **Search box**, and click the **Start Searching arrow**.

- Regardless of the technique you choose, Access will display a message indicating that it is searching Microsoft Office Online. (Help is not available locally, and this can be a problem with a slow Internet connection.)

- You should see a task pane with the results of the search as shown in Figure 1.4l. Click the link that is most appropriate (e.g., **About tables** in this example).

- A new window opens containing the detailed help information. Close the Help window. Close the task pane. Hide the Office Assistant.

- Exit Access if you do not want to continue with the next exercise at this time.

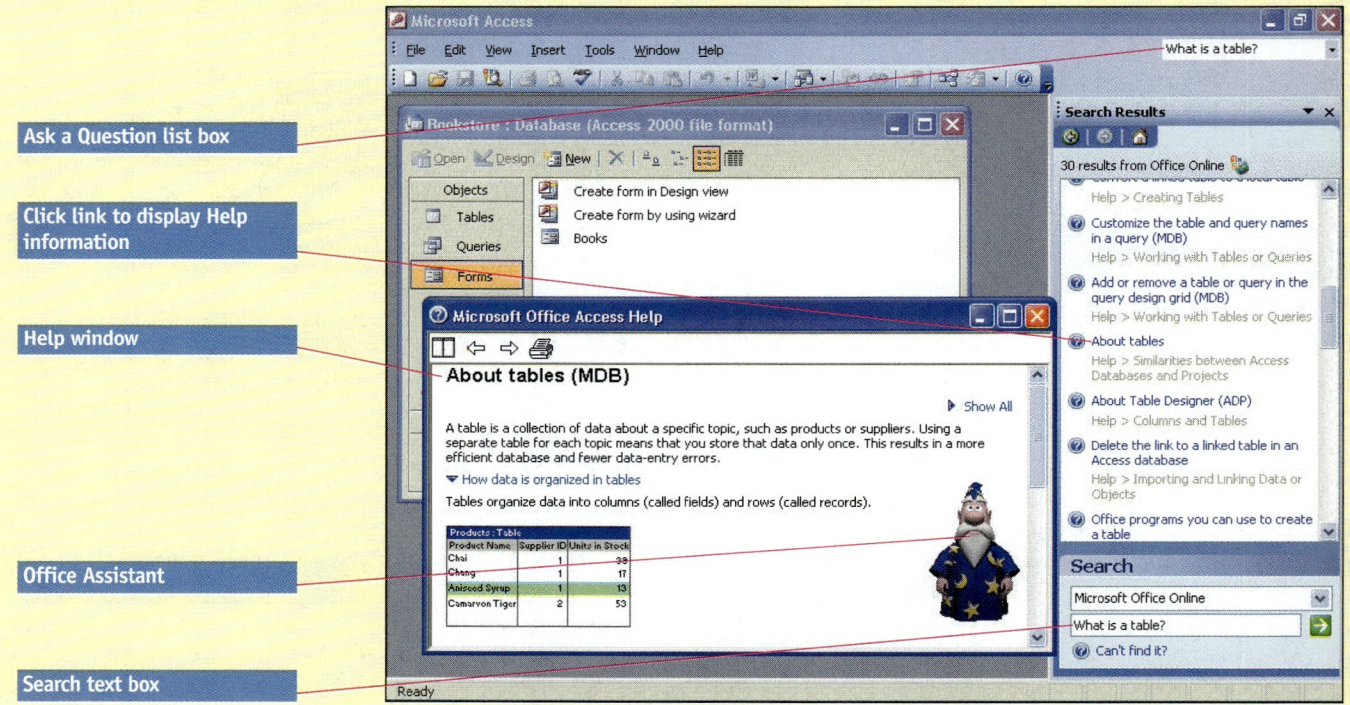

Ask a Question list box

Click link to display Help information

Help window

Office Assistant

Search text box

(l) Help with Access (step 12)

FIGURE 1.4   Hands-on Exercise 1 (*continued*)

CHOOSE YOUR OWN ASSISTANT

Pull down the Help menu, click the command to Show the Office Assistant, click the Office Assistant when it appears, then click the Options button to display the Office Assistant dialog box. Click the Gallery tab, then click the Next button repeatedly to cycle through the available characters. Click OK to accept the character of your choice. You're still in control, however. Pull down the Help menu and click the command to Hide the Office Assistant if it becomes annoying.

The exercise just completed described how to use an existing report to obtain information from the database. But what if you are in a hurry and don't have the time to create the report? There is a faster way. You can open the table in the Datasheet view, then apply a filter and/or a sort to the table to display selected records in any order. A ***filter*** displays a subset of records from the table according to specified criteria. A ***sort*** lists those records in a specific sequence, such as alphabetically by last name or by EmployeeID. We illustrate both of these concepts in conjunction with Figure 1.5.

Figure 1.5a displays an employee table with 14 records. Each record has 8 fields. The records in the table are displayed in sequence according to the EmployeeID, which is also the primary key (the field or combination of fields that uniquely identifies a record). The status bar indicates that there are 14 records in the table. What if, however, you wanted a partial list of those records, such as employees with a specific title?

Figure 1.5b displays a filtered view of the same table in which we see only the Account Reps. The status bar shows that this is a filtered list, and that there are 8 records that satisfy the criteria. (The employee table still contains the original 14 records, but only 8 records are visible with the filter in effect.) The table has also been sorted so that the selected employees are displayed in alphabetical order, as opposed to EmployeeID order.

Two operations are necessary to go from Figure 1.5a to Figure 1.5b—filtering and sorting, and they can be performed in either order. The easiest way to implement a filter is to click in any cell that contains the value of the desired criterion (such as any cell that contains "Account Rep" in the Title field), then click the ***Filter by Selection*** button on the Database toolbar. To sort the table, click in the field on which you want to sequence the records (the LastName field in this example), then click the ***Sort Ascending*** button on the Database toolbar. The ***Sort Descending*** button is appropriate for numeric fields such as salary, if you want to display the records with the highest value listed first.

The operations can be done in any order; that is, you can filter a table to show only selected records, then you can sort the filtered table to display the records in a different order. Conversely, you can sort a table and then apply a filter. It does not matter which operation is performed first, and indeed, you can go back and forth between the two. You can also filter the table further, by applying a second (or third) criterion; for example, click in a cell containing "Good," then click the Filter by Selection button a second time to display the Account Reps with good performance. You can also click the ***Remove Filter*** button at any time to display all of the records in the complete table.

Figure 1.5c illustrates an alternate and more powerful way to apply a filter known as ***Filter by Form***, in which you can select the criteria from a drop-down list, and/or apply multiple criteria simultaneously. However, the real advantage of the Filter by Form command extends beyond these conveniences to two additional capabilities. First, you can specify relationships within a criterion; for example, you can select employees with a salary greater than (or less than) $40,000. Filter by Selection, on the other hand, requires you to specify criteria equal to an existing value. Figure 1.5d displays the filtered table of Chicago employees earning more than $40,000.

A second advantage of the Filter by Form command is that you can specify alternative criteria (such as employees in Chicago *or* employees who are account reps) by clicking the Or tab. (The latter capability is not implemented in Figure 1.5.) Suffice it to say, however, that the availability of the various filter and sort commands enables you to obtain information from a database quickly and easily without having to create a query or report.

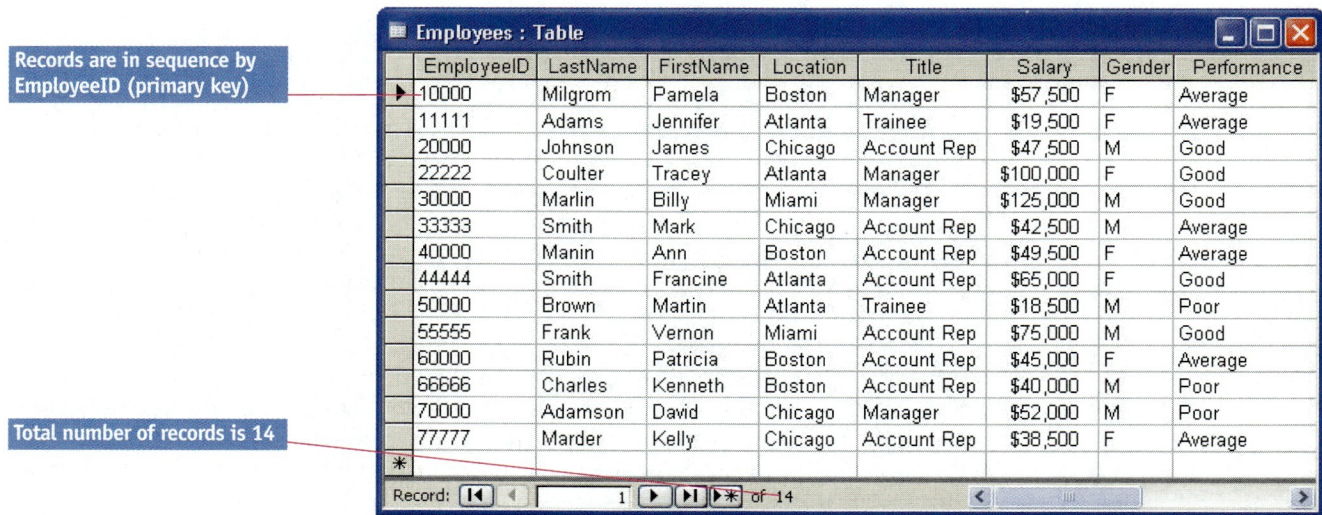

Records are in sequence by EmployeeID (primary key)

Total number of records is 14

(a) The Employees Table (by EmployeeID)

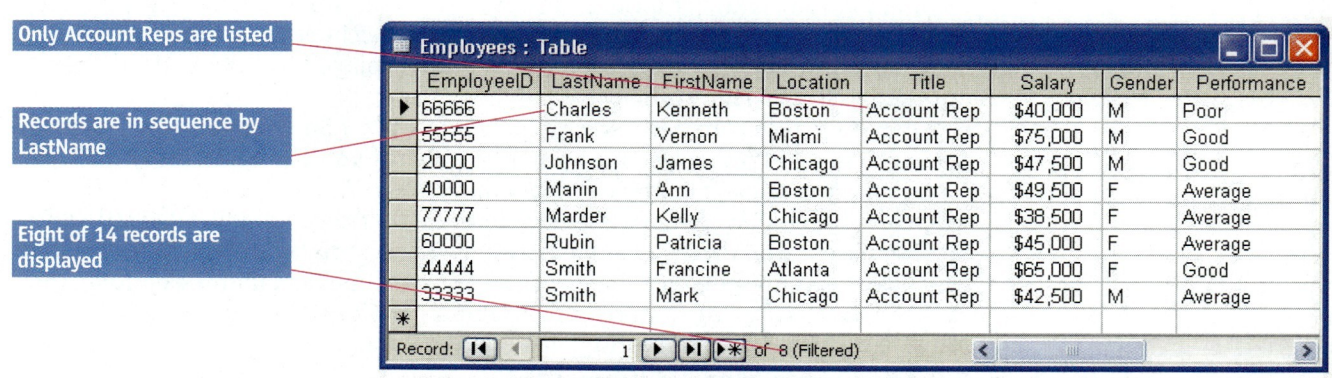

Only Account Reps are listed

Records are in sequence by LastName

Eight of 14 records are displayed

(b) Filtered List (Account Rep by last name)

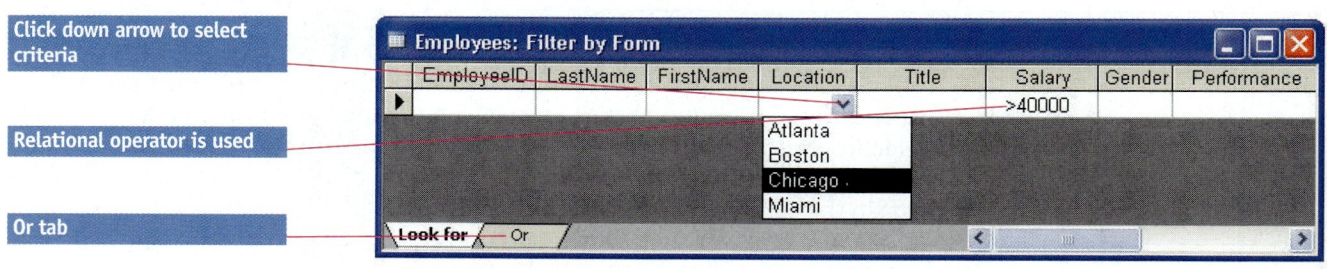

Click down arrow to select criteria

Relational operator is used

Or tab

(c) Filter by Form

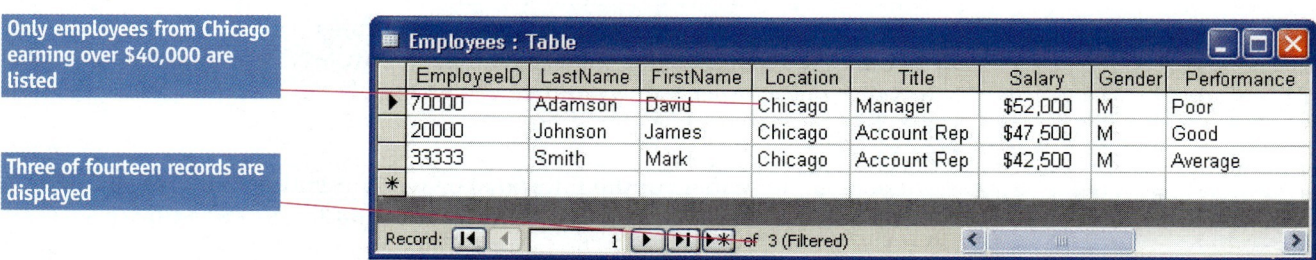

Only employees from Chicago earning over $40,000 are listed

Three of fourteen records are displayed

(d) Filtered List (Chicago employees earning more than $40,000)

FIGURE 1.5 Filters and Sorting

2   Filters and Sorting

Objective   To display selected records within a table by applying the Filter by Selection and Filter by Form criteria; to sort the records in a table. Use Figure 1.6 as a guide in the exercise.

Step 1:   **Open the Employees Table**

- Start Access as you did in the previous exercise, but this time you will open a different database. Pull down the **File menu** and click the **Open command** to display the Open dialog box.

- Click the **down arrow** in the Look In box to select the drive (**drive C** is recommended rather than drive A) and folder (**Exploring Access**) that contains the **Employee database**.

- Click the **Open button** in the Open dialog box to open the database, then click the **Open button** within the Security Warning dialog box if you see a warning message.

- Click the **Forms button** in the Database window, then double click the **Employees form** to open the form as shown in Figure 1.6a. Click the **Maximize button** so that the Employee form fills the Access window.

- Click the **Add Record button**, then enter data for yourself, using **12345** as the EmployeeID, and your first and last name. You have been hired as an **Account Rep**. Your salary is **$40,000**, you will work in **Miami**, and your performance is **Good**.

- Click the **Print Record button** to print the record containing your data. Click the **Close Form button** to return to the Database window.

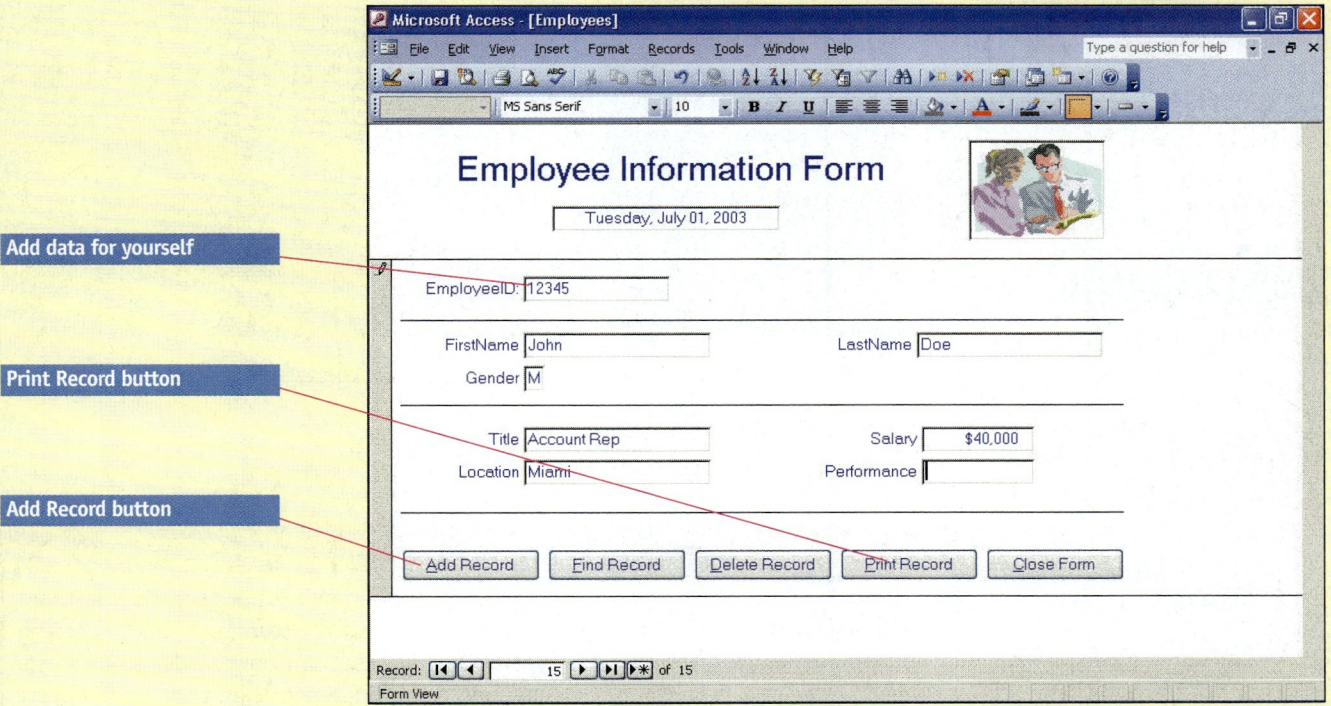

(a) Open the Employees Table (step 1)

FIGURE 1.6   Hands-on Exercise 2

Step 2: **Filter by Selection**

- Click the **Tables button** in the Database window. Double click the **Employees table** to open the table, which should contain 15 records, including the record you added for yourself.

- Click in the Title field of any record that contains the title **Account Rep**, then click the **Filter by Selection button**.

- You should see 9 employees, all of whom are Account Reps, as shown in Figure 1.6b. The status bar indicates that there are 9 records (as opposed to 15) and that there is a filter condition in effect.

- Click in the performance field of any employee with a Good performance (we clicked in the Performance field of the first record), then click the **Filter by Selection button** a second time.

- This time you see 4 employees, each of whom is an Account Rep with a performance evaluation of Good. The status bar indicates that 4 records satisfy this filter condition.

- Click the **Print button** to print the filtered table.

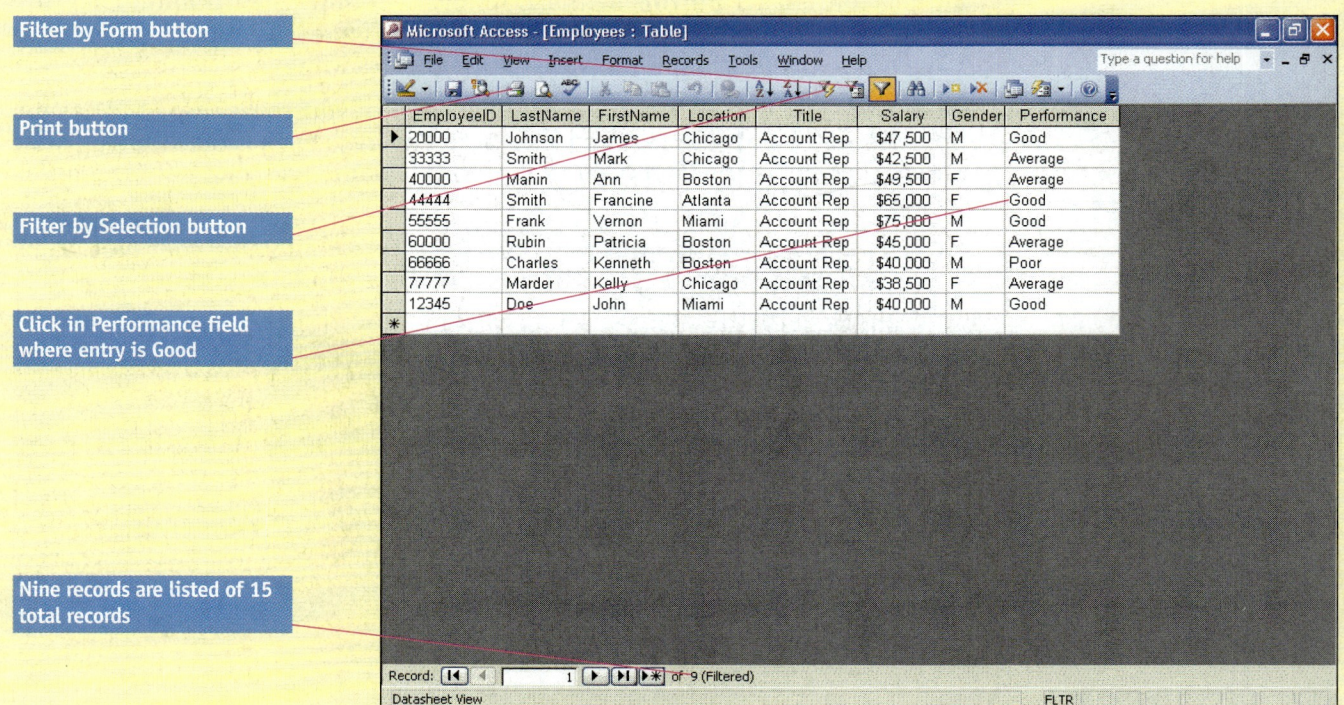

(b) Filter by Selection (step 2)

FIGURE 1.6 Hands-on Exercise 2 (*continued*)

FILTER EXCLUDING SELECTION

The Filter by Selection button on the Database toolbar selects all records that meet the designated criterion. The Filter Excluding Selection command does just the opposite and displays all records that do not satisfy the criterion. First, click the Remove Filter button to remove any filters that are in effect, then click in the appropriate field of any record that contains the value you want to exclude. Pull down the Records menu, click (or point to) the Filter command, then click the Filter Excluding Selection command to display the records that do not meet the criterion.

Step 3:   **Filter by Form**

- Click the **Filter by Form button** to display the form in Figure 1.6c, where you can enter or remove criteria in any sequence. Each time you click in a field, a drop-down list appears that displays all of the values for the field that occur within the table.

- Click in the columns for **Title** and **Performance** to remove the criteria that were entered in the previous step. Select the existing entries individually and press the **Del key** as each entry is selected.

- Click in the cell underneath the **Salary field** and type **>30000** (as opposed to selecting a specific value). Click in the cell underneath the **Location Field**, click the **down arrow**, and select **Chicago**.

- Click the **Apply Filter button** to display the records that satisfy these criteria. (You should see 4 records.)

- Click the **Print button** to print the table.

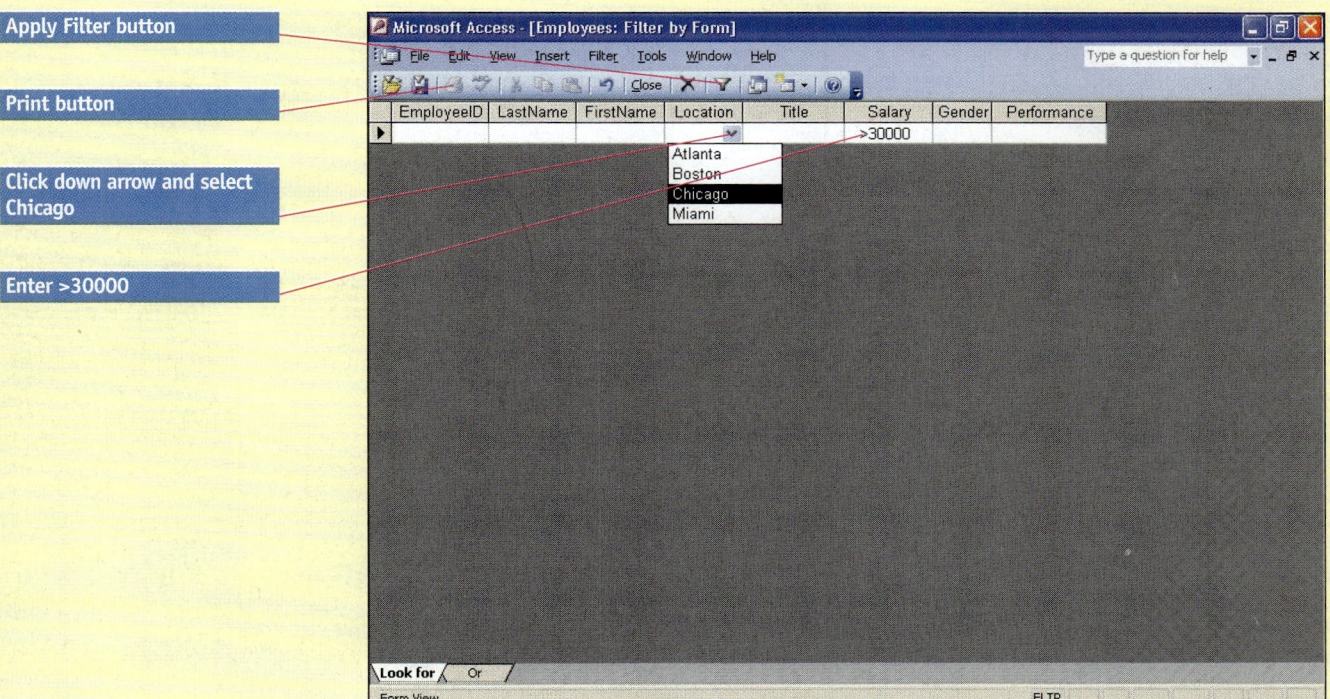

(c) Filter by Form (step 3)

FIGURE 1.6   Hands-on Exercise 2 (*continued*)

FILTER BY FORM VERSUS FILTER BY SELECTION

The Filter by Form command has all of the capabilities of the Filter by Selection command, and provides two additional capabilities. First, you can use relational operators such as >, >=, <, or <=, as opposed to searching for an exact value. Second, you can search for records that meet one of several conditions (the equivalent of an "Or" operation). Enter the first criterion as you normally would, then click the Or tab at the bottom of the window to display a second form in which you enter the alternate criteria. (To delete an alternate criterion, click the associated tab, then click the Delete button on the toolbar.)

Step 4: Sort the Table

■ Click the **Remove Filter button** to display the complete table, which contains 15 employee records.

■ Click in the **LastName field** of any record, then click the **Sort Ascending button**. The records are displayed in alphabetical (ascending) order by last name as shown in Figure 1.6d.

■ Click in the **Salary field** of any record, then click the **Sort Descending button**. The records are in descending order of salary; that is, the employee with the highest salary is listed first.

■ Click in the **Location field** of any record, then click the **Sort Ascending button** to display the records by location, although the employees within a location are not in any specific order.

■ You can sort on two fields at the same time, provided the fields are next to each other, as described in the next step.

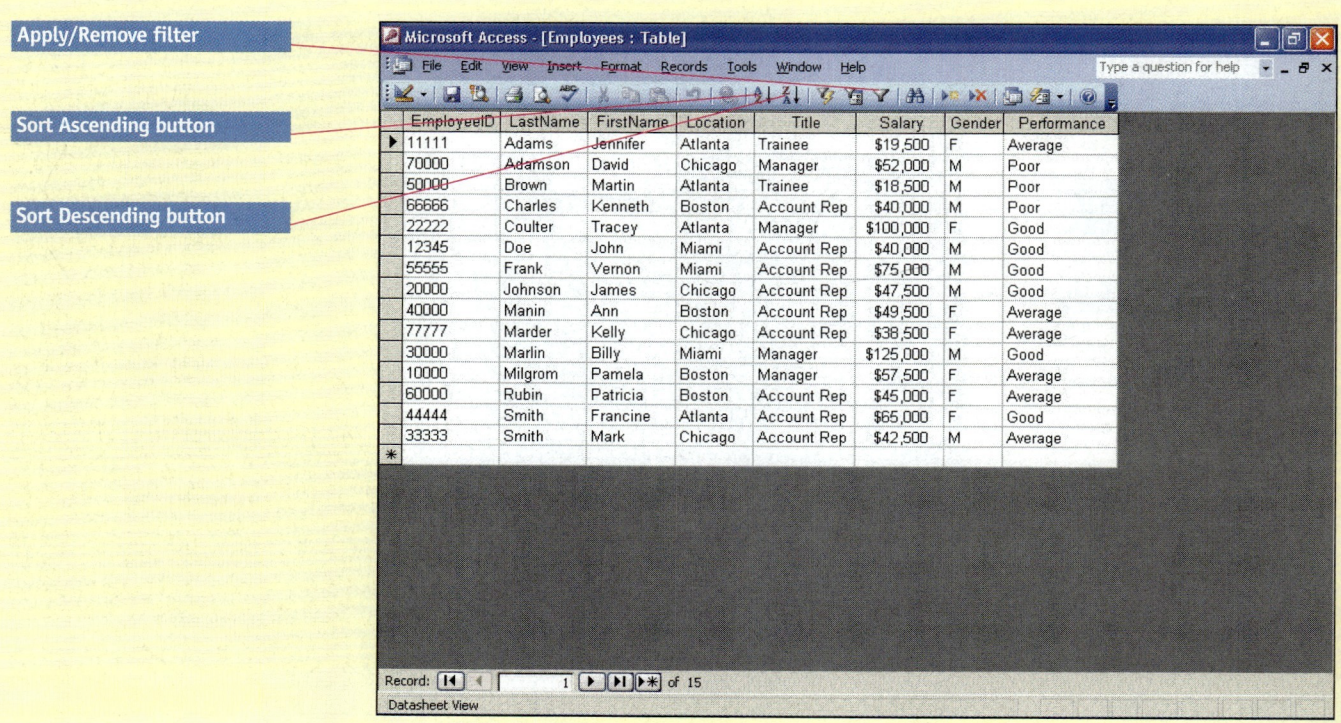

Apply/Remove filter

Sort Ascending button

Sort Descending button

(d) Sort the Table (step 4)

FIGURE 1.6 Hands-on Exercise 2 (*continued*)

THE SORT OR FILTER—WHICH IS FIRST?

It doesn't matter whether you sort a table and then apply a filter, or filter first and then sort. The operations are cumulative. Thus, once a table has been sorted, any subsequent display of filtered records for that table will be in the specified sequence. Alternatively, you can apply a filter, then sort the filtered table by clicking in the desired field and clicking the appropriate sort button. Remember, too, that all filter commands are cumulative, and hence you must remove the filter to see the original table.

Step 5: **Sort on Two Fields**

- Click the header for the **Location field** to select the entire column. Click and drag the **Location header** so that the Location field is moved to the left of the LastName field.

- Click anywhere to deselect the column, then click on the **Location header** and click and drag to select both the Location header and the LastName Header as shown in Figure 1.6e.

- Click the **Sort Ascending button**. The records are sorted by location and alphabetically within location. (You could extend the sort to three fields such as Location, LastName, and FirstName by selecting all three fields prior to clicking the Sort button.)

- Print the table for your instructor. Close the table, saving the changes when prompted to do so.

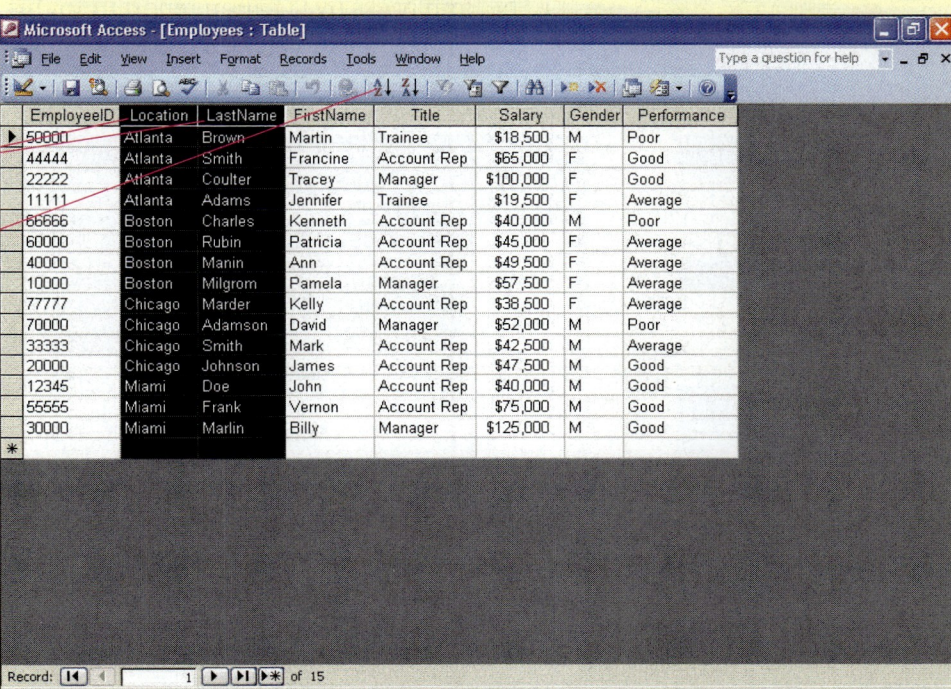

Click Location header area and drag to select LastName as well

Sort Ascending button

(e) Sort on Two Fields (step 5)

FIGURE 1.6 Hands-on Exercise 2 (*continued*)

REMOVING VERSUS DELETING A FILTER

Removing a filter displays all of the records that are in a table, but it does not delete the filter because the filter is stored permanently with the table. To delete the filter entirely is more complicated than simply removing it. Pull down the Records menu, click Filter, then click the Advanced Filter/Sort command to display a grid containing the criteria for the filter. Clear the Sort and Criteria rows by clicking in any cell containing an entry and deleting that entry, then click the Apply Filter button when all cells are clear to return to the Datasheet view. The Apply Filter button should be dim, indicating that the table does not contain a filter.

Step 6: Print a Report

- Click the **Reports button** in the Database window. Double click the icon for **Employees by Location report**.

- Click the **Maximize button** in the Report Window so that the report takes the entire screen as shown in Figure 1.6f.

- Click the **Zoom button** to toggle to 100% so that you can read the report. The report displays the employees in the same order as the sorted table from step 5. (The sequence for the report is contained in its design specification and does not depend on the sequence of the underlying table.)

- Click the **Print button** on the Report toolbar to print the report for your instructor. Submit all of the printed information to your instructor:
  - ❏ The employee form from step 1
  - ❏ The filtered table from steps 2 and 3
  - ❏ The sorted table from step 5
  - ❏ The Employees by Location report from this step

- Close the report. Exit Access if you do not want to continue with the next exercise at this time.

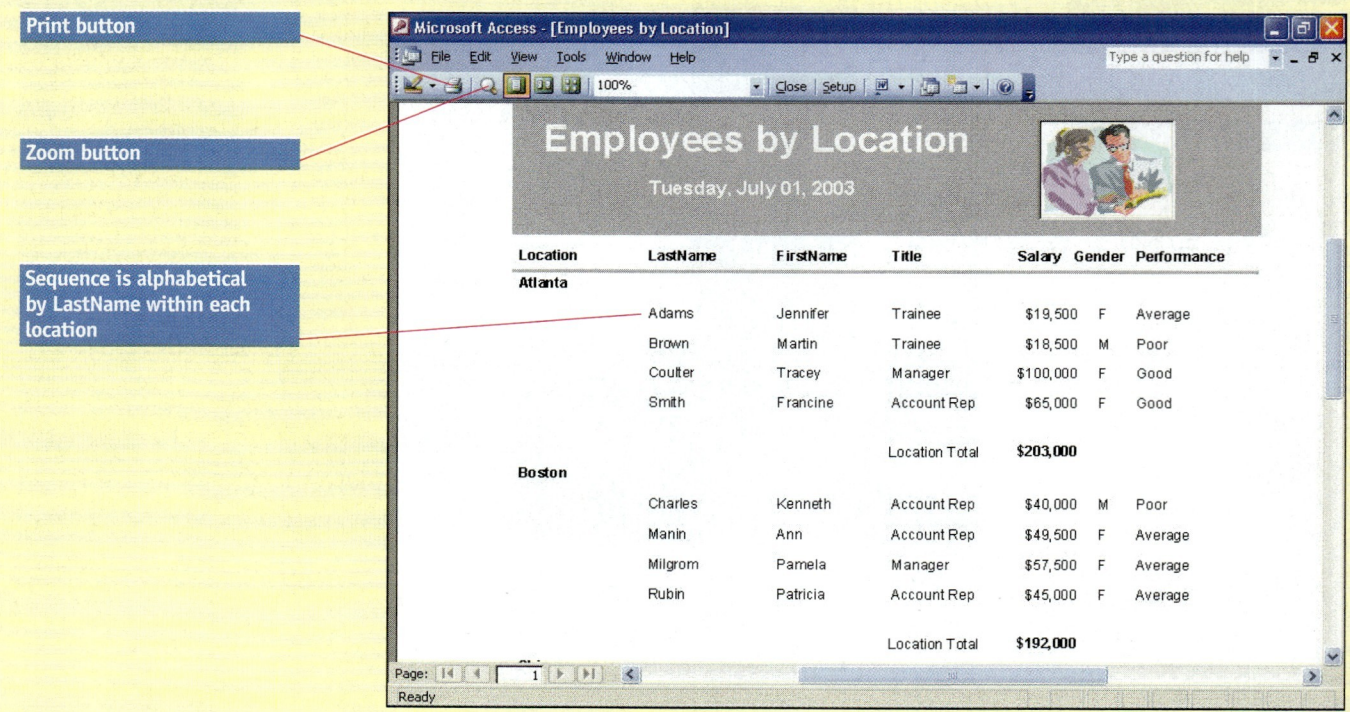

Print button

Zoom button

Sequence is alphabetical by LastName within each location

(f) Print a Report (step 6)

FIGURE 1.6 Hands-on Exercise 2 (*continued*)

DATA VERSUS INFORMATION

Data and information are not synonymous although the terms are often used interchangeably. Data is the raw material and consists of the table (or tables) that comprise a database. Information is the finished product. Data is converted to information by selecting (filtering) records, by sequencing (sorting) the selected records, and/or by summarizing data from multiple records. Decisions in an organization are based on information that is compiled from multiple records, as opposed to raw data.

LOOKING AHEAD: A RELATIONAL DATABASE

The Bookstore and Employee databases are both examples of simple databases in that they each contained only a single table. The real power of Access, however, is derived from multiple tables and the relationships between those tables. This type of database is known as a ***relational database*** and is illustrated in Figure 1.7. This figure expands the original Employee database by adding two tables, for locations and titles, respectively.

The Employees table in Figure 1.7a is the same table we used at the beginning of the previous exercise, except for the substitution of a LocationID and TitleID for the location and title, respectively. The Locations table in Figure 1.7b has all of the fields that pertain to each location: LocationID, Location, Address, State, Zipcode, and OfficePhone. One field, the LocationID, appears in both Employees and Locations tables and links the two tables to one another. In similar fashion, the Titles table in Figure 1.7c has the information for each title: the TitleID, Title, Description, EducationRequired, and Minimum and MaximumSalary. The TitleID appears in both the Employees and Titles tables to link those tables to one another.

EmployeeID	LastName	FirstName	LocationID	TitleID	Salary	Gender	Performance
10000	Milgrom	Pamela	L02	T02	$57,500	F	Average
11111	Adams	Jennifer	L01	T03	$19,500	F	Average
20000	Johnson	James	L03	T01	$47,500	M	Good
22222	Coulter	Tracey	L01	T02	$100,000	F	Good
30000	Marlin	Billy	L04	T02	$125,000	M	Good
33333	Smith	Mark	L03	T01	$42,500	M	Average
40000	Manin	Ann	L02	T01	$49,500	F	Average
44444	Smith	Francine	L01	T01	$65,000	F	Good
50000	Brown	Mark	L01	T03	$18,500	M	Poor
55555	Frank	Vernon	L04	T01	$75,000	M	Good
60000	Rubin	Patricia	L02	T01	$45,000	F	Average
66666	Charles	Kenneth	L02	T01	$40,000	M	Poor
70000	Adamson	David	L03	T02	$52,000	M	Poor
77777	Marder	Kelly	L03	T01	$38,500	F	Average

(a) The Employees Table

LocationID	Location	Address	State	Zipcode	OfficePhone
L01	Atlanta	450 Peachtree Road	GA	30316	(404) 333-5555
L02	Boston	3 Commons Blvd	MA	02190	(617) 123-4444
L03	Chicago	500 Loop Highway	IL	60620	(312) 444-6666
L04	Miami	210 Biscayne Blvd	FL	33103	(305) 787-9999

(b) The Locations Table

TitleID	Title	Description	EducationRequired	MinimumSalary	MaximumSalary
T01	Account Rep	A marketing ...	Four year degree	$25,000	$75,000
T02	Manager	A supervisory ...	Four year degree	$50,000	$150,000
T03	Trainee	An entry-level ...	Two year degree	$18,000	$25,000

(c) The Titles Table

FIGURE 1.7 A Relational Database

To obtain information about a specific employee's title or location, you go to the Employees table, then use the LocationID and TitleID to locate the appropriate records in the Locations and Titles tables, respectively. The tables are color coded to emphasize the relationships between them. It sounds complicated, but it is really quite simple and very elegant. More importantly, it enables you to obtain detailed information about any employee, location, or title. To show how it works, we will ask a series of questions that require you to look in one or more tables for the answer. Consider:

Query: At which location does Pamela Milgrom work? What is the phone number of her office?

Answer: Pamela works in the Boston office, at 3 Commons Blvd., Boston, MA, 02190. The phone number is (617) 123-4444.

Did you answer the question correctly? You had to search the Employees table for Pamela Milgrom to obtain the LocationID (L02 in this example) corresponding to her office. You then searched the Locations table for this LocationID to obtain the address and phone number for that location. The process required you to use both the Locations and Employees tables, which are linked to one another through a ***one-to-many relationship***. One location can have many employees, but a specific employee can work at only one location. Let's try another question:

Query: Which employees are managers?

Answer: There are four managers: Pamela Milgrom, Tracey Coulter, Billy Marlin, and David Adamson.

The answer to this question is based on the one-to-many relationship that exists between titles and employees. One title can have many employees, but a given employee has only one title. To answer the query, you search the Titles table for "manager" to determine its TitleID (T02). You then go to the Employees table and select those records that have this value in the TitleID field.

The design of a relational database enables us to extract information from multiple tables in a single query. Equally important, it simplifies the way data is changed in that modifications are made in only one place. Consider:

Query: Which employees work in the Boston office? What is their phone number?

Answer: There are four employees in Boston: Pamela Milgrom, Ann Manin, Patricia Rubin, and Kenneth Charles, each with the same number (617-123-4444).

Once again, we draw on the one-to-many relationship between locations and employees. Thus, we begin in the Locations table where we search for "Boston" to determine its LocationID (L02) and phone number (617 123-4444). Then we go to the Employees table to select those records with this value in the LocationID field.

Query: What change(s) are necessary to accommodate a new telephone number for the Boston office?

Answer: Only one change is necessary. One would open the Locations table, locate the record for Boston, and change the phone number.

This query illustrates the ease with which changes are made to a relational database. There are four employees in Boston, but each employee record contains the LocationID (L02), rather than the actual information for the Boston office. Thus, changing the contents of the appropriate record in the Locations table automatically changes the information for the employees in that location.

We're ready for our next hands-on exercise in which we illustrate the true power of an Access database and its ability to work with multiple tables in a relational database. (The exercise uses the same data as the tables in Figure 1.7.)

3 A Look Ahead

Objective To open a database with multiple tables; to identify the one-to-many relationships within the database; and to produce reports based on those relationships. Use Figure 1.8 as a guide in the exercise.

Step 1: **Open the Relationships Window**

- Start Access. Pull down the **File menu** and click the **Open command**. Open the **Look Ahead database** in the **Exploring Access folder**.

- Pull down the **Tools menu** and click the **Relationships command** to open the Relationships window as shown in Figure 1.8a. Pull down the **Relationships menu** and click the **Show Table command** to display the Show Table dialog box.

- Click (select) the **Locations table** (within the Show Table dialog box), then click the **Add button** to add this table to the Relationships window.

- Double click the **Titles** and **Employees tables** to add these tables to the Relationships window. Close the Show Table dialog box.

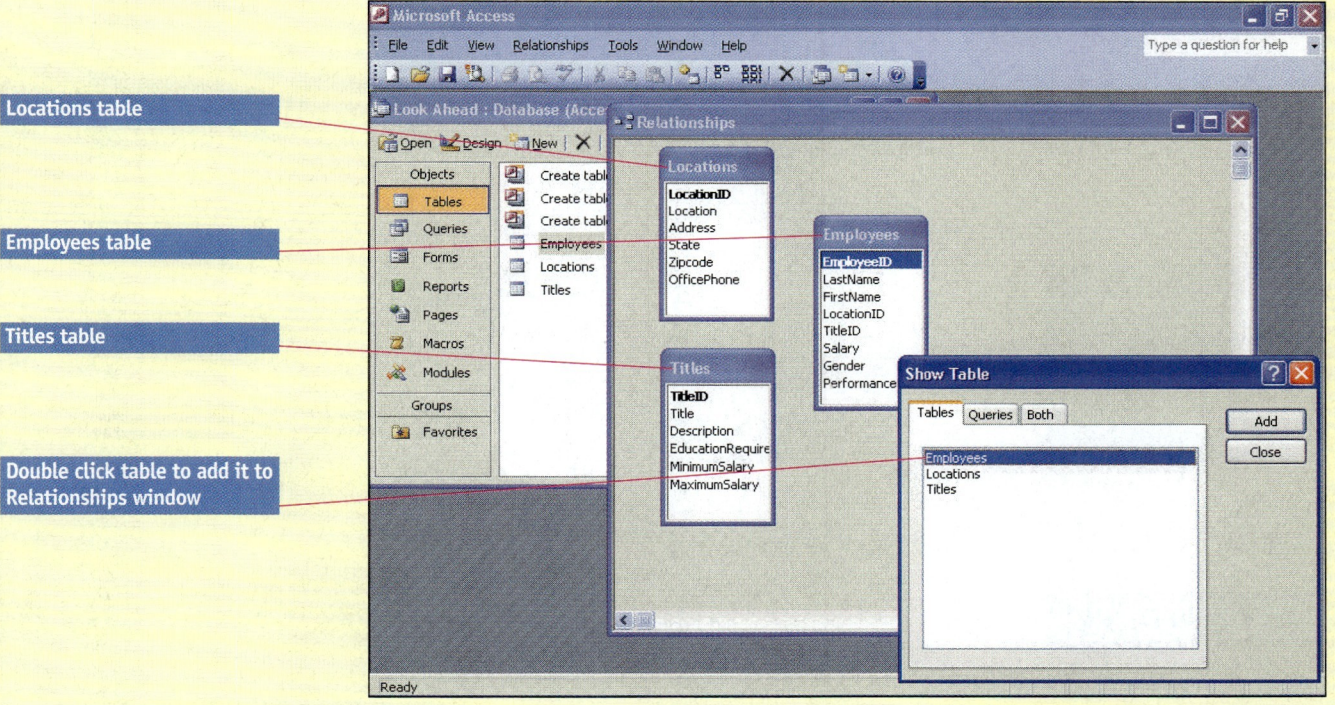

Locations table

Employees table

Titles table

Double click table to add it to Relationships window

(a) Open the Relationships Window (step 1)

FIGURE 1.8 Hands-on Exercise 3

WORK ON DRIVE C

Even in a lab setting, it is preferable to work on the local hard drive, as opposed to a floppy disk. The hard drive is much faster, which is significant when working with the large files associated with Access. More importantly, the capacity of the floppy disk is limited, so that you are likely to crash as the database expands. Work on drive C throughout the exercise, then use Windows Explorer at the end of the exercise to copy the database to a floppy disk that you can take with you.

Step 2: Create the Relationships

■ Maximize the Relationships windows so that you have more room in which to work. Click and drag the title bar of each table so that the positions of the tables match those in Figure 1.8b.

■ Click and drag the bottom (and/or right) border of each table so that you see all of the fields in each table.

■ Click and drag the **LocationID field** in the Locations table field list to the **LocationID field** in the Employees field list. Release the mouse button. You will see the Edit Relationships dialog box.

■ Check the box to **Enforce Referential Integrity**. Click the **Create button** to create the relationship.

■ Click and drag the **TitleID field** in the Titles table field list to the **TitleID field** in the Employees field list. Release the mouse button. You will see the Edit Relationships dialog box.

■ Check the box to **Enforce Referential Integrity** as shown in Figure 1.9b. Click the **Create button** to create the relationship.

■ Click the **Save button** on the Relationships toolbar to save the Relationships window, then close the Relationships window.

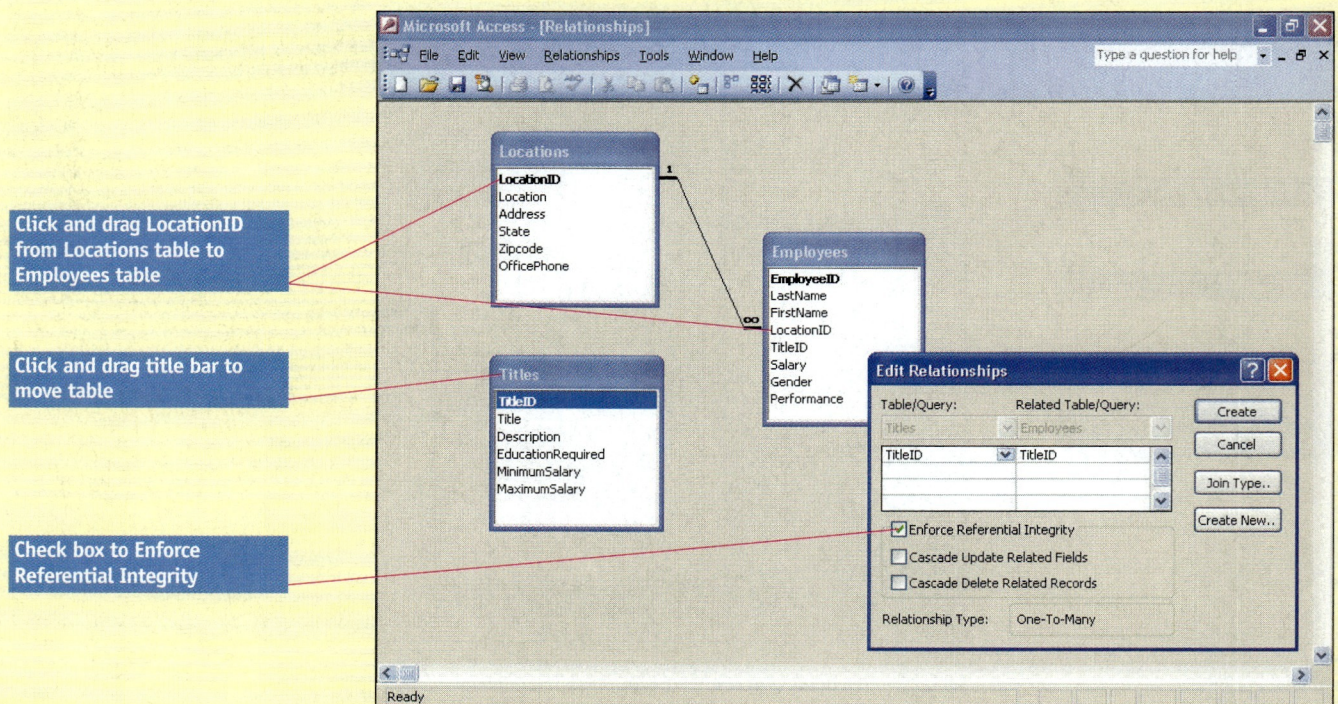

(b) Create the Relationships (step 2)

FIGURE 1.8 Hands-on Exercise 3 (*continued*)

THE RELATIONSHIPS ARE VISUAL

The tables in an Access database are created independently, then related to one another through the Relationships window. The number 1 and the infinity symbol (∞) appear at the ends of the lines to indicate the nature of the relationship—for example, a one-to-many relationship between the Locations and Employees tables.

Step 3: Referential Integrity

- Double click the **Employees table** to open the table. Maximize the window. Pull down the **Insert** menu and click the **New Record command** (or click the **New Record button** on the Table Datasheet toolbar).

- Enter data for yourself, using 12345 as the EmployeeID, and your first and last name as shown in Figure 1.8c. Enter an invalid LocationID (e.g., **L44**), then complete the record as shown in the figure.

- Press the **Enter key** when you have completed the data entry, then click **OK** when you see the error message. Access prevents you from entering a location that does not exist.

- Click in the **LocationID field** and enter **L04**, the LocationID for Miami. Press the **down arrow key** to move to the next record, which automatically saves the current record.

- Close the Employees table.

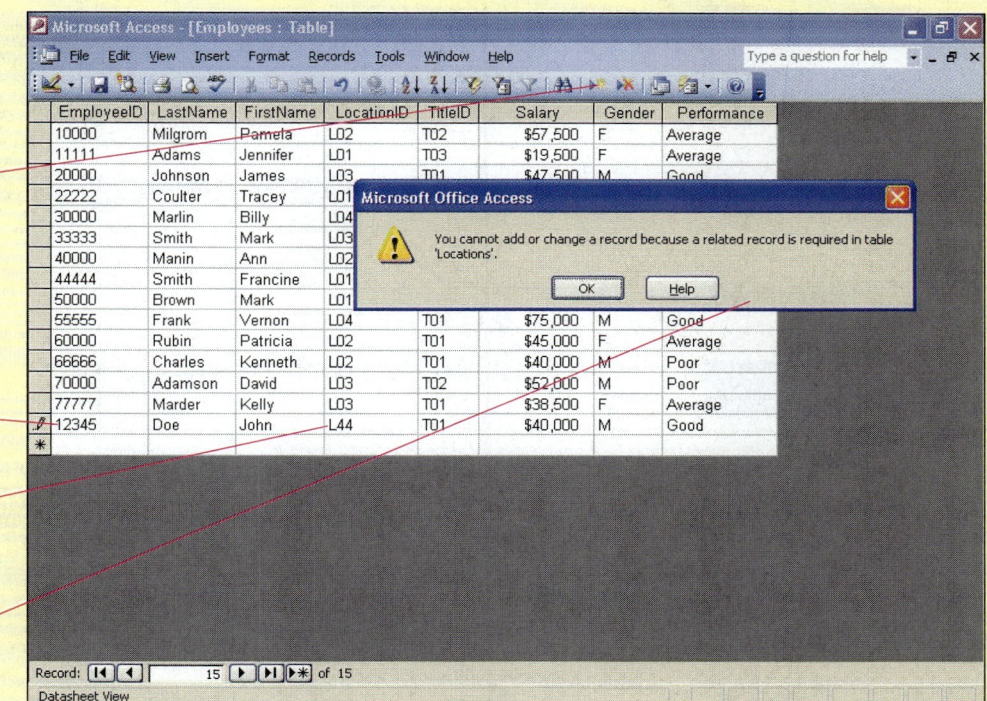

(c) Referential Integrity (step 3)

FIGURE **1.8** Hands-on Exercise 3 (*continued*)

REFERENTIAL INTEGRITY

The tables in a database must be consistent with one another, a concept known as referential integrity. Thus, Access automatically implements certain types of data validation to prevent such errors from occurring. You cannot, for example, enter a record in the Employees table that contains an invalid value for either the LocationID or the TitleID. Nor can you delete a record in the Locations or Titles table if it has related records in the Employees table. Think for a moment what the consequences would be if this type of validation was not imposed on the database.

Step 4: Simplified Data Entry

- Click the **Forms button** in the Database window, then double click the **Employees form** to open this form as shown in Figure 1.8d.

- Click the **Add Record button** (or use the **Alt+A** keyboard shortcut), then click in the text box for the EmployeeID.

- Enter the data for **Bob Grauer** one field at a time, pressing the **Tab key** to move from one field to the next. Click the **down arrow** when you come to the location field to display the available locations, then select (click) **Miami**.

- Press the **Tab key** to move to the Title field, click the **down arrow**, and choose **Account Rep**.

- Complete the data for Bob's record by entering **$150,000**, **M**, and **Excellent** in the Salary, Gender, and Performance fields, respectively.

- Click the **Close Form button** (or use the **Alt+C** keyboard shortcut) when you have finished entering the data.

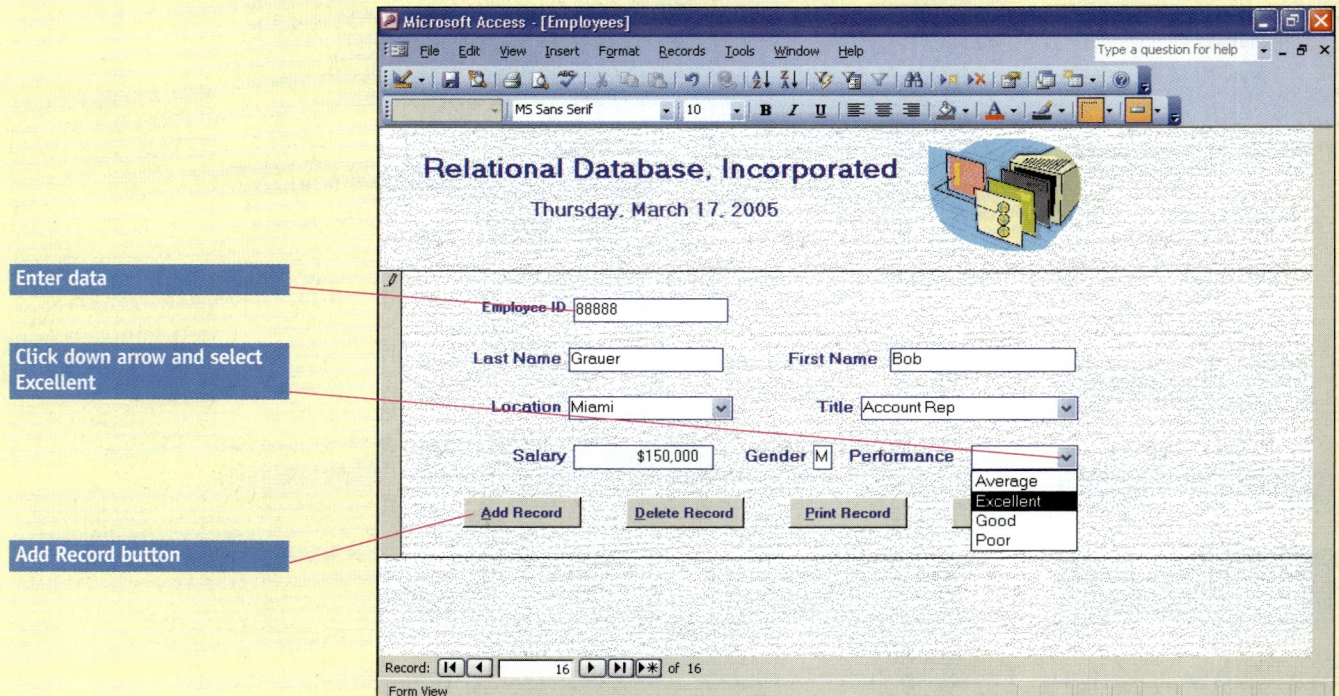

(d) Simplified Data Entry (step 4)

FIGURE 1.8 Hands-on Exercise 3 (*continued*)

APPLY A FILTER TO A FORM

A filter can be applied in either Datasheet view or Form view to display a subset of records according to specified criteria. Open any form and note the number of records in the underlying table (16 in our example). Now click the Filter by Form button on the Form View toolbar to display a blank form, enter the desired criteria; e.g., Boston and "Account Rep" for location and title respectively, and then click the Apply Filter button to see the selected records. The status bar at the bottom of the screen indicates three records followed by the word "filtered". See practice exercise 9 at the end of the chapter.

Step 5: **Print the Employee Master List**

- Click the **Reports button** in the Database window. Double click the **Employee Master List** report to open the report as shown in Figure 1.8e.

- Click the **Maximize button** in the Report window so that the report takes the entire desktop. Click the **Zoom button** to view the report at **100%**.

- The report displays selected fields for every employee in the Employees table. The two new employees, you and Bob Grauer, appear in alphabetical order. Both employees are in the Miami office.

- The fields for each employee are taken from different tables in the database:
  - ❏ The values for last name, first name, salary, and performance are from the Employees table.
  - ❏ The name of the location and the office phone are from the Locations table, which is related to the Employees table through the LocationID field that appears in both tables.
  - ❏ The employee's title is taken from the Titles table, which is related to the Employees table through the TitleID field that appears in both tables.

- Click the **Print button** to print the report. Close the Report window.

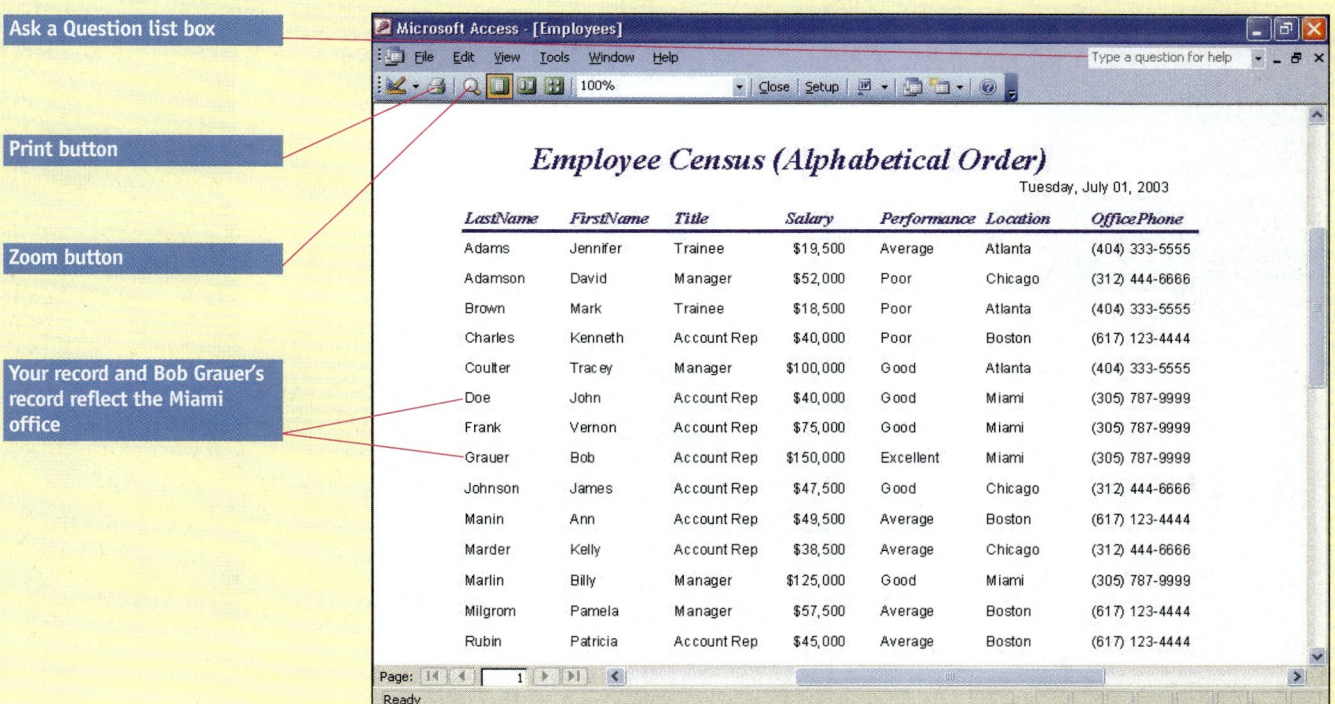

Ask a Question list box

Print button

Zoom button

Your record and Bob Grauer's record reflect the Miami office

Employee Census (Alphabetical Order)

Tuesday, July 01, 2003

LastName	FirstName	Title	Salary	Performance	Location	OfficePhone
Adams	Jennifer	Trainee	$19,500	Average	Atlanta	(404) 333-5555
Adamson	David	Manager	$52,000	Poor	Chicago	(312) 444-6666
Brown	Mark	Trainee	$18,500	Poor	Atlanta	(404) 333-5555
Charles	Kenneth	Account Rep	$40,000	Poor	Boston	(617) 123-4444
Coulter	Tracey	Manager	$100,000	Good	Atlanta	(404) 333-5555
Doe	John	Account Rep	$40,000	Good	Miami	(305) 787-9999
Frank	Vernon	Account Rep	$75,000	Good	Miami	(305) 787-9999
Grauer	Bob	Account Rep	$150,000	Excellent	Miami	(305) 787-9999
Johnson	James	Account Rep	$47,500	Good	Chicago	(312) 444-6666
Manin	Ann	Account Rep	$49,500	Average	Boston	(617) 123-4444
Marder	Kelly	Account Rep	$38,500	Average	Chicago	(312) 444-6666
Marlin	Billy	Manager	$125,000	Good	Miami	(305) 787-9999
Milgrom	Pamela	Manager	$57,500	Average	Boston	(617) 123-4444
Rubin	Patricia	Account Rep	$45,000	Average	Boston	(617) 123-4444

Page: 1

Ready

(e) Print the Employee Master List (step 5)

FIGURE 1.8 Hands-on Exercise 3 (*continued*)

ASK A QUESTION

Click in the "Ask a Question" list box that appears at the right of the document window, enter the text of a question such as "How do I print a report?", press Enter, and Access returns a list of potential Help topics. Click any topic that appears promising to display the detailed information. You can ask multiple questions during an Access session, then click the down arrow in the list box to return to an earlier question, which will return you to the Help topics.

Step 6:   **Change the Locations Table**

- Click the **Tables button** in the Database window, then double click the **Locations table** to open this table as shown in figure 1.8f. Maximize the window if necessary.

- Click the **plus sign** next to location L04 (Miami) to view the employees in this office. The plus sign changes to a minus sign as the employee records for this location are shown.

- Your name appears in this list as does Bob Grauer's. Click the **minus sign** and the list of related records disappears.

- Click and drag to select **Miami** (the current value in the Location field). Type **Orlando** and press the **Tab key**. Enter the corresponding values for the other fields: **1000 Kirkman Road, FL, 32801**, and **(407) 555-5555** for the address, state, zip code, and office phone, respectively.

- Close the **Locations table**. You have effectively moved the Miami Office to Orlando; i.e., all employees who were assigned to the Miami Office are now working out of Orlando.

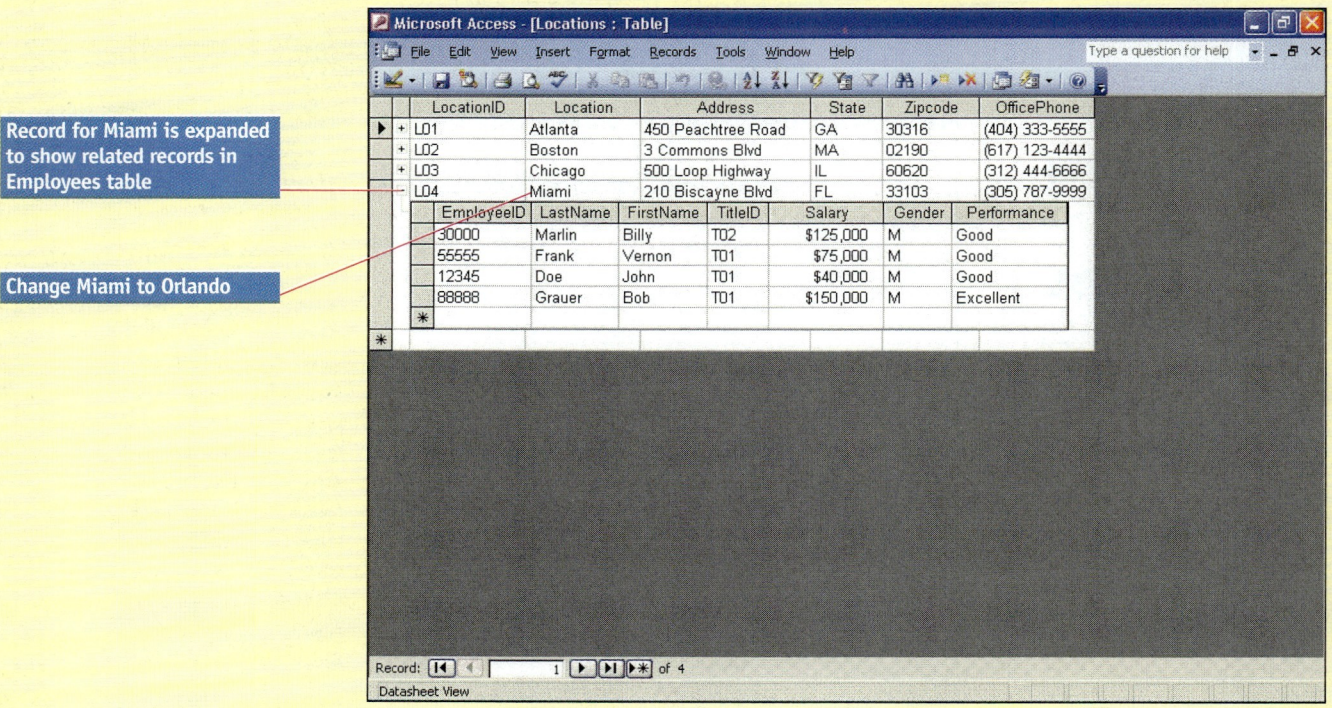

Record for Miami is expanded to show related records in Employees table

Change Miami to Orlando

(f) Change the Locations Table (step 6)

FIGURE 1.8   Hands-on Exercise 3 (*continued*)

ADD AND DELETE RELATED RECORDS

Take advantage of the one-to-many relationship between locations and employees (or titles and employees) to add and/or delete records in the Employees table. Open the Locations table, then click the plus sign next to the location where you want to add or delete an employee record. To add a new employee, click in any employee record, click the New Record navigation button, then add the new data. To delete a record, click the record, then click the Delete Record button on the Table Datasheet toolbar. Click the minus sign to close the employee list.

Step 7: **Print the Employees by Title Report**

- Click the **Reports button** in the Database window, then double click the **Employees by Title report** to open the report shown in Figure 1.8g.

- Click the **Maximize button** in the Report window so that the report takes the entire desktop. Click the **Zoom button** to view the report at **100%**.

- This report lists employees by title, rather than alphabetically. Note that you and Bob Grauer are both listed as Account Reps in the Orlando office; that is, the location of the office was changed in the Locations table, and that change is automatically reflected for all employees assigned to that office.

- Pull down the **File menu** and click the **Page Setup command**. Click the **Margins tab**, then change the left and right margins to **.75 inch** each, so that the report fits on one page. Click **OK**. Print the report for your instructor to show you completed the exercise.

- Close the Report window. Close the Database window. Exit Access. Welcome to the world of relational databases.

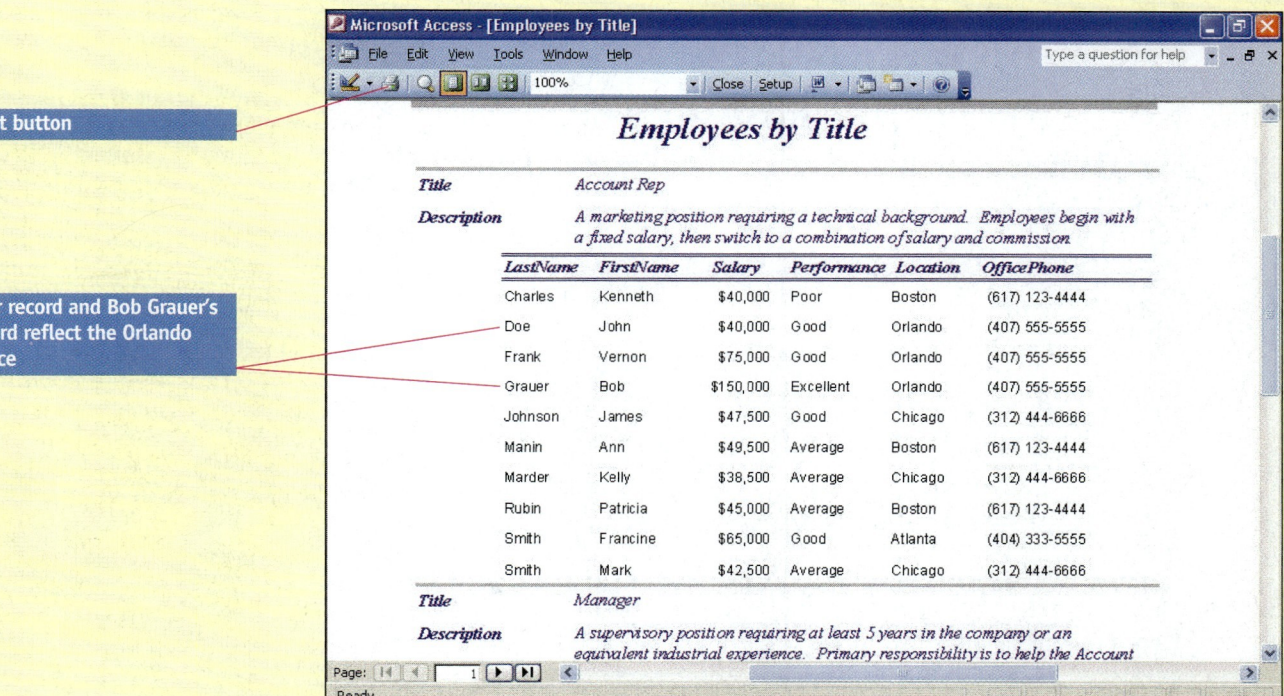

(g) Print the Employees by Title Report (step 7)

FIGURE 1.8 Hands-on Exercise 3 (*continued*)

BACK UP YOUR WORK

We cannot overemphasize the importance of adequate backup and urge you to back up your important files at every opportunity. Exit Access, start Windows Explorer, then copy the database from drive C to a floppy disk, CD, memory stick, or Zip drive. Remember, you can always get another copy of Microsoft Office, but your data files are irreplaceable. Make duplicate copies of any files that you cannot afford to lose, and then store those files away from your computer. Develop a backup strategy and follow it faithfully!

SUMMARY

An Access database has seven types of objects—tables, forms, queries, reports, pages, macros, and modules. The database window displays these objects and enables you to open an existing object or create a new object.

Each table in the database is composed of records, and each record is in turn composed of fields. Every record in a given table has the same fields in the same order. The primary key is the field (or combination of fields) that makes every record in a table unique. A table can have only one primary key.

A table is displayed in multiple views. The Design view is used to define the table initially and to specify the fields it will contain. The Datasheet view is the view you use to add, edit, or delete records. The PivotTable view is similar in concept to an Excel pivot table and provides a convenient way to summarize data about groups of records. The PivotChart view creates a chart from the associated PivotTable view. (The PivotTable and PivotChart views are discussed in Chapter 4.)

A record selector symbol is displayed next to the current record in Datasheet view and signifies the status of that record. A triangle indicates that the record has been saved. A pencil indicates that the record has not been saved and that you are in the process of entering (or changing) the data. An asterisk appears next to the blank record present at the end of every table, where you add a new record to the table.

Access automatically saves any changes in the current record as soon as you move to the next record or when you close the table. The Undo Current Record command cancels (undoes) the changes to the previously saved record.

A filter is a set of criteria that is applied to a table to display a subset of the records in that table. Microsoft Access lets you filter by selection or filter by form. The application of a filter does not remove the records from the table, but simply suppresses them from view. The records in a table can be displayed in ascending or descending sequence by clicking the appropriate button on the Database toolbar.

No system, no matter how sophisticated, can produce valid output from invalid input. Data validation is thus a critical part of any system. Access automatically imposes certain types of data validation during data entry. Additional checks can be implemented by the user.

A relational database contains multiple tables and enables you to extract information from those tables in a single query. The related tables must be consistent with one another, a concept known as referential integrity. Thus, Access automatically implements additional data validation to ensure the integrity of a database.

Adequate backup is essential when working with an Access database (or any other Office application). A duplicate copy of the database should be created at the end of every session and stored off site (away from the computer).

KEY TERMS

AutoCorrect 11	Filter by Selection 19	Referential Integrity 31
Current record 4	Find command 12	Relational database 27
Database 2	Form 5	Remove filter 19
Database window 3	GIGO (garbage in, garbage out) . . . 2	Replace command 12
Data validation 15	One-to-many relationship 28	Report 5
Datasheet view 4	PivotChart view 4	Sort 19
Design view 4	PivotTable view 4	Sort Ascending 19
Field 2	Primary key 4	Sort Descending 19
Filter 19	Query 5	Table 2
Filter by Form 19	Record 2	Undo command 13

MULTIPLE CHOICE

1. Which sequence represents the hierarchy of terms, from smallest to largest?

    (a) Database, table, record, field

    (b) Field, record, table, database

    (c) Record, field, table, database

    (d) Field, record, database, table

2. Which of the following is true regarding movement within a record (assuming you are not in the first or last field of that record)?

    (a) Press Tab or the right arrow key to move to the next field

    (b) Press Shift+Tab or the left arrow key to return to the previous field

    (c) Both (a) and (b)

    (d) Neither (a) nor (b)

3. You're performing routine maintenance on a table within an Access database. When should you execute the Save command?

    (a) Immediately after you add, edit, or delete a record

    (b) Periodically during a session—for example, after every fifth change

    (c) Once at the end of a session

    (d) None of the above since Access automatically saves the changes as they are made

4. Which of the following objects are contained within an Access database?

    (a) Tables and forms

    (b) Queries and reports

    (c) Macros and modules

    (d) All of the above

5. Which of the following is true about the views associated with a table?

    (a) The Design view is used to create a table

    (b) The Datasheet view is used to add or delete records

    (c) Both (a) and (b)

    (d) Neither (a) nor (b)

6. Which of the following is true of an Access database?

    (a) Every record in a table has the same fields as every other record

    (b) Every table contains the same number of records as every other table

    (c) Both (a) and (b)

    (d) Neither (a) nor (b)

7. Which of the following is *false* about the Open Database command?

    (a) It can be executed from the File menu

    (b) It can be executed by clicking the Open button on the Database toolbar

    (c) It loads a database from disk into memory

    (d) It opens the selected table from the Database window

8. Which of the following is true regarding the record selector symbol?

    (a) A pencil indicates that the current record has already been saved

    (b) A triangle indicates that the current record has not changed

    (c) An asterisk indicates the first record in the table

    (d) All of the above

9. Which view is used to add, edit, and delete records in a table?

    (a) The Design view

    (b) The Datasheet view

    (c) Either (a) or (b)

    (d) Neither (a) nor (b)

10. What does GIGO stand for?

    (a) Gee, I Goofed, OK

    (b) Global Input, Global Output

    (c) Garbage In, Garbage Out

    (d) Gospel In, Gospel Out

... c o n t i n u e d

11. Which of the following will be accepted as valid during data entry?

    (a) Adding a record with a duplicate primary key
    (b) Entering text into a numeric field
    (c) Entering numbers into a text field
    (d) Omitting a required field

12. The find and replace values in a Replace command must be:

    (a) The same length
    (b) The same case
    (c) Both (a) and (b)
    (d) Neither (a) nor (b)

13. An Access table containing 10 records, and 10 fields per record, requires two pages for printing. What, if anything, can be done to print the table on one page?

    (a) Print in Landscape rather than Portrait mode
    (b) Decrease the left and right margins
    (c) Both (a) and (b)
    (d) Neither (a) nor (b)

14. Which of the following capabilities is available through Filter by Selection?

    (a) The imposition of a relational condition
    (b) The imposition of an alternate (OR) condition
    (c) Both (a) and (b)
    (d) Neither (a) nor (b)

15. Which of the following best describes the relationship between locations and employees as implemented in the Look Ahead database within the chapter?

    (a) One to one
    (b) One to many
    (c) Many to many
    (d) Impossible to determine

16. A corporate database has a one-to-many relationship between its branch offices and its employees. The Atlanta branch, which currently has 50 employees, is relocating. Where do you enter the new address and phone number?

    (a) In the employee record of the Atlanta branch manager
    (b) In the employee record of every employee who works in Atlanta
    (c) In the Atlanta record in the Branch Office table
    (d) All of the above

17. Which of the following commands can be used to replace all existing occurrences of the abbreviation CIS with Computer Information Systems?

    (a) Find and Replace
    (b) AutoCorrect
    (c) Both AutoCorrect and Find and Replace
    (d) Neither AutoCorrect nor Find and Replace

18. You are looking at an Employee table in Datasheet view. Which of the following requires an ascending sort?

    (a) To list the employees alphabetically by their last name
    (b) To list the employees according to their age with the youngest employee appearing first (an employee's birth date is stored in the table rather than the employee's age)
    (c) Both (a) and (b)
    (d) Neither (a) nor (b)

ANSWERS

1. b	7. d	13. c
2. c	8. b	14. d
3. d	9. b	15. b
4. d	10. c	16. c
5. c	11. c	17. a
6. a	12. d	18. a

PRACTICE WITH ACCESS

1. **The Oscars:** The Academy Awards®, also known as the Oscars®, are given out each year to honor the best efforts in motion pictures for the previous year. We enjoy the movies and we have created a database that contains the Oscar winners in the major categories. Your first task is to update the table in our database to include any additional awards since the publication of our text. Proceed as follows:

   a. Open the *Chapter 1 Practice 1* database in the Exploring Access folder. Click the Forms button and open the Award Winners form shown in Figure 1.9. Maximize the form. Use the navigation bar at the bottom of the form to go to the last record to determine the last year in our table.

   b. Skip this step if the database is current; otherwise, click the hyperlink in the Award Winners form to go to the Oscars site and determine the winners for the years since we published our text. Use the existing form to enter the winners for the six major awards (best picture, best actor and actress, best director, and best supporting actor and actress) into the Award Winners table.

   c. The form should display the most recent year for which data is available. Click the selection area at the left of the form to select this record. Pull down the File menu, click the Print command, then click the option button to print the selected record. Click OK. (You can also click the Print button on the form to print only the current record.) Close the form.

   d. Return to the Database window, click the Tables button and open the Award Winners table. Adjust the column widths (if necessary) so that you see all of the information for each field in each column. Pull down the File menu, click the Page Setup command, and change to landscape printing with one-half-inch margins all around. Use the Print Preview button to see how the table will appear prior to actually printing the table. Unless you change to a font that is too small to read, the data for one year will not fit on one page. Do not print the table. Close the Print Preview window, then close the table.

   e. Return to the Database window. Click the Reports button. Open the Major Winners by Year report and print the first page. (All of the data for a given year appears on the same page.) Close the report.

   f. Add a cover sheet, then submit the form and report to your instructor.

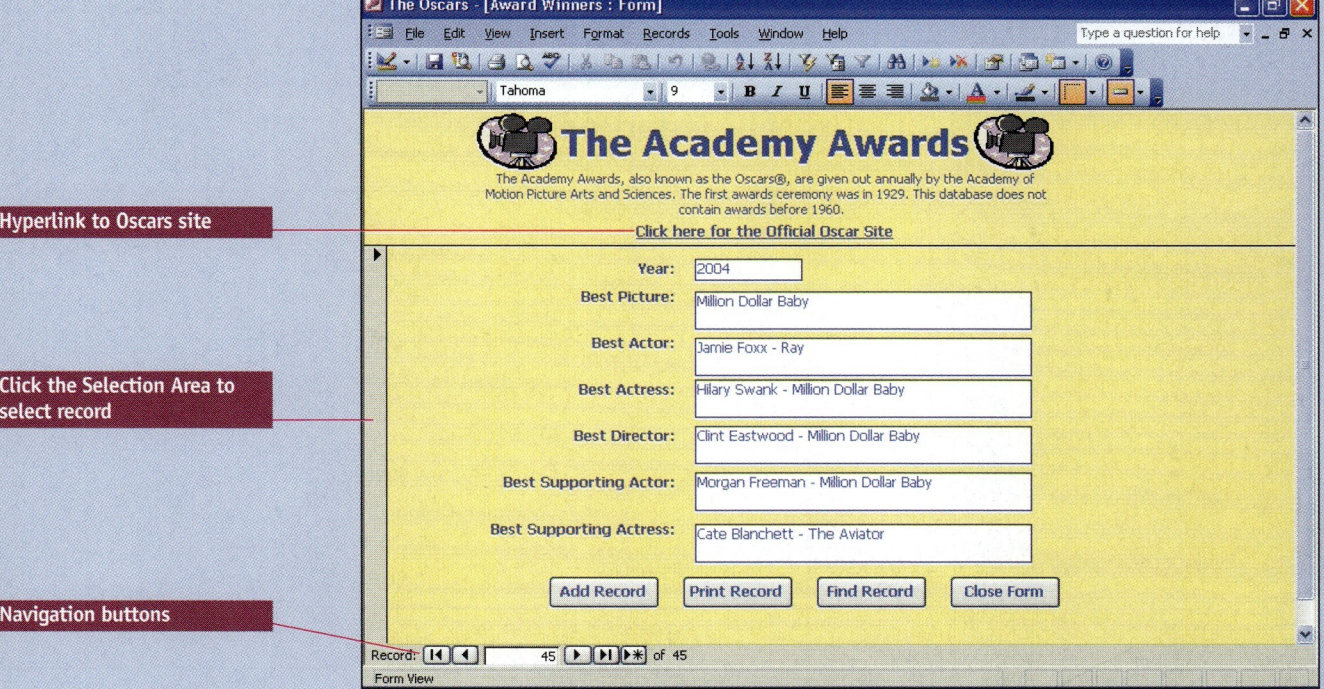

FIGURE 1.9 The Oscars (exercise 1)

2. **Definitely Needlepoint:** The Definitely Needlepoint boutique is owned and operated by four friends who wanted a friendly place to sit and stitch. They opened their store three years ago and it has grown quickly. The friends created a simple database to maintain customer records. It is your job to test the various objects in that database. You are to add, edit, and delete customer records and then view the results of those transactions in reports and queries. Open the *Chapter 1 Practice 2* database in the Exploring Access folder and proceed as follows:

    a. Open the Customers form, maximize the form, and click the Add Record button. Enter data for yourself as shown in Figure 1.10. Use customer number C1000 as shown in the figure. Indicate that you are a guild member and that you want to receive all mailings. Print the completed form for your instructor.

    b. Open the Guild Members query and uncheck the Guild Member box for Diane Battle, indicating that she is no longer a guild member. Delete the record for Anita Brockway. Close the query.

    c. Run the Guild Members report, which is based on the modified Guild Members query. Diane Battle is not listed on the report, as she is no longer a guild member. Anita Brockway is not listed either because her record has been permanently deleted from the table. Print the report for your instructor. Close the report.

    d. Open the Customers table. Filter the list by selection so that only the customers from Coral Gables are displayed. Sort the filtered list so that the customers are displayed in alphabetical order by last name. Print the filtered list. Further filter the list so that only the customers from Coral Gables who are priority 1 on the mailing list are displayed. Print this list as well. Submit both filtered lists to your instructor.

    e. Click the Filter by Form tool and delete the existing filters. Use the Filter by Form to filter the list so that only mailing list priority 1 or 2 is shown, but not priority 3. Sort the filtered list in ascending order by zip code. Print the filtered list for your instructor.

    f. Add a cover sheet to identify the assignment and submit all items to your instructor to show you completed the assignment.

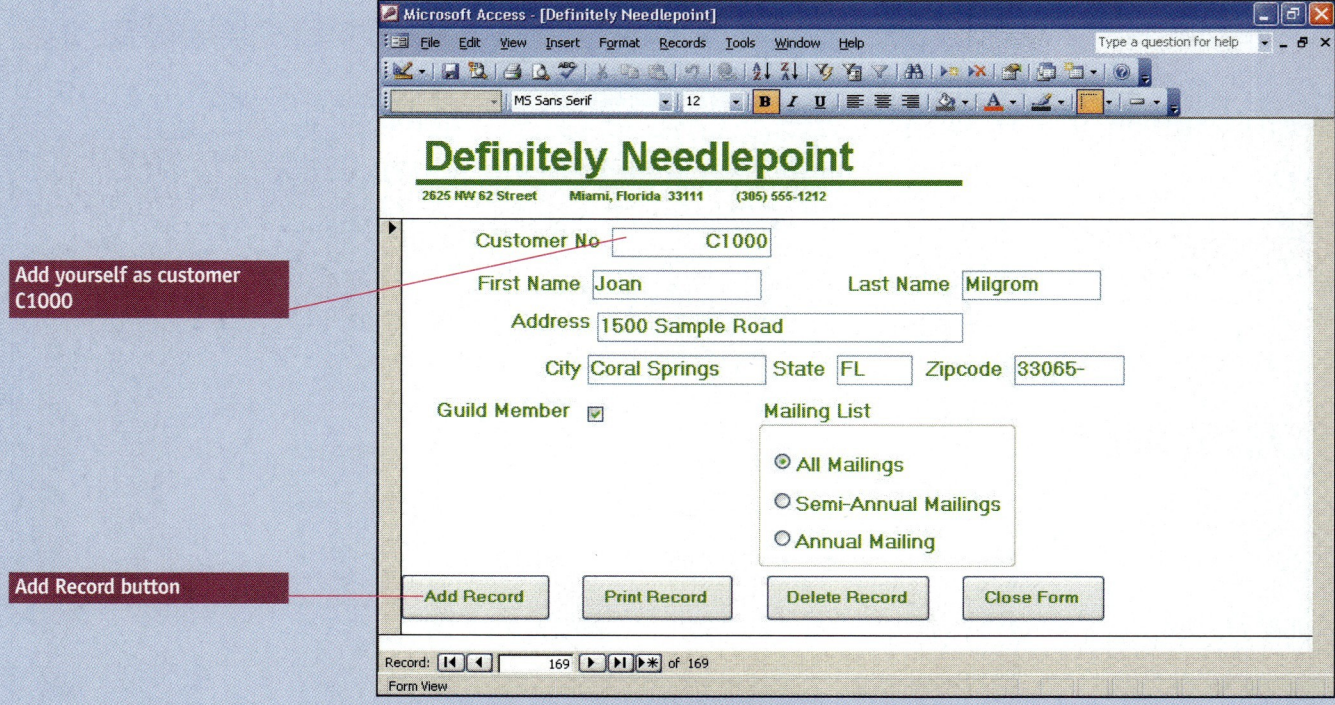

FIGURE 1.10 Definitely Needlepoint (exercise 2)

3. **The United States:** Figure 1.11 displays a table from the *Chapter 1 Practice 3* database in the Exploring Access folder. The database contains statistical data about all 50 states and enables you to create various reports such as the 10 largest states in terms of population or area.

a. Open the *Chapter 1 Practice 3* database, and then open the States table, as shown in Figure 1.11. Pull down the File menu and click the Page Setup command to display the associated dialog box. Select landscape printing and decrease the left and right margins to half an inch. Click the Print Preview button to check that all of the fields for one record fit on one page. Print the table with all fifty records. (The table itself will take two pages because there are 50 records in the table.)

b. Return to the Datasheet view. Click in the Population field of any state, and then click the Sort Descending button to list the states in descending order by population. Click and drag to select the first ten records so that you have selected the ten most populous states.

c. Change to landscape printing, and then click the Print Preview button to check that all of the fields for one record fit on one page. Pull down the File menu, click the Print command, then click the option button to print the selected records (the ten states with the largest population).

d. Return to the table and print the 10 states with the largest area. Which states (if any) appear on both listings? Close the table.

e. Click the Queries button and open the Population Density Query. Which field is present in the query that is not present in the underlying States table? How is this field computed? How many records are displayed? What is the sequence for the displayed records? Close the query.

f. Click the Reports button and print the Population Density Report. How does the information in this report compare to the Population Density Query? Which format do you prefer? Close the report.

g. Print any other reports that are in the database. Are these reports based on a table or a query?

h. Create a cover sheet. Submit the table of all 50 states, the 10 largest states by population, the 10 largest states by area, the Population Density report, as well as any additional reports that were in the database.

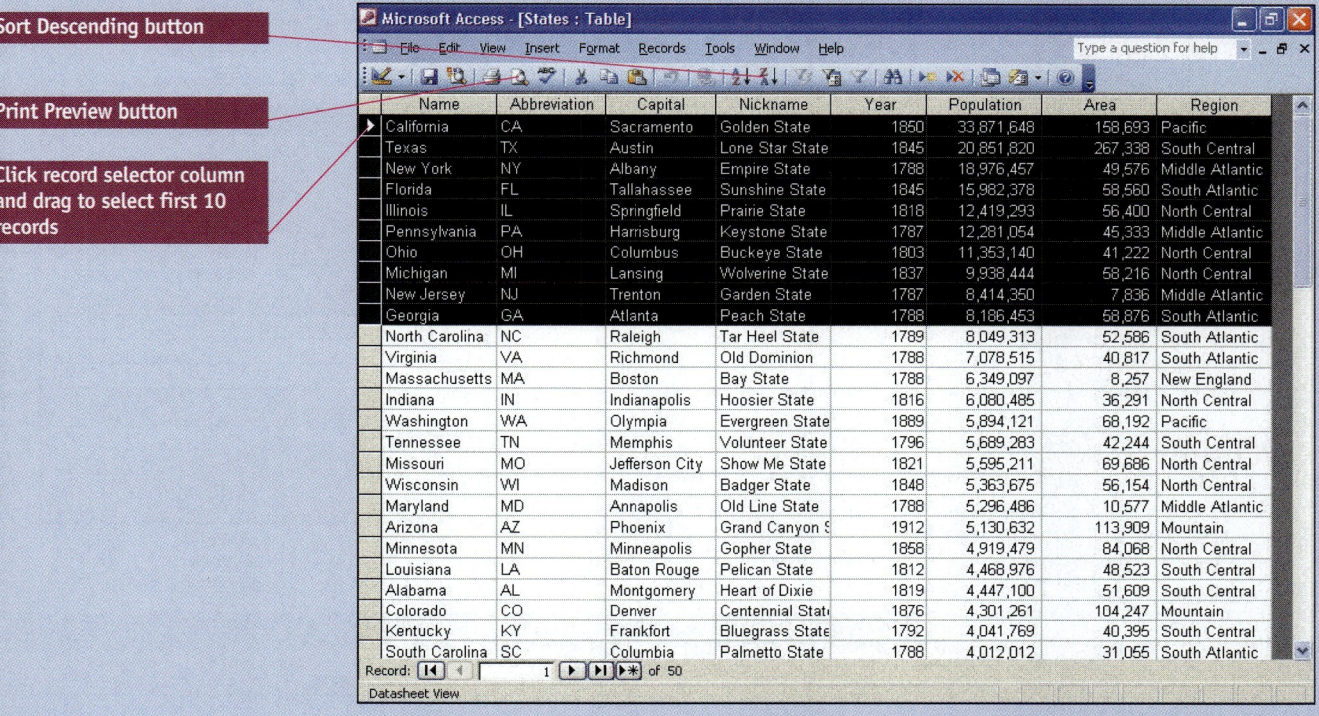

FIGURE 1.11 The United States (exercise 3)

practice exercises

4. **Large Databases:** Figure 1.12 displays a filtered list from the *Chapter 1 Practice 4* database that is found in the Exploring Access folder. The database is similar to the Employee database that was used in the second hands-on exercise, except that it contains more than 300 records. The purpose of this exercise, however, is to provide experience working with a larger database. It also introduces the Format Datasheet command to change the default formatting for an Access table.

   a. Open the *Chapter 1 Practice 4* database and add your name as the last record in the Employees table. Assume that you are employed as an Account Rep in Boston. Your salary is $55,000, and your performance has been rated excellent. Use your own name and an EmployeeID of 99999.

   b. Filter the Employee table to display only the employees who are Account Reps in Boston as shown in Figure 1.12. Sort the filtered list by last name.

   c. Pull down the Format menu and click the Datasheet command to display the Format Datasheet dialog box in Figure 1.12. Note that the default formatting provides for both horizontal and vertical gridlines in silver. Clear the box to print vertical gridlines, and then change the color of the gridlines to dark blue. Click OK to apply the changes to the table.

   d. Pull down the File menu, click the Page Setup command, click the Page tab, and then change to landscape printing. Click the Print Preview button to be sure that the filtered table will fit on a single sheet of paper. Print the table.

   e. Remove the existing filter, then impose a new filter to display only those employees who are managers. Arrange this filtered list in sequential order by employee number. Print the list of managers.

   f. Pull down the Format menu and explore the additional commands that are available to change the appearance of a table. Do the Hide, Unhide, Freeze, and Unfreeze Column commands seem familiar? How do these commands compare to similar commands in Excel? Do you think that the additional formatting enhances the appearance of a table, or are you better off to stick with the default formatting?

   g. Create a cover sheet for this assignment. Submit the printed tables together with your responses to the discussion question to your instructor.

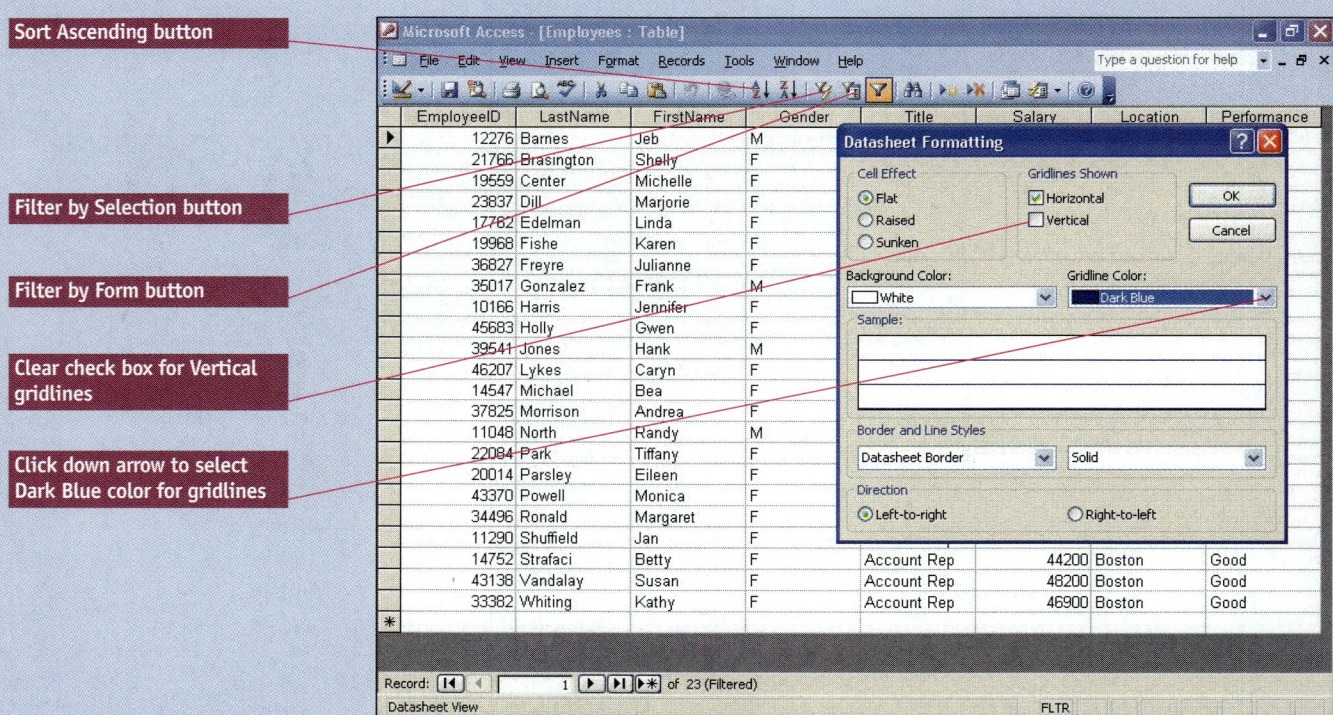

FIGURE 1.12 Large Databases (exercise 4)

5. **The Look Ahead Database:** The Look Ahead database that was introduced at the end of the chapter is a relational database that contains three tables—for employees, locations, and titles. This type of database facilitates data entry in that any change to a specific location or title is made in only one place, in the Locations or Titles tables, respectively, as opposed to having to change every employee record individually. Complete the third hands-on exercise in the chapter, and then make the following additional changes to the database.

   a. Open the *Look Ahead* database, open the Locations table, and add a new location. Use L05, Los Angeles, 1000 Rodeo Drive, CA, 90210, and (213) 666-6666 for the LocationID, Location, Address, State, ZipCode, and OfficePhone fields, respectively. Close the Locations table.

   b. Open the Titles table and change the title "Manager" to "Supervisor". Change the education requirement for a supervisor to a graduate degree. Close the Titles table.

   c. Open the Employees table. Delete the records for Kenneth Charles and David Adamson. Change the location for Bob Grauer and Francine Smith to the Los Angeles Office (location L05). Change Bob's title code to T02 so that Bob becomes the supervisor of the new office. Close the Employees table.

   d. Open the Employees form and use it to add two employees, Linda Laquer and Paul Frank, to the Los Angeles office. Both employees are Account Reps and start at $50,000. These are new employees, so no performance data is available. Assign a unique EmployeeID to each person. Is it easier to use the Employees table or the Employees form to modify data?

   e. Print all three reports in the database after the changes to the various tables have been made. (The second page of the Employees by Location report is shown in Figure 1.13 after the changes to the various tables have been made.) Submit all three reports to your instructor.

   f. Create a new report that displays the relationships within the database. Pull down the Tools menu and click Relationships to open the Relationships window, then pull down the File menu and click the Print Relationships command to display the Print Preview screen of a report that displays the contents of the Relationships window. Print this report for your instructor.

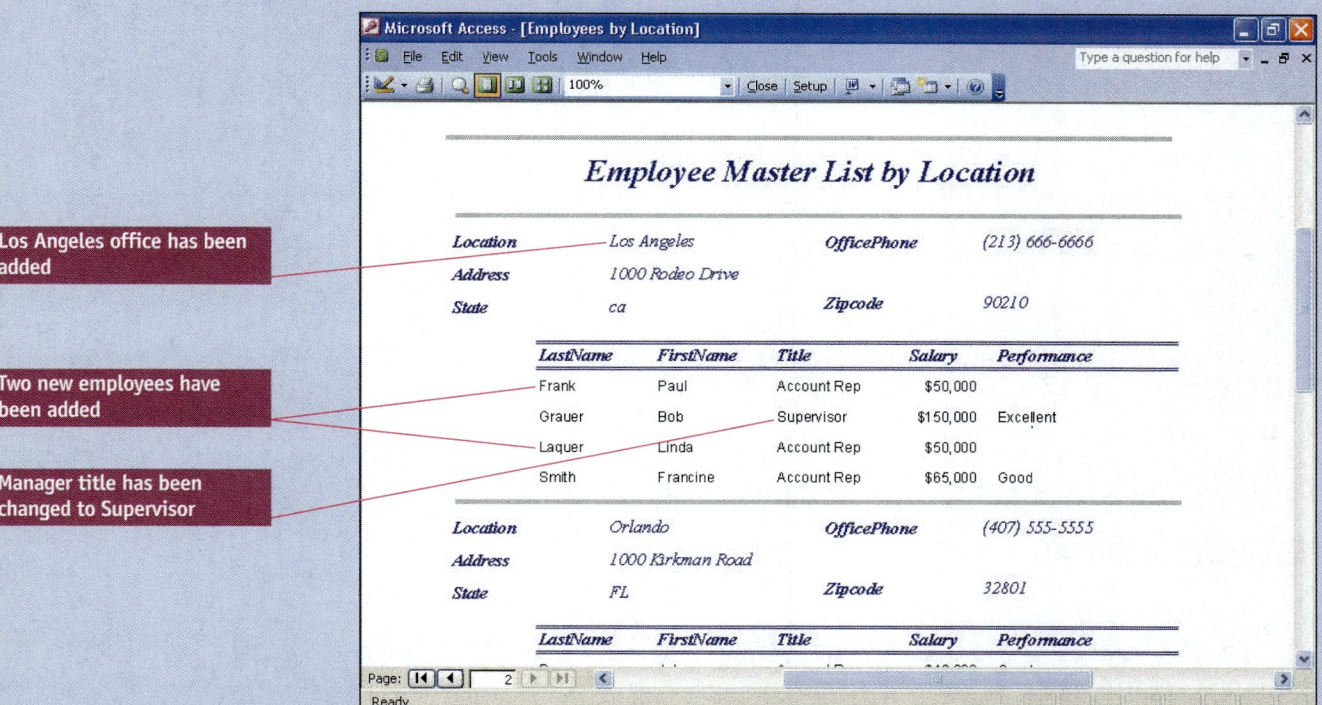

FIGURE 1.13   The Look Ahead Database (exercise 5)

6. **Peppy's Restaurants:** The Peppy's Restaurant chain is operated by individual franchisees throughout the state of Florida. Each restaurant offers the same menu, but differs in the size of the restaurant and the type of service offered. The data about all of the restaurants is maintained at corporate headquarters in an Access database. Your assignment is to open the *Chapter 1 Practice 6* database in the Exploring Access folder and test the various objects. Proceed as follows:

   a. Open the Restaurants form as shown in Figure 1.14. Add R0011 to the table, entering your name as the franchisee. Use any data that you think is appropriate. Print the record that you just added for your restaurant by clicking the Print button within the form. Close the form.

   b. Open the Restaurants table. Change the annual sales for restaurant R0003 to $1,000,000. Delete restaurant R0007.

   c. Print the Restaurants table for your instructor. Does all of the information for each restaurant fit on one page? Close the table. Return to the Database window, click the Report tab, and print the All Restaurants report. Does all of the information for each restaurant fit on one page? Do you see the restaurant that you just added in both places? Close the report.

   d. Click the Queries button in the Database window, then open both queries. Do both queries display all of the records in the Restaurants table? Does either query contain a field that is not present in the Restaurants table? Close the queries.

   e. Click the Reports button and print the two reports that correspond to the queries in part (d) for your instructor. Which is the more attractive way to display information, a query or a report?

   f. Return to the Database window. Pull down the File menu, click the Database Properties command, and then click the Contents tab. Which objects are in the database? How does this information compare to the information that is displayed in the Database Window?

   g. Submit all of the printed information to your instructor together with your answers to the discussion questions. Add a cover sheet to complete the assignment.

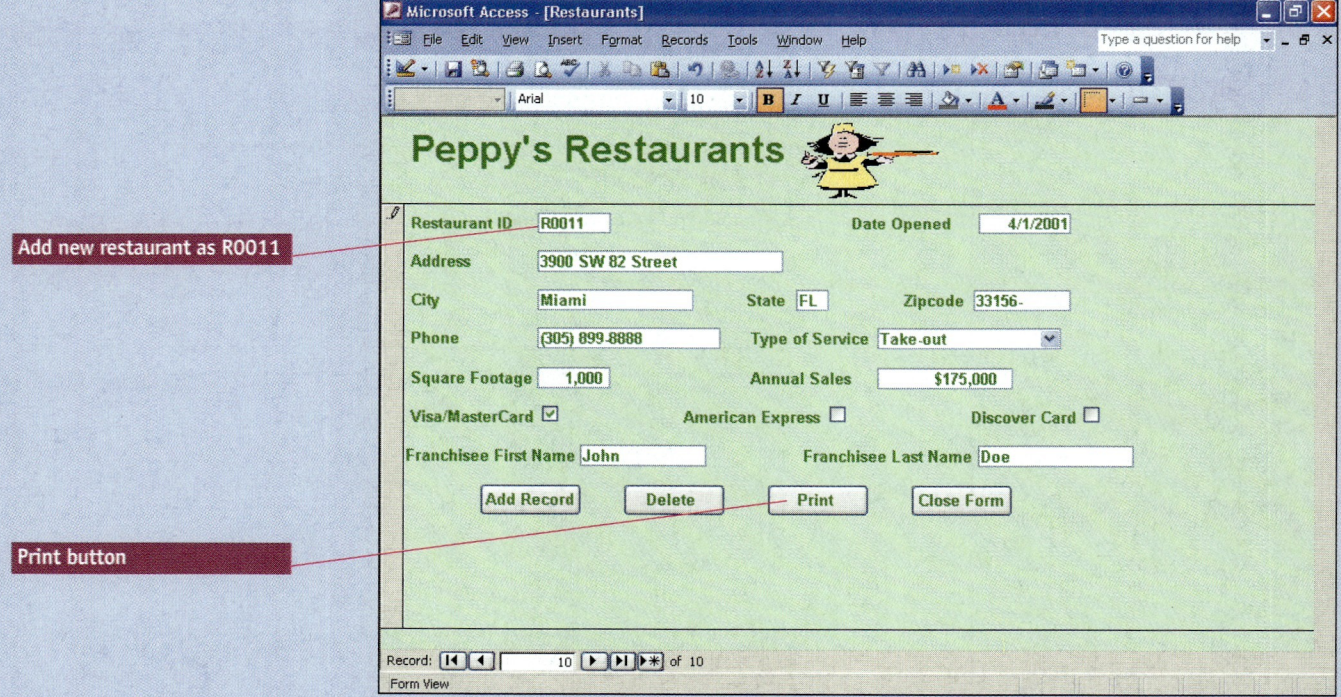

FIGURE 1.14 Peppy's Restaurants (exercise 6)

7. **Peppy's Relational Database:** The Peppy's Restaurant chain has replaced the database from the previous exercise with a relational database that contains separate tables for restaurants and franchisees. We have created a new database for you, as opposed to asking you to convert the previous database to a relational format. Nevertheless, there is still work for you to do. Accordingly, open the *Chapter 1 Practice 7* database and do the following:

a. Create the one-to-many relationship between franchisees (i.e., owners) and restaurants as shown in Figure 1.15. The company encourages individuals to operate more than one restaurant, but a specific restaurant is run by only one franchisee.

b. Open the Franchisees form and add yourself as Franchisee F008. Use any data that you deem appropriate. (You do not have to enter the same information as in the previous problem.)

c. Open the Restaurants form and add restaurant R0011, using any data that you deem appropriate. You must, however, assign yourself (F008) as the franchisee.

d. Change the FranchiseeID in restaurants 9 and 10 to F008 so that you will be associated with these restaurants as well.

e. Print the Master Restaurant List report, which displays all restaurants in order of Restaurant ID. Print the Restaurant by Franchisee report, which lists the franchisees in order together with the restaurants they operate. Submit both reports to your instructor as proof you did the exercise.

f. Create a new report that displays the relationships within the database. Pull down the Tools menu and click Relationships to open the Relationships window, then pull down the File menu and click the Print Relationships command to display the Print Preview screen of a report that displays the contents of the Relationships window. Print this report for your instructor.

g. What is referential integrity and how does it pertain to Peppy's Relational Database? What happens if you assign a restaurant to a franchisee that does not exist? What happens if you attempt to delete a franchisee who owns multiple restaurants? Submit all of the printed information to your instructor together with the answers to the discussion questions.

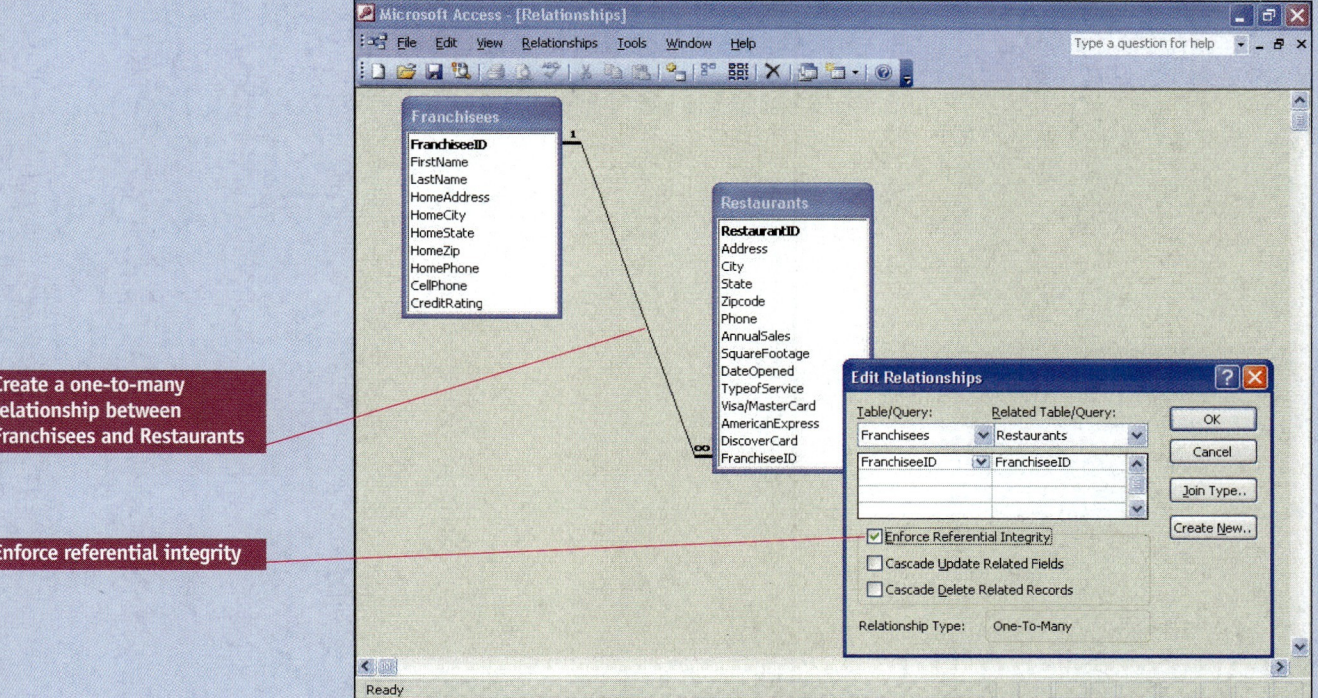

FIGURE 1.15 Peppy's Relational Database (exercise 7)

8. **Metro Zoo:** The newly opened Metro Zoo is the pride of your city. A relational database has been created with three tables: exhibits, trainers, and animals. There is a one-to-many relationship between exhibits and animals. One exhibit can have many different animals, but a specific animal is assigned to only one exhibit. A one-to-many relationship also exists between trainers and animals. One trainer can have many animals, but a specific animal has only one trainer. Open the *Chapter 1 Practice 8* database and proceed as follows:

   a. Pull down the Tools menu, click the Relationships command, and create the one-to-many relationships that exist in the system. Be sure to enforce referential integrity for both relationships.

   b. Open the Trainers form. Add yourself as a new trainer, using any information you deem appropriate. (Do not enter the TrainerID as this number is entered automatically.)

   c. Open the Animals form to add the record for the mountain tapir as shown in Figure 1.16. (Do not enter the AnimalID as this value is entered automatically.) Assign the tapir to the Americas exhibit and assign yourself as the trainer. Locate the Galapagos tortoise, black rhinoceros, and gorilla (AnimalID of 3, 11, and 12, respectively), and assign yourself as the trainer for these animals as well. Close the form.

   d. Click the Reports button in the database and print all four reports to verify that you have entered the data correctly. Which of these reports is based on data from more than one table?

   e. Create a fifth report that displays the relationships within the database. Pull down the Tools menu and click Relationships to open the Relationships window, then pull down the File menu and click the Print Relationships command to display the Print Preview screen of a report that displays the contents of the Relationships window. Print this report for your instructor.

   f. What is referential integrity, and how does it apply to the Metro Zoo database? What happens, for example, if you attempt to assign an animal to an exhibit that does not exist? What happens if you attempt to delete a trainer who has several employees? Submit all of the printed information to your instructor.

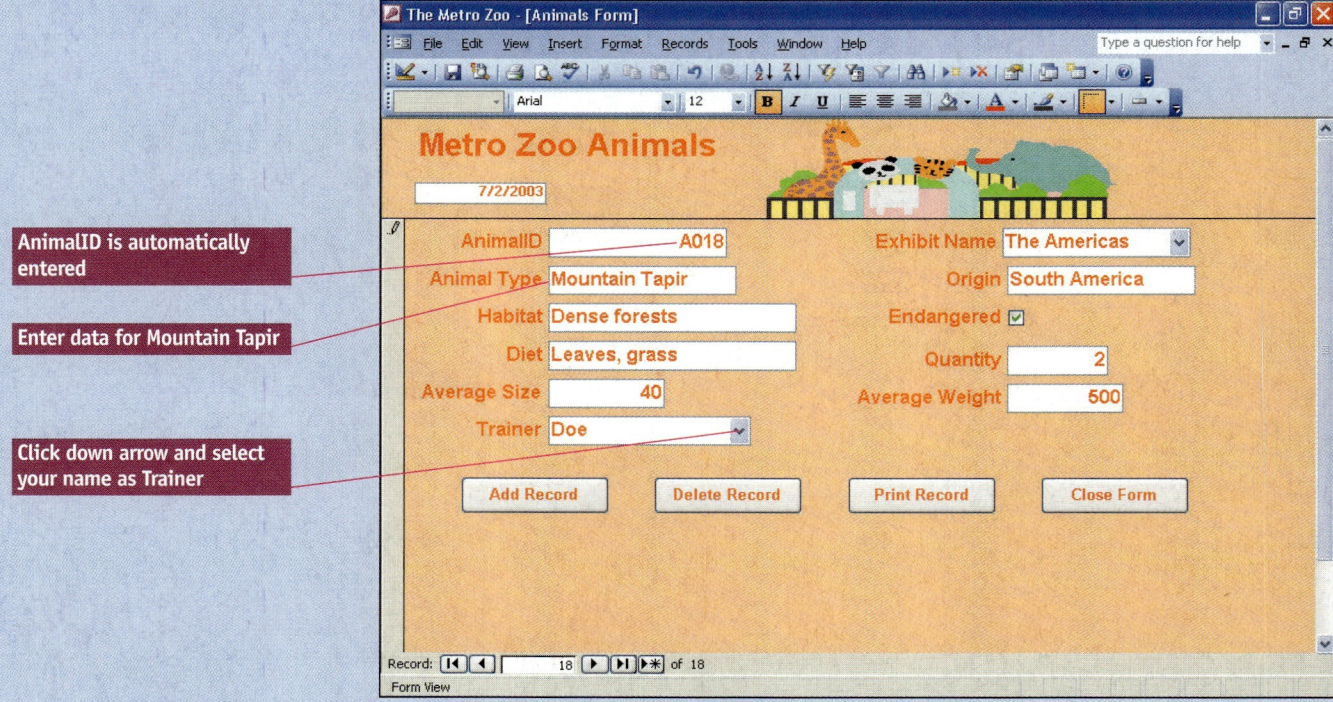

FIGURE 1.16 Metro Zoo (exercise 8)

practice exercises

9. **Finding a Physician:** A filter is a quick and easy way to query a table and identify records that meet a specified set of criteria. The filter may be applied in Datasheet view as it was in earlier exercises, or it may be applied in Form view as shown in Figure 1.17. Proceed as follows:

   a. Open the *Chapter 1 Practice 9—Finding a Physician* database in the Exploring Access folder. Click the Tables button, open the Physicians table, then move to the last record and enter data for Ken Grauer. Ken practices in Miami, his specialty is internal medicine, he is accepting new patients, and he was board certified on July 1 last year. (The Physician ID is entered automatically as soon as you begin to enter the last name.)

   b. Click the Filter by Form button. Specify Miami as the city and Internal Medicine as the specialty, then apply the filter. Nine physicians satisfy the criteria. Click in the Last Name field for any record, then click the Sort Ascending button to list the physicians alphabetically by last name. Click the Print Preview button to be sure that the table will fit on one page. (You may switch to landscape printing, change the left and right margins, and/or change the column widths.) Print the filtered table for your instructor. Remove the filter. Close the table.

   c. Open the Physicians form and click the Filter by Form button. Specify Miami as the city and Internal Medicine as the specialty as before, then expand the criteria to include your preference for a male or female physician, and limit the selection to physicians who are accepting new patients. Apply this filter. You should see two qualified physicians (regardless of the gender you specified). Print the form for each physician.

   d. The database contains three different reports: a master list that lists every physician in alphabetical order, a second report that lists physicians by specialty, and a third report that lists physicians by city. Choose any one of these reports and print it. How does the information contained in that report support the results that were obtained earlier through a filter?

   e. Submit all of the printed information to your instructor: the filtered table in part (b), the two forms from part (c), and the selected report from part (d).

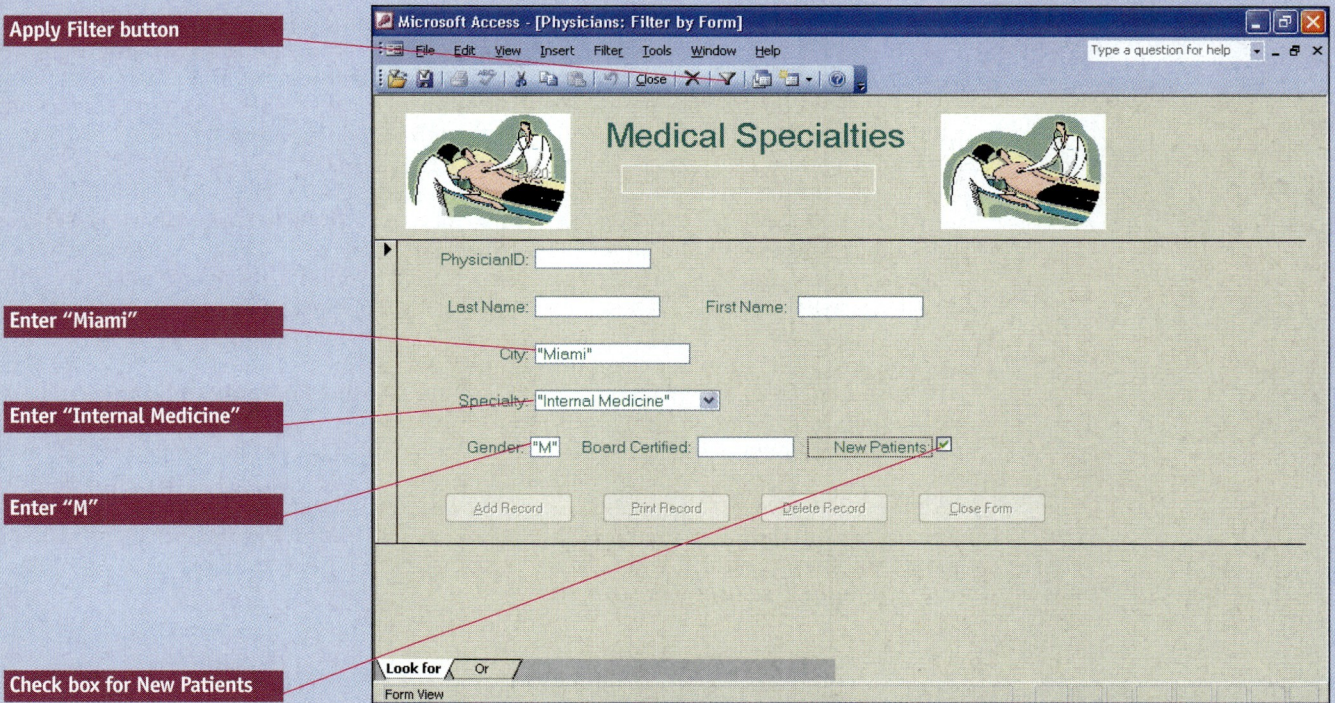

FIGURE 1.17 Finding a Physician (exercise 9)

MINI CASES

Online Study Guide

Every chapter in the Exploring Office series has an online component that enables you to review the conceptual material in the chapter. Go to our Web site, www.prenhall.com/grauer, after you have completed the chapter and click the icon for the Office 2003 book to go to the home page for this series. Click the appropriate title in the left pane, then click the down arrow in the list box at the top of the screen to select the appropriate chapter, such as Access Chapter 1. Click the link to online study guide in the left pane and take the quiz that consists of objective questions (multiple choice, true/false, and matching).

Click the "Submit Answers for Grading" button at the bottom of the quiz so that you can see your results. Scroll to the bottom of the answer screen, and then e-mail the results to yourself in HTML format. (If you send the results as text instead of HTML, you will get too many pages of output.) Start your e-mail program, print the e-mail message that contains your results, and submit to your instructor.

Garbage In, Garbage Out

Your excellent work in this course has earned you an internship in the registrar's office. Your predecessor has created a student database that appears to work well, but in reality it has several problems in that the report on student grade point averages does not produce the expected information. Open the *Chapter 1 Mini Case GIGO* database in the Exploring Access folder and print the report. Study the results to see if you can determine the errors in the underlying data that create the erroneous output. What would you do in the future to prevent similar errors from reoccurring?

Chapter Recap—Natalie's Cuppa Joe

Natalie's Cuppa Joe is a locally famous coffee shop that is known for its large and very creative selection of signature espresso drinks for coffee enthusiasts. The owner, Natalie Anderson, has always believed that variety is the spice of life and that there is much more to coffee than just cream and sugar. Natalie insists on good customer relations, and her staff is expected to know regular customers by their first name. Customers are also encouraged to submit suggestions for additional signature selections.

To make it easier on her employees, Natalie has built a database with information about her customers. New customers are asked to complete a questionnaire the first time they come into the shop as they wait for their drink to be prepared. Customers provide the standard name and address information, indicate whether they want to be included on a mailing list, and whether they wish to purchase the discount "Cuppa Card." This data is then entered into the database within three to four days.

You have just been hired by Natalie's Cuppa Joe and are expected to become knowledgeable about its customers and proficient at brewing the wild coffee drinks for which they are famous. Natalie has given you time away from the front counter to become familiar with the database, to enter recent customer information, and to generate two reports that will reflect the new data.

Your assignment is to review the chapter, paying special attention to each of the hands-on exercises. You will then open the *Chapter 1 Ending Case Study—Natalie's Cuppa Joe* database, and examine each of its objects (tables, forms, queries, and reports). You will use the existing Customers form to enter data about yourself as a new customer. Indicate that you want to be on the mailing list, but that you have not yet purchased the discount card. Be sure to suggest a specialty drink in the space provided. Print the completed form containing your data, and then print both of the reports within the database. (Your name should appear on both if you followed our instructions correctly.) Submit all of the printed information to your instructor.

Tables and Forms:
Design, Properties, Views, and Wizards

OBJECTIVES

After reading this chapter you will:

1. Discuss in general terms how to design a table.
2. Describe several data types and the associated properties.
3. Set the primary key of a table.
4. Use the Table Wizard to create a table; modify a table in Design view.
5. Describe how data validation is implemented in a table.
6. Use the Form Wizard to create a form; modify a form in Design view.
7. Distinguish between a bound control, an unbound control, and a calculated control.
8. Add a combo box and command buttons to a form.
9. Use a form to add, edit, and delete records in the underlying table.

hands-on exercises

1. CREATING A TABLE
   Input: None
   Output: My First Database

2. CREATING A FORM
   Input: My First Database (modified after exercise 1)
   Output: My First Database (modified)

3. A MORE SOPHISTICATED FORM
   Input: My First Database (modified after exercise 2)
   Output: My First Database (modified)

CASE STUDY
DEBBIE'S FINE FASHIONS

Debbie Berridge, a talented clothing designer, recently opened a boutique that carries her own line of fine fashions, as well as those of other local designers. Business has been taking off, and she is enjoying both the challenges and joys of owning her own business. One of Debbie's biggest successes is the semi-annual fashion show that features models drawn from her existing clients. Prior to each show, Debbie and her staff make personal calls to each of her customers, inviting them to the show. The calls are very time consuming, but they always produce a good turnout.

The detailed tracking of each customer's individual data has created quite a paper trail, and Debbie has decided to store the data electronically. She will start by collecting simple demographics (name, address, telephone number, and so on). She also wants to store the customer's dress size (P, S, M, L, XL), whether the customer wants to be on her mailing list, whether the customer wants to attend fashion shows, and whether the customer is interested in modeling for these special events. Debbie also plans to add a notes section to keep track of any special preferences for each client. All of this information will help her to reduce the number of calls she has to make prior to each show. ■

Your assignment is to read the chapter and create a database for Debbie. You can use the Table Wizard to create a Customers table, but you will have to modify the table to include all of the required data as per the case description, and further to set the properties of the individual fields as appropriate. You will also need to create a form in which to enter the data. The Form Wizard is a good place to start, but you will have to modify the result to include command buttons, a suitable piece of clip art in the form header, and appropriate formatting throughout. Use the completed form to enter data about your instructor, indicating whether or not he/she wishes to attend a fashion show.

A STUDENT DATABASE

This chapter introduces a new case study, that of a student database, which we use to present the basic principles of table and form design. Tables and forms are used to input data into a system from which information can be produced. The value of that information depends entirely on the quality of the underlying data, which must be both complete and accurate. We begin, therefore, with a conceptual discussion emphasizing the importance of proper design and develop essential guidelines that are used throughout the book.

After the design has been developed, we turn our attention to implementing that design in Access. We show you how to create a table using the Table Wizard, then show you how to refine its design by changing the properties of various fields within the table. We also stress the importance of data validation during data entry.

The second half of the chapter introduces forms as a more convenient way to enter and display data. We introduce the Form Wizard to create a basic form, then show you how to modify that form to include command buttons, a list box, a check box, and an option group.

As a student you are well aware that your school maintains all types of data about you. They have your Social Security number. They have your name and address and phone number. They know whether or not you are receiving financial aid. They know your major and the number of credits you have completed. Think for a moment about the information your school requires, then write down all of the data needed to produce that information. This is the key to the design process. You must visualize the output the end user will require to determine the input to produce that output. Think of the specific fields you will need. Try to characterize each field according to the type of data it contains (such as text, numbers, or dates) as well as its size (length).

Our solution is shown in Figure 2.1, which may or may not correspond to what you have written down. The order of the fields within the table is not significant. Neither are the specific field names. What is important is that the table contain all necessary fields so that the system can perform as intended.

Field Name	Type
SSN	Text
FirstName	Text
LastName	Text
Address	Text
City	Text
State	Text
PostalCode	Text
PhoneNumber	Text
Major	Text
BirthDate	Date/Time
FinancialAid	Yes/No
Gender	Text
Credits	Number
QualityPoints	Number
DateAdmitted	Date/Time
E-mail	Text
International	Yes/No
HomePage	Hyperlink

FIGURE 2.1 The Students Table

Figure 2.1 may seem obvious upon presentation, but it does reflect the results of a careful design process based on three essential guidelines:

1. Include all of the necessary data

2. Store data in its smallest parts

3. Do not use calculated fields

Each guideline is discussed in turn. As you proceed through the text, you will be exposed to many applications that help you develop the experience necessary to design your own systems. Design is an important skill. Yes, you want to learn how to use Access, but you must first understand how to design a database and its tables if you are to use Access effectively.

Include the Necessary Data

How do you determine the necessary data? The best way is to create a rough draft of the reports you will need, then design the table so that it contains the fields necessary to create those reports. In other words, ask yourself what information will be expected from the system, then determine the data required to produce that information. Consider, for example, the type of information that can and cannot be produced from the table in Figure 2.1:

- You can contact a student by mail or by telephone. You cannot, however, contact the student's parents if the student lives on campus or has an address different from that of his or her parents.

- You can calculate a student's grade point average (GPA) by dividing the quality points by the number of credits. You cannot produce a transcript listing the courses a student has taken.

- You can calculate a student's age from his or her date of birth. You cannot determine when the student declared a major because that date is not included in the table.

Whether or not these omissions are important depends on the objectives of the system. Suffice it to say that you must design a table carefully, so that you are not disappointed when the database is implemented. *You must be absolutely certain that the data entered into a system is sufficient to provide all necessary information.* Think carefully about all of the reports you are likely to want, then be sure to capture the data to create those reports.

DESIGN FOR THE NEXT 100 YEARS

Your system will not last 100 years, but it is prudent to design as though it will. It is a fundamental law of information technology that systems evolve continually and that information requirements will change. Try to anticipate the future needs of the system, then build in the flexibility to satisfy those demands. Include the necessary data at the outset, and be sure that the field sizes are large enough to accommodate future expansion.

Store Data in Its Smallest Parts

The design in Figure 2.1 divides a student's name into two fields (first name and last name) to reference each field individually. You might think it easier to use a single field consisting of both the first and last name, but that approach is inadequate. Consider, for example, the list shown on the next page in which the student's name is stored as a single field:

Allison Foster
Brit Reback
Carrie Graber
Danielle Ferrarro
Evelyn Adams
Frances Coulter

List is in alphabetical order by first name

The first problem in this approach is one of flexibility, in that you cannot separate a student's first name from her last name. You could not, for example, create a salutation of the form "Dear Allison" or "Dear Ms. Foster" because the first and last name are not accessible individually. (In actuality you could write a procedure to divide the name field in two, but that is well beyond the capability of the Access novice.)

A second difficulty is that the list of students cannot be put into true alphabetical order because the last name begins in the middle of the field. Indeed, whether you realize it or not, the names in the list are already in alphabetical order (according to the design criteria of a single field) because sorting always begins with the leftmost position in a field. Thus the "A" in Allison comes before the "B" in Brit, and so on. The proper way to sort the data is on the last name, which can be done only if the last name is stored as a separate field. This illustrates the importance of storing data in its smallest parts.

CITY, STATE, AND ZIP CODE: ONE FIELD OR THREE?

The city, state, and zip code should always be stored as separate fields. Any type of mass mailing requires you to sort on zip code to take advantage of bulk mail. Other applications may require you to select records from a particular state or zip code, which can be done only if the data is stored as separate fields. The guideline is simple—store data in its smallest parts.

Avoid Calculated Fields

A *calculated field* is a field whose value is derived from a formula or function that references an existing field or combination of fields. Calculated fields should not be stored in a table because they are subject to change, waste space, and are otherwise redundant.

A student's Grade Point Average (GPA) is an example of a calculated field since it is computed by dividing the number of quality points by the number of credits. Thus it is unnecessary to store GPA in the Students table, because the table contains the fields on which the GPA is based. In other words, Access is able to calculate the GPA from these fields whenever it is needed, which is much more efficient than doing it manually. Imagine, for example, having to manually enter new values for credits and quality points and then having to recalculate the GPA for 10,000 students each semester.

BIRTH DATE VERSUS AGE

A person's age and date of birth provide equivalent information, as one is calculated from the other. It might seem easier, therefore, to store the age rather than the birth date, and thus avoid the calculation. That would be a mistake because age changes continually (and would need to be updated continually), whereas the date of birth remains constant. Similar reasoning applies to an employee's length of service versus date of hire.

There are two ways to create a table. The easier way is to use the **Table Wizard**, an interactive coach that lets you choose from many predefined tables. The Table Wizard asks you questions about the fields you want to include in your table, then creates the table for you. Alternatively, you can create a table yourself by defining every field in the table. Regardless of how a table is created, you can modify it to include a new field or to delete an existing field.

Every field has a **field name** to identify the data that is entered into the field. The field name should be descriptive of the data and can be up to 64 characters in length, including letters, numbers, and spaces. We do not, however, use spaces in our field names, but use uppercase letters to distinguish the first letter of a new word. This is consistent with the default names provided by Access in its predefined tables.

Every field also has a **data type** that determines the type of data that can be entered and the operations that can be performed on that data. Access recognizes nine data types:

- A **Number field** contains a value that can be used in a calculation, such as the number of credits a student has earned. The contents of a number field are restricted to numbers, a decimal point, and a plus or minus sign.

- A **Text field** stores alphanumeric data, such as a student's name or address. It can contain alphabetic characters, numbers, and/or special characters (e.g., an apostrophe in O'Malley). Fields that contain only numbers but are not used in a calculation (e.g., Social Security Number, telephone number, or zip code) should be designated as text fields. A text field can hold up to 255 characters.

- A **Memo field** can be up to 65,535 characters long. Memo fields are used to hold lengthy, descriptive data (several sentences or paragraphs).

- A **Date/Time field** holds formatted dates or times (e.g., mm/dd/yy) and allows the values to be used in date or time arithmetic.

- A **Currency field** can be used in a calculation and is used for fields that contain monetary values.

- A **Yes/No field** (also known as a Boolean or Logical field) assumes one of two values, such as Yes or No, or True or False, or On or Off.

- An **OLE Object field** contains an object created by another application. OLE objects include pictures, sounds, or graphics.

- An **AutoNumber field** is a special data type that causes Access to assign the next consecutive number each time you add a record. The value of an AutoNumber field is unique for each record in the file, and thus AutoNumber fields are frequently used as the primary key.

- A **Hyperlink field** stores a Web address (URL). All Office documents are Web-enabled so that you can click a hyperlink and display the associated Web page.

Primary Key

The **primary key** is a field (or combination of fields) that makes each record in a table unique. The primary key is not required, but is highly recommended. There can be only one primary key per table.

A person's name is not used as the primary key because names are not unique. A Social Security number, on the other hand, is unique and is a frequent choice for the primary key, as in the Students table in this chapter. The primary key emerges naturally in many applications, such as a part number in an inventory system, or the ISBN in the Books table of Chapter 1. If there is no apparent primary key, a new field can be created with the AutoNumber field type.

Views

A table has multiple views. The Datasheet view is the view you used in Chapter 1 to add, edit, and delete records. The Design view is the view you will use in this chapter to create (and modify) a table. The *PivotTable view* provides a convenient way to summarize data about groups of records. The *PivotChart view* displays a chart of the associated PivotTable view. (The PivotTable view and PivotChart view were introduced in Access 2002 and did not exist in previous versions. Both views are discussed in detail in Chapter 4.)

Figure 2.2a shows the Datasheet view corresponding to the table in Figure 2.1. (The horizontal scroll bar indicates that not all of the fields are visible.) The *Datasheet view* displays the record selector symbol for the current record (a pencil or a triangle). It also displays an asterisk in the record selector column next to the blank record at the end of the table.

Figure 2.2b shows the Design view of the same table. The *Design view* displays the field names in the table, the data type of each field, and the properties of the selected field. The Design view also displays a key indicator next to the field (or combination of fields) designated as the primary key.

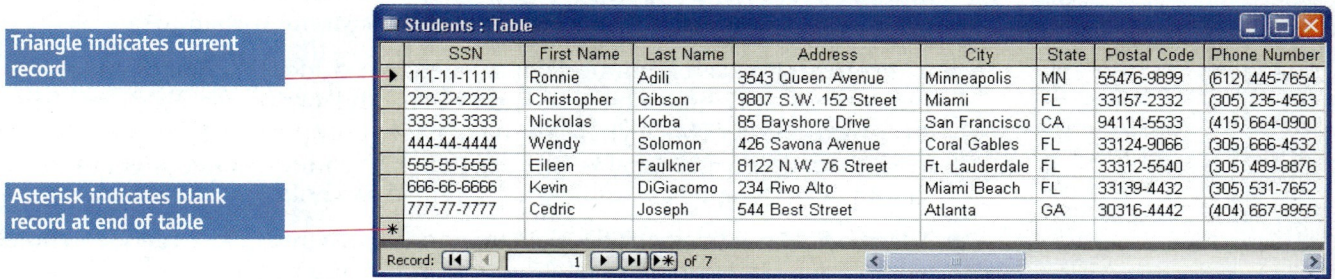

(a) Datasheet View

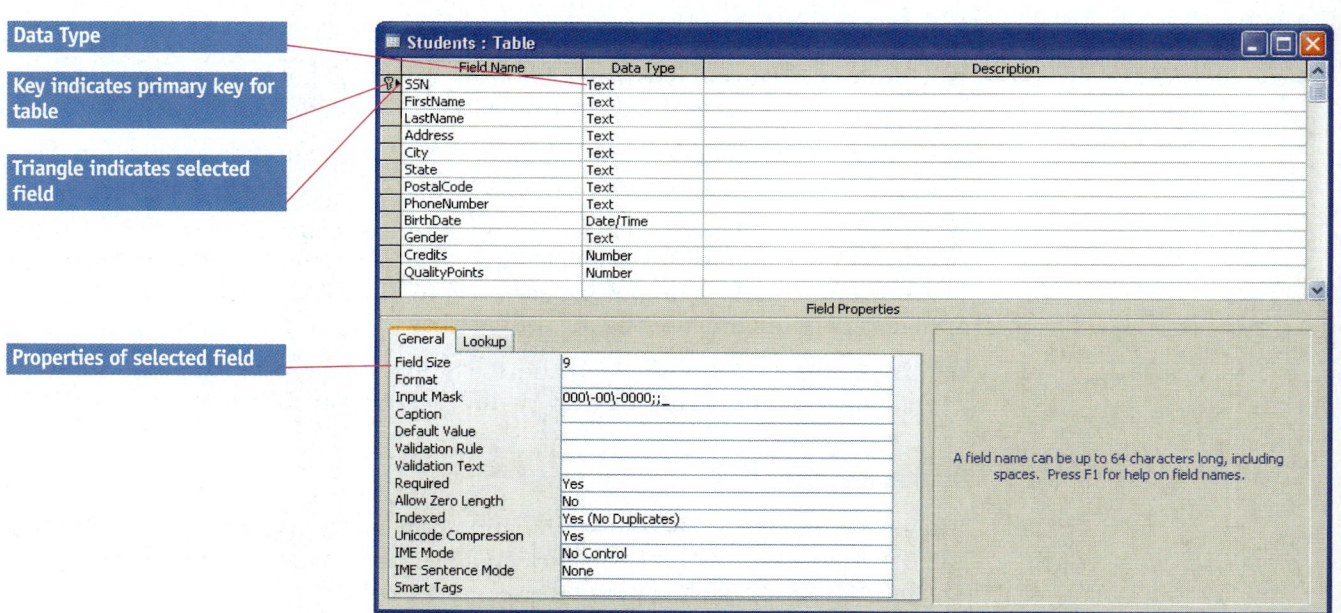

(b) Design View

FIGURE 2.2 The Views of a Table

Properties

A *property* is a characteristic or attribute of an object that determines how the object looks and behaves. Every Access object (tables, forms, queries, and reports) has a set of properties that determine the behavior of that object. The properties for an object are displayed and/or changed in a *property sheet*, which is described in more detail later in the chapter.

Each field has its own set of properties that determine how the data in the field is stored and displayed. The properties are set to default values according to the data type, but can be modified as necessary. The properties are displayed in the Design view and described briefly below:

- The *Field Size property* adjusts the size of a text field or limits the allowable value in a number field. Microsoft Access uses only the amount of space it needs even if the field size allows a greater number.

- The *Format property* changes the way a field is displayed or printed, but does not affect the stored value.

- The *Input Mask property* facilitates data entry by displaying literal characters, that are displayed but not stored, such as hyphens in a Social Security number or slashes in a date. It also imposes data validation by ensuring that the data entered by the user fits within the mask.

- The *Caption property* specifies a label other than the field name for forms and reports.

- The *Default Value property* automatically enters a designated (default) value for the field in each record that is added to the table.

- The *Validation Rule property* rejects any record in which the data entered does not conform to the specified rules for data entry.

- The *Validation Text property* specifies the error message that is displayed when the validation rule is violated.

- The *Required property* rejects any record that does not have a value entered for this field.

- The *Allow Zero Length property* allows text or memo strings of zero length.

- The *Indexed property* increases the efficiency of a search on the designated field. (The primary key in a table is always indexed.)

- The *Unicode Compression property* is set to "Yes" by default for Text, Memo, and Hyperlink fields to store the data more efficiently.

- The *IME Mode* and *IME Sentence Mode properties* refer to the Input Method Editor for East Asian languages and are not discussed further.

There is no need to memorize the list of properties because they are readily available in the Design view of a table. And, as you may have guessed, it's time for our next hands-on exercise, in which you create a new database. We begin with the Table Wizard, then switch to the Design view to add additional fields and modify selected properties of various fields within the table.

CHANGE THE DEFAULT FOLDER

The default folder is the folder Access uses to retrieve (and save) a database unless it is otherwise instructed. To change the default folder, pull down the Tools menu, click Options, then click the General tab in the Options dialog box. Enter the name of the default database folder (e.g., C:\Exploring Access), then click OK to accept the settings and close the Options dialog box. The next time you access the File menu, the default folder will reflect the change.

1 Creating a Table

Objective	To create a new database; to use the Table Wizard to create a table; to add and delete fields of an existing table. Use Figure 2.3 as a guide.

Step 1: **Create a New Database**

- Click the **Start button**, click the **All Programs button**, click **Microsoft Office**, then click **Microsoft Access** to start the program.

- Click **Create a new file** at the bottom of the Getting Started task pane, then click **Blank database** in the New File task pane. (If the task pane is not open, click the **New button** on the toolbar.)

- You should see the File New Database dialog box shown in Figure 2.3a.

- Click the **drop-down arrow** on the Save In list box and select the appropriate drive. Double click the **Exploring Access folder**.

- Click in the **File Name text box** and drag to select **db1**. Type **My First Database** as the name of the database you will create. Click the **Create button**.

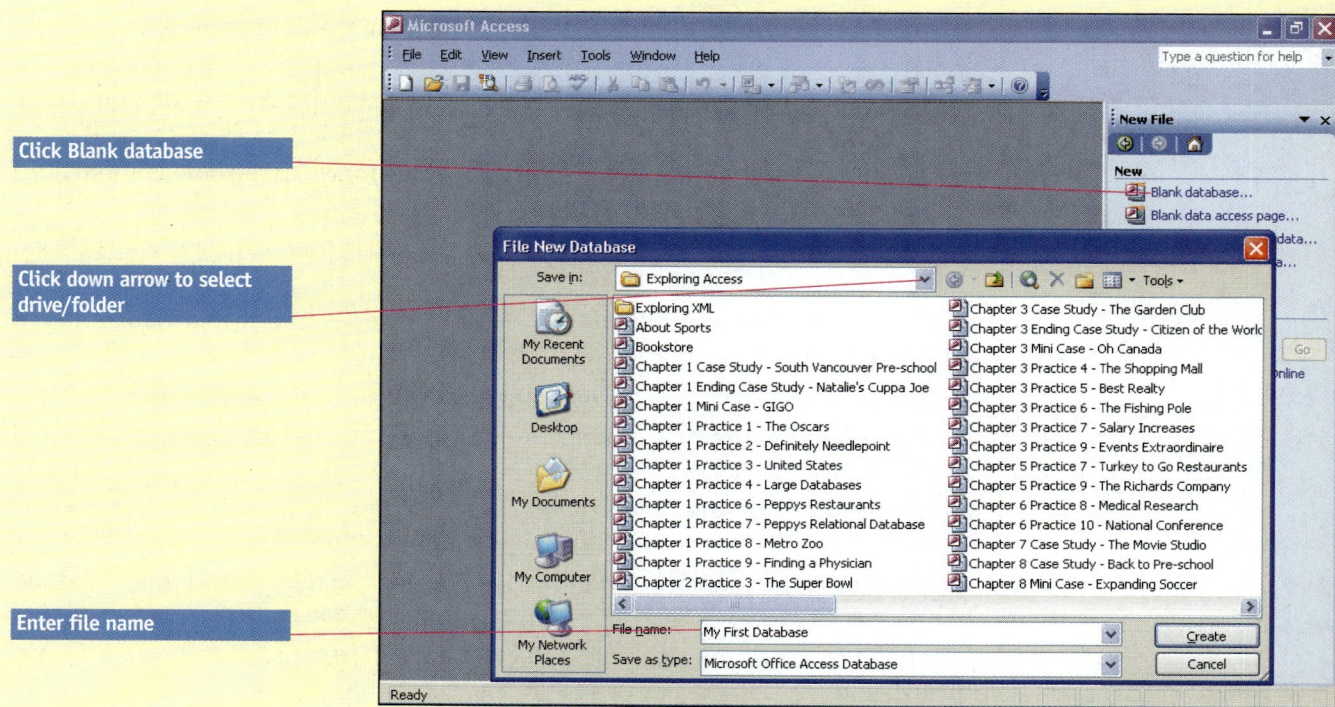

Click Blank database

Click down arrow to select drive/folder

Enter file name

(a) Create a New Database (step 1)

FIGURE 2.3 Hands-on Exercise 1

FILE FORMATS

Access 2002 (Office XP) introduced a new file format that was continued in Access 2003. Access 2000, however, cannot read the new format; thus, it is convenient to save files in the older Access 2000 format to maintain compatibility with anyone using Microsoft Office 2000. Pull down the Tools menu, click Options, click the Advanced tab, and change the Default File Format to Access 2000. Use Help to learn about converting from one file format to another.

Step 2: **The Table Wizard**

■ The Database window for My First Database should appear on your monitor. The Tables button is selected by default.

■ Double click the icon to **Create table by using wizard** to start the Table Wizard as shown in Figure 2.3b. Click the **Business option button**.

■ Click the **down arrow** on the Sample Tables list box to scroll through the available tables until you can select (click) the **Students table**. (The Students table is found near the bottom of the list.)

■ The **StudentID field** is already selected in the Sample Fields list box. Click the **> button** to enter this field into the list of fields for the new table.

■ Enter the additional fields for the new table by selecting the field and clicking the **> button** (or by double clicking the field). The fields to enter are **FirstName, LastName, Address, City**, and **StateOrProvince**.

■ Click the **Rename Field button** after adding the StateOrProvince field to display the Rename Field dialog box. Enter **State** to shorten the name of this field. Click **OK** to accept the new name and close the dialog box.

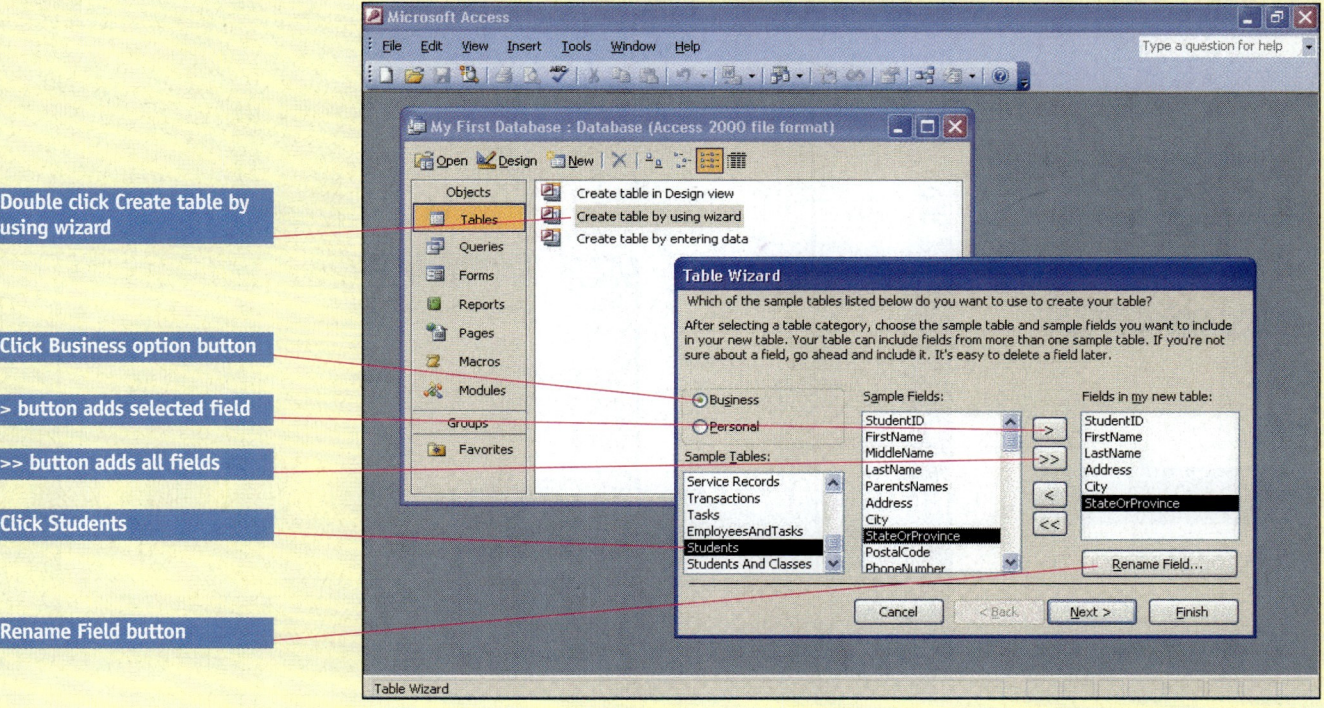

Double click Create table by using wizard

Click Business option button

> button adds selected field

>> button adds all fields

Click Students

Rename Field button

(b) The Table Wizard (step 2)

FIGURE 2.3   Hands-on Exercise 1 (*continued*)

WIZARDS AND BUTTONS

Many wizards present you with two open list boxes and expect you to copy some or all fields from the list box on the left to the list box on the right. The > and >> buttons work from left to right. The < and << buttons work in the opposite direction. The > button copies the selected field from the list box on the left to the box on the right. The >> button copies all of the fields. The < button removes the selected field from the list box on the right. The << removes all of the fields.

Step 3: **The Table Wizard Continued**

- Add **PostalCode** and **PhoneNumber** (you may need to click the **down arrow** to scroll). Click **Next**.

- The next screen in the Table Wizard asks you to name the table and determine the primary key.
  - ❏ Accept the Wizard's suggestion of **Students** as the name of the table.
  - ❏ Make sure that the option button **Yes**, **set a primary key for me** is selected as shown in Figure 2.3c.
  - ❏ Click **Next** to accept both of these options.

- The final screen in the Table Wizard asks what you want to do next.
  - ❏ Click the option button to **Modify the table design**.
  - ❏ Click the **Finish command button**.

- The Students table should appear in Design view. Pull down the **File menu** and click **Save** (or click the **Save button** on the Table Design toolbar) to save the table within the database.

- The Table Wizard provided an easy way to create the table initially. You can now modify the table in Design view as described in the next several steps.

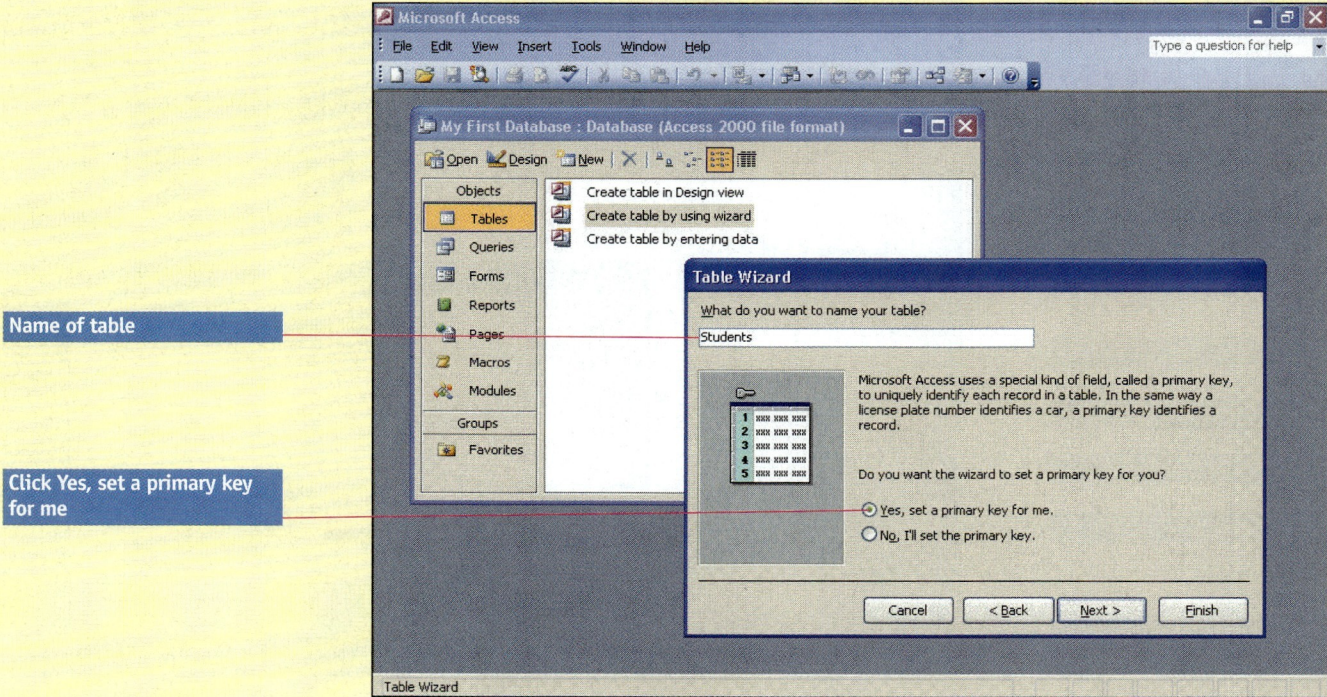

Name of table

Click Yes, set a primary key for me

(c) The Table Wizard Continued (step 3)

FIGURE 2.3 Hands-on Exercise 1 (*continued*)

YOU DON'T HAVE TO USE THE TABLE WIZARD

There is no requirement to use the Table Wizard, especially if you are creating a table that is very different from those available through the wizard. Go to the Database window, click the Tables button, then double click the option to Create Table in Design view. Enter the field name for the first field, select the field type, then modify the field properties as necessary. Continue to work in this fashion as you enter the remaining fields into the table. See practice exercises 4, 6, 8, and 10 at the end of the chapter.

Step 4: Add the Additional Fields

- Click the **Maximize button** to give yourself more room to work. Click the cell immediately below the last field in the table (PhoneNumber). Type **BirthDate** as shown in Figure 2.3d.

- Press the **Tab key** to move to the Data Type column. Click the **down arrow** on the drop-down list box. Click **Date/Time.** (You can also type the first letter of the field type such as **D** for Date/Time, **T** for Text, or **N** for number.)

- Add the remaining fields to the Students table.
  - ❏ Add **Gender** as a Text field.
  - ❏ Add **Credits** as a Number field.
  - ❏ Add **QualityPoints** as a Number field. (There is no space in the field name.)

- The additional fields are unique to our application and were not available in the wizard.

- Click the **Save button** to save the table.

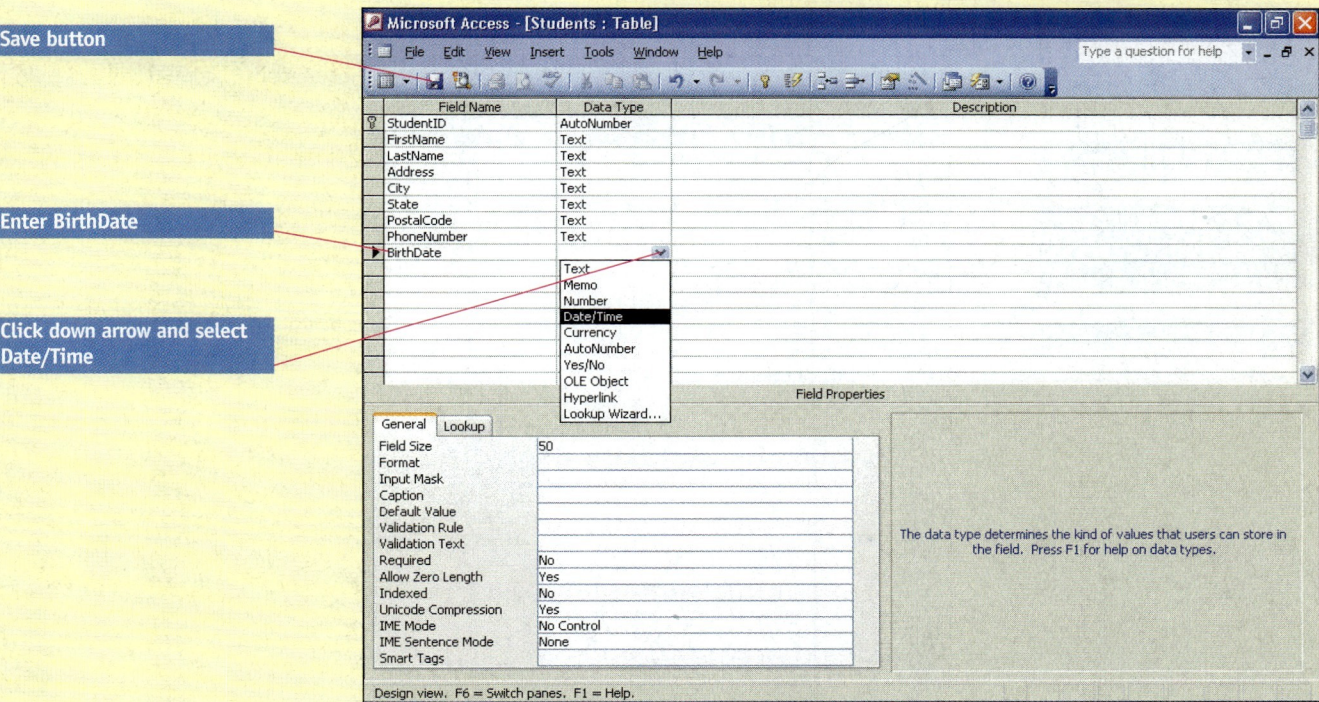

(d) Add the Additional Fields (step 4)

FIGURE 2.3 Hands-on Exercise 1 (*continued*)

NUMBERS AS TEXT FIELDS

The numeric field type should be restricted to fields on which you perform calculations, such as a student's credits or quality points. This implies that fields such as Social Security number, zip code, and telephone number are defined as text fields even though they contain numbers, as opposed to alphabetic characters. Look closely within the Students table that was created by the Table Wizard and you will see that PostalCode and PhoneNumber have been defined as text fields. (The additional characters that appear within a field, such as hyphens in a Social Security number, are entered as an input mask and are not stored within the field.)

Step 5: **Change the Primary Key**

- Point to the first field in the table and click the **right mouse button** to display the shortcut menu in Figure 2.3e. Click **Insert Rows**.

- Click the **Field Name column** in the newly inserted row. Type **SSN** (for Social Security Number) as the name of the new field. Press **Enter**. The data type will be set to Text by default.

- Click the **Required box** in the Properties area. Click the **drop-down arrow** and select **Yes**.

- Click in the Field Name column for **SSN**, then click the **Primary Key button** on the Table Design toolbar to change the primary key to Social Security Number. The primary key symbol has moved to SSN.

- Point to the **StudentID field** in the second row. Click the **right mouse button** to display the shortcut menu. Click **Delete Rows** to remove this field from the table definition.

- Save the table.

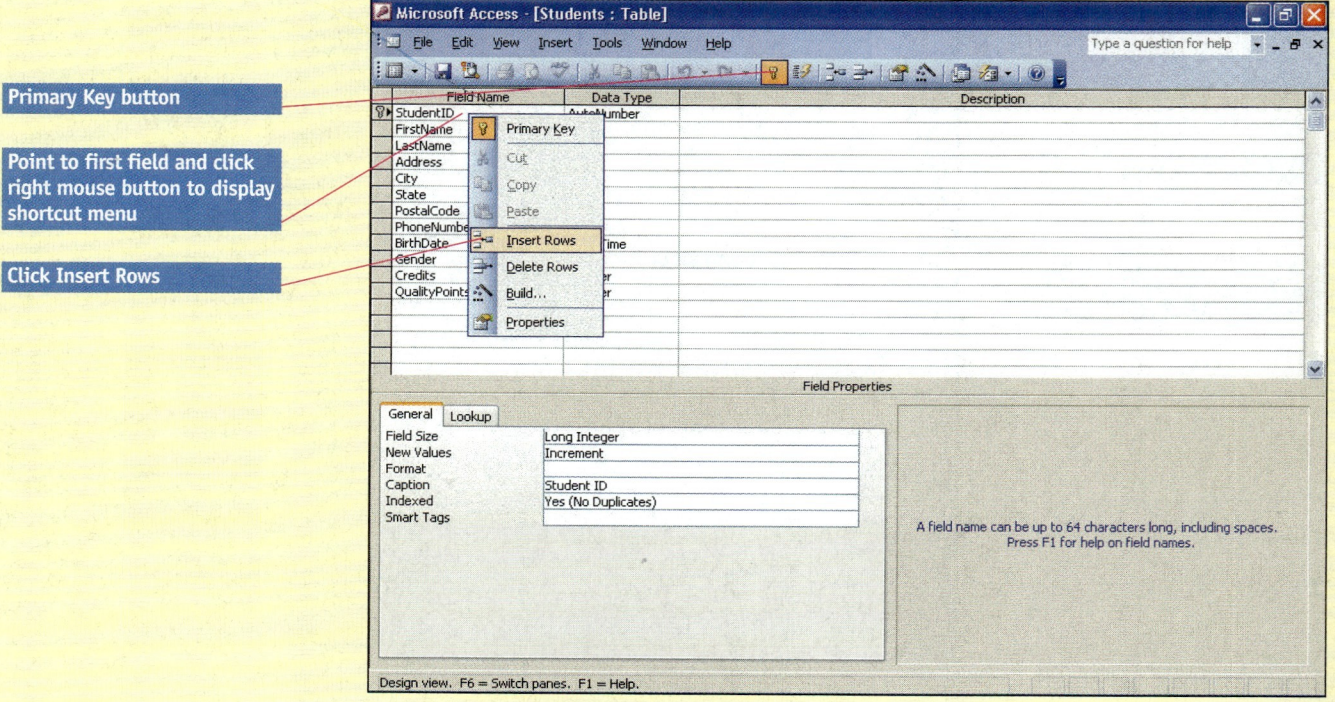

(e) Change the Primary Key (step 5)

FIGURE 2.3 Hands-on Exercise 1 (*continued*)

INSERTING OR DELETING FIELDS

To insert or delete a field, point to an existing field, then click the right mouse button to display a shortcut menu. Click Insert Rows or Delete Rows to add or remove a field as appropriate. To insert (or delete) multiple fields, point to the field selector to the left of the field name, click and drag the mouse over multiple rows to extend the selection, then click the right mouse button to display a shortcut menu.

Step 6: **Create an Input Mask**

- Click the field selector column for **SSN**. Click the **Input Mask box** in the Properties area. (The box is currently empty.)
- Click the **Build button** to display the Input Mask Wizard. Click **Yes** if asked to save the table. Click **Social Security Number** in the Input Mask Wizard dialog box as shown in Figure 2.3f.
- Click the **Try It** text box and enter a Social Security number to see how the mask works. If necessary, press the **left arrow key** until you are at the beginning of the text box, then enter a Social Security number (digits only). Click the **Finish command button** to accept the input mask. Click in the text box for the Field Size property and change the field size to **9**.
- Click the field selector column for **BirthDate**, then follow the steps detailed above to add an input mask. (Choose the **Short Date** format.) Click **Yes** if asked whether to save the table.
- Set an appropriate input mask for the telephone number as well. Change the field size to **10**.
- Save the table.

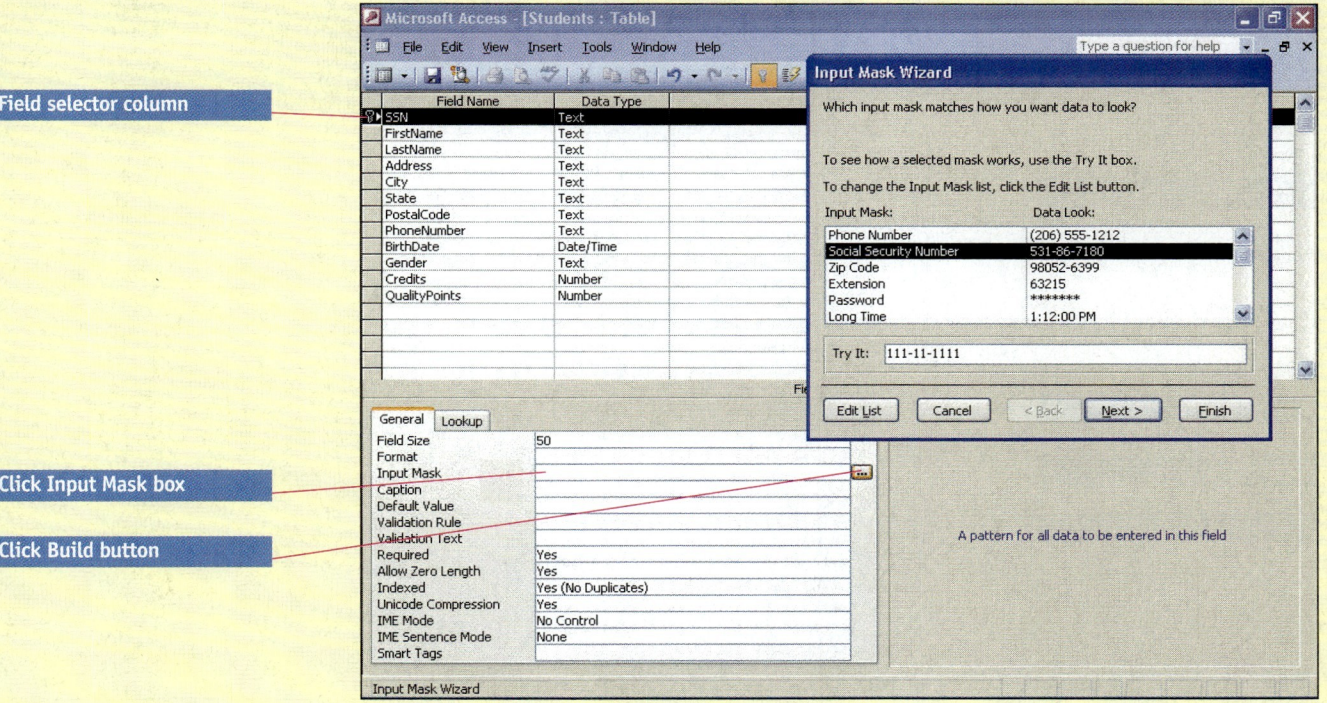

(f) Create an Input Mask (step 6)

FIGURE 2.3 Hands-on Exercise 1 (*continued*)

CREATE YOUR OWN INPUT MASK

The Input Mask imposes character-by-character data validation by requiring that data be entered in a specific way. The Social Security mask, for example, 000\-00\-0000, specifies a zero to require a numeric value from 0 to 9. The character following the slash (a hyphen in this example) is an insertion character and appears within the field during data entry but is not stored. You can create your own input masks for text fields by using the characters "L" to require a letter, or "A" to require either a letter or a digit. Use the Help command for additional information.

Step 7: **Change the Field Properties**

- Click the field selector column for the **FirstName field**. Click in the text box for the **Field Size property** and change the field size to **15**. Change the **Required property** to **Yes**.

- Select the **LastName field**. Set the **Field Size property** to **20** and the **Required property** to **Yes**.

- Select the **State field**. Set the **Field Size property** to two. Click the **Format box** in the Properties Area. Type a > sign to display the data in uppercase as shown in Figure 2.3g. Click in the **InputMask property** and type **LL** to require letters, as opposed to digits.

- Select the **Credits field**. Click the **Field Size box** in the Properties area, click the **down arrow** to display the available field sizes, then click **Integer**. Click in the **Default property box** and delete the default value of zero.

- Set the Field Size and Default properties for the **QualityPoints field** to match those of the Credits field.

- Save the table.

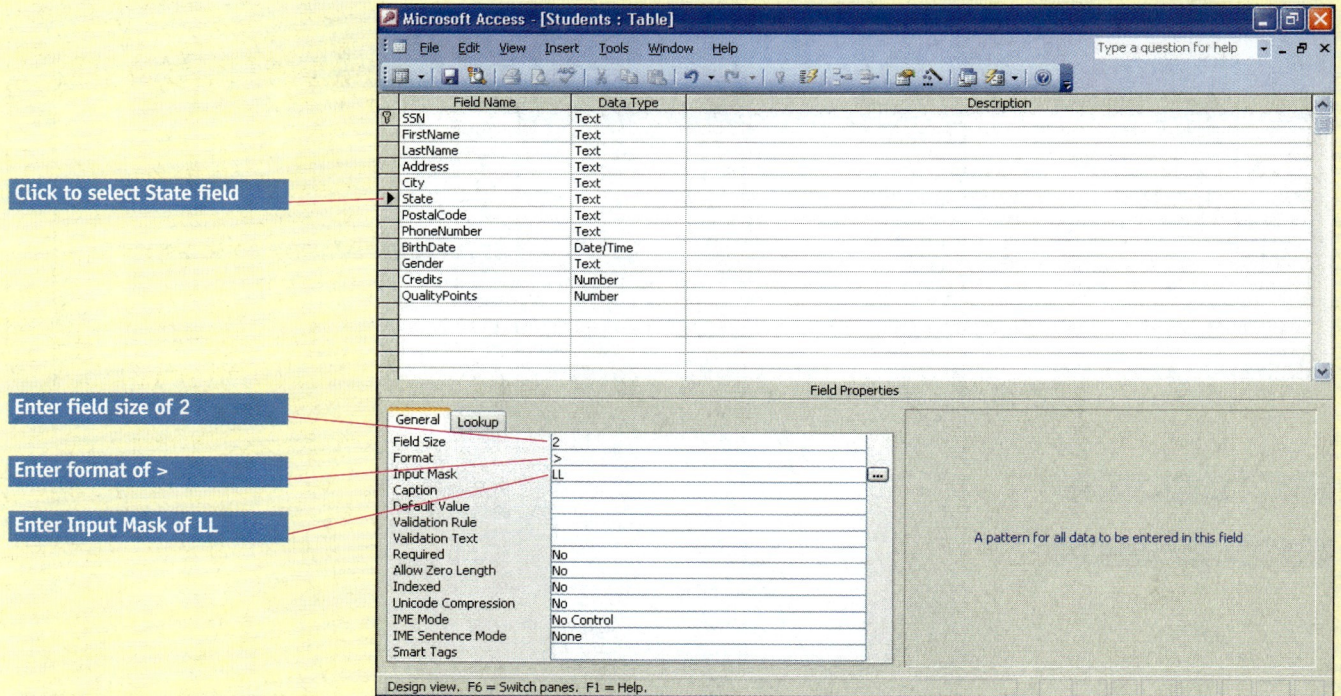

(g) Change the Field Properties (step 7)

FIGURE 2.3 Hands-on Exercise 1 (*continued*)

THE FIELD SIZE PROPERTY

The field size property should be set to the smallest possible setting because smaller data sizes are processed more efficiently. A text field can hold from 0 to 255 characters (50 is the default). Number fields which do not contain a decimal value can be set to Byte, Integer, or Long Integer field sizes, which hold values up to 255, 32,767, or 2,147,483,647, respectively. (Click in the Field Size box for a Number field and press F1 for more information.)

Step 8:   **Add a Validation Rule**

■ Data validation is implemented in several ways. You can set the Required property to Yes to ensure that a value is entered and/or you can create an input mask to accept only certain characters. You can also set the Validation Rule property.

■ Select the **Gender field** as shown in Figure 2.3h. Click the **Field Size box** and change the field size to **1**.

■ Click the **Format box** in the Properties area. Type a **>** sign to display the data in uppercase letters.

■ Click the **Validation Rule box**. Type **="M" or "F"** to accept only these values on data entry. Click the **Validation Text box**, and type **You must specify M or F**. (This message explains the error to the user.)

■ Check that the required property is set to "No" so that gender is not required. If the user enters a value, however, it must be "M" or "F".

■ Save the table.

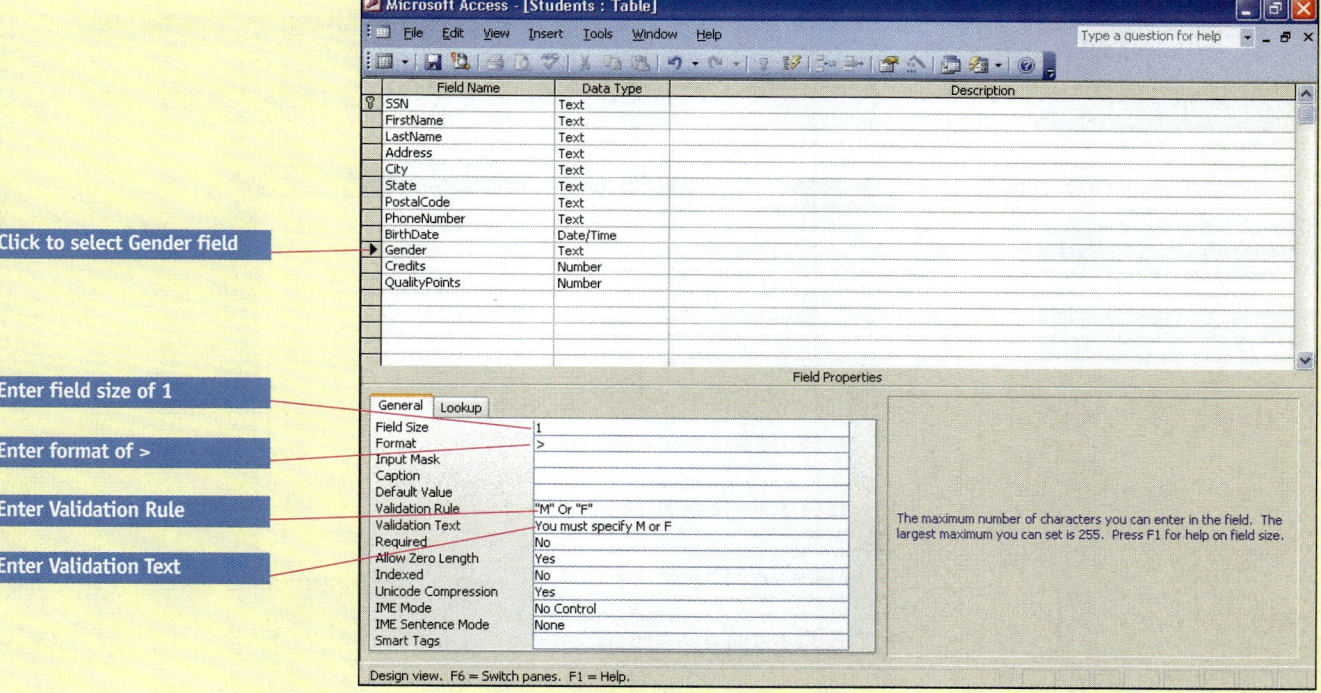

(h) Add a Validation Rule (step 8)

FIGURE 2.3   Hands-on Exercise 1 (*continued*)

VALIDATE THE INCOMING DATA

No system, no matter how sophisticated, can produce valid output from invalid input—in other words, "garbage in, garbage out." It is absolutely critical, therefore, that you take the time to validate the data as it is entered to ensure the quality of the output. Some validation is already built in by Access. You cannot, for example, enter duplicate values for a primary key, nor can you enter text into a numeric field. Other validation is built in at the initiative of the developer by setting various field properties in Design view.

Step 9: **Print the Students Table**

- Pull down the **View menu** and click **Datasheet View** to change to the Datasheet view as shown in Figure 2.3i. Enter data for yourself, but use a hypothetical Social Security number such as **123-45-6789**. (Note the input mask that appears.)

- Pull down the **File menu** and click the **Page Setup command** to display the Page Setup dialog box. Click the **Page tab** and change to **Landscape printing**.

- Click the **Margins tab**. Change the left and right margins to **.5 inch**. Click **OK**.

- Click the **Print Preview button** to view the table to check that it fits on one page. (If not, return to the Datasheet view and reduce the column widths as necessary.)

- Pull down the **File menu**, click the **Print command**, and click **OK** to print the table. Close the Print Preview window. Close the Students table. Click **Yes** if prompted to save the changes to the table.

- Pull down the **File menu** and click the **Exit command** if you do not want to continue with the next exercise at this time.

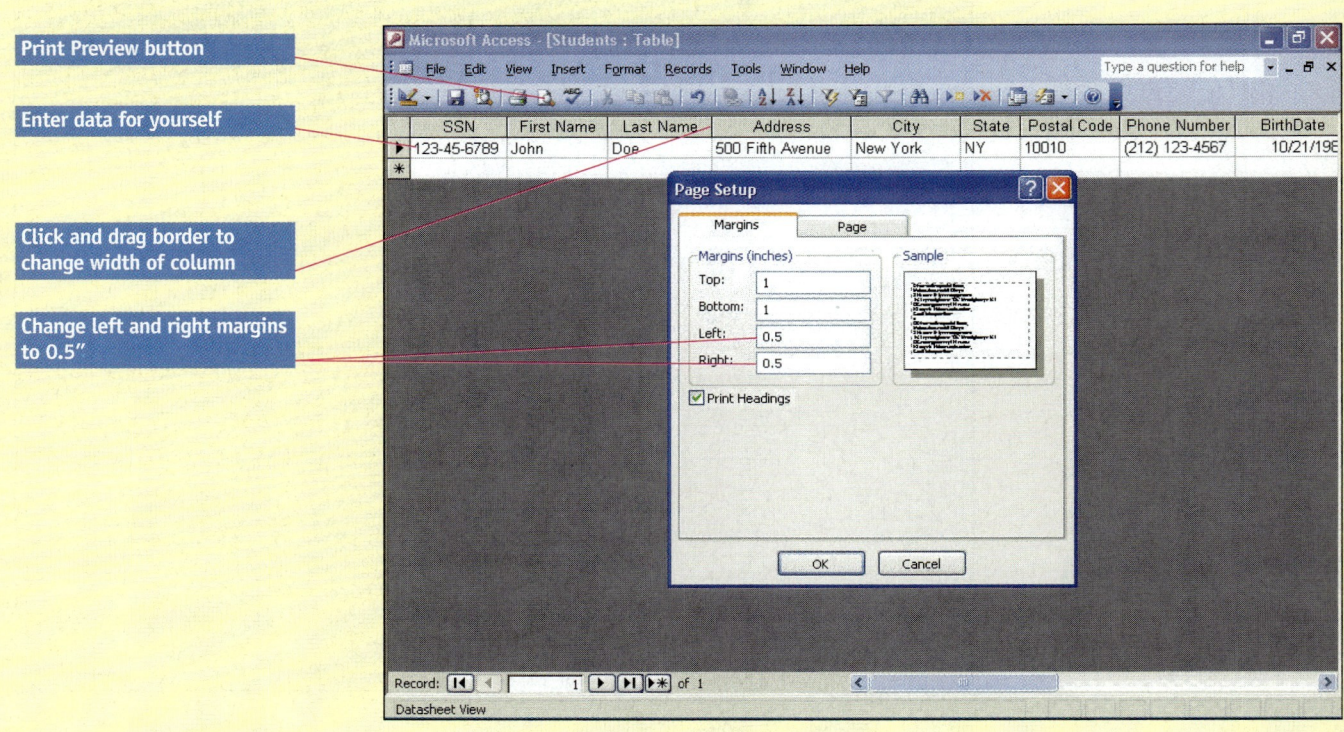

(i) Print the Students Table (step 9)

FIGURE 2.3 Hands-on Exercise 1 (*continued*)

CHANGE THE FIELD WIDTH—ACCESS AND EXCEL

Drag the border between field names to change the displayed width of a column. You can also double click the right border of a field name to change the width of the column to accommodate the widest entry in that column. This is the same convention that is followed in Microsoft Excel. Look for other similarities between the two applications. For example, you can click within a field, then click the Sort Ascending or Sort Descending buttons (in tables with multiple records) on the toolbar to display the records in the indicated sequence.

A **form** provides an easy way to enter and display the data stored in a table. You type data into a form, such as the one in Figure 2.4, and Access stores the data in the corresponding (underlying) table in the database. One advantage of using a form (as opposed to entering records in the Datasheet view) is that you can see all of the fields in a single record without scrolling. A second advantage is that a form can be designed to resemble a paper form, and thus provide a sense of familiarity for the individuals who actually enter the data.

A form has different views, as does a table. The **Form view** in Figure 2.4a displays the completed form and is used to enter or modify the data in the underlying table. The **Design view** in Figure 2.4b is used to create or modify the form. A form also provides access to the PivotTable view and PivotChart view.

All forms contain **controls** (objects) that accept and display data, perform a specific action, decorate the form, or add descriptive information. There are three types of controls—bound, unbound, and calculated. A **bound control** (such as the text boxes in Figure 2.4a) has a data source (a field in the underlying table) and is used to enter or modify the data in that table.

An **unbound control** has no data source. Unbound controls are used to display titles, labels, lines, graphics, or pictures. Note, too, that every bound control in Figure 2.4a is associated with an unbound control (or label to identify the control). The bound control for Social Security number, for example, is preceded by a label (immediately to the left of the control) that indicates to the user the value that is to be entered. An unbound control is also used for the title of the form.

A **calculated control** has as its data source an expression rather than a field. An **expression** is a combination of operators (e.g., +, −, *, and /), field names, constants, and/or functions. A student's Grade Point Average (GPA in Figure 2.4a) is an example of a calculated control because it is computed by dividing the number of quality points by the number of credits.

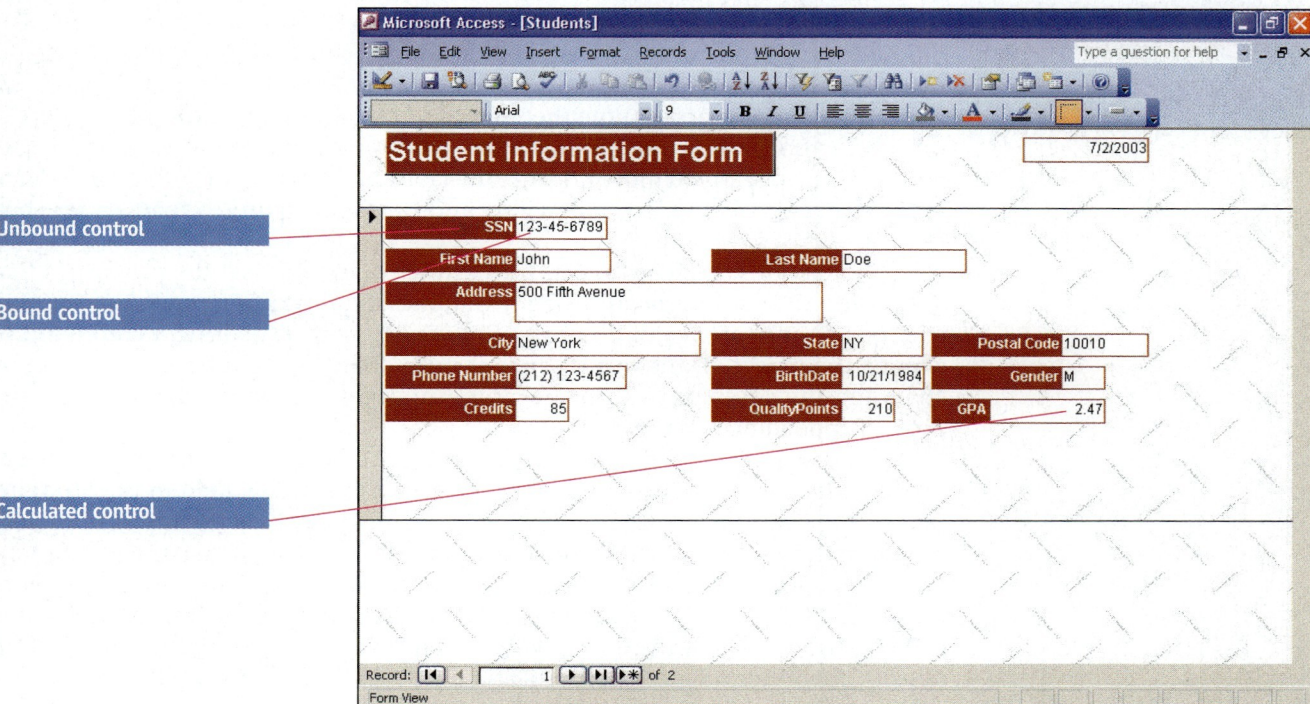

(a) Form View

FIGURE 2.4 Forms

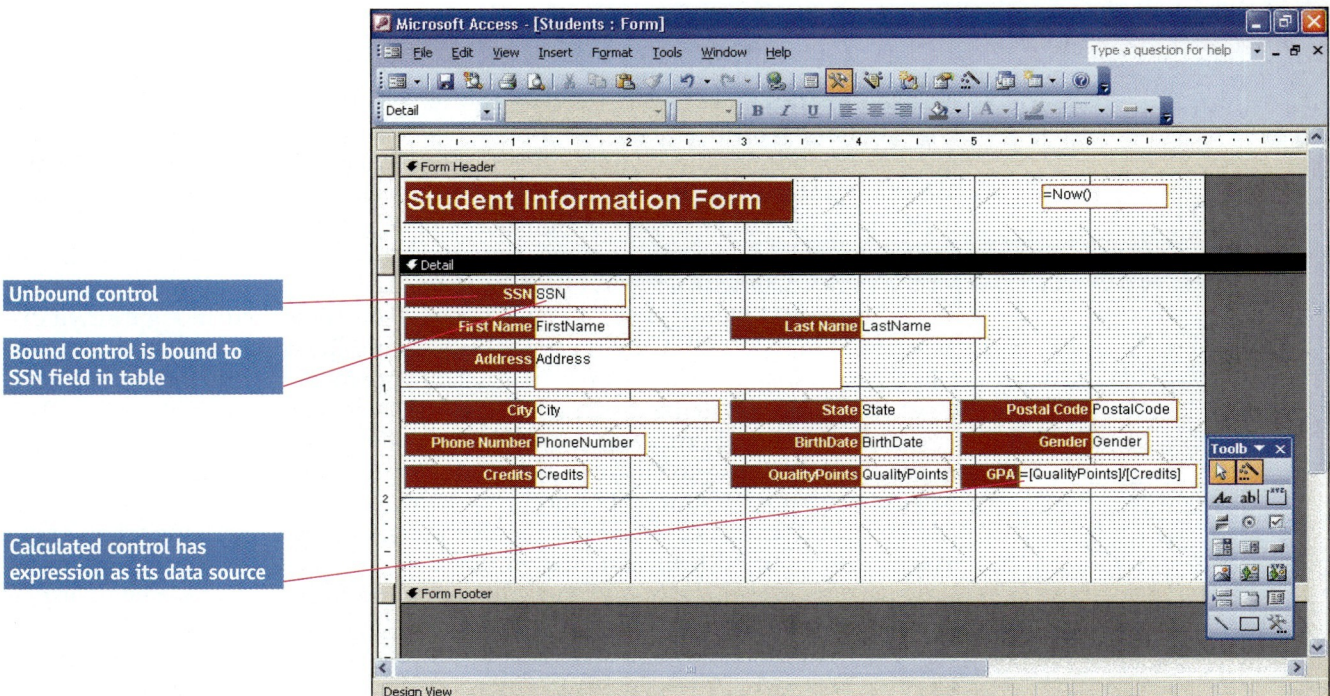

Unbound control

Bound control is bound to SSN field in table

Calculated control has expression as its data source

(b) Design View

FIGURE 2.4 Forms (*continued*)

Properties

As previously stated, a property is a characteristic or attribute of an object that determines how the object looks and behaves. Every control in a form has its own set of properties, just as every field in a table has its own set of properties. The properties for a control are displayed in a property sheet, as shown in Figure 2.5.

Figure 2.5a displays the property sheet for the Form Header Label. There are many different properties (note the vertical scroll bar) that control every aspect of the label's appearance. The properties are determined automatically as the object is created; that is, as you move and size the label on the form, the properties related to its size and position (Left, Top, Width, and Height in Figure 2.5a) are established for you.

Other actions, such as various formatting commands, set the properties that determine the font name and size (Arial and 18 point in Figure 2.5a). You can change the appearance of an object in two ways—by executing a command to change the object on the form, which in turn changes the property sheet, *or* by changing the property within the property sheet, which in turn changes the object's appearance on the form.

Figure 2.5b displays the property sheet for the bound SSN control. The name of the control is SSN. The source for the control is the SSN field in the Students table. Thus, various properties of the SSN control, such as the input mask, are inherited from the SSN field in the underlying table. Note, too, that the list of properties in Figure 2.5b, which reflects a bound control, is different from the list of properties in Figure 2.5a for an unbound control. Some properties, however (such as Left, Top, Width, and Height, which determine the size and position of an object), are present for every control and determine its location on the form.

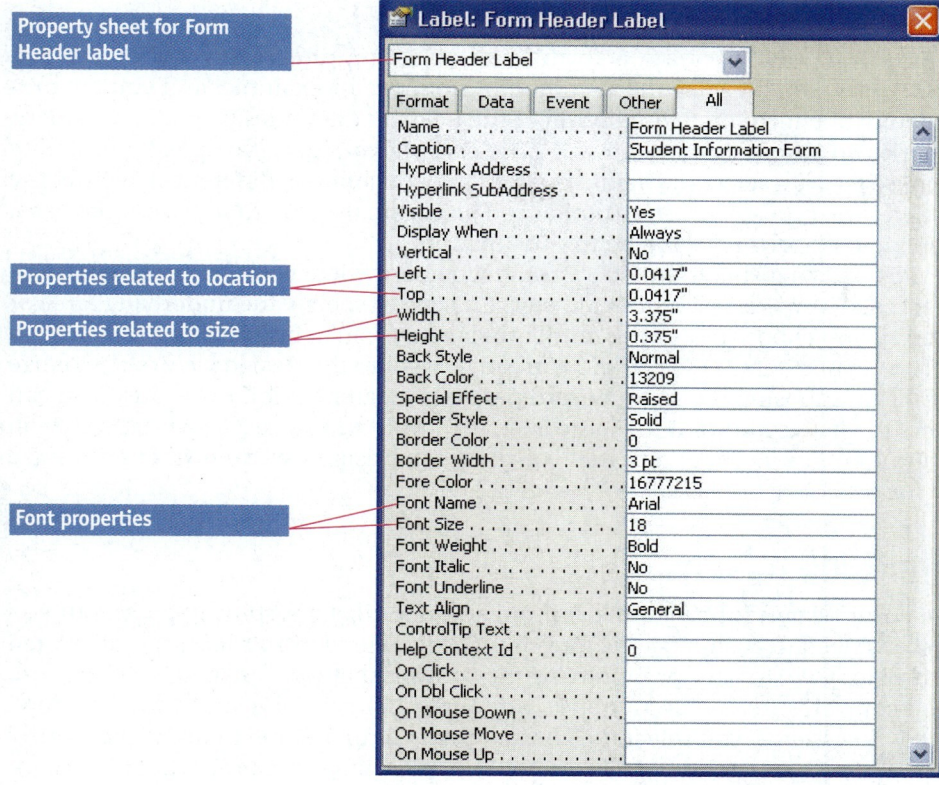

Property sheet for Form Header label

Properties related to location

Properties related to size

Font properties

(a) From Header Label (unbound control)

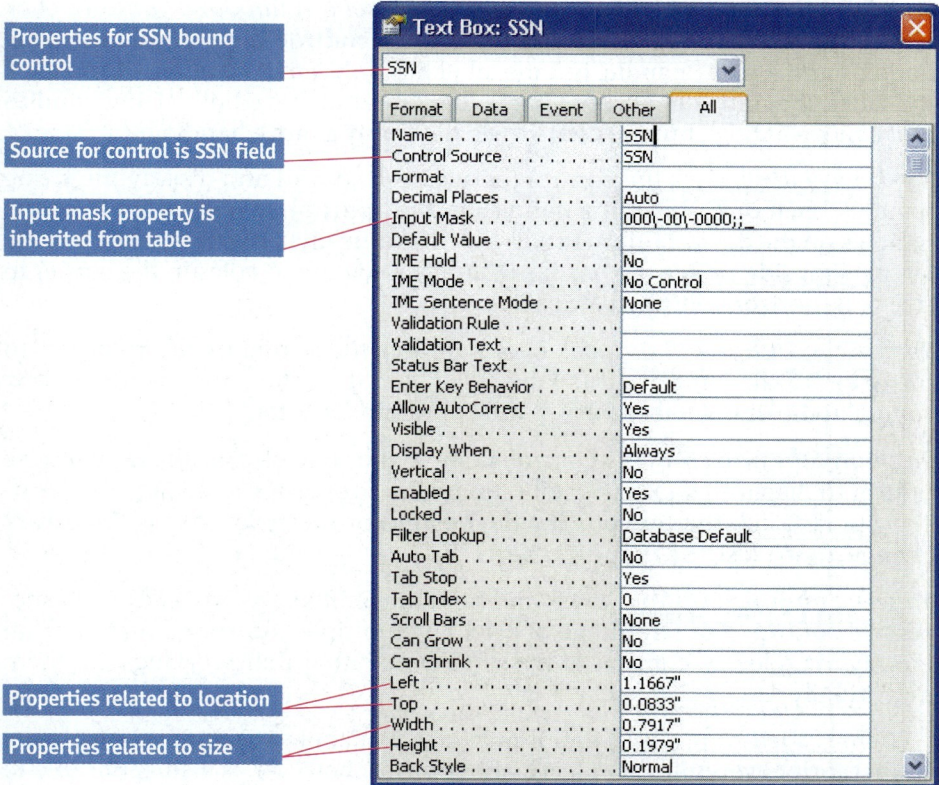

Properties for SSN bound control

Source for control is SSN field

Input mask property is inherited from table

Properties related to location

Properties related to size

(b) SSN Text Box (bound control)

FIGURE 2.5 Property Sheets

AutoForms and the Form Wizard

The easiest way to create a form is by selecting one of several predefined *AutoForms*. Double click the Columnar Autoform, for example, and you are presented with a form that contains all of the fields in the underlying table or query. (Queries are discussed in Chapter 3.) The *Form Wizard* gives you greater flexibility because you can select the fields you want and/or choose a different style from the default style provided by the AutoForm. The wizard asks you a series of questions, then builds the form according to your answers.

Figure 2.6a displays the New Form dialog box, where you choose AutoForm or select the Form Wizard, but either way you have to specify the underlying table or query. If you choose one of the AutoForm layouts, you're finished; that is, the form will be created automatically, and you can go right to the Design view to customize the form. Choosing the Form Wizard provides greater flexibility because you can select the fields you want in Figure 2.6b, the layout in Figure 2.6c, and the style in Figure 2.6d. It is at that point that you go to the Design view to further customize the form.

Modifying a Form

The Form Wizard (or an AutoForm) provides an excellent starting point, but you typically need to customize the form by adding other controls (e.g., the calculated control for GPA) and/or by modifying the controls that were created by the wizard. Each control is treated as an object, and moved or sized like any other Windows object. In essence, you select the control, then click and drag to resize the control or position it elsewhere on the form. You can also change the properties of the control through buttons on the various toolbars or by displaying the property sheet for the control and changing the appropriate property. Consider:

■ *To select a bound control and its associated label (an unbound control),* click either the control or the label. If you click the control, the control has sizing handles and a move handle, but the label has only a move handle. If you click the label, the opposite occurs; that is, the label will have both sizing handles and a move handle, but the control will have only a move handle.

■ *To size a control,* click the control to select the control and display the sizing handles, then drag the sizing handles in the appropriate direction. Drag the handles on the top or bottom to size the box vertically. Drag the handles on the left or right side to size the box horizontally. Drag the handles in the corner to size both horizontally and vertically.

■ *To move a control and its label,* click and drag the border of either object. To move either the control or its label, click and drag the move handle (a tiny square in the upper left corner) of the appropriate object.

■ *To change the properties of a control,* point to the control, click the right mouse button to display a shortcut menu, then click Properties to display the property sheet. Click the text box for the desired property, make the necessary change, then close the property sheet.

■ *To select multiple controls,* press and hold the Shift key as you click each successive control. The advantage of selecting multiple controls is that you can modify the selected controls at the same time rather than working with them individually.

There is a learning curve, and it may take you a few extra minutes to create your first form. Everything you learn about forms, however, is also applicable to reports. Subsequent exercises will go much faster. And, as you may have guessed, it's time for our next hands-on exercise.

Form Wizard

AutoForms can be used instead of Form Wizard

Available field list

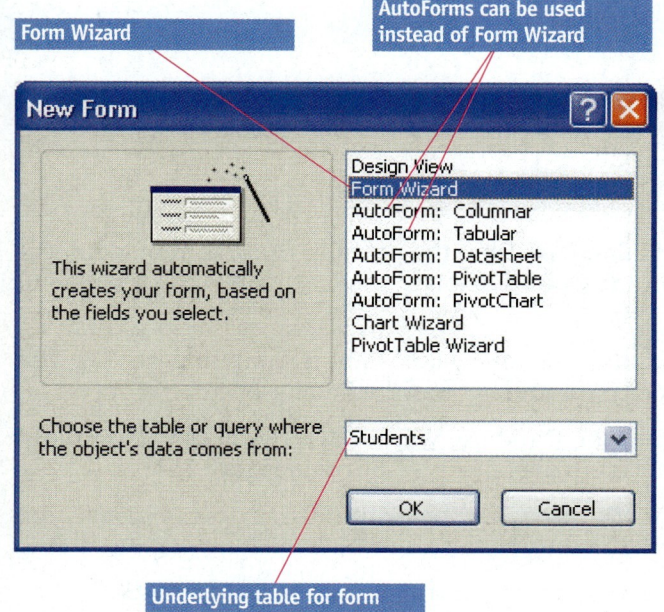

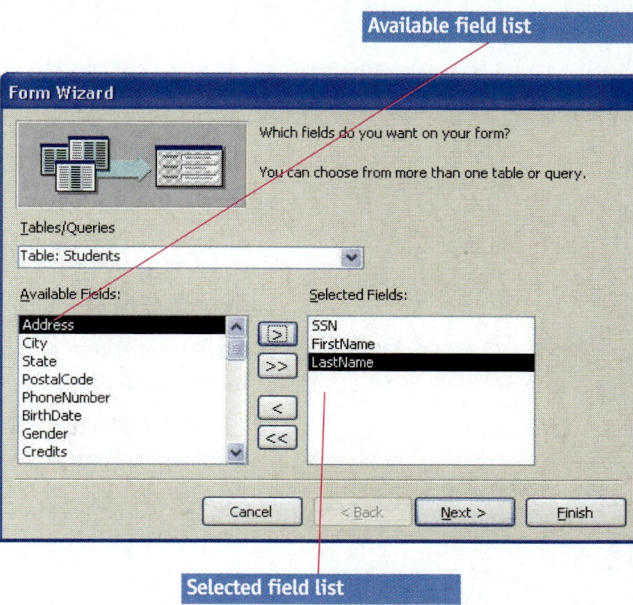

Underlying table for form

Selected field list

(a) Specify the Underlying Table

(b) Select the Fields

Preview of layout

Selected layout

Preview of style

Selected style

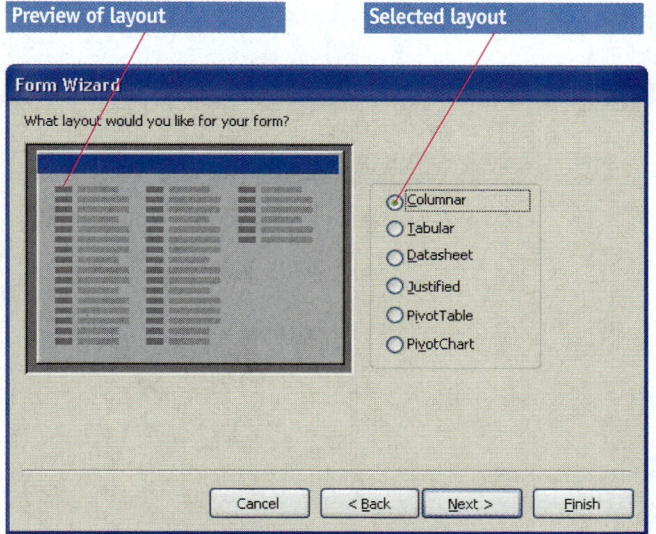

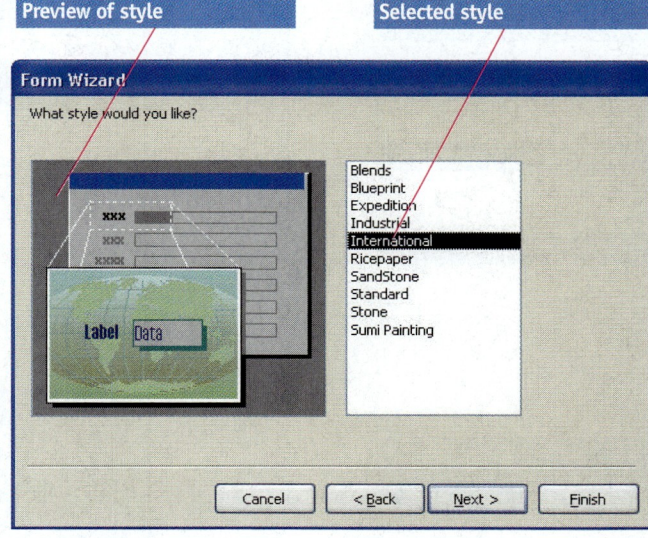

(c) Choose the Layout

(d) Choose the Style

FIGURE 2.6 The Form Wizard

TRY THE AUTOFORM FIRST

Go to the Database window, click the Forms button, then click the New button to display the New Form dialog box. Click the drop-down arrow in the Table or Query list box to select the object on which the form is based, then double click one of the AutoForm entries to create the form. If you don't like the result, don't bother to save the form. You have lost all of 30 seconds and can start again with the Form Wizard.

2 Creating a Form

Objective To use the Form Wizard to create a form; to move and size controls within a form; to use the completed form to enter data into the associated table.

Step 1: **Open the Database**

- Start Access. The **My First database** from the previous exercise should appear in the list of databases in the Open section in the task pane. Click the link to open the database.

- If the database is not listed or the task pane is not open, pull down the **File menu**, and click the **Open command** to open the database.

- Click the **Forms button** in the Database window. Click the **New command button** to display the New Form dialog box as shown in Figure 2.7a.

- Click **Form Wizard** in the list box. Click the **drop-down arrow** to display the available tables and queries in the database on which the form can be based.

- Click **Students** to select the table from the previous exercise. Click **OK**.

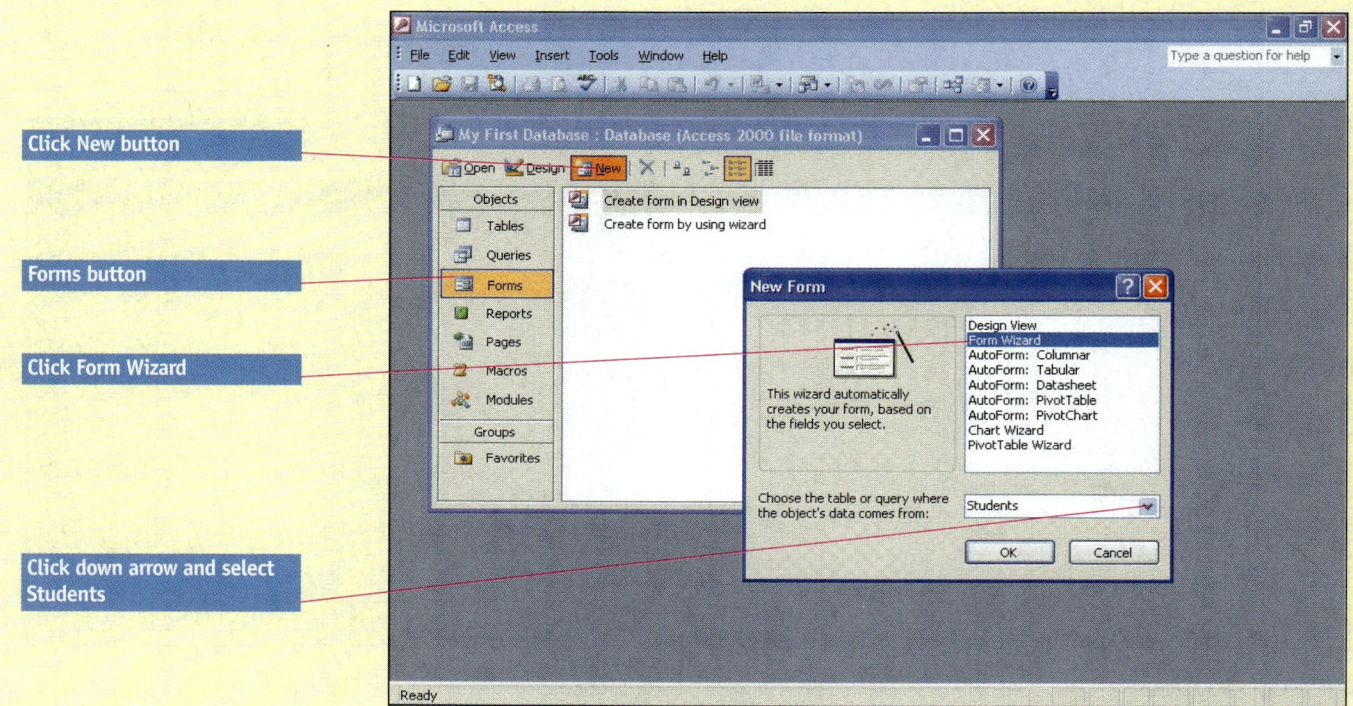

Click New button

Forms button

Click Form Wizard

Click down arrow and select Students

(a) Open the Database (step 1)

FIGURE 2.7 Hands-on Exercise 2

ANATOMY OF A FORM

A form is divided into one or more sections. Virtually every form has a detail section to display or enter the records in the underlying table. You can, however, increase the effectiveness or visual appeal of a form by adding a header and/or footer. Either section may contain descriptive information about the form, such as a title, instructions for using the form, or a graphic or logo.

Step 2: The Form Wizard

- You should see the dialog box in Figure 2.7b, which displays all of the fields in the Students table. Click the **>> button** to enter all of the fields in the table on the form. Click the **Next command button**.

- The **Columnar layout** is already selected. (The various layouts correspond to the different AutoForms.) Click the **Next command button**.

- Click **Industrial** as the style for your form. Click the **Next command button**.

- The Form Wizard will ask you for the title of the form and what you want to do next.
  - ❏ The Form Wizard suggests **Students** as the title of the form. Keep this entry.
  - ❏ Click the option button to **Modify the form's design**.

- Click the **Finish command button** to display the form in Design view. The wizard has created the initial form for you. You will now modify the form in Design view as described in the next several steps.

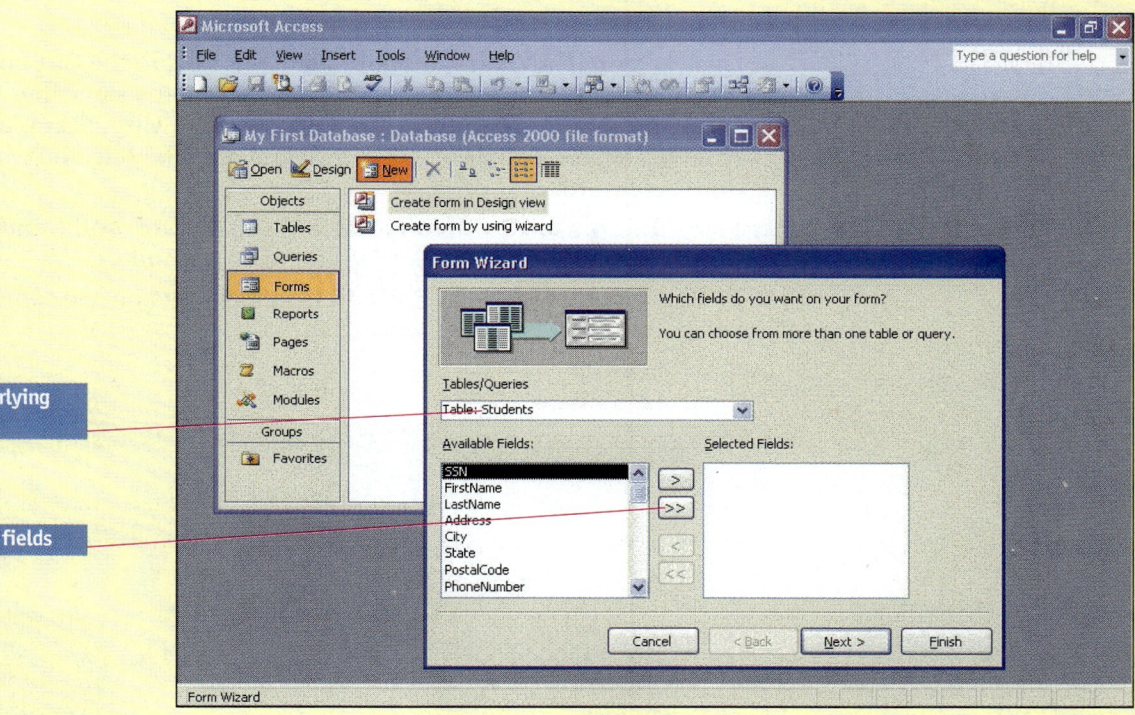

Students is the underlying table

Click >> to select all fields

(b) The Form Wizard (step 2)

FIGURE 2.7 Hands-on Exercise 2 (*continued*)

FLOATING TOOLBARS

A toolbar is typically docked (fixed) along the edge of the application window, but it can be displayed as a floating toolbar within the application window. To move a docked toolbar, drag the toolbar background (or the toolbar's move handle). To move a floating toolbar, drag its title bar. To size a floating toolbar, drag any border in the direction you want to go. And finally, you can double click the background of any floating toolbar to dock it.

Step 3: Move the Controls

- If necessary, click the **Maximize button** so that the form takes the entire screen as shown in Figure 2.7c. Close the field list. The Form Wizard has arranged the controls in columnar format, but you need to rearrange the controls.

- Click the **Credits control** to select it. Press the **Shift key** as you click the **QualityPoints control** to select it as well. Click and drag the border of either control (the pointer changes to a hand) to move them out of the way.

- Click the **LastName control** to select the control and display the sizing handles. (Be sure to select the text box and *not* the attached label.) Click and drag the **border** of the control (the pointer changes to a hand) so that the LastName control is on the same line as the FirstName control. Use the grid to space and align the controls.

- Click and drag the **Address control** under the FirstName control (to take the space previously occupied by the last name).

- Click and drag the **right border** of the form to **7 inches** so that the City, State, and PostalCode controls will fit on the same line. (Click and drag the title bar of the Toolbox toolbar to move the toolbar out of the way.)

- Click and drag the **State control** so that it is next to the City control, then click and drag the **PostalCode control** so that it is on the same line as the other two. Press and hold the **Shift key** as you click the **City**, **State**, and **PostalCode** **controls** to select all three, then click and drag the selected controls under the Address control.

- Place the controls for **PhoneNumber**, **BirthDate**, and **Gender** on the same line. Move the controls under City, State, PostalCode.

- Place the controls for **Credits** and **QualityPoints** on the same line. Move the controls under PhoneNumber.

- Save the form.

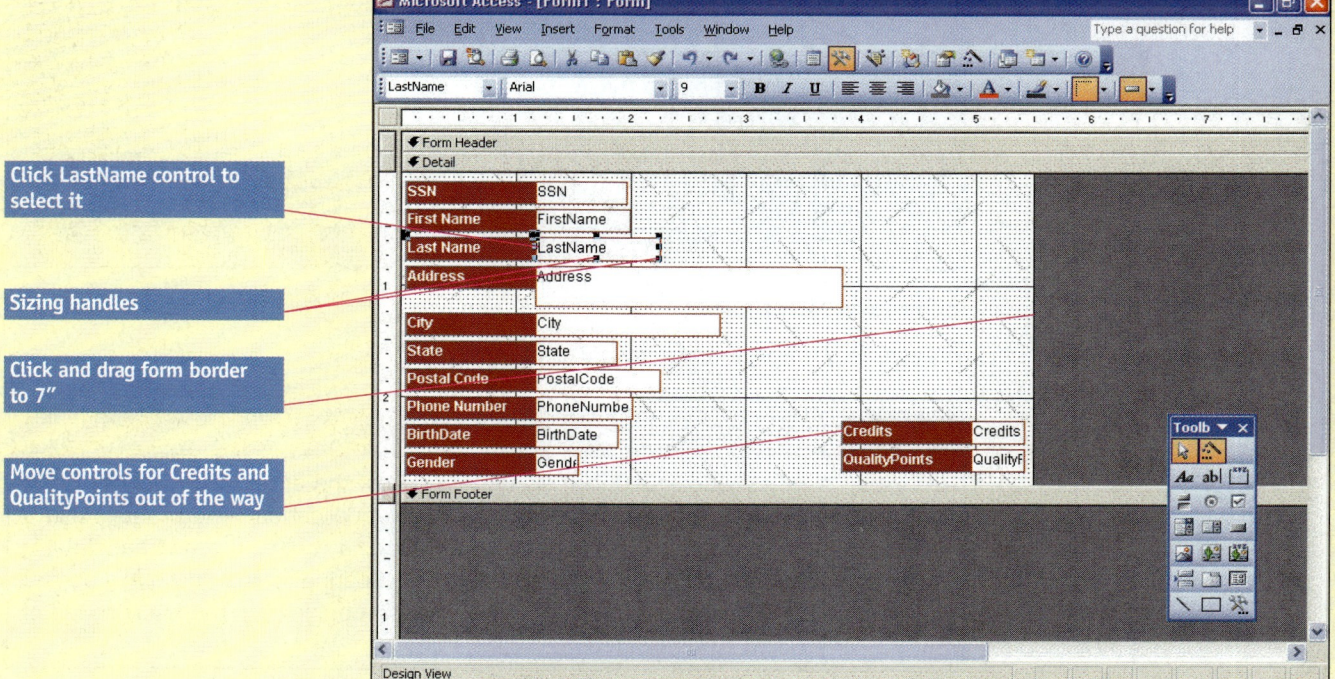

Click LastName control to select it

Sizing handles

Click and drag form border to 7"

Move controls for Credits and QualityPoints out of the way

(c) Move the Controls (step 3)

FIGURE 2.7 Hands-on Exercise 2 (*continued*)

Step 4: **Add a Calculated Control (GPA)**

- Click the **Text Box tool** in the toolbox as shown in Figure 2.7d. The mouse pointer changes to a tiny crosshair with a text box attached.

- Click and drag in the form where you want the text box (the GPA control) to go. Release the mouse. You will see an Unbound control and an attached label containing a field number (e.g., Text24) as shown in Figure 2.7d.

- Click in the **text box** of the control. The word Unbound will disappear. Enter **=[QualityPoints]/[Credits]** to calculate a student's GPA. You must enter the field names *exactly* as they were defined in the table; that is, do *not* include a space between Quality and Points.

- Select the attached label (**Text24**), then click and drag to select the text in the attached label. Type **GPA** as the label for this control and press **Enter**.

- Size the label appropriately for GPA. Size the bound control as well. Move either control as necessary.

- Save the form.

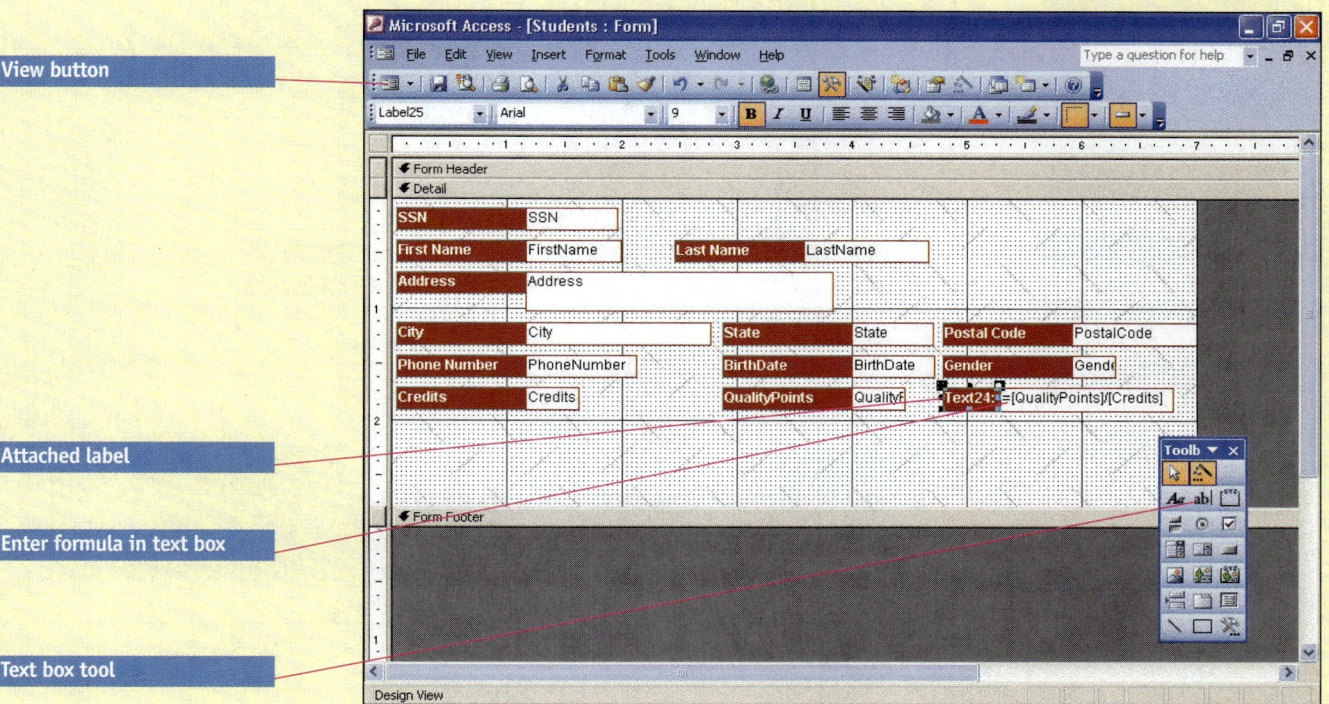

(d) Add a Calculated Control (step 4)

FIGURE 2.7 Hands-on Exercise 2 (*continued*)

SIZING OR MOVING A CONTROL AND ITS LABEL

A bound and/or an unbound control is created with an attached label. Select (click) the control, and the control has sizing handles and a move handle, but the label has only a move handle. Select the label (instead of the control), and the opposite occurs; the control has only a move handle, but the label will have both sizing handles and a move handle. To move a control and its label, click and drag the border of either object. To move either the control or its label, click and drag the move handle (a tiny square in the upper left corner) of the appropriate object.

Step 5: **Modify the Property Sheet**

- Point to the GPA bound control and click the **right mouse button** to display a shortcut menu. Click **Properties** to display the Properties dialog box.

- If necessary, click the **All tab** as shown in Figure 2.7e. The Control Source text box contains the entry =[QualityPoints]/[Credits] from the preceding step.

- Click the **Name text box**. Replace the original name (e.g., Text24) with **GPA**.

- Click the **Format box**. Click the **drop-down arrow**, then scroll until you can select **Fixed**.

- Click the box for the **Decimal places**. Click the **drop-down arrow** and select **2** as the number of decimal places.

- Close the Properties dialog box to accept these settings and return to the form.

- Save the form.

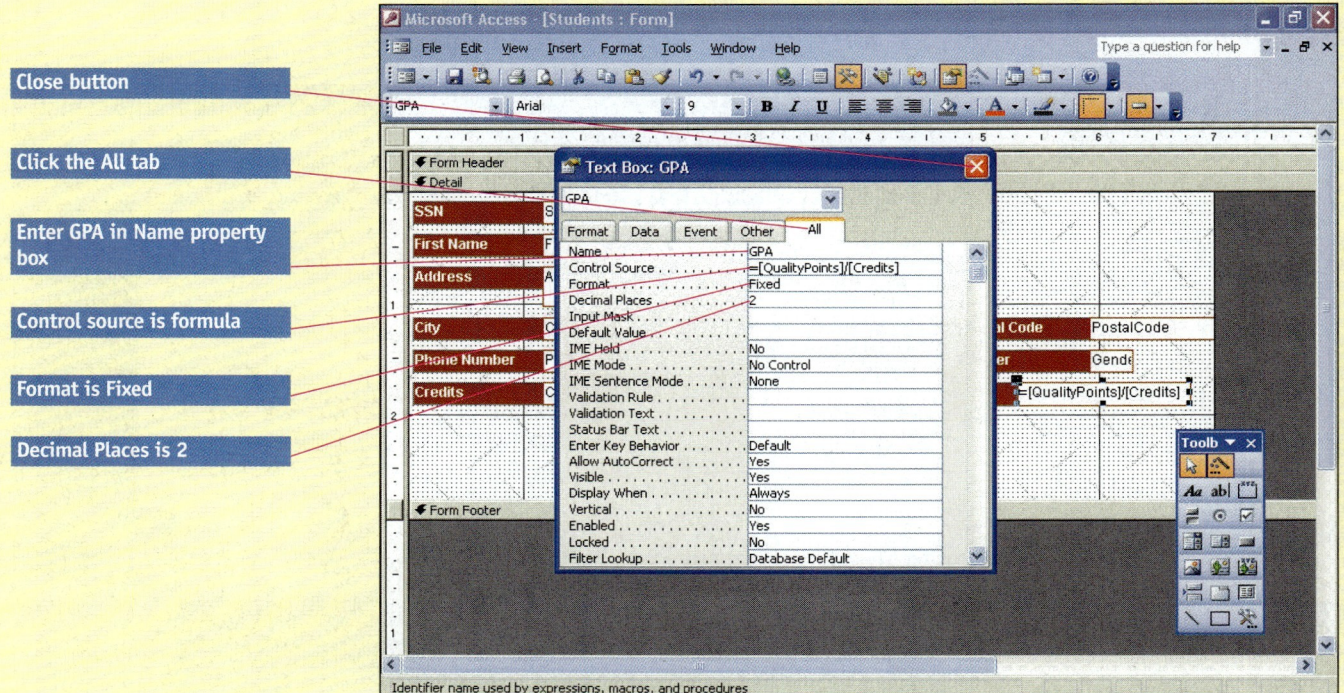

Close button

Click the All tab

Enter GPA in Name property box

Control source is formula

Format is Fixed

Decimal Places is 2

(e) Modify the Property Sheet (step 5)

FIGURE 2.7 Hands-on Exercise 2 (*continued*)

USE THE PROPERTY SHEET

You can change the appearance or behavior of a control in two ways—by changing the actual control on the form itself or by changing the underlying property sheet. Anything you do to the control automatically changes the associated property, and conversely, any change to the property sheet is reflected in the appearance or behavior of the control. In general, you can obtain greater precision through the property sheet, but we find ourselves continually switching back and forth between the two techniques. Every object in an Access database has its own property sheet.

Step 6: **Align the Controls**

■ Click the label for SSN, then press and hold the **Shift key** as you click the labels for the other controls on the form. This enables you to select multiple controls at the same time to apply uniform formatting to the selected controls.

■ All labels should be selected as shown in Figure 2.7f. Click the **Align Right button** on the Formatting toolbar to move the text to the right so that the text in each label is closer to its associated control.

■ Click anywhere on the form to deselect the controls, then fine-tune the form as necessary to make it more attractive. (Use the Undo command anytime the results of a command are not what you expect.)

■ Make additional changes as necessary. We moved LastName to align it with State. We also made the PostalCode and GPA controls smaller.

■ Save the form.

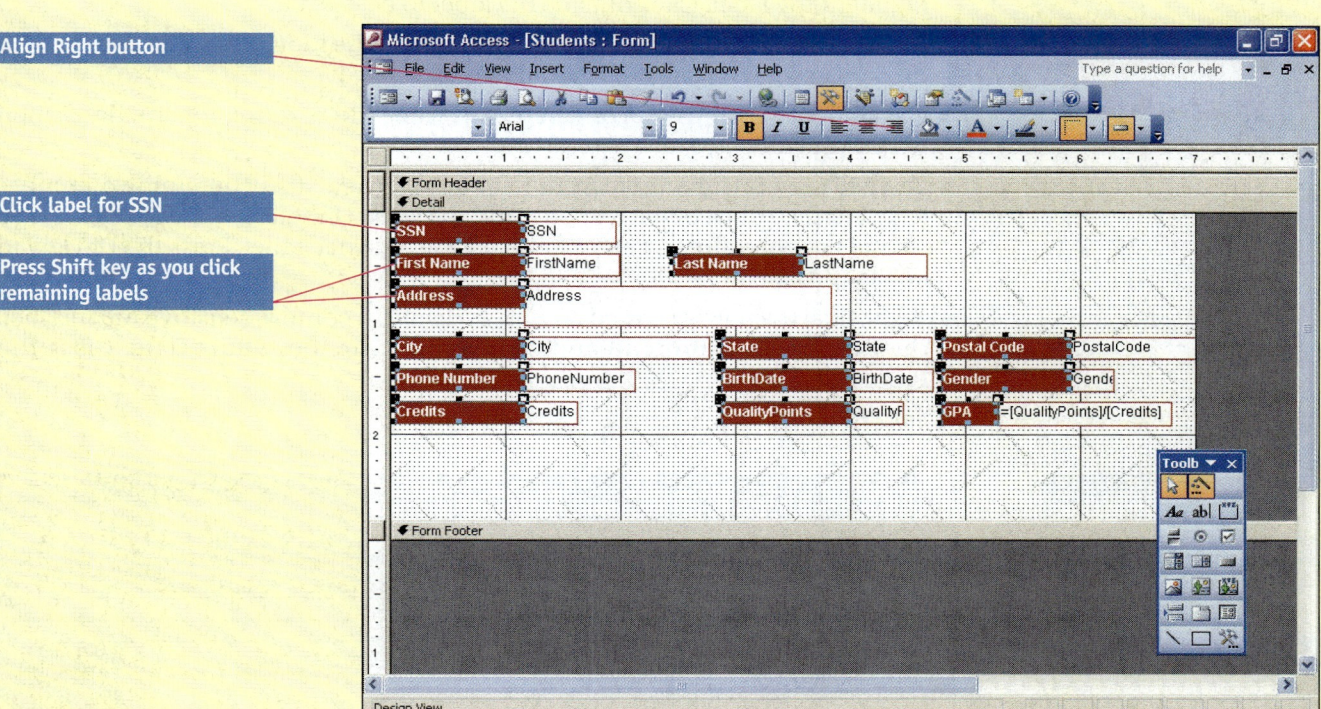

Align Right button

Click label for SSN

Press Shift key as you click remaining labels

(f) Align the Controls (step 6)

FIGURE 2.7   Hands-on Exercise 2 (*continued*)

ALIGN THE CONTROLS

To align controls in a straight line (horizontally or vertically), press and hold the Shift key and click the labels of the controls to be aligned. Pull down the Format menu, click Align, then select the edge to align (Left, Right, Top, and Bottom). Click the Undo command if you are not satisfied with the result. It takes practice to master the Design view, but everything you learn about forms also applies to reports. (Reports are covered in Chapter 3.)

Step 7: Create the Form Header

- Click and drag the line separating the border of the Form Header and Detail sections to provide space for a header as shown in Figure 2.7g.

- Click the **Label tool** on the Toolbox toolbar (the mouse pointer changes to a cross hair combined with the letter A). Click and drag the mouse pointer to create a label within the header. The insertion point (a flashing vertical line) is automatically positioned within the label.

- Type **Student Information Form**. Do not be concerned about the size or alignment of the text at this time. Click outside the label when you have completed the entry, then click the control to select it.

- Click the **drop-down arrow** on the **Font Size list box** on the Formatting toolbar. Click **18**. The size of the text changes to the larger point size.

- Click the **drop-down arrow** next to the **Special Effect button** on the Formatting toolbar to display the available effects. Click the **Raised button** to highlight the label. Click outside the label to deselect it.

- Click the **Textbox tool** on the Toolbox toolbar. The mouse pointer changes to a tiny crosshair with a text box attached.

- Click and drag in the form where you want the text box for the date, then release the mouse.

- You will see an Unbound control and an attached label containing a number (e.g., Text27). Click in the text box, and the word Unbound will disappear. Type =**Now( )** to enter the current date. Click the attached label. Press the **Del key** to delete the label.

- Right click the newly created control to display a context-sensitive menu. Click the **Properties command** and change the format to **Short Date**. Close the Properties sheet.

- Save the form.

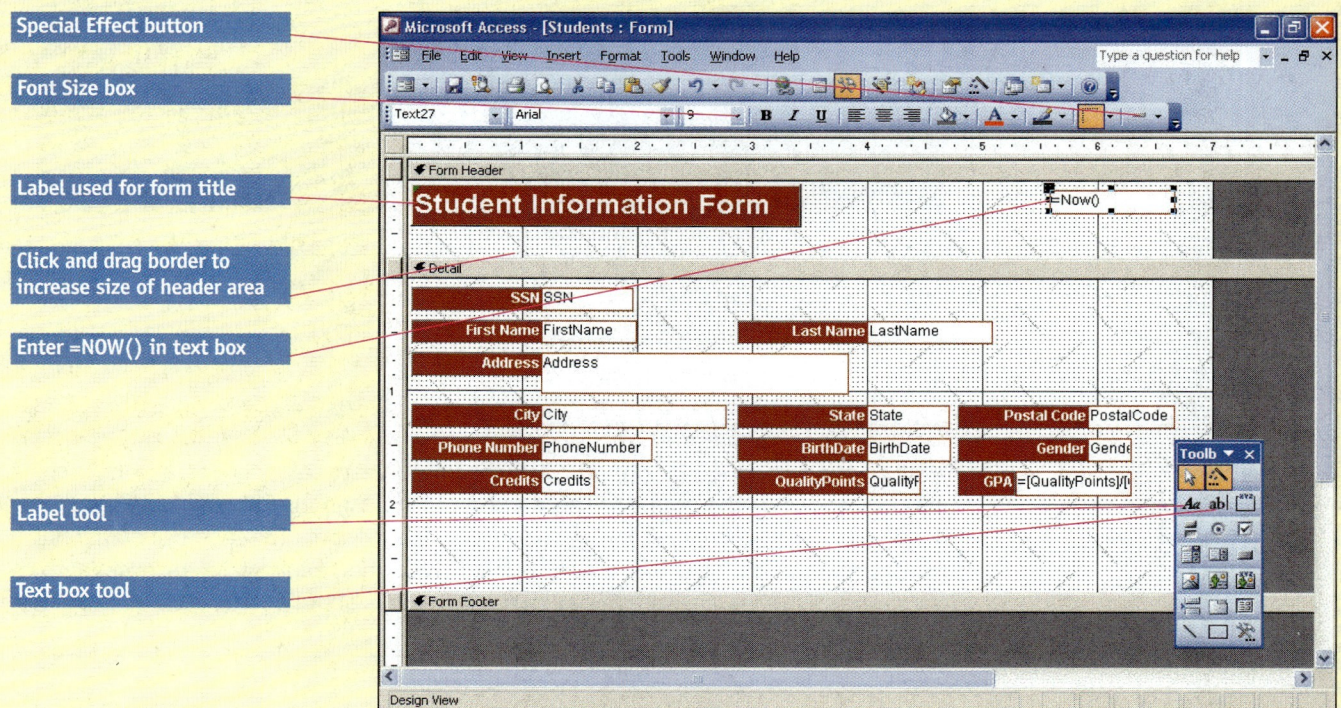

(g) Create the Form Header (step 7)

FIGURE 2.7 Hands-on Exercise 2 (*continued*)

Step 8: The Finished Form

- Click the **View button** to switch to the Form view. You will see the first record in the table that was created in the previous exercise.

- Click the **New Record button** to move to the end of the table to enter a new record as shown in Figure 2.7h. Enter data for a classmate:
  - ❏ The record selector symbol changes to a pencil as you begin to enter data as shown in Figure 2.7h.
  - ❏ Press the **Tab key** to move from one field to the next within the form. All properties (masks and data validation) have been inherited from the Students table created in the first exercise.
  - ❏ There are now two records in the table.

- Pull down the **File menu** and click **Close** to close the form. Click **Yes** if asked to save the changes to the form.

- Pull down the **File menu** and click **Close** to close the database and remain in Access. Pull down the **File menu** a second time and click **Exit** if you do not want to continue with the next exercise at this time.

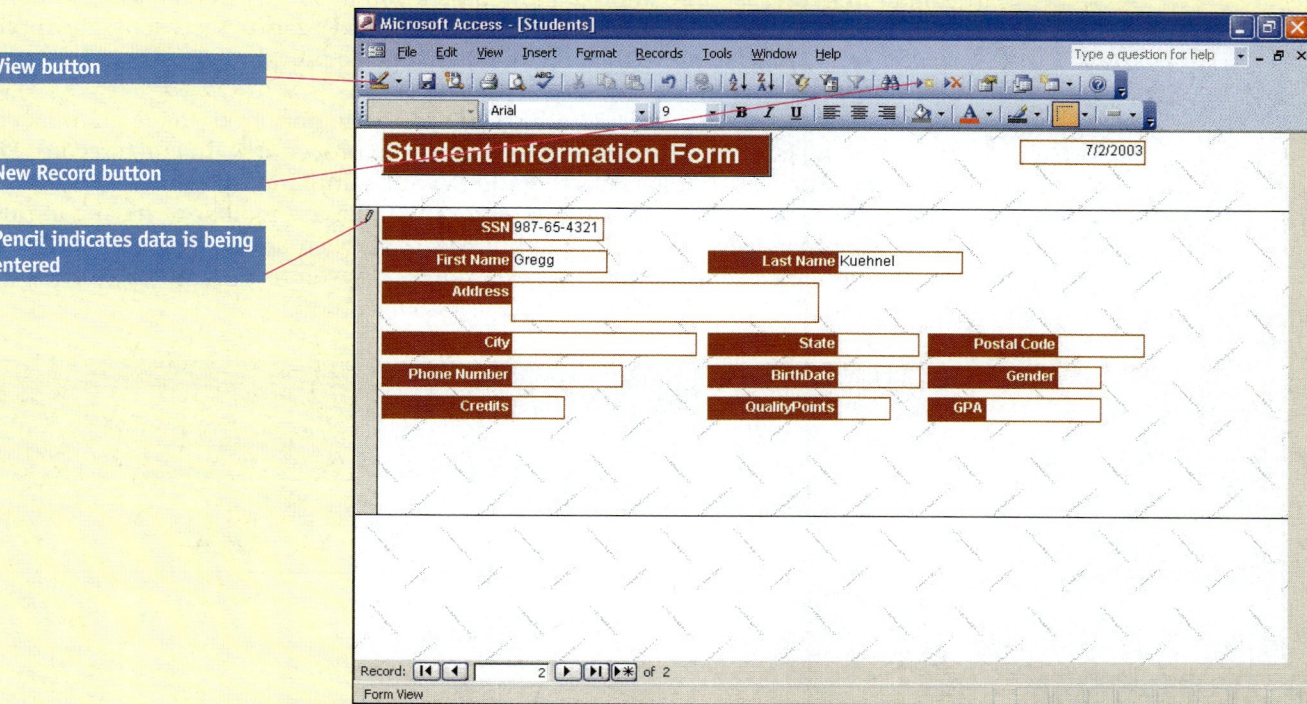

View button

New Record button

Pencil indicates data is being entered

(h) The Finished Form (step 8)

FIGURE 2.7 Hands-on Exercise 2 (*continued*)

ERROR MESSAGES—#NAME? OR #ERROR?

The most common reason for either message is that the control source references a field that no longer exists, or a field whose name is misspelled. Go to the Design view, right click the control, click the Properties command, then click the All tab within the Properties dialog box. Look at the Control Source property and check the spelling of every field. Be sure there are brackets around each field in a calculated control—for example, =[QualityPoints]/[Credits].

The Form Wizard provides an excellent starting point but stops short of creating the form you really want. The exercise just completed showed you how to add controls to a form that were not in the underlying table, such as the calculated control for the GPA. The exercise also showed how to move and size existing controls to create a more attractive and functional form.

Consider now Figure 2.8, which further improves on the form from the previous exercise. Three additional controls have been added—for major, financial aid, and campus—to illustrate other ways to enter data than through a text box. The student's major is selected from a *drop-down list box*. The indication of financial aid (a Yes/No field) is entered through a *check box*. The student's campus is selected from an *option group*, in which you choose one of three mutually exclusive options.

The form in Figure 2.8 also includes clip art in the header. The way in which clip art is added to a form (or report) in Access differs from the way it is done in the other Office applications, in that the Insert Picture command does not link to the Clip Organizer as it does with Word, Excel, and PowerPoint. Execution of the command in Access is more limited and requires you to specify the file that contains the clip art image. (You can, however, start the Clip Organizer as a separate application, copy the clip art to the clipboard, then paste the contents of the clipboard into Access.)

Command buttons have also been added to the bottom of the form to facilitate the way in which the user carries out certain procedures. To add a record, for example, the user simply clicks the Add Record command button, as opposed to having to click the New Record button on the Database toolbar or having to pull down the Insert menu. Additional buttons have been added to find or delete a record and to close the form. The next exercise has you retrieve the form you created in Hands-on Exercise 2 to add these enhancements.

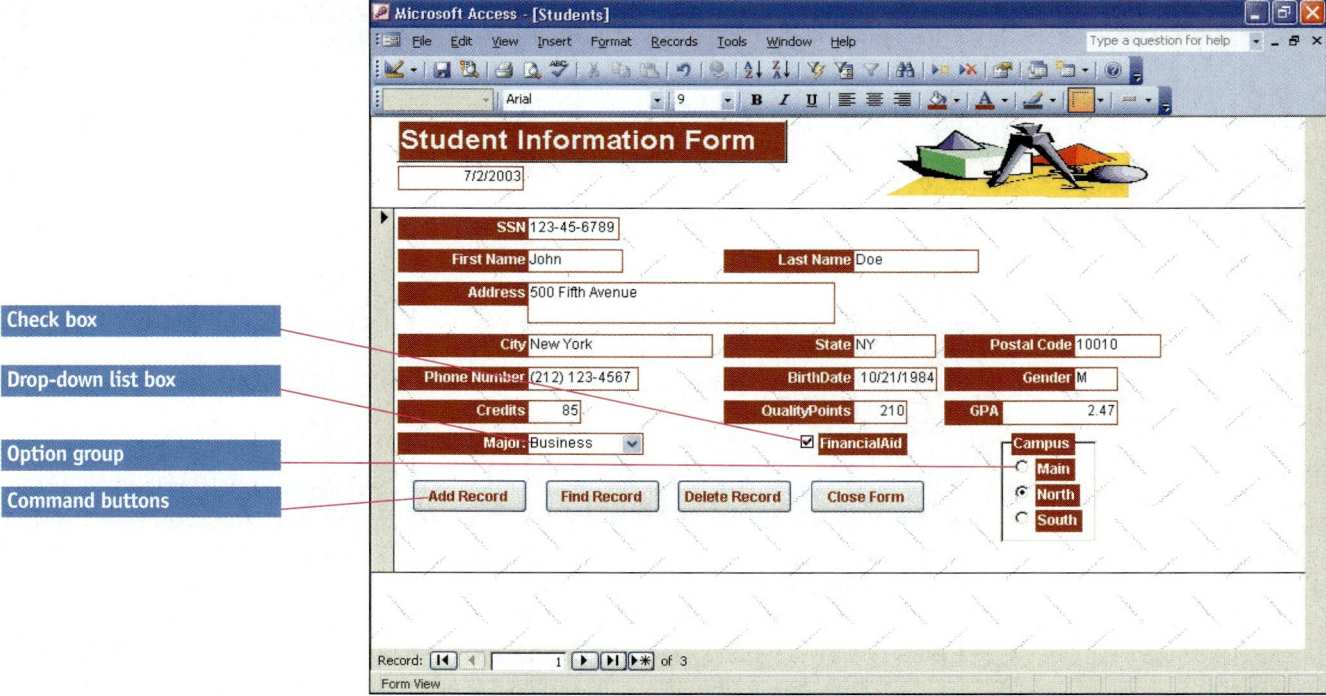

FIGURE 2.8 A More Sophisticated Form

3   A More Sophisticated Form

Objective   To add fields to an existing table; to use the Lookup Wizard to create a combo box; to add controls to an existing form to demonstrate inheritance; to add command buttons to a form. Use Figure 2.9 as a guide in the exercise.

Step 1:   Modify the Table

- Open **My First Database** that we have been using throughout the chapter. If necessary, click the **Tables button** in the Database window. The **Students table** is already selected since that is the only table in the database.

- Click the **Design command button** to open the table in Design view as shown in Figure 2.9a. (The FinancialAid, Campus, and Major fields have not yet been added.) Maximize the window.

- Click the **Field Name box** under QualityPoints. Enter **FinancialAid** as the name of the new field. Press the **Enter (Tab,** or **right arrow) key** to move to the Data Type column. Type **Y** (the first letter in a Yes/No field) to specify the data type.

- Click the **Field Name box** on the next row. Type **Campus.** (There is no need to specify the Data Type since Text is the default.)

- Press the **down arrow key** to move to the Field Name box on the next row. Enter **Major.** Press the **Enter (Tab,** or **right arrow) key** to move to the Data Type column. Click the **drop-down arrow** to display the list of data types as shown in Figure 2.9a. Click **Lookup Wizard.**

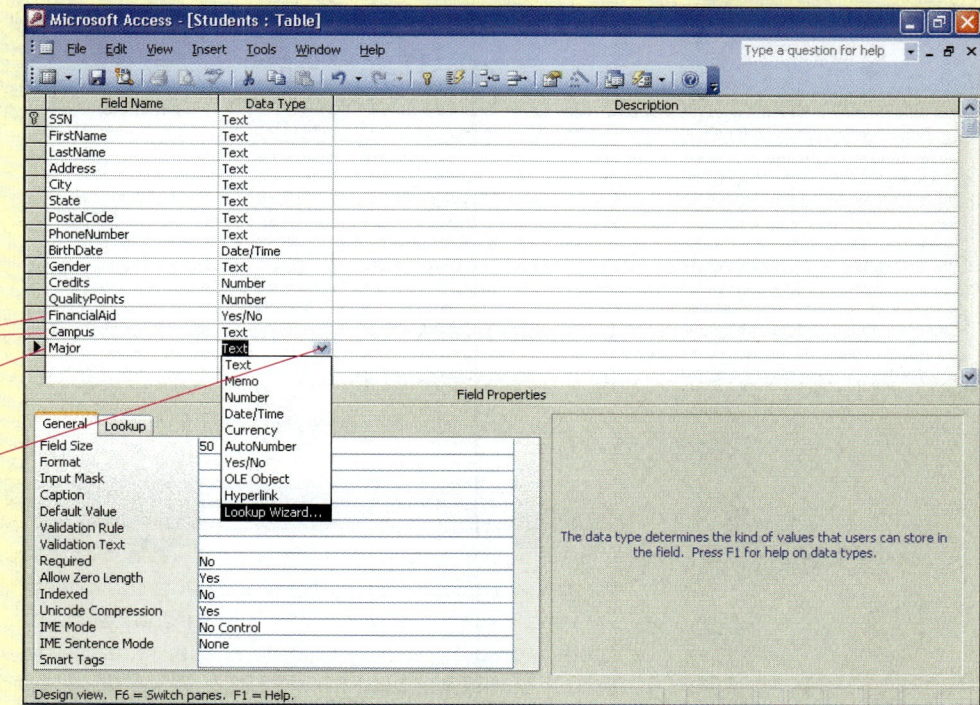

Enter new fields

Enter Major

Click down arrow and select Lookup Wizard

(a) Modify the Table (step 1)

FIGURE 2.9   Hands-on Exercise 3

Step 2: **The Lookup Wizard**

- The first screen in the Lookup Wizard asks how you want to look up the data. Click the option button that indicates **I will type in the values that I want**. Click **Next**.

- You should see the dialog box in Figure 2.9b. The number of columns is already entered as 1. Click the **text box** to enter the first major. Type **Business**. Press **Tab** or the **down arrow key** (do *not* press the Enter key) to enter the next major.

- Complete the entries shown in Figure 2.9b. Click **Next**. The wizard asks for a label to identify the column. (Major is already entered.)

- Click **Finish** to exit the wizard and return to the Design view.

- The data type has been set to Text as a result of the entries you made using the Lookup Wizard.

- Click the **Save button** to save the table. Close the table.

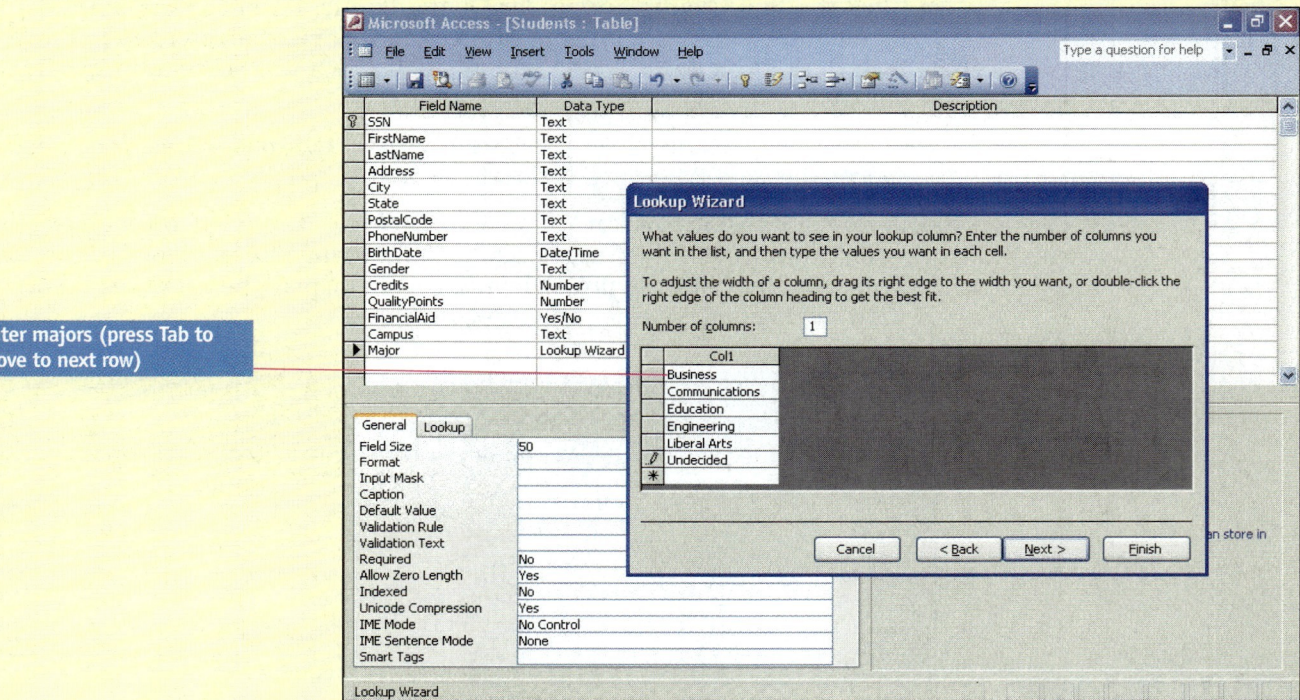

Enter majors (press Tab to move to next row)

(b) The Lookup Wizard (step 2)

FIGURE 2.9 Hands-on Exercise 3 (*continued*)

RELATIONAL DATABASES—MORE SOPHISTICATED APPLICATIONS

The simplest way to use the Lookup Wizard is to type the potential values directly into the associated field. It's more powerful, however, to instruct the wizard to look up the values in a table, which in turn necessitates the creation of that table, in effect creating a relational database. Indeed, the true power of Access comes from databases with multiple tables, as was demonstrated in the Look Ahead database of Chapter 1. We develop this topic further, beginning in Chapter 4 and continue through the remaining chapters in the text.

Step 3: **Add the New Controls**

- Click the **Forms button** in the Database window. If necessary, click the **Students form** to select it.

- Click the **Design command button** to open the form from the previous exercise. If necessary, click the **Maximize button** so that the form takes the entire window.

- If the field list is not displayed, pull down the **View menu**. Click **Field List** to display the field list for the table on which the form is based. You can move and size the field list just like any other Windows object.
  - ❑ Click and drag the **title bar** of the field list to the position in Figure 2.9c.
  - ❑ Click and drag a **corner** or **border** of the field list so that you can see all of the fields at the same time.

- Fields can be added to the form from the field list in any order. Click and drag the **Major field** from the field list to the form. The Major control is created as a combo box because of the lookup list in the underlying table.

- Click and drag the **FinancialAid field** from the list to the form. The FinancialAid control is created as a check box because FinancialAid is a Yes/No field in the underlying table.

- Move and size the labels and bound controls as necessary. Save the form.

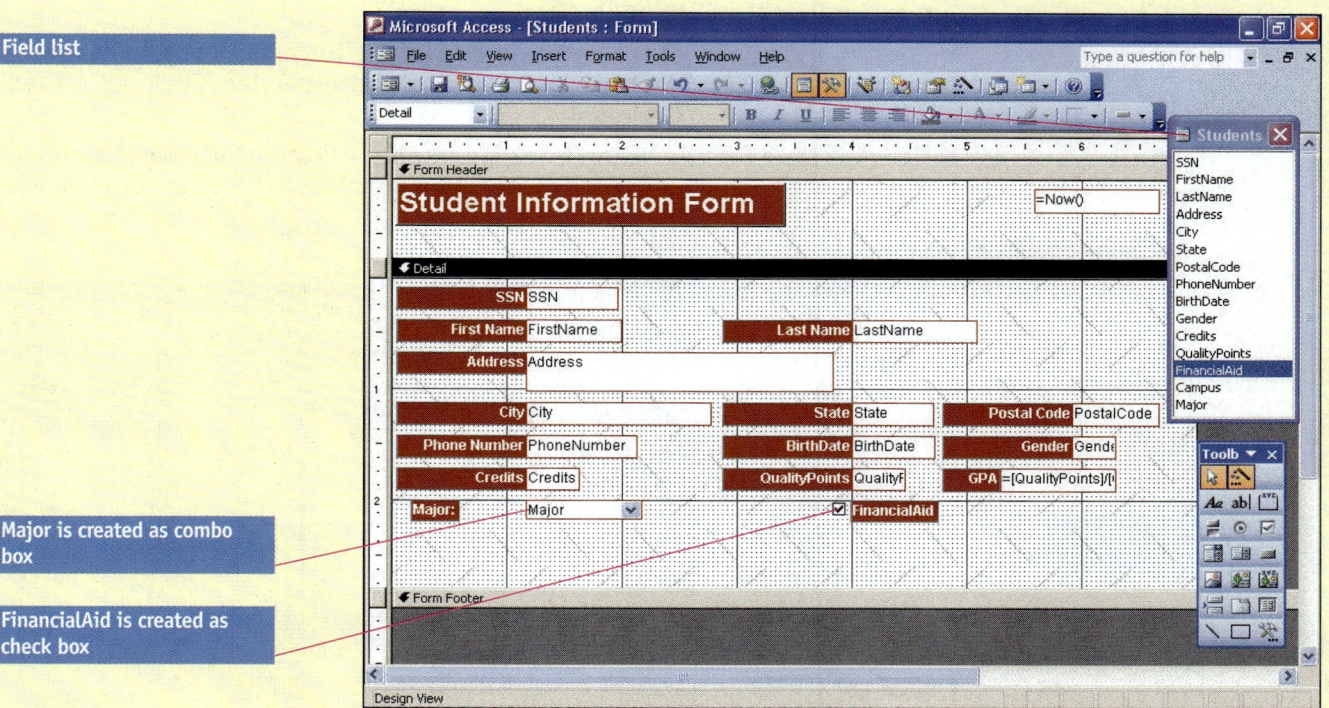

(c) Add the New Controls (step 3)

FIGURE 2.9   Hands-on Exercise 3 (*continued*)

INHERITANCE

A bound control inherits its properties from the associated field in the underlying table. A check box, for example, appears automatically for any field that was defined as a Yes/No field. In similar fashion, a drop-down list appears for any field that was defined through the Lookup Wizard. All of the other properties of the control are also inherited from the underlying table.

Step 4: **Create an Option Group**

- Click the **Option Group button** on the Toolbox toolbar. The mouse pointer changes to a tiny crosshair. Click and drag in the form where you want the option group to go, then release the mouse.

- You should see the Option Group Wizard as shown in Figure 2.9d. Enter **Main** as the label for the first option, then press the **Tab key** to move to the next line. Type **North** and press **Tab** to move to the next line. Enter **South** as the third and last option. Click **Next**.

- The option button to select Main (the first label that was entered) as the default is selected. Click **Next**.

- Main, North, and South will be assigned the values 1, 2, and 3, respectively. (Numeric entries are required for an option group.) Click **Next**.

- Click the **drop-down arrow** to select the field in which to store the value selected through the option group, then scroll until you can select **Campus**. Click **Next**.

- Make sure the Option button is selected as the type of control.

- Click the Option button for the **Sunken style** to match the other controls on the form. Click **Next**.

- Enter **Campus** as the caption for the group. Click the **Finish command button** to create the option group on the form. Click and drag the option group to position it on the form under the GPA control.

- Point to the border of the option group on the form, click the **right mouse button** to display a shortcut menu, and click **Properties**. Click the **All tab**. Change the name to **Campus**.

- Click the label for the **Option Group** (Campus). Click the **Fill Color button** on the Formatting toolbar to change the fill color to match that of the other labels.

- Close the dialog box. Close the field list. Save the form.

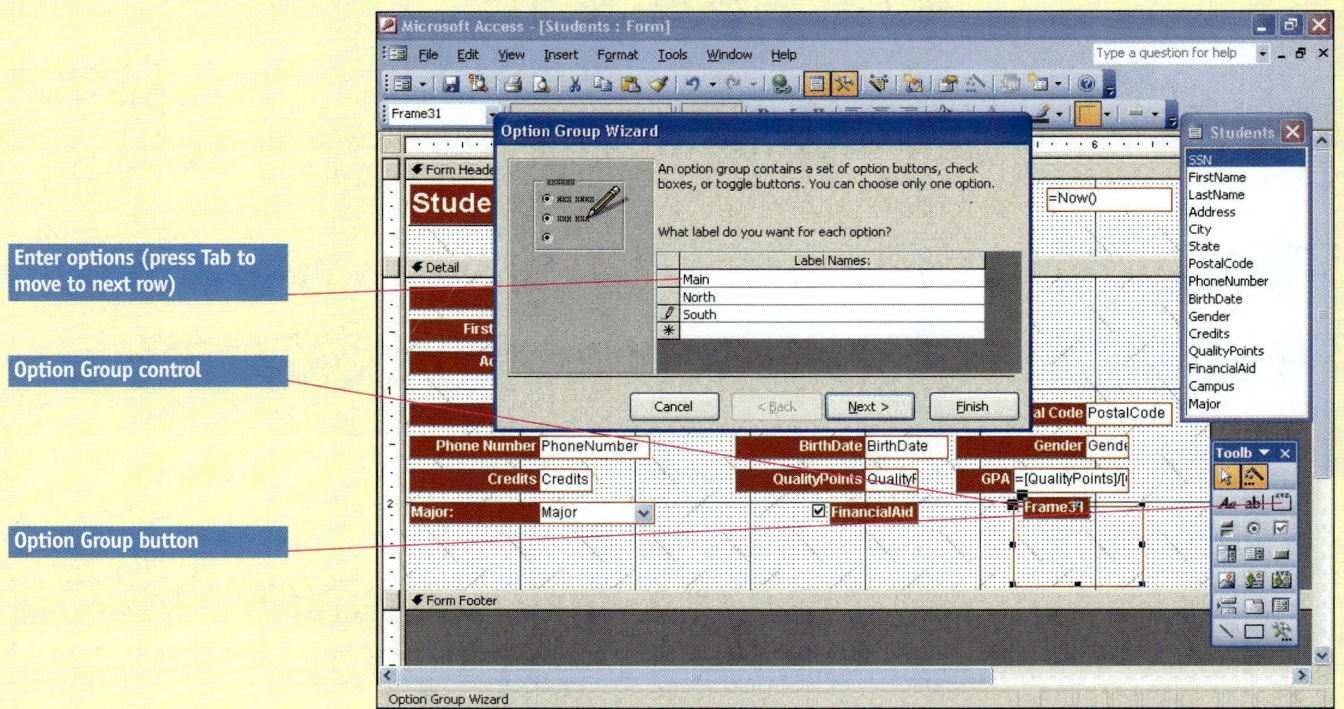

(d) Create an Option Group (step 4)

FIGURE 2.9 Hands-on Exercise 3 (*continued*)

Step 5:   **Add the Command Buttons**

- Click the **Command Button tool**. The mouse pointer changes to a tiny crosshair that is attached to a command button when you point anywhere in the form.

- Click and drag in the form where you want the button to go, then release the mouse. This draws a button and simultaneously opens the Command Button Wizard as shown in Figure 2.9e. (The number in your button may be different from ours.)

- Click **Record Operations** in the Categories list box. Choose **Add New Record** as the operation. Click **Next**.

- Click the **Text option button** in the next screen. Click **Next**.

- Type **Add Record** as the name of the button, then click the **Finish command button**. The completed command button should appear on your form.

- Repeat these steps to add the command buttons to find a record (Record Navigation), to delete a record (Record Operations), and to close the form (Form Operations). We will adjust the size and alignment of all four buttons in the next step.

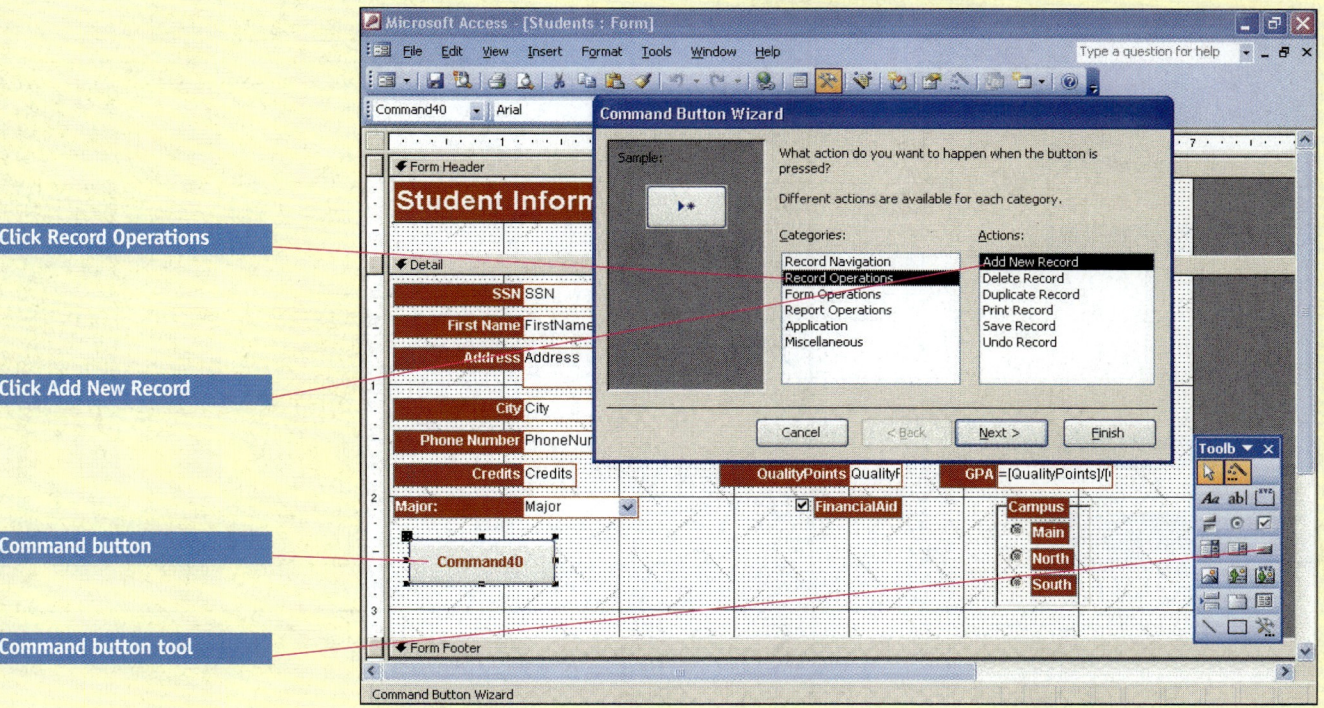

(e) Add the Command Buttons (step 5)

FIGURE 2.9   Hands-on Exercise 3 (*continued*)

WINDOWS THEMES AND ROUNDED COMMAND BUTTONS

It's a subtle difference, but we prefer the sleeker look of rounded command buttons in our forms, as opposed to the rectangular buttons that are created by default. Pull down the Tools menu, click the Options command, click the Forms/Reports tab, and check the box to use Windows Themed Controls on forms. Click the Apply button, then close the dialog box. Save the form you are working on, close the form, and then reopen it. You should see rounded buttons.

Step 6: Align the Command Buttons

- Select the four command buttons that were created in the previous step by pressing and holding the **Shift key** as you click each button. Release the Shift key when all buttons are selected.

- Pull down the **Format menu**. Click **Size** to display the cascade menu shown in Figure 2.9f. (Click the **double arrow** at the bottom of the menu if you don't see the Size command.) Click **To Widest** to set a uniform width.

- Pull down the **Format menu** a second time, click **Size**, then click **To Tallest** to set a uniform height.

- Pull down the **Format menu** again, click **Horizontal Spacing**, then click **Make Equal** so that each button is equidistant from the other buttons.

- Pull down the **Format menu** a final time, click **Align**, then click **Bottom** to complete the alignment.

- Save the form.

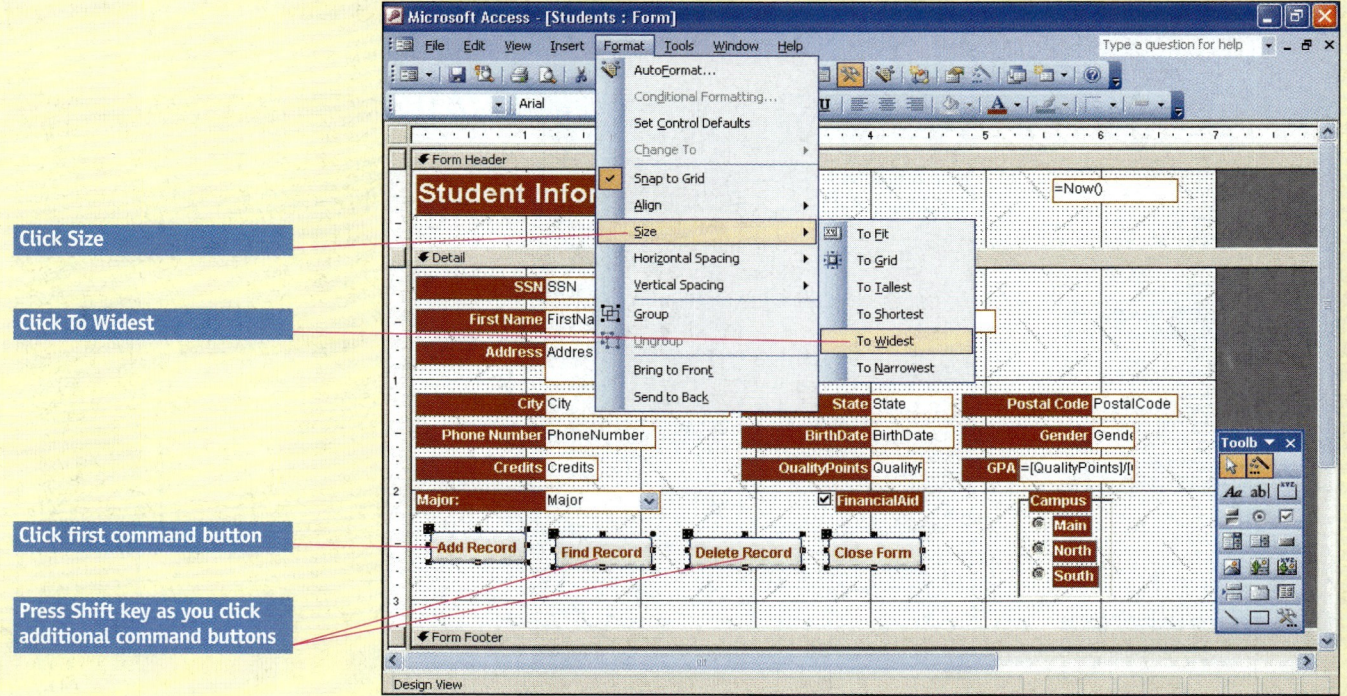

Click Size

Click To Widest

Click first command button

Press Shift key as you click additional command buttons

(f) Align the Command Buttons (step 6)

FIGURE 2.9 Hands-on Exercise 3 (*continued*)

MULTIPLE CONTROLS AND PROPERTIES

Press and hold the Shift key as you click one control after another to select multiple controls. To view or change the properties for the selected controls, click the right mouse button to display a shortcut menu, then click Properties to display a property sheet. If the value of a property is the same for all selected controls, that value will appear in the property sheet; otherwise the box for that property will be blank. Changing a property when multiple controls are selected changes the property for all selected controls.

Step 7: **Reset the Tab Order**

■ Click anywhere in the Detail section. Pull down the **View menu**. Click **Tab Order** to display the Tab Order dialog box in Figure 2.9g. (Click the **double arrow** at the bottom of the menu if you don't see the Tab Order command.)

■ Click the **Auto Order command button** so that the Tab key will move to fields in left-to-right, top-to-bottom order as you enter data in the form. Click **OK** to close the Tab Order dialog box.

■ Right click the **GPA control**, click **Properties** to display the Properties sheet, click the **All tab**, set the **Tab Stop** property to **No**, and close the property sheet.

■ Check the form one more time to make any last-minute changes. (We had to right align the label for major.)

■ Save the form.

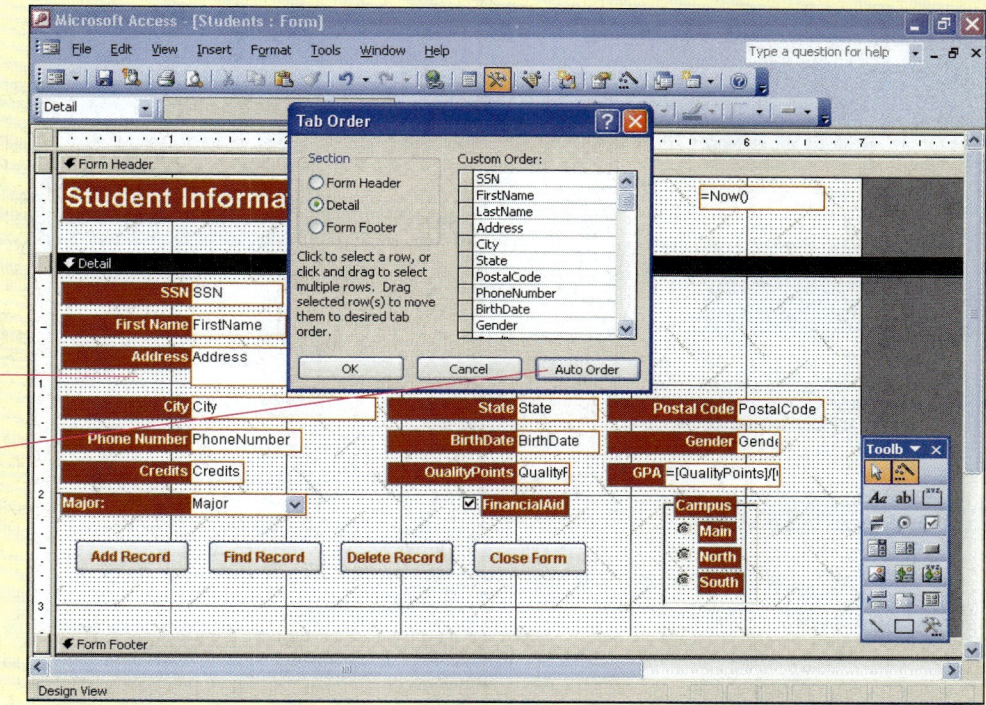

Click in Detail section

Click Auto Order button

(g) Reset the Tab Order (step 7)

FIGURE 2.9 Hands-on Exercise 3 (*continued*)

THE TAB STOP PROPERTY

The Tab key provides a shortcut in the finished form to move from one field to the next. Calculated controls, such as GPA, are not entered explicitly, however, and can be bypassed by setting the Tab Stop property to no. AutoNumber fields can be bypassed in similar fashion. Note, too, that the order in which fields are selected corresponds to the sequence in which the controls were entered onto the form, and need not correspond to the physical appearance of the actual form. To restore a left-to-right, top-to-bottom sequence, pull down the View menu, click Tab Order, select AutoOrder, then click OK to close the Tab Order dialog box.

Step 8: Insert the Clip Art

- Click in the Form Header area. Pull down the **Insert menu** and click the **Picture command** to display the Insert Picture dialog box as shown in Figure 2.9h.

- Change to the **Exploring Access folder**. Click the **Views button** repeatedly until you see the **Thumbnails Views**.

- Select (click) a picture, then click **OK** to insert the picture on the form. Right click the newly inserted object to display a shortcut menu, then click **Properties** to display the Properties dialog box.

- Select the **Size Mode property** and select **Stretch** from the associated list. Close the dialog box.

- Click and drag the sizing handles on the frame to size the object appropriately for the header area. Size the form header as necessary. Move the picture and other controls in the header until you are satisfied with its appearance.

- Save the form.

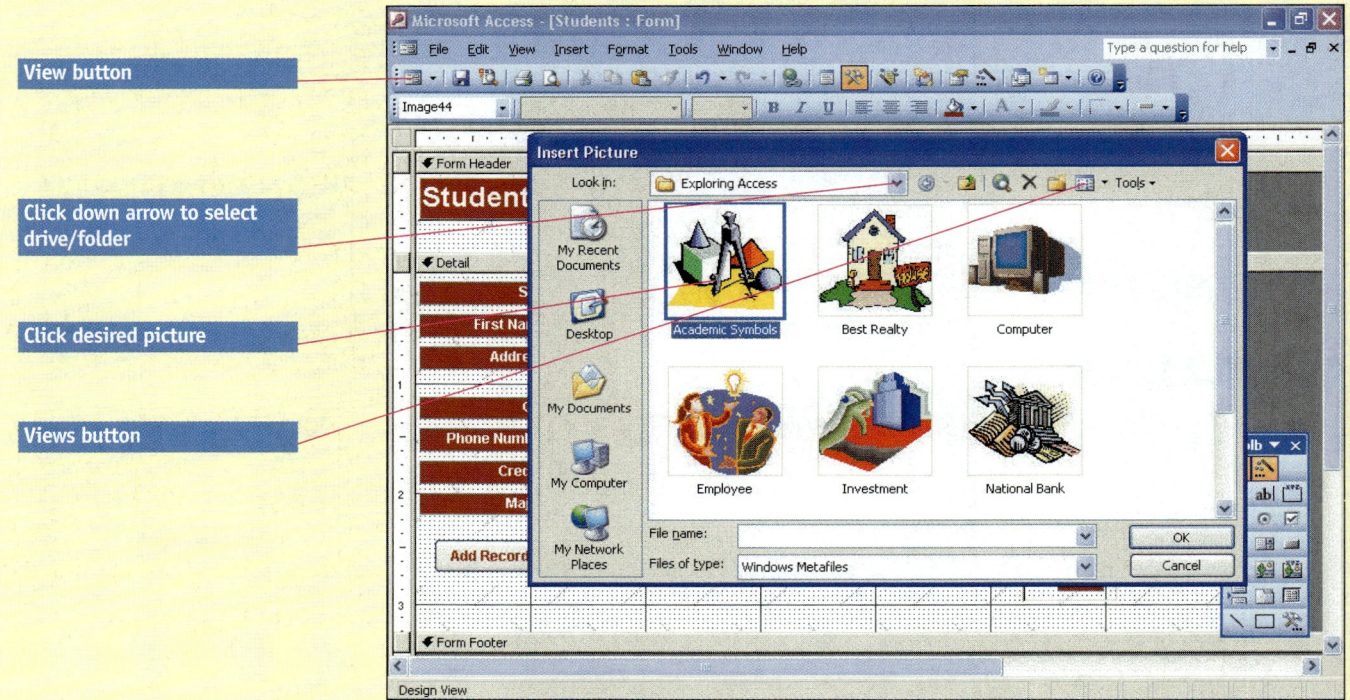

(h) Insert the Clip Art (step 8)

FIGURE 2.9 Hands-on Exercise 3 (*continued*)

MISSING TASK PANE

The Insert Picture command functions differently in Access than in the other Office applications since it does not display the Clip Art task pane. You can still search for clip art explicitly, however, by starting the Clip Organizer as a separate application. Click the Start button, click the All Programs button, click Microsoft Office Tools, then start the Clip Organizer. Select a clip art image from within the Clip Organizer, and click the Copy button. Use the Windows taskbar to return to Access, open the form in Design view, and click the Paste button.

Step 9: **The Completed Form**

■ Click the **View button** to switch to the Form view. Click the **Add Record command button** to create a new record. Click the text box for **Social Security Number**. Add the record shown in Figure 2.9i.

■ Click the **selection area** (the thin vertical column to the left of the form) to select the current record. The record selector changes to an arrow. The selection area is shaded to indicate that the record has been selected.

■ Pull down the **File menu**. Click **Print** to display the Print dialog box. Click the option button to print **Selected Record**. Click **OK**.

■ Examine your printed output to be sure that the form fits on a single page.

■ If it doesn't, you need to adjust the margins of the form itself and/or change the margins using the Page Setup command in the File menu, then print the form a second time.

■ Click the **Close Form command button** on the form after you have printed the record for your instructor.

■ Click **Yes** if you see a message asking to save changes to the form design.

■ Pull down the **File menu**. Click **Exit** to leave Access.

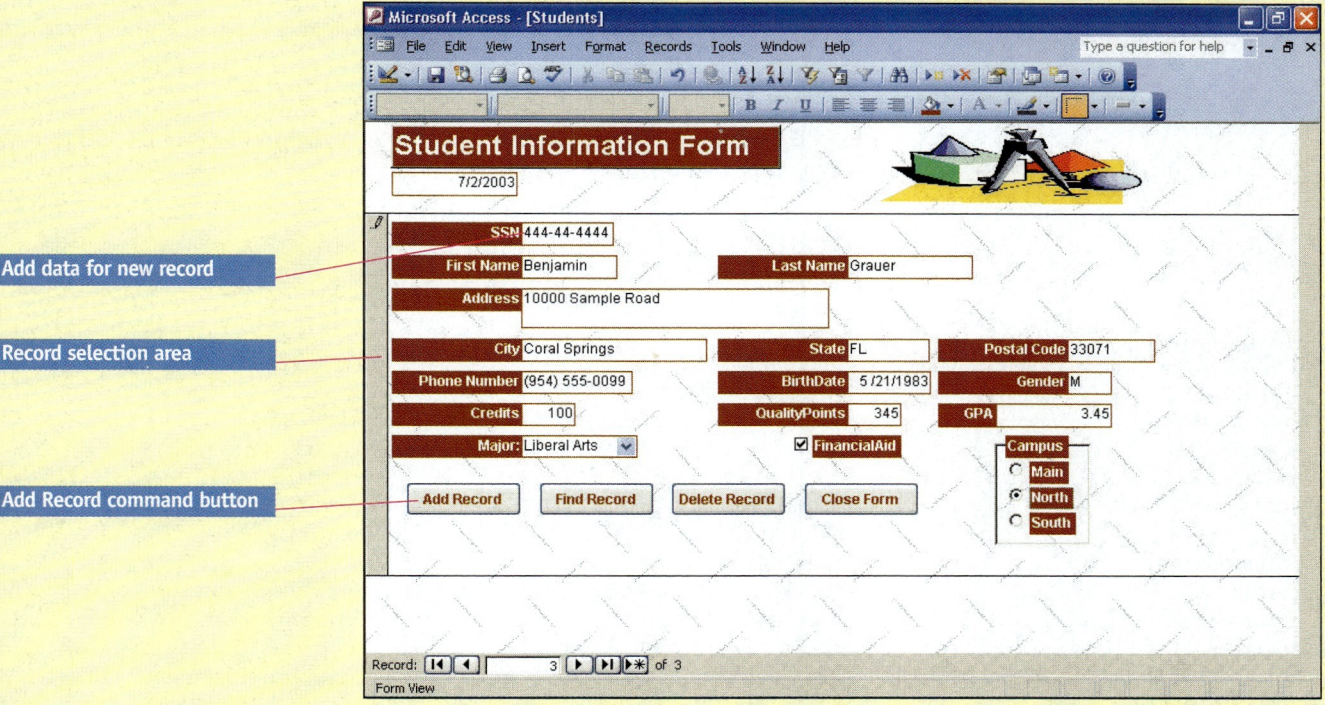

(i) The Completed Form (step 9)

FIGURE 2.9 Hands-on Exercise 3 (*continued*)

REMOVE THE WIZARD'S BACKGROUND

The Form (Report) Wizard is the fastest way to create these objects. One complaint about either wizard is the less-than-perfect design that is inserted as the background, but it's easy to eliminate. Go to Design view, then right click the Form (Report) selector button, click Properties, click the All tab, and then scroll until you find the Picture property. Select the entry (bitmap), press the Delete key, then click Yes when asked if you want to remove the picture.

SUMMARY

Access should be considered as a means to an end, rather than an end in itself. The real objective is to obtain useful information from a database, and that can be accomplished only if the database contains the necessary data to produce that information. Thus, one starts with a list of desired reports (or output), then determines the data (or input) to produce that information, after which the table can be created. The data within a table should be divided into the smallest possible units, such as separate fields for first and last name. Calculated fields should be avoided.

A table has different views—the Design view and the Datasheet view. The Design view is used to create the table and determine the fields within the table, as well as the data type and properties of each field. The Datasheet view is used after the table has been created to add, edit, and delete records. (The PivotTable view and PivotChart view display summary data and are discussed in Chapter 4.)

The Table Wizard is the easiest way to create a table. It lets you choose from a series of business or personal tables, asks you questions about the fields you want, then creates the table for you. The wizard creates the initial table for you, after which you can modify the table in Design view.

A form provides a user-friendly way to enter and display data, in that it can be made to resemble a paper form. AutoForms and the Form Wizard are easy ways to create a form. The Design view enables you to modify an existing form.

A form consists of objects called controls. A bound control has a data source such as a field in the underlying table. An unbound control has no data source. A calculated control contains an expression. Controls are selected, moved, and sized the same way as any other Windows object.

A property is a characteristic or attribute of an object that determines how the object looks and behaves. Every Access object (e.g., tables, fields, forms, and controls) has a set of properties that determine the behavior of that object. The properties for an object are displayed in a property sheet.

KEY TERMS

Allow Zero Length property 55
AutoForm 68
AutoNumber field 53
Bound control 65
Calculated control 65
Calculated field 52
Caption property 55
Check box 78
Command button 78
Control 65
Currency field 53
Data type 53
Datasheet view 54
Date/Time field 53
Default Value property 55
Design view 54
Drop-down list box 78

Expression 65
Field name 53
Field Size property 55
Form 65
Form view 65
Form Wizard 68
Format property 55
Hyperlink field 53
IME Mode property 55
IME Sentence Mode property . . . 55
Indexed property 55
Input Mask property 55
Memo field 53
Number field 53
OLE Object field 53
Option group 78
PivotChart view 54

PivotTable view 54
Primary key 53
Property 55
Property sheet 55
Required property 55
Tab Order 85
Tab Stop property 85
Table Wizard 53
Text field 53
Unbound control 65
Unicode Compression
    property 55
Validation Rule property 55
Validation Text property 55
Yes/No field 53

MULTIPLE CHOICE

1. Which of the following is true?

   (a) The Table Wizard must be used to create a table

   (b) The Form Wizard must be used to create a form

   (c) Both (a) and (b)

   (d) Neither (a) nor (b)

2. Which of the following is implemented automatically by Access?

   (a) Rejection of a record with a duplicate value of the primary key

   (b) Rejection of numbers in a text field

   (c) Both (a) and (b)

   (d) Neither (a) nor (b)

3. Social Security number, phone number, and zip code should be designated as:

   (a) Number fields

   (b) Text fields

   (c) Yes/No fields

   (d) Any of the above depending on the application

4. Which of the following is true of the primary key?

   (a) Its values must be unique

   (b) It must be defined as a text field

   (c) It must be the first field in a table

   (d) It can never be changed

5. Social Security number rather than name is used as a primary key because:

   (a) The Social Security number is numeric, whereas the name is not

   (b) The Social Security number is unique, whereas the name is not

   (c) The Social Security number is a shorter field

   (d) All of the above

6. Which of the following is true regarding buttons within the Form Wizard?

   (a) The > button copies a selected field from a table onto a form

   (b) The < button removes a selected field from a form

   (c) Both (a) and (b)

   (d) Neither (a) nor (b)

7. Which of the following was *not* a suggested guideline for designing a table?

   (a) Include all necessary data

   (b) Store data in its smallest parts

   (c) Avoid calculated fields

   (d) Designate at least two primary keys

8. Which of the following are valid parameters for use with a form?

   (a) Portrait orientation, a width of 6 inches, left and right margins of $1\frac{1}{4}$ inch

   (b) Landscape orientation, a width of 9 inches, left and right margins of 1 inch

   (c) Both (a) and (b)

   (d) Neither (a) nor (b)

9. Which view is used to add, edit, or delete records in a table?

   (a) The Datasheet view

   (b) The Design view

   (c) The PivotTable view

   (d) The PivotChart view

10. Which of the following is true?

    (a) Any field added to a table after a form has been created is automatically added to the form as a bound control

    (b) Any calculated control that appears in a form is automatically inserted into the underlying table

    (c) Every bound and unbound control in a form has an underlying property sheet

    (d) All of the above

11. In which view will you see the record selector symbols of a pencil and a triangle?

    (a) Only the Datasheet view

    (b) Only the Form view

    (c) The Datasheet view and the Form view

    (d) The Form view, the Design view, and the Datasheet view

... continued

m u l t i p l e   c h o i c e

12. To move a control (in the Design view), you select the control, then:

(a) Point to a border (the pointer changes to an arrow) and click and drag the border to the new position

(b) Point to a border (the pointer changes to a hand) and click and drag the border to the new position

(c) Point to a sizing handle (the pointer changes to an arrow) and click and drag the sizing handle to the new position

(d) Point to a sizing handle (the pointer changes to a hand) and click and drag the sizing handle to the new position

13. Which fields are commonly defined with an input mask?

(a) Social Security number and phone number

(b) First name, middle name, and last name

(c) City, state, and zip code

(d) All of the above

14. Which data type appears as a check box in a form?

(a) Text field

(b) Number field

(c) Yes/No field

(d) All of the above

15. Which properties would you use to limit a user's response to two characters, and automatically convert the response to uppercase?

(a) Field Size and Format

(b) Input Mask, Validation Rule, and Default Value

(c) Input Mask and Required

(d) Field Size, Validation Rule, Validation Text, and Required

16. Which of the following is true with respect to an individual's hire date and years of service, both of which appear on a form that is based on an employee table?

(a) Hire date should be a calculated control; years of service should be a bound control

(b) Hire date should be a bound control; years of service should be a calculated control

(c) Both should be bound controls

(d) Both should be calculated controls

17. What is the best way to store an individual's name in a table?

(a) As a single field consisting of the last name, first name, and middle initial, in that order

(b) As a single field consisting of the first name, last name, and middle initial, in that order

(c) As three separate fields for first name, last name, and middle initial

(d) All of the above are equally suitable

18. Which of the following would *not* be a good primary key?

(a) Student number

(b) Social Security number

(c) An e-mail address

(d) A 9-digit zip code

ANSWERS

1. d	**7.** d	**13.** a
2. a	**8.** c	**14.** c
3. b	**9.** a	**15.** a
4. a	**10.** c	**16.** b
5. b	**11.** c	**17.** c
6. c	**12.** b	**18.** d

PRACTICE WITH ACCESS

1. **A Modified Student Form:** Open the *My First Database* used in the chapter and modify the Student form created in the hands-on exercises to match the form in Figure 2.10. (The form contains three additional controls that must be added to the Students table, prior to modifying the form.)

   a. Open the Students table in Design view. Add DateAdmitted and EmailAddress as a date and a text field, respectively. Add a Yes/No field to indicate whether the student is an international student.

   b. Open the Students form in Design view. Add controls for the additional fields as shown in Figure 2.10.

   c. Modify the State field in the underlying Students table to use the Lookup Wizard, and set CA, FL, NJ, and NY as the values for the list box. (These are the most common states in the student population.) The control in the form will not, however, inherit the list box because it was added to the table after the form was created. Hence, you have to delete the existing control in the form, display the field list, then click and drag the State field from the field list to the form.)

   d. Add a hyperlink in the form header that contains the Web address of your school or university. It's easy—just click the Insert Hyperlink button on the Form Design toolbar, then enter the text and associated address in the ensuing dialog box. Click and drag the control containing the hyperlink to the appropriate place on the form.

   e. Change the Caption property in each command button to include an ampersand in front of the underlined letter (e.g., &Add Record). The resulting command button is shown with an underline under the letter (e.g., <u>A</u>dd Record). This in turn lets you use a shortcut, Alt+A (where A is the underlined letter), to activate the command button.

   f. Resize the control in the Form Header so that *Your School or University Student Information Form* takes two lines. Press Ctrl+Enter to force a line break within the control. Resize the Form Header.

   g. Change the tab order to reflect the new fields in the form.

   h. Use the Page Setup command to change the margins and/or orientation of the page to be sure that the form fits on one page. Click the record selector column to select your record, then print the form for your instructor.

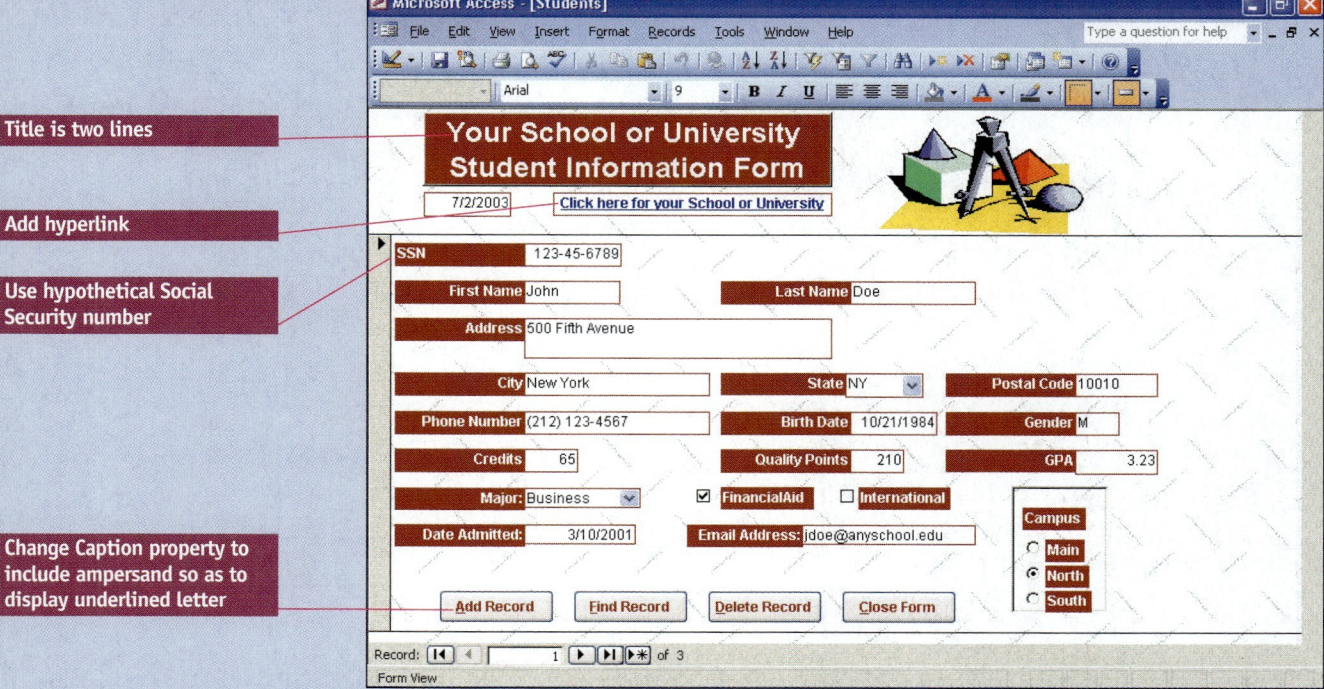

FIGURE 2.10 Modified Student Form (exercise 1)

practice exercises

2. **The United States Database:** This assignment builds on the United States database that was used for an earlier exercise in Chapter 1. Your assignment is to build a form similar to the one in Figure 2.11. You do not have to match our form exactly. You do, however, have to duplicate the functionality. Proceed as follows:

a. Open the *Chapter 1 Practice 3* database in the Exploring Access folder. Click the Tables button in the Database window and open the States table in Design view. Insert a new field at the end of the table, using WebPage and hyperlink as the field name and field type, respectively.

b. Use the Form Wizard to create the form initially, based on the States table (select all of the fields). Select the columnar layout and choose any style. Open the form in Design view to complete the form. Move and size the various controls as shown in Figure 2.11.

c. Add clip art to the form header that contains an image representing the United States. (Change the Size Mode property of the clip art to Stretch.) Insert a hyperlink to the White House (www.whitehouse.gov) underneath the image. Add your name and date in the form header.

d. Create a calculated control for the population density (population/area). Set the Tab Stop property to No.

e. Add the indicated command buttons, using the Caption property to implement the keyboard shortcut; for example, &Find Record will underline the letter "F" and enable the Alt+F keyboard shortcut to activate the button.

f. Pull down the View menu, click the Tab Order command to display the Tab Order dialog box, and then click the Auto Order button to set the tab order to match the physical arrangement of the controls in the form.

g. Go to the Form view. Use the navigation buttons to locate your home state (or any state if you are an international student). Enter the address of the state's Web page, using an address of the form www.state.*abbreviation*.us (e.g., www.state.fl.us for Florida).

h. Use the Page Setup command to change the margins and/or orientation of the page to be sure that the form fits on one page. Click the record selector column to select your state and print this record for your instructor. Click the hyperlink for your state's Web page and print that page for your instructor as well.

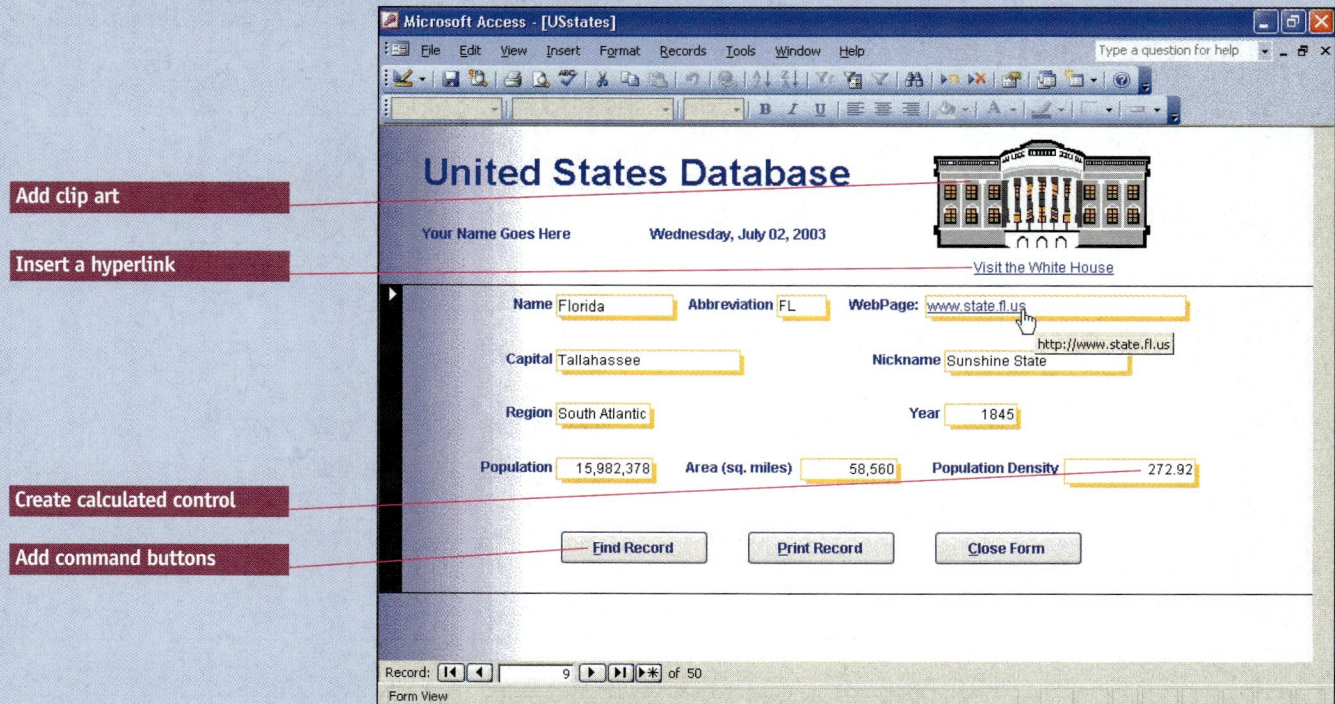

FIGURE 2.11 The United States Database (exercise 2)

practice exercises

3. **The Super Bowl:** Figure 2.12 displays a Web page (or Data Access page) that can be used to view and/or enter data in an underlying Access database. Look closely and you will see that the form is displayed in Internet Explorer, as opposed to Access, because the form was created as a Web page within Access. Proceed as follows:

a. Open the *Chapter 2 Practice 3* database in the Exploring Access folder. Click the Pages tab in the Database window, and then double click the option to create the Data Access page using the wizard. The wizard will prompt you for the information it needs in a series of screens. The first screen asks you to choose the table or query (Previous Games) and the fields within that table (All). Click Next.

b. You do not need grouping or sorting, but you should check the box to apply a theme (to make the form more attractive). End the wizard by viewing the page in Design view. Enter a title as indicated by the Click here prompt. Insert a hyperlink to the Super Bowl Web site (www.superbowl.com).

c. Pull down the File menu, click the Save command, then save the page in the Exploring Access folder. You will be warned that you have specified an absolute path and that the network may not be able to reconnect in the future. Click OK.

d. Close the database and exit Access. Go to the Exploring Access folder and open the Web page (HTML document) that you just created to view the records in the Super Bowl table as shown in Figure 2.12. (The HTML document exists as a separate document outside of the Access database.)

e. Click the New button to add a record for any games that are not in our table. (You can click the link to the Super Bowl Web site to obtain the scores of the additional games.) Print the record of the most recent game from Internet Explorer. Close Internet Explorer.

f. Start Access and reopen the *Chapter 2 Practice 3* database. Click the Tables button, open the Previous Games table, and go to the last record in the table, which should contain the data that you just entered. Now think about what you have accomplished. You were able to add a record to an Access database using a Web page as the "front end" for the database. You can continue to add, edit, or delete records using the Web page, and all changes will be reflected in the underlying Access table.

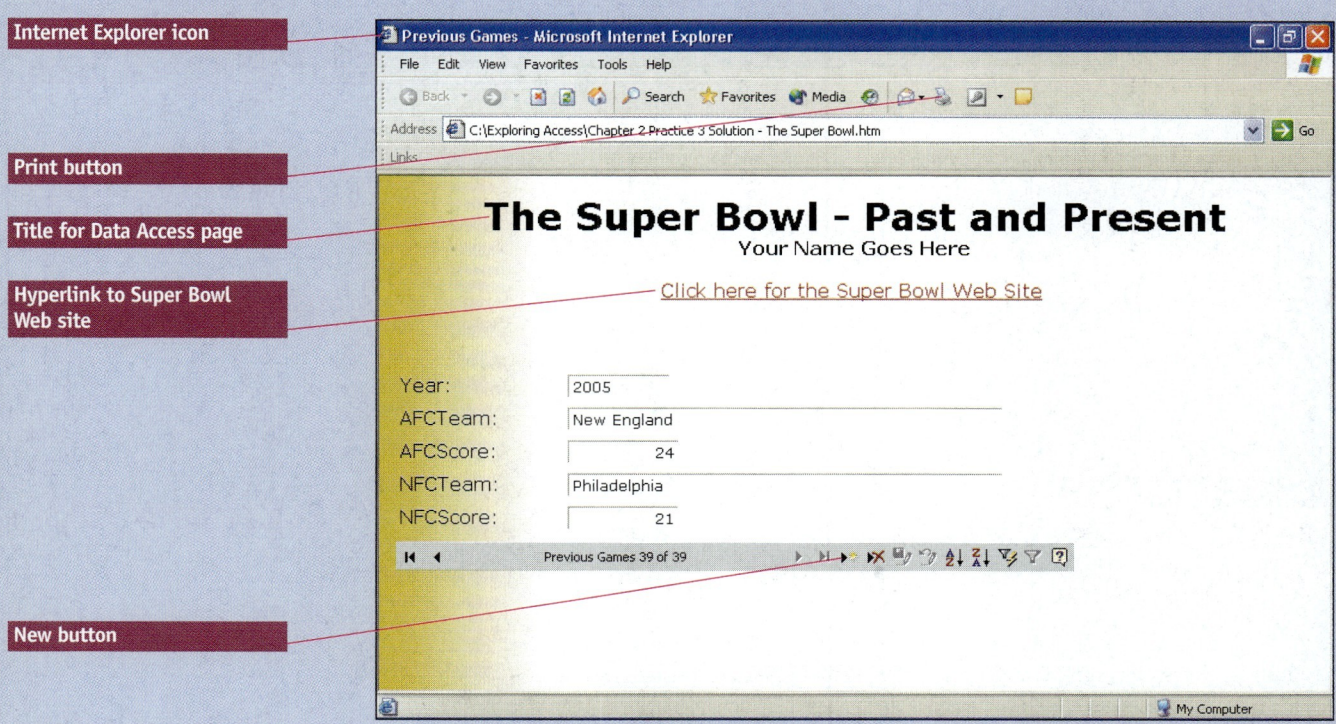

FIGURE 2.12 The Super Bowl (exercise 3)

4. **The Fishing Pole:** You have been asked by a marine hardware store to create a database that will be used to track its customers. In essence, you are to create the table in Figure 2.13 without benefit of the Table Wizard. Proceed as follows:

a. Start Access and create a new (blank) database. Click the Tables button in the Database window and double click the option to create a new table in Design view. To enter a new field, click in the Field Name column and type the name of the field (do not use spaces in the field name). Move to the Data Type column and choose the field type.

b. Create all of the fields in Figure 2.13. (The BoatType should be specified using the Lookup Wizard, and include Fishing, Power, and Sail as the boat types to be listed.) Save the table as Customers.

c. The CustomerNumber is to be the primary key. It should be an AutoNumber data type, and the Format should be \C0000, which will automatically produce a Customer Number that begins with the letter C, followed by a four-digit number each time a record is added to the table.

d. Establish input masks for the customer's zip code and phone number, as well as the initial purchase date. The initial purchase date should also have a short date format.

e. Use the Format property so that the state is displayed in uppercase letters, regardless of how it is entered.

f. Set appropriate field sizes for all text fields. Eliminate the default value of 0 and set a currency format with 2 decimal places for the initial purchase amount.

g. Set the Required property for the LastName and FirstName fields to Yes.

h. Set the Validation Rule property for the MailingList field to restrict values to 1, 2, or 3. Set the Validation Text property to display an appropriate message if the user attempts to enter invalid data.

i. Enter one record into the completed table, entering your name as the customer name. Print the table only if you are not doing the next exercise. The table will require two pages, even if you change to landscape printing.

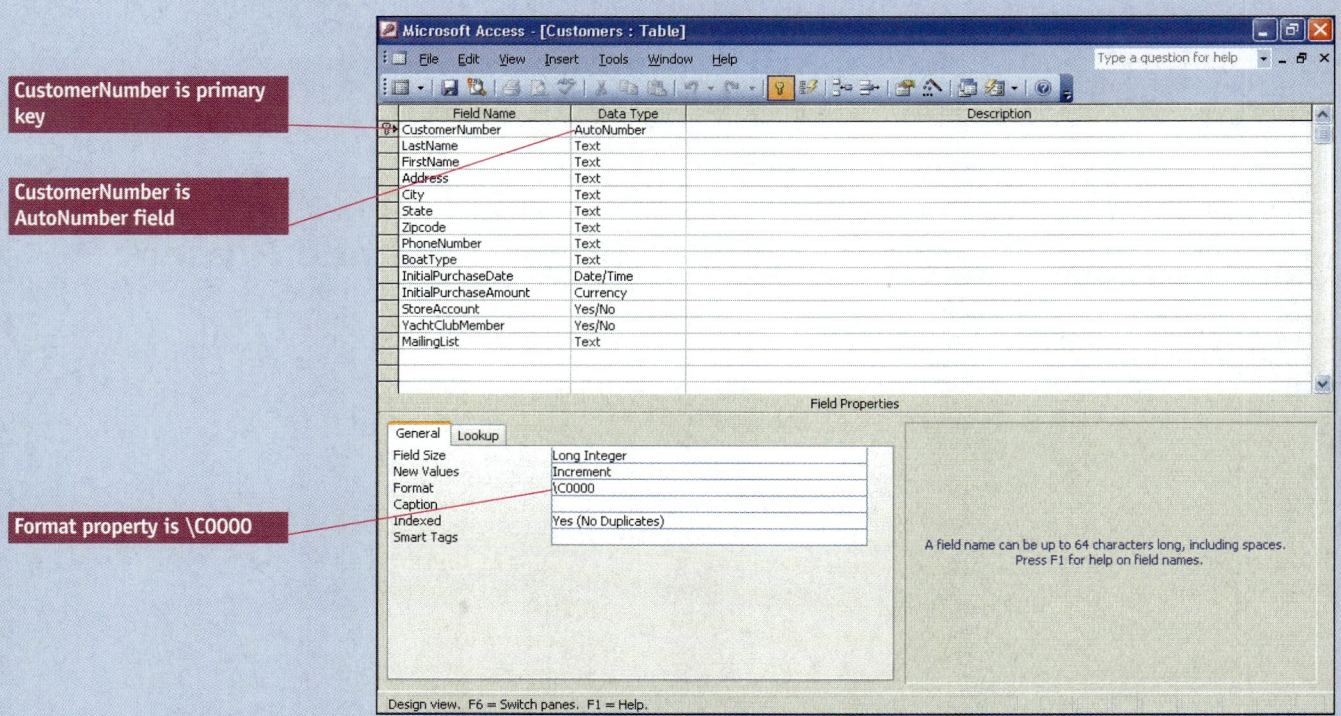

FIGURE 2.13 The Fishing Pole (exercise 4)

5. **A Form for the Fishing Pole:** Your assignment is to create a form similar to the one in Figure 2.14 that is based on the Fishing Pole database created in the previous exercise. The design of your form can be different from ours, but you must duplicate the functionality in our figure. Start with the Form Wizard, and then modify the resulting form as necessary so that your finished form accommodates all of the following:

a. The form should contain a control for every field in the underlying table. Move, format, align, and size the controls as necessary. Change the tab order of the controls so that the user tabs through the controls from left to right, top to bottom. Set the Tab Stop property of the Customer Number to No because the user does not input this value.

b. Use a different background color for the required fields (such as the customer's first and last name) to emphasize that these fields must be entered. Include a note at the bottom of the form to explain the color change.

c. Insert a form header with clip art (you do not have to use the same clip art as in our figure) and an appropriate title as shown in Figure 2.14. Set the Size Mode property of the clip art to Stretch.

d. Add command buttons as indicated. The command buttons should be a uniform size with equal spacing between them. Test each command button to be sure that it works as intended.

e. Use the Page Setup command to be sure that the form will fit on a single page when printed. Change the margins and/or orientation of the form as necessary. The completed form should display the data that you entered for yourself when you created the table in the previous problem. Print this form for your instructor.

f. Click the Add Record button to add a new record to the Customers table. Use your instructor's name as the customer's name, and supply other information as you see fit. Click the record selector column to select your instructor's record. Pull down the File menu, click the Print command, then select the option button to print the selected record. Submit both forms to your instructor to show that you completed this assignment.

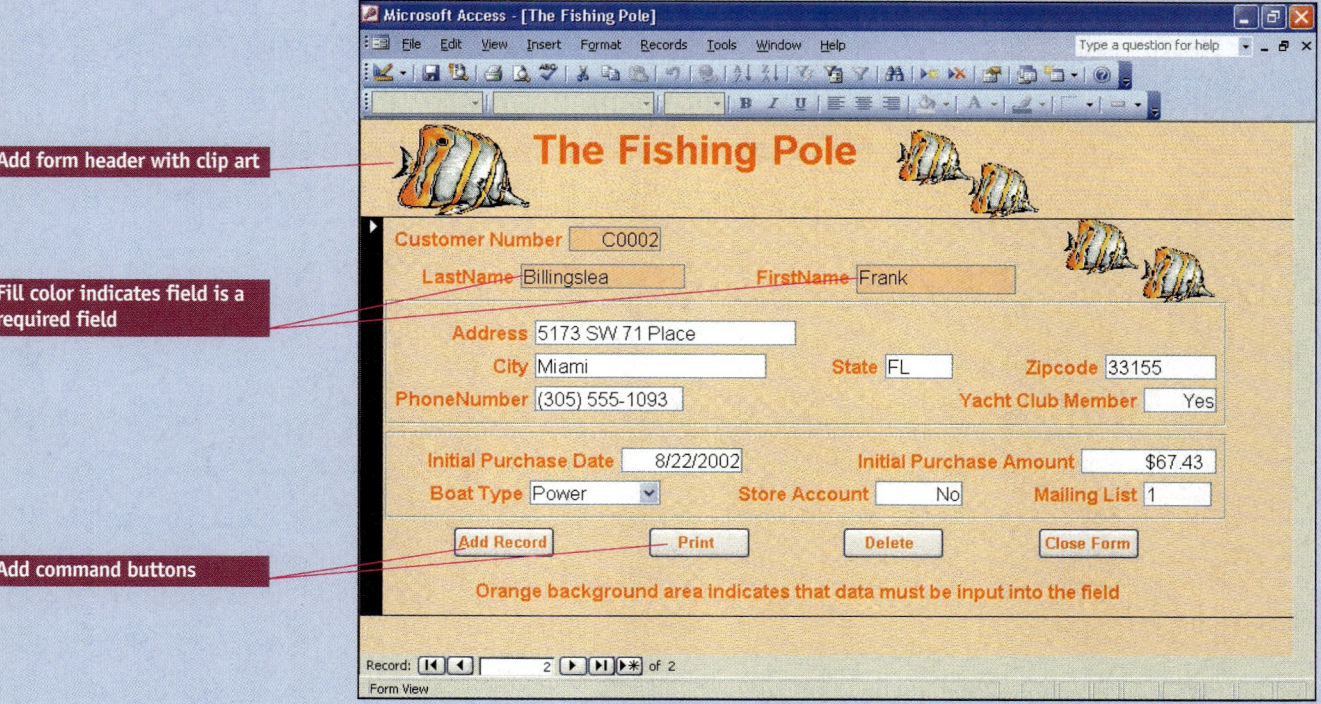

FIGURE 2.14 A Form for the Fishing Pole (exercise 5)

6. **The Shopping Mall:** You have been hired as a consultant for a shopping mall to create a database that is to track all of the stores in the mall. You have met with the mall manager several times and have decided on the various fields that need to be included in the Stores table. The results of your discussion can be summarized by the Design view of the table as shown in Figure 2.15.

   a. Create the table without benefit of the Table Wizard. Start Access and specify that you will create a new database. The database should be called Shopping Mall and it should be stored in your Exploring Access folder.

   b. Click the Tables button in the Database window and double click the option to create a new table in Design view. To enter a new field, click in the Field Name column and type the name of the field (do not use spaces in the field name). Move to the Data Type column and choose the field type. The fields in your table should match those in Figure 2.15.

   c. The StoreID is to be the primary key. Use the validation rule that is specified in the figure, which requires that the file begin with the letter S followed by four digits to indicate the store unit number.

   d. The StoreType should be specified using the Lookup Wizard, and include Clothing, Jewelry, Furniture, Home Accessories, Restaurant, and Shoes as the store types to be listed.

   e. Establish input masks for the manager's phone number, as well as the lease start date and lease end date. The latter two fields require short date formats.

   f. Set appropriate field sizes for all text fields. Eliminate the default values of 0 and set appropriate formats for the currency fields. The PricePerSquareFt is the rent per square foot and should allow two decimal places. The StoreRevenue field should be formatted without any decimal places.

   g. The StoreID, StoreName, and StoreType are required fields.

   h. Enter one record into the completed table. Use StoreID S0001 and use your name as the manager. Change to landscape printing and adjust the column width and/or the margins, so that the records fit on a single sheet of paper. Print this record for your instructor.

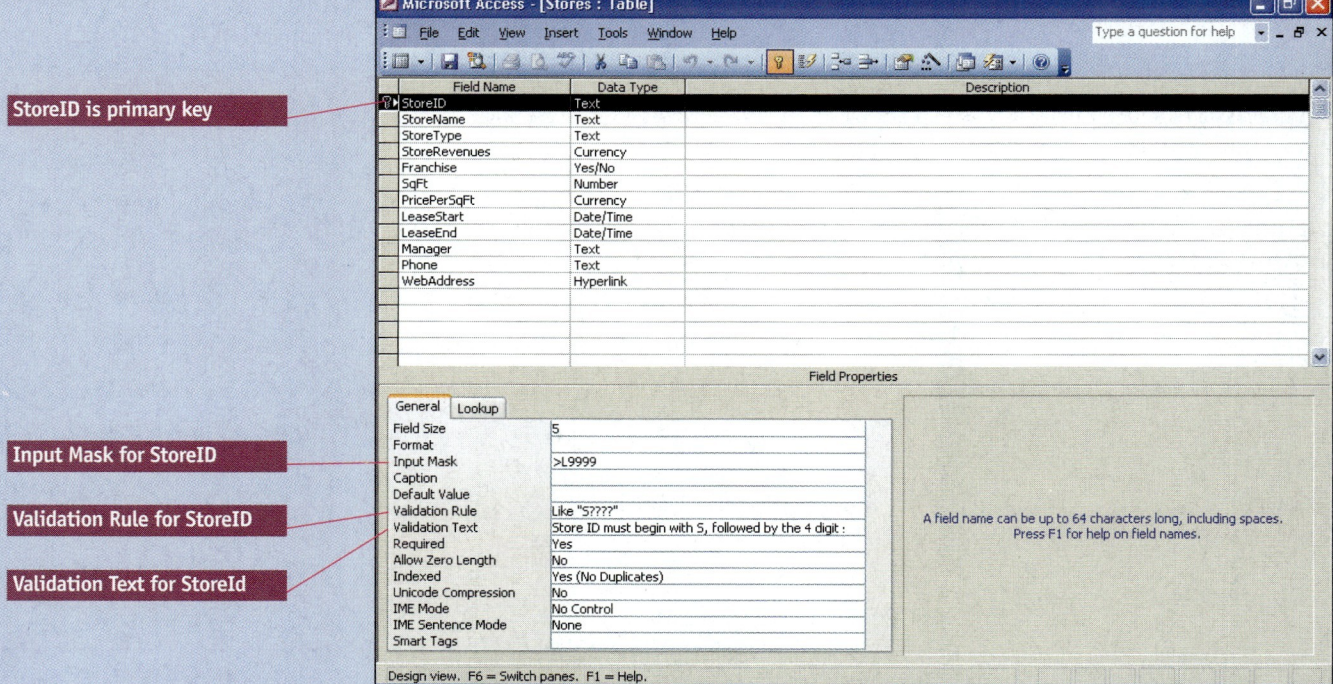

FIGURE 2.15 The Shopping Mall (exercise 6)

7. **A Form for the Shopping Mall:** Your assignment is to create a form similar to the one in Figure 2.16 that is based on the Shopping Mall database created in the previous exercise. The design of your form can be different from ours, but you must duplicate the functionality in our figure. Start with the Form Wizard, and then modify the resulting form as necessary so that your finished form accommodates all of the following:

a. The form should contain a control for every field in the underlying table. Format, move, size, and align the controls as necessary. Change the tab order of the controls so that the user tabs through the controls from left to right, top to bottom.

b. Include a calculated control to determine the monthly rent, which is equal to the number of square feet times the price per square foot. Change the format of this control to currency. Set the Tab Stop property to No.

c. Use a different background for the required fields (such as the StoreID and StoreType) to emphasize that the data for these fields is required. Include a note at the bottom of the form that explains the color change.

d. Insert a form header with clip art (you do not have to use the same clip art as in our figure) and an appropriate title. Set the Size Mode property of the clip art to Stretch.

e. Add command buttons as indicated. The command buttons should be a uniform size with equal spacing between them. Test each command button to be sure that it works as intended.

f. Use the Page Setup command to be sure that the form will fit on a single page when printed. The completed form should display the data that you entered for store number S0001 when you created the table in the previous problem. Print this form for your instructor.

g. Click the Add Record button to add a new record with StoreID S0002. Use your instructor's name as the store manager, and supply other information as you see fit. Click the record selector column to select your instructor's record. Pull down the File menu, click the Print command, then select the option button to print the selected record. Submit both forms to your instructor to show that you completed this assignment.

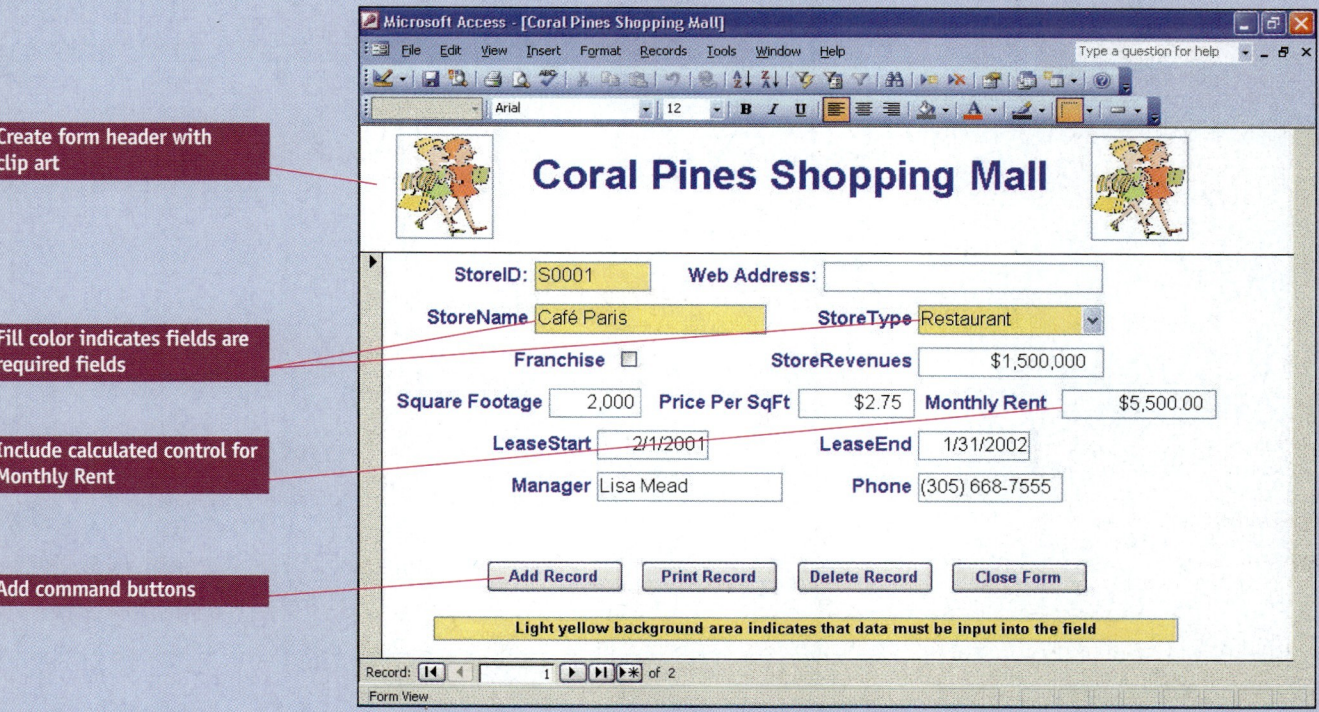

FIGURE 2.16 A Form for the Shopping Mall (exercise 7)

8. **Best Realty:** Best Realty is a real estate agency that specializes in the listing/selling of homes, including single-family dwellings as well as multiple-family dwellings. You have recently been hired by Best Realty to develop a database to track their property listings. After much thought and planning, you have decided upon the fields shown in Figure 2.17. Proceed as follows:

a. Create the table shown *without* using the Table Wizard. After you start Access, specify that you will create a new database—then assign the name Best Realty and save it in the Exploring Access folder.

b. Click the Tables button in the Database window and double click the option to create a new table in the Design view. To enter a new field, click in the Field Name column and type the name of the field (do not use spaces in the field name). Move to the Data Type column and choose the field type. The fields in your table should match those in Figure 2.17.

c. The PropertyID should be designated as the primary key. Be sure to include a validation rule that specifies that the ID should be composed of the letter P followed by four digits.

d. The PropertyType should be created using the Lookup Wizard, and include Single-Family, Townhome, Duplex, and Condominium.

e. Set appropriate field sizes for all text fields. Eliminate the default values of 0 and set appropriate formats for the number fields.

f. Create an input mask and format for the DateListed and DateSold fields.

g. The PropertyID, Address, AskingPrice, and AgentLastName should be specified as required fields.

h. Enter one record into the completed table. Use P0001 as the PropertyID and use your name as the agent. Change to landscape printing and adjust the column width and/or the margins so that the record fits on a single sheet of paper. Print this record for your instructor.

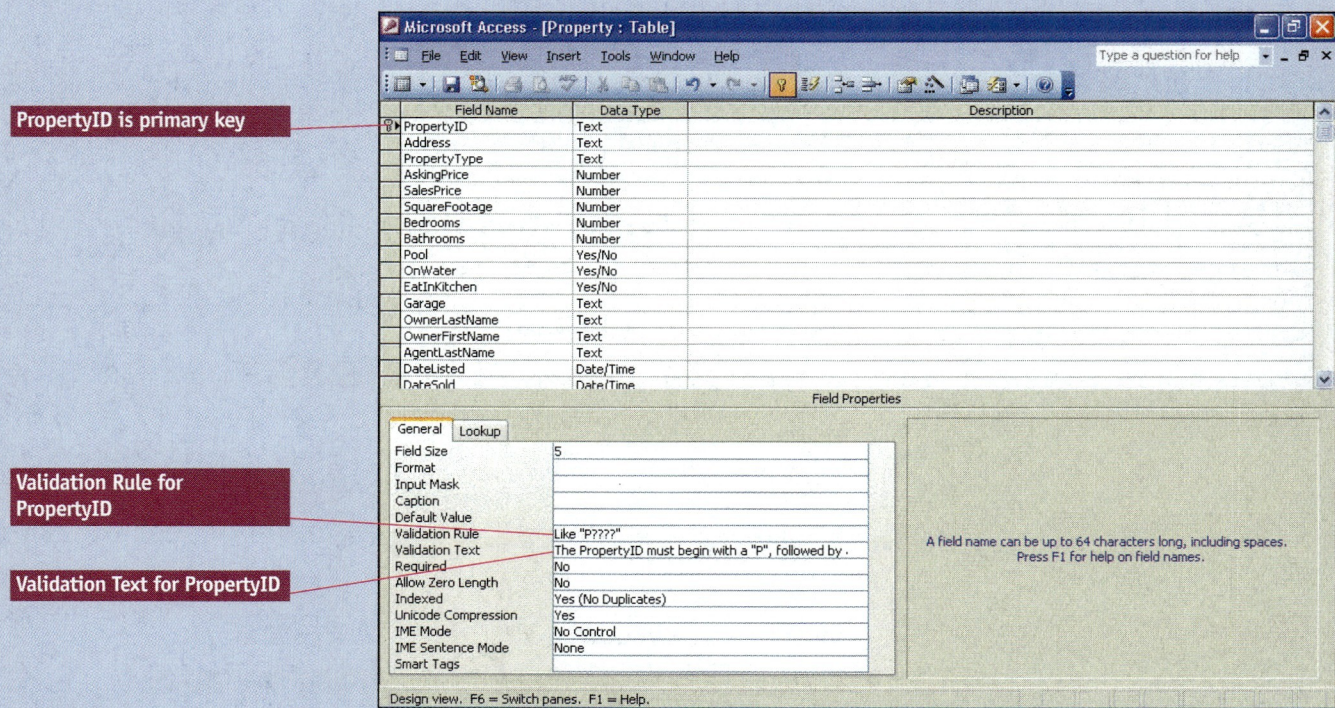

FIGURE 2.17   Best Realty (exercise 8)

9. **A Form for Best Realty:** Your assignment is to create a form similar to the one in Figure 2.18 that is based on the Best Realty database created in the previous exercise. The design of your form can be different from ours, but you must duplicate the functionality in our figure. Start with the Form Wizard, and then modify the resulting form as necessary so that your finished form accommodates all of the following:

a. The form should contain a control for every field in the underlying table. Format, move, size, and align the controls as necessary. Change the tab order of the controls so that the user tabs through the controls from left to right, top to bottom.

b. Add a calculated control to determine the price per square foot, which is equal to the sales price divided by the number of square feet. Change the format of this control to currency. Set the Tab Stop property to No.

c. Use a different background for the required fields (such as the PropertyID and Address) to emphasize that the data for these fields is required. Include a note at the bottom of the form to explain the color change.

d. Insert a form header with clip art (you do not have to use the same clip art as in our figure) and an appropriate title. Set the Size Mode property of the clip art to Stretch.

e. Add command buttons as indicated. The command buttons should be a uniform size with equal spacing between them. Test each command button to be sure that it works as intended.

f. Use the Page Setup command to be sure that the form will fit on a single page when printed. The completed form should display the data that you entered for the first property when you created the table in the previous problem. Print this form for your instructor.

g. Click the Add Record button to add a new record with PropertyID P0002. Use your instructor's name as the owner, and supply other information as you see fit. Click the record selector column to select this record. Pull down the File menu, click the Print command, then select the option button to print the selected record. Submit both forms to your instructor to show that you completed this assignment.

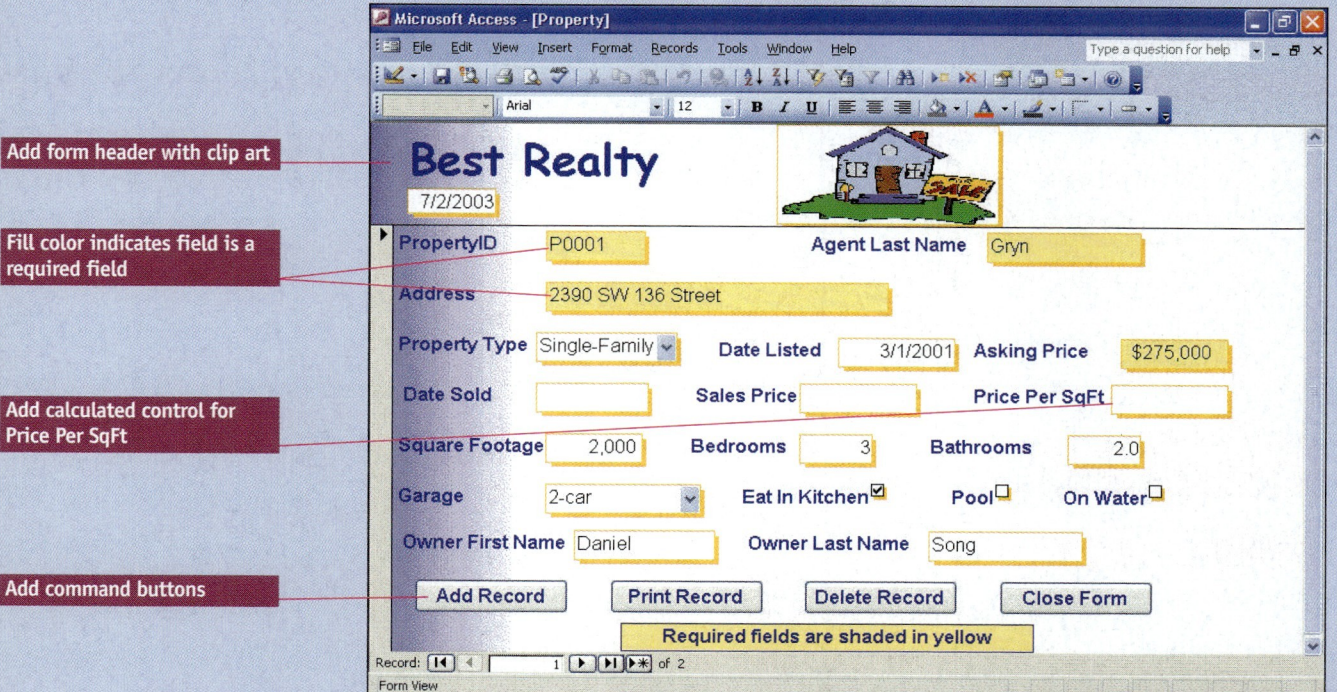

FIGURE 2.18   A Form for Best Realty (exercise 9)

10. **Events Extraordinaire:** A close friend, who has started his own event planning business, has asked for your help in creating an Access database. The database is to track the events that your friend's company will coordinate. Your first task is to create the database and associated table as shown in Figure 2.19. The table is to be developed without benefit of the Table Wizard. Proceed as follows:

a. Start Access and create a new database. Click the Tables button in the Database window and double click the option to Create table in Design view.

b. Enter all of the fields and associated field types as shown in Figure 2.19. (To enter a new field, click in the Field Name column and type the name of the field. Do not use spaces in the field name.) Move to the Data Type column and choose the field type. Note that the EventScope should be created using the Lookup Wizard, and should specify Local, State, National, and International as the event scopes to be listed. Save the table as Events.

c. Designate the EventID as the primary key (it was established as an AutoNumber field type). Set the Format property to \E000, which will automatically display an EventID that begins with the letter E, followed by a four-digit number. The Event IDs will be generated automatically each time a record is added.

d. Establish input masks for the sponsor's contact phone number, the starting date, and the ending date. Establish the short date format for both dates.

e. Set appropriate field sizes for all text fields; for example, change the field size of the Sponsor Contact's Last Name to 15 from the default value of 50.

f. Select the currency format with zero decimal places for both the cost per person and the planning fee.

g. Set the Required property to "Yes" for the Event Name, Sponsor, Sponsor Contact First Name, Sponsor Contact Last Name, Start Date, and End Date.

h. Set the Validation Rule property for the Start Date and End Date to specify a date at least 30 days from today (>Now()+30). Set the Validation Text property to display an appropriate message if the user attempts to enter invalid data.

i. Enter one record into the completed table using your name as the sponsor contact. Print the table only if you are not doing the next exercise. The table will require two or three pages, even if you change to landscape printing.

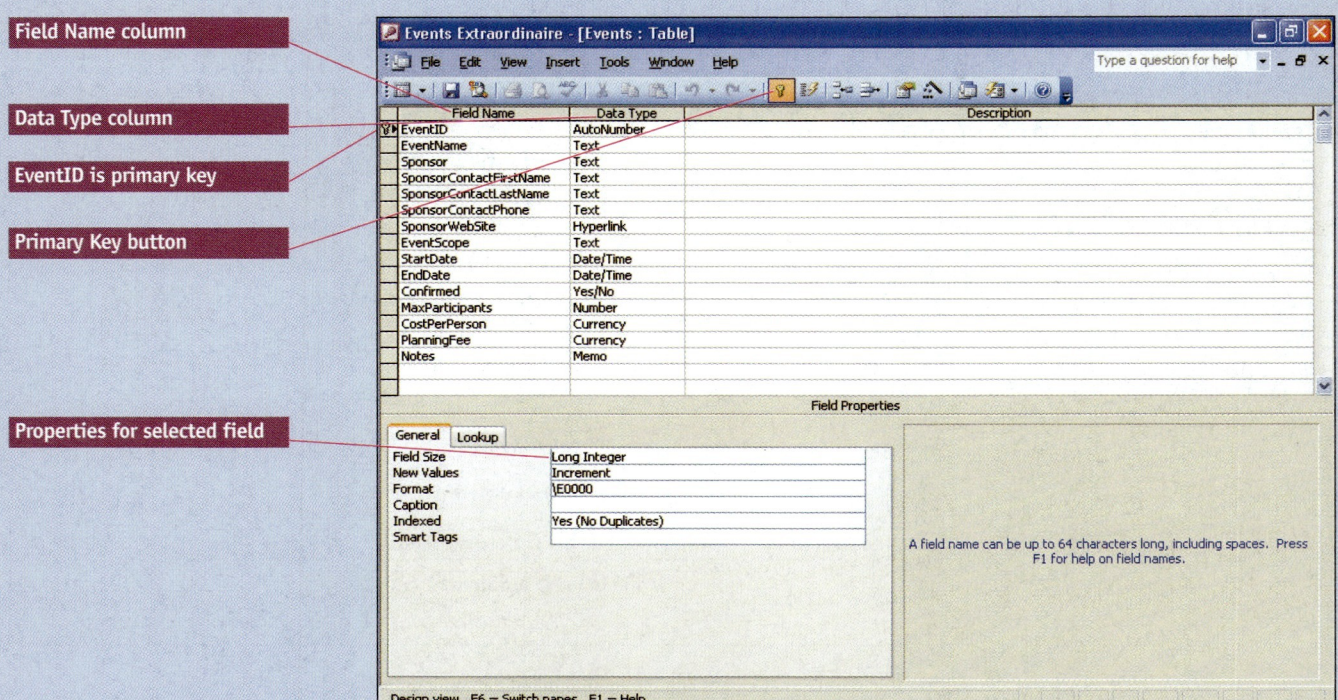

FIGURE 2.19 Events Extraordinaire (exercise 10)

11. **A Form for Events Extraordinaire (with Tab Controls):** The form in Figure 2.20 uses tab controls to create a multiple-page form. This is a convenient technique to display additional information on a form without extensive scrolling. You do not have to follow our design exactly, but you are to include the underlying functionality. Proceed as follows:

a. Open the Events Extraordinaire database from the previous exercise, click the Forms button, double click the icon to Create form in Design view, right click the Form selector tab in the upper-left corner, click Properties, click the All tab, and choose the Events table as the record source. The field list should appear automatically. Close the property sheet.

b. The form has to contain a control for every field in the underlying table. Click and drag the indicated fields to the top part of the form as shown. Do not be concerned about formatting or position at this time.

c. Click the Tab Control tool in the Toolbox, then click and drag where you want the tabbed control to go. Two tabs are created by default (the page numbers do not matter as we will change them later). Click and drag the Sponsor fields (first and last name, contact, and Web site) to the first tab. Click the second tab, then click and drag the remaining fields as shown in Figure 2.20. Create the Potential Revenue control, which is a calculated control equal to the maximum number of participants times the cost per person.

d. Right click the tab for the first page, click Properties, then change the name to Sponsor Details. Change the name of the second tab as well.

e. Move, size, and format the controls on the main form and both tabs. Pull down the View menu, then click the command for Form Header/Footer to open the form header. Create the form title and insert the clip art. Close the footer since it is not used.

f. Add the indicated command buttons at the bottom of the form. Move, size, and align the buttons as shown. Pull down the View menu, click Tab Order, then choose AutoOrder.

g. Save the form, then go to Form view. Use the Page Setup command to be sure that the form will fit on a single page when printed. Click the Print button to print the record you added in the previous exercise.

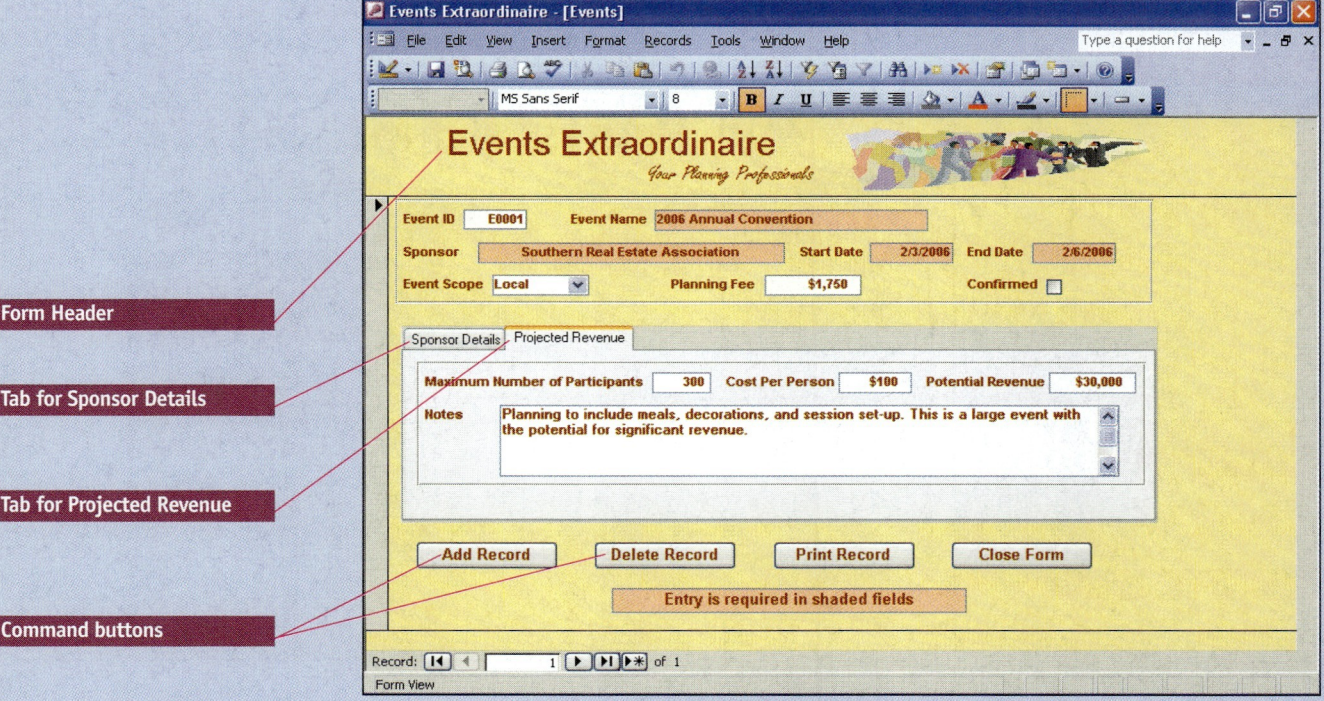

FIGURE 2.20 A Form for Events Extraordinaire (exercise 11)

12. **Paw Prints:** The form in Figure 2.21 is based on a simple table with nine fields, one of which is defined as an OLE object, which enables us to store a picture within each each record. The picture is a "nice touch" but it comes with a price—a substantial increase in the size of the database. The photo can be linked or embedded into the underlying table, but embedding is simpler because the image becomes part of the database and travels with it. The disadvantage is that you must embed a bitmapped image (as opposed to JPEG files), which rapidly increases the size of the database. Proceed as follows:

a. Start a new database. Create the Animals table, which is composed of the fields in Figure 2.21. Be sure to specify AnimalID as an AutoNumber field.

b. Set the properties of the other fields as you see fit. The AnimalType field is to be taken from a list box that accepts "dog", "cat", or "other". Size is also taken from a list box that contains, "toy", "small", "medium", or "large". The Gender field should accept only "M" or "F". Save the table design.

c. Create a form based on the Animals table similar to the form in Figure 2.21. (You do not have to follow our design exactly.) Right click the control for the photo, click Properties to display the associated property sheet, then click the All tab. Change the Size Mode property to Stretch. Change the Border Style property to Solid.

d. Add the indicated command buttons. Set the tab order appropriately. Check that the width of the form does not exceed 7.5 inches. Pull down the File menu, click the Page Setup command, then change the left and right margins to half an inch each, so that the form fits on one sheet of paper. Save the form.

e. Use the finished form to enter the data for Buster and Daisy, a dog and cat, respectively. Buster's data is visible in Figure 2.21, whereas you can make up Daisy's data. To enter the picture, pull down the Insert menu and click the Object command. Click the Create from File option button. Click the Browse button to locate the picture of each animal in the Exploring Access folder. Click OK twice to insert the picture.

f. Print the two completed forms for your instructor. Add a cover sheet to submit with the assignment.

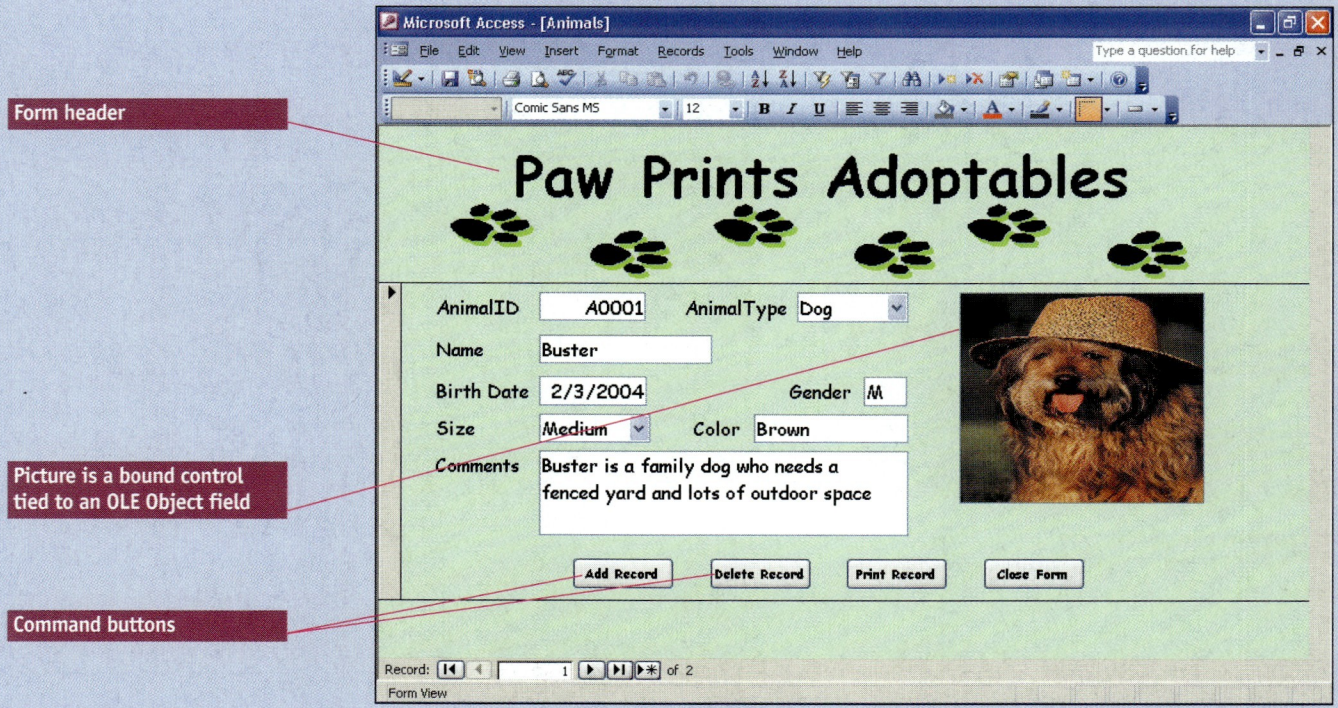

FIGURE 2.21   Paw Prints (exercise 12)

13. **About Our Students:** Figure 2.22 illustrates a form that we create for all of our databases that appears automatically when the database is opened. The form is not based on a table within the database; that is, the form contains descriptive information about the database such as a version number, serial number, logo, and/or copyright notice. You can use our design and wording and/or you can modify either element as you see fit. Proceed as follows:

a. Open the *My First Database* that you have used throughout the chapter. Click the Forms button, then double click the command to create a form in Design view. Click and drag the borders of the form so that the size of the form is approximately 3½ inches by 3½ inches.

b. Display the Toolbox toolbar. Use the Label tool to add the various text boxes that appear on the form. We suggest an 8-point sans serif typeface (Arial, Tahoma, or MS Sans Serif).

c. Insert the clip art logo that you used earlier for the Students form. (Set the Size Mode property to Stretch so that the clip art is not truncated.)

d. Use the Command Button Wizard to insert a button to close the form. Change the text of the button to "OK" as shown in Figure 2.22.

e. You have to change the properties of the form itself to suppress the scroll bars, record selector, and navigation buttons because the form is not based on an underlying table. Go to Design view, right click the Form Selector button (the tiny square in the upper-left corner) to display a context-sensitive menu, choose Properties to display the Property sheet for the form, and then look for the appropriate properties.

f. Save the form as About Our Students. (The name of the form will appear automatically in the title bar when the form is displayed.) Go to the Form view to see the completed form. Return to Design view to make changes as necessary. Print the completed form for your instructor.

g. The Startup property can be used to display the form automatically when the database is open. Pull down the Tools menu, click the Startup command, select About Our Students in the Display Form/Page list box, and click OK. Close the database, then reopen it to see your form.

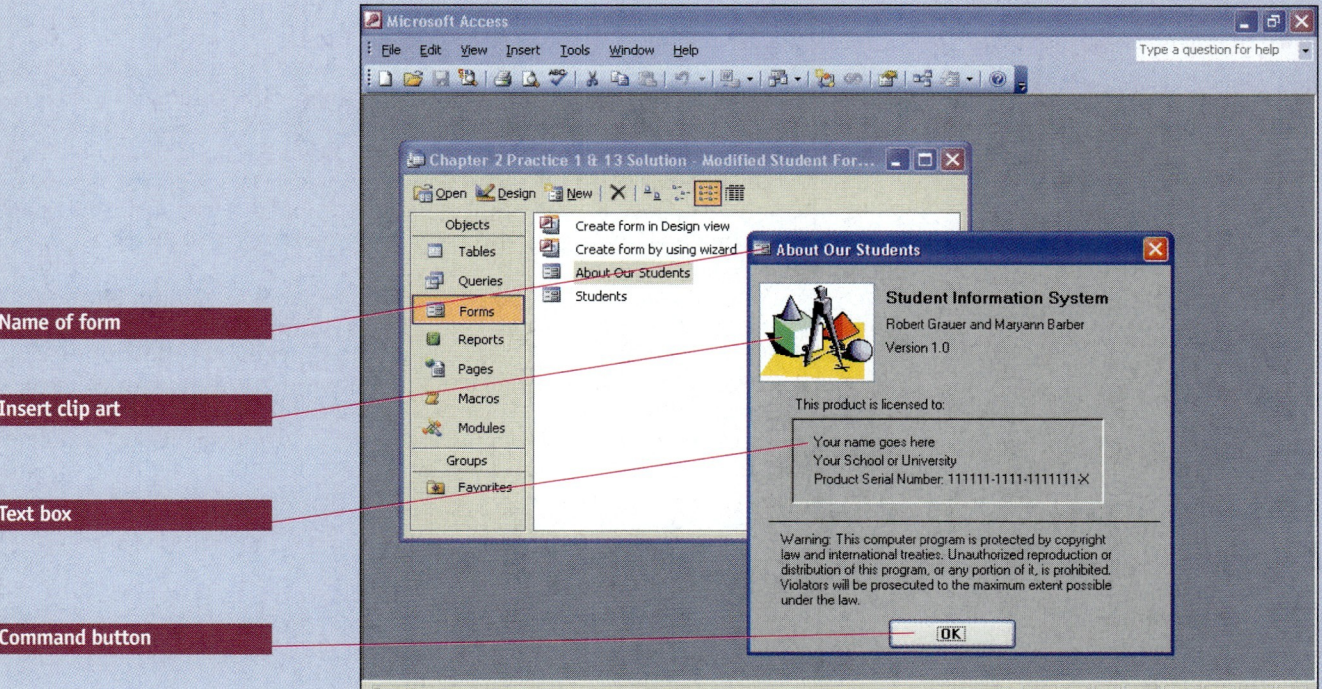

FIGURE 2.22 About Our Students (exercise 13)

MINI CASES

Employee Compensation

You have been hired as the Personnel Director for a medium-sized firm (500 employees) and are expected to implement a system to track employee compensation. You want to be able to calculate the age of every employee as well as the length of service. You want to know each employee's most recent performance evaluation. You want to be able to calculate the amount of the most recent salary increase, both in dollars and as a percentage of the previous salary. You also want to know how long the employee had to wait for that increase—that is, how much time elapsed between the present and previous salary. Design a table capable of providing this information. Create a supporting form.

The Stockbroker

A good friend has come to you for help. He is a new stockbroker whose firm provides computer support for existing clients, but does nothing in the way of data management for prospective clients. Your friend wants to use a PC to track the clients he is pursuing. He wants to know when he last contacted a person, how the contact was made (by phone or through the mail), and how interested the person was. He also wants to store the investment goals of each prospect, such as growth or income, and whether a person is interested in stocks, bonds, and/or a retirement account. And finally, he wants to record the amount of money the person has to invest. Design a table suitable for the information requirements. Create a supporting form, then use that form to enter data for two clients.

Chapter Recap—Kahakai Villas

Kahakai Villas, owned and operated by Kahakai Development, Inc. in Kona, Hawaii, has just broken ground on the construction of a 156-unit condominium. Kahakai Villas promises its future residents the ultimate in oceanside living, with unobstructed ocean views from every unit, in a lush tropical setting to create a true spirit of aloha. Residents choose from one, two, or three bedrooms. The base price ranges from $150,000 to $350,000, with the final price determined by the location and amenities selected. A carport is standard, whereas a garage is optional. Approximately half of the villas are adjacent to the private beach owned by the development company. The complex will also contain a spectacular swimming pool with units close to the pool paying a premium.

Joseph Murray, the project sales manager, wants to create an Access database to track the sales prospects who visit the site. He has created a simple questionnaire to capture demographic data (name, address, telephone, and so on) as well as the client's preferences in a villa. Joseph inquires about the client's price range, preferred floor, number of bedrooms, if they want a garage or carport, how soon they would be interested in moving (6 months, 9 months, 1 year, and 1 year plus), and if they would be living in the villa year-round or would be interested in offering their villa up for rental. He also leaves a space to make notes for himself.

Your assignment is to review the chapter and create a database for Mr. Murray. You can use the Table Wizard as the basis of your Customers (Prospects) table, but you will have to modify the table to include all of the required data as per the case description, and further to set the properties of the individual fields as appropriate. You will also need to create a form in which to enter the data. The Form Wizard is a good place to start, but you will have to modify the result to include command buttons, a suitable piece of clip art in the form header, and appropriate formatting throughout. Use the completed form to enter information about your instructor and the villa that he or she desires.

3

Information from the Database:
Reports and Queries

OBJECTIVES

After reading this chapter you will:

1. Describe the reports available through the Report Wizard.

2. Describe the similarities between forms and reports with respect to the underlying controls.

3. List the sections in a report.

4. Use conditional formatting in a report.

5. Differentiate between a query and a table; define a dynaset.

6. Use the design grid to create and modify a select query.

7. Explain the use of multiple criteria rows in a query.

8. Use concatenation to combine fields in a query or report.

9. Use an immediate If statement to create a calculated control.

10. Define an action query.

11. Create a crosstab query.

hands-on exercises

1. THE REPORT WIZARD
   Input: Our Students
   Output: Our Students (modified)

2. CREATING A SELECT QUERY
   Input: Our Students (after Hands-on Exercise 1)
   Output: Our Students (modified)

3. GROUPING RECORDS
   Input: Our Students (after Hands-on Exercise 2)
   Output: Our Students (modified)

4. CROSSTAB AND ACTION QUERIES
   Input: Our Students (after Hands-on Exercise 3)
   Output: Our Students (modified)

CASE STUDY
THE GARDEN CLUB

The Coral Springs Garden Club is a highly regarded civic organization known for its community projects that are funded in part by the members opening up their homes for an annual garden tour of eight to ten gardens. Lauren Schur, your favorite aunt, has been an active member for several years, and she was just elected president. It is a prestigious position, but Lauren needs your help. The membership has gown significantly, yet fund raising is down, and the club has had to cut back on its projects. Your aunt is convinced that the club's enthusiasm is as strong as ever and that all she needs is an efficient way to reach out to its membership.

The club is automated to the extent that it has an Access database with a members table and associated form. The data entry works well, but little if any information is generated from that data; that is, the database contains only a single membership report. Your aunt would like several additional reports, and she has asked you to take a Saturday afternoon to mine the available data. In particular, she wants to know which members have indicated a willingness to open their homes for the garden tour so that she can begin to plan next year's event. Lauren also wants a list of members who have donated more than $25 to the club. You love your aunt, and as she stated jokingly, it is one way to get your hands dirty! ■

Your assignment is to read the chapter and focus on how to create queries and reports that generate specific information. You will then open the *Chapter 3 Case Study—The Garden Club* database and use the existing form to add yourself as a member, indicate that your home is available for garden tours, that your last donation was $100, and that you would like to be included on every mailing. You will then create the reports (and associated queries) that were requested by your aunt. Use the existing report as a guide in the design of the new reports. Print a copy of the two reports you created (your name should appear on both) and submit them to your instructor as proof you completed the case study.

Chapters 1 and 2 described how to enter and maintain data through the use of tables and forms. This chapter shows how to convert the data into information through queries and reports. Queries enable you to ask questions about the database. Reports provide presentation quality output and display detail as well as summary information about the records in a database.

As you read the chapter, you will see that the objects in an Access database (tables, forms, reports, and queries) have many similar characteristics. We use these similarities to build on what you have learned in previous chapters. You already know, for example, that the controls in a form inherit their properties from the corresponding fields in a table. The same concept applies to the controls in a report. You also know that there are three types of controls—bound controls, unbound controls, and calculated controls. And since you know how to move and size controls within a form, you also know how to move and size the controls in a report. As you read the chapter, look for these similarities to apply your existing knowledge to new material.

Reports

A *report* is a printed document that displays information from a database. Figure 3.1 shows several sample reports, each of which will be created in this chapter. The reports were created with the *Report Wizard* and are based on the Students table that was presented in Chapter 2. (The table has been expanded to 24 records.) As you view each report, ask yourself how the data in the table was rearranged to produce the information in the report.

The *columnar (vertical) report* in Figure 3.1a is the simplest type of report. It lists every field for every record in a single column (one record per page) and typically runs for many pages. The records in this report are displayed in the same sequence (by Social Security number) as the records in the table on which the report is based.

The *tabular report* in Figure 3.1b displays fields in a row rather than in a column. Each record in the underlying table is printed in its own row. Unlike the previous report, only selected fields are displayed, so the tabular report is more concise than the columnar report of Figure 3.1a. Note, too, that the records in the report are listed in alphabetical order rather than by Social Security number.

The report in Figure 3.1c is also a tabular report, but it is very different from the report in Figure 3.1b. The report in Figure 3.1c lists only a selected set of students (those students with a GPA of 3.50 or higher), as opposed to the earlier reports, which listed every student. The students are listed in descending order according to their GPA.

The report in Figure 3.1d displays the students in groups, according to their major, then computes the average GPA for each group. The report also contains summary information (not visible in Figure 3.1d) for the report as a whole, which computes the average GPA for all students. The individual fields within a student record are considered data. A list of students on the Dean's list, however, is information that has been produced from the data about the individual students. In similar fashion, the average GPA for each major is also information rather than data.

DATA VERSUS INFORMATION

Data and information are not synonymous although the terms are often interchanged. Data is the raw material and consists of the table (or tables) that comprise a database. Information is the finished product. Data is converted to information by selecting records, performing calculations on those records, and/or changing the sequence in which the records are displayed. Decisions in an organization are based on information rather than raw data.

Student Roster

SSN	111-11-1111
First Name	Ronnie
Last Name	Adili
Address	3543 Queen Avenue
City	Minneapolis
State	MN
Postal Code	55476-9899
Phone Number	(612) 445-7654
BirthDate	6/1/1985
Gender	F
Credits	60
QualityPoints	155
FinancialAid	No
Campus	3
Major	Business

Sunday, July 06, 2003   Page 1 of 24

(a) Columnar Report

Student Master List

Last Name	First Name	Phone Number	Major
Adili	Ronnie	(612) 445-7654	Business
DiGiacomo	Kevin	(305) 531-7652	Business
Gibson	Christopher	(305) 235-4563	Business
Ramsay	Robert	(212) 223-9889	Business
Watson	Ana	(305) 561-2334	Business
Faulkner	Eileen	(305) 489-8876	Communications
Joseph	Cedric	(404) 667-8955	Communications
Ortiz	Frances	(303) 575-3211	Communications
Price	Lori	(310) 961-2323	Communications
Slater	Erica	(312) 545-6978	Communications
Korba	Nickolas	(415) 664-0900	Education
Zimmerman	Kimberly	(713) 225-3434	Education
Berlin	Jared	(803) 223-7868	Engineering
Heltzer	Peter	(305) 753-4533	Engineering
Solomon	Wendy	(305) 666-4532	Engineering
Camejo	Oscar	(716) 433-3321	Liberal Arts
Parulis	Christa	(410) 877-6565	Liberal Arts
Watson	Ana	(305) 595-7877	Liberal Arts
Weissman	Kimberly	(904) 388-8605	Liberal Arts
Coe	Bradley	(415) 235-6543	Undecided
Cornell	Ryan	(404) 755-4490	Undecided
Frazier	Steven	(410) 995-8755	Undecided
Huerta	Carlos	(212) 344-5654	Undecided
Zacco	Michelle	(617) 884-3434	Undecided

7/6/2003   Page 1 of 1

(b) Tabular Report

Dean's List

First Name	Last Name	Major	Credits	Quality Points	GPA
Peter	Heltzer	Engineering	25	100	4.00
Cedric	Joseph	Communications	45	170	3.78
Erica	Slater	Communications	105	390	3.71
Kevin	DiGiacomo	Business	105	375	3.57
Wendy	Solomon	Engineering	50	175	3.50

Sunday, July 06, 2003   Page 1 of 1

(c) Dean's List

GPA by Major

Major	Last Name	First Name	GPA
Business			
	Adili	Ronnie	2.58
	DiGiacomo	Kevin	3.57
	Gibson	Christopher	1.71
	Ramsay	Robert	3.24
	Watson	Ana	2.50
	Average GPA for major		2.72
Communications			
	Faulkner	Eileen	2.67
	Joseph	Cedric	3.78
	Ortiz	Frances	2.14
	Price	Lori	1.75
	Slater	Erica	3.71
	Average GPA for major		2.81
Education			
	Korba	Nickolas	1.66
	Zimmerman	Kimberly	3.29
	Average GPA for major		2.48
Engineering			
	Berlin	Jared	2.50
	Heltzer	Peter	4.00
	Solomon	Wendy	3.50
	Average GPA for major		3.33
Liberal Arts			
	Camejo	Oscar	2.80
	Parulis	Christa	1.80
	Watson	Ana	2.79
	Weissman	Kimberly	2.63
	Average GPA for major		2.51
Undecided			
	Coe	Bradley	2.75
	Cornell	Ryan	1.78
	Frazier	Steven	1.29
	Huerta	Carlos	2.67
	Zacco	Michelle	3.24
	Average GPA for major		2.35

Sunday, July 06, 2003   Page 1 of 2

(d) Summary Report

FIGURE 3.1   Report Types

Anatomy of a Report

All reports are based on an underlying table or query within the database. (Queries are discussed later in the chapter.) A report, however, displays the data or information in a more attractive fashion because it contains various headings and/or other decorative items that are not present in either a table or a query.

The easiest way to learn about reports is to compare a printed report with its underlying design. Consider, for example, Figure 3.2a, which displays the tabular report, and Figure 3.2b, which shows the underlying design. The latter shows how a report is divided into sections, which appear at designated places when the report is printed. There are seven types of sections, but a report need not contain all seven.

The *Report Header* appears once, at the beginning of a report. It typically contains information describing the report, such as its title and the date the report was printed. (The report header appears above the page header on the first page of the report.) The *Report Footer* appears once at the end of the report, above the page footer on the last page of the report, and displays summary information for the report as a whole.

The *Page Header* appears at the top of every page in a report and can be used to display page numbers, column headings, and other descriptive information. The *Page Footer* appears at the bottom of every page and may contain page numbers (when they are not in the page header) or other descriptive information.

A *Group Header* appears at the beginning of a group of records to identify the group. A *Group Footer* appears after the last record in a group and contains summary information about the group. Group headers and footers are used only when the records in a report are sorted (grouped) according to a common value in a specific field. These sections do not appear in the report of Figure 3.2, but were shown earlier in the report of Figure 3.1d.

The *Detail section* appears in the main body of a report and is printed once for every record in the underlying table (or query). It displays one or more fields for each record in columnar or tabular fashion, according to the design of the report.

The Report Wizard

The Report Wizard is the easiest way to create a report, just as the Form Wizard is the easiest way to create a form. The Report Wizard asks you questions about the report you want, then builds the report for you. You can accept the report as is, or you can customize it to better suit your needs.

Figure 3.3a displays the New Report dialog box, from which you can select the Report Wizard. The Report Wizard, in turn, requires you to specify the table or query on which the report will be based. The report in this example will be based on an expanded version of the Students table that was created in Chapter 2.

After you specify the underlying table, you select one or more fields from that table, as shown in Figure 3.3b. The Report Wizard then asks you to select a layout (e.g., Tabular in Figure 3.3c.) and a style (e.g., Soft Gray in Figure 3.3d). This is all the information the Report Wizard requires, and it proceeds to create the report for you. The controls on the report correspond to the fields you selected and are displayed in accordance with the specified layout.

Apply What You Know

The Report Wizard provides an excellent starting point, but typically does not create the report exactly as you would like it to be. Accordingly, you can modify a report created by the Report Wizard, just as you can modify a form created by the Form Wizard. The techniques are the same, and you should look for similarities between forms and reports so that you can apply what you already know. Knowledge of one is helpful in understanding the other.

Report Header

Page Header

Detail section

Page Footer

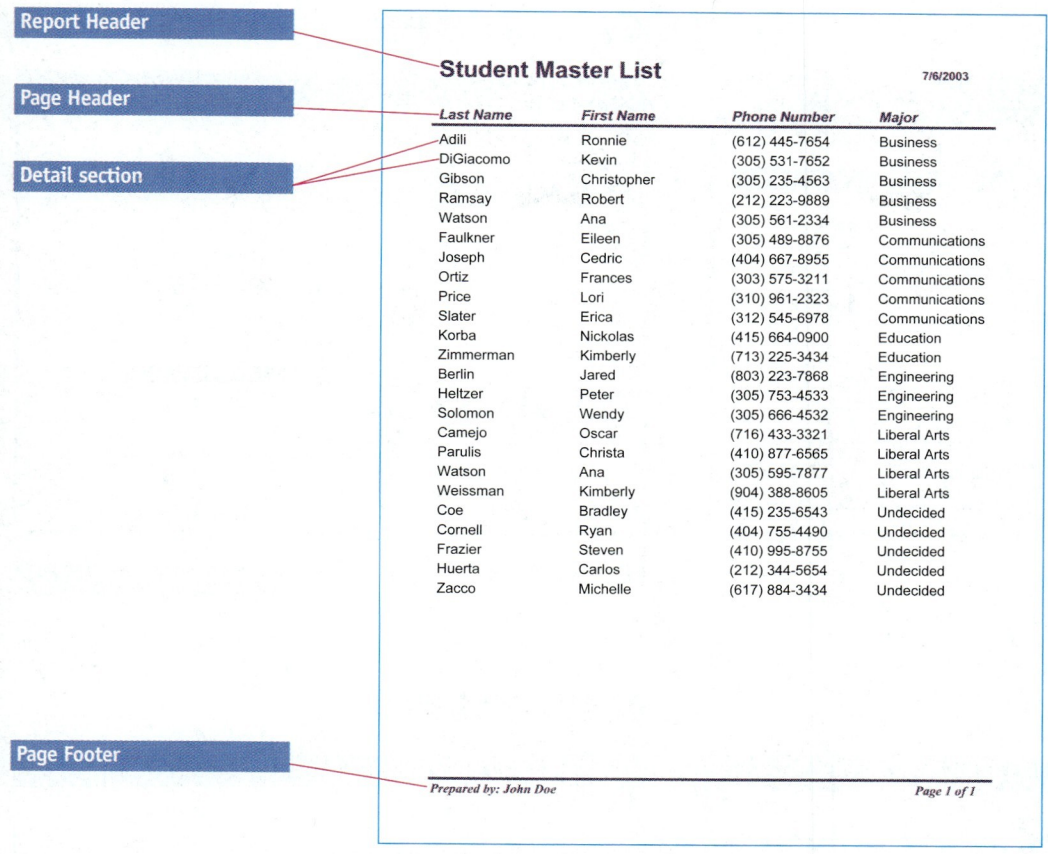

(a) The Printed Report

Report Header

Page Header

Detail section

Page Footer

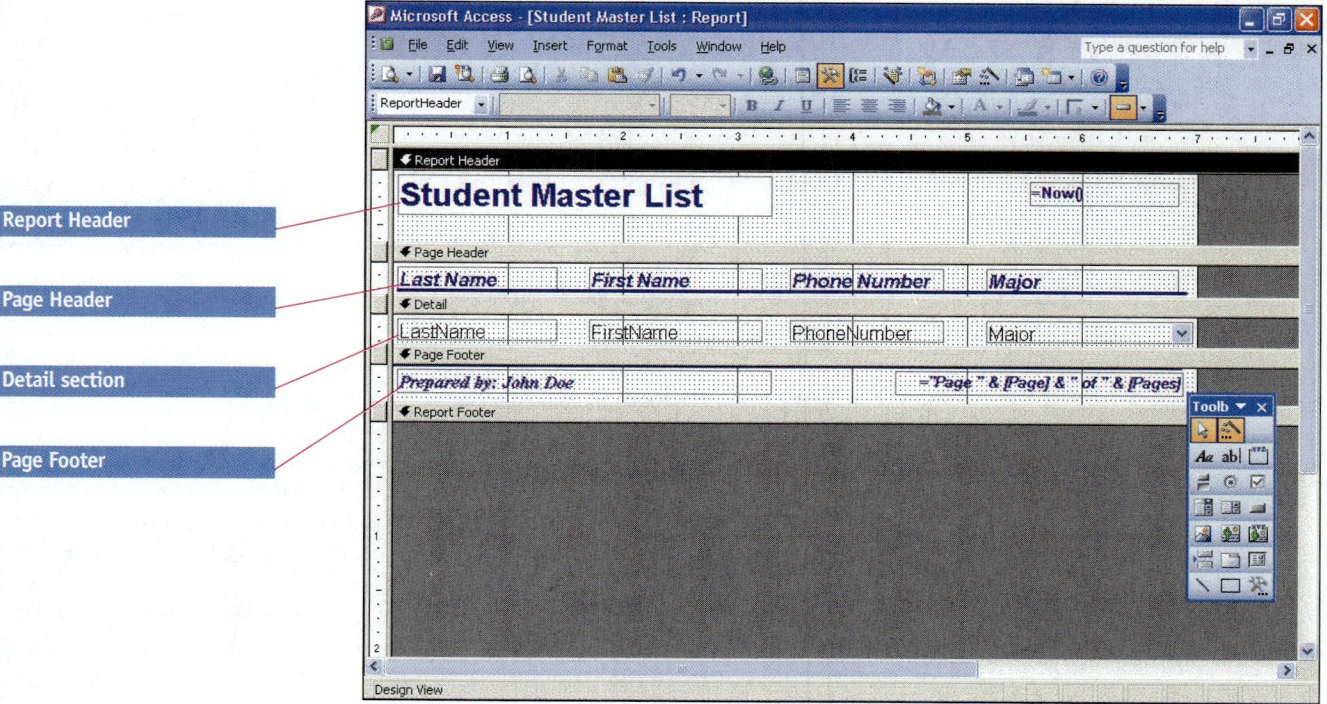

(b) Design View

FIGURE 3.2 Anatomy of a Report

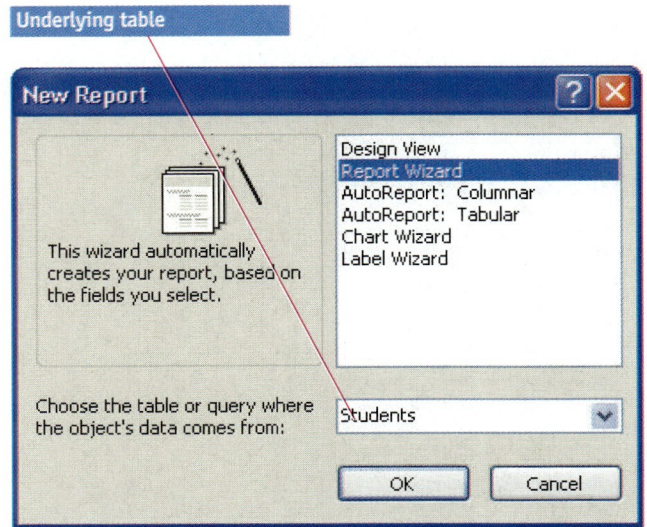

Underlying table

(a) Select the Underlying Table

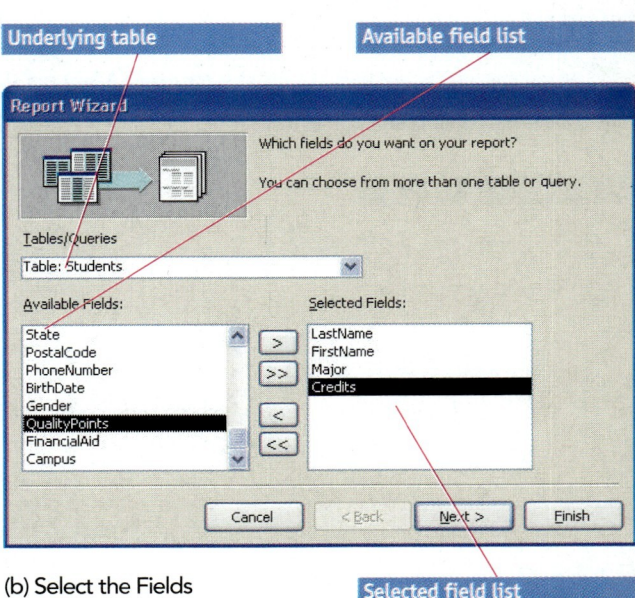

Underlying table **Available field list**

Selected field list

(b) Select the Fields

Selected layout

(c) Choose the Layout

Selected style

(d) Choose the Style

FIGURE 3.3 The Report Wizard

Bound, Unbound, and Calculated Controls

Controls appear in a report just as they do in a form, and the same definitions apply. A ***bound control*** has as its data source a field in the underlying table. An ***unbound control*** has no data source and is used to display titles, labels, lines, rectangles, and graphics. A ***calculated control*** has as its data source an expression rather than a field. A student's Grade Point Average is an example of a calculated control since it is computed by dividing the number of quality points by the number of credits. The means for selecting, sizing, moving, aligning, and deleting controls are the same, regardless of whether you are working on a form or a report. And, as you may have guessed, it is time for our next hands-on exercise.

1   The Report Wizard

Objective   To use the Report Wizard to create a new report; to modify an existing report by adding, deleting, and/or modifying its controls. Use Figure 3.4 as a guide in the exercise.

Step 1:   **Open the Our Students Database**

- Start Access. Pull down the **File menu** and click the **Open command** or click the link to **More . . .** if the task pane is open.

- Open the **Our Students database** in the Exploring Access folder. Click **Open** in response to the security warning.

- The Our Students database has the identical design as the database you created in Chapter 2. We have, however, expanded the Students table so that it contains 24 records to enable you to create more meaningful reports and queries from the database.

- Click the **Reports button** in the Database window, then click the **New command button** to display the New Report dialog box in Figure 3.4a. Select the **Report Wizard** as the means of creating the report.

- Click the **drop-down arrow** to display the tables and queries in the database in order to select the one on which the report will be based. (There are currently two tables and no queries.)

- Click **Students**, then click **OK** to start the Report Wizard, which prompts you for the information it needs to create a report.

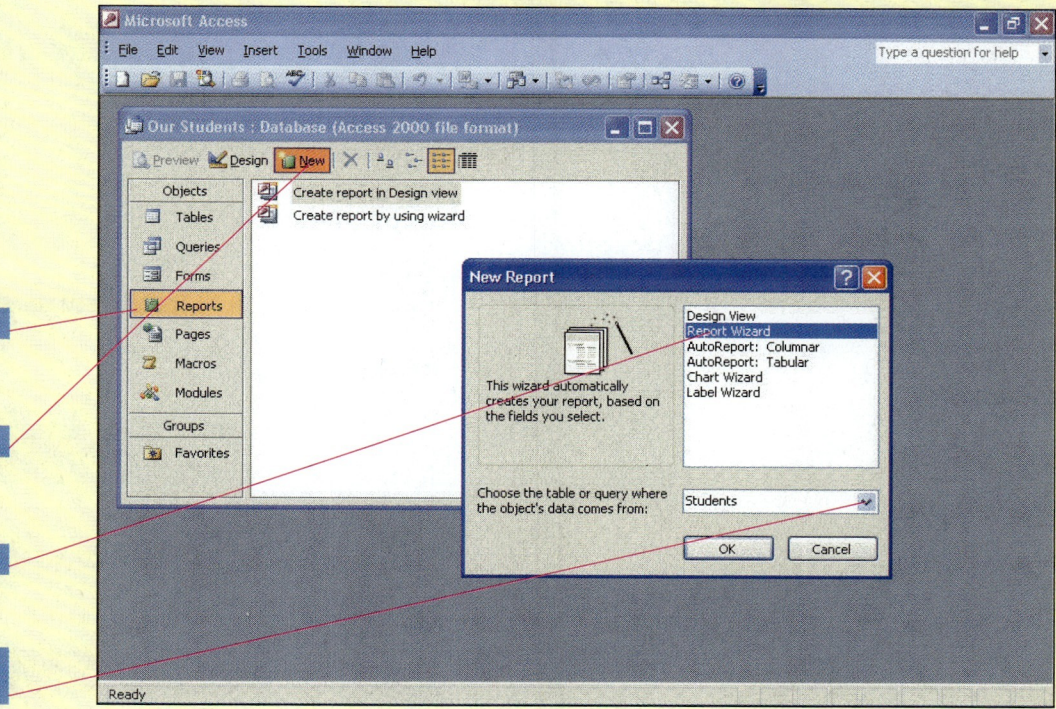

Click Reports button

Click New command button

Click Report Wizard

Click down arrow and select Students

(a) Open the Our Students Database (step 1)

FIGURE 3.4   Hands-on Exercise 1

Step 2: **The Report Wizard**

- You should see the dialog box in Figure 3.4b, which displays all of the fields in the Students table. Double click the **LastName field** in the Available Fields list box, as shown in Figure 3.4b.

- Enter the remaining fields (**FirstName**, **PhoneNumber**, and **Major**) one at a time by double clicking the field name. Click **Next**.

- The Report Wizard displays several additional screens asking about the report you want to create. The first screen asks whether you want to choose any grouping levels. Click **Next** without specifying a grouping level.

- The next screen asks whether you want to sort the records. Click the **drop-down arrow** to display the available fields, then select **LastName**. Click **Next**.

- The **Tabular layout** is selected, as is **Portrait orientation**. Be sure the box is checked to **Adjust field width so all fields fit on a page**. Click **Next**.

- Choose **Corporate** as the style. Click **Next**.

- Enter **Student Master List** as the title for your report. The option button to **Preview the Report** is already selected.

- Click the **Finish button** to exit the Report Wizard and view the report.

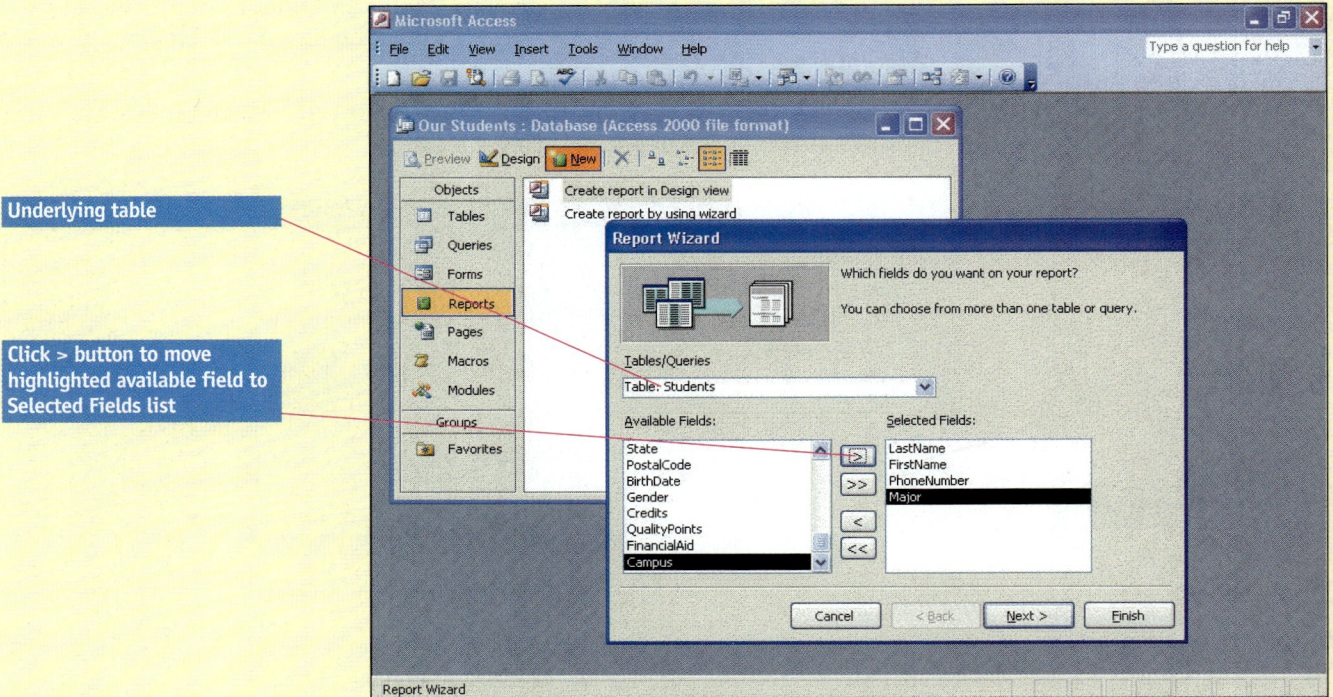

Underlying table

Click > button to move highlighted available field to Selected Fields list

(b) The Report Wizard (step 2)

FIGURE 3.4 Hands-on Exercise 1 (*continued*)

WHAT THE REPORT WIZARD DOESN'T TELL YOU

The fastest way to select a field is by double clicking; that is, double click a field in the Available Fields list box, and it is automatically moved to the Selected Fields list for inclusion in the report. The process also works in reverse; that is, you can double click a field in the Selected Fields list to remove it from the report.

Step 3: **Preview the Report**

■ Click the **Maximize button** so the report takes the entire window as shown in Figure 3.4c.
  ❏ There is a Report Header (the title of the report) at the beginning of the report, a Page Header (column headings) at the top of the page, and a Page Footer at the bottom of the page.
  ❏ There is also a detail line for every record in the underlying table.

■ Click the **drop-down arrow** on the Zoom box so that you can view the report at different magnifications. We chose 75%.

■ Click the **scroll arrows** on the vertical scroll bar to view the names of additional students. Click and drag the horizontal scroll bar to position the report within the window.

■ Click the **Close button** to close the Print Preview window and change to the Report Design view. The next step describes how to modify the report so that the controls are spaced more attractively.

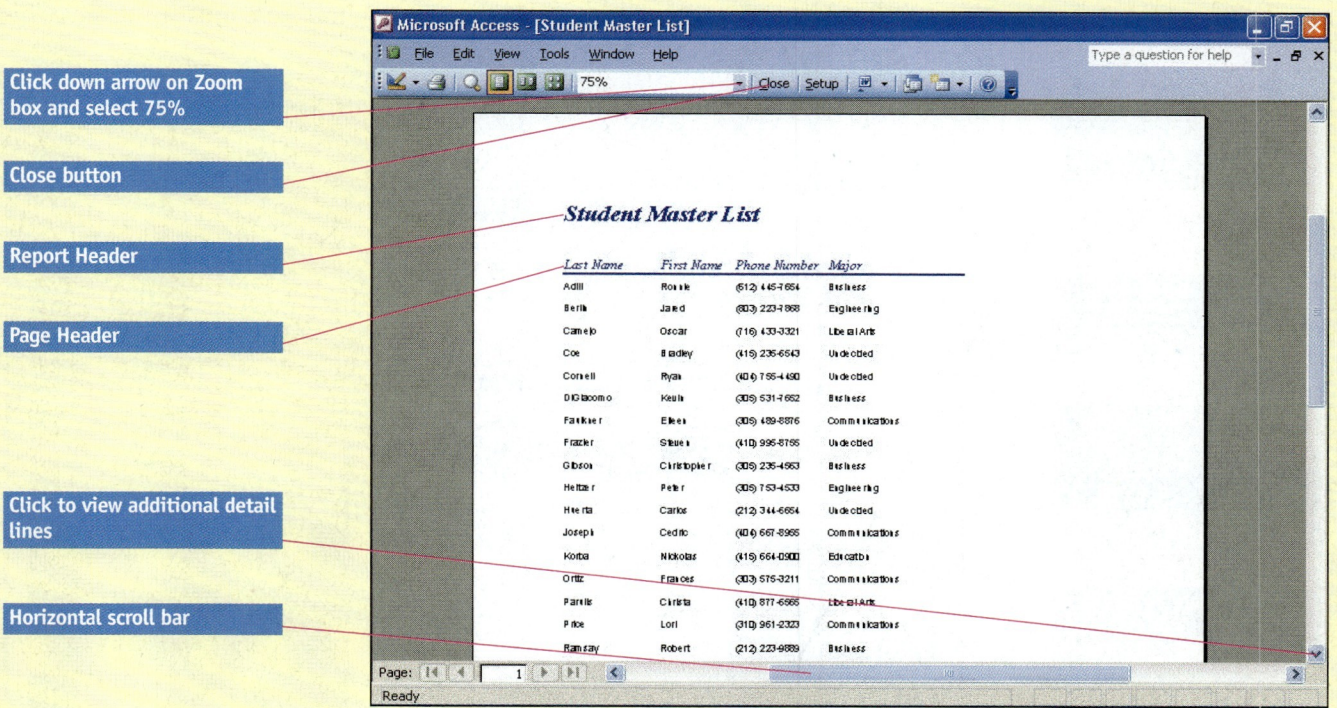

(c) Preview the Report (step 3)

FIGURE 3.4 Hands-on Exercise 1 (*continued*)

THE PRINT PREVIEW WINDOW

The Print Preview window enables you to preview a report in various ways. Click the One Page, Two Pages, or Multiple Pages buttons for different views of a report. Use the Zoom button to toggle between the full page and zoom (magnified) views, or use the Zoom box to choose a specific magnification. The Navigation buttons at the bottom of the Print Preview window enable you to preview a specific page, while the vertical scroll bar at the right side of the window lets you scroll within a page.

Step 4: **Modify an Existing Control**

- Click the **Major control** in the Detail section, then press the **Shift key** as you click its label in the Page Header. Point to the border of either control, then drag the controls to the right. Move the **PhoneNumber** and **FirstName** controls in similar fashion so that the fields are spaced attractively across the width of the report.

- Click the **blue line** in the Page Header to select the line. Press the **Shift key** (to retain a horizontal line) as you drag the sizing handle to the right side of the page.

- Click and drag the border of the control containing the **Now function** from the Report Footer to the Report Header as shown in Figure 3.4d.

- Size the control as necessary, then check that the control is still selected and click the **Align Right button** on the Formatting toolbar.

- Point to the control, then click the **right mouse button** to display a shortcut menu, and click **Properties** to display the Properties sheet.

- Click the **Format tab** in the Properties sheet, click the **Format property**, then click the **drop-down arrow** to display the available formats. Click **Short Date**, then close the Properties sheet.

- Pull down the **File menu** and click **Save** (or click the **Save button**) to save the modified design

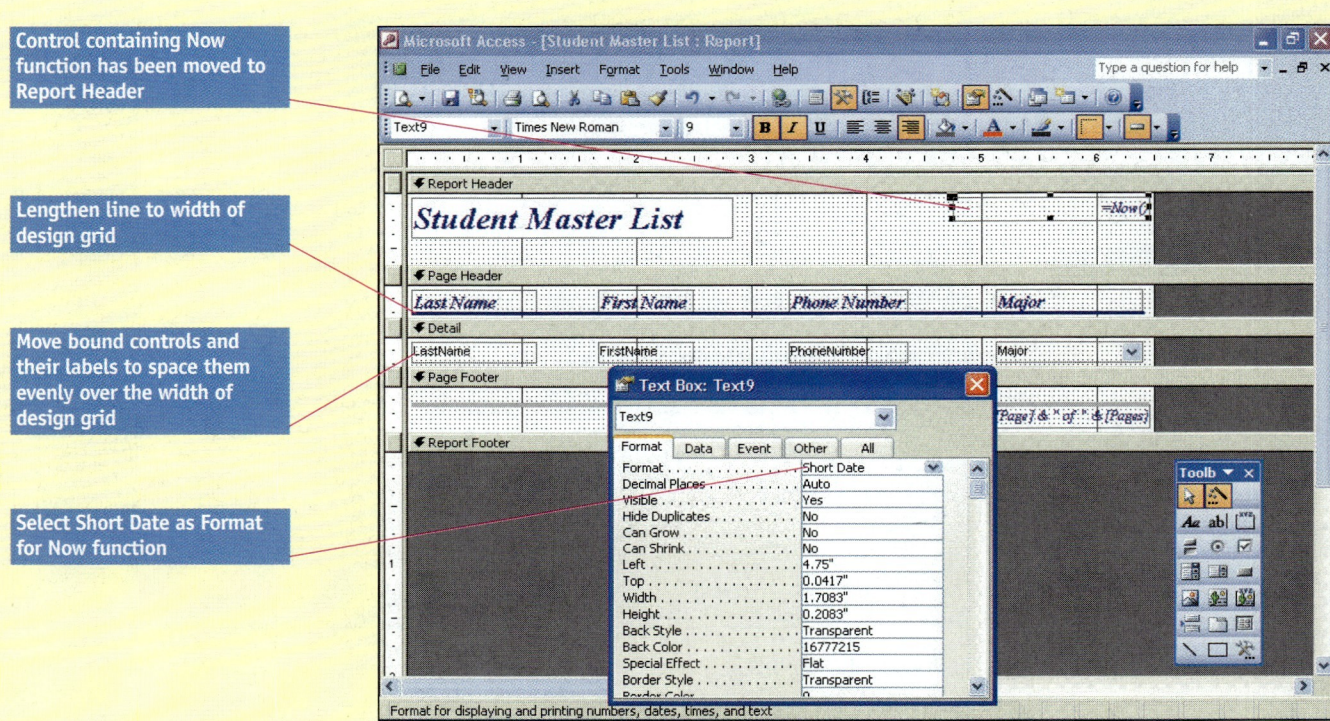

Control containing Now function has been moved to Report Header

Lengthen line to width of design grid

Move bound controls and their labels to space them evenly over the width of design grid

Select Short Date as Format for Now function

(d) Modify an Existing Control (step 4)

FIGURE 3.4   Hands-on Exercise 1 (*continued*)

THE REPORT WIZARD, FUNCTIONS, AND FIELDS

The Report Wizard automatically inserts the Now function and the Page and Pages fields to enhance the appearance of a report. The Now function returns the current date and time. The Page and Pages fields return the specific page number and the total number of pages, respectively. You can also add these controls explicitly by creating a text box, then replacing the default unbound control by an equal sign, followed by the function or field—for example, =Now() to insert the current date and time.

Step 5: Add an Unbound Control

- Click the **Label tool** on the Toolbox toolbar, then click and drag in the Report Footer where you want the label to go and release the mouse. You should see a flashing insertion point inside the label control. (If you see the word *Unbound* instead of the insertion point, it means you selected the Text Box tool rather than the Label tool; delete the text box and begin again.)

- Type **Prepared by** followed by your name as shown in Figure 3.4e. Press **Enter** to complete the entry and also select the control.

- You will see a green triangle in the upper-left corner of the control and an exclamation point icon to indicate a potential error. Point to the icon, click the **down arrow** to display the list of potential errors, then click **Ignore Error**.

- Point to the control, click the **right mouse button** to display the shortcut menu, then click **Properties** to display the Properties dialog box.

- Click the **down arrow** on the scroll bar, then scroll until you see the Font Size property. Click in the **Font Size box**, click the **drop-down arrow**, then scroll until you can change the font size to **9**. Close the Property sheet.

- Save the report.

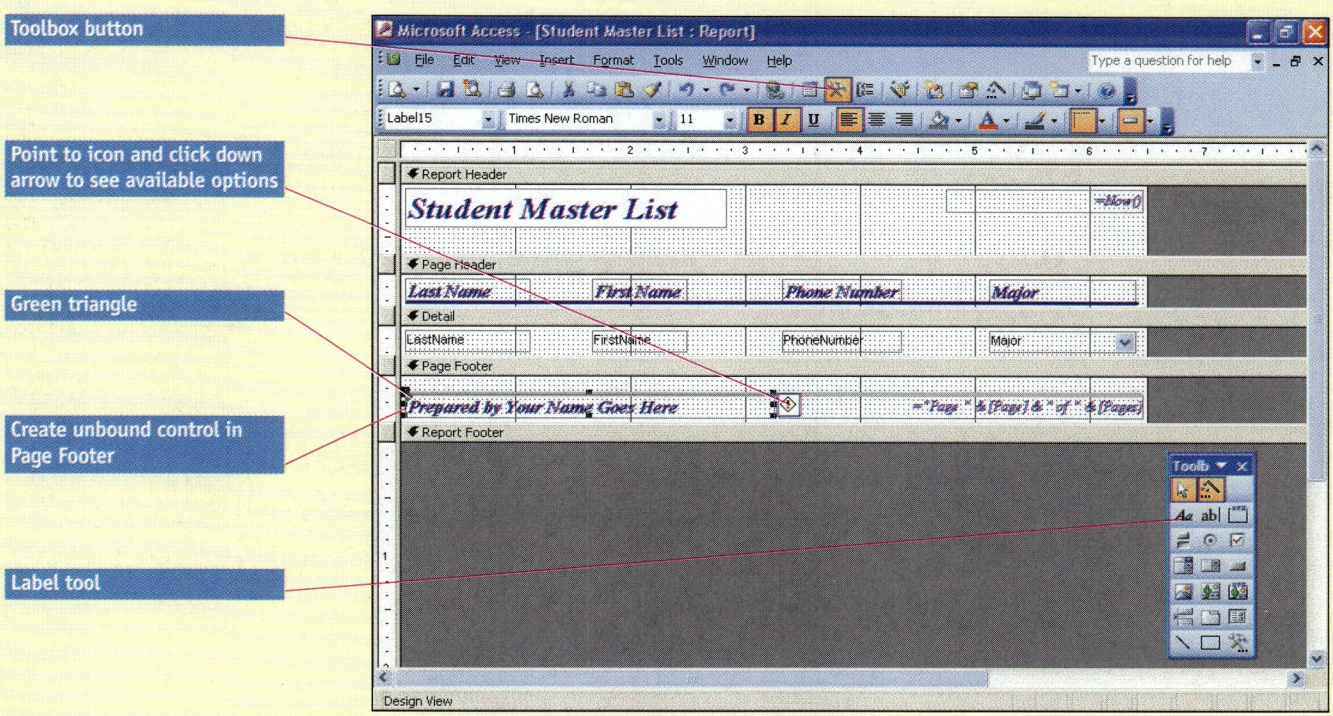

Toolbox button

Point to icon and click down arrow to see available options

Green triangle

Create unbound control in Page Footer

Label tool

(e) Add an Unbound Control (step 5)

FIGURE 3.4 Hands-on Exercise 1 (*continued*)

MISSING TOOLBARS

The Report Design, Formatting, and Toolbox toolbars appear by default in the Report Design view, but any (or all) of these toolbars may be hidden at the discretion of the user. If any of these toolbars does not appear, point to any visible toolbar, click the right mouse button to display a shortcut menu, then click the name of the toolbar you want to display. You can also click the Toolbox button on the Report Design toolbar to display (hide) the Toolbox toolbar.

Step 6: Change the Sort Order

- Pull down the **View menu**. Click the **Sorting and Grouping command** to display the Sorting and Grouping dialog box in Figure 3.4f. The students are currently sorted by last name.

- Click the **drop-down arrow** in the Field Expression box. Click **Major**. (The ascending sequence is selected automatically.)

- Click on the next line in the Field Expression box, click the **drop-down arrow** to display the available fields, then click **LastName** to sort the students alphabetically within major.

- Close the Sorting and Grouping dialog box. The students will now be listed by major and alphabetically by last name within each major when you view the report in step 7.

- Save the report.

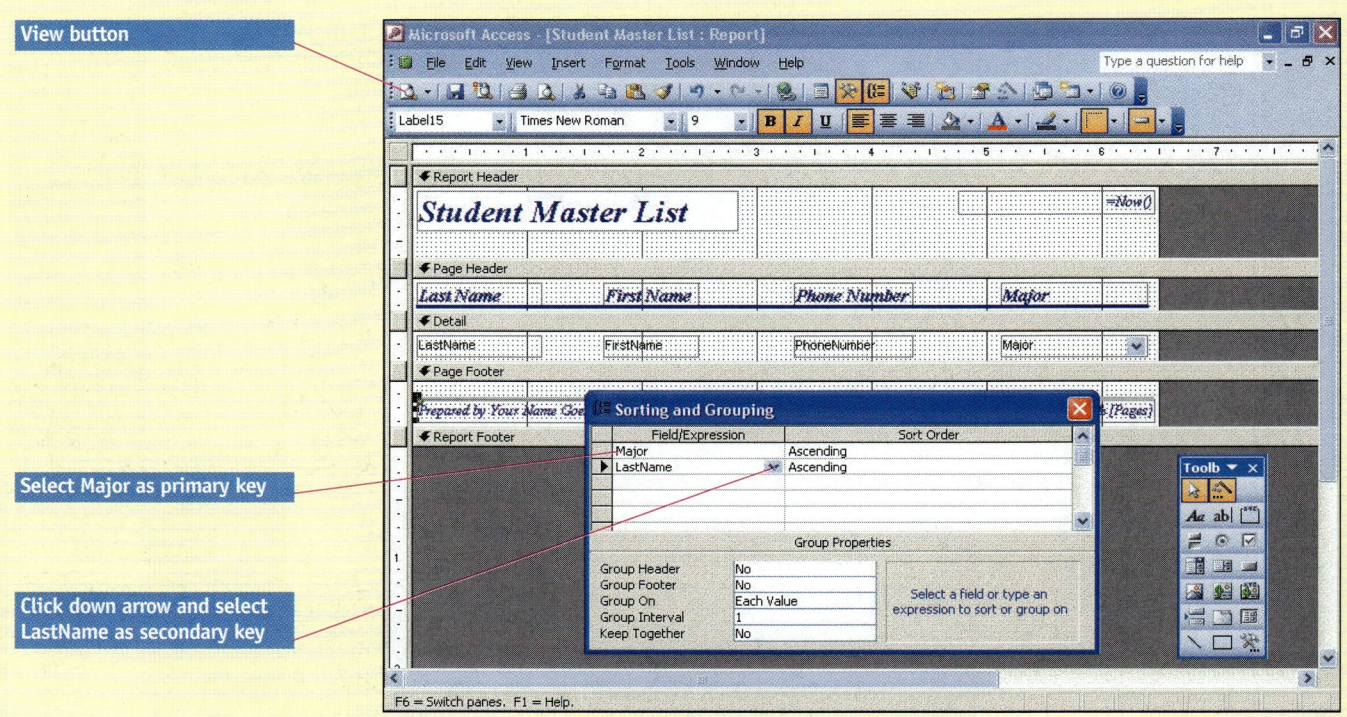

(f) Change the Sort Order (step 6)

FIGURE 3.4 Hands-on Exercise 1 (*continued*)

ADDING A GROUP HEADER OR FOOTER

You can add or remove a Group Header or Footer after a report has been created. Pull down the View menu and click the Sorting and Grouping command to display the associated dialog box. Click the line containing the field for which you want to add or remove the element, then enter Yes or No, respectively, in the Group Properties area and close the dialog box. The newly created header or footer is initially empty, and thus you will have to insert the necessary controls to complete the report.

Step 7: View the Modified Report

■ Click the **View button** to preview the finished report. If necessary, click the **Zoom button** on the Print Preview toolbar so that the display on your monitor matches Figure 3.4g. The report has changed so that:

❏ The date appears in the Report Header (as opposed to the Report Footer). The format of the date has changed to a numbered month, and the day of the week has been eliminated.

❏ The controls are spaced attractively across the page.

❏ The students are listed by major and, within each major, alphabetically according to last name.

❏ Your name appears in the Report Footer. Click the **down arrow** on the vertical scroll bar to move to the bottom of the page to see your name.

■ Click the **Print button** to print the report and submit it to your instructor. Click the **Close button** to exit the Print Preview window.

■ Click the **Close button** in the Report Design window. Click **Yes** if asked whether to save the changes to the Student Master List report.

■ Close the database. Exit Access if you do not want to continue with the next exercise at this time.

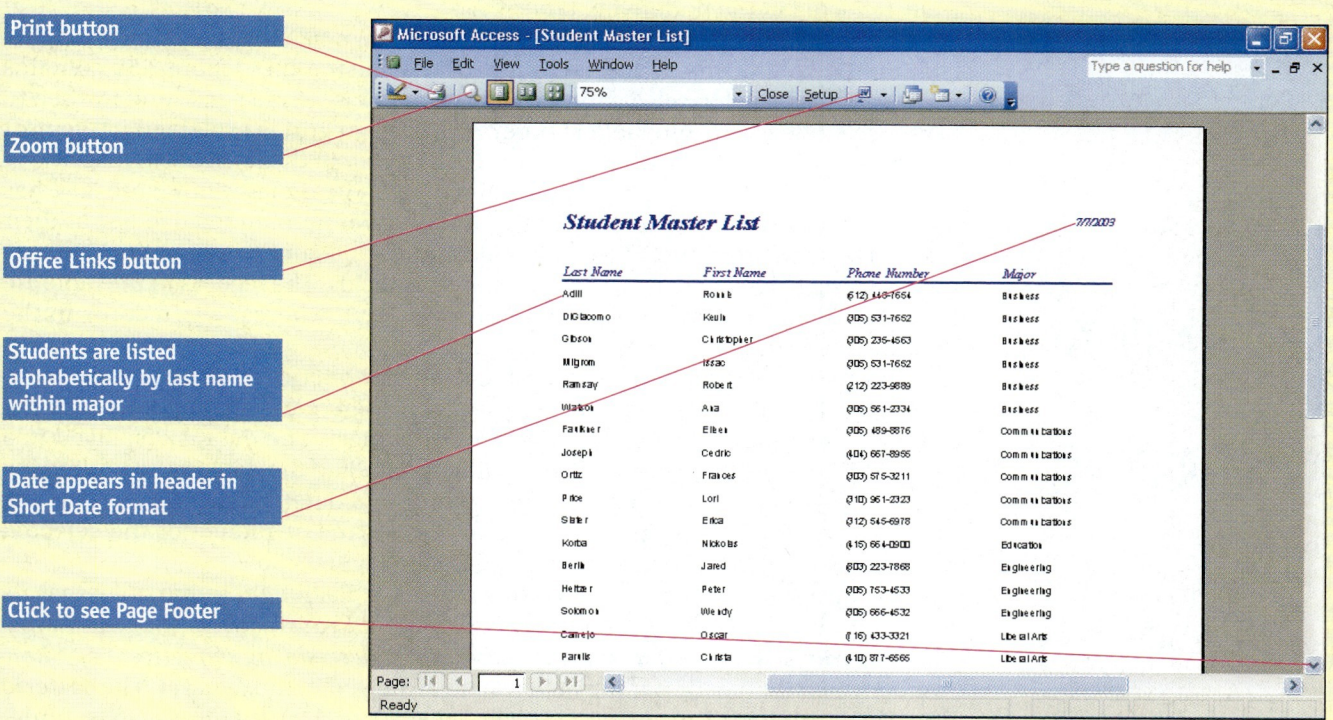

(g) View the Modified Report (step 7)

FIGURE 3.4   Hands-on Exercise 1 (*continued*)

LINK TO WORD OR EXCEL

Click the down arrow on the Office Links button to display links to Word and Excel. Click either link to start the associated application, where you can take advantage of the extended editing or analysis (including chart) capabilities in Word and Excel, respectively. You can save the report as either a Word document or Excel workbook, but any subsequent changes to the Access report are static and will not be reflected in the other applications.

INTRODUCTION TO QUERIES

The report you just created displayed every student in the underlying table. What if, however, we wanted to see just the students who are majoring in Business? Or the students who are receiving financial aid? Or the students who are majoring in Business *and* receiving financial aid? The ability to ask questions such as these, and to see the answers to those questions, is provided through a query. Queries represent the real power of a database.

A *query* lets you see the data you want in the sequence that you want it. It lets you select specific records from a table (or from several tables) and show some or all of the fields for the selected records. It also lets you perform calculations to display data that is not explicitly stored in the underlying table(s), such as a student's GPA.

The query is created by the **Simple Query Wizard** or directly in Design view. The results of the query are displayed in a **dynaset**, which contains the records that satisfy the criteria specified in the query.

A dynaset looks and acts like a table, but it isn't a table; it is a *dyna*mic sub*set* of a table that selects and sorts records as specified in the query. A dynaset is similar to a table in appearance and, like a table, it enables you to enter a new record or modify or delete an existing record. Any changes made in the dynaset are automatically reflected in the underlying table.

Figure 3.5a displays the Students table we have been using throughout the chapter. (We omit some of the fields for ease of illustration.) Figure 3.5b contains the design grid used to select students whose major is "Undecided" and further, to list those students in alphabetical order. (The design grid is explained in the next section.) Figure 3.5c displays the answer to the query in the form of a dynaset.

The table in Figure 3.5a contains 24 records. The dynaset in Figure 3.5c has only five records, corresponding to the students who are undecided about their major. The table in Figure 3.5a has 15 fields for each record (some of the fields are hidden). The dynaset in Figure 3.5c has only four fields. The records in the table are in Social Security number order (the primary key), whereas the records in the dynaset are in alphabetical order by last name.

The query in Figure 3.5 is an example of a **select query**, which is the most common type of query. A select query searches the underlying table (Figure 3.5a in the example) to retrieve the data that satisfies the query. The data is displayed in a dynaset (Figure 3.5c), which can be modified to update the data in the underlying table(s). The specifications for selecting records and determining which fields will be displayed for the selected records, as well as the sequence of the selected records, are established within the design grid of Figure 3.5b.

The design grid consists of columns and rows. Each field in the query has its own column and contains multiple rows. The **Field row** displays the field name. The **Sort row** enables you to sort in **ascending** or **descending sequence**. The **Show row** controls whether or not the field will be displayed in the dynaset. The **Criteria row(s)** determines the records that will be selected, such as students with an undecided major.

REPORTS, QUERIES, AND TABLES

Every report is based on either a table or a query. The design of the report may be the same with respect to the fields that are included, but the actual reports will be very different with respect to the information they provide. A report based on a table contains every record in the table. A report based on a query contains only the records that satisfy the criteria in the query.

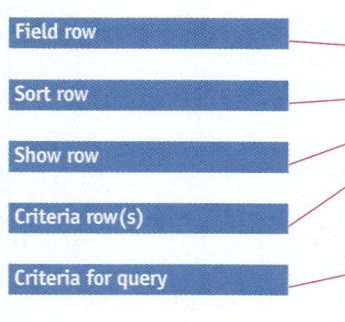

Students are listed in order of primary key (SSN)

Twenty-four records are in the table

Students : Table

SSN	First Name	Last Name	BirthDate	Gender	Credits	QualityPoints	Major
111-11-1111	Ronnie	Adili	6/1/1985	F	60	155	Business
112-12-1212	Peter	Heltzer	3/8/1983	M	25	100	Engineering
222-22-2222	Christopher	Gibson	3/12/1983	M	35	60	Business
223-34-2323	Kimberly	Zimmerman	4/18/1980	F	120	395	Education
233-33-4444	Robert	Ramsay	5/1/1984	M	50	162	Business
333-22-1111	Steven	Frazier	9/9/1978	M	35	45	Undecided
333-33-3333	Nickolas	Korba	11/11/1981	M	100	166	Education
333-33-3334	Kimberly	Weissman	11/11/1984	F	63	166	Liberal Arts
334-44-4444	Christa	Parulis	7/15/1982	F	50	90	Liberal Arts
444-43-4343	Jared	Berlin	1/15/1982	M	100	250	Engineering
444-44-4443	Oscar	Camejo	3/10/1979	M	100	280	Liberal Arts
444-44-4444	Wendy	Solomon	1/31/1985	F	50	175	Engineering
446-66-7777	Ana	Watson	4/18/1985	F	30	75	Business
555-55-5555	Eileen	Faulkner	9/12/1985	F	30	80	Communications
555-55-5557	Ana	Watson	8/1/1985	F	70	195	Liberal Arts
556-66-7777	Frances	Ortiz	2/3/1984	F	28	60	Communications
666-33-1111	Bradley	Coe	8/22/1981	M	52	143	Undecided
666-66-6666	Kevin	DiGiacomo	5/31/1982	M	105	375	Business
666-77-7766	Erica	Slater	5/1/1982	F	105	390	Communications
777-77-7777	Cedric	Joseph	4/12/1984	M	45	170	Communications
777-88-8888	Ryan	Cornell	9/30/1984	M	45	80	Undecided
888-77-7777	Lori	Price	7/1/1982	F	24	42	Communications
888-88-8888	Michelle	Zacco	10/24/1985	F	21	68	Undecided
999-99-9999	Carlos	Huerta	6/18/1985	M	15	40	Undecided

Record: 1 of 24

(a) Students Table

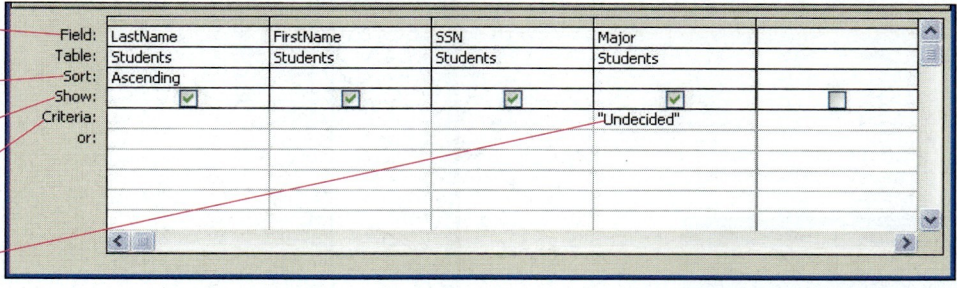

Field row

Sort row

Show row

Criteria row(s)

Criteria for query

Field:	LastName	FirstName	SSN	Major	
Table:	Students	Students	Students	Students	
Sort:	Ascending				
Show:	☑	☑	☑	☑	☐
Criteria:				"Undecided"	
or:					

(b) Design Grid

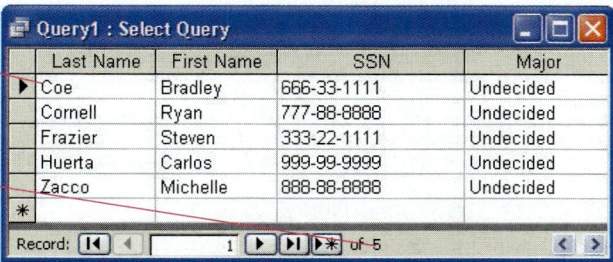

Students are listed in alphabetical order by Last Name

Five records meet the criterion

Query1 : Select Query

Last Name	First Name	SSN	Major
Coe	Bradley	666-33-1111	Undecided
Cornell	Ryan	777-88-8888	Undecided
Frazier	Steven	333-22-1111	Undecided
Huerta	Carlos	999-99-9999	Undecided
Zacco	Michelle	888-88-8888	Undecided

Record: 1 of 5

(c) Dynaset

FIGURE 3.5 Queries

Query Design View

A select query is created by the Simple Query Wizard and/or in Design view as shown in Figure 3.6. The upper portion of the Design View window contains the field list for the table(s) on which the query is based (the Students table in this example). The lower portion of the window displays the ***design grid***, which is where the specifications for the select query are entered. A field is added to the design grid by dragging it from the field list.

The data type of a field determines the way in which the criteria are specified for that field. The criterion for a text field is enclosed in quotation marks. The criteria for number, currency, and counter fields are shown as digits with or without a decimal point. (Commas and dollar signs are not allowed.) Dates are enclosed in pound signs and are entered in the mm/dd/yy format. The criterion for a Yes/No field is entered as Yes (or True) or No (or False).

Access accepts values for text and date fields in the design grid in multiple formats. The value for a text field can be entered with or without quotation marks (Undecided or "Undecided"). A date can be entered with or without pound signs (1/1/97 or #1/1/97#). Access converts your entries to standard format as soon as you move to the next cell in the design grid. Thus, text entries are always shown in quotation marks, and dates are enclosed in pound signs.

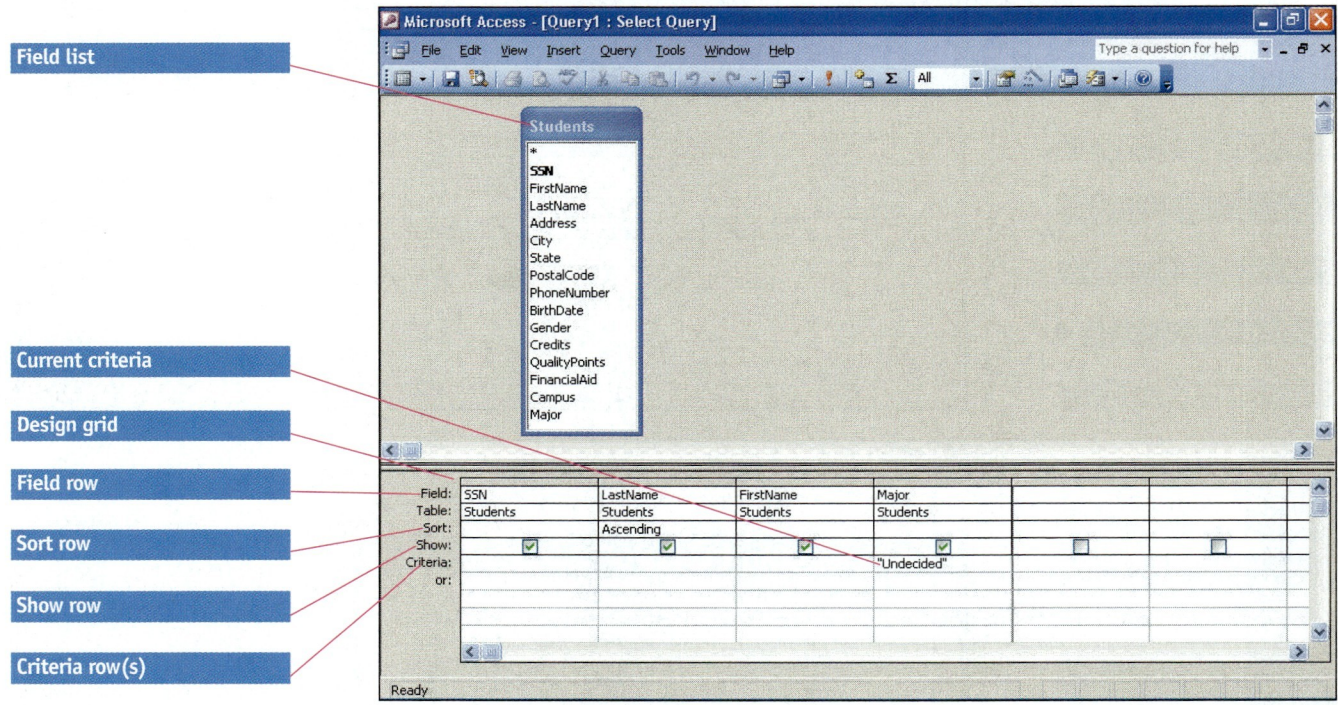

FIGURE 3.6 Query Design View

WILD CARDS

Select queries recognize the question mark and asterisk wild cards that enable you to search for a pattern within a text field. A question mark stands for a single character in the same position as the question mark; thus H?ll will return Hall, Hill, and Hull. An asterisk stands for any number of characters in the same position as the asterisk; for example, S*nd will return Sand, Stand, and Strand. (Access will change the format of any entry with a wild card to include the Like operator; for example, S*nd is converted to Like "S*nd" in the Design grid.)

Selection Criteria

To specify selection criteria in the design grid, enter a value or expression in the Criteria row of the appropriate column. Figure 3.7 contains several examples of simple criteria and provides a basic introduction to select queries.

The criterion in Figure 3.7a selects the students majoring in Business. The criteria for text fields are case insensitive. Thus, *"Business"* is the same as *"business"* or *"BUSINESS"*.

Values entered into multiple columns of the same Criteria row implement an ***AND operator*** in which the selected records must meet *all* of the specified criteria. The criteria in Figure 3.7b select students who are majoring in Business *and* who are from the state of Florida. The criteria in Figure 3.7c select Communications majors who are receiving financial aid.

Values entered into different Criteria rows are connected by an ***OR operator*** in which the selected records may satisfy *any* of the indicated criteria. The criteria in Figure 3.7d select students who are majoring in Business *or* who are from Florida or both.

Field:	LastName	State	Major	BirthDate	FinancialAid	Credits	
Sort:							
Show:	☑	☑	☑	☑	☑	☑	
Criteria:			"Business"				
or:							

(a) Business Majors

Field:	LastName	State	Major	BirthDate	FinancialAid	Credits	
Sort:							
Show:	☑	☑	☑	☑	☑	☑	
Criteria:		"FL"	"Business"				
or:							

(b) Business Majors from Florida

Field:	LastName	State	Major	BirthDate	FinancialAid	Credits	
Sort:							
Show:	☑	☑	☑	☑	☑	☑	
Criteria:			"Communications"		Yes		
or:							

(c) Communications Majors Receiving Financial Aid

Field:	LastName	State	Major	BirthDate	FinancialAid	Credits	
Sort:							
Show:	☑	☑	☑	☑	☑	☑	
Criteria:		"FL"					
or:			"Business"				

(d) Business Majors or Students from Florida

FIGURE 3.7 Selection Criteria

Relational operators (>, <, >=, <=, =, and <>) are used with date or number fields to return records within a designated range. The criteria in Figure 3.7e select Engineering majors with fewer than 60 credits.

The **Like operator** identifies those records that match a pattern; e.g., Like "Business" to identify Business majors. You can enter the complete pattern or you can use wild card characters as shown in Figure 3.7f; e.g., Like "Bus*" will select "Bus", "Business" and anything in between.

Other functions enable you to impose still other criteria. The **Between operator** selects records that fall within a range of values. The criterion in Figure 3.7g selects students who have between 60 and 90 credits. The **NOT operator** selects records that do not contain the designated value. The criterion in Figure 3.7h selects students with majors other than Liberal Arts.

Field:	LastName	State	Major	BirthDate	FinancialAid	Credits
Sort:						
Show:	✓	✓	✓	✓	✓	✓
Criteria:			"Engineering"			<60
or:						

(e) Engineering Majors with Fewer than 60 Credits

Field:	LastName	State	Major	BirthDate	FinancialAid	Credits
Table:	Students	Students	Students	Students	Students	Students
Sort:						
Show:	✓	✓	✓	✓	✓	✓
Criteria:			Like "Bus"			
or:						

(f) Business Majors (will select "Bus", "Business", and anything in between)

Field:	LastName	State	Major	BirthDate	FinancialAid	Credits
Sort:						
Show:	✓	✓	✓	✓	✓	✓
Criteria:						Between 60 and 90
or:						

(g) Students with between 60 and 90 Credits

Field:	LastName	State	Major	BirthDate	FinancialAid	Credits
Sort:						
Show:	✓	✓	✓	✓	✓	✓
Criteria:			Not "Liberal Arts"			
or:						

(h) Students with Majors Other than Liberal Arts

FIGURE 3.7 Selection Criteria (*continued*)

Creating a Select Query

Objective To create a select query using the Simple Query Wizard; to show how changing values in a dynaset changes the values in the underlying table; to create a report based on a query. Use Figure 3.8 as a guide in the exercise.

Step 1: **The Simple Query Wizard**

- Start Access and open the **Our Students database** from the previous exercise. Click **Open** in response to the security warning.

- Click the **Queries button** in the Database window. Double click the icon next to **Create query by using wizard** to start the Simple Query Wizard as shown in Figure 3.8a.

- The Students table should be already selected from the Tables/Queries list box. (If not, click the **drop-down arrow** in this list box and select the **Students table**.)

- Select the **LastName field** from the field list at the left, then click the **> button** to add this field to the Selected Fields list. (Use the **< button** if necessary to remove a field from the Selected Fields list.)

- Add the **FirstName**, **PhoneNumber**, **Major**, and **Credits fields** in that order to the Selected Fields list. (You can double click a field name to add it to the field list.) Click **Next**.

- The option button for a **Detail query** is selected. Click **Next**.

- Enter **Undecided Major** as the name of the query. Click the option button that says you want to **Modify the query design**. Click **Finish**.

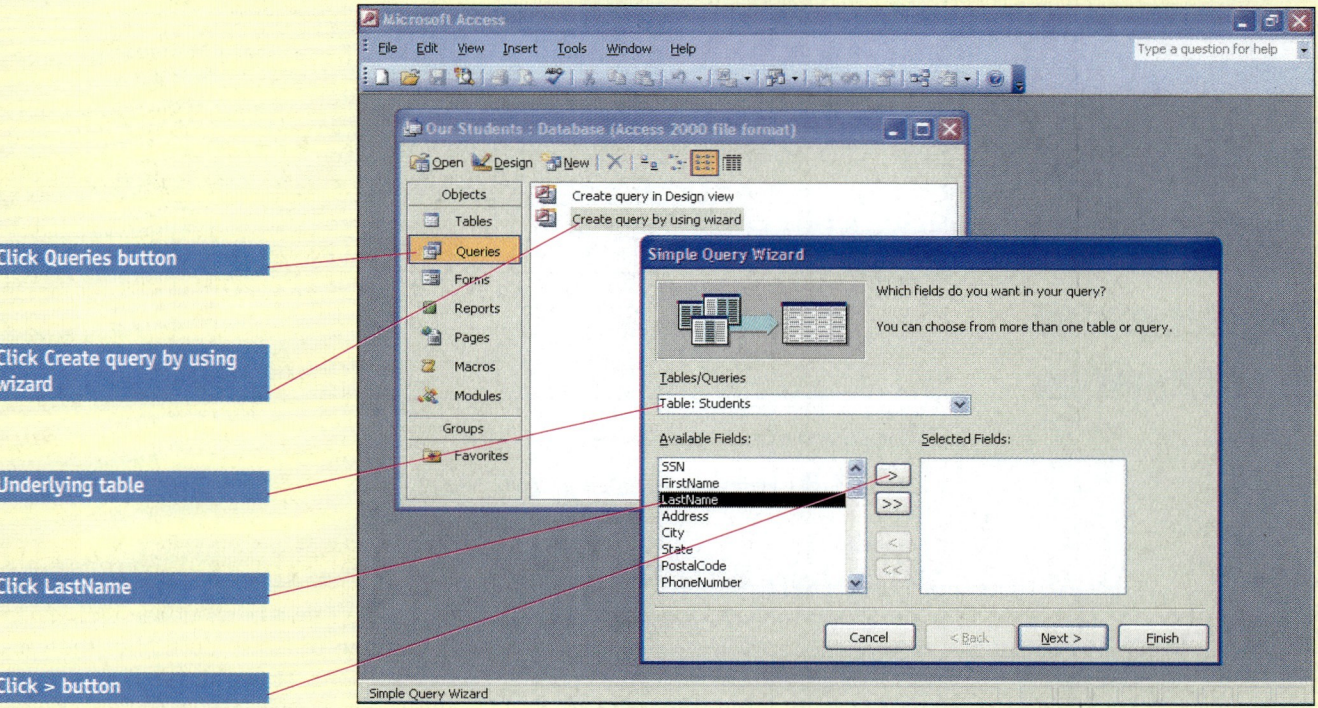

(a) The Simple Query Wizard (step 1)

FIGURE 3.8 Hands-on Exercise 2

Step 2: **Complete the Query**

- You should see the Query Design window as shown in Figure 3.8b. (Your query has not yet been completed, however, and so your figure does not match ours at this time.) Click the **Maximize button** so that the Design window takes the entire screen.

- Click and drag the border between the upper and lower portions of the window to give you more room in the upper half. Click and drag the bottom of the field list so that you can see all of the fields in the Students table.

- Check that you have all of the necessary fields in the lower half of the window. You can click and drag any missing field from the field list to the grid, and/or you can select a column, then drag it within the grid to rearrange the order of the fields.

- Click the **Criteria row** for **Major**. Type **Undecided**.

- Click the **Sort row** under the LastName field, click the **drop-down arrow**, then select **Ascending** as the sort sequence.

- Click the **Save button** to save the query.

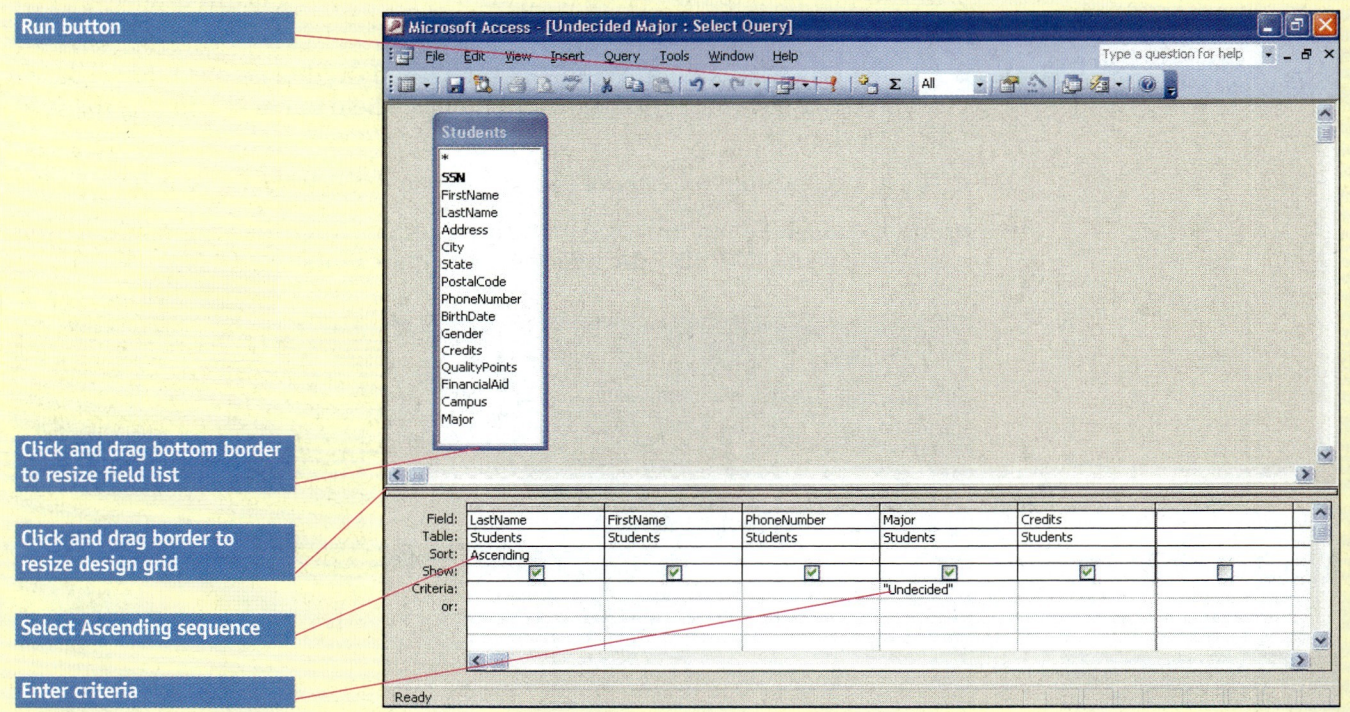

(b) Complete the Query (step 2)

FIGURE 3.8 Hands-on Exercise 2 (*continued*)

CUSTOMIZE THE QUERY WINDOW

The Query window displays the field list and design grid in its upper and lower halves, respectively. To increase (decrease) the size of either portion of the window, drag the line dividing the upper and lower sections. Drag the title bar to move a field list. You can also size a field list by dragging a border just as you would size any other window. Press the F6 key to toggle between the upper and lower halves as you work in the Design view.

Step 3: **Run the Query**

- Pull down the **Query menu** and click **Run** (or click the **Run button**) to run the query and change to the Datasheet view.

- You should see the five records in the dynaset of Figure 3.8c. Change Ryan Cornell's major to Business by clicking in the **Major field**, clicking the **drop-down arrow**, then choosing **Business** from the drop-down list.

- Click the **View button** to return to the Design view in order to rerun the query. Click the **Run button**.

- You should now see four students. Ryan Cornell no longer appears because he has changed his major.

- Change to the Design view.

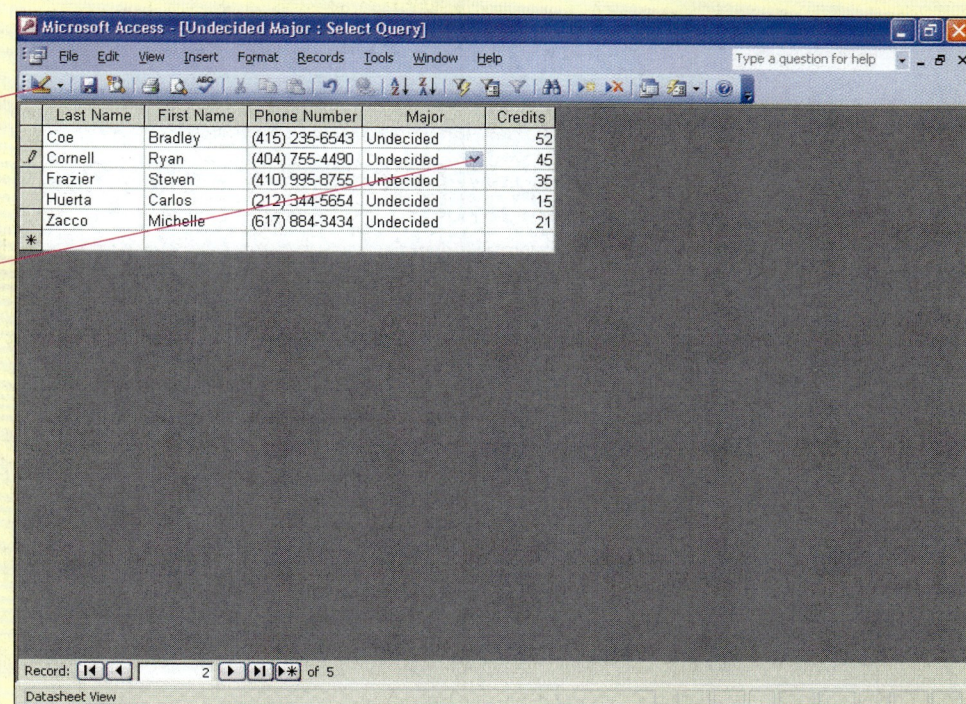

(c) Run the Query (step 3)

FIGURE 3.8 Hands-on Exercise 2 (*continued*)

THE DYNASET

A query represents a question and an answer. The question is developed by using the design grid in the Query Design view. The answer is displayed in a dynaset that contains the records that satisfy the criteria specified in the query. A dynaset looks and acts like a table, but it isn't a table; it is a dynamic subset of a table that selects and sorts records as specified in the query. A dynaset is like a table in that you can enter a new record or modify or delete an existing record. It is dynamic because the changes made to the dynaset are automatically reflected in the underlying table.

Step 4:   **Modify the Query**

- Click the **Show check box** in the Major field to remove the check as shown in Figure 3.8d. The Major field will be used to select students, but it will not appear in the dynaset.

- Click the **Criteria row** under credits. Type **>30** to select only the Undecided majors with more than 30 credits.

- Pull down the **File menu** and click the **Save As command** to save the revised query as shown. Click **OK**. Click the **Run button** to run the revised query.

- This time there are only two records (Bradley Coe and Steven Frazier) in the dynaset, and the major is no longer displayed.

- Carlos Huerta and Michelle Zacco do not appear because they do not have more than 30 credits.

- Close the query.

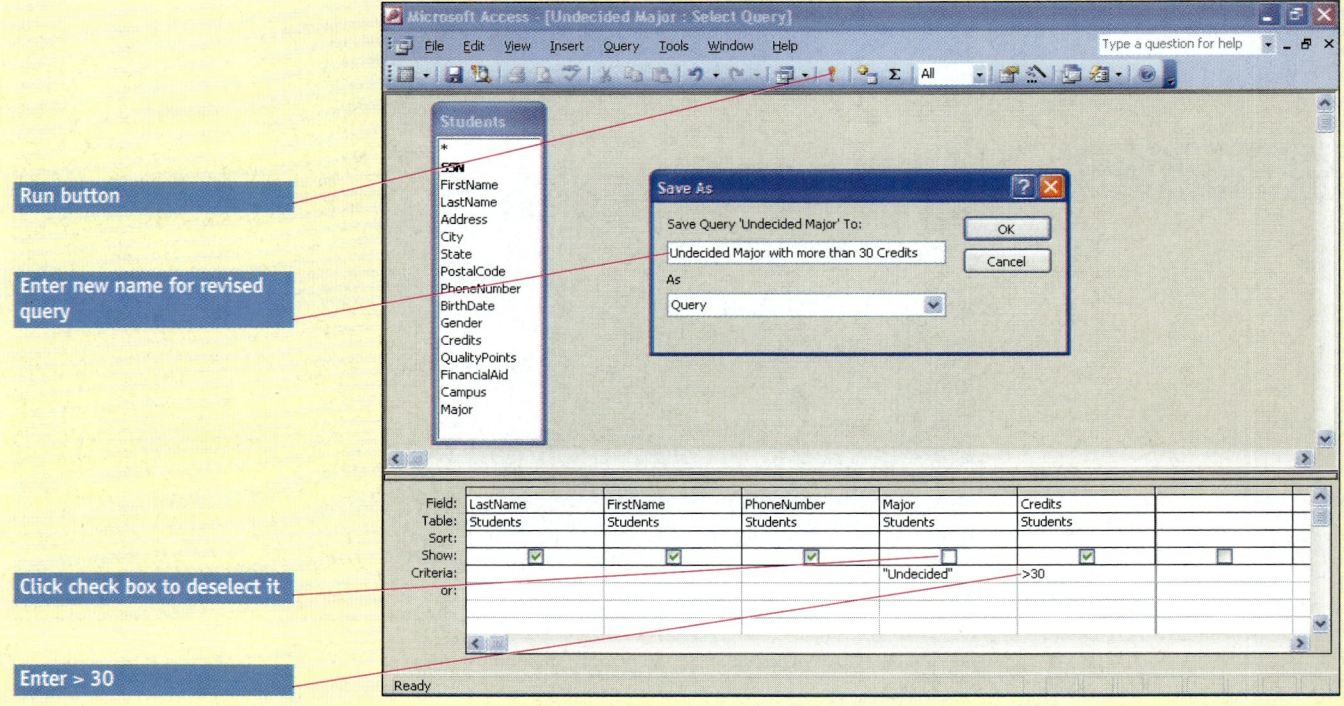

Run button

Enter new name for revised query

Click check box to deselect it

Enter > 30

(d) Modify the Query (step 4)

FIGURE 3.8   Hands-on Exercise 2 (*continued*)

FLEXIBLE CRITERIA

Access offers a great deal of flexibility in the way you enter the criteria for a text field. Quotation marks and/or an equal sign are optional. Thus, "Undecided", Undecided, =Undecided, or ="Undecided" are all valid, and you may choose any of these formats. Access will convert your entry to standard format ("Undecided" in this example) after you have moved to the next cell. Numeric fields, however, are always entered without quotation marks.

Step 5: Create a Report

■ You should see the Database window in Figure 3.8e. Click the **Reports button**, then double click the icon next to **Create report by using wizard**.

■ Click the **drop-down arrow** on the **Tables/Queries** list box and select **Query:Undecided Major with more than 30 credits**. All of the visible fields (major has been hidden) are displayed.

■ Click the **>> button** to select all of the fields in the query for the report. Click **Next** to continue.

■ You do not want to choose additional grouping levels. Click **Next** to move to the next screen.

■ There is no need to specify a sort sequence. Click **Next**.

■ The **Tabular layout** is selected, as is **Portrait orientation**. Be sure the box is checked to **Adjust field width so all fields fit on a page**. Click **Next**.

■ Choose **Soft Gray** as the style. Click **Next**.

■ If necessary, enter **Undecided Major with more than 30 credits** as the title. The option button to **Preview the report** is already selected.

■ Click the **Finish command button** to exit the Report Wizard and view the report and check your progress.

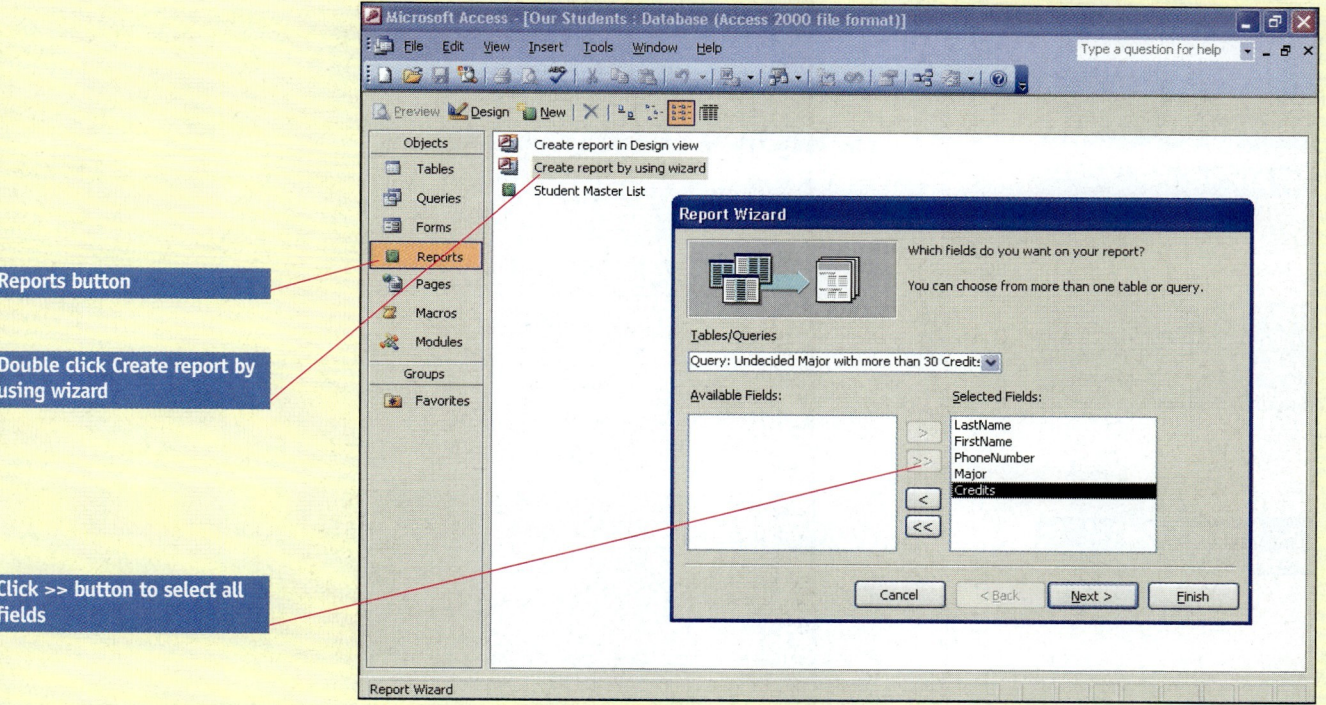

(e) Create a Report (step 5)

FIGURE 3.8 Hands-on Exercise 2 (*continued*)

THE BACK BUTTON

The Back button is present on every screen within the Report Wizard and enables you to recover from mistakes or simply to change your mind about how you want the report to look. Click the Back button at any time to return to the previous screen, then click it again if you want to return to the screen before that. Alternatively, you can click Cancel and start over.

Step 6:   Complete the Report

- Change to Design view. Change the font size of the title to **16 points**. Add a second label containing your name and format it appropriately.

- Click in the Report Header, pull down the **Insert menu**, and click the **Picture command** to display the Insert Picture dialog box. Change to the **Exploring Access folder**. Select the **Academic Symbols picture**, then click **OK**.

- Right click the picture to display a context-sensitive menu, then click **Properties** to display the Properties Dialog box. Click the **Size Mode property**, click the **down arrow**, and click **Stretch**.

- Close the Properties sheet. Move and size the picture as shown in Figure 3.8f.

- Click in the page header (above and to the right of the Credits label), then drag the mouse to select all of the objects in the Page Header and Detail sections. Release the mouse (the objects will be selected), then click and drag the selected objects to the right to center them.

- Pull down the **File menu** and click the **Page Setup command**, then adjust the left and right margins so that the report fits on one page. Print the report, which contains two students (Coe and Frazier).

- Close the report.

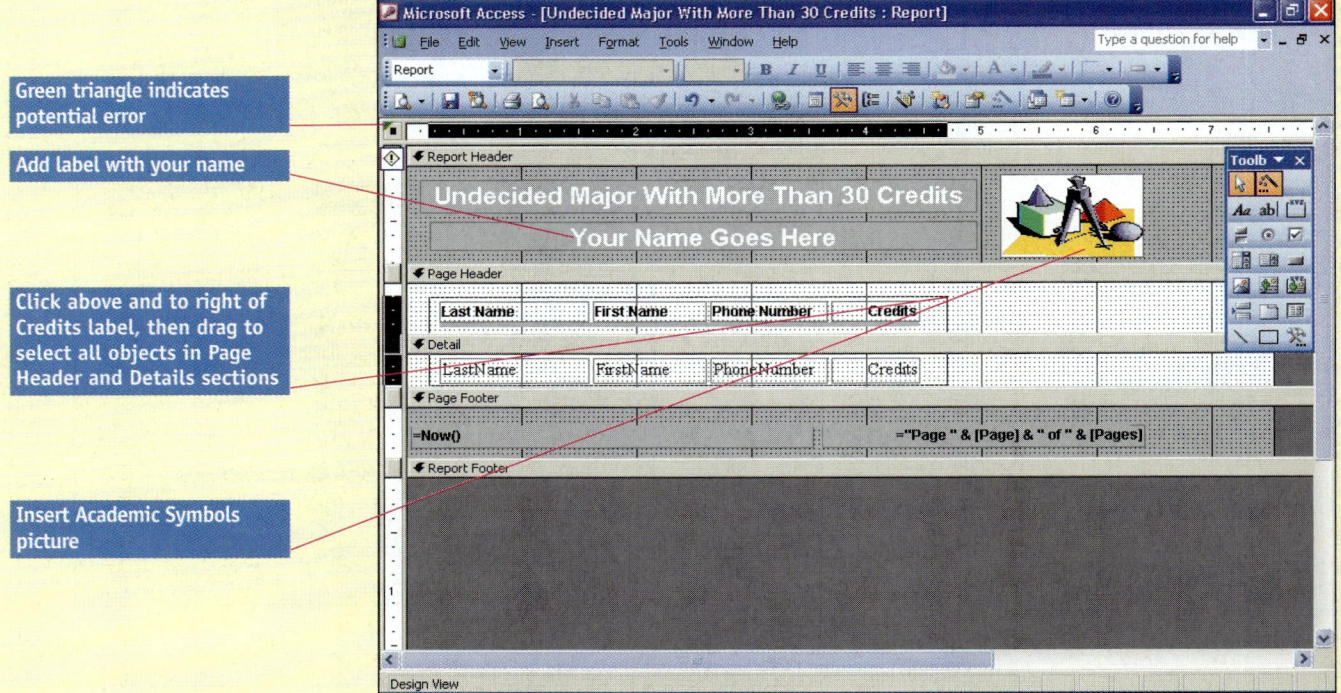

Green triangle indicates potential error

Add label with your name

Click above and to right of Credits label, then drag to select all objects in Page Header and Details sections

Insert Academic Symbols picture

(f) Complete the Report (step 6)

FIGURE 3.8   Hands-on Exercise 2 (*continued*)

THE GREEN TRIANGLE

The green triangle will appear in the Design view of either a form or report and is Access' way of indicating a potential error. Click the object containing the triangle (the report selector in this example), click the exclamation point that appears, and then correct the indicated error. Microsoft Excel follows a similar convention.

Step 7: **Apply a Filter to a Form**

■ You can also search for selected records by applying a filter. Click the **Forms button** in the Database window. Open the **Students form**.

■ Click the **Filter by Form button** to display the form as shown in Figure 3.8g. (The Filter by Form button is no longer visible after you click the button; you can, however, still access the command by pulling down the **Filter menu**.)

■ Enter the criteria for **business majors** receiving **financial aid**, then click the **Apply Filter button**. The status bar should indicate that you are looking at one of three records and that the list is filtered.

■ Click in the **Last Name control**, then click the **Sort Ascending button**. Kevin DiGiacomo should now appear as the first record. Click the **Print Record button** to print this form.

■ Submit the printed report from the previous step together with Kevin's form to your instructor. Close the Our Students database.

■ Exit Access if you do not wish to continue with the next exercise at this time.

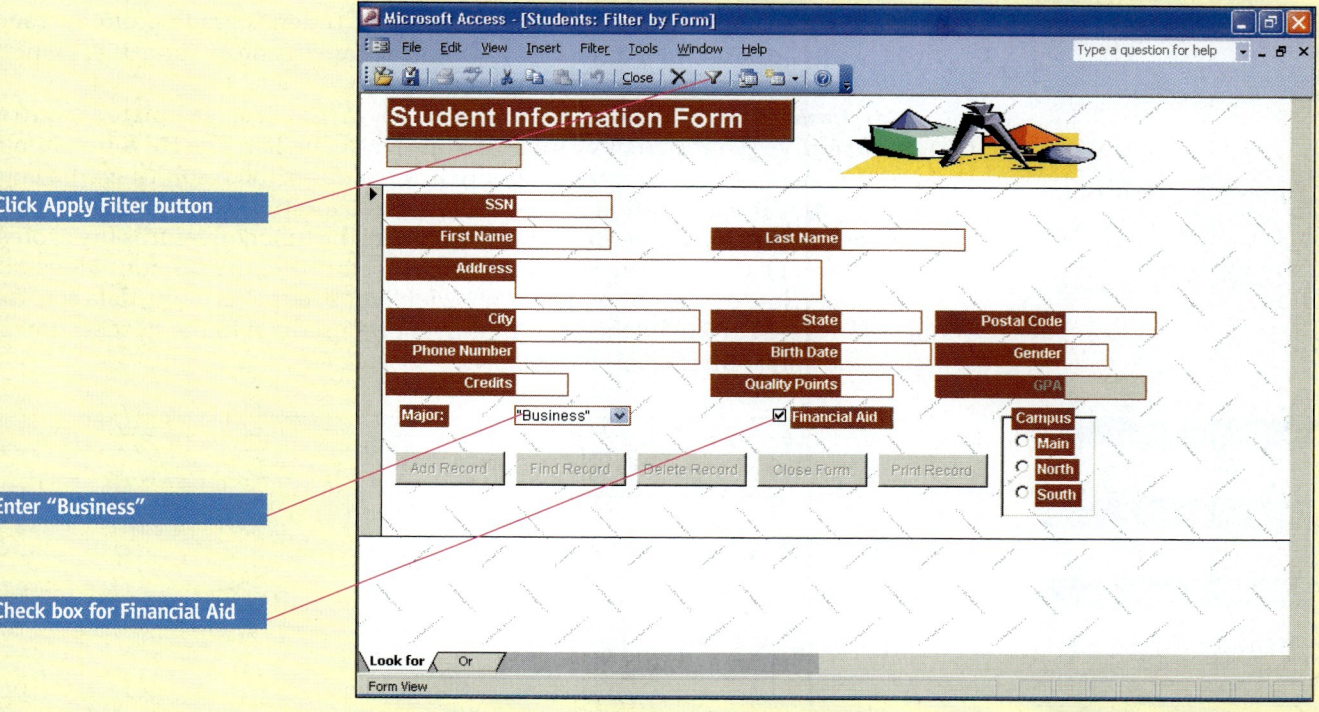

(g) Apply a Filter to a Form (step 7)

FIGURE 3.8 Hands-on Exercise 2 (*continued*)

APPLY A FILTER FROM A QUERY

You can leverage the existing queries in a database by using an existing query as a filter. Open the existing form; click Filter by Form on the Form View toolbar, which in turn displays the Filter/Sort toolbar. Click the Load from Query button (which is at the extreme left of the toolbar), choose the desired filter (query), click OK, and then apply the filter. You will find this technique especially useful if you want to filter based on a calculated field because you cannot enter data into a calculated control such as GPA; that is, you must create a query to filter on a calculated control.

ACCESS FUNCTIONS AND CALCULATED CONTROLS

A report, and/or the query on which it is based, can be enhanced through the use of Access functions to create calculated controls. Figure 3.9a displays a query in Design view, whereas Figure 3.9b shows (a portion of) the corresponding dynaset. The students appear in alphabetical order according to their major, and then alphabetically by last name within each major. Three of the controls in the query (Major, QualityPoints, and Credits) are from the underlying Students table as can be seen from the corresponding entries in the Table row. The other controls (Name, GPA, and Distinction) are calculated and thus, are not contained in an underlying table; that is, the entries in the Table row for these fields are blank.

Syntactically, the name of a calculated control is followed by a colon, a space, and then the expression. The first calculated control, Name, uses the ampersand to **concatenate** (join together) three components of a student's name: the last name, a comma followed by a space, and the first name. The result can be seen in the dynaset—for example, "Adili, Ronnie" for the first student in the table. Notice how the concatenated field is more visually appealing than displaying the two name fields individually.

The next calculated control, GPA, uses simple division (the quality points divided by the number of credits) to compute a student's grade point average. Jared Berlin, for example, has quality points and credits of 250 and 100, respectively, resulting in a calculated GPA of 2.50.

An **Immediate IF (IIF) function** is used in the last calculated control (Distinction) to determine if a student is on the Dean's list. The IIF function has three arguments—a condition that is either true or false, the result when the condition is true, and an (optional) result when the condition is false. Thus, in this example, if the GPA is greater than or equal to 3.50, the function returns the expression "Dean's List". If, however, the condition is not true, the function does not return any value; that is, the control will be left blank in the resulting data set. The query in Figure 3.9 will be the basis of the report described in the next section as well as the hands-on exercise that follows.

Concatenated fields

Calculated control

Immediate IF function

Field:	Major	Name: [LastName] & ", " & [FirstName]	QualityPoints	Credits	GPA: [QualityPoints]/[Credits]	Distinction: IIf([GPA]>=3.5,"Dean's List")
Table:	Students		Students	Students		
Sort:	Ascending	Ascending				
Show:	☑	☑	☑	☑	☑	☑
Criteria:						
or:						

(a) Design View

Students are listed alphabetically by last name within major

Student's last name and first name have been concatenated

GPA has been calculated to 2 decimals

Dean's List is indicated only where GPA is >= 3.5

Major	Name	QualityPoints	Credits	GPA	Distinction
Business	Adili, Ronnie	155	60	2.58	
Business	Cornell, Ryan	80	45	1.78	
Business	DiGiacomo, Kevin	375	105	3.57	Dean's List
Business	Gibson, Christopher	60	35	1.71	
Business	Ramsay, Robert	162	50	3.24	
Business	Watson, Ana	75	30	2.50	
Communications	Faulkner, Eileen	80	30	2.67	
Communications	Joseph, Cedric	170	45	3.78	Dean's List
Communications	Ortiz, Frances	60	28	2.14	
Communications	Price, Lori	42	24	1.75	
Communications	Slater, Erica	390	105	3.71	Dean's List
Education	Korba, Nickolas	166	100	1.66	

(b) Dynaset

FIGURE 3.9 Access Functions

The report in Figure 3.10 is based on the query just discussed; that is, look closely, and you will see that the report contains the same business majors as previously. The GPA is calculated as before, and it illustrates **conditional formatting**; that is, the format (in this case, the font color) depends on the value of the GPA control. A GPA greater than 3.5 is printed in blue, a GPA less than 2.0 is printed in red, and all other values are printed in black.

The report in Figure 3.10a, for example, groups students according to their major, sorts them alphabetically according to last name within each major, then calculates the average GPA for all students in each major. A Group Header appears before each group of students to identify the group and display the major. A Group Footer appears at the end of each group and displays the average GPA for students in that major.

Figure 3.10b displays the Design view of the report in Figure 3.10a, which determines the appearance of the printed report. Look carefully at the design to relate each section to the corresponding portion of the printed report:

- The **Report Header** contains the title of the report and appears once, at the beginning of the printed report.

- The **Page Header** contains the column headings that appear at the top of each page. The column headings are labels (or unbound controls) and are formatted in bold.

- The **Group Header** consists of a single bound control that displays the value of the major field prior to each group of detail records.

- The **Detail section** consists of bound controls that appear directly under the corresponding heading in the Page Header. The Detail section is printed once for each record in each group.

- The **Group Footer** appears after each group of detail records. It consists of an unbound control (Average GPA for Major:) followed by a calculated control that computes the average GPA for each group of students.

- The **Page Footer** appears at the bottom of each page and contains the date, page number, and total number of pages in the report.

- The **Report Footer** appears at the end of the report. It consists of an unbound control (Average GPA for All Students:) followed by a calculated control that computes the average GPA for all students.

Grouping records within a report enables you to perform calculations on each group, as was done in the Group Footer of Figure 3.10. The calculations in our example made use of the **Avg function**, but other types of calculations are possible:

- The **Sum function** computes the total for a specific field for all records in the group.

- The **Min function** determines the minimum value for all records in the group.

- The **Max function** determines the maximum value for all records in the group.

- The **Count function** counts the number of records in the group.

Look closely at the page footer to see the inclusion of three additional functions—Now, Page, and Pages—that display the current date, the current page, and total number of pages, respectively. The Report Wizard builds the Page Footer automatically, but you can learn from the wizard and incorporate these functions in other reports that you create.

The following exercise has you create the report in Figure 3.10. The Report Wizard is used to design the basic report, but additional modifications are necessary to create the Group Header and Group Footer.

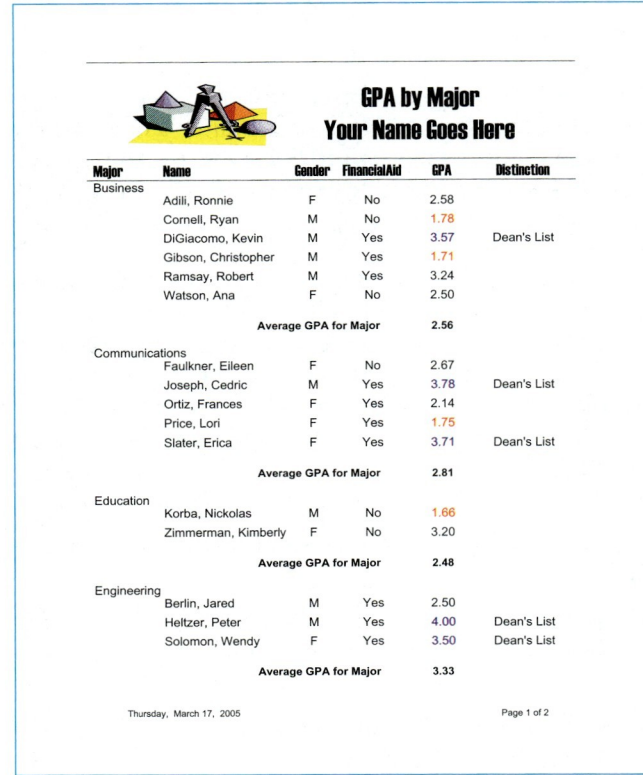

(a) The Printed Report

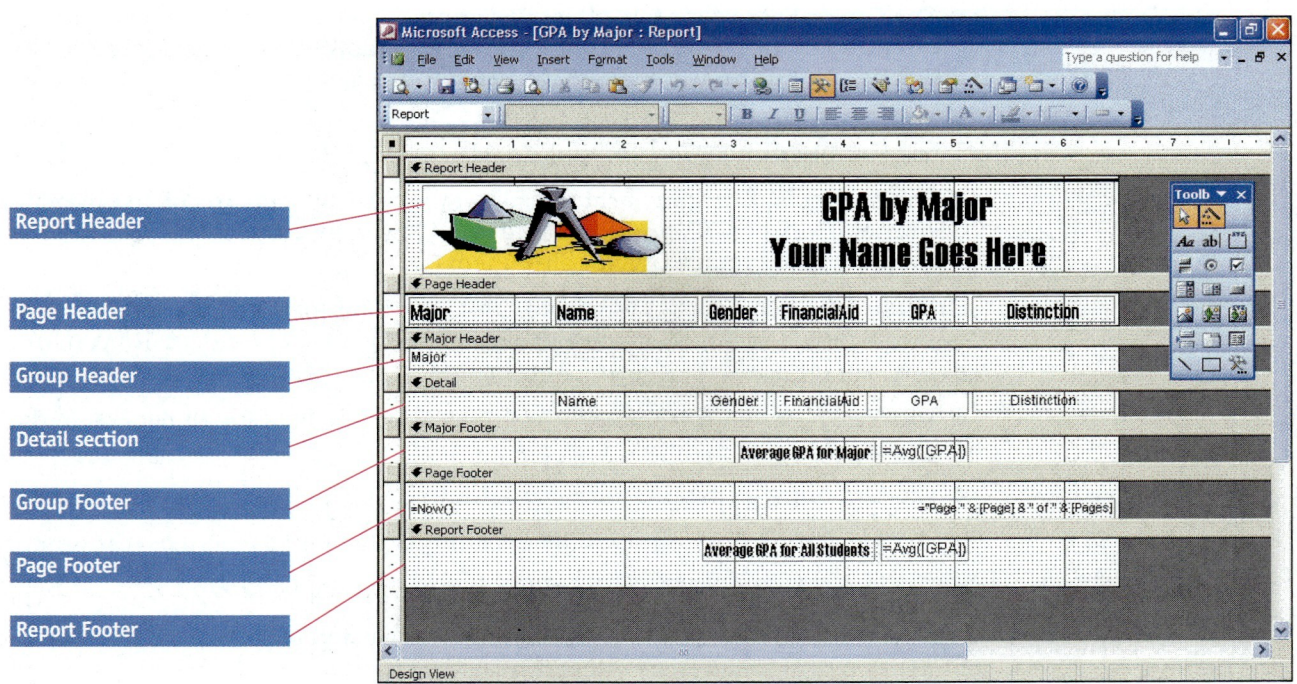

Report Header

Page Header

Group Header

Detail section

Group Footer

Page Footer

Report Footer

(b) Design View

FIGURE 3.10 The Summary Report

3   Grouping Records

Objective	To create a query containing a calculated control, then create a report based on that query; to use the Sorting and Grouping command to add a Group Header and Group Footer to a report. Use Figure 3.11 as a guide.

Step 1:   Create the Query

- Start Access and open the **Our Students database** from the previous exercise. Click **Open** in response to the security warning.

- Click the **Queries button** in the Database window. Double click **Create query in Design view** to display the Query Design window and bypass the Simple Query Wizard.

- The Show Table dialog box appears; the **Tables tab** is already selected, as is the **Students table**. Click the **Add button** to add the table to the query. Click **Close** to close the Show Table dialog box.

- Click the **Maximize button** so that the window takes up the entire screen as shown in Figure 3.11a. Drag the border between the upper and lower portions of the window to give yourself more room in the upper portion. Make the field list larger, to display more fields at one time.

- Scroll (if necessary) within the field list, then click and drag the **Major field** from the field list to the query. Click and drag the **Gender**, **FinancialAid**, **QualityPoints**, and **Credits fields** (in that order).

- Click the **Sort row** for the Major field. Click the **down arrow** to open the drop-down list box. Click **Ascending**.

- Click **Save** to display the dialog box in Figure 3.11a. Enter **GPA by Major** as the query name. Click **OK**.

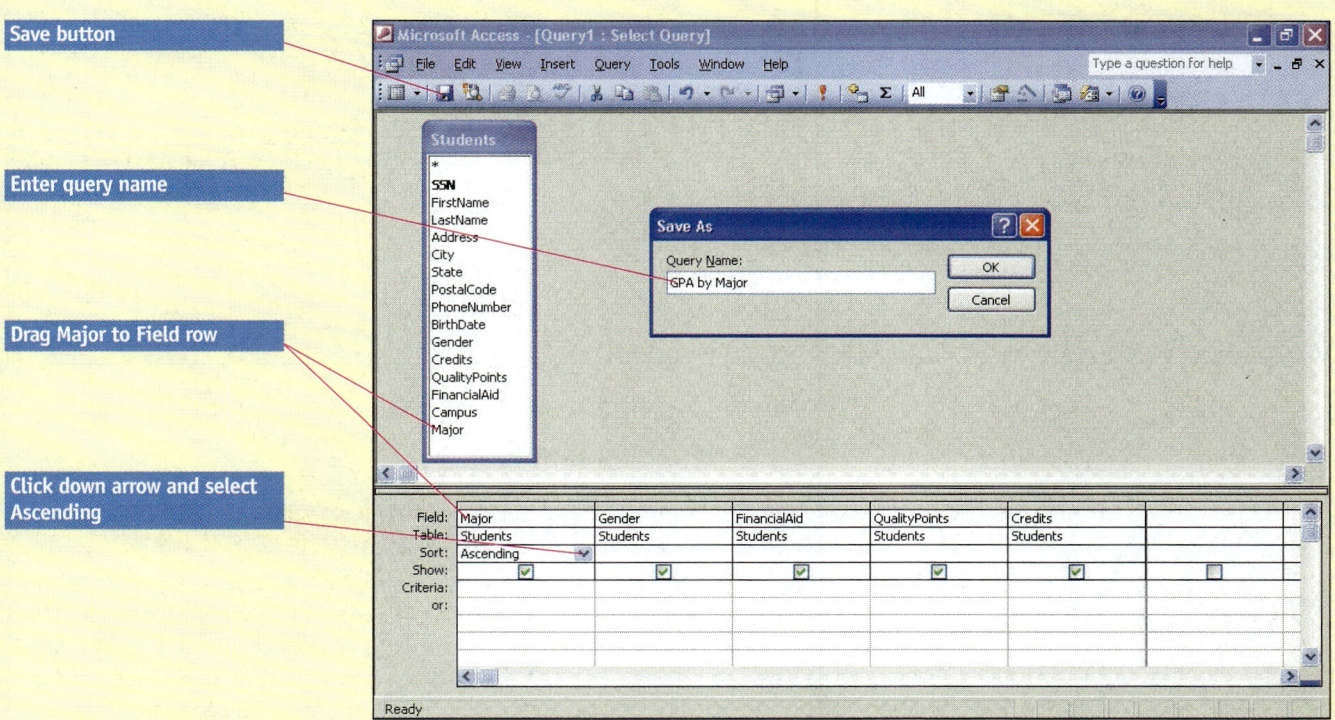

(a) Create the Query (step 1)

FIGURE 3.11   Hands-on Exercise 3

Step 2: **Add the Calculated Controls**

- Click anywhere in the **Gender column**. Pull down the **Insert menu** and click **Columns** to insert a blank column to the left of the Gender field.

- Click in the **Field row** of the newly inserted column to enter a calculated control. Type **Name: LastName & ", " & FirstName**, and press **Enter**. (Be sure to leave a space after the comma.) The ampersand concatenates (joins together) the various components in the name field.

- Be sure to spell the fields correctly (there are no spaces in "LastName" or "FirstName"). You are concatenating (joining together) the last name, a comma and a space, and the first name into a single field called Name.

- Click in the **Sort row** under the newly created Name control. Click the **down arrow** and choose an **Ascending** sequence as shown in Figure 3.11b.

- Click in the **Field row** of the first blank column. Type **GPA: QualityPoints/Credits**, and press **Enter**. Be sure to spell the field names correctly.

- Change the column widths as necessary. Save the query.

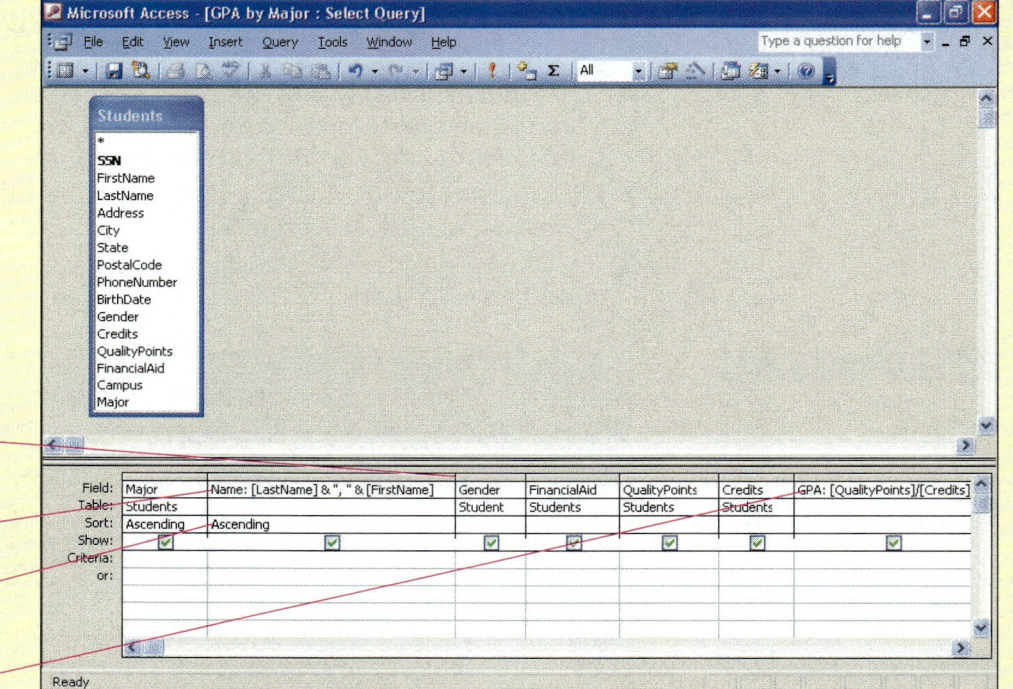

Click and drag border to change column width

Click in Field row and enter calculated control for Name

Select Ascending sequence

Click in Field row and enter calculated control for GPA

(b) Add the Calculated Controls (step 2)

FIGURE 3.11 Hands-on Exercise 3 (*continued*)

THE TOP VALUES PROPERTY

The Top Values property lets you display a specified percentage or number of the top or bottom records in a list. Remove any sort keys in the query, then sort the table according to the desired sequence, ascending or descending, to get the lowest or highest values, respectively. Click the down arrow in the Top Values list box to choose the number of records, such as 5 or 5% to show the top five or five percent, respectively. Save the query, then run it. See practice exercise 3 at the end of the chapter.

Step 3: **Run the Query**

- Pull down the **Query menu** and click **Run** (or click the **Run button** on the Query Design toolbar). You will see the dynaset in Figure 3.11c, which displays the records that satisfy the query.

- Students are listed by major and alphabetically by last name within major. (Access sorts from left to right according to the way in which the fields appear in the Design grid. Thus, the Major field must appear to the left of the LastName field within the Design view.)

- Change column widths as necessary by dragging the border between adjacent column headings.

- A total of seven fields appear in the dynaset, corresponding to the controls that were added to the design grid in Design view. The GPA is displayed to too many decimal places.

- Click the **View button** to modify the query.

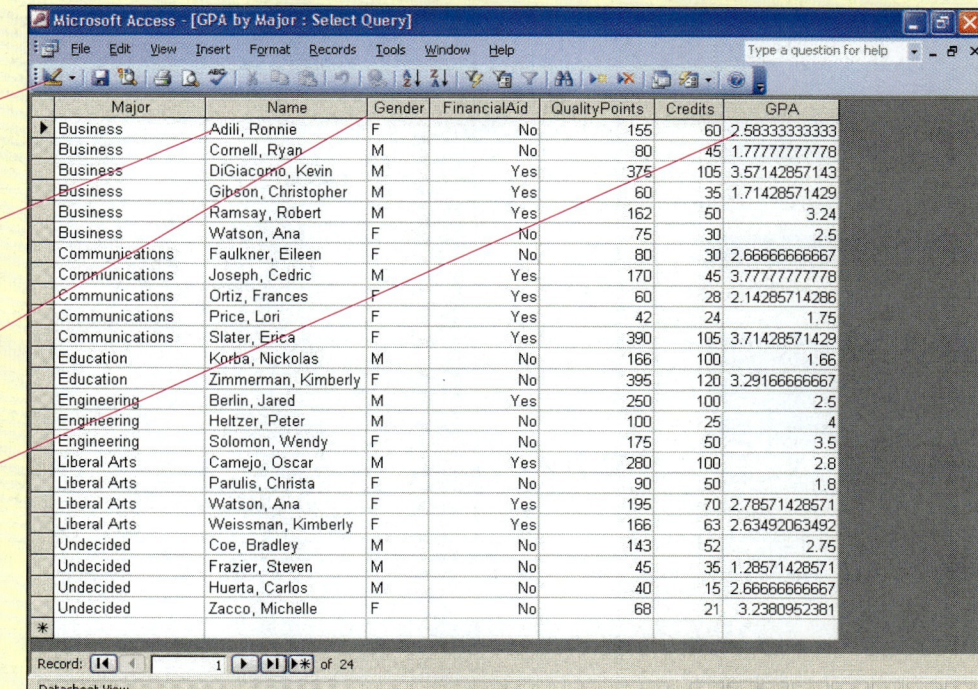

(c) Run the Query (step 3)

FIGURE 3.11 Hands-on Exercise 3 (*continued*)

ADJUST THE COLUMN WIDTH

Point to the right edge of the column you want to resize, then drag the mouse in the direction you want to go; drag to the right to make the column wider or to the left to make it narrower. Alternatively, you can double click the column selector line (right edge) to fit the longest entry in that column. Adjusting the column width in the Design view does not affect the column width in the Datasheet view, but you can use the same technique in both views.

Step 4: **Modify the Query**

- Point to the GPA column and click the **right mouse button** to display a shortcut menu. Click the **Properties command** to display the Field Properties dialog box in Figure 3.11d.

- Click the **General tab** if necessary. Click the **Format text box**. Click the **drop-down arrow** to display the available formats. Click **Fixed**. Close the Field Properties dialog box.

- We will add another calculated control that will display "Dean's List" if the student has earned this distinction. Click in the **Field row** in the first blank column of the design grid.

- Enter **Distinction: IIF(GPA>=3.5, "Dean's List")** for the new control as shown in Figure 3.11d. This expression will display the literal "Dean's List" if the student has a GPA greater than or equal to 3.5.

- Click the **Save button** to save the modified query.

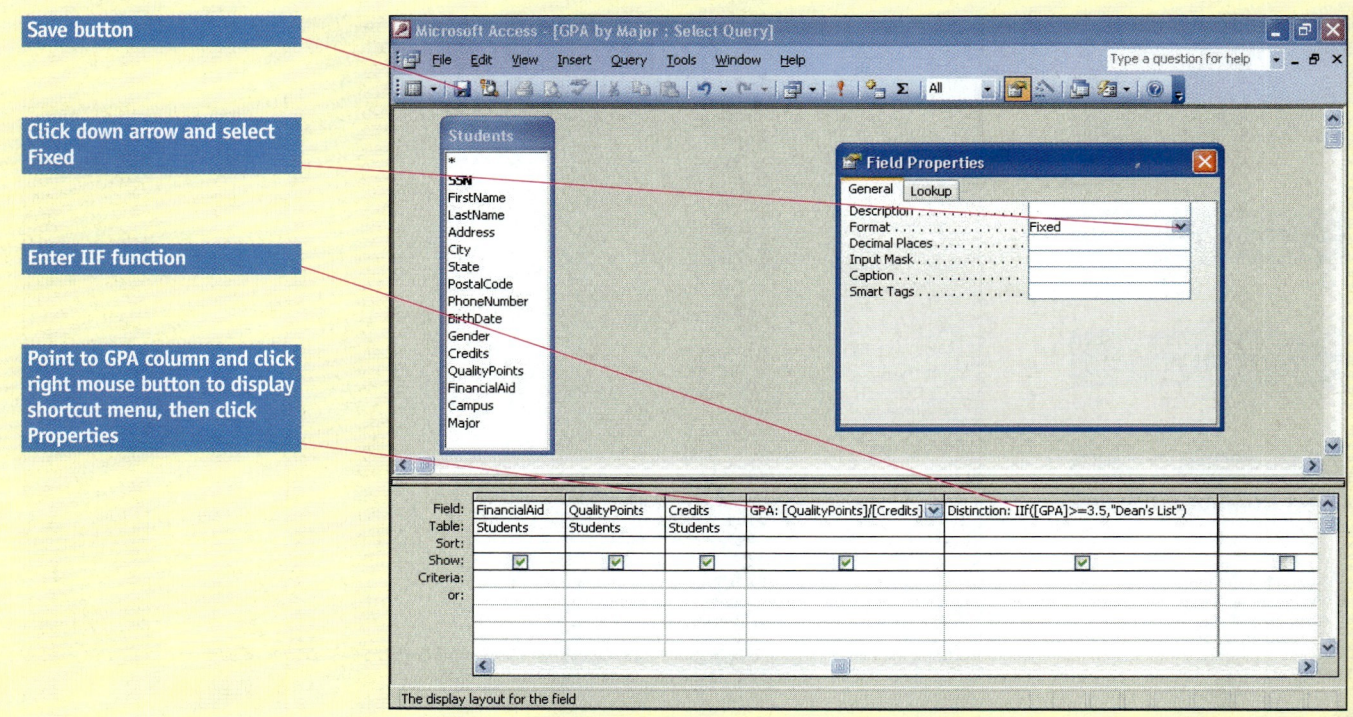

Save button

Click down arrow and select Fixed

Enter IIF function

Point to GPA column and click right mouse button to display shortcut menu, then click Properties

(d) Modify the Query (step 4)

FIGURE 3.11 Hands-on Exercise 3 (*continued*)

NESTED IF STATEMENTS

A "nested If" (or an If within an If) is a common logic structure in every programming language. It could be used in this example to implement more complicated logic such as displaying either "Dean's List" or "Probation", depending on the GPA. The IIF function has three arguments—a condition, the result if the condition is true, and the result if the condition is false. A nested If replaces either condition with another If. Thus, you could enter IIF(GPA>=3.5, "Dean's List", IIF(GPA<2.0, "Probation","N/A")).

Step 5: **Rerun the Query**

- Click the **Run button** to run the modified query. You will see a new dynaset corresponding to the modified query as shown in Figure 3.11e. Resize the column widths (as necessary) within the dynaset.
    - ❑ Students are still listed by major and alphabetically within major.
    - ❑ The GPA is calculated to two decimal places and appears under the GPA field.
    - ❑ Dean's List is indicated for those students with a GPA of 3.5 or above.

- Click the **QualityPoints field** for Christopher Gibson. Replace 60 with **70**. Press **Enter**. The GPA changes automatically to 2.

- Pull down the **Edit menu** and click **Undo Current Field/Record** (or click the **Undo button** on the Query toolbar). The GPA returns to its previous value.

- Tab to the **GPA field** for Christopher Gibson. Type **2**. Access will beep and prevent you from changing the GPA because it is a calculated field as indicated on the status bar.

- Click the **Close button** to close the query and return to the Database window. Click **Yes** if asked whether to save the changes.

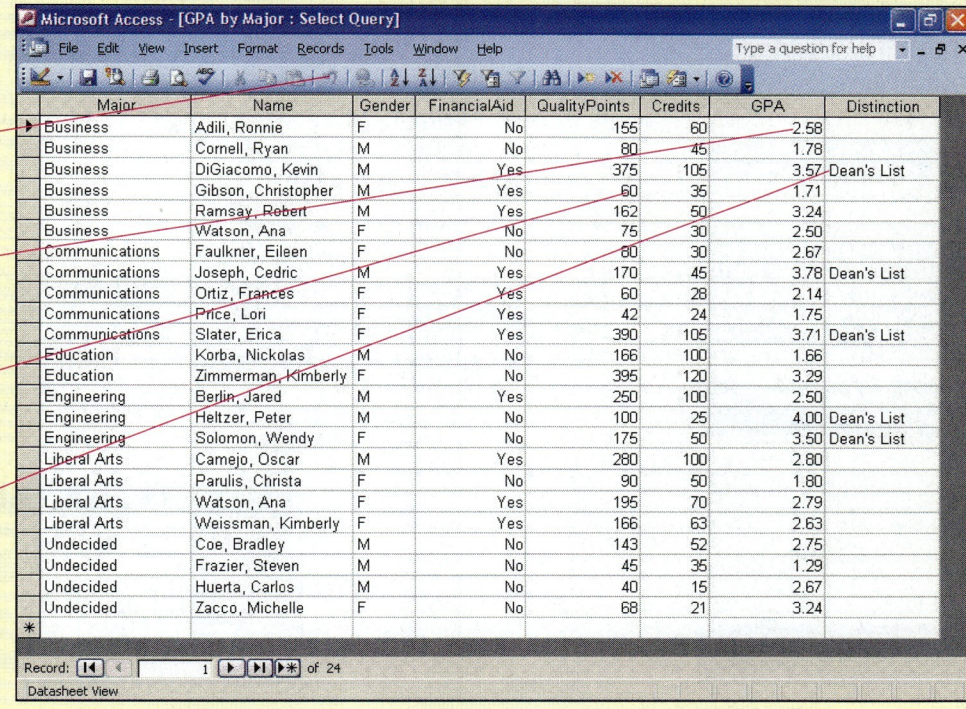

(e) Rerun the Query (step 5)

FIGURE 3.11 Hands-on Exercise 3 (*continued*)

USE WHAT YOU KNOW

An Access table or dynaset not only resembles an Excel worksheet in appearance, but it also accepts many of the same commands and operations. The Sort Ascending and Sort Descending buttons function identically to their Excel counterparts. You can also double click the right border of a column heading to adjust the column width. The Format menu enables you to change the row width or column height, hide or unhide columns, or freeze and unfreeze columns.

Step 6:

The Report Wizard

- You should see the Database window. Click the **Reports button**, then double click **Create report by using the wizard** to start the Report Wizard.

- Select **GPA by Major** from the Tables/Queries drop-down list. The Available Fields list displays all of the fields in the GPA by Major query.
  - ❑ Click the **Major field** in the Available Fields list box. Click the **> button**.
  - ❑ Add the **Name, Gender, FinancialAid, GPA**, and **Distinction fields** one at a time. The easiest way to add a field is to double click the field name.
  - ❑ Do not include the QualityPoints or Credits fields. Click **Next**.

- You should see the screen asking whether you want to group the fields. Click the **Major field**, then click the **> button** to display the screen in Figure 3.11f.

- The Major field appears above the other fields to indicate that the records will be grouped according to the value of the Major field. Click **Next**.

- The next screen asks you to specify the order for the detail records. Click the **drop-down arrow** on the list box for the first field. Click **Name** to sort the records alphabetically by last name within each major. Click **Next**.

- The **Stepped Option button** is already selected for the report layout, as is **Portrait orientation**. Be sure the box is checked to **Adjust field width so all fields fit on a page**. Click **Next**.

- Choose **Compact** as the style. Click **Next**.

- **GPA by Major** (which corresponds to the name of the underlying query) is already entered as the name of the report. Click the Option button to **Modify the report's design**.

- Click **Finish** to exit the Report Wizard.

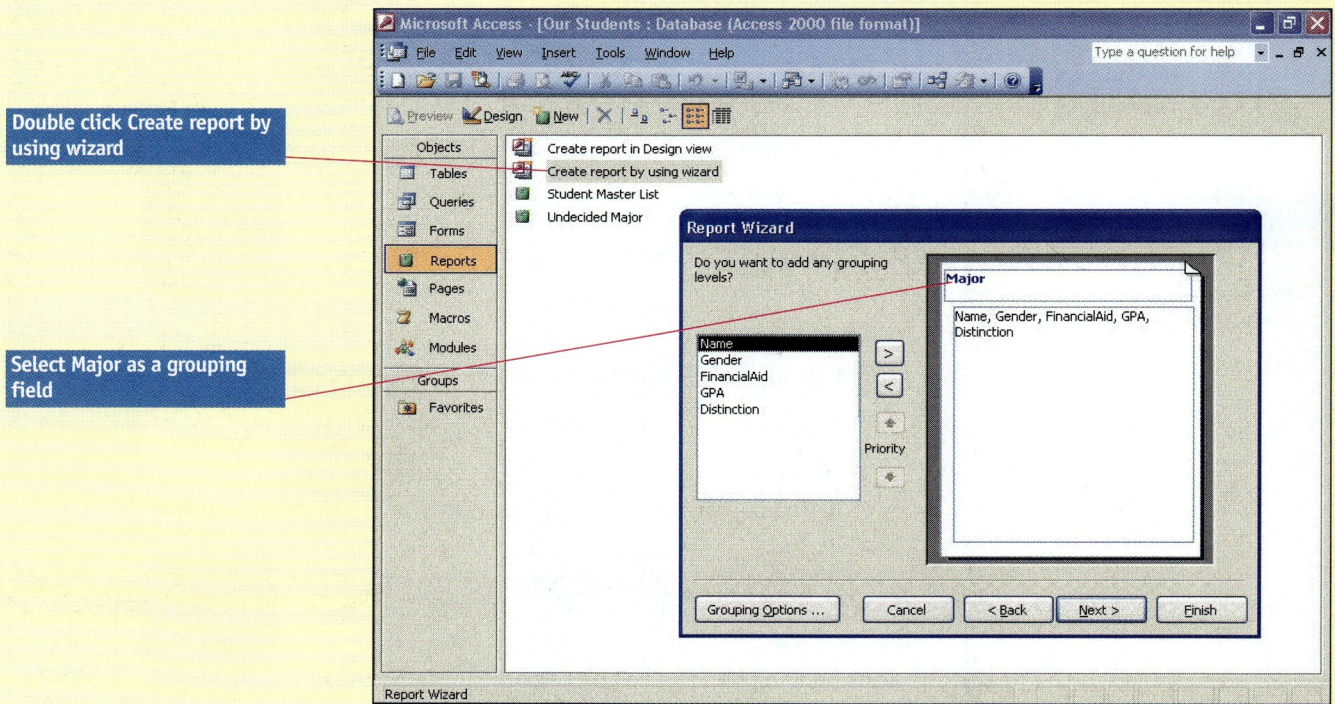

(f) The Report Wizard (step 6)

FIGURE 3.11 Hands-on Exercise 3 (*continued*)

Step 7: **Sorting and Grouping**

- Click and drag the right border of the label in the Report Header to the right to increase the size of the label. Press **Shift+Enter** to force a line break. Enter your name as shown in Figure 3.11g.

- Click the **Center button** to center the text within the unbound control. Click outside the label, then click and drag the label to the right.

- Move, size, and align the column headings and bound controls. You may have to go back and forth between Design view and Report Preview until you are satisfied.

- Pull down the **View menu**. Click **Sorting and Grouping** to display the Sorting and Grouping dialog box.

- The **Major field** should already be selected. Click the **Group Footer** property, click the **drop-down arrow**, then click **Yes** to create a Group Footer for the Major field.

- Click the down arrow for the **Keep Together** property. Click **Whole Group**. Close the dialog box. The Major footer has been added to the report.

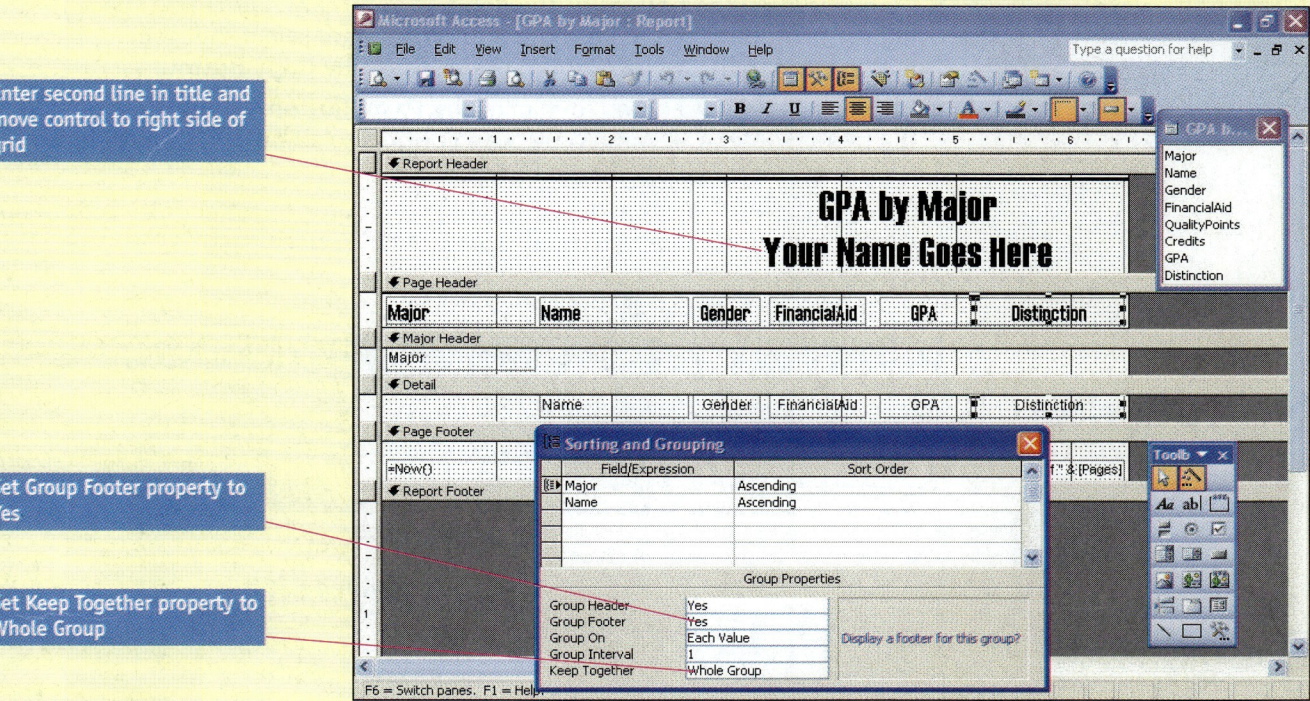

Enter second line in title and move control to right side of grid

Set Group Footer property to Yes

Set Keep Together property to Whole Group

(g) Sorting and Grouping (step 7)

FIGURE 3.11 Hands-on Exercise 3 (*continued*)

SELECTING MULTIPLE CONTROLS

Select (click) a column heading in the Page Header, then press and hold the Shift key as you select the corresponding bound control in the Detail section. This selects both the column heading and the bound control and enables you to move and size the objects in conjunction with one another. Continue to work with both objects selected as you apply formatting through various buttons on the Formatting toolbar, or change properties through the property sheet. Click anywhere on the report to deselect the objects when you are finished.

Step 8: **Create the Group and Report Footers**

- Click the **Text Box button** on the Toolbox toolbar. The mouse pointer changes to a tiny crosshair with a text box attached.
- Click and drag in the Major Footer where you want the text box (which will contain the average GPA) to go. Release the mouse.
- You will see an Unbound control and an attached label containing a field number (e.g., Text 18).
- Click in the **text box** control (Unbound will disappear). Enter **=Avg(GPA)** to calculate the average of the GPA for all students in this group as shown in Figure 3.11h.
- Click in the attached unbound control, click and drag to select the text (Text 18), then type **Average GPA for Major** as the label for this control. Size, move, and align the label as shown in the figure.
- Point to the **Average GPA control**, click the **right mouse button** to display a shortcut menu, then click **Properties** to display the Properties dialog box.
- Click the **Format tab**. Change the format to **Fixed** and the number of decimal places to **2**. Close the Properties sheet.
- Click and drag the bottom of the Report Footer down to create space for the Report Footer. Press and hold the **Shift key** as you select the label and associated control in the Major (Group) footer. Click the **Copy Button**.
- Click in the Report Footer, then click the **Paste button** to copy the controls to the report footer. Click and drag both controls to align them under the corresponding controls in the Major footer.
- Change the text of the label in the Report Footer to reflect **all students** as shown in Figure 3.11h. Move and size the label as necessary.
- Save the report.

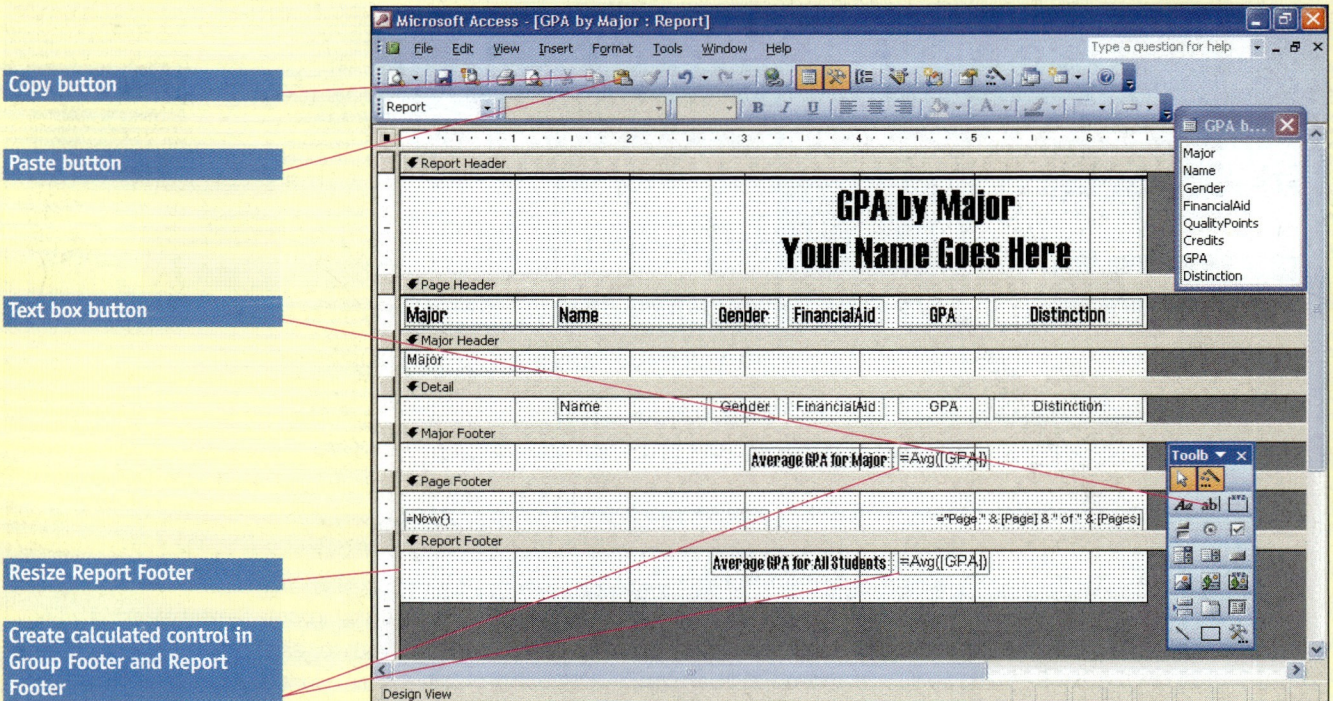

(h) Create the Group and Report Footers (step 8)

FIGURE 3.11 Hands-on Exercise 3 (*continued*)

Step 9: The Finishing Touches

- Click in the Report Header. Pull down the **Insert menu** and click the **Picture command** to display the Insert Picture dialog box. Change to the **Exploring Access folder**. Select the **Academic Symbols picture**, then click **OK**.

- **Right click** the picture to display a context-sensitive menu, then click **Properties** to display the Properties Dialog box. Click the **Size Mode property**, click the **down arrow**, and click **Stretch**. Close the Properties sheet.

- Click and drag to size the picture. Resize the Report Header as appropriate.

- Select the **GPA control** in the Detail section. Pull down the **Format menu** and click the **Conditional Formatting command** to display the associated dialog box.

- Enter the first condition as shown in Figure 3.11i. Click the **down arrow** on the font color button and click **blue**.

- Click the **Add button**, then enter the second condition, this time selecting a font color of **red**. Click **OK** to accept both conditions and close the dialog box.

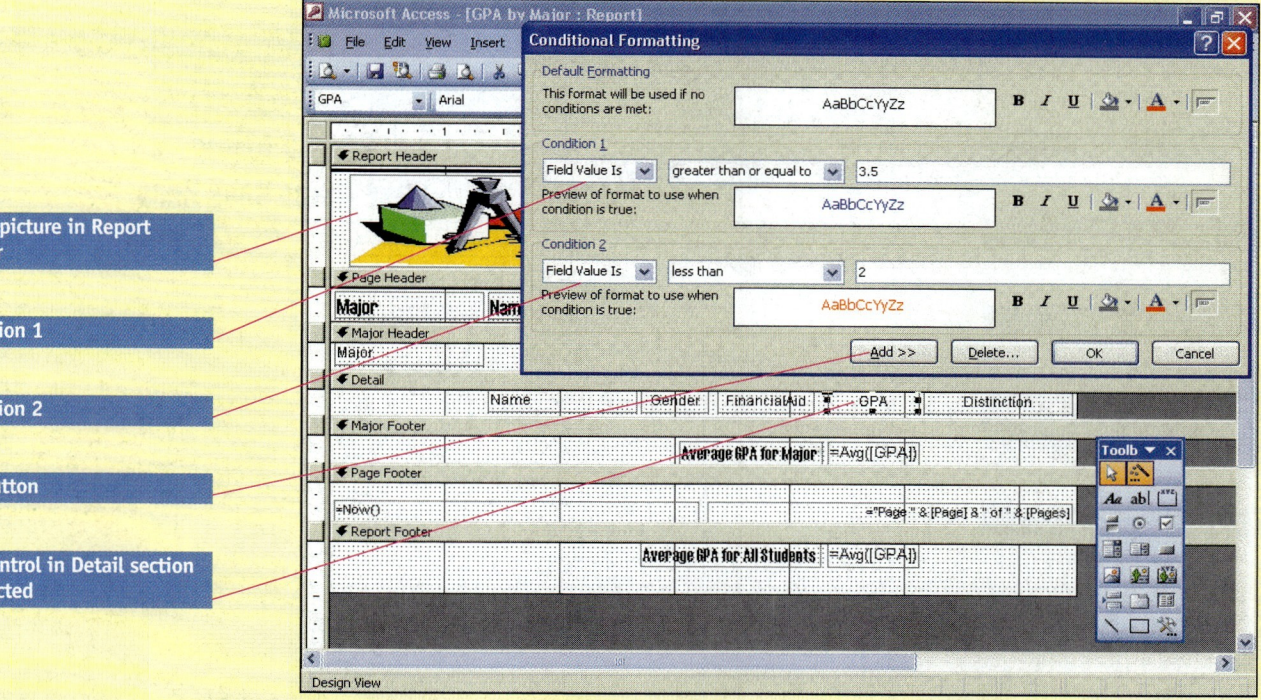

Insert picture in Report Header

Condition 1

Condition 2

Add button

GPA control in Detail section is selected

(i) The Finishing Touches (step 9)

FIGURE 3.11 Hands-on Exercise 3 (*continued*)

MISSING TASK PANE

The Insert Picture command functions differently in Access than in the other Office applications because it does not display the Clip Art task pane. You can still search for clip art explicitly, however, by starting the Clip Organizer as a separate application. Click the Start button, click the All Programs button, click Microsoft Office, click Microsoft Office Tools, then start the Microsoft Clip Organizer. Select a clip art image from within the Clip Organizer, and click the Copy button. Use the Windows taskbar to return to Access, open the form or report in Design view, and click the Paste button.

Step 10: The Completed Report

- Click the **Print Preview button** to view the completed report as shown in Figure 3.11j. The status bar shows you are on Page 1 of the report.

- Click the **Zoom button** to see the entire page. Click the **Zoom button** a second time to return to the higher magnification, which lets you read the report.

- Be sure that you are satisfied with the appearance of the report and that all controls align properly with their associated labels. If necessary, return to the Design view to modify the report.

- Pull down the **File menu** and click **Print** (or click the **Print button**) to display the Print dialog box. The **All option button** is already selected under Print Range. Click **OK** to print the report.

- Pull down the **File menu** and click **Close** to close the GPA by Major report. Click **Yes** if asked to save design changes to the report.

- Close the **Our Students database**. Exit Access if you do not want to continue with the next exercise at this time.

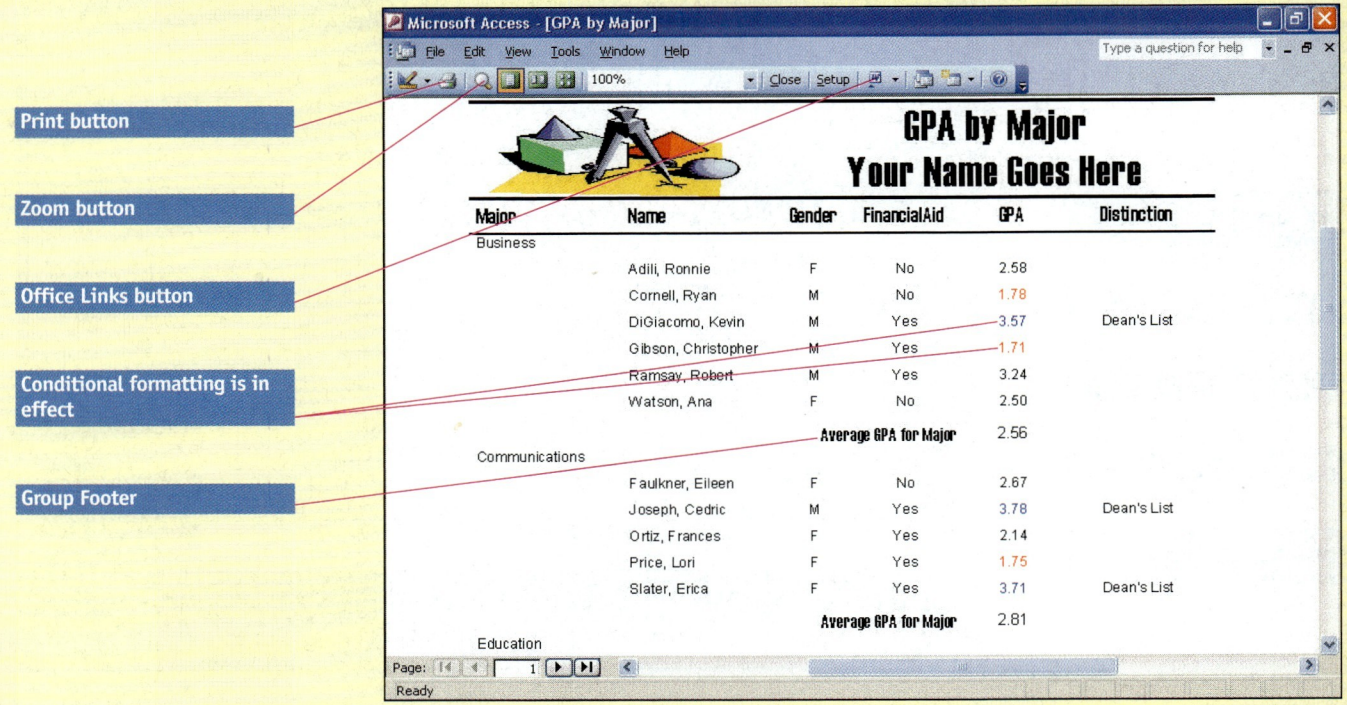

(j) The Completed Report (step 10)

FIGURE 3.11 Hands-on Exercise 3 (*continued*)

THE PRINT PREVIEW TOOLBAR

The Print Preview toolbar has several useful tools to preview a report. Click the One page, Two pages, or Multiple pages buttons, to see the indicated number of pages, and/or use the Zoom button to toggle between different magnifications. And finally, you can use the Office Links button to convert the report to a Word document or Excel workbook.

CROSSTAB QUERIES

A *crosstab query* consolidates data from an Access table and presents the information in a row and column format (similar to a pivot table in Excel). Figure 3.12 shows a crosstab query that displays the average GPA for all students by major and gender. A crosstab query aggregates (sums, counts, or averages) the values of one field (e.g., GPA), then groups the results according to the values of another field listed down the left side of the table (major), and a set of values listed across the top of the table (gender).

A crosstab query can be created in the Query Design view, but it is easier to use the Crosstab Query Wizard, as you will see in the next hands-on exercise. The wizard allows you to choose the table (or query) on which the crosstab query is based, then prompts you for the fields to be used for the row and column values (major and gender in our example). You then select the field that will be summarized (GPA), and choose the desired calculation (average). It's easy and you get a chance to practice in the hands-on exercise that follows shortly.

Major is in the rows

Gender is in the columns

Calculation is average GPA

Major	F	M
Business	2.54	2.66
Communications	2.57	3.78
Education		1.66
Engineering	3.50	3.25
Liberal Arts	2.41	2.80
Undecided	2.96	2.23

FIGURE 3.12 Crosstab Query

ACTION QUERIES

Queries are generally used to extract information from a database. A special type of query, however, known as an *action query*, enables you to update the database by changing multiple records in a single operation. There are four types of action queries: update, append, delete, and make-table.

An *update query* changes multiple records within a table. You could, for example, create an update query to raise the salary of every employee by 10 percent. You can also use criteria in the update query; for example, you can increase the salaries of only those employees with a specified performance rating.

An *append query* adds records from one table to the end of another table. It could be used in the context of the student database to add transfer students to the Students table, given that the transfer records were stored originally in a separate table. An append query can include criteria, so that it adds only selected records from the other table, such as those students with a designated GPA.

A *delete query* deletes one or more records from a table according to designated criteria. You could, for example, use a delete query to remove employees who are no longer working for a company, students who have graduated, or products that are no longer kept in inventory.

A *make-table query* creates a new table from records in an existing table. This type of query is especially useful prior to running a delete query in that you can back up (archive) the records you are about to delete. Thus, you could use a make-table query to create a table containing those students who are about to graduate (e.g., those with 120 credits or more), then run a delete query to remove the graduates from the Students table. You're ready for another hands-on exercise.

4   Crosstab and Action Queries

Objective   To use action queries to modify a database; to create a crosstab query to display summarized values from a table. Use Figure 3.13 as a guide in completing the exercise.

Step 1:   **Create the Make-Table Query**

■ Start Access and open the **Our Students database**. Click **Open** in response to the security warning. Click the **Queries button** in the Database window, then double click **Create query in Design view**.

■ The Show Table dialog box appears automatically with the Tables tab already selected. If necessary, select the **Students table**, then click the **Add button** to add the table to the query as shown in Figure 3.13a. Close the Show Table dialog box. Maximize the query window, then resize the top portion of the window as well as the field list.

■ Click the **SSN** (the first field) in the Students table. Press and hold the **Shift key**, then scroll (if necessary) until you can click **Major** (the last field) in the table. Click and drag the selected fields (i.e., every field in the table) from the field list to the design grid in Figure 3.13a.

■ Scroll in the design grid until you can see the Credits field. Click in the **Criteria row** for the Credits field and enter **>=120**.

■ Click the **drop-down arrow** next to the **Query Type button** on the toolbar and select (click) the **Make-Table query** as shown in Figure 3.13a. Enter **Graduating Seniors** as the name of the table you will create.

■ Verify that the option button for Current Database is selected, then click **OK**.

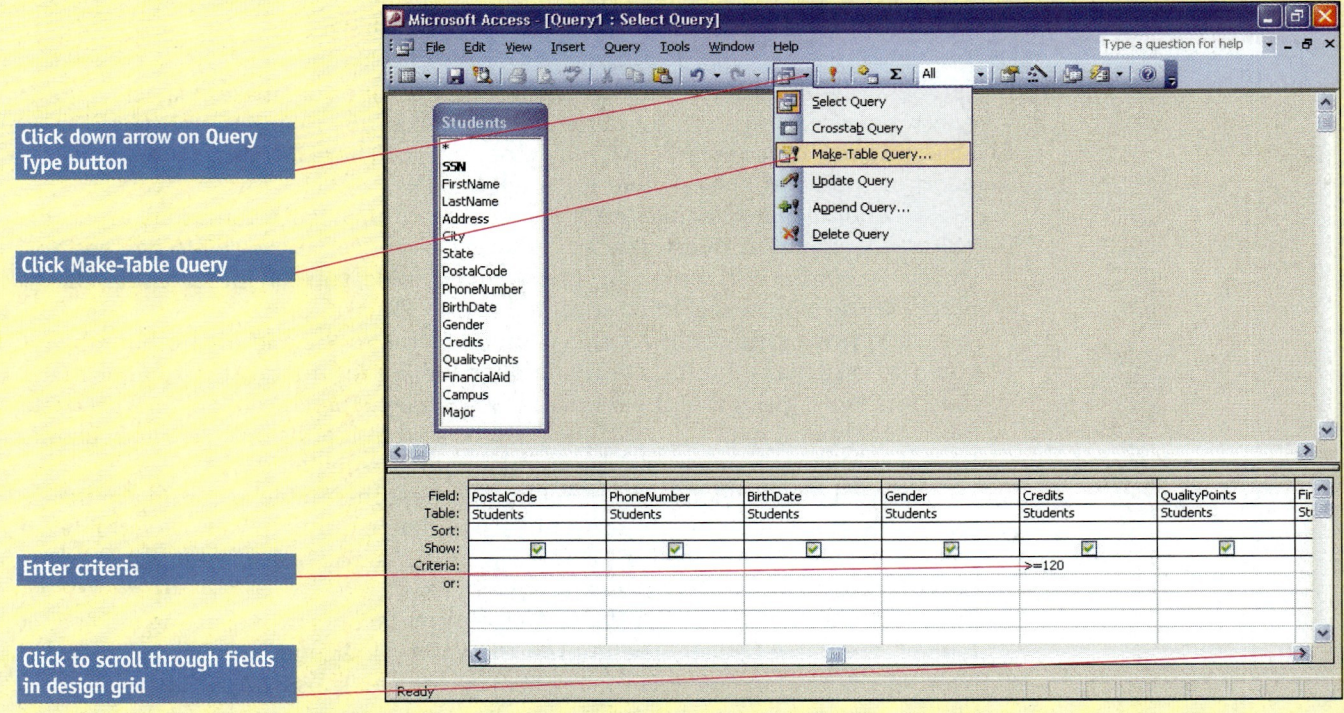

(a) Create the Make-Table Query (step 1)

FIGURE 3.13   Hands-on Exercise 4

Step 2: Run the Make-Table Query

- Click the **Run button** to run the Make-Table query. Click **Yes** in response to the message in Figure 3.13b indicating that you are about to paste one record (for the graduating seniors) into a new table.

- Do not be concerned if you do not see the Graduating Seniors table at this time; unlike a select query, you remain in the Design view after executing the Make-Table query.

- Close the Make-Table query. Save the query as **Archive Graduating Seniors**.

- Click the **Tables button** in the Database window, then open the **Graduating Seniors table** you just created. The table should contain one record (for Kim Zimmerman) with 120 or more credits.

- Close the table.

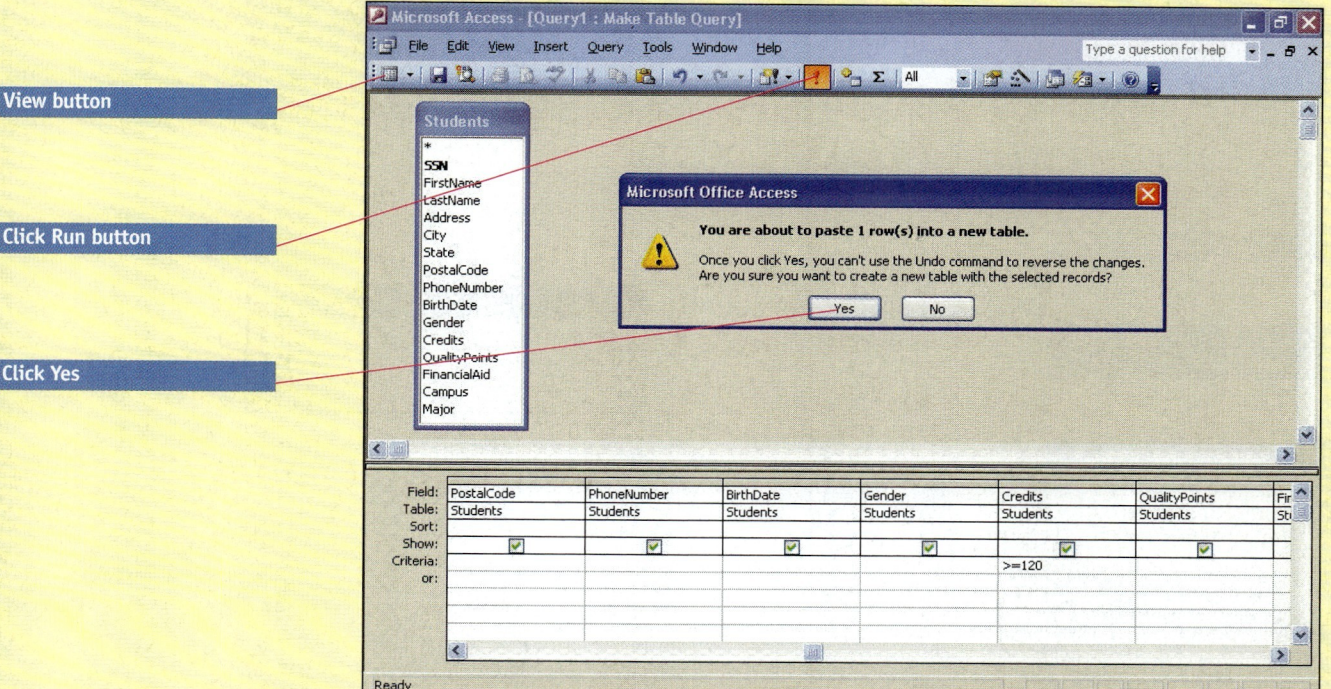

(b) Run the Make-Table Query (step 2)

FIGURE 3.13 Hands-on Exercise 4 (*continued*)

LOOK BEFORE YOU LEAP

The result of an action query is irreversible; that is, once you click Yes in the dialog box displayed by the query, you cannot undo the action. You can, however, preview the result before creating the query by clicking the View button at the left of the Query Design toolbar. Click the button and you see the results of the query displayed in a dynaset, then click the View button a second time to return to the Design view. Click the Run Query button to execute the query, but now you can click Yes with confidence since you have seen the result.

Step 3: **Create the Delete Query**

- Click the **Queries button** in the Database window, then click the **Archive Graduating Seniors query** to select the query.

- Pull down the **Edit menu** and click **Copy** to copy the query to the clipboard. (You can also click the Copy button on the Database toolbar.)

- Pull down the **Edit menu** a second time, then click the **Paste command** to display the Paste As dialog box in Figure 3.13c. (You can also click the Paste button on the Database toolbar.)

- Type **Purge Graduating Seniors** as the name of the query, then click **OK**.

- The Database window contains the original query (Archive Graduating Seniors) as well as the copied version (Purge Graduating Seniors) that you just created.

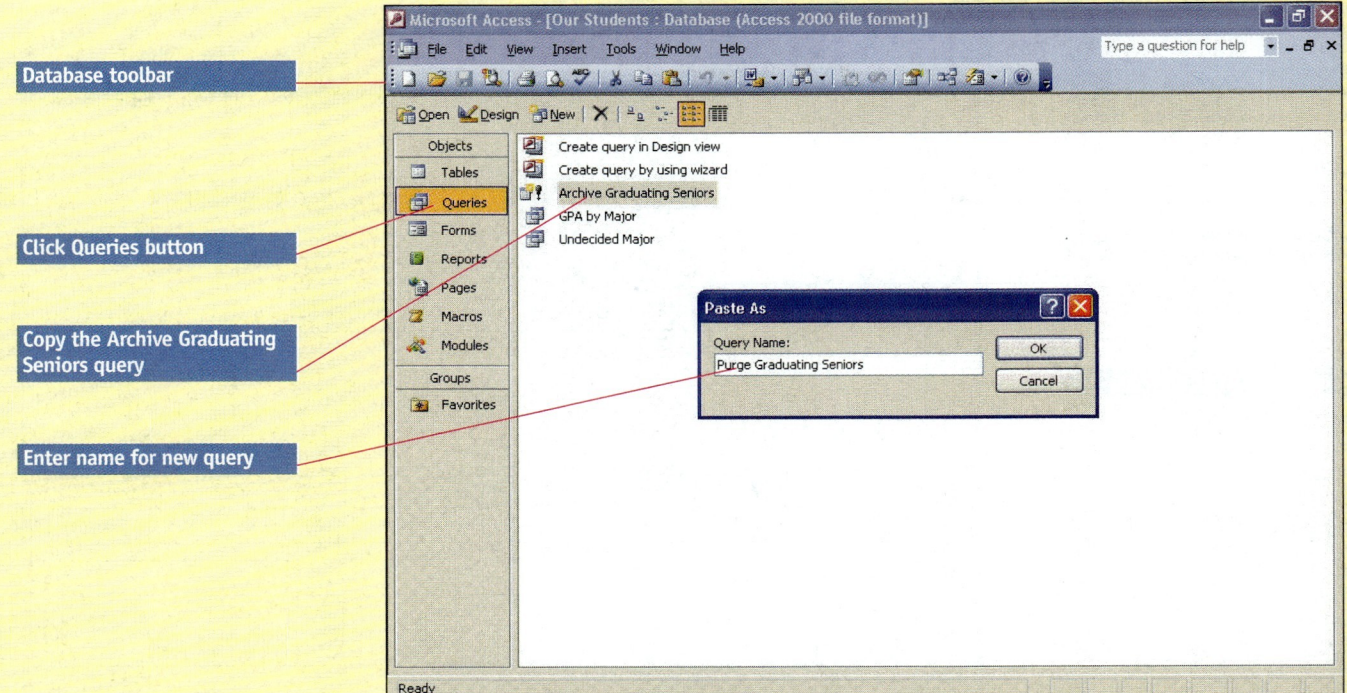

Database toolbar

Click Queries button

Copy the Archive Graduating Seniors query

Enter name for new query

(c) Create the Delete Query (step 3)

FIGURE 3.13 Hands-on Exercise 4 (*continued*)

COPY, RENAME, OR DELETE AN ACCESS OBJECT

Use the Copy and Paste commands in the Database window to copy any object in an Access database. To copy an object, select the object, pull down the Edit menu, and click Copy (or use the Ctrl+C keyboard shortcut). Pull down the Edit menu a second time and select the Paste command (or use the Ctrl+V shortcut), then enter a name for the copied object. To delete or rename an object, point to the object, then click the right mouse button to display a shortcut menu and select the desired operation.

Step 4: Complete and Run the Delete Query

■ Open the newly created query in the Design view. Maximize the window. Click the **drop-down arrow** next to the **Query Type button** on the toolbar and select (click) the **Delete Query**.

■ Click and drag the box on the horizontal scroll bar until you can see the **Credits field** as shown in Figure 3.13d. The criterion, >= 120, is already entered because the Delete query was copied originally from the Make-Table query, and the criteria are identical.

■ Click the **Run button** to execute the query. Click **Yes** when warned that you are about to delete one record from the specified table. Once again, you remain in the Design view after the query has been executed.

■ Close the Query window. Click **Yes** if asked to save the changes.

■ Open the **Students table**. The record for Kim Zimmerman is no longer there.

■ Close the Students table.

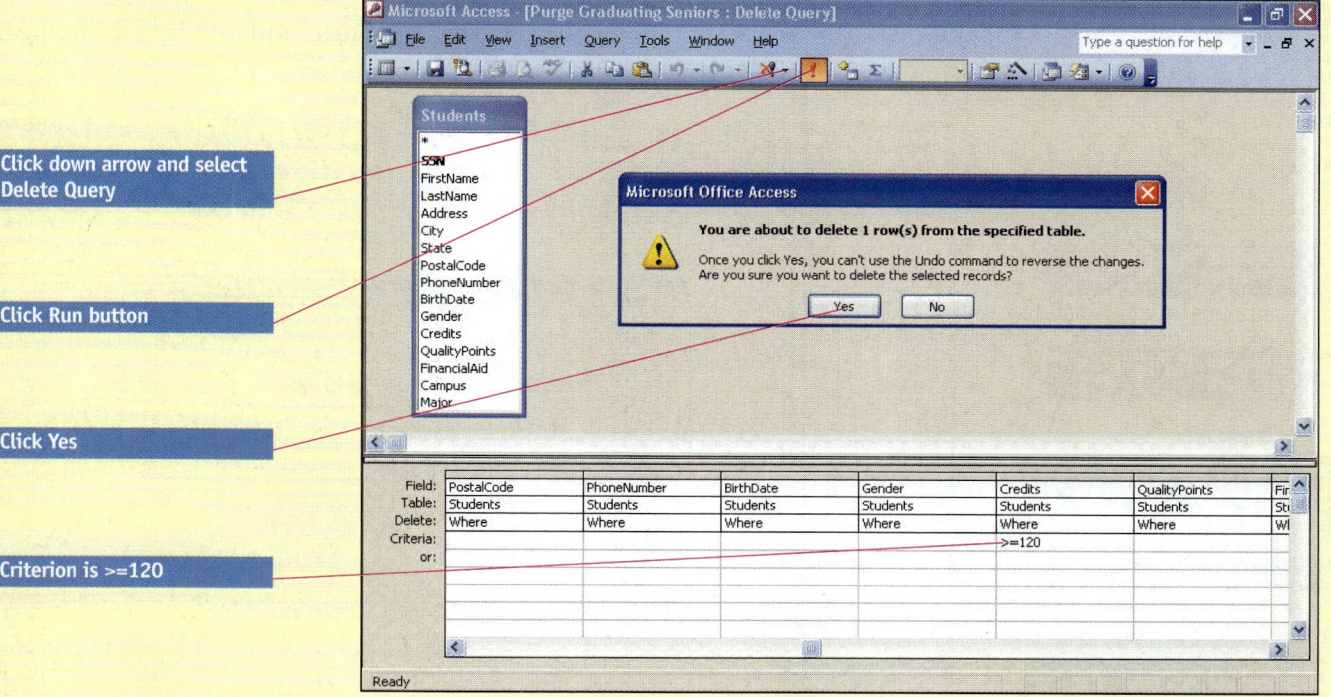

Click down arrow and select Delete Query

Click Run button

Click Yes

Criterion is >=120

(d) Complete and Run the Delete Query (step 4)

FIGURE 3.13 Hands-on Exercise 4 (*continued*)

PLAN FOR THE UNEXPECTED

Deleting records is cause for concern in that once the records are removed from a table, they cannot be restored. This may not be a problem, but it is comforting to have some means of recovery. Accordingly, we always execute a Make-Table query, with the identical criteria as in the Delete query, prior to running the latter. The deleted records from the original table can be restored through an Append query should it be necessary.

Step 5:   Create the Append Query

- Click the **Queries button**, then double click **Create query in Design view**. The Show Tables dialog box opens and contains the following tables:
    - ❑ The Students table that you have used throughout the chapter.
    - ❑ The Graduating Seniors table that you just created.
    - ❑ The Transfer Students table that will be appended to the Students table.

- Select the **Transfer Students table**, then click the **Add button** to add this table to the query. Close the Show Table dialog box. Maximize the window. Click and drag the **asterisk** from the field list to the **Field row** in the query design grid.

- Click the **drop-down arrow** next to the **Query Type button** on the toolbar and select (click) **Append Query** to display the Append dialog box. Click the **drop-down arrow** on the Append to Table Name list box and select the **Students table** as shown in Figure 3.13e. Click **OK**.

- Click the **Run button**. Click **Yes** when warned that you are about to add 4 rows (from the Transfer Students table) to the Students table.

- Save the query as **Append Transfer Students**. Close the query window.

- Open the **Students table**. Four records have been added (Liquer, Thomas, Rudolph, Milgrom). Close the table.

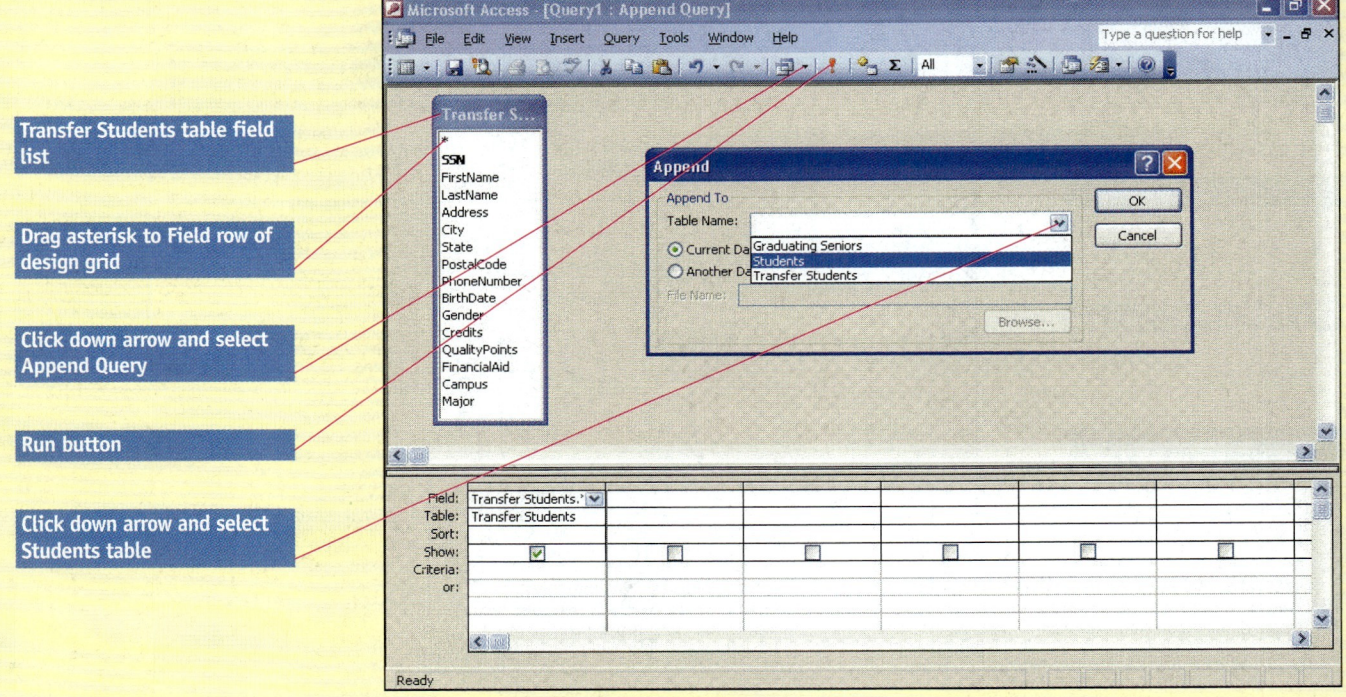

Transfer Students table field list

Drag asterisk to Field row of design grid

Click down arrow and select Append Query

Run button

Click down arrow and select Students table

(e) Create the Append Query (step 5)

FIGURE 3.13 Hands-on Exercise 4 (*continued*)

THE ASTERISK VERSUS INDIVIDUAL FIELDS

Click and drag the asterisk in the field list to the design grid to add every field in the underlying table to the query. The advantage to this approach is that it is quicker than selecting the fields individually. The disadvantage is that you cannot sort or specify criteria for individual fields.

Step 6: Create an Update Query

■ Click the **Queries button** in the Database window. Select (click) the **GPA by Major query**, press **Ctrl+C** to copy the query, then press **Ctrl+V** to display the Paste As dialog box. Enter **Update Financial Aid**. Click **OK**.

■ Open the newly created query in the Design view as shown in Figure 3.13f. Click the **drop-down arrow** next to the **Query Type button** on the toolbar and select (click) **Update Query**. The design grid changes to include an Update To row, and the Sort row disappears.

■ Click in the **Criteria row** for the **GPA field** and enter **>=3**. Click in the **Update To row** for the **FinancialAid field** and enter **Yes**. The combination of these entries will change the value of the Financial Aid field to "yes" for all students with a GPA of 3.00 or higher.

■ Click the **Run button** to execute the query. Click **Yes** when warned that you are about to update nine records. Close the query window.

■ Click **Yes** if asked whether to save the changes.

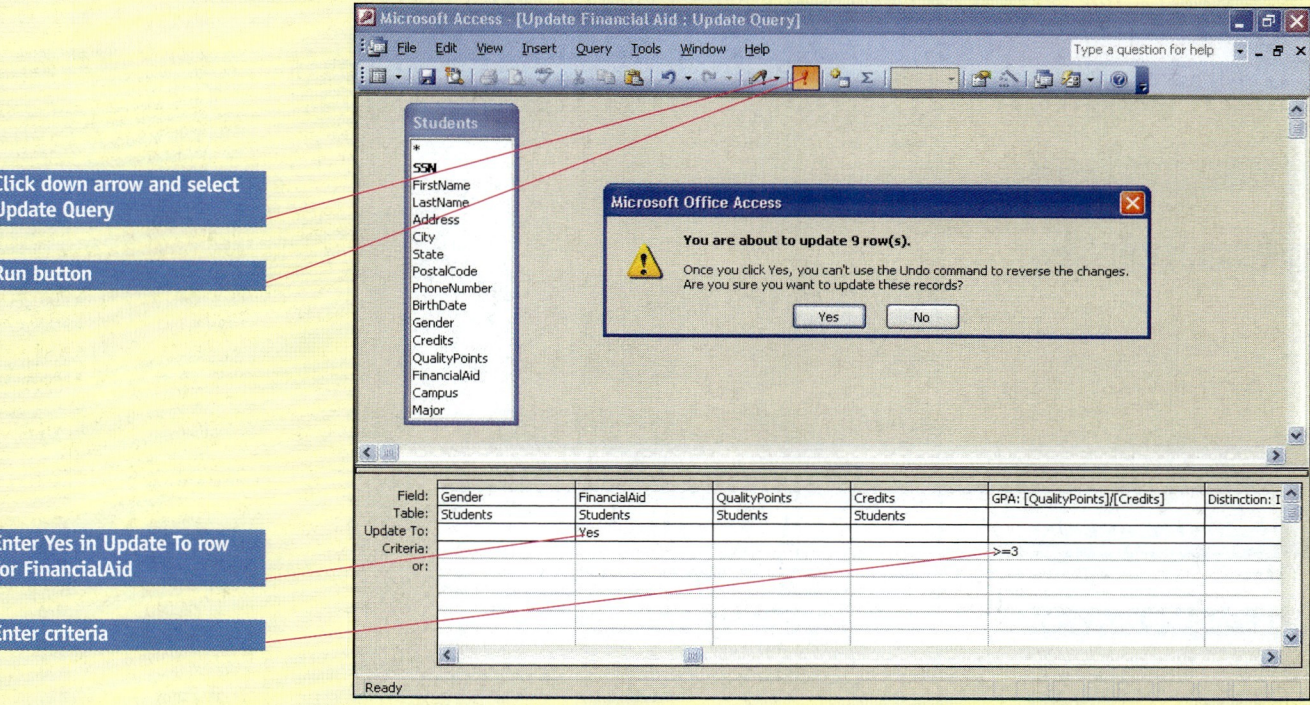

(f) Create an Update Query (step 6)

FIGURE 3.13 Hands-on Exercise 4 (*continued*)

VERIFY THE RESULTS OF THE UPDATE QUERY

You have run the Update Query, but are you sure it worked correctly? Press the F11 key to return to the Database window, click the Queries button, and rerun the GPA by Major query that was created earlier. Click in the GPA field for the first student, then click the Sort Descending button to display the students in descending order by GPA. Every student with a GPA of 3.00 or higher should be receiving financial aid.

Step 7: Check Results of the Action Queries

■ Click the **Tables button** in the Database window. Open (double click) the **Students, Graduating Seniors**, and **Transfer Students tables** one after another. You have to return to the Database window each time you open a table.

■ Pull down the **Window menu** and click the **Tile Vertically command** to display the tables as shown in Figure 3.13g. The arrangement of your tables may be different from ours.

■ Check your progress by comparing the tables to one another:
   ❑ Check the first record in the Transfer Students table, Lindsey Liquer, and note that it has been added to the Students table via the Append Transfer Students query.
   ❑ Check the record in the Graduating Seniors table, Kim Zimmerman, and note that it has been removed from the Students table via the Purge Graduating Seniors query.
   ❑ The Students table reflects the current student database. The other two tables function as backup.

■ Close the Students, Transfer Students, and Graduating Seniors tables.

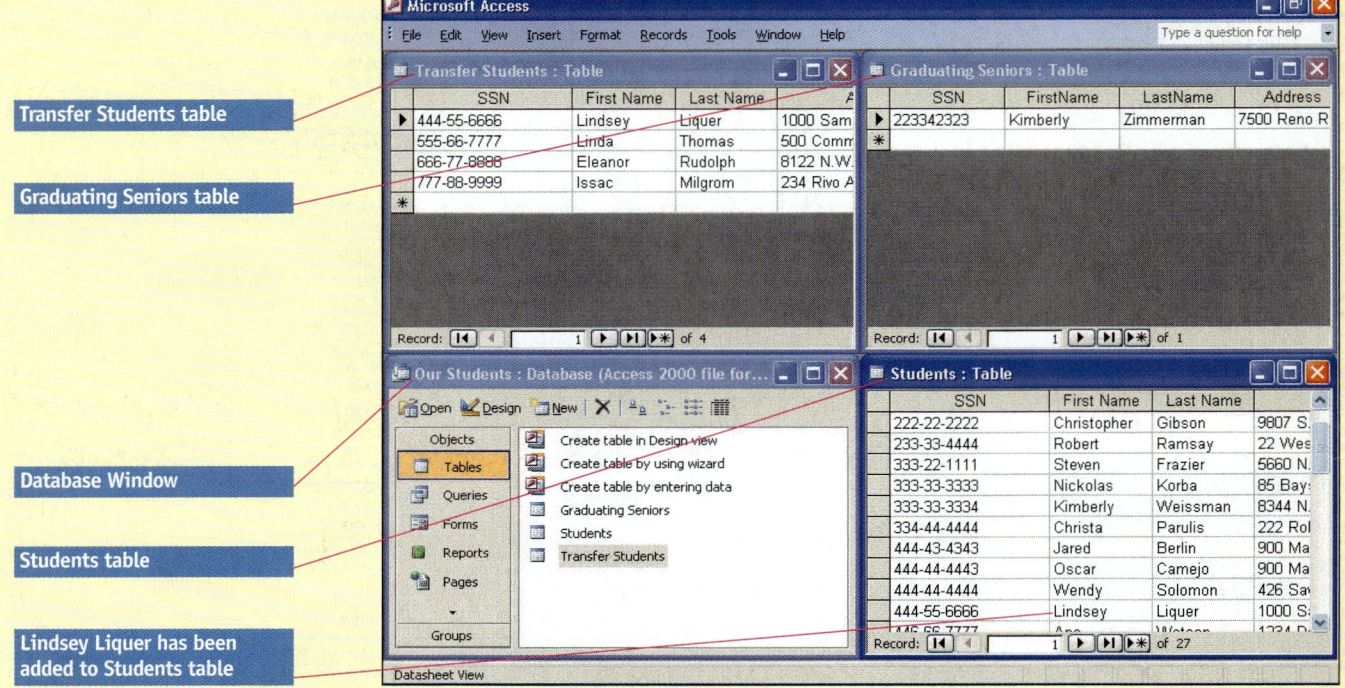

(g) Check Results of the Action Queries (step 7)

FIGURE 3.13 Hands-on Exercise 4 *(continued)*

DATABASE PROPERTIES

The buttons within the Database window display the objects within a database, but show only one type of object at a time. You can, for example, see all of the reports or all of the queries, but you cannot see the reports and queries at the same time. There is another way. Pull down the File menu, click Database Properties, then click the Contents tab to display the contents (objects) in the database.

Step 8: Create a Crosstab Query

- Click the **Queries button** in the Database window, click **New**, click the **Crosstab Query Wizard** in the New Query dialog box, and click **OK** to start the wizard.

- Click the **Queries option button** and select the **GPA by Major query**. Click **Next** to continue.
  - ❑ Click **Major** in the Available Fields list, then click **>** to place it in the Selected Fields list. Click **Next**.
  - ❑ Click **Gender** as the field for column headings. Click **Next**.
  - ❑ Click **GPA** as the field to calculate and select the **Avg function** as shown in Figure 3.13h. Clear the check box to include row sums. Click **Next**.
  - ❑ The name of the query is suggested for you, as is the option button to view the query. Click **Finish**.

- The results of the crosstab query are shown. The query lists the average GPA for each combination of major and gender. The display is awkard, however, in that the GPA is calculated to an unnecessary number of decimal places.

- Click the **View button** to display the Design view for this query. Right click in the **GPA column** to display a context-sensitive menu, click **Properties** to display the Field Properties dialog box, click in the **Format row**, and select **Fixed**. Set the number of decimals to **two**.

- Click the **Run button** to re-execute the query. This time the GPA is displayed to two decimal places. Save the query. Close the Query window.

- Close the Our Students database.

- Exit Access.

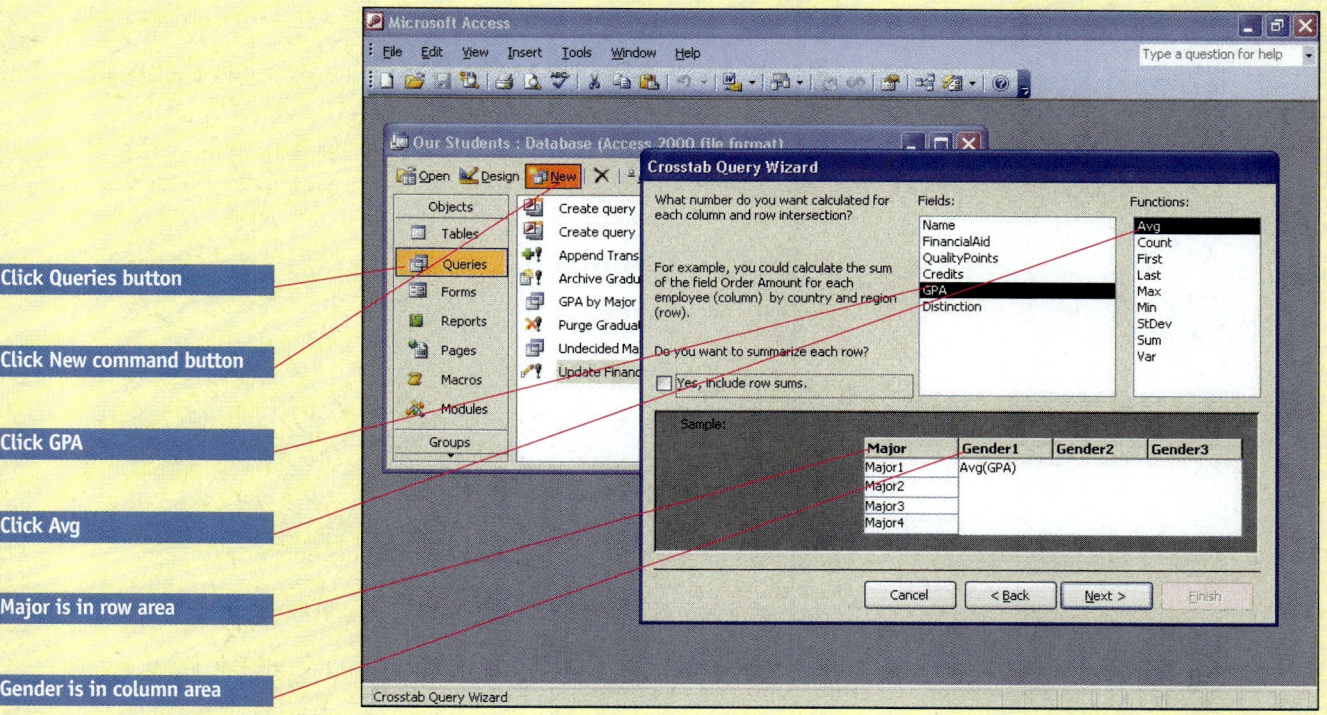

Click Queries button

Click New command button

Click GPA

Click Avg

Major is in row area

Gender is in column area

(h) Create a Crosstab Query (step 8)

FIGURE 3.13 Hands-on Exercise 4 (*continued*)

SUMMARY

Data and information are not synonymous although the terms are often interchanged. Data is the raw material and consists of the table (or tables) that comprise a database. Information is the finished product. Data is converted to information by selecting records, performing calculations on those records, and/or changing the sequence in which the records are displayed. Decisions in an organization are based on information rather than raw data.

A report is a printed document that displays information from the database. Reports are created through the Report Wizard, then modified as necessary in the Design view. A report is divided into sections. The Report Header (Footer) occurs at the beginning (end) of the report. The Page Header (Footer) appears at the top (bottom) of each page. The Detail section is found in the main body of the report and is printed once for each record in the report.

Each section is composed of objects known as controls. A bound control has a data source such as a field in the underlying table. An unbound control has no data source. A calculated control contains an expression. Controls are selected, moved, and sized the same way as any other Windows object.

Every report is based on either a table or a query. A report based on a table contains every record in that table. A report based on a query contains only the records satisfying the criteria in the query.

A query enables you to select records from a table (or from several tables), display the selected records in any order, and perform calculations on fields within the query. A select query is the most common type of query. It is created using the Simple Query Wizard and/or in Design view. A select query displays its output in a dynaset that can be used to update the data in the underlying table(s).

The records in a report are often grouped according to the value of a specific field within the record. A Group Header appears before each group to identify the group. A Group Footer appears at the end of each group and can be used to display the summary information about the group.

An action query modifies one or more records in a single operation. There are four types of action queries: update, append, delete, and make-table. An update query changes multiple records within a table. An append query adds records from one table to the end of another table. A delete query deletes one or more records from a table according to designated criteria. A make-table query creates a new table from records in an existing table.

A crosstab query displays aggregated information, as opposed to individual records. It can be created directly in the Query Design view, but is created more easily through the Crosstab Query Wizard.

KEY TERMS

Action query 143	Detail section 108	Query window 124
AND operator 121	Dynaset 118	Relational operators 122
Append query 143	Field row 118	Report 106
Ascending sequence 118	Filter (with form) 129	Report Footer 108
Avg function 131	Group Footer 108	Report Header 108
Between operator 122	Group Header 108	Report Wizard 106
Bound control 110	Immediate IF function 130	Select query 118
Calculated control 110	Like operator 122	Show row 118
Columnar report 106	Make-table query 143	Simple Query Wizard 118
Concatenate 130	Max function 131	Sort row 118
Conditional formatting 131	Min function 131	Sorting and Grouping 139
Count function 131	NOT operator 122	Sum function 131
Criteria row 118	OR operator 121	Tabular report 106
Crosstab query 143	Page Footer 108	Top Values property 134
Delete query 143	Page Header 108	Unbound control 110
Descending sequence 118	Print Preview 142	Update query 143
Design grid 120	Query 118	

MULTIPLE CHOICE

1. Why might a report be based on a query rather than a table?

   (a) To limit the report to selected records
   (b) To include a calculated field in the report
   (c) Both (a) and (b)
   (d) Neither (a) nor (b)

2. An Access database may contain:

   (a) One or more tables
   (b) One or more queries
   (c) One or more reports
   (d) All of the above

3. Which of the following is true regarding the names of objects within an Access database?

   (a) A form or report may have the same name as the underlying table
   (b) A form or report may have the same name as the underlying query
   (c) Both (a) and (b)
   (d) Neither (a) nor (b)

4. The dynaset created by a query may contain:

   (a) A subset of records from the associated table
   (b) A subset of fields from the associated table for every record
   (c) Both (a) and (b)
   (d) Neither (a) nor (b)

5. Which toolbar contains a button to display the properties of a selected object?

   (a) The Query Design toolbar
   (b) The Report Design toolbar
   (c) Both (a) and (b)
   (d) Neither (a) nor (b)

6. Which of the following does *not* have a Design view and a Datasheet view?

   (a) Tables
   (b) Forms
   (c) Queries
   (d) Reports

7. Which of the following is true regarding the wild card character?

   (a) A question mark stands for a single character in the same position as the question mark
   (b) An asterisk stands for any number of characters in the same position as the asterisk
   (c) Both (a) and (b)
   (d) Neither (a) nor (b)

8. Which of the following will print at the top of every page?

   (a) Report header
   (b) Group header
   (c) Both (a) and (b)
   (d) Neither (a) nor (b)

9. Which of the following must be present in every report?

   (a) A report header and a report footer
   (b) A page header and a page footer
   (c) Both (a) and (b)
   (d) Neither (a) nor (b)

10. A query, based on the Our Students database within the chapter, contains two fields from the Student table (QualityPoints and Credits) as well as a calculated field (GPA). Which of the following is true?

    (a) Changing the value of Credits or QualityPoints in the query's dynaset automatically changes these values in the underlying table
    (b) Changing the value of GPA automatically changes its value in the underlying table
    (c) Both (a) and (b)
    (d) Neither (a) nor (b)

... continued

multiple choice

11. Which of the following may be included in a report as well as in a form?

    (a) Bound control

    (b) Unbound control

    (c) Calculated control

    (d) All of the above

12. The navigation buttons ▶ and ◀ will:

    (a) Move to the next or previous record in a table

    (b) Move to the next or previous page in a report

    (c) Both (a) and (b)

    (d) Neither (a) nor (b)

13. Assume that you created a query based on an Employee table, and that the query contains fields for Location and Title. Assume further that there is a single criteria row and that New York and Manager have been entered under the Location and Title fields, respectively. The dynaset will contain:

    (a) All employees in New York

    (b) All managers

    (c) Only the managers in New York

    (d) All employees in New York and all managers

14. You have decided to modify the query from the previous question to include a second criteria row. The Location and Title fields are still in the query, but this time New York and Manager appear in *different* criteria rows. The dynaset will contain:

    (a) All employees in New York

    (b) All managers

    (c) Only the managers in New York

    (d) All employees in New York and all managers

15. Which of the following is true about a query that lists employees by city and alphabetically within city?

    (a) The design grid should specify a descending sort on both city and employee name

    (b) The City field should appear to the left of the employee name in the design grid

    (c) Both (a) and (b)

    (d) Neither (a) nor (b)

16. Which of the following is *not* an example of an action query?

    (a) Delete query

    (b) Append query

    (c) Select query

    (d) Make-table query

17. You want to create a query that will select all managers in New York earning less than $80,000, and all managers in San Francisco earning less than $60,000. How many criteria rows will you need in the Design grid?

    (a) 1

    (b) 2

    (c) 3

    (d) 4

18. Which of the following expressions will display a student's last name, a comma and a space, followed by the student's first name?

    (a) LastName, FirstName

    (b) "LastName, FirstName"

    (c) LastName & ", " & FirstName

    (d) LastName, " " FirstName

ANSWERS

1. c		**7.** c		**13.** c	
2. d		**8.** d		**14.** d	
3. c		**9.** d		**15.** b	
4. c		**10.** a		**16.** c	
5. d		**11.** d		**17.** b	
6. d		**12.** c		**18.** c	

PRACTICE WITH ACCESS

1. **The Oscars:** Figure 3.14 displays the first of three reports that you are to create for the Oscars database, which was introduced in Chapter 1. Your first task is to update the database to include the additional awards (if any) since the publication of our text. Open the *Chapter 1 Practice 1* database, open the existing form, and go to the last record to see if the data is current. If not, go to the Oscars Web site (www.oscar.com) to obtain the winners in the six major categories—Best Picture, Best Director, Best Actor and Actress, and Best Supporting Actor and Actress—for any years that are not in the database. You can then create the required reports. Proceed as follows:

   a. Use the Report Wizard to create the report in Figure 3.14, which is based on the Awards Winners table. The wizard creates a basic report with four sections—the Report Header, Page Header, Detail, and Page Footer. It will ask whether you want to group the records (no) and whether to sort the records (select year, then click the Ascending button to change to a descending sort.) Choose any layout, style, and title when prompted.

   b. Exit the wizard and go to Design view. You do not have to duplicate our design exactly, but you are to use a clip art image in the Report Header. The width of your report should not exceed 6½ inches. Close the report.

   c. Go to the Database window and select the report that you just created. Press Ctrl+C to copy the report, then press Ctrl+V to display the Paste As dialog box. Enter *Best Actor and Actress* as the name of the new report.

   d. Open *Best Actor and Actress* report in Design view (which currently has the best picture and director information). Change the labels in the Report and Page Headers as necessary. Delete the Best Picture and Best Director controls from the Detail section. Pull down the View menu and click the Field List command to display the Award Winners table. Click and drag the BestActor control to its appropriate place in the Detail section, then delete the associated label. Click and drag the BestActress control in similar fashion. Move and size the controls as needed.

   e. Close the report. Return to the Database window. Copy the *Best Actor and Actress* report that you just created to a new *Best Supporting Actor and Actress* report, then modify that report accordingly. Print all three reports for your instructor.

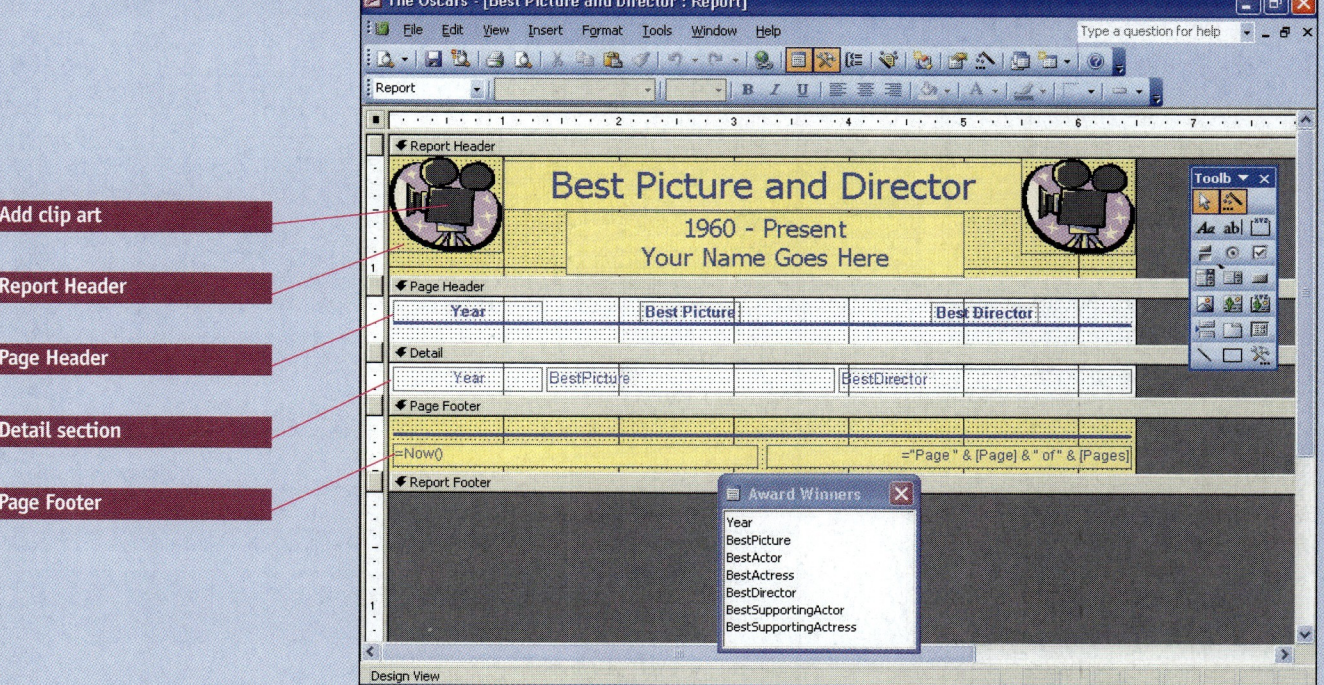

FIGURE 3.14 The Oscars (exercise 1)

2. **The United States:** The report in Figure 3.15 contains one example of every type of report section (a Report Header and Report Footer, a Page Header and Page footer, a Group header and Group footer, and a Detail section). It is based on the United States database from Chapter 1, and it computes the population and area totals for each region of the country. The report also contains a population density field that divides a state's population by its area. Open the *Chapter 1 Practice 3* database and proceed as follows:

a. Use the Report Wizard to create the report in Figure 3.15, which is based on the Population Density query that is already in the database. The report is to be sorted by region and then sorted by the name of each state within each region. Click the Summary Options button (in the same step where you specify the sorting sequence), check the boxes to sum the Population and Area fields, and click the option button for Detail and Summary information. Check the box to adjust field width so that all fields fit on one page. Choose a stepped layout and soft gray as the style. Name the report United States by Region, click the option button to modify the report's design, then click Finish.

b. You will see a report similar to Figure 3.15, but there is a lot of work to do. Start in the Region footer and change the contents to match Figure 3.15. You will have to delete an existing label, add new labels, increase font sizes, and move and align the various controls. You will have to further modify the footer so that it displays the average population density for each region. Click the Text Box tool, create an unbound control, then click in the control and enter the formula, =Sum([Population])/Sum([Area]). Click the button to preview the report. If you entered the formula correctly, the density for the Middle Atlantic region should be 396.54 (after you change the formatting properties of the control).

c. Enter a similar control =Sum([Population])/Sum([Area]) in the Report Footer to compute the population density for the country as a whole.

d. Change the formatting of the report and/or the contents of the various labels as you see fit. You do not have to match our design exactly, but be sure to add your name to the Report Header. Print the completed report for your instructor. The width of the report should not exceed 6½ inches.

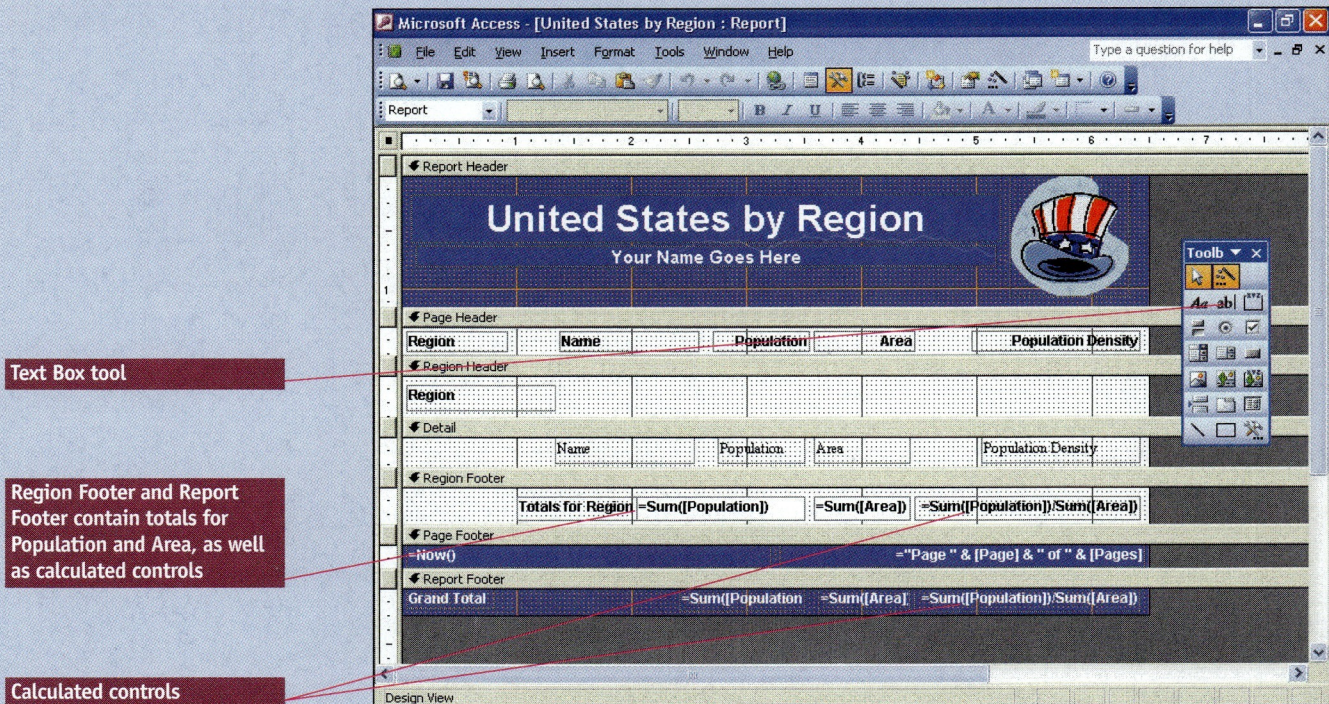

Text Box tool

Region Footer and Report Footer contain totals for Population and Area, as well as calculated controls

Calculated controls

FIGURE 3.15 The United States (exercise 2)

3. **The Super Bowl:** Figure 3.16 displays a History of the Super Bowl report that will be the basis of two subsequent reports that you will create in this exercise. Your first task is to update the database to include the additional games (if any) since the publication of our text. The database was introduced in Chapter 2 when we asked you to create a Web page for data entry. Proceed as follows:

a. Open the *Chapter 2 Practice 3* database, open the existing table, and see if the data is current. If not, go to the Super Bowl Web site (www.superbowl.com) to obtain the results for any years that are not in the database.

b. Go to the Database window. Click the Reports button. Modify the existing History of the Super Bowl report to include your name. Print this report.

c. Click the Queries Button. Select the History of the Super Bowl query, press Ctrl+C to copy the query, then press Ctrl+V to display the Paste As dialog box. Enter Biggest Blowouts as the name of the query, then open the query in Design view. Change the sort sequence to display the records in descending sequence by margin of victory. Click in the Margin column, then click the down arrow on the Top Value list box and choose 5 (to list the five games with the highest margin.) Run the query to be sure it is correct.

d. Click the Reports button. Select the History of the Super Bowl report, press Ctrl+C to copy the report, then press Ctrl+V to display the Paste As dialog box. Enter Biggest Blowouts as the name of the report. Open the report in Design view. Change the report properties so that the report is based on the Biggest Blowouts query. (Right click the Report Selector box in the upper left corner, click Properties to display the property sheet for the report as a whole, and click the All tab. Click the down arrow in the Record Source box and select the Biggest Blowouts query. Close the property sheet.) Change the report title to The Super Bowl's Biggest Blowouts. Print this report for your instructor.

e. Repeat the process in steps (c) and (d) to create a query and associated report that shows the games in which your favorite team participated. Print this report. Add a cover sheet, then submit all three reports (History of the Super Bowl, Biggest Blowouts, and My Favorite Team) to your instructor.

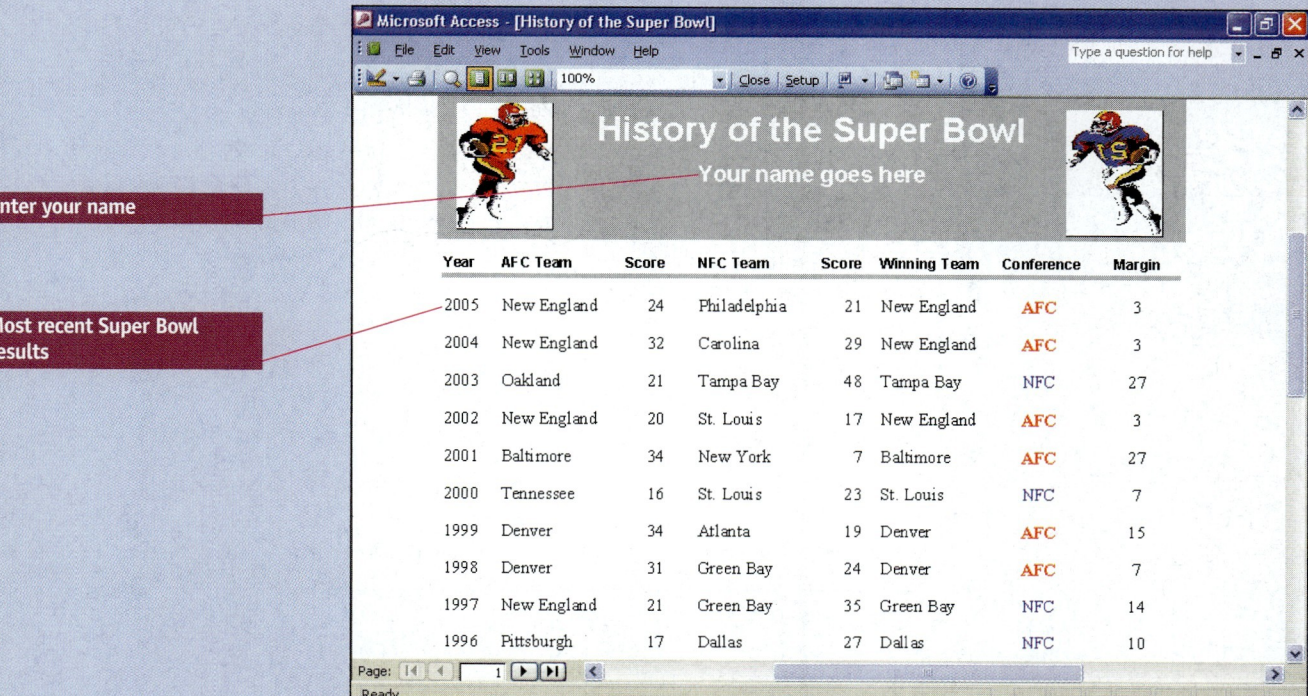

FIGURE 3.16 The Super Bowl (exercise 3)

4. **The Shopping Mall:** The partially completed *Chapter 3 Practice 4* database contains our version of the Shopping Mall database from Chapter 2. You will find a Stores table with 10 to 15 records, a form to enter data, and a form that describes the Shopping Mall database. Your assignment is to create the various reports that are described below. Each of the reports is based on an underlying query that contains a calculated control, selection criteria, and/or a sorting sequence. You should create the query first, display the associated dynaset to be sure the information is correct, then proceed to create the report. Use the Report Wizard to create the initial report, then modify the result in Design view. Proceed as follows:

a. Create the report in Figure 3.17 that lists all stores with a monthly rental greater than $5,000. The stores are to be listed in descending order of the monthly rent. Your report should contain all of the fields that appear in our report, but you need not match the design.

b. Create a report that shows all stores whose leases end in 2005. The stores are to be listed in chronological order by the ending date, with the earliest date shown first. Use the same design for your report as in Figure 3.17 and include all of the following fields: StoreID, StoreName, StoreType, LeaseStartDate, and LeaseEndDate.

c. Create a report that displays all clothing stores in alphabetical order. Include the store revenue, monthly rent, manager's name, and phone number.

d. Create a report listing those stores for which no manager has been assigned. List the stores in alphabetical order by the name of the store. The report should include the StoreID, the name of the store, whether or not it is a franchise, and the lease start and end dates.

e. Print each of the reports and turn them in to your instructor. You may need to change the page orientation and/or margins to ensure that each report fits on one page. Add a cover sheet to complete the assignment.

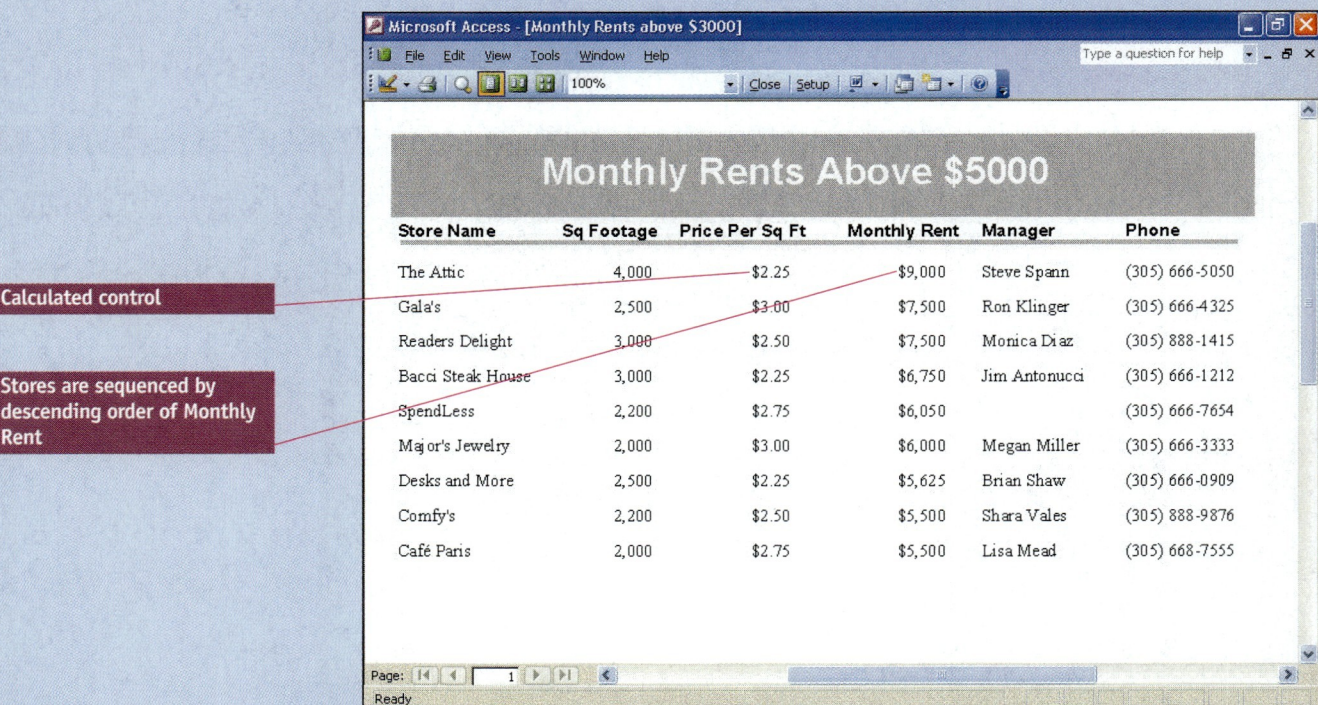

FIGURE 3.17 The Shopping Mall (exercise 4)

5. **Best Realty:** The partially completed *Chapter 3 Practice 5* database contains our version of the Best Realty database from Chapter 2. You will find a Property table with 10 to 15 records, a form to enter data, and a form that describes the Best Realty database. Your assignment is to create the various reports that are described below:

   a. The report in Figure 3.18 that shows all properties that have been sold to date. The report is based on a query that contains two calculated fields: the price per square foot (based on the selling price, as opposed to the asking price) and the number of days that the property was on the market. Your report should contain all of the fields that appear in our report, but you need not match the design.

   b. A report listing properties with an asking price of more than $250,000. The properties are to be listed from most expensive to least expensive. Include the Asking Price, PropertyID, Address, Agent's Last Name, Property Type, and Date Listed. This report should contain only properties that are available (i.e., properties that have not been sold).

   c. A report listing the available properties that are on the water. List the properties in alphabetical order by the owner's last name. Include in the report the owner's last name, the address, the asking price, the number of bedrooms and bathrooms, and whether or not the property has a pool.

   d. A report listing the available properties that have more than 3 bedrooms. List the properties in order from the one with the most to fewest bedrooms. The report should include the number of bedrooms, the agent's last name, the address, the property type, the garage information, and the date listed.

   e. Choose a different format for each report to experiment with the different designs that are available. You may need to change the page orientation and/or margins to ensure that each report fits on one page.

   f. Print each of the reports and turn them in to your instructor. Add a cover sheet to complete the assignment.

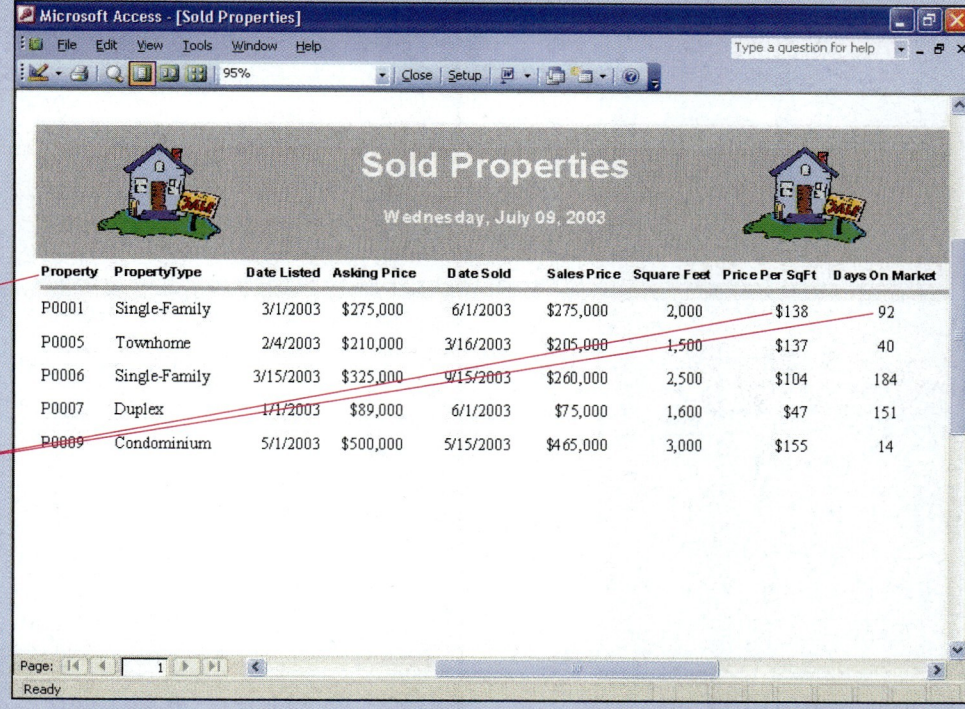

FIGURE 3.18 Best Realty (exercise 5)

6. **The Fishing Pole:** The partially completed *Chapter 3 Practice 6* database builds on an earlier example from Chapter 2. Your present assignment is to create the various reports that are described below, each of which requires its own query. We provide a Customers table with 60 records. Proceed as follows:

   a. Create a report similar to Figure 3.19 that lists all customers whose initial purchase was more than $500. The customers are to be listed in descending order of the initial purchase amount. Your report should contain all of the fields that appear in our report, but you need not match our design exactly. We suggest you start with the Report Wizard, and then modify the report in Design view.

   b. Create a report that shows all customers who own a fishing boat, listing the customers in alphabetical order by last name. Your report should include the customer's first and last name, the boat type, phone number, store account, and an indication of whether the customer is a yacht club member.

   c. Create a report that displays all the long-term customers (people who have been customers for at least two years). This report is based on an underlying query that contains a calculated field to determine the number of years since the customer's initial purchase. (You will need to use the Integer function to truncate the decimal portion of the field. Use the function Int((Now()-[InitialPurchaseDate])/365)to determine the number of years.) The report should include the customer's name, address (on two lines), and initial purchase date, as well as the number of years since the initial purchase.

   d. Create a report that groups customers by mailing list priority. List the customers in alphabetical order by last name within each group. (The mailing list priority will appear in the group header.) The Detail section should include the customer's number, name, address, city, state, zip code, and phone number.

   e. Print each of the reports and turn them in to your instructor. Change the page orientation and/or margins if necessary to ensure that all of the fields for one record fit on one page.

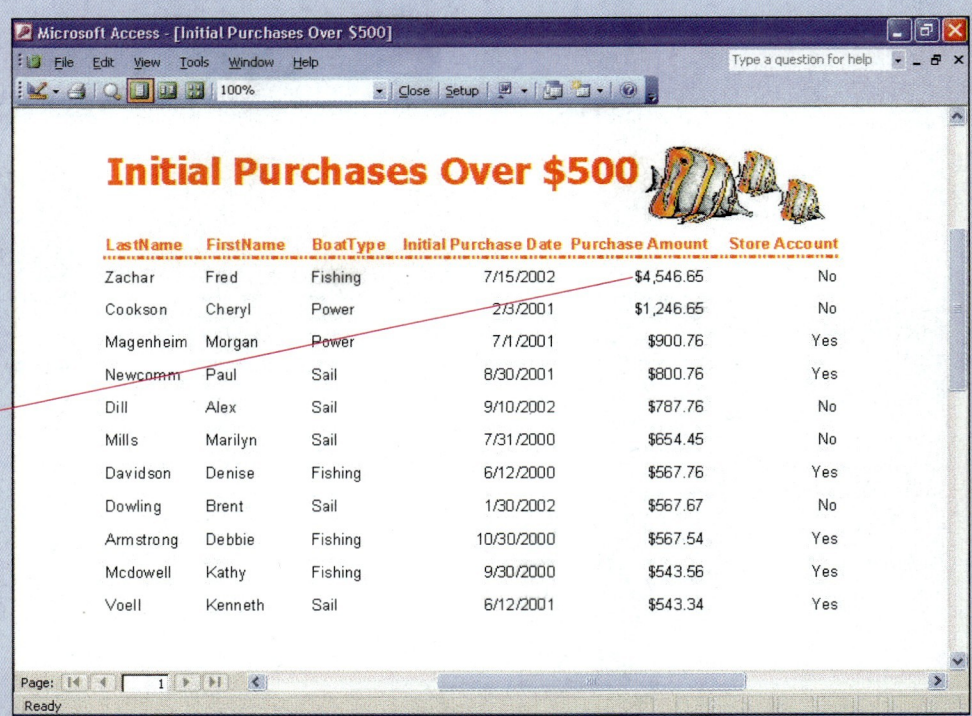

FIGURE 3.19 The Fishing Pole (exercise 6)

7. **Salary Increases:** The report in Figure 3.20 displays salary information for employees grouped by the location where they work. The easiest way to create this report is to use the Report Wizard, then modify the result in the Design view as necessary. You don't have to match our design exactly, but you are to include the identical information in your report. Proceed as follows:

a. Open the *Chapter 3 Practice 7* database in the Exploring Access folder. Use the Report Wizard to create the initial version of the report in Figure 3.20. Group the data by location, and sort the records by last name. Do not specify summary options at this time. Choose a stepped layout and any style that appeals to you.

b. Go to the Design view. Pull down the View menu, click the Sorting and Grouping command, select Location in the Field/Expression list box, then click Yes to display the Group Footer. Click in the location footer, then use the Text box to add an unbound control with the formula, =Sum(Salary). Change the label of the control to "Total Salaries for Location". Copy these controls to the Report Footer.

c. Add clip art to the Report Header. You can copy the clip art that appears in the Report Header from either the Employees form or the Employee Census report that is included in the database. Open either object in Design view, select the clip art, and click the Copy button. Open the Employee by Location report in Design view, click in the Report Header, click the Paste button, then move and size the image as necessary. Save the report. Print the report.

d. Create a parallel report that displays employees by title rather than location. The easiest way to create this report is to copy the location report, then modify the copied report as necessary. Go to the Database window and click the Reports button. Select the Employees by Location report. Press Ctrl+C to copy the report, then press Ctrl+V to duplicate the report as Employees by Title.

e. Open the Employees by Title report in Design view. Pull down the View menu, click the Sorting and Grouping command, and change the grouping order from location to title. Modify the report title, column headings, and bound controls within the report as necessary. Save the report, then print it for your instructor. Add a cover sheet to complete the assignment.

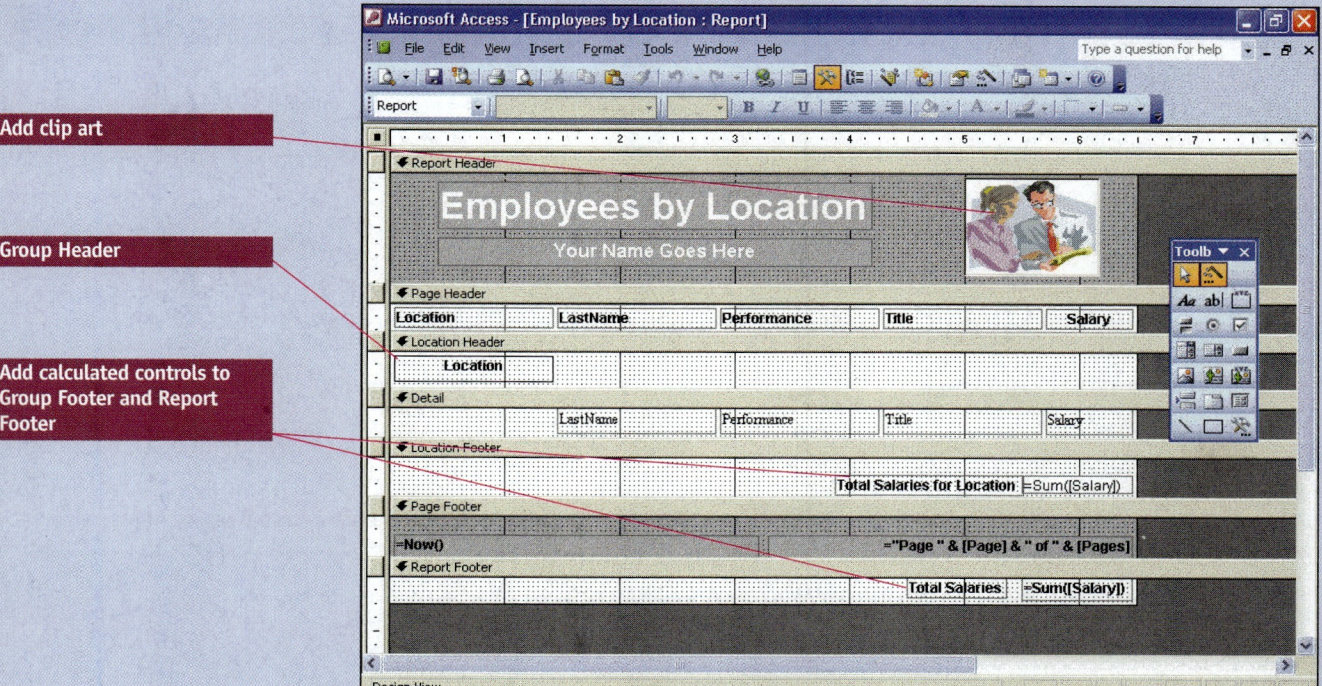

FIGURE 3.20   Salary Increases (exercise 7)

8. **Action Queries:** This problem asks you to create several action queries, after which you are to rerun a report from the previous exercise to see the effects of the action queries on the original data. Realize, however, that action queries will modify the original Employees table, and hence it is good practice to duplicate the table before you begin. Proceed as follows:

   a. Open the *Chapter 3 Practice 7* database in the Exploring Access folder. Go to the Database window, select the Employees table, pull down the Edit menu, and click the Copy command (or use the Ctrl+C keyboard shortcut). Pull down the Edit menu and click the Paste command (or use the Ctrl+V shortcut). Click the option button to copy the data and the structure. Name the copied table "Original Employees" and keep it as backup should you need to return to the original data.

   b. Create a Delete query (based on the Employees table) to delete all employees with poor performance. Run the query.

   c. Create an Update query to give all employees with Average performance a 5% raise. (The Update To row in the Salary column should contain the entry [Salary]*1.05). Be sure to run this query only once.

   d. Create two additional Update queries to give employees who had a performance of Good or Excellent, increases of 10% and 15%, respectively. Be sure to run each query only once. (If there are no employees that satisfy the criteria, the query will not update any records.)

   e. Use the Crosstab Query Wizard to create the query in Figure 3.21, which displays the total salary for each location-gender-title combination, after all of the action queries have been run. Print the query for your instructor.

   f. Rerun the Employee by Location report from the previous exercise and compare the results to the earlier version. The Atlanta manager now has a salary of $110,000, which reflects the 10% increase for Good performance. Note, too, there is only one sales coordinator in Atlanta (Bowles). Her salary is $31,500, which reflects a 5% raise ($1,500) for Average performance. Brown, the other sales coordinator in Atlanta (in the previous exercise) was terminated because of Poor performance.

   g. Add a cover sheet and submit all printouts to your instructor.

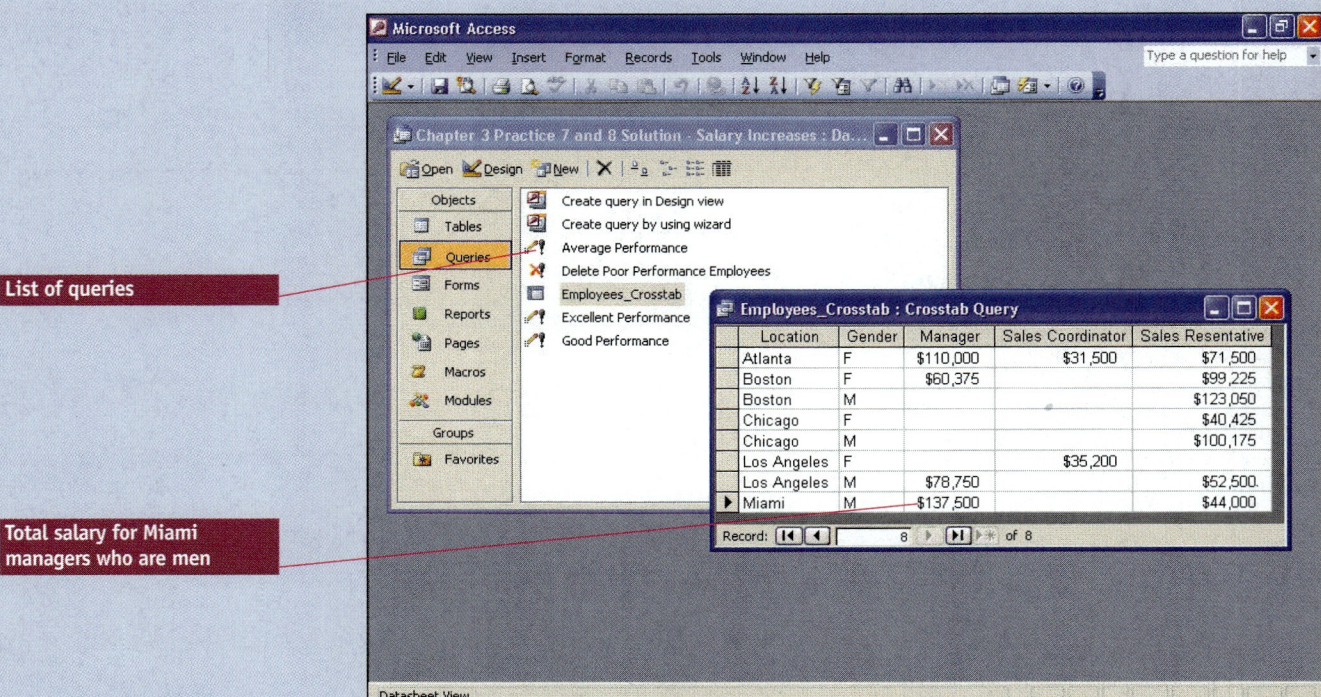

FIGURE 3.21   Action Queries (exercise 8)

9. **Events Extraordinaire:** The partially completed *Chapter 3 Practice 9—Events Extraordinaire* database builds on the database from Chapter 2. This database contains an Events table with 12 records that is the basis of four reports that are described below. (Only one report is shown in Figure 3.22.) All four reports are to have the same overall design and logo, but you need not match our design. Each report is required to have a page footer that displays today's date, the page number, and the number of pages in the complete report (e.g., "Page 1 of 2"). You may start with the Report Wizard and then modify the report in Design view, or you may create each report directly in Design view. Proceed as follows:

a. The first report is to display every event in the database in ascending sequence according to the starting date. This report is to include five fields for each event: Event ID, Sponsor, the event name, the start date, and the planning fee. You are also asked to add a calculated control to the report footer that shows the number of the events (12 in our database).

b. The second report is to display all local events in alphabetical sequence according to the sponsor's name. The report is to include sponsor, event name, start and end dates, and the maximum number of participants. (This report requires an underlying query.)

c. The third report is to display the confirmed events in sequence by the starting date. The report is to include the start date, event name, sponsor, contact name (as a concatenated field that includes the first and last name), and the contact phone number. (This report requires an underlying query.)

d. The fourth report is the group total report that is displayed in Figure 3.22. The Potential Revenues field is a calculated field that is equal to the maximum number of participants times the cost per person. The report can be based on a query, or you can add a calculated control in Design view. The group footer should show the potential revenue for each group. The report footer should show the total potential revenues for all events.

e. Print each of the reports and turn them in to your instructor. Change the page orientation and/or margins if necessary to ensure that all of the fields for one record fit on one page.

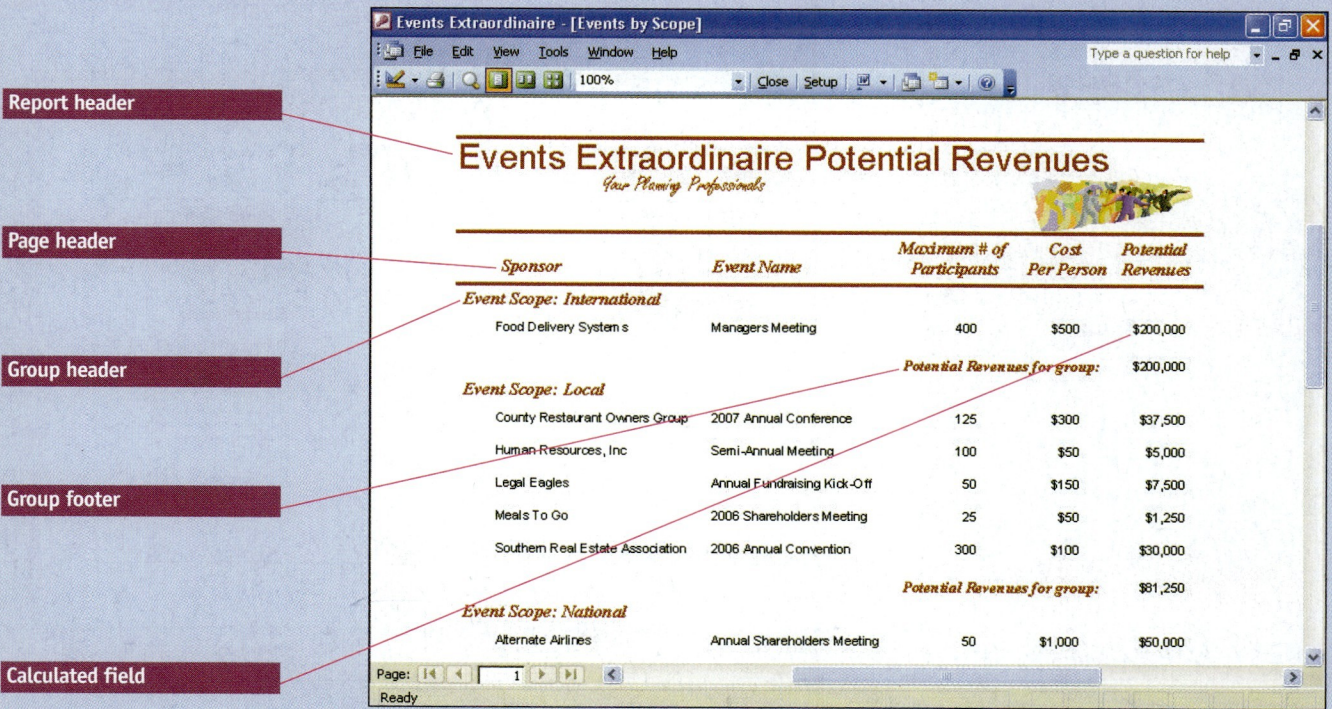

FIGURE 3.22 Events Extraordinaire (exercise 9)

10. **Paw Prints:** The report in Figure 3.23 continues the development of the Paw Prints database that was introduced in Chapter 2. This report is different from previous examples in that it displays a photograph for each record in the underlying table. You do not have to match our report exactly, but you are to include a photograph. In addition, the information for each animal is to appear on a separate page. Proceed as follows:

a. Create the Paw Prints database as described in the *Chapter 2 Practice 12* exercise at the end of that chapter. The form is not required, but you must create the Animals table in order to create the report. Refer to the earlier exercise for information about the various field properties, and then enter two records into the Animals table, one for Buster and one for Daisy. The pictures of Buster and Daisy are found in the Exploring Access folder.

b. Create the report in Design view without benefit of the Report Wizard. Right click the Report selector box in the upper-left corner, click Properties, then specify the Animals table as the record source. The field list should open automatically, and you will need to drag all of the fields from the Field List to the Details section of the report.

c. Right click the control for the photograph, click Properties to display the associated property sheet, then click the All tab. Change the Size Mode property to Stretch. Move, size, and format the controls as needed.

d. The report requires both a Page Header and a Page Footer. The Page Header should contain the title of the report as well as the clip art. The Page Footer should include today's date, the current page number, and the total number of pages. (You may want to look at the Design view of another report to see how these controls are entered.)

e. The report for each animal is to begin on the top of a new page, which requires you to insert a page break into the Detail section after the last field. Click the Page Break tool on the Toolbox, and then click below the Comments field. Make sure that there is no blank space under the Page Break or you will get a blank page at the end of the report.

f. Check the width of your report to be sure that it does not exceed 6 ½ inches. Print the completed report for your instructor.

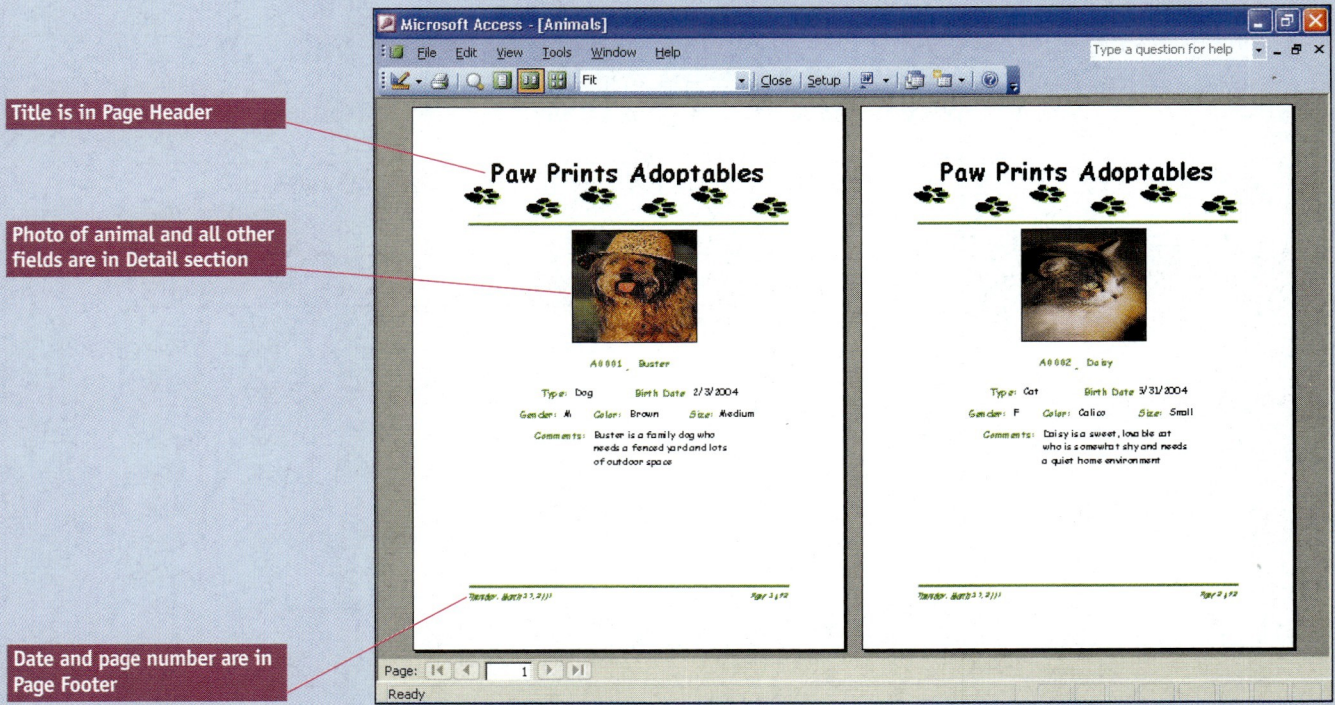

FIGURE 3.23 Paw Prints (exercise 10)

MINI CASES

Mail Merge

A mail merge takes the tedium out of sending form letters, as it creates the same letter many times, changing the name, address, and other information as appropriate from letter to letter. The form letter is created in a word processor (e.g., Microsoft Word), but the data file may be taken from an Excel workbook or an Access table or query. Use the *Our Students* database that you have worked with throughout the chapter as the basis for two different form letters that are to be sent to two different groups of students. The first letter is to congratulate students on the Dean's list (GPA of 3.50 or higher). The second letter is a warning to students on academic probation (GPA of less than 2.00).

We have created the form letters for you as the Word documents *Chapter 3 Mini Case Study—Probation Letter* and *Chapter 3 Mini Case Study—Dean's List,* with both documents stored in the Exploring Access folder. Open the Access database and create the required queries, then select each query individually, pull down the Tools menu, click Office Links, and click the command to Merge it with Microsoft Word. Word provides step-by-step assistance, and you should be able to complete the mail merge without difficulty. Print the first form letter for each query to show your instructor that you have completed the assignment.

Oh Canada

If you ask the average Canadian how many states there are in the United States, you are very likely to get the correct answer. If you reverse the question and ask the average American about Canadian provinces, the response is far less accurate. This assignment enables you to learn about our neighbor to the North. Open the *Chapter 3 Mini Case Study—Oh Canada* database in the Exploring Access folder. You will find a single table with four fields—the name of the province or territory, the estimated population for 2002 (in thousands), the area in square kilometers, and an indication of whether the data pertains to a province or territory.

Your assignment is to create a report that parallels the Population Density report in the United States database that was described in practice exercise 2. Your first task will be to create a query to compute the population density, after which you can create a report based on that query. The report should be grouped by province or territory, with population and area totals for each group, the average population density for each group, as well as statistics for Canada as a whole.

The Oh Canada database also contains an About Canada form that cites the source of the statistics that appear in the database. The form contains a map of Canada that you are asked to copy to the report you create. Last, but not least, modify the About Canada form so that it contains your name and student number. Print the completed form and report for your instructor.

Compacting versus Compressing

An Access database becomes fragmented, and thus unnecessarily large, as objects (e.g., reports and forms) are modified or deleted. It is important, therefore, to periodically compact a database to reduce its size (enabling you to back it up more easily). Choose a database with multiple objects, such as the Our Students database used in this chapter. Use the Windows Explorer to record the file size of the database as it presently exists. Start Access, open the database, pull down the Tools menu, and select Database Utilities to compact the database, then record the size of the database after compacting. You can also compress a compacted database (using a standard Windows utility such as WinZip) to further reduce the requirement for disk storage. Use Windows Explorer to record the size of the compressed database. Summarize your findings in a short report to your instructor. Try compacting and compressing at least two different databases to better appreciate these techniques. Be sure to mention that a smaller database is also uploaded (downloaded) more quickly. (Note, too, that WinZip is essential if you want to e-mail a database to a colleague because Outlook blocks Access attachments.)

Chapter Recap—Citizen of the World

Jodi McPherson, a student intern at the World Health Organization, was asked to conduct a study on overcrowding in countries around the world. The premise of the study is that we share one planet, that we are all "citizens of the world," and that we must work together to develop a global environmental policy. The study is to focus on population density, which is defined as the number of people per square kilometer. Jodi's supervisor has asked for a report that shows the twenty countries with the highest population density in descending order of that statistic. He has also requested two additional reports that show the twenty largest countries by area and the twenty largest countries by population. All three reports are to have a similar design with attractive formatting and a uniform logo.

Thus far, Jodi's internship has been terrific. She has a nicely equipped cubicle with a beautiful view and a state-of-the art computer with the latest version of Microsoft Access. She spent the first two weeks of her internship gathering data about each country, including its capital, area, and population. Once this was accomplished, Jodi entered the data into a table within an Access database and now needs to create various reports to analyze the data she has collected.

Your assignment is to put yourself in Jodi's place and develop the required reports based on the Access database, *Chapter 3 Ending Case Study—Citizen of the World*. The database also contains an "About Citizen of the World" form that cites the source of the data. You are to review the chapter and pay special attention to Hands-on Exercises 2 and 3 that describe how to create a select query and how to create a report based on that query. Your next task will be to create a query that contains population density as a calculated field and that sorts the records in descending order of population density. You can then set the Top Values property to display the twenty countries with the highest population density. (In actuality, you will need three queries, one for each report.) Print a copy of each report for your instructor.

4

Proficiency:
Relational Databases, Pivot Charts, and the Switchboard

OBJECTIVES

After reading this chapter you will:

1. Import data from an Excel workbook for inclusion in an Access database
2. Use the Relationships window to create a one-to-many relationship; define referential integrity.
3. Create a report that contains a relationships diagram
4. Create and modify a multiple-table select query.
5. Create a totals query.
6. Use Microsoft Graph to create a chart for inclusion in a report.
7. Create a pivot table and associated pivot chart.
8. Create and modify a switchboard.
9. Show the object dependencies that exist within a database.
10. Compact and repair a database; back up a database.

hands-on exercises

1. IMPORTING DATA FROM EXCEL
Input: Investment Data workbook; Investment database (Access)
Output: Investment Data workbook (modified); Investment database (modified)

2. TOTAL QUERIES, CHARTS, AND PIVOT TABLES
Input: Investment database (after exercise 1)
Output: Investment database (modified)

3. THE SWITCHBOARD MANAGER
Input: Investment database (after exercise 2)
Output: Investment database (modified)

CASE STUDY
THE DISC JOCKEY

Tim Bozik has loved music as long as he can remember, from rock to rap, from disco to classical. He is very successful professionally, but what he really enjoys are his "weekend gigs" as a disc jockey. It began innocently enough—he would spin records at fraternity parties and family gatherings. Then a friend submitted his name as a guest DJ on local radio, which led to a regular spot at "The Parthenon." Tim would gladly do it for free, but the fact that he is paid makes it even better.

Tim has an extensive music collection on various media that he wants to catalog within an Access database. He envisions three tables—artists, albums, and songs—with the appropriate one-to-many relationships between artists and albums, and between albums and songs. Tim wants the Songs table to include an OLE field whereby he can store a "clip" of the actual song. The Albums table should contain the title of the album, the genre, the media type, the year of release, the name of the label, and the price that Tim paid for the album. The Artists table should contain the artist's name and notes about the artist. (For the sake of simplicity, Tim has decided on one artist per album.) Tim has asked you to help him implement the design. Be sure to include all necessary fields in each table and to set the properties appropriately.

Your assignment is to read the chapter, paying special attention on how to create a one-to-many relationship and enforce referential integrity. You will then create a new database with the required tables for the Disc Jockey database. (You do not have to enter data into all of the tables.)

Your database should also include a basic switchboard, an About form, and a relationships diagram. Use a common clip art image and consistent design elements for each object in the database. Print the switchboard form, the table of switchboard items, the relationships diagram, and the About form for your instructor.

Each application in Microsoft Office is independent of the others, but it is often necessary or advantageous to share data between the applications. Data may be collected in Excel, imported or linked to an Access database to take advantage of its relational capability, then exported back to Excel for data analysis, or to Microsoft Word for a mail merge. This chapter describes how to share data between applications in the context of a database for an investment firm.

The Investment database is a relational database with two tables, one for clients, and one for financial consultants. Data from both tables can be displayed in a single query that contains fields from each table, and therein lies the real power of Microsoft Access. The chapter also introduces the concept of a total query to produce summary information. The results of a total query are then presented in graphical form through Microsoft Graph. The last portion of the chapter describes the creation of a user interface (or switchboard) that lets a nontechnical person move easily from one object to another by clicking a menu item. The switchboard is created through the Switchboard Manager, one of several utilities in Microsoft Access.

The database in Figure 4.1 is designed for an investment firm that monitors its clients and their financial consultants. The firm requires the typical data for each client—name, birth date, telephone, assets under management, and so on. The firm also stores data about its employees who are the financial consultants that service the clients. Each entity (clients and consultants) requires its own table in the database in order to add, edit, and/or delete data for individual clients and consultants, independently of one another.

If, for example, you wanted to know (or change) the account type and assets for Bradley Adams, you would search the Clients table for Bradley's record, where you would find the account type (Retirement), and assets ($90,000). In similar

Bradley Adams' record

ConsultantID points to Andrea Carrion (ConsultantID of 1)

SSN	FirstName	LastName	ConsultantID	BirthDate	Gender	Account Type	Assets
100-00-0000	Eileen	Marder	2	9/12/1935	F	Standard	$14,000
111-11-1111	Bradley	Adams	1	8/22/1961	M	Retirement	$90,000
111-22-2333	Linda	Laquer	3	3/16/1981	F	Corporate	$25,000
200-00-0000	Kevin	Stutz	3	5/31/1972	M	Retirement	$150,000
222-22-2222	Nickolas	Gruber	2	11/11/1961	M	Corporate	$90,000
300-00-0000	Cedric	Stewart	4	4/12/1974	M	Retirement	$90,000
333-33-3333	Lori	Graber	3	7/1/1972	F	Deluxe	$120,000
400-00-0000	Ryan	Yanez	1	9/30/1974	M	Standard	$18,000
444-44-4444	Christopher	Milgrom	4	3/12/1953	M	Corporate	$100,000
444-55-5666	Jessica	Benjamin	1	10/31/1973	F	Deluxe	$125,000
500-00-0000	Erica	Milgrom	2	5/1/1972	F	Retirement	$150,000
555-55-5555	Peter	Carson	1	3/8/1953	M	Standard	$12,000
600-00-0000	Michelle	Zacco	2	10/24/1975	F	Deluxe	$90,000
666-66-6666	Kimberly	Coulter	2	11/11/1974	F	Corporate	$180,000
700-00-0000	Steven	Frazier	4	9/9/1968	M	Retirement	$150,000
777-77-7777	Ana	Johnson	3	4/18/1948	F	Standard	$12,000
800-00-0000	Christa	Parulis	1	7/15/1972	F	Corporate	$120,000
888-88-8888	David	James	4	8/1/1945	M	Deluxe	$100,000
900-00-0000	Ronnie	Jones	2	6/1/1949	F	Standard	$12,000
999-99-9999	Wendy	Simon	1	1/31/1945	F	Retirement	$10,000

(a) The Clients Table

Andrea Carrion has ConsultantID of 1

ConsultantID	FirstName	LastName	Phone	DateHired	Status
1	Andrea	Carrion	(954) 346-1980	9/1/1995	Partner
2	Ken	Grauer	(954) 346-1955	9/1/1999	Associate
3	Robert	Arnold	(954) 346-1958	10/18/2000	Associate
4	Issac	Milgrom	(954) 346-1961	3/16/2002	Partner

(b) The Consultants Table

FIGURE 4.1 The Investments Database

fashion, you could search the Consultants table for Andrea Carrion and learn that she was hired on September 1, 1995, and that she is a partner in the firm. You could also use the ConsultantID field in Bradley Adams' record to learn that Andrea Carrion is Bradley's financial consultant.

The investment firm imposes a ***one-to-many relationship*** between financial consultants and their clients. One consultant can have many clients, but a given client is assigned to only one consultant. This relationship is implemented in the database by including a common field, ConsultantID, in both tables. The ConsultantID is the ***primary key*** (the field or combination of fields that ensures each record is unique) in the Consultants table. It also appears as a ***foreign key*** (the primary key of another table) in the Clients table in order to relate the two tables to one another.

The data from both tables can be combined through this relationship to provide complete information about any client and the consultant who serves him/her, or about any consultant and the clients he or she services. For example, to determine the name, telephone number, and status of Bradley Adams' financial consultant, you would search the Clients table to determine the ConsultantID assigned to Bradley (consultant number 1). You would then search the Consultants table for that consultant number and retrieve the associated data.

Multiple-table Queries

You have just seen how to manually relate data from the Clients and Consultants tables to one another. As you might expect, it can also be done automatically through the creation of a multiple-table query as shown in Figure 4.2. Figure 4.2a shows the Design view, whereas Figure 4.2b displays the associated dynaset. Bradley Adams appears first in the dynaset since the query lists clients in alphabetical order by last name. Note, too, that Carrion appears as Bradley's financial consultant, which is the same conclusion we reached when we looked at the tables initially.

The one-to-many relationship between consultants and clients is shown graphically in the Query window. The tables are related through the ConsultantID

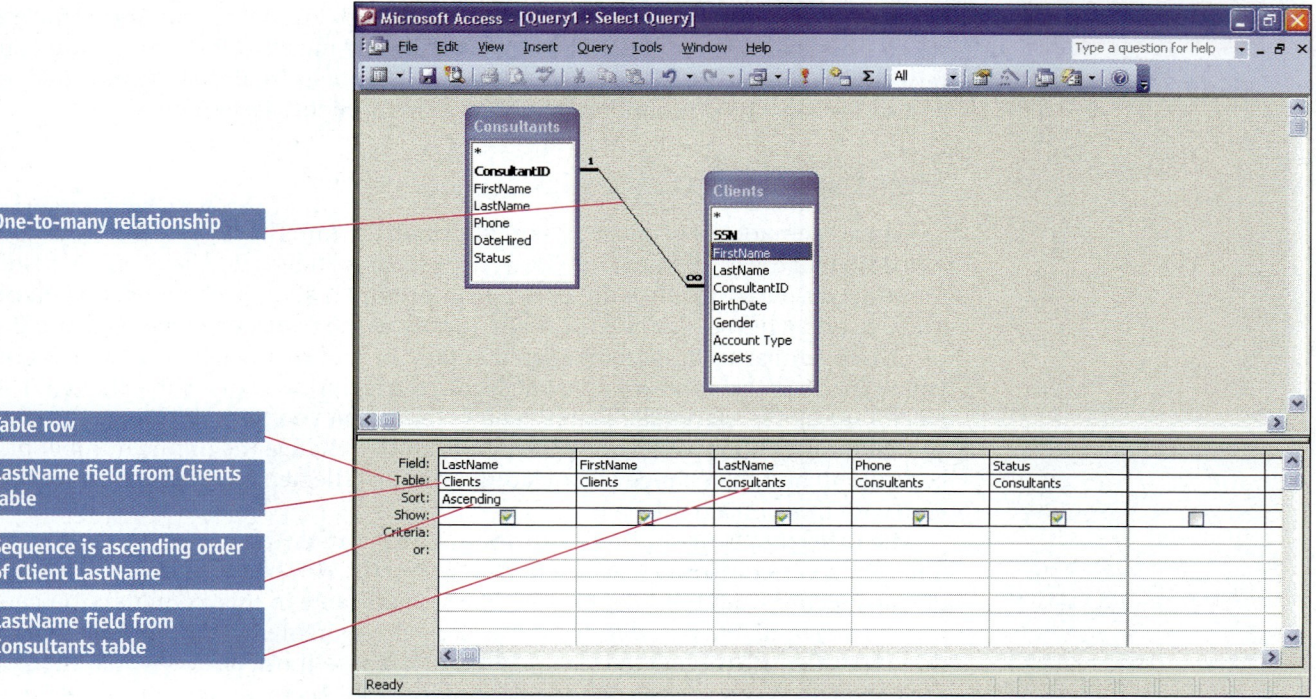

(a) Design View

FIGURE **4.2**   Multiple-table Query

Clients.LastName	FirstName	Consultants.LastName	Phone	Status
Adams	Bradley	Carrion	(954) 346-1980	Partner
Benjamin	Jessica	Carrion	(954) 346-1980	Partner
Carson	Peter	Carrion	(954) 346-1980	Partner
Coulter	Kimberly	Grauer	(954) 346-1955	Associate
Frazier	Steven	Milgrom	(954) 346-1961	Partner
Graber	Lori	Arnold	(954) 346-1958	Associate
Gruber	Nickolas	Grauer	(954) 346-1955	Associate
James	David	Milgrom	(954) 346-1961	Partner
Johnson	Ana	Arnold	(954) 346-1958	Associate
Jones	Ronnie	Grauer	(954) 346-1955	Associate
Laquer	Linda	Arnold	(954) 346-1958	Associate
Marder	Eileen	Grauer	(954) 346-1955	Associate
Milgrom	Erica	Grauer	(954) 346-1955	Associate
Milgrom	Christopher	Milgrom	(954) 346-1961	Partner
Parulis	Christa	Carrion	(954) 346-1980	Partner
Simon	Wendy	Carrion	(954) 346-1980	Partner
Stewart	Cedric	Milgrom	(954) 346-1961	Partner
Stutz	Kevin	Arnold	(954) 346-1958	Associate
Yanez	Ryan	Carrion	(954) 346-1980	Partner
Zacco	Michelle	Grauer	(954) 346-1955	Associate

Sequence is alphabetical order by Client LastName

Consultant LastName

(b) Dynaset

FIGURE 4.2   Multiple-table Query (*continued*)

field that appears in both tables. ConsultantID is the primary key of the "one" table (the Consultants table in this example), but it is also a field in the "many" table (the Clients table). This in turn links the tables to one another, making it possible to join data from the two tables in a single query.

The lower half of the Query window is similar to the queries you created in Chapter 3. The difference is that the design grid contains a *Table row* to indicate the table from where the field was taken. The client's last name and first name are taken from the Clients table. The consultant's last name, phone, and status are taken from the Consultants table. The records appear in alphabetical order (in ascending sequence) according to the value of the client's last name.

Maintaining the Database

You have seen how easy it is to obtain information from the investment database. The design of the investment database, with separate tables for clients and consultants, makes it easy to add, edit, or delete information about a client or consultant. Thus, to add a new client or consultant, just go to the respective table and add the record. In similar fashion, to change the data for an existing client or consultant, you again go to the appropriate table, locate the record, and make the change. The advantage of the relational database, however, is that you have to change the consultant information in only one place; for example, change the phone number of a consultant, and the change will be automatically reflected for every client associated with that consultant.

Realize, too, that the tables in the database must be consistent with one another, a concept known as *referential integrity*. For example, you can always delete a record from the Clients table (the "many" table in this example). You cannot, however, delete a record from the Consultants table (the "one" table) when there are clients assigned to that consultant, because those clients would then be assigned to a financial consultant who did not exist. Access monitors the relationships that are in effect and prevents you from making changes that do not make sense. It will enforce referential integrity automatically.

It is important to realize that data is data regardless of where it originates. You may prefer to work in Access, but others in the organization may use Excel or vice versa. In any event, there is a need to send data back and forth between applications. The **Get External Data command** imports or links data from an external source into Access. The data may come from an Excel workbook (as in our next hands-on exercise), or from a text file that was created by an application outside of Microsoft Office. The **Export command** does the reverse and copies an Access database object to an external destination.

The **Import Spreadsheet Wizard** is illustrated in Figure 4.3. The Wizard asks you a series of questions, then it imports the Excel worksheet into the Access table. You select the worksheet in Figure 4.3a, designate the Excel column headings and Access field names in Figure 4.3b, and specify the primary key in Figure 4.3c. You can then view and/or modify the resulting table as shown in Figure 4.3d.

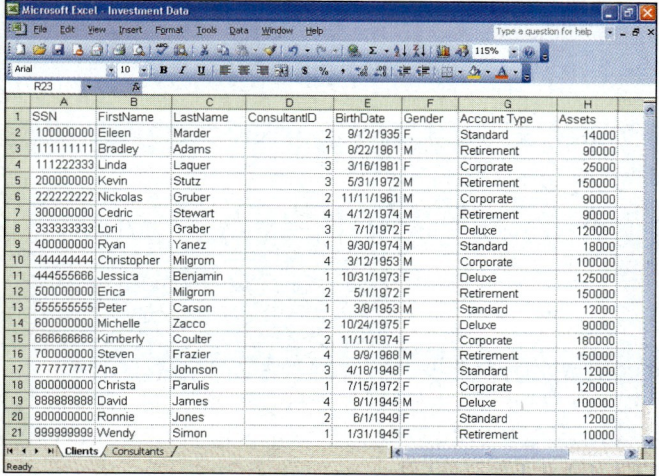

(a) The Excel Workbook

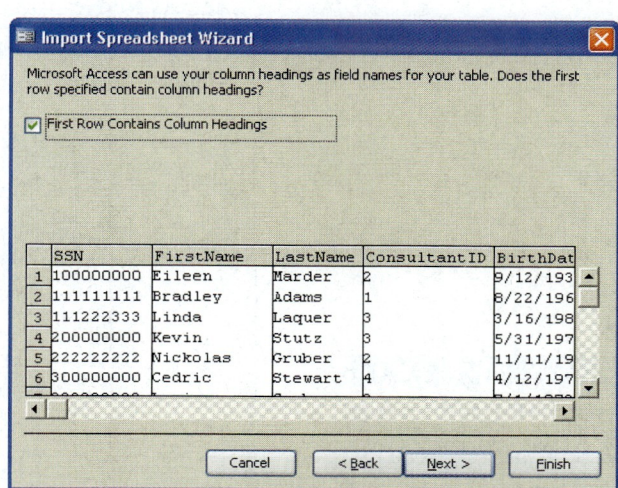

(b) Designate Column Headings (field names)

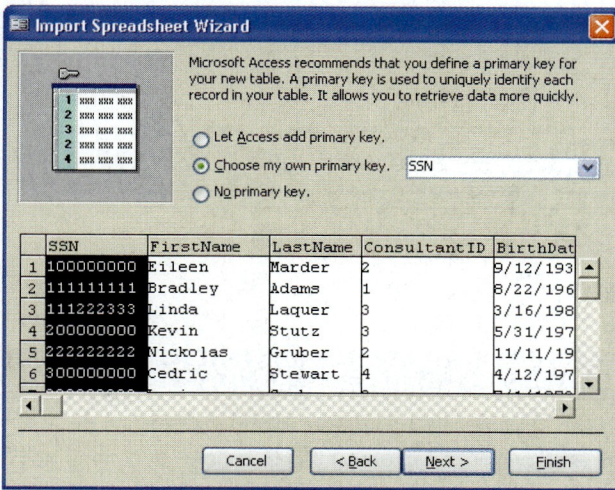

(c) Choose the Primary Key

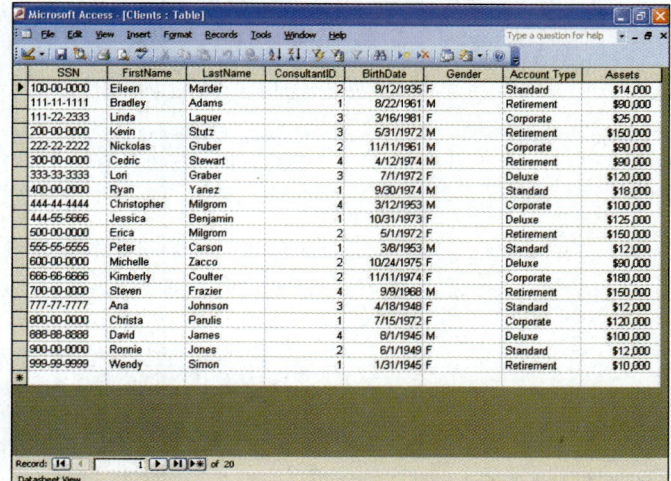

(d) The Clients Table

FIGURE 4.3   The Import Spreadsheet Wizard

1   Importing Data from Excel

Objective   To import an Access table from an Excel workbook; to create a one-to-many relationship; to create a multiple-table query.

Step 1:   **Import the Excel Worksheet**

- Start Access. Click the link to **More . . .** in the task pane, or pull down the **File menu** and click the **Open command**. Open the **Investment database** in the **Exploring Access folder**. Click **Open** in response to the security warning. If necessary, click the **Tables button**.

- Pull down the **File menu**, click (or point to) the **Get External Data command**, then click **Import** to display the Import dialog box in Figure 4.4a.

- Click the **down arrow** on the Look in list box and change to the **Exploring Access folder** (the same folder that contains the Access databases).

- Click the **down arrow** on the Files of type list box and select **Microsoft Excel**. Select the **Investment Data workbook**. Click the **Import button**.

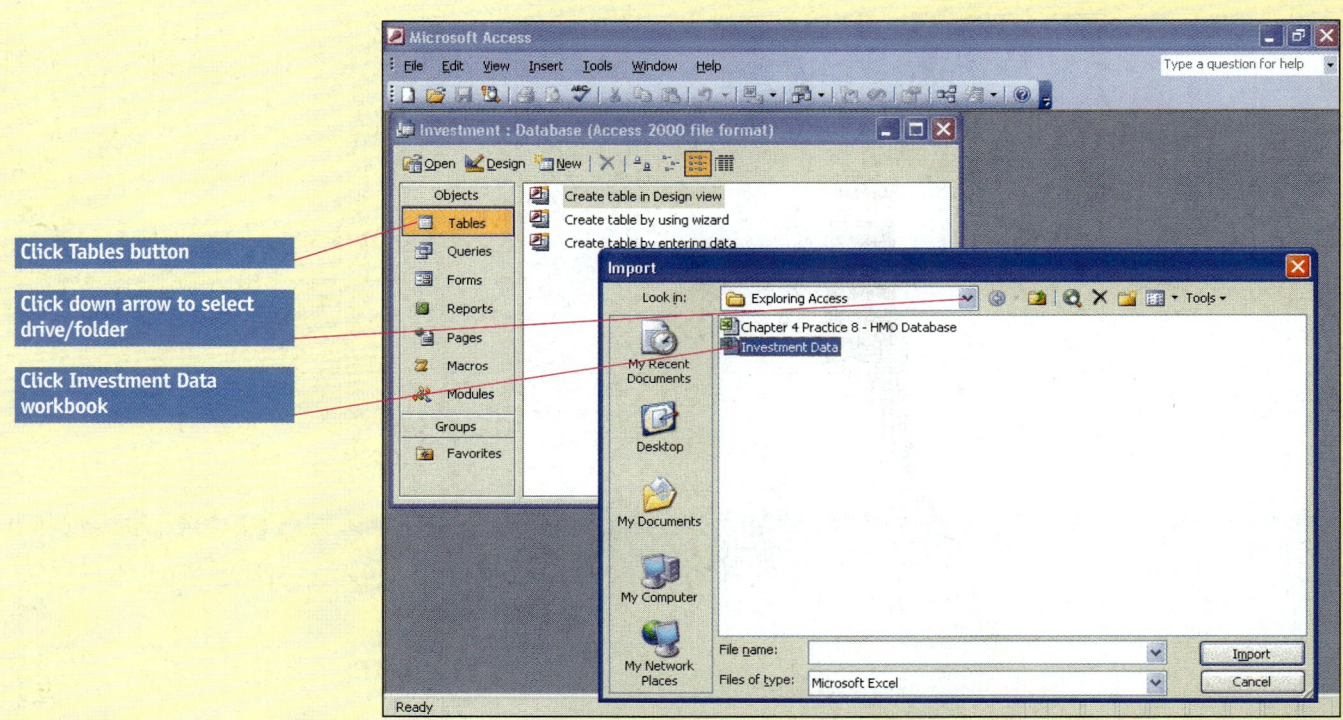

Click Tables button

Click down arrow to select drive/folder

Click Investment Data workbook

(a) Import the Excel Worksheet (step 1)

FIGURE 4.4   Hands-on Exercise 1

IMPORTING VERSUS LINKING

The Get External Data command displays a cascaded menu to import or link tables. Importing a table brings a copy of the table into the database and does not maintain a tie to the original data. Linking, on the other hand, does not bring the table into the database but only a pointer to the data source. Any changes to the data are made in the original data source and are reflected automatically in any database that is linked to that source.

Step 2: The Import Spreadsheet Wizard

- You should see the first step in the Import Spreadsheet Wizard as shown in Figure 4.4b. The option button to **Show Worksheets** is selected. The Clients worksheet is also selected. Click **Next**.

- Access will use the column headings in the Excel workbook as field names in the Access table, provided you check the box indicating that the first row contains column headings. Click **Next**.

- Select the option button to store the data in a new table. Click **Next**.

- You do not need information about the individual fields. Click **Next**.

- Select the option to choose your own primary key. Click the **drop-down arrow** on the list box, and select **SSN**. Click **Next**.

- Access indicates that it will import the data to a Clients table. Click the **Finish button**, then click **OK** when the wizard indicates it has finished importing the data. The Clients table appears within the Database window.

- Repeat the steps to import the **Consultants table** into the Investment database from the Investment Data workbook. Use the **ConsultantID field** as the primary key for this table.

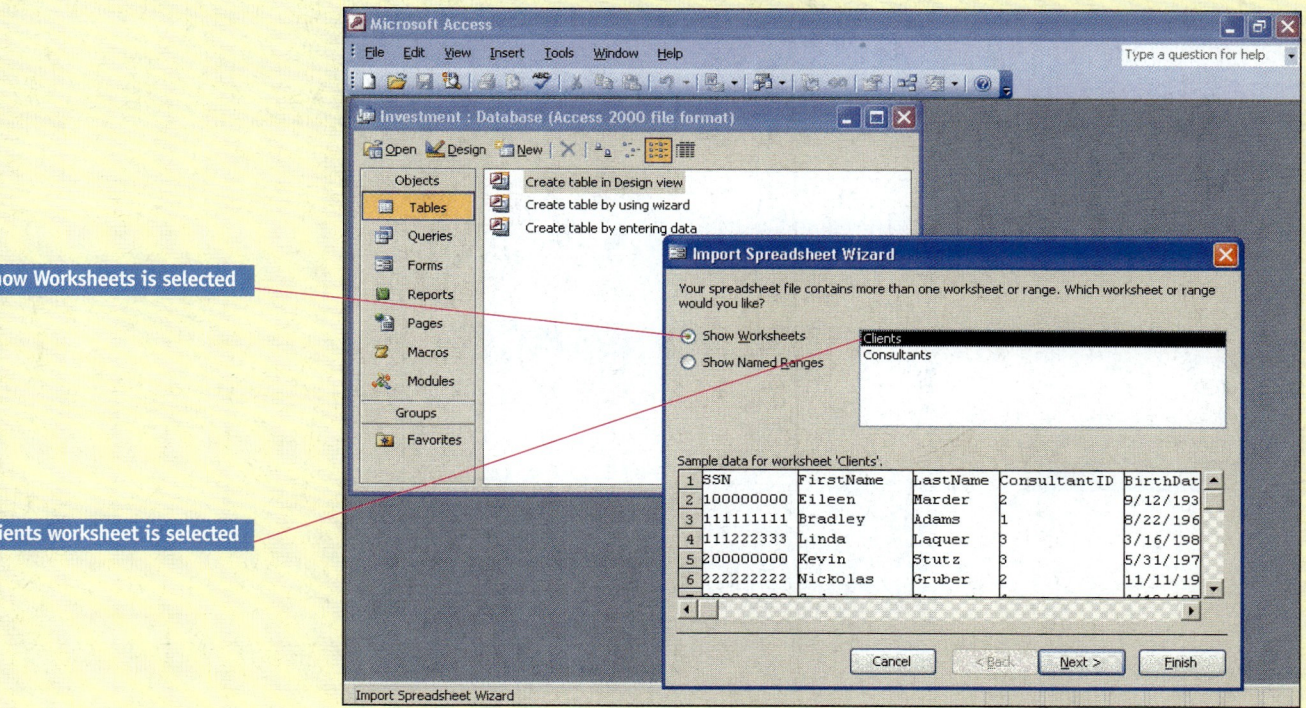

Show Worksheets is selected

Clients worksheet is selected

(b) The Import Spreadsheet Wizard (step 2)

FIGURE 4.4 Hands-on Exercise 1 (*continued*)

THE IMPORT TEXT WIZARD

The most common format for data originating outside of Microsoft Office is a text (or ASCII) file that stores the data without formatting of any kind. Pull down the File menu, click the Get External Data command, click Import, and specify Text Files as the file format to start the Import Text Wizard.

Step 3: **Create the Relationship**

- Pull down the **Tools menu** and click the **Relationships command** to open the Relationships window in Figure 4.4c. (The tables are not yet visible.)

- Pull down the **Relationships menu** and click the **Show Table command** to display the Show Table dialog box. Click (select) the **Clients table** (within the Show Table dialog box), then click the **Add button**.

- Double click the **Consultants table** to add this table to the Relationships window. Close the Show Table dialog box. Click and drag the title bar of each table so that the positions of the tables match those in Figure 4.4c.

- Click and drag the bottom (and/or right) border of each table so that you see all of the fields in each table.

- Click and drag the **ConsultantID field** in the Consultants table field list to the **ConsultantID field** in the Clients field list. You will see the Edit Relationships dialog box.

- Check the box to **Enforce Referential Integrity**. Click the **Create button** to create the relationship.

- Click the **Save button** to save the Relationships window.

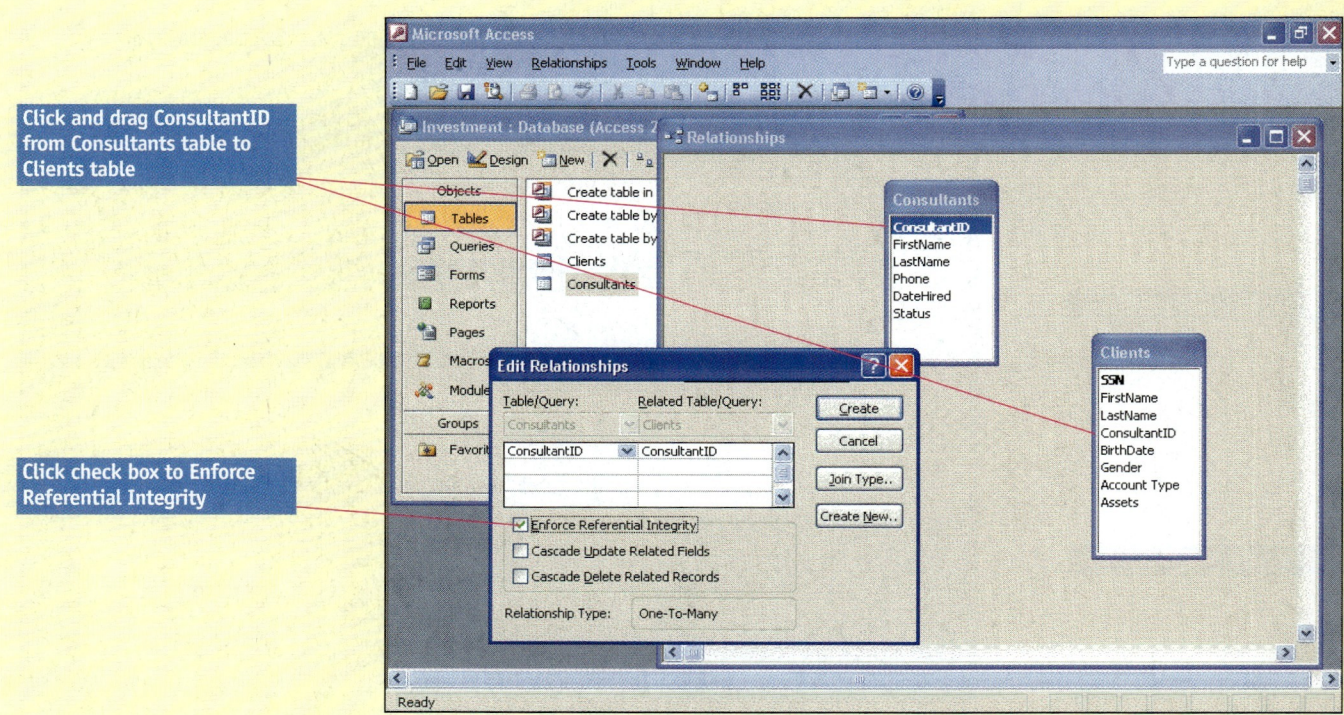

Click and drag ConsultantID from Consultants table to Clients table

Click check box to Enforce Referential Integrity

(c) Create the Relationship (step 3)

FIGURE 4.4 Hands-on Exercise 1 (*continued*)

REFERENTIAL INTEGRITY

The tables in a database must be consistent with one another, a concept known as referential integrity. Thus, Access automatically implements certain types of data validation to prevent errors of inconsistency from occurring. You cannot, for example, enter a record in the Clients table that references a Consultant who does not exist. Nor can you delete a record in the Consultants table if it has related records in the Clients table.

Step 4: **Print the Relationship**

- Pull down the **File menu** and click the **Print Relationships command**. You will see the Print Preview screen of a report. Maximize the window.

- Click the **View button** to change to the Design view as shown in Figure 4.4d. If necessary, click the **Toolbox button** to display the Toolbox toolbar.

- Click the **Label tool** on the Toolbox toolbar, then click and drag in the Report Header section of the report to create an unbound control.

- The insertion point is positioned automatically within the label you just created. Type **Prepared by:** followed by your name. Size the labels within the header as necessary.

- Click the **Save button** to display the Save As dialog box. Change the name of the report to **Relationships Diagram**, then click **OK**.

- Click the **View button** to change to the **Print Preview** view of the report. Click the **Print button**. Close the Print Preview window.

- Close the Report window. Close the Relationships window.

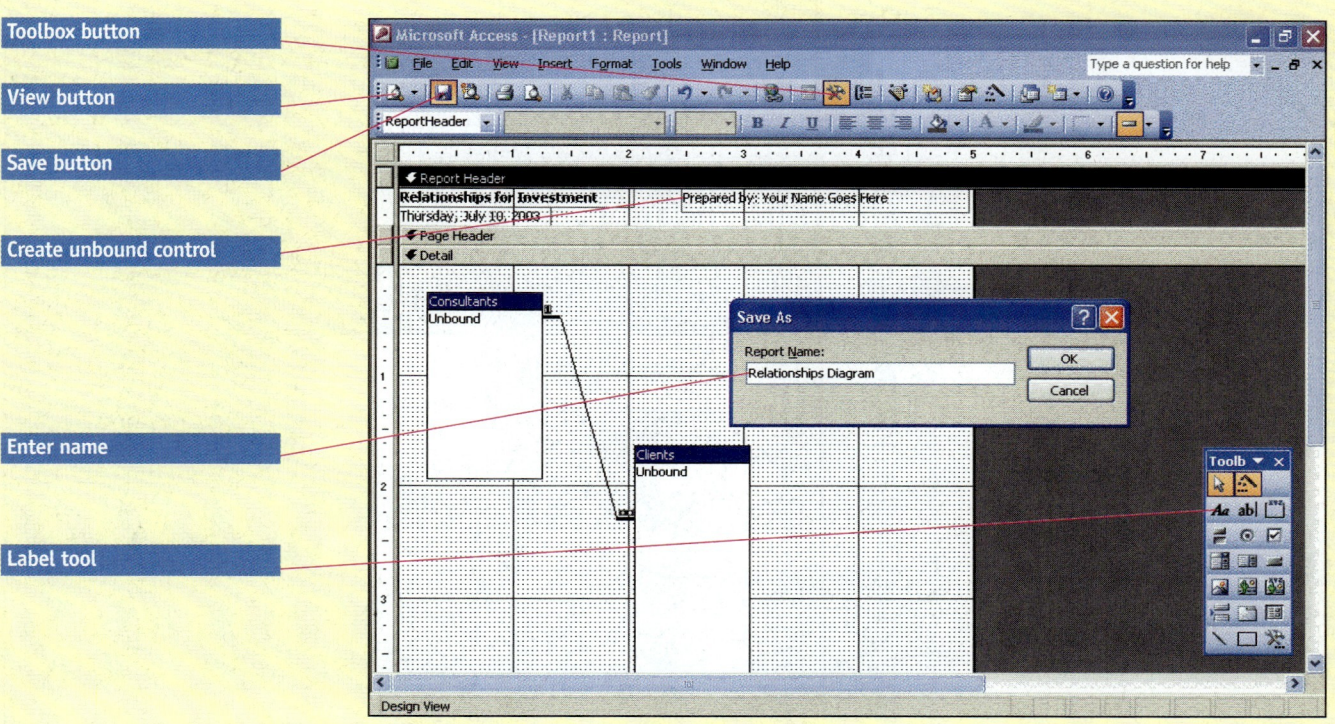

Toolbox button

View button

Save button

Create unbound control

Enter name

Label tool

(d) Print the Relationship (step 4)

FIGURE 4.4 Hands-on Exercise 1 (*continued*)

DISPLAY THE CURRENT DATE

A report typically displays one of two dates—the date it was created, or the current date (i.e., the date on which it is printed). We prefer the latter, which is obtained through the Now() function. Click in the Report header and delete the control containing today's (fixed) date. Click the Text Box tool, click and drag where you want the date to appear, then release the mouse. Click in the text box and enter the function =Now(). Save the report. The next time you open the report, it will display the current date.

Step 5: Add Your Own Record

- Click the **Forms button** in the Database window, then double click the **Consultants form** to open the form.

- Click the **Add Record button** and enter the data for your instructor. Enter **5** as the ConsultantID, enter your **instructor's name**, and use today's date as the date of hire. Your instructor is a **partner**. Close the form.

- Double click the **Clients form** in the Database window to open the form as shown in Figure 4.4e. Click the **Add Record button**, then enter the appropriate data for yourself.
  - ❑ Enter **987-65-4321** as your *hypothetical* Social Security number.
  - ❑ Click the **down arrow** on the Consultants list box, then select your instructor (Barber in our example) as your financial consultant.
  - ❑ Enter **Standard** as the Account Type.
  - ❑ Enter **$25,000** in the Assets field.

- Click the **Print Record button** to print the form.

- Click the **Close Form button**.

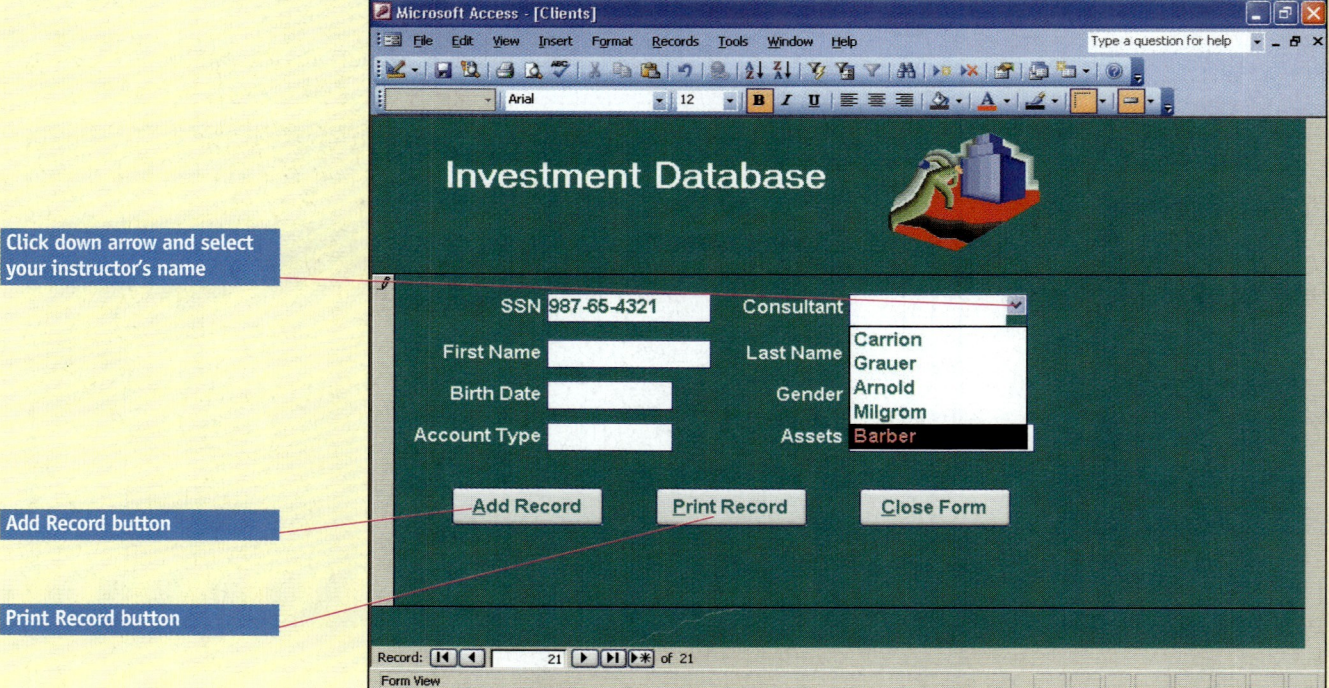

Click down arrow and select your instructor's name

Add Record button

Print Record button

(e) Add Your Own Record (step 5)

FIGURE 4.4 Hands-on Exercise 1 (*continued*)

ADD A HYPERLINK

You can enhance the appeal of your form through inclusion of a hyperlink. Open the form in Design view, then click the Insert Hyperlink button to display the Insert Hyperlink dialog box. Enter the Web address and click OK to close the dialog box and return to the Design view. Right click the hyperlink to display a shortcut menu, click the Properties command to display the Properties dialog box, then change the caption, font, and/or point size as appropriate.

Step 6: **Create the Multiple-table Query**

- Click the **Queries button** in the Database window. Double click the icon to **Create query in design view** to open the Design window. The Show Table dialog box appears automatically.

- Press and hold the **Ctrl key** to select the Clients and Consultants tables, then click the **Add button** to add these tables to the query. Close the Show Table dialog box.

- Click the **Maximize button** so that the Query Design window takes the entire desktop. Point to the line separating the field lists from the design grid (the mouse pointer changes to a cross), then click and drag in a downward direction. This gives you more space to display the field lists.

- Click and drag the title bars of each table to arrange the tables as shown in Figure 4.4f. Click and drag the bottom of each field list until you can see all of the fields in the table.

- You are ready to complete the query, which will contain fields from both the Clients and Consultants tables.

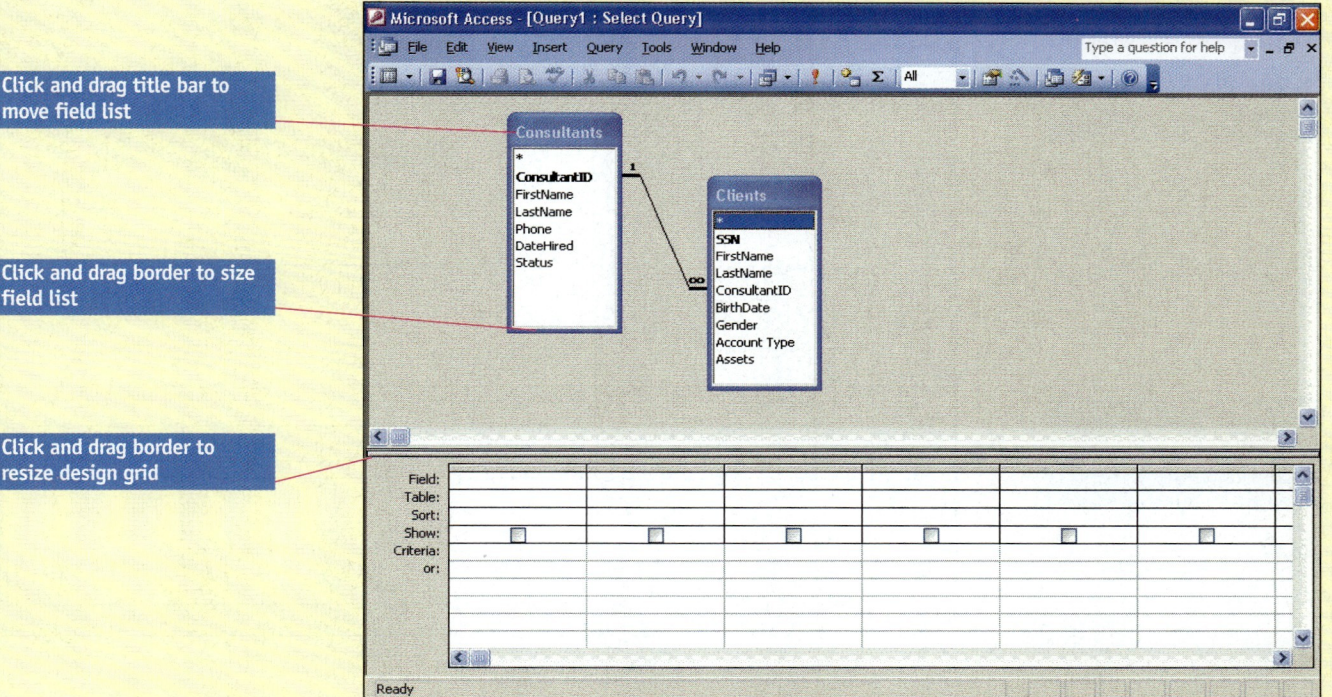

(f) Create the Multiple-table Query (step 6)

FIGURE 4.4 Hands-on Exercise 1 (*continued*)

THE JOIN LINE

Access joins the tables in a query automatically if a relationship exists between the tables within the database. Access will also join the tables (even if no relationship exists) if both tables have a field with the same name and data type, and if one of the fields is a primary key. And finally, you can create the join yourself by dragging a field from one table to the other, but this type of join applies only to the query in which it was created.

Step 7: Complete the Multiple-table Query

- The Table row should be visible within the design grid. If not, pull down the **View menu** and click **Table Names** to display the Table row in the design grid as shown in Figure 4.4g.

- Double click the **LastName** and **Status fields** from the Consultants table to add these fields to the design grid. Double click the **LastName**, **Assets**, and **Account Type fields** from the Clients table to add these fields as well.

- Click the **Sort row** under the **LastName field** from the **Consultants table**, then click the **down arrow** to open the drop-down list box. Click **Ascending**.

- Click the **Save button** on the Query Design toolbar to display the Save As dialog box. Save the query as **Assets Under Management**. Click **OK** to save the query.

- Click the **Run button** (the exclamation point) to run the query. The results are displayed on a dynaset.

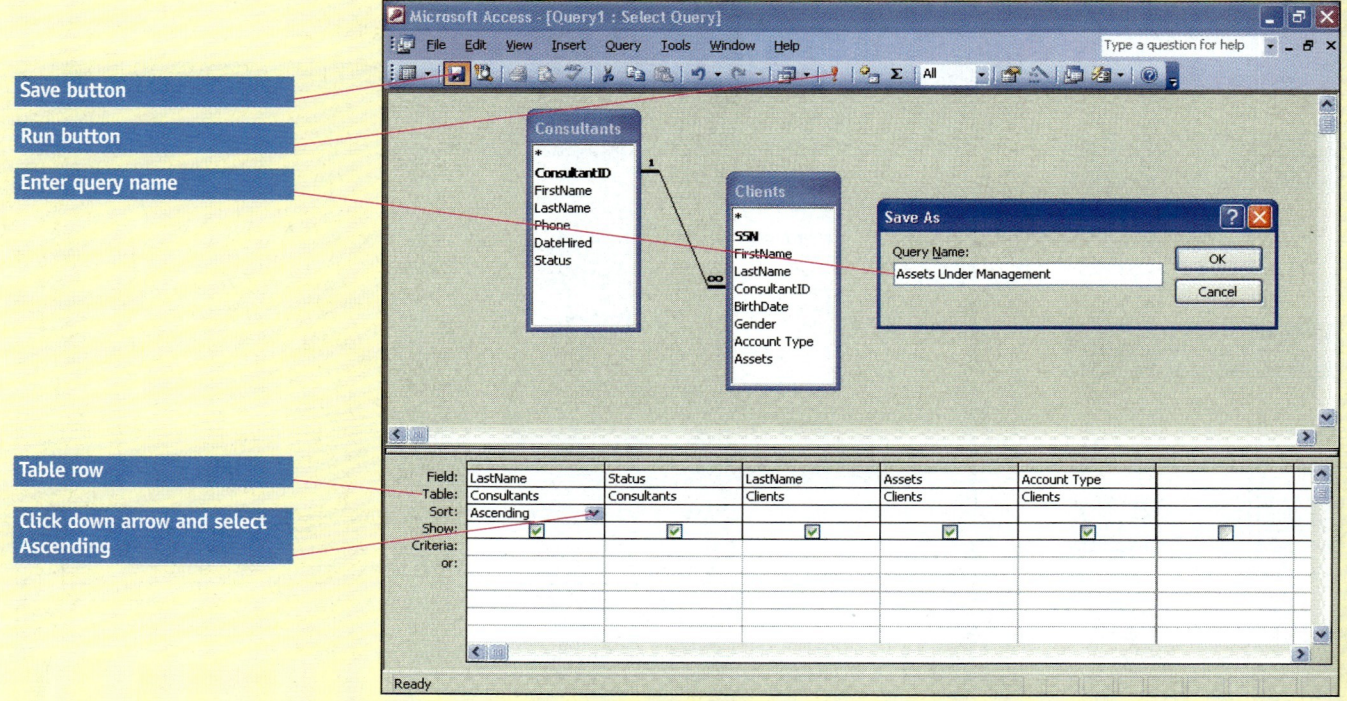

(g) Complete the Multiple-table Query (step 7)

FIGURE 4.4 Hands-on Exercise 1 (*continued*)

SORT ON MULTIPLE FIELDS

A query can be sorted on multiple fields (e.g., by consultant, and by client's last name within consultant), provided the fields are in the proper order within the design grid. Access sorts from left to right (the leftmost field is the most important field), so the consultant's last name must appear to the left of the client's last name. To move a field within the design grid, click the column selector above the field name to select the column, then drag the column to its new position. Click the Sort row for both fields and choose the ascending sequence.

Step 8: **Export the Query**

- You should see the dynaset created by the query as shown in Figure 4.4h. The query lists all of the client records grouped by the last name of the financial consultant. There should be one record for your instructor.

- Pull down the **File menu**, click (or point to) the **Export command** to display the Export Query dialog box. Click the **down arrow** in the Save as type list box to select **Microsoft Excel 97-2003**.

- Select the **Investment Data workbook** and click the **Export All button** to save the query as a worksheet in the Investment Data workbook. Click **Yes** if asked whether to replace the file. Close the Query window.

- Click the **Tables button** in the Database window. Select the **Clients table**, pull down the **File menu**, click the **Export command**, and change the file type to **Microsoft Excel 97-2003**. Select (click) the **Investment Data workbook**. Click **Export**. Click **Yes** if asked to replace the file.

- Export the **Consultants table** in similar fashion.

- Start Excel. Open the **Investment Data workbook** in the **Exploring Access folder**. The workbook should contain Clients, Consultants, and Assets under Management worksheets.

- If the workbook contains two Client worksheets (Clients and Clients1), it is because you did not replace the original worksheet. Delete that worksheet now.

- Format the individual worksheets as necessary, and then print the completed workbook for your instructor. Use the **Page Setup command** to show row and column headings. Include a **custom footer** with your name, the name of the worksheet, and today's date. Exit Excel.

- Exit Access if you do not want to continue with the next exercise at this time.

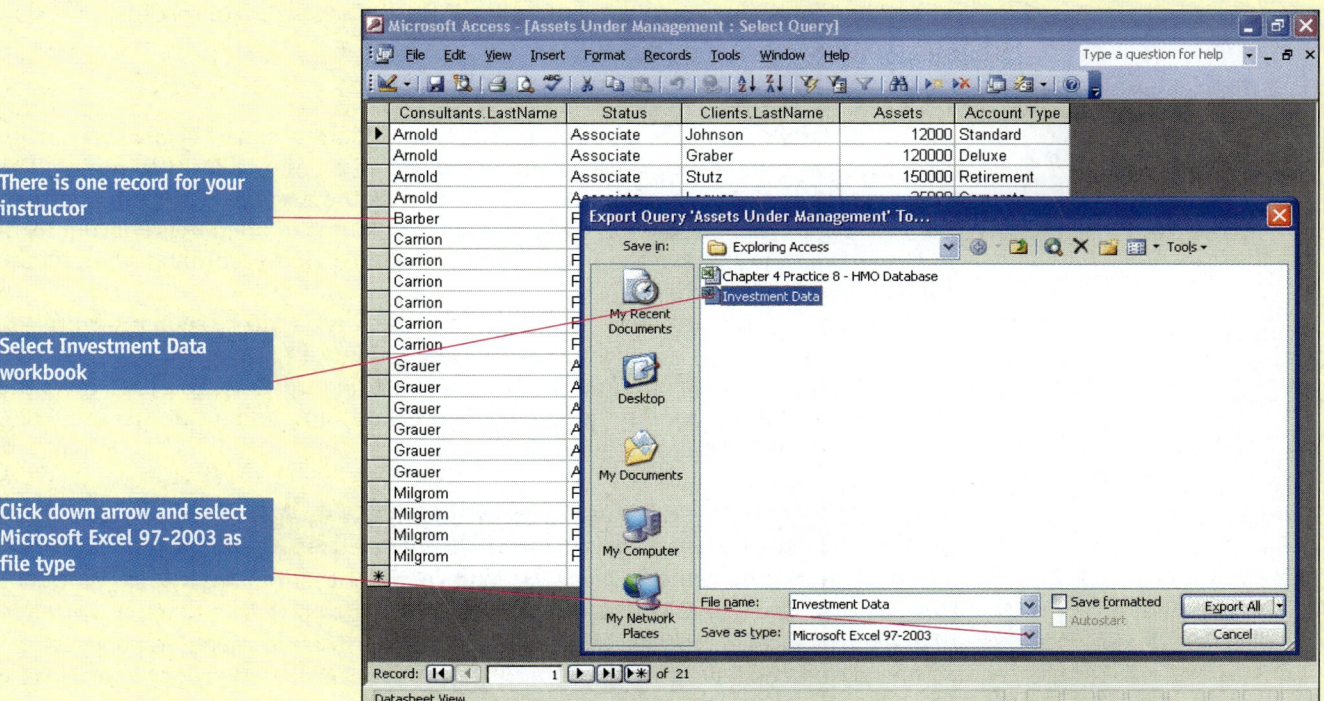

(h) Export the Query (step 8)

FIGURE 4.4 Hands-on Exercise 1 (*continued*)

Chapter 3 described several types of queries, including a select query, various action queries, and a crosstab query. Now we present a *total query*, which performs calculations on a group of records using one of several *aggregate (summary) functions* available within Access. These include the Sum, Count, Avg, Max, and Min functions to determine the total, number, average, maximum, and minimum values, respectively. Figure 4.5 shows a total query to compute the total assets under management for each financial consultant.

Figure 4.5a displays the results of a select query similar to the query created in the first hands-on exercise. The records are displayed in alphabetical order according to the last name of the financial consultant. The dynaset contains one record for each client in the Clients table and enables us to verify the results of the total query in Figure 4.5c. Arnold, the first consultant listed, has four clients (Johnson, Graber, Stutz, and Laquer). The total assets that Arnold has under management are $307,000, which is obtained by adding the Assets field in the four records.

Figure 4.5b shows the Design view of the total query to calculate the total assets managed by each consultant. The query contains three fields, the LastName (from the Consultants table), followed by the LastName and Assets fields from the Clients table. The design grid also displays a *Total row* in which each field in the query has either a Group By or aggregate entry. The *Group By* entry under the consultant's last name indicates that the records in the dynaset are to be grouped (aggregated) according to the like values of the consultant's last name; that is, there will be one record in the total query for each consultant. The *Count function* under the client's last name indicates that the query is to count the number of records for each consultant. The *Sum function* under the Assets field specifies that the values in this field are to be summed for each consultant.

The dynaset in Figure 4.5c displays the result of the total query and contains *aggregate* records, as opposed to *individual* records. There are four records for Arnold in Figure 4.5a, but only one record in Figure 4.5c. This is because each record in a total query contains a calculated result for a group of records.

Microsoft Graph

Microsoft Office includes a supplementary application called *Microsoft Graph* that enables you to create a graph (or chart) within an Access form or report. The chart can be based on any table or query, such as the Assets Under Management query in Figure 4.5. The easiest way to create the chart is to open the report or form in Design view, pull down the Insert menu, click the Chart command, then let the *Chart Wizard* take over.

The Chart Wizard guides you every step of the way as can be seen in Figure 4.6. The wizard asks you to choose the table or query (Figure 4.6a), the fields within the table or query (Figure 4.6b), and the type of chart (Figure 4.6c). You then have the chance to preview or modify the chart (Figure 4.6d) and add a title (Figure 4.6e). Figure 4.6f displays the completed chart.

EMPHASIZE YOUR MESSAGE

A graph is used to deliver a message, and you want that message to be as clear as possible. One way to help put your point across is to choose a title that will lead the audience. A neutral title, such as "Assets Under Management," is nondescriptive and requires the audience to reach its own conclusion. A better title might be, "Grauer Leads All Consultants," if the objective is to emphasize an individual's performance.

Arnold is the consultant for
first four clients

Arnold's total assets under
management is $307,000

Barber's total assets under
management has increased to
$100,000

Consultants.LastName	Status	Clients.LastName	Assets	Account Type
Arnold	Associate	Johnson	12000	Standard
Arnold	Associate	Graber	120000	Deluxe
Arnold	Associate	Stutz	150000	Retirement
Arnold	Associate	Laquer	25000	Corporate
Barber	Partner	Doe	100000	Standard
Carrion	Partner	Yanez	18000	Standard
Carrion	Partner	Benjamin	125000	Deluxe
Carrion	Partner	Carson	12000	Standard
Carrion	Partner	Parulis	120000	Corporate
Carrion	Partner	Simon	10000	Retirement
Carrion	Partner	Adams	90000	Retirement
Grauer	Associate	Jones	12000	Standard
Grauer	Associate	Marder	14000	Standard
Grauer	Associate	Gruber	90000	Corporate
Grauer	Associate	Milgrom	150000	Retirement
Grauer	Associate	Coulter	180000	Corporate
Grauer	Associate	Zacco	90000	Deluxe
Milgrom	Partner	Stewart	90000	Retirement
Milgrom	Partner	Milgrom	100000	Corporate
Milgrom	Partner	Frazier	150000	Retirement
Milgrom	Partner	James	100000	Deluxe

(a) Detail Records

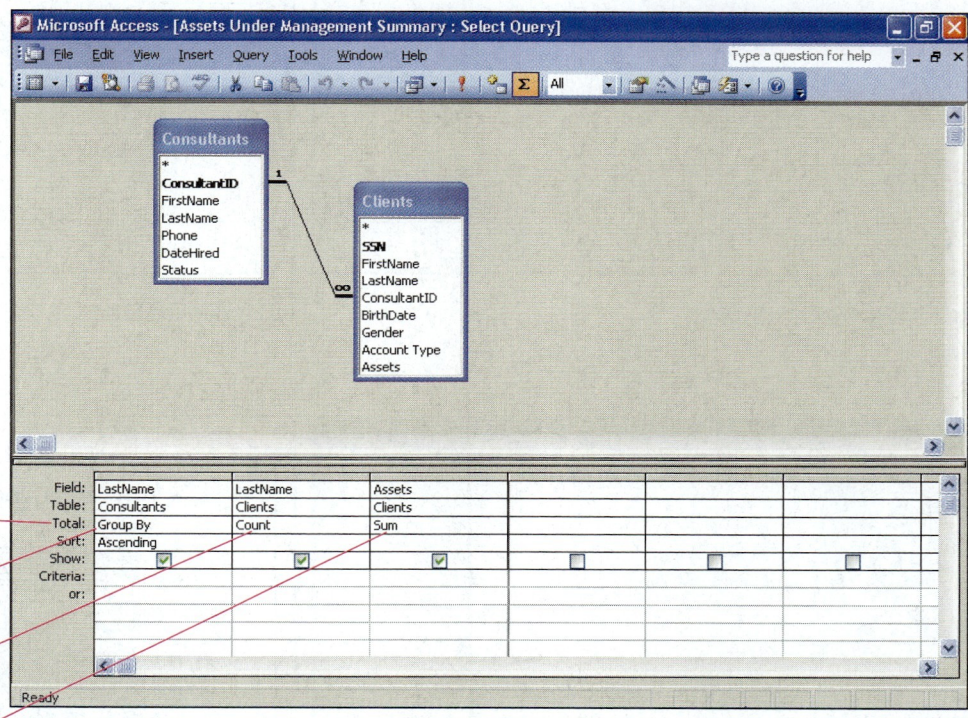

Total row

Group by Consultant's
LastName

Count function will count
clients for each consultant

Sum function will sum assets
for each consultant

(b) Detail Grid

One aggregate record for
Arnold shows 4 clients with a
total of $307,000 in assets
under management

LastName	CountOfLastName	SumOfAssets
Arnold	4	$307,000
Barber	1	$100,000
Carrion	6	$375,000
Grauer	6	$536,000
Milgrom	4	$440,000

(c) Summary Totals

FIGURE 4.5 A Total Query

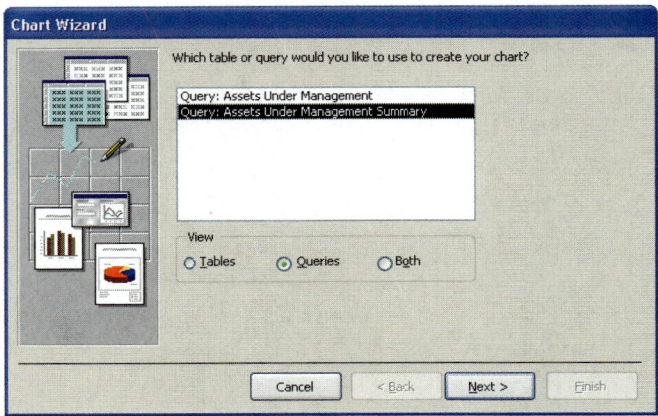

(a) Choose the Query

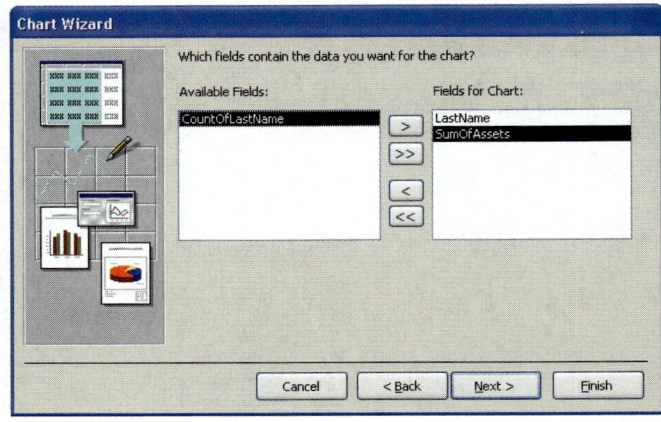

(b) Choose the Fields

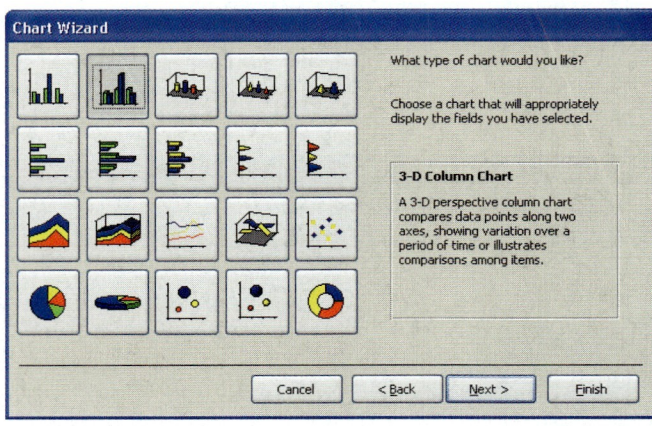

(c) Choose the Chart Type

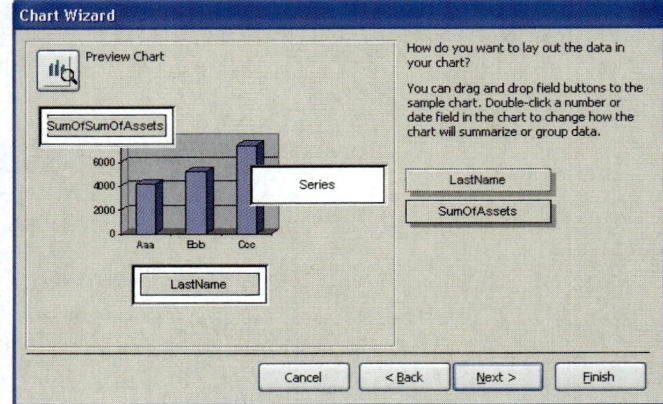

(d) Preview the Chart

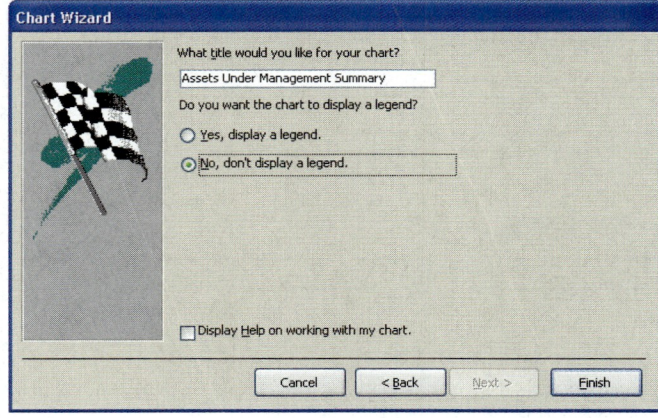

(e) Title the Chart

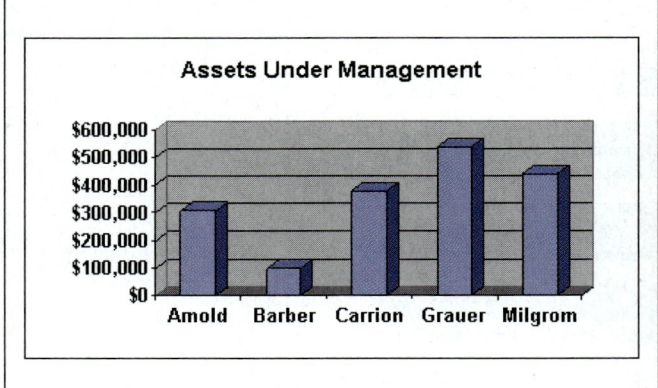

(f) The Completed Chart

FIGURE 4.6 The Chart Wizard

Microsoft Graph is a simple and effective way to visualize the data in a table or query. Pivot tables and the associated pivot charts provide a more powerful way of analyzing the same data as can be seen in Figure 4.7. A ***pivot table*** computes summary statistics for the records in a table (or query) according to the parameters you supply. A ***pivot chart*** provides the same information in graphical form.

The pivot table in Figure 4.7a displays the assets under management for each combination of consultant and account type within the Investment database. Arnold, for example, has $307,000 under management that is distributed over the different account types. In similar fashion, Barber and Carrion have assets under management of $100,000 and $375,000, respectively. The combined assets for all consultants are $1,758,000. The columns show the total assets for each account type as distributed over the various consultants. The combined assets for all account types also total to $1,758,000.

A pivot table is very flexible in that the fields in the row and column areas, Consultant's LastName and Account Type in this example, can be expanded or collapsed to show detail or summary statistics. We have elected to suppress the details for all consultants except Carrion to illustrate the distinction. Carrion, for example, has two retirement accounts of $10,000 and $90,000, and the individual amounts are displayed, as opposed to the total.

There is additional flexibility in that you can display (remove) data for any consultant or account type, by clicking the down arrow in the field name and checking (or clearing) the box for the specific value of the field. Note, too, the third dimension in the pivot table (the filter area) that indicates all of the records in the database. The Status field in this example (is from the Consultant's table, and it) contains one of two values, Partner or Associate, to indicate the status of the consultant. As with the row and column fields, you can click the down arrow to filter the table to display or hide the records according to the value of the Status field.

You can also change the overall structure of the pivot table to add or remove fields by dragging the field names on or off the table. You can switch the orientation (pivot the table) by dragging a field to or from the row, column, or filter area. You can change the means of calculation by switching to the Average, Minimum, or Maximum value, as opposed to the Sum function value in the present table. And finally, you can change the data in the underlying table, then refresh the pivot table to reflect the changes in the table.

Best of all, a pivot table is very easy to create. You may recall that a table (or query) has four different views: Datasheet view, Design view, Pivot Table view, and Pivot Chart view. The pivot table is created within the Pivot Table view. In essence, all you do is click and drag a field from the ***field list*** to the indicated drop area. The Consultant's LastName, Account Type, and Status fields, for example, have been dragged to the row, column, and filter areas, respectively. The Assets field is dragged to the body of the table, and the row and column totals are specified.

The Pivot Chart view in Figure 4.7b displays the graphical equivalent of the associated pivot table. The pivot chart is created automatically when you create the associated pivot table. You can pivot the chart just as you can pivot the table, and any changes made to the pivot chart are automatically reflected in the pivot table and vice versa. You can filter the data to display (hide) selected records. You could, for example, click the down arrow next to Account Type field, then clear the check box that appears next to any of the account types to suppress these values. And finally, you can change the properties of any of the chart's components to display different fonts, formatting, styles, and so on.

Pivot tables have been available for several years in Microsoft Excel, but they are still a well-kept secret in that many otherwise knowledgeable individuals do not know of their existence. Pivot tables and charts are relatively new to Microsoft Access, however, as they were first introduced in Office XP.

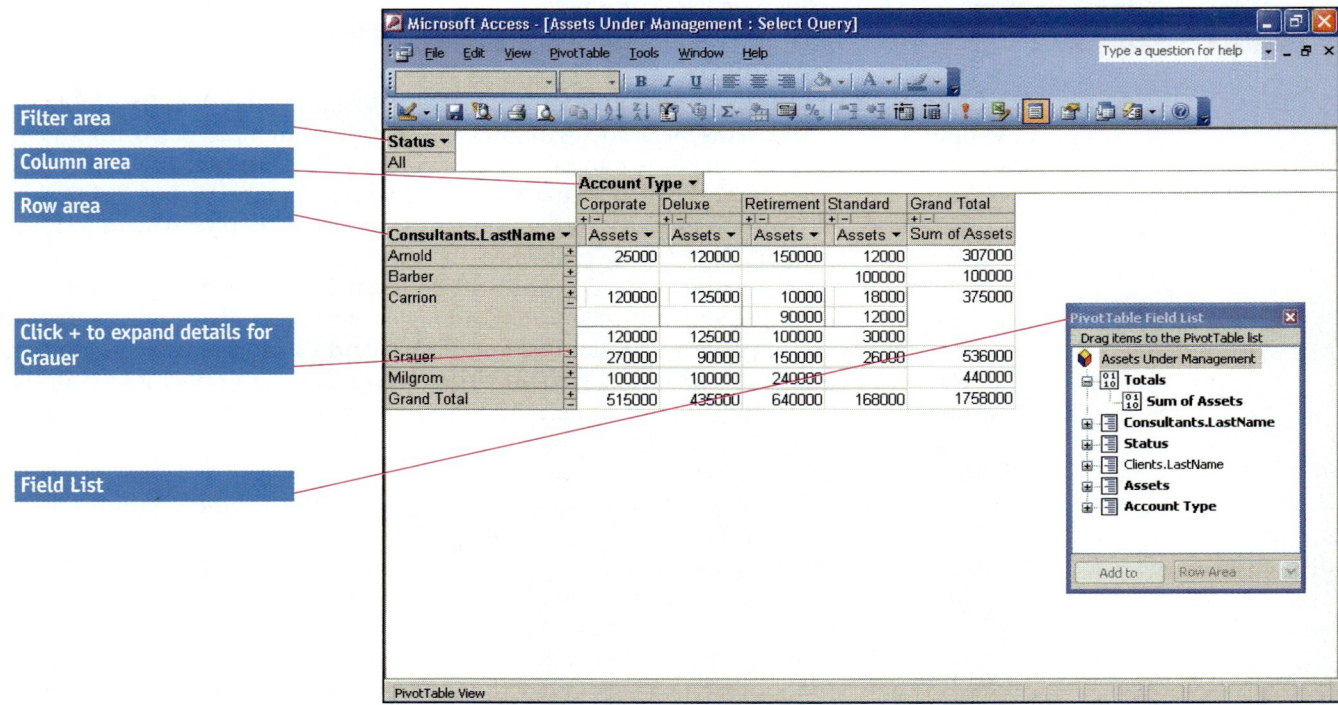

Filter area

Column area

Row area

Click + to expand details for Grauer

Field List

(a) Pivot Table

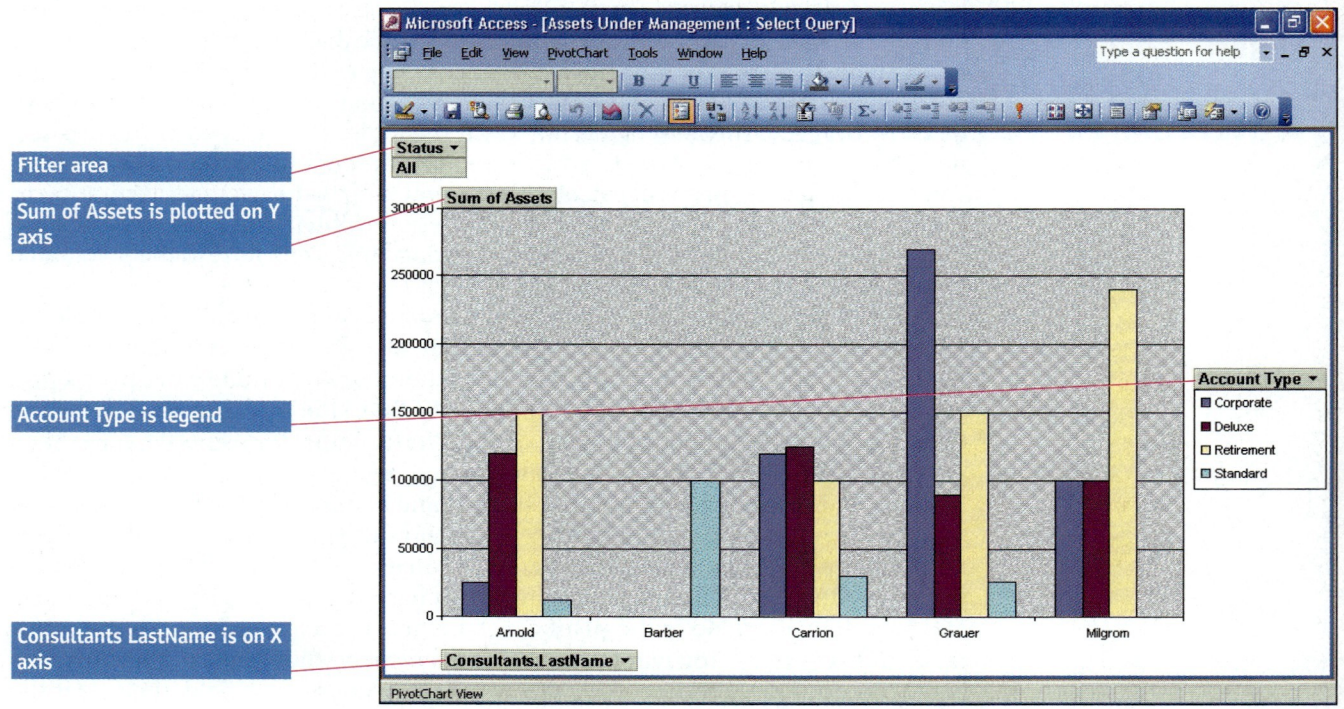

Filter area

Sum of Assets is plotted on Y axis

Account Type is legend

Consultants LastName is on X axis

(b) Pivot Chart

FIGURE 4.7 Pivot Tables and Pivot Charts

Total Queries, Charts, and Pivot Tables

Objective   To create a total query; to use Microsoft Graph to present data from an Access object in graphical form. Use Figure 4.8 as a guide.

Step 1:   **Copy the Assets Under Management Query**

- Open the **Investment database**. Click the **Queries button** in the Database window and select the **Assets Under Management query** that was created earlier.

- Click the **Copy button** on the Database toolbar (or press **Ctrl+C**) to copy the query to the clipboard. Click the **Paste button** (or press **Ctrl+V**) to display the Paste As dialog box in Figure 4.8a.

- Enter **Assets Under Management Summary** as the name of the new query. Click **OK**. There are now two queries in the database window, the original query that was created in the previous exercise, as well as a copy of that query that you will modify in this exercise.

- Select (click) the **Assets Under Management Summary query** that was just created via the Copy and Paste commands. Click the **Design button** to open the query in Design view.

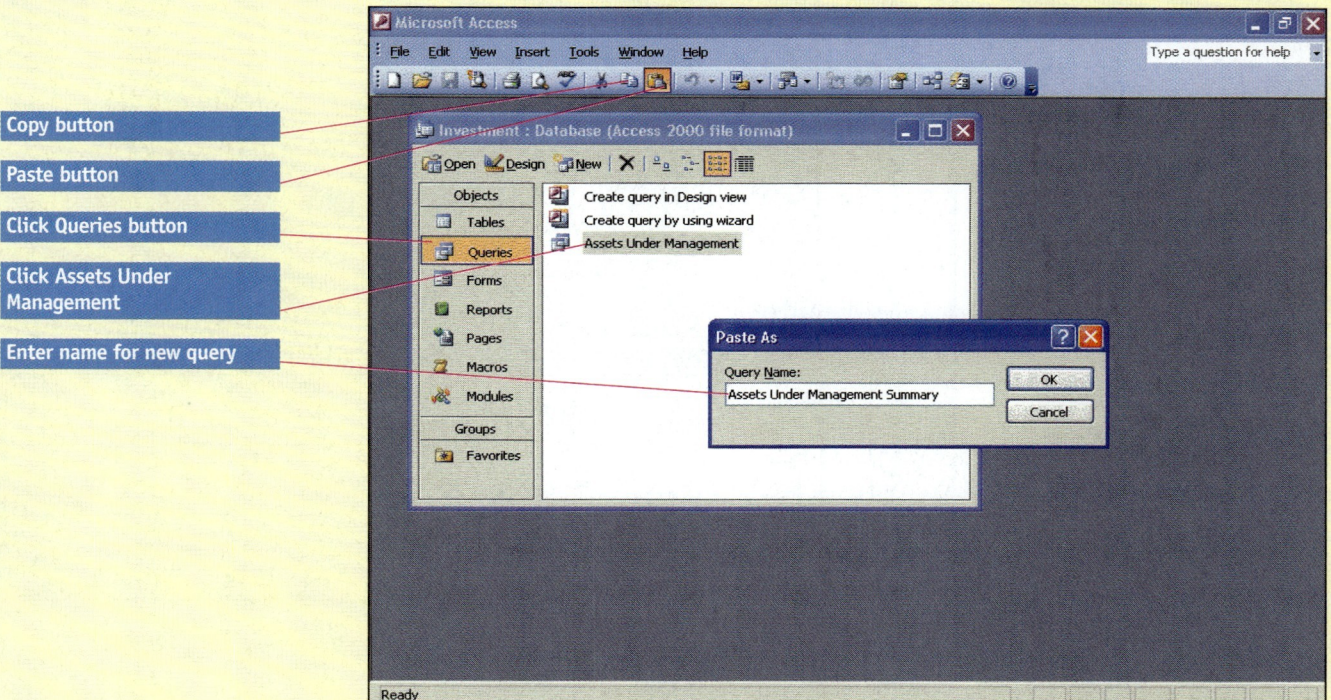

(a) Copy the Assets Under Management Query (step 1)

FIGURE 4.8   Hands-on Exercise 2

KEYBOARD SHORTCUTS—CUT, COPY, AND PASTE

Ctrl+X, Ctrl+C, and Ctrl+V are shortcuts to cut, copy, and paste, respectively, and apply to all applications in the Office suite as well as to Windows applications in general. The shortcuts are easier to remember when you realize that the operative letters X, C, and V are next to each other at the bottom left side of the keyboard.

Step 2: **Create the Total Query**

- You should see the Assets Under Management Summary in Design view as shown in Figure 4.8b. Maximize the window. Pull down the **View menu** and click **Totals** to display the Total row.

- Click the **Total row** under the **Client's LastName field**, click the **down arrow** to display the list of summary functions, then click the **Count function**.

- Click the **Total row** under the Assets field, click the **down arrow** to display the list of summary functions, then click the **Sum function**.

- Click the column selector for the **Consultants Status field** to select the entire column, then press the **Del key** to remove the column from the query. Delete the column containing the **Client's Account Type field** in similar fashion. Your query should now contain three fields.

- Pull down the **Query menu** and click **Run** (or click the **Run button**) to run the query. You should see a dynaset with five records, one for each financial consultant. Each record contains the total assets for one consultant.

- Save the query. Close the query.

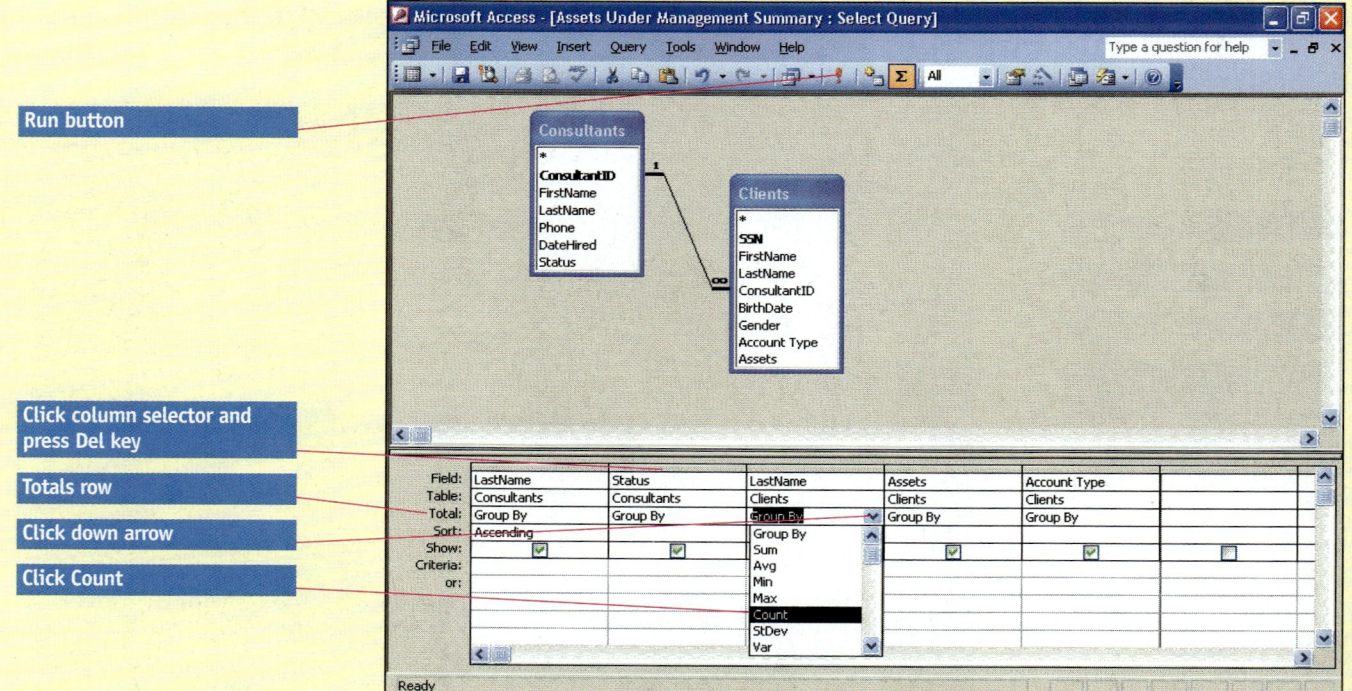

(b) Create the Total Query (step 2)

FIGURE 4.8 Hands-on Exercise 2 (*continued*)

THE UNMATCHED QUERY WIZARD

Any business wants all of its employees to be productive, and our hypothetical financial services concern is no exception. The Unmatched Query Wizard identifies records in one table (e.g., Consultants) that do not have matching records in another table (e.g., clients). In other words, it will tell you which consultants (if any) do not have any clients. Click the Queries button in the Database window, click the New button, select the Find Unmatched Query Wizard, and click OK. Answer the prompts to create the query and see the results.

Step 3: **Start the Chart Wizard**

- Click the **Reports button** in the Database window. Double click the **Assets Under Management report** to run the report. Click the **View button** to switch to Design view.

- You should see the Assets Under Management report in Design view as shown in Figure 4.8c. Click and drag the **Report Header** down in the report to increase the size of the Report Header.

- Click the control that is to contain the name of the person who prepared the report and enter your name. Arrange and format the controls in the Report Header as shown.

- Pull down the **Insert menu** and click the **Chart command**. The mouse pointer changes to a tiny crosshair. Click and drag in the **Report Header** to draw the outline of the chart as shown in Figure 4.8c.

- The Chart Wizard starts automatically and asks for the table or query on which to base the chart. Click the **Queries button**, click the **Assets Under Management Summary query**, and click **Next**.

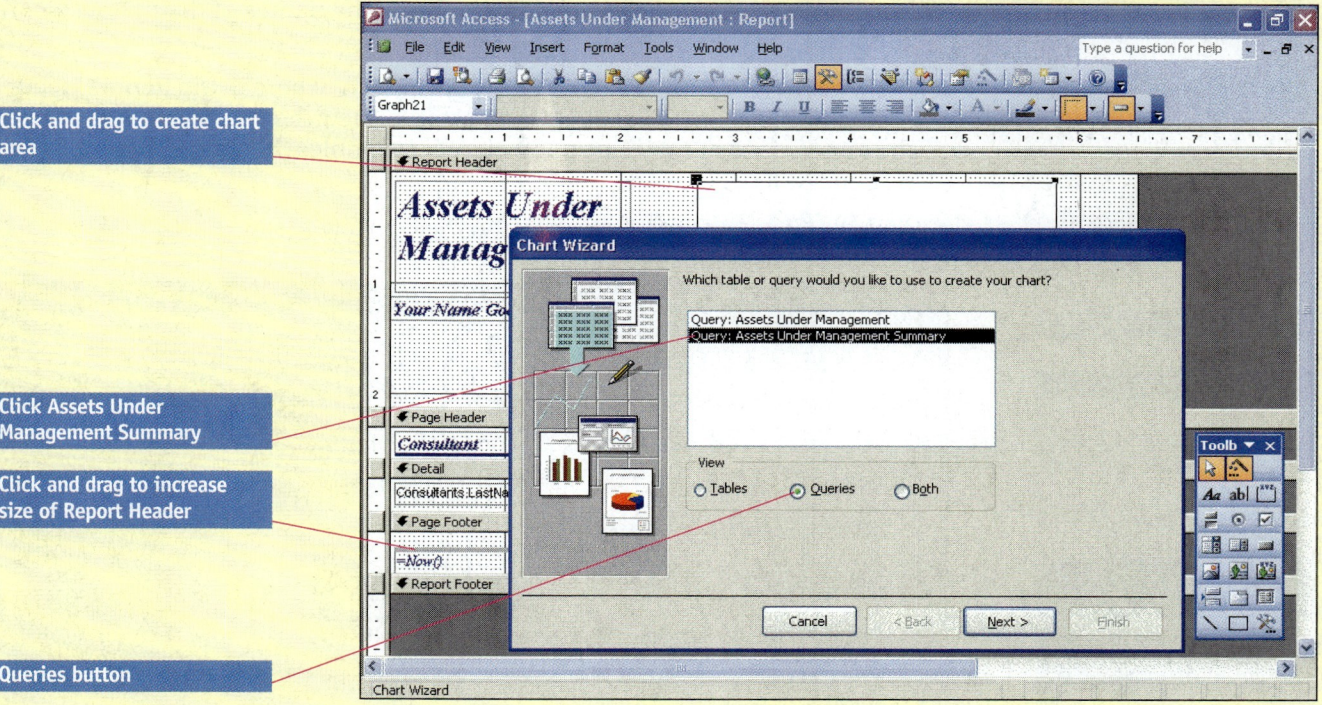

Click and drag to create chart area

Click Assets Under Management Summary

Click and drag to increase size of Report Header

Queries button

(c) Start the Chart Wizard (step 3)

FIGURE 4.8 Hands-on Exercise 2 (*continued*)

ANATOMY OF A REPORT

All reports are divided into sections that print at designated times. The Report Header and Report Footer are each printed once at the beginning and end of the report. The Page Header appears under the Report Header on the first page and at the top of every page thereafter. The Page Footer appears at the bottom of every page in the report, including the last page, where it appears after the Report Footer. The Detail section is printed once for each record in the underlying query or table.

Step 4:   **Complete the Chart Wizard**

- Answer the questions posed by the Chart Wizard to complete the chart.

- Double click the **LastName** and **SumOfAssets fields** to move these fields from the list of Available fields to the list containing the fields for the chart. Click **Next** to continue.

- Select the **3-D Column Chart** as the chart type. Click **Next**.

- The Chart Wizard lays out the chart for you, with the SumOfAssets field on the Y axis and the LastName field on the X axis. Click **Next**.

- The chart should not change from record to record because we are plotting the total for each consultant. Thus, click the **down arrow** in both the Report Fields list and the Chart Fields list and select No Field. Click **Next**.

- Assets Under Management Summary is entered automatically as the title for the chart. Click the option button that indicates you do not want to display a legend. Click **Finish**.

- The completed chart appears in the report as shown in Figure 4.8d. Do not be concerned that the values along the Y axis do not match the Asset totals or that the labels on the X axis do not correspond to the names of the financial consultants.

- Click the **Save button** to save the report. Click anywhere in the **Report Header** to deselect the chart. Click the **View button** to view the chart within the report. The appearance of the chart more closely resembles the finished product, but the chart still needs work.

- Click the **View button** to return to the Design view.

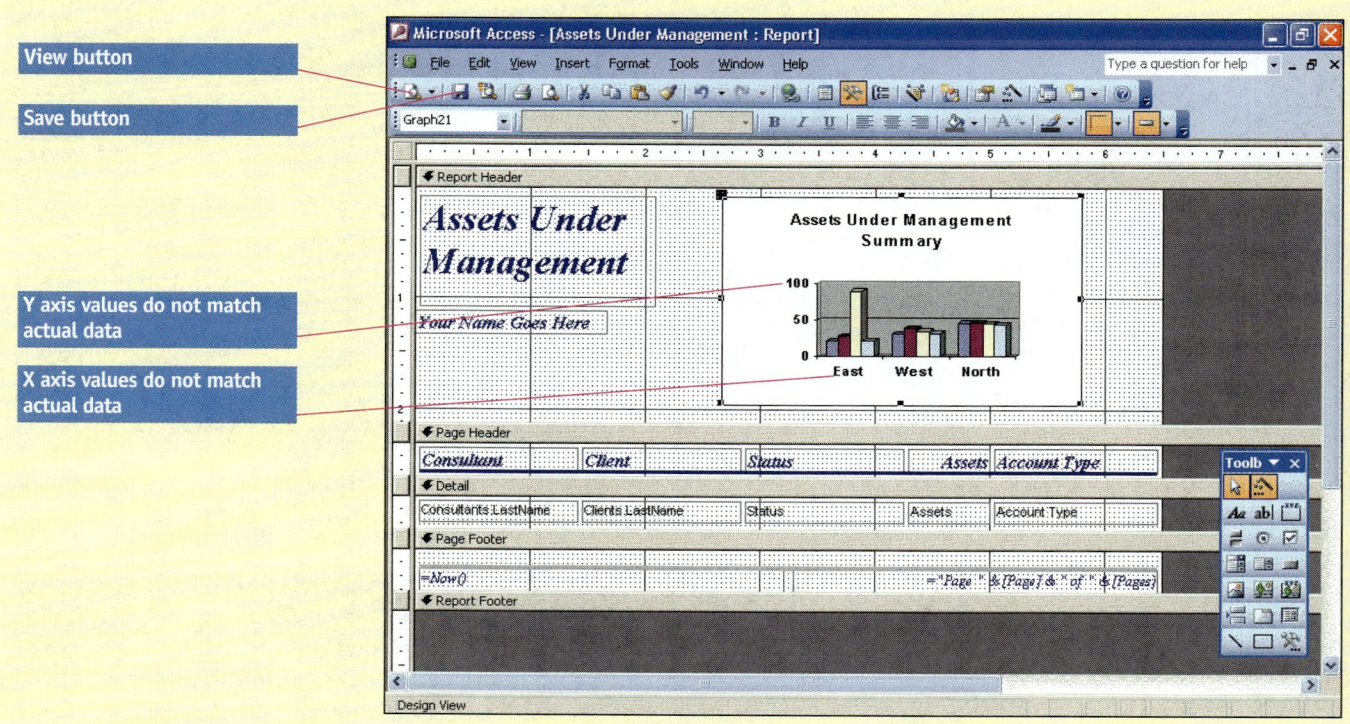

(d) Complete the Chart Wizard (step 4)

FIGURE 4.8   Hands-on Exercise 2 (*continued*)

Step 5: **Increase the Plot Area**

■ Click anywhere in the chart to display the sizing handles, then (if necessary) drag the sizing handle on the right border to increase the width of the chart.

■ You might also want to drag the Report Header down (to increase the size of the header), then click and drag the bottom border of the chart to make it deeper. The chart area should be large enough so that you will be able to see the names of all the financial consultants along the X axis.

■ Click off the chart to deselect it, then double click within the chart to display the hashed border as shown in Figure 4.8e.

■ Close the chart datasheet if it appears. Click (select) the title of the chart and press the **Del key**.

■ Right click the **Y axis**, click **Format Axis**, click the **Number tab**, and set to **Currency format** with **zero** decimals. Click **OK**.

■ Click off the chart to deselect the chart, then click the **View button**. Continue to move back and forth between the Design view and the finished report, until you can see all of the consultants' names along the X axis.

■ Close the report. Click **Yes** if asked whether to save the changes to the report.

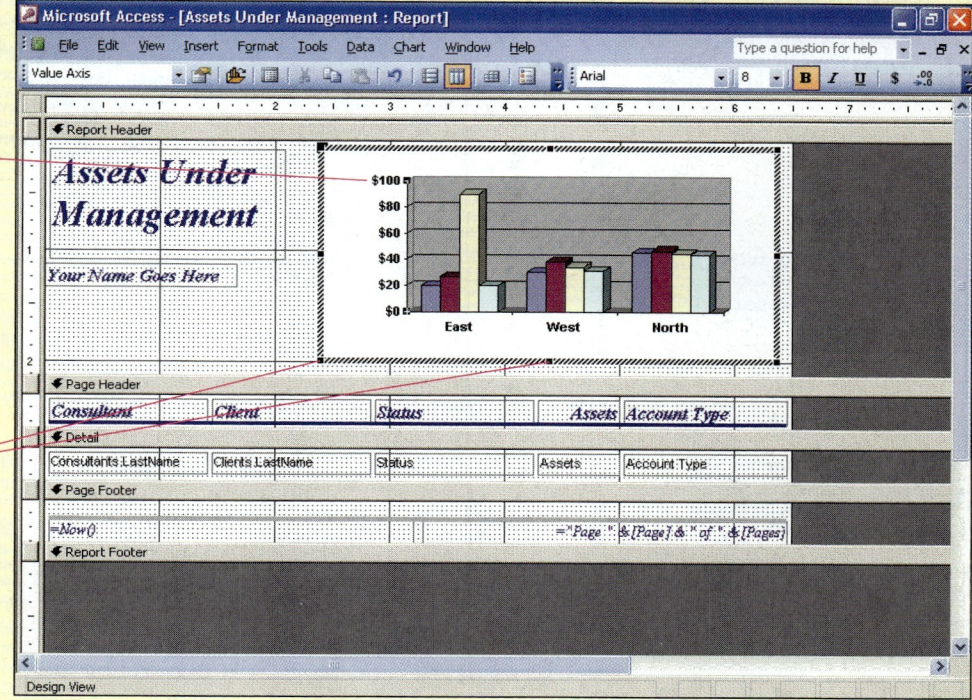

(e) Increase the Plot Area (step 5)

FIGURE 4.8 Hands-on Exercise 2 (*continued*)

TO CLICK OR NOT TO CLICK

Click anywhere on the chart to select the chart and display the sizing handles; this allows you to move and/or size the chart within the report. Click off the chart to deselect it, then double click the chart to start the Microsoft Graph in order to modify the chart itself.

Step 6: The Completed Report

- Click the **Forms button**, open the **Clients form**, locate your record, and change your assets to **$100,000**. Click the ▶ **button** to record your changes and move to the next record. Close the Clients form.

- Click the **Queries button**, then double click the **Assets Under Management Summary query** to rerun the query. The increased value of your account should be reflected in the Assets Under Management of your instructor. Close the query.

- Click the **Reports button**, and double click the **Assets Under Management report** to open the report as shown in Figure 4.7f.

- The detailed information for your account (Doe in this example) appears within the detailed records in the body of the report. The value of your account ($100,000) is reflected in the total for your instructor.

- Click the **Setup button** and change all margins to **one-half an inch**. Click the **Print button** to print the report for your instructor. Close the Report window.

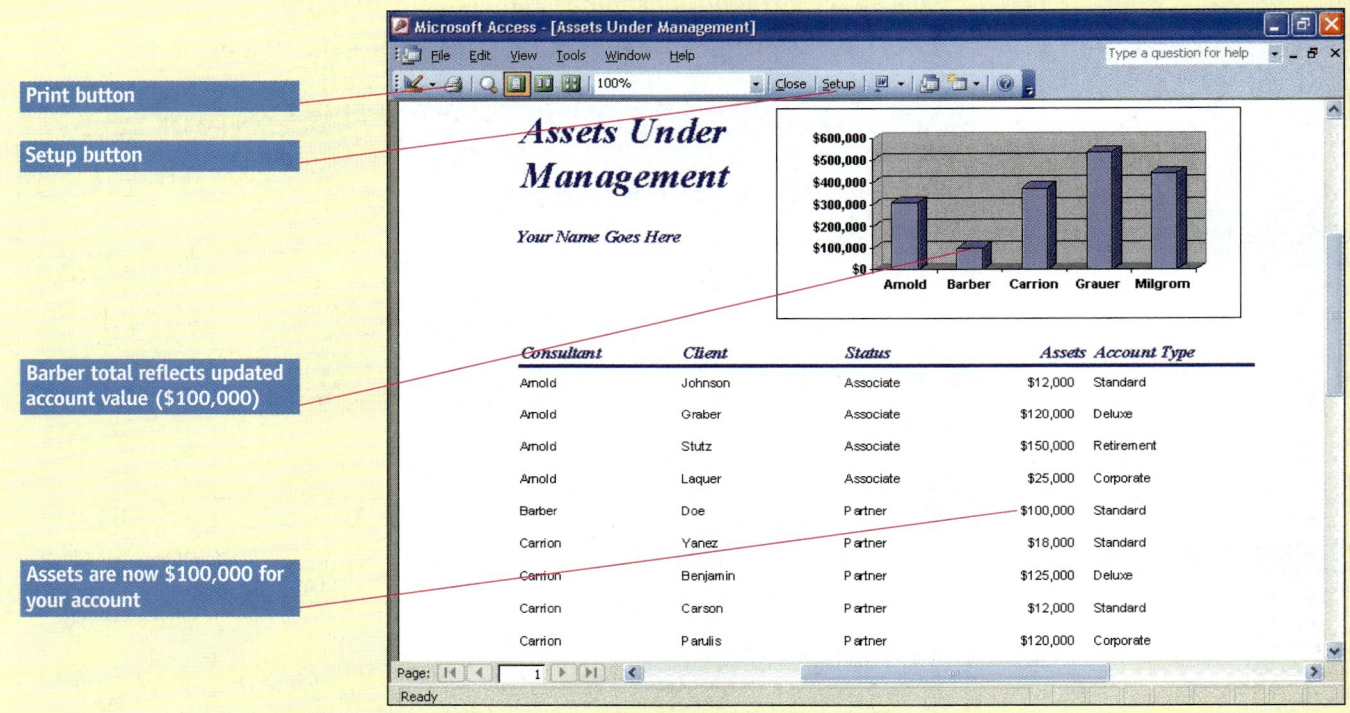

Print button

Setup button

Barber total reflects updated account value ($100,000)

Assets are now $100,000 for your account

(f) The Completed Report (step 6)

FIGURE 4.8 Hands-on Exercise 2 (*continued*)

OPEN THE SUBDATASHEET

Take advantage of the one-to-many relationship that exists between consultants and clients to add and/or delete records in the Clients table while viewing the information for the associated consultant. Go to the Database window, open the Consultants table in Datasheet view, then click the plus sign next to the consultant. You now have access to all of the client records for that consultant and can add, edit, or delete a record as necessary. Click the minus sign to close the client list.

Step 7: Create the Pivot Table

- Open the **Assets Under Management query**. Pull down the **View menu** and select the **PivotTable View** to display an empty pivot table. If necessary, pull down the **View menu** a second time and click the **Field List command** (or simply click the **Field List button** on the Pivot Table toolbar) to display the field list.

- Click and drag the **Consultants.LastName field** to the row area as shown in Figure 4.8g. Click and drag the **Account Type field** to the column area and the **Status field** to the filter area.

- Click and drag the **Assets field** to the Totals or Detail Fields area as shown in Figure 4.8g. You should see the total assets for each consultant, account type, and the database as a whole. Click the **Save button**. Close the field list.

- Right click on the **25,000** Corporate Assets for Arnold. Click **AutoCalc**; click **Sum**. You will see the sum of each client's assets in the Grand Total column.

- Click the **minus sign** next to each consultant's name to show just the totals for each consultant in each Account Type category.

- Pull down the **File menu**, click the **Print command**, and click **OK** (or click the **Print button** on the PivotTable toolbar) to print the pivot table.

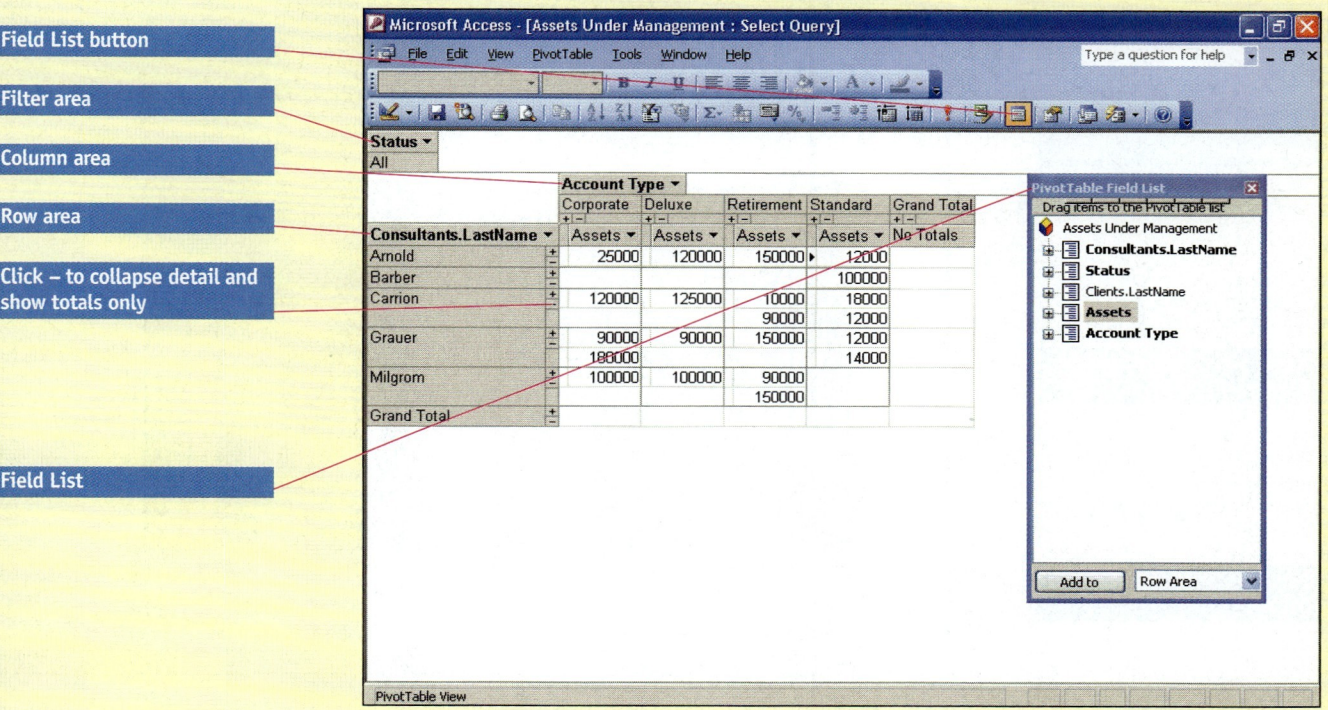

Field List button
Filter area
Column area
Row area
Click – to collapse detail and show totals only
Field List

(g) Create the Pivot Table (step 7)

FIGURE 4.8 Hands-on Exercise 2 (*continued*)

CHANGE THE ORDER

Click within any row or column, then click the Ascending or Descending button on the PivotChart toolbar to display the entries in the selected sequence. Click in the Consultants.LastName column, for example, and click the Ascending button to display the rows alphabetically. Click a single cell in the Grand Total column, then click the Descending button to display the consultant with the highest assets first.

Step 8: **The Pivot Chart**

- Pull down the **View menu** and select the **PivotChart view** to display the pivot chart in Figure 4.8h. The chart corresponds to the pivot table you just created. Close the Field list.

- Pull down the **PivotChart menu** and click the **Show Legend command** (or click the **Show Legend button** on the PivotChart toolbar) to display the legend. The names of the different account types appear as a legend.

- Pull down the **PivotChart menu** and click the **By Row/By Column command** to reverse the rows and columns. The Account Types now appear as the category names, and the names of the consultants appear in the legend.

- The label "Axis Title" does not enhance either the X or Y axis. Click the label on either axis, then press the **Delete key**. Delete the other label in similar fashion.

- Pull down the **File menu**, click the **Page Setup command**, click the **Page tab**, change to **Landscape printing**, and click **OK**. Click the **Print button** on the PivotTable toolbar to print the pivot table.

- Close the query. Click **Yes** when asked whether to save the changes. Exit Access if you do not want to continue with the next exercise at this time.

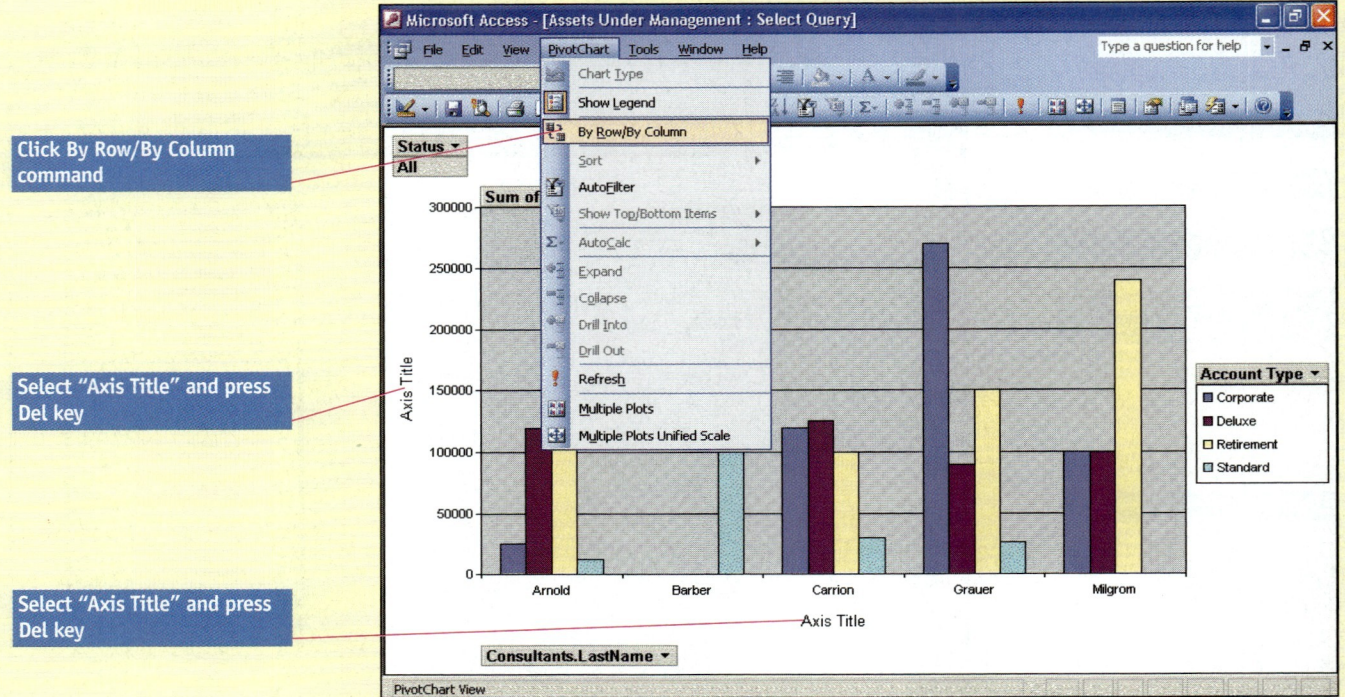

(h) The Pivot Chart (step 8)

FIGURE 4.8 Hands-on Exercise 2 (*continued*)

IMPOSE OR CLEAR A FILTER

Click the down arrow next to any field name to display all of the values for that field, then check or clear the boxes next to the field values. Click the down arrow next to the Account Type field, for example, then clear the box for the Corporate account type. Click OK and the associated column disappears from the table. There is no Undo command, but you can restore the column by reversing the process. And remember, any changes to the pivot chart are automatically reflected in the associated pivot table.

The Investment database has grown in sophistication throughout the chapter. It contains two tables, for clients and consultants. There is a one-to-many relationship between consultants and clients, and referential integrity is enforced. There is a form to enter data into each table. There are also queries and reports based on these tables. You are proficient in Access and are familiar with its Database window to the extent that you can select different objects to accomplish the work you have to do. But what if the system is to be used by a nontechnical user who might not know how to open the various forms and reports within the system?

It is important, therefore, to create a user interface that ties the objects together so that the database is easy to use. The interface displays a menu (or series of menus) enabling a nontechnical person to open the various objects within the database, and to move easily from one object to another. This type of interface is called a *switchboard*, and it is illustrated in Figure 4.9. The switchboard itself is stored as a form within the database, but it is subtly different from the forms you have developed in previous chapters. Look closely and note that the record selector and navigation buttons have been suppressed because the switchboard is not used for data entry, but rather as a menu for the user.

The switchboard is intuitive and easy to use. Click About Investments, the first button on the switchboard in Figure 4.9a, and the system displays the informational screen we like to include in all of our applications. Click any other button, and you display the indicated form or report. Close the form or report, and you will be returned to the switchboard, where you can select another item.

You should try to develop a switchboard that will appeal to your users. Speak in depth to the people who will use your application to determine what they expect from the system. Identify the tasks they consider critical, and be sure you have an easily accessible menu option for those tasks.

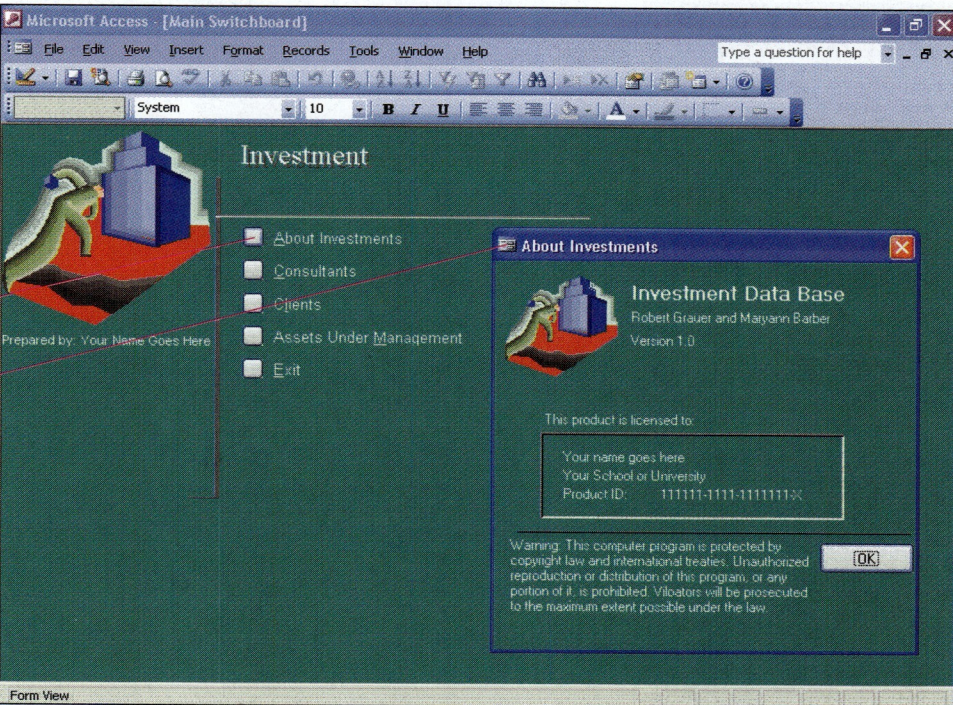

Click button to open About Investments form

About Investments form

(a) The Switchboard

FIGURE 4.9   The Switchboard

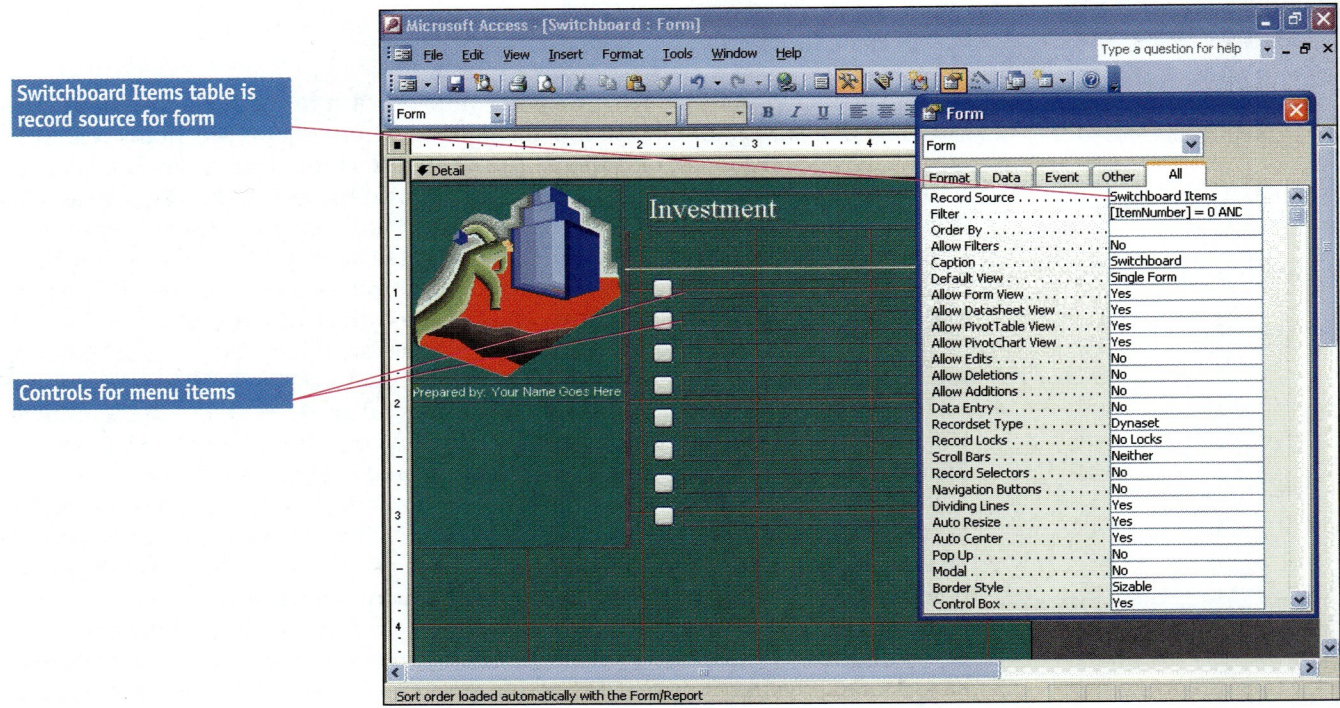

Switchboard Items table is record source for form

Controls for menu items

(b) Design View

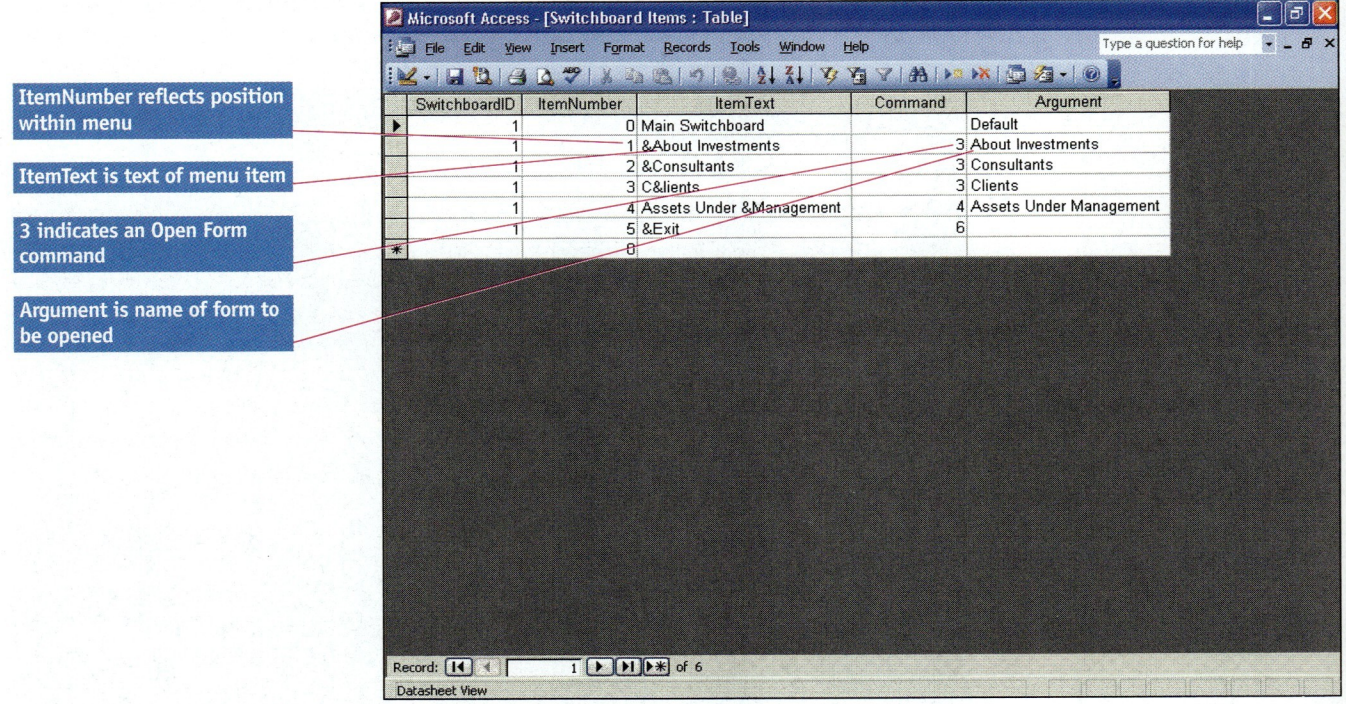

ItemNumber reflects position within menu

ItemText is text of menu item

3 indicates an Open Form command

Argument is name of form to be opened

(c) The Switchboard Items Table

FIGURE 4.9 The Switchboard (*continued*)

The Switchboard Manager

The switchboard is quite powerful, but it is also very easy to create. All of the work is done by the *Switchboard Manager*, an Access utility that prompts you for information about each menu. You supply the text of the item, as it is to appear on the switchboard (e.g., Clients), together with the underlying command (e.g., Open Clients Form). Access does the rest. It creates the switchboard form and an associated *Switchboard Items table* that is the basis for the switchboard. Figure 4.9b displays the Design view of the switchboard in Figure 4.9a.

At first, the two views do not appear to correspond to one another, in that text appears next to each button in the Form view, but it is absent in the Design view. This, however, is the nature of a switchboard, because the text for each button is taken from the Switchboard Items table in Figure 4.9c, which is the record source for the form, as can be inferred from the Form property sheet shown in Figure 4.9b. In other words, each record in the Switchboard Items table has a corresponding menu item in the switchboard form.

The Switchboard Items table is created automatically and need never be modified explicitly. It helps, however, to have an appreciation for each field in the table. The SwitchboardID field identifies the number of the switchboard, which becomes important in applications with more than one switchboard. Access limits each switchboard to eight items, but you can create as many switchboards as you like, each with a different value for the SwitchboardID. Every database has a main switchboard by default, which can in turn display other switchboards as necessary.

The ItemNumber and ItemText fields identify the position and text of the item, respectively, as it appears on the switchboard form. (The & that appears within the ItemText field will appear as an underlined letter on the switchboard to enable a keyboard shortcut; for example, &Consultants is displayed as Consultants and recognizes the Alt+C keyboard shortcut in lieu of clicking the button.) The Command and Argument fields determine the action that will be taken when the corresponding button is clicked. Command number 3, for example, opens a form.

Other Access Utilities

The *Convert Database command* changes the file format of an Access 2003 database to the format used by earlier versions. Think, for a moment, why such a command is necessary. Access 2003 is the current release of Microsoft Access, and thus it is able to read files that were created in all previous versions. The converse is not true, however. Access 2000, for example, cannot read an Access 2003 database because the latter uses a file format that was unknown when Access 2000 was developed. The Convert Database command solves the problem by translating an Access 2003 database to the earlier format. (Access 2003 also enables you to create and modify databases in the Access 2000 format, without going through the conversion process.)

The *Compact and Repair Database command* serves two functions, as its name suggests. The compacting process eliminates the fragmentation and wasted disk space that occur during development as you add, edit, and delete the various objects in a database. Compacting can be done when the database is open or closed. Compacting a database when it's open saves the database under the same name. Compacting a database when it is closed is safer, however, since the compacted database is stored as a new file (enabling you to return to the original file should anything go wrong). The Repair function takes place automatically if Access is unable to read a database when the database is opened initially.

The *Back Up Database command* compacts the open database, and then it saves the compacted database under a different name that contains the date the backup was created. Thus, if you were to back up a database named "Investment", the backup copy would be named "Investment_2003-07-16", given that the backup was created on July 16, 2003.

3   The Switchboard Manager

Objective   To create a switchboard and user interface; to compact a database. Use Figure 4.10 as a guide in the exercise.

Step 1:   **Start the Switchboard Manager**

- Open the **Investment database**. Minimize the Database window to give yourself more room in which to work.
- Pull down the **Tools menu**, click the **Options command**, click the **Forms/Report tab** to display the associated dialog box, then check the box to **Use Windows Themed Controls on Forms**.
- Pull down the **Tools menu**, click the **Database Utilities command**, and choose **Switchboard Manager**.
- Click **Yes** if you see a message indicating that there is no valid switchboard and asking if you want to create one. You should see the Switchboard Manager dialog box as shown in Figure 4.10a.
- Click the **Edit command button** to edit the Main Switchboard, which displays the Edit Switchboard Page dialog box. Click the **New command button** to add an item to this page, which in turn displays the Edit Switchboard item dialog box. Add the first switchboard item as follows.
  - ❑ Click in the **Text list box** and type **&About Investments**, which is the name of the command, as it will appear in the switchboard.
  - ❑ Click the **drop-down arrow** on the Command list box and choose the command to Open the Form in either the Add or Edit mode.
  - ❑ Click the **down arrow** in the Form list box and choose **About Investments**.
- Click **OK** to create the switchboard item. The Edit Switchboard Item dialog box closes, and the item appears in the Main Switchboard page.

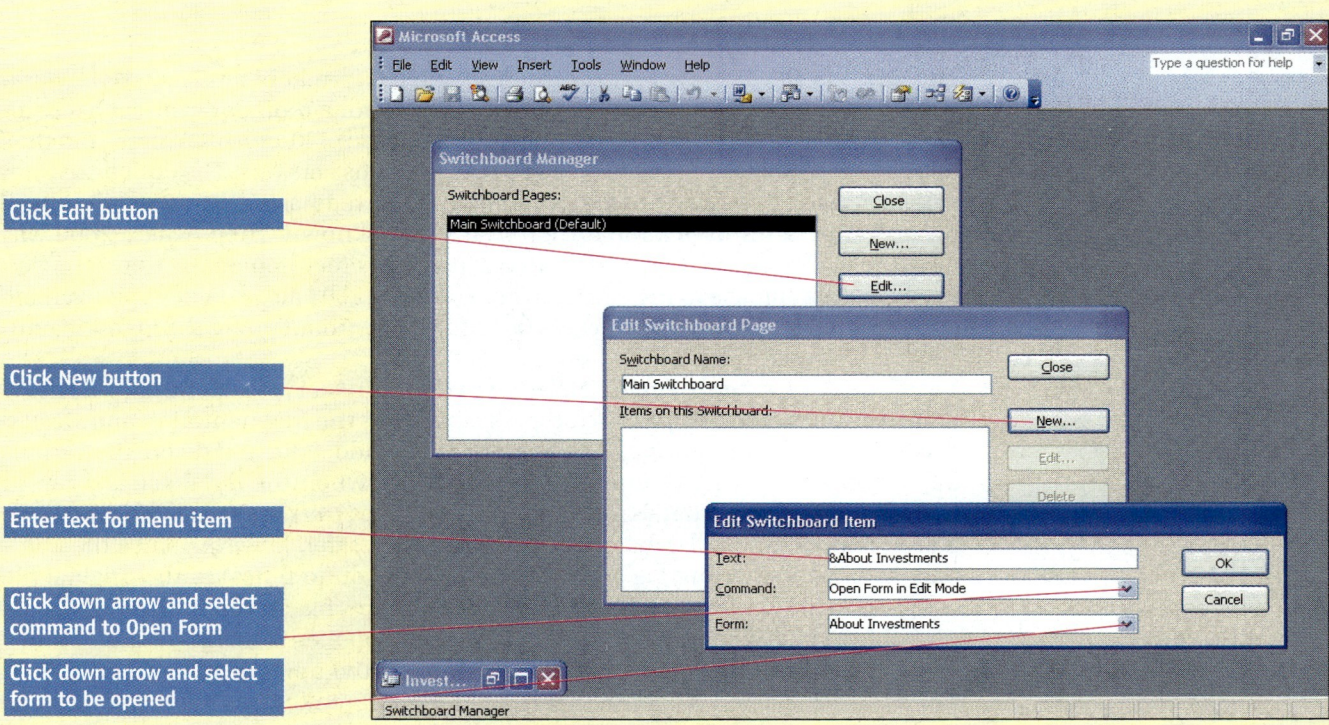

(a) Start the Switchboard Manager (step 1)

FIGURE 4.10   Hands-on Exercise 3

Complete the Switchboard

- Click the **New command button** in the Edit Switchboard Page dialog box to add a second item to the switchboard.

- Click in the **Text list box** and type **&Consultants**. Click the **drop-down arrow** on the Command list box and choose **Open Form in Edit Mode**. Click the **drop-down arrow** in the Form list box and choose **Consultants**. Click **OK**.

- The &Consultants command appears as an item on the switchboard (The switchboard will display <u>C</u>onsultants to indicate a keyboard shortcut—see boxed tip.)

- Add the remaining items to the switchboard as shown in Figure 4.10b. The menu items are as follows:
  - ❏ **C&lients**—Opens the Clients form in Edit mode.
  - ❏ **Assets Under &Management**—Opens the Assets report.
  - ❏ **&Exit**—Exits the application (closes the database but remains in Access).

- Click the **Close button** to close the Edit Switchboard Page dialog box after you have added the last item. Close the Switchboard Manager dialog box.

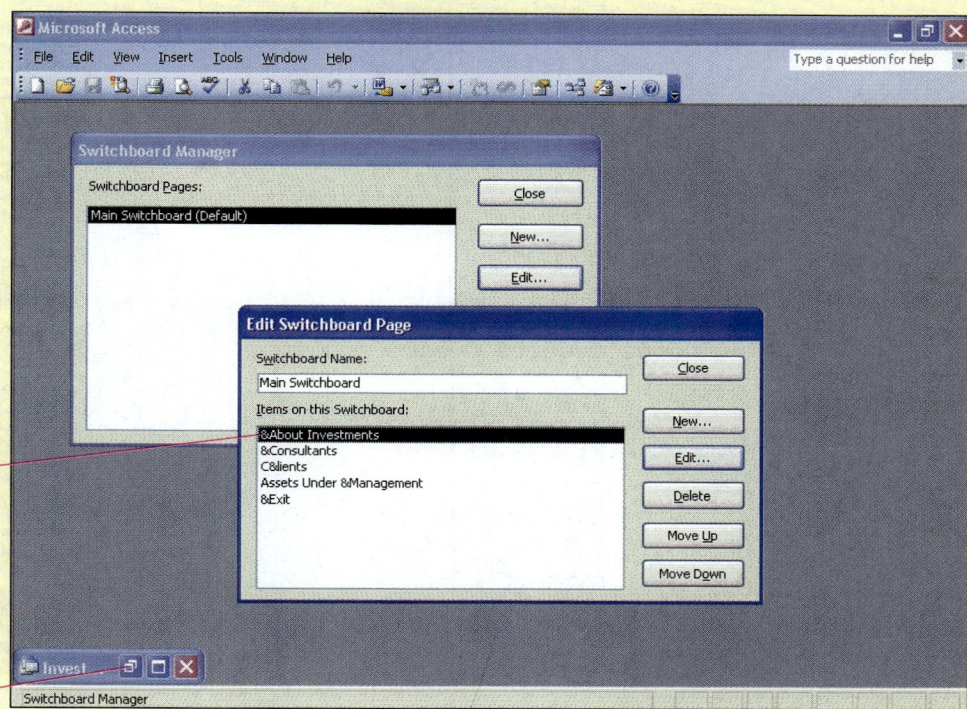

Menu Items

Click Restore button

(b) Complete the Switchboard (step 2)

FIGURE **4.10**   Hands-on Exercise 3 (*continued*)

CREATE A KEYBOARD SHORTCUT

The & has special significance when used within the name of an Access object because it creates a keyboard shortcut to that object. Enter "&About Investments", for example, and the letter A (the letter immediately after the ampersand) will be underlined and appear as "<u>A</u>bout Investments" on the switchboard. From there, you can execute the item by clicking its button, or you can use the Alt+A keyboard shortcut (where "A" is the underlined letter in the menu option).

Step 3: **Test the Switchboard**

- Click the **Restore button** in the Database window to view the objects in the database, then click the **Forms button**. The Switchboard Manager has created the Switchboard form automatically.

- Double click the **Switchboard form** to open the Main Switchboard. Do not be concerned about the design of the switchboard at this time, as your immediate objective is to make sure that the buttons work.

- Click the **About Investments button** (or use the **Alt+A** shortcut) to display the About Investments form as shown in Figure 4.10c. Click the **OK button** to close the form.

- Click the **Consultants button** (or use the **Alt+C** keyboard shortcut) to open the Consultants form. Click the **Close Form button** on the form to close this form and return to the switchboard.

- Test the remaining items on the switchboard (except the Exit button). You can click the button and/or use the keyboard shortcut as you see fit.

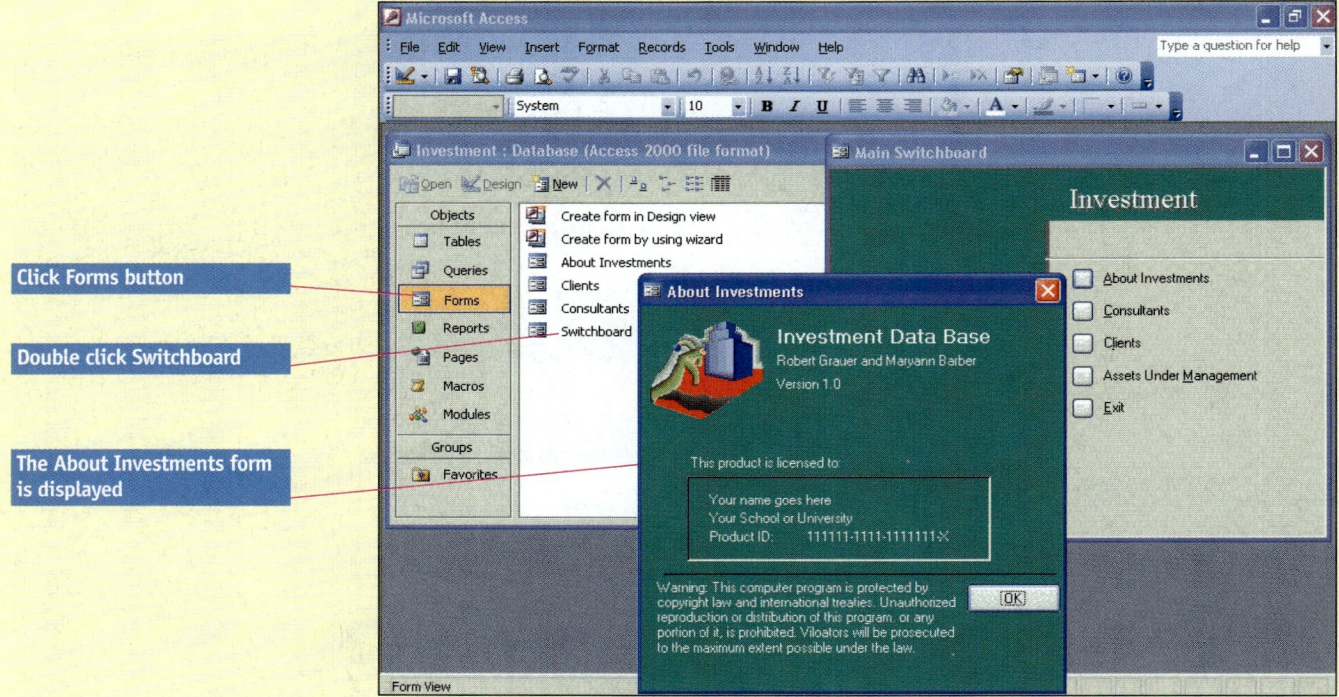

Click Forms button

Double click Switchboard

The About Investments form is displayed

(c) Test the Switchboard (step 3)

FIGURE 4.10 Hands-on Exercise 3 (*continued*)

THE SWITCHBOARD ITEMS TABLE

You can modify an existing switchboard in one of two ways—by using the Switchboard Manager or by making changes directly in the underlying table of switchboard items. Press the F11 key to display the Database window, click the Tables button, then open the Switchboard Items table where you can make changes to the various entries on the switchboard. We encourage you to experiment, but start by changing one entry at a time. The ItemText field is a good place to begin.

Step 4: Insert the Clip Art

- Change to Design view. Maximize the window so that you have more room to work. Click in the left side of the switchboard. Pull down the **Insert menu** and click the **Picture command** to display the Insert Picture dialog box as shown in Figure 4.10d.

- Select the **Exploring Access folder**. Click the **Views button** repeatedly until you see the **Thumbnails View**. Select (click) a picture. Click **OK**.

- Move and/or size the image as necessary. Do not be concerned if you do not see the entire image as you change its size and position.

- Right click the clip art after it has been sized to display a shortcut menu, then click **Properties** to display the Properties dialog box. Select (click) the **Size Mode property**, click the **down arrow**, and select **Stretch** from the associated list. Close the dialog box.

- Click to the right of the picture in the Detail (gray) area of the form. Click the **drop-down arrow** on the **Fill/Back Color button** on the Formatting toolbar to display a color palette. Select the same shade as the rest of the form (the fifth square from the left in the second row).

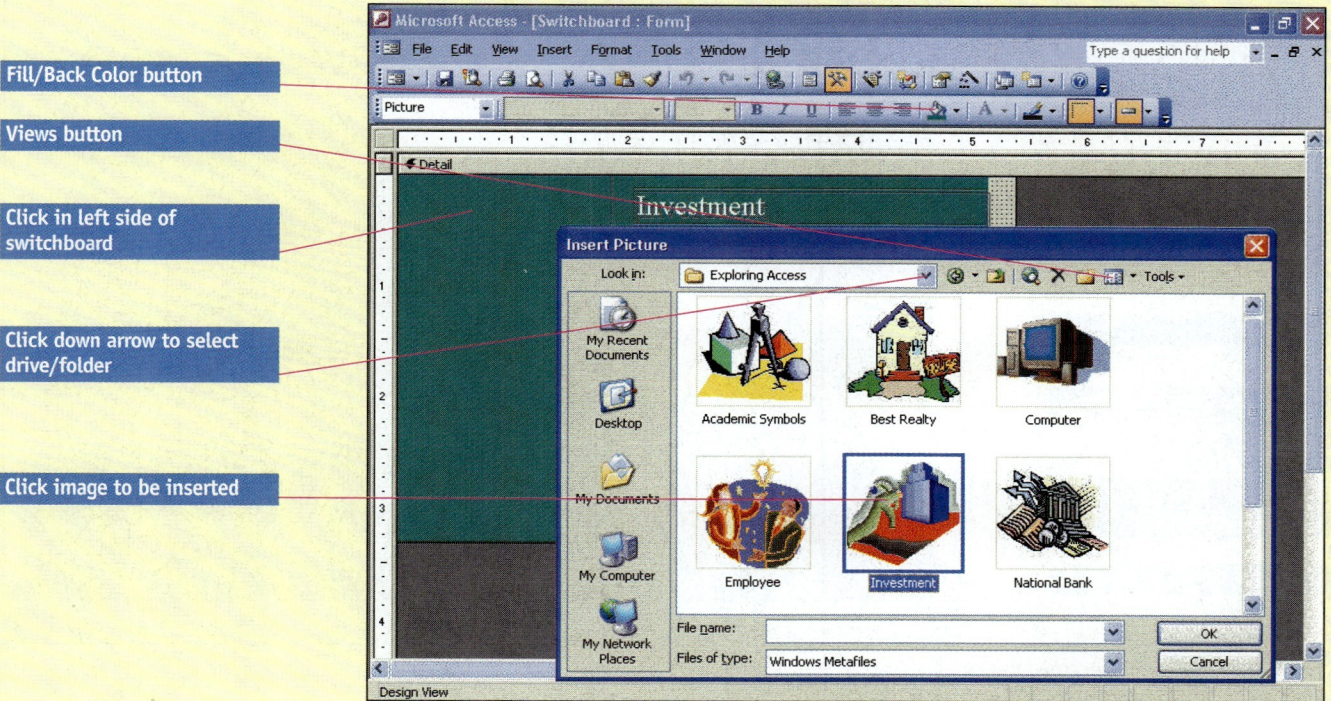

Fill/Back Color button

Views button

Click in left side of switchboard

Click down arrow to select drive/folder

Click image to be inserted

(d) Insert the Clip Art (step 4)

FIGURE 4.10 Hands-on Exercise 3 (*continued*)

SEARCHING FOR CLIP ART

The Insert Picture command functions differently in Access than in the other Office applications since it does not display the Clip Art task pane. You can still search for clip art explicitly, however, by starting the Clip Organizer as a separate application. Click the Start button, click the All Programs button, click Microsoft Office, click Microsoft Office Tools, then start the Microsoft Clip Organizer. Select a clip art image from within the Clip Organizer, and click the Copy button. Use the Windows taskbar to return to Access, open the form in Design view, and click the Paste button.

Step 5: **Complete the Design**

- If necessary, click the **Toolbox tool** to display the toolbox. Click the **Label tool**, then click and drag to create a text box under the picture.

- Enter your name in an appropriate font, point size, and color. Move and/or size the label containing your name as appropriate.

- Press and hold the **Shift button** as you click each text box in succession. Be sure that you select all eight, even if you do not have eight menu choices.

- Click the **drop-down arrow** on the Font/Fore color button and change the font to white as shown in Figure 4.10e. Change the font and point size to **Arial** and **10 pt**, respectively.

- Click the **Save button** to save the changes, then switch to the Form view to see the modified switchboard. Return to the Design view as necessary and make final adjustments to the switchboard. Save the form.

- Click the **View button** to see the switchboard.

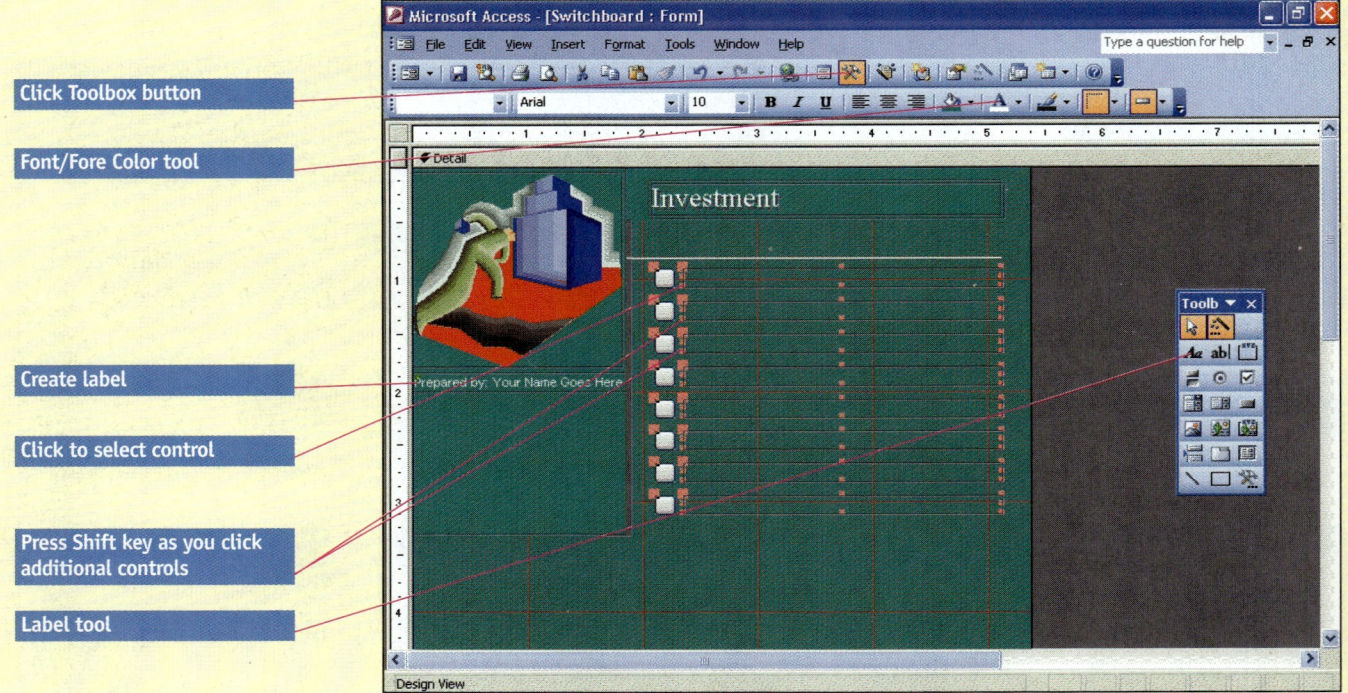

Click Toolbox button

Font/Fore Color tool

Create label

Click to select control

Press Shift key as you click additional controls

Label tool

(e) Complete the Design (step 5)

FIGURE 4.10 Hands-on Exercise 3 (*continued*)

THE STARTUP COMMAND

The ideal way to open a database is to present the user with the main switchboard, without the user having to take any special action. Pull down the Tools menu, click Startup to display the Startup dialog box, click the drop-down arrow in the Display Form/Page list box, and select the Switchboard as the form to open. Add a personal touch to the database by clicking in the Application Title text box and entering your name. Click OK to accept the settings and close the Startup dialog box. The next time the database is opened, the switchboard will be displayed automatically.

Step 6: **The Completed Switchboard and Object Dependencies**

- You should see the completed switchboard in Figure 4.10f. Click the **Maximize button** so that the switchboard takes the entire screen.

- Press **Alt+L** (when the switchboard is active) to open the Clients form. Locate your record. Change the Assets to $2,000,000 (wishful thinking). Close the Clients form and return to the switchboard.

- Press **Alt+M** to open the Assets Under Management report. The chart should reflect the increased value of your account. Close the report.

- Pull down the **View menu** and click the **Object Dependencies command** to open the task pane in Figure 4.10f. Click the option button that says **Objects that I depend on**.

- If necessary, click the **plus sign** that appears next to Tables within the task pane. You should see the Switchboard Items table indicating that the switchboard is dependent on an underlying table.

- Click the **Close button** at the extreme right of the menu bar to close the switchboard but leave the database open.

Object Dependencies task pane

Switchboard form is dependent on Switchboard Items table

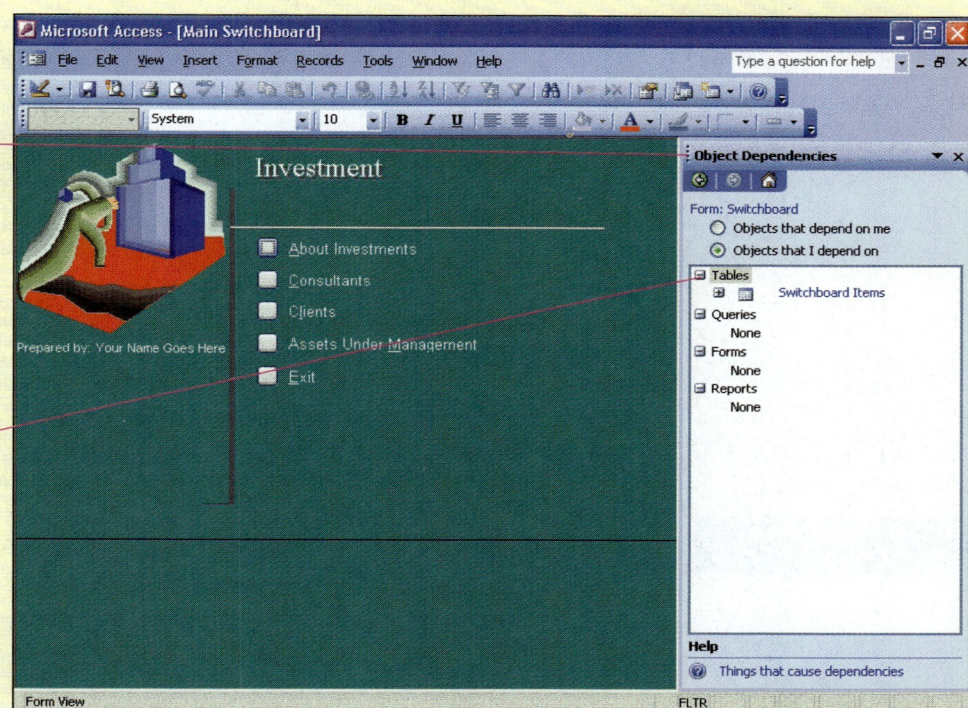

(f) The Completed Switchboard and Object Dependencies (step 6)

FIGURE 4.10 Hands-on Exercise 3 (*continued*)

OBJECT DEPENDENCIES

The objects in an Access database depend on one another; for example, a report is based on an underlying query, which in turn is based on a table. Over time, the report may become obsolete, so you delete the report and the underlying query, but if the same query were the basis of another report, the latter object would no longer function. The ability to view object dependencies can prevent this type of error from occurring. Select the object in the Database window, pull down the View menu, and click Object Dependencies to open the task pane and view the objects that depend on the selected object.

Step 7: **Compact and Back Up the Database**

- Pull down the **Tools menu**, click (or point to) the **Database Utilities command**, and then click the **Compact and Repair Database command**.

- The system pauses as it compacts the database, closes it, then reopens it, which in turn displays the Security Warning dialog box. Click the **Open button** to open the database. You should see the Database window for the Investment database.

- Pull down the **Tools menu**, click the **Database Utilities command**, and then click the **Back Up Database command** to display the Save Backup As dialog box as shown in Figure 4.10g.

- Access supplies a default file name consisting of the original name of the database followed by the date on which the backup was made (July 7, 2003 in our example). Click the **Save button**.

- The system pauses as it backs up the Investment database, closes the backup copy, then reopens the original Access database, which in turn displays the Security Warning dialog box.

- Click **Cancel** since we are finished working. Close Access. Congratulations on a job well done.

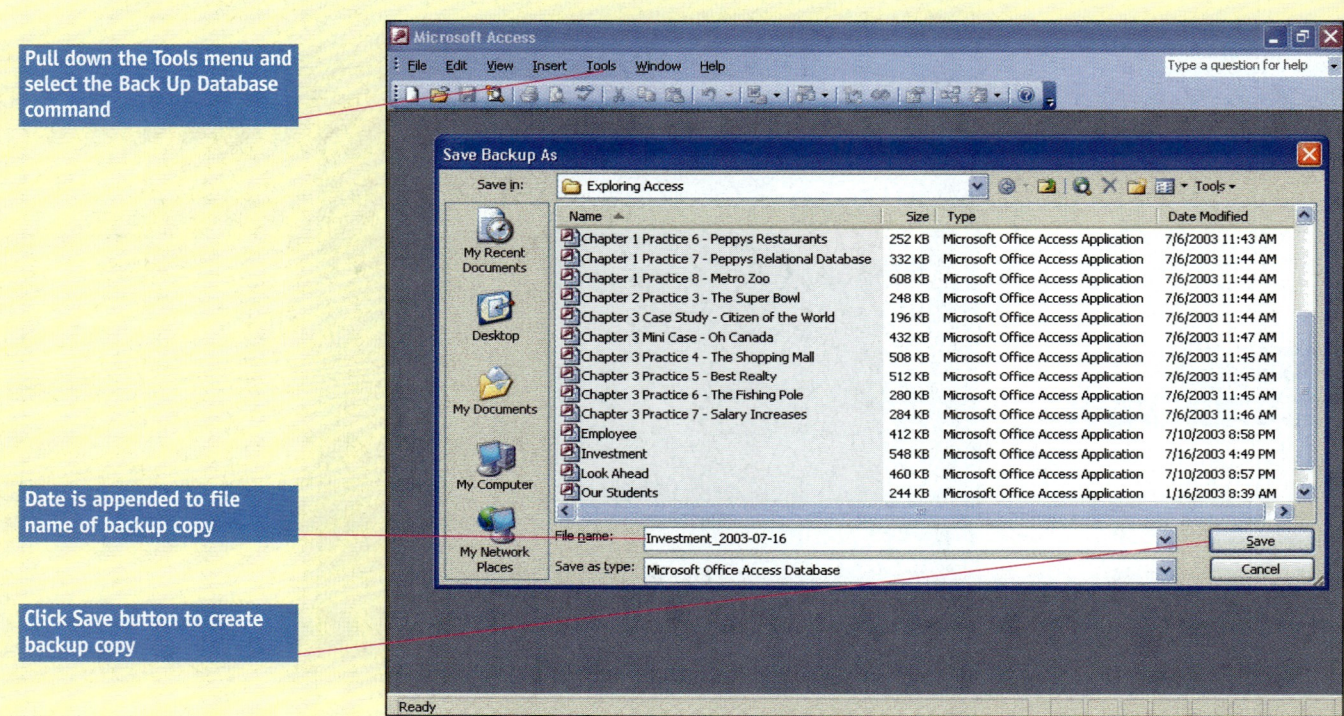

(g) Compact and Back Up the Database

FIGURE 4.10 Hands-on Exercise 3 (*continued*)

A FALSE SENSE OF SECURITY

The backup copy you just created helps to protect you against the accidental deletion or corruption of the Investment database. It does not, however, protect you against damage to your hard drive (if both copies are on the same drive). Nor does it protect you against the loss of your system due to theft or natural disaster. It is important, therefore, that you store the backup copy (or copies) offsite, away from your computer. Note, too, that any backup copy is static and that frequent backup is necessary to retain the most recent copy of your database.

SUMMARY

A relational database contains multiple tables. Each table stores data about a specific entity in the physical system, such as clients and consultants in the Investment database. The tables are related to one another through a one-to-many relationship; for example, one consultant can have many clients, as in the database from this chapter. The relationship is created in the Relationships window by dragging the join field from the one table to the related table. Referential integrity ensures that all of the data in the two tables are consistent.

A select query can contain fields from multiple tables. The relationship between those tables is shown graphically in the Query Design view. The Tables row displays the name of the table that contains each field in the query.

The Get External Data command starts a wizard that will import (or link) data from an external source—such as an Excel workbook—into an Access database. The Export command does the reverse and copies an Access object to an external destination.

A total query performs calculations on a group of records using one of several summary (aggregate) functions. Execution of the query displays a summary record for each group, and individual records do not appear. The results of a total query can be input to Microsoft Graph to display the information graphically in a form or report.

A pivot table is a very flexible way to display summary statistics for the records in a table (or query) according to the parameters you supply. A pivot chart provides the same information as the corresponding pivot table in graphical form. Any changes to the pivot table are automatically reflected in the associated pivot chart and vice versa.

A switchboard is a user interface that enables a nontechnical person to open the objects in an Access database by selecting commands from a menu. The switchboard is created through the Switchboard Manager, a tool that prompts you for the information about each menu item. The switchboard itself is stored as a form within the database that reads data from an underlying table of switchboard items.

The Convert Database command changes the file format of an Access database to the format used by earlier versions of the program. The Compact and Repair Database command serves two functions, as its name suggests. The compacting process eliminates the fragmentation and wasted disk space that occur during development as you add, edit, and delete the various objects in a database. The Repair function takes place automatically if Access is unable to read a database when the database is opened initially. The Back Up Database command compacts the open database, and then it saves the compacted database under a different name that contains the date the backup was created.

The Object Dependencies command (in the View menu) enables you to see the dependencies in an Access database. The dependencies can be viewed in two directions (the objects that depend on you, and the objects you depend on). Thus, it will show all of the objects that depend on a selected object, such as all of the forms and reports that depend on a specific table. It will also show all of the objects that a current object depends on, such as the queries and underlying tables that are the basis of a report.

KEY TERMS

Aggregate functions 180
Back Up Database command 195
Chart Wizard 180
Compact and Repair
    Database command 195
Convert Database command 195
Count function 180
Export command 171
Field list .183
Foreign key 169

Get External Data command 171
Group By .180
Import Spreadsheet Wizard 171
Microsoft Graph 180
Object Dependencies 201
One-to-many relationship 169
Pivot chart 183
Pivot table 183
Primary key 169
Referential integrity 170

Startup command 200
Sum function 180
Switchboard 193
Switchboard Items table 195
Switchboard Manager 195
Table row .170
Total query 180
Total row .180

MULTIPLE CHOICE

1. A database has a one-to-many relationship between physicians and patients (one physician can have many patients). Which of the following is true?

   (a) The PhysicianID will appear in the Patients table
   (b) The PatientID will appear in the Physicians table
   (c) Both (a) and (b)
   (d) Neither (a) nor (b)

2. You are creating a database for an intramural league that has a one-to-many relationship between teams and players. Which of the following describes the correct database design?

   (a) Each record in the Teams table should contain the PlayerID field
   (b) Each record in the Players table should contain the TeamID field
   (c) Both (a) and (b)
   (d) Neither (a) nor (b)

3. Which of the following will create a problem of referential integrity in the Investments database that was developed in the chapter?

   (a) The deletion of a consultant record with a corresponding client record
   (b) The deletion of a consultant record that does not have any client records
   (c) The deletion of a client record who is assigned to a consultant
   (d) All of the above

4. Which of the following is true about a select query?

   (a) It may reference fields from more than one table
   (b) It may have one or more criteria rows
   (c) It may sort on one or more fields
   (d) All of the above

5. Which of the following is a true statement about Access tables?

   (a) An Access query can be exported to an Excel workbook
   (b) An Excel worksheet can be imported as an Access table
   (c) Both (a) and (b)
   (d) Neither (a) nor (b)

6. The Get External Data command will:

   (a) Import a worksheet from an Excel workbook as a new Access table
   (b) Import a text file as a new Access table
   (c) Both (a) and (b)
   (d) Neither (a) nor (b)

7. An Excel worksheet has been imported into an Access database as a new table, after which the data has been modified. Which of the following is *false*?

   (a) The Excel worksheet will be updated to reflect the modified table
   (b) A query run after the table has been modified will reflect the new data
   (c) A report run after the table has been modified will reflect the new data
   (d) All of the above

8. Which of the following is true about the rows in the Query Design grid?

   (a) The Total row can contain different functions for different fields
   (b) The Table row can reflect different tables
   (c) The Sort row can include entries for multiple fields
   (d) All of the above

9. Which of the following is available as an aggregate function within a query?

   (a) Sum and Avg
   (b) Min and Max
   (c) Both (a) and (b)
   (d) Neither (a) nor (b)

10. Which of the following is true about clicking and double clicking a chart within a report?

    (a) Clicking the chart selects the chart, enabling you to change the size of the chart, click and drag it to a new position, or delete it altogether
    (b) Double clicking the chart opens the underlying application (Microsoft Graph), enabling you to change the appearance of the chart
    (c) Both (a) and (b)
    (d) Neither (a) nor (b)

... continued

11. Which of the following is created by the Switchboard Manager?

   (a) A switchboard form

   (b) A Switchboard Items table

   (c) Both (a) and (b)

   (d) Neither (a) nor (b)

12. How do you insert clip art into a switchboard?

   (a) Start the Switchboard Manager, then use the Insert Clip Art command

   (b) Open the switchboard form in Design view, then add the clip art using the same techniques as for any other form

   (c) Both (a) and (b)

   (d) Neither (a) nor (b)

13. Which of the following is true about compacting a database?

   (a) Compacting a database when the database is open saves the compacted database under the original file name

   (b) Compacting a closed database saves the compacted database under a different file name

   (c) Both (a) and (b)

   (d) Neither (a) nor (b)

14. Which of the following best describes how to create a pivot chart?

   (a) Use the Get External Data command to import an Excel worksheet into an Access database

   (b) Use Microsoft Graph to create a multicolumn chart, then convert that chart to a pivot chart

   (c) Use the Import Spreadsheet Wizard command to convert a worksheet to a pivot chart

   (d) None of the above

15. The database of a commercial bank has a one-to-many relationship between Customers and Loans; that is, one customer can have many loans, but a specific loan is associated with only one customer. Which table(s) should contain the LoanID?

   (a) Only the Loans table

   (b) Only the Customers table

   (c) Both the Loans table and the Customers table

   (d) None of the above; the LoanID is not relevant to the database

16. The database of a commercial bank has a one-to-many relationship between Customers and Loans; that is, one customer can have many loans, but a specific loan is associated with only one customer. Which table(s) should contain the CustomerID?

   (a) Only the Loans table

   (b) Only the Customers table

   (c) Both the Loans table and the Customers table

   (d) None of the above; the CustomerID is not relevant to the database

17. Which of the following was suggested as essential to a backup strategy?

   (a) Backing up data files at the end of every session

   (b) Storing the backup file(s) at another location

   (c) Both (a) and (b)

   (d) Neither (a) nor (b)

18. Which of the following is an advantage of a pivot table?

   (a) You can add or remove fields by dragging the field names on or off the table.

   (b) You can switch the orientation by dragging a field to or from the row, column, or filter area.

   (c) You can change the means of calculation by changing the average value to sum, minimum, or maximum value.

   (d) All of the above

ANSWERS

1. a	**7.** a	**13.** c
2. b	**8.** d	**14.** d
3. a	**9.** c	**15.** a
4. d	**10.** c	**16.** c
5. c	**11.** c	**17.** c
6. c	**12.** b	**18.** d

PRACTICE WITH ACCESS

1. **The Oscars:** The switchboard in Figure 4.11 contains seven commands, three of which reference reports that were created in an end-of-chapter exercise in Chapter 3. You can do this exercise even if you did not create the reports, since the other objects are already in the database. You do, however, have to create the About the Oscars form, which is best accomplished by importing (and modifying) the similar form from the Investment database.

   a. Open the *Chapter 1 Practice 1* database in the Exploring Access folder. Click the Forms button in the Database window, pull down the File menu, click the Get External Data command, click Import, and then import the About Investments form from the Investment database. Return to the Database window. Right click the newly imported form, and change the name of the form to About the Oscars, then open that form in Design view. Change the clip art, labels, and colors as necessary. And finally, right click the form selector button, click Properties, select the Caption property and change the text to reflect the Oscars.

   b. Use the Switchboard Manager to create the switchboard in Figure 4.11. The Award Winners form, which is used to enter Oscar data, is already in the database (open the form in Edit mode). The report to list the major winners by year is also in the database, but the availability of the additional reports depends on whether you completed the end-of-chapter exercise in Chapter 3. Format the switchboard so that its appearance is consistent with Figure 4.11.

   c. Test each button on the switchboard to be sure that the commands work properly. Click the button to enter Oscar data, and then view the last record in the table to see the most recent awards. If necessary, click the link on the form to go to the Oscars Web site to obtain the additional awards (if any) since the publication of our book. Enter that data into the database.

   d. Click the appropriate button to view, and then print each report in the database.

   e. Pull down the Tools menu, and click the Startup command. Select the switchboard as the form to display when the database is opened. Click OK to close the Startup dialog box. Pull down the Tools menu, click Database Utilities, and then click the Compact and Repair Database command. The database should compact itself and reopen with the switchboard displayed automatically.

   f. Print the Switchboard form and Switchboard Items table for your instructor.

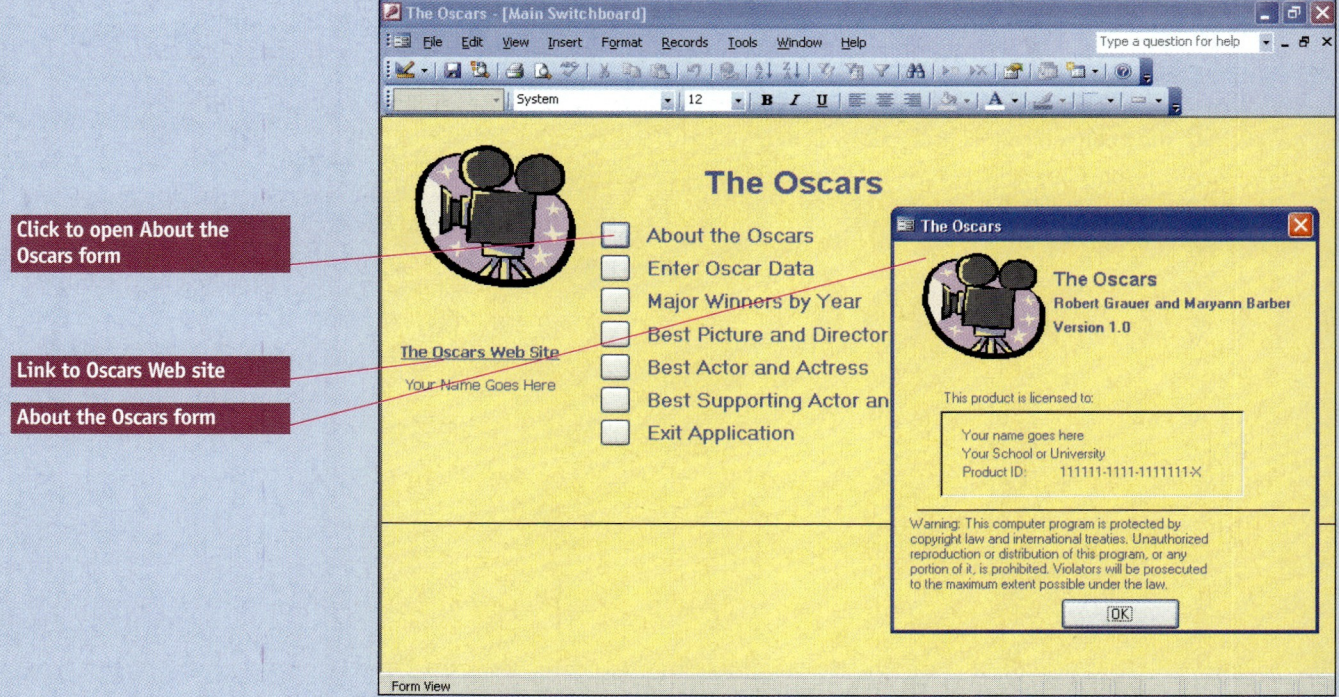

Click to open About the Oscars form

Link to Oscars Web site

About the Oscars form

FIGURE 4.11 The Oscars (exercise 1)

2. **Employee Health Plans:** Figure 4.12 displays the relationships diagram of a database that tracks employees, the cities in which they work, and the health plans to which they subscribe. The database contains the typical data for every employee (name, birth date, salary, and so on) and for every office location (address, telephone, and so on). The database also stores data about the available health plans such as the name and description of the plan, the monthly contribution, the deductible each employee is required to pay, and the percent of expenses that an employee will be reimbursed. Your task is to create the tables (you do not have to enter any data), implement the relationships, and create a simple switchboard. Note the following:

a. Each employee is assigned to one city, but a given city has multiple employees. In similar fashion, each employee chooses one health plan, but a given health plan has multiple employees. An employee cannot be hired without being assigned to a city. New employees have 30 days, however, to decide on a health plan.

b. The report in Figure 4.12 is created from the Relationships window after the relationships have been specified. Pull down the Tools menu and click Relationships to open the Relationships window, then pull down the File menu and click the Print Relationships command to display the Print Preview screen of a report that displays the contents of the Relationships window. Change to the Design view to modify the report to include your name and an appropriate clip art image.

c. Create a simple About the Employee Health Plans form similar to the other forms in this chapter.

d. Create a switchboard with three menu options—a button to display the About Employee Health Plans form, a button to print the relationships diagram, and a button to exit the application. The switchboard should contain the same clip art as the relationships diagram. Use the Startup property to display the switchboard automatically when the database is opened.

e. Test the switchboard thoroughly to be sure it works correctly. Use the Startup property in the Tools menu to display the switchboard automatically when the database is opened initially. Print the relationships diagram, the Switchboard form, and the Switchboard Items table for your instructor.

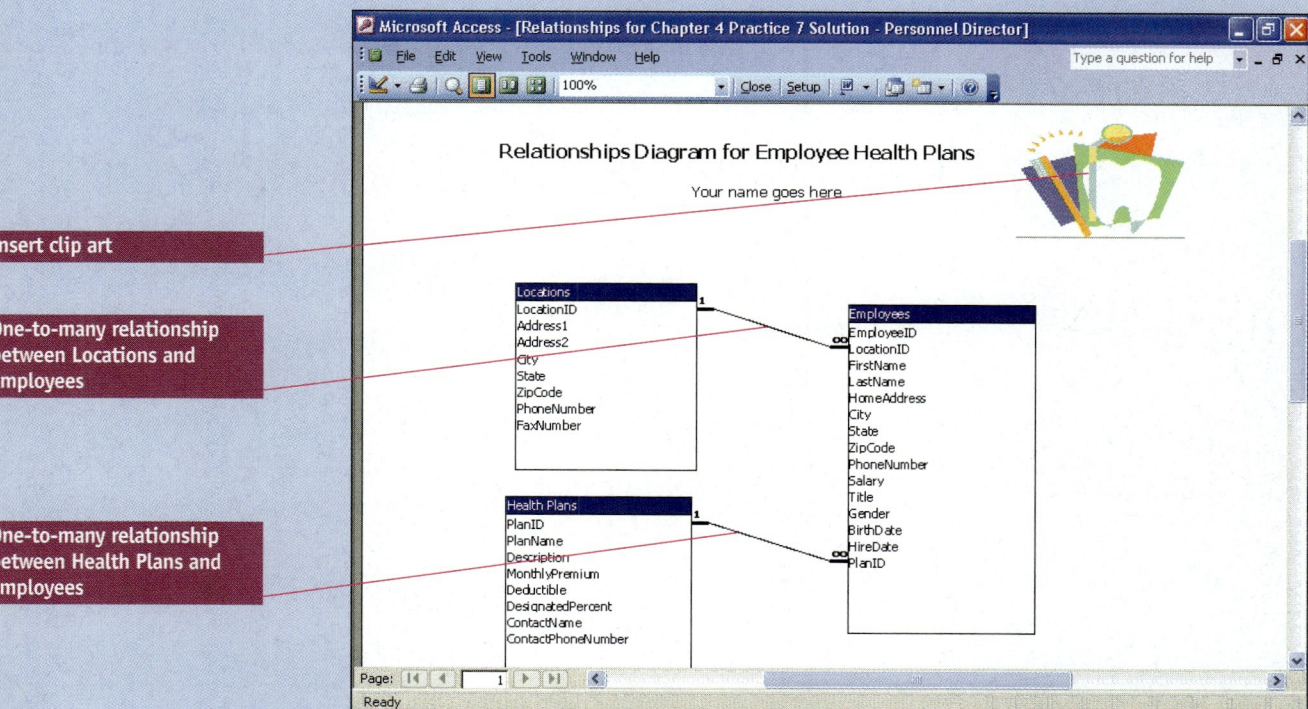

FIGURE 4.12 Employee Health Plans (exercise 2)

3. **The Metro Zoo:** The switchboard in Figure 4.13 is based on the Metro Zoo database that was introduced in Chapter 1. You do not have to match our design exactly, but you are required to duplicate the functionality. All of the objects (i.e., the forms and reports) have been created for you and are found in the database. Proceed as follows:

a. Open the *Chapter 1 Practice 8* database and complete that exercise if you have not already done so. Pull down the Tools menu, click the Relationships command, and create the one-to-many relationships that exist in the system. Enforce referential integrity for every relationship.

b. Start the Switchboard Manager, which will display the Switchboard Manager dialog box. Click New to create a new switchboard (in addition to the main switchboard that is created by default). Enter Report Menu as the name of the new switchboard page, then click OK.

c. You will return to the Switchboard Manager dialog box. Select the Main Switchboard, click Edit, and build the items for the main switchboard as shown in Figure 4.13. Be sure to open all of the forms in the Edit mode. After you have built the main switchboard, click Close on the Edit Switchboard Page dialog box to return to the Switchboard Manager dialog box.

d. Select the Report Menu switchboard, and click Edit. Build the items for the Report Menu, which consist of a separate command for each report plus a command to return to main menu. (The latter is a Go To Switchboard command that opens the Main switchboard.) Close the switchboard page. Close the Switchboard Manager.

e. Open the Switchboard form in Design view to format the switchboard as shown in Figure 4.13. You do not have to match our design exactly.

f. Test both switchboards to be sure that they work correctly. Verify that the data entry operations for the Trainer and Animal tables have been implemented correctly as described in Chapter 1. Use the report menu to print each report in the database.

g. Which report is based on a query rather than a table? How many tables are referenced in that query? Go to the Database window and print the dynaset for the underlying query for the report in question. Print the Switchboard form and Switchboard Items table and then submit all items to your instructor.

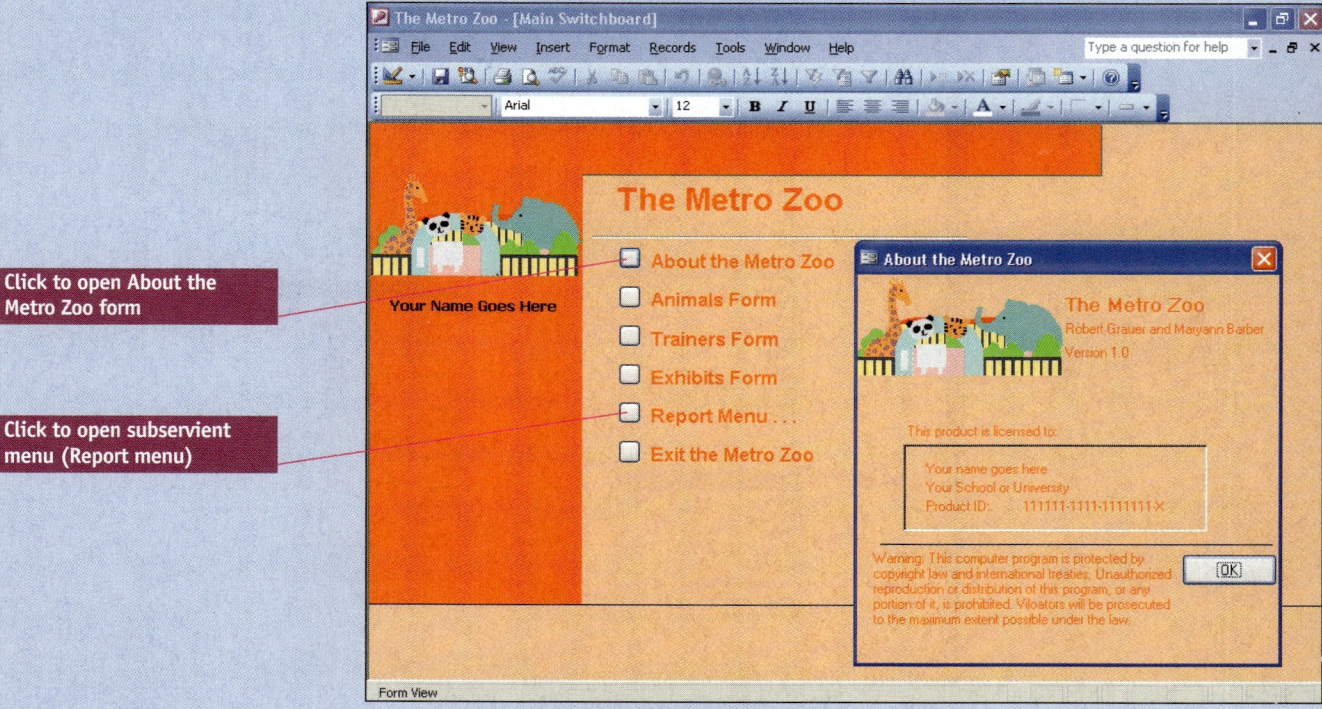

FIGURE 4.13 The Metro Zoo (exercise 3)

4. **The Shopping Mall (secondary switchboard):** Figure 4.14 displays a switchboard for the Shopping Mall database that has been developed in previous chapters, most recently in Chapter 3. Your present assignment is to create the switchboard in Figure 4.14, which includes an option to display a report menu. The latter is a second (subsidiary) switchboard that includes commands to print all of the reports that were created in Chapter 3, as well as an option to return to the Main Menu. Proceed as follows:

a. Start the Switchboard Manager. At the Switchboard Manager dialog box, click New to create a new switchboard. In the Create New dialog box, enter a name for the new switchboard, such as Report Menu, then click OK.

b. You will return to the Switchboard Manager dialog box. Select the Main Switchboard, click Edit, and build the items for the Main Switchboard (open the "About the Mall" form, open the Coral Pines Shopping Mall form to enter/edit data, go to the Report Menu switchboard, and Exit). After you have built the main switchboard, click Close on the Edit Switchboard Page dialog box to return to the Switchboard Manager.

c. Select the Report Menu switchboard, and click Edit. Build the items for the Report Menu (one each to open the individual reports and one to return to the Main Menu—which is actually a Go To Switchboard command that opens the Main Switchboard).

d. Open the Switchboard form in Design view to format the switchboard in an attractive fashion. You do not have to match our design exactly, but your switchboard should enhance the default design.

e. Use the Startup property in the Tools menu to display the switchboard automatically when the database is opened initially. Pull down the Tools menu, click the Database Utilities command, then click the command to Compact and Repair the Database. Access will close, and then reopen, the database; the switchboard should be displayed automatically.

f. Be sure you test both switchboards completely to be sure that they work correctly. Print the Switchboard form and the Switchboard Items table for your instructor.

g. Take a minute to reflect on what you have accomplished over the last several chapters. You created the database and designed a table and associated form in Chapter 2, you created various reports in Chapter 3, and you put everything together via the switchboard in this exercise. Well done!

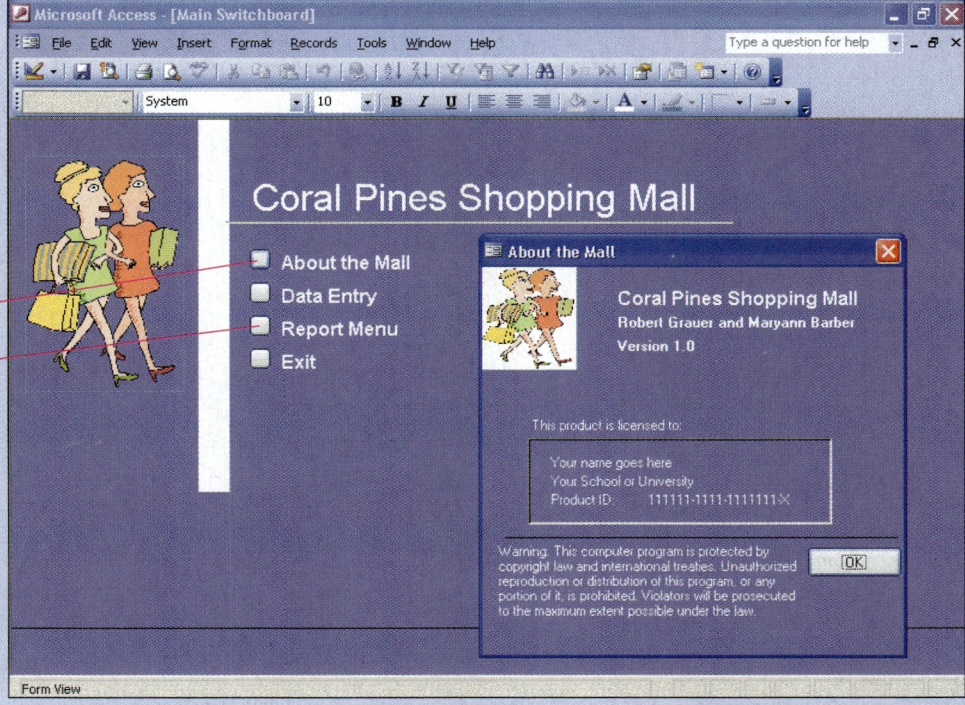

Click to open About the Mall form

Click to open Report menu

FIGURE 4.14 The Shopping Mall (exercise 4)

5. **Best Realty (secondary switchboard):** Figure 4.15 displays a switchboard for the *Best Realty* database that has been developed in previous chapters, most recently in Chapter 3. Your present assignment is to create the switchboard shown in Figure 4.15, which includes an option to display a report menu. The latter is a second (subsidiary) switchboard that includes commands to print all of the reports that were created in Chapter 3, as well as an option to return to the Main Menu. The technique for creating the subsidiary menu was described in the previous problem.

   a. Create the switchboards as indicated in Figure 4.15. You do not have to copy our design exactly, but you are to incorporate all of the indicated functionality. Format the switchboard in an attractive way and include clip art. The report menu is to provide access to all of the reports that were created in Chapter 3.

   b. Go to the main menu, and open the form to modify the property data. Use the form to indicate that property P0008 has sold for $140,000. Use today's date as the date the property was sold.

   c. Go to the Report menu, and open the report that shows the properties that have been sold. This report should include the property from part (b). Print this report for your instructor.

   d. Use the Startup property in the Tools menu to display the switchboard automatically when the database is opened initially. Pull down the Tools menu, click the Database Utilities command, then click the command to Compact and Repair the Database. Access will close, and then reopen, the database; the switchboard should be displayed automatically.

   e. Be sure that you test both switchboards completely to be sure that they work correctly. Print the switchboard form and table of Switchboard Items. Use landscape printing if necessary to be sure that each item fits on one page. Add a cover sheet and submit everything to your instructor.

   f. Take a minute to reflect on what you have accomplished over the last several chapters. You created the database and designed a table and associated form in Chapter 2, you created various reports in Chapter 3, and you put everything together via the switchboard in this exercise. Well done!

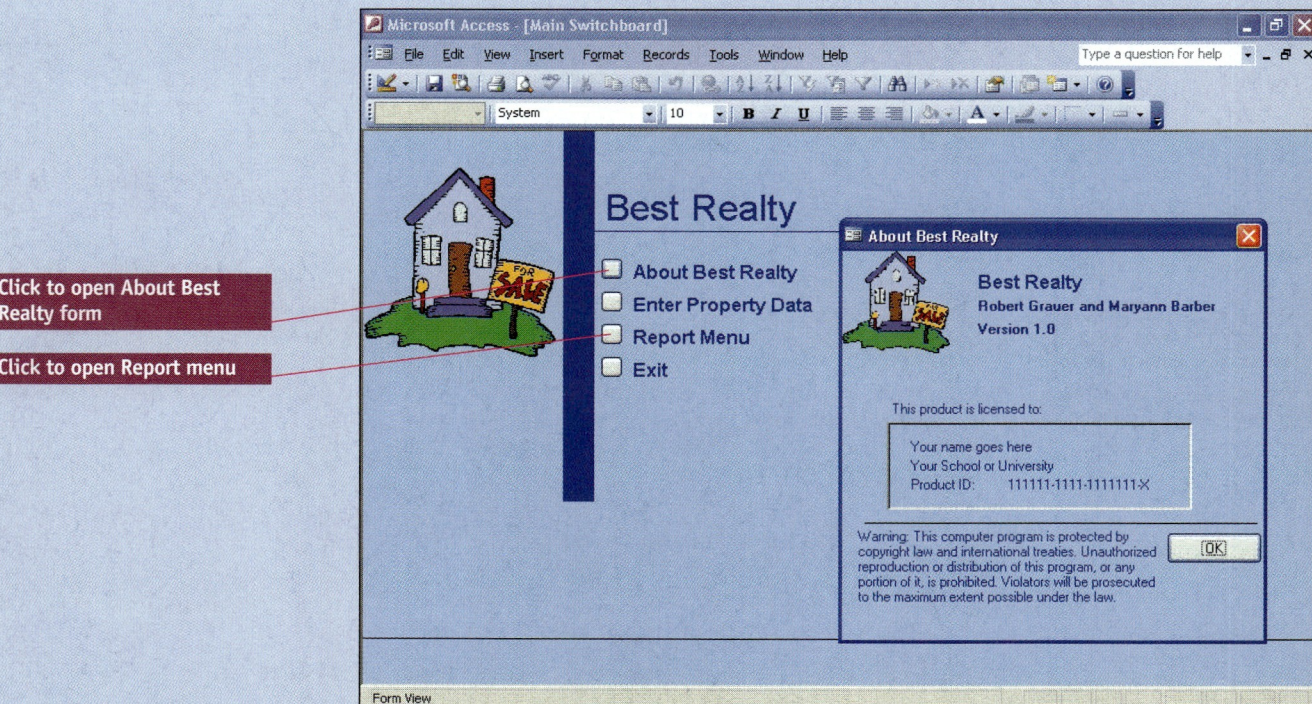

FIGURE 4.15   Best Realty (exercise 5)

6. **The Fishing Pole:** Figure 4.16 displays a switchboard for the Fishing Pole database that has been developed in previous chapters. Your assignment is to create a comparable switchboard that includes an option to display a report menu. The latter is a second (subsidiary) switchboard that includes commands to print all of the reports in the database, as well as an option to return to the Main Menu. Open the *Chapter 3 Practice 6* database in the Exploring Access folder and proceed as follows:

   a. Start the Switchboard Manager, which will display the Switchboard Manager dialog box. Click New to create a new switchboard (in addition to the main switchboard that is created by default). Enter Report Menu as the name of the new switchboard page, then click OK.

   b. You will return to the Switchboard Manager dialog box. Select the Main Switchboard, click Edit, and build the items for the main switchboard (open the About the Fishing Pole form, which is included in the database, open the Customers form in edit mode, open the Report Menu switchboard, and exit the application). After you have built the main switchboard, close the Switchboard Page dialog box to return to the Switchboard Manager dialog box.

   c. Select the Report Menu switchboard, and click Edit. Build the items for the Report Menu, which consist of a separate command for each report in the database, plus a command to return to main menu. (The latter is a Go To Switchboard command that opens the Main switchboard.) Close the switchboard page. Close the Switchboard Manager.

   d. Open the Switchboard form in Design view to format the switchboard as shown in Figure 4.16. You do not have to match our design exactly, but your switchboard should enhance the default design.

   e. Use the Startup property in the Tools menu to display the switchboard automatically when the database is opened initially. Pull down the Tools menu, click the Database Utilities command, then click the command to Compact and Repair the Database. Access will close, and then reopen; the database and the switchboard should be displayed automatically. Test both switchboards completely.

   f. Print the Switchboard form and Switchboard Items table for your instructor.

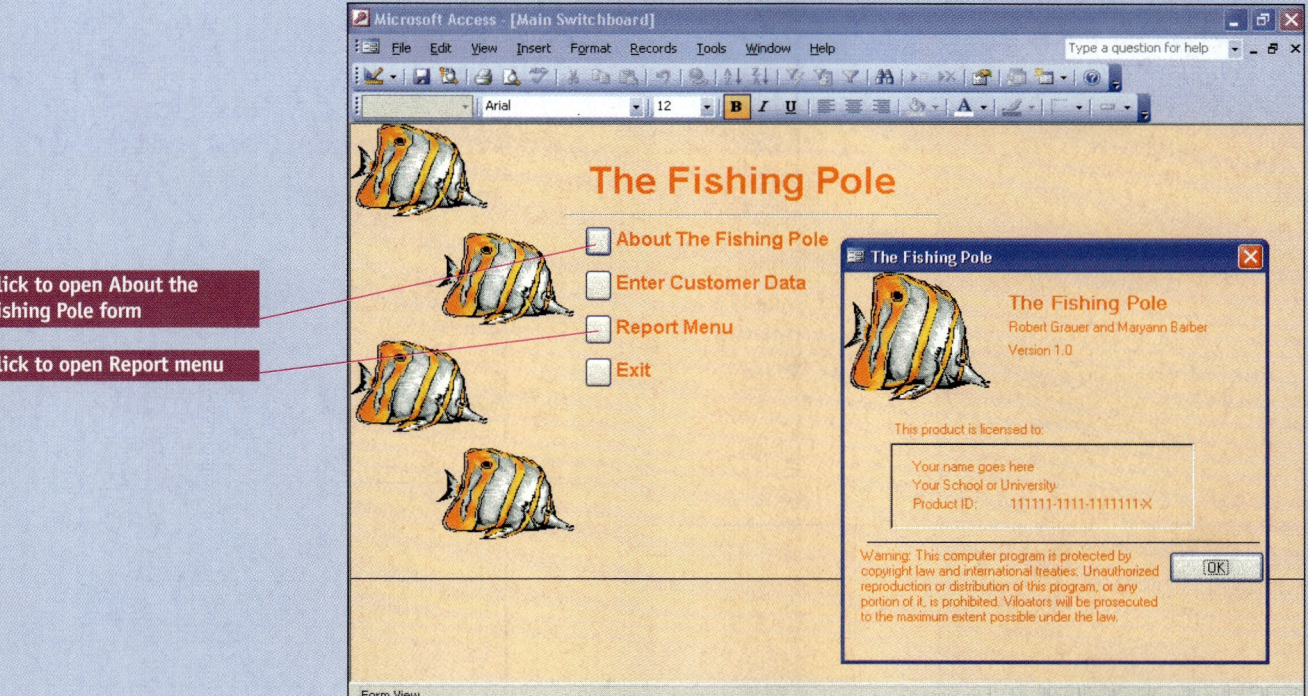

FIGURE 4.16 The Fishing Pole (exercise 6)

7. **Events Extraordinaire Report Switchboard:** Figure 4.17 displays a switchboard for the Events Extraordinaire database that has been developed in the preceding three exercises. Your assignment is to create a comparable switchboard that includes an option to display a report menu. The latter is a second (subsidiary) switchboard that includes commands to print all of the reports in the database, as well as an option to return to the Main Menu. Open the *Chapter 3 Additional Practice 1* database from the previous exercise and proceed as follows:

   a. Start the Switchboard Manager, which will display the Switchboard Manager dialog box. Click New to create a new switchboard (in addition to the main switchboard that is created by default). Enter "Report Menu" as the name of the new switchboard page, then click OK.

   b. You will return to the Switchboard Manager dialog box. Select the Main Switchboard, click Edit, and build the items for the main switchboard (open the About Events Extraordinaire form, which has been provided for you; open the Events form in Edit mode; go to the Report Menu switchboard; and exit the application). After you have built the main switchboard, close the Edit Switchboard Page dialog box to return to the Switchboard Manager dialog box.

   c. Select the Report Menu switchboard and click Edit. Build the items for the Report Menu, which consists of a separate command to open each report in the database, plus a command to return to the main menu. (The latter is a Go To Switchboard command that opens the Main switchboard.) Close the Edit Switchboard Page dialog box. Close the Switchboard Manager.

   d. Open the Switchboard form in Design view to format the switchboard as shown in Figure 4.17. You do not have to match our design exactly, but your switchboard should be consistent with the design of your forms and reports.

   e. Use the Startup property in the Tools menu to display the switchboard automatically when the database is opened initially. Pull down the Tools menu, click the Database Utilities command, then click the command to Compact and Repair the Database. Access will close the database and then reopen the database and display the switchboard. Test both switchboards completely to be sure that they work correctly.

   f. Print the Switchboard form and Switchboard Items table for your instructor.

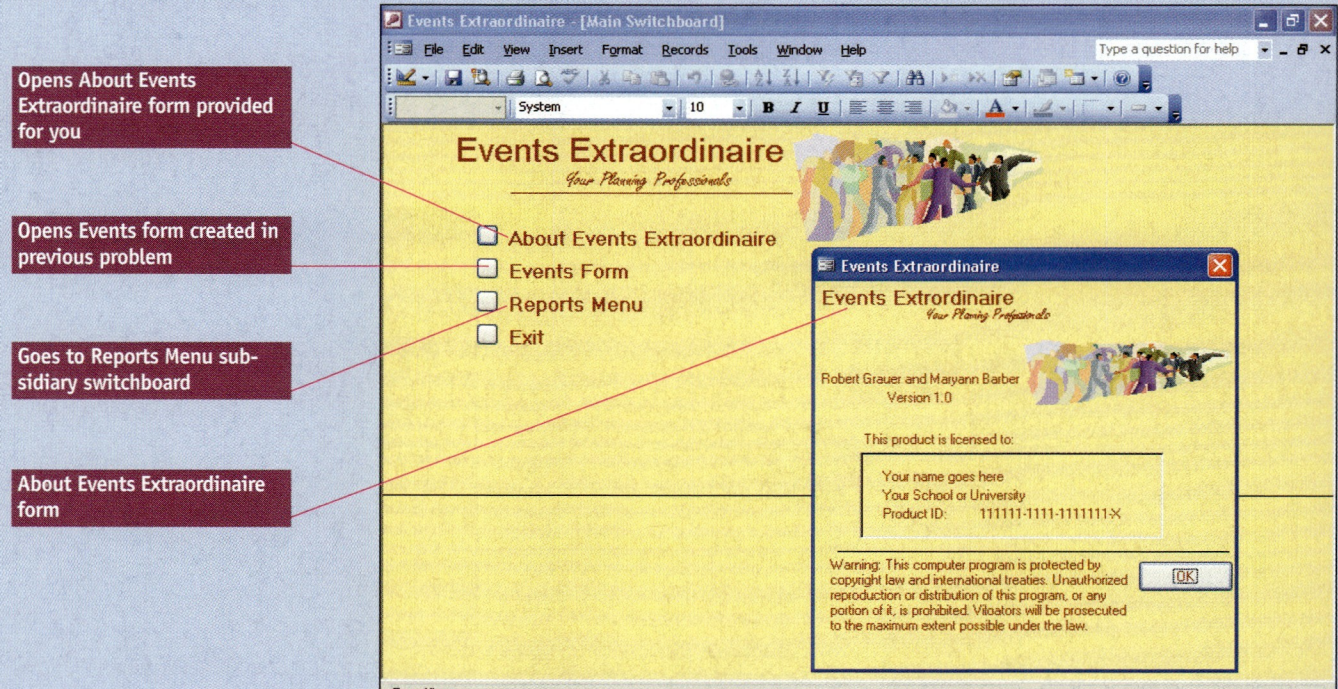

FIGURE 4.17 Events Extraordinaire Report Switchboard (exercise 7)

8. **Access Jeopardy:** How well do you know Microsoft Access? The presentation in Figure 4.18 contains a Jeopardy game with 25 answers and questions that review material from Chapters 1 through 4. All you have to do is open the presentation and play the game. Thus, open the *Chapter 4 Practice 8—Access Jeopardy* presentation and proceed as follows:

a. Pull down the Slide Show menu and click the View Show command (or click the F5 key) to view the slide show, which begins with the title slide. Click the mouse to move to slide 2 (the board). The names of the categories will appear one after another, after which you can select any question in any category. Each dollar amount is a hyperlink to another slide in the presentation.

b. Select (click) a question, such as the $400 question in the Tables and Forms category, to display the clue, "Recommended field type for phone numbers and zip codes". Click the mouse to display the answer "What is a text field?" (that appears in the form of a question), then click the answer to return to slide 2 (the board). Before you click, be sure you see the tiny hand indicating that you are clicking the hyperlink, as opposed to clicking the background of the slide.

c. You should be back on slide 2, the Jeopardy board. Look closely and you will see that the color of the text (i.e., the 400) has changed, indicating that the hyperlink has been followed. Select a different question, view the answer, and return to the game board so that you can be sure of the navigation.

d. Select a classmate and play the game. There is no buzzer, so you have to determine an equitable way to gain control of the board and keep score. We leave the details to you.

e. Print the presentation in a variety of ways. Select the first two slides, pull down the File menu, click the Print command, choose the option button for Selection, and select Slides in the Print What list box. Click OK to print. Pull down the Print menu a second time and print the entire presentation in Outline view. Study the outline and be sure that you can answer all of the questions.

f. You will find additional games for the other Office applications (PowerPoint, Excel, and Word) in the appropriate folders after downloading the practice files from our Web site. The Excel game, for example, is found in the Exploring Excel folder and reviews material from Chapters 1 through 4 in the Excel section.

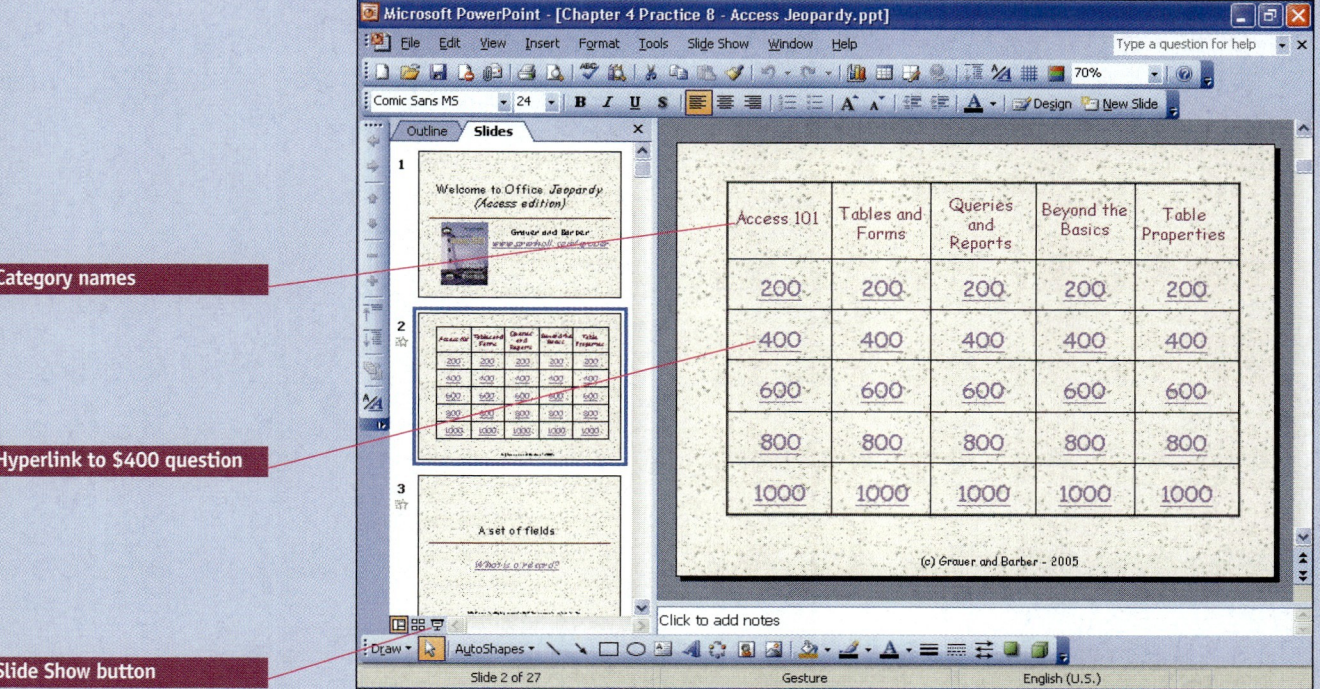

FIGURE 4.18 Access Jeopardy (exercise 8)

9. **The Database Wizard:** The switchboard in Figure 4.19 is for a contact management database that maintains information about the individuals contacted and the associated telephone calls. There is nothing remarkable in the switchboard per se, except that it and the underlying database (the tables, forms, queries, and reports) were created in a matter of minutes using one of several Database Wizards that are built into Microsoft Access. Proceed as follows:

a. Start Access. Pull down the File menu and select the New command to open the task pane. Click the link to Other templates on My Computer to display the Templates dialog box. Click the Databases tab, then double click the Contact Management database to start the Database Wizard. You should see the File New Database dialog box in which you specify the name of the database (use Contact Management) and the folder where to store the database (use the Exploring Access folder). Click Create.

b. You will see several screens that prompt you for information about the database that you want to create. The first screen tells you that the database stores contact and call information. Click Next.

c. The next screen displays the tables in the database. You have to accept all of the tables, but you have the option of adding or removing fields within each table. Accept all fields for all of the tables. Click Next.

d. The third and fourth screens let you choose the style for your forms and reports, respectively. These choices parallel those for the Form and Report Wizards. Select any style and click Next at each screen.

e. The next two screens ask you for the title of your database (as it is to appear in the switchboard) and also give you the option of including a picture on the forms and reports. Check the option to start the database after it is built, and click the Finish button to display a switchboard similar to Figure 4.19.

f. Explore the functionality of the database that was just created. Write a paragraph or two to your instructor describing whether the database is useful and what additional information you would like to see included. Are you able to modify the database to include the additional features you suggested?

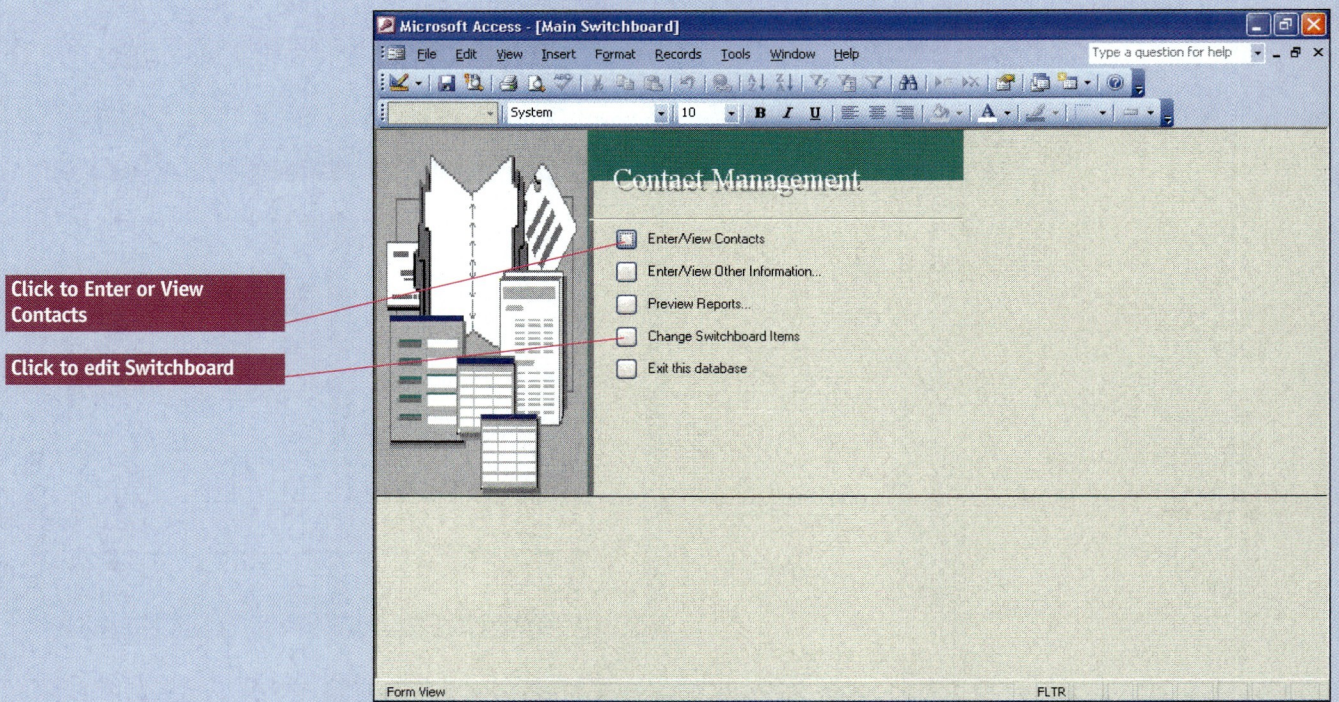

FIGURE 4.19 The Database Wizard (exercise 9)

MINI CASES

Study Break—Access Crossword Puzzle

We enjoy a good puzzle and with that in mind, we have created a unique crossword puzzle that reviews the material from Chapters 1 to 4. Many of the clues are taken from the end-of-chapter list of key terms and concepts, but additional clues come from elsewhere in the chapter. Open the *Chapter 4 Mini Case—Access Crossword Puzzle* Word document in the Exploring Access folder, give yourself one hour, and do your best to complete the puzzle. Add your name at the top of the page, and submit the puzzle to your instructor. Our students find this exercise to be an excellent review for an exam.

Recreational Sports League

Design a database for a recreational sports league to maintain data on the league's teams, players, coaches, and sponsors. There can be any number of teams in the league. Each team has multiple players, but a specific player is associated with only one team. A team may have multiple coaches, but a given coach is associated with only one team. The league also depends on local businesses to sponsor various teams to offset the cost of uniforms and referees. One business can sponsor many teams, but a team cannot have more than one sponsor.

Design a database with four tables, for teams, players, coaches, and sponsors. You do not have to enter data into any of the tables, but you do need to design the tables in order to create a relationships diagram. Your database should also include a basic switchboard, an About form, and a relationships diagram. Use a common clip art image and consistent design elements for each object in the database. Print the switchboard form, the table of switchboard items, the relationships diagram, and the About form for your instructor.

The Franchise

The management of a national restaurant chain is automating its procedure for monitoring its restaurants, restaurant-owners (franchisees), and the contracts that govern the two. Each restaurant has one owner (franchisee), but a given individual can own multiple restaurants.

The payment from the franchisee to the company varies according to the contract in effect for the particular restaurant. The company offers a choice of contracts, which vary according to the length of the contract, the franchise fee, and the percentage of the restaurant's sales paid to the company for marketing and royalty fees. Each restaurant has one contract, but a given contract may pertain to many restaurants.

The company needs a database capable of retrieving all data for a given restaurant, such as its annual sales, location, phone number, owner, and type of contract in effect. It would also like to know all restaurants owned by one person as well as all restaurants governed by a specific contract type.

Design a database with the necessary tables. You do not have to enter data into any of the tables, but you do need to design the tables in order to create a relationships diagram. Your database should also include a basic switchboard, an About form, and a relationships diagram. Use a common clip art image and consistent design elements for each object in the database. Print the switchboard form, the table of switchboard items, the relationships diagram, and the About form for your instructor.

The Loan Officer

You are working in the IT department of a commercial bank and have been asked to design a database for customer loans. The bank needs to track its customers, the loans for each customer, the loan officer who approved the individual loan, and the payments received for each loan. One customer can have multiple loans, but a specific loan is associated with only one customer. A loan officer (who is an employee of the bank) must approve each loan before it is made.

One critical report is the list of all loans for each loan officer. Another important report is the list of all payments for each loan, which contains the amount of the payment and the date the payment was received. You do not have to enter data into any of the tables, but you do need to create the tables in order to create a relationships diagram and associated report. Be sure to set the required property properly for the various fields in different tables. You should not, for example, be able to create a new record in the Loans table unless that loan has been assigned to a customer and was approved by a loan officer.

Your database should also include a basic switchboard, an About form, and a relationships diagram. Use a common clip art image and consistent design elements for each object in the database. Print the switchboard form, the table of switchboard items, the relationships diagram, and the About form for your instructor.

Chapter Recap—Attorneys for Athletes

Matt Denham was always a blue-chip athlete, and it came as no surprise when he went in the second round of the most recent NFL draft. Matt was very distrustful of professional agents and asked you to negotiate his first contract, given your recent graduation from law school at the top of your class. Matt is your best friend, and he also asked you to represent three teammates who were drafted by teams in other cities.

Your reputation for negotiating huge signing bonuses spread quickly and you now represent more than 100 athletes. As your business grew, you began to hire other attorneys, so that you have offices in several cities, each of which employs multiple attorneys. The downside is that your business has grown so quickly that it is becoming more difficult to provide the quality service of which you are so proud. A consultant has recommended that you create a relational database to store the data for your offices, attorneys, and the athletes they represent. The consultant has submitted a preliminary design in the form of a simple database that includes the required tables and the associated relationships diagram. The consultant has also chosen a logo (clip art) and color scheme, and has created a descriptive form to show the visual design.

Your assignment is to review the chapter and focus on the one-to-many relationships that exist within the database. Put yourself in the place of the consultant and create the initial version of the database, including the switchboard. You will need three tables to track offices, attorneys, and athletes. There is a one-to-many relationship between offices and attorneys (one office has several attorneys, but a given attorney works in only one office). There is a second one-to-many relationship between attorneys and athletes (one attorney represents many athletes, but a specific athlete is represented by only one attorney). Your switchboard should contain three menu items: to display an About Attorneys for Athletes form, to print the relationships diagram, and to exit the application. The visual design is important. Print the relationships diagram, the Switchboard form, and the Switchboard Items table for your instructor.

5

One-to-many Relationships:
Subforms and Multiple-table Queries

OBJECTIVES

After reading this chapter you will:

1. Distinguish between a primary key and a foreign key.
2. Define referential integrity.
3. Use the Relationships window to create a one-to-many relationship.
4. Explain how the AutoNumber field type simplifies data entry.
5. Distinguish between a main form and a subform.
6. Create a multiple-table query, then use the query to create a report.
7. Create a main form with linked subforms.

hands-on exercises

1. ONE-TO-MANY RELATIONSHIPS
   Input: National Bank
   Output: National Bank (modified)

2. CREATING A SUBFORM
   Input: National Bank (from exercise 1)
   Output: National Bank (modified)

3. QUERIES AND REPORTS
   Input: National Bank (from exercise 2)
   Output: National Bank (modified)

4. LINKED SUBFORMS
   Input: National Bank (from exercise 3)
   Output: National Bank (modified)

CASE STUDY
THE RESIDENTIAL COLLEGES

Maryann Barber made the suggestion to convert the student dorms to residential colleges at a Board of Trustees meeting three years ago. At the time, the dorms were only 80% occupied, and indeed that was only because the university required that freshmen live in the dorms. Maryann proposed that two faculty members and their families move into each dorm as Master and Assistant Master. The objective would be to create a "home away from home" for students while simultaneously creating a learning environment outside the classroom to promote intellectual curiosity as well as personal growth and development.

The experiment has proven to be an overwhelming success, and today the residential colleges are an integral part of student life. Maryann is in the process of creating an Access database for ease of administration and has come to you for help. You will need three tables: one for students, one for faculty, and one for the residential colleges. There is a one-to-many relationship between the residence halls and students (one hall has many students). There is a second one-to-many relationship between the residence halls and faculty. Each faculty member is given his or her own apartment within the residence hall. Students, however, live in rooms, as opposed to apartments. ◼

Your assignment is to read the chapter, paying special attention on how to create a one-to-many relationship and enforce referential integrity. You will then create a new database that contains the various tables for the Residential Halls database. You do not have to enter data into any of the tables, but you are to include all necessary fields and set the properties appropriately. Your database should also include a basic switchboard, an About form, a relationships diagram, and templates for the reports and forms that will be used in the database. Use a common clip art image and consistent design elements for each object in the database. Print the switchboard form, the table of switchboard items, the relationships diagram, and both templates for your instructor.

The real power of Access stems from its use as a relational database that contains multiple tables and the objects associated with those tables. We introduced this concept at the end of Chapter 1 when we looked briefly at a database that had three tables. We revisited the concept in the previous chapter when we looked at a second relational database. This chapter presents an entirely new case study that focuses on a relational database.

Let us assume that you are in the Information Systems department of a commercial bank and are assigned the task of implementing a system for consumer loans. The bank needs complete data about every loan (the amount, interest rate, term, and so on). It also needs data about the customers holding those loans (name, address, telephone, etc.). The problem is how to structure the data so that the bank will be able to obtain all of the information it needs from its database. The system must be able to supply the name and address of the person associated with a loan. The system must also be able to retrieve all of the loans for a specific individual. We present two alternative solutions.

The first solution is based on an expanded loans table as shown in Figure 5.1. At first glance this solution appears to be satisfactory. You can, for example, search for a specific loan (e.g., L0006) and determine that Lori Sangastiano is the customer associated with that loan. You can also search for a particular customer (e.g., Michelle Zacco) and find all of her loans (L0007, L0008, L0009, and L0021). The database is able to provide information about every loan and/or every customer.

LoanID	Loan Data	Customer Data
L0001	Loan data for loan L0001	Customer data for Wendy Solomon
L0002	Loan data for loan L0002	Customer data for Wendy Solomon
L0003	Loan data for loan L0003	Customer data for Alex Rey
L0004	Loan data for loan L0004	Customer data for Wendy Solomon
L0005	Loan data for loan L0005	Customer data for Ted Myerson
L0006	Loan data for loan L0006	Customer data for Lori Sangastiano
L0007	Loan data for loan L0007	Customer data for Michelle Zacco
L0008	Loan data for loan L0008	Customer data for Michelle Zacco
L0009	Loan data for loan L0009	Customer data for Michelle Zacco
L0010	Loan data for loan L0010	Customer data for Eileen Faulkner
L0011	Loan data for loan L0011	Customer data for Scott Wit
L0012	Loan data for loan L0012	Customer data for Alex Rey
L0013	Loan data for loan L0013	Customer data for David Powell
L0014	Loan data for loan L0014	Customer data for Matt Hirsch
L0015	Loan data for loan L0015	Customer data for Benjamin Grauer
L0016	Loan data for loan L0016	Customer data for Eileen Faulkner
L0017	Loan data for loan L0017	Customer data for Eileen Faulkner
L0018	Loan data for loan L0018	Customer data for Benjamin Grauer
L0019	Loan data for loan L0019	Customer data for Scott Wit
L0020	Loan data for loan L0020	Customer data for Benjamin Grauer
L0021	Loan data for loan L0021	Customer data for Michelle Zacco
L0022	Loan data for loan L0022	Customer data for Matt Hirsch
L0023	Loan data for loan L0023	Customer data for Benjamin Grauer
L0024	Loan data for loan L0024	Customer data for Wendy Solomon
L0025	Loan data for loan L0025	Customer data for Lori Sangastiano

FIGURE 5.1   Single-table Solution

There is a problem, however, in that certain customer data are duplicated throughout the database. If, for example, one customer has multiple loans, the customer's name, address, and other data are stored multiple times. Maintaining the data in this form is a time-consuming and error-prone procedure, because any change to the customer's data has to be made in many places.

A second problem arises if you were to enter data for a new customer before a loan has been approved. The bank receives the customer's application data prior to granting a loan, and it wants to retain the customer data even if a loan is turned down. Adding a customer to the database in Figure 5.1 is awkward, however, because it requires the creation of a "dummy" loan record to hold the customer data.

The deletion (payoff) of a loan creates a third type of problem. What happens, for example, when Ted Myerson pays off loan L0005? The loan record would be deleted, but so too would Ted's data as he has no other outstanding loans. The bank might want to contact Mr. Myerson about another loan in the future, but it would lose his data with the deletion of the existing loan.

The database in Figure 5.2 represents a much better design because it eliminates all three problems. It uses two different tables, a Loans table and a Customers table. Each record in the Loans table has data about a specific loan (LoanID, Date, Amount, Interest Rate, Term, Type, and CustomerID). Each record in the Customers table has data about a specific customer (CustomerID, First Name, Last Name, Address, City, State, Zip Code, and Phone Number). Each record in the Loans table is associated with a matching record in the Customers table through the CustomerID field common to both tables. This solution may seem complicated, but it is really quite simple and elegant.

Consider, for example, how easy it is to change a customer's address. If Michelle Zacco were to move, you would go into the Customers table, find her record (Customer C0008), and make the necessary change. You would not have to change any of the records in the Loans table, because they do not contain customer data, but only a CustomerID that indicates who the customer is. In other words, you would change Michelle's address in only one place, and the change would be automatically reflected for every associated loan.

The addition of a new customer is done directly in the Customers table. This is much easier than the approach of Figure 5.1, which required an existing loan in order to add a new customer. And finally, the deletion of an existing loan is also easier than with the single-table organization. A loan can be deleted from the Loans table without losing the corresponding customer data.

The database in Figure 5.2 is composed of two tables in which there is a ***one-to-many relationship*** between customers and loans. One customer (Michelle Zacco) can have many loans (Loan numbers L0007, L0008, L0009, and L0021), but a specific loan (e.g., L0007) is associated with only one customer (Michelle Zacco). The tables are related to one another by a common field (CustomerID) that is present in both the Customers and the Loans table.

Access enables you to create the one-to-many relationship between the tables, then uses that relationship to answer questions about the database. It can retrieve information about a specific loan, such as the name and address of the customer holding that loan. It can also find all loans for a particular customer.

Use the tables in Figure 5.2 to answer the queries below and gain an appreciation for the power of a relational database.

Query: What are the name, address, and phone number of the customer associated with loan number L0003?

Answer: Alex Rey, at 3456 Main Highway is the customer associated with loan L0003. His phone number is (303) 555-6666.

To determine the answer, Access searches the Loans table for loan L0003 to obtain the CustomerID (C0005 in this example). It then searches the Customers table for the customer with the matching CustomerID and retrieves the name, address, and phone number. Consider a second example.

LoanID	Date	Amount	Interest Rate	Term	Type	CustomerID
L0001	1/15/2003	$475,000	6.90%	15	M	C0004
L0002	1/23/2003	$35,000	7.20%	5	C	C0004
L0003	1/25/2003	$10,000	5.50%	3	C	C0005
L0004	1/31/2003	$12,000	9.50%	10	O	C0004
L0005	2/8/2003	$525,000	6.50%	30	M	C0006
L0006	2/12/2003	$10,500	7.50%	5	O	C0007
L0007	2/15/2003	$35,000	6.50%	5	O	C0008
L0008	2/20/2003	$250,000	8.80%	30	M	C0008
L0009	2/21/2003	$5,000	10.00%	3	O	C0008
L0010	2/28/2003	$200,000	7.00%	15	M	C0001
L0011	3/1/2003	$25,000	10.00%	3	C	C0002
L0012	3/1/2003	$20,000	9.50%	5	O	C0005
L0013	3/3/2003	$56,000	7.50%	5	C	C0009
L0014	3/10/2003	$129,000	8.50%	15	M	C0010
L0015	3/11/2003	$200,000	7.25%	15	M	C0003
L0016	3/21/2003	$150,000	7.50%	15	M	C0001
L0017	3/22/2003	$100,000	7.00%	30	M	C0001
L0018	3/31/2003	$15,000	6.50%	3	O	C0003
L0019	4/1/2003	$10,000	8.00%	5	C	C0002
L0020	4/15/2003	$25,000	8.50%	4	C	C0003
L0021	4/18/2003	$41,000	9.90%	4	C	C0008
L0022	4/22/2003	$350,000	7.50%	15	M	C0010
L0023	5/1/2003	$150,000	6.00%	15	M	C0003
L0024	5/3/2003	$350,000	8.20%	30	M	C0004
L0025	5/8/2003	$275,000	9.20%	15	M	C0007

(a) Loans Table

CustomerID	First Name	Last Name	Address	City	State	Zip Code	Phone Number
C0001	Eileen	Faulkner	7245 NW 8 Street	Minneapolis	MN	55346	(612) 894-1511
C0002	Scott	Wit	5660 NW 175 Terrace	Baltimore	MD	21224	(410) 753-0345
C0003	Benjamin	Grauer	10000 Sample Road	Coral Springs	FL	33073	(305) 444-5555
C0004	Wendy	Solomon	7500 Reno Road	Houston	TX	77090	(713) 427-3104
C0005	Alex	Rey	3456 Main Highway	Denver	CO	80228	(303) 555-6666
C0006	Ted	Myerson	6545 Stone Street	Chapel Hill	NC	27515	(919) 942-7654
C0007	Lori	Sangastiano	4533 Aero Drive	Santa Rosa	CA	95403	(707) 542-3411
C0008	Michelle	Zacco	488 Gold Street	Gainesville	FL	32601	(904) 374-5660
C0009	David	Powell	5070 Battle Road	Decatur	GA	30034	(301) 345-6556
C0010	Matt	Hirsch	777 NW 67 Avenue	Fort Lee	NJ	07624	(201) 664-3211

(b) Customers Table

FIGURE 5.2   Multiple-table Solution

Query: Which loans are associated with Wendy Solomon?

Answer: Wendy Solomon has four loans: loan L0001 for $475,000, loan L0002 for $35,000, loan L0004 for $12,000, and loan L0024 for $350,000.

This time Access begins in the Customers table and searches for Wendy Solomon to determine the CustomerID (C0004). It then searches the Loans table for all records with a matching CustomerID.

The AutoNumber Field Type

Every table requires a ***primary key***, a field (or combination of fields) that makes every record in the table unique. The selection of the primary key in certain applications may be obvious, such as a Social Security Number in an employee database. Even so, it is always possible, and often convenient, to create a new field and assign that field the ***AutoNumber field*** type to generate the primary key for you. In other words, the AutoNumber specification will automatically assign the next sequential number to the primary key of a new record.

The records in both the Customer and Loans tables of Figure 5.2 are numbered consecutively: C0001, C0002, or L0001, L0002, and so on. The C (or L) and the associated leading zeros that appear are *not* part of the fields themselves, but are displayed through the ***Format property*** associated with the field.

Referential Integrity

Microsoft Access automatically implements certain types of data validation during data entry to ensure that the database will produce accurate information. Access always lets you enter a record in the "one" table, the Customers table in this example, provided that all existing rules for data validation are met. You cannot, however, enter a record in the "many" table (the Loans table in this example) if that record contains an invalid (nonexistent) value for the CustomerID. This type of data validation is known as ***referential integrity*** and it guarantees that the tables within a database are consistent with one another. Consider:

Query: Can you add a loan to the Loans table (as it presently exists) for Customer C0001? Can you add a loan for Customer C0020?

Answer: Yes, you can add a loan for Customer C0001, provided that the other rules for data validation are met. You cannot add a loan for Customer C0020 because that customer is not in the table.

Implementation in Access

Figure 5.3a displays the ***Relationships window*** that is used to create the one-to-many relationship between customers and loans. Each table stores data about a specific subject, such as customers or loans. CustomerID is the primary key in the Customers table. LoanID is the primary key in the Loans table.

The one-to-many relationship between the tables is based on the fact that the same field (CustomerID) appears in both tables. The CustomerID is the primary key in the Customers table, where its values are unique, but it is a ***foreign key*** in the Loans table, where its values are not unique. (A foreign key is simply the primary key of another table.) In other words, multiple records in the Loans table can have the same CustomerID to implement the one-to-many relationship between customers and loans.

To create a one-to-many relationship, you open the Relationships window in Figure 5.3a and add the necessary tables. You then drag the field on which the relationship is built from the field list of the "one" table (Customers) to the matching field in the related table (Loans). Once the relationship has been established, you will see a ***relationship line*** connecting the tables that indicates the one and many sides of the relationship.

Figure 5.3b displays the Customers table after the one-to-many relationship has been created. A plus (or minus) sign appears to the left of the CustomerID to indicate that there are corresponding records in a related table. You can click the plus sign next to any customer record to display the related records (called a ***subdatasheet***) for that customer. Conversely, you can click the minus sign (after the related records have been displayed) and the records are hidden. Look carefully at the related records for customer C0004 (Wendy Solomon) and you will see the answer to one of our earlier queries.

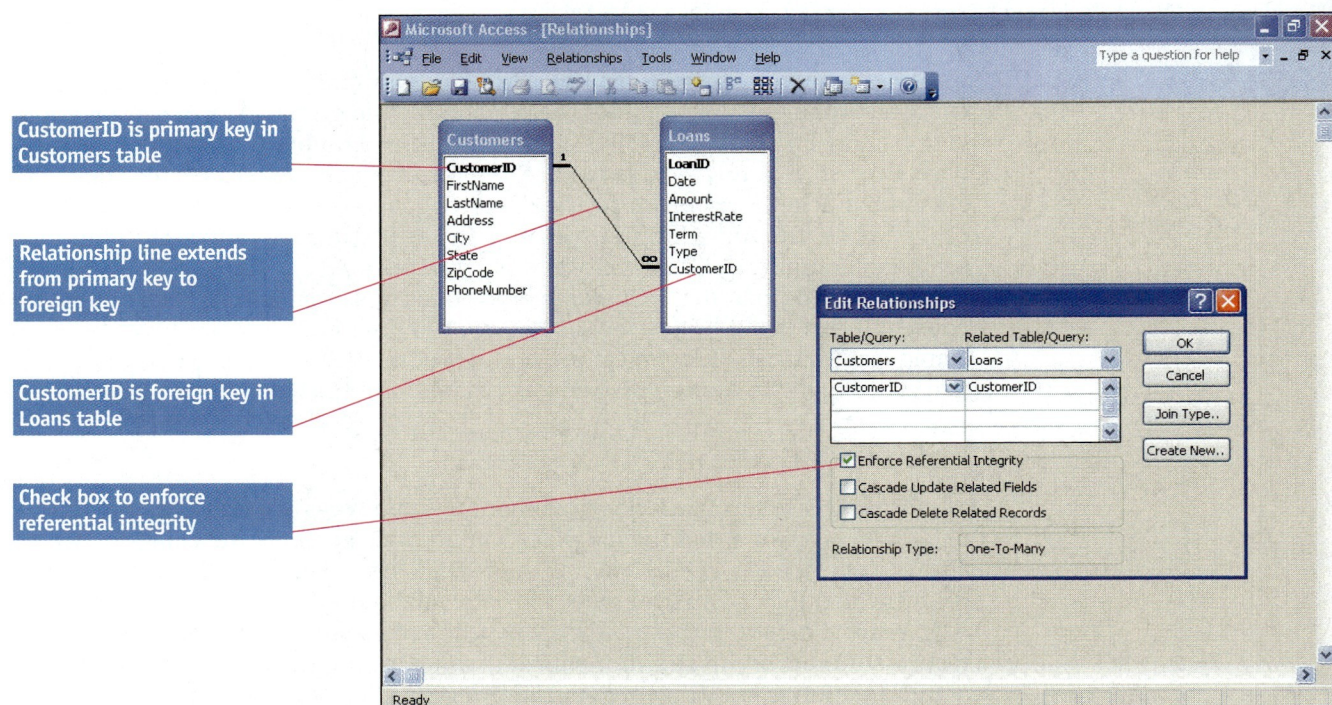

CustomerID is primary key in Customers table

Relationship line extends from primary key to foreign key

CustomerID is foreign key in Loans table

Check box to enforce referential integrity

(a) The Relationships Window

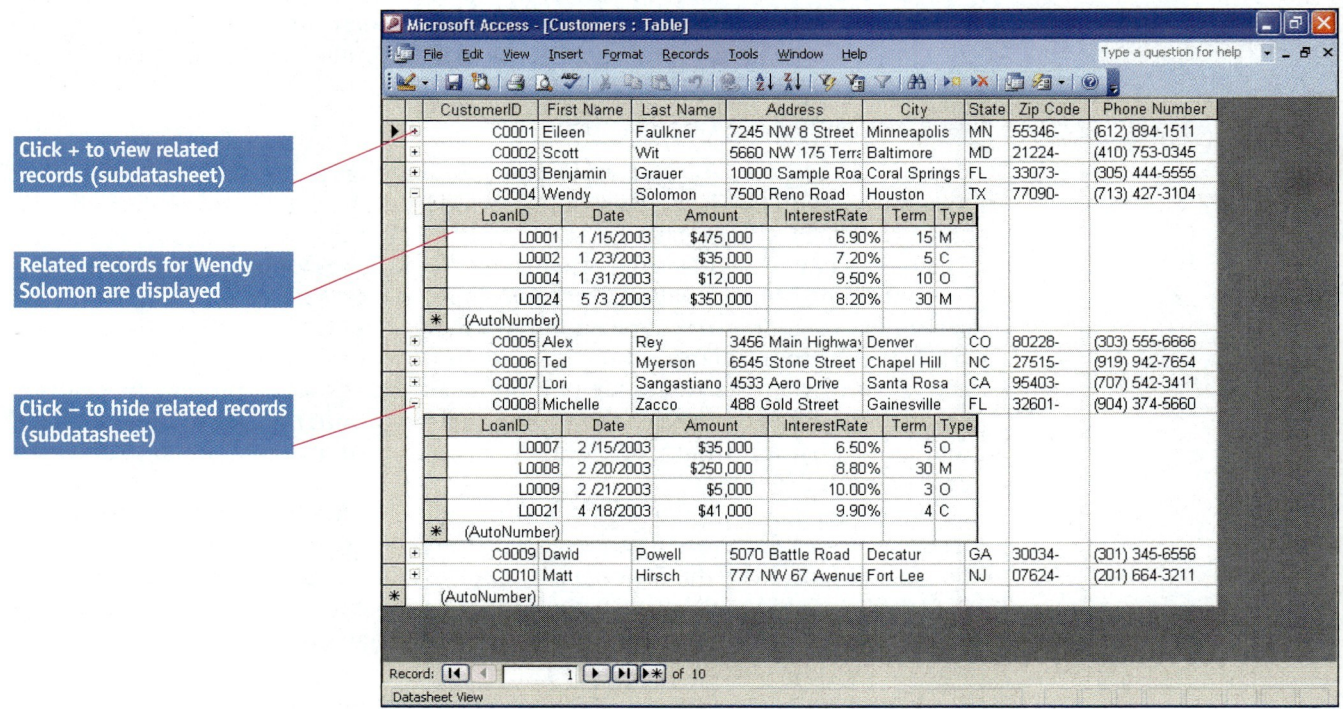

Click + to view related records (subdatasheet)

Related records for Wendy Solomon are displayed

Click – to hide related records (subdatasheet)

(b) The Customers Table with Related Records

FIGURE 5.3   One-to-many Relationship

One-to-many Relationships

Objective To create a one-to-many relationship between existing tables in a database; to demonstrate referential integrity between the tables in a one-to-many relationship. Use Figure 5.4 as a guide in the exercise.

Step 1: **The Relationships Window**

- Start Access. Open the **National Bank database** in the **Exploring Access folder**. The database contains three tables: for Customers, Loans, and Payments. (The Payments table will be used later in the chapter.)

- Pull down the **Tools menu** and click **Relationships** to open the Relationships window as shown in Figure 5.4a. (The Customers and Loans tables are not yet visible.) If you do not see the Show Table dialog box, pull down the **Relationships menu** and click the **Show Table command**.

- The **Tables tab** is selected within the Show Table dialog box. Click (select) the **Customers table**, then click the **Add Command button**.

- Click the **Loans table**, then click the **Add Command button** (or simply double click the **Loans table**) to add this table to the Relationships window. Do *not* add the Payments table at this time. Close the Show Table dialog box.

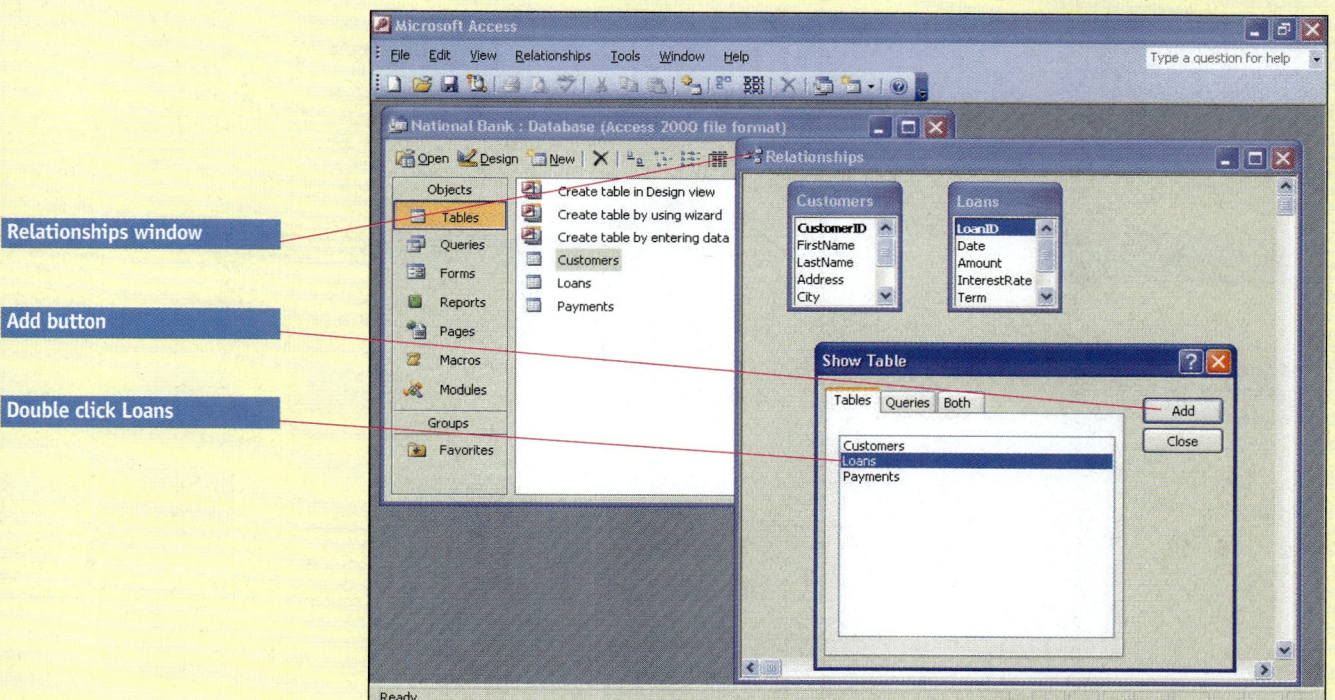

Relationships window

Add button

Double click Loans

(a) The Relationships Window (step 1)

FIGURE 5.4 Hands-on Exercise 1

DATABASE DESIGN

Each entity in a relational database requires its own table. Each table in turn requires a primary key to ensure that the records in the table are unique. The physical order of the rows (records) and columns (fields) in the table is immaterial. See Appendix A for additional examples of database design.

Step 2: **Create the Relationship**

- Maximize the Relationships window. Point to the bottom border of the **Customers field list** (the mouse pointer changes to a double arrow), then click and drag the border until all of the fields are visible.

- Click and drag the bottom border of the **Loans field list** until all of the fields are visible. Click and drag the title bar of the **Loans field list** so that it is approximately one inch away from the Customers field list.

- Click and drag the **CustomerID field** in the Customers field list to the **CustomerID field** in the Loans field list. You will see the Relationships dialog box in Figure 5.4b.

- Check the **Enforce Referential Integrity** check box. (If necessary, clear the check boxes to Cascade Update Related Fields and Cascade Delete Related Records.)

- Click the **Create command button** to establish the relationship and close the Relationships dialog box. You should see a line indicating a one-to-many relationship between the Customers and Loans tables.

- Close the Relationships window. Click **Yes** to save the layout changes.

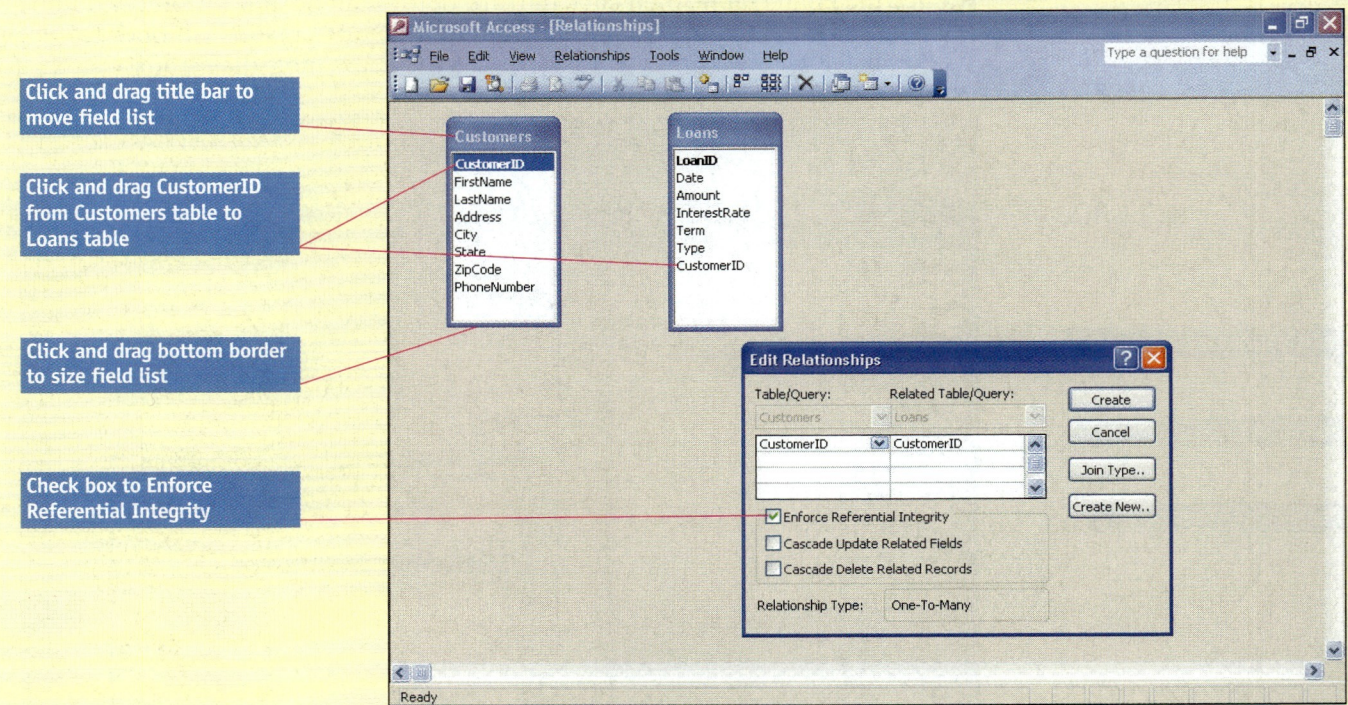

(b) Create the Relationship (step 2)

FIGURE 5.4 Hands-on Exercise 1 (*continued*)

RELATED FIELDS AND DATA TYPES

The fields on both sides of a relationship must have the same data type; for example, both fields should be text fields or both fields should be number fields. In addition, Number fields must also have the same field size. The exception is an AutoNumber field in the primary table, which is joined to a Number field with a field size of Long Integer in the related table.

Step 3: Add a Customer Record

- The Database window is again visible with the Tables button selected. Open the **Customers table**. If necessary, click the **Maximize button** to give yourself additional room when adding a record. Widen the fields as necessary.

- Click the **New Record button** on the toolbar, which moves the record selector to the last record (record 11). You are positioned in the CustomerID field.

- You do not enter the field, however, because the value of an AutoNumber field is entered automatically. Press **Tab** to move to the First Name field. You should see C0011 appear automatically in the CustomerID field as soon as you begin to enter the name as shown in Figure 5.4c.

- Enter data for yourself (Brian Frew in our Figure) as the new customer. Data validation has been built into the Customers table, so you must enter the data correctly.

- Press **Enter** when you have completed your record.

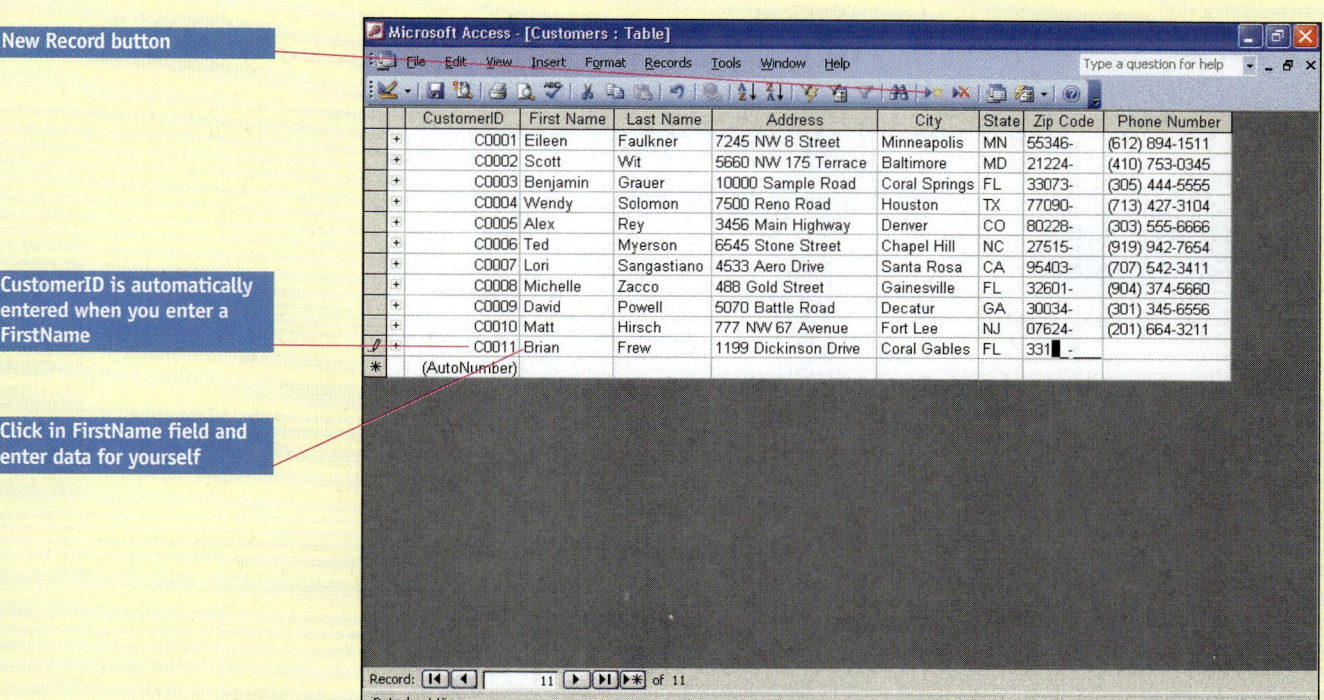

New Record button

CustomerID is automatically entered when you enter a FirstName

Click in FirstName field and enter data for yourself

(c) Add a Customer Record (step 3)

FIGURE 5.4 Hands-on Exercise 1 *(continued)*

THE AUTONUMBER VALUES REMAIN CONSTANT

The values in an AutoNumber field type are permanent and are not affected by deletions to the table. If, for example, there are 10 records initially, with AutoNumber values of 1 to 10 inclusive, and you delete record 6, the remaining records retain the AutoNumber values of 7 to 10. The next record will be given an AutoNumber of 11. Note, too, that if you attempt to add a new record and are unsuccessful for any reason, the value (the next sequential number) will not appear in the table. Regardless of whether the actual numbers are consecutive or not, however, the inclusion of an AutoNumber field ensures a set of unique values for the primary key.

Step 4: **Add a Loan Record**

- Click the **plus sign** next to the record selector for customer C0003 (Benjamin Grauer). The plus sign changes to a minus sign and you see the related records. Click the **minus sign** and it changes back to a plus sign. The related records for this customer are no longer visible.

- Click the **plus sign** next to your customer record (record C0011 in our figure). The plus sign changes to a minus sign but there are no loans as yet. Enter data for a new loan record as shown in Figure 5.4d.

- The LoanID will be entered automatically since it is an AutoNumber field. Thus, click in the Date field for the first loan and enter today's date. The next available loan number (L0026) is entered automatically as you begin to enter the date.

- Data validation has been built into the Loans table. The term of the loan, for example, cannot exceed 30 years. The interest rate must be entered as a decimal. The type of the loan must be C, M, or O for Car, Mortgage, or Other. Enter **C** for a car loan.

- Press **Enter** when you have completed the loan record.

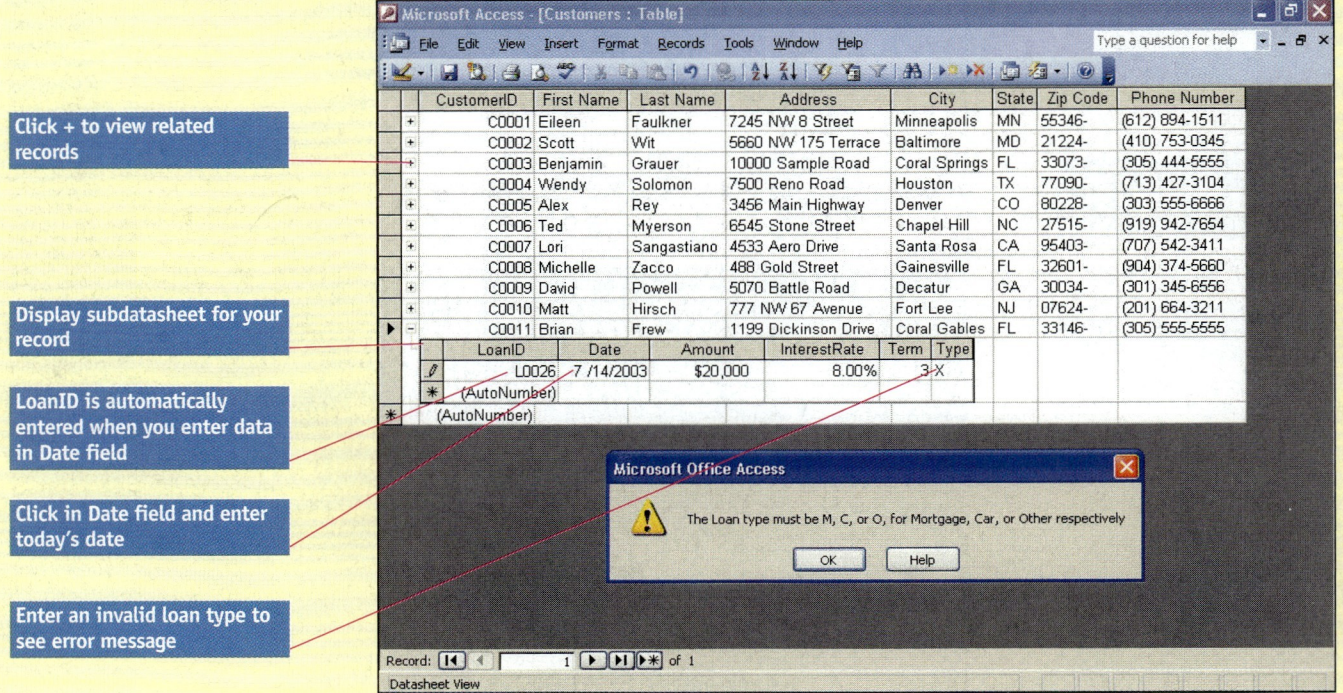

Click + to view related records

Display subdatasheet for your record

LoanID is automatically entered when you enter data in Date field

Click in Date field and enter today's date

Enter an invalid loan type to see error message

(d) Add a Loan Record (step 4)

FIGURE 5.4 Hands-on Exercise 1 *(continued)*

ADD AND DELETE RELATED RECORDS

Take advantage of the one-to-many relationship that exists between Customers and Loans to add or delete records in the Loans table from within the Customers table. Open the Customers table, then click the plus sign next to the Customer for whom you want to add or delete a loan record. To add a Loan, click in the blank row marked by the asterisk, then enter the new data. To delete a loan, select the Loan record, then click the Delete Record button on the Standard toolbar.

Step 5:   **Referential Integrity**

- Click the **plus sign** next to the record selector for Customer C0009 (David Powell). Click in the **CustomerID field** for this customer, then click the **Delete Record button** to (attempt to) delete this customer.

- You will see the error message in Figure 5.4e indicating that you cannot delete the customer record because there are related loan records. Click **OK**.

- Click in the **LoanID field** for L0013 (the loan for this customer). Click the **Delete Record button**. Click **Yes** when warned that you will not be able to undo this operation. The loan is deleted.

- Click in the **CustomerID field**, click the **Delete Record button**, then click **Yes** to delete the record. The deletion was permitted because there were no longer any related records in the Loans table.

- Close the Customers table. Close the National Bank database. Exit Access if you do not want to continue with the next exercise at this time.

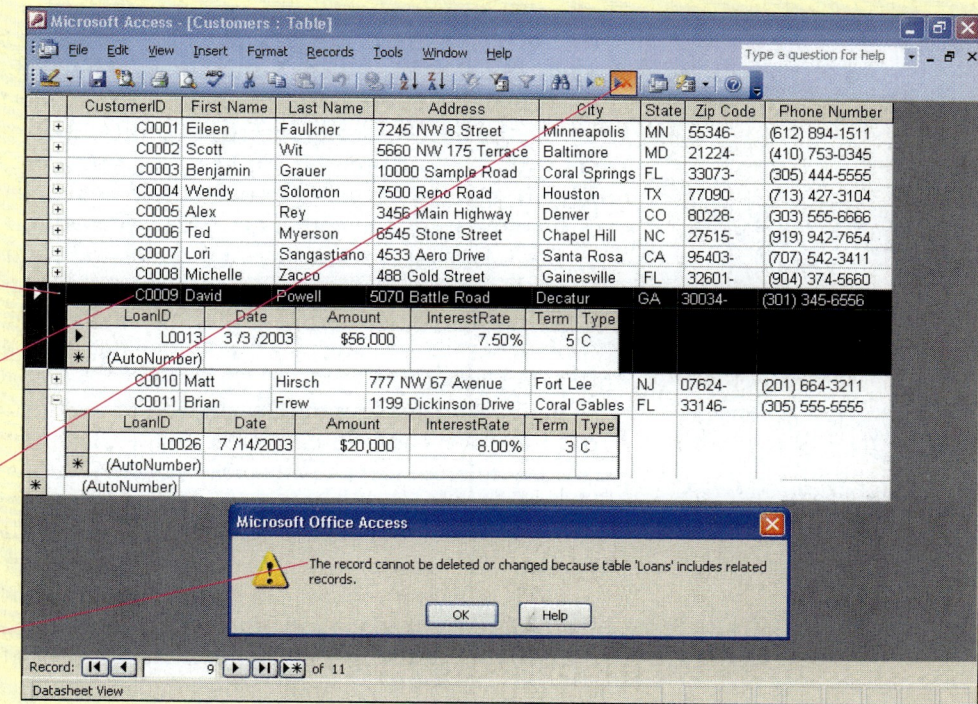

(e) Referential Integrity (step 5)

FIGURE 5.4   Hands-on Exercise 1 (*continued*)

CASCADE DELETED RECORDS

The enforcement of referential integrity prevents the deletion of a record in the primary (Customers) table if there is a corresponding record in the related (Loans) table. In other words, in order to delete a customer, you first have to delete all of the loans for that customer. This restriction can be relaxed if you modify the relationship by checking the Cascade Delete Related Records option in the Relationships dialog box. The Cascade Delete option may make sense in some applications, but not here since the bank wants the loan to remain on the books.

A *subform* is a form within a form. It appears inside a main form to display records from a related table. A main form and its associated subform, to display the loans for one customer, are shown in Figure 5.5. The *main form* (also known as the primary form) is based on the primary table (the Customers table). The subform is based on the related table (the Loans table).

The main form and the subform are linked to one another so that the subform displays only the records related to the record currently displayed in the main form. The main form shows the "one" side of the relationship (the customer). The subform shows the "many" side of the relationship (the loans). The main form displays the customer data for one record (Eileen Faulkner with CustomerID C0001). The subform shows the loans for that customer. The main form is displayed in the *Form view*, whereas the subform is displayed in the *Datasheet view*. (A subform can also be displayed in the Form view, in which case it would show one loan at a time.)

Each form in Figure 5.5a has its own status bar and associated navigation buttons. The status bar for the main form indicates that the active record is record 1 of 10 records in the Customers table. The status bar for the subform indicates record 1 of 3 records. (The latter shows the number of loans for this customer rather than the number of loans in the Loans table.) Click the navigation button to move to the next customer record, and you will automatically see the loans associated with that customer. If, for example, you were to move to the last customer record (C0011, which contains the data you entered in the first hands-on exercise), you would see your customer and loan information.

The Loans form also contains a calculated control, the payment due, which is based on the loan parameters. Loan L0010, for example (a $200,000 mortgage at 7% with a 15-year term), has a monthly payment of $1,797.66. The amount of the payment is calculated using a predefined function, as will be described in the next hands-on exercise.

Figure 5.5b displays the Design view of the Customers form in Figure 5.5a. The Loans subform control is an object on the Customers form and can be moved and sized (or deleted) just like any other object. It should also be noted that the Loans subform is a form in and of itself, and can be opened in either the Datasheet view or the Form view. It can also be opened in the Design view (to modify its appearance) as will be done in the next hands-on exercise.

Note, too, that reports can be linked to one another in exactly the same way that forms are linked to each other. Thus, you could create a main report/subreport combination to display the same information as the forms in Figure 5.5a. The choice between a form and a report depends on the information requirements of the system. Access, however, gives you the capability to create both. There is a learning curve, but everything that you learn about creating a subform also pertains to creating a subreport.

THE PMT FUNCTION

The PMT function is one of several predefined functions built into Access. It calculates the payment due on a loan based on the principal, interest rate, and term and is similar to the PMT function in Excel. The PMT function is reached most easily through the Expression Builder and can be entered onto any form, query, or report. (The periodic payment is a calculated field and thus it is used in a query rather than a table.)

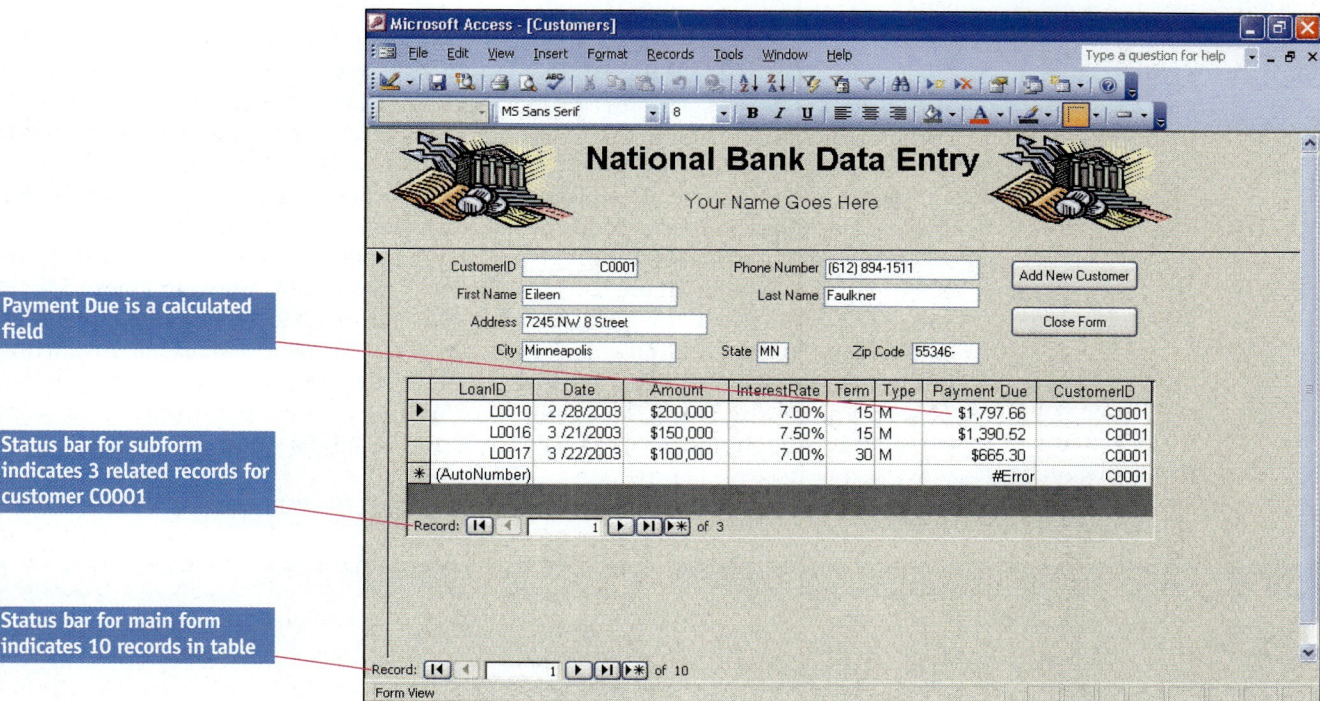

Payment Due is a calculated field

Status bar for subform indicates 3 related records for customer C0001

Status bar for main form indicates 10 records in table

(a) Form View

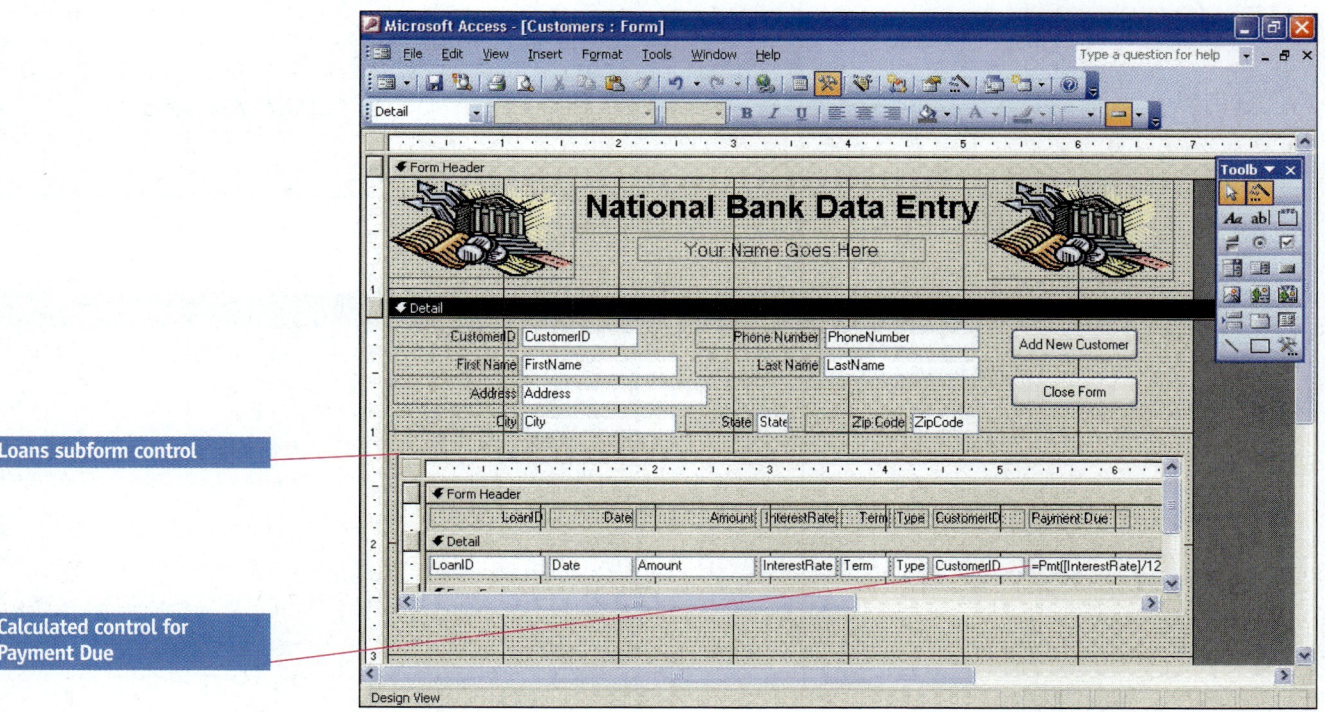

Loans subform control

Calculated control for Payment Due

(b) Design View

FIGURE 5.5 A Main Form and a Subform

The Form Wizard

A subform is created in different ways depending on whether or not the main form already exists. The easiest way is to create the two forms at the same time by using the Form Wizard as depicted in Figure 5.6. The wizard starts by asking you which fields you want to include in your form. You will need to select fields from the Customers table, as shown in Figure 5.6a, as well as from the Loans table as shown in Figure 5.6b, since these tables are the basis for the main form and subform, respectively.

The wizard will do the rest. It gives you the opportunity to view the records by customer, as shown in Figure 5.6c. (Additional screens, not shown in Figure 5.6, let you choose the style of the forms.) Finally, you save each form as a separate object as shown in Figure 5.6d. You will find that the wizard provides an excellent starting point, but you usually have to customize the forms after they have been created. This is done in the Form Design view using the identical techniques that were presented earlier to move and size controls and/or modify their properties.

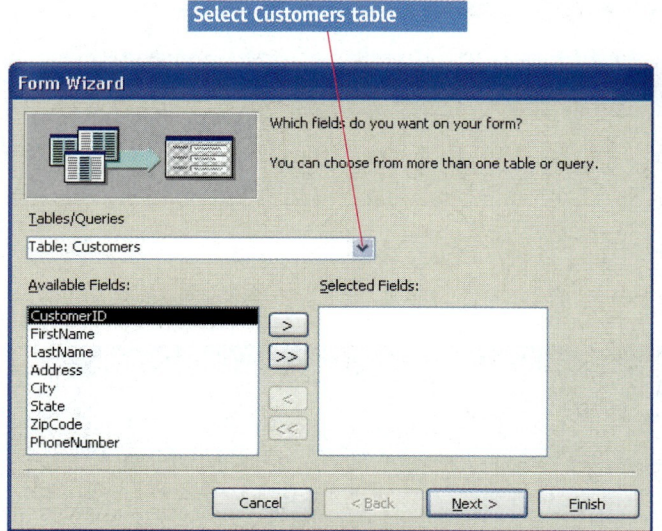

(a) The Customers Table

(b) The Loans Table

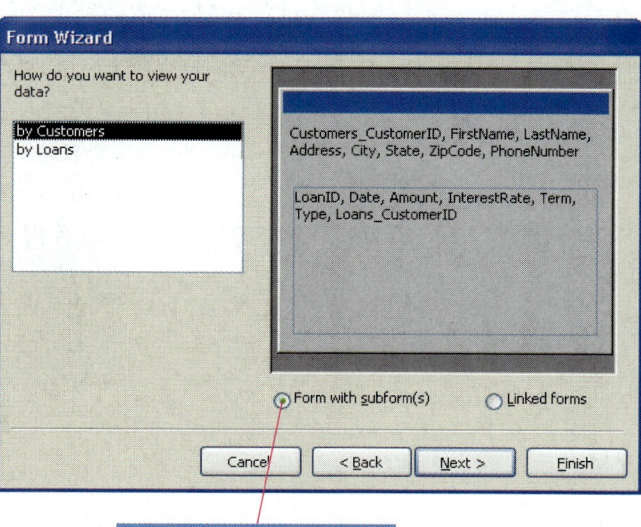

(c) View Data by Customers

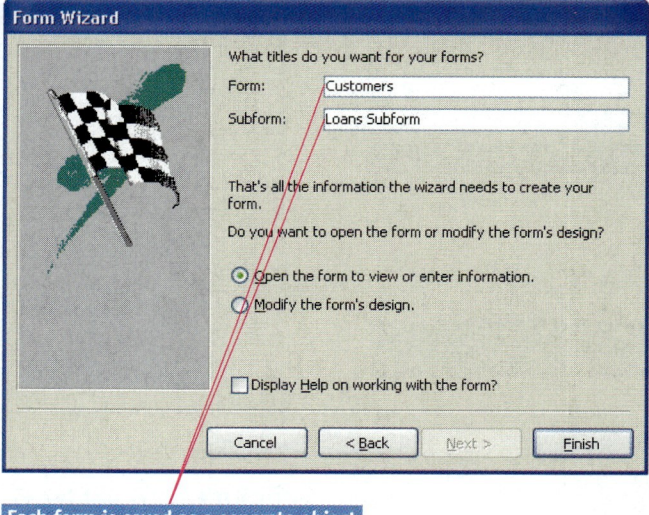

(d) Save the Form

FIGURE 5.6 The Form Wizard

2 Creating a Subform

Objective To create a subform that displays the many records in a one-to-many relationship; to move and size controls in an existing form; to enter data in a subform. Use Figure 5.7 as a guide in doing the exercise.

Step 1: **Start the Form Wizard**

■ Open the **National Bank database** from the previous exercise. Click the **Forms button** in the Database window, then double click the **Create form by using wizard button** to start the Form Wizard.

■ You should see the Form Wizard dialog box in Figure 5.7a, except that no fields have been selected.

■ The Customers table is selected by default. Click the **>> button** to enter all of the fields in the Customers table on the form.

■ Click the **drop-down arrow** in the Tables/Queries list box to display the tables and queries in the database.

■ Click **Loans** to select the Loans table as shown in Figure 5.7a. Click the **>> button** to enter all of the fields in the Loans table on the form.

■ Be sure that the Selected Fields area contains the fields from both the Loans form and the Customers form.

■ Click **Next** to continue with the Form Wizard.

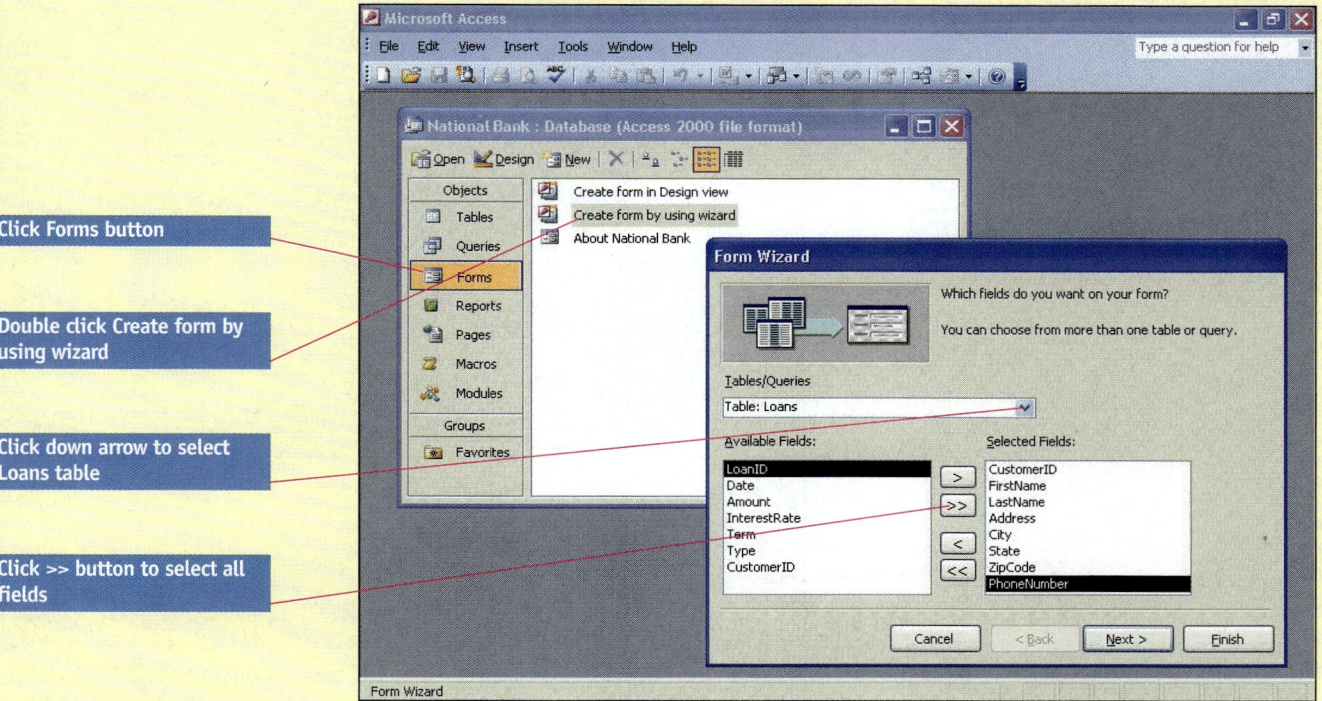

(a) Start the Form Wizard (step 1)

FIGURE 5.7   Hands-on Exercise 2

Step 2: Complete the Form

■ The wizard will prompt you for the additional information it needs to create the Customers form and the associated Loans subform. The next screen suggests that you view the data by customers and that you are going to create a form with subforms. Click **Next**.

■ The Datasheet option button is selected as the default layout for the subform. Click **Tabular**. Click **Next**.

■ Click **Standard** as the style for your form. Click **Next**.

■ You should see the screen in Figure 5.7b, in which the Form Wizard suggests **Customers** as the title of the form and **Loans Subform** as the title for the subform.

■ Click the option button to **Modify the form's design**, then click the **Finish command button** to create the form and exit the Form Wizard.

■ You should be in the Design view of the Customer form you just created. Click the **Save button** to save the form and continue working.

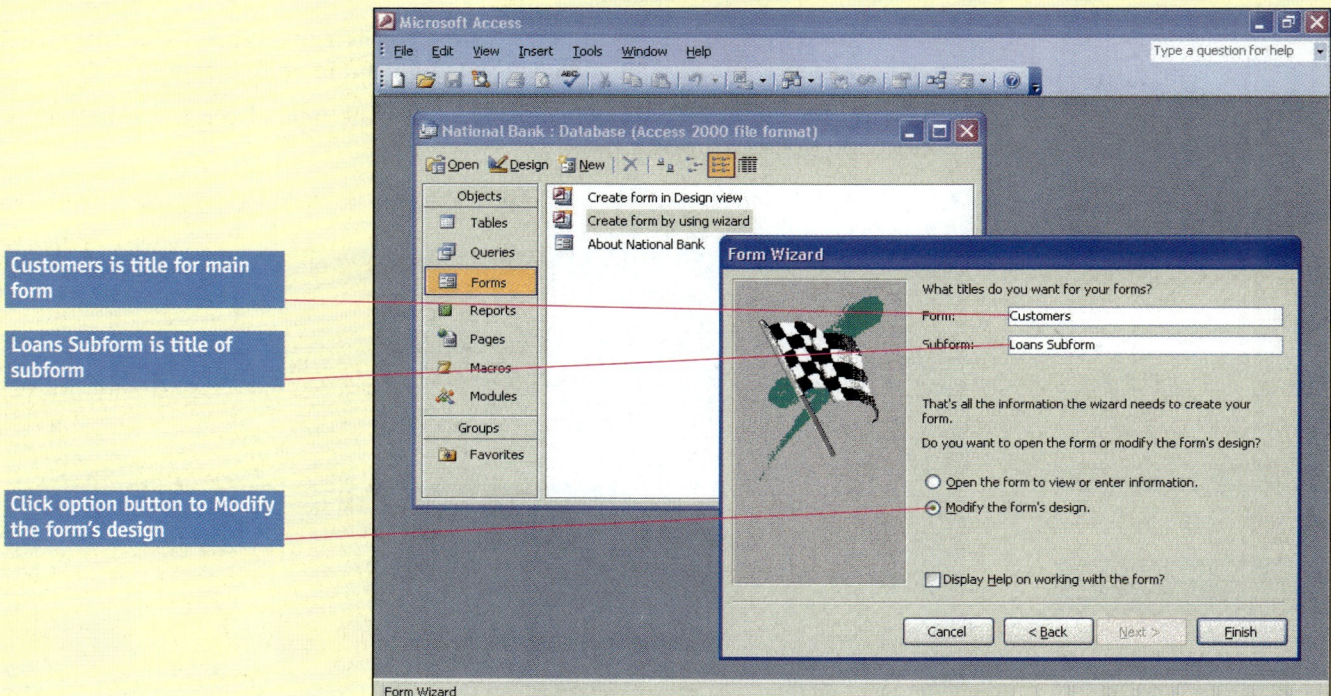

Customers is title for main form

Loans Subform is title of subform

Click option button to Modify the form's design

(b) Complete the Form (step 2)

FIGURE 5.7 Hands-on Exercise 2 (*continued*)

THE NAME'S THE SAME

The Form Wizard automatically assigns the name of the underlying table (or query) to each form (subform) it creates. The Report Wizard works in similar fashion. The intent of the similar naming convention is to help you select the proper object from the Database window when you want to subsequently open the object. This becomes increasingly important in databases that contain a large number of objects.

Step 3: **Modify the Customers Form**

■ You should see the Customers form in Figure 5.7c. The appearance of your form will be different from our figure, however, as you need to rearrange the position of the fields on the form. Maximize the form window.

■ Click and drag the bottom of the Detail section down to give yourself additional room in which to work.

■ It takes time (and a little practice) to move and size the controls within a form. Try the indicated command, then click the **Undo button** if you are not satisfied with the result.
  ❑ Move the **State, ZipCode, and PhoneNumber** to the bottom of the detail section. (This is only temporary, but we need room to work.)
  ❑ Increase the width of the form to **seven inches**. Click the **LastName control** to select the control and display the sizing handles, then drag the **LastName control** and its attached label so that it is next to the FirstName control. Align the tops of the LastName and FirstName controls.
  ❑ Move the **Address control** up. Place the controls for **City, State**, and **ZipCode** on the same line, then move these controls under the Address control. You may need to size some of the other labels to fit everything on one line. Align the tops of these controls as well.
  ❑ Click and drag the control for **PhoneNumber** to the right of the CustomerID field. Align the tops of the controls.
  ❑ Right align all of the labels so that they appear close to the bound control they identify. Size and move controls as needed.

■ Your form should now match Figure 5.7c. Click the label attached to the subform control and press the **Del key**. Be sure you delete only the label and not the control for the subform.

■ Save the form.

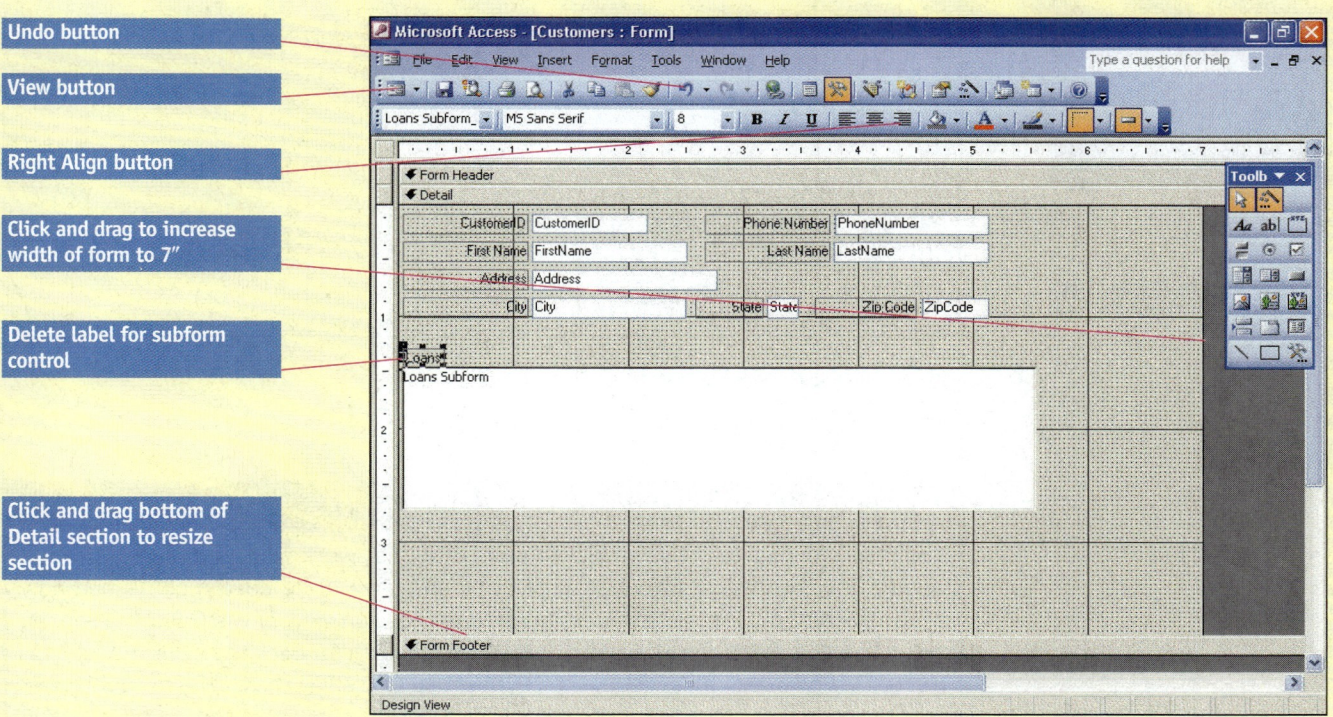

Undo button

View button

Right Align button

Click and drag to increase width of form to 7″

Delete label for subform control

Click and drag bottom of Detail section to resize section

(c) Modify the Customers Form (step 3)

FIGURE 5.7 Hands-on Exercise 2 (*continued*)

Step 4: View the Customers Form

- Click the **View button**. You should see the Customers form in the Form view as in Figure 5.7d. Do not be concerned about the column widths in the subform or the fact that you may not see all of the fields at this time. Our objective is simply to show the relationship between the main form and the subform.
  - ❏ The customer information for the first customer (C0001) is displayed in the main portion of the form. The loans for that customer are in the subform.
  - ❏ The status bar at the bottom of the window (corresponding to the main form) displays record 1 of 10 records (you are looking at the first record in the Customers table).
  - ❏ The status bar for the subform displays record 1 of 3 records (you are on the first of three loan records for this customer).

- Click the ▶ **button** on the status bar for the main form to move to the next customer record. The subform is updated automatically to display the two loans belonging to this customer.

- Close the Customers form. Click **Yes** if asked to save the changes.

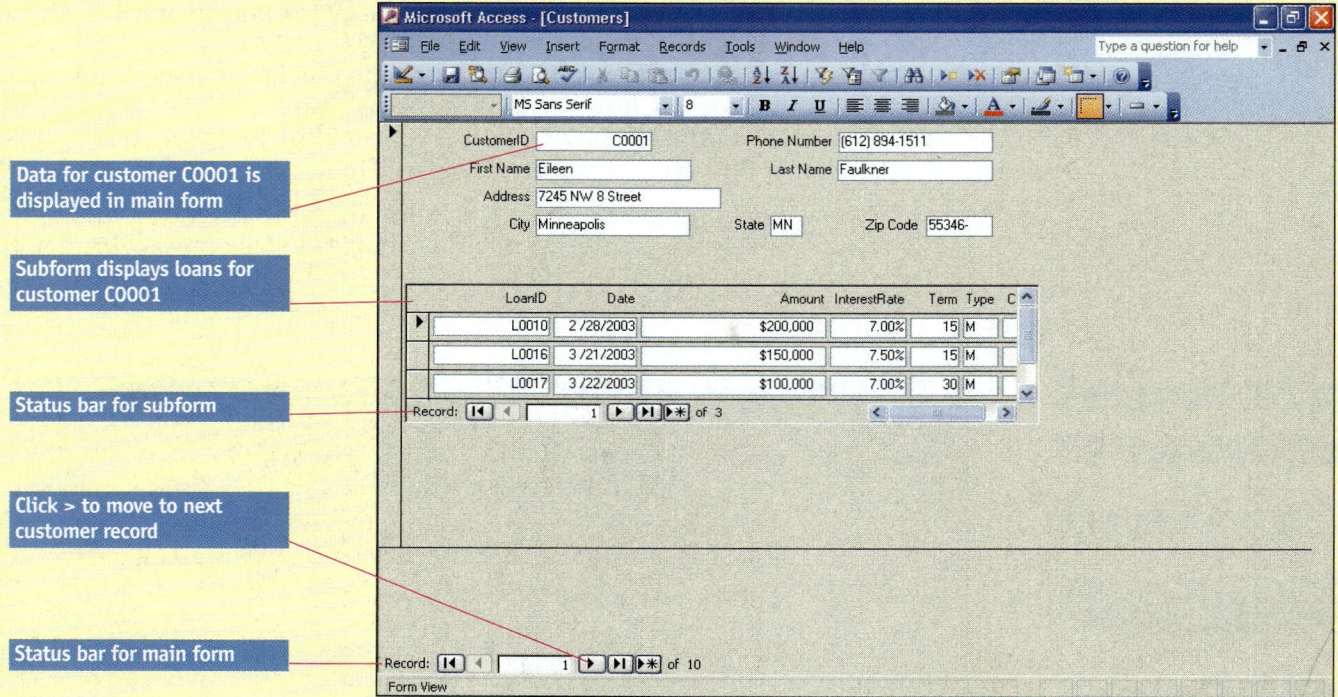

Data for customer C0001 is displayed in main form

Subform displays loans for customer C0001

Status bar for subform

Click > to move to next customer record

Status bar for main form

(d) View the Customers Form (step 4)

FIGURE 5.7 Hands-on Exercise 2 (*continued*)

WHY IT WORKS

The main form (Customers) and subform (Loans) work in conjunction with one another so that you always see all of the loans for a given customer. To see how the link is actually implemented, change to the Design view of the Customers form and point anywhere on the border of the Loans subform. Click the right mouse button to display a shortcut menu, click Properties to display the Subform/Subreport properties dialog box, and, if necessary, click the All tab within the dialog box. You should see CustomerID next to two properties (Link Child Fields and Link Master Fields).

Step 5: Add the Payment Amount

- Click the **Forms button** in the Database window. Open the **Loans subform** in Design view. Click and drag the right edge of the form to **7 inches**.

- Right click the **Form Selector button** to display a context-sensitive menu, then click **Properties** to display the Properties sheet for the form. Click the **All Tab**, click in the **Default View** text box, then select **Datasheet**. Close the Property sheet.

- Click the **Label button** on the Toolbox toolbar, then click and drag in the **Form Header** to create an unbound control. Enter **Payment Due** as the text for the label as shown in Figure 5.7e. Size and align the label.

- Click the **Text Box button**, then click and drag in the **Detail section** to create an unbound control that will contain the amount of the monthly payment. Click the label for the control (e.g., Text 15), then press the **Del key**.

- Point to the unbound control, click the **right mouse button**, then click **Properties** to open the Properties dialog box. Click the **All tab**. Click the **Name property**. Enter **Payment Due** in place of the existing label.

- Click the **Control Source property**, then click the **Build (…) button**.
  - ❑ Double click **Functions** (if there is a plus sign in its icon), then click **Built-In Functions**. Click **Financial** in the second column, then double click **Pmt**.
  - ❑ You need to replace each of the arguments in the Pmt function with the appropriate field names from the Loans table. Select the arguments one at a time and enter the replacement as shown in Figure 5.7e. Click **OK**.

- Click the **Format property**, click the **down arrow**, and specify **Currency**. Click the **Decimal Places property**, click the **down arrow**, and select **2**.

- Close the Properties dialog box. Change to the **Datasheet view**, and check the column widths, making adjustments as necessary. Close the Loans subform. Click **Yes** to save the changes.

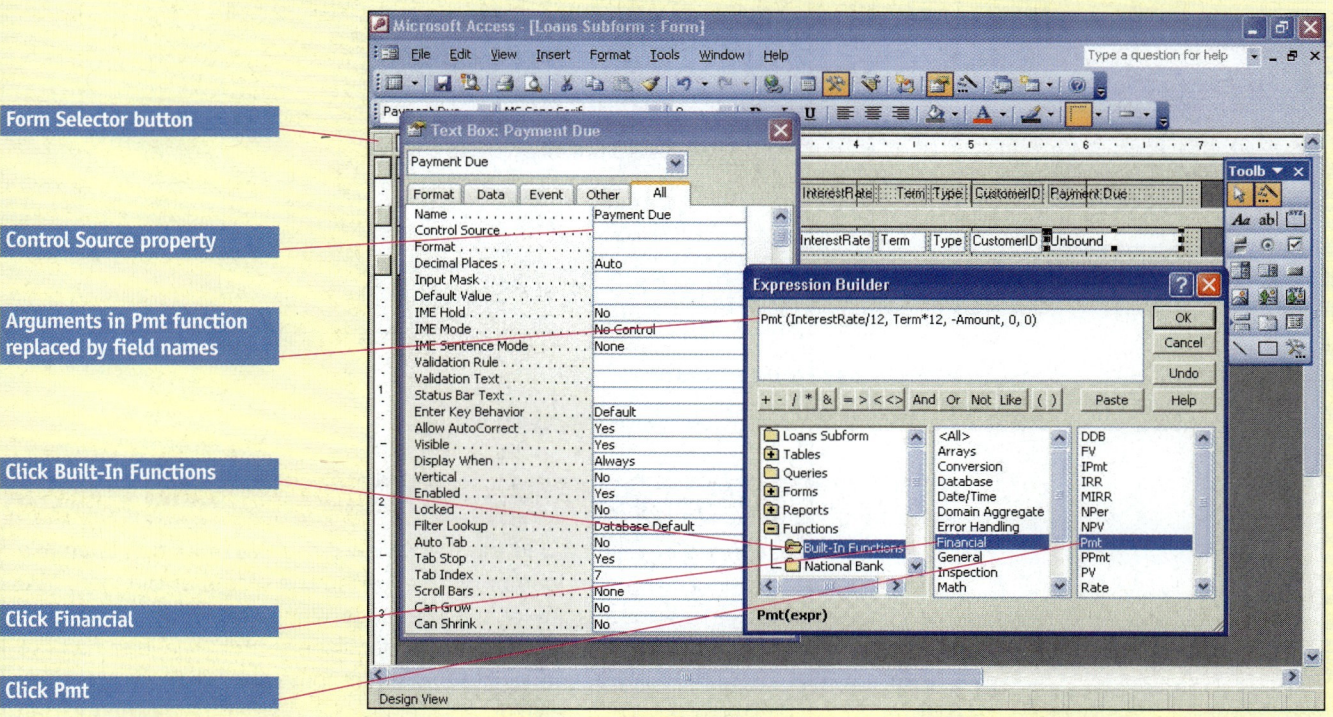

(e) Add the Payment Amount (step 5)

FIGURE 5.7 Hands-on Exercise 2 (*continued*)

Step 6: Check Your Progress

- Open the **Customers form**. You should see the first customer in the database, together with the associated loan information as shown in Figure 5.7f. As before, you are on customer 1 of 10, and loan 1 of 3 for that customer. (The CustomerID appears in the Loans subform to check that the forms are linking correctly. We will delete the control from the subform in the next step.)

- The payment for each loan has been added to the subform, but you may have to adjust the column widths. You can drag the border between column headings, just as you would adjust the columns in an Excel worksheet.

- You may also have to adjust the size or position of the subform within the main form. Change to **Design view**.
  - ❑ Click the **subform control** to select it, then click and drag a sizing handle to change the size of the subform within the main form.
  - ❑ Click and drag a border of the control to change its position.

- You may have to switch back and forth between the Form and Design views to get the correct size and position. Save the completed form.

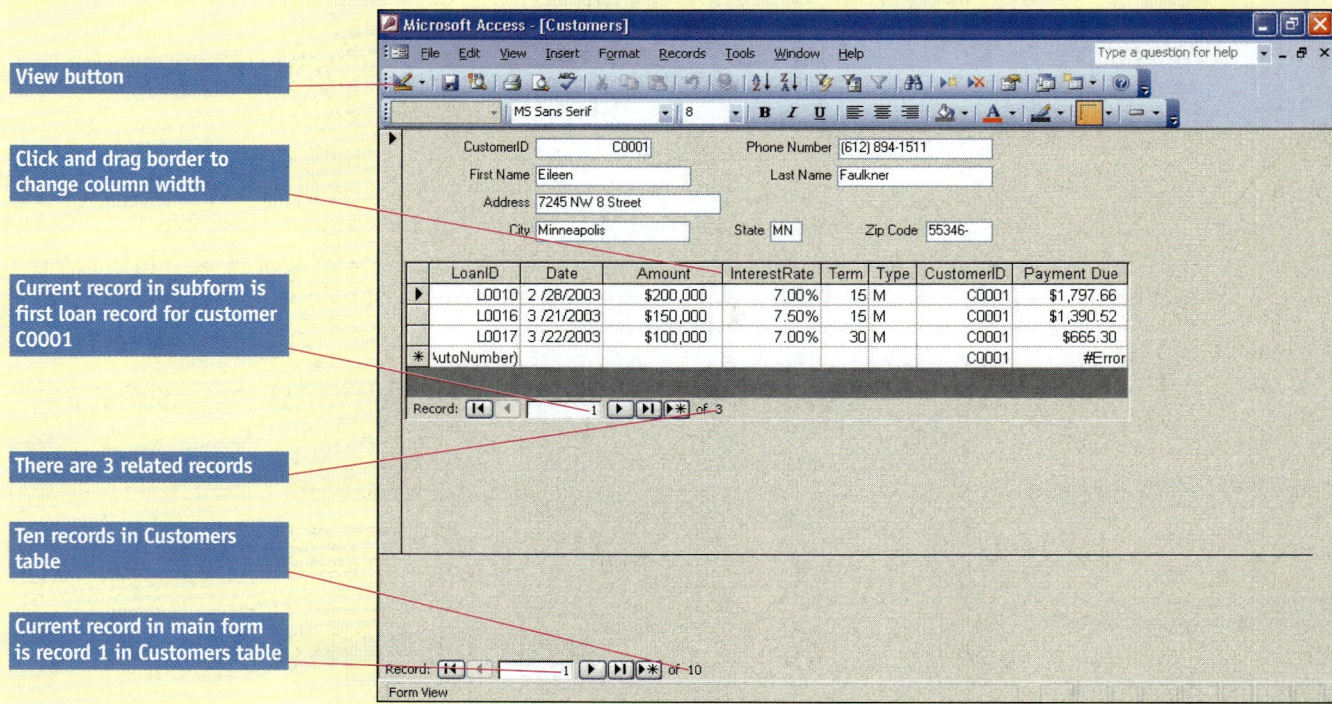

(f) Check Your Progress (step 6)

FIGURE 5.7 Hands-on Exercise 2 (*continued*)

ERROR AND HOW TO AVOID IT

A # Error message will be displayed in the Form view if the PMT function is unable to compute a payment for a new loan prior to entering the terms of the loan. You can, however, suppress the display of the message using the IIF (Immediate If) function to test for a null argument. In other words, if the term of the loan has not been entered, do not display anything; otherwise compute the payment. Use the IIF function, =IIF(Term Is Null," ",PMT(InterestRate/12, Term*12, -Amount)) as the control source for the payment amount.

Step 7: **Complete the Customers Form**

- Return to **Design view**. Click and drag the bottom of the **Form Header** down in the form to create room in which to work. Click in the Form Header.
- Pull down the **Insert menu**, click **Picture**, select the **Exploring Access folder** in the Look in box, select the **National Bank clip art** image, and click **OK**.
- Move and size the clip art as shown. Right click the clip art, click **Properties**, click **Size Mode**, click the **down arrow**, then choose **Stretch**, so that the clip art fills the placeholder. Close the Properties sheet.
- Select the clip art, click the **Copy button**, then click the **Paste button** to duplicate the image. Drag the copied image to the right side of the form.
- Use the **Label tool** to create unbound controls for the title of the form and your name. Move, size, and format the labels. Size the form header appropriately.
- Use the **Command Button Wizard** to create command buttons to **Add New Customer** and **Close the Form** as shown in Figure 5.7g.
- Press and hold the **Shift key** to select both command buttons. Use the **Format command** to size and align the buttons. Right click either button, click Properties, then set the **Tab Stop property** to **No** so that the Tab key skips both buttons in Form view. Close the Properties sheet.
- Pull down the **View menu**, click the **Tab Order command**, click the **AutoOrder button** to set the order in which the controls are selected (top to bottom, left to right), then click **OK** to accept the settings and close the dialog box.
- You're almost finished. Click the **CustomerID control** in the Loans subform and press the **Del key**. Delete the label for the control as well. The CustomerID field is still in the Loans table, but it need not appear in the Loans form, since its value corresponds to the CustomerID in the main form.
- Move the payment control and its label to the left. Size and move the subform control as necessary. Save the completed form.

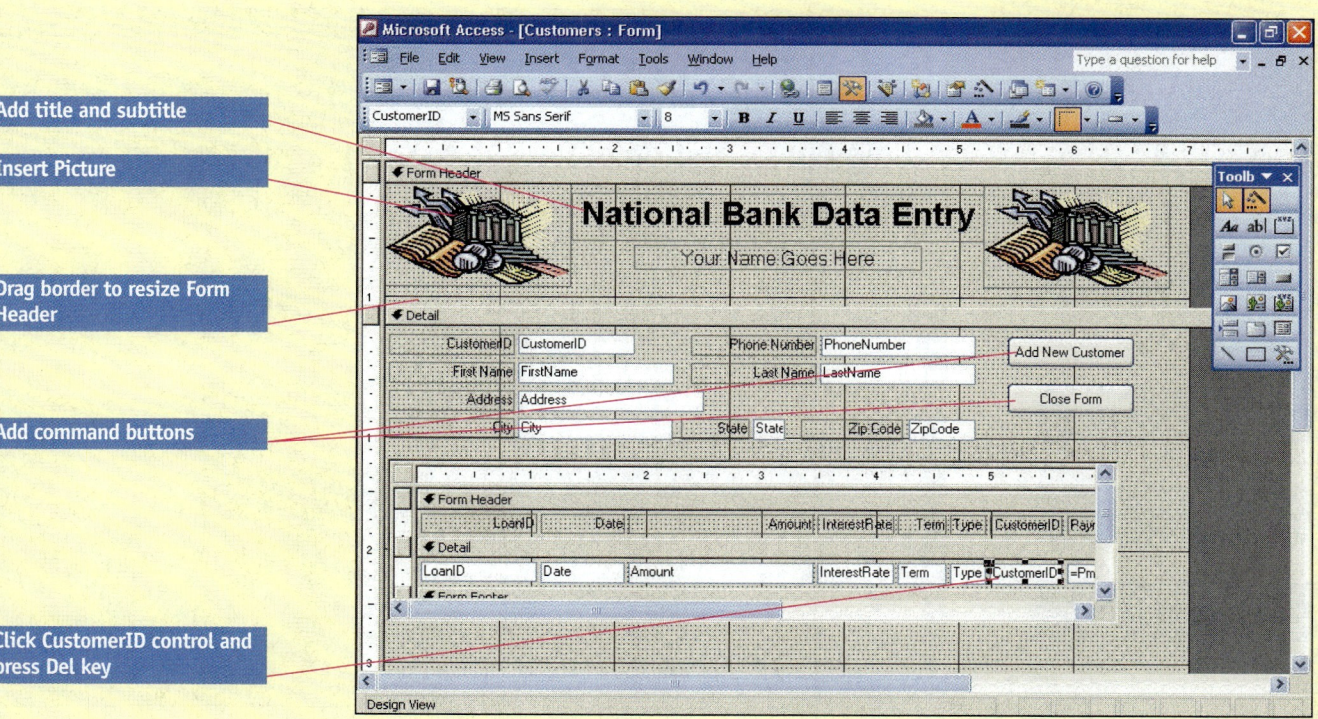

(g) Complete the Customers Form (step 7)

FIGURE 5.7 Hands-on Exercise 2 (continued)

Step 8: Enter a New Loan

- Click the **View button** to switch to the Form view as shown in Figure 5.7h. You should see the form Header. The CustomerID has also disappeared from the subform.

- Click the ▶ on the status bar of the main form to move to the last record (customer C0011), which is the record you entered in the previous exercise. (Click the **PgUp key** if you are on a blank record.)

- Click in the **Date field** for the blank record in the subform. Enter data for the new loan as shown in Figure 5.7h.

- The LoanID is entered automatically because it is an AutoNumber field. (It should be L0027 if you have followed the exercise exactly.) The payment due will be computed automatically as soon as you complete the Term field.

- Press the **down arrow** when you have entered the last field (Type), which saves the data in the current record. (The record selector symbol changes from a pencil to a triangle.)

- Check that you are still on the record for customer 11 (the record containing your data), then click the **selection area** at the left of the form.

- Pull down the **File menu** and click **Print** (or click the **Print button**) to display the Print dialog box. Click the **Selected Record(s) option button**. Click **OK**. (It may be necessary to use the **Page Setup command** to change the margins so that the form fits on one page.)

- Close the Customers form. Click **Yes** if asked to save the changes to the form or subform. Close the National Bank database.

- Exit Access if you do not want to continue with the next hands-on exercise at this time.

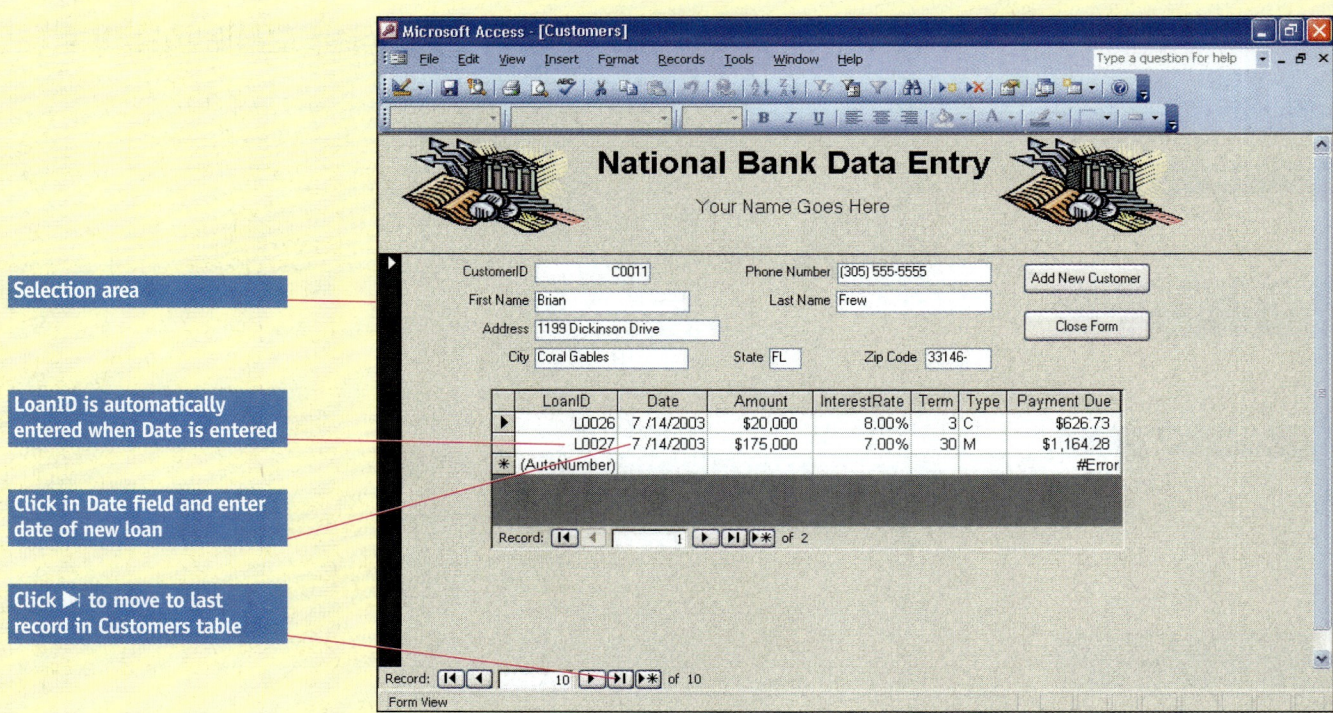

(h) Enter a New Loan (step 8)

FIGURE 5.7 Hands-on Exercise 2 (*continued*)

MULTIPLE-TABLE QUERIES

The chapter began with a conceptual view of the National Bank database, in which we described the need for separate tables to store data for customers and loans. We created a database with sample data, asked several questions about various customers and their loans, then intuitively drew on both tables to derive the answers. Access simply automates the process through creation of a *multiple-table query*. This type of query was introduced in the previous chapter, but it is reviewed in this section because of its importance.

Let's assume that you wanted to know the name of every customer who held a 15-year mortgage that was issued after April 1, 2003. To answer that question, you would need data from both the Customers table and the Loans table, as shown in Figure 5.8. You would create the query using the same grid as for a simple select query, but you would have to add fields from both tables to the query. The Design view of the query is shown in Figure 5.8a. The resulting dynaset is displayed in Figure 5.8b.

The Query window contains the Field, Sort, Show, and Criteria rows that appear in simple select queries. The *Table row* is necessary only in multiple-table queries and indicates the table where the field originates. The customer's last name and first name are taken from the Customers table. All of the other fields are from the Loans table. The one-to-many relationship between the Customers table and the Loans table is shown graphically within the Query window. The tables are related through the CustomerID field, which is the primary key in the Customers table and a foreign key in the Loans table. The line between the two field lists is called a *join line*, and its properties determine how the tables will be accessed within the query.

Figure 5.8 extends the earlier discussion on multiple-table queries to include the SQL statement in Figure 5.8c and the Join Properties dialog box in Figure 5.8d. This information is intended primarily for the reader who is interested in the theoretical concepts of a relational database. *Structured Query Language* (SQL) is the universal way to access a relational database, meaning that the information provided by any database is obtained through SQL queries. Access simplifies the creation of an SQL query, however, by providing the Design grid, then converting the entries in the grid to the equivalent SQL statements. You can view the SQL statements from within Access as we did in Figure 5.8c, by changing to the SQL view, and in so doing you can gain a better appreciation for how a relational database works. (You can also ignore the SQL view and work exclusively from the Design grid.)

The concept of a "join" is also crucial to a relational database. In essence, Access, or any other relational database, combines (joins) all of the records in the Customers table with all of the records in the Loans table to create a temporary working table. The result is a very large table in which each record contains all of the fields from both the Customers table and the Loans table. The number of records in this table is equal to the product of the number of Customer records times the number of Loans records; for example, if there were 10 records in the Customers table, and 30 records in the Loans table, there would be 300 records in the combined table. However, Access displays only those records wherein the value of the joined field (CustomerID) is the same in both tables. It sounds complicated (it is), but Access does the work for you. And as we said earlier, you need only to master the Design grid in Figure 5.8a and let Access do the rest.

The power of a relational database is its ability to process multiple-table queries, such as the example in Figure 5.8. The forms and reports within a database also become more interesting when they contain information based on multiple-table queries. Our next exercise has you create a query similar to the one in Figure 5.8, then create a report based on that query.

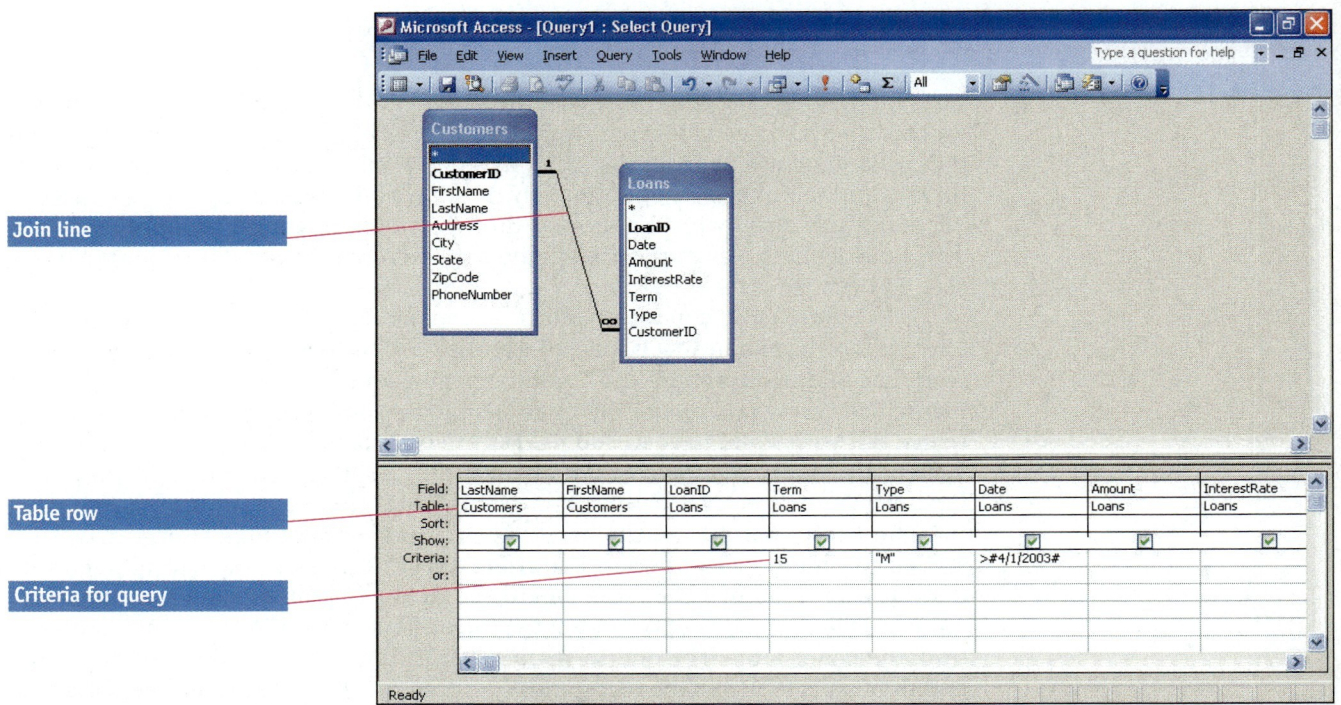

Join line

Table row

Criteria for query

(a) Query Window

	Last Name	First Name	LoanID	Term	Type	Date	Amount	InterestRate
▶	Hirsch	Matt	L0022	15	M	4 /22/2003	$350,000	7.50%
	Grauer	Benjamin	L0023	15	M	5 /1 /2003	$150,000	6.00%
	Sangastiano	Lori	L0025	15	M	5 /8 /2003	$275,000	9.20%
*			(AutoNumber)					

(b) Dynaset

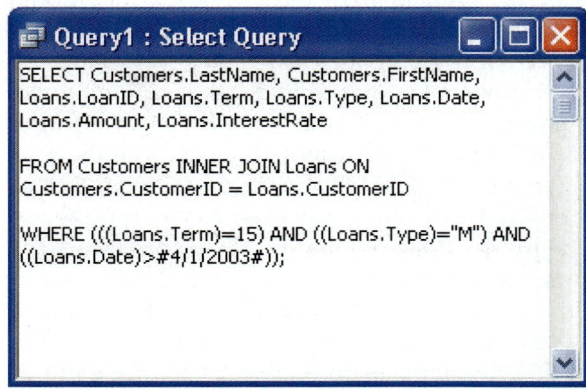

```
SELECT Customers.LastName, Customers.FirstName,
Loans.LoanID, Loans.Term, Loans.Type, Loans.Date,
Loans.Amount, Loans.InterestRate

FROM Customers INNER JOIN Loans ON
Customers.CustomerID = Loans.CustomerID

WHERE (((Loans.Term)=15) AND ((Loans.Type)="M") AND
((Loans.Date)>#4/1/2003#));
```

(c) SQL View

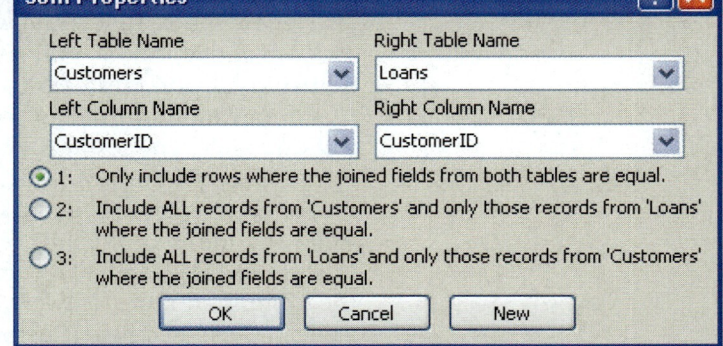

(d) Join Properties

FIGURE 5.8   A Multiple-table Query

3 Queries and Reports

Objective   To create a query that relates two tables to one another, then create a report based on that query; to use the query to update the records in the underlying tables. Use Figure 5.9 as a guide in the exercise.

Step 1:   **Add the Tables**

■ Open the **National Bank database** from the previous exercise.

■ Click the **Queries button** in the Database window. Double click **Create query in Design view**.

■ The Show Table dialog box appears as shown in Figure 5.9a, with the Tables tab already selected.

■ Click the **Customers table**, then click the **Add button** (or double click the **Customers table**) to add the Customers table to the query.

■ Double click the **Loans table** to add the Loans table to the query.

■ Click **Close** to close the Show Table dialog box.

Customers table and Loans table have been added

Add button

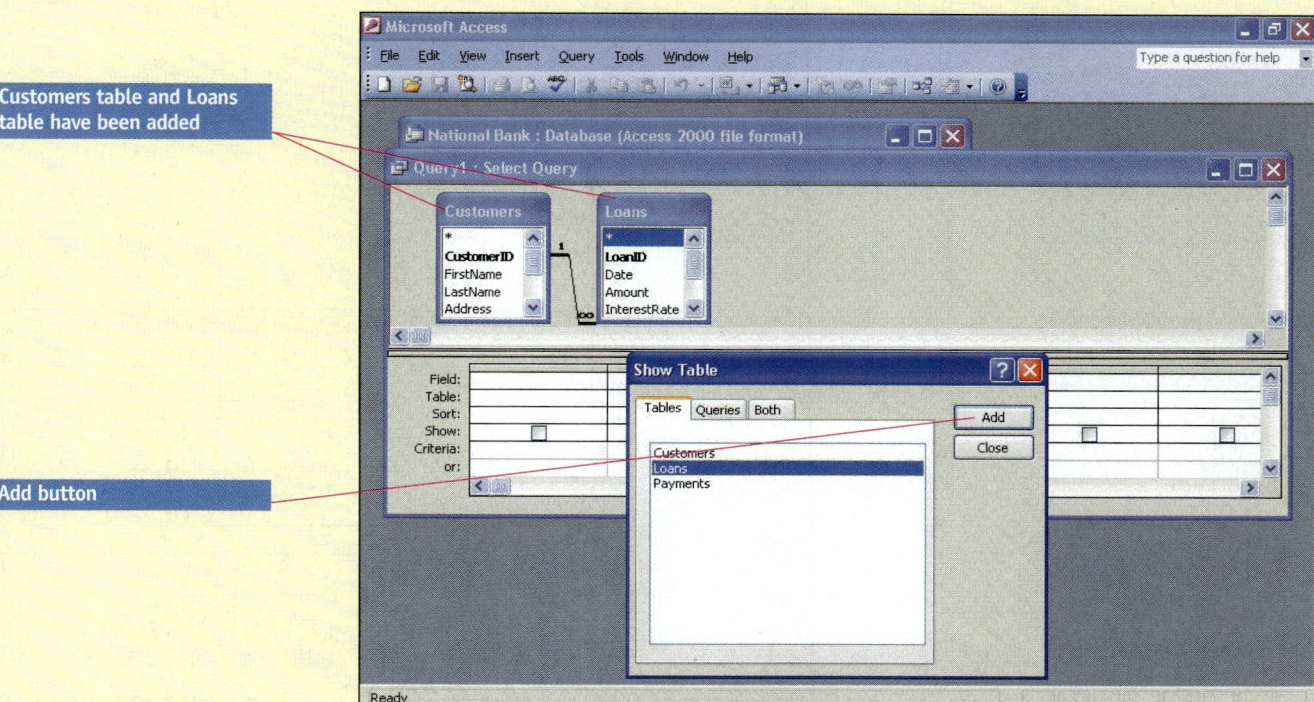

(a) Add the Tables (step 1)

FIGURE 5.9   Hands-on Exercise 3

ADDING AND DELETING TABLES

To add a table to an existing query, pull down the Query menu, click Show Table, then double click the name of the table from the Table/Query list. To delete a table, click anywhere in its field list and press the Del key, or pull down the Query menu and click Remove Table.

Step 2: **Move and Size the Field Lists**

- Click the **Maximize button** so that the Query Design window takes the entire desktop.

- Point to the line separating the field lists from the design grid (the mouse pointer changes to a cross), then click and drag in a downward direction. This gives you more space to display the field lists for the tables in the query as shown in Figure 5.9b.

- Click and drag the bottom of the **Customers table field list** until you can see all of the fields in the Customers table.

- Click and drag the bottom of the **Loans table field list** until you can see all of the fields in the Loans table.

- Click and drag the title bar of the **Loans table** to the right until you are satisfied with the appearance of the line connecting the tables.

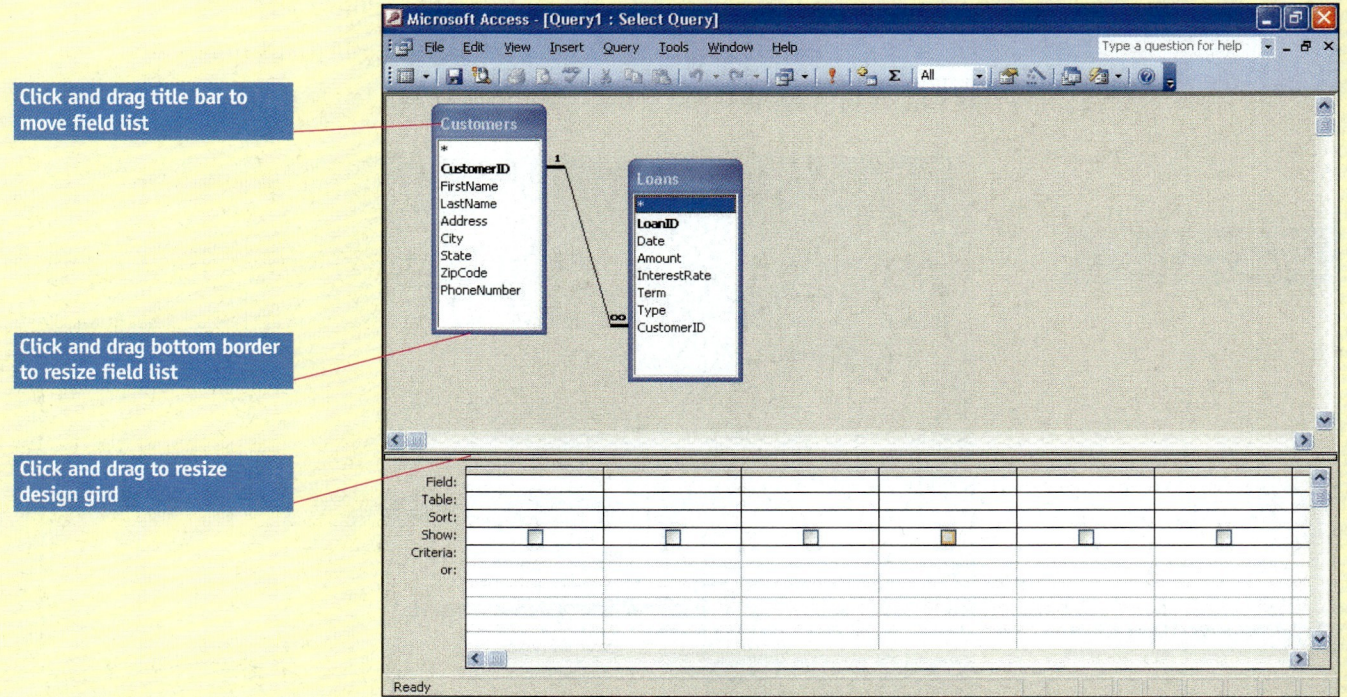

Click and drag title bar to move field list

Click and drag bottom border to resize field list

Click and drag to resize design gird

(b) Move and Size the Field Lists (step 2)

FIGURE 5.9 Hands-on Exercise 3 (*continued*)

CONVERSION TO STANDARD FORMAT

Access is flexible in accepting text and date expressions in the Criteria row of a select query. A text entry can be entered with or without quotation marks (e.g., M or "M"). A date entry can be entered with or without pound signs (you can enter 1/1/03 or #1/1/03#). Access does, however, convert your entries to standard format as soon you move to the next cell in the design grid. Thus, text entries are always displayed in quotation marks, and dates are always enclosed in pound signs.

Step 3: **Create the Query**

- The Table row should be visible within the design grid. If not, pull down the **View menu** and click **Table Names** to display the Table row in the design grid as shown in Figure 5.9c.

- Double click the **LastName** and **FirstName fields**, in that order, from the Customers table to add these fields to the design grid.

- Double click the **title bar** of the Loans table to select all of the fields, then drag the selected group of fields to the design grid.

- Enter the selection criteria (scrolling if necessary) as follows:
  - ❏ Click the **Criteria row** under the **Date field**. Type **Between 1/1/03 and 3/31/03**. (You do not have to type the pound signs.)
  - ❏ Click the **Criteria row** for the **Amount field**. Type **>200000**.
  - ❏ Type **M** in the Criteria row for the **Type field**. (You do not have to type the quotation marks.)

- Select all of the columns in the design grid by clicking the column selector in the first column, then pressing and holding the **Shift key** as you scroll to the last column and click its column selector.

- Double click the right edge of any column selector to adjust the column width of all the columns simultaneously.

- Click the **Sort row** under the LastName field, then click the **down arrow** to open the drop-down list box. Click **Ascending**.

- Click the **Save button** on the Query Design toolbar. Save the query as **First Quarter 2003 Jumbo Loans**.

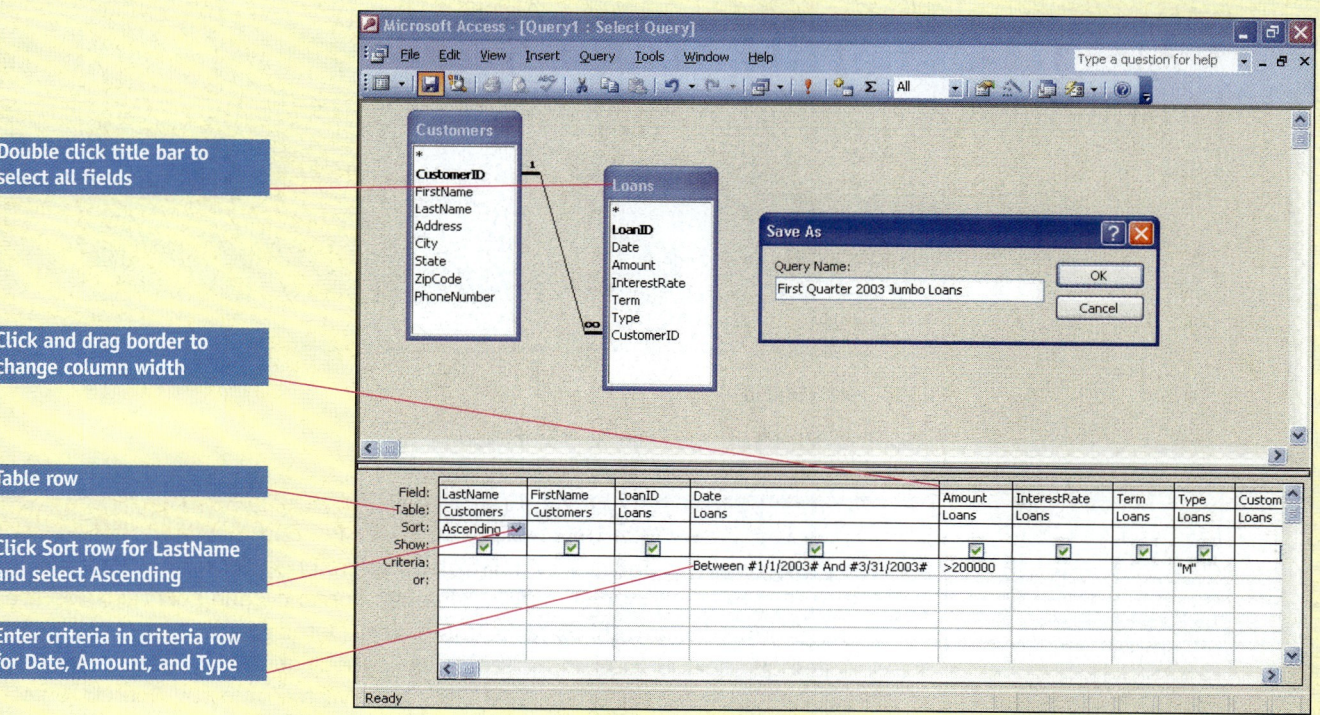

(c) Create the Query (step 3)

FIGURE 5.9 Hands-on Exercise 3 (*continued*)

Step 4: **The Dynaset**

- Click the **Run button** (the exclamation point) to run the query and create the dynaset in Figure 5.9d. Three jumbo loans are listed. The loans appear in alphabetical order according to the customer's last name.

- Click the **Amount field** for loan L0008. Enter **100000** as the corrected amount and press **Enter**. (This will reduce the number of jumbo loans in subsequent reports to two.)

- Click the **View button** to return to the Design view in order to rerun the query.

- This time, only two loans are listed, because loan L0008 is no longer a jumbo loan. Changing a value in a dynaset automatically changes the underlying table.

- Click the **Close button** to close the query. Click **Yes** if asked whether to save the changes to the query.

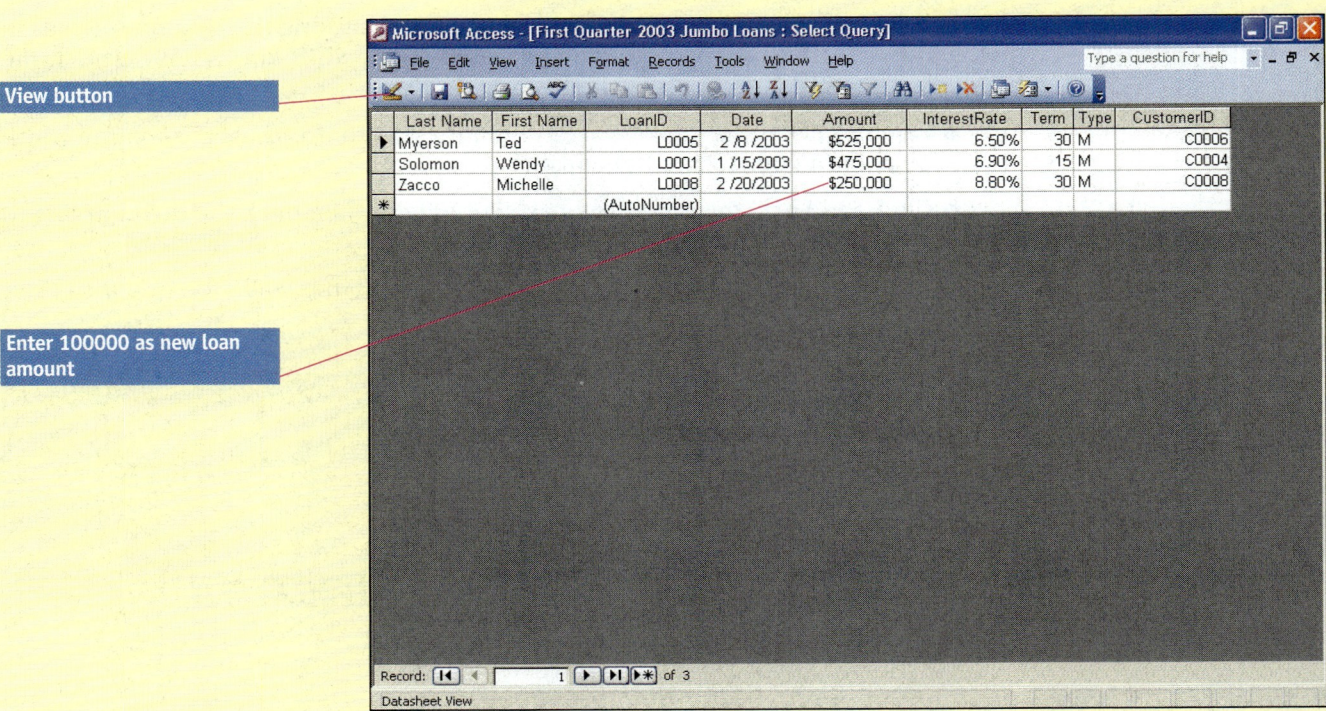

(d) The Dynaset (step 4)

FIGURE 5.9 Hands-on Exercise 3 (*continued*)

DATA TYPE MISMATCH

The data type determines the way in which criteria appear in the design grid. A text field is enclosed in quotation marks. Number, currency, and counter fields are shown as digits with or without a decimal point. Dates are enclosed in pound signs. A Yes/No field is entered as Yes or No without quotation marks. Entering criteria in the wrong format produces a Data Type Mismatch error when attempting to run the query.

Step 5: **Create a Report**

- The National Bank database should still be open (although the size of your window may be different from the one in the figure).

- Click the **Reports button** in the Database window. Double click **Create report by using wizard**.

- Click the **drop-down arrow** to display the tables and queries in the database to select the one on which the report will be based.

- Select **First Quarter 2003 Jumbo Loans** (the query you just created) as the basis of your report as shown in Figure 5.9e.

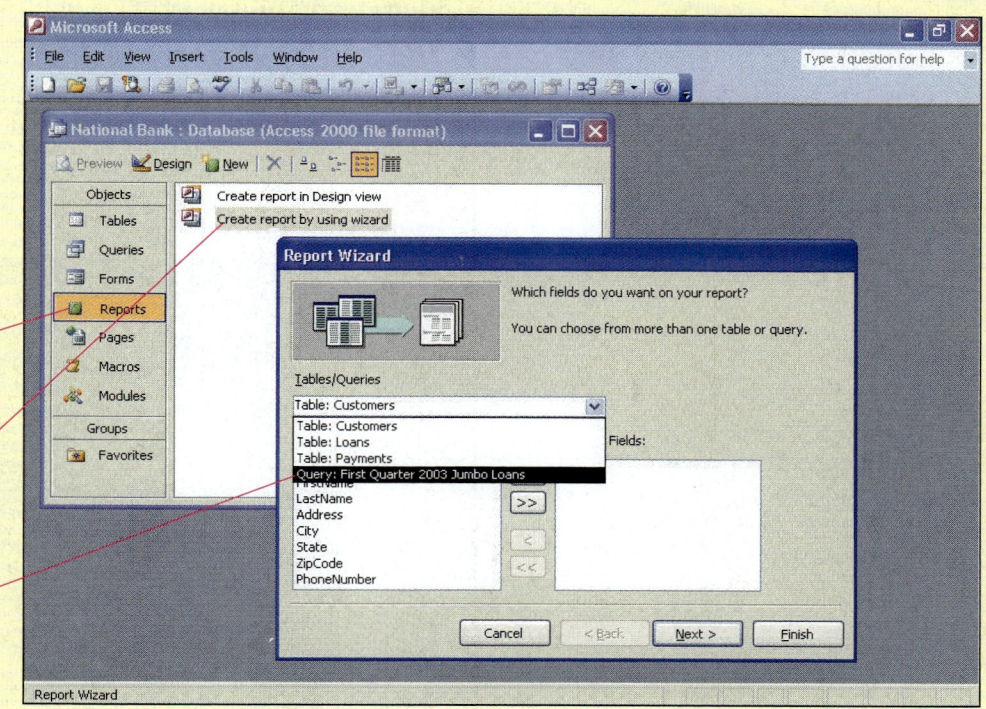

Click Reports button

Double click Create report by using wizard

Click First Quarter 2003 jumbo Loans

(e) Create a Report (step 5)

FIGURE 5.9 Hands-on Exercise 3 (*continued*)

CHANGE THE REPORT PROPERTIES

Do you want the Page Header or Page Footer to appear on every page of a report, or would you prefer to suppress the information on pages where there is a Report Header or Footer? You can customize a report to accommodate this and other subtleties by changing the report properties. Open the report in Design view, right click the Report Selector button (the solid square in the upper-left corner), then click the Properties command to display the property sheet for the report. Click the All tab, locate the Page Header or Page Footer property, and make the appropriate change.

Step 6:   The Report Wizard

- Double click **LoanID** from the Available Fields list box to add this field to the report. Add the **LastName, FirstName, Date**, and **Amount fields** as shown in Figure 5.9f. Click **Next**.

- You will be asked how you want to view your data, by Customers or by Loans. Select **Loans**. Click **Next**.

- There is no need to group the records. Click **Next**.

- There is no need to sort the records. Click **Next**.

- The **Tabular layout** is selected, as is **Portrait orientation**. Be sure the box is checked to **Adjust field width so all fields fit on a page**. Click **Next**.

- Choose **Soft Gray** as the style. Click **Next**.

- Enter **First Quarter 2003 Jumbo Loans** as the title for your report. The option button to **Preview the Report** is already selected.

- Click the **Finish Command button** to exit the Report Wizard and preview the report.

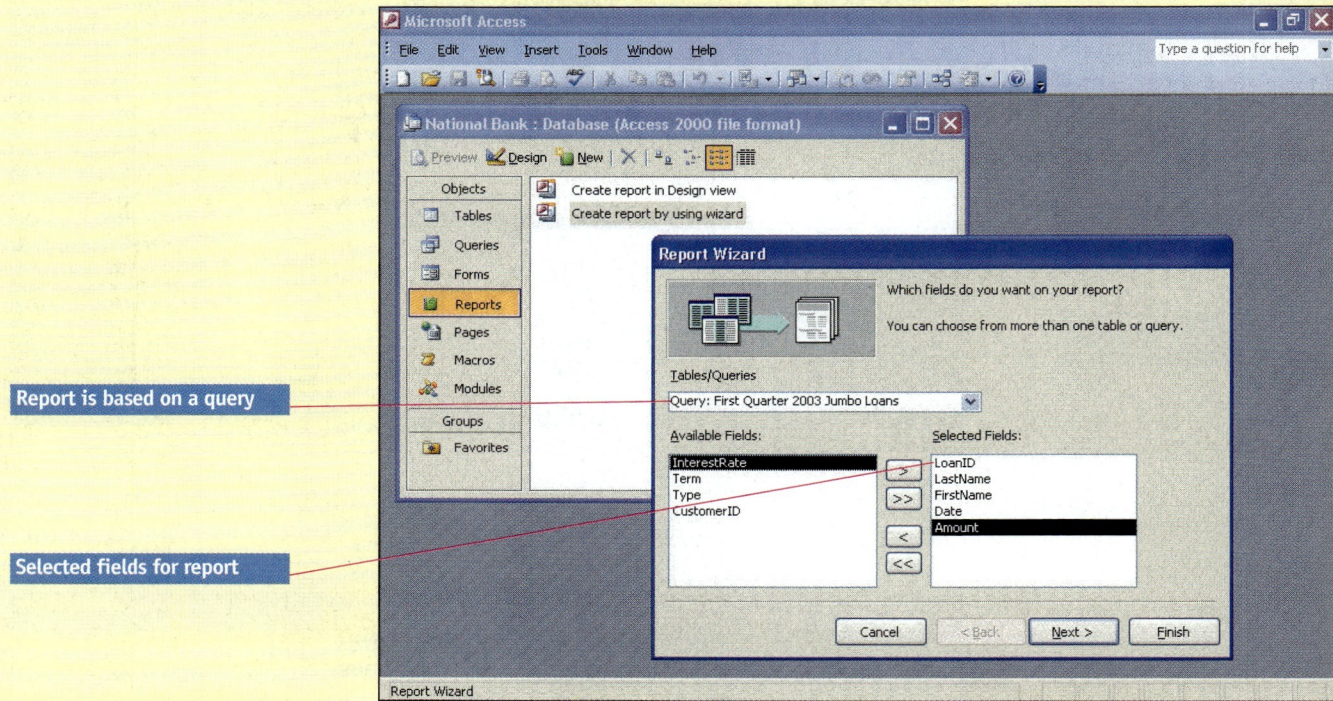

Report is based on a query

Selected fields for report

(f) The Report Wizard (step 6)

FIGURE 5.9   Hands-on Exercise 3 (*continued*)

GROUPING RECORDS WITHIN A REPORT

What if you wanted a report that showed all of the customers in a database, and for each customer, all of the loans for that customer? Start the Report Wizard, select fields from the Customers table (name, telephone, and so on), then select additional fields from the Loans table. Access will ask you how to view the report (specify by customer) and how to sort the records (specify LoanID). Go to Design view when the wizard is finished to add a logo and/or modify the formatting. See practice exercise 4 at the end of the chapter.

Step 7: Print the Completed Report

- Change to Design view. Modify the Form Header so that it is similar to the report in Figure 5.9g. (Use the same clip art image as in the Customers form for consistency within the application.)

- Move, size, and align the controls in the Detail section as necessary. Save the modified report.

- Click the **Print Preview button** to view the report and see the customers with jumbo loans. (Return to Design view to make additional changes if necessary.)

- The report in Figure 5.9g is based on the query created earlier. Michelle Zacco is *not* in the report because the amount of her loan was updated in the query's dynaset in step 4.

- Click the **Print button** to print the report. Close the Preview window, then close the Report window. Click **Yes** if asked to save the changes.

- Close the National Bank database and exit Access if you do not want to continue with the next exercise at this time.

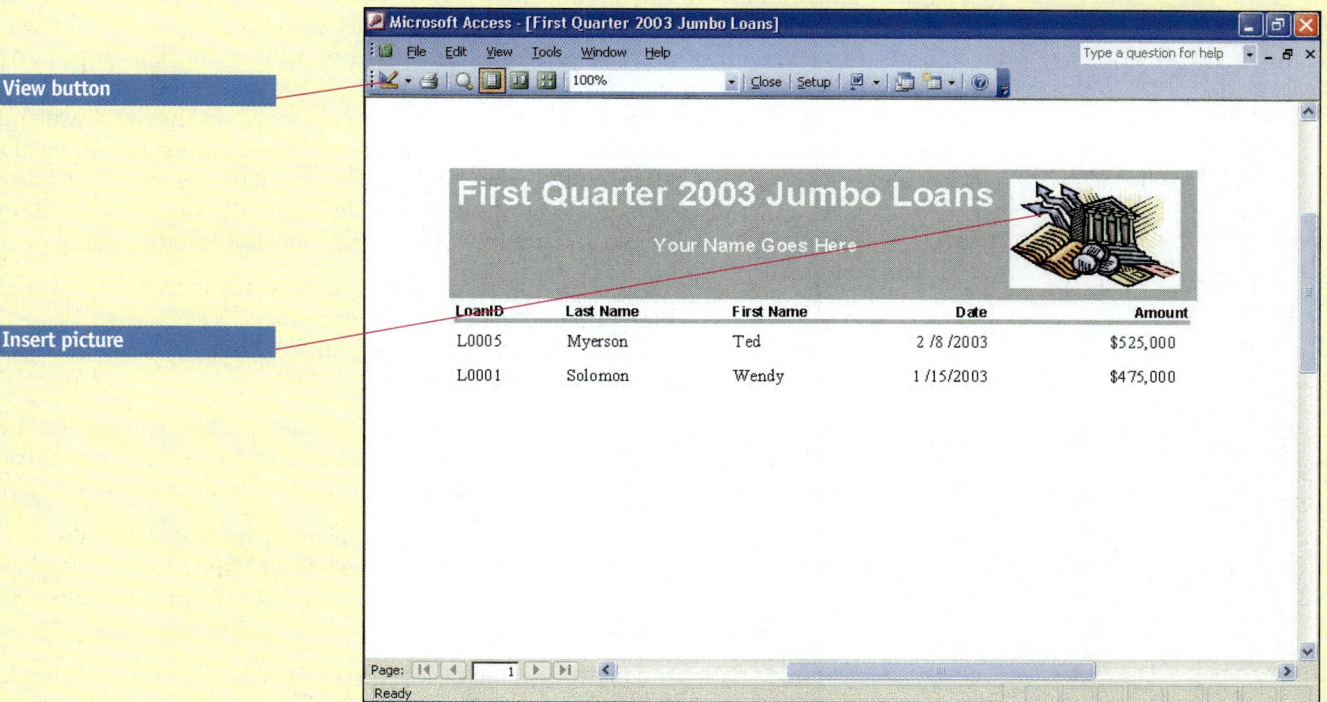

(g) Print the Completed Report (step 7)

FIGURE 5.9   Hands-on Exercise 3 (*continued*)

COMPACT AND REPAIR THE DATABASE

Access databases tend to grow very quickly, especially as you create and edit new forms and reports, and thus you should always compact a database before you exit. Pull down the Tools menu; click Database Utilities, then click Compact and Repair Database. The database will close and then reopen, after the compacting process has eliminated the fragmentation that occurs as you work on a database. Compacting is different from compressing; that is, you can use WinZip (or a similar utility) to further reduce the file size of a compacted database.

The database we have used throughout the chapter contained only two tables; a Customers table and a Loans table. A relational database can be easily expanded, however, to include additional data without disturbing the existing tables. Thus, we expand the National Bank database to include a Payments table as shown in Figure 5.10. Recall that the original database had a one-to-many relationship between customers and loans. The expanded database will contain a second one-to-many relationship between loans and payments. One loan has many payments, but a specific payment is associated with only one loan. The primary key of the Loans table (LoanID) will appear as a foreign key in the Payments table.

The Payments table in Figure 5.10c contains four fields for each record: PaymentID, LoanID, PaymentDate (the date the payment was received), and the AmountReceived. The PaymentID is the primary key, and it has been designated as an AutoNumber field. Thus, the payments are numbered sequentially according to the order they were received by the bank. (An alternate design would be to eliminate the PaymentID in favor of a primary key consisting of both the LoanID and PaymentDate. Although there are multiple records in the Payments table with the same loan number, as well as multiple records with the same payment date, the *combination* of LoanID and PaymentDate is unique, assuming that multiple payments for the same loan are not received on the same date. We prefer the PaymentID with the AutoNumber field type.)

We began the chapter by showing you hypothetical records in the database and asking you to answer queries based on that data. We end the chapter the same way, by asking you to consider several queries in conjunction with the data in Figure 5.10. Realize, too, that while you go through the tables manually, Access will obtain the information automatically for you when you create a multiple-table query.

Query: How many payments have been received for loan L0002? What was the date of the most recent payment?

Answer: Three payments have been received for loan L0002. The most recent payment was received on 4/15/2003.

This query is answered with reference to just the Payments table. You search the Payments table for all records containing the designated LoanID, sort these records in ascending order (earliest date first), and then select the last record.

Query: How many payments have been received from Matt Hirsch?

Answer: Only one payment has been received from Matt Hirsch. The payment was for $1,270.31 and was received on April 10, 2003 for LoanID L0014.

This requires data from all three tables. First you look in the Customers table to determine the CustomerID for Matt Hirsch (C0010), then you search the Loans table for all loans for this customer (L0014 and L0022), and finally you go to the Payments table to retrieve the payments for the indicated loans. Note that loan L0022 was granted on April 22 and thus no payments have been made.

Query: Can you add a payment to the Payments table for LoanID L0100? Can you add a payment to the Payments table without specifying the LoanID?

Answer: The answer to the first question is always no because the loan does not exist. The answer to the second question is also no, provided LoanID is a *required field* in the Payments table. Referential integrity prevents you from adding a payment record with an *invalid* LoanID, but lets you omit the LoanID. Since this does not make sense in the physical environment, the LoanID should be specified as a required field in the Payments table.

LoanID	Date	Amount	Interest Rate	Term	Type	CustomerID
L0001	1/15/2003	$475,000	6.90%	15	M	C0004
L0002	1/23/2003	$35,000	7.20%	5	C	C0004
L0003	1/25/2003	$10,000	5.50%	3	C	C0005
L0004	1/31/2003	$12,000	9.50%	10	O	C0004
L0005	2/8/2003	$525,000	6.50%	30	M	C0006
L0006	2/12/2003	$10,500	7.50%	5	O	C0007
L0007	2/15/2003	$35,000	6.50%	5	O	C0008
L0008	2/20/2003	$250,000	8.80%	30	M	C0008
L0009	2/21/2003	$5,000	10.00%	3	O	C0008
L0010	2/28/2003	$200,000	7.00%	15	M	C0001
L0011	3/1/2003	$25,000	10.00%	3	C	C0002
L0012	3/1/2003	$20,000	9.50%	5	O	C0005
L0013	3/3/2003	$56,000	7.50%	5	C	C0009
L0014	3/10/2003	$129,000	8.50%	15	M	C0010
L0015	3/11/2003	$200,000	7.25%	15	M	C0003
L0016	3/21/2003	$150,000	7.50%	15	M	C0001
L0017	3/22/2003	$100,000	7.00%	30	M	C0001
L0018	3/31/2003	$15,000	6.50%	3	O	C0003
L0019	4/1/2003	$10,000	8.00%	5	C	C0002
L0020	4/15/2003	$25,000	8.50%	4	C	C0003
L0021	4/18/2003	$41,000	9.90%	4	C	C0008
L0022	4/22/2003	$350,000	7.50%	15	M	C0010
L0023	5/1/2003	$150,000	6.00%	15	M	C0003
L0024	5/3/2003	$350,000	8.20%	30	M	C0004
L0025	5/8/2003	$275,000	9.20%	15	M	C0007

(a) Loans Table

CustomerID	First Name	Last Name	Address	City	State	Zip Code	Phone Number
C0001	Eileen	Faulkner	7245 NW 8 Street	Minneapolis	MN	55346	(612) 894-1511
C0002	Scott	Wit	5660 NW 175 Terrace	Baltimore	MD	21224	(410) 753-0345
C0003	Benjamin	Grauer	10000 Sample Road	Coral Springs	FL	33073	(305) 444-5555
C0004	Wendy	Solomon	7500 Reno Road	Houston	TX	77090	(713) 427-3104
C0005	Alex	Rey	3456 Main Highway	Denver	CO	80228	(303) 555-6666
C0006	Ted	Myerson	6545 Stone Street	Chapel Hill	NC	27515	(919) 942-7654
C0007	Lori	Sangastiano	4533 Aero Drive	Santa Rosa	CA	95403	(707) 542-3411
C0008	Michelle	Zacco	488 Gold Street	Gainesville	FL	32601	(904) 374-5660
C0009	David	Powell	5070 Battle Road	Decatur	GA	30034	(301) 345-6556
C0010	Matt	Hirsch	777 NW 67 Avenue	Fort Lee	NJ	07624	(201) 664-3211

(b) Customers Table

PaymentID	LoanID	Payment Date	Amount Received	PaymentID	LoanID	Payment Date	Amount Received
P0001	L0001	2/15/2003	$4,242.92	P00016	L0012	4/1/2003	$420.04
P0002	L0002	2/15/2003	$696.35	P00017	L0005	4/8/2003	$3,318.36
P0003	L0003	2/25/2003	$301.96	P00018	L0014	4/10/2003	$1,270.31
P0004	L0004	2/28/2003	$155.28	P00019	L0015	4/11/2003	$1,825.73
P0005	L0005	3/8/2003	$3,318.36	P00020	L0006	4/12/2003	$210.40
P0006	L0006	3/12/2003	$210.40	P00021	L0001	4/15/2003	$4,242.92
P0007	L0001	3/15/2003	$4,242.92	P00022	L0002	4/15/2003	$696.35
P0008	L0002	3/15/2003	$696.35	P00023	L0007	4/15/2003	$684.82
P0009	L0007	3/15/2003	$684.82	P00024	L0008	4/20/2003	$1,975.69
P0010	L0008	3/20/2003	$1,975.69	P00025	L0009	4/21/2003	$161.34
P0011	L0009	3/21/2003	$161.34	P00026	L0016	4/21/2003	$1,390.52
P0012	L0003	3/25/2003	$301.96	P00027	L0017	4/22/2003	$665.30
P0013	L0010	3/28/2003	$1,797.66	P00028	L0003	4/25/2003	$301.96
P0014	L0004	3/31/2003	$155.28	P00029	L0010	4/28/2003	$1,797.66
P0015	L0011	4/1/2003	$806.68	P00030	L0004	4/30/2003	$155.28

(c) Partial Payments Table

FIGURE 5.10 Expanding the Database

Multiple Subforms

Subforms were introduced earlier in the chapter as a means of displaying data from related tables. Figure 5.11 continues the discussion by showing a main form with two levels of subforms. The main (Customers) form has a one-to-many relationship with the first (Loans) subform. The Loans subform in turn has a one-to-many relationship with the second (Payments) subform. The Customers form and the Loans subform are the forms that you created in the second hands-on exercise. (The Loans subform is displayed in the Form view, as opposed to the Datasheet view.) The Payments subform is new and will be developed in our next hands-on exercise.

The records displayed in the three forms are linked to one another according to the relationships within the database. There is a one-to-many relationship between customers and loans so that the first subform displays all of the loans for one customer. There is also a one-to-many relationship between loans and payments so that the second subform (Payments) displays all of the payments for the selected loan. Click on a different loan (for the same customer), and the Payments subform is updated automatically to show all of the payments for that loan.

The status bar for the main form indicates record 5 of 10, meaning that you are viewing the fifth of 10 Customer records. The status bar for the Loans subform indicates record 1 of 2, corresponding to the first of two loan records for the fifth customer. The status bar for the Payments subform indicates record 1 of 5, corresponding to the first of five payment records for this loan for this customer.

The three sets of navigation buttons enable you to advance to the next record(s) in any of the forms. The records move in conjunction with one another. Thus, if you advance to the next record in the Customers form, you will automatically display a different set of records in the Loans subform, as well as a different set of Payment records in the Payments subform. Note, too, the command buttons that appear in the upper-right portion of the form to add a new customer and to close the Customers form.

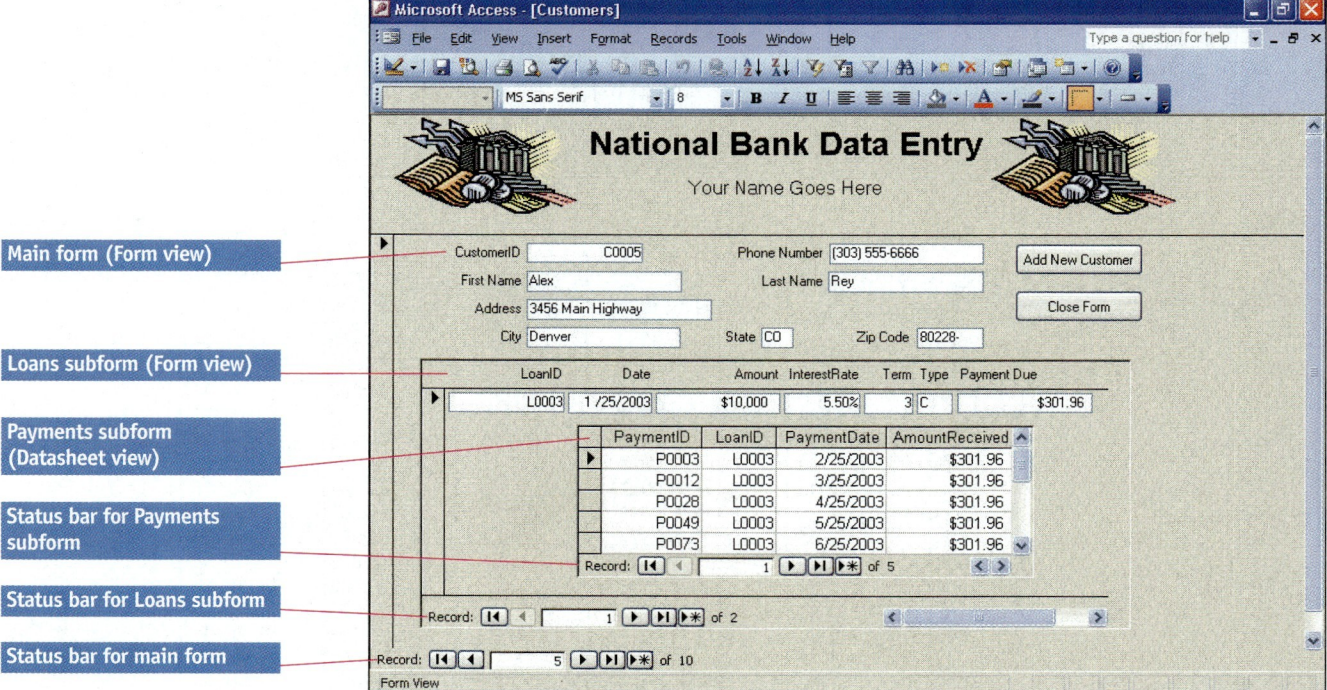

FIGURE 5.11 Multiple Subforms

Linked Subforms

Objective To create a main form with two levels of subforms; to display a subform in Form view or Datasheet view. Use Figure 5.12 as a guide.

Step 1: **Add a Relationship**

- Open the **National Bank database**. Pull down the **Tools menu**. Click **Relationships** to open the Relationships window as shown in Figure 5.12a.

- Maximize the Relationships window. Pull down the **Relationships menu**. Click **Show Table** to display the Show Table dialog box.

- The **Tables tab** is selected within the Show Table dialog box. Double click the **Payments table** to add the table to the Relationships window. Close the Show Table dialog box.

- Click and drag the title bar of the **Payments Field list** so that it is positioned approximately one inch from the Loans table.

- Click and drag the **LoanID field** in the Loans field list to the **LoanID field** in the Payments field list. You will see the Relationships dialog box.

- Check the **Enforce Referential Integrity** check box. (If necessary, clear the check boxes to Cascade Update Related Fields and Cascade Delete Related Records.)

- Click the **Create button** to establish the relationship. You should see a line indicating a one-to-many relationship between the Loans and Payments tables.

- Click the **Save button**, then close the Relationships window.

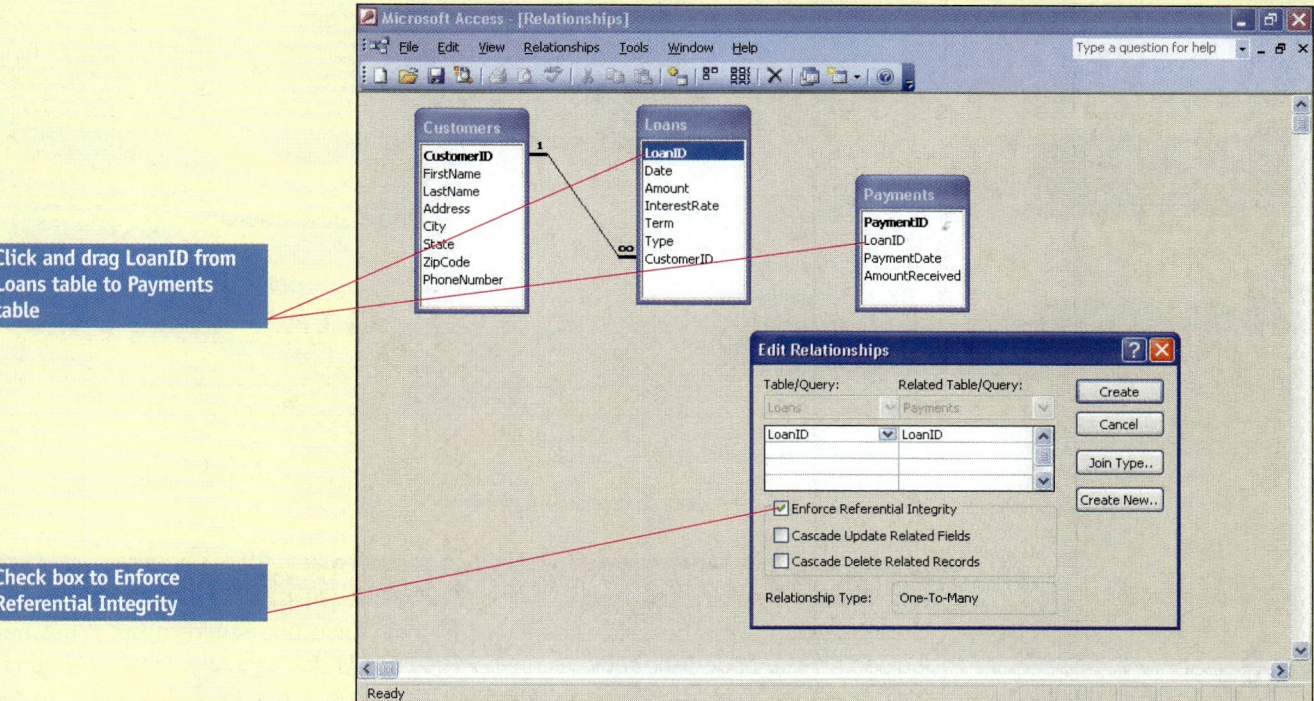

Click and drag LoanID from Loans table to Payments table

Check box to Enforce Referential Integrity

(a) Add a Relationship (step 1)

FIGURE 5.12 Hands-on Exercise 4

Step 2: **Create the Payments Subform**

- You should be back in the Database window. Click the **Forms button**, then open the **Loans subform** in Design view as shown in Figure 5.12b.

- Click and drag the bottom edge of the **Details section** so that you have approximately 2 to 2½ inches of blank space in the Detail section.

- Click the **Subform/Subreport button** on the Toolbox toolbar, then click and drag in the **Loans form** to create the Payments subform. Release the mouse.

- The **Use Existing Tables and Queries option button** is selected, indicating that we will build the subform from a table or query. Click **Next**. You should see the Subform/Subreport dialog box in Figure 5.12b.

- Click the **drop-down arrow** on the Tables and Queries list box to select the **Payments table**. Click the **>> button** to add all of the fields in the Payments table to the subform. Click **Next**.

- The Subform Wizard asks you to define the fields that link the main form to the subform. The option button to **Choose from a list** is selected, as is **Show Payments for each record in Loans using LoanID**. Click **Next**.

- **Payments subform** is entered as the name of the subform. Click **Finish**.

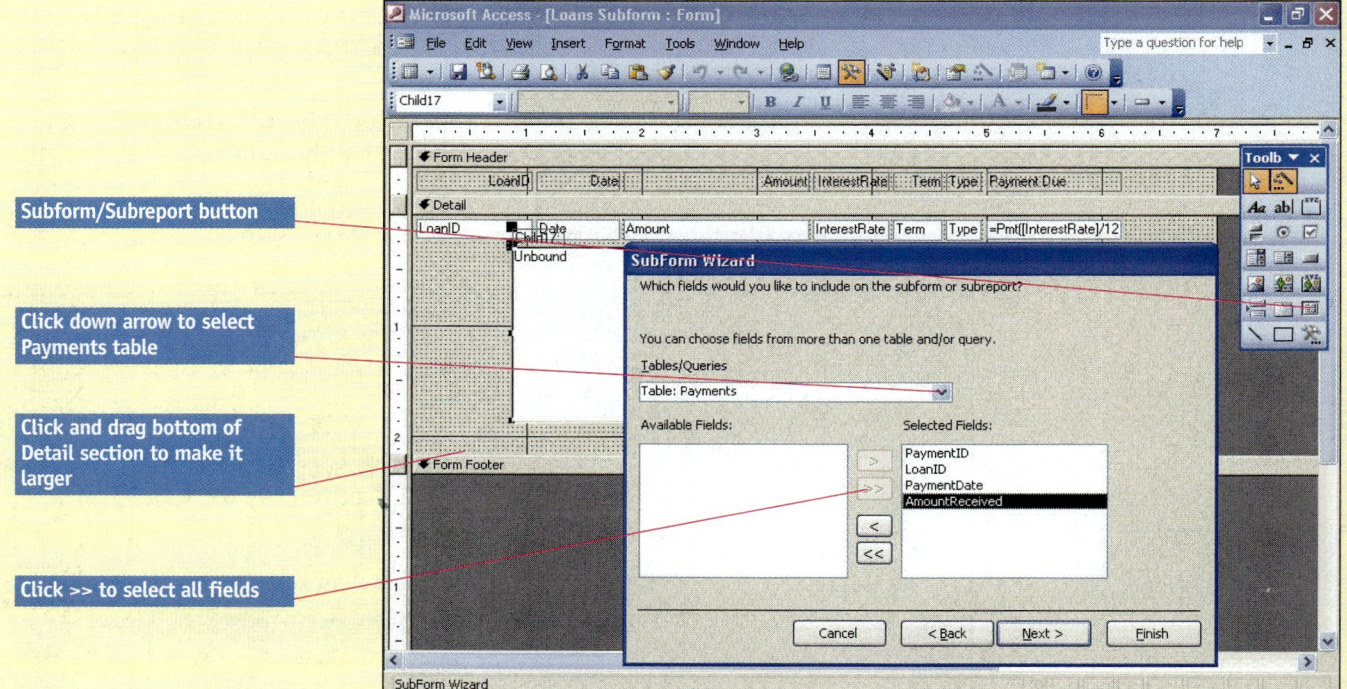

(b) Create the Payments Subform (step 2)

FIGURE 5.12 Hands-on Exercise 4 (*continued*)

LINKING FIELDS, FORMS, AND SUBFORMS

Linking fields do not have to appear in the main form and subform but must be included in the underlying table or query. The LoanID, for example, links the Loans form and the Payments form and need not appear in either form. We have, however, chosen to display the LoanID in both forms to emphasize the relationship between the corresponding tables.

Step 3: **Change the Loans Subform**

- Maximize the window. Point to the **Form Selector box** for the Loans subform in the upper-left corner of the Design window and click the **right mouse button** to display a shortcut menu.

- Click **Properties** to display the Form Properties dialog box in Figure 5.12c.

- The property sheet pertains to the form as a whole, as can be seen from the title bar. Click in the **Default View box**, click the **drop-down arrow** to display the views, then click **Single Form**. Close the Properties dialog box.

- Select the label for the Payments subform control, then press the **Del key** to delete the label.

- Save the form.

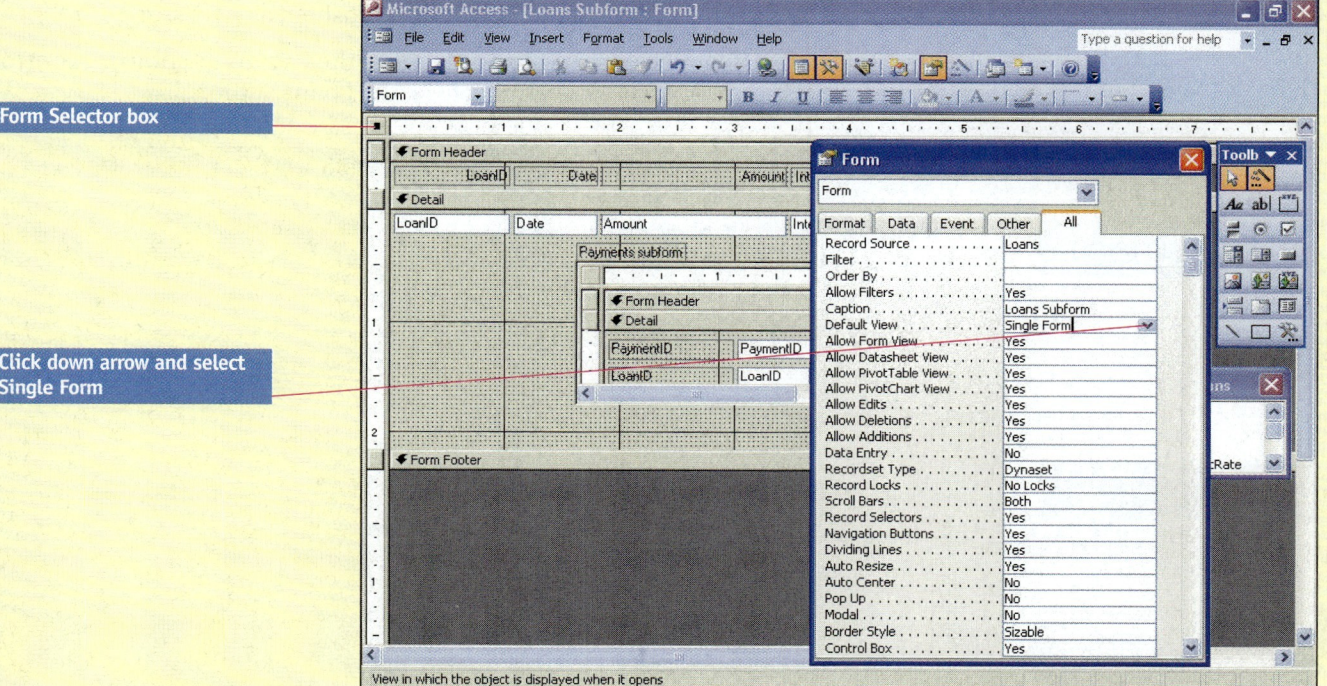

Form Selector box

Click down arrow and select Single Form

(c) Change the Loans Subform (step 3)

FIGURE 5.12 Hands-on Exercise 4 (*continued*)

THE DEFAULT VIEW PROPERTY

The Default View property determines how a form is dislayed initially and is especially important when working with multiple forms. In general, the highest level form(s) is (are) displayed in the Single Form view and the lowest level in the Datasheet view. In this example, the Customers and Loans forms are both set to the Single Form view, whereas the Payment form is set to the Datasheet view. To change the default view, right click the Form Selector box to display the property sheet for the form as a whole, click the All tab, then change the entry in the Default View property.

Step 4: **The Loans Subform in Form View**

- Click the **drop-down arrow** next to the **View button** to switch to the Form view for the Loans subform as shown in Figure 5.12d.

- Do not be concerned if the size and/or position of your Payments subform is different from ours as you can return to the Design view to make the necessary changes.
  - ❏ The status bar of the Loans subform indicates record 1 of 26, meaning that you are positioned on the first of 26 records in the Loans table.
  - ❏ The status bar for the Payments subform indicates record 1 of 5, corresponding to the first of five payment records for this loan.

- Pull down the **View menu**, click **Datasheet** to change to the Datasheet view of the Loans subform. Click the **plus sign** next to the first loan record to expand the record and see its associated payments.

- Change the column widths in the Payments datasheet as necessary.

- Change to the **Design view** to size and/or move the Payments subform control within the Loans subform. Save, then close, the Loans subform.

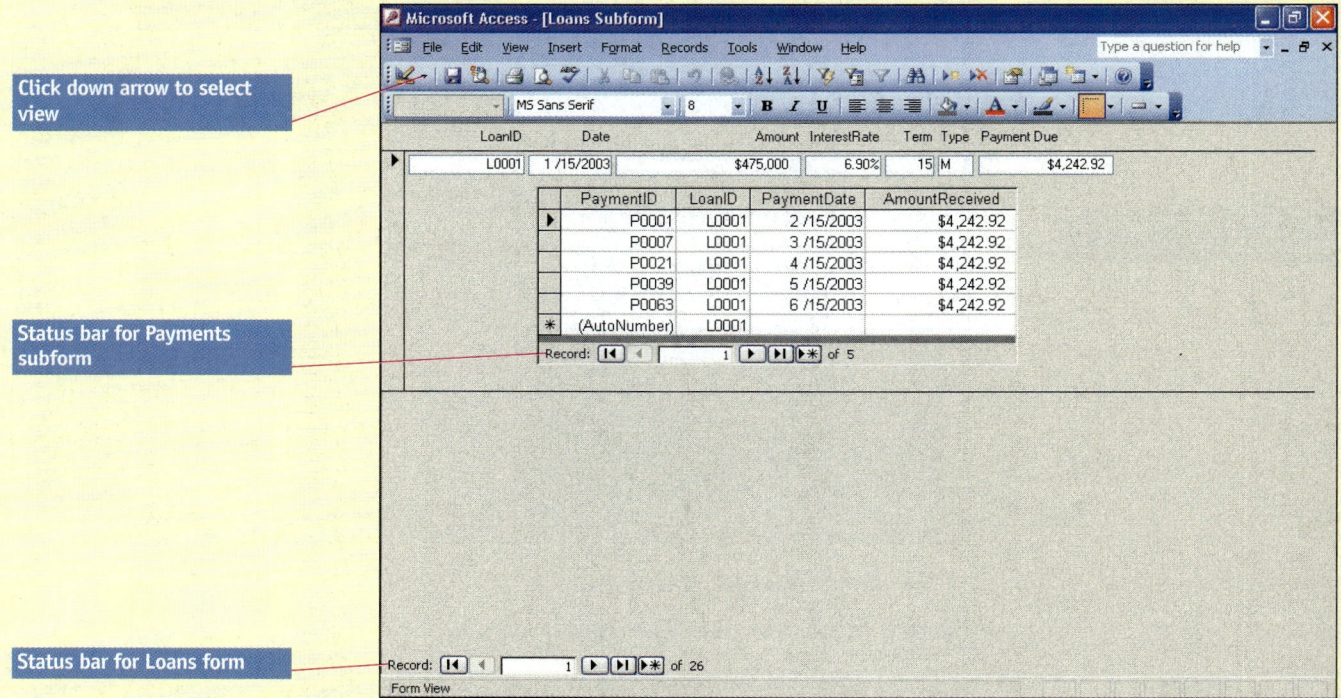

Click down arrow to select view

Status bar for Payments subform

Status bar for Loans form

(d) The Loans Subform in Form View (step 4)

FIGURE 5.12 Hands-on Exercise 4 (*continued*)

USER-FRIENDLY FORMS

The phrase "user-friendly" appears so frequently that we tend to take it for granted. The intention is clear, however, and you should strive to make your forms as clear as possible so that the user is provided with all the information he or she may need. It may be obvious to the designer that one has to click the navigation buttons to move to a new loan, but a novice unfamiliar with Access may not know that. Adding a descriptive label to the form goes a long way toward making a system successful.

Step 5:

The Customers Form

■ You should be back in the Database window. Click the **Forms button** (if necessary), then open the **Customers form** as shown in Figure 5.12e.

■ Do not be concerned if the sizes of the subforms are different from ours as you can return to the Design view to make the necessary changes.

■ The status bar of the Customers form indicates record 1 of 10, meaning that you are positioned on the first of 10 records in the Customers table.

■ The status bar for the Loans subform indicates record 1 of 3, corresponding to the first of three records for this customer.

■ The status bar for the Payments subform indicates record 1 of 4, corresponding to the first of four payments for this loan.

■ Change to the **Design view** to move and/or size the control for the Loans subform as described in step 6.

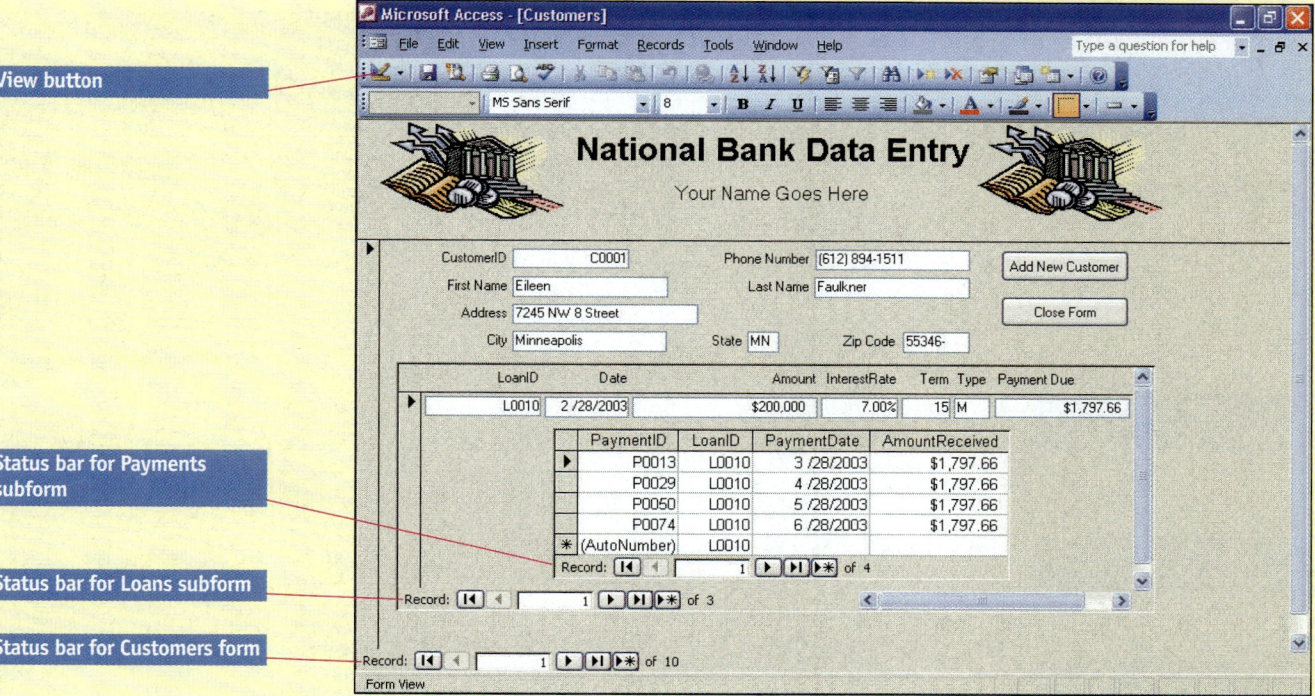

(e) The Customers Form (step 5)

FIGURE 5.12 Hands-on Exercise 4 *(continued)*

THE STARTUP COMMAND

The Startup command determines how a database will appear when it is opened. One very common option is to open a form automatically so that the user is presented with the form without having to navigate through the Database window. Pull down the Tools menu, click Startup to display the Startup dialog box, then click the drop-down arrow in the Display Form/Page list box. Select the desired form, such as the Customers form created in this exercise, then click OK. The next time you open the database the designated form will be opened automatically.

Step 6: **The Finishing Touches**

- You may need to increase the size of the Loans subform control. Click and drag the bottom edge of the **Detail section** in Figure 5.12f to make the section larger. You may also have to click and drag the **Loans subform** to the left, then click and drag its right border to make it wider.

- We also found it necessary to decrease the size of the Amount field within the Loans subform. Click the label for the **Amount field** in the Form Header.

- Press and hold the **Shift key** as you select the bound control for the Amount field in the Detail section, then click and drag the right border to make both controls narrower.

- Click the **Interest Rate label**. Press and hold the **Shift key** as you select the remaining controls to the left of the Amount field, then click and drag these fields to the left.

- Move and size the subform control as necessary. Save the changes.

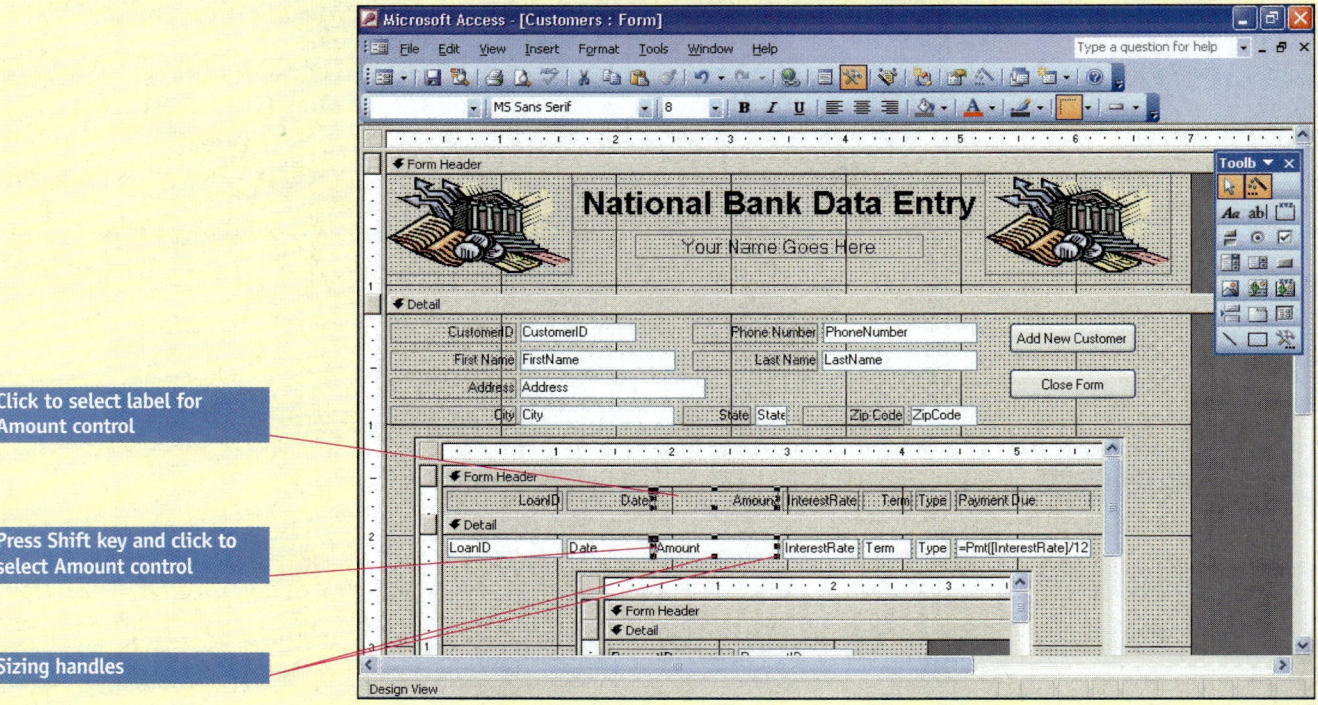

(f) The Finishing Touches (step 6)

FIGURE 5.12 Hands-on Exercise 4 (*continued*)

MULTIPLE CONTROLS AND PROPERTIES

Press and hold the Shift key as you click one control after another to select multiple controls. To view or change the properties for the selected controls, click the right mouse button to display a shortcut menu, then click Properties to display a property sheet. If the value of a property is the same for all selected controls, that value will appear in the property sheet; otherwise the box for that property will be blank. Changing a property when multiple controls are selected changes the property for all selected controls.

Step 7: **Make Your Payments**

- Change to the **Form view**. Click the ▶| on the status bar for the Customers form to move to the last record as shown in Figure 5.12g. This should be Customer C0011 (your record) that you entered in the earlier exercises in this chapter. You currently have two loans, L0026 and L0027, the first of which is displayed.

- Click in the **PaymentDate field** of **Payments subform**. Enter the date of your first payment, press **Tab**, then enter the amount paid. (The PaymentID and LoanID are entered automatically.)

- Press **Enter** to move to the next payment record and enter this payment as well. Press **Enter** and enter a third payment.

- Click the **selection area** at the left of the form to select this record. Pull down the **File menu** and click **Print** to display the Print dialog box. Click the **Selected Records option button**. Click **OK** to print the selected form.

- Close the Customers form. Click **Yes** if asked to save the changes to the form.

- Close the National Bank database. Exit Access.

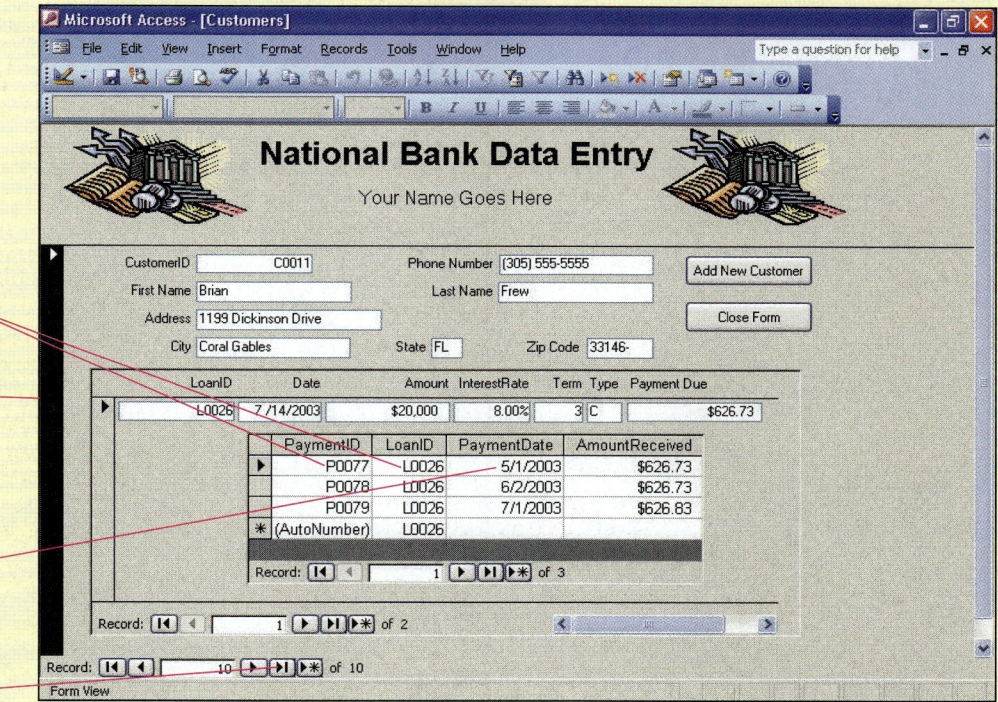

(g) Make Your Payments (step 7)

FIGURE 5.12 Hands-on Exercise 4 (*continued*)

THREE SETS OF NAVIGATION BUTTONS

Each form or subform has its own set of navigation buttons. Thus, in this example you are looking at record 10 of 10 in the Customers form, loan 1 of 2 in the Loans form for this customer, and payment 3 of 3 in the Payments form for this loan. Click the next or previous button in the Customers form and you will be taken to the next or previous customer record, respectively. Click the next button in the Loans form, however, and you are taken to the next loan for the current customer. In similar fashion, clicking the next button in the Payments form takes you to the next payment for the current loan for the current customer.

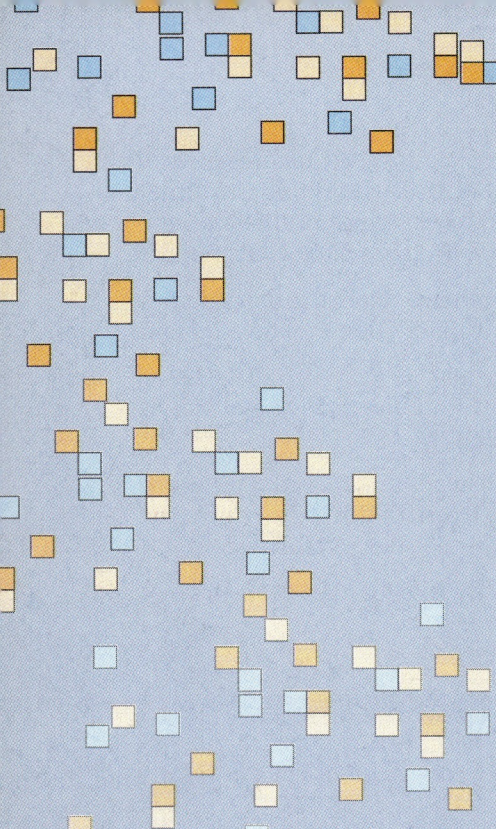

SUMMARY

An Access database may contain multiple tables. Each table stores data about a specific subject. Each table has a primary key, which is a field (or combination of fields) that uniquely identifies each record. A one-to-many relationship uses the primary key of the "one" table as a foreign key in the "many" table. (A foreign key is simply the primary key of the related table.) The Relationships window enables you to graphically create a one-to-many relationship by dragging the join field from one table to the other.

The AutoNumber field type automatically assigns the next sequential number to the primary key of a new record. The values in an AutoNumber field type are permanent and are not affected by deletions to the table. The Format property can be used to display an AutoNumber field with high-order zeros and/or a letter; e.g. a format of \C0000 will display customer numbers as C0001, C0002, and so on.

Referential integrity ensures that the tables in a one-to-many relationship (such as the Customers and Loans tables used throughout the chapter) are consistent with one another. Thus, it prevents you from adding a record to the "many" table if that record contains an invalid reference to the "one" table; for example, you cannot add a record to the Loans table that contains a value of CustomerID that does not exist in the Customers table. Referential integrity will also prevent you from deleting a record in the "one" table if there are corresponding records in the "many" table; for example, you cannot delete a record from the Customers table if there are loan records for that customer.

Referential integrity does not prevent you from adding a record to the "many" table that omits the reference to the primary table; for example, it would allow you to add a record to the Loans table without specifying a customer. Since this does not make sense in the physical system, the CustomerID should be specified as a required field in the Loans table.

A subform is a form within a form and is used to display data from a related table. It is created most easily with the Form Wizard, then modified in the Form Design view just as any other form. A main form can have any number of subforms. Subforms can extend to two levels, enabling a subform to be created within a subform.

The power of a select query lies in its ability to include fields from several tables. The Design view of a query shows the relationships that exist between the tables by drawing a join line that indicates how to relate the data. The Tables row displays the name of the table containing the corresponding field. Once created, a multiple table query can be the basis for a form or report.

The results of a query are displayed in a dynaset, a dynamic subset of the underlying tables that contains the records that satisfy the criteria within the query. Any changes to the dynaset are automatically reflected in the underlying table(s).

Tables can be added to a relational database without disturbing the data in existing tables. A database can have several one-to-many relationships. All relationships are created in the Relationships window.

KEY TERMS

AutoNumber field 221
Datasheet view 228
Foreign key 221
Form view 228
Form Wizard 230
Format property 221
Join line 239

Main form 228
Multiple-table query 239
One-to-many relationship 219
Pmt function 228
Primary key 221
Referential integrity 221
Relationship line 221

Relationships window 221
Startup command 255
Structured Query
    Language (SQL) 239
Subdatasheet 221
Subform 228
Table row .239

MULTIPLE CHOICE

1. Which of the following will cause a problem of referential integrity?

   (a) The deletion of a customer record that has corresponding loan records

   (b) The deletion of a customer record that has no corresponding loan records

   (c) The deletion of a loan record with a corresponding customer record

   (d) All of the above

2. Which of the following will cause a problem of referential integrity?

   (a) The addition of a new customer prior to entering loans for that customer

   (b) The addition of a new loan that references an invalid customer

   (c) Both (a) and (b)

   (d) Neither (a) nor (b)

3. Which of the following is true about a database that monitors players and the teams to which those players are assigned?

   (a) The PlayerID will be defined as a primary key within the Teams table

   (b) The TeamID will be defined as a primary key within the Players table

   (c) The PlayerID will appear as a foreign key within the Teams table

   (d) The TeamID will appear as a foreign key within the Players table

4. Which of the following relationships exist in the expanded *National Bank* database?

   (a) A one-to-many relationship between customers and loans

   (b) A one-to-many relationship between loans and payments

   (c) Both (a) and (b)

   (d) Neither (a) nor (b)

5. Which of the following is true about a query?

   (a) It may reference fields in one or more tables

   (b) It may have one or more Criteria rows

   (c) It may sort on one or more fields

   (d) All of the above

6. A database has a one-to-many relationship between branches and employees (one branch can have many employees). Which of the following is a true statement about that database?

   (a) The EmployeeID is the primary key within the Branches table

   (b) The BranchID will be defined as a primary key within the Employees table

   (c) The EmployeeID will appear as a foreign key within the Branches table

   (d) The BranchID will appear as a foreign key within the Employees table

7. Every table in an Access database:

   (a) Must be related to every other table

   (b) Must have one or more foreign keys

   (c) Both (a) and (b)

   (d) Neither (a) nor (b)

8. Which of the following is true of a main form and subform that are created in conjunction with the one-to-many relationship between customers and loans?

   (a) The main form should be based on the Customers table

   (b) The subform should be based on the Loans table

   (c) Both (a) and (b)

   (d) Neither (a) nor (b)

9. Which of the following is true regarding the navigation buttons for a main form and its associated subform?

   (a) The navigation buttons pertain to just the main form

   (b) The navigation buttons pertain to just the subform

   (c) There are separate navigation buttons for each form

   (d) There are no navigation buttons at all

10. Which of the following is true?

    (a) A main form may contain multiple subforms

    (b) A subform may contain another subform

    (c) Both (a) and (b)

    (d) Neither (a) nor (b)

... continued

11. The status bar of the main form shows record 1 of 10 while the status bar of the subform displays record 2 of 3. What happens if you click the next record button on the status bar for the main form?

    (a) The status bar for the main form will show record 2 of 10

    (b) The status bar for the subform will show record 3 of 3

    (c) The status bar for the main form will show record 2 of 10 and the status bar for the subform will show record 3 of 3

    (d) None of the above

12. The status bar of the main form shows record 1 of 10 while the status bar of the subform displays record 2 of 3. What happens if you click the next record button on the status bar for the subform?

    (a) The status bar for the main form will show record 2 of 10

    (b) The status bar for the subform will show record 3 of 3

    (c) The status bar for the main form will show record 2 of 10 and the status bar for the subform will show record 3 of 3

    (d) None of the above

13. Which of the following describes how to move and size a field list within the Relationships window?

    (a) Click and drag the title bar to size the field list

    (b) Click and drag a border or corner to move the field list

    (c) Both (a) and (b)

    (d) Neither (a) nor (b)

14. Which of the following is true regarding the Criteria row of a query?

    (a) A text field may be entered with or without quotation marks

    (b) A date may be entered with or without surrounding number (pound) signs

    (c) Both (a) and (b)

    (d) Neither (a) nor (b)

15. A report may be based on:

    (a) A table

    (b) A query

    (c) Both (a) and (b)

    (d) Neither (a) nor (b)

16. You are working with an investment database. The Brokers and Clients tables are joined in a one-to-many relationship. If referential integrity is enforced, which records can you delete?

    (a) A client, regardless of the records in the Brokers table

    (b) A client, only if there are no corresponding records in the Brokers table

    (c) A broker, regardless of the records in the Clients table

    (d) A broker, only if there are corresponding records in the Clients table

17. You are working with an investment database. The Brokers and Clients tables are joined in a one-to-many relationship. The BrokerID is a required field in the Clients table. If referential integrity is enforced, which of the following actions can you take?

    (a) Add a client without specifying the broker

    (b) Delete a broker, regardless of the records in the Clients table

    (c) Add a broker, regardless of the records in the Clients table

    (d) None of the above

18. Which combination of views would you select to see all clients for a specific broker, given that you were looking at a main and subform based on the Brokers and Clients tables, respectively?

    (a) The main form in Form view and the subform in Datasheet view

    (b) The main form in Datasheet view and the subform in Form view

    (c) Both the main and subform in Datasheet view

    (d) Both the main and subform in Form view

ANSWERS

1. a	7. d	13. d
2. b	8. c	14. c
3. d	9. c	15. c
4. c	10. c	16. a
5. d	11. a	17. c
6. d	12. b	18. a

PRACTICE WITH ACCESS

1. **Understanding Database Design:** The presentation in Figure 5.13 represents a *hypothetical* assignment for a group project in which the group is asked to present the design for their project to the class as a whole. We have created a similar presentation for you to illustrate what we mean; your only task is to view our presentation, which in turn will help you to review the *National Bank* database that was developed in the chapter. Your instructor may want to extend the assignment and ask you to create a parallel presentation for a different database, which he or she may assign as an actual group project. Proceed as follows:

   a. Start PowerPoint. Open the *Chapter 5 Practice 1* presentation in the Exploring Access folder. This is a PowerPoint presentation, but you do not have to know PowerPoint to complete this exercise. Pull down the View menu and change to the Normal view. If necessary, click the Slide tab to see the miniature slides instead of the outline.

   b. There are nine slides in the complete presentation. The left pane shows the slide miniatures. The right pane shows a larger view of the selected slide (slide one in this example). The slide describes the hypothetical assignment, which is to create a 10-minute presentation to the class describing the physical problem and the associated database design.

   c. Select (click) the first slide. Pull down the View menu and click the Slide Show command (or click the Slide Show button above the status bar). Click the mouse continually to move through the slide show. You will see a recap of the *National Bank* database, its design, and several suggested queries.

   d. Press the Esc button at the end of the show. Pull down the File menu, and click the Print command. Select the All option button in the Print Range area. Click the down arrow in the Print What area, and select handouts. Choose 6 slides per page. Be sure to check the box to frame the slides. Click OK to print the presentation. Print the presentation a second time, but this time print only the title slide (as a full slide) to use as a cover sheet for your assignment.

   e. Review the printed presentation. Do you see how the discipline provided by this assignment can help to ensure the accuracy of the design?

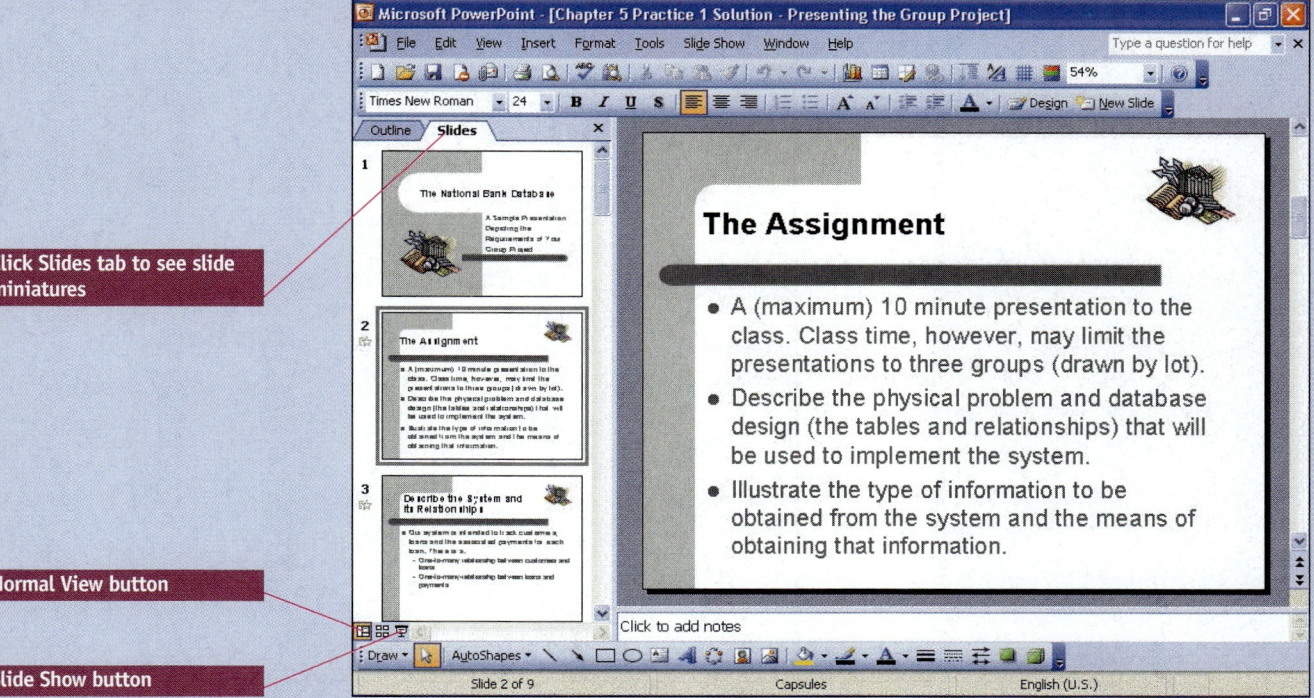

FIGURE 5.13 Understanding Database Design (exercise 1)

2. **Widgets of America (database design):** Figure 5.14 displays the relationships diagram in the *Widgets of America* database that tracks the orders generated by the company's sales staff. Your task is to implement the design in Figure 5.14 by creating the indicated tables and establishing the necessary relationships. Proceed as follows:

   a. Start Access and create a new database. You do not have to enter data into any of the tables, but you have to create the tables and set all of the field properties in each table. Pay particular attention to the required property as it pertains to the related fields in the various tables. Note that a customer must have an assigned sales representative in order to place an order. In addition, the company will not accept an order unless it (the order) is associated with a specific customer.

   b. Pull down the Tools menu and click the Relationships command to establish the relationships in Figure 5.14. Stay in the Relationships window, pull down the File menu, and then click the Print Relationships command to preview the report containing the relationships diagram. Change to the Design view to modify the Report Header to include a title, today's date, your name, and an appropriate clip art image. (The clip art can be used as a logo for the other objects in the database.)

   c. Create a simple About Widgets of America form that is similar to the other forms that were presented in the previous chapter. Use the same clip art as in the relationships diagram.

   d. Create a simple switchboard with three menu options—a button to display the About Widgets of America, a button to print the relationships diagram, and a button to exit the application. The switchboard should contain the same clip art, color scheme, and fonts as the relationships diagram.

   e. Test the switchboard thoroughly to be sure it works correctly. Use the Startup property in the Tools menu to display the switchboard automatically when the database is opened initially.

   f. Print the relationships diagram, the switchboard form, and the Switchboard Items table for your instructor. Add a cover sheet to complete the assignment.

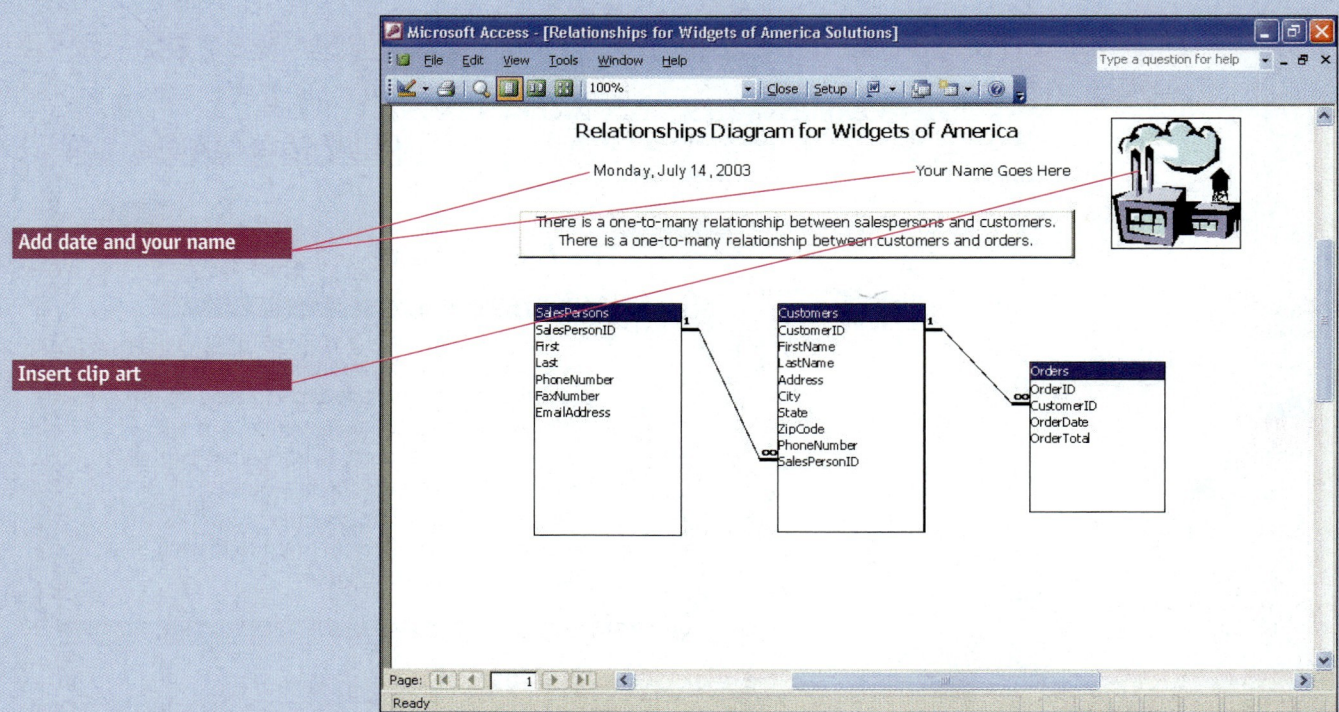

FIGURE 5.14 Widgets of America (database design) (exercise 2)

3. **Expanding National Bank:** Expand the *National Bank* database to include a table for Loan Officers, the bank employees who approve each loan before it is granted. One officer is assigned to many loans, but a specific loan is approved by only one officer, and the loan cannot be granted until the officer approves. Complete the four hands-on exercises in the chapter, then proceed as follows:

a. Open the *National Bank* database after completing the fourth hands-on exercise. Go to the Database window, click the Tables button, and create the Loan Officers table. The table contains only four fields—LoanOfficerID, LastName, FirstName, and DateHired. The LoanOfficerID should be an AutoNumber field. Set the Format property to \O0000 to be consistent with the other tables in the database. Add two records, Robert Grauer and Maryann Barber, as loan officers one and two, respectively.

b. Modify the Loans table to include a field for the LoanOfficerID. Set the Format property to \O0000. Switch to the Datasheet view, display the loans by LoanID (if they are not yet in this sequence), then assign each loan to an officer by typing 1 or 2 in the LoanOfficerID field. Assign all loans with a LoanID of 10 or less to Bob. Assign the other loans to Maryann.

c. Change to the Design view of the Loans table and make the LoanOfficerID a required field. This ensures that all subsequent loans will be approved by a loan officer.

d. Open the Relationships window and create the one-to-many relationship between loan officers and loans. Enforce referential integrity.

e. Open the existing Loans subform in Design view and insert a control for the Loan Officer as shown in Figure 5.15. The control should be created as a combo box so that a user can select the loan officer by name, as opposed to having to enter the LoanOfficerID. Pull down the View menu and use the Tab Order command to adjust the order in which the data is entered.

f. Open the Customer form. Click the navigation button to go to the last customer record (it should be Customer C0011 with the data you entered for yourself during the hands-on exercises). Click the record selector, pull down the File menu, click the Print command, select the option to print the selected record, and print this form for your instructor.

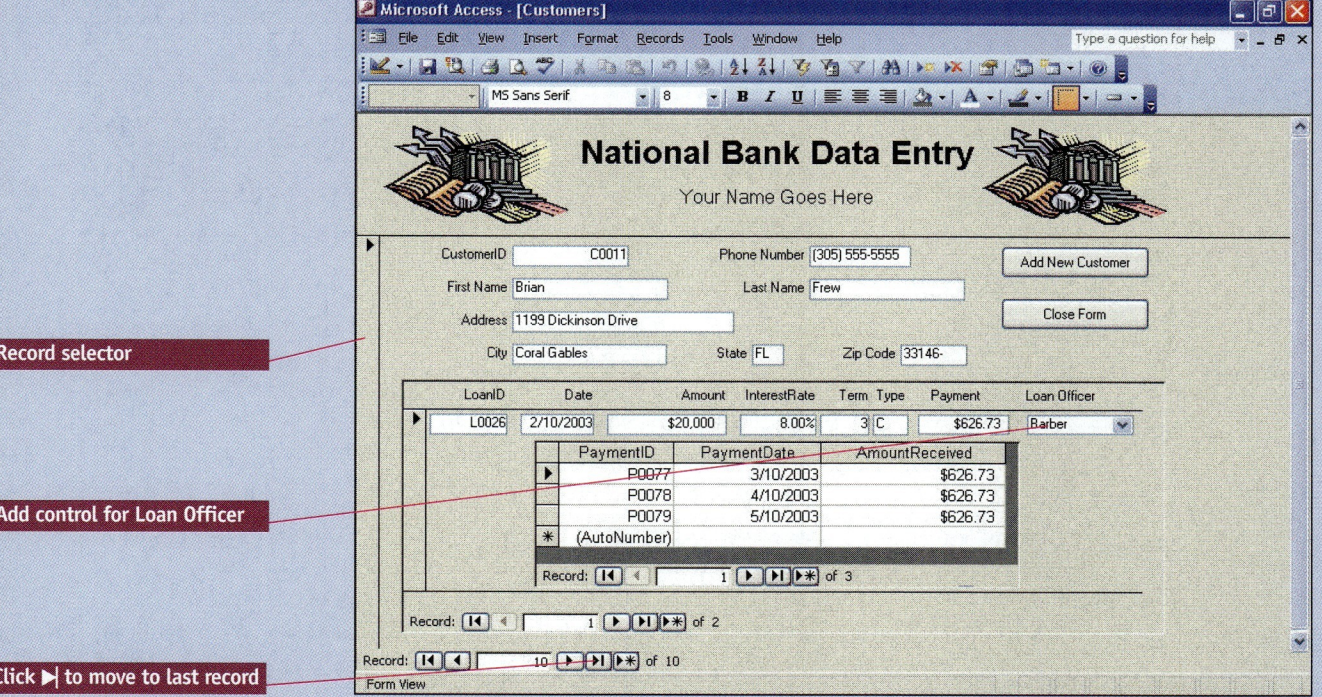

FIGURE 5.15 Expanding National Bank (exercise 3)

4. **National Bank Customer List:** The report in Figure 5.16 reflects the newly entered information about loan officers from the previous exercise. The Report Wizard does a good job creating the basic report, but it is up to you to format the report in an attractive fashion. You do not have to match our design exactly, but your report is to contain all of the indicated data. Proceed as follows:

a. Open the *National Bank* database from the previous exercise. Click the Reports button and double click the icon to Create report by using wizard. Select the Customers table in the Tables/Query list box and choose all of the fields for inclusion in the report. Select the Loans table and choose all of the fields *except* the CustomerID and the LoanOfficerID. Now choose the LoanOfficers table and choose the officer's last name. Click Next.

b. Group the report by customers. Click Next. There are no additional grouping requirements. Click Next. Sort the report by LoanID. Click Next.

c. Choose the Align Left 1 layout. Be sure to choose this layout, or else the data for one customer will not fit on one page. Choose portrait orientation. Check the box to force the fields to fit on one page. Click Next.

d. Choose Soft Gray for the style. Click Next. Enter Customer List as the name of the report. Click Finish to preview the report. You should see the same data as in Figure 5.16, but the formatting needs improvement. Go to Design view. The easiest modification is the Report Header. Use the Insert Picture command to insert the National Bank logo in the Report Header. Change the title of the report and add your name.

e. We suggest that you eliminate the borders that appear around all of the controls in the customer information. Press and hold the Shift key to select multiple controls, right click any of the selected controls, click Properties, then change the Border Style property to transparent. Close the property sheet. Click anywhere in the report to deselect the controls.

f. We also removed the double lines above and below the loan information for each customer and added a line immediately above the Customer data. Change the label for Loan Officer Last Name to Loan Officer. Experiment with formatting, sizing, and alignment as you see fit. Print the completed report for your instructor.

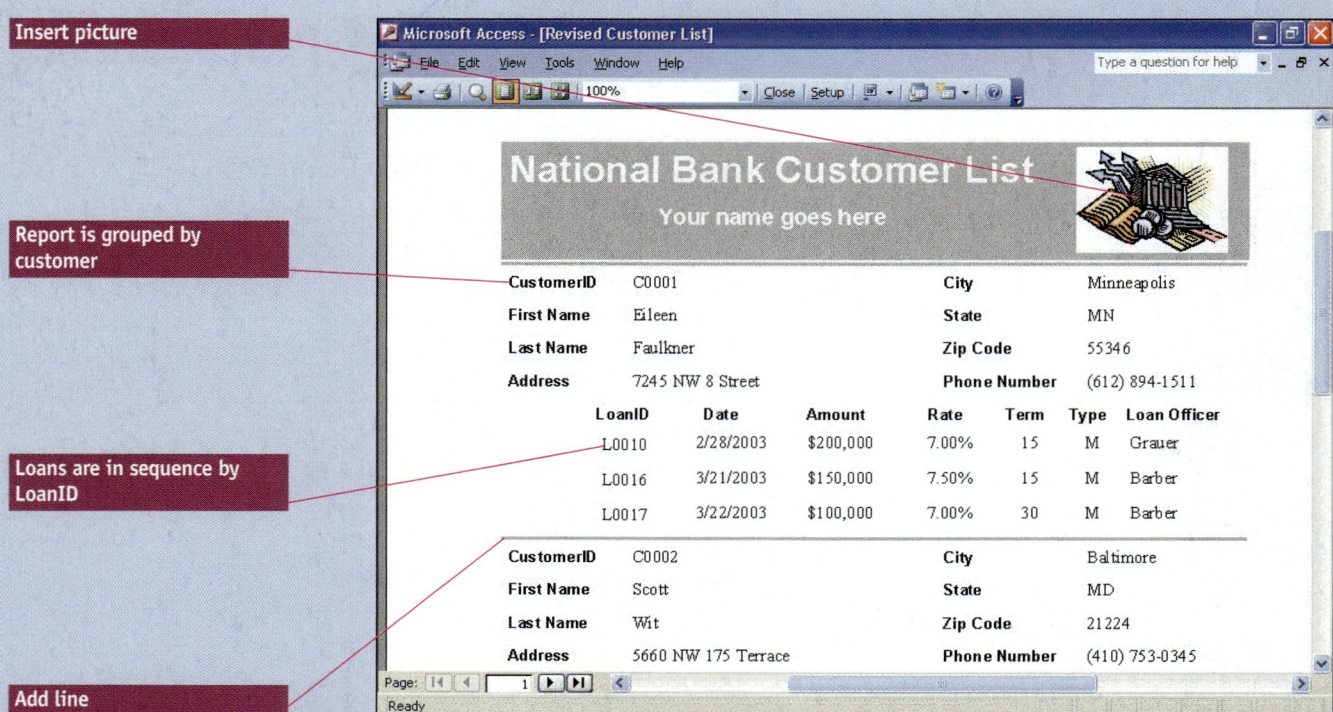

FIGURE 5.16 National Bank Customer List (exercise 4)

5. **Customer Payment Information:** The report in Figure 5.17 lists all of the payments that were received from a specific customer in the order in which the payments were received. The report is based on a parameter query that requests the customer's first and last name, after which the payments are displayed. (Use Help to learn more about this powerful query.) Open the *National Bank* database and proceed as follows:

a. Click the Queries tab in the Database window, then double click the icon to Create query in Design view. Add the Customers, Loans, and Payments tables to the query. Recall that there is a one-to-many relationship between customers and loans, and a second one-to-many relationship between loans and payments.

b. Add the LastName and FirstName fields from the Customers table, the LoanID field from the Loans table, and the PaymentDate and AmountReceived fields from the Payments table.

c. Click in the Criteria row under the LastName field and added the bracketed entry, [Enter Customer's Last Name]. Add a similar entry under the FirstName field as well. Click in the Sort row of the Payment Date field and specify an ascending sequence. Save the query as Customer Payment Query.

d. Run the query. Enter the customer's first and last name when prompted. You should see the same data as in Figure 5.17. Close the query.

e. Click the Reports button in the Database window, then use the Report Wizard to create a report based on the query you just created. Select the option to view the report by Customers.

f. Grouping is not required, but the report should be in ascending sequence by Payment date. Select the stepped layout and the Soft Gray style.

g. Enter the customer's first and last name when prompted. You should see the same information as in Figure 5.17, but the report requires some modification.

h. Press and hold the Shift key to select the FirstName and LastName controls from the group header, then drag these fields to the Report Header. Right click either control, click Properties, then change the border property to transparent. Delete the corresponding labels from the Page Header. Move and align the remaining controls and their labels. Add clip art to the Report Header, then print the completed report.

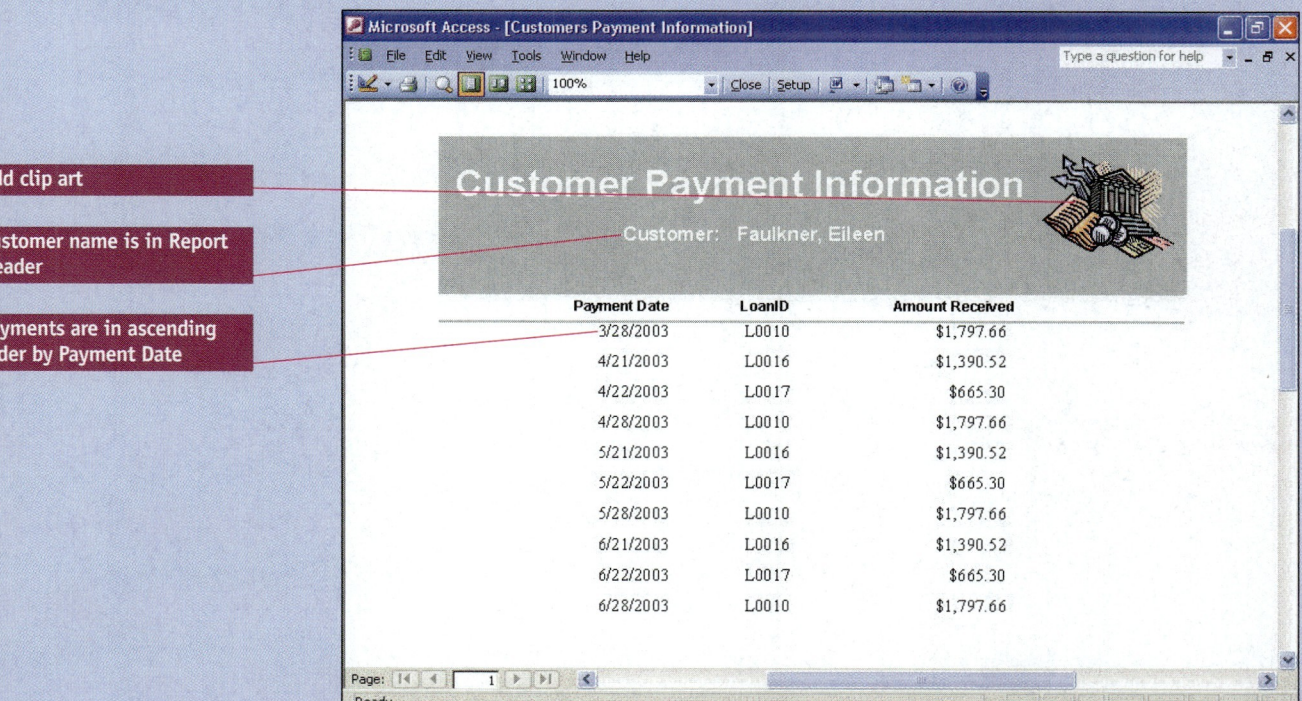

FIGURE 5.17 Customer Payment Information (exercise 5)

6. **National Bank Switchboard:** Figure 5.18 displays a switchboard for the *National Bank* database that encompasses all of the hands-on exercises in the chapter as well as the three previous exercises. Your present assignment is to create the main switchboard, a subsidiary switchboard with buttons to display the various reports that already exist, as well as a new report that will be created in this exercise. You also have to create the relationships diagram. Proceed as follows:

   a. The About National Bank form is included with the original database. All you have to do is modify the text on this form to include your name instead of Bob and Maryann's. Close the form.

   b. Open the Relationships window, pull down the File menu, click the Print Relationships command, and then view the completed report in Design view. Modify the report to include a title, date, your name and the National Bank logo that has been used for other objects in the database.

   c. Use the Report Wizard to create a new report that displays the existing automobile loans. The report should contain the customer's first and last name, address, telephone number, and amount of the loan. The customers should be listed alphabetically by last name. The address should appear on two lines; i.e., the street address on one line, and the city, state, and zip code on a second line. (Create the associated query before creating the report.)

   d. Use the Switchboard Manager to create the main switchboard and the subsidiary report switchboard as shown in Figure 5.18. The latter should contain four reports (the First Quarter Jumbo Loans report from Hands-on Exercise 3, the Customer List from practice exercise 3, the Customer Payment information from the previous exercise, and the Report on Car Loans that you just created). The report switchboard should also have a button to return to the main menu.

   e. Use the StartUp property to display the switchboard automatically when the database is opened. Test both switchboards completely to be sure that they work correctly. Print the Switchboard Items table, the switchboard form, the relationships diagram, and the Report on Car Loans. Add a cover sheet and submit the completed assignment.

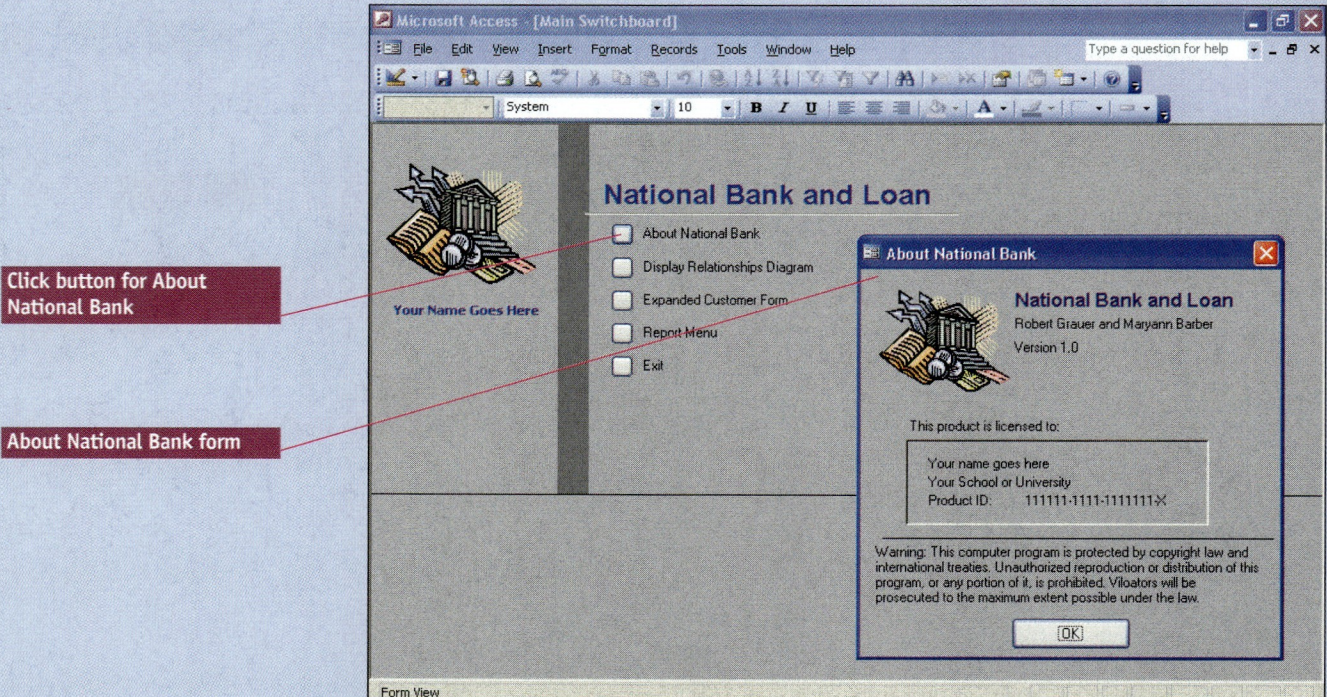

Click button for About National Bank

About National Bank form

FIGURE 5.18 National Bank Switchboard (exercise 6)

7. **Turkeys To Go Restaurants:** Turkeys To Go Restaurants is a small regional company that builds restaurants to order for individuals seeking a turn-key franchise operation. The company encourages its franchisees to own many restaurants, but a specific restaurant is associated with only one person. Your predecessor at the company has started a database to keep track of restaurants and franchisees, but left unexpectedly, so it is up to you to complete the work. Proceed as follows:

   a. Open the *Chapter 5 Practice 7* database in the Exploring Access folder. The Restaurants and Franchisees tables have already been created, and data has been entered into both tables. The RestaurantID and FranchiseeID have been set as AutoNumber fields in their respective tables. Note that the FranchiseeID is a required field in the Restaurants table because the company will not build a restaurant unless a franchisee has already been approved for that restaurant.

   b. Open the Relationships window and create the one-to-many relationship between franchisees and restaurants. Enforce referential integrity.

   c. Your first task is to create a main form/subform combination that is similar to Figure 5.19. The forms contain all of the fields in both the Franchisees and Restaurants tables, and thus all data entry can be accomplished from this screen. Start the Form Wizard. Select the Franchisee table and include all of the fields in this table. Now select the Restaurants table and include all of the fields except the FranchiseeID; this field need not appear in the subform because it is already in the main form. View the data by Franchisees, choose datasheet as the layout for the subform, select a style (we chose standard), then modify the completed form in Design view.

   d. You do not have to match our design exactly, but you are to include all of the indicated controls. Your name should appear in the Form Header. Add the commands buttons to the main form as shown in Figure 5.19.

   e. Use the completed form to enter data for yourself. You will automatically be assigned a Franchisee number (F0008). Add two restaurants once you have completed your personal data. The restaurant numbers will be assigned automatically as well. You can use any address and restaurant information that you deem appropriate. The annual sales of each restaurant should exceed $500,000. Print the completed form for your instructor.

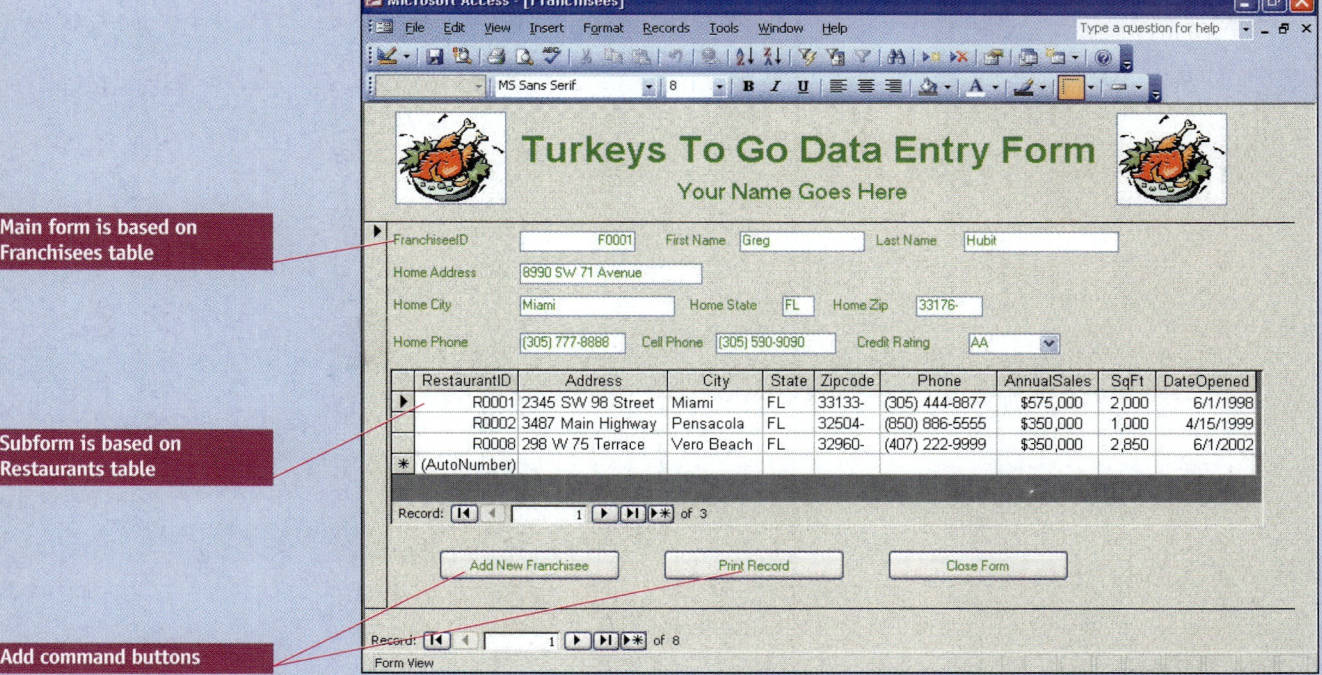

Main form is based on Franchisees table

Subform is based on Restaurants table

Add command buttons

FIGURE 5.19 Turkeys To Go Restaurants (exercise 7)

8. **Turkeys To Go Switchboard:** This assignment asks you to continue the development of the *Turkeys To Go* database by creating the switchboard in Figure 5.20. The Data Entry form referenced in the switchboard is the form you created in the previous exercise. The About form is included in the original database, but you have to modify the text on this form to include your name instead of Bob and Maryann's. All of the other objects that are referenced on the switchboard have to be created, however, before you can create the switchboard. Proceed as follows:

a. Open the Relationships window, pull down the File menu, click the Print Relationships command, and then view the completed report in Design view. Modify the report to include your name and the turkey logo.

b. Three additional reports are required as can be seen by looking at the switchboard. We leave the design and exact content of each report to you, but try to achieve a uniform look (design) for all of your reports. Use the company logo on all reports. (You can copy the clip art from the About form that is already in the database.)

c. Use the Switchboard Manager to create the switchboard in Figure 5.20. You do not have to match our design exactly, but you are required to have all of the menu options; further, the design of the switchboard should be consistent with the About form that is in the database.

d. Set the Startup property to display the switchboard automatically when the database is opened. Pull down the Tools menu, click the Database Utilities command, and then compact and repair the database. This does two things—first, it compacts the database, which is always a good idea. Second, it tests the Startup property; that is, the database should open immediately after compacting and display the switchboard.

e. Test the switchboard completely to be sure that it works correctly. Print the Switchboard Items table, the switchboard form, the relationships diagram, and each of the indicated reports. Add a cover sheet and submit the completed assignment to your instructor.

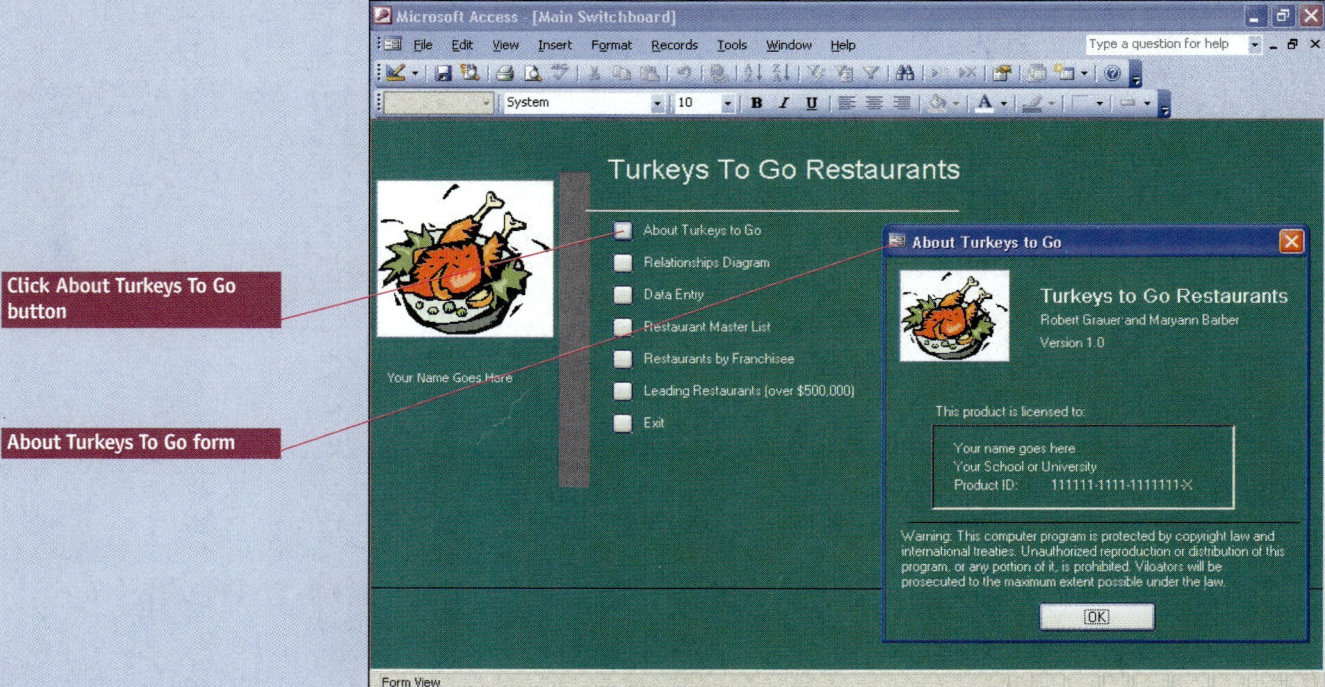

FIGURE 5.20 Turkeys To Go Switchboard (exercise 8)

9. **The Richards Company:** The Richards Company maintains a relational database that tracks its employees, the locations in which they work, and the various positions to which they have been assigned. There is a one-to-many relationship between locations and employees (one location can have many employees, but a specific employee is assigned to only one location). There is a second one-to-many relationship between titles and employees (one title can have many employees, but a specific employee is assigned only one title). Your assignment is to open the partially completed *Chapter 5 Practice 9* database and develop the necessary forms for data entry. The tables have been created for you, and sample data has been entered into each table. Proceed as follows:

a. Open the Relationships window, display all three tables, and then implement the one-to-many relationships that exist in the system.

b. Create a main form/subform combination that is similar to the form in Figure 5.21. The easiest way to create the form is to use the Form Wizard. Select all of the fields from the Locations table, as well as all fields from the Employees table except the LocationID. View the data by locations, choose datasheet as the layout for the subform, select a style (we chose Blueprint), then modify the completed form in Design view.

c. You do not have to match our design exactly, but you are to include all of the indicated controls. Your name should appear in the Form Header. Add the commands buttons to the main form as shown in Figure 5.21. Close the Locations form, then open the Employees subform in Design view. Substitute a combo box for the TitleID, so that you can enter an employee's title by selecting its description.

d. Open the Locations form and use it to add a new location for New York City. The address is 580 5th Avenue, New York, NY, 10036. The phone number is (212) 333-4444. Add an employee record for yourself (EmployeeID 88888) as a new account rep. Add a second record for your instructor as a manager (EmployeeID 99999). Print the form for New York with both employees.

e. Create a parallel main form/subform combination for the Title and Employee tables. The title information will appear in the main form and the employee information in the subform. Go to the first record in the Titles table (Account Reps) and print the associated form for your instructor.

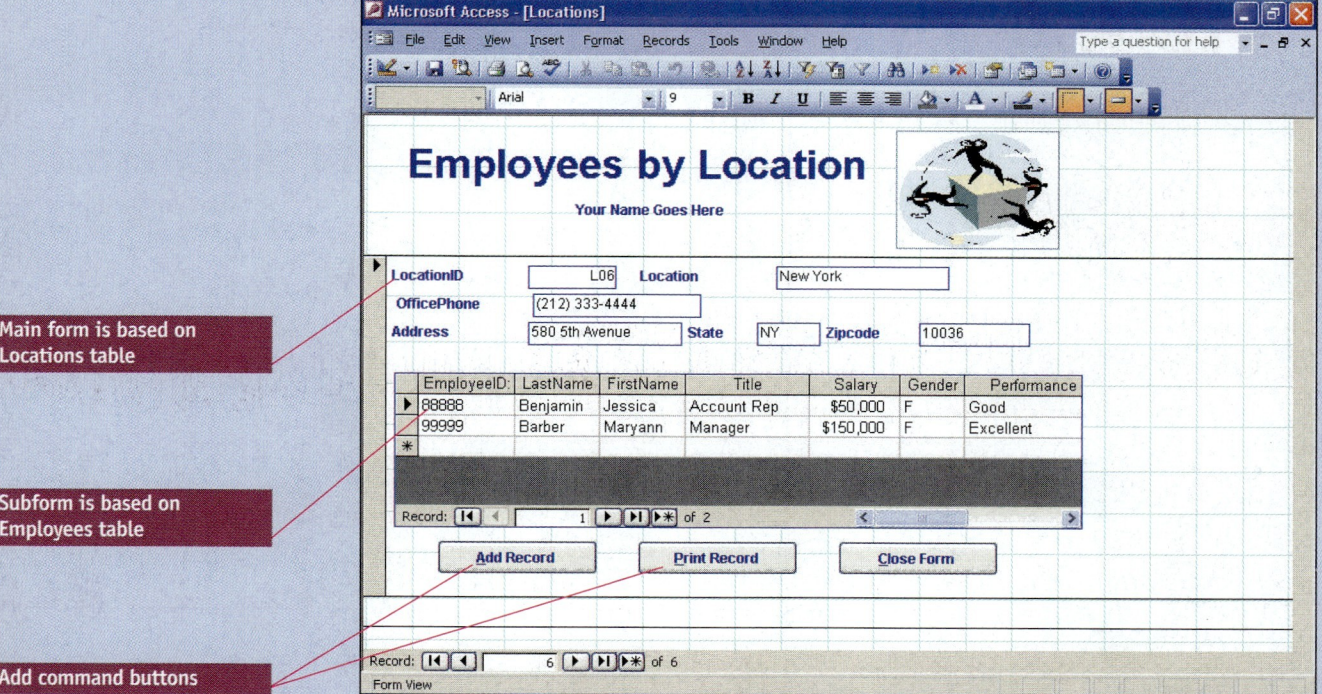

Main form is based on Locations table

Subform is based on Employees table

Add command buttons

FIGURE 5.21 The Richards Company (exercise 9)

10. **The Richards Company Switchboard:** This assignment asks you to continue the development of the *Richards Company* database by creating the switchboard in Figure 5.22. The Employees by Location and Employees by Title forms that are referenced in the switchboard are the forms you created in the previous exercise. The About form is included in the original database, but you have to modify the text on this form to include your name instead of Bob and Maryann's. All of the other objects have to be created, however, before you can create the switchboard. Proceed as follows:

a. Open the Relationships window, pull down the File menu, click the Print Relationships command, and then view the completed report in Design view. Modify the report to include a title, your name, and the company logo.

b. Three additional reports are required as can be seen by looking at the switchboard. We leave the design and exact content of each report to you, but try to achieve a uniform look (design) for all of your reports. (You may also have to create a query for one or more of the reports.) Include the clip art from the About form in the Report Header to create a sense of continuity in the application.

c. Start the switchboard manager and use it to create the switchboard. You do not have to match our design exactly, but you are required to have all of the menu options.

d. Set the Startup property to display the switchboard automatically when the database is opened. Pull down the Tools menu, click the Database Utilities command, and then compact and repair the database. This does two things—first, it compacts the database, which is always a good idea. Second, it tests the startup property; that is, the database should open immediately after compacting and display the switchboard.

e. Test the switchboard completely to be sure that it works correctly. Print the Switchboard Items table, the switchboard form, the relationships diagram, and each of the indicated reports. Add a cover sheet and submit the completed assignment to your instructor.

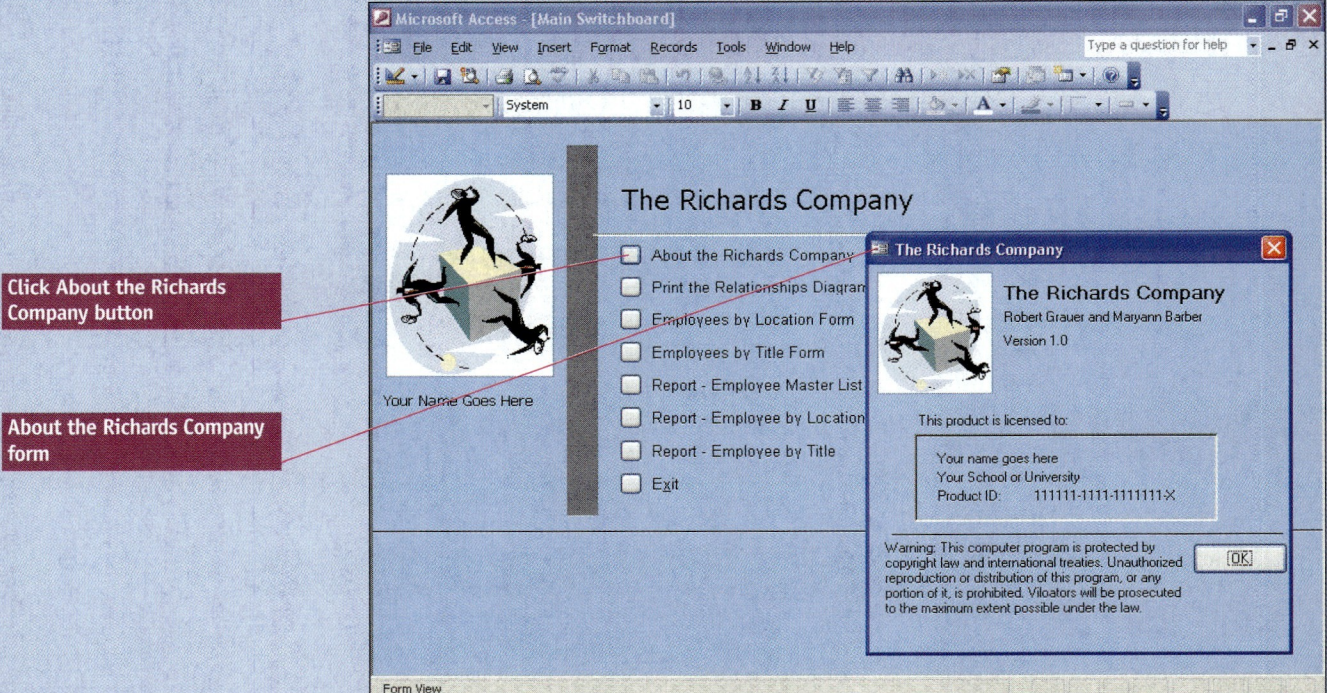

FIGURE 5.22 The Richards Company Switchboard (exercise 10)

MINI CASES

University Apartments

You have just signed your lease for next year at University Apartments, where you have the opportunity to design a database for the complex and thereby save on your rent. The complex has 500 apartments, which are divided into various categories as determined by the number of bedrooms, and additional amenities such as a washer/dryer, patio, and so on. There are many apartments in each category, but a given apartment falls into only one category.

Your database is to track all apartments in the complex and the students who live in those apartments. Each apartment is leased to one or more students, who sign the identical lease with the same rent and the same starting date for the lease. The lease information is stored within the Apartment record, but each student pays his or her rent individually. The database is to store every payment for every student in a separate payments table. Your database should produce a report showing the total rent received for each apartment and another report showing the total rent paid by each student.

Design a database that will satisfy the information requirements. You do not have to enter data into the tables, but you do have to create the tables in order to create the relationships diagram, which you will submit to your instructor. (You do not have to be concerned about the individual field properties at this time.) Create a simple switchboard with three menu options—a button to display an "About the Apartments" form describing the database, a button to print the relationships diagram, and a button to exit the application. The switchboard should contain the same clip art as the relationships diagram. Use the Startup property to display the switchboard when the database is opened. Print the Switchboard and Switchboard Items table for your instructor. Add a cover sheet to complete the assignment.

The Automobile Dealership

You have been retained as a database consultant for a local automobile dealership. The dealership has been in the community for fifty years, and it places a premium on customer loyalty, as the typical customer has made repeated purchases over time. The dealership maintains the usual data about its customers—name, address, phone number, credit rating, and so on. It also maintains the usual data about its sales staff. The dealership is large and has several sales managers, each of whom is responsible for multiple salespersons.

The key to the design of the database is the Automobiles table, which contains a record for every car that passes through the dealership. The table contains fields to indicate the date the car was received and the dealer cost. It also contains fields for the sale price and sale date, information that is entered when the car is sold. The Automobiles table also contains additional fields that describe the vehicle such as the make, model, year, and color.

Only one salesperson gets credit for each sale, and that is the individual who closes the deal. The salesperson receives a commission based on the difference between the sale price and dealer cost. Managers receive an override based on all sales generated by their sales staff.

Design a database that will enable the dealership to track its sales by customer, salesperson, and manager. You do not have to enter data into the tables, but you do have to create the tables in order to create the relationships diagram, which you will submit to your instructor. (You do not have to be concerned about the individual field properties at this time.)

Create a simple switchboard with three menu options—a button to display an "About the Dealership" form describing the database, a button to print the relationships diagram, and a button to exit the application. The switchboard should contain the same clip art as the relationships diagram. Use the Startup property to display the switchboard when the database is opened. Print the Switchboard and Switchboard Items table for your instructor. Add a cover sheet to complete the assignment.

Chapter Recap—Evergreen Flying Club

The Evergreen Flying Club is a 45-year-old, nonprofit flying club whose members fly and maintain antique airplanes. The airplanes are delicate and require hangar storage, as opposed to being left out in the open air. The club has affiliations with several private airports in the tri-state area in order to provide timely information to its members as new hangar space becomes available. Each airport has multiple hangars, but a specific hangar is associated with only one airport. Most club members lease space in more than one airport; they may own more than one airplane, and/or they may lease a hangar at different airports so that they will be able to store their plane overnight when they take trips.

Frank Barber, the president of Evergreen, maintains all information about the club on paper, but this is no longer practical. The membership has grown, as has the number of affiliated airports as well as the number of hangars in individual airports. Frank needs an Access database and has come to you for help in return for flying lessons. This is an exciting project and you cannot wait to get started.

Your assignment is to review the chapter, paying special attention on how to create a one-to-many relationship and enforce referential integrity. You will then create a new database with the required tables for the Evergreen Flying Club. You do not have to enter data into any of the tables, but you are to include all necessary fields and set the properties appropriately. Frank suggests three tables for airports, members, and hangars.

The Hangars table is especially important and should include the HangarID, AirportID, CustomerID, length, width, height, the date the lease begins, the date the lease ends, and the monthly rental. The design of the Airports and Customers tables is left to you. Your database should also include a basic switchboard, an About form, and a relationships diagram. Use a common clip art image and consistent design elements for each object in the database. Print the switchboard form, the table of switchboard items, the relationships diagram, and the About form for your instructor.

Many-to-many Relationships:
A More Complex System

OBJECTIVES

After reading this chapter you will:

1. Use the AutoNumber field type as the primary key for a new record.
2. Explain the field types required when an AutoNumber field is in a relationship.
3. Implement a many-to-many relationship in Access.
4. Use the Cascade Update and Cascade Delete options in a relationship.
5. Create a main form and sub-form based on a query.
6. Create a parameter query.
7. Use aggregate functions in a select query to perform calculations on groups of records.
8. Use the Get External Data command to add tables from another database.

hands-on exercises

1. RELATIONSHIPS AND REFERENTIAL INTEGRITY
   Input: Computer Store
   Output: Computer Store (modified)

2. SUBFORMS AND MULTIPLE-TABLE QUERIES
   Input: Computer Store (from exercise 1)
   Output: Computer Store (modified)

3. ADVANCED QUERIES
   Input: Computer Store (from exercise 2)
   Output: Computer Store (modified)

4. EXPANDING THE DATABASE
   Input: Salespersons database; Computer Store (from exercise 2)
   Output: Computer Store (modified)

CASE STUDY
AT YOUR SERVICE

The idea came to Chip Gillikin as he was leaving his upscale New York City apartment to embark on several errands. Life would be so much easier if he could simply leave instructions at the front desk rather than doing the chores himself. Such a service would cost dearly, but Chip is convinced there is a market. He recently read that the median price of an apartment in New York City exceeded $500,000 and that prices in excess of $1,000,000 are common. He reasoned that these wealthy tenants expect a variety of services and are willing to pay to get what they want.

Chip's concept is very simple and requires that he sign up buildings and vendors (i.e., service providers), each of whom will pay a commission based on the revenue that is generated. The management of a building will provide Chip with a list of tenants as well as a concierge desk in the lobby. The tenants (clients) will engage the concierge to contract for the individual services; that is, the concierge does not perform the actual service but contracts with an approved vendor. There is one-to-many relationship between buildings and tenants, but a many-to-many relationship between vendors and tenants. The fee is applied when the service is booked.

Your assignment is to read the chapter, paying special attention on how to create a many-to-many relationship and enforce referential integrity. You will then create a new database that contains the various tables for the At Your Service agency that Chip proposes. You do not have to enter data into any of the tables, but you are to include all necessary fields and set the properties appropriately. Your database should also include a basic switchboard, an About form, a relationships diagram, and templates for the reports and forms that will be used in the database. Use a common clip art image and consistent design elements for each object in the database. Print the switchboard form, the table of switchboard items, the relationships diagram, and both templates for your instructor.

This chapter introduces a new case study to give you additional practice in database design. The system extends the concept of a relational database to include both a one-to-many and a many-to-many relationship. The case solution reviews earlier material on establishing relationships in Access and the importance of referential integrity. Another point of particular interest is the use of an AutoNumber field to facilitate the addition of new records.

The chapter extends what you already know about subforms and queries, and uses both to present information from related tables. The forms created in this chapter are based on multiple-table queries rather than tables. The queries themselves are of a more advanced nature. We show you how to create a parameter query, where the user is prompted to enter the criteria when the query is run. We also review queries that use the aggregate functions built into Access to perform calculations on groups of records.

The case study in this chapter is set within the context of a computer store that requires a database for its customers, products, and orders. The store maintains the usual customer data (name, address, phone, etc.). It also keeps data about the products it sells, storing for each product a ProductID, description, quantity on hand, quantity on order, and unit price. And finally, the store has to track its orders. It needs to know the date an order was received, the customer who placed it, the products that were ordered, and the quantity of each product.

Think, for a moment, about the tables that are necessary and the relationships among those tables, then compare your thoughts to our solution in Figure 6.1. You probably have no trouble recognizing the need for the Customers, Products, and Orders tables. Initially, you may be puzzled by the Order Details table, but you will soon appreciate why it is there and how powerful it is.

You can use the Customers, Products, and Orders tables individually to obtain information about a specific customer, product, or order, respectively. For example:

Query: What is Jeffrey Muddell's phone number?
Answer: Jeffrey Muddell's phone is (305) 253-3909.

Query: What is the price of a Pentium IV notebook? How many are in stock?
Answer: A Pentium IV notebook sells for $2,599. Fifteen systems are in stock.

Query: When was order O0003 placed?
Answer: Order O0003 was placed on April 18, 2003.

Other queries require you to relate the tables to one another. There is, for example, a ***one-to-many relationship*** between customers and orders. One customer can place many orders, but a specific order can be associated with only one customer. The tables are related through the CustomerID, which appears as the ***primary key*** in the Customers table and as a foreign key in the Orders table. Consider:

Query: What is the name of the customer who placed order number O0003?
Answer: Order O0003 was placed by Jeffrey Muddell.

Query: How many orders were placed by Jeffrey Muddell?
Answer: Jeffrey Muddell placed five orders: O0003, O0014, O0016, O0024, and C0025.

These queries require you to use two tables. To answer the first query, you would search the Orders table to find order O0003 and obtain the CustomerID (C0006 in this example). You would then search the Customers table for the customer with this CustomerID and retrieve the customer's name. To answer the

(a) Customers Table

Customer ID	First Name	Last Name	Address	City	State	Zip Code	Phone Number
C0001	Benjamin	Lee	1000 Call Street	Tallahassee	FL	33340	(904) 327-4124
C0002	Eleanor	Milgrom	7245 NW 8 Street	Margate	FL	33065	(305) 974-1234
C0003	Neil	Goodman	4215 South 81 Street	Margate	FL	33065	(305) 444-5555
C0004	Nicholas	Colon	9020 N.W. 75 Street	Coral Springs	FL	33065	(305) 753-9887
C0005	Michael	Ware	276 Brickell Avenue	Miami	FL	33131	(305) 444-3980
C0006	Jeffrey	Muddell	9522 S.W. 142 Street	Miami	FL	33176	(305) 253-3909
C0007	Ashley	Geoghegan	7500 Center Lane	Coral Springs	FL	33070	(305) 753-7830
C0008	Serena	Sherard	5000 Jefferson Lane	Gainesville	FL	32601	(904) 375-6442
C0009	Luis	Couto	455 Bargello Avenue	Coral Gables	FL	33146	(305) 666-4801
C0010	Derek	Anderson	6000 Tigertail Avenue	Coconut Grove	FL	33120	(305) 446-8900
C0011	Lauren	Center	12380 S.W. 137 Avenue	Miami	FL	33186	(305) 385-4432
C0012	Robert	Slane	4508 N.W. 7 Street	Miami	FL	33131	(305) 635-3454

(a) Customers Table

(b) Products Table

Product ID	Product Name	Units In Stock	Units On Order	Uni tPrice
P0001	Celeron® at 2.0GHz	50	0	$899.00
P0002	Pentium® IV at 2.6GHz	25	5	$1,099.00
P0003	Pentium® IV at 3.0GHz	125	15	$1,399.00
P0004	Pentium® III Notebook at 800 MHz	25	50	$1,599.00
P0005	Pentium® IV Notebook at 2.0GHz	15	25	$2,599.00
P0006	17" CRT Monitor	50	0	$499.00
P0007	19" CRT Monitor	25	10	$899.00
P0008	21" CRT Monitor	50	20	$1,599.00
P0009	2 Years On Site Service	15	20	$299.00
P0010	4 Years On Site Service	25	15	$399.00
P0011	Multi Media Projector	10	0	$1,245.00
P0012	Digital Camera - 2.0 megapixels	40	0	$249.00
P0013	Digital Camera - 4.0 megapixels	50	15	$449.95
P0014	HD Floppy Disks (50 pack)	500	200	$9.99
P0015	CD-R (25 pack spindle)	100	50	$14.79
P0016	Digital Scanner	15	3	$179.95
P0017	Serial Mouse	150	50	$69.95
P0018	Trackball	55	0	$59.95
P0019	Joystick	250	100	$39.95
P0020	Wireless broadband router	35	10	$189.95
P0021	Fax/Modem 56 Kbps	20	0	$65.95
P0022	Digital Photography Package	100	15	$1,395.00
P0023	Ink Jet Printer	50	50	$249.95
P0024	Laser Printer (personal)	125	25	$569.95
P0025	Windows® XP Home Edition	400	200	$95.95
P0026	Antivirus/Firewall Upgrade	150	50	$75.95
P0027	Tax Preparaton Software	150	50	$115.95
P0028	Typing Tutor	75	25	$29.95
P0029	Microsoft Office Home Edition	250	100	$129.95
P0030	Learning Adventure	25	10	$59.95
P0031	Surge Protector	15	0	$45.95

(b) Products Table

(c) Orders Table

OrderID	CustomerID	Order Date
O001	C0004	4/15/2003
O002	C0003	4/18/2003
O003	C0006	4/18/2003
O004	C0007	4/18/2003
O005	C0001	4/20/2003
O006	C0001	4/21/2003
O007	C0002	4/21/2003
O008	C0002	4/22/2003
O009	C0001	4/22/2003
O010	C0002	4/22/2003
O011	C0001	4/24/2003
O012	C0007	4/24/2003
O013	C0004	4/24/2003
O014	C0006	4/25/2003
O015	C0009	4/25/2003
O016	C0006	4/26/2003
O017	C0011	4/26/2003
O018	C0011	4/26/2003
O019	C0012	4/27/2003
O020	C0012	4/28/2003
O021	C0010	4/29/2003
O022	C0010	4/29/2003
O023	C0008	4/30/2003
O024	C0006	5/1/2003
O025	C0006	5/1/2003

(c) Orders Table

(d) Order Details Table

OrderID	ProductID	Quantity
O0001	P0013	1
O0001	P0014	4
O0001	P0027	1
O0002	P0001	1
O0002	P0006	1
O0002	P0020	1
O0002	P0022	1
O0003	P0005	1
O0003	P0020	1
O0003	P0022	1
O0004	P0003	1
O0004	P0010	1
O0004	P0022	2
O0005	P0003	2
O0005	P0012	2
O0005	P0016	2
O0006	P0007	1
O0006	P0014	10
O0007	P0028	1
O0007	P0030	3
O0008	P0001	1
O0008	P0004	3
O0008	P0008	4
O0008	P0011	2
O0008	P0012	1
O0009	P0006	1
O0010	P0002	2
O0010	P0022	1
O0010	P0023	1
O0011	P0016	2
O0011	P0020	2
O0012	P0021	10
O0012	P0029	10
O0012	P0030	10
O0013	P0009	4
O0013	P0016	10
O0013	P0024	2
O0014	P0019	2
O0014	P0028	1
O0015	P0018	1
O0015	P0020	1
O0016	P0029	2
O0017	P0019	2
O0018	P0009	1
O0018	P0025	2
O0018	P0026	2
O0019	P0014	25
O0020	P0024	1
O0021	P0004	1
O0022	P0027	1
O0023	P0021	1
O0023	P0028	1
O0023	P0029	1
O0024	P0007	1
O0024	P0013	5
O0024	P0014	3
O0024	P0016	1
O0025	P0012	2
O0025	P0029	2

(d) Order Details Table

FIGURE 6.1 Super Store Database

second query, you would begin in the Customers table and search for Jeffrey Muddell to determine the CustomerID (C0006), then search the Orders table for all records with this CustomerID.

The system is more complicated than earlier examples in that there is a ***many-to-many relationship*** between orders and products. One order can include many products, and at the same time a specific product can appear in many orders. The implementation of a many-to-many relationship requires an additional table, the Order Details table, containing (at a minimum) the primary keys of the individual tables.

The Order Details table will contain many records with the same OrderID because there is a separate record for each product in a given order. It will also contain many records with the same ProductID because there is a separate record for every order containing that product. However, the *combination* of OrderID and ProductID is unique, and this ***combined key*** becomes the primary key in the Order Details table. The Order Details table also contains an additional field (Quantity), whose value depends on the primary key (the *combination* of OrderID and ProductID). Thus:

Query: How many units of product P0014 are in order O0001?
Answer: Order O0001 included four units of product P0014. (The order also included one unit of Product P0013 and one unit of P0027.)

The Order Details table has four records with a ProductID of P0014. It also has three records with an OrderID of O0001. There is, however, only one record with a ProductID P0014 *and* an OrderID O0001, which is for four units.

The Order Details table makes it possible to determine all products in a given order or all orders for a given product. You can also use the Products table in conjunction with the Order Details table to determine the names of those products. Consider:

Query: Which orders include a Celeron 2.0GHz desktop system?
Answer: A Celeron 2.0GHz system is found in orders O0002 and O0008.

Query: Which products were included in Order O0003?
Answer: Order O0003 consisted of products P0005 (a Pentium IV notebook), P0020 (a wireless router), and P0022 (a digital photography package).

To answer the first query, you would begin in the Products table to find the ProductID for the Celeron system (P0001). You would then search the Order Details table for records containing a ProductID of P0001, which in turn identifies orders O0002 and O0008. The second query is processed in similar fashion except that you would search the Order Details table for an OrderID of O0003. This time you would find three records with ProductIDs P0005, P0020, and P0022, respectively. You would then go to the Products table to look up the ProductIDs to return the name of each product.

We've emphasized that the power of a relational database comes from the inclusion of multiple tables and the relationships between those tables. As you already know, you can use data from several tables to compute the answer to more complex queries. For example:

Query: What is the total cost of order O0006? Which products are in the order and how many units of each product?
Answer: The total cost of order O0006 is $998.90. The order consists of one 19-inch monitor at $899 and ten boxes of HD floppy disks at $9.99 each.

To determine the cost of an order, you must first identify all of the products associated with that order, the quantity of each product, and the price of each product. The previous queries have shown how you would find the products in an order and the associated quantities. The price of a specific product is obtained from the Products table, which enables you to compute the invoice by multiplying the price of each product by the quantity. Thus, the total cost of order O0006 is $998.90. (One unit of P0007 at $899.00 and ten units of product P0014 at $9.99.)

The AutoNumber Field Type

Look carefully at the Customer, Order, and Product numbers in their respective tables and note that each set of numbers is consecutive. This is accomplished by specifying the *AutoNumber field* type for each of these fields in the design of the individual tables. The AutoNumber specification automatically assigns the next sequential number to the primary key of a new record. If, for example, you were to add a new customer to the existing Customers table, that customer would be assigned the number 13. In similar fashion, the next order will be order number 26, and the next product will be product number 32. (Deleting a record does not, however, renumber the remaining records in the table; that is, once a value is assigned to a primary key, the primary key will always retain that value.)

The C, O, and P that appear as the initial character of each field, as well as the high-order zeros, are *not* part of the fields themselves, but are displayed through the *Format property* associated with each field. Our Customers table, for example, uses the format \C0000, which displays a "C" in front of the field and pads it with high-order zeros. The Format property determines how a value is displayed, but does not affect how it is stored in the table. Thus, the CustomerID of the first customer is stored as the number 1, rather than C0001. The zeros provide a uniform appearance for that field throughout the table.

The Relationships Window

The *Relationships window* in Figure 6.2 shows the Computer Store database as it will be implemented in Access. The database contains the Customers, Orders, Products, and Order Details tables as per the previous discussion. The field lists display the fields within each table, with the primary key shown in bold. The OrderID and ProductID are both shown in bold in the Order Details table, to indicate that the primary key consists of the combination of these fields.

The many-to-many relationship between Orders and Products is implemented by a *pair* of one-to-many relationships. There is a one-to-many relationship between the Orders table and the Order Details table. There is a second one-to-many relationship between the Products table and the Order Details table. In other words, the Orders and Products tables are related to each other through the pair of one-to-many relationships with the Order Details table.

The *relationship lines* show the relationships among the tables. The number 1 appears next to the Products table on the relationship line connecting the Products table and the Order Details table. The infinity symbol appears at the end of the relationship line next to the Order Details table. The one-to-many relationship between these tables means that each record in the Products table can be associated with many records in the Order Details table. Each record in the Order Details table, however, is associated with only one record in the Products table.

In similar fashion, there is a second one-to-many relationship between the Orders table and the Order Details table. The number 1 appears on the relationship line next to the Orders table. The infinity symbol appears at the end of the line next to the Order Details table. Thus, each record in the Orders table can be associated with many records in the Order Details table, but each record in the Order Details table is associated with only one order.

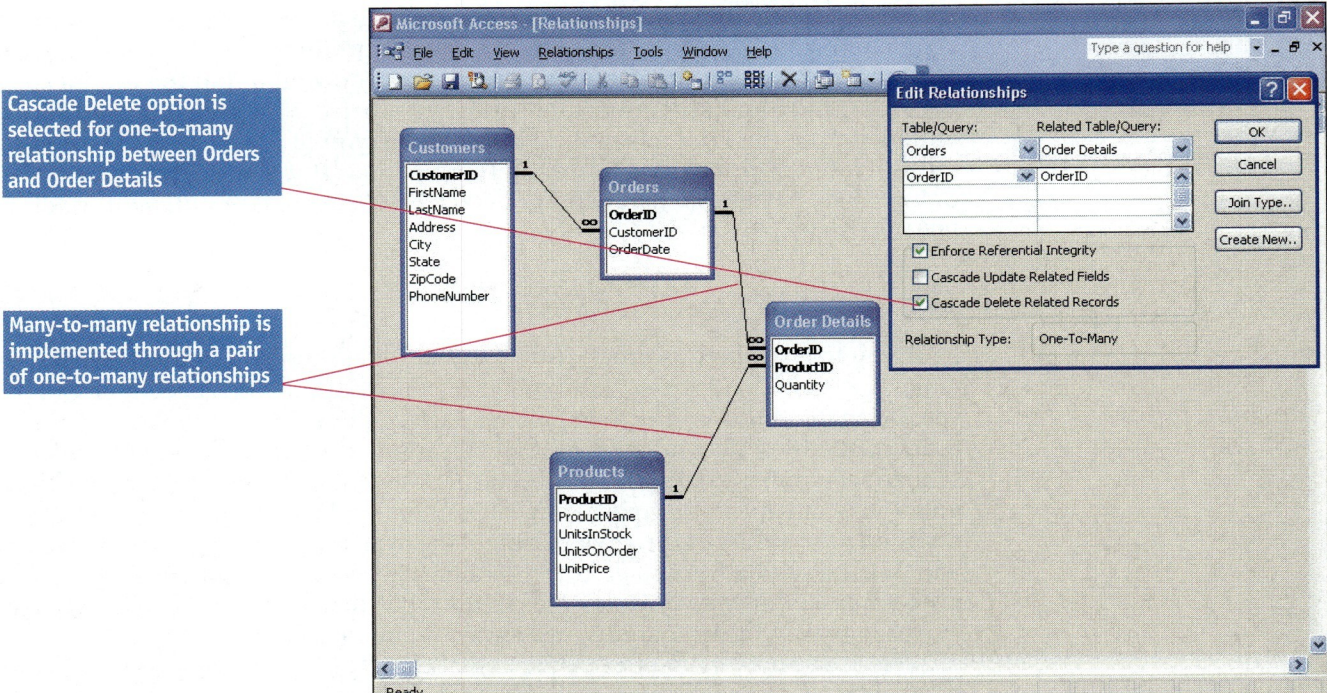

Cascade Delete option is selected for one-to-many relationship between Orders and Order Details

Many-to-many relationship is implemented through a pair of one-to-many relationships

FIGURE 6.2 The Relationships Window

Referential integrity ensures that the records in related tables are consistent with one another by preventing you from adding a record to a related table with an invalid foreign key. You could not, for example, add a record to the Order Details table that referenced a nonexistent order in the Orders table. The enforcement of referential integrity will also prevent you from deleting a record in the primary (Orders) table when there are corresponding records in the related (Order Details) table.

There may be times, however, when you want to delete an order and simultaneously delete the corresponding records in the Order Details table. This is accomplished by enabling the ***cascaded deletion*** of related records (as shown in Figure 6.2), so that when you delete a record in the Orders table, Access automatically deletes the associated records in the Order Details table. If, for example, you were to delete order number O0006 from the Orders table, any records with this OrderID in the Order Details table would be deleted automatically.

You might also want to enable the ***cascaded updating*** of related fields to correct the value of an OrderID. Enforcement of referential integrity would ordinarily prevent you from changing the value of the OrderID field in the Orders table when there are corresponding records in the Order Details table. You could, however, specify the cascaded updating of related fields so that if you were to change the OrderID in the Orders table, the corresponding fields in the Order Details table would also change.

PRACTICE WITH DATABASE DESIGN

An Access database contains multiple tables, each of which stores data about a specific entity. To use Access effectively, you must be able to relate the tables to one another, which in turn requires knowledge of database design. Appendix A provides three additional examples that enable you to master the principles of a relational database.

Relationships and Referential Integrity

Objective To create relationships between existing tables in order to demonstrate referential integrity; to edit an existing relationship to allow the cascaded deletion of related records. Use Figure 6.3 as a guide in the exercise.

Step 1: **Add a Customer Record**

- Start Access as you have throughout the text. Open the **Computer Store database** in the **Exploring Access folder**.

- Click the **Tables button** in the Database window. Open the **Customers table**, then click the **Maximize button** (if necessary) so that the table takes the entire screen as shown in Figure 6.3a.

- Click the **New Record button**, then click in the **FirstName field**. Enter the first letter of your first name (e.g., "J" as shown in the figure):
  - ❏ The record selector changes to a pencil to indicate that you are in the process of entering a record.
  - ❏ The CustomerID is assigned automatically as soon as you begin to enter data. *Remember your customer number as you will use it throughout the chapter.* (Your CustomerID is 13, not C0013. The prefix and high-order zeros are displayed through the Format property.)

- Complete your customer record, pressing the **Tab key** to move from one field to the next. Press **Tab** after you have entered the last field (phone number) to complete the record.

- Close the Customers table.

New Record button

CustomerID is automatically entered as soon as you begin to enter data in FirstName field

Click in FirstName field and enter first letter of your first name

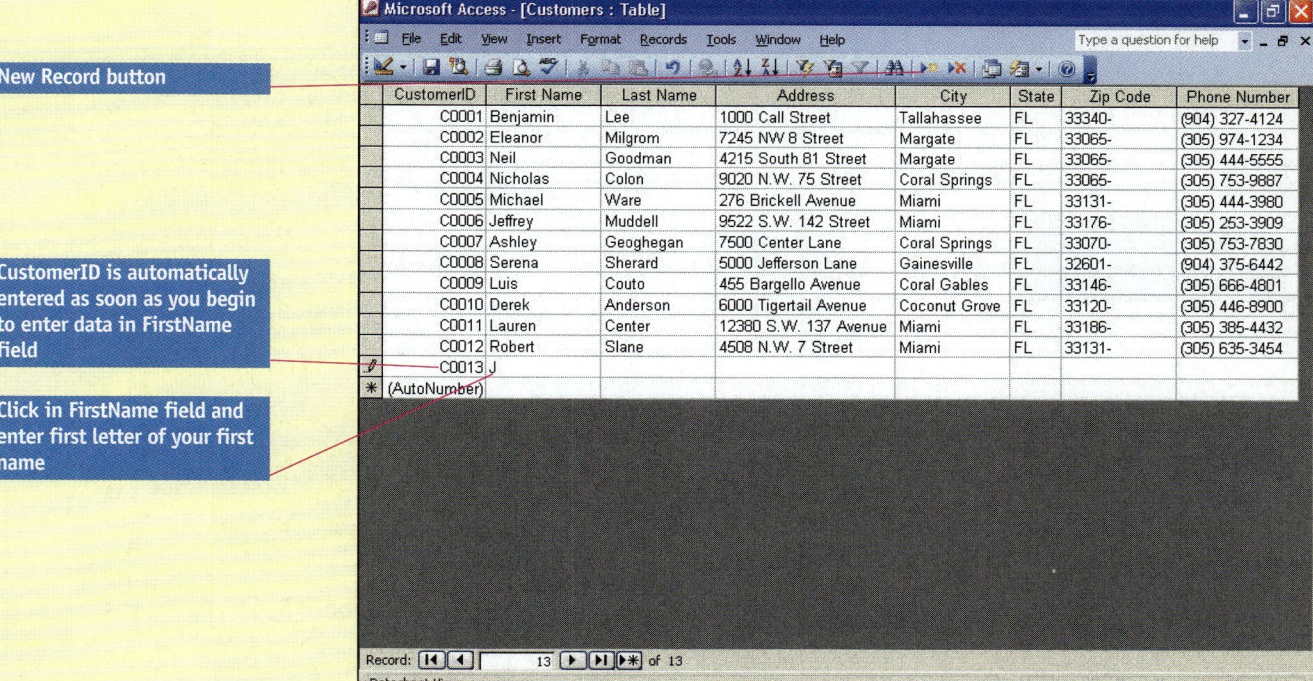

(a) Add a Customer Record (step 1)

FIGURE 6.3 Hands-on Exercise 1

Step 2: **Create the Relationships**

- Pull down the **Tools menu** and click **Relationships** to open the Relationships window as shown in Figure 6.3b. Maximize the Relationships window.

- Pull down the **Relationships menu** and click **Show Table** (or click the **Show Table button**) to display the Show Table dialog box.

- The **Tables tab** is selected within the Show Table dialog box, and the **Customers table** is selected. Click the **Add Command button**.

- Add the **Order Details**, **Orders**, and **Products** tables in similar fashion. Close the Show Table dialog box.

- Point to the bottom border of the **Customers field list**, then click and drag the border until all of the fields are visible.

- If necessary, click and drag the bottom border of the other tables until all of their fields are visible. Click and drag the title bars to move the field lists.

- Click and drag the **CustomerID field** in the Customers field list to the **CustomerID field** in the Orders field list. You will see the Relationships dialog box in Figure 6.3b when you release the mouse.

- Click the **Enforce Referential Integrity** check box. Click the **Create Command button** to establish the relationship.

- Click and drag the **OrderID field** in the Orders field list to the **OrderID field** in the Order Details field list. Click the **Enforce Referential Integrity** check box, then click the **Create Command button**.

- Click and drag the **ProductID field** in the Products field list to the **ProductID field** in the Order Details field list. Click the **Enforce Referential Integrity** check box, then click the **Create Command button**.

- Click the **Save button**. Close the Relationships window.

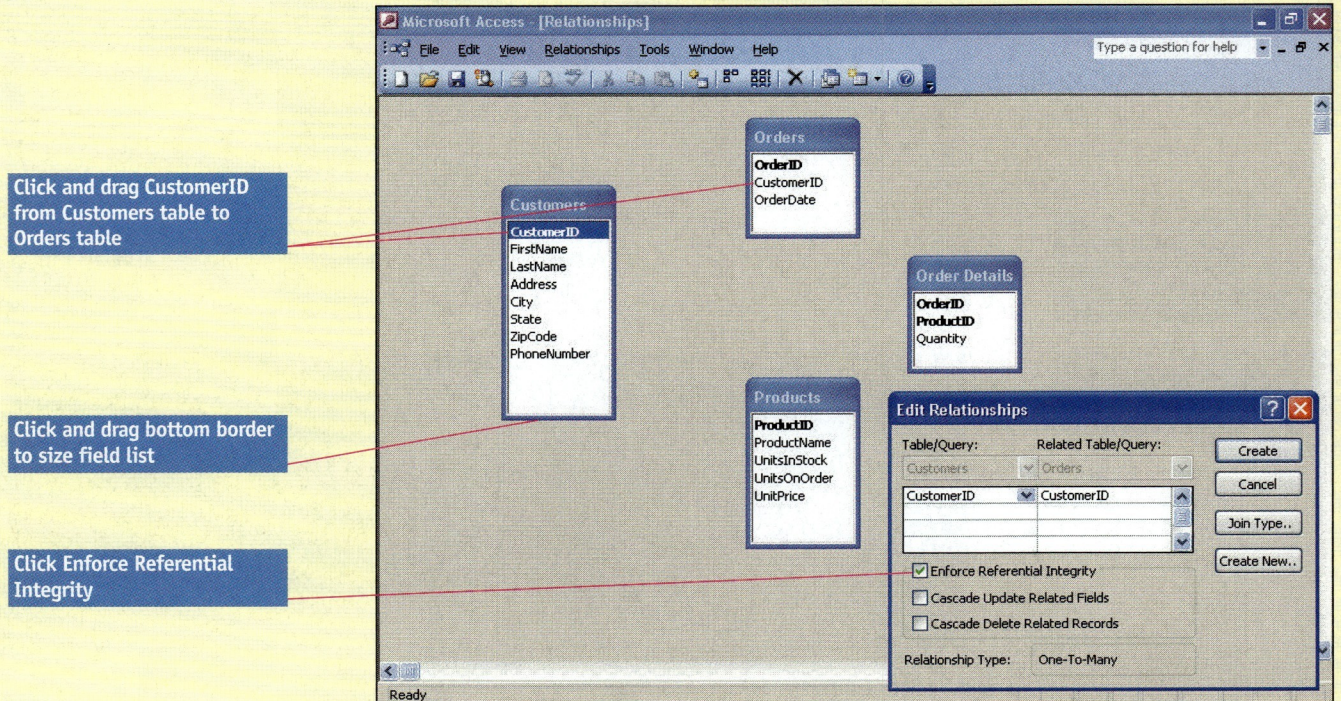

Click and drag CustomerID from Customers table to Orders table

Click and drag bottom border to size field list

Click Enforce Referential Integrity

(b) Create the Relationships (step 2)

FIGURE 6.3 Hands-on Exercise 1 (*continued*)

Step 3: **Delete an Order Details Record**

- You should be in the Database window. If necessary, click the **Tables button**, then open the **Orders table** as shown in Figure 6.3c.

- Click the **plus sign** next to order O0005. The plus sign changes to a minus sign, and you see the order details for this record. Click the **row selector column** to select the Order Details record for product **P0016** in order **O0005**.

- Press the **Del key**. You will see a message indicating that you are about to delete one record. Click **Yes**. The Delete command works because you are deleting a "many" record in a one-to-many relationship.

- Click the **minus sign** next to **Order O0005**. The minus sign changes to a plus sign, and you no longer see the order details. Click the **row selector column** to select the record, then press the **Del key** to (attempt to) delete the record.

- You will see a message indicating that you cannot delete the record. The Delete command does not work because you are attempting to delete the "one record" in a one-to-many relationship. Click **OK** to close the dialog box. The record for order O0005 is not deleted.

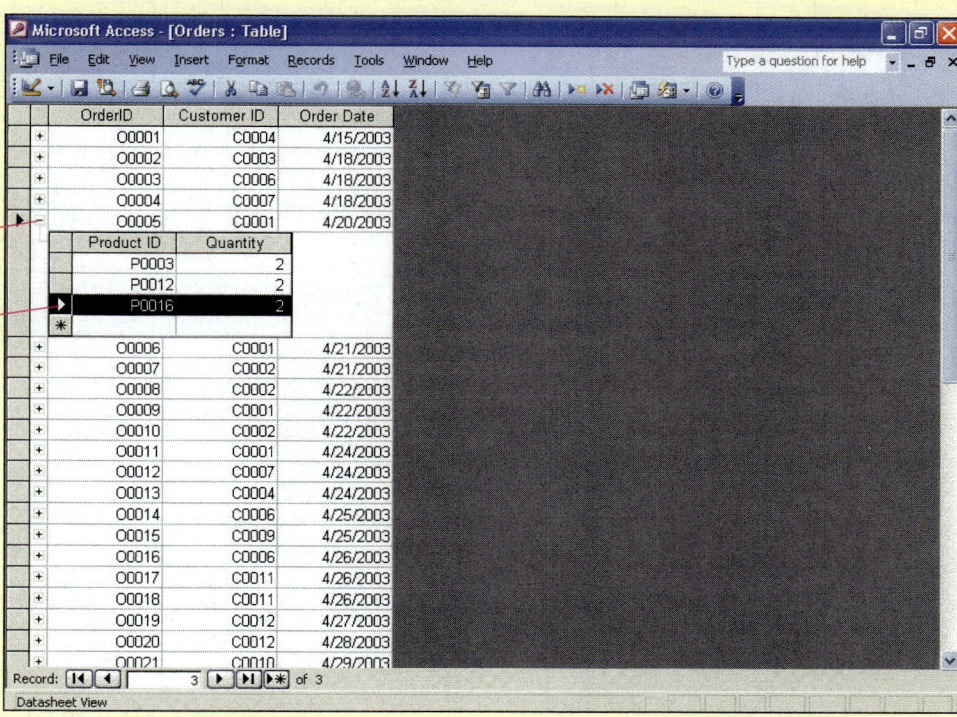

Click + (which becomes a −) to display related records

Click record selector column and press Del key

(c) Delete an Order Details Record (Step 3)

FIGURE 6.3 Hands-on Exercise 1 (*continued*)

WHAT YOU CAN AND CANNOT DELETE

You can always delete a record from the "many" table, such as the Order Details table in this example. The enforcement of referential integrity, however, will prevent you from deleting a record in the "one" table (i.e., the Orders table) when there are related records in the "many" table (i.e., the Order Details table). Thus, you may want to modify the relationship to permit the cascaded deletion of related records, in which case deleting a record from the "one" table will automatically delete the related records.

Step 4: **Edit a Relationship**

- Close the Orders table. (The tables in a relationship must be closed before the relationship can be edited.)

- Pull down the **Tools menu** and click **Relationships** to reopen the Relationships window (or click the **Relationships button** on the toolbar). Maximize the window.

- Point to the line connecting the Orders and Order Details tables, then click the **right mouse button** to display a shortcut menu. Click **Edit Relationship** to display the Relationships dialog box in Figure 6.3d.

- Check the box to **Cascade Delete Related Records**, then click **OK** to accept the change and close the dialog box. Click the **Save button** on the Relationships toolbar to save the edited relationship.

- Close the Relationships window.

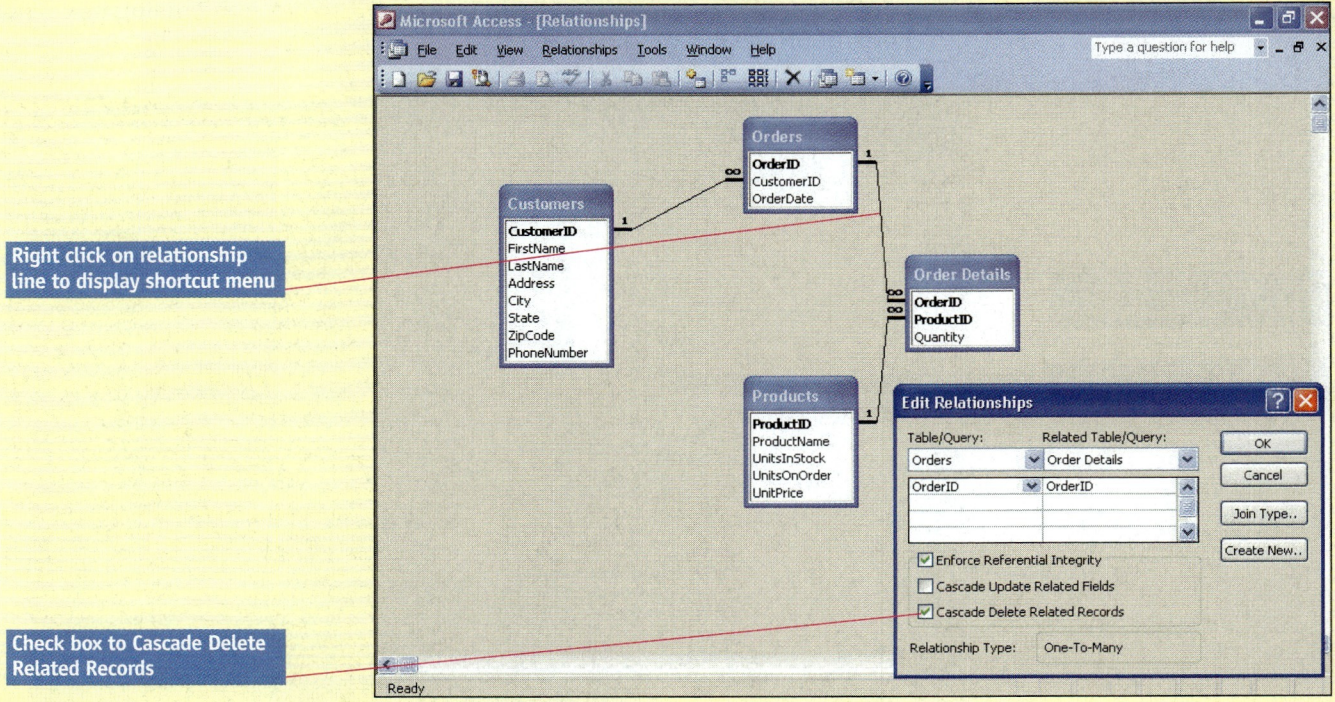

Right click on relationship line to display shortcut menu

Check box to Cascade Delete Related Records

(d) Edit a Relationship (step 4)

FIGURE 6.3 Hands-on Exercise 1 (*continued*)

RELATED FIELDS AND DATA TYPE

The related fields on both sides of a relationship must be the same data type—for example, both number fields or both text fields. (Number fields must also have the same field size setting.) You cannot, however, specify an AutoNumber field on both sides of a relationship. Accordingly, if the related field in the primary table is an AutoNumber field, the related field in the related table must be specified as a number field, with the Field Size property set to Long Integer.

Step 5: **Delete a Record in the Orders Table**

- You should be back in the Database window. Open the **Orders table**. Click the **record selector column** for **Order O0005**. Press the **Del key**.

- Record O0005 is deleted from the table (although you can cancel the deletion by clicking No in response to the message that is displayed on your screen). We want you to delete the record, however. Thus, click **Yes** in response to the message in Figure 6.3e.

- Order O0005 is permanently deleted from the Orders table as are the related records in the Order Details table. The Delete command works this time (unlike the previous attempt in step 3) because the relationship was changed to permit the deletion of related records.

- Close the Orders table. Close the database. Click **Yes** if prompted to save the tables or relationships.

- Exit Access if you do not want to continue with the next exercise at this time.

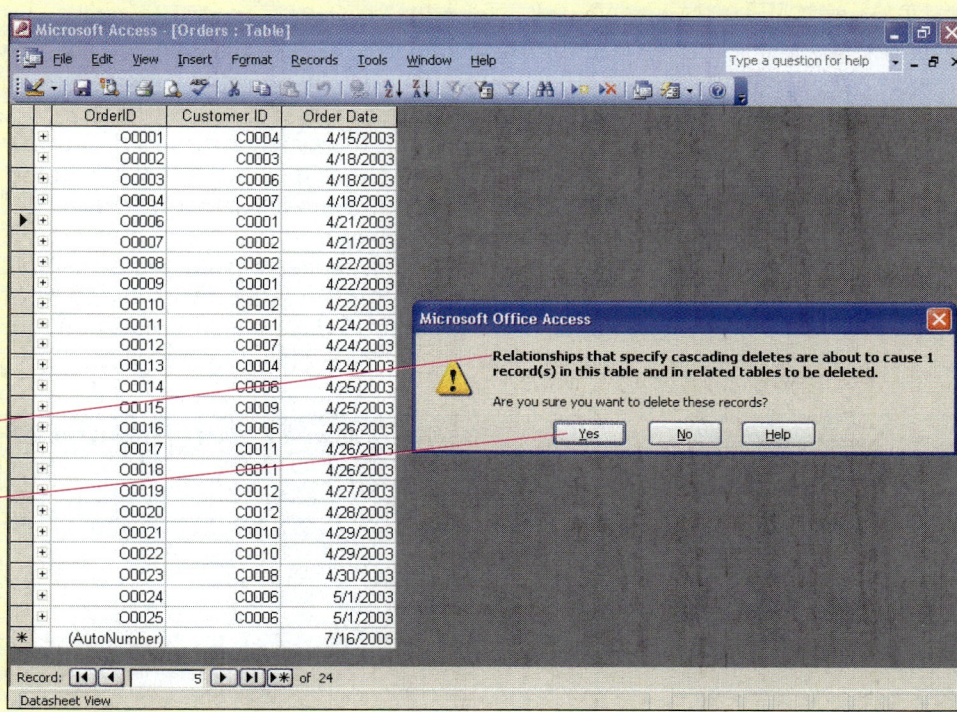

Message indicates related records will be deleted as well

Click Yes to confirm deletion

(e) Delete a Record in the Orders Table (step 5)

FIGURE 6.3 Hands-on Exercise 1 (*continued*)

USE WITH CAUTION

The cascaded deletion of related records relaxes referential integrity and eliminates errors that would otherwise occur during data entry. That does not mean, however, that the option should always be selected, and in fact, most of the time it is disabled. What would happen, for example, in an employee database with a one-to-many relationship between branch offices and employees, if cascade deleted records was in effect and a branch office was deleted?

The main and subform combination in Figure 6.4 is used by the store to enter a new order for an existing customer. The forms are based on queries (rather than tables) for several reasons. A query enables you to display data from multiple tables, to display a calculated field, and to take advantage of AutoLookup, a feature that is explained shortly. A query also lets you display records in a sequence other than by primary key.

The **main form** contains fields from both the Orders table and the Customers table. The OrderID, OrderDate, and CustomerID (the join field) are taken from the Orders table. The other fields are taken from the Customers table. The query is designed so that you do not have to enter any customer information other than the CustomerID; that is, you enter the CustomerID, and Access will automatically look up **(AutoLookup)** the corresponding customer data.

The **subform** is based on a second query containing fields from the Order Details table and the Products table. The OrderID, Quantity, and ProductID (the join field) are taken from the Order Details table. The ProductName and UnitPrice fields are from the Products table. AutoLookup works here as well so that when you enter the ProductID, Access automatically displays the Product Name and Unit Price. You then enter the quantity, and the amount (a calculated field) is determined automatically.

The queries for the main form and subform are shown in Figures 6.5a and 6.5b, respectively. The upper half of the Query window displays the field list for each table and the relationship between the tables. The lower half of the Query window contains the design grid.

The following exercise has you create the main and subform in Figure 6.4. We supply the query for the main form (Figure 6.5a), but we ask you to create the query for the subform (Figure 6.5b). Once both queries are available, you can proceed to create the Super Store Order form.

OrderID, CustomerID, and Order Date are from Orders table

Remaining fields in main form are from Customers table

ProductID and Quantity are from Order Details table; Product Name and UnitPrice are from Products table

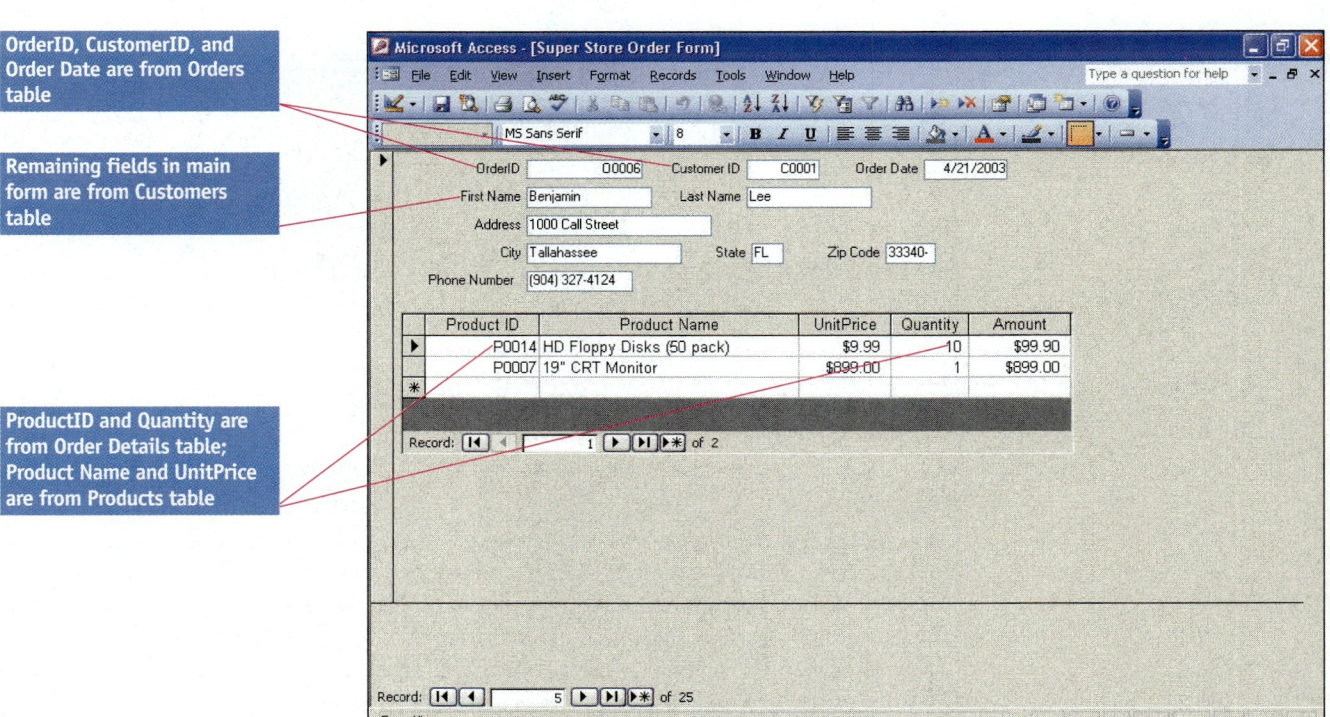

FIGURE 6.4   The Super Store Order Form

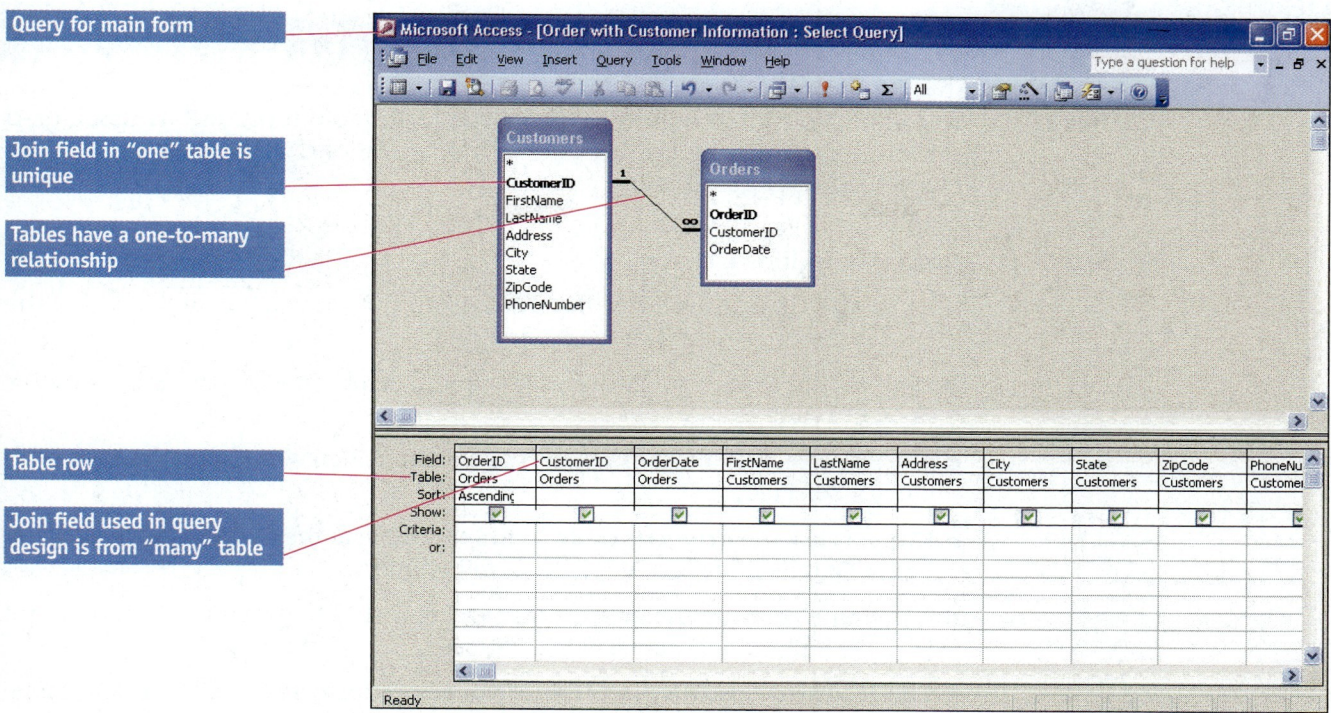

Query for main form

Join field in "one" table is unique

Tables have a one-to-many relationship

Table row

Join field used in query design is from "many" table

(a) Order with Customer Information Query (used for the main form)

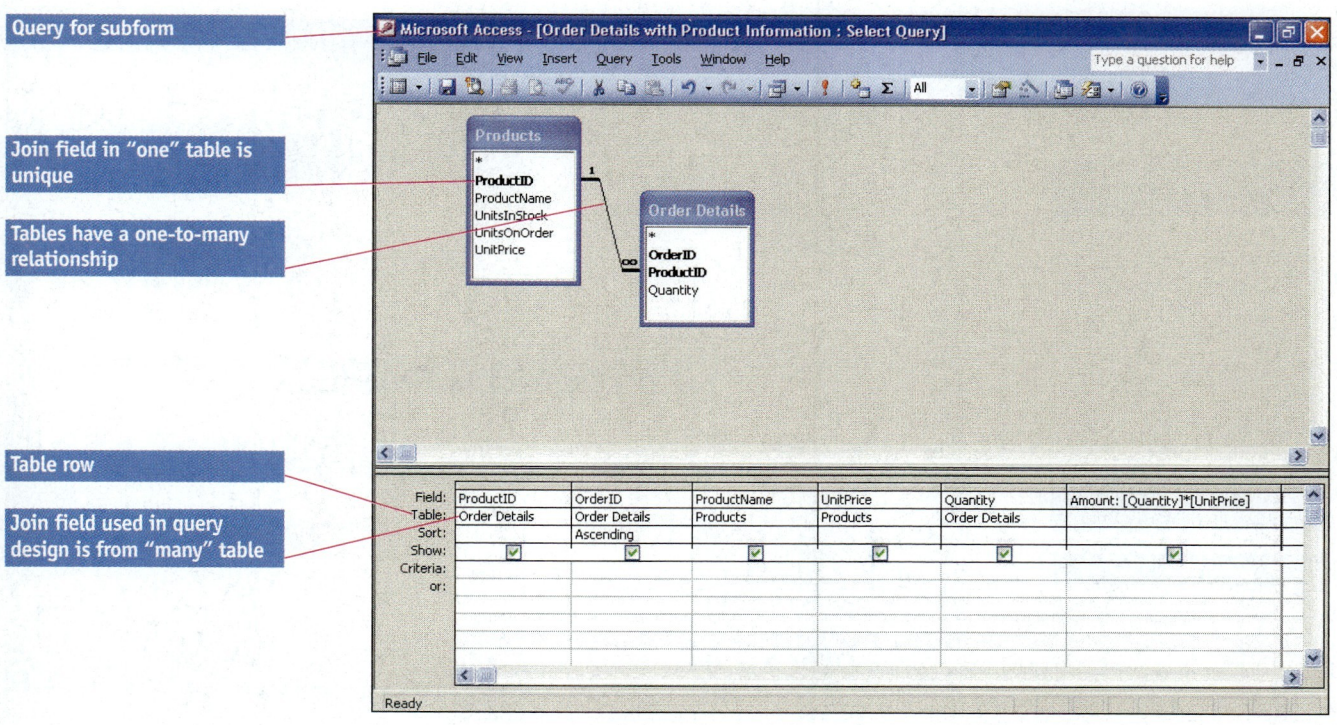

Query for subform

Join field in "one" table is unique

Tables have a one-to-many relationship

Table row

Join field used in query design is from "many" table

(b) Order Details with Product Information Query (used for subform)

FIGURE 6.5 Multiple-table Queries

2 Subforms and Multiple-table Queries

Objective To use multiple-table queries as the basis for a main form and its associated subform; to create the link between a main form and subform manually. Use Figure 6.6 as a guide in the exercise.

Step 1: **Create the Subform Query**

- Open the **Computer Store database** from the previous exercise. Click the **Queries button** in the Database window.

- Double click **Create query in Design view** to display the Query Design window in Figure 6.6c.

- The Show Table dialog box appears as shown in Figure 6.6a with the Tables tab already selected.

- Double click the **Products table** to add this table to the query. Double click the **Order Details table** to add this table to the query.

- A join line showing the one-to-many relationship between the Products and Order Details tables appears automatically.

- Click **Close** to close the Show Table dialog box. If necessary, click the **Maximize button**. Resize the field lists as necessary.

- Click and drag the border separating the two parts of the query window to better display the field list. You are ready to create the query.

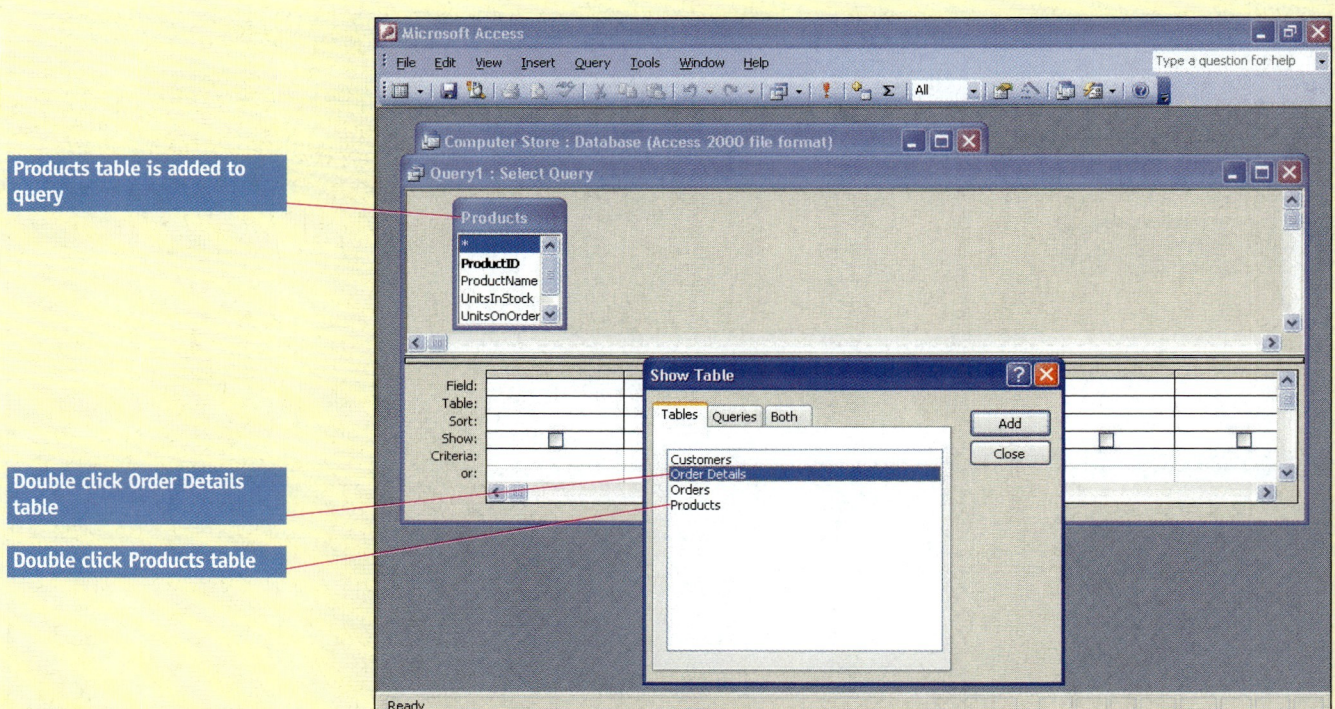

Products table is added to query

Double click Order Details table

Double click Products table

(a) Create the Subform Query (step 1)

FIGURE 6.6 Hands-on Exercise 2

Step 2: **Create the Subform Query (continued)**

- Add the fields to the query as follows:
    - ❏ Double click the **ProductID** and **OrderID fields** in that order from the Order Details table.
    - ❏ Double click the **ProductName** and **UnitPrice fields** in that order from the Products table.
    - ❏ Double click the **Quantity field** from the Order Details table.

- Click the **Sort row** under the **OrderID field**. Click the **drop-down arrow**, then specify an **ascending** sequence.

- Click the first available cell in the Field row. Type **=[Quantity]*[UnitPrice]**. Do not be concerned if you cannot see the entire expression.

- Press **Enter**. Access has substituted Expr1: for the equal sign you typed. Drag the column boundary so that the entire expression is visible as in Figure 6.6b. (You may need to make the other columns narrower to see all of the fields in the design grid.)

- Click and drag to select **Expr1**. (Do not select the colon.) Type **Amount** to substitute a more meaningful field name.

- Point to the expression and click the **right mouse button** to display a shortcut menu. Click **Properties** to display the Field Properties dialog box in Figure 6.6b.

- Click the box for the **Format property**. Click the **drop-down arrow**, then scroll until you can click **Currency**. Close the Properties dialog box.

- Save the query as **Order Details with Product Information**. Click the **Run button** to test the query so that you know the query works prior to using it as the basis of a form.

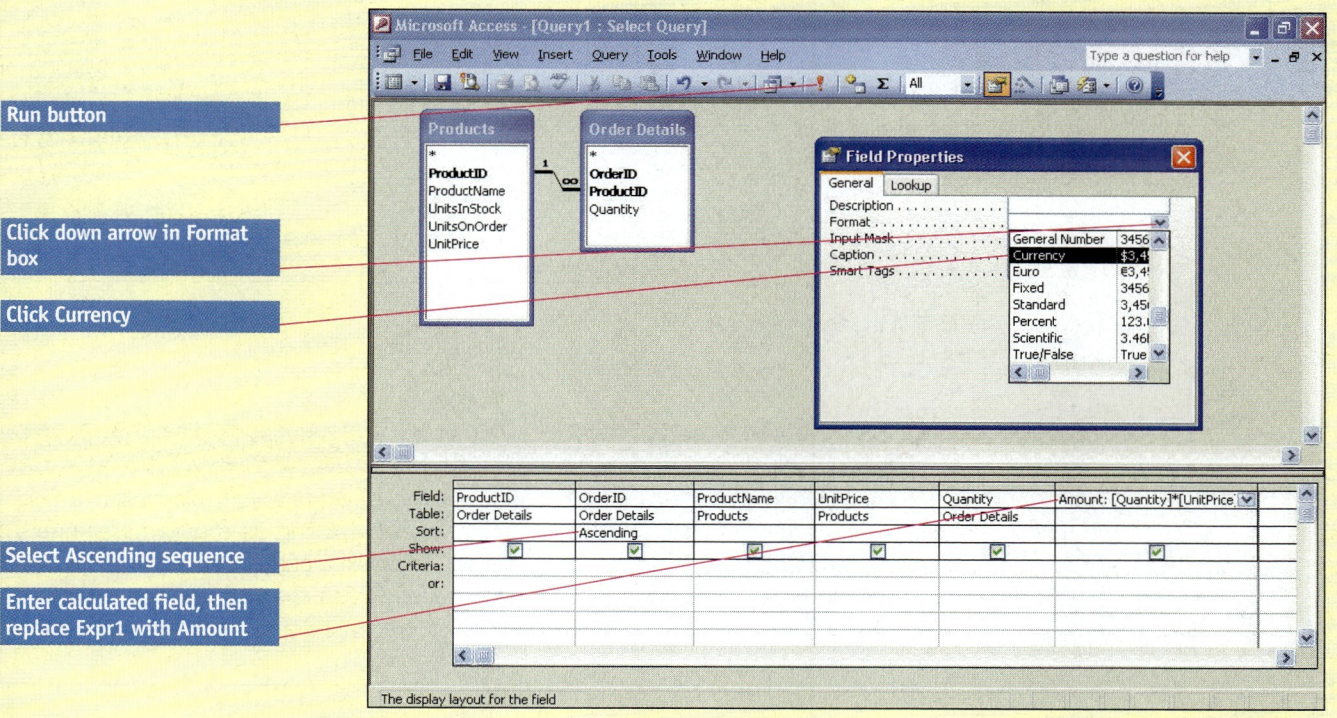

(b) Create the Subform Query (continued) (step 2)

FIGURE 6.6 Hands-on Exercise 2 *(continued)*

Step 3: **Test the Query**

- You should see the dynaset shown in Figure 6.6c. (See the boxed tip if the dynaset does not appear.)

- Enter **1** (not P0001) to change the ProductID to 1 (from 14) in the very first record. (The Format property automatically displays the letter P and the high-order zeros.)

- Press **Enter**. The Product Name changes to a Celeron® at 2.0GHz system as you hit the Enter key. The unit price also changes, as does the computed amount.

- Click the **Undo button** to cancel the change. The ProductID returns to P0014, and the Product Name changes back to HD Floppy Disks (50 pack). The unit price also changes, as does the computed amount.

- Close the query. Save the changes to the query design if prompted to do so.

Undo button

Enter 1 as ProductID

Product data will change when you press Enter key, as will calculated amount

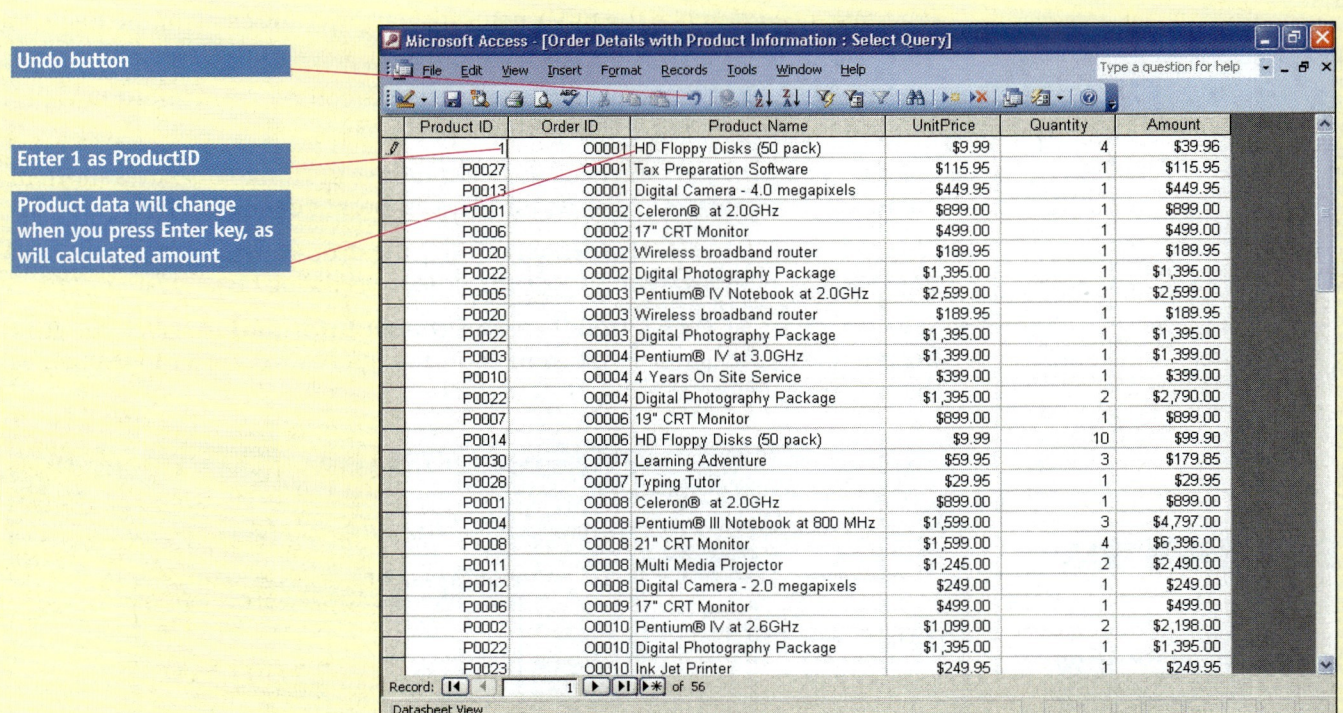

(c) Test the Query (step 3)

FIGURE 6.6 Hands-on Exercise 2 (*continued*)

A PUZZLING ERROR

If you are unable to run a query, it is most likely because you misspelled a field name in the design grid. Access interpets the misspelling as a parameter query (discussed later in the chapter) and asks you to enter a parameter value (the erroneous field name is displayed in the dialog box). Press the Esc key and return to the Design view. Click the field row for the problem field and make the necessary correction.

Step 4:   Create the Orders Form

- Click the **Forms button** in the Database window, then double click the **Create form by using wizard icon** to start the Form Wizard. You should see the dialog box in Figure 6.6d except that no tables have been selected at this time.

- Click the **drop-down arrow** on the Tables/Queries list box to display the tables and queries in the database. Select **Order with Customer Information** (the query we provided), then click the **>> button** to enter all of the fields from the query onto the form.

- Click the **drop-down arrow** to redisplay the tables and queries in the database. Click **Order Details with Product Information** to select this query as shown in Figure 6.6d. Select every field *except* OrderID.

- Be sure that the Selected Fields area contains the selected fields from both queries. Click **Next**. The wizard will prompt you for the additional information it needs to create the form and its associated subform:
  - ❑ The next screen suggests that you view the data by **Order with Customer Information** and that you create a form with subforms. Click **Next**.
  - ❑ The **Datasheet option button** is selected as the default layout for the subform. Click **Next**.
  - ❑ Click **Standard** as the style for your form. Click **Next**.
  - ❑ Enter **Super Store Order form** as the title of the form, but accept the wizard's suggestion for the name of the subform (**Order Details with Product Information subform**).
  - ❑ Click the option button to **Modify the form's design**, then click the **Finish command button** to create the form and exit the Form Wizard.

- You should be in the Design view of the Super Store Order form you just created. Click the **Save button** to save the form and continue working.

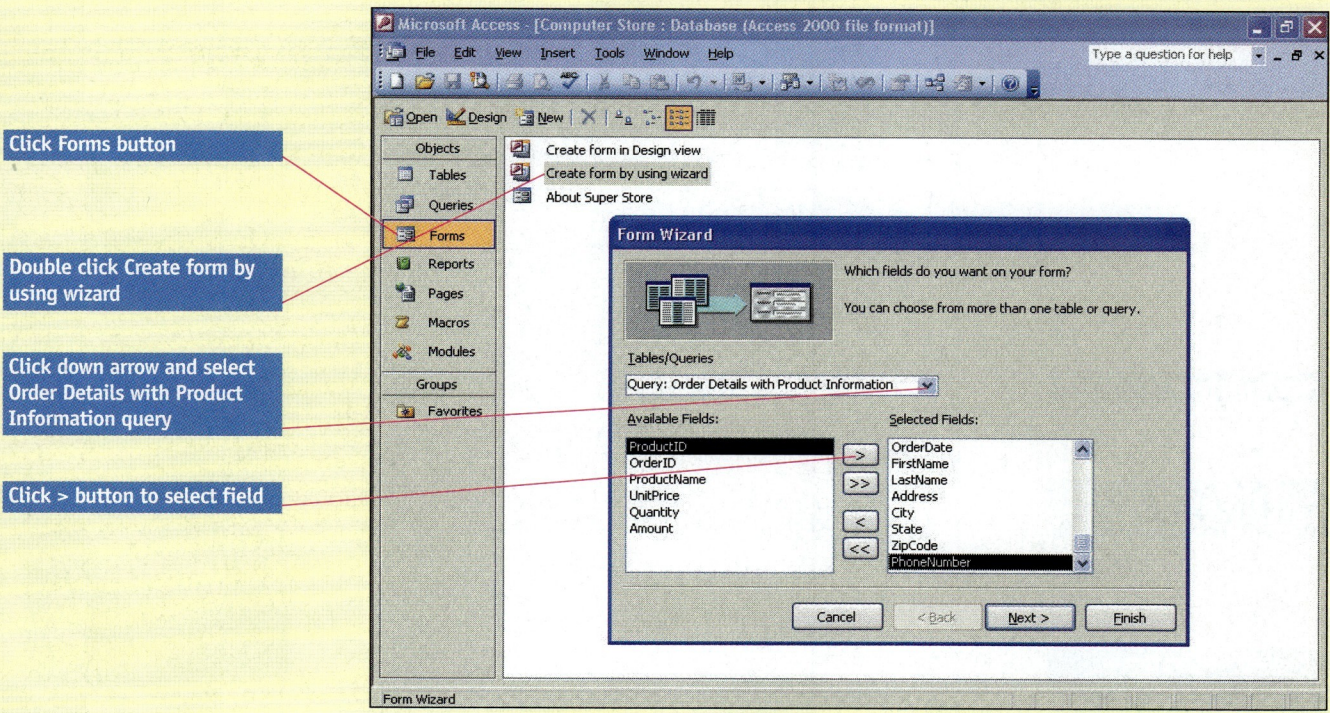

Click Forms button

Double click Create form by using wizard

Click down arrow and select Order Details with Product Information query

Click > button to select field

(d) Create the Orders Form (step 4)

FIGURE 6.6   Hands-on Exercise 2 (*continued*)

Step 5: **Modify the Orders Form**

- You are in the Design view. Maximize the window (if necessary), then **click and drag the bottom of the Details section** down to give yourself additional room in which to work.

- It takes time (and a little practice) to move and size the controls within a form. Try the indicated command, then click the **Undo button** if you are not satisfied with the result.

- Click and drag the control for the subform and its label toward the Form Footer. Select the label of the subform control, then press the **Del key** to delete the label as shown in Figure 6.6e. Click and drag the left border of the subform control toward the left to make the subform wider.

- Click the **PhoneNumber control** to select the control and display the sizing handles, then drag the control above the subform control.

- Click and drag the controls for **City**, **State**, and **ZipCode** (one at a time) on the line above the PhoneNumber control.

- Click and drag the **LastName control** so that it is next to the FirstName control. Click and drag the **Address control** under the control for FirstName.

- Move the **CustomerID control** to the right of the OrderID control. Click and drag the **OrderDate control** so that it is next to the CustomerID. The width of the form will change automatically if the form is not wide enough. You may, however, need to extend the width a little further when you release the mouse.

- Select the **Page Break tool**, then click below the subform control to insert a page break on the form. The page break will print one order per page.

- Adjust the size, spacing, and alignment of the labels and bound controls as necessary, switching back and forth between Form view and Design view.

- Save the form.

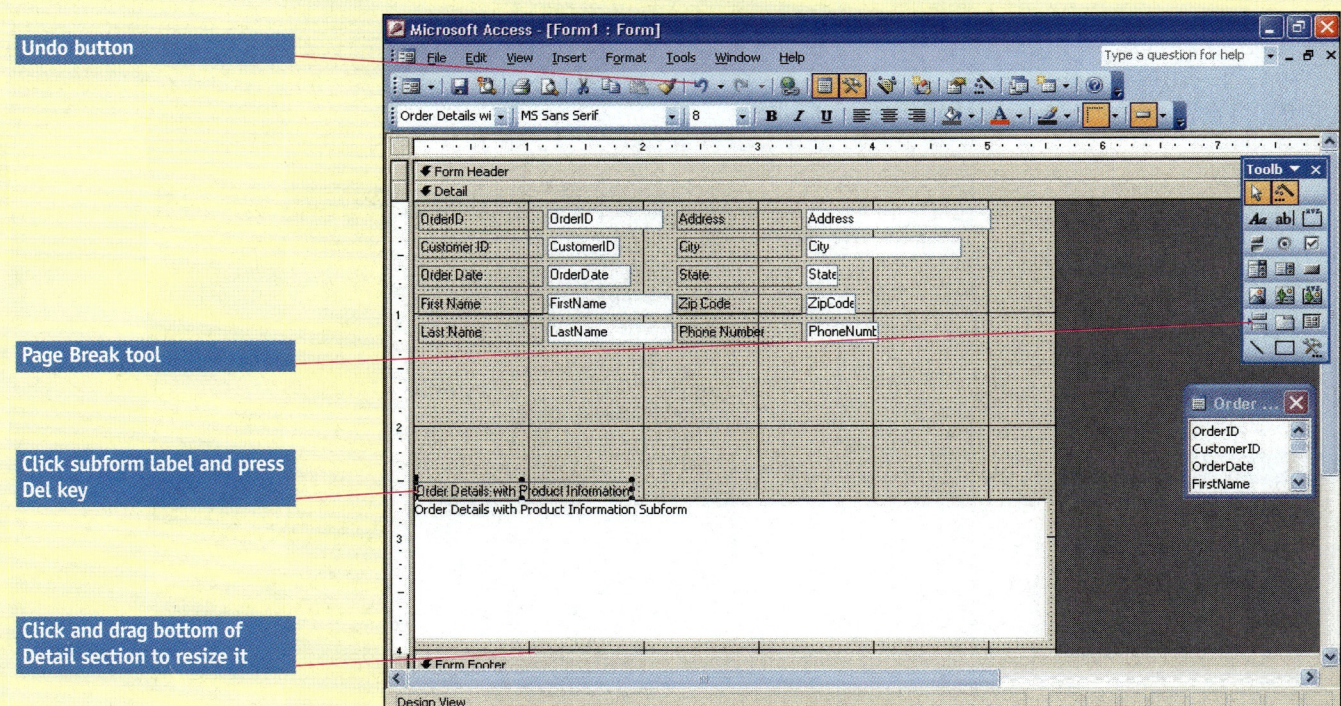

(e) Modify the Orders Form (step 5)

FIGURE 6.6 Hands-on Exercise 2 (*continued*)

Step 6: Change the Column Widths

- Click the **View button** to change to the Form view. You should see the first order in the database together with the associated product information. You may, however, have to adjust the width of the columns within the subform and/or change the size and position of the subform within the main form.

- To change the width of the columns within the subform:
  - ❑ Click the **down arrow** on the **View button** and change to the **Datasheet view**. Click the **plus sign** next to the OrderID column for the first order to display the related records as shown in Figure 6.6f.
  - ❑ Click and drag the border of the various column headings until you can read all of the information. Click the **Save button** to save the new layout, then close the form. You must close the main form, then reopen the form for the changes in the subform to be visible.
  - ❑ You should be back in the Database window. Double click the **Super Store Order form** to reopen the form and check the width of the columns in the subform. If necessary, click the **down arrow** on the **View button** to return to the Datasheet view to further adjust the columns.

- It may also be necessary to change the size or position of the subform within the main form. Click the **View button** and change to the **Design view**.

- Click and drag a sizing handle to change the size of the subform control. Click and drag the subform control to change its position. If necessary, extend the width of the form.

- The process is one of trial and error, but it should take only a few minutes to size the subform properly.

- Save the completed form.

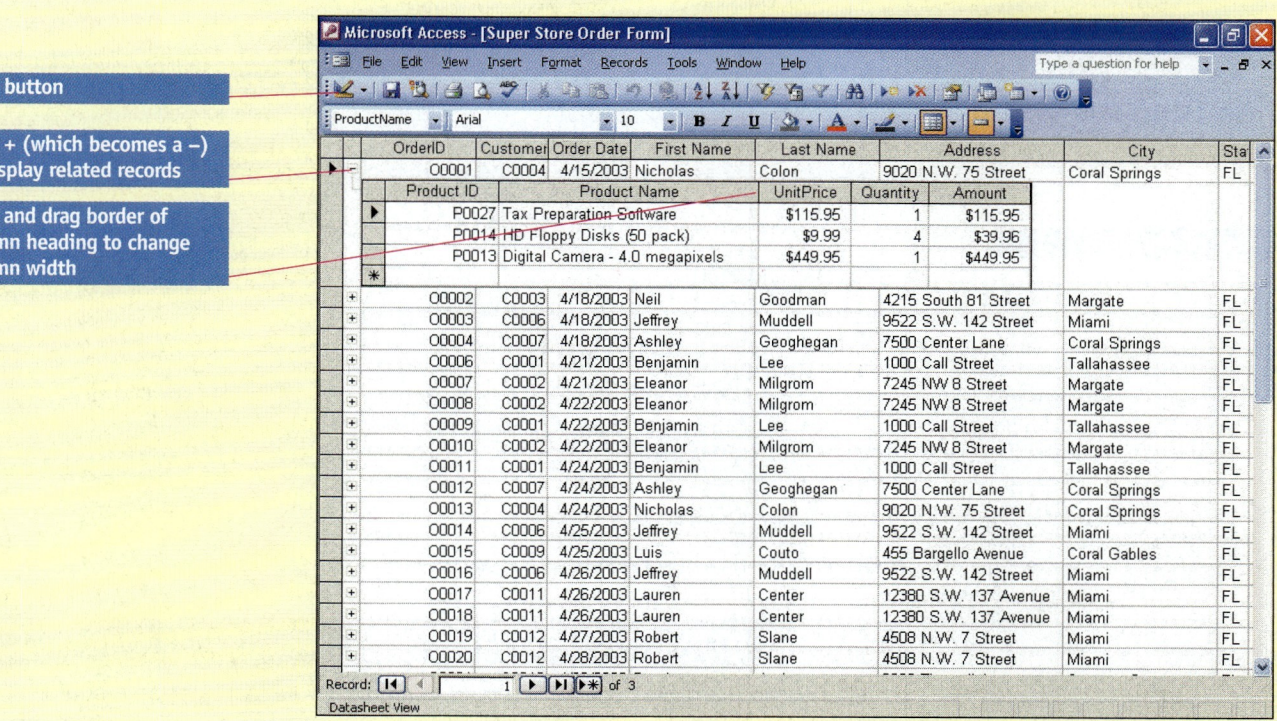

(f) Change the Column Widths (step 6)

FIGURE 6.6 Hands-on Exercise 2 (*continued*)

Step 7: **Enter a New Order**

- Change to the **Form view** of the Super Store Order form as shown in Figure 6.6g. The navigation buttons on the main form move from one order to the next. The navigation buttons on the subform move between products in an order.
- Click the **New Record button** on the main form to display a blank form so that you can place an order. Click in the **CustomerID** text box. Enter **13** (your customer number from exercise 1), then press the **Tab** or **Enter key**.
  - ❏ The OrderID is entered automatically since it is an AutoNumber field.
  - ❏ All of your customer information is entered automatically because of the AutoLookup feature that is built into the underlying query.
  - ❏ Today's date is entered automatically as the default value.
- Click the **ProductID** text box in the subform. Enter **1** (not P0001) and press the **Enter key**. The Product Name and Unit Price are entered automatically.
- Press the **Tab key** twice to move to the Quantity field, enter **1**, and press the **Tab key** twice more to move to the ProductID field for the next item. (The amount is calculated automatically.)
- Complete your order as shown in Figure 6.6g. Print this order. Close the form.
- Exit Access if you do not want to continue with the next exercise at this time.

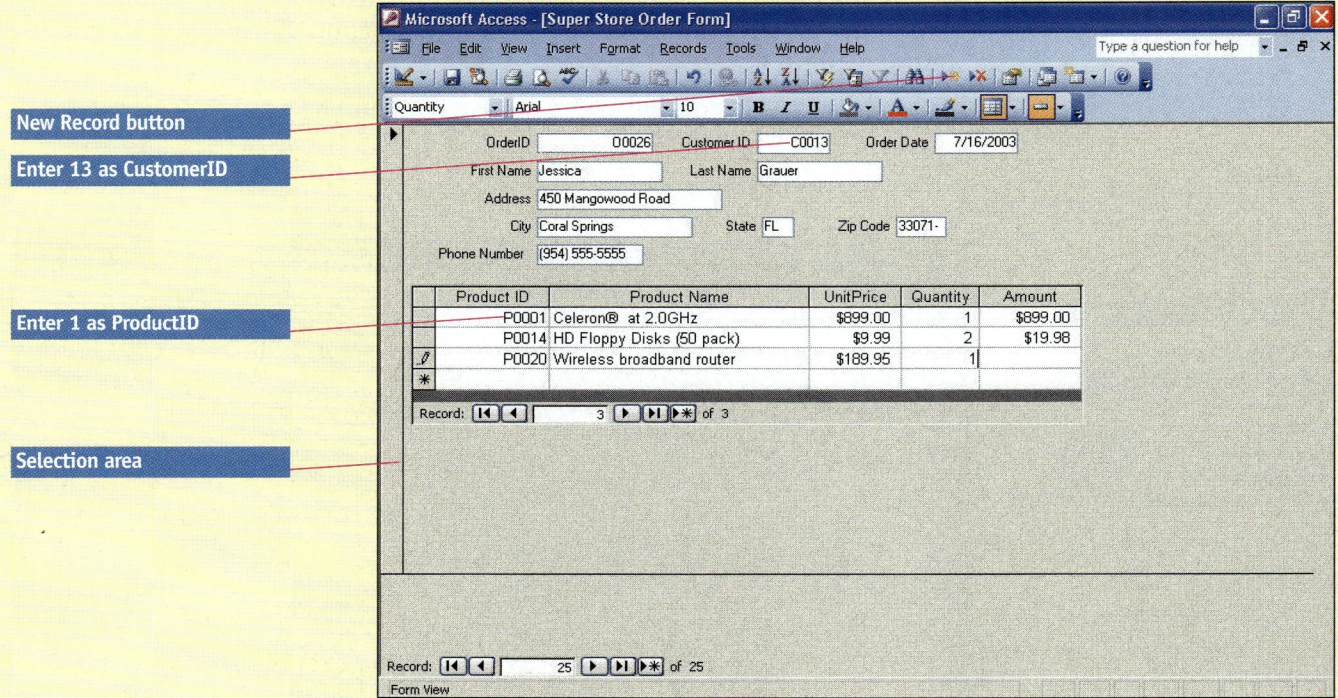

(g) Enter a New Order (step 7)

FIGURE 6.6 Hands-on Exercise 2 (*continued*)

SUBREPORTS AND SUBFORMS—USE WHAT YOU KNOW

A subreport is a report that is inserted into another report, just as a subform is a form inserted onto another form. There are multiple ways to create either type of object; for example, you can use the Form or Report Wizard and select fields from two tables or queries, and let the Wizard do the work. You can also start with a main form or report, then use the Subform/Subreport tool in Design view to create the dependent object. See practice exercise 5 at the end of the chapter.

PARAMETER QUERIES

A select query, powerful as it is, has its limitations. It requires you to enter the criteria directly into the query, which means you have to change the query every time you vary the criteria. What if you wanted to use a different set of criteria (e.g., a different customer's name) every time you ran the "same" query?

A *parameter query* prompts you for the criteria each time you execute the query. It is created in similar fashion to a select query and is illustrated in Figure 6.7. The difference between a parameter query and an ordinary select query is the way in which the criteria are specified. A select query contains the actual criteria. A parameter query, however, contains a *prompt* (message) that will request the criteria when the query is executed.

The design grid in Figure 6.7a creates a parameter query that will display the orders for a particular customer. The query does not contain the customer's name, but a prompt for that name. The prompt is enclosed in square brackets and is displayed in a dialog box in which the user enters the requested data when the query is executed. Thus, the user supplies the customer's name in Figure 6.7b, and the query displays the resulting dynaset in Figure 6.7c. This enables you to run the same query with different criteria; that is, you can enter a different customer name every time you execute the query. (You can also omit the customer name by pressing Enter immediately, in which case you will see every record in the underlying table.)

A parameter query may prompt for any number of variables (parameters), which are entered in successive dialog boxes. The parameters are requested in order from left to right, according to the way in which they appear in the design grid.

TOTAL QUERIES

A *total query* performs calculations on a *group* of records using one of several summary (aggregate) functions available within Access. These include the Sum, Count, Avg, Max, and Min functions to determine the total, number of, average, maximum, and minimum values, respectively. Figure 6.8 illustrates the use of a total query to compute the total amount for each order.

Figure 6.8a displays the dynaset from a select query with fields from both the Products and Order Details tables. (The dynaset contains one record for each product in each order and enables us to verify the results of the total query in Figure 6.8c.) Each record in Figure 6.8a contains the price of the product, the quantity ordered, and the amount for that product. There are, for example, three products in order O0001. The first product costs $449.95, the second product costs $39.96 (four units at $9.99 each), and the third product costs $115.95). The total for the order comes to $605.86, which is obtained by (manually) adding the amount field in each of the records for this order.

Figure 6.8b shows the Design view of the total query to calculate the cost of each order. The query contains only two fields, OrderID and Amount. The QBE grid also displays a *Total row* in which each field in the query has either a Group By or aggregate entry. The *Group By* entry under OrderID indicates that the records in the dynaset are to be grouped (aggregated) according to the like values of OrderID; that is, there will be one record in the total query for each distinct value of OrderID. The *Sum function* specifies the arithmetic operation to be performed on that field for each group of records.

The dynaset in Figure 6.8c displays the result of the total query and contains *aggregate* records, as opposed to *individual* records. There are three records for order O0001 in Figure 6.8a, but only one record in Figure 6.8c. This is because each record in a total query contains a calculated result for a group of records. In similar fashion, there are four detail records for order O0002 but only one summary record.

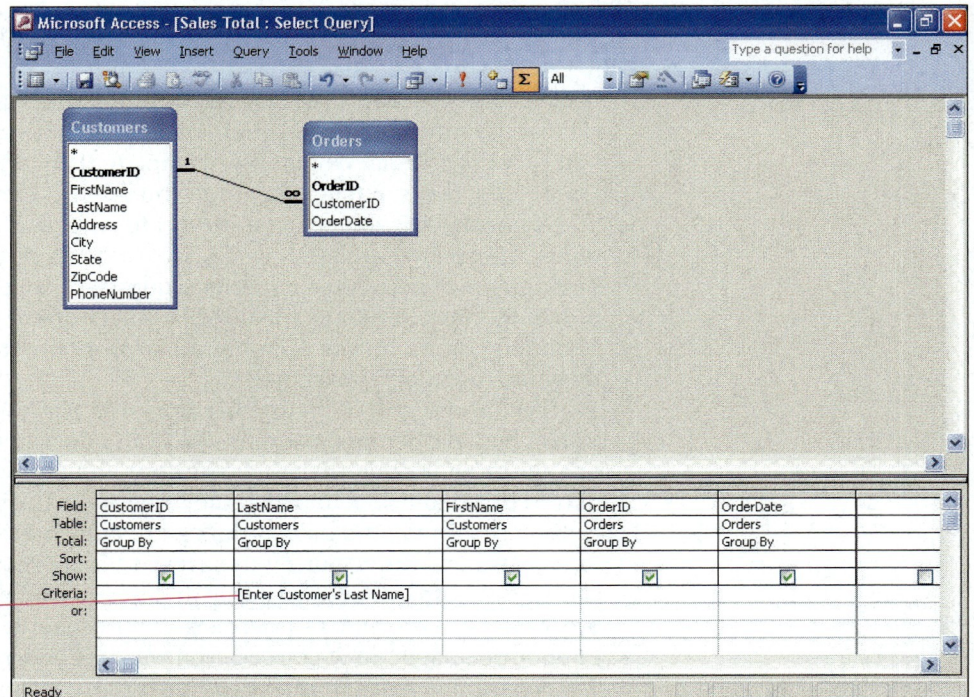

Prompt is entered in Criteria row between square brackets

(a) Design grid

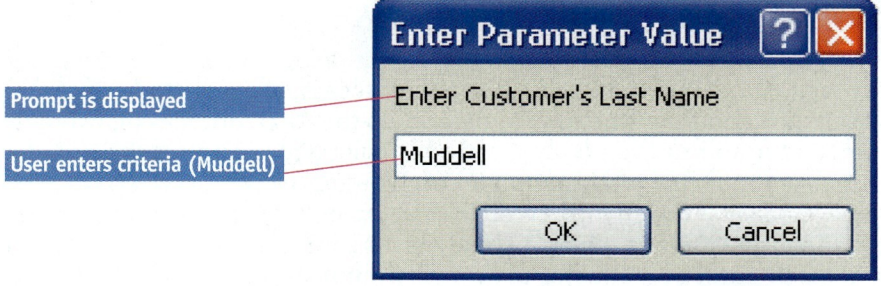

Prompt is displayed

User enters criteria (Muddell)

(b) Dialog Box

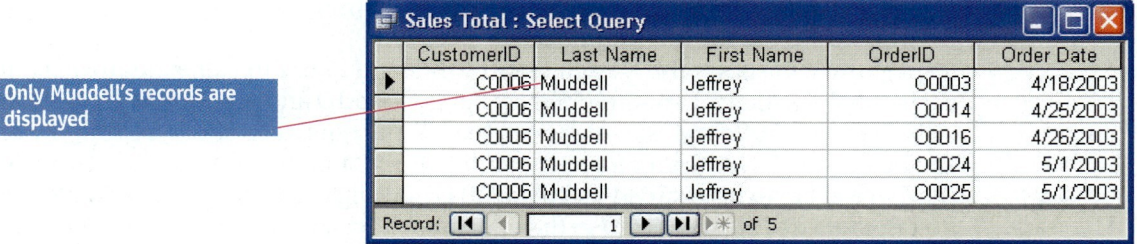

Only Muddell's records are displayed

(c) Dynaset

FIGURE 6.7 Parameter Query

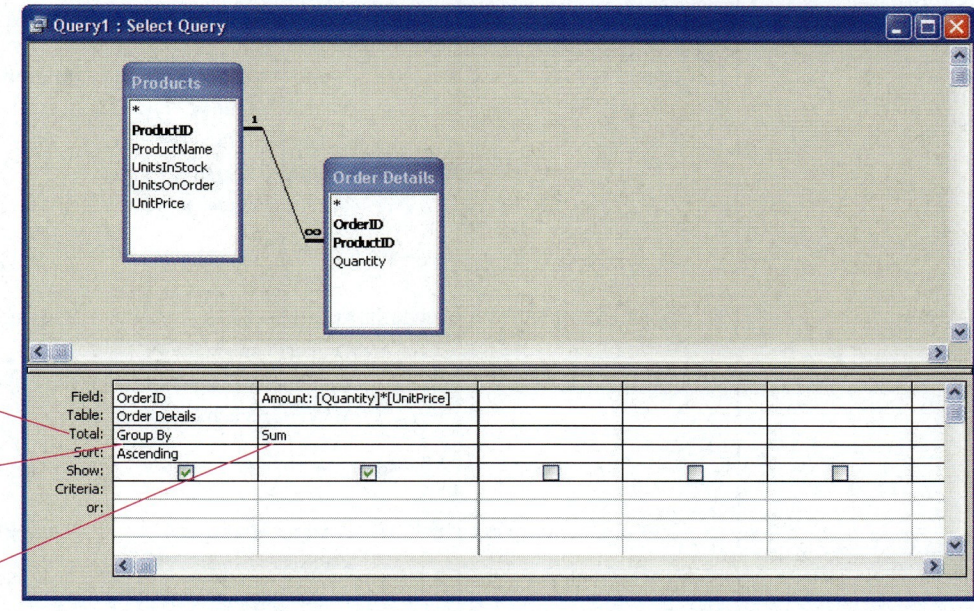

Three products are included in order 00001

Amount of each product in order 00001 is shown

OrderID	Product ID	Product Name	UnitPrice	Quantity	Amount
00001	P0013	Digital Camera - 4.0 megapixels	$449.95	1	$449.95
00001	P0014	HD Floppy Disks (50 pack)	$9.99	4	$39.96
00001	P0027	Tax Preparation Software	$115.95	1	$115.95
00002	P0001	Celeron® at 2.0GHz	$899.00	1	$899.00
00002	P0006	17" CRT Monitor	$499.00	1	$499.00
00002	P0020	Wireless broadband router	$189.95	1	$189.95
00002	P0022	Digital Photography Package	$1,395.00	1	$1,395.00
00003	P0005	Pentium® IV Notebook at 2.0GHz	$2,599.00	1	$2,599.00
00003	P0020	Wireless broadband router	$189.95	1	$189.95
00003	P0022	Digital Photography Package	$1,395.00	1	$1,395.00
00004	P0003	Pentium® IV at 3.0GHz	$1,399.00	1	$1,399.00
00004	P0010	4 Years On Site Service	$399.00	1	$399.00
00004	P0022	Digital Photography Package	$1,395.00	2	$2,790.00
00006	P0007	19" CRT Monitor	$899.00	1	$899.00
00006	P0014	HD Floppy Disks (50 pack)	$9.99	10	$99.90
00007	P0028	Typing Tutor	$29.95	1	$29.95
00007	P0030	Learning Adventure	$59.95	3	$179.85
00008	P0001	Celeron® at 2.0GHz	$899.00	1	$899.00
00008	P0004	Pentium® III Notebook at 800 MHz	$1,599.00	3	$4,797.00
00008	P0008	21" CRT Monitor	$1,599.00	4	$6,396.00
00008	P0011	Multi Media Projector	$1,245.00	2	$2,490.00
00008	P0012	Digital Camera - 2.0 megapixels	$249.00	1	$249.00

Record: 1 of 59

(a) Order Details with Product Information Dynaset

Total row

Records are grouped by OrderID

Calculation to be performed on group is Sum of Amount field

Field:	OrderID	Amount: [Quantity]*[UnitPrice]			
Table:	Order Details				
Total:	Group By	Sum			
Sort:	Ascending				
Show:	☑	☑	☐	☐	☐
Criteria:					
or:					

(b) Design grid

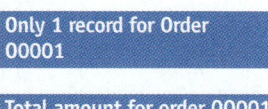

Only 1 record for Order 00001

Total amount for order 00001

Order ID	Amount
00001	$605.86
00002	$2,982.95
00003	$4,183.95
00004	$4,588.00
00006	$998.90
00007	$209.80
00008	$14,831.00

Record: 1

(c) Dynaset

FIGURE 6.8 Total Query

The exercise that follows begins by having you create the report in Figure 6.9. The report is a detailed analysis of all orders, listing every product in every order. The report is based on a query containing fields from the Orders, Customers, Products, and Order Details tables. The exercise also provides practice in creating parameter queries and total queries. Note, too, the attractive formatting throughout the report in addition to the clip art in the report header.

Sales Analysis by Order
Prepared by: Your Name Goes Here

O0001 Colon	4 /15/2003	Product Name	Quantity	Unit Price	Amount
		Digital Camera - 4.0 megapixels	1	$449.95	$449.95
		HD Floppy Disks (50 pack)	4	$9.99	$39.96
		Tax Preparation Software	1	$115.95	$115.95
				Sum	$605.86

O0002 Goodman	4 /18/2003	Product Name	Quantity	Unit Price	Amount
		17" CRT Monitor	1	$499.00	$499.00
		Celeron® at 2.0GHz	1	$899.00	$899.00
		Digital Photography Package	1	$1,395.00	$1,395.00
		Wireless broadband router	1	$189.95	$189.95
				Sum	$2,982.95

O0003 Muddell	4 /18/2003	Product Name	Quantity	Unit Price	Amount
		Digital Photography Package	1	$1,395.00	$1,395.00
		Pentium® IV Notebook at 2.0GHz	1	$2,599.00	$2,599.00
		Wireless broadband router	1	$189.95	$189.95
				Sum	$4,183.95

O0004 Geoghegan	4 /18/2003	Product Name	Quantity	Unit Price	Amount
		4 Years On Site Service	1	$399.00	$399.00
		Digital Photography Package	2	$1,395.00	$2,790.00
		Pentium® IV at 3.0GHz	1	$1,399.00	$1,399.00
				Sum	$4,588.00

O0006 Lee	4 /21/2003	Product Name	Quantity	Unit Price	Amount
		19" CRT Monitor	1	$899.00	$899.00
		HD Floppy Disks (50 pack)	10	$9.99	$99.90
				Sum	$998.90

Wednesday, July 16, 2003   Page 1 of 5

FIGURE 6.9 Sales Analysis by Order

3   Advanced Queries

Objective   To copy an existing query; to create a parameter query; to create a total query using the Aggregate Sum function. Use Figure 6.10 as a guide.

Step 1:   **Create the Query**

- Open the **Computer Store database** from the previous exercise. Click the **Queries button** in the Database window. Double click **Create query in Design view** to display the Query Design window.

- By now you have had sufficient practice creating a query, so we will just outline the steps:
  - Add the **Customers**, **Orders**, **Products**, and **Order Details** tables. Move and size the field lists within the Query window to match Figure 6.10a. Maximize the window.
  - Add the **OrderID** field from the Orders table. Add the additional fields to the design grid as shown in Figure 6.10a. Be sure to take each field from the appropriate table.
  - Add the calculated field to compute the amount by multiplying the quantity by the unit price. Point to the expression, click the **right mouse button** to display a shortcut menu, then change the Format property to **Currency**.
  - Check that your query matches Figure 6.10a. Save the query as **Sales Analysis by Order**.

- Click the **Run button** (the exclamation point) to run the query. The dynaset contains one record for every item in every order.

- Close the query.

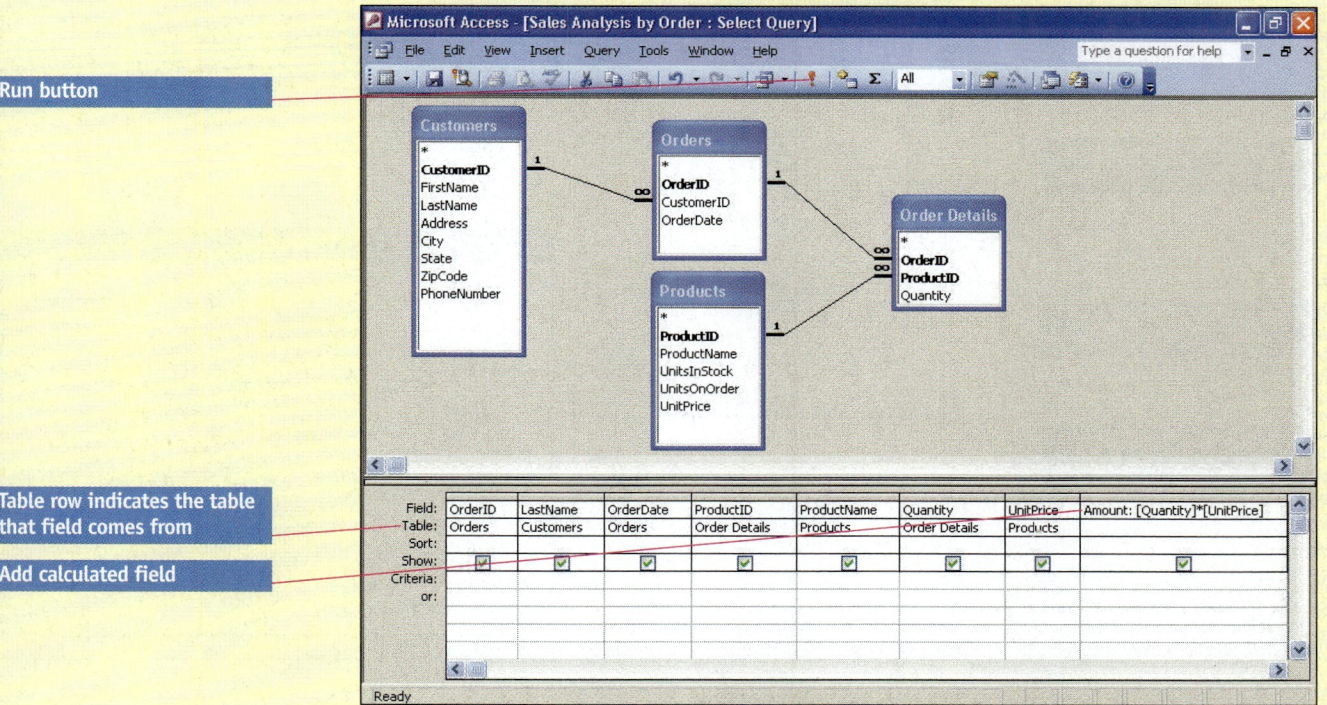

Run button

Table row indicates the table that field comes from

Add calculated field

(a) Create the Query (step 1)

FIGURE 6.10   Hands-on Exercise 3

Step 2: The Report Wizard

- Click the **Reports button** in the Database window. Double click the **Create report by using wizard** icon to start the Report Wizard.

- Click the **drop-down arrow** to display the tables and queries in the database, then select **Sales Analysis by Order** (the query you just created).

- By now you have had sufficient practice using the Report Wizard, so we will just outline the steps:
  - ❏ Select all of the fields in the query *except* the ProductID. Click the **>> button** to move every field in the Available Fields list box to the Selected Fields list.
  - ❏ Select the **ProductID field** in the Selected Fields list and click the **< button** to remove this field. Click **Next**.
  - ❏ Group the report by **OrderID**. Click **Next**.
  - ❏ Sort the report by **ProductName**. Click the **Summary Options button** to display the Summary Options dialog box in Figure 6.10b. Check **Sum** under the Amount field. The option button to **Show Detail and Summary** is selected. Click **OK** to close the Summary Options dialog box. Click **Next**.
  - ❏ The **Stepped Layout** is selected, as is **Portrait orientation**. Be sure the box is checked to **Adjust field width so all fields fit on a page**. Click **Next**.
  - ❏ Choose **Soft Gray** as the style. Click **Next**.
  - ❏ **Sales Analysis by Order** is entered as the title of the report. The option button to **Preview the Report** is selected. Click **Finish**.

- The report you see approximates the finished report, but requires several modifications to improve the formatting. The OrderDate and LastName, for example, are repeated for every product in an order, when they should appear only once in the Group (OrderID) Header.

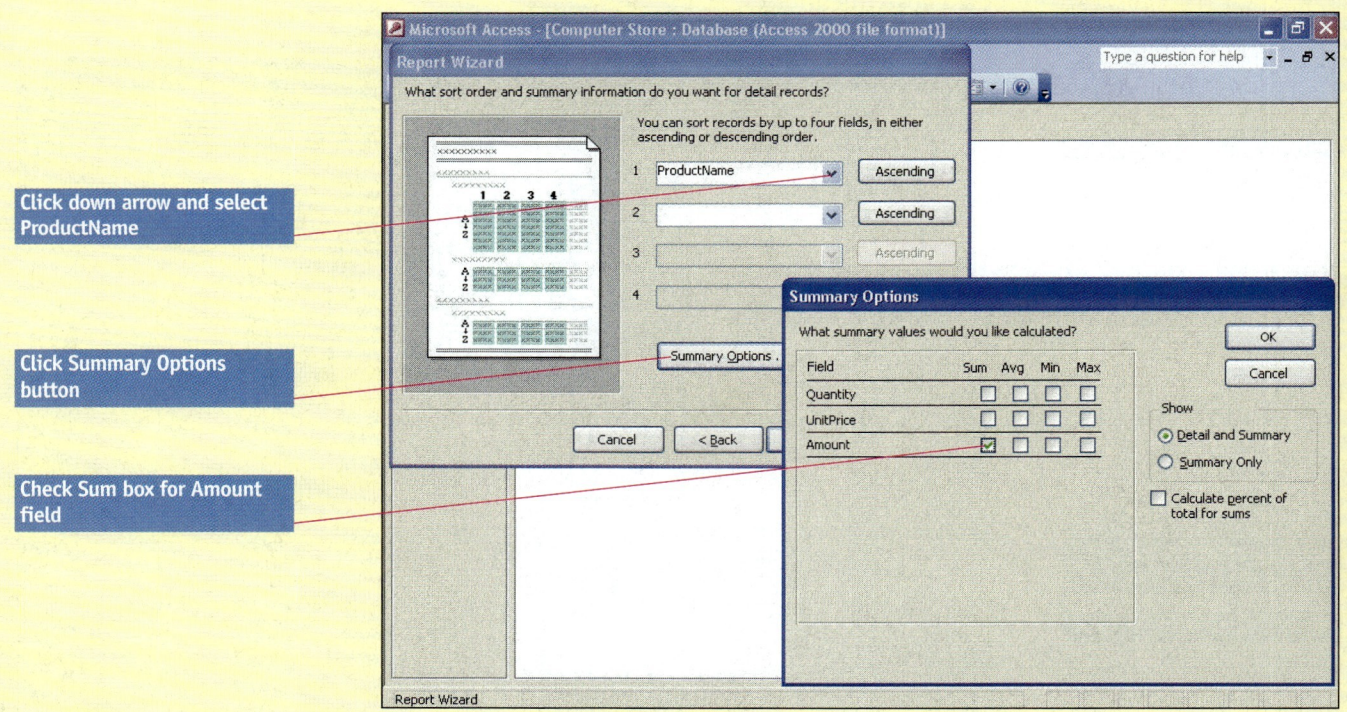

Click down arrow and select ProductName

Click Summary Options button

Check Sum box for Amount field

(b) The Report Wizard (step 2)

FIGURE 6.10 Hands-on Exercise 3 (*continued*)

Step 3: Modify the Report Design

- Change to **Design view**. Pull down the **View menu** and click the **Sorting and Grouping command** to display the dialog box in Figure 6.10c.

- Click in the **OrderID** box under Field/Expression. Click the **down arrow** in the **Keep Together property** and choose **Whole Group**. Close the dialog box.

- Press and hold the **Shift key** as you click the **LastName** and **OrderDate controls** in the Detail Area, then drag the controls to the Group Header next to the OrderID. Click anywhere to deselect the controls.

- Press and hold the **Shift key** to select the **OrderID**, **LastName**, and **OrderDate** labels in the Page Header. Press the **Del key** to delete the labels.

- Click and drag the **Product Name label** from the Page Header to the OrderID header. Press and hold the **Shift key** to select the remaining labels (**Quantity**, **UnitPrice**, and **Amount**) in the Page Header and drag them to the OrderID header. Move, size, and align the labels as necessary.

- Click the **OrderID control** in the Group Header. Click the **right mouse button**, click **Properties**, and change the Border Style to **Transparent**. Close the Properties dialog box. Move, size, and align the controls as necessary.

- Select (click) the first control in the OrderID footer (which begins with the literal ="Summary for). Press the **Del key**.

- Click and drag the unbound control containing the word **Sum** to the right of the Group Footer so that the label is next to the computed total for each order. Change the font size for the label and calculated control to **10 points**. Do the same for the **Grand Total** label in the Report Footer.

- Save the report, then click the **Report View button** to preview the report.

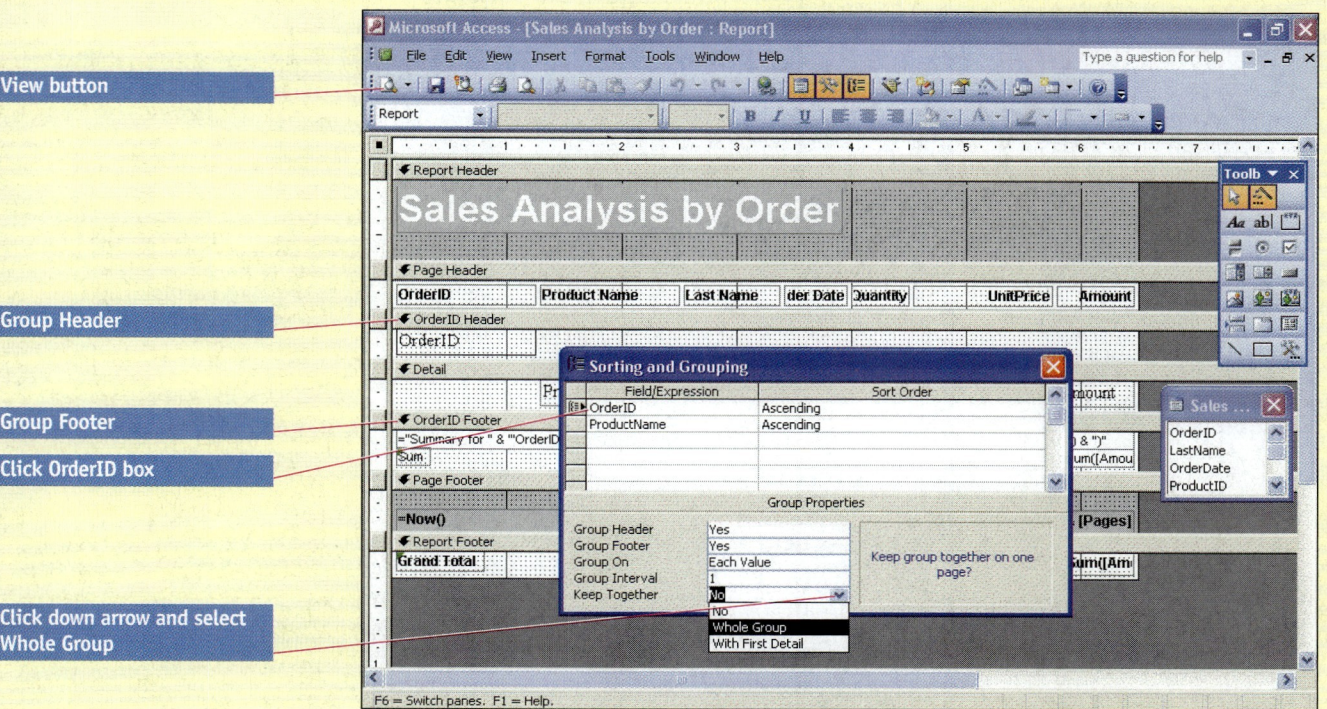

(c) Modify the Report Design (step 3)

FIGURE 6.10 Hands-on Exercise 3 (*continued*)

Step 4: **Complete the Report Design**

- Return to **Design view** as shown in Figure 6.10d. This is our goal, but do not be concerned if you do not duplicate our report exactly.

- Press and hold the **Shift key** to select the **OrderID**, **LastName**, and **OrderDate controls** in the OrderID header. These are controls and not labels. Change to **9 point bold Arial** to match the formatting of the labels in this header.

- Move and size the **ProductName**, **Quantity**, **UnitPrice**, and **Amount controls** in the Detail area so they are under their respective labels in the OrderID header. Change back and forth between Design view and Print Preview to check your work.

- Click the **Line tool**. Click at the bottom of the OrderID footer, then press and hold the **Shift key** as you drag the mouse to draw a line of approximately one inch. Right click the line, click the **Properties command**, then change the **width** to **6.5 inches**. Close the Properties sheet.

- Look closely and you will see a gray line in the Page Header. Select the line and click the **Del key**. Close the Page Header.

- Click in the Report Header. Use the **Label tool** to enter your name. Pull down the **Insert menu** and click the **Picture command** to display the Insert Picture dialog box. Change to the **Exploring Access folder**.

- Select the **Computer picture**, then click **OK** to insert the picture into the report. Be sure you insert the picture in the Report Header.

- **Right click** the picture to display a context-sensitive menu, then click **Properties** to display the Property dialog box. Click the **Size Mode property**, click the **down arrow**, and click **Stretch**. Close the Properties sheet.

- Click and drag to size the picture. Resize the Report Header as appropriate. View the report. Make additional corrections as necessary.

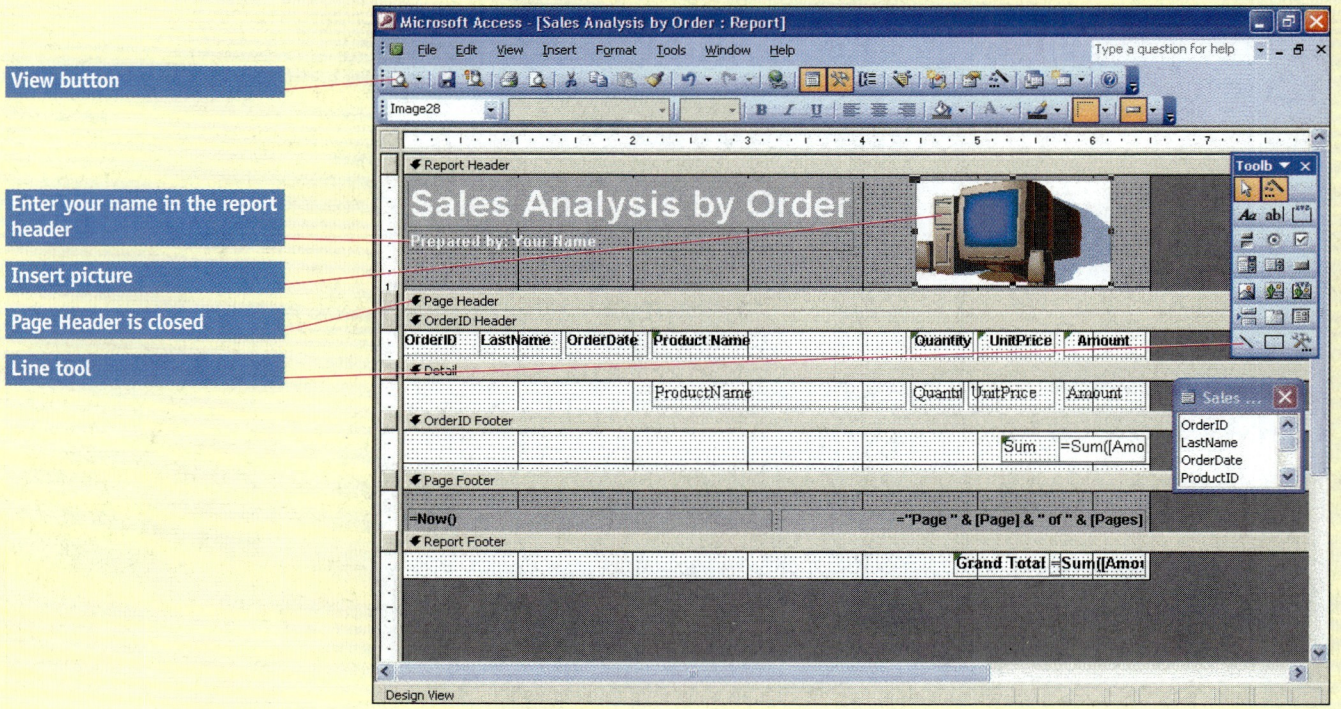

(d) Complete the Report Design (step 4)

FIGURE 6.10 Hands-on Exercise 3 (*continued*)

Step 5: **Print the Report**

- You should see the report in Figure 6.10e, which groups the reports by OrderID. The products are in alphabetical order within each order.

- Click the **Zoom button** to see the entire page. Click the **Zoom button** a second time to return to the higher magnification.

- Use the navigation buttons at the bottom of the window to see other pages in the report.

- Click the **Printer button** if you are satisfied with the appearance of the report, or return to the Design view to make any needed changes.

- Pull down the **File menu** and click **Close** to close the report. Click **Yes** if asked whether to save the changes.

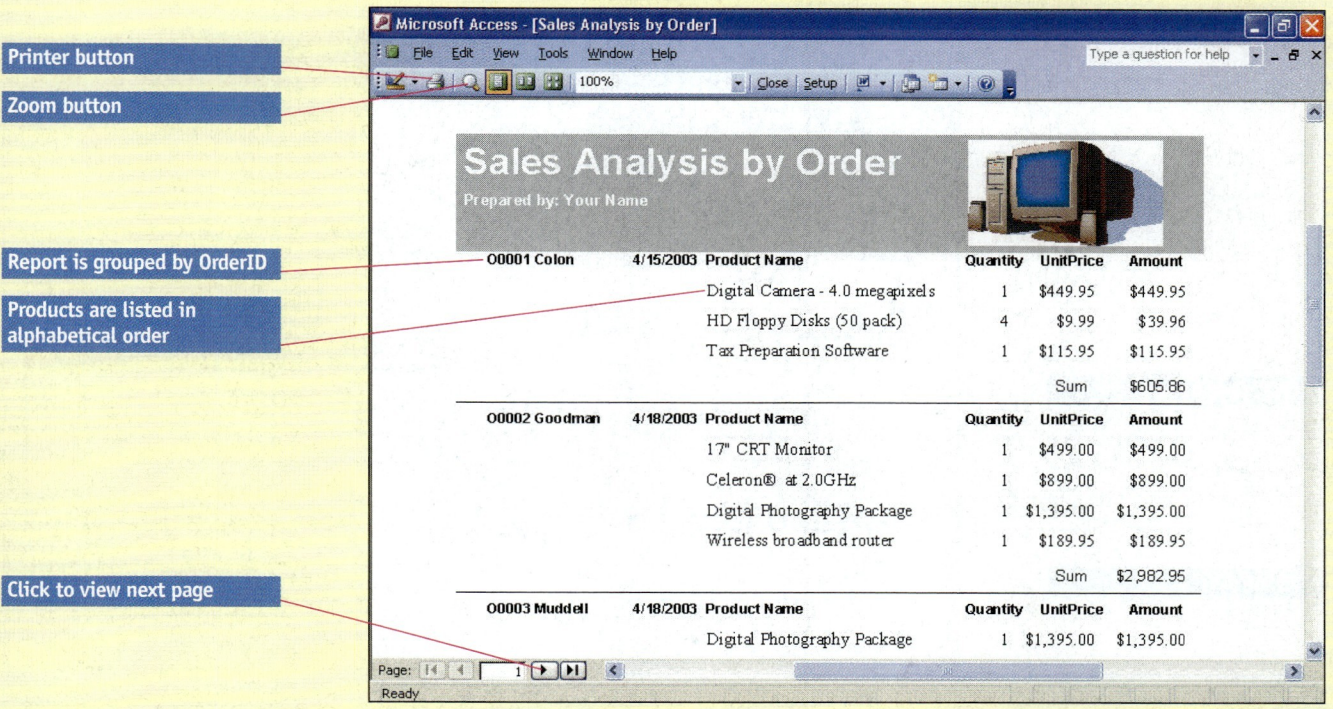

(e) Print the Report (step 5)

FIGURE 6.10 Hands-on Exercise 3 (*continued*)

THE UNMATCHED QUERY WIZARD

The cost of inventory is a significant expense for every business. It is one thing to maintain inventory of products that are selling well, and quite another to stock products that have never been ordered. The Unmatched Query Wizard identifies records in one table (such as the Products table) that do not have matching records in another table (such as the Order Details table). In other words, it will tell you which products (if any) have never been ordered. See exercise 2 at the end of the chapter.

Step 6: Create a Total Query

- Open the **Sales Analysis by Order** query in Design view as shown in Figure 6.10f. (The Save As dialog box is not yet visible.)

- Click the **column selector** for the **OrderDate field** to select the column. Press the **Del key** to delete the field from the query. Delete the **ProductID**, **ProductName**, **Quantity**, and **UnitPrice fields** in similar fashion.

- Pull down the **View menu** and click **Totals** to display the Total row (or click the **Totals button** on the toolbar).

- Click the **Total row** under the Amount field, then click the **drop-down arrow** to display the summary functions. Click **Sum** as shown in the figure.

- Pull down the **File menu** and click the **Save As command** to display the associated dialog box. Enter **Sales Total** as the name of the query. Click **OK**.

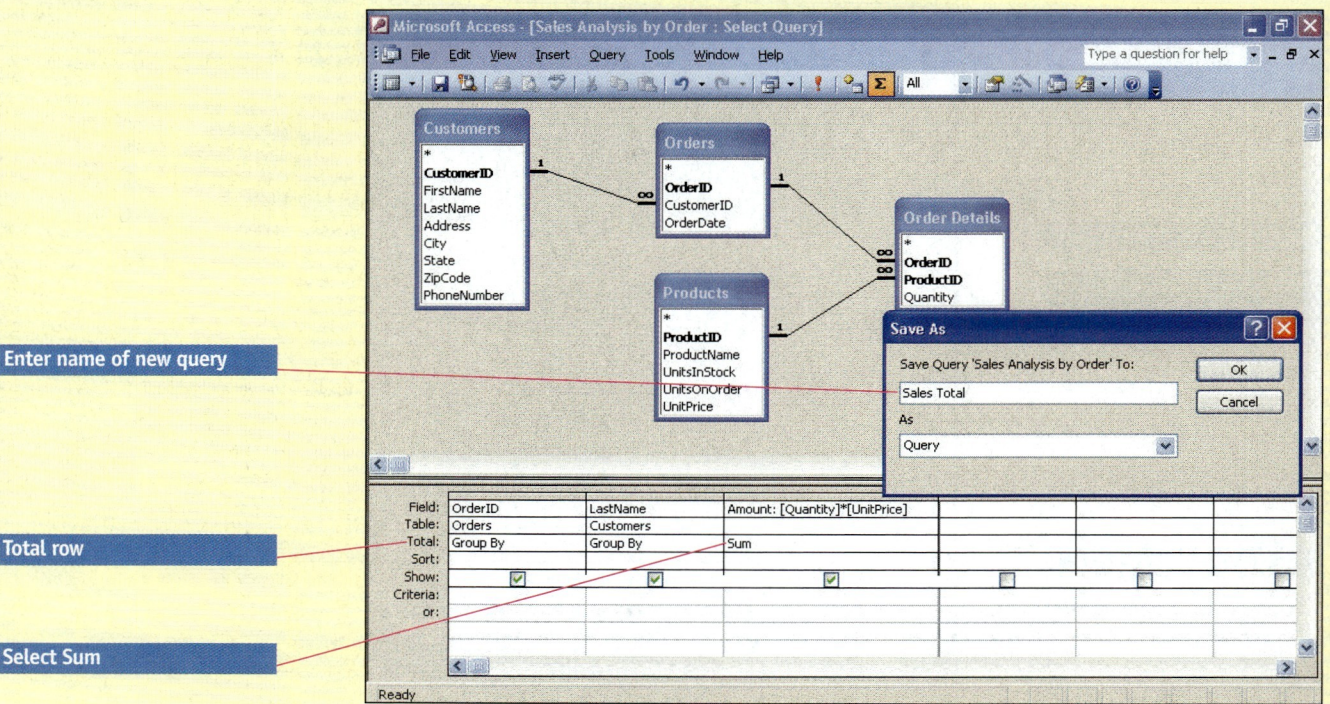

(f) Create a Total Query (step 6)

FIGURE 6.10 Hands-on Exercise 3 (*continued*)

THE DESCRIPTION PROPERTY

A working database will contain many different objects of the same type, making it all too easy to forget the purpose of the individual objects. The Description property helps you to remember. Point to any object within the Database window, click the right mouse button to display a shortcut menu, click Properties to display the Properties dialog box, enter an appropriate description, then click OK to close the Properties sheet. Once a description has been created, you can right click any object in the Database window, then click the Properties command from the shortcut menu to display the information.

Step 7: Run the Query

- Pull down the **Query menu** and click **Run** (or click the **Run button**) to run the query. You should see the datasheet in Figure 6.10g, which contains one record for each order with the total amount of that order.

- Click any field and attempt to change its value. You will be unable to do so as indicated by the beep.

- Print the dynaset for your instructor to show that you have successfully created the totals query.

- Click the **View button** to return to the Query Design view.

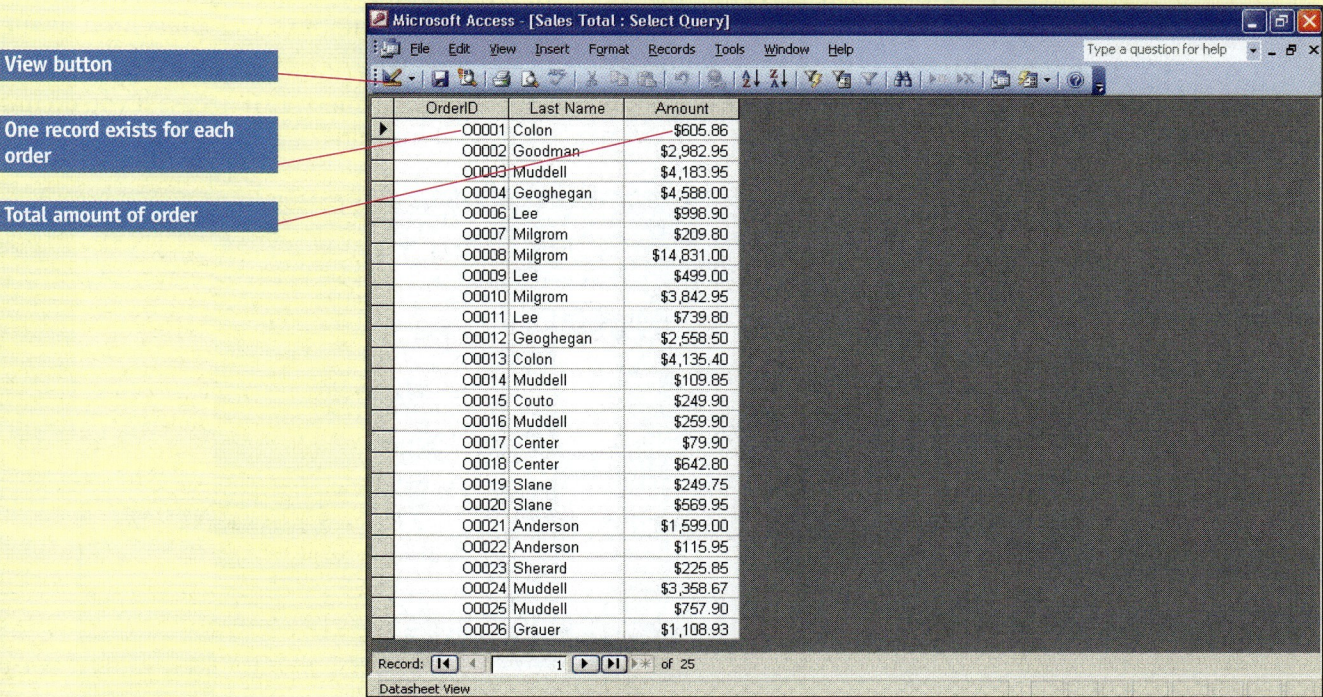

View button

One record exists for each order

Total amount of order

(g) Run the Query (step 7)

FIGURE 6.10 Hands-on Exercise 3 (*continued*)

UPDATING THE QUERY

The changes made to a query's dynaset are automatically made in the underlying table(s). Not every field in a query is updatable, however, and the easiest way to determine if you can change a value is to run the query, view the dynaset, and attempt to edit the field. Access will prevent you from updating a calculated field, a field based on an aggregate function (such as Sum or Count), or the join field on the "one side" of a one-to-many relationship. If you attempt to update a field you cannot change, the system will beep.

Step 8: **Create a Parameter Query**

- Add the **OrderDate** and **PhoneNumber** fields to the query as shown in Figure 6.10h.

- Click the **Criteria row** under **LastName**. Type [**Enter Customer's Last Name**]. Be sure to enclose the entry in square brackets.

- Pull down the **file menu**. Click **Save As**. Enter **Customer Parameter Query** in the Save Query "Sales Total" To box. Click **OK**.

- Run the query. Access will display the dialog box in Figure 6.10h, asking for the Customer's last name. Type **Muddell** and press **Enter**.

- Access displays the five orders for Jeffrey Muddell. (This is the same information that you retrieved manually when the database was presented at the beginning of the chapter.)

- Print the dynaset for your instructor. Close the query. Exit Access if you do not want to continue with the next exercise at this time.

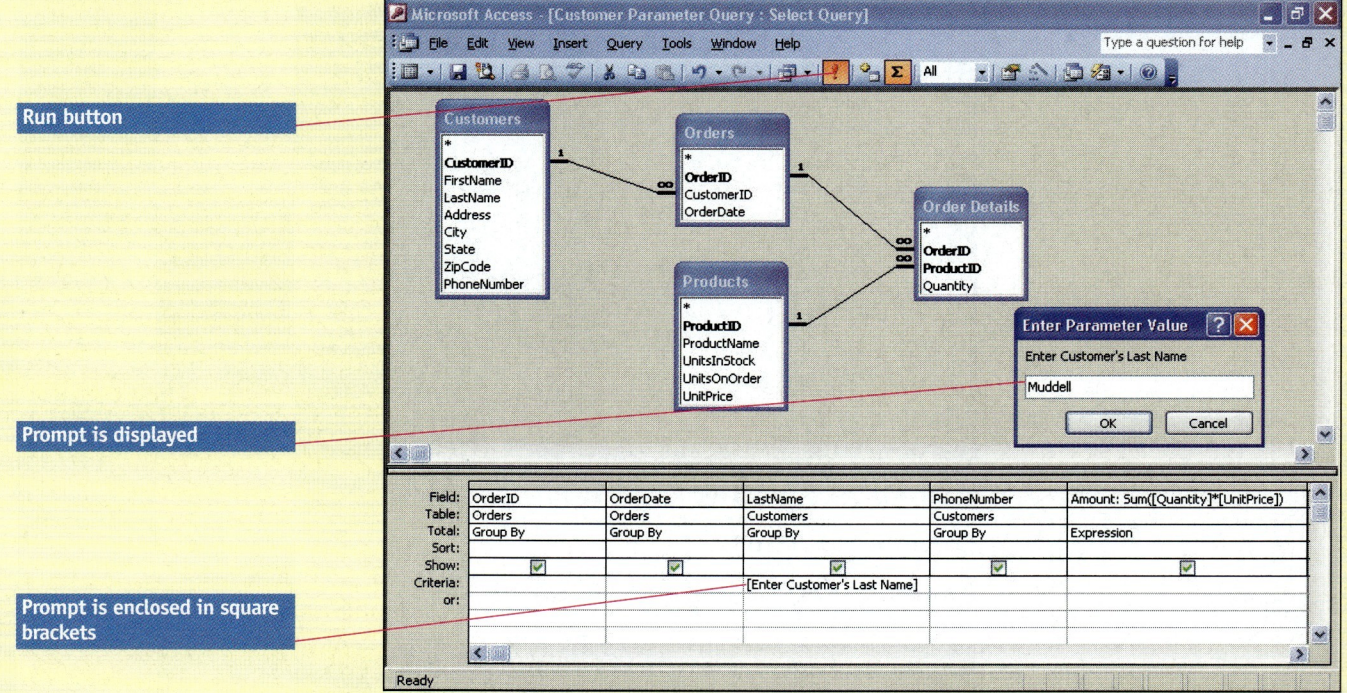

(h) Create a Parameter Query (step 8)

FIGURE 6.10 Hands-on Exercise 3 (*continued*)

THE TOPVALUES PROPERTY

The TopValues property returns a designated number of records rather than the entire dynaset. Open the query in Design view, then click the right mouse button *outside* the design grid to display a shortcut menu. Click Properties, click the box for TopValues, and enter the desired value as either a number or a percent; for example, 5 to list the top five records, or 5% to display the records that make up the top five percent. The dynaset must be in sequence according to the desired field for the TopValues property to work properly.

One of the advantages of an Access database is that it can be easily expanded to include additional data without disturbing the existing tables. The database used throughout the chapter consisted of four tables: a Customers table, a Products table, an Orders table, and an Order Details table. Figure 6.11 extends the Computer Super Store database to include a Sales Persons table with data about each member of the sales staff.

The salesperson helps the customer as he or she comes into the store, then receives a commission based on the order. There is a one-to-many relationship between the salesperson and orders. One salesperson can generate many orders, but an order can have only one salesperson. (One customer can work with a different salesperson each time he or she enters the store; i.e., there is no direct relationship between customers and the sales staff.) The Sales Persons and Orders tables are joined by the SalesPersonID field, which is common to both tables.

Figure 6.11 is similar to Figure 6.1 at the beginning of the chapter except that the Sales Persons table has been added and the Orders table has been expanded to include a SalesPersonID. This enables management to monitor the performance of the sales staff. Consider:

Query: How many orders has Cori Rice taken?
Answer: Cori has taken five orders.

The query is straightforward and easily answered. You would search the Sales Persons table for Cori Rice to determine her SalesPerson ID (S03). You would then search the Orders table and count the records containing S03 in the SalesPersonID field.

The Sales Persons table is also used to generate a report listing the commissions due to each salesperson. The store pays a 5% commission on every sale. It's easy to determine the salesperson for each order. It's more complicated to compute the commission. Consider:

Query: Which salesperson is associated with order O0003? When was this person hired?
Answer: Cori Rice is the salesperson for order O0003. Ms. Rice was hired on March 15, 1999.

The determination of the salesperson is straightforward, as all you have to do is search the Orders table to locate the order and obtain the SalesPerson ID (S03). You then search the Sales Persons table for this value (S03) and find the corresponding name (Cori Rice) and hire date (3/15/99).

Query: What is the commission on order O0003?
Answer: The commission on order O0003 is $209.20.

The calculation of the commission requires a fair amount of arithmetic. First, you need to compute the total amount of the order. Thus, you would begin in the Order Details table, find each product in order O0003, and multiply the quantity of that product by its unit price. The total cost of order O0003 is $4,183.95, based on one unit of product P0005 at $2,599, one unit of product P0020 at $189.95, and one unit of product P0022 at $1,395. (You can also refer to the sales report in Figure 6.9 that was developed in the previous exercise to check these calculations.)

Now that you know the total cost of the order, you can compute the commission, which is 5% of the total order, or $209.20 (.05 × $4,183.95). The complete calculation is lengthy, but Access does it automatically, and therein lies the beauty of a relational database.

(a) Customers Table

Customer ID	First Name	Last Name	Address	City	State	Zip Code	Phone Number
C0001	Benjamin	Lee	1000 Call Street	Tallahassee	FL	33340	(904) 327-4124
C0002	Eleanor	Milgrom	7245 NW 8 Street	Margate	FL	33065	(305) 974-1234
C0003	Neil	Goodman	4215 South 81 Street	Margate	FL	33065	(305) 444-5555
C0004	Nicholas	Colon	9020 N.W. 75 Street	Coral Springs	FL	33065	(305) 753-9887
C0005	Michael	Ware	276 Brickell Avenue	Miami	FL	33131	(305) 444-3980
C0006	Jeffrey	Muddell	9522 S.W. 142 Street	Miami	FL	33176	(305) 253-3909
C0007	Ashley	Geoghegan	7500 Center Lane	Coral Springs	FL	33070	(305) 753-7830
C0008	Serena	Sherard	5000 Jefferson Lane	Gainesville	FL	32601	(904) 375-6442
C0009	Luis	Couto	455 Bargello Avenue	Coral Gables	FL	33146	(305) 666-4801
C0010	Derek	Anderson	6000 Tigertail Avenue	Coconut Grove	FL	33120	(305) 446-8900
C0011	Lauren	Center	12380 S.W. 137 Avenue	Miami	FL	33186	(305) 385-4432
C0012	Robert	Slane	4508 N.W. 7 Street	Miami	FL	33131	(305) 635-3454

(b) Products Table

Product ID	Product Name	Units In Stock	Units On Order	Uni tPrice
P0001	Celeron® at 2.0GHz	50	0	$899.00
P0002	Pentium® IV at 2.6GHz	25	5	$1,099.00
P0003	Pentium® IV at 3.0GHz	125	15	$1,399.00
P0004	Pentium® III Notebook at 800 MHz	25	50	$1,599.00
P0005	Pentium® IV Notebook at 2.0GHz	15	25	$2,599.00
P0006	17" CRT Monitor	50	0	$499.00
P0007	19" CRT Monitor	25	10	$899.00
P0008	21" CRT Monitor	50	20	$1,599.00
P0009	2 Years On Site Service	15	20	$299.00
P0010	4 Years On Site Service	25	15	$399.00
P0011	Multi Media Projector	10	0	$1,245.00
P0012	Digital Camera - 2.0 megapixels	40	0	$249.00
P0013	Digital Camera - 4.0 megapixels	50	15	$449.95
P0014	HD Floppy Disks (50 pack)	500	200	$9.99
P0015	CD-R (25 pack spindle)	100	50	$14.79
P0016	Digital Scanner	15	3	$179.95
P0017	Serial Mouse	150	50	$69.95
P0018	Trackball	55	0	$59.95
P0019	Joystick	250	100	$39.95
P0020	Wireless broadband router	35	10	$189.95
P0021	Fax/Modem 56 Kbps	20	0	$65.95
P0022	Digital Photography Package	100	15	$1,395.00
P0023	Ink Jet Printer	50	50	$249.95
P0024	Laser Printer (personal)	125	25	$569.95
P0025	Windows® XP Home Edition	400	200	$95.95
P0026	Antivirus/Firewall Upgrade	150	50	$75.95
P0027	Tax Preparaton Software	150	50	$115.95
P0028	Typing Tutor	75	25	$29.95
P0029	Microsoft Office Home Edition	250	100	$129.95
P0030	Learning Adventure	25	10	$59.95
P0031	Surge Protector	15	0	$45.95

(c) Orders Table

OrderID	CustomerID	Order Date	SalesPersonID
O001	C0004	4/15/2003	S01
O002	C0003	4/18/2003	S02
O003	C0006	4/18/2003	S03
O004	C0007	4/18/2003	S04
O006	C0001	4/21/2003	S05
O007	C0002	4/21/2003	S01
O008	C0002	4/22/2003	S02
O009	C0001	4/22/2003	S03
O010	C0002	4/22/2003	S04
O011	C0001	4/24/2003	S05
O012	C0007	4/24/2003	S01
O013	C0004	4/24/2003	S02
O014	C0006	4/25/2003	S03
O015	C0009	4/25/2003	S04
O016	C0006	4/26/2003	S05
O017	C0011	4/26/2003	S01
O018	C0011	4/26/2003	S02
O019	C0012	4/27/2003	S03
O020	C0012	4/28/2003	S04
O021	C0010	4/29/2003	S05
O022	C0010	4/29/2003	S01
O023	C0008	4/30/2003	S02
O024	C0006	5/1/2003	S03
O025	C0006	5/1/2003	S04

(d) Order Details Table

OrderID	ProductID	Quantity
O0001	P0013	1
O0001	P0014	4
O0001	P0027	1
O0002	P0001	1
O0002	P0006	1
O0002	P0020	1
O0002	P0022	1
O0003	P0005	1
O0003	P0020	1
O0003	P0022	1
O0004	P0003	1
O0004	P0010	1
O0004	P0022	2
O0006	P0007	1
O0006	P0014	10
O0007	P0028	1
O0007	P0030	3
O0008	P0001	1
O0008	P0004	3
O0008	P0008	4
O0008	P0011	2
O0008	P0012	1
O0009	P0006	1
O0010	P0002	2
O0010	P0022	1
O0010	P0023	1
O0011	P0016	2
O0011	P0020	2
O0012	P0021	10
O0012	P0029	10
O0012	P0030	10
O0013	P0009	4
O0013	P0016	10
O0013	P0024	2
O0014	P0019	2
O0014	P0028	1
O0015	P0018	1
O0015	P0020	1
O0016	P0029	2
O0017	P0019	2
O0018	P0009	1
O0018	P0025	2
O0018	P0026	2
O0019	P0014	25
O0020	P0024	1
O0021	P0004	1
O0022	P0027	1
O0023	P0021	1
O0023	P0028	1
O0023	P0029	1
O0024	P0007	1
O0024	P0013	5
O0024	P0014	3
O0024	P0016	1
O0025	P0012	2
O0025	P0029	2

(e) Sales Persons Table

SalesPersonID	First Name	Last Name	Work Phone	Hire Date
S01	Linda	Black	(305) 284-6105	2/3/2000
S02	Michael	Vaughn	(305) 284-3993	2/10/2001
S03	Cori	Rice	(305) 284-2557	3/15/1999
S04	Karen	Ruenheck	(305) 284-4641	11/24/2002
S05	Richard	Linger	(305) 284-4662	1/21/2003

FIGURE 6.11 Super Store Database

The Sales Commission Query

Figure 6.12a displays the design view of a parameter query to calculate the commissions for a specific sales person. (This query determines the commissions for Cori Rice, which you computed manually in the previous discussion.) Enter the last name of the sales associate, Rice, and the query returns the dynaset in Figure 6.12b, showing all of her commissions. Note, too, that the commission returned for order O0003 is $209.20, which corresponds to the amount we arrived at earlier.

The query in Figure 6.12a includes fields from all five tables in the database. The relationships are shown graphically in the top half of the query window and reflect the earlier discussion—for example, the one-to-many relationship between salespersons and orders. These tables are joined through the SalesPersonID field, which is the primary key in the Sales Persons table but a foreign key in the Orders table. (The Orders table has been modified to include this field.)

The query can easily be modified to show the sales commission on every order by removing the criteria under the salesperson's last name. The resulting query will then compute the commissions for every salesperson and can be used as the basis of the sales commission report in Figure 6.12c.

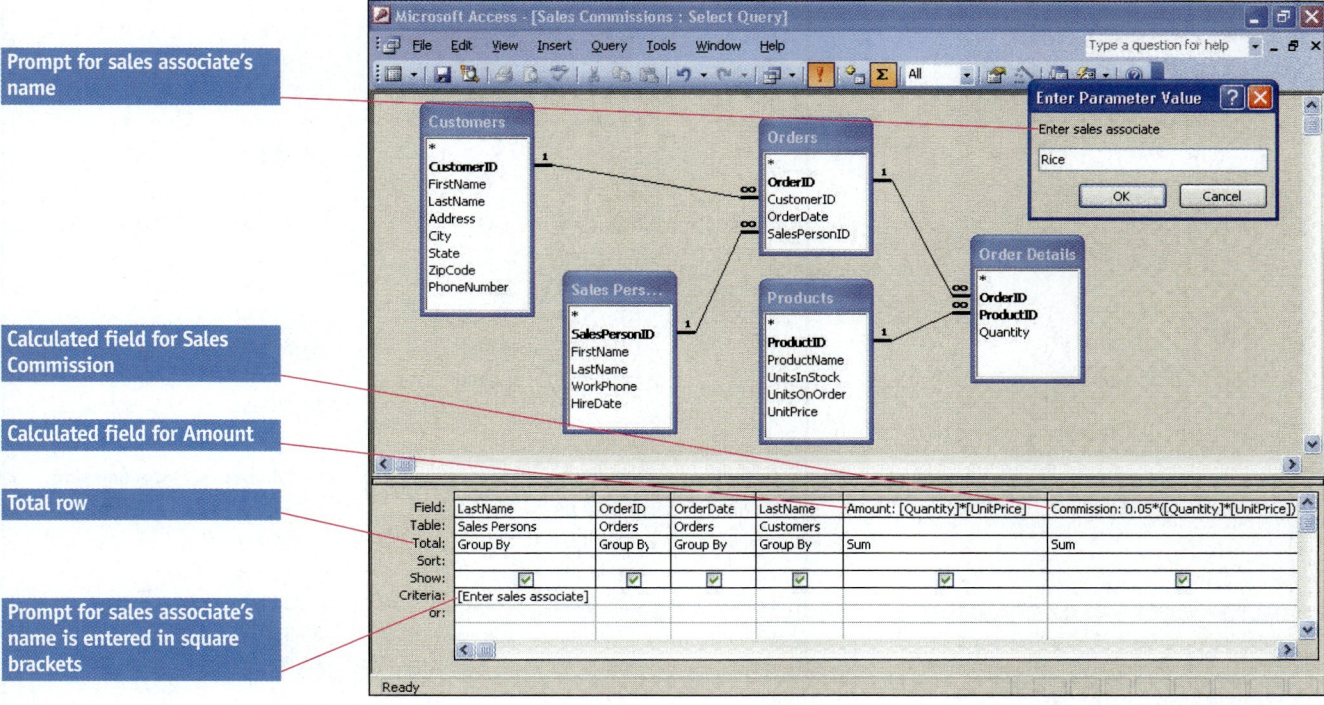

Prompt for sales associate's name

Calculated field for Sales Commission

Calculated field for Amount

Total row

Prompt for sales associate's name is entered in square brackets

(a) Design View

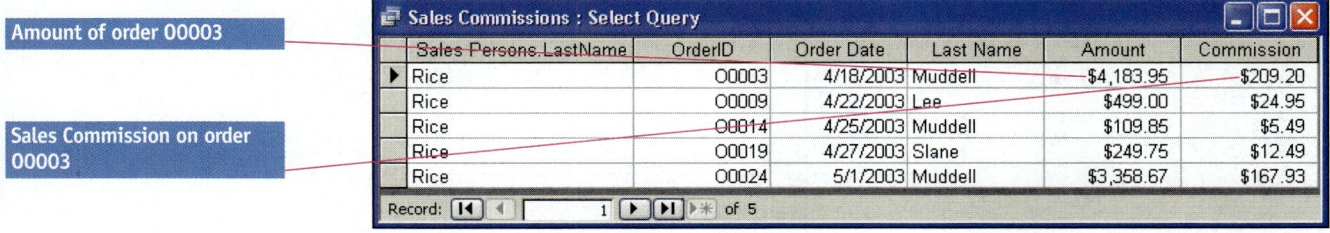

Amount of order O0003

Sales Commission on order O0003

(b) Dynaset

FIGURE 6.12 Sales Commissions

The report in Figure 6.12c parallels the sales analysis report of Figure 6.9 that was developed in the previous hands-on exercise. This time, however, the entries in the report are grouped by salesperson and sorted by OrderID for each salesperson. The total sales and commission for each salesperson are also calculated.

The exercise that follows has you import the Sales Persons table from another database. It then directs you to modify the existing Orders table to include a SalesPersonID, which references the records in the Sales Persons table, and finally to modify the Computer Store Order form to include the salesperson data. The sales commission report is left to you as an end-of-chapter exercise.

Sales Commission Report
Prepared by: Your Name Goes Here

Black	OrderID	Order Date	Last Name	Amount	Commission
	O0001	4/15/2003	Colon	$605.86	$30.29
	O0007	4/21/2003	Milgrom	$209.80	$10.49
	O0012	4/24/2003	Geoghegan	$2,558.50	$127.93
	O0017	4/26/2003	Center	$79.90	$4.00
	O0022	4/29/2003	Anderson	$115.95	$5.80
	O0027	7/17/2003	Grauer	$2,698.00	$134.90
			Total:	$6,268.01	$313.40

Linger	OrderID	Order Date	Last Name	Amount	Commission
	O0006	4/21/2003	Lee	$998.90	$49.95
	O0011	4/24/2003	Lee	$739.80	$36.99
	O0016	4/26/2003	Muddell	$259.90	$13.00
	O0021	4/29/2003	Anderson	$1,599.00	$79.95
	O0026	7/16/2003	Grauer	$1,108.93	$55.45
			Total:	$4,706.53	$235.33

Rice	OrderID	Order Date	Last Name	Amount	Commission
	O0003	4/18/2003	Muddell	$4,183.95	$209.20
	O0009	4/22/2003	Lee	$499.00	$24.95
	O0014	4/25/2003	Muddell	$109.85	$5.49
	O0019	4/27/2003	Slane	$249.75	$12.49
	O0024	5/1/2003	Muddell	$3,358.67	$167.93
			Total:	$8,401.22	$420.06

Ruenheck	OrderID	Order Date	Last Name	Amount	Commission
	O0004	4/18/2003	Geoghegan	$4,588.00	$229.40
	O0010	4/22/2003	Milgrom	$3,842.95	$192.15
	O0015	4/25/2003	Couto	$249.90	$12.50
	O0020	4/28/2003	Slane	$569.95	$28.50
	O0025	5/1/2003	Muddell	$757.90	$37.90
			Total:	$10,008.70	$500.44

Thursday, July 17, 2003   Page 1 of 2

(c) Sales Commission Report

FIGURE 6.12   Sales Commissions (*continued*)

hands-on exercise
4   Expanding the Database

Objective   To import a table from another database; to modify the design of an existing table. Use Figure 6.13 as a guide in the exercise.

Step 1:   **Import the Sales Persons Table**

- Open the **Computer Store database**. Click the **Tables button**. Pull down the **File menu**. Click **Get External Data**, then click the **Import command**.

- Click (select) the **Sales Persons database** from the **Exploring Access folder**, then click **Import** to display the Import Objects dialog box in Figure 6.13a.

- If necessary, click the **Tables button**, click **SalesPersons** (the only table in this database), then click **OK**.

- A dialog box will appear briefly on your screen as the Sales Persons table is imported into the Computer Store database.

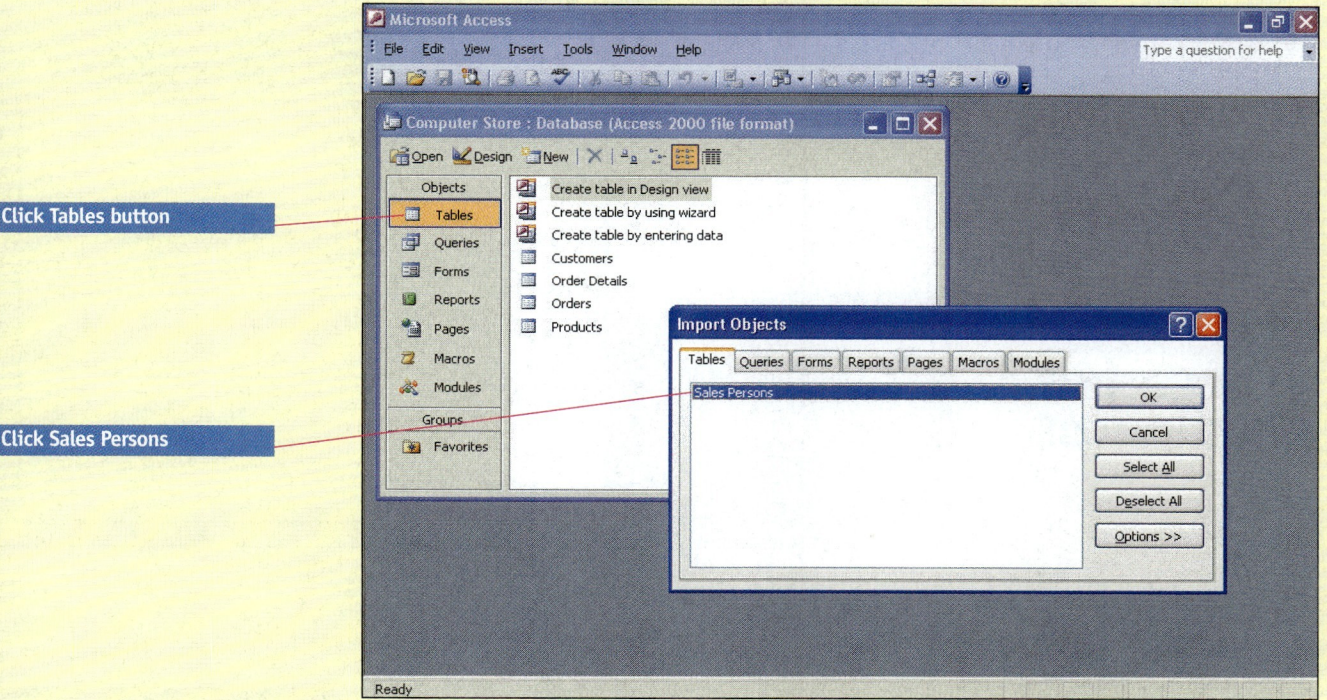

(a) Import the Sales Persons Table (step 1)

FIGURE 6.13   Hands-on Exercise 4

THE DOCUMENTS SUBMENU

The My Recent Documents menu in Windows XP contains shortcuts to the last 15 files that were opened. Click the Start button, click (or point to) the My Recent Documents menu, then click the document you wish to open (e.g., Computer Store), assuming that it appears on the menu. Windows will start the application, then open the indicated document.

Step 2: Modify the Orders Table Design

- Select the **Orders table** from the Database window as shown in Figure 6.13b. Click the **Design button**.

- Click in the first available row in the **Field Name** column. Enter **SalesPersonID** as shown in Figure 6.13b. Choose **Number** as the data type. The Field Size property changes to Long Integer by default.

- Click the **Format** property. Enter **\S00**.

- Click the **Default Value** property and delete the **0**.

- Click the **Save button** to save the modified design of the Orders table. You will enter data for the new field in the next step.

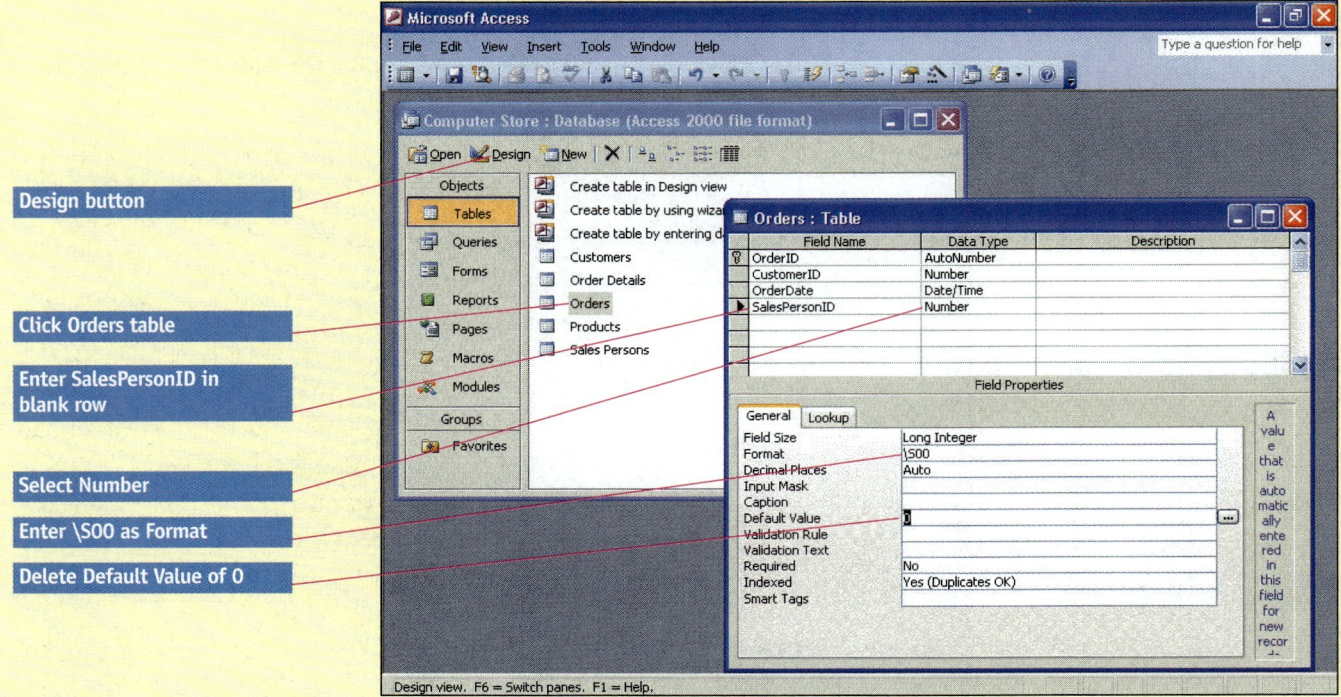

Design button

Click Orders table

Enter SalesPersonID in blank row

Select Number

Enter \S00 as Format

Delete Default Value of 0

(b) Modify the Orders Table Design (step 2)

FIGURE 6.13 Hands-on Exercise 4 (*continued*)

RELATIONSHIPS AND THE AUTONUMBER FIELD TYPE

The join fields on both sides of a relationship must be the same data type—for example, both number fields or both text fields. The AutoNumber field type, however, cannot be specified on both sides of a relationship. Thus, if the join field (SalesPersonID) in the primary table (Sales Persons) is an AutoNumber field, the join field in the related table (Orders) must be specified as a Number field, with the Field Size property set to Long Integer.

Step 3: Add the Sales Person to Existing Orders

- Click the **Datasheet View button** to change to the Datasheet view as shown in Figure 6.13c. Maximize the window.

- Enter the **SalesPersonID** for each existing order as shown in Figure 6.13c.

- Enter only the number (e.g., 1, rather than S0001) as the S and leading zeros are displayed automatically through the Format property. We are adding the data in random fashion so that we will be able to generate meaningful reports later on in the exercise.

- You should now set the Required property for the SalesPersonID in the Orders table to **Yes** to make this a required field for new orders.

- Close the Orders table. Click **Yes** if prompted to save the table. Click **Yes** to retain the changes to the data integrity rules.

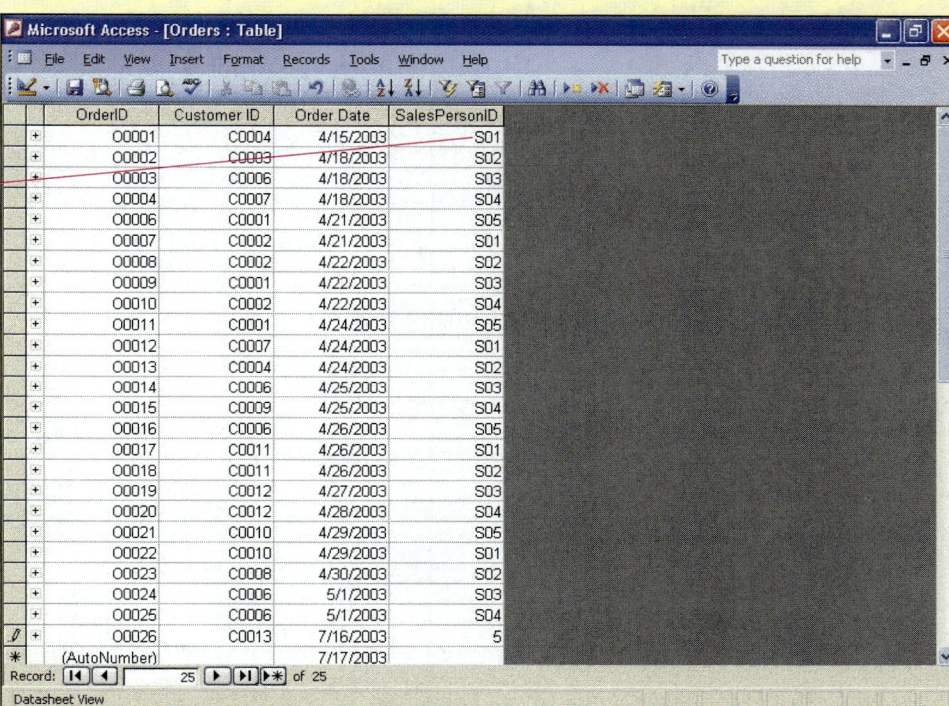

Enter SalesPersonID for each order (enter 1,2,3,4, or 5 only)

(c) Add the Sales Person to Existing Orders (step 3)

FIGURE 6.13 Hands-on Exercise 4 (*continued*)

HIDE THE WINDOWS TASKBAR

The Windows taskbar is great for novices because it makes task switching as easy as changing channels on a TV. It also takes up valuable real estate on the desktop, and hence you may want to hide the taskbar when you don't need it. Point to an empty area on the taskbar, click the right mouse button to display a shortcut menu, and click Properties to display the Taskbar Properties dialog box. Click the Taskbar tab (if necessary), check the box to Autohide the taskbar, and click OK. The taskbar should disappear. Now point to the bottom of the screen (or the edge where the taskbar was last displayed), and it will reappear.

Step 4: Create the Relationship

■ Pull down the **Tools menu**. Click **Relationships** to open the Relationships window as shown in Figure 6.13d. (The Sales Persons table is not yet visible.) Click the **Maximize button**.

■ If necessary, drag the bottom border of the **Orders table** until you see the SalesPersonID (the field you added in step 2).

■ Pull down the **Relationships menu**. Click **Show Table**. Click the **Tables button** if necessary, select the **Sales Persons table**, then click the **Add button**. Close the Show Table dialog box.

■ Drag the title bar of the **Sales Persons table** to position the table as shown in Figure 6.13d. Drag the **SalesPersonID field** from the Sales Persons table to the SalesPersonID in the Orders table.

■ Check the box to **Enforce Referential Integrity**. Click the **Create button** to create the relationship. Click the **Save button** to save the Relationships window.

■ Close the Relationships window.

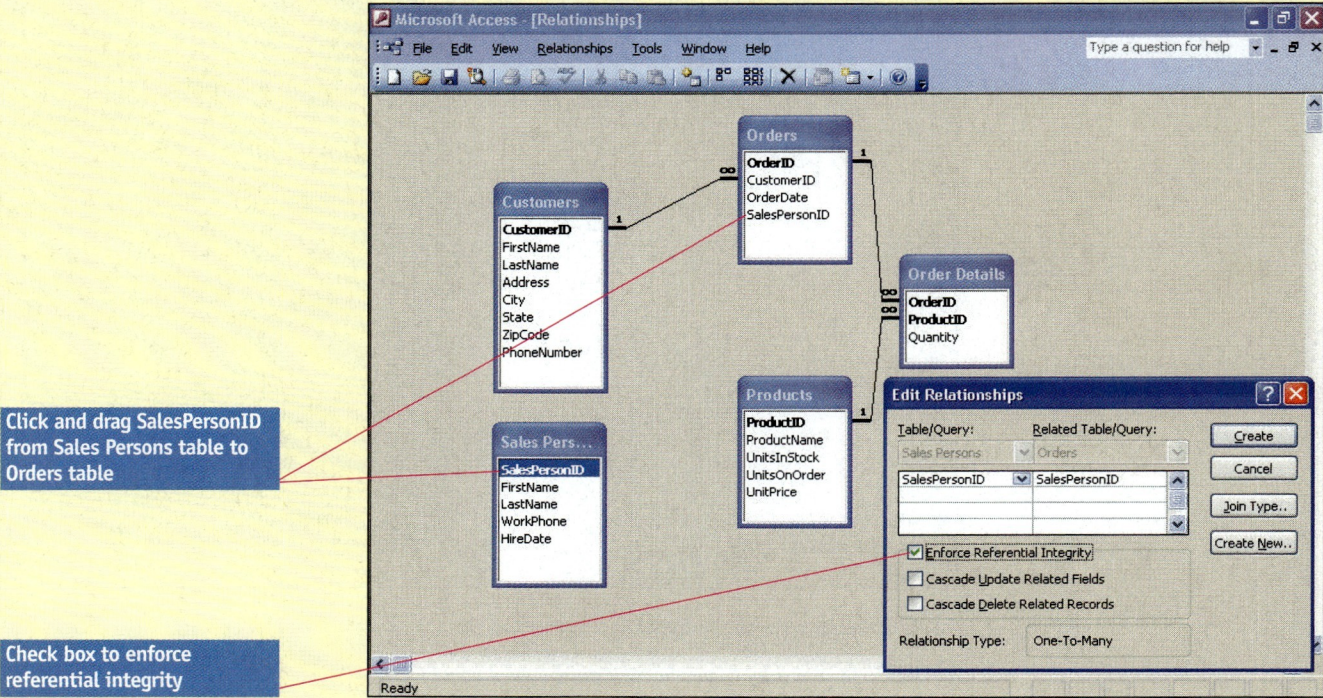

Click and drag SalesPersonID from Sales Persons table to Orders table

Check box to enforce referential integrity

(d) Create the Relationship (step 4)

FIGURE 6.13 Hands-on Exercise 4 (*continued*)

PRINT THE RELATIONSHIPS

Pull down the Tools menu and click the Relationships command to open the Relationships window, then pull down the File menu and click the Print Relationships command. You will see the Print Preview screen of a report that displays the contents of the Relationships window. Click the Print button to print the report, or change to the Design view to modify the report, perhaps by adding your name. Save the report after printing so that it will be available at a later time.

Step 5: **Modify the Order with Customer Information Query**

- You should be back in the Database window. Click the **Queries button**, select the **Order with Customer Information query**, then click the **Design button** to open the query in the Design view as shown in Figure 6.13e.

- If necessary, click and drag the border of the **Orders table** so that the newly added SalesPersonID field is displayed. Click the **horizontal scroll arrow** until a blank column in the design grid is visible.

- Click and drag the **SalesPersonID** from the Orders table to the first blank column in the design grid.

- Save the query. Close the query.

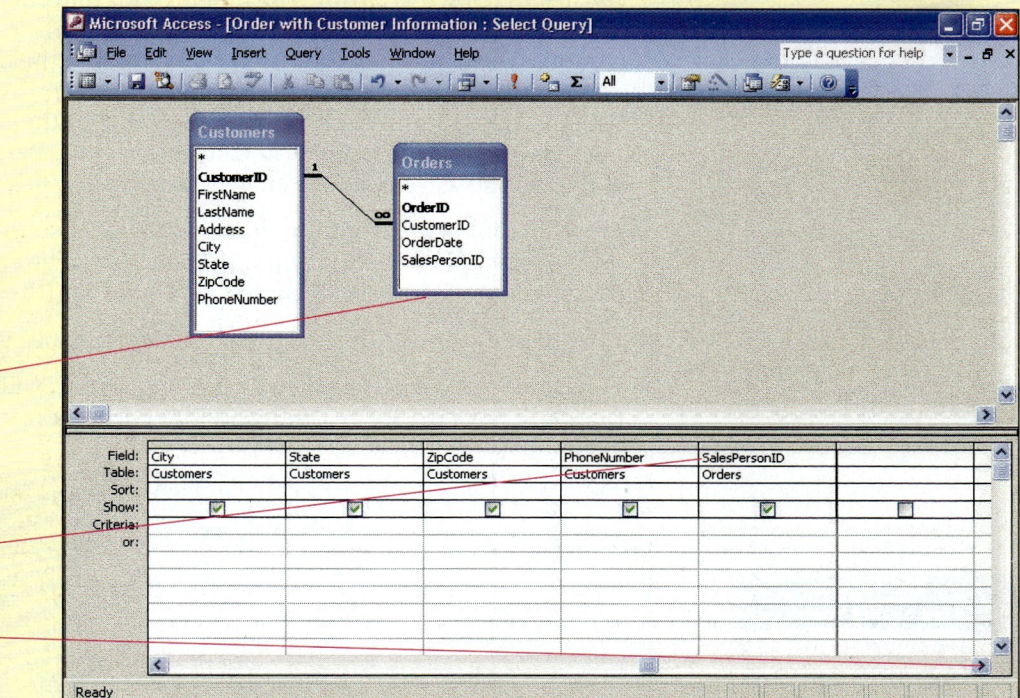

(e) Modify the Order with Customer Information Query (step 5)

FIGURE 6.13 Hands-on Exercise 4 (*continued*)

OPTIMIZE QUERIES USING INDEXES

The performance of a database becomes important as you progress from a "student" database with a limited number of records to a real database with large tables. Thus, it becomes advantageous to optimize the performance of individual queries by creating indexes in the underlying tables. Indexes should be specified for any criteria field in a query, as well as for any field that is used in a relationship to join two tables. To create an index, open the table in Design view and set the indexed property to Yes.

Step 6: **Modify the Order Form**

- You should be back in the Database window. Click the **Forms button**, select the **Super Store Order Form**, then click the **Design button**.

- Move and size the controls on the first line to make room for the SalesPersonID as shown in Figure 6.13f.

- Click the **Combo Box tool**, then click and drag in the form where you want the combo box to go. Release the mouse to start the Combo Box Wizard.
  - ❑ Check the option button that indicates you want the combo box to look up values in a table or query. Click **Next**.
  - ❑ Choose the **Sales Persons table** in the next screen. Click **Next**.
  - ❑ Select the **SalesPersonID** and **LastName**. Click **Next**.
  - ❑ Click the **down arrrow** in the first text box and click **Last Name** to sort the list alphabetically by last name. Click **Next**.
  - ❑ Adjust the column width if necessary. Be sure the box to hide the key column is checked. Click **Next**.
  - ❑ Click the option button to store the value in the field. Click the **drop-down arrow** to display the fields and select the **SalesPersonID field**. Click **Next**.
  - ❑ Enter **Sales Person** as the label for the combo box. Click **Finish**.

- Move and/or size the combo box and its label so that it is spaced attractively on the form. Point to the combo box, click the **right mouse button** to display a shortcut menu, and click **Properties**. Click the **Other tab**.

- Change the name of the box to **Sales Person**. Close the dialog box.

- Pull down the **View menu** and click **Tab Order**. Click the **AutoOrder button**. Click **OK**. Save the form. Change to the **Form view**.

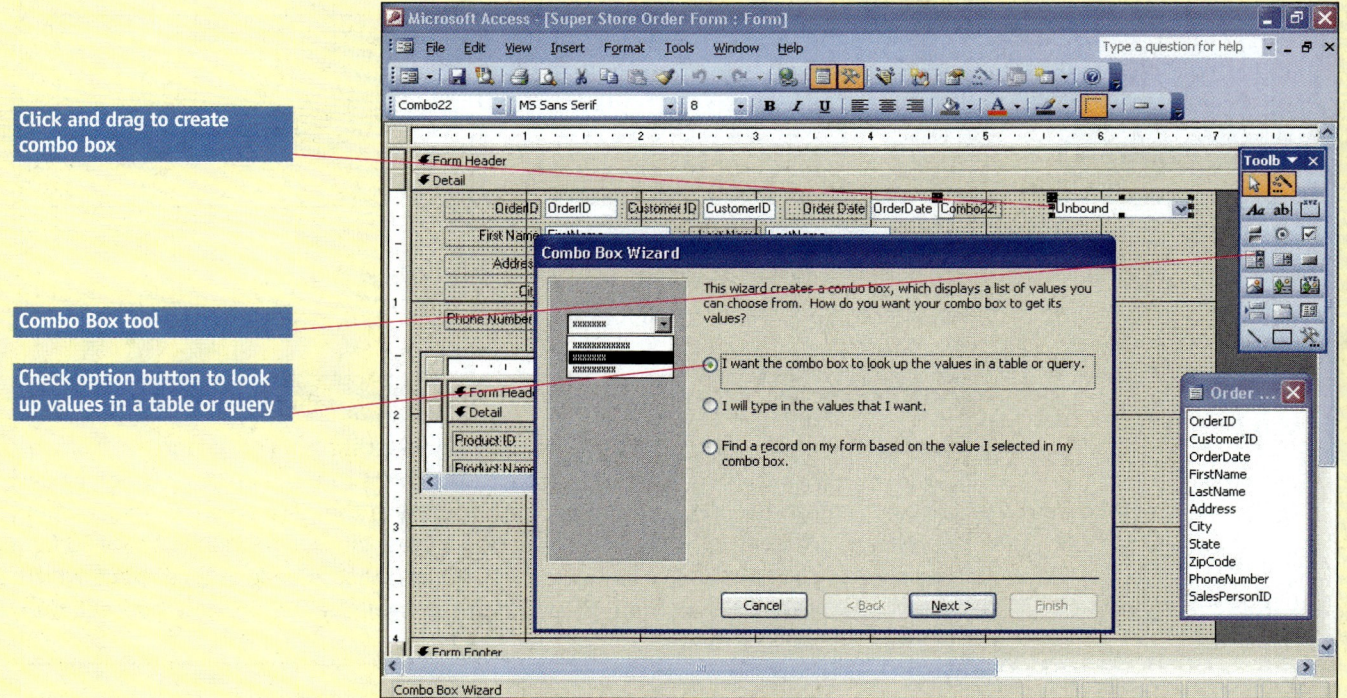

(f) Modify the Order Form (step 6)

FIGURE 6.13   Hands-on Exercise 4 (*continued*)

Step 7: The Completed Order Form

- You should see the completed form as shown in Figure 6.13g. Click the **New Record button** on the Form View toolbar to display a blank form.

- Click in the **Customer ID text box**. Enter **13** (your customer number from the first exercise), then press the **Tab key** to move to the next field.

- The OrderID is entered automatically as it is an AutoNumber field. Your customer information is entered automatically because of the AutoLookup feature. Today's date is entered automatically as the order date.

- Click the **drop-down arrow** on the Sales Person combo box. Select **Black** (or click in the box and type **B**), and the complete name is entered automatically.

- Click the **ProductID text box** in the subform. Enter **2** (not P0002) and press **Enter**. The Product Name and Unit Price are entered automatically.

- Press the **Tab key** twice to move to the Quantity field. Enter **1**. The amount is computed automatically. Close the Order form.

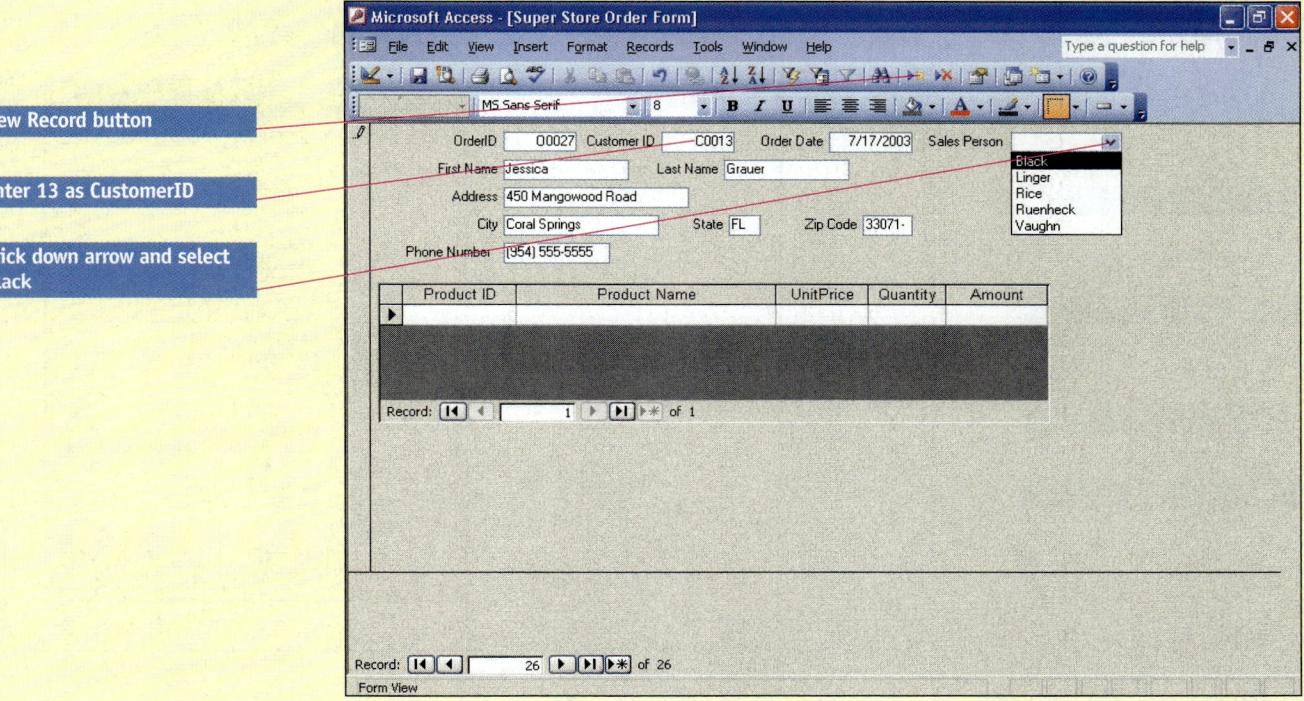

New Record button

Enter 13 as CustomerID

Click down arrow and select Black

(g) The Completed Order Form (step 7)

FIGURE 6.13   Hands-on Exercise 4 (*continued*)

ENTER A NEW CUSTOMER

The Order form is based on a query that contains required fields from both the Customers table and the Orders table, enabling you to add a new customer at the same time you enter his or her order. Click the New Record button to add a new order. Skip the OrderID, CustomerID, and Order Date fields, and then select the Sales Person. Click in the First Name text box, enter a value, press Tab, and notice that a value has been entered into the CustomerID field for the new customer. Continue to add the customer information, and then complete the order in the usual fashion. See exercise 3 at the end of the chapter.

Step 8: **Database Properties**

- You should be back in the Database window. Pull down the **File menu** and click **Database Properties** to display the dialog box in Figure 6.13h.

- Click the **Contents tab** to display the contents of the Computer Store database.
  - ❑ There are five tables (Customers, Order Details, Orders, Products, and Sales Persons).
  - ❑ There are five queries, which include the Total and Parameter queries you created in Hands-on Exercise 3.
  - ❑ There are three forms—the main form, which you have completed in this exercise, the associated subform, and an About Super Store form for use in an end-of-chapter exercise.
  - ❑ There is one report, the report you created in exercise 3.

- Click **OK** to close the dialog box. Close the Computer Store database. Exit Access. Congratulations on a job well done.

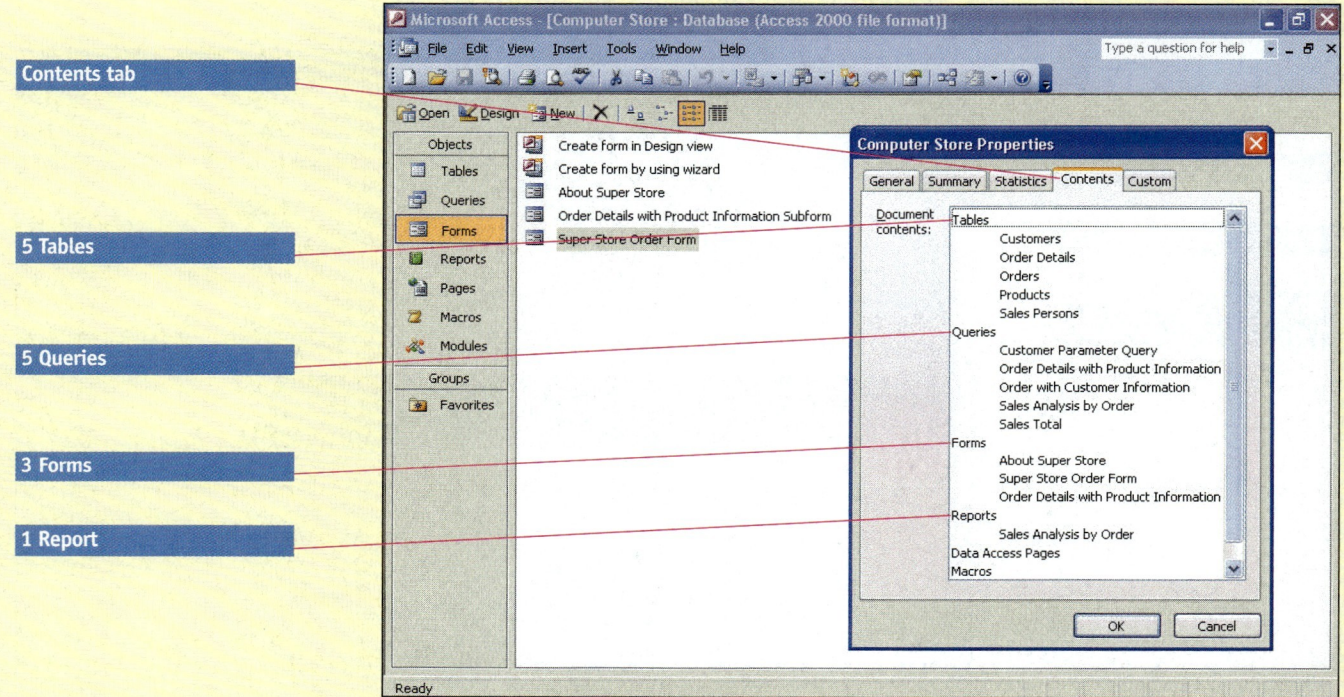

(h) Database Properties (step 8)

FIGURE 6.13 Hands-on Exercise 4 (*continued*)

OBJECT DEPENDENCIES

The objects in an Access database depend on one another; for example, a report is created from a query, which in turn is created from a table. Over time, the report may become obsolete, so you delete the report and the underlying query; but if the same query were the basis of another report, the latter object would no longer function. The ability to view object dependencies can prevent this type of error from occurring. Select the object in the Database window, pull down the View menu, and click Object Dependencies. Click OK if prompted to turn the feature on. The task pane will open, and you will see the objects that depend on the selected object.

SUMMARY

The implementation of a many-to-many relationship requires an additional table whose primary key consists of (at least) the primary keys of the individual tables. The many-to-many table may also contain additional fields whose values are dependent on the combined key. All relationships are created in the Relationships window by dragging the join field from the primary table to the related table. A many-to-many relationship in the physical system is implemented by a pair of one-to-many relationships in an Access database.

Enforcement of referential integrity prevents you from adding a record to the related table if that record contains an invalid value of the foreign key. (You cannot, for example, add a record to the Orders table that contains an invalid value for CustomerID.) Referential integrity also prevents the deletion and/or updating of records on the "one" side of a one-to-many relationship when there are matching records in the related table. The deletion (updating) can take place, however, if the relationship is modified to allow the cascaded deletion (updating) of related records (fields).

Referential integrity does not prevent you from adding a record to the "many" table that omits a value for the field from the "one" table. You could, for example, add a record to the Orders table that omitted CustomerID. If this does not make sense in the physical situation, then you have to make the CustomerID a required field in the Orders table.

There are several reasons to base a form (or subform) on a query rather than a table. A query can contain a calculated field; a table cannot. A query can contain fields from more than one table and take advantage of AutoLookup. A query can also contain selected records from a table and/or display those records in a different sequence from that of the table on which it is based.

A parameter query prompts you for the criteria each time you execute the query. The prompt is enclosed in square brackets and is entered in the Criteria row within the Query Design view. Multiple parameters may be specified within the same query.

Aggregate functions (Avg, Min, Max, Sum, and Count) perform calculations on groups of records. Execution of the query displays an aggregate record for each group, and individual records do not appear. Updating of individual records is not possible in this type of query.

Tables may be added to an Access database without disturbing the data in existing tables. The Get External Data command enables you to import an object(s) from another database.

KEY TERMS

AutoLookup 284	Main form .284	Relationships window 277
AutoNumber field 277	Many-to-many relationship 276	Subform 284
Cascaded deletion 278	Object Dependencies 316	Subreport 292
Cascaded updating 278	One-to-many relationship 274	Sum function 293
Combined key 276	Parameter query 293	TopValues property 304
Description property 302	Primary key 274	Total query .293
Format property 277	Prompt 293	Total row 293
Group By 293	Referential integrity 278	Unmatched Query Wizard 301
Keep Together property 299	Relationship lines 277	

MULTIPLE CHOICE

1. Which table(s) is(are) necessary to implement a many-to-many relationship between students and the courses they take?

   (a) A Students table

   (b) A Courses table

   (c) A Students–Courses table

   (d) All of the above

2. Which of the following would be suitable as the primary key in a Students–Courses table, where there is a many-to-many relationship between Students and Courses, and further, when a student is allowed to repeat a course?

   (a) The combination of StudentID and CourseID

   (b) The combination of StudentID, CourseID, and semester

   (c) The combination of StudentID, CourseID, semester, and grade

   (d) All of the above are equally appropriate

3. Which of the following is necessary to add a record to the "one" side in a one-to-many relationship in which referential integrity is enforced?

   (a) A unique primary key for the new record

   (b) One or more matching records in the many table

   (c) Both (a) and (b)

   (d) Neither (a) nor (b)

4. Which of the following is necessary to add a record to the "many" side in a one-to-many relationship in which the join field is a required field in the "many" table?

   (a) A unique primary key for the new record

   (b) A matching record in the primary table

   (c) Both (a) and (b)

   (d) Neither (a) nor (b)

5. Under which circumstances can you delete a "many" record in a one-to-many relationship?

   (a) Under all circumstances

   (b) Under no circumstances

   (c) By enforcing referential integrity

   (d) By enforcing referential integrity with the cascaded deletion of related records

6. Under which circumstances can you delete the "one" record in a one-to-many relationship?

   (a) Under all circumstances

   (b) Under no circumstances

   (c) By enforcing referential integrity

   (d) By enforcing referential integrity with the cascaded deletion of related records

7. Which of the following would be suitable as the primary key in a Patients–Doctors table, where there is a many-to-many relationship between patients and doctors, and where the same patient can see the same doctor on different visits?

   (a) The combination of PatientID and DoctorID

   (b) The combination of PatientID, DoctorID, and the date of the visit

   (c) Either (a) or (b)

   (d) Neither (a) nor (b)

8. How do you implement the many-to-many relationship between patients and doctors described in the previous question?

   (a) Through a one-to-many relationship between the Patients table and the Patients–Doctors table

   (b) Through a one-to-many relationship between the Doctors table and the Patients–Doctors table

   (c) Both (a) and (b)

   (d) Neither (a) nor (b)

9. A database has a one-to-many relationship between teams and players. Which data type and field size should be assigned to the TeamID field in the Players table, if TeamID is defined as an AutoNumber field in the Teams table?

   (a) AutoNumber and Long Integer

   (b) Number and Long Integer

   (c) Text and Long Integer

   (d) Lookup Wizard and Long Integer

10. Which of the following is true about a main form and an associated subform?

    (a) The main form can be based on a query

    (b) The subform can be based on a query

    (c) Both (a) and (b)

    (d) Neither (a) nor (b)

... continued

11. A parameter query:

   (a) Displays a prompt within brackets in the Criteria row of the query

   (b) Is limited to a single parameter

   (c) Both (a) and (b)

   (d) Neither (a) nor (b)

12. Which of the following is available as an aggregate function within a select query?

   (a) Sum and Avg

   (b) Min and Max

   (c) Both (a) and (b)

   (d) Neither (a) nor (b)

13. The Relationships window is displayed, and you notice that one of the tables has two fields shown in bold. What does this mean?

   (a) The primary key for the table consists of both fields

   (b) The table is joined to two others in two many-to-many relationships

   (c) The table has both primary and foreign keys

   (d) Those two fields allow cascaded updating and deleting

14. Which of the following can be imported from another Access database?

   (a) Tables and forms

   (b) Queries and reports

   (c) Both (a) and (b)

   (d) Neither (a) nor (b)

15. Which of the following is true of the TopValues query property?

   (a) It can be used to display the top 10 records in a dynaset

   (b) It can be used to display the top 10 percent of the records in a dynaset

   (c) Both (a) and (b)

   (d) Neither (a) nor (b)

16. You are working with a bookstore database. The Publishers and Books tables are joined in a one-to-many relationship. If referential integrity is enforced, which records can you delete?

   (a) A book, regardless of the records in the Publishers table

   (b) A book, only if there are no corresponding records in the Publishers table

   (c) A publisher, regardless of the records in the Books table

   (d) A publisher, only if there are corresponding records in the Books table

17. You are working with a bookstore database. The Publishers and Books tables are joined in a one-to-many relationship. The PublisherID is a required field in the Books table. If referential integrity is enforced, which of the following actions can you take?

   (a) Add a book without specifying the publisher

   (b) Delete a publisher, regardless of the records in the Books table

   (c) Add a publisher, regardless of the records in the Books table

   (d) None of the above

18. You are working with a bookstore database. The Publishers and Books tables are joined in a one-to-many relationship. The options to cascade updated or deleted records are both in effect. Which of the following actions is *prevented*?

   (a) Adding a book that references a publisher not found in the Publishers table

   (b) Changing the primary key of a record in the Publishers table if there are matching records in the Books table

   (c) Both (a) and (b)

   (d) Neither (a) nor (b)

ANSWERS

1. d	**7.** b	**13.** a
2. b	**8.** c	**14.** c
3. a	**9.** b	**15.** c
4. c	**10.** c	**16.** a
5. a	**11.** a	**17.** c
6. d	**12.** c	**18.** a

PRACTICE WITH ACCESS

1. **Understanding Database Design:** The presentation in Figure 6.14 represents a *hypothetical* assignment for a group project in which the group is asked to present the design for their project to the class as a whole. We have created a similar presentation for you to illustrate what we mean; your only task is to view our presentation, which in turn will help you to review the *Computer Store* database that was developed in the chapter. (Your instructor may want to extend the assignment and ask you to create a parallel presentation for a different database, which he or she may assign as an actual group project.) Proceed as follows:

   a. Start PowerPoint. Open the *Chapter 6 Practice 1* presentation in the Exploring Access folder. This is a PowerPoint presentation, but you do not have to know PowerPoint to complete this exercise. Pull down the View menu and change to the Normal view. If necessary, click the Slide tab to see the miniature slides instead of the outline.

   b. There are nine slides in the complete presentation. The left pane shows the slide miniatures. The right pane shows a larger view of the selected slide (slide one in this example). The slide describes the hypothetical assignment, which is to create a 10-minute presentation to the class describing the physical problem and the associated database design.

   c. Select (click) the first slide. Pull down the View menu and click the Slide Show command (or click the Slide Show button above the status bar). Click the mouse continually to move through the slide show. You will see a recap of the *Computer Store* database, its design, and several suggested queries.

   d. Press the Esc button at the end of the show. Pull down the File menu, and click the Print command. Select the All option button in the Print Range area. Click the down arrow in the Print What area and select handouts. Choose 6 slides per page. Be sure to check the box to frame the slides. Click OK to print the presentation. Print the presentation a second time, but this time print only the title slide (as a full slide) to use as a cover sheet for your assignment.

   e. Review the printed presentation. Do you see how the discipline provided by this assignment can help to ensure the accuracy of the design?

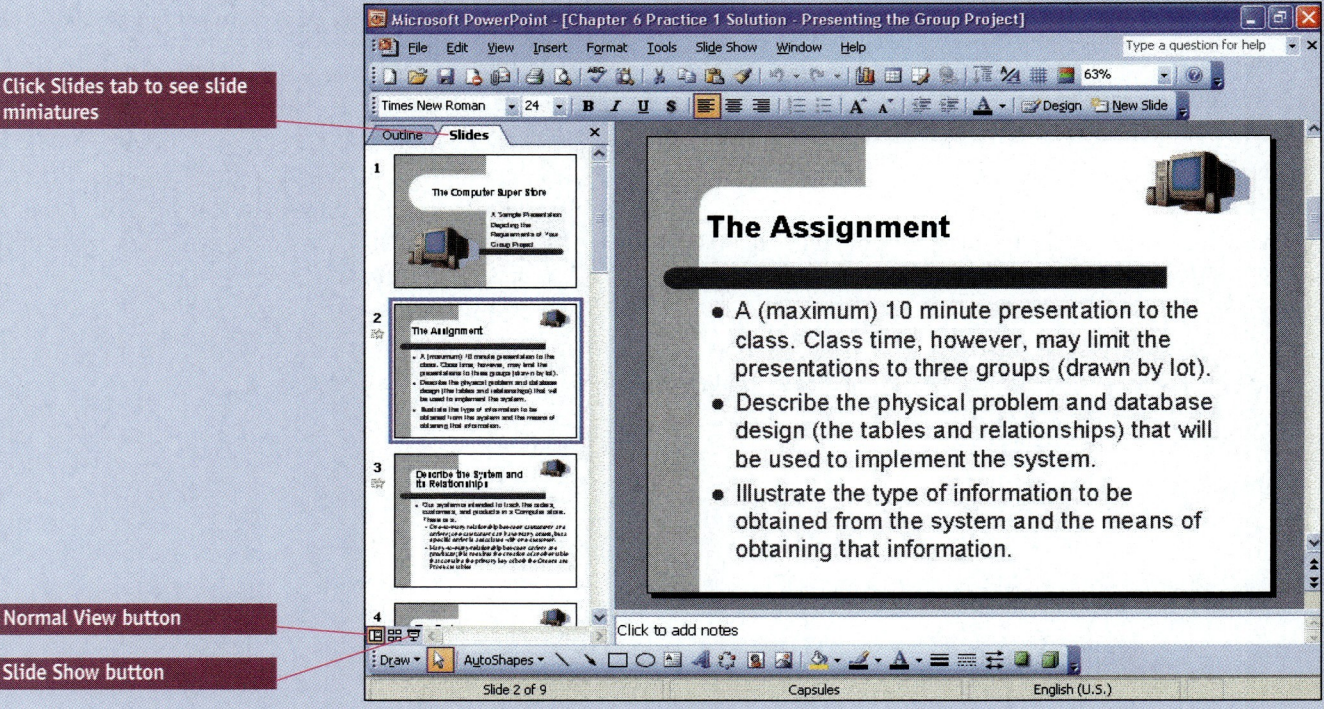

FIGURE 6.14 Understanding Database Design (exercise 1)

2. **Unmatched Query Wizard:** The report in Figure 6.15 is based on a query that was created by the Unmatched Query Wizard, and indicates the products that have never been purchased. This type of information is very valuable to management, which can realize significant cost savings by eliminating these products from inventory. In essence, the query takes each record in the Products table and searches for a matching entry in the Order Details table. Any products that do not appear in the latter table are "unmatched entries" and correspond to a product that has never been ordered. Proceed as follows:

   a. Open the *Computer Store* database that you have used throughout the chapter. Click the Queries button in the Database window. Click the New button, select the Find Unmatched Query Wizard and click OK. Choose Products as the table whose records you want to see in the query results. Click Next. Choose Order Details as the table that contains the related records.

   b. Product ID is selected automatically as the matching field. Click Next. Select every field from the Available Fields list. Click Next. The Wizard enters Products without Matching Order Details as the name of the query.

   c. Click Finish to display a list of the products (if any) that have never been purchased. You should see the same data as in Figure 6.15. Close the query.

   d. Use the Report Wizard to create a report based on the query you just created. Grouping is not required but the report should be sorted by ProductID. Choose the tabular layout and the Soft Gray style.

   e. Modify the report in Design view. You will (most likely) have to modify the column headings and associated controls so that they are spaced more attractively. (You may find it useful to press and hold the Shift key to select both the column heading and associated control in order to move and/or size both objects simultaneously. The Format Align command is also useful.)

   f. Modify the report header to include your name and clip art as shown in Figure 6.15. You do not have to match our design exactly.

   g. Print the completed report for your instructor. What advice would you give to management regarding the inventory of these items?

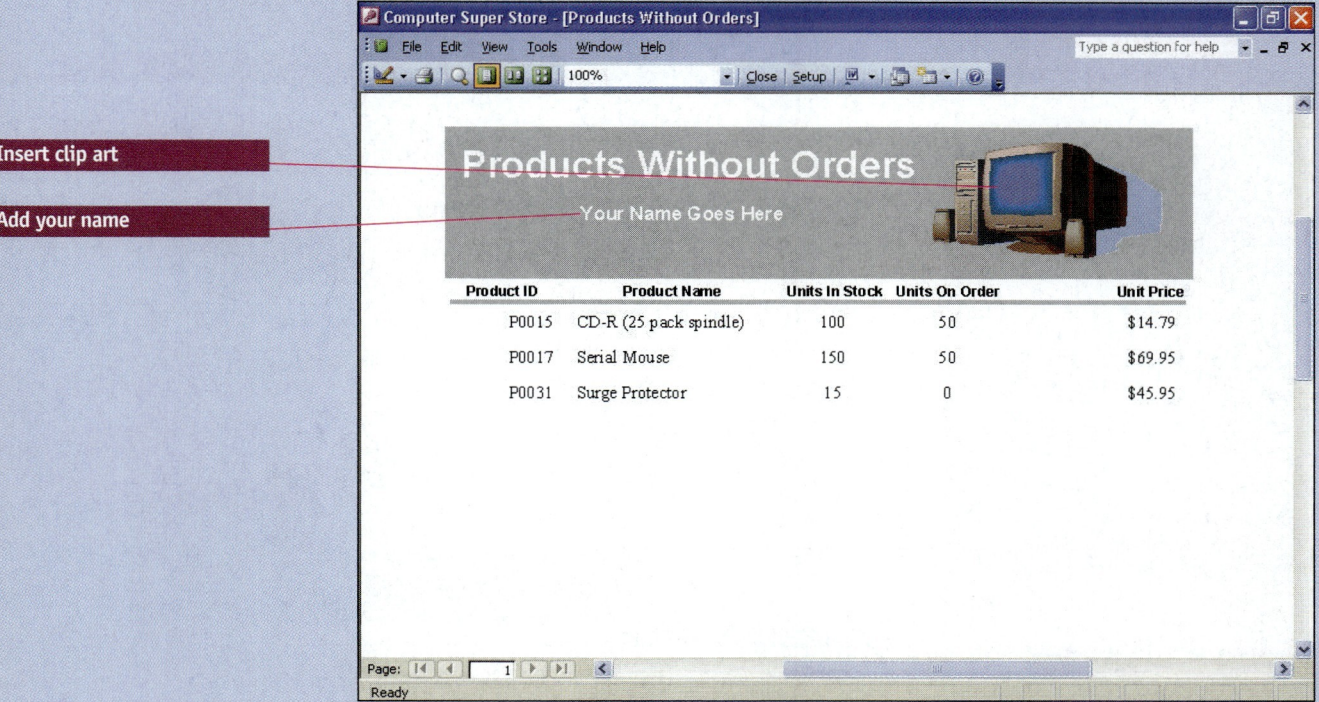

FIGURE 6.15 Unmatched Query Wizard (exercise 2)

3. **An Improved Order Form:** The order form in Figure 6.16 builds on the form that was developed in the fourth hands-on exercise in the chapter. A header has been added that includes clip art and a label for your name and three command buttons have also been added. The most significant change, however, is the inclusion of a Product Name combo box on the subform in place of the ProductID.

a. Open the *Computer Store* database. Click the Forms button in the Database window and open the Order Details with Product Information subform in Design view. Delete the controls and associated labels for ProductID and Product Name. Click the Combo Box Wizard tool, then click and drag in the Detail area of the subform to create a combo box.

b. Click the option button to indicate that you want the Combo box to look up values in a table or query. Click Next. Specify the Products table. Click Next. Select the ProductID and ProductName fields. Click Next. Click the down arrow in the text box and select Product Name to sort the list alphabetically. Adjust the column width of the ProductName field. Click Next. Click the option button to store the value in a field and specify ProductID. Click Finish.

c. Right click the combo box, click Properties, and change the name of the combo box to ProductName. Pull down the View menu, click the Tab Order command and specify AutoOrder. Click OK. Save the subform. Close the subform.

d. Open the Computer Store Order form in Design view. Add command buttons to add a new order, close the form, and print a record. Press and hold the Shift key to select all three buttons. Use the Format Size and Format Align commands to size and align the buttons as shown. Pull down the View menu, click the Tab Order command and specify AutoOrder.

e. Add a form header. You do not have to match our design exactly, but you are to include your name and a clip art image. Save the form. Go to Form view.

f. Click the button to add a new order, but skip the OrderID, CustomerID, and date fields. Click in the list box for the salesperson and choose anyone. The OrderID is created and today's date appears as the order date. Click in the First Name text box, enter your instructor's first name, and press Tab to create a new CustomerID. Complete the address and other information for your instructor, then click in the subform to create the actual order. Print the record for your instructor. Close the form.

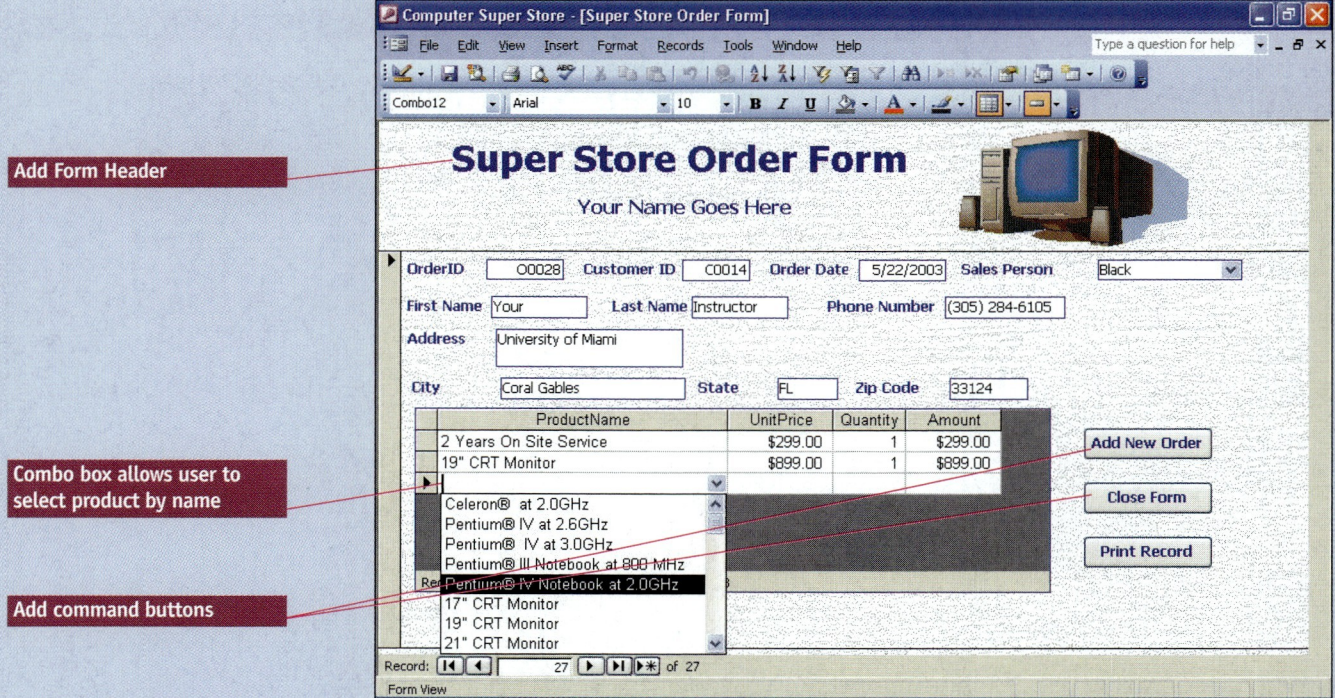

FIGURE 6.16 An Improved Order Form (exercise 3)

p r a c t i c e   e x e r c i s e s

4. **The Order Total:** The order form in Figure 6.17 looks very much like the form that was used throughout the chapter with one significant change; the total of the order is computed directly on the main form. This is a sophisticated change that is easily accomplished when you know how. In essence, you add a calculated control to the footer of the subform, then you reference that control on the main form. Proceed as follows:

a. Open the Order Details with Product Information Subform in Design view. Click and drag to open the Form Footer. Click in the Form Footer, then click and drag the Text box tool to create an unbound control. Enter =Sum([Amount]) to convert it to a calculated control. Right click the control, click Properties, click the All tab, then enter OrderTotal as the name of this control. Save the subform.

b. Click the down arrow on the View button to go to Form view to check the results. You should see a large number, in excess of $50,000, which represents the total of every order. Close the form.

c. Open the Super Store Order form in Design view. Move the phone number from the bottom of the main form next to the last name to give yourself more room in which to work. Move the subform up in the main form.

d. Click below the subform and use the Text Box tool to create an unbound control. Enter the expression =[Order Details with Product Information Subform].Form!OrderTotal. Be sure you enter the control correctly. The bracketed entry is the name of the subform. This is followed by a period, the word Form to indicate the type of object, an exclamation point, followed by OrderTotal (the name of the control on the subform).

e. Right click the control, click Properties, and then change the format to Currency with two decimals. Save the form. Go to Form view and view the first order. You should see a total of $605.86. Delete the digital camera from the first order, and the total changes to $155.91. Add the digital camera back in, and the total is again $605.86.

f. Return to Design view to add the finishing touches; for example, move, size, and/or format the control and its associated label. Pull down the View menu, click Tab Order, and then click AutoOrder. Save the form. Exit Access.

Move Phone Number next to Last Name

Move subform control up in the main form

Create calculated control for Order Total

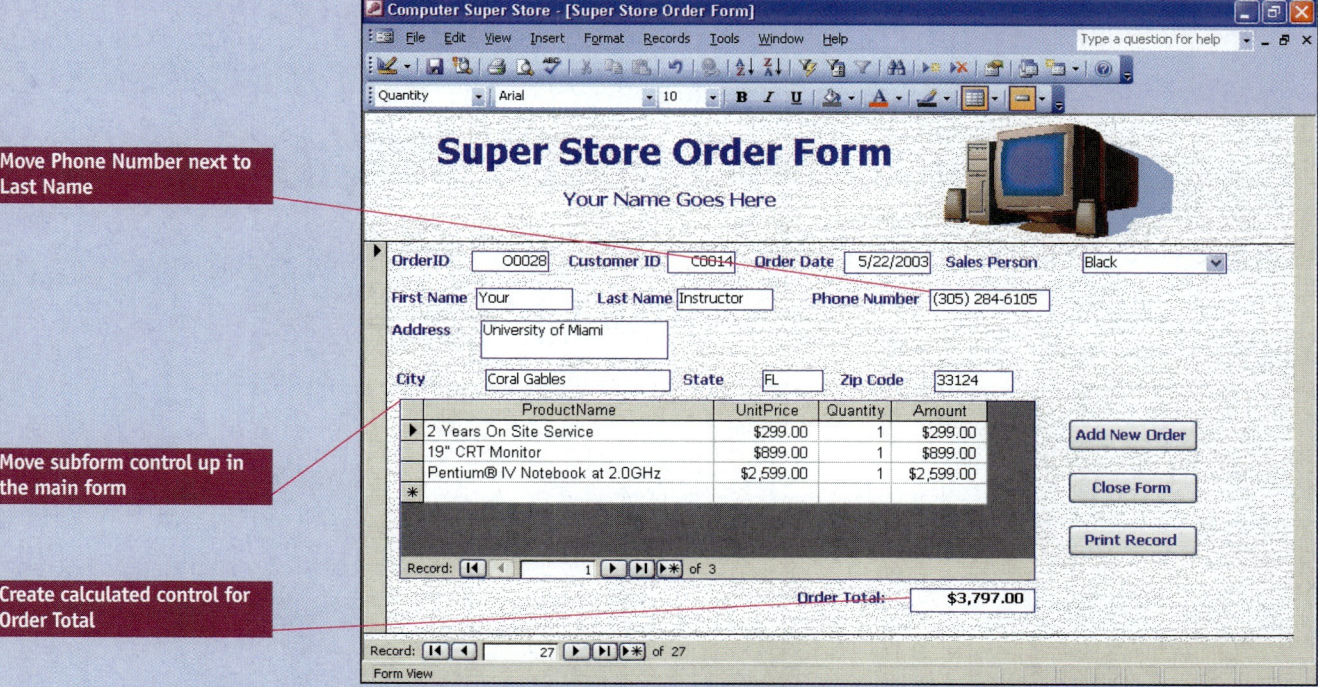

FIGURE 6.17   The Order Total (exercise 4)

MICROSOFT OFFICE ACCESS 2003 REVISED   323

practice exercises

5. **The Products Master List (using a subreport):** The report in Figure 6.18 lists all products by ProductID, and within each product, a list of orders that contained that product. The report can be created in different ways, one of which is to create a subreport. Proceed as follows:

   a. Open the partially completed Products Master List report (which we provide) in Design view. Click and drag the bottom of the Detail section to increase its size in order to accommodate the subreport.

   b. Click and drag the Subform/Subreport tool to start the Subreport Wizard. Click the option button to Use Existing Tables and Queries. Click Next.

   c. Select the Order Details with Product Information Query, then select every field except the ProductName. Click Next.

   d. Click the option button to Define my own link. Select the ProductID field from both reports. Click Next. Order Details with Product Information subreport is selected as the name of the report. Click Finish.

   e. You are back in Design view. Delete the label that appears above the subreport, then if necessary move the subreport up within the Detail section. Click and drag to reduce the width of the subreport, then reduce the width of the report to 6.5 inches. Click the Preview button.

   f. The ProductID field is redundant within the subreport, but it had to be selected or else the link would not have been possible. Close the Product Master List report. Click Yes when asked whether to save the report.

   g. Open the Order Details with Product Information subreport in Design view. Delete the ProductID in the Report Header and Detail section, then move the remaining items to the left. Reduce the width of the Quantity and Amount fields. Save the report.

   h. Open the Products Master List report to view the changes. Print the first page of this report for your instructor.

   i. The equivalent report can also be created using the Report Wizard. The process is basically the same except for the beginning, where you need to start the Wizard, then select the appropriate fields from the Products table and the Order Details with Product Information query. Which technique to you prefer?

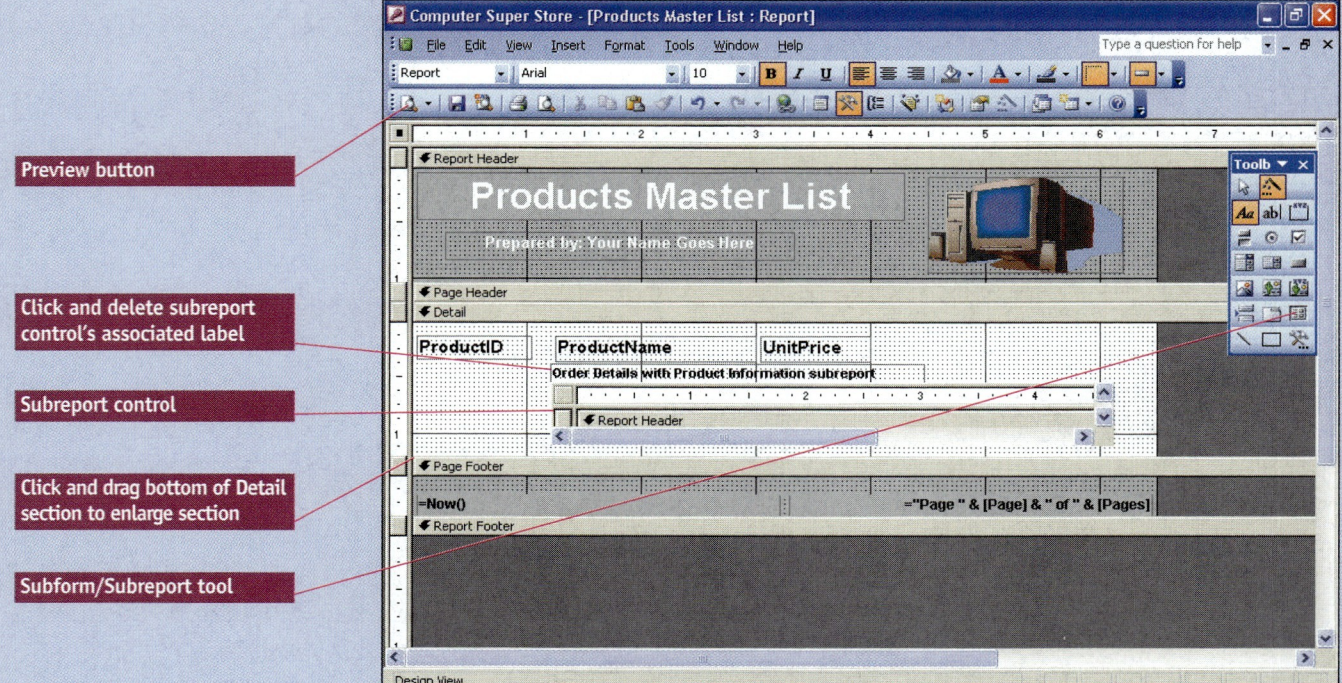

FIGURE 6.18 The Products Master List (exercise 5)

6. **Parameter Queries and Reports:** The report in Figure 6.19 is based on the parameter query that was created in the third hands-on exercise. The user is prompted to enter the name of a specific customer, after which the orders for that customer are displayed. The original query has been modified, however, to return every customer if the user omits the customer's name when prompted. Proceed as follows:

   a. Open the Customer Parameter query in Design view. Click the Run button, then click OK immediately when prompted to enter the customer's last name. The dynaset is empty because there are no records without a last name. Return to Design view to modify the query.

   b. Click in the Criteria row under LastName and change the existing entry to the following: Like ([Enter Customer's Last Name]) & "*". Run the new query to be sure that it works. Enter "Muddell" as before, and you get all of the orders for this customer. Run the query again, but this time omit the customer name, and you will get every order. The Like operator looks for a matching pattern; for example, if you enter "Muddell" you get Like "Muddell*" which returns every rep whose last name begins with Muddell. And if you omit the name, you get Like "*" which returns every record.

   c. Use the Report Wizard to create the report in Figure 6.19 based on the query you just created. The wizard will create the Page Header, Detail, and Page Footer sections automatically, but you have to create the Report Header yourself. The easiest way to do that is to open the report from the previous exercise in Design view, select the elements in its Report Header, click the Copy button, click the Report Header of this report, and click the Paste button. Change the title of the report, then save the report as Orders for Selected Customer. Close the report to return to the Database window.

   d. Print two different versions of this report for your instructor. The first version should show the orders for Muddell (or any customer you choose); the second version should show every customer. Compact and repair the database before closing it. Add a cover sheet to complete the assignment.

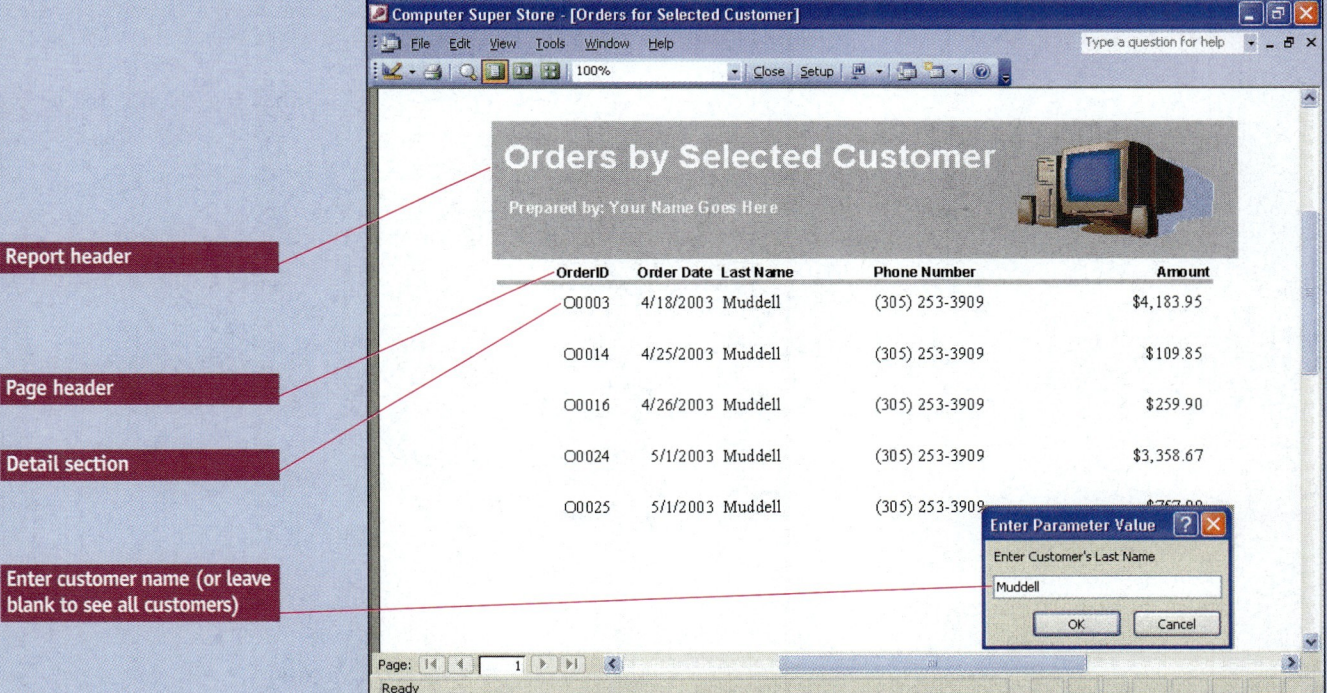

FIGURE 6.19 Parameter Queries and Reports (exercise 6)

7. **Computer Store Switchboard:** Implementation of the switchboard in Figure 6.20 completes the *Computer Store* database that you have worked on throughout the chapter. All of the objects referenced in the switchboard have already been created with the exception of the Sales Commission report that was described in the chapter (see Figure 6.12c to see the completed report). Your first task is to create that report, after which you can complete the switchboard. Proceed as follows:

a. Open the *Computer Store* database from the previous exercise. Click the Queries button in the Database window to create the Sales Commission query, which computes the total amount for each order and the commission on that order (5% of the total). The query is identical to the query in Figure 6.12a except that it omits the prompt under salesman's last name, so as to show commissions for every sales person, as opposed to a specific sales person.

b. Use the Report Wizard to create the initial version of the Sales Commission report (Figure 6.12c), based on the query that you just created, and then modify the report in Design view. You need not match our design exactly, but you have to display equivalent information. (Use steps 3 and 4 in Hands-on Exercise 3 as a guide in modifying the report design.)

c. The About Computer Store form is already in the database. Open the form in Design view and substitute your name in place of ours.

d. Use the Switchboard Manager to create the switchboard in Figure 6.20. All of the objects were created in the hands-on exercises and/or the previous end-of-chapter problems. You do not have to match our design exactly, but you have to include all of the command buttons as well as a logo.

e   Change the Startup property to display the switchboard automatically when the database is opened. Pull down the Tools menu, click the Database and Utilities command, then choose the Compact and Repair command. The database should close, and then reopen with the switchboard visible.

f. Print the completed switchboard for your instructor as well as the table of switchboard items. Include a printed version of each object referenced in the switchboard. Add a cover sheet, then submit all of the printed information to your instructor.

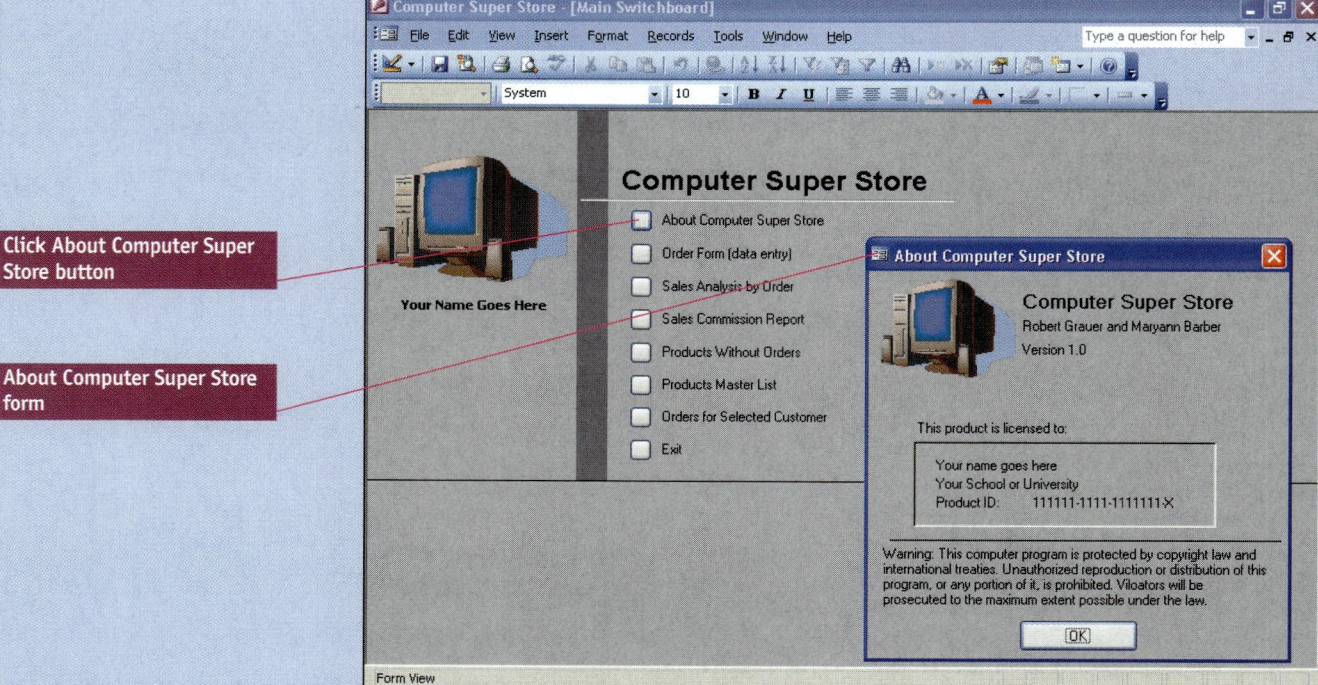

Click About Computer Super Store button

About Computer Super Store form

FIGURE 6.20 Computer Store Switchboard (exercise 7)

8. **Medical Research Database Design:** Your first assignment as an intern in the School of Medicine is to design a database that will track research studies, the physicians who work on those studies, and the volunteers (subjects) who participate. The system is required to produce multiple reports, such as the volunteers and physicians assigned to a specific study, as well as a list of physicians who are not assigned to a research study. Additional specifications are provided below:

a. There is a one-to-many relationship between studies and volunteers; that is, one study requires several subjects, but a specific subject may participate in only one study. Physicians, however, can work on multiple studies, and one study will have multiple physicians assigned to it. Each physician is designated as either a primary or a secondary investigator. (The same physician may be a primary investigator in one study and a secondary investigator in a different study.)

b. The Volunteers table stores all data about a specific volunteer (subject) such as name, birth date, gender, height, weight, blood pressure, cholesterol level, and so on. The Physicians table holds basic data about each physician. The Studies table contains all characteristics associated with a particular study such as the title, beginning date, ending date, and so on.

c A preliminary database design is shown in Figure 6.21. Your assignment is to open the partially completed *Chapter 6 Practice 8* database and create the relationships diagram that is shown in the figure. The tables have been created for you, and data has been entered into those tables to enable you to create various forms and reports as described in the next exercise. The relationships diagram should contain an appropriate logo or clip art image that will be used throughout the database.

d. You are also to create a simple switchboard with three menu options—a button to display an "About Medical Research" form describing the database, a button to print the relationships diagram, and a button to exit the application. The switchboard should contain the same clip art as the relationships diagram. (You can copy the clip art from the About form that is already in the database.) Use the Startup property to display the switchboard when the database is opened. Print the relationships diagram for your instructor.

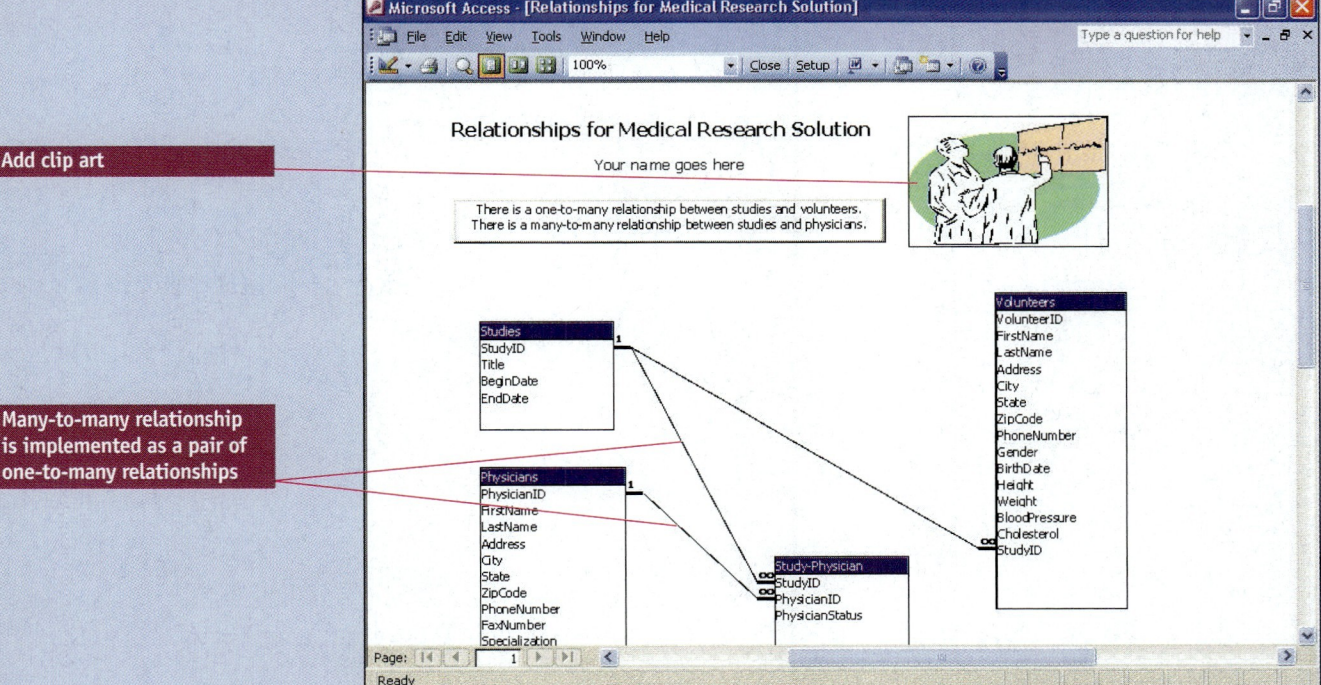

FIGURE 6.21 Medical Research Database Design (exercise 8)

9. **Medical Research Switchboard:** Implementation of the switchboard in Figure 6.22 completes the *Medical Research* database that was introduced in the previous exercise. The main switchboard provides access to various forms that enable you to add, edit, and/or delete records in every table within the database. The Report menu provides buttons to print the relationships diagram as well as each of the reports in parts (c), (d), and (e) below. Proceed as follows:

a. Use the Form Wizard to create a simple form to enter or modify data in the Studies table. Use the Form Wizard to create a second form for the Volunteers table. Open the Volunteers form in Design view, remove the StudyID, and replace it with a combo box that lets the user select the Study title (but store the StudyID).

b. Use the Form Wizard to create a main form/subform combination that enables data entry for the physicians and the studies in which they will participate. The main form should contain every field in the Physicians table so that a physician can be added using this form. The subform should be based on a query that uses the StudyID from the StudyPhysicians table so that you can assign a physician to a study. (Delete the StudyID and replace it with a combo box that lets the user select the Study title but store the StudyID.) Print the form for Dr. Holly Davis.

c. Use the Unmatched Query Wizard to create a query that lists physicians that have not been assigned to a study. Use the Report Wizard to create a report based on that query. Print the completed report.

d. Create a parameter query that requests the number of a specific study, then lists all of the volunteers for that study. Use the Report Wizard to create a report based on that query. Print the completed report.

e. Create a master list that displays all studies (in sequence by StudyID) and the associated volunteers in each study. The report should be grouped by StudyID and should display the name of the study and the start and end dates. The volunteers for each study should be listed in alphabetical order together with their telephone and address. Print the completed report.

f. Print the switchboard form and table of switchboard items for your instructor. Add a cover sheet, then submit all of the printed information to your instructor.

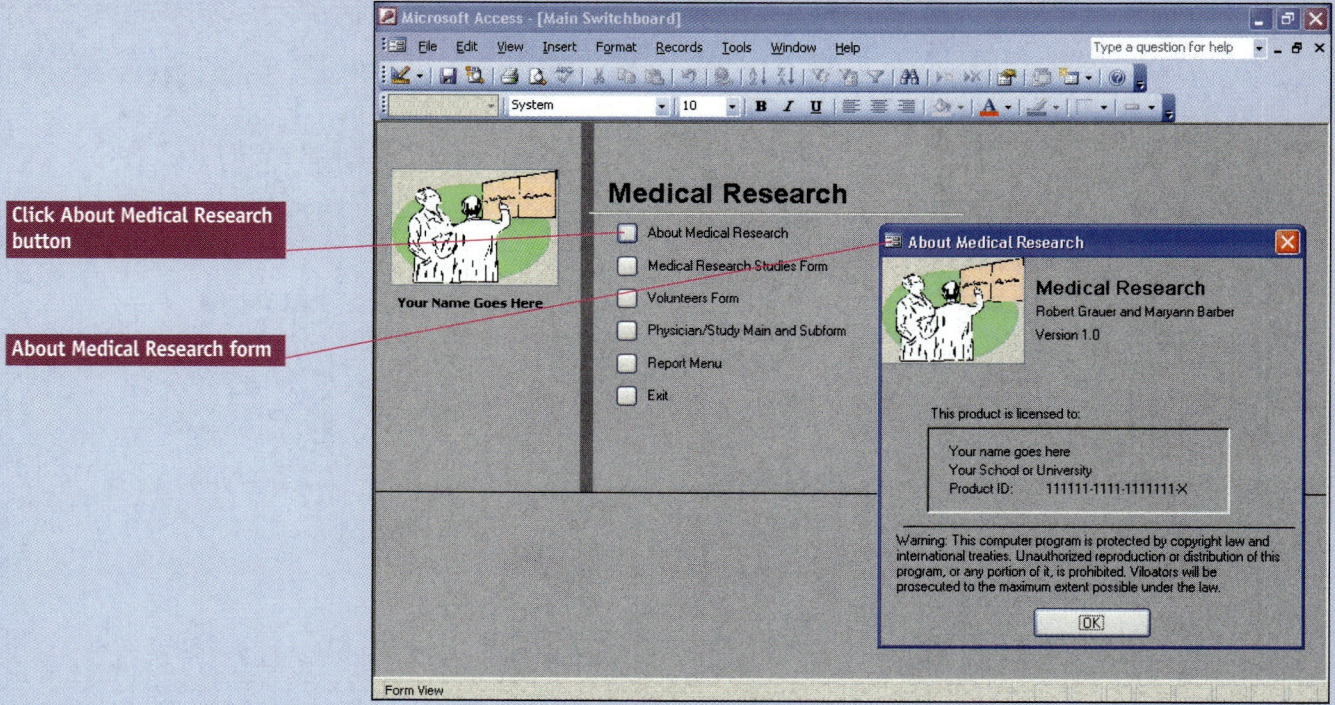

FIGURE 6.22 Medical Research Switchboard (exercise 9)

10. **National Conference Database Design:** You have been retained as a consultant to design a database for the national conference for a professional organization. This is an annual event, and the planning is extensive. The database is to track the speakers that come to the conference, the sessions at which they speak, and the rooms in which the sessions are held. The most important report produced by the system is the conference program, which is a master list of sessions and speakers. Additional specifications are provided below:

a. There is a many-to-many relationship between sessions and speakers; that is, one speaker can participate in many sessions, and one session can have many speakers. The Speakers table stores data for every speaker (name, address, telephone, e-mail, and so on). The Sessions table stores data for every session (the title, a more detailed synopsis of up to 500 words, the date, starting time, duration, and the room).

b. The database also tracks the rooms within the hotel to facilitate the session assignments. One room will host many sessions during the conference, but a particular session will be held in only one room. The Rooms table stores the capacity of each room as well as the special facilities within the room (e.g., large screens, the ability to serve refreshments, and so on).

c. A preliminary database design is shown in Figure 6.23. Your assignment is to open the partially completed *Chapter 6 Practice 10* database and create the relationships diagram that is shown in the figure. The tables have been created for you, and data has been entered into those tables to enable you to create various forms and reports as described in the next exercise. The relationships diagram should contain an appropriate logo or clip art image that will be used throughout the database.

d. You are also to create a simple switchboard with three menu options—a button to display an "About the Conference" form describing the database, a button to print the relationships diagram, and a button to exit the application. The switchboard should contain the same clip art as the relationships diagram. (You can copy the clip art from the About form that is already in the database.) Use the Startup property to display the switchboard when the database is opened. Print the relationships diagram for your instructor.

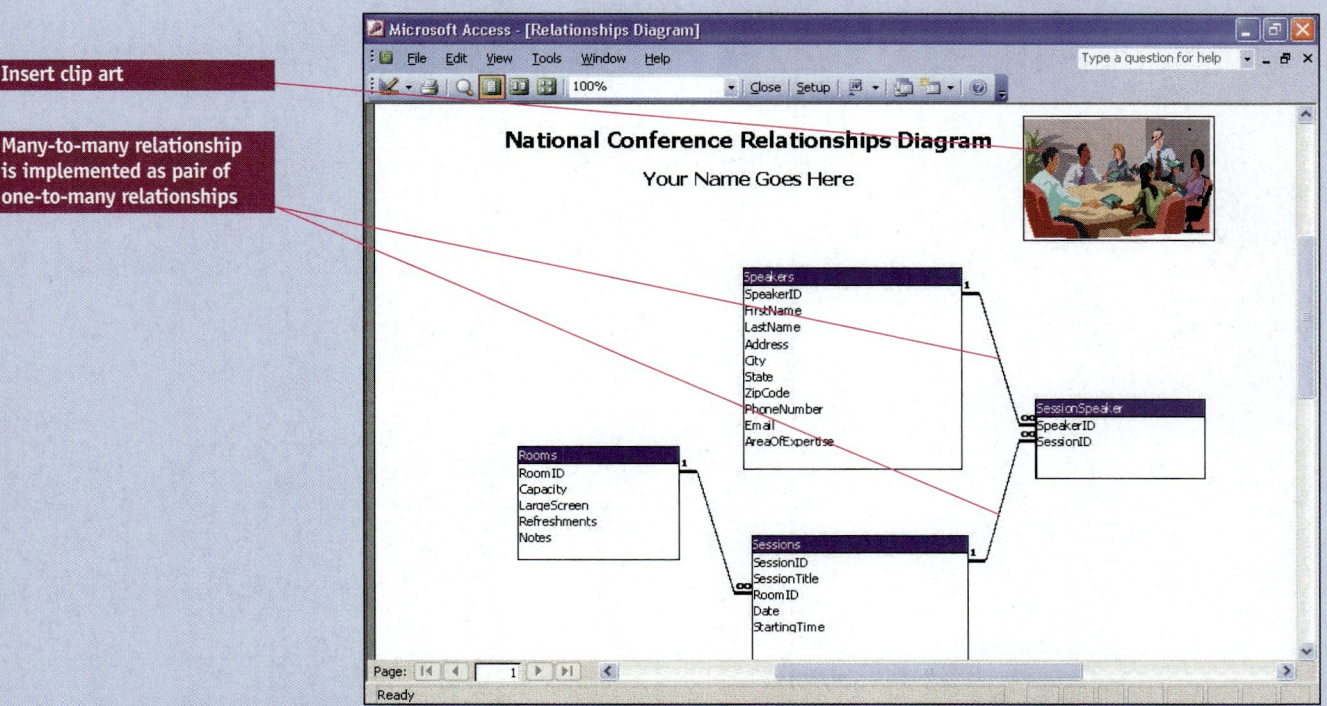

FIGURE 6.23 National Conference Database Design (exercise 10)

11. **National Conference Switchboard:** Implementation of the switchboard in Figure 6.24 completes the *National Conference* database that was introduced in the previous exercise. The main switchboard provides access to various forms that enable you to add, edit, and/or delete records in every table within the database. The Report menu provides buttons to print the relationships diagram as well as each of the reports in parts (c), (d), and (e) below. Proceed as follows:

a. Use the Form Wizard to create a simple form to add or modify data to the Rooms table. Use the wizard a second time to create a form for the Sessions table. (Replace the RoomID field with a combo box that enables the user to select the room for the session from the existing Rooms table.)

b. Use the Form Wizard to create a main form/subform combination that enables data entry for the speakers and the sessions they will participate in. The main form should contain every field in the Speakers table so that speakers can be added using this form. The subform should be based on a query that uses the SpeakerID from the SessionSpeaker table so that you can assign a speaker to a session. (Delete the SessionID and replace it with a combo box that lets the user select the Session title but store the SessionID.) Print the completed form to show the sessions for Cheryl Ashley.

c. Use the Unmatched Query Wizard to create a query that lists rooms that do not have sessions scheduled. Use the Report Wizard to create a report based on that query. Print the completed report.

d. Create a parameter query that requests a speaker's last name, then lists all of the sessions for that speaker. Use the Report Wizard to create a report based on that query. Print the completed report.

e. Create a report that shows the master schedule for the conference. The report contains data from both the Sessions and Speakers tables. It should group the report by session and display the name, time, and room of every session in sequence by session number, together with the speakers for that session, their phone number, and their e-mail address. Print the completed report.

f. Print the switchboard form and table of switchboard items for your instructor. Add a cover sheet, then submit all of the printed information to your instructor.

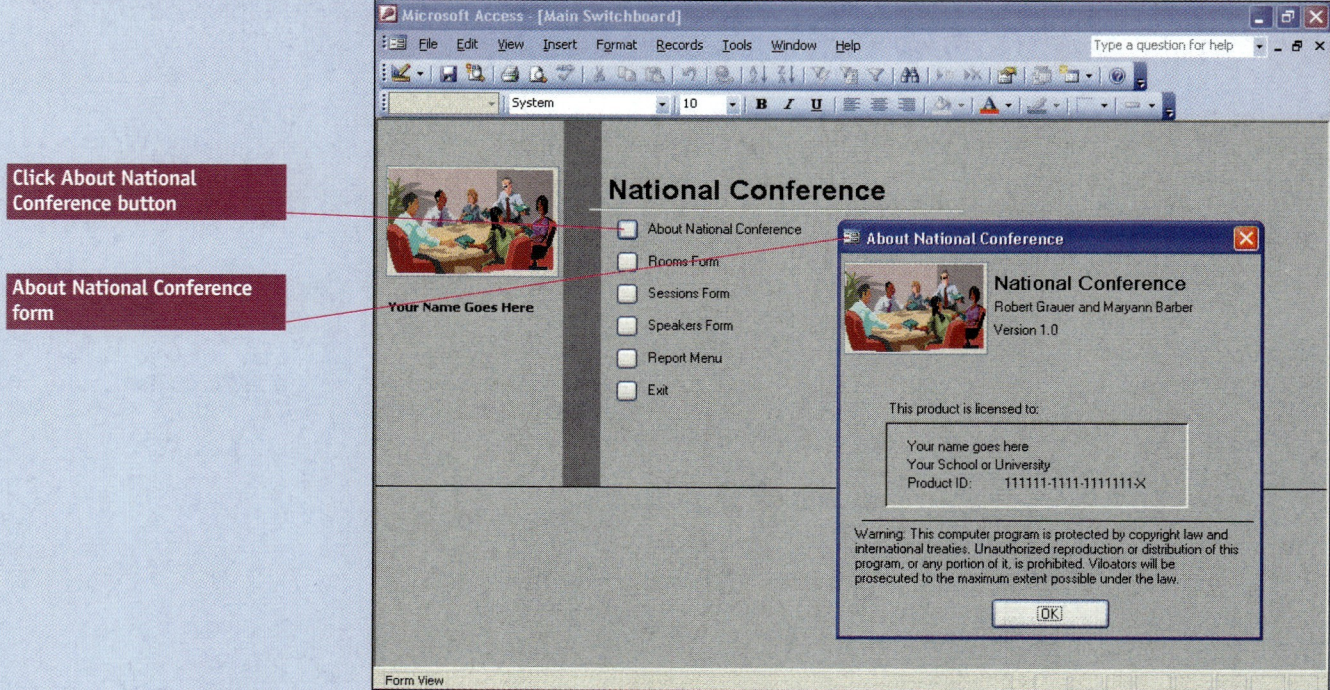

FIGURE 6.24 National Conference Switchboard (exercise 11)

MINI CASES

Health Clubs

Your interest in physical fitness has led to a part-time job at a local health club, where you have been asked to design a database for its members and trainers. The health club runs promotions periodically, and so individuals join under different membership plans. Each plan specifies the initial fee (if any), monthly payment (if any), and duration (in months). One plan can have many members, but a specific member has only one plan.

The health club needs to track the number of hours that each employee works, which is accomplished through time cards that record the date, time in, and time out. The health club also wants to know how often members work out, and which trainer they use—thus, all members complete a simple workout form each time they are at the club that contains the member's identification number, the date, the time in and the time out of the work-out, and the trainer seen. The workout form also indicates the specific facilities that were used in that session. One member can work out with different trainers, and one trainer will work out with many different members.

The database should be capable of computing the total revenue that is received by the health club. One report should show the sum of all initial fees that have been paid by all members. A second report should show the projected revenue each month, based on the monthly payment due from each member.

Print the report containing the relationships diagram for your instructor as proof that you completed this exercise. Create a simple switchboard with three menu options—a button to display an "About the Health Clubs" form describing the database, a button to print the relationships diagram, and a button to exit the application. The switchboard should contain the same clip art as the relationships diagram. Use the Startup property to display the switchboard when the database is opened.

The Morning Paper

We take the delivery of our morning paper for granted, but there is a lot of planning to ensure that we receive it each day. You are to design a database for a large metropolitan newspaper that is printed at a central location within the area. Once printed, the papers are delivered to multiple warehouses. Each warehouse services multiple carriers, each of whom goes to the assigned warehouse to pick up the requisite number of papers for his or her customers. One carrier has many customers, but a particular customer has only one carrier.

The database is further complicated by the fact that the newspaper has several editions such as a Spanish edition, a daily (Monday through Saturday) edition, and a Sunday edition. One edition can go to many customers, and one customer can order many editions. There is a specific price associated with each edition. You are to design a database that will enable the paper to determine how many of each edition is to be sent to each warehouse. The database should also be capable of producing a report that shows the total amount of business that each carrier brings in.

Print the report containing the relationships diagram for your instructor as proof that you completed this exercise. Create a simple switchboard with three menu options—a button to display an "About the Morning Paper" form describing the database, a button to print the relationships diagram, and a button to exit the application. The switchboard should contain the same clip art as the relationships diagram. Use the Startup property to display the switchboard when the database is opened.

The College Bookstore

The manager of a college bookstore has asked for your help in improving its database. The bookstore needs to know which books are used in which courses. One course may require several books, and the same book can be used in different courses. A book may be required in one course and merely recommended in another. The only course information that is required by the bookstore is the course number, the name of the course, and the faculty coordinator.

The design of this database begins with the creation of a Books table that contains the ISBN for each book, its title and author, year of publication, price, and publisher. Books are ordered directly from the publisher, so it is necessary to know the address and telephone for each publisher. One publisher has many books, but a specific book has only one publisher.

The bookstore places multiple orders with each publisher. One order can specify many books, and the same book can appear in multiple orders. The manager must know the date that each order was placed and the total cost of each order. The manager must also be able to create a report showing the books that are used in each course and its status for that course (i.e., whether the book is required or suggested). Your assignment is to design a database that will fulfill all of the requirements of the bookstore manager.

Print the report containing the relationships diagram for your instructor as proof that you completed this exercise. Create a simple switchboard with three menu options—a button to display an "About the Bookstore" form describing the database, a button to print the relationships diagram, and a button to exit the application. The switchboard should contain the same clip art as the relationships diagram. Use the Startup property to display the switchboard when the database is opened.

Chapter Recap—University Career Placement Center

The director of the University Career Placement Center has asked you to design a database that will keep track of the interviews that are being conducted in the Career Center. The director has to track which companies are conducting on-campus interviews at the Center, which students are being interviewed, and by which company. In designing the database, keep in mind that a company can interview many students and that a student has the option of interviewing with as many companies as he/she wishes. In addition, each student is assigned to one of the Center's three advisors, and that advisor will work with that student until he/she graduates.

The system you design must be able to generate reports on the advisors (name, office, phone number, fax number), students (name, campus address, campus phone number, major, GPA, graduation date), and companies (name, interviewer, address, phone number, industry). It should also be able to create reports that list the students interviewed by a given company, the companies that a given student has interviewed with, and the students assigned to a given advisor.

Your assignment is to review the chapter, paying special attention to the discussion of many-to-many relationships and referential integrity. You will then create a new database with the required tables for the Placement Center. You do not have to enter data into any of the tables, but you are to include all necessary fields and set the properties appropriately. You are also to implement the relationships within the system.

Your database should include a basic switchboard, an About form, and a relationships diagram. You should also use a common clip art image and consistent design elements for each object in the database. Print the switchboard form, the table of switchboard items, the relationships diagram, and the About form for your instructor.

7

Building Applications: Macros and a Multilevel Switchboard

CASE STUDY
THE MOVIE STUDIO

Maggie Moylan is majoring in Motion Pictures within the Communication Department and is studying for her bachelor's degree. The program at her university is unique in that it focuses on the business end of the movie industry. The capstone course in the program requires every student to design a database that will track the movies made by a hypothetical studio and the associated actors and directors. It is an interesting as well as a challenging project, and Maggie is eager to get started.

The professor divides the class into two-person teams. Maggie has been assigned to work with Cheryl Garner, who has submitted an initial design to Maggie for comments. Cheryl has determined that there is a one-to-many relationship between directors and movies; that is, one director will (over time) work on many movies, but a specific movie has only one director. Cheryl has also suggested a many-to-many relationship between actors and movies; one actor works on many movies, and one movie has many actors. The database is to contain the basic data about every director and every actor. It should also contain the director's salary (which may differ depending on the movie), as well as each actor's salary, which is also dependent on the specific movie. ■

Your assignment is to read the chapter, complete the hands-on exercises, then open the partially completed *Chapter 7 Case Study—Movie Studio*, and review the existing table design and relationships diagram. Your main task, however, is to develop an application prototype in the form of a two-level switchboard that will provide the "look and feel" of the completed application.

The main switchboard should include an About form, a relationships diagram, a form template, a button to display the report switchboard, and an option to exit. The second level (report) switchboard should contain the report template and various hypothetical reports. The visual design is very important, and you should include common clip art and design elements throughout. Use macros where appropriate such as the AutoExec and Prototype macros that were developed in the chapter.

This chapter revisits the concept of a user interface (or switchboard) that ties the objects in a database together, so that the database is easy to use. The switchboard displays a menu, often a series of menus, which enables a nontechnical person to move easily from one Access object to another. Any database containing a switchboard is known as an application and, unlike an ordinary Access database, it does not require knowledge of Microsoft Access on the part of the user.

The development of an application may also entail the splitting of a database into two files—one containing the tables and the other containing the remaining objects (the forms, reports, queries, and macros). The tables are then linked to the other objects through the Link Tables command. It sounds complicated, but this approach has several advantages, as you will see.

The chapter also covers macros and prototypes, two techniques that are used by developers in creating applications. A macro automates common command sequences and further simplifies the system for the end user. Prototypes are used in conjunction with developing the various switchboards to demonstrate the "look and feel" of an application, even before the application is complete.

You have probably played in a sports league at one time or another, whether in Little League as a child or in an intramural league at school or work. Whatever the league, it had teams, players, and coaches. The typical league registers the players and coaches individually, then holds a draft among the coaches to divide the players into teams according to ability. The league may have been organized informally, with manual procedures for registering the participants and creating the teams. Now we automate the process.

Let's think for a moment about the tables and associated relationships that will be necessary to create the database. There are three tables, one each for players, coaches, and teams. There is a one-to-many relationship between teams and players (one team has many players, but a player is assigned to only one team). There is also a one-to-many relationship between teams and coaches (one team has many coaches, but a coach is assigned to only one team).

In addition to the tables, the database will contain multiple forms, queries, and reports based on these tables. A Players form is necessary in order to add a new player, or edit or delete the record of an existing player. A similar form should exist for Coaches. There might also be a sophisticated main and subform combination for the Teams table that displays the players and coaches on each team, and through which data for any table (Team, Player, or Coach) can be added, edited, or deleted. And, of course, there will be a variety of reports and queries.

Let's assume that this database has been created. It would not be difficult for a person knowledgeable in Access to open the database and select the various objects as the need arose. He or she would know how to display the Database window and how to select the various buttons to open the appropriate objects. But what if the system is to be used by someone who does not know Access, which is typically the case? You can see that the user interface becomes the most important part of the system, at least from the viewpoint of the end user. An interface that is intuitive and easy to use will be successful. Conversely, a system that is difficult to use or visually unappealing is sure to fail.

Figure 7.1a displays the *switchboard* that will be created for this application. We have added a soccer ball as a logo, but the application applies to any type of recreational sports league. The interface is intuitive and easy to use. Click the About Sports button, the first button on our menu, and the system displays the informational screen we like to include in all of our applications. Click any other button, and you display the indicated form. Click the Teams button, for example, and you see the form in Figure 7.1b, where you can add a new team, view, edit, or print the data for any existing team, then click the Close Form button to return to the main menu.

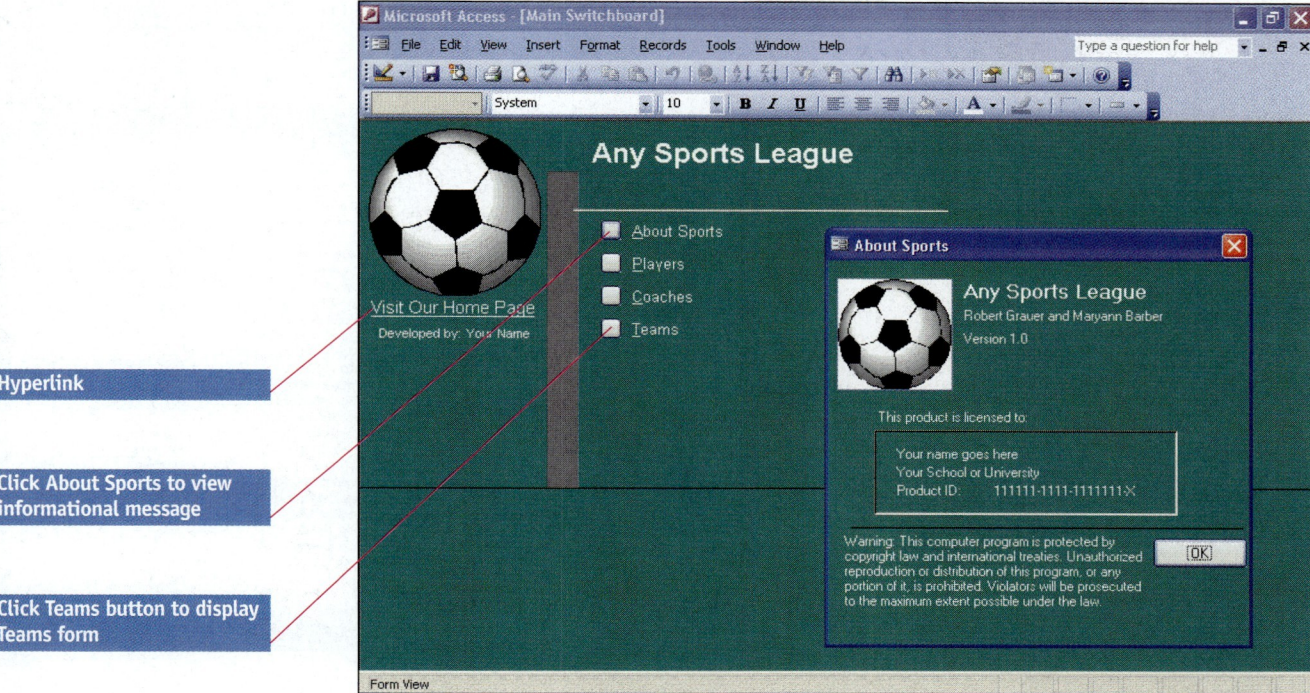

Hyperlink

Click About Sports to view informational message

Click Teams button to display Teams form

(a) The Main Menu

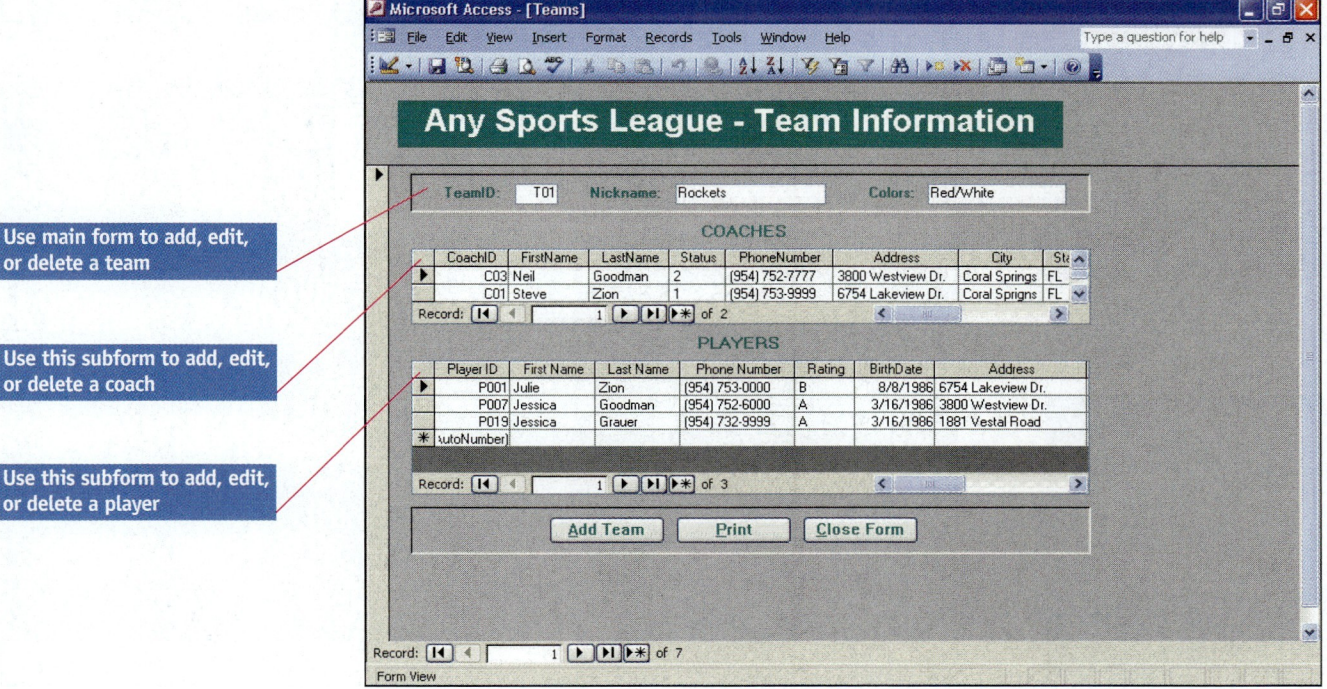

Use main form to add, edit, or delete a team

Use this subform to add, edit, or delete a coach

Use this subform to add, edit, or delete a player

(b) The Teams Form

FIGURE 7.1   Building a User Interface

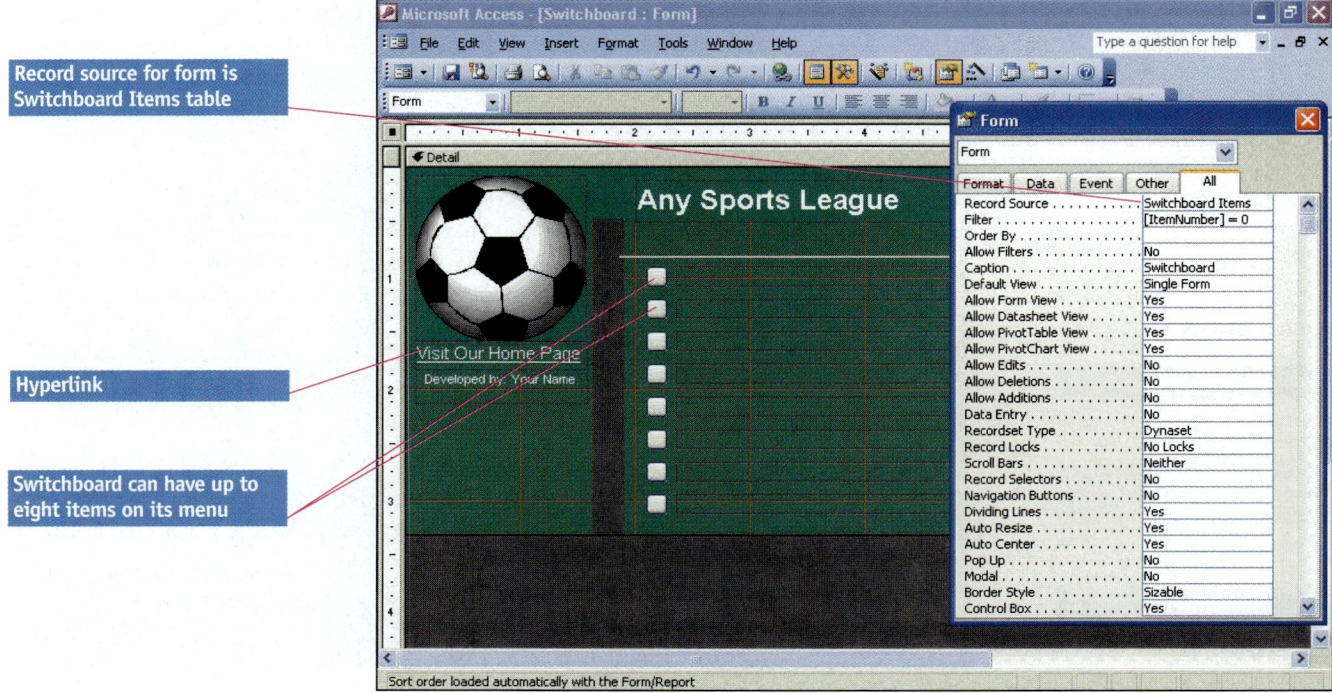

Record source for form is Switchboard Items table

Hyperlink

Switchboard can have up to eight items on its menu

(c) Design View

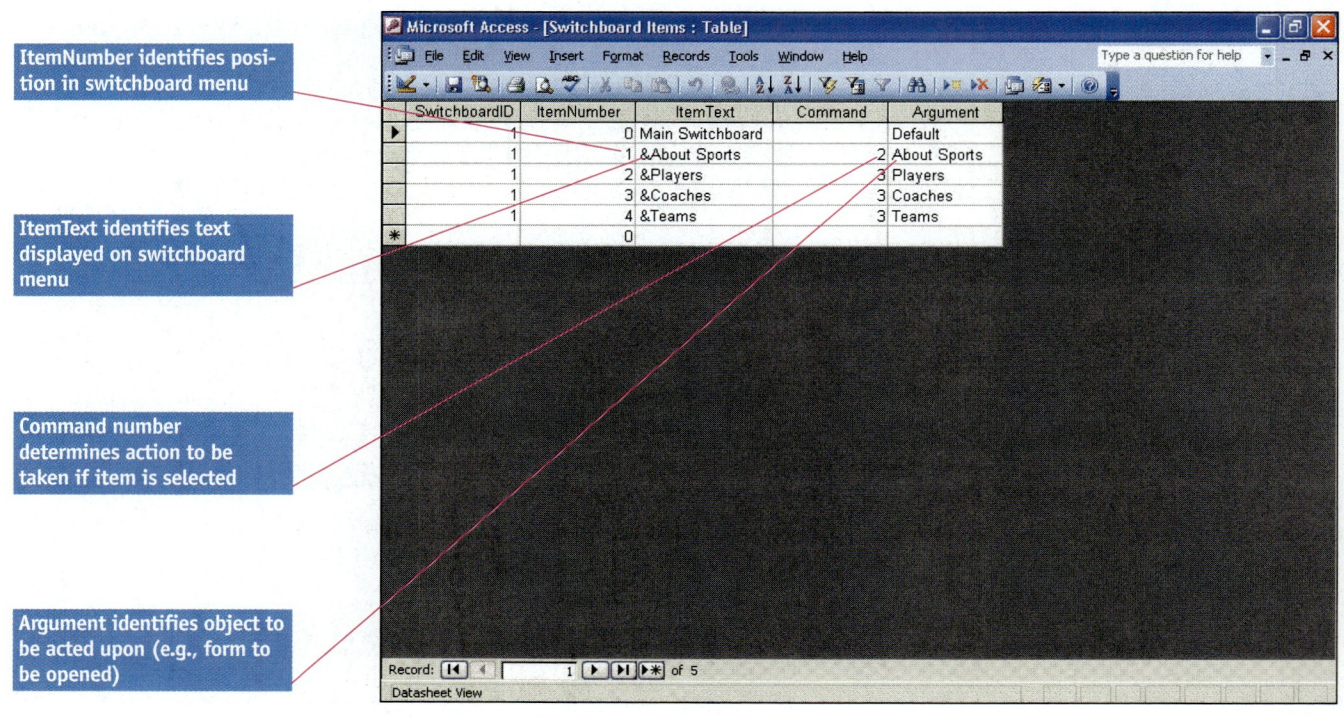

ItemNumber identifies position in switchboard menu

ItemText identifies text displayed on switchboard menu

Command number determines action to be taken if item is selected

Argument identifies object to be acted upon (e.g., form to be opened)

(d) Switchboard Items

FIGURE 7.1 Building a User Interface (*continued*)

The switchboard in Figure 7.1a exists as a form within the database. Look closely, however, and you will see it is subtly different from the forms you have developed in previous chapters. The record selector and navigation buttons, for example, have been suppressed because they are not needed. In other words, this form is not used for data entry, but as the basis of a menu for the user. You can even visit the league's Web site by clicking the indicated hyperlink.

The essence of the form, however, lies in the command buttons that enable the user to open the other objects in the database. Thus, when a user clicks a button, Access interprets that action as an *event* and responds with an action that has been assigned to that event. Clicking the Teams button, for example, causes Access to open the Teams form. Clicking the Players button is a different event, and causes Access to open the Players form.

The Switchboard Manager

The *Switchboard Manager* creates a switchboard automatically by prompting you for information about each menu item. You supply the text of the item as it is to appear on the switchboard, together with the underlying command. Access does the rest. It creates a *switchboard form* that is displayed to the user and a *Switchboard Items table* that stores information about each command.

The switchboard form is shown in both the Form view and the Design view, in Figures 7.1a and 7.1c, respectively. At first, the views do not appear to correspond to one another, in that text appears next to each button in the Form view, but it is absent in the Design view. This, however, is the nature of a switchboard, because the text for each button is taken from the Switchboard Items table in Figure 7.1d, which is the record source for the form, as can be inferred from the Form property sheet. In other words, each record in the Switchboard Items table has a corresponding menu item in the switchboard form. Note, too, that you can modify the switchboard form after it has been created, perhaps by inserting a picture or a hyperlink as was done in Figure 7.1.

As indicated, the Switchboard Items table is created automatically and can be modified through the Switchboard Manager or by directly opening the table. It helps, therefore, to have an appreciation for each field in the table. The SwitchboardID field identifies the number of the switchboard, which becomes important in applications with more than one switchboard. Access limits each switchboard to eight items, but you can create as many switchboards as you like, each with a different value for the SwitchboardID. Every application has a main switchboard by default, which can in turn display other switchboards as necessary.

The ItemNumber and ItemText fields identify the position and text of the item, respectively, as it appears on the switchboard form. (The & that appears within the ItemText field will appear as an underlined letter on the switchboard to enable a keyboard shortcut; for example, &Teams is displayed as T̲eams and recognizes the Alt+T keyboard shortcut in lieu of clicking the button.) The Command and Argument fields determine the action that will be taken when the corresponding button is clicked. Command number 3, for example, opens a form.

The Linked Tables Manager

Every application consists of tables *and* objects (forms, queries, reports, macros, and modules) based on those tables. The tables and objects may be stored in the same database (as has been done throughout the text), or they may be stored in separate databases, as will be done for the soccer application. Look closely at the Database window in Figure 7.2a. The title bar displays "Sports Objects" and indicates the name of the database that is currently open. Note, however, the arrows that appear next to the icons for the Players, Teams, and Coaches tables to indicate that the tables are stored in a different database. The name of the second database, "Sports Tables," is seen in the Linked Table Manager dialog box in Figure 7.2b.

The tables and objects are associated with one another through the **Link Tables command** and/or through the **Linked Table Manager**. Once the linking has been established, however, it is as though the Players, Coaches, and Teams tables were in the Sports Objects database with respect to maintaining the data. In other words, you can add, edit, and delete a record in any of the three tables as if the tables were physically in the Sports Objects database.

The advantage to storing the tables and objects in separate databases is that you can enhance an application by creating a new version of the Sports Objects database, without affecting the underlying tables. The new version has the improved features, such as a new form or report, but attaches to the original data, and thus retains all of the transactions that have been processed.

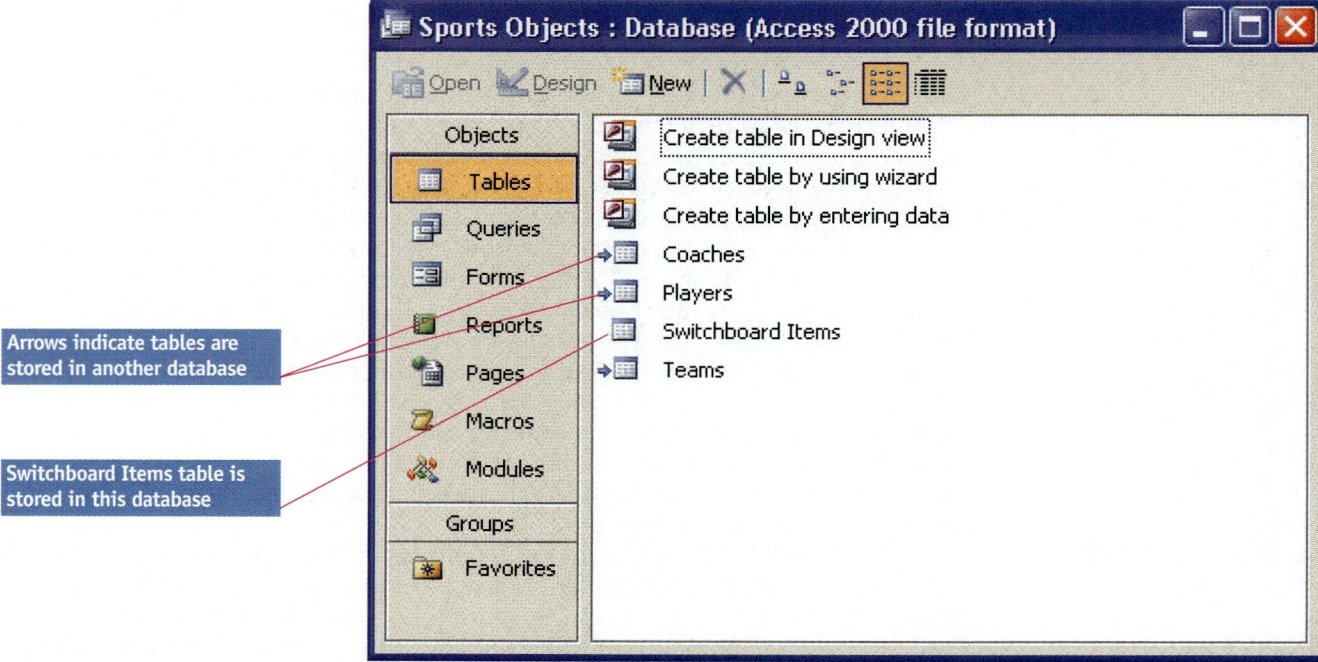

(a) The Database Window

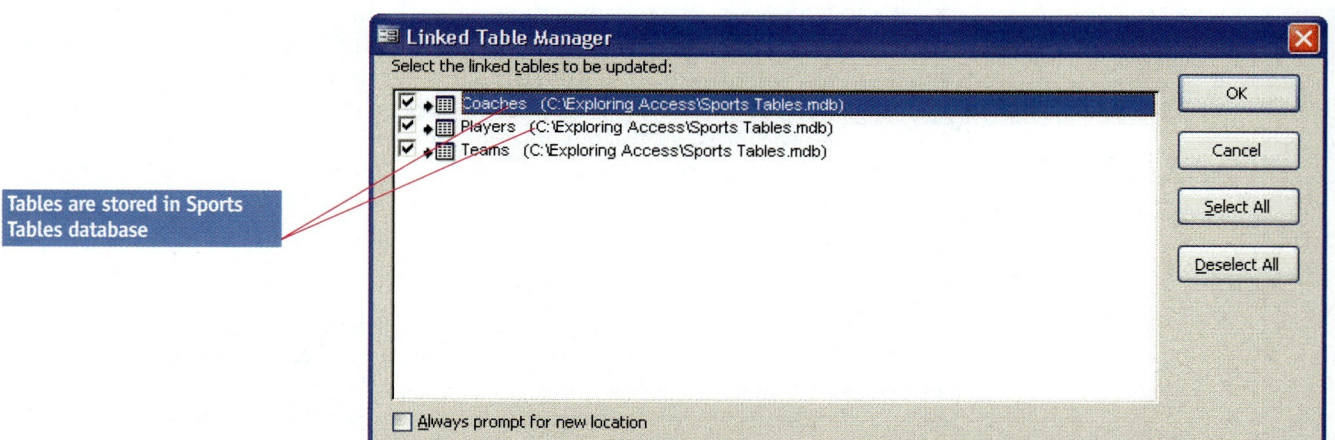

(b) The Linked Table Manager

FIGURE 7.2 Linking Tables

1 The Switchboard Manager

Objective   To create a switchboard; to use the Link Tables command to associate tables in one database with the objects in a different database. Use Figure 7.3 as a guide in the exercise.

Step 1:   **The Sports Objects Database**

■ Start Access. Change to the **Exploring Access folder** as you have been doing throughout the text.

■ Open the **Sports Objects database** as shown in Figure 7.3a, then click the various buttons in the Database window to view the contents of this database. This database contains the various objects (forms, queries, and reports) in the soccer application, but not the tables.
  ❑ Click the **Tables button**. There are currently no tables in the database.
  ❑ Click the **Queries button**. There is one query in the database.
  ❑ Click the **Forms button**. There are seven forms in the database.
  ❑ Click the **Reports button**. There is one report in the database.

■ Pull down the **File menu**, click **Database Properties**, then click the **Contents tab** to see the contents of the database as shown in Figure 7.3a. The Database Properties command enables you to see all of the objects on one screen.

■ Click the other tabs in the Properties dialog box to see the other information that is available.

■ Close the Properties dialog box.

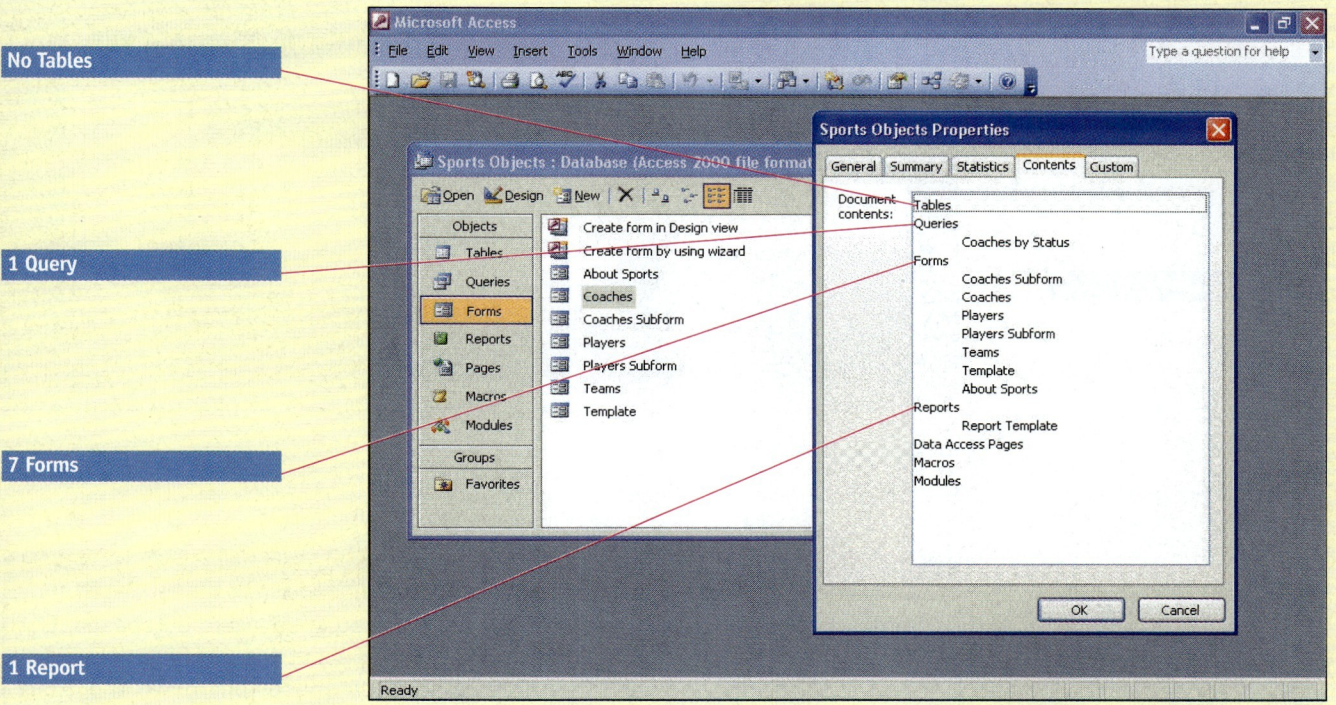

(a) The Sports Objects Database (step 1)

FIGURE 7.3   Hands-on Exercise 1

Step 2: The Link Tables Command

- Pull down the **File menu**. Click **Get External Data**, then click **Link Tables** from the cascaded menu. You should see the Link dialog box (which is similar in appearance to the Open dialog box).

- Select the **Exploring Access folder**, the folder you have been using throughout the text. Scroll (if necessary) until you can select the **Sports Tables database**, then click the **Link command button**.

- You should see the Link Tables dialog box in Figure 7.3b. Click the **Select All command button** to select all three tables, then click **OK**.

- The system (briefly) displays a message indicating that it is linking the tables, after which the tables should appear in the Database window.

- Click the **Tables button** in the Database window. The arrow next to each table indicates that the table physically resides in another database. (You may have to relink the tables if you move the database to another computer and/or to a different folder on this computer.)

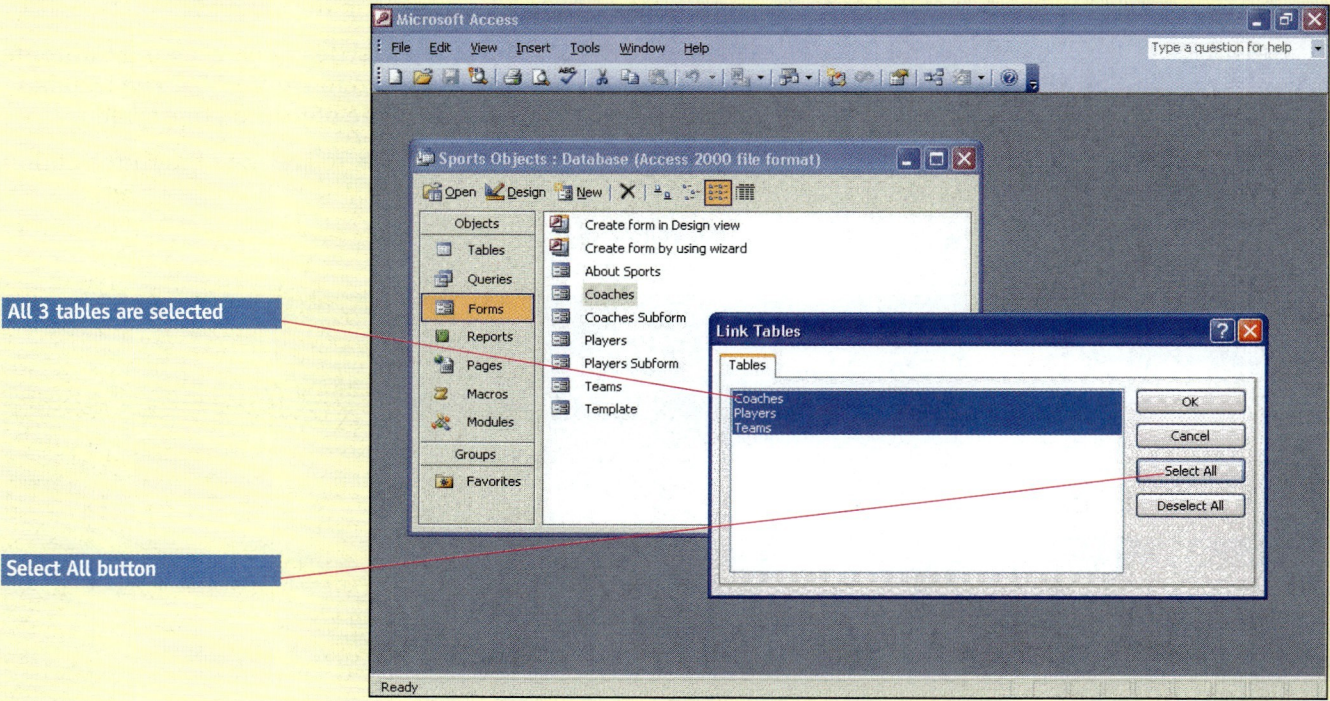

(b) The Link Tables Command (step 2)

FIGURE 7.3 Hands-on Exercise 1 (*continued*)

THE DATABASE SPLITTER

The tables and associated objects are typically stored in separate databases. But what if you created the application prior to learning about the ability to link tables and objects to one another? Open the existing database, pull down the Tools menu, click (or point to) the Database Utilities, select the Database Splitter command, and follow the onscreen instructions. You will wind up with two separate databases, a back end that contains the tables, and a front end that contains the other objects.

Step 3: **Start the Switchboard Manager**

- Minimize the Database window. Pull down the **Tools menu**, click the **Database Utilities command**, and choose **Switchboard Manager**.

- Click **Yes** if you see a message indicating that there is no valid switchboard. You should see the Switchboard Manager dialog box in Figure 7.3c.

- Click the **Edit command button** to display the Edit Switchboard Page dialog box. Click the **New command button** to add an item to this page, which in turn displays the Edit Switchboard Item dialog box.

- Click in the **Text** list box and type **&About Sports**, which is the name of the command as it will appear in the switchboard.

- Click the **drop-down arrow** on the Command list box. Choose the command to open the form in either Add or Edit mode (it doesn't matter for this form).

- Click the **drop-down arrow** in the Form list box and choose **About Sports**.

- Click **OK** to create the switchboard item. The Edit Switchboard Item dialog box closes and the About Sports item appears in the Main Switchboard.

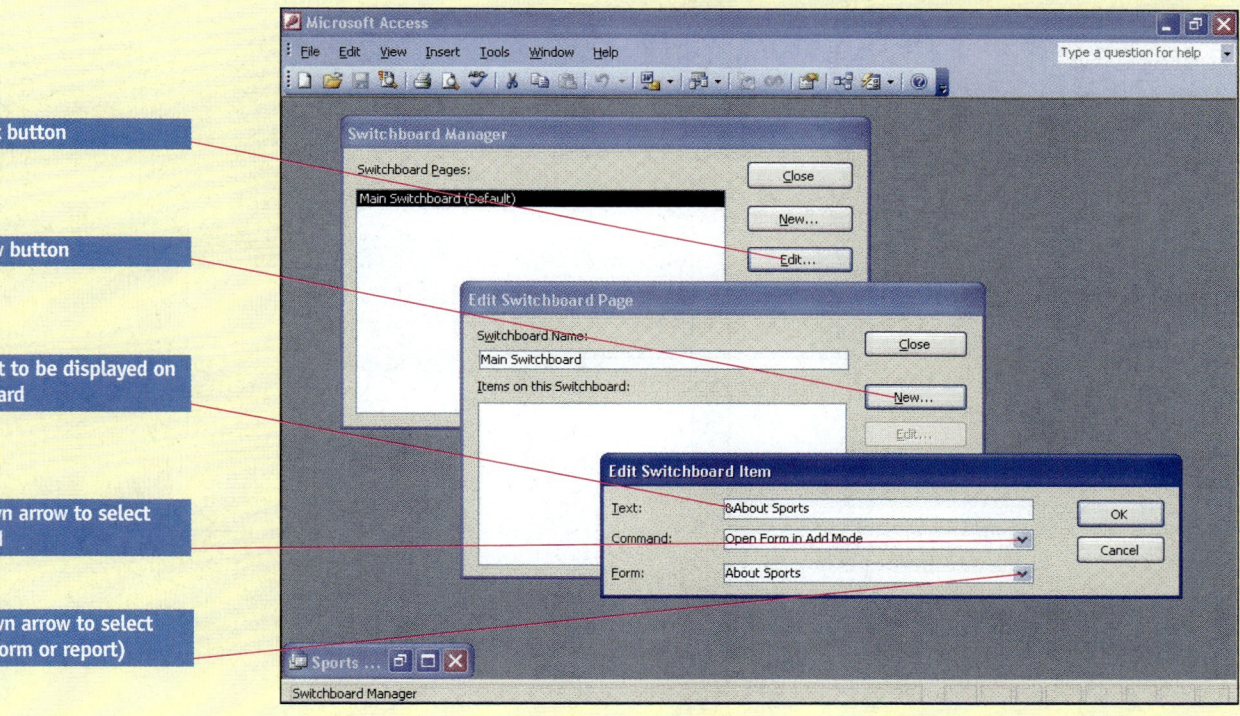

Click Edit button

Click New button

Enter text to be displayed on switchboard

Click down arrow to select command

Click down arrow to select object (form or report)

(c) Start the Switchboard Manager (step 3)

FIGURE 7.3 Hands-on Exercise 1 (*continued*)

CREATE A KEYBOARD SHORTCUT

The & has special significance when used within the name of an Access object because it creates a keyboard shortcut to that object. Enter "&About Sports", for example, and the letter A (the letter immediately after the ampersand) will be underlined and appear as "About Sports" on the switchboard. From there, you can execute the item by clicking its button, or you can use the Alt+A keyboard shortcut. Be sure to select a different shortcut (letter) for each menu item.

Step 4:   **Complete the Switchboard**

- Click the **New command button** in the Edit Switchboard Page dialog box to add a second item to the switchboard. Once again, you see the Edit Switchboard dialog box.

- Click in the **Text** list box and type **&Players**. Click the **drop-down arrow** on the Command list box and choose **Open Form in Edit Mode** (see boxed tip).

- Click the **drop-down arrow** in the Form list box and choose **Players** as the form.

- Click **OK** to close the Edit Switchboard Item dialog box. The &Players command appears as an item on the switchboard.

- Create two additional switchboard items for **&Coaches** and **&Teams** in similar fashion. Your switchboard should contain four items as shown in Figure 7.3d.

- Click **Close** to close the Edit Switchboard Page dialog box. Click **Close** to close the Switchboard Manager dialog box.

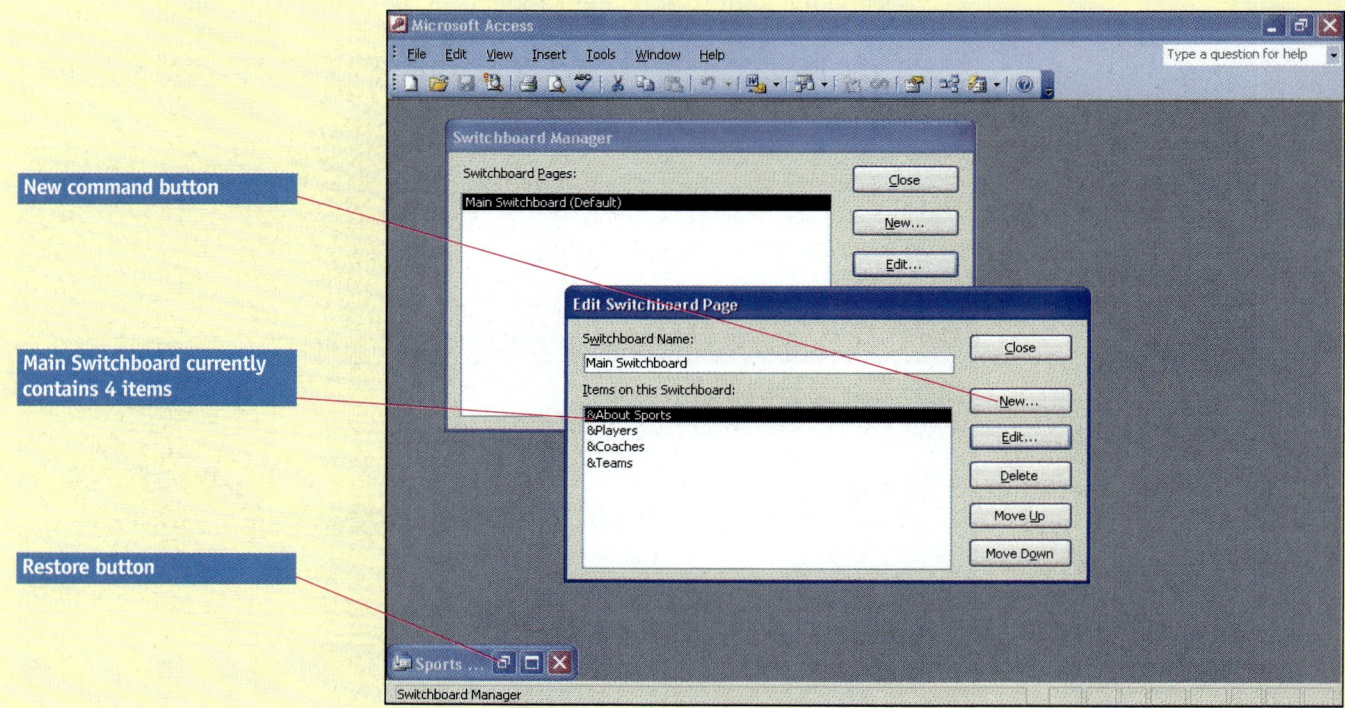

New command button

Main Switchboard currently contains 4 items

Restore button

(d) Complete the Switchboard (step 4)

FIGURE 7.3   Hands-on Exercise 1 (*continued*)

ADD MODE VERSUS EDIT MODE

It's easy to miss the difference between opening a form in the Add mode versus the Edit mode. The Add mode lets you add new records to a table, but it precludes you from viewing records that are already in the table. The Edit mode is more general and lets you add new records and/or edit existing records. Select the Add mode if you want to prevent a user from modifying existing data. Choose the Edit mode to give the user unrestricted access to the table.

Step 5: **Test the Switchboard**

- Click the **Restore button** in the Database window to view the objects in the database. Click the **Tables button**. The Switchboard Items table has been created for you (see boxed tip).

- Click the **Forms tab**. The Switchboard form has been created automatically by the Switchboard Manager. Double click the **Switchboard form** to open the Main Switchboard.

- Do not be concerned about the design of the switchboard at this time, as your immediate objective is to make sure that the buttons work. (We modify the design of the switchboard at the end of the exercise.) Maximize the window.

- Click the **About Sports button** (or use the **Alt+A** shortcut) to display the About Sports form as shown in Figure 7.3e. Click the **OK button** to close the form.

- Click the **Players button** (or use the **Alt+P** shortcut) to open the Players form. Click the **Maximize button** so that the Players form takes the entire window.

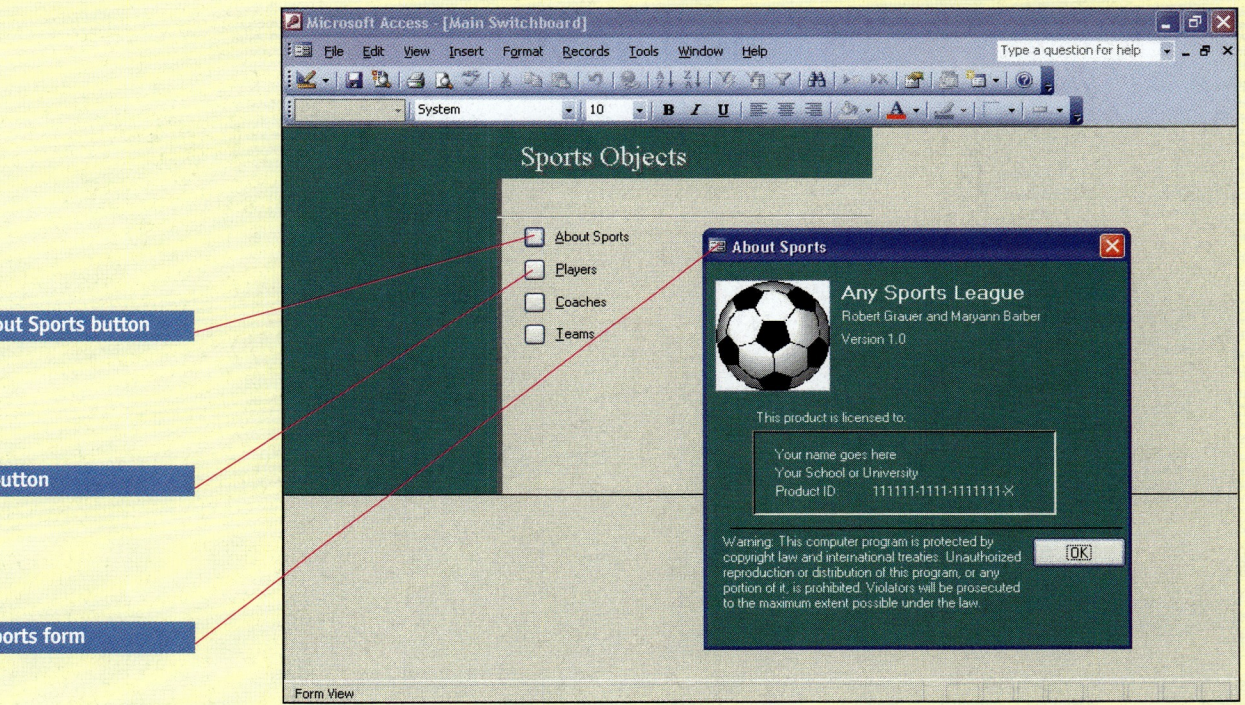

(e) Test the Switchboard (step 5)

FIGURE 7.3 Hands-on Exercise 1 (*continued*)

THE SWITCHBOARD ITEMS TABLE

You can modify an existing switchboard in one of two ways—by using the Switchboard Manager or by making changes directly in the underlying table of switchboard items. Press the F11 key to display the Database window, click the Tables button, then open the Switchboard Items table, where you can make changes to the various entries on the switchboard. We encourage you to experiment, but start by changing one entry at a time. The ItemText field is a good place to begin.

Step 6: Add Your Record

- Click the **Add Player button** on the bottom of the form (or use the **Alt+A** shortcut) to display a blank record where you will enter data for yourself as shown in Figure 7.3f.

- Click the **text box** to enter your first name. (The PlayerID is an AutoNumber field that is updated automatically.) Enter your name, then press the **Tab key** to move to the next field.

- Continue to enter the appropriate data for yourself, but please assign yourself to the **Comets team**. The team is entered via a drop-down list. Type **C** (the first letter in Comets) and Comets is entered automatically from the drop-down list for teams.

- The player rating is a required field (all players are evaluated for ability in order to balance the teams) and must be A, B, C, or D.

- Click the **Close Form button** to return to the switchboard.

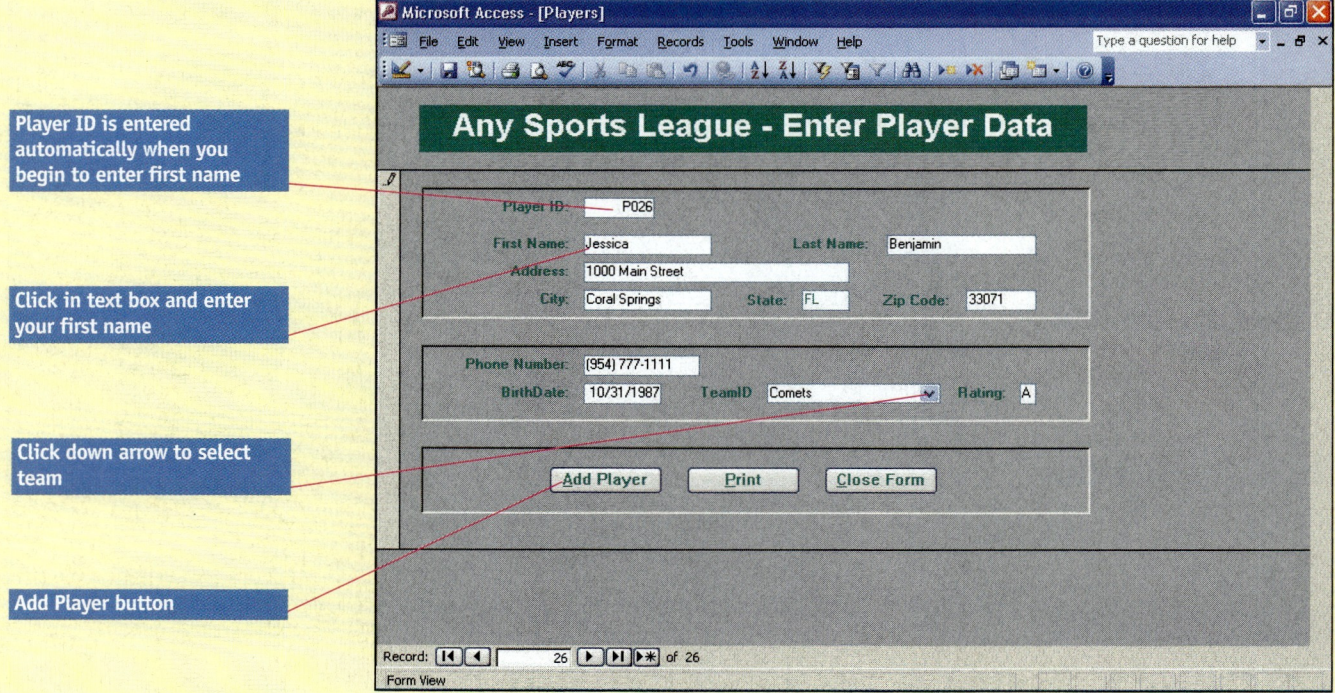

(f) Add Your Record (step 6)

FIGURE 7.3 Hands-on Exercise 1 (*continued*)

A LOOK AHEAD

The Add Record button in the Players form was created through the Command Button Wizard. The Wizard in turn creates a VBA *event procedure* that selects the blank record at the end of the underlying table and enables you to add a new player. The procedure does not, however, position you at a specific control within the Players form; that is, you still have to click in the First Name text box to start entering the data. You can, however, modify the event procedure by adding a VBA statement that automatically moves to the First Name control. See exercise 5 at the end of the chapter.

Step 7: Complete the Data Entry

- You should once again see the switchboard. Click the **Coaches button** (or use the **Alt+C** shortcut) to open the Coaches form.

- Click the **Add Coach button** at the bottom of the form. Click the **text box** to enter the coach's first name. (The CoachID is entered automatically since it is an AutoNumber field.)

- Enter data for your instructor as the coach. Click the appropriate **option button** to make your instructor a **Head Coach**. Assign your instructor to the Comets. Click the **Close Form button** to return to the switchboard.

- Click the **Teams command button** on the switchboard to open the Teams form and move to Team T02 (the Comets). You should see your instructor as the head coach and yourself as a player as shown in Figure 7.3g.

- Pull down the **Edit menu** and click **Select Record** (or click the selection area), then click the **Print button** to print the roster for your team.

- Click the **Close Form button** to return to the switchboard.

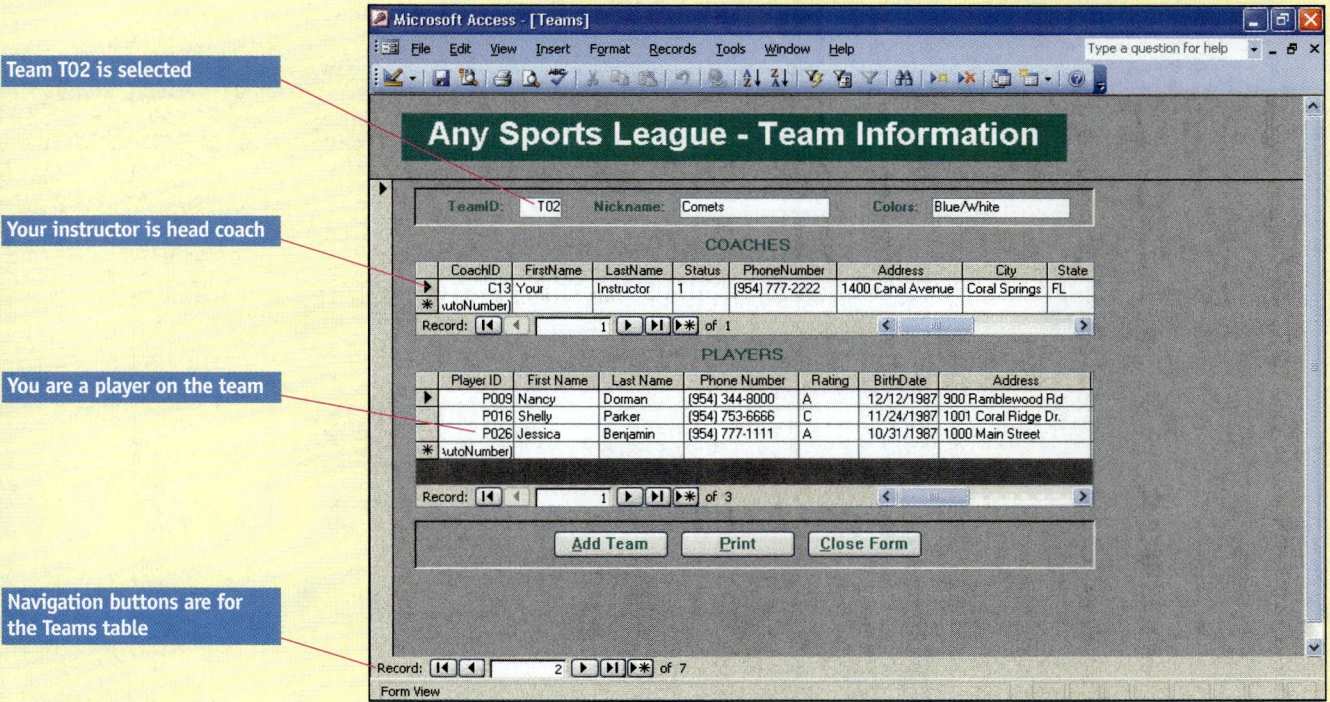

(g) Complete the Data Entry (step 7)

FIGURE 7.3   Hands-on Exercise 1 (*continued*)

THE DISPLAY WHEN PROPERTY

The Add, Print, and Close Form command buttons appear on the various forms (Team, Player, or Coach) when the forms are displayed on the screen, but not necessarily when the forms are printed. Open a form in Design view, point to an existing command button, then click the right mouse button to display a shortcut menu. Click the Properties command, click on the line for the Display When property, and choose when you want the button to appear—that is, when the form is displayed, printed, or both.

Step 8: **Insert the Clip Art**

- Change to the **Design view**. **Right click** in the Picture area of the form to display a context-sensitive menu, then click the **Properties command** to display the Properties sheet. Click the **All tab**.

- The Picture property is currently set to "none" because the default switchboard does not contain a picture. Click in the **Picture box**, then click the **Build button** to display the Insert Picture dialog box.

- Click the **down arrow** in the Look In box to change to the **Exploring Access folder**, then select the **SoccerBall** as shown in Figure 7.3h. Click **OK**.

- Size the picture as appropriate. The dimensions of the soccer ball should be changed to a square—for example, 1.5 inches × 1.5 inches. Close the property sheet.

- **Right click** below the picture in the Detail area of the form. Point to the **Fill/Back Color command** from the context-sensitive menu to display a color palette. Choose the same shade as appears on the rest of the form. (It is the fifth square from the left in the second row.)

- Click the **Undo button** if the color does not match. Save the form.

Click in Picture box and click Build button

Picture area

Click down arrow to select drive/folder

Select picture

(h) Insert the Clip Art (step 8)

FIGURE 7.3 Hands-on Exercise 1 (*continued*)

THE OBJECT BOX

The easiest way to familiarize yourself with the design of the switchboard is to click the down arrow on the Object box on the Formatting toolbar, scrolling as necessary to see the various objects. Select (click) any object in the Object box and it is selected automatically in the form. Right click the selected object to display its property sheet.

Step 9: **Complete the Design**

- Delete the label that contains the title of the switchboard, "Sports Objects". (You will have to delete two labels, because the switchboard manager automatically creates a shadow.)

- Click and drag the **Label tool** to create a new unbound control for the title of the switchboard. Enter **Any Sports League** as the title. Use **18 point Arial bold, in white** for the formatting.

- Click the **Label tool**, then click and drag to create a label under the picture. Enter your name in an appropriate font, point size, and color. Move and/or size the label containing your name as appropriate.

- Press and hold the **Shift key** as you click each text box in succession. The boxes appear to be empty, but the text will be drawn from the Switchboard Items table.

- Be sure that you selected all text boxes. Click the **drop-down arrow** on the Font/Fore Color button and change the color to white as shown in Figure 7.3i. Change the font and point size to **Arial** and **10pt**, respectively. Save the form.

- Change to the **Form view** to see the result of your changes. Exit Access if you do not want to continue with the next exercise at this time.

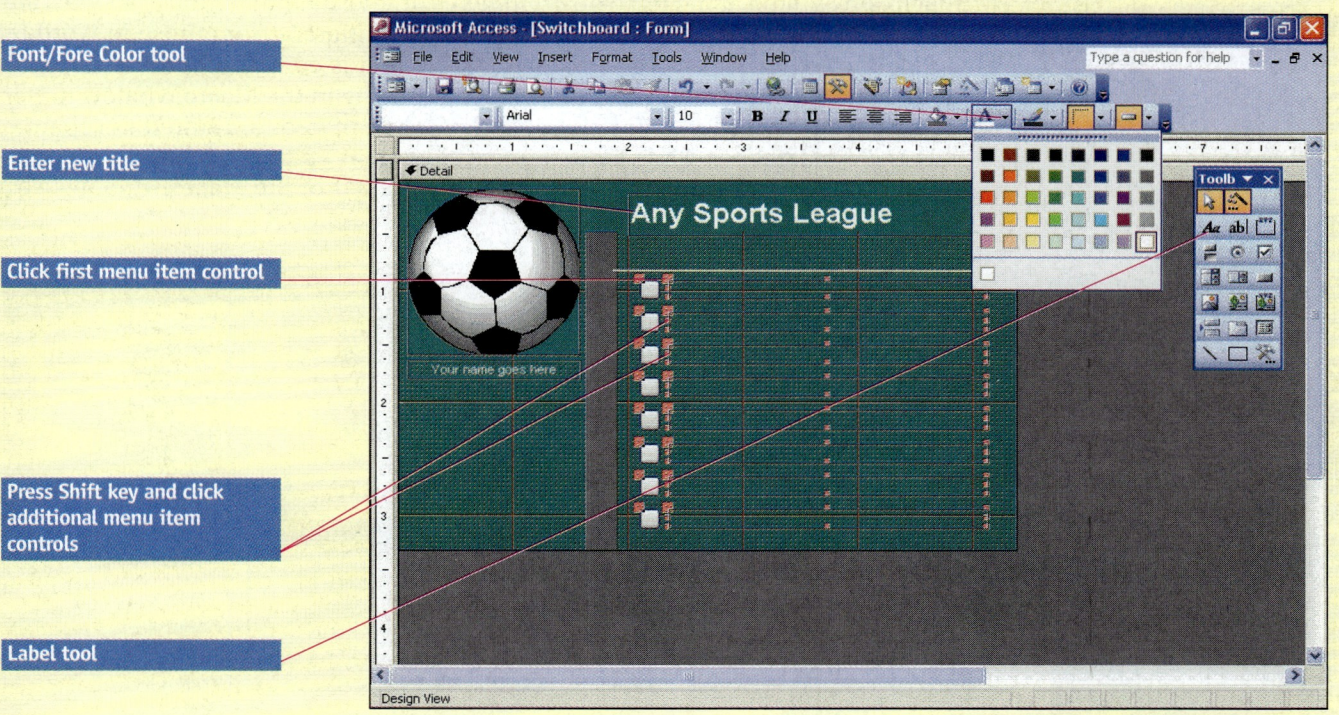

Font/Fore Color tool

Enter new title

Click first menu item control

Press Shift key and click additional menu item controls

Label tool

(i) Complete the Design (step 9)

FIGURE 7.3 Hands-on Exercise 1 (*continued*)

SET A TIME LIMIT

It's easy to spend an hour or more on the design of the switchboard, but that is counterproductive. The objective of this exercise was to develop a user interface that provides the "look and feel" of a system by selecting various menu options. That has been accomplished. Yes, it is important to fine-tune the interface, but within reason. Set a time limit for your design, then move on to the next exercise.

INTRODUCTION TO MACROS

The exercise just completed created a switchboard that enabled a nontechnical user to access the various tables within the database. It did not, however, automate the application completely in that the user still has to open the form containing the switchboard to get started, and further may have to maximize the switchboard once it is open. You can make the application even easier to use by including macros that perform these tasks automatically.

A **macro** automates a command sequence. Thus, instead of using the mouse or keyboard to execute a series of commands, you store the commands (actions) in a macro and execute the macro. You can create a macro to open a table, query, form, or report. You can create a macro to display an informational message, then beep to call attention to that message. You can create a macro to move or size a window, or to minimize, maximize, or restore a window. In short, you can create a macro to execute any command (or combination of commands) in any Access menu and thus make an application easier to use.

The Macro Window

A macro is created in the **Macro window**, as shown in Figure 7.4. The Macro window is divided into two sections. The **actions** (commands) that comprise the macro are entered at the top. The **arguments**, or information for those actions, are entered in the lower section. Access macros are different from those in Word or Excel, in that Access lacks the macro recorder that is common to those applications. Hence, you have to enter the actions explicitly in the Macro window rather than have the recorder do it for you. In any event, macros are stored as separate objects in a database. The macro name can contain up to 64 characters (letters, numbers, and spaces), and it appears in the title bar of the Macro window (e.g., Back up Your System in Figure 7.4).

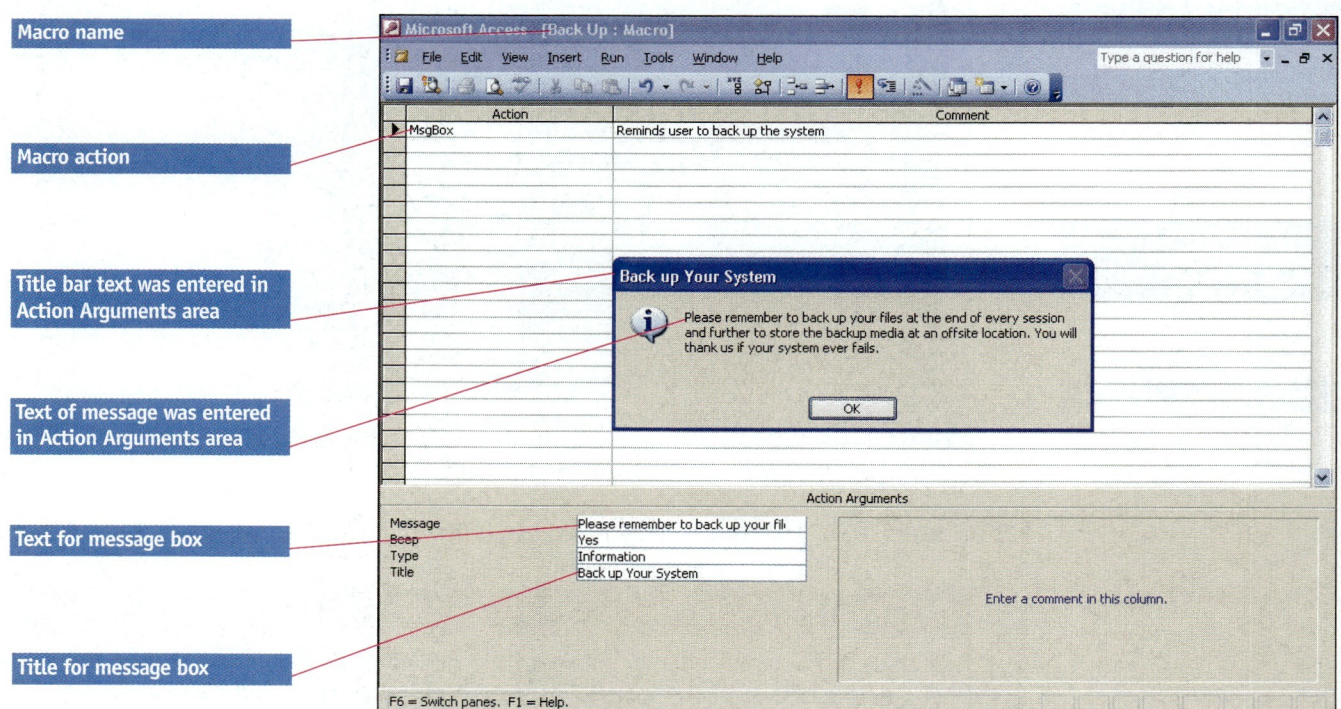

FIGURE 7.4 The Macro Window

To create a macro, select the Macros button in the Database window, then click the New button to display the Macro window. You add actions to a macro by clicking in the Action area, then choosing the action from a drop-down list, or by typing the name of the action. The arguments for an action are entered in similar fashion—that is, by choosing from a drop-down list (when available) or by typing the argument directly. The macro in Figure 7.4 consists of a single action with four arguments. As indicated, you specify the action, *MsgBox* in this example, in the top portion of the window, then you enter the values for the various arguments (Message, Beep, Type, and Title) in the bottom half of the window.

After the macro is created, you can execute it whenever the application is open. Execution of the macro in Figure 7.4, for example, will display the dialog box shown in the figure, to remind the user to back up his or her data. The contents of the dialog box are determined by the value of the arguments. The text of the dialog box is specified in the Message argument, only a portion of which is visible in the Macro window. The value of the Type argument determines the icon that is displayed within the dialog box (Information in this example). The Title argument contains the text that appears in the title bar of the dialog box.

The *macro toolbar* is displayed at the top of the Macro window and contains buttons that help create and test a macro. Many of the buttons (e.g., the Database window, Save, and Help buttons) are common to other toolbars you have used in conjunction with other objects. Other buttons are specific to the Macro window and are referenced in the hands-on exercises. As with other toolbars, you can point to a button to display its ScreenTip and determine its purpose.

The AutoExec Macro

The *AutoExec macro* is unique in that it is executed automatically whenever the database in which it is stored is opened. The macro is used to automate a system for the end user. It typically contains an OpenForm action to open the form containing the main switchboard. It may also perform other housekeeping chores, such as maximizing the current window.

Every database can have its own AutoExec macro, but there is no requirement for the AutoExec macro to be present. We recommend, however, that you include an AutoExec macro in every application to help the user get started.

Debugging

Writing a macro is similar to writing a program, in that errors occur if the actions and/or the associated arguments are specified incorrectly. Should Access encounter an error during the execution of a macro, it displays as much information as it can to help you determine the reason for the error.

Figure 7.5 contains an erroneous version of the AutoExec macro that attempts to open the Switchboard form. The macro contains two actions, Maximize and OpenForm. The Maximize action maximizes the Database window and affects all subsequent screens that will be displayed in the application. The OpenForm macro is intended to open the switchboard from the previous exercise. The name of the form is deliberately misspelled.

When the AutoExec macro is executed, Access attempts to open a form called "Switchboards", but is unable to do so, and hence it displays the informational message in the figure. Click OK, and you are presented with another dialog box, which attempts to step you through the macro and discover the cause of the error. As indicated, the error is due to the fact that the name of the form should have been "Switchboard" rather than "Switchboard*s*". The errors will not always be this easy to find, and hopefully, you will not make any. Should a bug occur, however, you will know where to begin the *debugging* process.

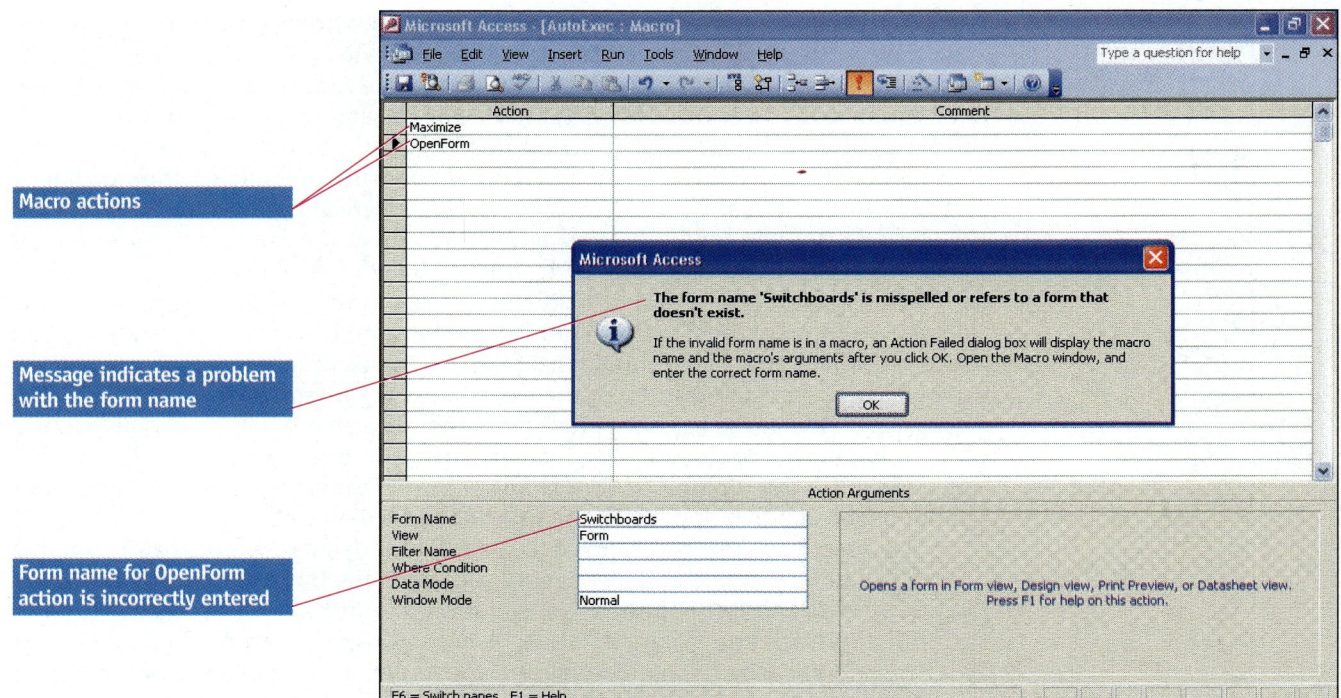

Macro actions

Message indicates a problem with the form name

Form name for OpenForm action is incorrectly entered

FIGURE 7.5 Debugging

APPLICATION DEVELOPMENT

Application development is an iterative process that entails continual dialog between the end user (client) and the developer. In essence, the developer presents the client with multiple versions of the application, with each successive version containing additional functionality. The user tests and evaluates each version and provides comments to the developer, who incorporates the feedback and delivers a new version (release) of the application. The process continues with each successive release containing increased functionality until the system is complete.

The user is presented with a working system (or ***prototype***) at every stage of testing that captures the "look and feel" of the finished application. The switchboard in Figure 7.6a, for example, is an updated version of the main switchboard from the first hands-on exercise. Two menu options have been added—a report menu that displays the report switchboard in Figure 7.6b and a player draft. (The latter is a form that is used to assign players to teams and is developed later in the chapter.) The Switchboard Manager creates both switchboards.

The reports, however, have not yet been created, nor do they need to be, because the user can click any of the buttons on the report switchboard and see the indicated message, which was created by a simple macro. The application is "complete" in the sense that every button on the switchboard works, but it is incomplete in that the reports have not been fully developed. Nevertheless, the prototype lets the user see a working system and enables the user to provide immediate feedback. He or she sees immediately all of the planned reports and can comment on whether any additional reports are required.

The Report switchboard also provides access to the report template. The purpose of the ***template*** is to provide additional feedback to the user with respect to the appearance of the eventual reports. It is just as easy to create an attractive report as an ugly one, and a uniform Report Header adds to the professional look of an application. The sooner the user communicates the requested changes to the developer, the easier (and less costly) it is for the developer to incorporate those changes.

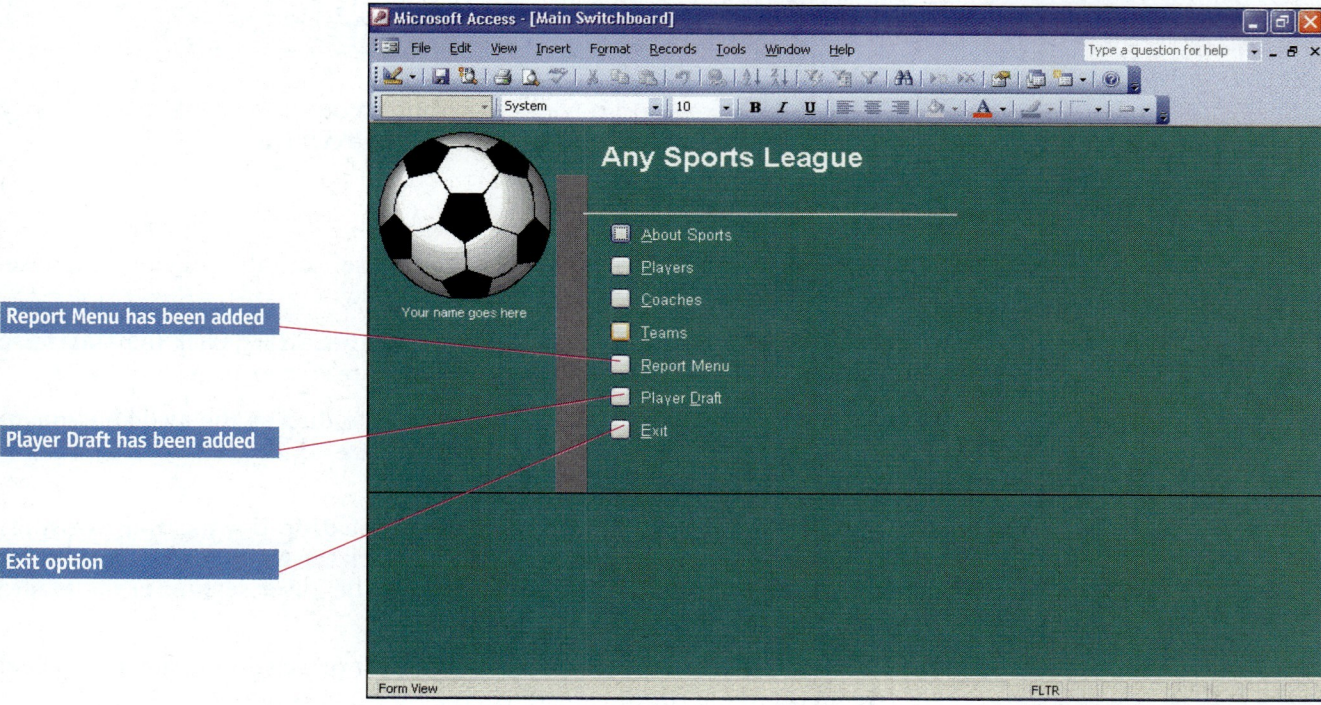

Report Menu has been added

Player Draft has been added

Exit option

(a) Main Switchboard

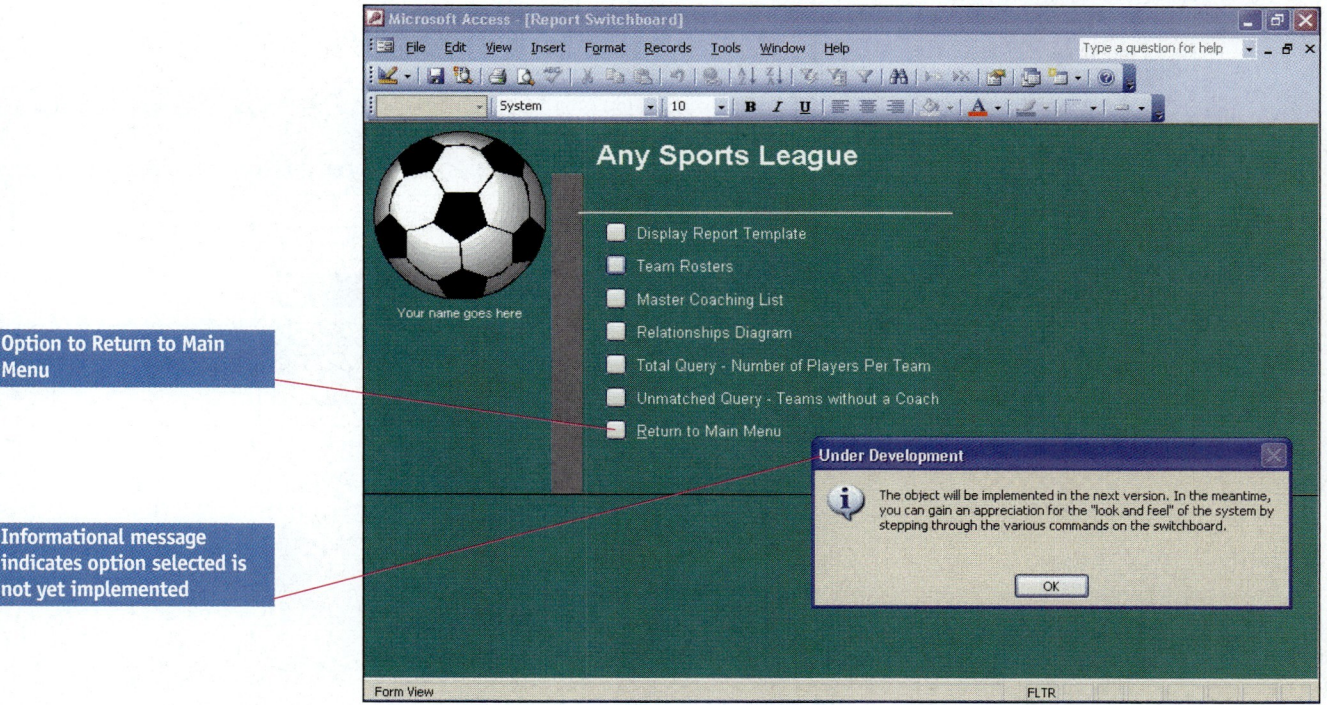

Option to Return to Main Menu

Informational message indicates option selected is not yet implemented

(b) Report Switchboard

FIGURE 7.6 Application Development

2 Macros and Prototyping

Objective To create an AutoExec and a Close Database macro; to create a subsidiary switchboard. Use Figure 7.7 as a guide in the exercise.

Step 1: **Create the AutoExec Macro**

- Start Access. Open the **Sports Objects database** from the previous exercise. Click the **Macros button** in the Database window.

- Click the **New button** to create a new macro. If necessary, click the **Maximize button** so that the Macro window takes the entire screen as in Figure 7.7a.

- Click the **drop-down arrow** in the Action box to display the available macro actions. Scroll until you can select the **Maximize** action. (There are no arguments for this action.)

- Click the **Action box** on the second line, click the **drop-down arrow** to display the macro actions, then scroll until you can click the **OpenForm action**. Click the text box for the **Form Name** argument in the lower section of the Macro window.

- Click the **drop-down arrow** to display the list of existing forms and select **Switchboard** (the form you created in the previous exercise).

- Click the **Save button** to display the Save As dialog box in Figure 7.7a. Type **AutoExec** as the macro name and click **OK**.

- Click the **Run button** to run the macro and open the switchboard.

- Close the switchboard. Close the AutoExec macro.

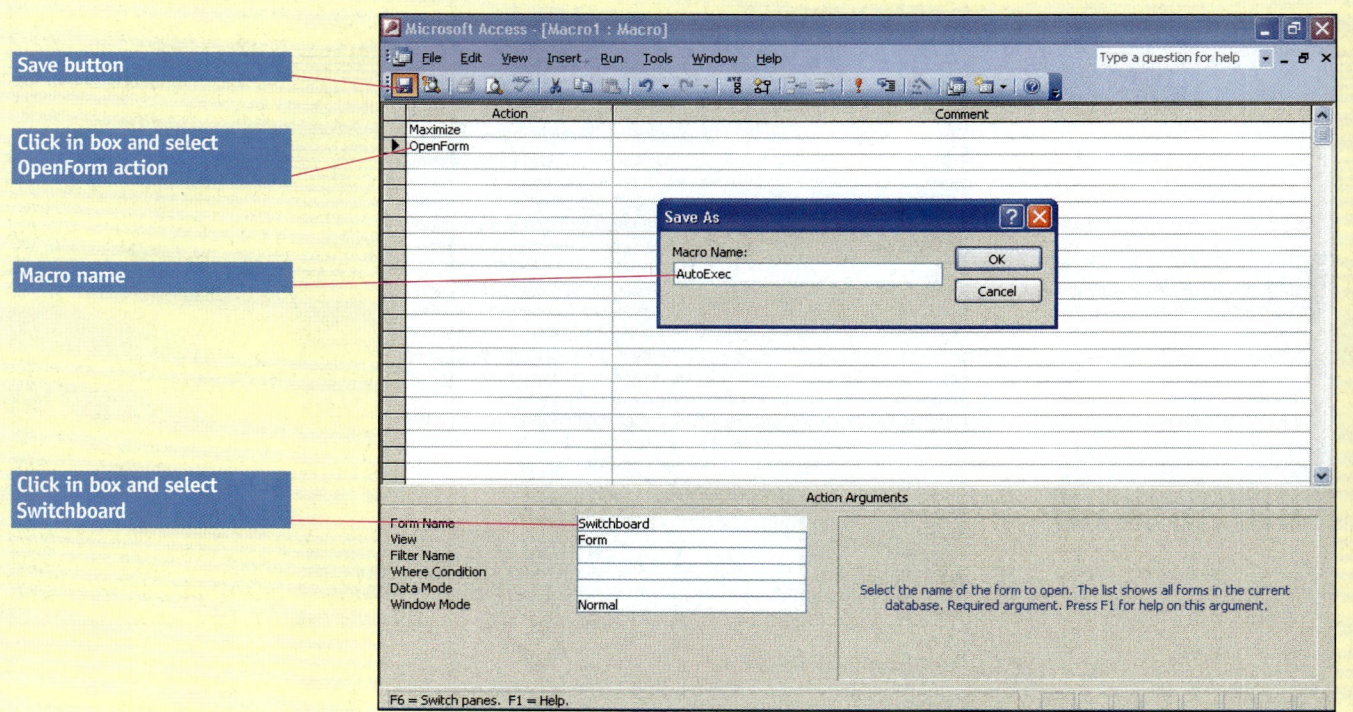

(a) Create the AutoExec Macro (step 1)

FIGURE 7.7 Hands-on Exercise 2

Step 2: Create the Prototype Macro

- You should be back in the Database window, which should display the name of the AutoExec macro. Click the **New button** to create a second macro.

- Type **Ms** (the first two letters in the MsgBox action), then press **Enter** to accept this action. Enter the comment shown in Figure 7.7b.

- Click the text box for the **Message** argument, then press **Shift+F2** to display the zoom box so that you can see the contents of your entire message. Enter the message in Figure 7.7b. Click **OK**.

- Click the text box for the **Type** argument, click the **drop-down arrow** to display the list of message types, and select **Information**.

- Click in the text box for the **Title** argument, and enter **Under Development**.

- Click the **Run button** to test the macro. You will see a message indicating that you have to save the macro. Click **Yes** to save the macro, type **Prototype** as the name of the macro, and click **OK**.

- You will see a dialog box containing the message you just created. Click **OK**. Close the macro.

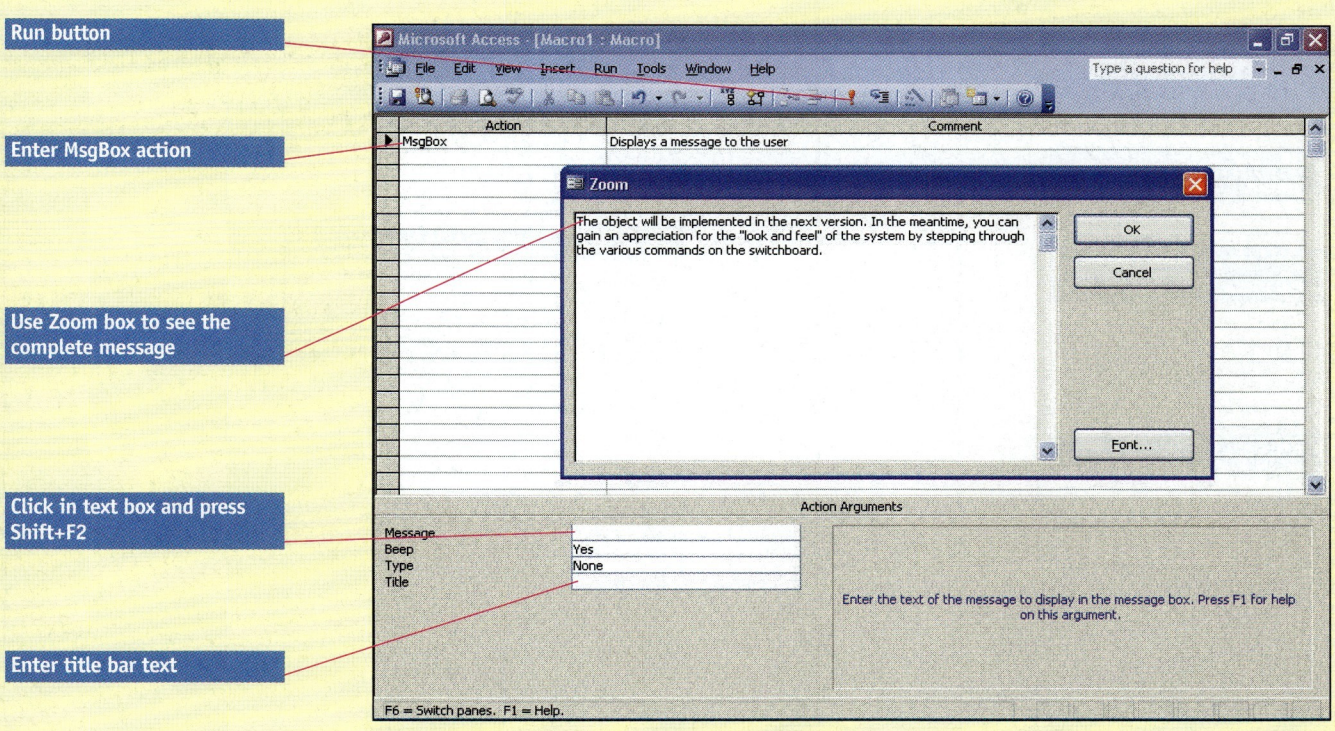

(b) Create the Prototype Macro (step 2)

FIGURE 7.7 Hands-on Exercise 2 (*continued*)

TYPE ONLY THE FIRST LETTER(S)

Click the Action box, then type the first letter of a macro action to move immediately to the first macro action beginning with that letter. Type an M, for example, and Access automatically enters the Maximize action. If necessary, type the second letter of the desired action; for example, type the letter i (after typing an M), and Access selects the Minimize action.

Step 3: **Create the Close Database Macro**

- Click the **New button** once again to create the third (and last) macro for this exercise. Specify the **MsgBox** action as the first command in the macro. Enter the comment shown in Figure 7.7c.

- Enter an appropriate message that stresses the importance of backup. Select Warning as the message type. Enter an appropriate title for the message box.

- Click the **Action box** on the second line. Type **Cl** (the first two letters in Close) and press **Enter**. Enter the indicated comment as shown in Figure 7.7c.

- Click the text box for the **Object Type** argument. Click the **drop-down arrow** and choose **Form** as the Object type. Click the **Object Name** argument, click the **drop-down arrow**, and choose **Switchboard** as the Object (form) name.

- Click the **Action box** on the third line. Type **Cl** (the first two letters in Close) and press **Enter**. Click the **comments line** for this macro action and enter the comment shown in the figure. No arguments are necessary.

- Save the macro as **Close Database**, then close the macro. If necessary, press the **F11 key** to return to the Database window, where you should see three macros: AutoExec, Close Database, and Prototype.

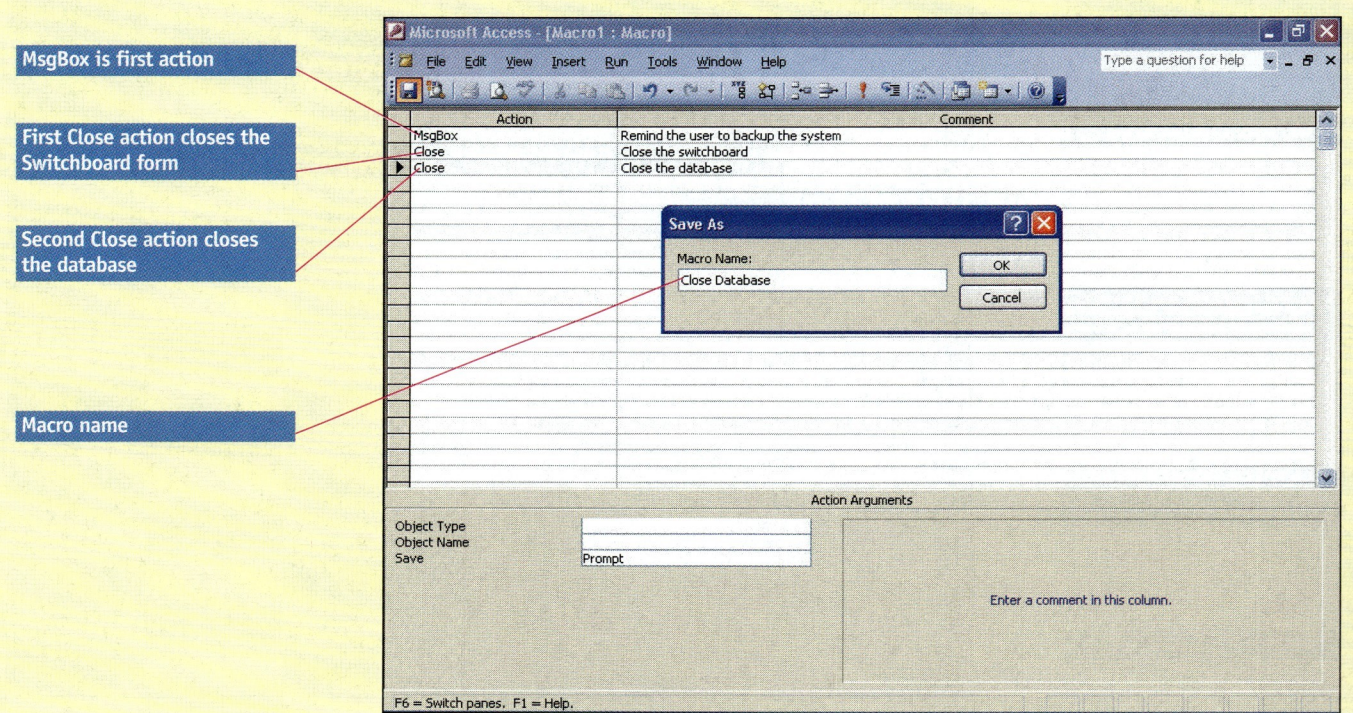

(c) Create the Close Database macro (step 3)

FIGURE 7.7 Hands-on Exercise 2 (*continued*)

USE KEYBOARD SHORTCUTS—F6, F11, AND SHIFT+F2

Use the F6 key to move back and forth between the top and bottom halves of the Macro window. Press Shift+F2 to display a zoom box that enables you to view long arguments in their entirety. Use the F11 key at any time to display the Database window.

Step 4: **Create the Report Switchboard**

- Minimize the Database window to give yourself more room in which to work. Pull down the **Tools menu**, click the **Database Utilities command**, and choose **Switchboard Manager** to display the Switchboard Manager dialog box.

- Click **New**. Enter **Report Switchboard** as the name of the switchboard page. Click **OK**. The Create New dialog box closes and the Report Switchboard page appears in the Switchboard Manager dialog box.

- Select the **Report Switchboard**, click **Edit** to open the Edit Switchboard Page dialog box. Click **New** to open the Edit Switchboard Item dialog box.

- Add the first switchboard item. Click in the **Text** list box and type **Display Report Template** as shown in Figure 7.7d.

- Press the **Tab key** to move to the Command list box and type **Open R** (the first several letters in Open Report). Press **Tab** to move to the Report list box and type **R** (the first letter in the report name, "Report Template").

- Click **OK** to create the switchboard item. The Edit Switchboard Item dialog box closes and Display Report Template appears on the Report Switchboard page.

- Add **Team Rosters** as the next switchboard item. Specify the **Run macro command** and choose **Prototype** as the macro. Add additional buttons for the **Master Coaching List** and **Relationships Diagram**, both of which run the Prototype macro.

- Add an additional item that will return the user to the main switchboard. Click **New** to open the Edit Switchboard Item dialog box. Click in the **Text** list box and type **"&Return to Main Menu..."**

- Press the **Tab key** to move to the Command list box, where the Go to Switchboard command is entered by default. Press the **Tab key** to move to the Switchboard list box, and type **M** (the first letter in the "Main Switchboard"). Click **OK** to create the switchboard item. Close the Edit Switchboard Page.

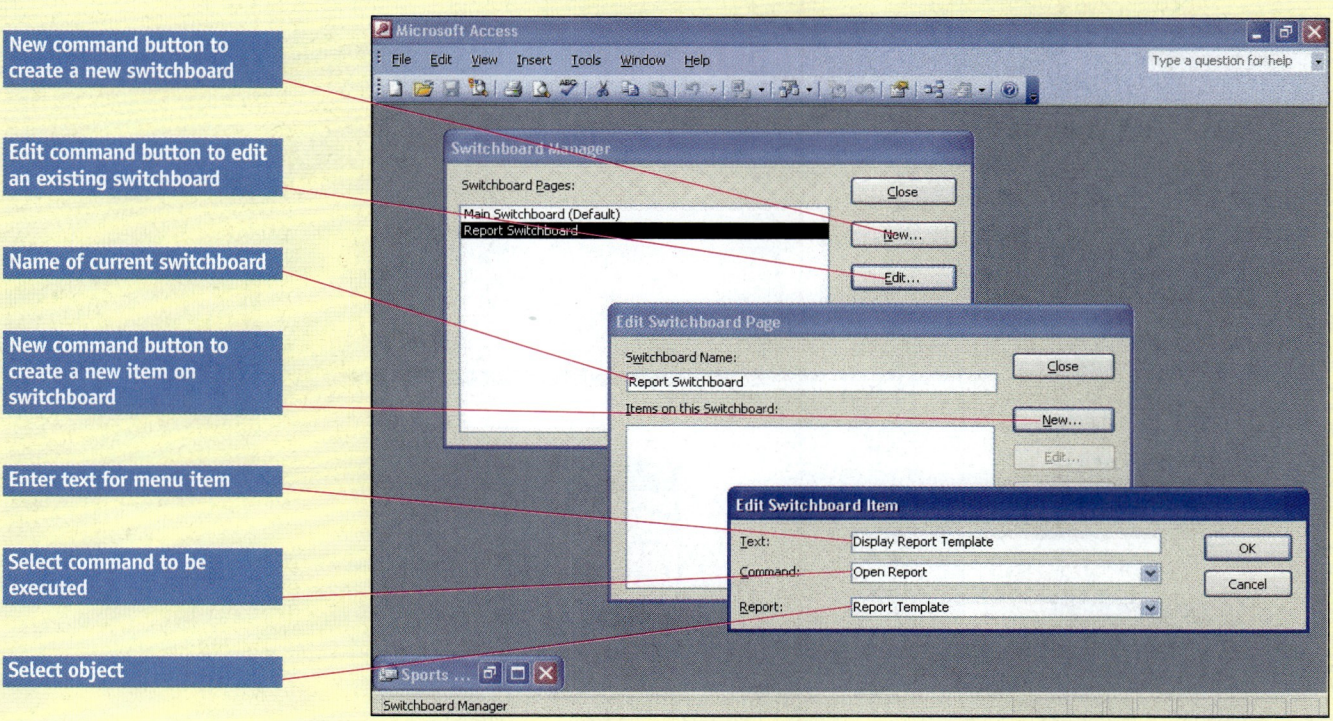

New command button to create a new switchboard

Edit command button to edit an existing switchboard

Name of current switchboard

New command button to create a new item on switchboard

Enter text for menu item

Select command to be executed

Select object

(d) Create the Report Switchboard (step 4)

FIGURE 7.7 Hands-on Exercise 2 (*continued*)

Step 5: Modify the Main Switchboard

- Select the **Main Switchboard** in the Switchboard Manager dialog box, click the **Edit button** to open the Edit Switchboard Page dialog box, then click **New** to open the Edit Switchboard Item dialog box as shown in Figure 7.7e.

- Add a new switchboard item to open the Report Switchboard. Click in the **Text** list box and type **"&Report Menu"**, the name of the command as it will appear in the switchboard.

- Press the **Tab key** to move to the Command list box, where "Go to Switchboard" is already entered, then press the **Tab key** a second time to move to the Switchboard list box. Type **R** (the first letter in the "Report Switchboard"). Click **OK** to create the switchboard item.

- The Edit Switchboard Item dialog box closes and "&Report Menu" appears on the main switchboard.

- The main switchboard needs one last command to close the database. Thus, click **New** to open the Edit Switchboard Item dialog box. Type **&Exit** as the name of the command.

- Press the **Tab key** to move to the Command list box and type **R** (the first letter in "Run Macro"). Press the **Tab key** a second time to move to the Macro list box, and type **C** (the first letter in the "Close Database" macro). Click **OK** to create the switchboard item.

- The main switchboard should contain six items—&About Sports, &Players, &Coaches, and &Teams from the first exercise, and &Report Menu and &Exit from this exercise.

- Close the Edit Switchboard Page dialog box. Close the Switchboard Manager.

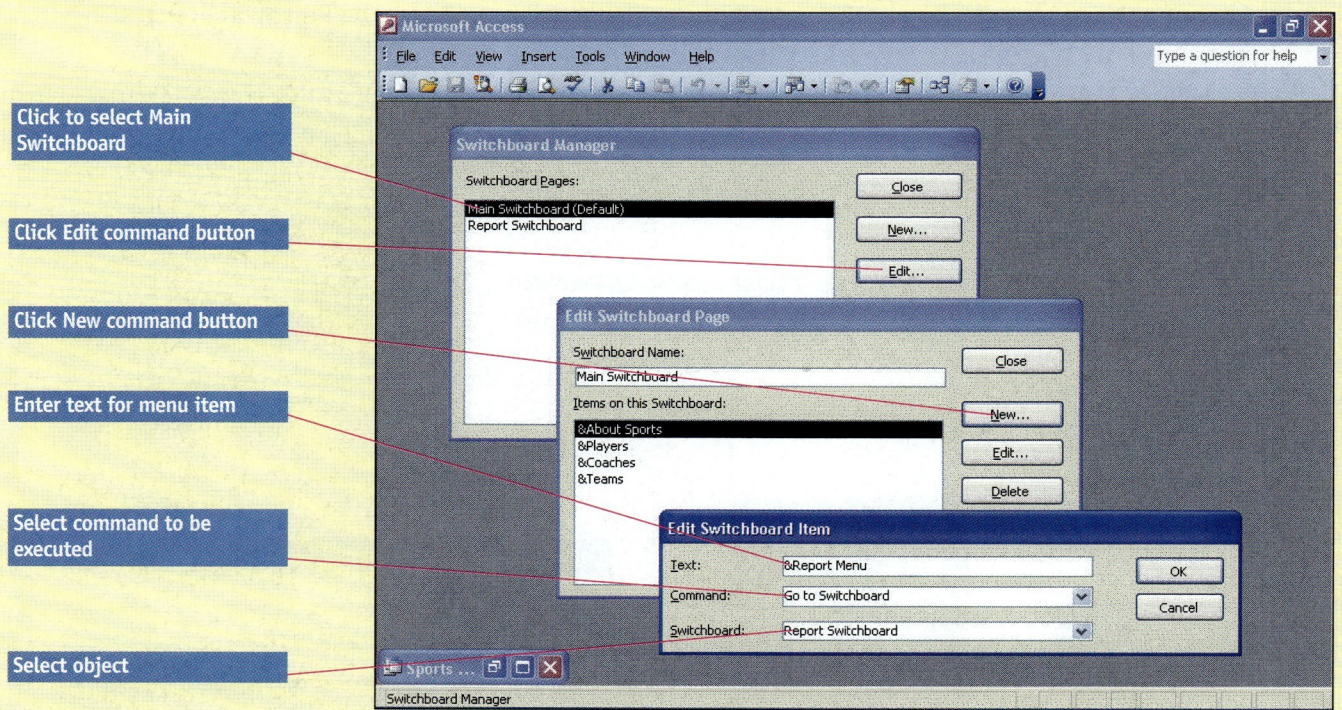

Click to select Main Switchboard

Click Edit command button

Click New command button

Enter text for menu item

Select command to be executed

Select object

(e) Modify the Main Switchboard (step 5)

FIGURE 7.7 Hands-on Exercise 2 *(continued)*

Step 6: Test the Main Switchboard

- Click the **Restore button** in the Database window to view the objects in the database, click the **Forms button**, then double click the **Switchboard form** to open the main switchboard.

- Click the **Exit button** (or use the **Alt+E** shortcut):
  - ❏ You should see an informational message similar to the one shown in Figure 7.7f. (The message is displayed by the MsgBox action in the Close Database macro.)
  - ❏ Click **OK** to accept the message. The Close Database macro then closes the database.

- Pull down the **File menu**, then click **Sports Objects** from the list of recently opened databases. Click **Open** in response to the security warning.

- The AutoExec macro executes automatically, maximizes the current window, and displays the main switchboard.

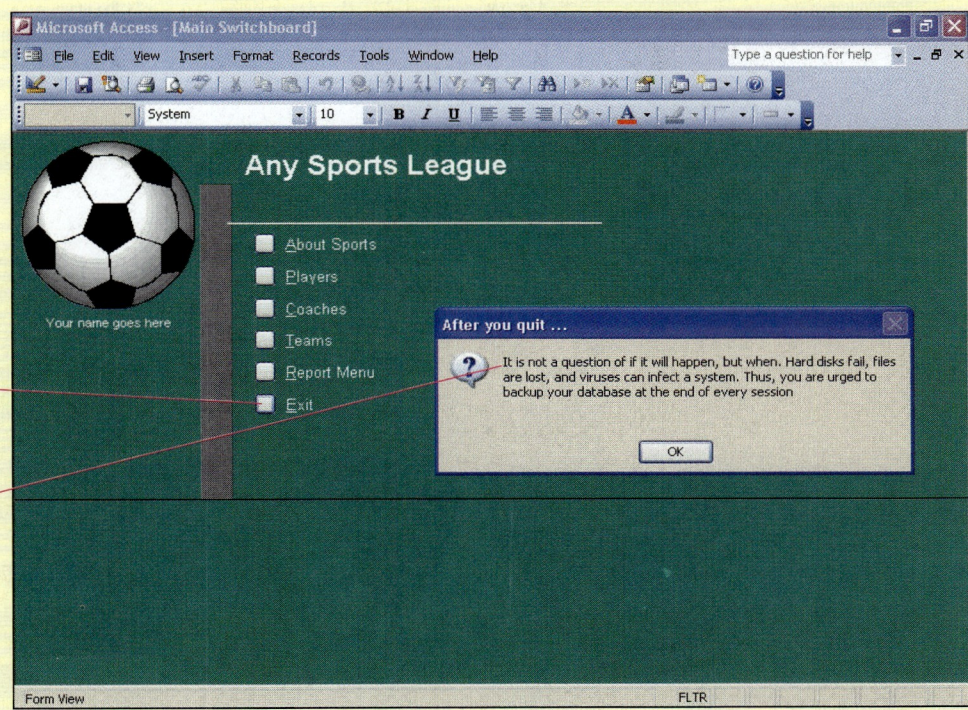

Click Exit button

Informational message is displayed

(f) Test the Main Switchboard (step 6)

FIGURE 7.7 Hands-on Exercise 2 (*continued*)

ADD A HYPERLINK

You can enhance the appeal of your switchboard through inclusion of a hyperlink. Open the switchboard form in Design view, then click the Insert Hyperlink button to display the Insert Hyperlink dialog box. Enter the text to be displayed and the Web address, then click OK to close the dialog box and return to the Design view. Right click the hyperlink to display a shortcut menu, click the Properties command to display the Properties dialog box, then change the font and/or point size as appropriate.

Step 7: Test the Report Switchboard

- Click the **Report Menu button** (or use the **Alt+R** keyboard shortcut) on the main switchboard to display the Report switchboard in Figure 7.7g.

- Click the button to **Display the Report Template**. Click the **Print button** to print a copy of this report for your instructor. Close the Report Preview window to return to the Report switchboard.

- Click the buttons for the other reports which should display the message in Figure 7.7g.

- Click the **Return to Main Menu button** to exit the Report Menu and return to the main switchboard.
  - ❏ To continue working, click the **Close button** on the title bar (or pull down the **File menu** and click the **Close command**) to close the form and continue working on this database. (You should not click the Exit command button as that would close the database.) You should be back in the Database window, where you can continue with the next hands-on exercise.
  - ❏ To close the database, click the **Exit button** (or use the **Alt+E** shortcut).

- Either way, you have demonstrated the "look and feel" of the system to the extent that you can step through the various menus. Good work.

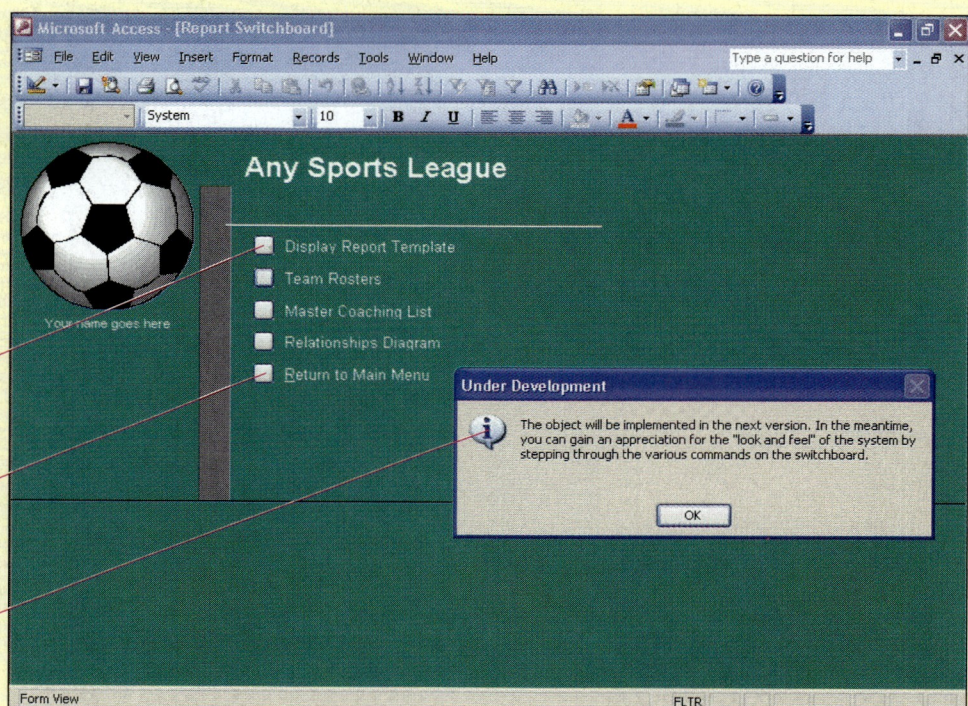

Click to display Report Template

Click to Return to Main Menu

Informational message displayed if button for a report is clicked

(g) Test the Report Switchboard (step 7)

FIGURE 7.7 Hands-on Exercise 2 (*continued*)

BE CONSISTENT

Consistency within an application is essential to its success. Similar functions should be done in similar ways to facilitate learning and build confidence in the application. The sports application, for example, has similar screens for the Players, Coaches, and Teams forms, each of which contains the identical buttons to add or print a record and close the form.

A player draft is essential to the operation of the league. Players sign up for the coming season at registration, after which the coaches meet to select players for their teams. All players are rated as to ability, and the league strives to maintain a competitive balance among teams. This is accomplished through a draft in which the coaches take turns selecting players from the pool of unassigned players.

The player draft is implemented through the form in Figure 7.8, which is based on a query that identifies players who have not yet been assigned to a team. The easiest way to create the underlying query is through the ***Unmatched Query Wizard*** that identifies records in one table (the Players table) that do not have matching records in another table (the Teams table). The wizard prompts you for the necessary information, then it creates the required query.

The query is displayed within a form as shown in Figure 7.8. The coaches will view the list of unassigned players during the actual draft and make the team assignments. A ***combo box*** within the query simplifies data entry in that a coach is able to click the drop-down list box to display the list of teams, rather than having to remember the TeamID.

In addition to displaying the list of unassigned players, the form in Figure 7.8 also contains three command buttons that are used during the player draft. The Find Player button moves directly to a specific player, and enables a coach to see whether a specific player has been assigned to a team, and if so, to which team. The Update List button refreshes the underlying query on which the list of unassigned players is based. It is used periodically during the draft as players are assigned to teams, to remove those players from the list of unassigned players. The End Draft button closes the form and returns to the switchboard. Note, too, that the appearance of the form matches the other forms in the application. This type of consistency is important to give your application a professional look.

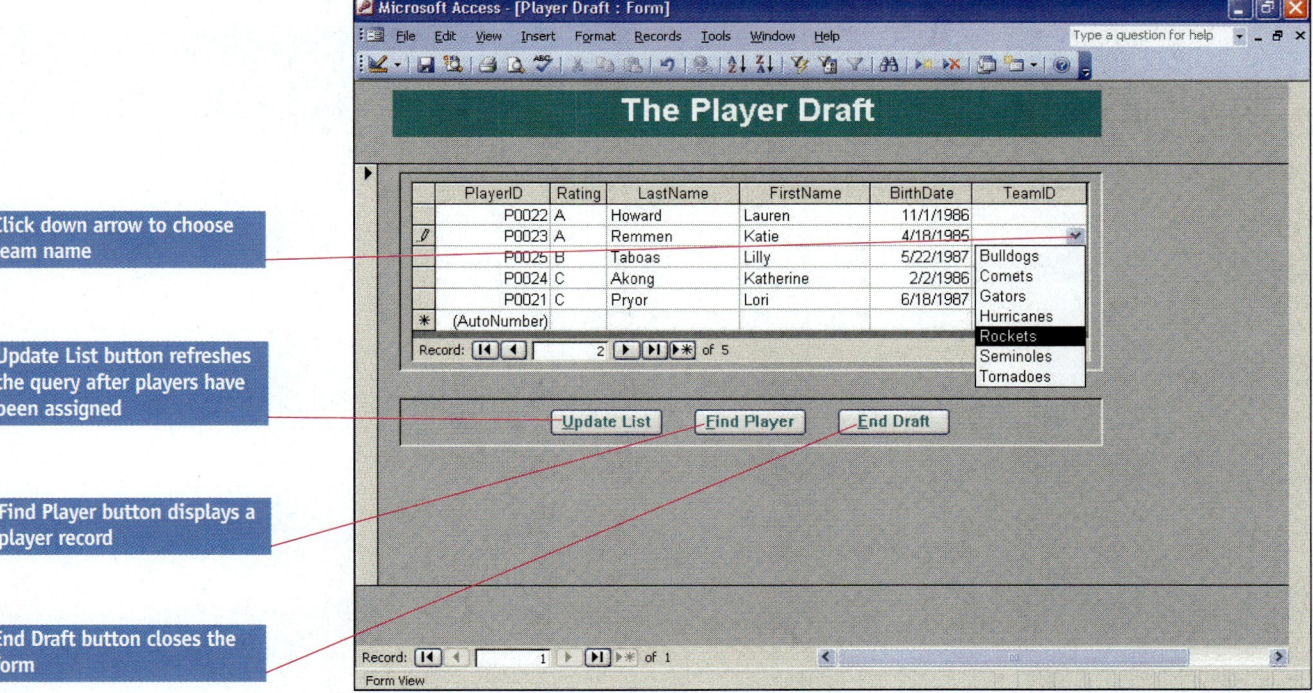

FIGURE 7.8 The Player Draft

Macro Groups

Implementation of the player draft requires three macros, one for each command button. Although you could create a separate macro for each button, it is convenient to create a ***macro group*** that contains the individual macros. The macro group has a name, as does each macro in the group. Only the name of the macro group appears in the Database window.

Figure 7.9 displays a Player Draft macro group containing three individual macros (Update List, Find Player, and End Draft), which run independently of one another. The name of each macro appears in the Macro Name column (which is displayed by clicking the Macro Names button on the Macro toolbar). The actions and comments for each macro are shown in the corresponding columns to the right of the macro name.

The advantage of storing related macros in a macro group, as opposed to storing them individually, is purely organizational. Large systems often contain many macros, which can overwhelm the developer as he or she tries to locate a specific macro. Storing related macros in macro groups limits the entries in the Database window, since only the (name of the) macro group is displayed. Thus, the Database window would contain a single entry (Player Draft, which is the name of the macro group), as opposed to three individual entries (Update List, Find Player, and End Draft, which correspond to the macros in the group).

Access must still be able to identify the individual macros so that each macro can be executed at the appropriate time. If, for example, a macro is to be executed when the user clicks a command button, the ***On Click property*** of that command button must specify both the individual macro and the macro group. The two names are separated by a period; for example, Player Draft.Update List to indicate the Update List macro in the Player Draft macro group.

As indicated, each macro in Figure 7.9 corresponds to a command button in the Player Draft form. The macros are created in the following hands-on exercise that implements the player draft.

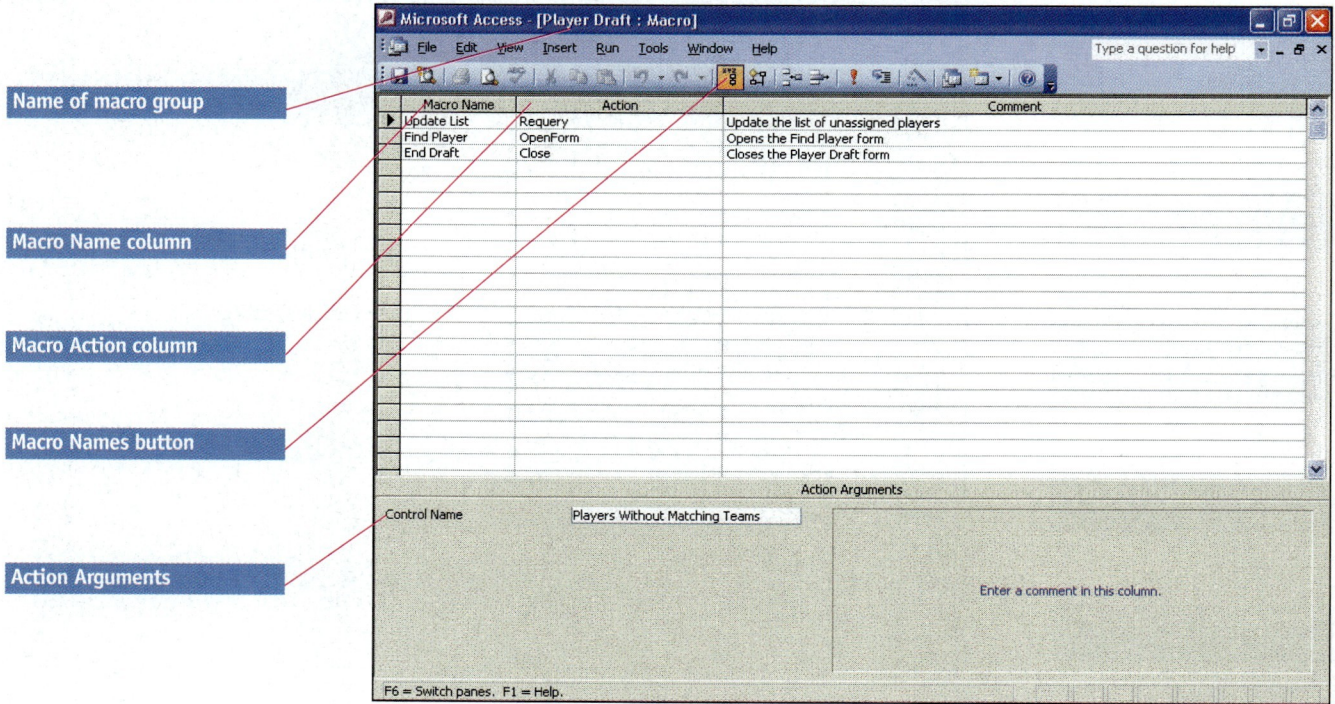

FIGURE 7.9 Macro Group

3   The Player Draft

Objective   Use the Unmatched Query Wizard, then create a form based on the resulting query. Create a macro group containing three macros to implement a player draft. Use Figure 7.10 as a guide in the exercise.

Step 1:   **The Unmatched Query Wizard**

- Start Access and open the **Sports Objects database**. Pull down the **File menu** and click **Close** (or click the **Close button**) to close the Main Menu form but leave the database open.

- Click the **Queries button** in the Database window. Click **New**, select the **Find Unmatched Query Wizard**, then click **OK** to start the wizard:
  - ❑ Select **Players** as the table whose records you want to see in the query results. Click **Next**.
  - ❑ Select **Teams** as the table that contains the related records. Click **Next**.
  - ❑ **TeamID** is automatically selected as the matching field. Click **Next**.
  - ❑ Select the following fields from the Available Fields list: **PlayerID, Rating, LastName, FirstName, BirthDate**, and **TeamID**. Click **Next**.
  - ❑ **Players Without Matching Teams** is entered as the name of the query. Check that the option button to **View the results** is selected, then click **Finish** to exit the wizard and see the results of the query.

- You should see a dynaset containing five players (Pryor, Howard, Remmen, Akong, and Taboas) as shown in Figure 7.10a.

- The TeamID field for each of these players is blank, indicating that these players have not yet been assigned.

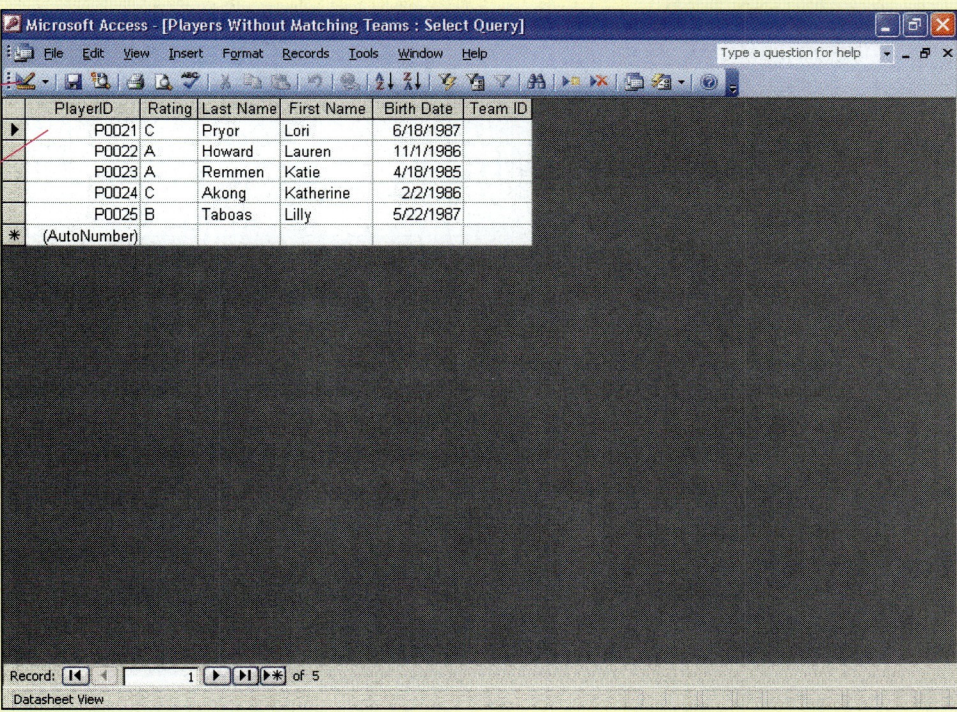

(a) The Unmatched Query Wizard (step 1)

FIGURE 7.10   Hands-on Exercise 3

Step 2: Modify the Query

- Change to **Design view** to see the underlying query as displayed in Figure 7.10b.

- Click and drag the line separating the upper and lower portions of the window. If necessary, click and drag the field lists to match the figure.

- Click in the **Sort row** for **Rating**, then click **Ascending** from the drop-down list. Click in the **Sort row** for **LastName**, then click **Ascending** from the drop-down list.

- Click the **Run button** to view the revised query, which lists players according to their player rating and alphabetically within rating.

- Close the query. Click **Yes** if asked whether to save the changes to the Players Without Matching Teams query.

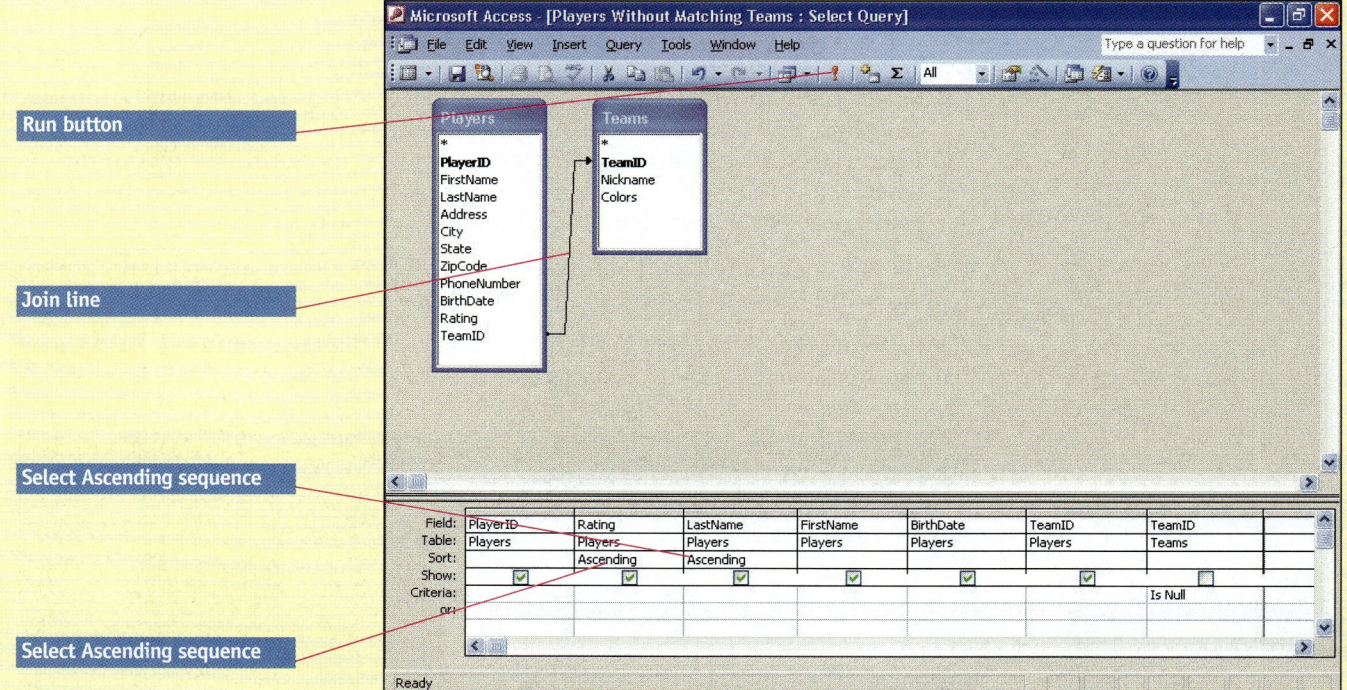

(b) Modify the Query (step 2)

FIGURE 7.10 Hands-on Exercise 3 *(continued)*

THE IS NULL CRITERION

The Is Null criterion selects those records that do not have a value in the designated field. It is the essence of the Unmatched Query Wizard, which uses the criterion to identify the records in one table that do not have a matching record in another table. The NOT operator can be combined with the Is Null criterion to produce the opposite effect; that is, the criterion Is Not Null will select records with any type of entry (including spaces) in the specified field.

Step 3: **Create the Unmatched Players Form**

- Click the **Forms button** in the Database window, click **New**, and select **AutoForm:Tabular**. Click the **drop-down arrow** to choose a table or query. Select the **Players Without Matching Teams** query. Click **OK**.

- Maximize the window if necessary, then change to the **Design view**. Select the **TeamID control** in the Detail section, then press the **Del key**.

- Click the **Combo Box tool**. Click and drag in the **Detail section**, then release the mouse to start the Combo Box Wizard:
  - ❏ Check the option button that indicates you want the combo box to **look up values in a table or query**. Click **Next**.
  - ❏ Choose the **Teams table** in the next screen. Click **Next**.
  - ❏ Select the **TeamID** and **Nickname fields**. Click **Next**.
  - ❏ Select **Nickname** as the field on which to sort. Click **Next**.
  - ❏ Adjust the column width if necessary. Be sure the box to **Hide the key column** is checked. Click **Next**.
  - ❏ Click the option button to store the value in the field. Click the **drop-down arrow** to display the fields and select the **TeamID field**. Click **Next**.
  - ❏ Enter **Team** as the label for the combo box. Click **Finish**.

- Click (select) the label next to the control you just created. Press the **Del key**. Point to the combo box, click the **right mouse button** to display a shortcut menu, and click **Properties**. Change the name of the control to **TeamID**.

- Click the **Form Selector box**. Click the **Default View** text box, click the **drop-down arrow**, and select **Datasheet**. Close the Properties sheet.

- Click the **Save button** to display the Save As dialog box in Figure 7.10c. Click **OK** to save the form, then close the form.

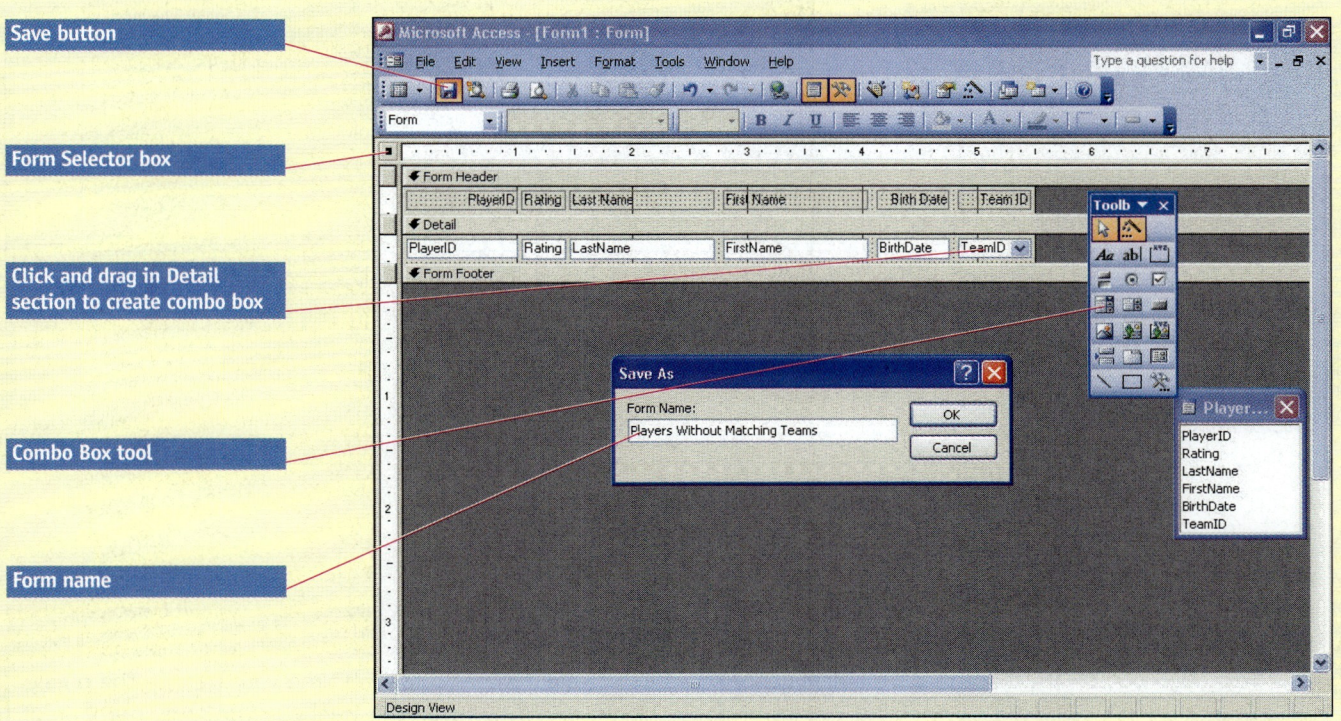

(c) Create the Unmatched Players Form (step 3)

FIGURE 7.10 Hands-on Exercise 3 (*continued*)

Step 4:   **Create the Find Player Query**

- Click the **Queries button** in the Database window. Double click the icon to **Create Query in Design view**. Add the **Players table**. Close the Show Table dialog box.

- Click and drag all of the fields from the Players table to the Design grid. Click the **Criteria row** of the LastName field and type **[Enter Player's Last Name]** as shown in Figure 7.10d. Save the query as **Find Player**. Close the query.

- Click the **Forms button** in the Database window. Select the **Players form**, press **Ctrl+C** to copy the form, then press **Ctrl+V** to display the Paste As dialog box. Enter **Find Player** as the name of the form and click **OK**.

- Open the **Find Player** form in Design view. Right click the **Form Selector box** in the upper-left corner, click **Properties** to display the property sheet for the form as a whole, and click the **All tab**.

- Click the **down arrow** in the Record Source box and select the **Find Player query** that you just created. Close the property sheet. Save the form.

- Go to **Form view**, enter your last name when prompted, then click **OK**. You should see a form that displays your record. Close the form.

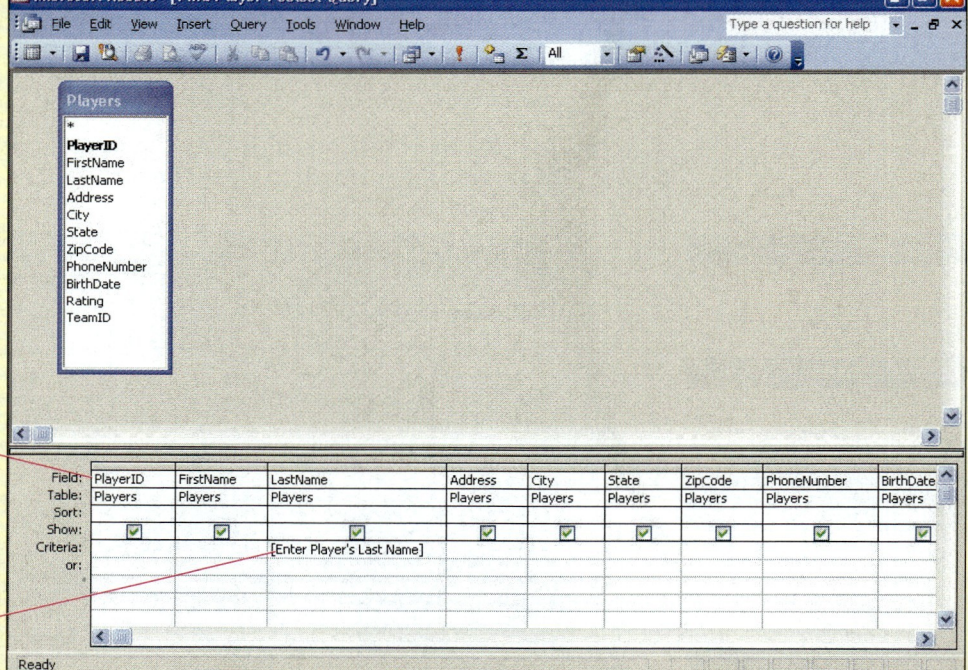

Drag all of the fields from field list to field row

Enter prompt within square brackets

(d) Create the Find Player Query (step 4)

FIGURE 7.10   Hands-on Exercise 3 *(continued)*

BE FLEXIBLE—CREATE A PARAMETER QUERY

A parameter query prompts you for the criteria each time you execute the query, enabling you to change the criteria whenever the query is run. Any number of prompts may be specified; the prompts are read from left to right when the query is run. A form and/or a report can be based on a parameter query, in which case the user is asked for the criteria prior to generating the form or report.

Step 5: **Create the Player Draft Macro Group**

- Click the **Macros button** in the Database window. Click **New** to create a new macro. Click the **Maximize button** to maximize the Macro window.

- If you do not see the Macro Names column, pull down the **View menu** and click **Macro Names** to display the column.

- Enter the macro names, comments, and actions, as shown in Figure 7.10e.
  - ❏ The Requery action (in the UpdateList macro) has a single argument in which you specify the control name (the name of the query). Type **Players Without Matching Teams**, which is the query you created in step 1.
  - ❏ The FindPlayer macro requires you to open the **Find Player** form that was created earlier.
  - ❏ The arguments for the End Draft macro are visible in Figure 7.10d. The Player Draft form will be created in the next step. (You must enter the name manually since the form has not yet been created.)

- Save the Macro group as **Player Draft**. Close the Macro window.

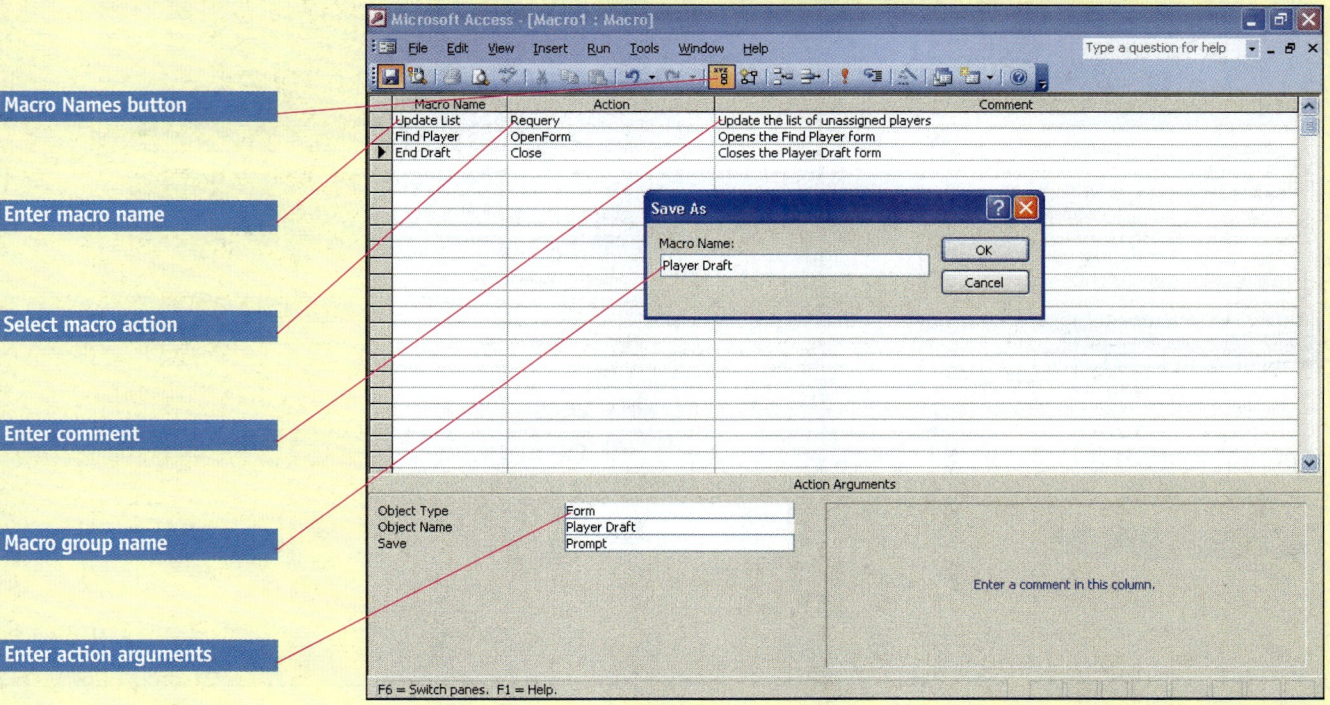

(e) Create the Player Draft Macro Group (step 5)

FIGURE 7.10   Hands-on Exercise 3 (*continued*)

REQUERY COMMAND NOT AVAILABLE

The macros in the Player Draft group are designed to run only when the Player Draft form is open. Do not be concerned, therefore, if you attempt to test the macros at this time and the Action Failed dialog box appears. The macros will work correctly at the end of the exercise, when all of the objects for the player draft have been created.

Step 6: **Create the Player Draft Form**

- Click the **Forms button** in the Database window. Select the **Template form** and click the **Copy button** to copy the form to the clipboard.

- Click the **Paste button** to complete the copy operation. Type **Player Draft** as the name of the copied form. Click **OK**.

- Open the **Player Draft** form in Design view. Pull down the **Window menu** and click **Tile Horizontally** to arrange the windows as shown in Figure 7.10f. (If necessary, close any open windows besides the two in our figure, then retile the windows.)

- Click in the **Player Draft** form. Delete the labels and text boxes for fields 1 and 2.

- Click in the **Database window**. Click and drag the **Players Without Matching Teams** form into the Detail section of the Player Draft form as shown in Figure 7.10f. Maximize the Player Draft window.

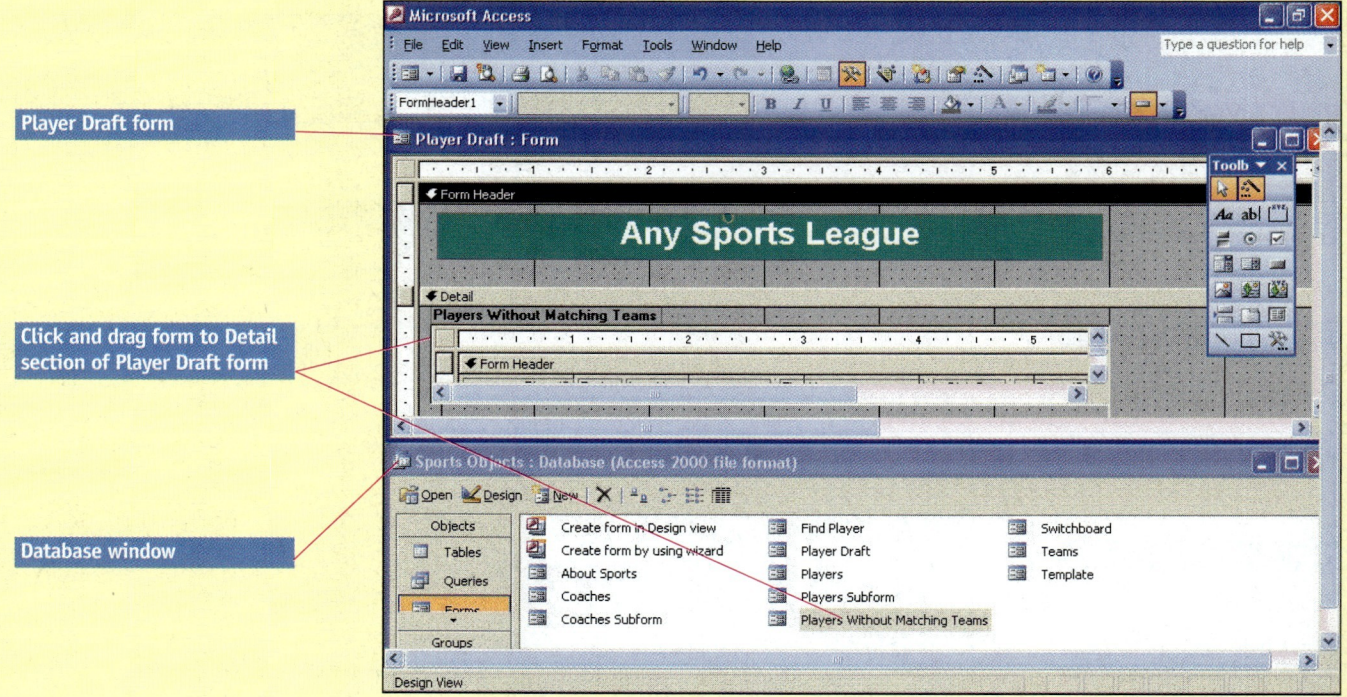

(f) Create the Player Draft Form (step 6)

FIGURE 7.10 Hands-on Exercise 3 (*continued*)

USE A TEMPLATE

Avoid the routine and repetitive work of creating a new form by basing all forms for a given application on the same template. A template is a partially completed form or report that contains graphic elements and other formatting specifications. A template does not, however, have an underlying table or query. We suggest that you create a template for your application and store it within the database, then use that template whenever you need to create a new form. It saves you time and trouble. It also promotes a consistent look that is critical to the application's overall success.

Step 7: **Modify the Player Draft Form**

- Click and drag the decorative box so that it is larger than the Players Without Matching Forms control. Move the control within the decorative box.

- Select the control for the form, then click and drag the **sizing handles** in the Players Without Matching Team form so that its size approximates the form in Figure 7.10g.

- Select (click) the label, **Players Without Matching Teams**, as shown in Figure 7.10g, then press the **Del key** to remove the label. Change the text in the Form Header to say **The Player Draft**.

- Change to the **Form view**. You should see the Form view of the subform, which displays the players who have not yet been assigned to a team. Change the column widths if necessary.

- Return to the **Form Design view** to change the width of the subform. Continue to switch back and forth between the Form view and the Design view until you are satisfied.

- Save the form.

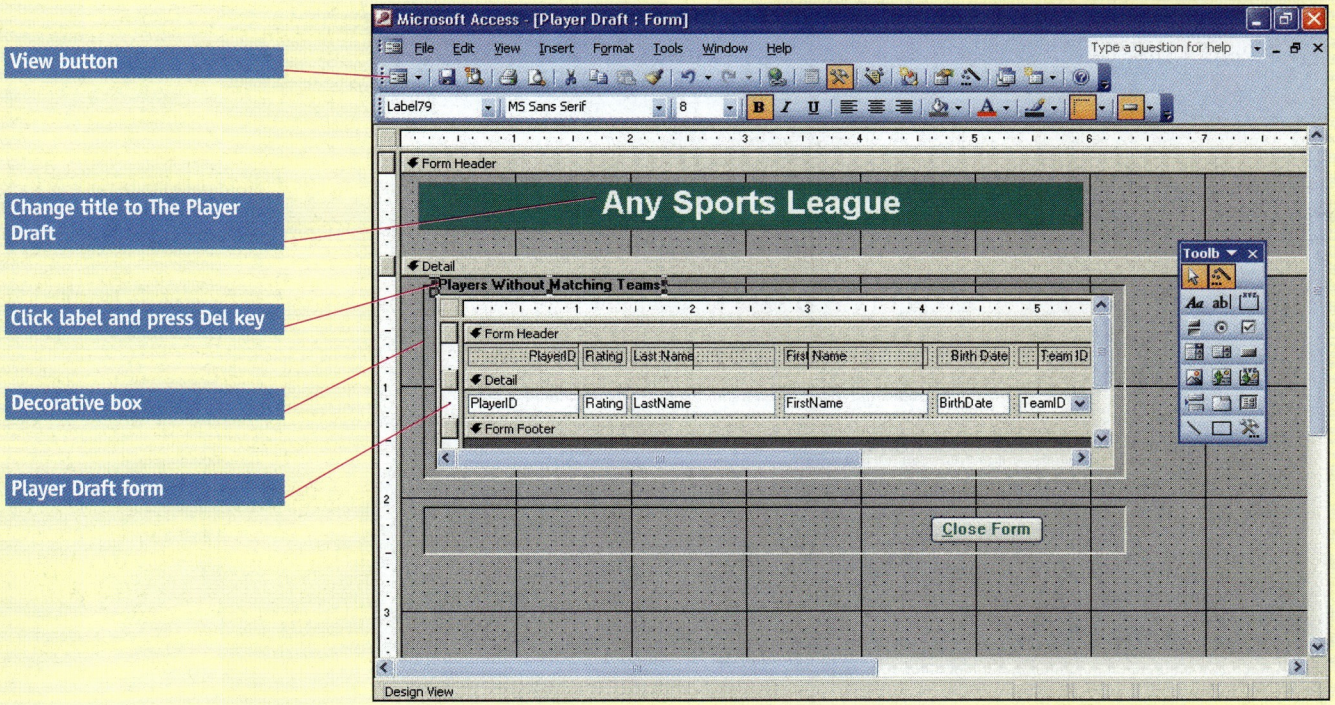

(g) Modify the Player Draft Form (step 7)

FIGURE 7.10 Hands-on Exercise 3 (*continued*)

SUPPRESS THE RECORD SELECTOR AND NAVIGATION BUTTONS

On the Player Draft form you can suppress the Record Selector and navigation buttons, which have no active function and only confuse the user. Change to the Design view, right click the Form Selector box to the left of the ruler, then click the Properties command to display the Properties dialog box. Click the Record Selectors text box and click No to disable it. Click the Navigation Buttons text box and click No to disable it. Close the Properties dialog box, then return to the Form view to see the effect of these changes, which are subtle but worthwhile.

Step 8: **Add the Command Buttons**

- Click and drag the **Command Button tool** to create a command button, as shown in Figure 7.10h. Click **Miscellaneous** in the Categories list box. Select **Run Macro** from the list of actions. Click **Next**.

- Select **Player Draft.Update List** from the list of existing macros. Click **Next**.

- Click the **Text option button**. Click and drag to select the default text (Run Macro), then type **&Update List** as the text to display. Click **Next**.

- Enter **Update List** (in place of the button number). Click **Finish**.

- Create a second command button to find a player. The caption of the button should be **&Find Player** and it should run the FindPlayer macro.

- Change the caption property of the existing button on the template that closes the form to **&End Draft**.

- Size, align, space, and color the command buttons. Use the **Format Painter button** so that all of the buttons have the same appearance. Save the form.

- Change to the **Form view**. Click the **End Draft button** to close the form.

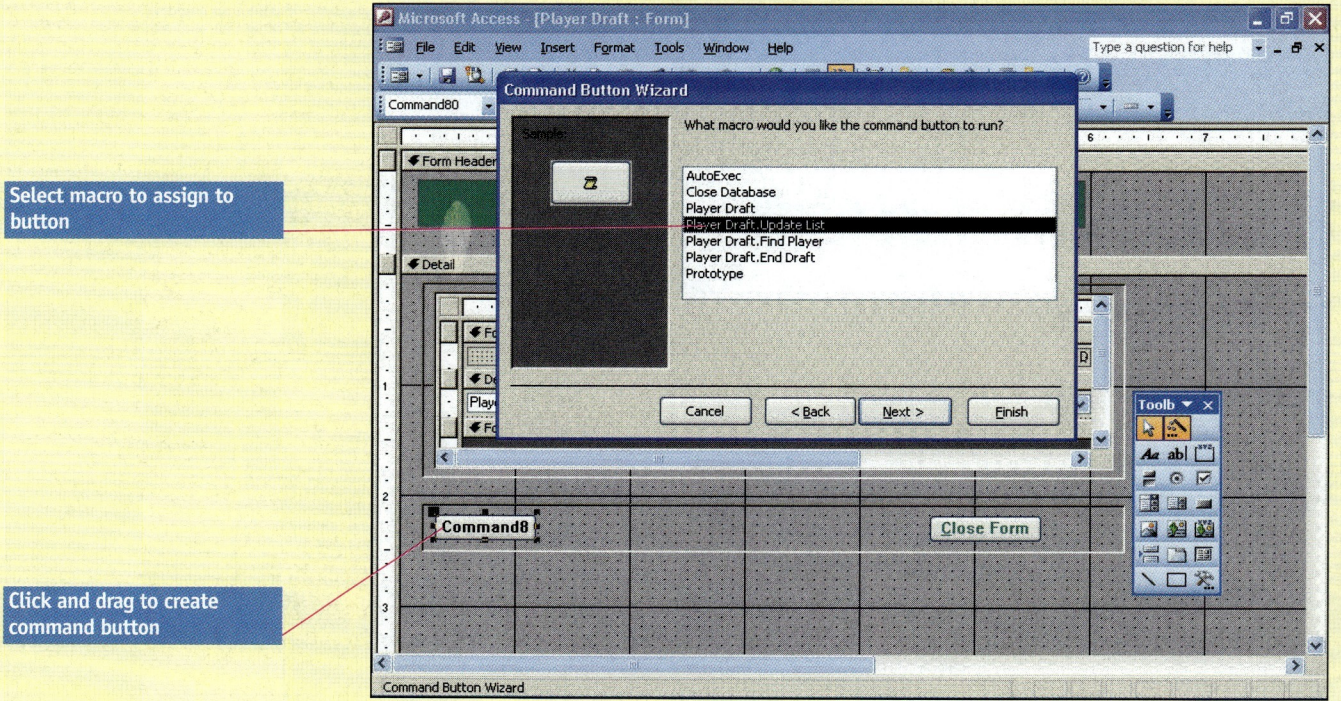

(h) Add the Command Buttons (step 8)

FIGURE 7.10 Hands-on Exercise 3 (*continued*)

ASSIGN MACROS TO CONTROLS AND COMMAND BUTTONS

Right click any command button or control to display a context-sensitive menu in which you click the Properties command, then click the Event tab in the resulting property sheet. Click in the text box of the desired event, then click the down arrow to assign an existing macro to the control or command button. Note, too, that you can click the Build button, instead of the down arrow, to select the Macro Builder and create a macro if it does not yet exist.

Step 9: **Modify the Main Switchboard**

- Pull down the **Tools menu**, click the **Database Utilities command**, and choose **Switchboard Manager**. Select the **Main Switchboard** in the Switchboard Manager dialog box, then click the **Edit button**.

- Click **New** to open the Edit Switchboard Item dialog box. Click in the **Text** list box and type **Player &Draft**. (The ampersand in front of the letter "D" establishes Alt+D as a shortcut for this button.)

- Press the **Tab key** to move to the Command list box. Select the command to open the form in the **Edit mode**. Press the **Tab key** to move to the Form list box and select the **Player Draft form** as shown in Figure 7.10i.

- Click **OK** to create the switchboard item. The Edit Switchboard Item dialog box closes and Player &Draft appears on the Main Switchboard. Select the **Player &Draft** entry, then click the **Move Up button** to move this command above the &Exit command.

- Close the Edit Switchboard page, then close the Switchboard Manager.

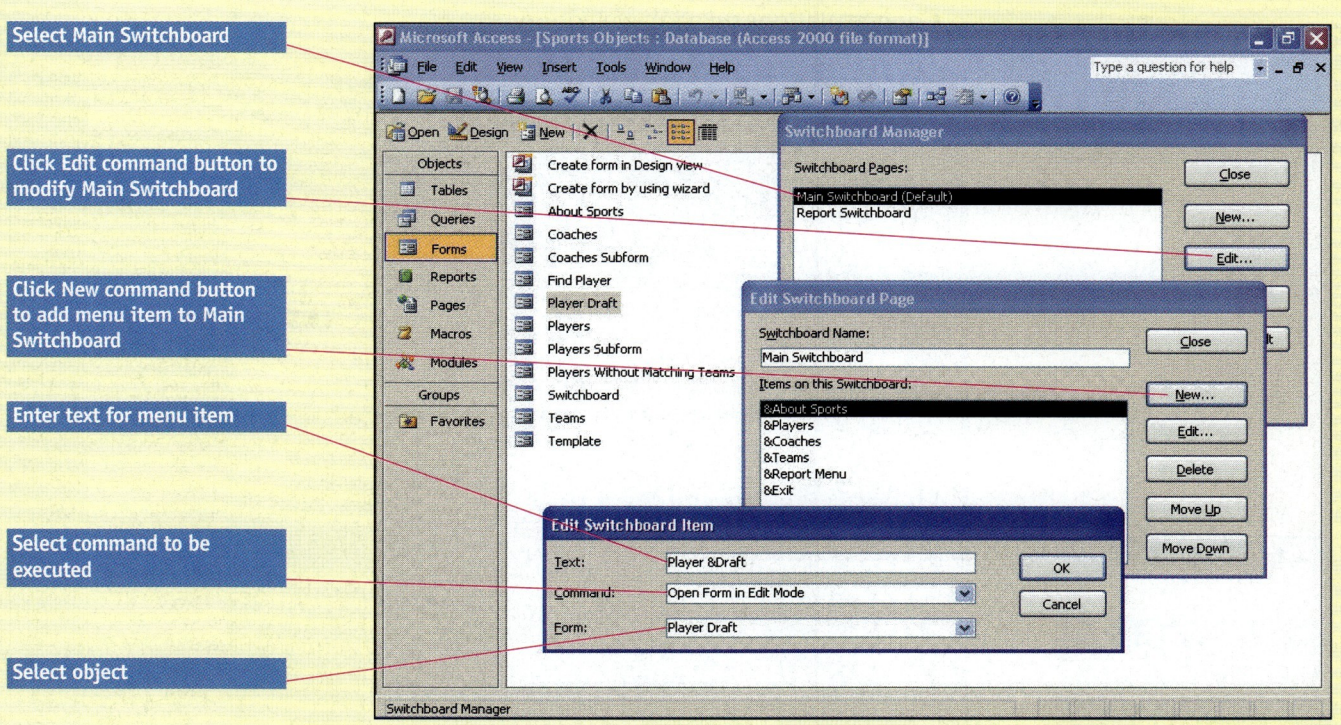

(i) Modify the Main Switchboard (step 9)

FIGURE 7.10 Hands-on Exercise 3 (*continued*)

COMPACT AND REPAIR THE DATABASE

Access databases tend to grow very quickly, especially as you create and edit new forms and reports, and thus you should always compact a database before you exit. Pull down the Tools menu, click Database Utilities, then click Compact and Repair database. The database will close, then reopen, after the compacting process has eliminated the fragmentation that occurs as you work on a database. Compacting is different from compressing; that is, you can use WinZip (or a similar utility) to further reduce the file size of a compacted database.

Step 10: **Test the Completed Switchboard**

■ Click the **Macros button** in the Database window. Double click the **AutoExec macro** to execute this macro, as though you just opened the database.

■ Click the **Player Draft button** on the Main Switchboard to display the form you just created, as shown in Figure 7.10j.

■ Click the **TeamID field** for Katie Remmen. Type **R** (the first letter in Rockets) and Katie is assigned automatically to this team. Click the **Update List command button**. Katie disappears from the list of unassigned players.

■ Click the **Find Player button**. Enter **Remmen** when prompted for the player's last name, and click **OK**. You will see a player form for Katie Remmen, indicating that she has been assigned to the Rockets. Click the **Close Form button**. Click the **End Draft button**.

■ Click the **Teams command button** to view the team rosters. Team T01 (Rockets) is the first team you see, and Katie Remmen is on the roster. Click the **Close Form button** to return to the switchboard.

■ Click the **Exit button**. Click **OK** in response to the message for backup. Congratulations on a job well done.

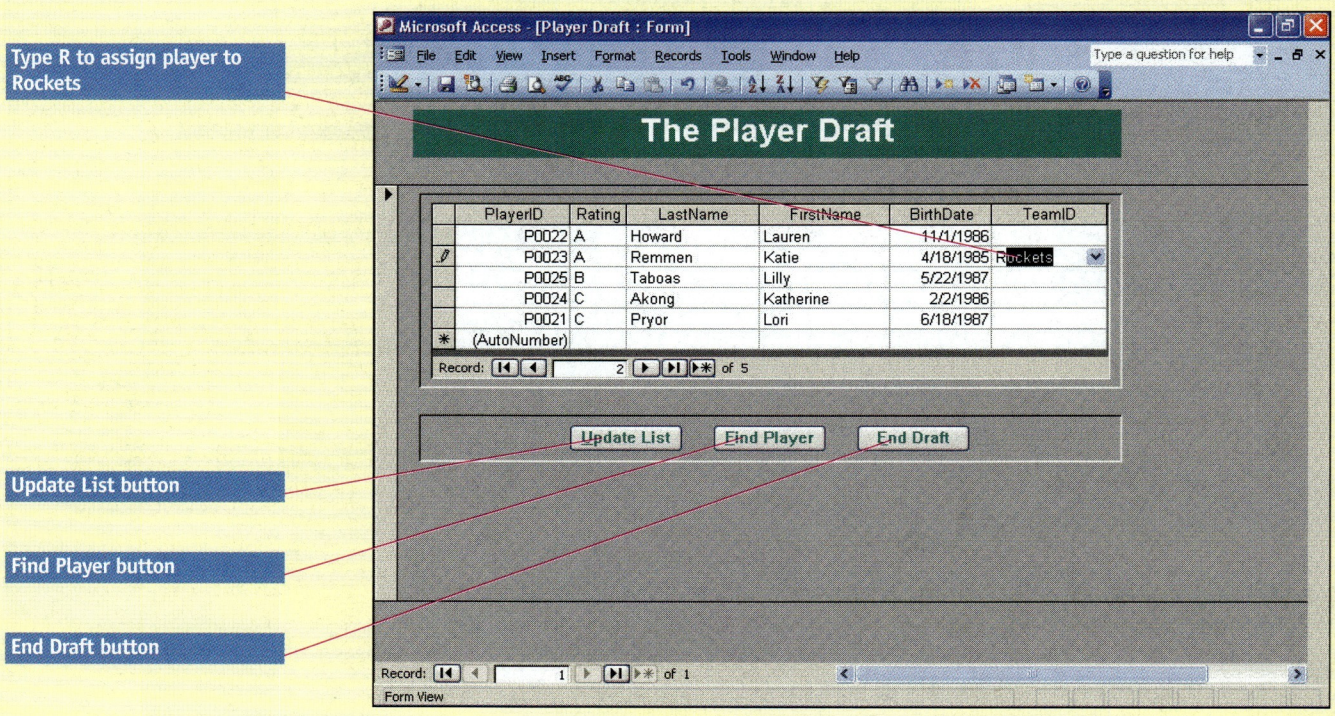

Type R to assign player to Rockets

Update List button

Find Player button

End Draft button

(j) Test the Completed Switchboard (step 10)

FIGURE 7.10   Hands-on Exercise 3 (*continued*)

PASSWORD PROTECT A DATABASE

Protect your database from unauthorized access through imposition of a password. It's a two-step process. First, close the database, then pull down the File menu, click the Open command to display the Open dialog box, select the database, then click the drop-down Open button and choose Open Exclusive. Click Open in response to the security warning. Next, pull down the Tools menu, click Security, click Set Database password, and follow the onscreen prompts. Be careful, however, because you cannot open the database if you forget the password.

SUMMARY

An Access application is different from an ordinary database in that it contains an intuitive user interface known as a switchboard. The switchboard can be created automatically using the Switchboard Manager, a tool that prompts you for each item you want to include. You supply the text of the menu item, as it is to appear on the switchboard, together with the underlying command. Access does the rest and creates the switchboard form and associated table of switchboard items.

The tables in a database can be separated from the other objects to enable the distribution of updated versions of the application without disturbing the data. The tables are stored in one database and the objects in another. The Link Tables command associates the tables with the objects.

A template is a partially completed report or form that contains graphical elements and other formatting specifications. It is used as the basis for other objects and helps to promote a consistent look throughout an application.

A macro automates a command sequence and consists of one or more actions. The Macro window has two sections. The upper section contains the name (if any) of the macro and the actions (commands) that make up the macro. The lower section specifies the arguments for the various actions. A macro group consists of multiple macros and is used for organizational purposes.

The AutoExec macro is executed automatically whenever the database in which it is stored is opened. Each database can have its own AutoExec macro, but there is no requirement for an AutoExec macro to be present.

The Unmatched Query Wizard identifies the records in one table (e.g., the Players table) that do not have matching records in another table (e.g., the Teams table).

A prototype is a model (mockup) of a completed application that demonstrates the "look and feel" of the application. Prototypes can be developed quickly and easily through the use of simple macros containing the MsgBox action. Continual testing through prototyping is essential to the success of a system.

A database can be protected from unauthorized use through imposition of a password. Once a password has been implemented, the database cannot be opened without it.

KEY TERMS

Action 348	Get External Data command 340	Password protection 370
Argument 348	Is Null criterion 362	Prototype 350
AutoExec macro 349	Linked Table Manager 338	Requery command 365
Combo box 359	Link Tables command 338	Switchboard 334
Database properties 339	Macro 348	Switchboard form 337
Database splitter 340	Macro group 360	Switchboard Items table 337
Debugging 349	Macro toolbar 349	Switchboard Manager 337
Display When property 345	Macro window 348	Template 350
Event 337	MsgBox action 349	Unmatched Query Wizard 359
Event procedure 344	On Click property 360	

MULTIPLE CHOICE

1. Which of the following is created by the Switchboard Manager?
   (a) A form to hold the switchboard
   (b) A table containing the commands associated with the switchboard
   (c) Both (a) and (b)
   (d) Neither (a) nor (b)

2. Which of the following describes the storage of the tables and objects for the application developed in the chapter?
   (a) Each table is stored in its own database
   (b) Each object is stored in its own database
   (c) The tables are stored in one database and the objects in another
   (d) The tables and objects are stored in the same database

3. Which of the following is true regarding the Link Tables command as it was used in the chapter?
   (a) It was executed from the Sports Objects database
   (b) It was executed from the Sports Tables database
   (c) Both (a) and (b)
   (d) Neither (a) nor (b)

4. What happens when an Access database is opened initially?
   (a) Access executes the AutoExec macro if the macro exists
   (b) Access opens the AutoExec form if the form exists
   (c) Both (a) and (b)
   (d) Neither (a) nor (b)

5. Which statement is true regarding the AutoExec macro?
   (a) Every database must have an AutoExec macro
   (b) A database may have more than one AutoExec macro
   (c) Both (a) and (b)
   (d) Neither (a) nor (b)

6. Which of the following are examples of arguments?
   (a) MsgBox and OpenForm
   (b) Message type (e.g., critical) and Form name
   (c) Both (a) and (b)
   (d) Neither (a) nor (b)

7. Which of the following can be imported from another Access database?
   (a) Tables and forms
   (b) Queries and reports
   (c) Both (a) and (b)
   (d) Neither (a) nor (b)

8. How do you change the properties of a command button on a form?
   (a) Open the form in Form view, then click the left mouse button to display a shortcut menu
   (b) Open the form in Form view, then click the right mouse button to display a shortcut menu
   (c) Open the form in Form Design view, then click the left mouse button to display a shortcut menu
   (d) Open the form in Form Design view, then click the right mouse button to display a shortcut menu

9. Which of the following is true regarding the Unmatched Query Wizard with respect to the Sports league database?
   (a) It can be used to identify teams without players
   (b) It can be used to identify players without teams
   (c) Both (a) and (b)
   (d) Neither (a) nor (b)

10. Which of the following can be associated with the On Click property of a command button?
    (a) An event procedure created by the Command Button Wizard
    (b) A macro created by the user
    (c) Either (a) or (b)
    (d) Neither (a) nor (b)

. . . continued

11. Which of the following was suggested as essential to a backup strategy?

(a) Backing up files at the end of every session

(b) Storing the backup file(s) at another location

(c) Both (a) and (b)

(d) Neither (a) nor (b)

12. Which of the following is true if the On Click property of a command button contains the entry, *Player Draft. Update List*?

(a) Update List is an event procedure

(b) Player Draft is an event procedure

(c) Player Draft is a macro in the Update List macro group

(d) Update List is a macro in the Player Draft macro group

13. Which of the following is true?

(a) An existing database may be split into two separate databases, one containing the tables, and one containing the other objects

(b) Once the objects in a database have been linked to the tables in another database, the name and/or location of the latter database can never be changed

(c) Both (a) and (b)

(d) Neither (a) nor (b)

14. The F6 and F11 function keys were introduced as shortcuts. Which of the following is true about these keys?

(a) The F6 key switches between the top and bottom sections of the Macro window

(b) The F11 key makes the Database window the active window

(c) Both (a) and (b)

(d) Neither (a) nor (b)

15. Which of the following was suggested as a way to organize macros and thus limit the number of macros that are displayed in the Database window?

(a) Avoid macro actions that have only a single argument

(b) Avoid macros that contain only a single action

(c) Create a macro group

(d) All of the above

16. You are developing an Access application, which you expect to upgrade periodically. Which of the following statements is true?

(a) It will be easier to upgrade if the objects and tables are in the same database.

(b) It will be easier to upgrade if the objects are in one database and the tables in another.

(c) Every table should be in its own database.

(d) Every object should be in its own database.

17. Which macro is executed automatically when the database in which it is stored is opened?

(a) Switchboard

(b) AutoExec

(c) StartDatabase

(d) Startup

18. Which command is used to associate tables in one database with objects in another database?

(a) The Join Tables command

(b) The Link Tables command

(c) The Import Tables command

(d) The Get External Data command

ANSWERS

1. c		**7.** c		**13.** a
2. c		**8.** d		**14.** c
3. a		**9.** c		**15.** c
4. a		**10.** c		**16.** b
5. d		**11.** c		**17.** b
6. b		**12.** d		**18.** b

PRACTICE WITH ACCESS

1. **Understanding Database Design:** The presentation in Figure 7.11 represents a *hypothetical* assignment for a group project in which the group is asked to present the design for their project to the class as a whole. We have created a similar presentation for you to illustrate what we mean; your only task is to view our presentation, which in turn will help you to review the *Sports* database that was developed in the chapter. (Your instructor may want to extend the assignment and ask you to create a parallel presentation for a different database, which he or she may assign as an actual group project.) Proceed as follows:

   a. Start PowerPoint. Open the *Chapter 7 Practice 1* presentation in the Exploring Access folder. This is a PowerPoint presentation, but you do not have to know PowerPoint to complete this exercise. Pull down the View menu and change to the Normal view. If necessary, click the Slide tab to see the miniature slides instead of the outline.

   b. There are nine slides in the complete presentation. The left pane shows the slide miniatures. The right pane shows a larger view of the selected slide (slide one in this example). The slide describes the hypothetical assignment, which is to create a 10-minute presentation to the class describing the physical problem and the associated database design.

   c. Select (click) the first slide. Pull down the View menu and click the Slide Show command (or click the Slide Show button above the status bar). Click the mouse continually to move through the slide show. You will see a recap of the Sports database, its design, and several suggested queries.

   d. Press the Esc button at the end of the show. Pull down the File menu and click the Print command. Select the All option button in the Print Range area. Click the down arrow in the Print What area and select handouts. Choose six slides per page. Be sure to check the box to frame the slides. Click OK to print the presentation. Print the presentation a second time, but this time print only the title slide (as a full slide) to use as a cover sheet for your assignment.

   e. Review the printed presentation. Do you see how the discipline provided by this assignment can help to ensure the accuracy of the design?

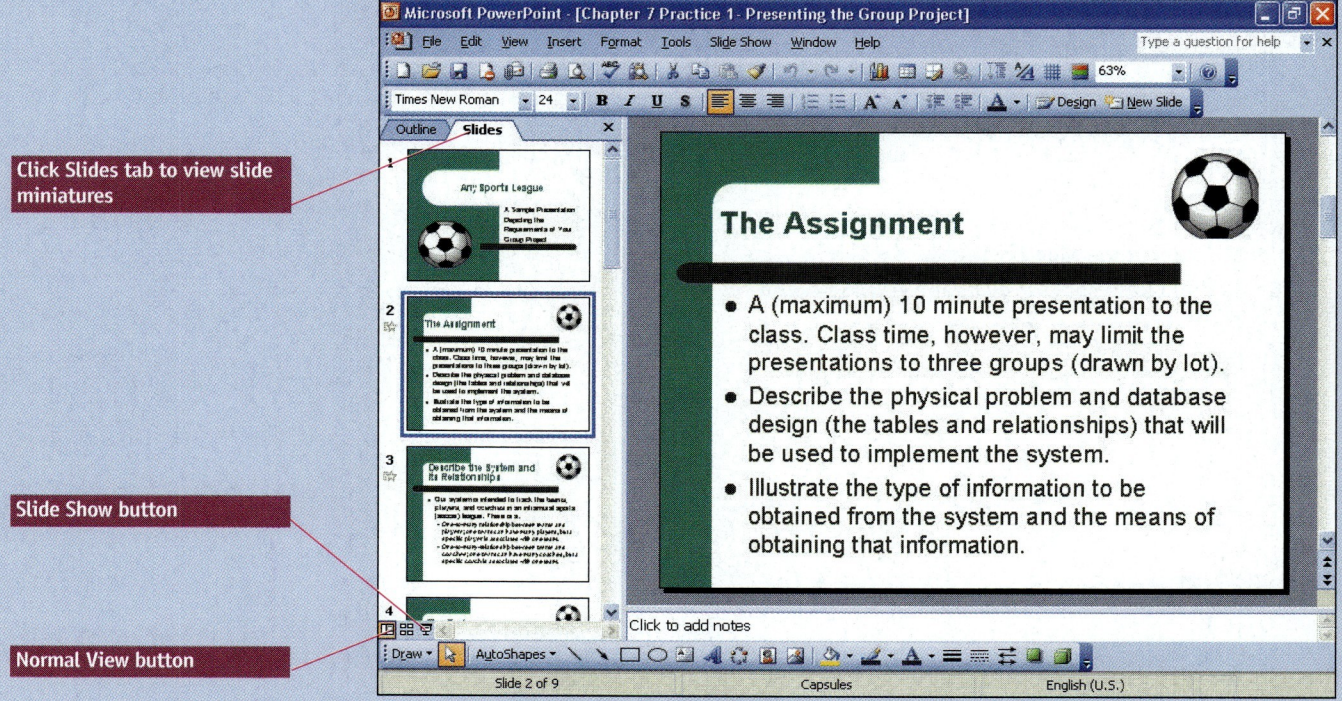

FIGURE 7.11 Understanding Database Design (exercise 1)

practice exercises

2. **Report Design:** Figure 7.12 displays the Design view of a report that prints the team rosters, showing all the players on each team, with their birth date and telephone number. The teams are listed alphabetically by team nickname, and by last name within each team. The report was created using a report template, as opposed to the Report Wizard, in order to maintain a consistent design throughout the application. Open the *Sports Objects* database and proceed as follows:

a. Create the Team Rosters query containing fields from the Teams table and the Players table. The query requires a concatenated field with the player's first and last name as follows, = LastName & ", " & FirstName. Assign "Player" as the name of this field, as opposed to the default name Expr1.

b. Click the Reports button. Select the Report Template, press Ctrl+C to copy the report, then press Ctrl+V to display the Paste As dialog box. Enter Team Rosters as the name of the report. Open the report in Design view. Right click the Report Selector box in the upper-left corner, click Properties to display the property sheet for the report as a whole, and click the All tab. Click the down arrow in the Record Source box and select the Team Rosters query that you just created. The field list should open automatically. Close the property sheet.

c. Pull down the View menu and click the Sorting and Grouping command to insert a Group Header for each team nickname as shown in Figure 7.12. Note the specification to keep the whole group together, which prevents a page break within a team; that is, all players on a given team are printed on the same page. Close the Sorting and Grouping dialog box.

d. Click and drag the Nickname field from the field list to the header you just created. Delete the attached label. Click and drag the remaining fields to the Detail area. Delete the attached labels because the template already contains formatted labels in the Page Header. You will have to change the text of each label to match the column headings in Figure 7.12. (The Page Header contains labels, as opposed to bound controls.) Move, size, and align the controls as needed.

e. Save the report. Print the completed report for your instructor.

Field list

Report Selector box

Nickname control is in Group Header

Click Nickname field

Select Yes to add a Group Header

Select Whole Group to keep whole group on one page

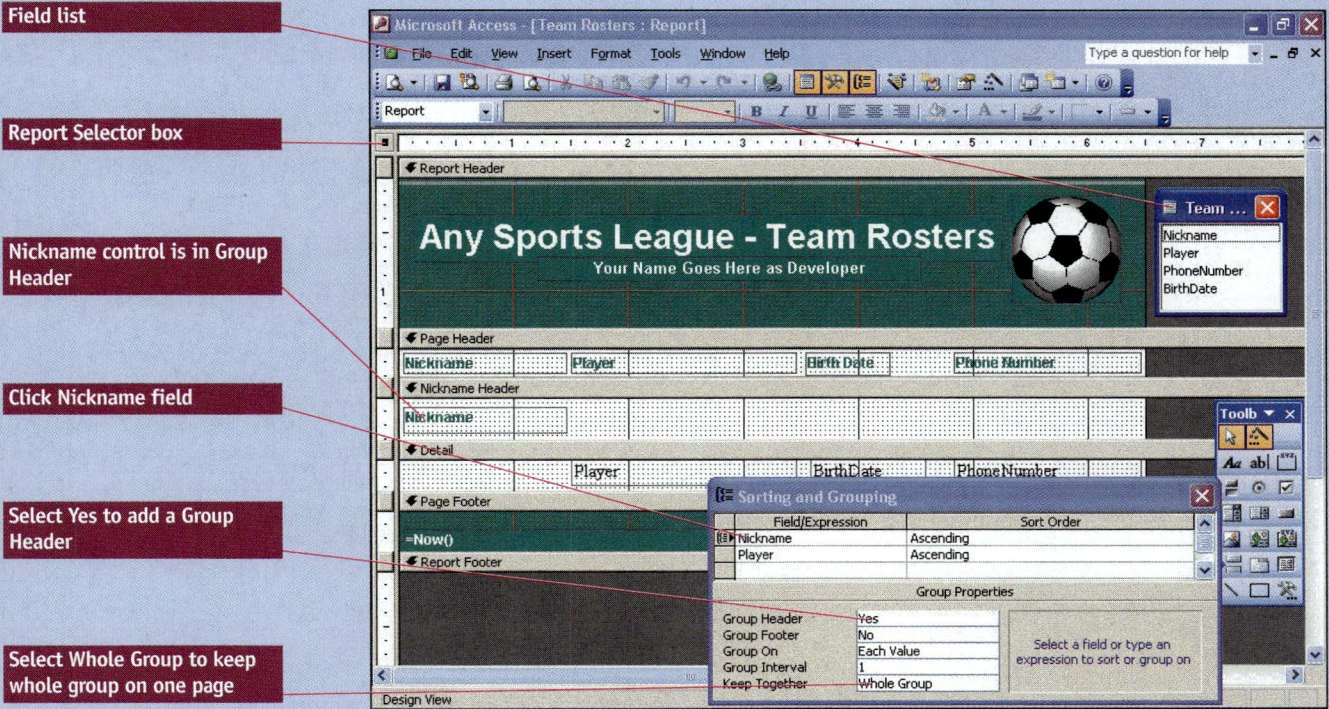

FIGURE 7.12   Report Design (exercise 2)

3. **Master Coaching List:** The query in Figure 7.13 is the basis of the Master Coaching List report. Your task is to create the query, and then create the associated report. The latter is based on the report template that is already in the database to ensure a consistent design throughout the application. Proceed as follows:

   a. Click the Queries button. Double click the icon to Create query in Design view. Add the Teams and Coaches table to the query. The join line should appear automatically as shown in Figure 7.13. Right click the join line, click Join Properties, and choose option 3, which will list every coach, regardless of whether the coach is assigned to a team.

   b. Click in the Field row of the leftmost column. Type LastName & ", " & FirstName and press Enter. Double click Expr1 (which is created automatically) and type Name in its place as the name of the expression. Click the Run button to verify that the expression works as intended.

   c. Complete the query as shown in Figure 7.13. The IIF (Immediate IF function) in the third field displays "Head Coach" or "Assistant" according to the value of the Status field in the Coaches table. Save the query as Master Coaching List.

   d. Click the Reports button. Select the Report Template, press Ctrl+C to copy the report, then press Ctrl+V to display the Paste As dialog box. Enter Master Coaching List as the name of the report. Open the report in Design view. Right click the Report Selector box in the upper-left corner, click Properties to display the property sheet for the report as a whole, and click the All tab. Click the down arrow in the Record Source box and select the Master Coaching List query. The field list should open automatically. Close the property sheet.

   e. Click and drag the first field (Name) from the field list to the Detail area. Click the label next to the control and press the Del key, then change the label in the Page Header from "Field Name" to "Name". Click and drag the remaining three fields (Nickname, Title, and PhoneNumber) to the Detail area, delete the attached label, and then change the label for each field in the Page Header.

   f. Move and/or size the controls so that they are aligned properly under their associated label in the Page Header. Save the report. Print the report.

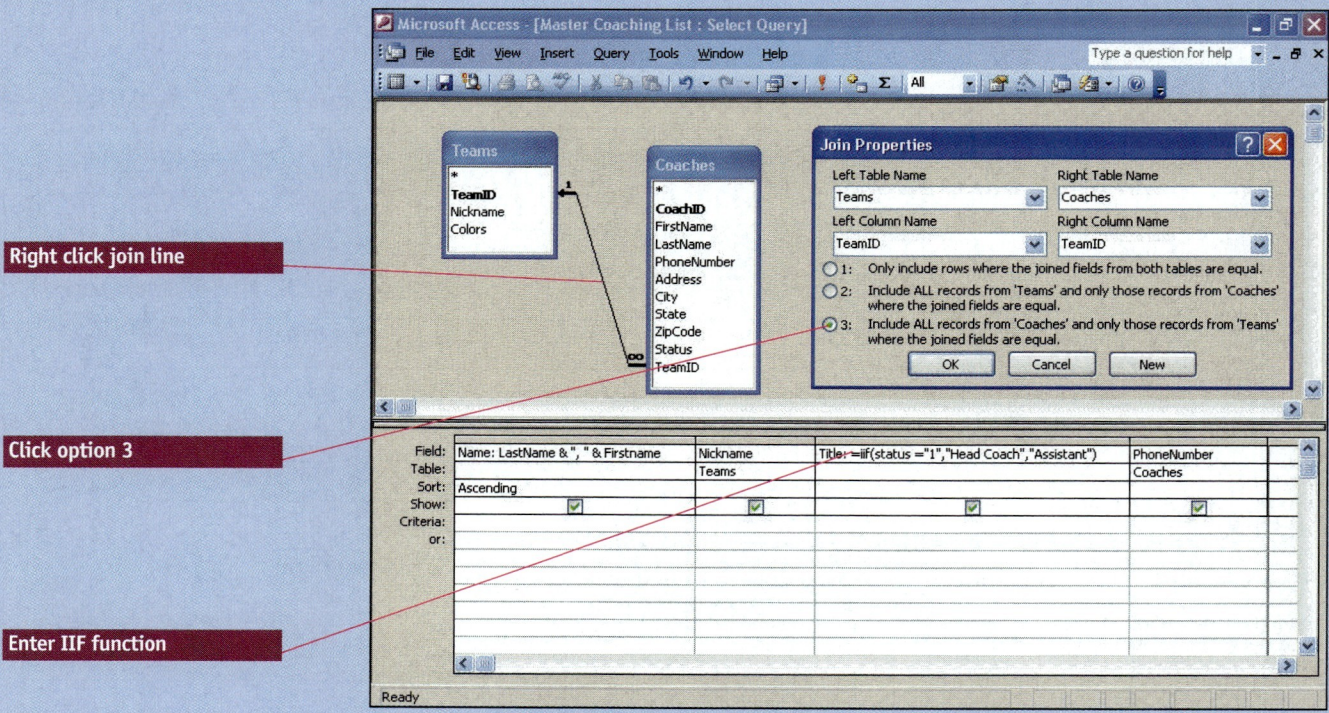

FIGURE 7.13 Master Coaching List (exercise 3)

4. **The Report Switchboard:** The switchboard in Figure 7.14 is an expanded version of the switchboard that was created in the third hands-on exercise. Your assignment is to create the indicated reports and queries, then modify the existing switchboard so that it matches Figure 7.14. (The Report Template, Team Rosters, and Master Coaches List have already been created in previous exercises.) Proceed as follows:

a. The Relationship Diagram is created from the Relationships window. Pull down the Tools menu, click the Relationships command, pull down the File menu, and then click the Print Relationships command. The report is created automatically for you. Change to Design view, and then modify the Report Header to contain your name and the clip art image of the soccer ball.

b. The totals query displays the number of players per team. It contains only two fields: the team nickname from the Teams table and the player's last name from the Players Table. The Count function is used in the Total row of the player's last name field to display the number of players on each team. Note, however, that you cannot run a query directly through the switchboard. Thus, you have to create a macro to open the query, and then run the macro from the switchboard.

c. Use the Unmatched Query Wizard to create a query that will list the teams that do not have a coach. Create a macro to open the query, then run the macro from the switchboard as described in part (b). (The master coaching list that was created in the previous exercise lists all coaches, including those that are not currently assigned to a team. You can use this report to find a coach for any team that does not have one.)

d. Once you have created the required objects, you can use the Switchboard Manager to modify the existing Report Switchboard from the hands-on exercises in the chapter to duplicate the switchboard in Figure 7.14.

e. Use the completed switchboard to print each report if you have not done so previously. Print the switchboard form itself as well as the table of switchboard items. Add a cover sheet and submit the completed assignment to your instructor. The Sports League application is complete.

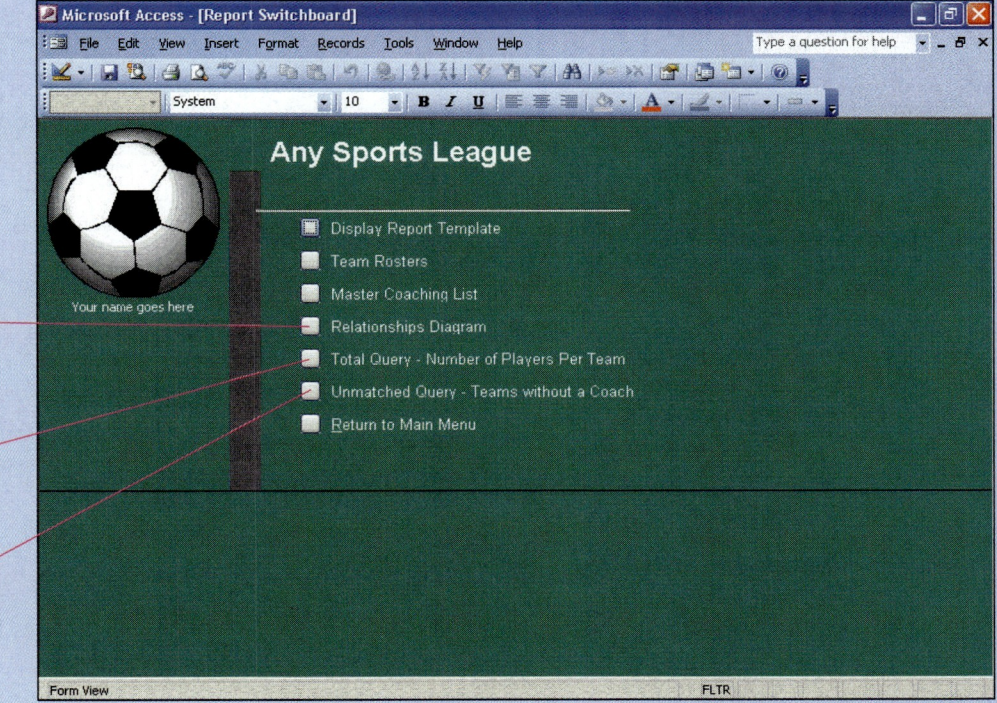

Click to display Relationships Diagram

Click to display Total Query

Click to display Unmatched Query

FIGURE 7.14   The Report Switchboard (exercise 4)

5. **A Look Ahead:** The Add Record button that appears on the Players form was created through the Command Button Wizard. Test the button to see how it works; i.e., open the Players form, click the button to add a player, then note that in order to add a player you must first click the First Name text box. You can automate the process by adding a statement to the event procedure that will position the user in the First Name text box automatically. Proceed as follows:

a. Open the Players form in Design view. Point to the Add Player command button, then click the right mouse button to display a shortcut menu. Click Properties to display the Properties dialog box. Click the down arrow on the vertical scroll bar until you can see the On Click property, which contains the entry [Event Procedure]. Click this entry, then click the Build Button (the three dots to the right of the box) to display the associated VBA code. Maximize the window. Click the Procedure View button at the bottom of the screen.

b. Click under the DoCmd statement and add the line FirstName.SetFocus as shown in Figure 7.15. This tells Access to go to the control called FirstName after inserting a new record. Click the Save button, then close the VBA window.

c. Click the Form View button to switch to Form view and test the Add Player macro. Click the Add Player command button. You should be positioned in the First Name box, where you can start typing immediately.

d. Click the Close Form command button when you have completed the record. Click Yes if prompted to save the changes to the Players form.

e. Open the Coaches form in Design view and make a similar modification to the Add Coach command button. This may seem like a lot of trouble, but the end user appreciates this type of convenience.

f. The programming statements that you have been working with are written in VBA (Visual Basic for Applications). VBA is a powerful programming language and is covered in the next chapter, where you will learn how to further enhance an Access application through VBA. Additional information on VBA is found in the "Getting Started with VBA" module at the end of the text.

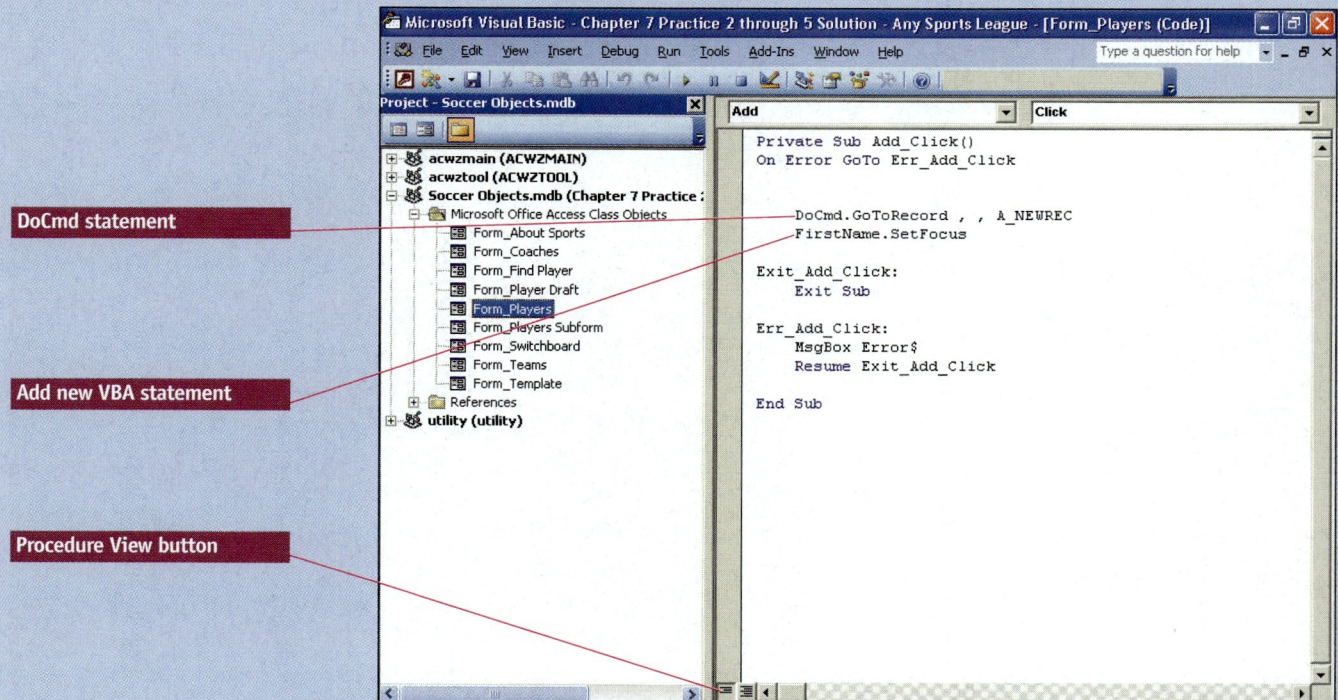

FIGURE 7.15   A Look Ahead (exercise 5)

6. **Class Scheduling:** The database design in Figure 7.16 is intended to implement a class scheduling application at a typical college or university. The scheduling process entails the coordination of course offerings as published in a registration schedule together with faculty assignments. The university may offer multiple sections of any given course at different times. The information about when a class meets is stored within the one-letter section designation; for example, section A meets from 9:00 to 9:50 on Mondays, Wednesdays, and Fridays. Note the following:

a. The database contains separate tables for courses, sections, and faculty as can be seen in Figure 7.16. There are many-to-many relationships between courses and sections, between courses and faculty, and between faculty and sections.

b. The key to the design is the creation of an additional Offerings table that includes the CourseID, SectionID, and FacultyID. The combination of these three fields could serve as the primary key of the Offerings table, but it is easier to add an additional field, the OfferingID with the AutoNumber field type. The additional fields in the Offerings table, Building and Room, provide information as to where the specific course will meet.

c. We have designed the database for you. Your task is to implement our design by creating a database that contains the indicated tables and associated relationships. You do not have to enter data into any of the tables, but you will need to create the tables in order to create a Relationships Diagram.

d. We have embellished the report containing the Relationships Diagram to include a Report Header, with modified font and clip art. (Use any appropriate image.) Print the completed report for your instructor. The clip art will also be used in the next two practice exercises that develop the switchboard and templates for the forms and reports in the database. The visual design of a system is an important consideration that should be given careful attention.

e. Would this design be applicable to the comparable database at your school or university? Summarize your thoughts in a short note to your instructor.

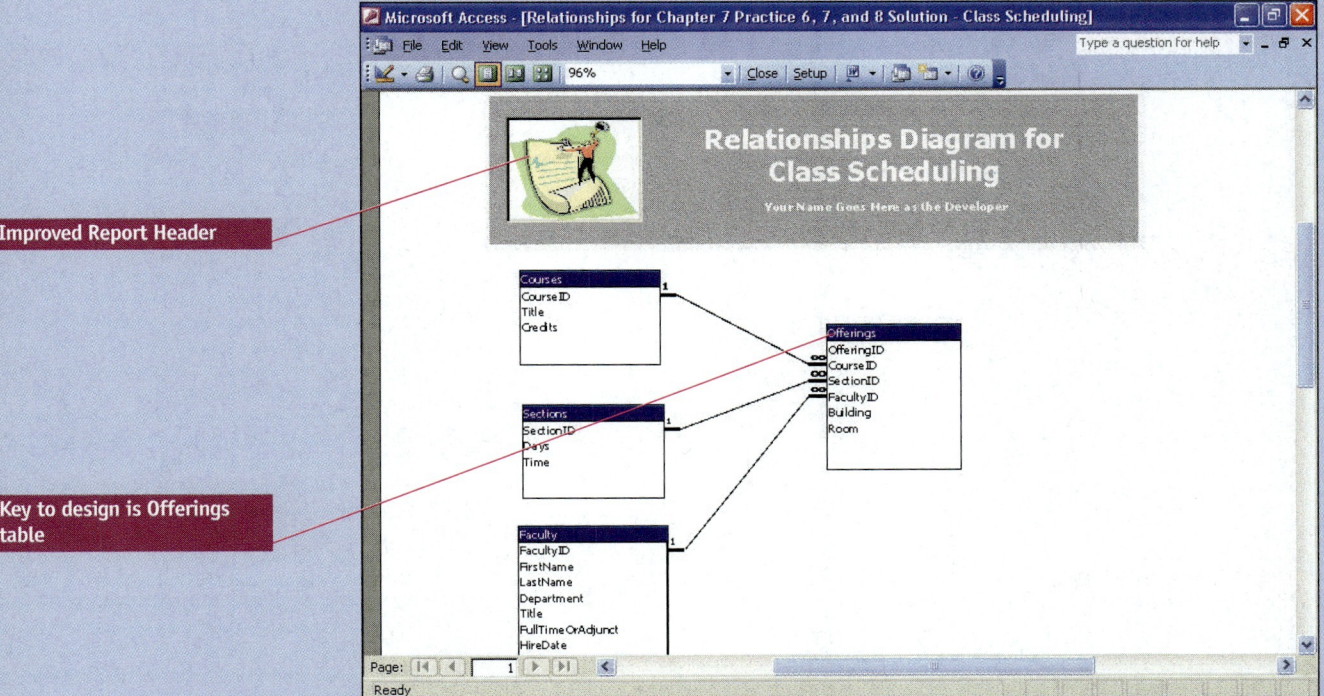

FIGURE 7.16 Class Scheduling (exercise 6)

7. **Class Scheduling Switchboard:** The switchboard in Figure 7.17 continues the development of the *Class Scheduling* database from the previous exercise and represents Version 1.0 of the completed system. You do not have to follow our design exactly, but you are required to include the indicated functionality. It is important, however, that you use a consistent design so that all of the objects in your database have a uniform look. This attention to detail enhances the visual appeal of a database and gives it a more professional appearance. Note the following:

a. The switchboard should open automatically whenever the database is opened. This can be accomplished through the Startup property or through the creation of an AutoExec macro.

b. The About Class Scheduling form contains the same logo that appears on the switchboard and is similar to the other About forms that have appeared throughout the text. The form should also contain your name and any other information required by your instructor.

c. The second menu option should print the report containing the Relationships Diagram from the previous exercise.

d. Create a prototype macro to indicate items under development as shown in Figure 7.17. The associated message box will appear upon clicking any of the next four items, which are not yet developed.

e. The Report Switchboard button should display a secondary switchboard that contains buttons for several reports that will be available in the completed system. Clicking any of the report buttons should also display the message from the prototype macro. The Report Switchboard must contain a button to return to the main switchboard.

f. The Exit button should run a macro that displays a message to the user to back up the system, then exits Access.

g. Print the switchboard and the table of switchboard items for your instructor. Add a cover sheet to complete the assignment. Does the switchboard in its present form provide the user with a meaningful understanding of the finished application?

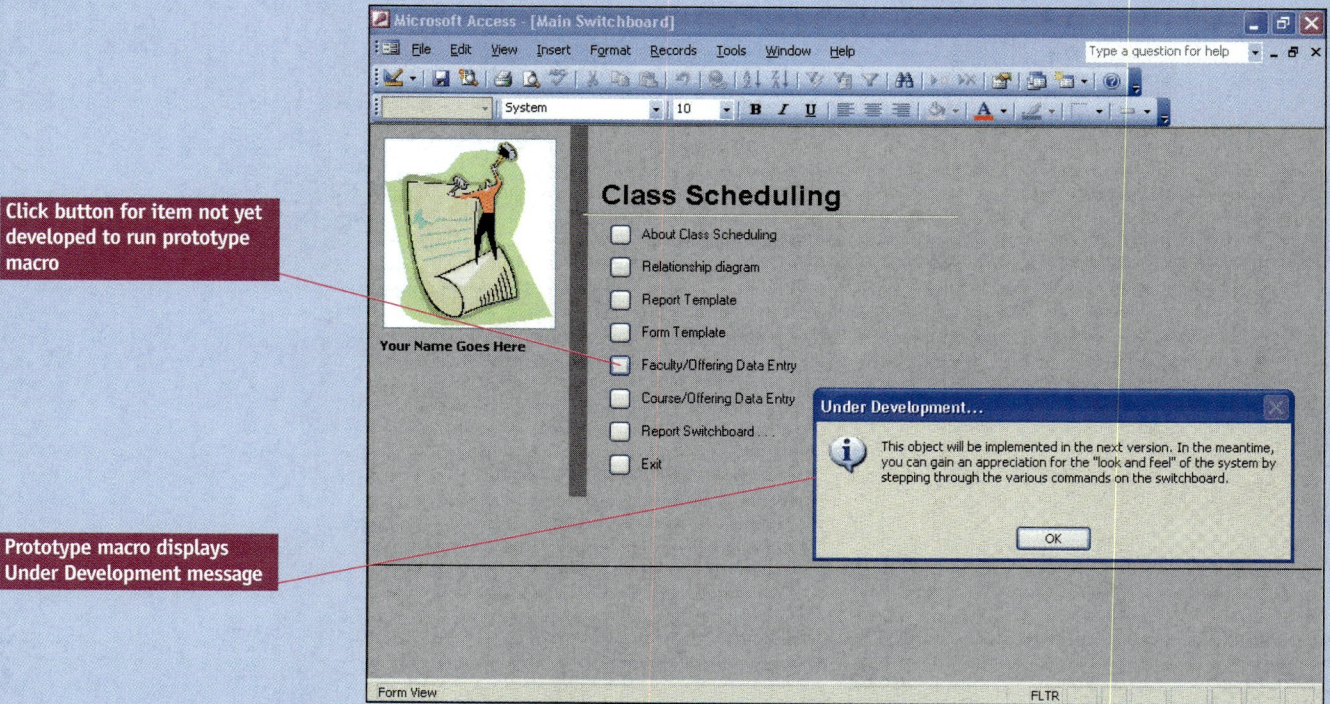

FIGURE 7.17 Class Scheduling Switchboard (exercise 7)

8. **Class Scheduling Templates:** The forms and reports within an application should have a consistent look that is also visually appealing. This exercise asks you to create the templates on which those objects will be based. The templates are created early in the development process so that the user has the opportunity to provide feedback as soon as possible in the event that changes are required. Proceed as follows:

   a. Click the Forms button in the Database window and then double click the icon to Create form in Design view. Enter a title for the form in the Form Header. Change the font, font size, and/or the color as you see fit. The formatting is important because it will appear in every subsequent form. Insert the same clip art that you used in the previous exercise for the switchboard and Relationships Diagram.

   b. Go to the Detail area and create two or three labels to identify the controls that will appear in the form. The text per se is not important; the formatting is. Use the Command Button Wizard to create a button to close the form. Add final changes as you see fit. Save the form as Form Template as shown in Figure 7.18. Print the completed template for your instructor.

   c. Click the Reports button in the Database window and then double click the icon to Create report in Design view. Enter a title for the report in the Report Header. Change the font, font size, and/or the color as you see fit. The formatting is important because it will appear in every subsequent report. Insert the same clip art that you used for the other objects.

   d. Click in the Page Header and enter the text for three or four labels (column headings). The text per se is not important; the formatting is. Create the Page Footer as a combination of text and fields. Our footer will print today's date, the page number, and the total number of pages in the report. Save the report as Report Template. Print the completed template for your instructor.

   e. Modify the main switchboard to display each template, as opposed to running the prototype macro. You have now completed Version 2.0 of the Class Scheduling application. The user has the opportunity to review both the technical design (the Relationships Diagram) and the visual design (the two templates you just created) within the context of a fully functional switchboard.

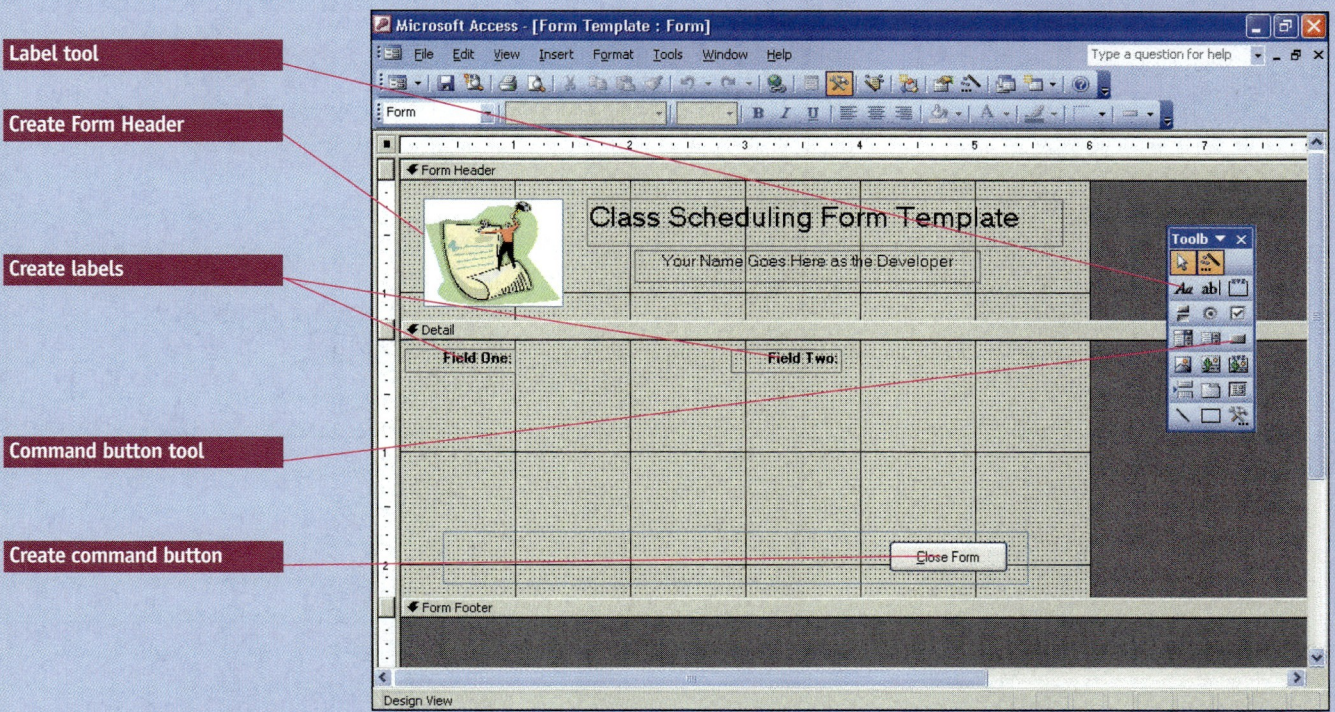

FIGURE 7.18 Class Scheduling Templates (exercise 8)

9. **The Video Store:** You have an internship at the local video store, which rents and/or sells tapes or DVDs to its customers. The store maintains the usual information about every customer (name, address, phone number, and so on.) It also has detailed information about every movie such as its duration, rating, rental price, and purchase price. There is a subtlety in the design because the video store stocks multiple copies (tapes and/or DVDs) of the same movie. Thus, a customer can rent a copy of the movie (from the Copies table), as opposed to renting a movie from the Movies table.

   a. The Movies table contains the detailed information about each movie. There is a one-to-many relationship between movies and copies; that is, one movie can have many copies, but a specific copy is associated with only one movie.

   b. There is a many-to-many relationship between customers and copies; that is, one customer can rent several copies, and the same copy will (over time) be rented to many customers. This in turn gives rise to the Rentals table as shown in Figure 7.19, which contains the additional fields as indicated.

   c. We have created the database design for you. Your task is to implement our design by creating a database that contains the indicated tables and associated relationships. You do not have to enter data into any of the tables, but you will need to create the tables in order to create a Relationships Diagram for your instructor.

   d. We have embellished the report containing the Relationships Diagram to include a Report Header, with a modified font and clip art (use any appropriate image). The elements will also be used in the next two practice exercises that develop the switchboard and templates for forms and reports. The visual design of a system is an important consideration that should be given careful attention. Print the completed report for your instructor.

   e. Would this design be applicable for the system in place at your local video store? Summarize your thoughts in a brief note to your instructor. Add a cover sheet to complete the assignment.

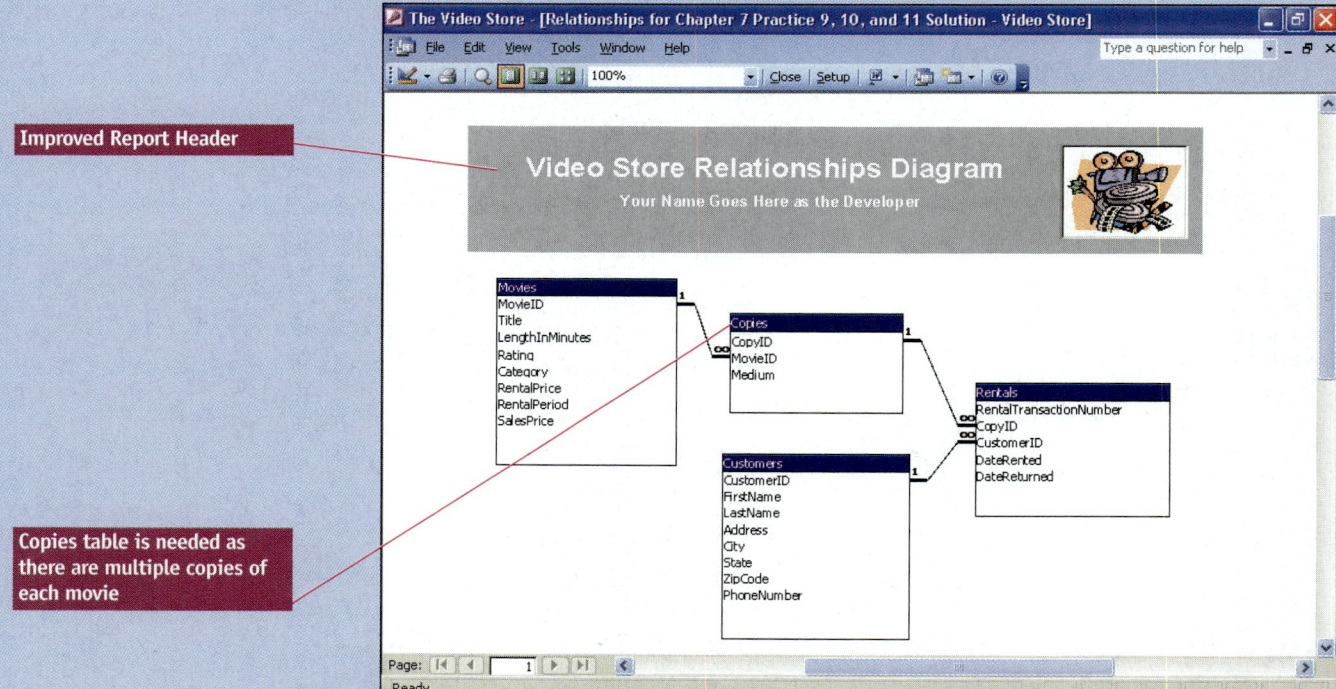

FIGURE 7.19 The Video Store (exercise 9)

10. **Video Store Switchboard:** The switchboard in Figure 7.20 continues the development of the *Video Store* database from the previous exercise and represents Version 1.0 of the completed system. You do not have to follow our design exactly, but you are required to include the indicated functionality. It is important, however, that you use a consistent design so that all of the objects in your database have a uniform look. This attention to detail enhances the visual appeal of a database and gives it a more professional appearance. Note the following:

a. The switchboard should open automatically whenever the database is opened. This can be accomplished through the Startup property or through the creation of an AutoExec macro.

b. The About Video Store form contains the same logo that appears on the switchboard and is similar to the other About forms that have appeared throughout the text.

c. The second menu option should print the report containing the relationships diagram from the previous exercise.

d. Create a prototype macro to indicate items under development as shown in Figure 7.20. The associated message box will appear upon clicking any of the next four items, which are not yet developed.

e. The Report Switchboard button should display a secondary switchboard that contains buttons for several reports that will be available in the completed system. Clicking any of the report buttons should also display the message from the prototype macro. The Report Switchboard must contain a button to return to the main switchboard.

f. The Exit button should run a macro that displays a message to the user to back up the system, then exits Access.

g. Print the switchboard and the table of switchboard items for your instructor. Add a cover sheet to complete the assignment. Does the switchboard in its present form provide a meaningful understanding of the finished application?

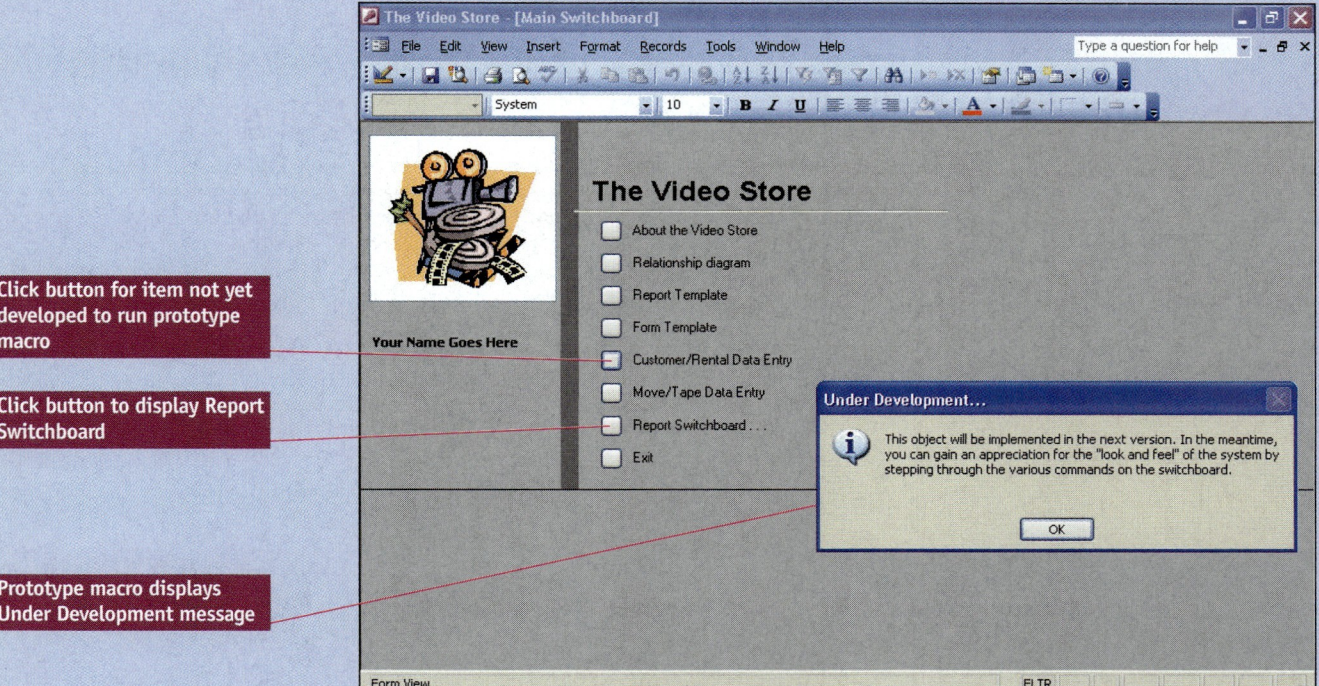

FIGURE 7.20 Video Store Switchboard (exercise 10)

11. **Video Store Templates:** The forms and reports within an application should have a consistent look that is also visually appealing. This exercise asks you to create the templates on which those objects will be based. The templates are created early in the development process so that the user has the opportunity to provide feedback as soon as possible in the event that changes are required. Proceed as follows:

   a. Click the Reports button in the Database window and then double click the icon to Create report in Design view. Enter a title for the report in the Report Header. Change the font, font size, and/or the color as you see fit. The formatting is important because it will appear in every subsequent report. Insert the same clip art that you used for the switchboard and Relationships Diagram.

   b. Click in the Page Header and enter the text for three or four labels (column headings). The text per se is not important; the formatting is. Create the Page Footer as a combination of text and fields. Our footer will print today's date, the page number, and the total number of pages in the report. Save the report as Report Template as shown in Figure 7.21. Print the completed template for your instructor.

   c. Click the Forms button in the Database window and then double click the icon to Create form in Design view. Enter a title for the form in the Form Header. Change the font, font size, and/or the color as you see fit. The formatting is important because it will appear in every subsequent form. Insert the same clip art that you used for the other objects.

   d. Go to the Detail area and create two or three labels to identify the controls that will appear in the form. The text per se is not important; the formatting is. Use the Command Button Wizard to create a button to close the form. Add final changes as you see fit. Save the form as Form Template. Print the completed template for your instructor.

   e. Modify the main switchboard to display each template, as opposed to running the prototype macro. You have now completed Version 2.0 of the Video Store application. The user has the opportunity to review both the technical design (the Relationships Diagram) and the visual design (the two templates you just created) within the context of a fully functional switchboard.

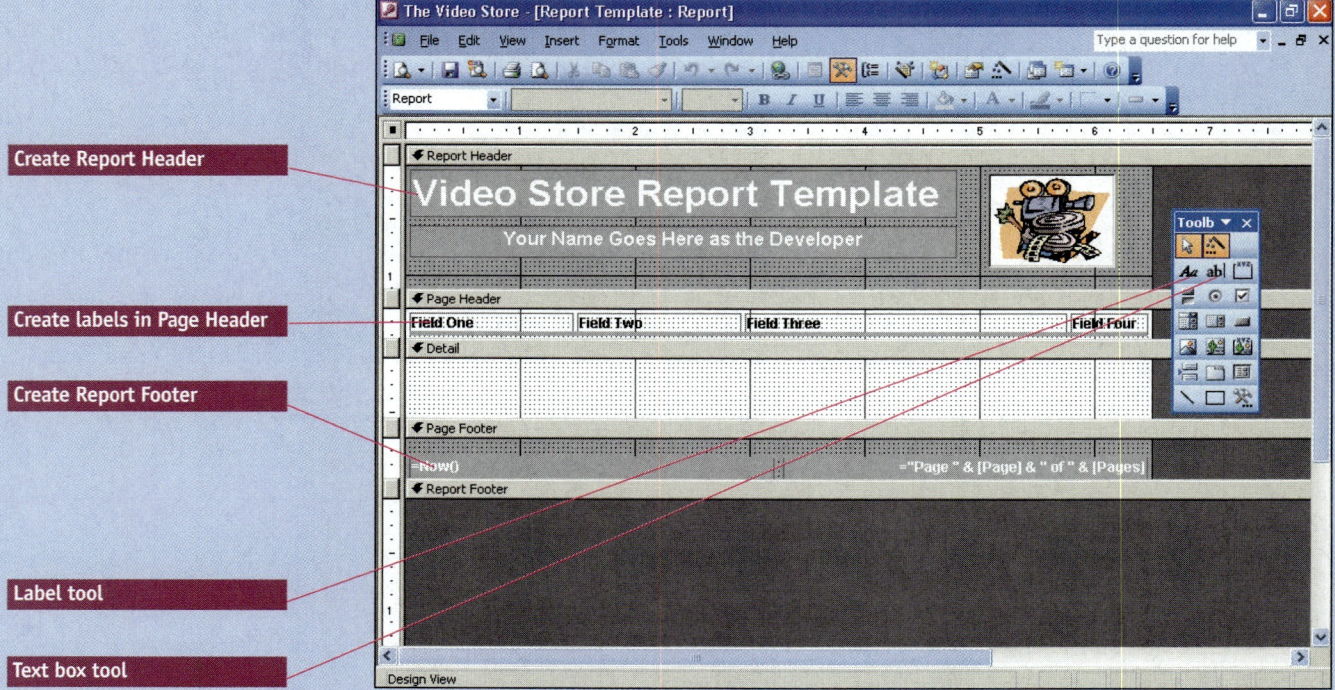

FIGURE 7.21 Video Store Templates (exercise 11)

MINI CASES

Computer Repair

The Director of Administrative Services has come to you for assistance in implementing a system to track the repairs associated with the computers on campus. The data about each computer, such as the make and model, operating system, location on campus, and so on, is stored in a Computers table within an Access database. The faculty or staff member assigned to that computer is also indicated. The data about the faculty/staff is stored in a separate table. One individual (a faculty or staff member) can be assigned to many computers, but a given computer is assigned to only one person.

Problems inevitably occur, and when they do, the faculty or staff member responsible for that computer calls the Director's office to report the problem. The nature of the problem is recorded, and a technician is assigned to fix it. (Technicians are employed as independent contractors and do not appear in the Faculty/Staff table.) One technician can work on many computers, and a specific computer may be worked on by different technicians. Your assignment is to design a database that will maintain this data and produce the associated reports. The database should be able to list all computers that are currently under repair. It should also provide a report that shows all completed repairs. Other reports might include all problems assigned to a specific technician, or all problems reported by a particular faculty or staff member.

A previous consultant has suggested four tables in all. You are to create each table, then create the Relationships Diagram, but you do not have to enter data into any of the tables. You have also been asked to create a simple switchboard with three menu options—a button to display an "About the Repair Service" form describing the database, a button to print the Relationships Diagram, and a button to exit the application. The switchboard should contain the same clip art as the Relationships Diagram and the About form. Use the Startup property to display the switchboard when the database is opened. Print the switchboard form, the table of switchboard items, the relationships diagram, and the About form.

Find a Mate Dating Service

The Find a Mate Dating Service employs dating counselors to match its clients to one another. Each counselor works with many clients, but a specific client always works with the same counselor. Each client completes an extensive questionnaire that describes themselves and the qualities they wish to find in a mate. The counselors evaluate this information and pair the agency's clients with one another to create a date. One client can have many dates, and a date has many (actually two) clients. Feedback is important, and each client is asked for his or her reaction to the date by rating it from one (a bad night) to five (outstanding).

Your assignment is to design a database that will track counselors, clients, and their dates. It should be able to list all dates for a specific client as well as all dates arranged by a specific counselor. A previous consultant has suggested four tables in all. You are to create each table and then create the Relationships Diagram, but you do not have to enter data into any of the tables. You have also been asked to create a simple switchboard with three menu options—a button to display an "About the Dating Service" form describing the database, a button to print the Relationships Diagram, and a button to exit the application. The switchboard should contain the same clip art as the Relationships Diagram and About form. Use the Startup property to display the switchboard when the database is opened. Print the switchboard form, the table of switchboard items, the Relationships Diagram, and the About form.

The Medical Practice

You have been asked to design a database for a small medical practice. Any patient may see any physician, and over time, one patient will see many physicians. This many-to-many relationship between physicians and patients is best expressed in a separate appointments table within the database that contains the PhysicianID, the PatientID, and the date and time of the appointment. A Procedures table has also been created for insurance and billing purposes; each record in this table contains the ProcedureID, a description of the procedure, and the associated fee.

A patient calls the office to make an appointment. (The patient sees only one physician per appointment.) The patient is billed for one or more procedures during that appointment—for example, a blood test and a chest x-ray. There is a many-to-many relationship between procedures and appointments; one appointment will reference multiple procedures, and the same procedure can be administered in multiple appointments.

You have been asked to design a database for the practice. A previous consultant has suggested five tables in all. You are to create each table and then create the Relationships Diagram, but you do not have to enter data into any of the tables. You have also been asked to create a simple switchboard with three menu options—a button to display an "About the Practice" form describing the database, a button to print the Relationships Diagram, and a button to exit the application. The switchboard should contain the same clip art as the Relationships Diagram and About form. Use the Startup property to display the switchboard when the database is opened. Print the switchboard form, the table of switchboard items, the Relationships Diagram, and the About form.

Chapter Recap—The EcoAdventures Cruise Line

The EcoAdventures Cruise Line, based in Victoria, British Columbia, is known for its exploration cruises on smaller ships that carry approximately 100 passengers. These specialty cruises appeal to the traveler who is seeking an expedition rather than a traditional cruise vacation, and who wants to go to the many places around the world where larger ships cannot venture. This ambition is reflected in the company's mission statement: *"EcoAdventures Cruise Lines—our job to make your cruise an adventure!"*

The cruise line is seeking more efficient ways of doing business and has hired you to complete the Access database that was started by your predecessor. The company needs to track its ships, the cruises for each ship, and the ports of call for each cruise. There is a one-to-many relationship between ships and cruises; that is, one ship will go on many cruises, but a specific cruise, such as Cruise Number 8012—Exploration Down Under, is assigned to only one ship. There is also a many-to-many relationship between cruises and ports; that is, a specific cruise will stop at many ports, whereas the same port will be a destination for many different cruises.

Your assignment is to review the chapter, complete the hands-on exercises, then open the partially completed *Chapter 7 Ending Case Study—The EcoAdventures Cruise Line,* and review the existing table design and relationships diagram. Your main task, however, is to develop an application prototype in the form of a two-level switchboard that will provide the "look and feel" of the completed application. The main switchboard should include an About form, a relationships diagram, a form template, a button to display the report switchboard, and an option to exit. The second level (report) switchboard should contain the report template and various hypothetical reports. The visual design is very important, and you should include common clip art and design elements throughout. Use macros where appropriate (e.g., AutoExec, Prototype, and CloseDatabase) that are similar to those contained in this chapter.

Creating More Powerful Applications:
Introduction to VBA

OBJECTIVES

After reading this chapter you will:

1. Describe the relationship of VBA to Microsoft Office.

2. Create an event procedure.

3. Describe the VBA editor.

4. Distinguish between the Procedure view and the Full Module view.

5. Create a combo box to locate a record on a form.

6. Describe the parameters associated with the MsgBox function.

7. Create a procedure to facilitate data entry through keyboard shortcuts.

8. Create a procedure to display application-specific error messages.

9. Describe several types of data validation and various ways of implementation.

hands-on exercises

1. CREATING A COMBO BOX AND ASSOCIATED VBA PROCEDURES
   Input: Introduction to VBA
   Output: Introduction to VBA (modified)

2. FACILITATING DATA ENTRY
   Input: Introduction to VBA (from exercise 1)
   Output: Introduction to VBA (modified)

3. ERROR TRAPPING
   Input: Introduction to VBA (from exercise 2)
   Output: Introduction to VBA (modified)

4. DATA VALIDATION
   Input: Introduction to VBA (from exercise 3)
   Output: Introduction to VBA (modified)

CASE STUDY
RETURN TO THE AUCTION

The South Vancouver Preschool case study was introduced in Chapter 1. At the time you did not realize the extent of your obligation when you volunteered to help the headmaster, Molly Riggs, with the upcoming auction. The auction is the major fund-raising event for the school, and it has grown every year. The work is not difficult, but the number of prospective donors has exceeded all expectations, and Molly has asked you to improve the database. She is leaving the specific changes to your discretion, but Molly would like you to focus on facilitating data entry. Molly would also like the reports in the database to be easier to read, and suggests that you shade the alternate lines in the "Items for Auction" report that is generated daily.

It will be necessary for you to develop some VBA code in order to make the necessary improvements to the database. Thankfully, you are enrolled in a more advanced computer applications course and have the skill set to comply with your supervisor's request. This project will increase your proficiency in Access, and it should help you to land a good job upon graduation. ■

Your assignment is to read the chapter, paying special attention to the many ways to enhance a database through VBA. You will then open *Chapter 8 Case Study—Back to the Auction* database and add procedures to the existing Donors form, basing your enhancements on the code that was developed in the chapter. Start by modifying the existing Add Record procedure to move directly to the appropriate field on the form, as opposed to having the user click in the text box. You should also include a Find Record combo box in the form to locate a specific donor, as well as shortcuts to enter the city, state, and zip code with a single keystroke combination. And finally, be sure to display a message that reminds the user to back up the system upon closing the database.

INTRODUCTION TO VBA

You can accomplish a great deal in Access without using Visual Basic. You can create an Access database consisting of tables, forms, queries, and reports, by executing commands from pull-down menus. You can use macros to create menus that tie those objects together so that the database is easier to use. Nevertheless, there comes a point where you need the power of a programming language to develop a truly useful application. Hence, this introduction to **Visual Basic for Applications** (or **VBA**), a subset of Visual Basic that is accessible from every application in Microsoft Office.

VBA is different from traditional programming languages in that it is event-driven. An **event** is any action that is recognized by Access. Opening or closing a form is an event. So is clicking a button in a form or entering data in a text box or other control on the form. The essence of VBA is the creation of **procedures** (or sets of VBA statements) that respond to specific events.

To enhance an application through VBA, you decide which events are significant and what is to happen when those events occur. Then you develop the appropriate event procedures. You can, for example, create an event procedure that displays a splash (introductory) screen for the application every time a user opens the database. You can write an event procedure that creates a keyboard shortcut for data entry that executes when the user presses a particular keystroke combination. You can create an event procedure to display a specific message in place of the standard error message supplied by Access. In all instances, the execution of your procedures depends entirely on the user, because he or she triggers the underlying events through an appropriate action.

You can also use VBA to modify the event procedures that Access has created for you. If, for example, you used the Command Button Wizard to create a button to close a form, Access created the event procedure for you. The user clicks the button, and the event procedure closes the form. You can, however, use VBA to improve the procedure created by Access by adding a statement that reminds the user to back up the database after closing the form.

This chapter provides a general introduction to VBA through four hands-on exercises that enhance an application in different ways. Our approach is very different from that of other texts that run several hundred pages and cover the subject in extended detail. Our objective is to provide you with an appreciation for what can be accomplished, rather than to cover VBA in detail. We will show you how to create and modify simple procedures. We will also provide you with the conceptual framework to explore the subject in greater detail on your own.

One last point before we begin is that VBA is common to every application in Microsoft Office, and thus anything that you learn about VBA from within Access is applicable to the other applications as well. If, for example, you create a macro in Word or Excel, the macro recorder captures the keystrokes and then generates a VBA procedure that is accessible through the Word document or Excel workbook, respectively. You can modify the procedure by changing existing statements and/or by adding additional statements using the techniques in this chapter.

GETTING STARTED WITH VBA

There are two ways to learn the rudiments of VBA. You can begin your study with this chapter, which has you look at typical VBA procedures within an Access form, then proceed to the VBA primer at the end of the text to study the syntax more precisely. Alternatively, you may want to start with the primer, then return to this chapter to see the application of the various VBA statements within Access. Either way, the two chapters reinforce each other and provide a solid foundation in this important programming language.

A BETTER STUDENT FORM

The form in Figure 8.1 will be used throughout the chapter as the basis of our VBA examples. The form itself is unremarkable and parallels many of the forms that were developed throughout the text. It was created initially through the Form Wizard, then modified by moving and sizing controls as appropriate. What then is so special about the form, and how does it utilize VBA?

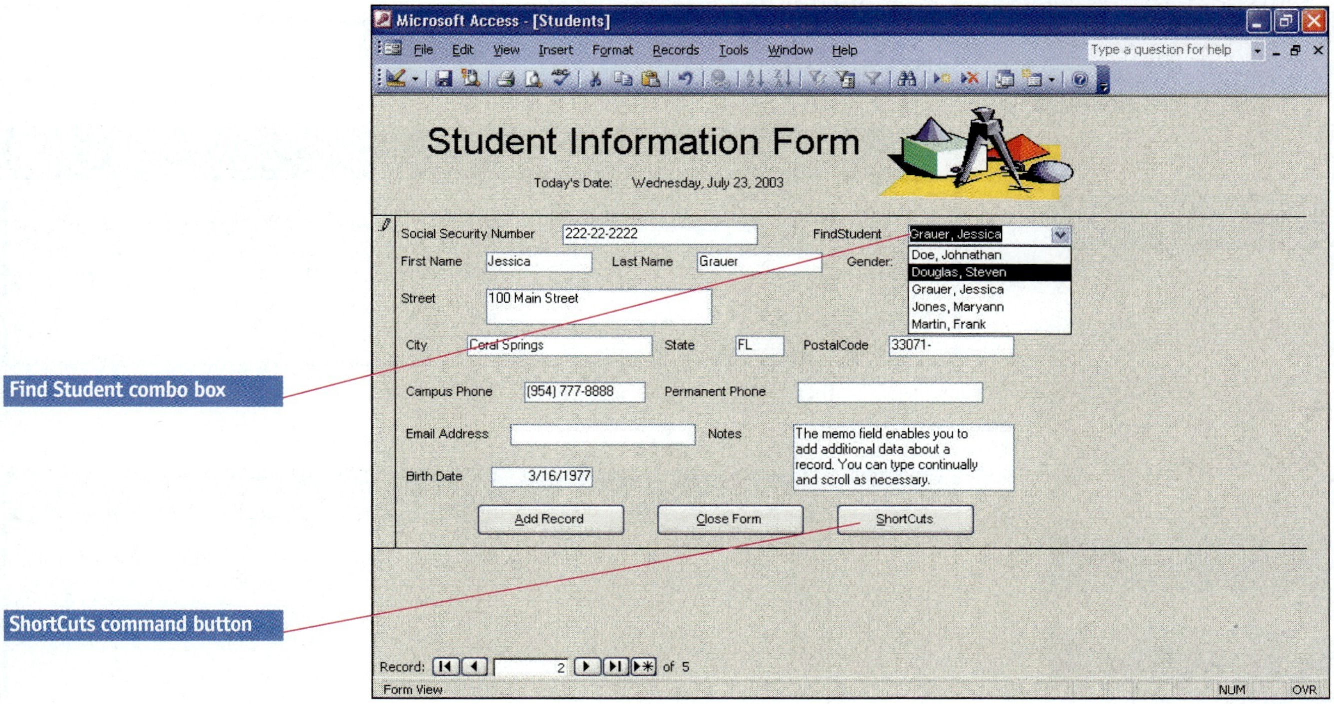

Find Student combo box

ShortCuts command button

FIGURE 8.1   A Better Student Form

The answer lies beneath the surface and is best explained in conjunction with the dialog boxes in Figure 8.2. At first glance the dialog boxes look like typical messages displayed by Microsoft Access. Look closely at the title bar of any message, however, and note that it has been changed to reflect the student or author's name. This is a subtle change that is easily implemented through VBA, and it gives your application a personal touch. Note, too, the different icons that are displayed in the various messages. This, too, is a subtle touch that further customizes the application and its messages.

Look closely at the content of each dialog box to learn more about the underlying VBA capability. The message in Figure 8.2a indicates that the user has omitted the e-mail address, then asks if the record should be saved anyway. This is an improvement over the built-in routines for data validation, which use the Required property to reject any record that omits the e-mail address. Should this occur, the user is notified that the field is required, but he or she cannot save the record unless a value is specified. Through VBA, however, the user has a choice and can opt to save the record even when there is no e-mail address.

The dialog box in Figure 8.2b is displayed as a result of clicking the ShortCuts command button on the form. The message implies that the user can use keyboard shortcuts to enter the city, state, and zip code for Miami or Coral Springs. True, the user could enter the data manually, but think how much time can be saved when there is extensive data entry.

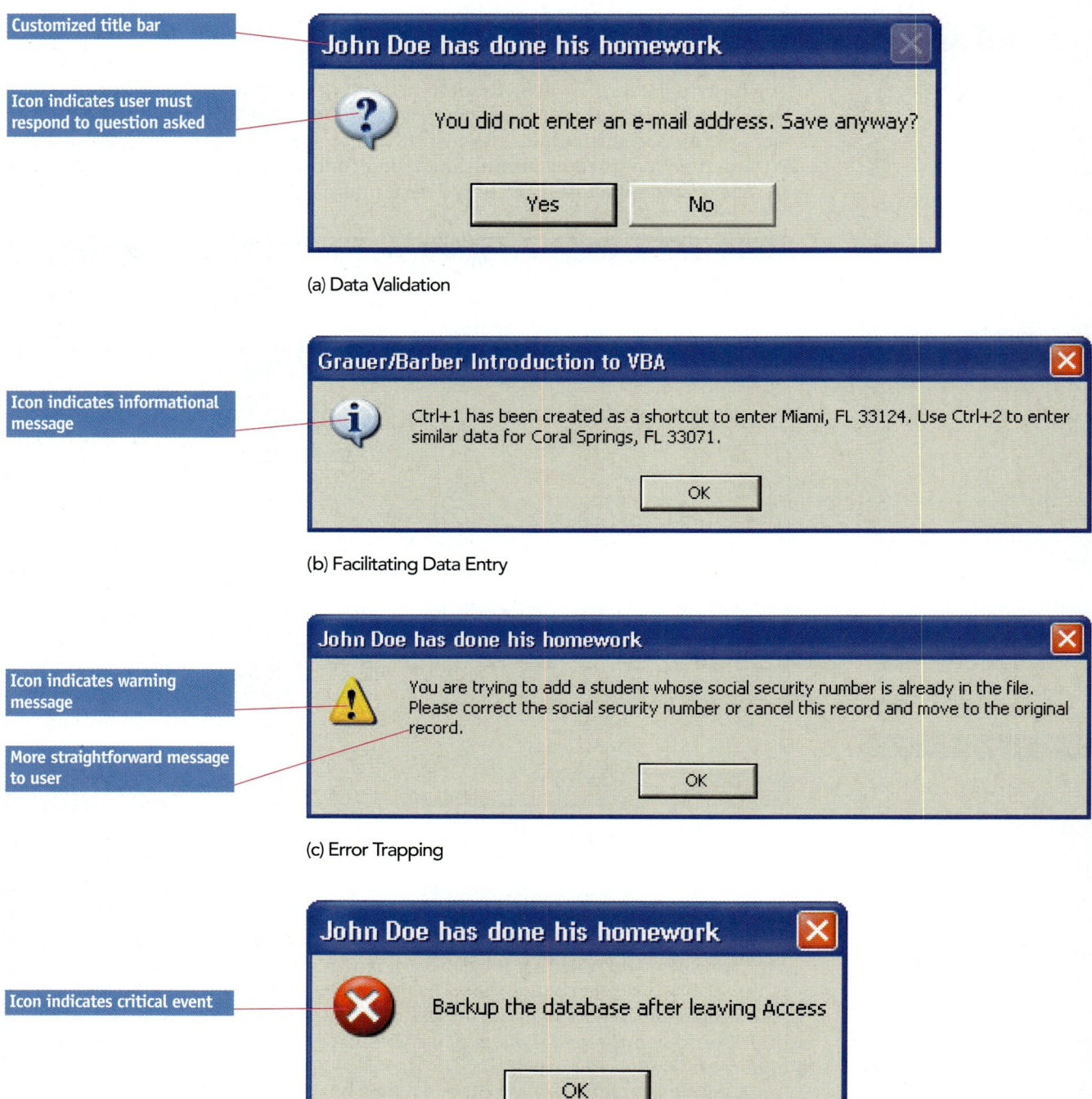

Customized title bar

Icon indicates user must respond to question asked

John Doe has done his homework

You did not enter an e-mail address. Save anyway?

Yes   No

(a) Data Validation

Icon indicates informational message

Grauer/Barber Introduction to VBA

Ctrl+1 has been created as a shortcut to enter Miami, FL 33124. Use Ctrl+2 to enter similar data for Coral Springs, FL 33071.

OK

(b) Facilitating Data Entry

Icon indicates warning message

More straightforward message to user

John Doe has done his homework

You are trying to add a student whose social security number is already in the file. Please correct the social security number or cancel this record and move to the original record.

OK

(c) Error Trapping

Icon indicates critical event

John Doe has done his homework

Backup the database after leaving Access

OK

(d) Enhanced Communication with User

FIGURE 8.2   Dialog Boxes

Figure 8.2c displays a message indicating that one is attempting to add a student whose Social Security number is already in the file. The text is very straightforward and that is exactly the point. The default Access error message would not be as clear, and would have indicated that changes to the table were not successful because they would have created a duplicate value of the primary key. In other words, we used VBA to first detect the error, and then substituted a more explicit message. Finally, the message in Figure 8.2d simply reminds the user to back up the database upon exiting Access.

Modules and Procedures

There are, in essence, two different ways to learn VBA. The first is to immerse yourself in the theory and syntax before you attempt to develop any applications on your own. The second, and the one we follow, is to start with an overall appreciation of what it can do, then plunge right in. You need some basic vocabulary, but after that you can model your procedures on ours and create some very powerful applications in the process. (You can also review the "Getting Started with VBA" module at the end of this text.)

Visual Basic code is developed in units called procedures. There are two types of procedures, general procedures and event procedures. *Event procedures* are the essence of an Access application and run automatically in response to an event such as clicking a button or opening a form. *General procedures* do not run automatically, but are called explicitly from within another procedure. We focus exclusively on event procedures.

All (general and event) procedures are stored in modules; that is, one module contains one or more procedures. Every form in an Access database has its own module (known as a *class module*), which contains the procedures for that form. A procedure is either public or private. A *private procedure* is accessible only from within the module in which it is contained. A *public procedure* is accessible from anywhere.

The procedures in a module are displayed and edited through the *Module window* within the Visual Basic editor. Figure 8.3, for example, displays the Module window for the student form shown earlier in Figure 8.1. Four different procedures are visible, each of which is associated with a different event. Each procedure begins with a procedure header that names the procedure. This is followed by the executable statements within the procedure, followed by the End Sub statement to mark the end of the procedure. Do not be concerned if you do not understand the precise syntax of every statement. Try, instead, to gain an overall appreciation for what the procedures do.

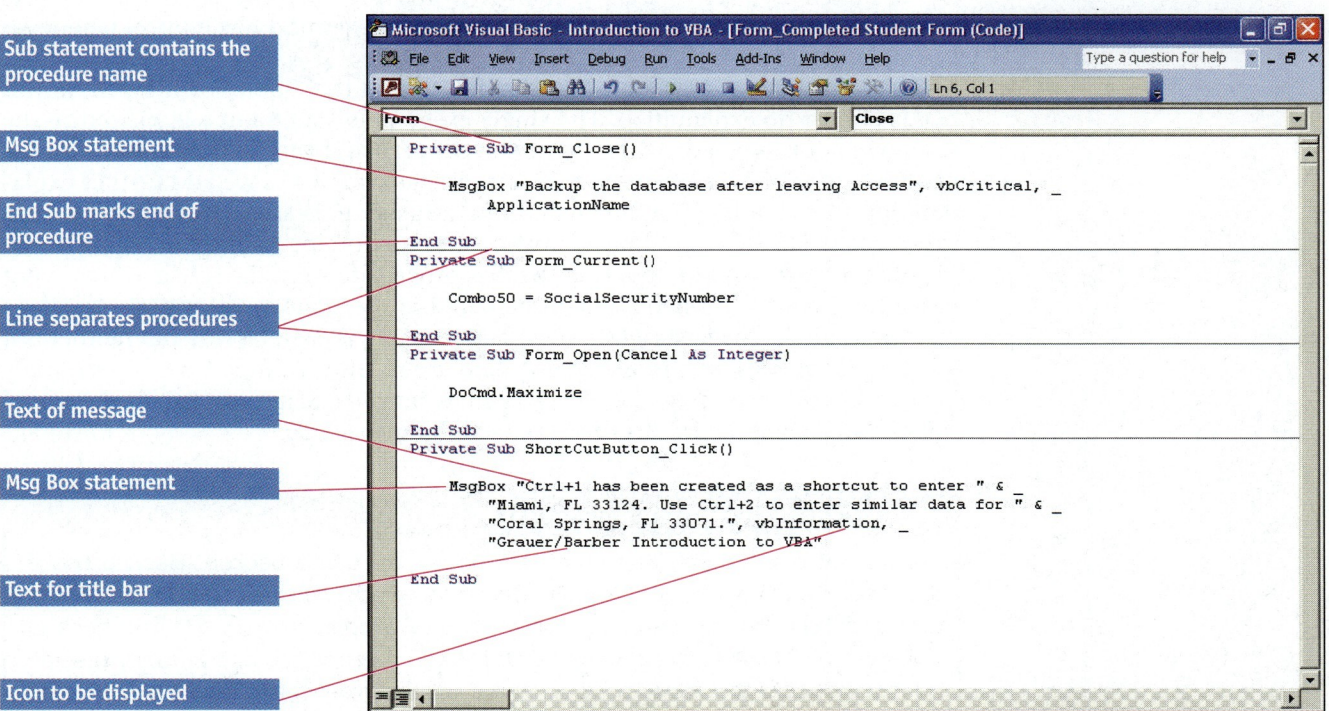

FIGURE 8.3 The Module Window

The first event procedure is for the **Close Form event**. The procedure header contains the keyword Sub, followed by the procedure name (Form_Close). The **MsgBox statement** within the procedure displays the message box (shown earlier in Figure 8.2d) when the event occurs. Thus, whenever the user closes the form, either by clicking the Close button on the form or by clicking the Close button in the document window, the event procedure is triggered and one is reminded to back up the database. (See boxed tip.)

The syntax of the MsgBox statement is typical of many VBA statements and is best understood if you view the statement as it might appear in a Help screen: *MsgBox (prompt, buttons, title)*. The various entries are known as **arguments** (or **parameters**) and determine the contents of the message box. The first argument is contained in quotation marks, and it specifies the prompt (or message text) that appears within the message box. The second argument indicates the type of command buttons (if any) and the associated icon that appear within the dialog box. This argument is specified as an **intrinsic** (or previously defined) **constant** (vbCritical in this example), and it determines the icon that is to appear in the message box. The third argument contains the text that appears in the title bar of the message box. It, too, appears in quotation marks.

The second event procedure is associated with the **Current event** of the form and is the focus of our first hands-on exercise. The nature of this procedure is much less intuitive than the previous example, yet this event procedure is critical to the success of the form. Return to the Student Form shown in Figure 8.1 and note the presence of a combo box to find a specific student. The user clicks the drop-down arrow on the combo box and selects a student from the displayed list, after which the data for that student is displayed in the form.

The combo box was created through the Combo Box Wizard, and it works well, but it does have one limitation. If the user elects to move from one record to the next by clicking a navigation button at the bottom of the form, the combo box is out of sync in that it does not reflect the name of the new student. Hence the need to write a VBA procedure for the Current event to change the value in the combo box to match the current record. In other words, the VBA procedure will move the SocialSecurityNumber of the current record to the combo box control whenever the record changes.

The third event procedure is associated with the Open Form event, and it needs almost no explanation. The single executable statement will maximize the form when it is opened. Again, do not be concerned if you do not understand the precise syntax of every statement in our initial examples as we add further explanation in the chapter. The fourth and final procedure is associated with the Click event of the ShortCut command button, and it contains another example of the MsgBox function. Note, too, that for this procedure to make sense, other event procedures have to be created to implement the shortcuts as described.

We would be misleading you if we said that VBA is easy. It's not, but neither is it as complicated as you might think. And more importantly, VBA is extremely powerful. We think you will be pleased with what you can accomplish by the end of this chapter. Once again, it is time for a hands-on exercise.

A SIMPLE STRATEGY FOR BACKUP

We cannot overemphasize the importance of adequate backup. Backup procedures are personal and vary from individual to individual as well as from installation to installation. Our suggested strategy is very simple, namely that you back up whatever you cannot afford to lose and that you do so at the end of every session. Be sure to store the backup at a different location from the original file. Develop a consistent strategy and follow it faithfully!

Creating a Combo Box and Associated VBA Procedure

Objective To create a combo box to locate a record; to create a VBA procedure to synchronize the combo box with the current record. Use Figure 8.4.

Step 1: **Open the Introduction to VBA Database**

- Start Access. Open the **Introduction to VBA database** in the **Exploring Access folder** as shown in Figure 8.4a.

- If necessary, click the **Forms button**. Select (click) the **Original Student Form**. Pull down the **Edit menu** and click the **Copy command** (or press **Ctrl+C** or click the **Copy button** on the Database toolbar). The form is copied to the clipboard.

- Pull down the **Edit menu** a second time and click the **Paste command** (or press **Ctrl+V** or click the **Paste button** on the Database toolbar) to display the Paste As dialog box. Type **Completed Student Form** and press **Enter**.

- The Database window contains two forms—the Original Student form and the Completed Student form you just created.

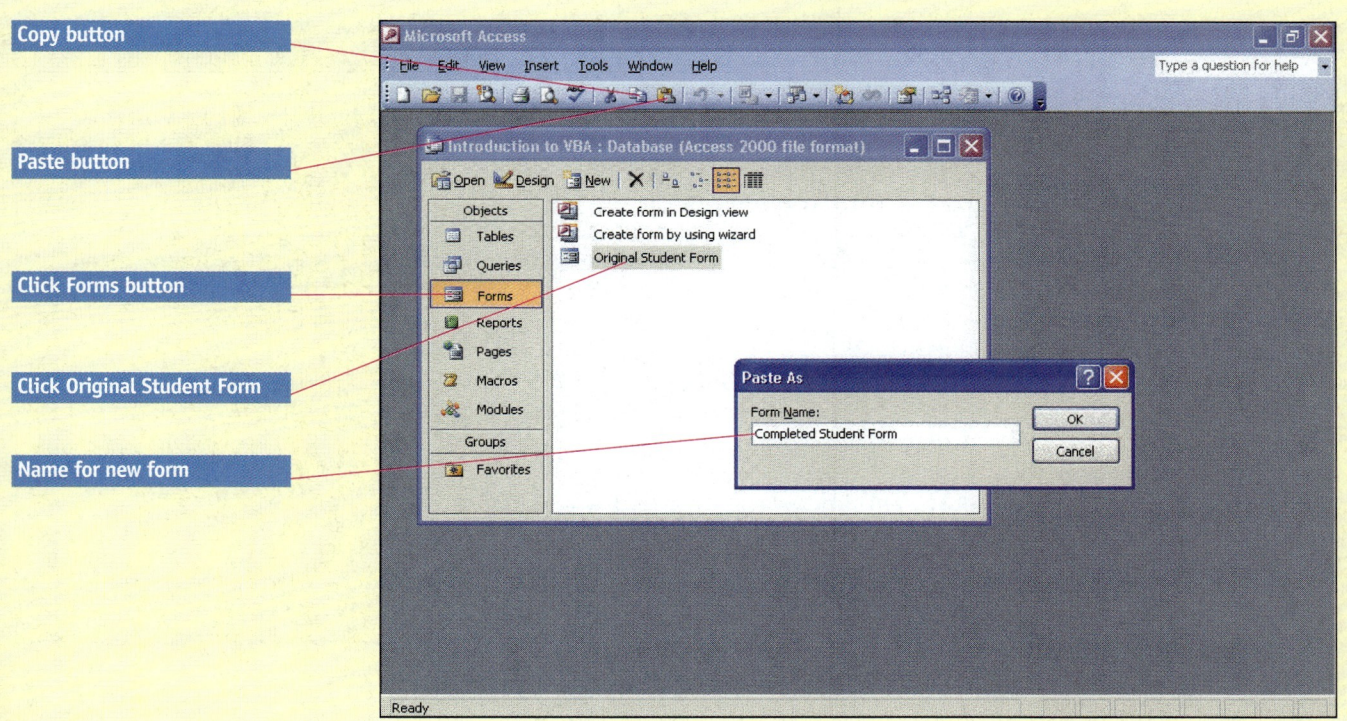

(a) Open the Introduction to VBA Database (step 1)

FIGURE 8.4 Hands-on Exercise 1

KEYBOARD SHORTCUTS—CUT, COPY, AND PASTE

Ctrl+X, Ctrl+C, and Ctrl+V are shortcuts to cut, copy, and paste, respectively, and apply to Windows applications in general. The shortcuts are easier to remember when you realize that the operative letters X, C, and V are next to each other at the bottom-left side of the keyboard.

Step 2:   **The Combo Box Wizard**

- Open the newly created **Completed Student Form** in Design view. Maximize the window.

- Click the **Combo Box tool** on the Toolbox toolbar, then click and drag on the form next to the SSN control to create a combo box and start the wizard.

- Select the option button to **Find a record on my form based on the value I selected in my combo box** as shown in Figure 8.4b. Click **Next**.

- Double click the **SocialSecurityNumber field** to move it from the list box of available fields (on the left of the Combo Box Wizard) to the list of selected fields. Double click the **LastName field** to move this field as well. Click **Next**.

- You should see the columns in the combo box as they will appear in the form. Be sure the Check box to Hide key column is checked. Click **Next**.

- Change the label of the combo box to **FindStudent** (do not use a space in the label). Click **Finish** to exit the Combo Box Wizard. The combo box should appear on the form.

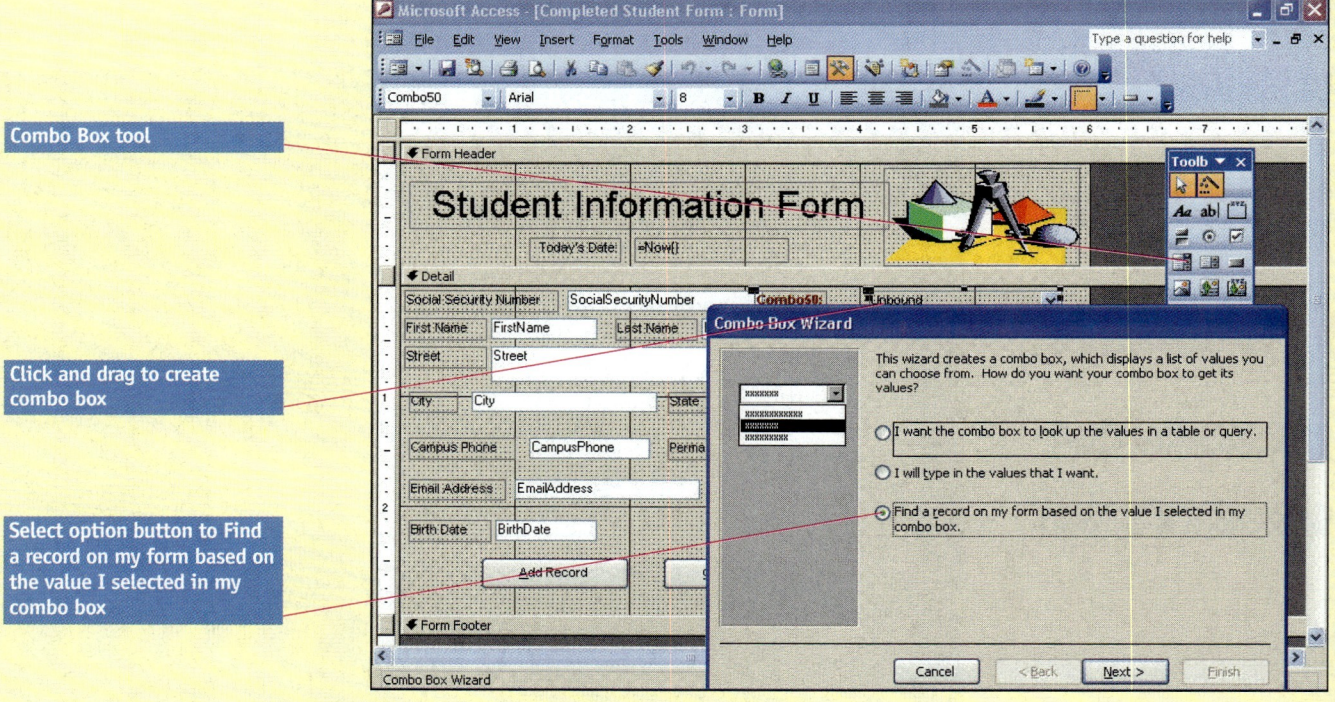

Combo Box tool

Click and drag to create combo box

Select option button to Find a record on my form based on the value I selected in my combo box

(b) The Combo Box Wizard (step 2)

FIGURE 8.4   Hands-on Exercise 1 (*continued*)

SIZING AND MOVING A COMBO BOX AND ITS LABEL

A combo box is always created with an attached label. Select (click) the combo box, and it will have sizing handles and a move handle, but the label has only a move handle. Select the label (instead of the combo box) and the opposite occurs. To move a combo box and its label, click and drag the border of either object. To move either the combo box or its label, click and drag the move handle (a tiny square in the upper-left corner) of the appropriate object. Use the Undo command if the results are not what you expect.

Step 3: **Move and Size the Combo Box**

- Move and size the newly created combo box to match the layout in Figure 8.4c. The Properties sheet is not yet visible. You will most likely have to decrease the size of the combo box and/or increase the size of the label.

- Change the format of the label to match the other labels on the form. (Use **Arial 8 point black** for the font.)

- To align the combo box and/or its label with the other controls on the same row of the form, press and hold the **Shift key** to select the controls you want to align. Pull down the **Format menu**, click **Align**, then click **Top** to align the top of all selected elements.

- Point to the combo box, click the **right mouse button** to display a shortcut menu, then click **Properties** to display the Properties dialog box in Figure 8.4c. If necessary, click the **All tab**.

- Write down the name of the combo box (Combo50 in our figure) as you will need it in step 7. The name of your control may be different from ours.

- Click the **Row Source property** to select it, then click the **Build button** (the button with three dots) that appears when the row is selected.

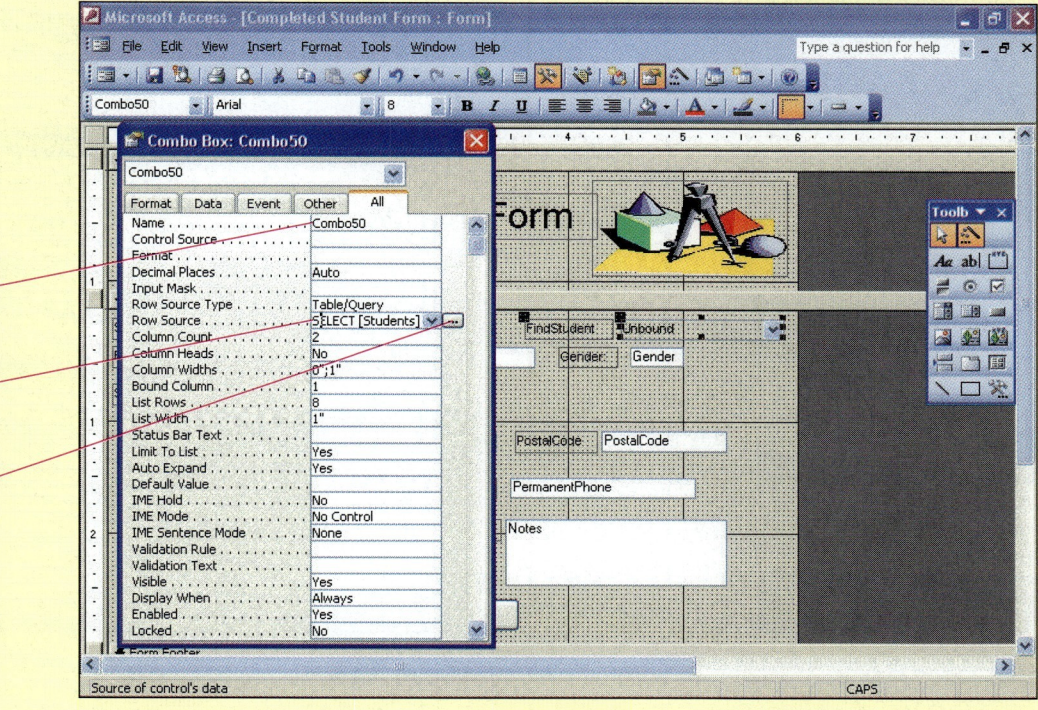

Name of combo box

Click Row Source property

Click Build button

(c) Move and Size the Combo Box (step 3)

FIGURE 8.4   Hands-on Exercise 1 (*continued*)

THE PROPERTY DIALOG BOX

You can change the appearance or behavior of a control in two ways—by changing the actual control on the form itself or by changing the underlying properties. Anything you do to the control automatically changes the associated property, and conversely, any change to the property sheet is reflected in the appearance or behavior of the control. We find ourselves continually switching back and forth between the two techniques.

Step 4: **Update the Row Source**

■ You should see the query in Figure 8.4d, except that your query has not yet been completed. Click in the second column of the Field row, immediately after the LastName control.

■ Press the **space bar**, then type **& ", " & FirstName**. Leave a space after the comma within the quotation marks. Press **Enter**.

■ Double click the border between this cell and the next to increase the column width so that you can see the entire expression. Note that Expr1: has been entered automatically in front of the expression.

■ Click in the **Sort row** of the same column, click the **down arrow** if necessary, then click **Ascending** to display the records in alphabetical order by last name. Close the Properties sheet.

■ Close the query. Click **Yes** when asked whether to save the changes that were made to the SQL statement.

■ Click the **View button** to return to Form view.

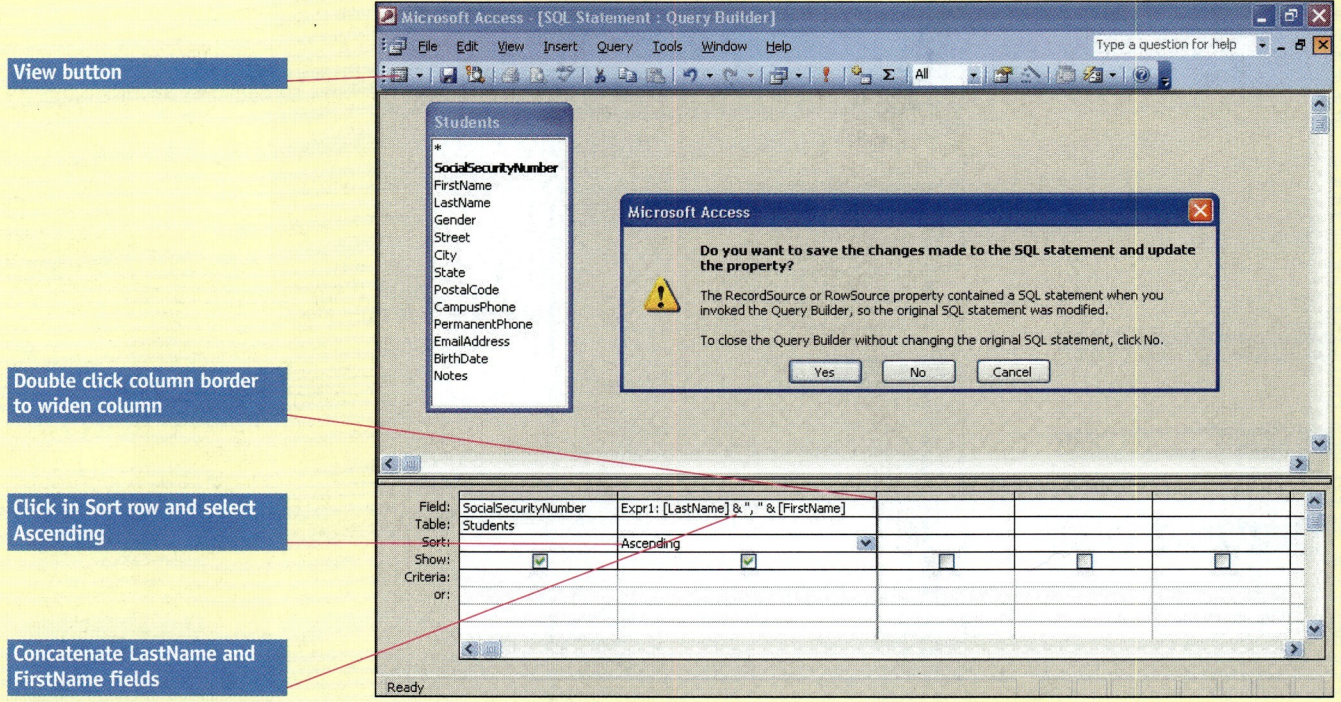

(d) Update the Row Source (step 4)

FIGURE 8.4 Hands-on Exercise 1 (*continued*)

CONCATENATING A STRING

The ampersand (&), or concatenation operator, indicates that the elements on either side of an expression are to appear adjacent to one another when the expression is displayed. You can also concatenate a literal and a field name such as "The employee's last name is " & LastName to display "The employee's last name is Smith," assuming that Smith is the current value in the LastName field. (Note the blank space that appears after the word "is" within the literal.)

Step 5: **Test the Find Student Combo Box**

- If necessary, click the **navigation button** above the status bar to return to the first record in the table, Maryann Jones, as shown in Figure 8.4e.

- Click the **drop-down arrow** on the combo box you just created to display a list of students in alphabetical order. (If you do not see the list of students, press **Esc** to cancel whatever operation is in effect, then return to Design view to repeat the instructions in the previous steps.)

- Select (click) **Grauer, Jessica** from the list of names in the combo box. The form is updated to display the information for this student.

- Click the **drop-down arrow** a second time and select **Douglas, Steven** from the combo box. Again the form is updated.

- Click the **navigation button** to return to the first student. The form displays the record for Maryann Jones, but the combo box is *not* updated; it still displays Douglas, Steven.

- Click the **View button** to return to Design view to create the required event procedure.

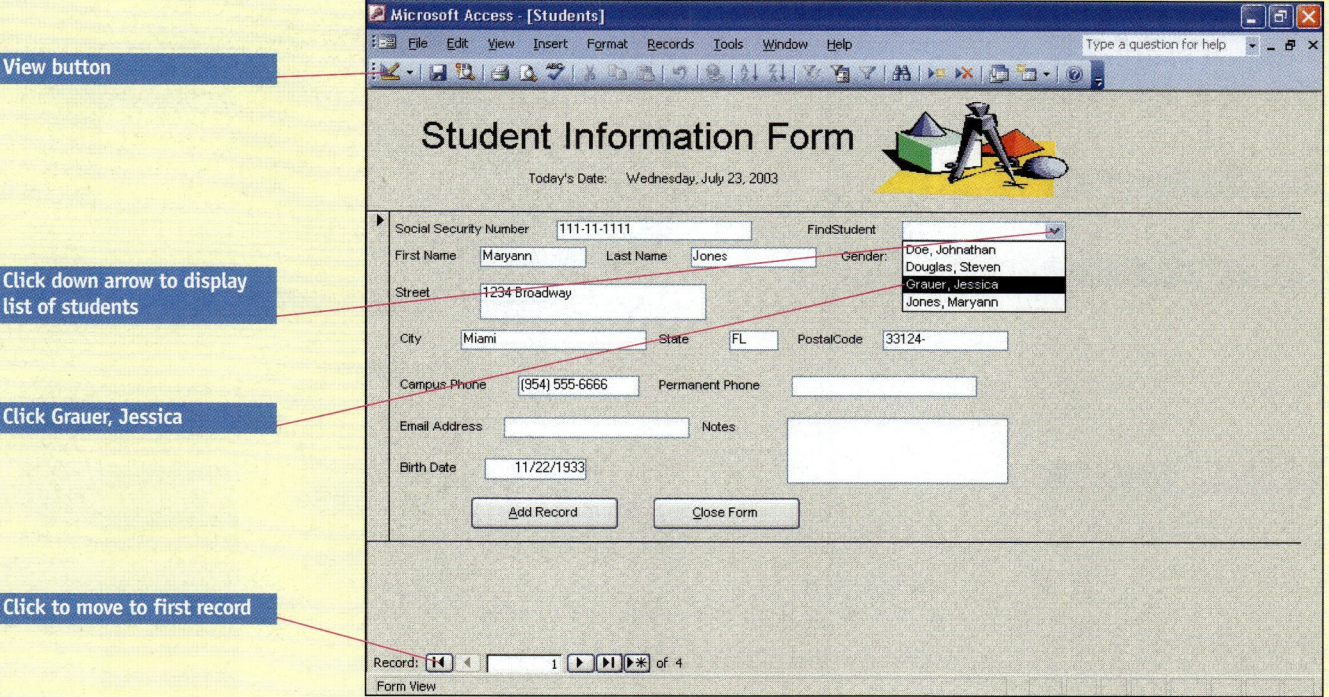

(e) Test the Find Student Combo Box (step 5)

FIGURE 8.4 Hands-on Exercise 1 (*continued*)

WHY USE VBA?

The combo box enables you to select a name from an alphabetical list, then updates the form to display the data for the corresponding record. All of this has been accomplished without the use of VBA. The problem is that the combo box is not updated automatically when records are selected via the navigation buttons. The only way to correct this problem is by writing a VBA procedure.

Step 6: Create an Event Procedure

- Point to the **Form Selector box** (the tiny square at the upper left of the form), click the **right mouse button** to display a shortcut menu, then click **Properties** to display the Form property sheet.

- Click the **Event tab**. Click the **On Current** event, then click the **Build button** to display the Choose Builder dialog box as shown in Figure 8.4f.

- Click (select) **Code Builder**, then click **OK**. A VBA window will open containing the module for the Completed Student Form.

- If necessary, maximize the VBA window and/or click the **Procedure View button** above the status bar. The insertion point is positioned automatically within a newly created event procedure.

- You should see a statement beginning Private Sub Form_Current( ) corresponding to the On Current event. You should also see the line ending End Sub, but no code appears between the Sub and End Sub statements.

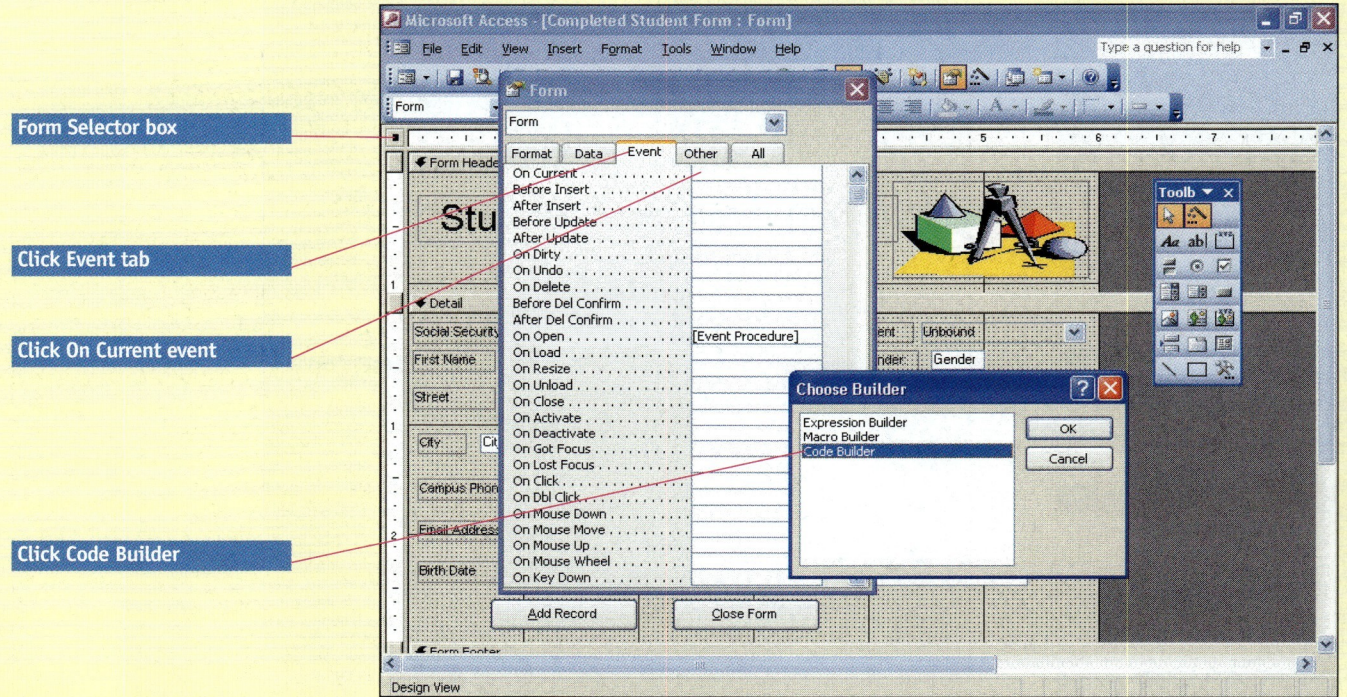

(f) Create an Event Procedure (step 6)

FIGURE 8.4 Hands-on Exercise 1 (*continued*)

CREATING AN EVENT PROCEDURE

There is only one correct way to create an event procedure, and that is the technique used in this exercise. Thus, you right click the Form Selector box to display the form properties, click the Event tab to select the desired event, click the Build button, and click the Code Builder. This in turn takes you to the VBA editor, where you enter the procedure. Do *not* create the event directly in the module window (without first clicking the Event tab). The latter technique appears reasonable, but it will not create the necessary association between the event and the code.

Step 7:   Complete the On Current Event Procedure

- The insertion point should be on a blank line, between the Sub and End Sub statements. If not, click on the blank line. Press the **Tab key** to indent the statements within the procedure. Indentation makes your code easier to read, but is not a syntactical requirement.

- Type **Combo50** (use the number of your combo box as determined in step 3).

- If you do not remember the name of the combo box, click the button on the taskbar to return to the Form window, click in the combo box and click the **All tab**. Look at the entry in the **Name property**.

- Press the **space bar** after you have entered the name of your combo box, type an **equal sign**, and press the **space bar** a second time. Type **Social** (the first several letters in the name of the SocialSecurityNumber control).

- Pull down the **Edit menu** and click **Complete Word** (or press **Ctrl+Space**) to display all of the objects, properties, and methods that start with these letters.

- SocialSecurityNumber is already selected as shown in Figure 8.4g. Press the **space bar** to copy the selected item and complete the statement.

- Click the **Save button** on the Visual Basic toolbar. Close the VBA window.

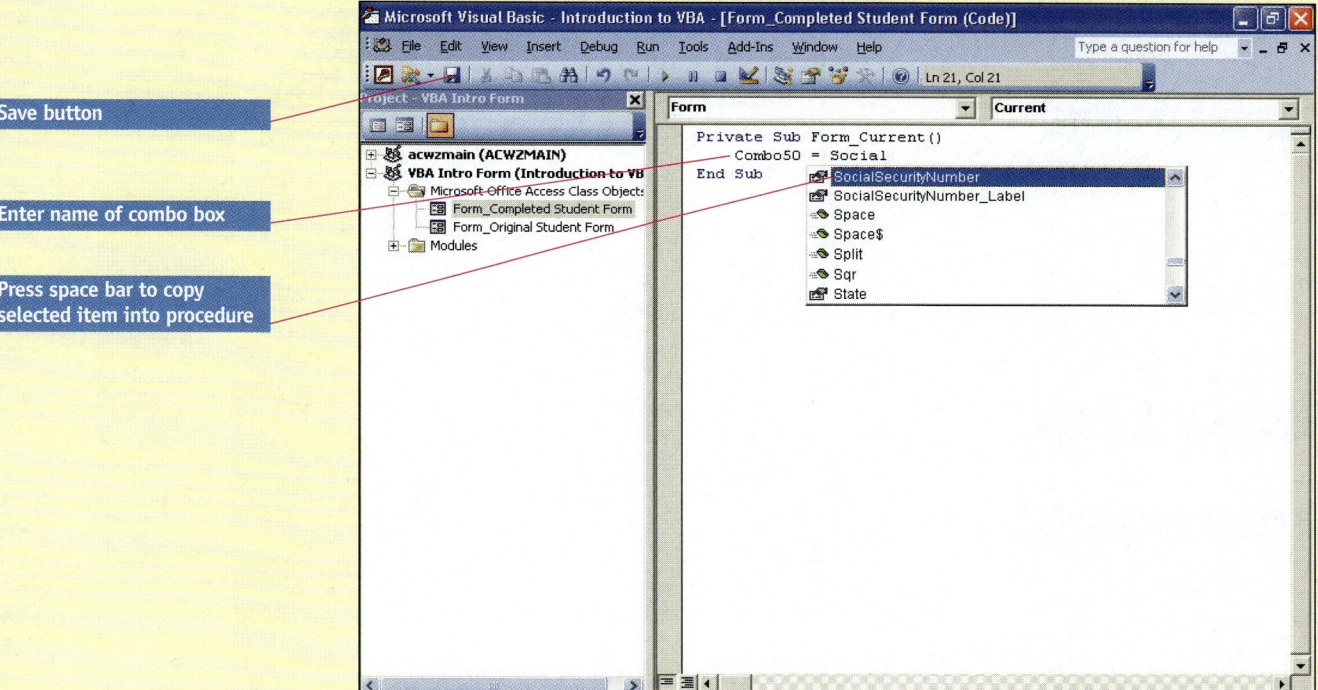

(g) Complete the On Current Event Procedure (step 7)

FIGURE 8.4   Hands-on Exercise 1 (*continued*)

USE THE RIGHT MOUSE BUTTON

The Quick Info and AutoList features are activated automatically as you create a VBA statement. The features can also be activated at any time by pulling down the Edit menu and selecting the Quick Info or List Properties/Methods commands, respectively. You can also point to any portion of a VBA statement and click the right mouse button to display a shortcut menu with options to display this information.

Step 8: **Add Your Record**

- If necessary, click the button for the Access form on the task bar. Close the Properties sheet. Click the **View button** to return to Form view.

- You should see the Student Information form. Click the **navigation button** to move to the next record. The data in the form and combo box is updated.

- Click the **navigation button** to return to the first record. Once again the data in the form is updated, as is the name in the combo box.

- Click the form's **Add Record command button**. You should see a blank form as shown in Figure 8.4h.

- Click in the **SocialSecurityNumber** text box and enter **999-88-7777** as your hypothetical Social Security number. Continue to enter your personal data. (You should never give anyone your real Social Security number unless it is absolutely necessary.)

- Close the form when you have finished entering data. Exit Access if you do not want to continue with the next exercise at this time.

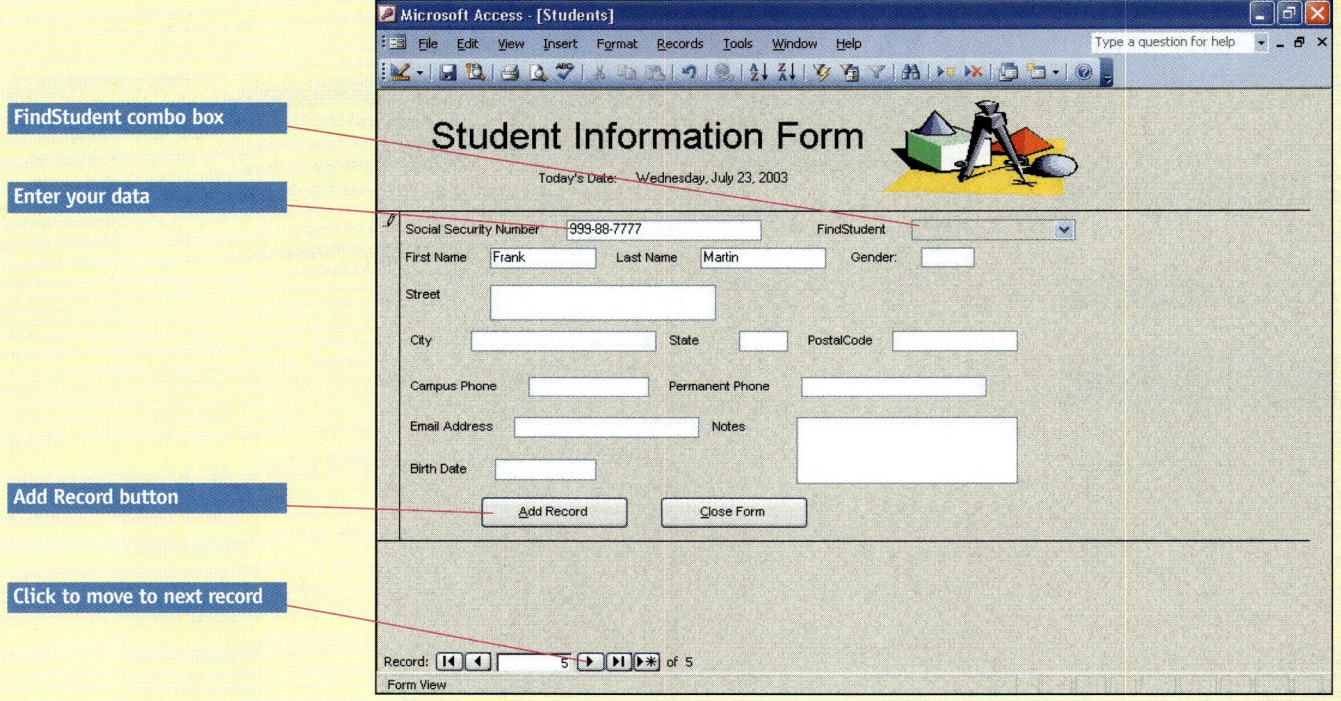

(h) Add Your Record (step 8)

FIGURE 8.4 Hands-on Exercise 1 (*continued*)

THE SET FOCUS METHOD

Ideally, clicking the Add Record button on the Student form should position you in the SocialSecurityNumber field, without your having to click in the field to begin entering data. Open the Student form in Design view, right click the Add Record button and display the Properties dialog box. Click the Event tab, click the On Click property, then click the Build button. Insert the statement SocialSecurityNumber.SetFocus immediately after the DoCmd statement. Go to Form view, then click the Add button. You should be positioned in the SocialSecurityNumber field.

FACILITATING DATA ENTRY

One of the most useful things you can accomplish through VBA is to provide the user with shortcuts for data entry. Many forms, for example, require the user to enter the city, state, and zip code for incoming records. In certain systems, such as a local store or company, this information is likely to be repeated from one record to the next. One common approach is to use the **Default property** in the table definition to specify default values for these fields, so that the values are automatically entered into a record.

What if, however, there are several sets of common values? Our local store, for example, may draw customers from two or three different cities, and we need to constantly switch among the different cities. The Default property is no longer effective because it is restricted to a single value. A better solution is to use VBA to provide a set of keyboard shortcuts such as Ctrl+1 for the first city, state, and zip code, Ctrl+2 for the next set of values, and so on. The user selects the appropriate shortcut, and the city, state, and zip code are entered automatically. The VBA code is shown in Figure 8.5.

Figure 8.5a displays the **KeyDown event** procedure to implement two shortcuts, Ctrl+1 and Ctrl+2, corresponding to Miami and Coral Springs, respectively. Figure 8.5b displays the **Click event** procedure for the shortcut button on the data entry form (which was shown in Figure 8.1). The user clicks the button, and a message is displayed that describes the shortcuts. The latter is very important because the system must communicate the availability of the shortcuts to the user, else how is he or she to know that they exist?

```
Private Sub Form_KeyDown(KeyCode As Integer, Shift As Integer)
'The Key Preview Property of the form must be set to Yes
    If KeyCode = vbKey1 And Shift = acCtrlMask Then 'Ctrl+1 was pressed
        City = "Miami"
        State = "FL"
        PostalCode = "33124"
        CampusPhone.SetFocus
    End If
    If KeyCode = vbKey2 And Shift = acCtrlMask Then 'Ctrl+2 was pressed
        City = "Coral Springs"
        State = "FL"
        PostalCode = "33071"
        CampusPhone.SetFocus
    End If
End Sub
```

KeyCode argument

SetFocus method

(a) Form KeyDown Event Procedure

```
Private Sub ShortCutButton_Click()
    MsgBox "Ctrl+1 has been created as a shortcut to enter " & _
        "Miami, FL 33124. Use Ctrl+2 to enter similar data for " & _
        "Coral Springs, FL 33071.", vbInformation, _
        "Grauer/Barber Introduction to VBA"
End Sub
```

MsgBox statement

Click event procedure

(b) ShortCutButton Click Event Procedure

FIGURE 8.5 Procedure for Exercise 2

Consider now the event procedure in Figure 8.5a and think about what it takes to implement a keyboard shortcut. In essence, the procedure must determine whether the user has used any of the existing shortcuts, and if so, enter the appropriate values in the form. There are different ways to accomplish this, the easiest being through a series of If statements, each of which checks for a specific shortcut. In other words, check to see if the user pressed Ctrl+1, and if so, enter the appropriate data. Then check to see if the user pressed Ctrl+2, etc. (If you have a previous background in programming, you may recognize alternate ways to implement this logic, either through the Else clause in the If statement, or through a Case statement. We explore these alternate structures later in the chapter, but for the time being, we want to keep our statements as simple as possible.)

Once again, we ask that you try to gain an overall appreciation for the procedure, as opposed to concerning yourself with every detail in every statement. You should recognize, for example, that the KeyDown event procedure requires two arguments, KeyCode and Shift, as can be seen from the parenthetical information in the *procedure header*. (The procedure header is created automatically as you shall see in the following hands-on exercise.)

The *KeyCode argument* tests for a specific number or letter; for example, KeyCode = vbKey1 determines whether the number 1 has been pressed by the user. (VBA defines several intrinsic constants such as vbKey1 or vbKeyA corresponding to the number 1 and letter A, respectively.) In similar fashion, the Shift argument tests for the Ctrl, Shift, or Alt key by checking for the intrinsic constants acCtrlMask, acShiftMask, and acAltMask, respectively. The And operator ensures that both keys (Ctrl and the number 1) have been pressed simultaneously.

Once a determination has been made as to whether a shortcut has been used, the corresponding values are moved to the indicated controls (City, State, and PostalCode) on the form. The *SetFocus method* then moves the insertion point to the CampusPhone control, where the user can continue to enter data into the form.

The Click event procedure in Figure 8.5b contains a single MsgBox statement, which displays information about the shortcuts to the user when he or she clicks the Shortcuts button. The MsgBox statement has three parameters—a literal that is continued over two lines containing the text of the message, an intrinsic constant (vbInformation) indicating the icon that is to be displayed with the message, and a second literal indicating the text that is to appear in the title bar of the message dialog box.

The statement is straightforward, but it does illustrate the rules for continuing a VBA statement from one line to the next. To continue a statement, leave a space at the end of the line to be continued, type the underscore character, then continue the statement on the next line. You may not, however, break a line in the middle of a character string. Thus, you need to complete the character string with a closing quotation mark, add an ampersand (as the concatenation operator to display this string with the character string on the next line), then leave a space followed by the underscore to indicate continuation.

BUILD CODE BY OBSERVATION AND INFERENCE

VBA is a powerful language with a subtle syntax and an almost endless variety of intrinsic constants. The expertise required to build the procedures for the keyboard shortcuts is beyond the novice, but once you are given the basic code, it is relatively easy to extend or modify the code to accommodate a specific application. Look at the code in Figure 8.5, for example, and decide how you would change the existing Ctrl+1 keyboard shortcut to reflect a different city. Can you add a third If statement to create a Ctrl+3 shortcut for a new city?

2 Facilitating Data Entry

Objective Create keyboard shortcuts to facilitate data entry. Use Figure 8.6 as a guide in the exercise.

Step 1: **Create the KeyDown Event Procedure**

- Open the **Introduction to VBA database** from the previous exercise. Click the **Forms button**, then open the **Completed Student Form** in Design view.

- Pull down the **View menu** and click **Code** (or click the **Code button** on the Database toolbar).

- If necessary, pull down the **View menu** and click **Project Explorer** to display the Project Explorer pane at the left of the window. If you are in Full Module view, click within any procedure, then click the **Procedure View button**.

- Click the **down arrow** in the Object list box and select **Form**.

- Click the **down arrow** in the Procedure list box to display the list of events for the form. Click **KeyDown** to create a procedure for this event.

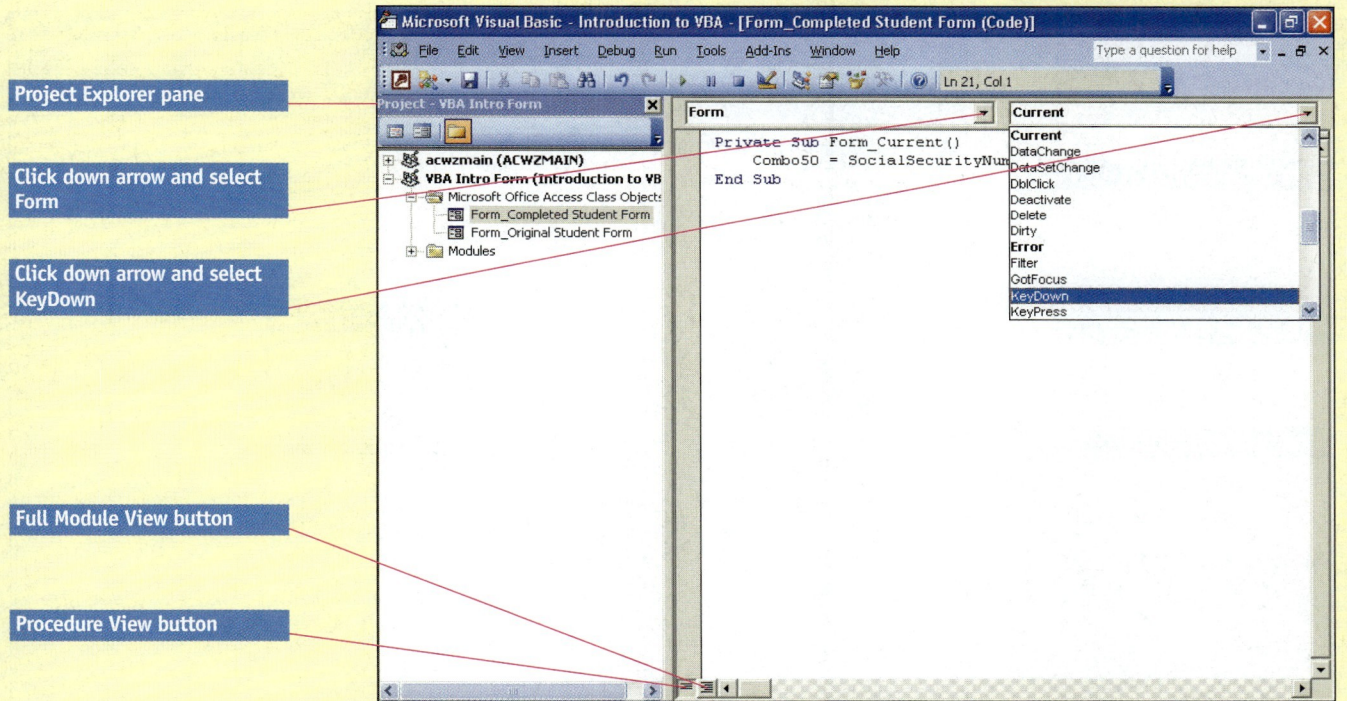

(a) Create the KeyDown Event Procedure (step 1)

FIGURE 8.6 Hands-on Exercise 2

PROCEDURE VIEW VERSUS FULL MODULE VIEW

Procedures can be displayed individually, or multiple procedures can be viewed simultaneously. Click the Procedure View button to display one procedure, or click the Full Module View button to show multiple procedures. Either way, you can press Ctrl+PgDn and Ctrl+PgUp to move between procedures in the Module window.

Step 2: Correct the Compile Error

■ The Procedure header and End Sub statements for the KeyDown event procedure are created automatically as shown in Figure 8.6b. The insertion point is positioned on the blank line between these two statements.

■ Type an **apostrophe** (to indicate a comment), then enter the text of the comment as shown in the figure. Press **Enter** when you have completed the comment. The line turns green to indicate it is a comment.

■ Press the **Tab key** to indent the first line of code, then enter the statement exactly as it appears in the figure. Press **Enter**.

■ You should see the error message in Figure 8.6b because we made a (deliberate) error in the If statement to illustrate what happens when you make an error.

■ Click **OK** if you know the reason for the error, or click **Help** to display a screen describing the error, then close the Help window.

■ Now return to the VBA statement, type a **space** at the end of the line, and add the key word **Then** to correct the error. Press **Enter** to move to the next line and complete the statement. The error message should not appear.

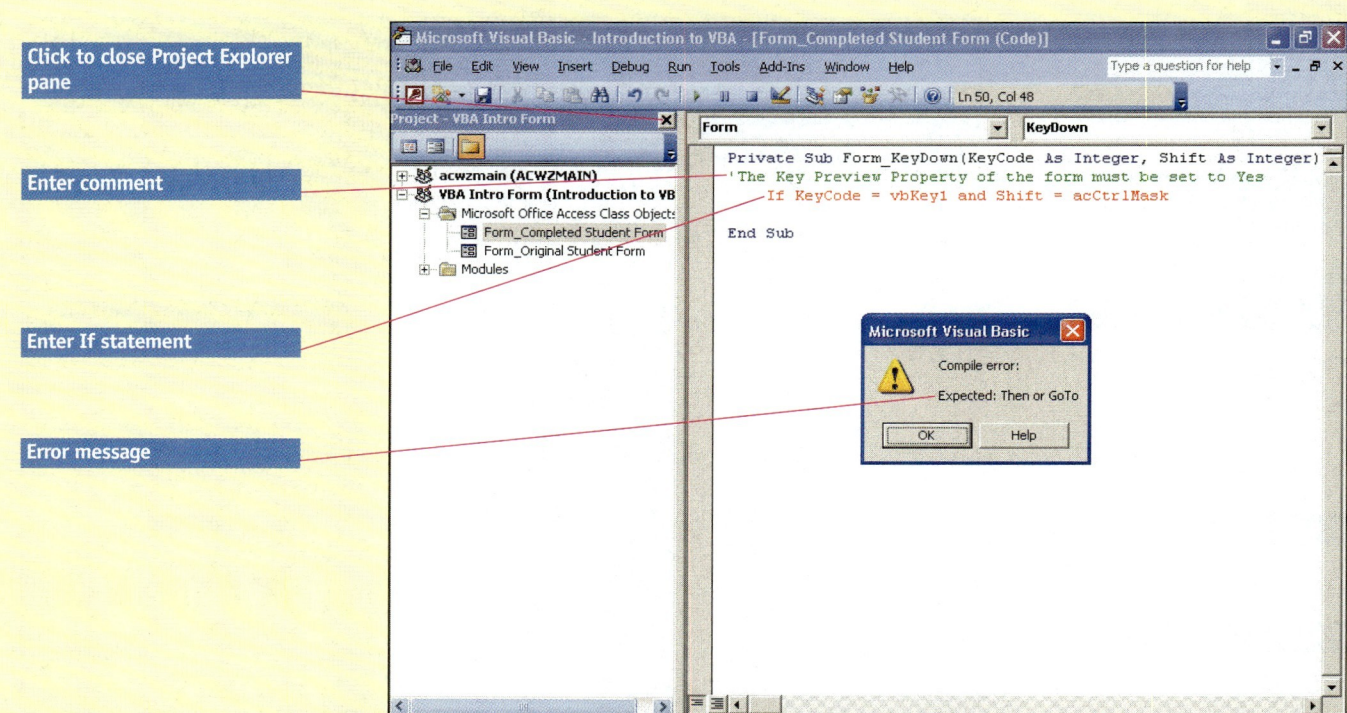

Click to close Project Explorer pane

Enter comment

Enter If statement

Error message

(b) Correct the Compile Error (step 2)

FIGURE 8.6 Hands-on Exercise 2 (*continued*)

RED, GREEN, AND BLUE

Visual Basic for Applications uses different colors for different types of statements (or a portion of those statements). Any statement containing a syntax error appears in red. Comments appear in green. Keywords, such as Sub and End Sub, appear in blue.

Step 3: **Complete the KeyDown Event Procedure**

■ Close the Project Explorer window and complete the KeyDown procedure as shown in Figure 8.6c. Use what you know about the Cut, Copy, and Paste commands to facilitate entering the code.

■ You could, for example, copy the first If statement, then modify the code as appropriate, rather then typing it from scratch. Select the statements to cut or copy to the clipboard, then paste them elsewhere in the module.

■ If the results are different from what you expected or intended, click the Undo command immediately to reverse the effects of the previous command.

■ Be sure that your code matches the code in Figure 8.6c. The indentation is not a syntactical requirement of VBA, per se, but is used to make the statements easier to read.

■ Click the **Save button** to save the module.

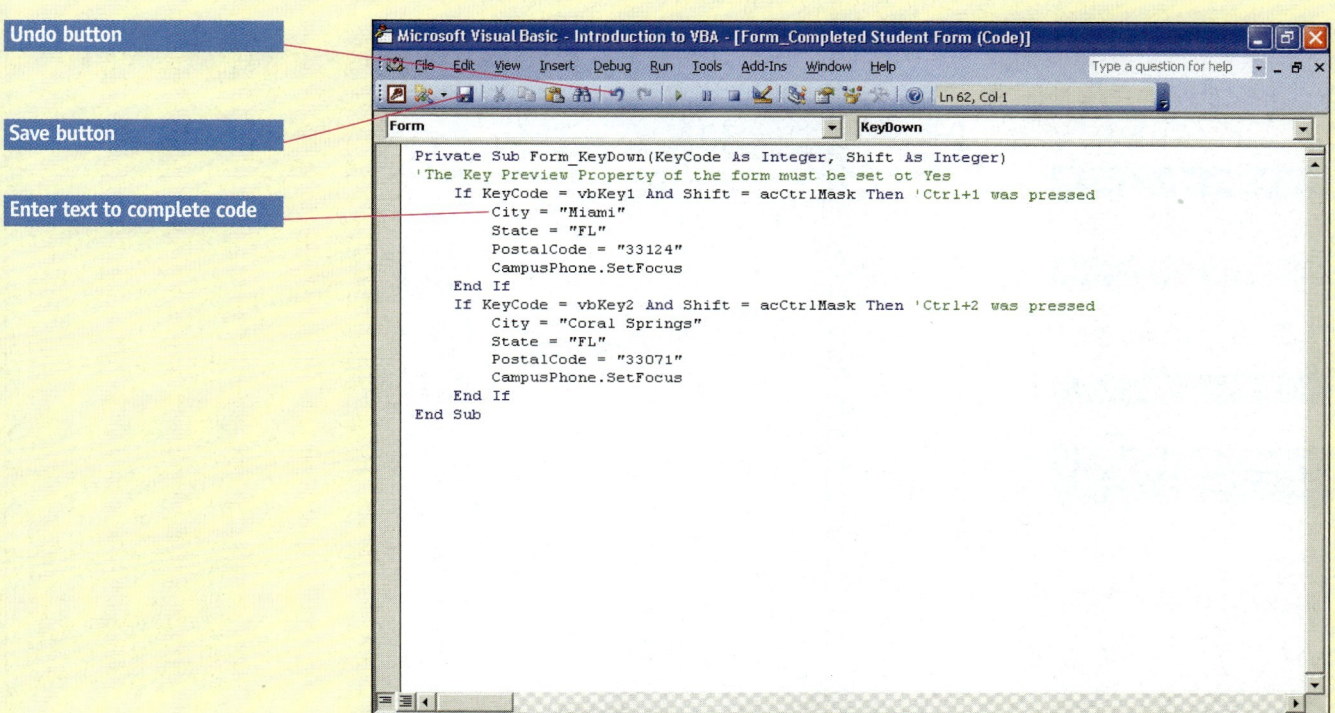

(c) Complete the KeyDown Event Procedure (step 3)

FIGURE 8.6 Hands-on Exercise 2 (*continued*)

THE COMPLETE WORD TOOL

You know that your form contains a control to reference the postal code, but you are not quite sure of the spelling. The Complete Word tool can help. Enter the first several characters, then press Ctrl+Space (or pull down the Edit menu and click Complete Word). VBA will complete the term for you if you have entered a sufficient number of letters, or it will display all of the objects, properties, and methods that begin with the letters you have entered. Use the down arrow to scroll through the list until you find the item, then press the space bar to complete the entry.

Step 4: Set the Key Preview Property

- The Key Preview property of the form must be set to **Yes** to complete the keyboard shortcut. Click the taskbar button to return to the **Completed Student Form**.

- Point to the **Form Selector box** (the tiny square at the upper left of the form). Click the **right mouse button** to display a context-sensitive menu with commands for the entire form.

- Click **Properties** to display the Form Properties dialog box. Click the **Event tab** and scroll until you can click the **Key Preview property**. If necessary, change the property to **Yes** as shown in Figure 8.6d.

- Close the Form Property dialog box. Save the form, which now contains the new procedure for the keyboard shortcut. The procedure should be tested as soon as it is completed.

- Click the **View button** on the Form Design toolbar to return to Form view.

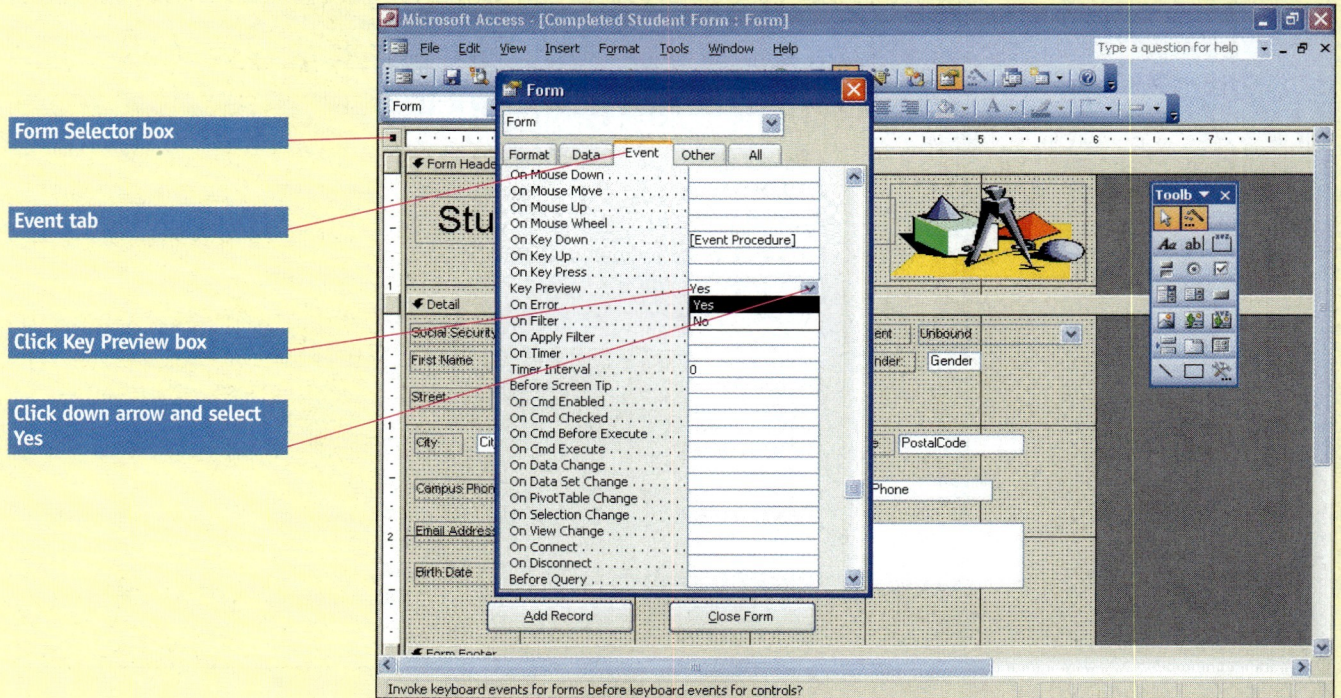

(d) Set the Key Preview Property (step 4)

FIGURE 8.6   Hands-on Exercise 2 (*continued*)

USE THE PROPERTY SHEET

Every object on a form has its own property sheet. This enables you to change the appearance or behavior of a control in two ways—by changing the control through application of a menu command or toolbar button, or by changing the underlying property sheet. Anything you do to the control changes the associated property, and conversely, any change to the property sheet is reflected in the appearance or behavior of the control.

Step 5: Test the Procedure

- Click the **navigation button** to move to the first record in the table as shown in Figure 8.6e. Press **Ctrl+2** to change the City, State, and Postal Code to reflect Coral Springs, as per the shortcut you just created.

- The data changes automatically, and you are automatically positioned on the CampusPhone field. The record selector changes to a pencil to indicate that the data has been edited, but not yet saved.

- If the shortcut does not work, return to step 4 and check that the Key Preview property has been set to Yes. If the shortcut still does not work, return to the module for the form and check the VBA statements.

- Press **Ctrl+1** to change the city to Miami. The data should change automatically, after which you are positioned in the CampusPhone field.

- Click the **View button** to return to the Design view of the form.

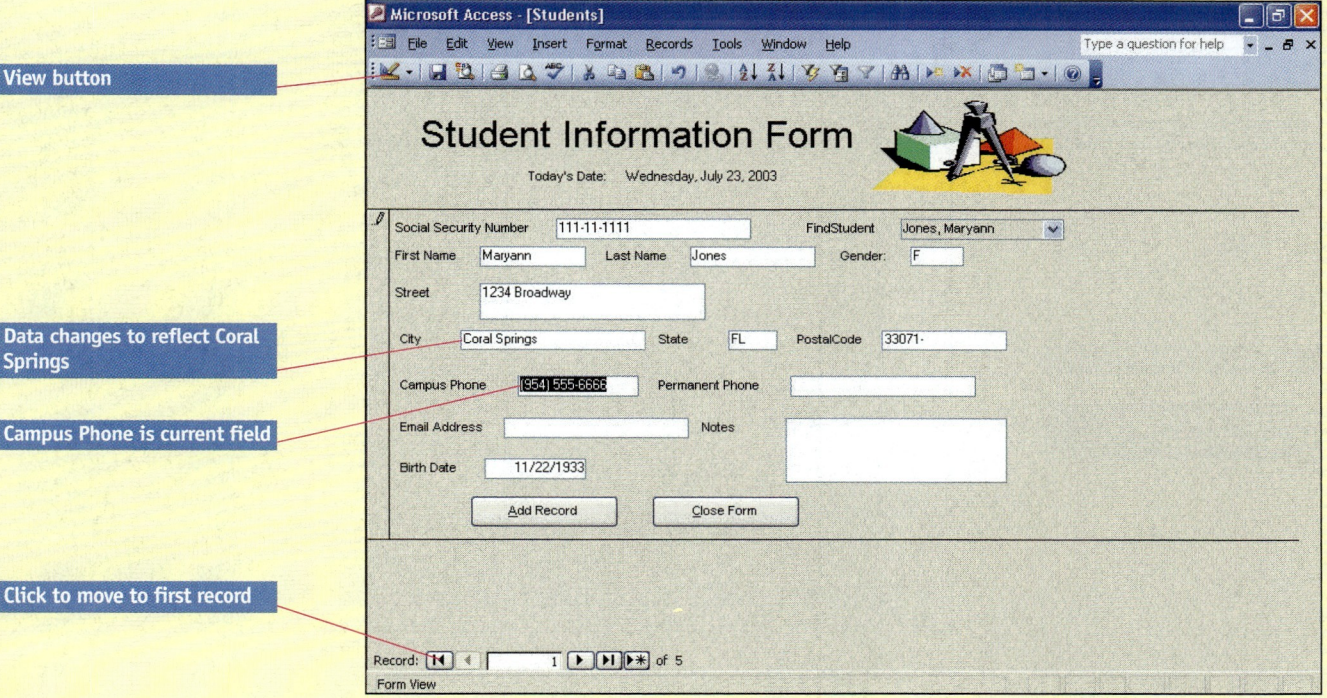

View button

Data changes to reflect Coral Springs

Campus Phone is current field

Click to move to first record

(e) Test the Procedure (step 5)

FIGURE 8.6 Hands-on Exercise 2 (*continued*)

CHANGE THE TAB ORDER

The Tab key provides a shortcut in the finished form to move from one field to the next; that is, you press Tab to move forward to the next field and Shift+Tab to return to the previous field. The order in which fields are selected corresponds to the sequence in which the controls were entered onto the form, and need not correspond to the physical appearance of the actual form. To restore a left-to-right, top-to-bottom sequence, pull down the View menu, click Tab Order, then select AutoOrder.

Step 6: **Create the ShortCut Command Button**

- Click and drag the **Command Button tool** on the Toolbox toolbar to create a new command button as shown in Figure 8.6f.

- The Command Button Wizard starts automatically. This time, however, you want to create the Click event procedure for this button yourself.

- Click the **Cancel button** as soon as you see the wizard. Right click the newly created command button and display its property sheet. Click the **All tab**.

- Change the Name property to **ShortCutButton**. Change the Caption property to **&ShortCuts**.

- Click the **Event tab**. Click the **On Click property**, click the **Build button**, click **Code Builder**, then click **OK** to display the Module window.

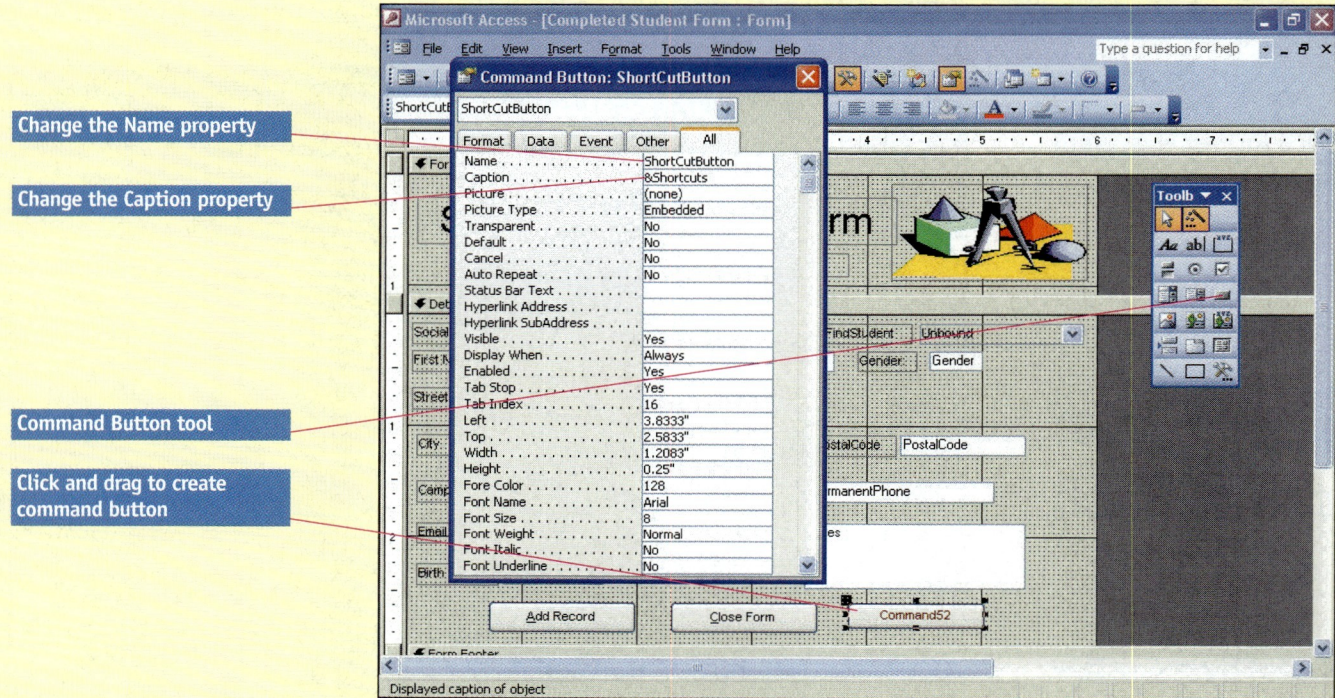

(f) Create the ShortCut Command Button (step 6)

FIGURE 8.6 Hands-on Exercise 2 (*continued*)

ACCELERATOR KEYS AND THE CAPTION PROPERTY

The Caption property enables you to create a keyboard shortcut for a command button. Right click the button in the Form Design view to display the Properties dialog box for the command button. Click the All tab, then modify the Caption property to include an ampersand immediately in front of the letter that will be used in the shortcut (e.g., &Help if you have a Help button). Close the dialog box, then go to Form view. The command button will contain an underlined letter (e.g., Help) that can be activated in conjunction with the Alt key (e.g., Alt+H) as a shortcut or accelerator key.

Step 7: Create the OnClick Procedure

■ You should be positioned in the ShortCutButton_Click procedure, as shown in Figure 8.6g. Press the **Tab key** to indent, then enter the VBA statement exactly as it is shown in the figure. Note the following:

❑ A tip (known as "Quick Info") appears as soon as you type the space after the MsgBox keyword. The tip displays the syntax of the statement and lists its arguments.

❑ Indentation is not a requirement of VBA per se, but is done to make the VBA code easier to read. Continuation is also optional and is done to make the code easier to read.

■ Complete the statement exactly as shown in the figure, except substitute your name for Grauer/Barber. Click the **Save button**. Close the Module window.

■ Return to the **Form Design view**. Close the property sheet. Size and align the new button. Change the text on the button to **8 point Arial**. Save the form.

■ Click the **View button** to change to Form view.

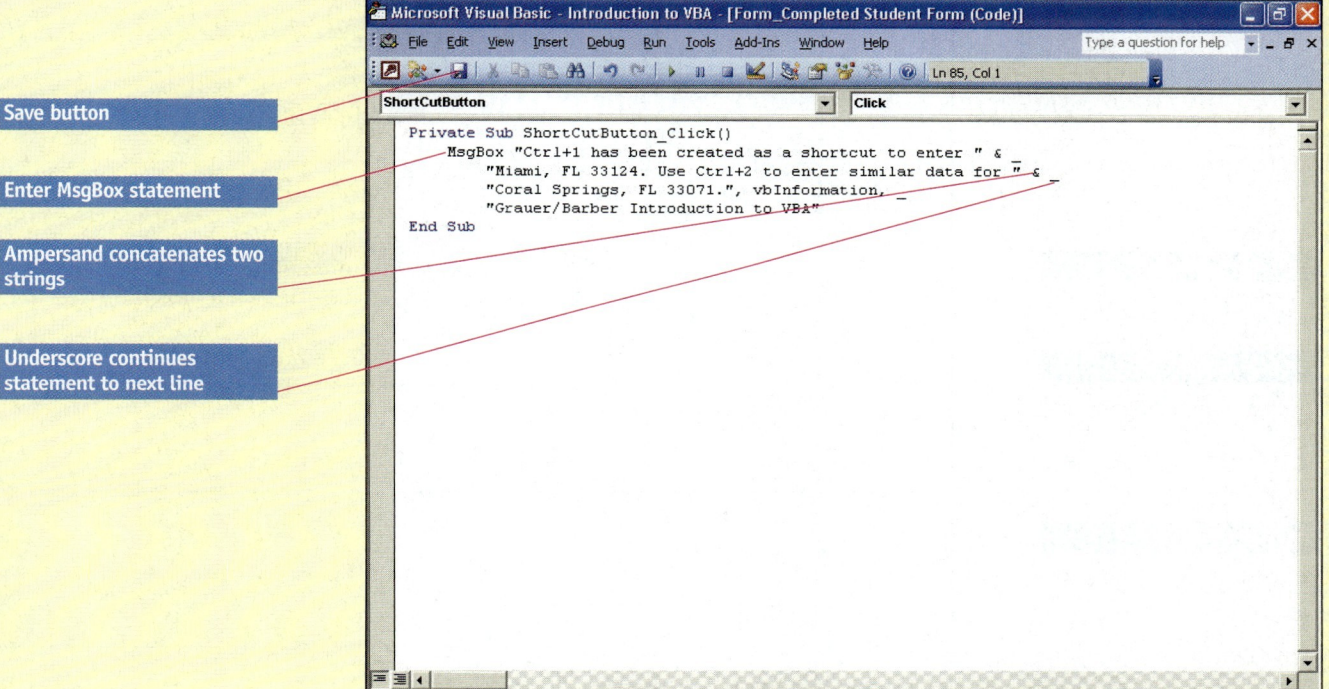

Save button

Enter MsgBox statement

Ampersand concatenates two strings

Underscore continues statement to next line

(g) Create the OnClick Procedure (step 7)

FIGURE 8.6   Hands-on Exercise 2 (*continued*)

THE MSGBOX STATEMENT

The MsgBox statement has three parameters—the text of the message to be displayed, an icon identifying the message type, and the text that appears on the title bar. The message itself is divided into multiple character strings, which continue from one line to the next. The ampersand concatenates the two character strings to display a single message. The underscore character indicates that the statement is continued to the next line.

Step 8: **Test the ShortCuts Button**

- Click the **ShortCuts button**. You can also use the keyboard shortcut, **Alt+S**, as indicated by the underlined letter on the button name that was established through the Caption property for the button.

- You should see the message box that is displayed in Figure 8.6h. Your name should appear in the title bar of the dialog box rather than ours. Click **OK** to close the dialog box.

- Try the other shortcuts that have been built into the form. Press **Ctrl+1** and **Ctrl+2** to switch back and forth between addresses in Miami and Coral Springs, respectively.

- Press **Alt+C** to close the form. Not everyone prefers the keyboard to the mouse, but you have nonetheless created a powerful set of shortcuts.

- Exit Access if you do not want to continue with the next exercise at this time.

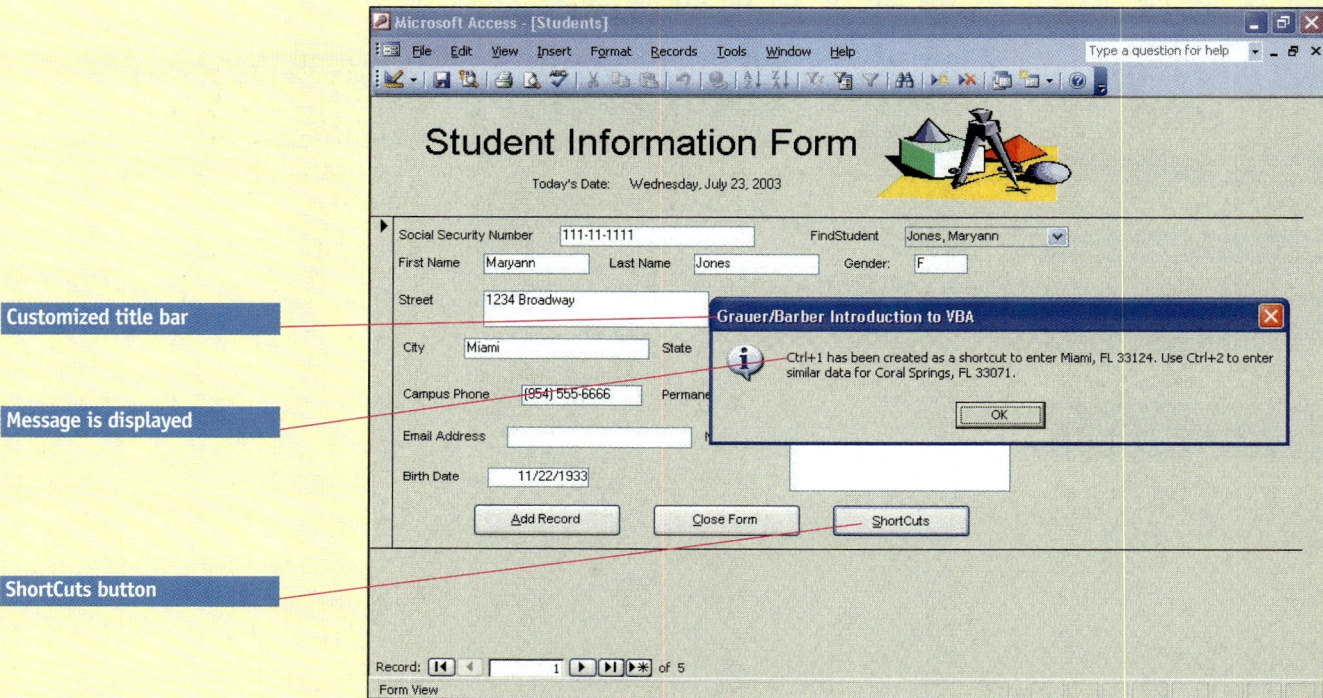

Customized title bar

Message is displayed

ShortCuts button

(h) Test the ShortCuts Button (step 8)

FIGURE 8.6 Hands-on Exercise 2 (*continued*)

CREATE UNIFORM COMMAND BUTTONS

A form is made more appealing if all of its command buttons have similar properties. Change to Design view, then press and hold the Shift key as you select each of the command buttons. Pull down the Format menu, click Size, then choose the desired parameter for all of the buttons such as widest and tallest. (You have to execute the command once for each parameter.) Leave the buttons selected, pull down the Format menu, select the Align command, then choose the desired alignment. Pull down the Format menu a final time, select the Horizontal Spacing command, then implement the desired (e.g., uniform) spacing for the buttons.

It is not a question of whether errors in data entry will occur, but rather how quickly a user will understand the nature of those errors in order to take the appropriate corrective action. If, for example, a user attempts to add a duplicate record for an existing customer, Access will display an error message of the form, "changes to the table were not successful because they would create duplicate values of the primary key." The issue is whether this message is clear to the nontechnical individual who is doing the data entry.

An experienced Access programmer will realize immediately that Access is preventing the addition of the duplicate record because another record with the same primary key (e.g., a Social Security or account number) is already in the file. A nontechnical user, however, may not understand the message because he or she does not know the meaning of "primary key." Wouldn't it be easier if the system displayed a message indicating that a customer with that Social Security or account number is already in the file? In other words, errors invariably occur, and it is important that the user sees a message which clearly indicates the problem so that it may be corrected promptly.

Figure 8.7 displays the event procedure that is developed in the next hands-on exercise to display application-specific error messages in place of the standard messages provided by Access. The procedure is triggered any time there is an error in data entry. Realize, however, that there are literally hundreds of errors, and it is necessary to test for each error for which we want a substitute message. Each error has a unique error number, and thus the first task is to determine the number associated with the error you want to detect. This is accomplished by forcing the error to occur, then printing the error number in the *Immediate window* (a special window within the VBA editor that enables you to display results of a procedure as it is executing). It's easier than it sounds, as you will see in the hands-on exercise.

Once you know the error numbers, you can complete the procedure by checking for the errors that you wish to trap, then displaying the appropriate error messages. One way to implement this logic is through a series of individual If statements, with one *If statement* for each error. It is more efficient, however, to use a Case statement as shown in Figure 8.7.

The *Case statement* tests the value of an incoming variable (DataErr in our example, which contains the error number), then goes to the appropriate set of statements, depending on the value of that variable. Our procedure tests for two errors, but it could be easily expanded to check for additional errors. Error 2237 occurs if the user attempts to find a record that is not in the table. Error 3022 results when the user attempts to add a duplicate record. Once an error is detected, the MsgBox statement is used to display the custom error message that we created, after which Access will continue normal processing without displaying the default error message.

Note, too, the last case (Else), which is executed when Access detects an error other than 2237 or 3022. This time we do not display our own message because we do not know the nature of the error. Instead we set the Response variable to the intrinsic constant acDataErrContinue, which causes Access to display the default error message for the error that occurred.

Figure 8.7b displays the *General Declarations section*, which contains statements that apply to every procedure in the form. The section defines the constant ApplicationName as a string and sets it to the literal value "John Doe did his homework." Note, too, how the two MsgBox statements in Figure 8.7a reference this constant as the third argument, and recall that this argument contains the text that is displayed on the title bar of the message box. In other words, we can change the value of the ApplicationName constant in one place, and have that change reflected automatically in every MsgBox statement.

```
Private Sub Form_Error(DataErr As Integer, Response As Integer)
' You need to determine the specific error number
'   1. Create the error in Access to determine the error number
'   2. Use the Print method of the Debug object to display the error
'   3. Press Ctrl+G to open the Immediate window where the error will be displayed

    Debug.Print "Error Number = ", DataErr

    Select Case DataErr
        Case 2237
            MsgBox "The student is not in our file. Please " & _
                "check the spelling and reenter correctly, or click the " & _
                "Add button to enter a new record.", vbInformation, _
                ApplicationName
            Response = acDataErrContinue
        Case 3022
            MsgBox "You are trying to add a student whose " & _
                "social security number is already in the file. Please " & _
                "correct the social security number or cancel this " & _
                "record and move to the original record.", vbExclamation, _
                ApplicationName
            Response = acDataErrContinue
        Case Else
            Response = acDataErrDisplay
    End Select
End Sub
```

Error number

Improved error message will be displayed

Default error message displayed for all other errors

(a) Form Error Event Procedure

```
Option Compare Database
Option Explicit

Const ApplicationName As String = "John Doe has done his homework"
```

Statement defines ApplicationName constant

(b) General Declarations Section

FIGURE 8.7 Procedures for Exercise 3

THE CASE STATEMENT

The Case statement tests the value of a variable, then branches to one of several sets of statements, depending on the value of that variable. You may not be able to write a Case statement intially, but once you see the statement, you can extend the code to accommodate any application. Look at the code in Figure 8.7, for example, and decide the required modifications to reflect employees rather than students. How would you extend the existing Case statement to include an additional error message?

3 Error Trapping

Objective To create an event procedure that substitutes application-specific messages for the standard Access error messages. Use Figure 8.8 as a guide.

Step 1: **Force the Error Message**

- Open the **Introduction to VBA database**. If necessary, click the **Forms button**, then open the **Completed Student Form** in Form view.

- Click and drag to select the name in the **Find Student** combo box. Type **XXXX** (an obviously invalid name). Press **Enter**. You should see the error message in Figure 8.8a, which may be confusing to a nontechnical user.

- Click **OK** to close the message box. Press the **Esc key** and erase the XXXX, since we are not interested in finding this student.

- Click the **View button** to change to **Design view**.

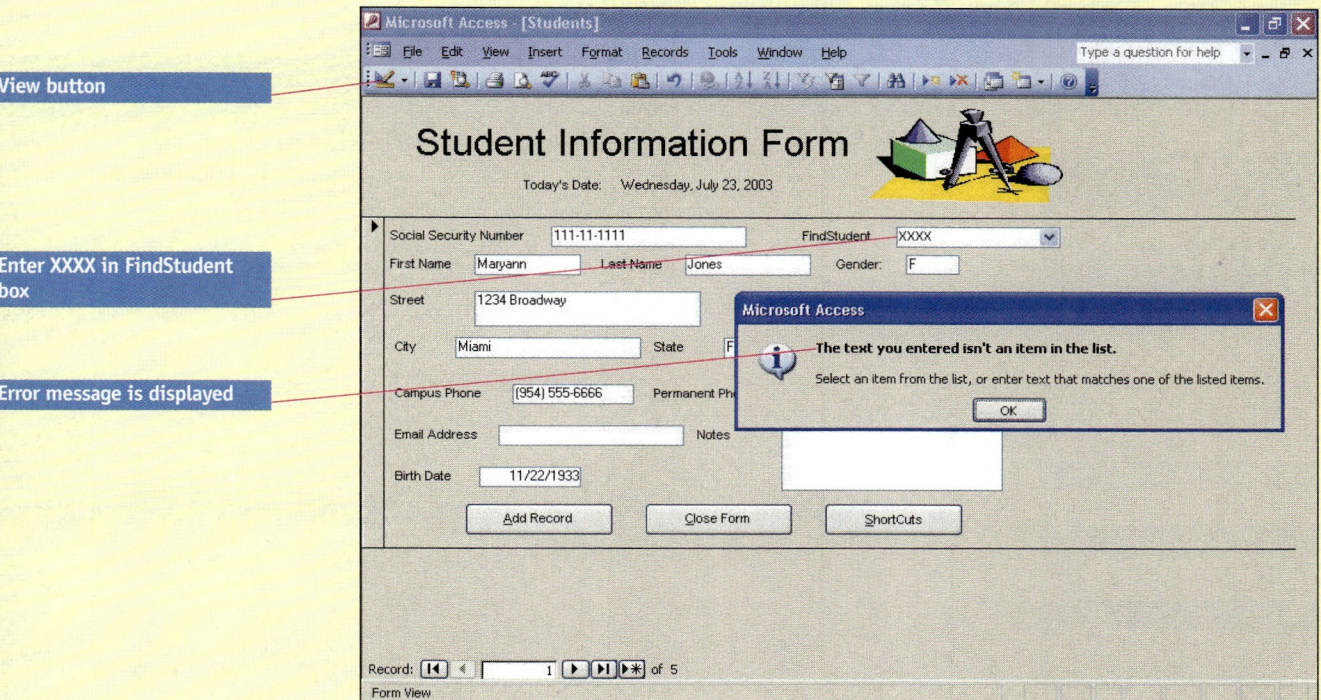

View button

Enter XXXX in FindStudent box

Error message is displayed

(a) Force the Error Message (step 1)

FIGURE 8.8 Hands-on Exercise 3 (*continued*)

EVENT-DRIVEN VERSUS TRADITIONAL PROGRAMMING

A traditional program is executed sequentially, beginning with the first line of code and continuing in order through the remainder of the program. VBA, however, is event-driven, meaning that its procedures are executed when designated events occur. Thus, it is the user, and not the program, who determines which procedures are executed and when. This exercise creates a procedure that will run if specified errors occur during data entry.

Step 2: **Determine the Error Number**

- Pull down the **View menu** and click **Code** (or click the **Code button** on the Form Design toolbar) to display the Module window. If necessary, click the **down arrow** for the Object box and select the **Form object**.

- Click the **down arrow** in the Procedure box and click **Error** to display the event procedure that will execute when an error occurs in the form. Click the **Procedure View button** as shown in Figure 8.8b.

- We created this procedure for you. It consists of a single executable statement, to print a literal, followed by the number of the error. The comments explain how to use the procedure.

- Pull down the **View menu** and click **Immediate Window** (or press **Ctrl+G**) to open the Immediate window. You should see number 2237.

- This is the error number reserved by Access to indicate that the value that was entered in the text portion of a combo box does not match any of the entries in the associated list.

- Close the Immediate window.

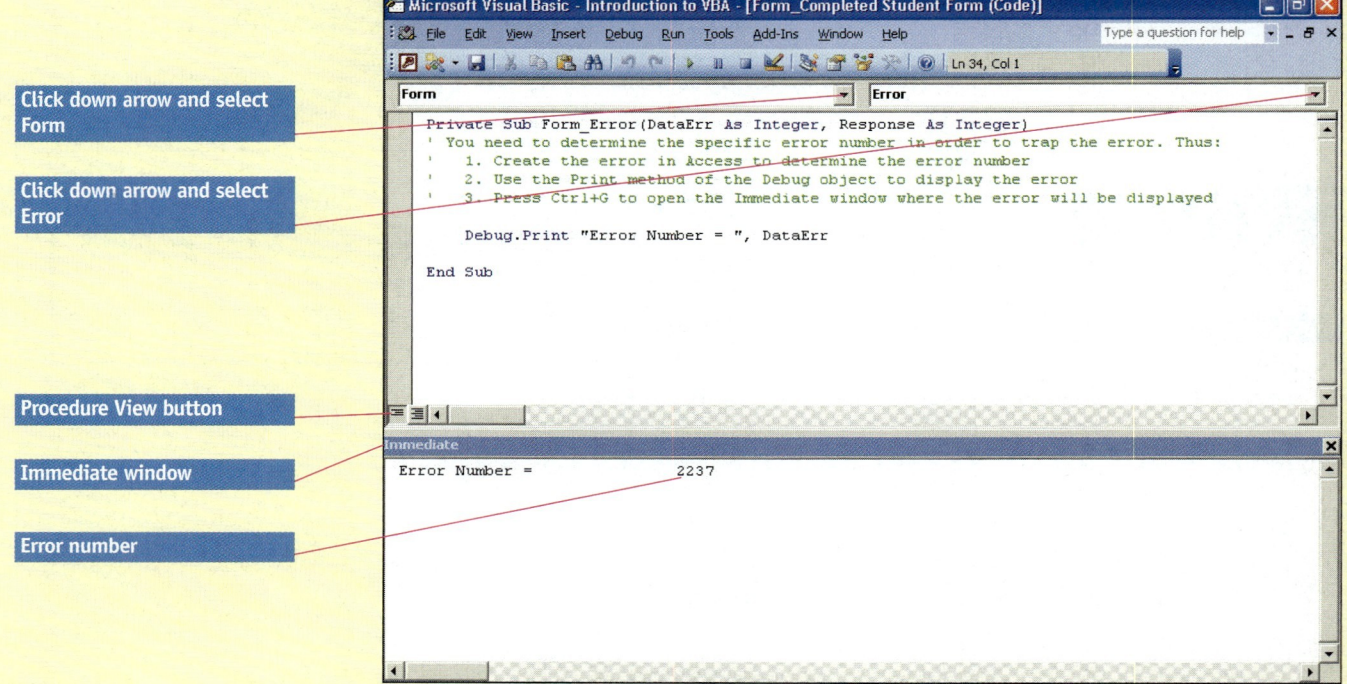

Click down arrow and select Form

Click down arrow and select Error

Procedure View button

Immediate window

Error number

(b) Determine the Error Number (step 2)

FIGURE 8.8 Hands-on Exercise 3 (*continued*)

INSTANT CALCULATOR

Use the Print method (action) in the Immediate window to use VBA as a calculator. Press Ctrl+G at any time to display the Immediate window. Type the statement Debug.Print, followed by your calculation, for example, Debug.Print 2+2, then press Enter. The answer is displayed on the next line in the Immediate window.

Step 3: Trap the First Error

■ Click in the event procedure at the end of the Debug statement, press the **Enter key** twice, then enter the VBA statements in Figure 8.8c. Note the following:
  ❏ Comments appear at the beginning of the procedure.
  ❏ The Case statement tests the value of an incoming variable (DataErr), then goes to the appropriate set of statements, depending on the value of that variable. The procedure currently tests for only one error, but it will be expanded later in the exercise to check for additional errors.
  ❏ The indentation and blank lines within the procedure are not requirements of VBA per se, but are used to make the code easier to read.
  ❏ A "Quick Info" tip appears as soon as you type the space after MsgBox. The tip displays the syntax of the statement.

■ Complete the procedure exactly as shown in Figure 8.8c. Click the **Save button** to save the procedure.

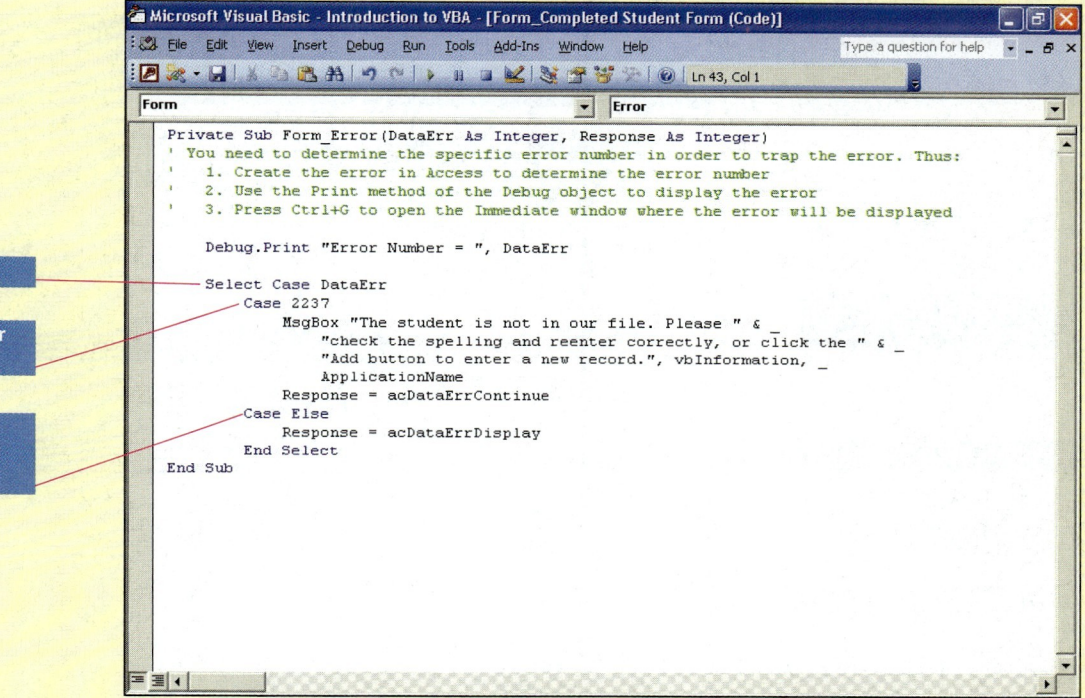

Enter VBA statements

Case tests for error number 2237

Case Else displays default error message for all other errors

(c) Trap the First Error (step 3)

FIGURE 8.8   Hands-on Exercise 3 (*continued*)

CONTINUING A VBA STATEMENT—THE & AND THE UNDERSCORE

A VBA statement can be continued from one line to the next by leaving a space at the end of the line to be continued, typing the underscore character, then continuing on the next line. You may not, however, break a line in the middle of a literal (character string). Thus, you need to complete the character string with a closing quotation mark, add an ampersand (as the concatenation operator to display this string with the character string on the next line), then leave a space followed by the underscore to indicate continuation.

Step 4: **Test the Error Event Procedure**

- Click the taskbar button to return to the **Completed Student Form**. Change to the **Form view** as shown in Figure 8.8d.

- Click and drag to select the name in the FindStudent combo box. Type **XXXX** (an obviously invalid name). Press **Enter**.

- This time you should see the error message in Figure 8.8d corresponding to the text you entered in the previous step. (Note the title bar on the dialog box indicating that your name goes here. We tell you how to modify the title bar later in the exercise.)

- Click **OK** to close the message box. Press the **Esc key** and erase the XXXX. Return to **Design view**.

- Pull down the **View menu** and click **Code** (or click the **Code button** on the Form Design toolbar) to display the Module window.

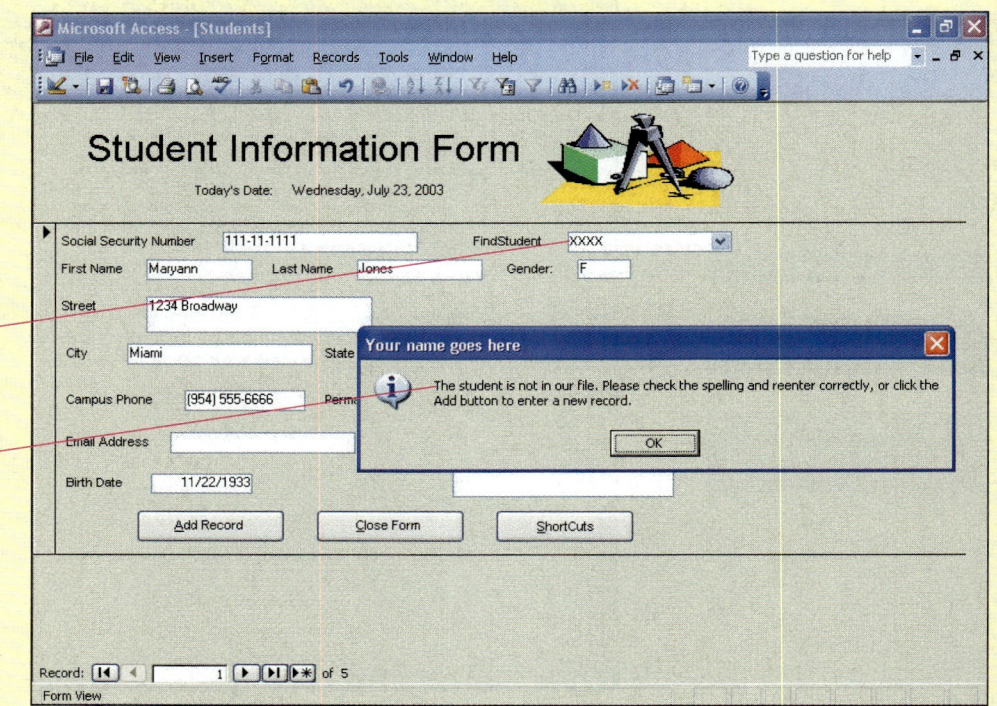

Enter XXXX in FindStudent box

Improved error message

(d) Test the Error Event Procedure (step 4)

FIGURE 8.8   Hands-on Exercise 3 (*continued*)

THE FIRST BUG

A bug is a mistake in a computer program; hence debugging refers to the process of finding and correcting program errors. According to legend, the first bug was an unlucky moth crushed to death on one of the relays of the electromechanical Mark II computer, bringing the machine's operation to a halt. The cause of the failure was discovered by Grace Hopper (at one point the oldest officer on active duty in the United States Navy), who promptly taped the moth to her logbook, noting, "First actual case of bug being found."

Step 5: **Change the Application Name**

■ Click the **down arrow** for the Object box and select **(General)** at the beginning of the list of objects.

■ We have defined the Visual Basic constant **ApplicationName**, and initialized it to "Your name goes here". This was the text that appeared in the title bar of the dialog box in the previous step.

■ Click and drag to select **Your name goes here**. Enter **John Doe has done his homework**, substituting your name for John Doe.

■ Pull down the **Edit menu**, click the **Find command** to display the Find dialog box. Enter **ApplicationName** in the Find What text box. Specify the option to search the **Current module** and specify **All** as the direction.

■ Use the **Find Next command button** to locate all occurrences of the ApplicationName constant. Can you appreciate the significance of this technique to customize your application?

■ Save the procedure.

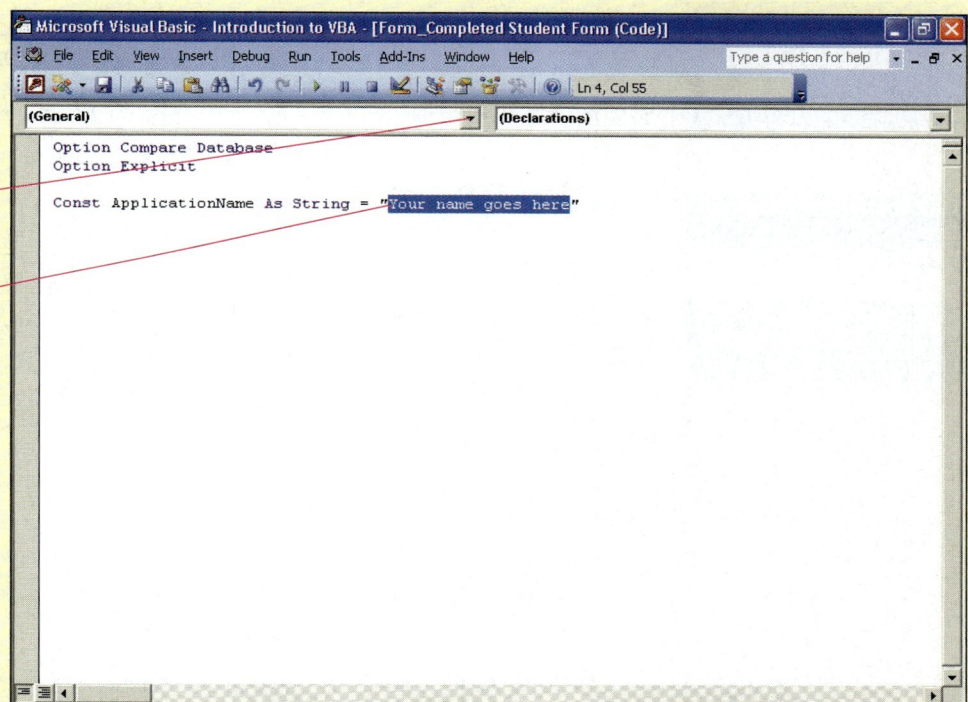

(e) Change the Application Name (step 5)

FIGURE 8.8   Hands-on Exercise 3 (*continued*)

THE MSGBOX STATEMENT—CONSTANTS VERSUS LITERALS

The third parameter in the MsgBox statement can be entered as a literal such as "John Doe's Application". It's preferable, however, to specify the argument as a constant such as ApplicationName, then define that constant in the Declarations section. That way, you can change the name of the application in one place, and have the change automatically reflected in every MsgBox statement that references the constant.

Step 6:   Complete the Error Event Procedure

- Click the **down arrow** for the Object box and select the **Form object**. Click the **down arrow** for the Procedure box and click the **Error procedure**.

- Click immediately before the Case Else statement, then enter the additional code shown in Figure 8.8f. Use the Copy and Paste commands to enter the second Case statement. Thus:
  - ❏ Click and drag to select the first Case statement, click the **Copy button**, click above the Case Else statement, and click the **Paste button**.
  - ❏ Modify the copied statements as necessary, rather than typing the statements from scratch. Use the **Ins key** to toggle between insertion and replacement. Be sure that your code matches ours.

- Click the **Save button** to save the procedure. Click the taskbar button to return to the **Completed Student Form**.

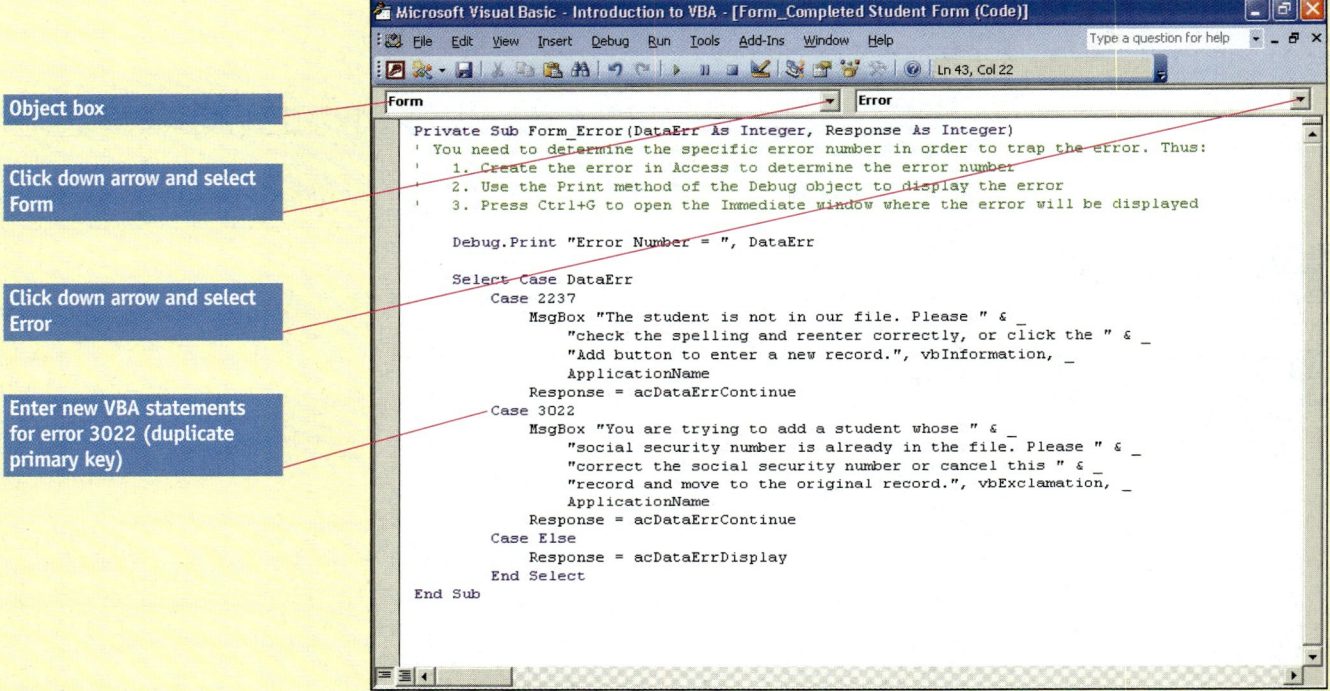

Object box

Click down arrow and select Form

Click down arrow and select Error

Enter new VBA statements for error 3022 (duplicate primary key)

```
Private Sub Form_Error(DataErr As Integer, Response As Integer)
' You need to determine the specific error number in order to trap the error. Thus:
'    1. Create the error in Access to determine the error number
'    2. Use the Print method of the Debug object to display the error
'    3. Press Ctrl+G to open the Immediate window where the error will be displayed

    Debug.Print "Error Number = ", DataErr

    Select Case DataErr
        Case 2237
            MsgBox "The student is not in our file. Please " & _
                "check the spelling and reenter correctly, or click the " & _
                "Add button to enter a new record.", vbInformation, _
                ApplicationName
            Response = acDataErrContinue
        Case 3022
            MsgBox "You are trying to add a student whose " & _
                "social security number is already in the file. Please " & _
                "correct the social security number or cancel this " & _
                "record and move to the original record.", vbExclamation, _
                ApplicationName
            Response = acDataErrContinue
        Case Else
            Response = acDataErrDisplay
    End Select
End Sub
```

(f) Complete the Error Event Procedure (step 6)

FIGURE 8.8   Hands-on Exercise 3 (*continued*)

THE OBJECT AND PROCEDURE BOXES

The Object box at the top left of the Module window displays the current object, such as a form or a control on the form. The Procedure box displays the name of the current procedure for the selected object. To create or navigate between events for a form, click the down arrow on the Object box to select the Form object, then click the down arrow on the Procedure box to display the list of events. Events that already have procedures appear in bold. Clicking an event that is not bold creates the procedure header and End Sub statements for that event.

Step 7: **Complete the Testing**

- You should be back in Design view of the Completed Student Form. Pull down the **View menu** and change to the **Datasheet view** as shown in Figure 8.8g. (You can also click the **down arrow** next to the View button on the Form Design view and select Datasheet view.)

- Enter **222-22-2222** as a duplicate Social Security number for the first record. Press the **down arrow** (or click the appropriate **navigation button**) to attempt to move to the next record.

- You should see the error message in Figure 8.8g which clearly explains the nature of the error. The title bar displays the value of the ApplicationName constant that was entered earlier in the exercise.

- Click **OK** (or press **Esc**) to close the dialog box. Press **Esc** to restore the original value of the Social Security number. Close the window.

- Exit Access if you do not want to continue with the next exercise at this time.

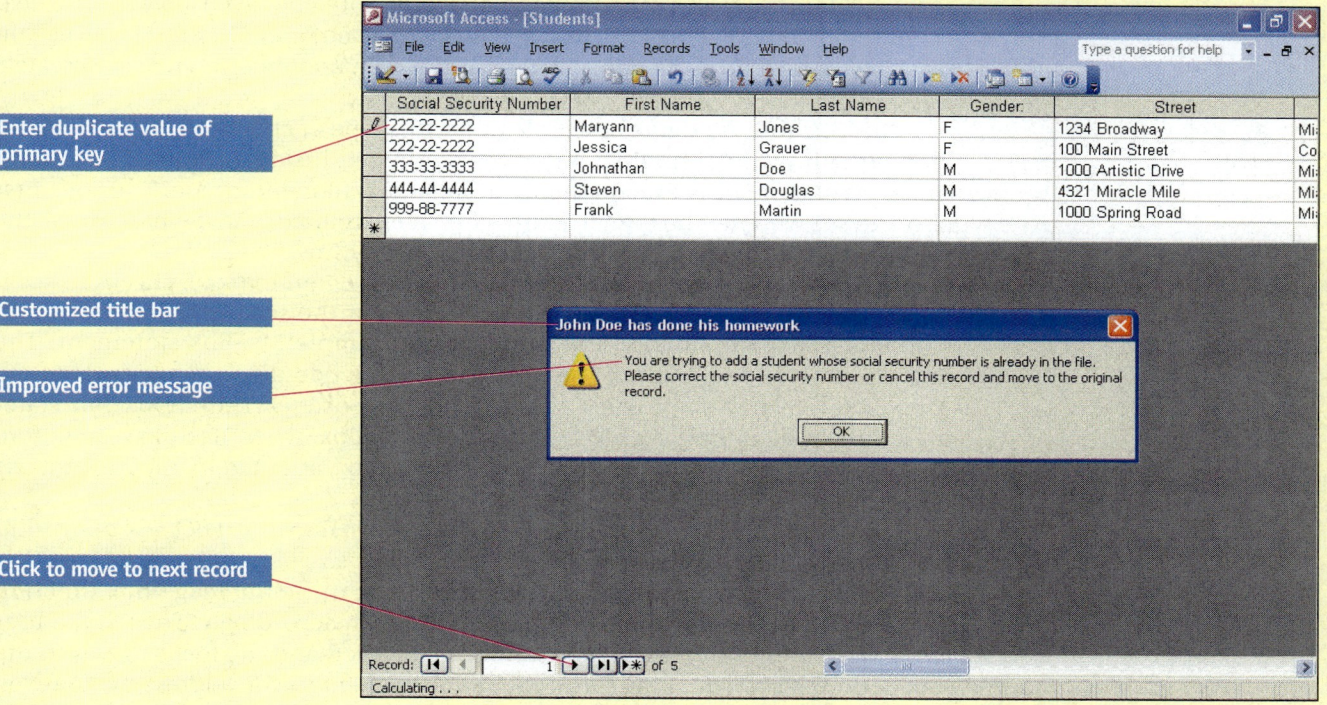

(g) Complete the Testing (step 7)

FIGURE 8.8 Hands-on Exercise 3 (*continued*)

DOCUMENT YOUR WORK

You understand your database completely, but the individual who (eventually) takes your position may not be as knowledgeable. It helps, therefore, to leave a written record of your work to explain what you have done. Access helps to automate the process. Pull down the Tools menu, click Analyze, then click Documenter to display the associated dialog box where you select the objects for which you want documentation. Be careful, however, because a few mouse clicks can generate a hundred pages or more. See practice exercise 6 at the end of the chapter.

DATA VALIDATION

Data validation is a crucial component of any system. The most basic type of validation is implemented automatically, without any additional effort on the part of the developer. A user cannot, for example, enter data that does not conform to the designated field type. The user cannot enter text into a numeric field, nor can one enter an invalid date—such as February 30—into a date field. Access also prevents you from entering a duplicate record (i.e., a record with the same primary key as another record).

Other validation checks are implemented by the developer for the specific application, at either the field or record level. The former performs the validation as soon as you move from one field to the next within a table or form. The latter waits until all of the fields have been completed, then checks the entire record prior to updating the record. Both types of validation are essential to prevent invalid data from corrupting the system.

The developer can also use VBA to extend the data validation capabilities within Access. You can, for example, write an event procedure to remind the user that a field is empty and ask whether the record should be saved anyway. The field is not required and hence the Required property is not appropriate. However, you do not want to ignore the omitted field completely, and thus you need to create a VBA procedure.

The VBA code in Figure 8.9 implements this type of check through a **nested If statement** in which one If statement is contained inside another. The second (inner) If statement is executed only if the first statement is true. Thus, we first check to see whether the e-mail address has been omitted, and if it has, we ask the user whether he or she wants to save the record anyway.

The outer If statement in Figure 8.9, *If IsNull (EmailAddress),* checks to see if the e-mail address is blank, and if it is, it executes the second If statement that contains a MsgBox function, as opposed to a simple MsgBox statement. The difference between the two is that the MsgBox function displays a prompt to the user, then returns a value (such as which button a user clicked). A MsgBox statement, however, simply displays a message. MsgBox, when used as a function, requires parentheses around the arguments. MsgBox, as a statement, does not use parentheses.

Look carefully at the second argument, *vbYesNo + vbQuestion* within Figure 8.9. The intrinsic constant vbYesNo displays two command buttons (Yes and No) within the message box. The If in front of the message box function enables VBA to test the user's response and branch accordingly. Thus, if the user clicks the No button, the save operation is cancelled and the focus moves to the EmailAddress control in the form, where the user enters the address. If, however, the user clicks the Yes button, the If statement is false, and the record is saved without the e-mail address.

Nested If statement

MsgBox function

vbYesNo displays Yes and No command buttons in dialog box

```
Private Sub Form_BeforeUpdate(Cancel As Integer)
    If IsNull(EmailAddress) Then
        If MsgBox("You did not enter an e-mail address. Save anyway?", _
            vbYesNo + vbQuestion, ApplicationName) = vbNo Then
            Cancel = True
            EmailAddress.SetFocus
        End If
    End If
End Sub
```

FIGURE 8.9 Procedure for Exercise 4

4   Data Validation

Objective   To use Field and Table properties to implement different types of data validation. Use Figure 8.10 as a guide in the exercise.

Step 1:   **Set the Field Properties**

- Open the **Introduction to VBA database**. Click the **Tables button**, then open the **Students table** in Design view as shown in Figure 8.10a.

- Click the field selector column for the **Gender**. Click the **Validation Rule box**. Type =**"M" or "F"** to accept only these values on data entry.

- Click the **Validation Text box**. Type **Please enter either M or F as the gender.**

- Click the **Required property** and change its value to **Yes**.

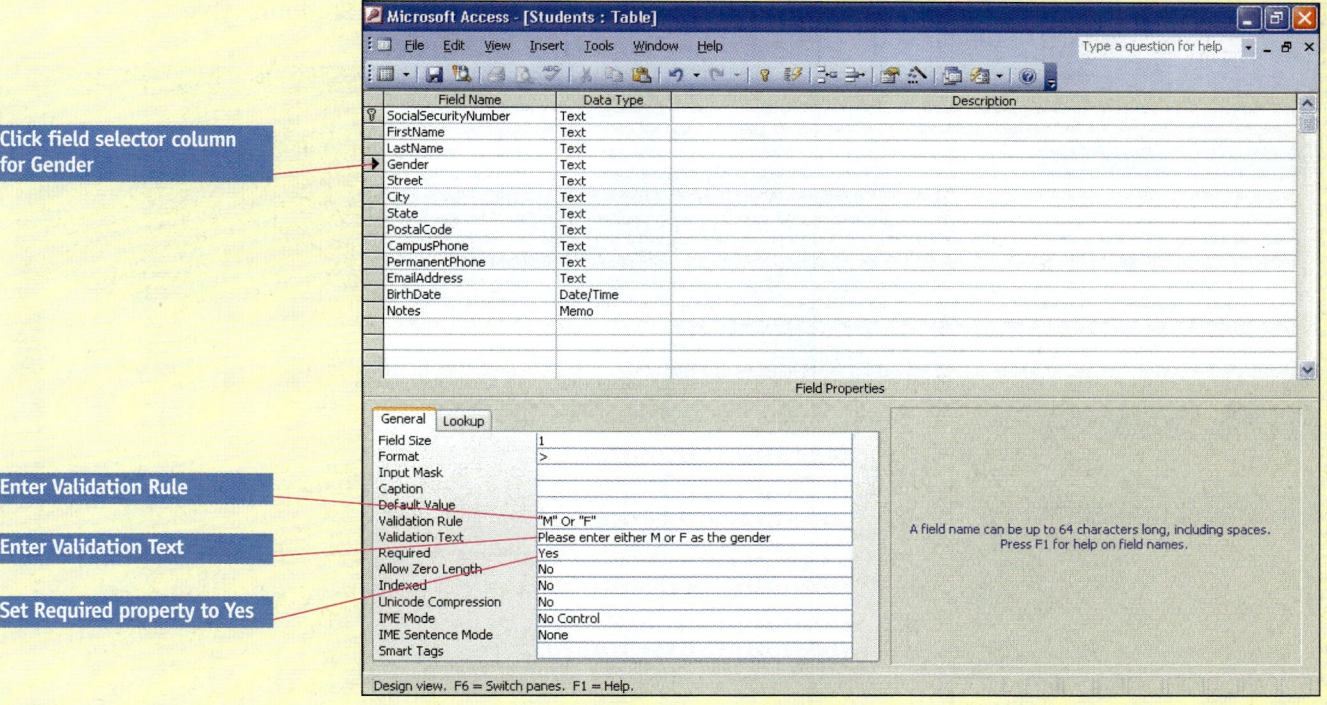

(a) Set the Field Properties (step 1)

FIGURE 8.10   Hands-on Exercise 4

OPTIMIZE DATA TYPES AND FIELD SIZES

The data type property determines the data that can be accepted into a field and the operations that can be performed on that data. Any field that is intended for use in a calculation should be given the numeric data type. You can, however, increase the efficiency of an Access database by specifying the appropriate value for the Field Size property of a numeric field. The Byte, Integer, and Long Integer field sizes hold values up to 256; 32,767; and 2,147,483,648, respectively. Use the appropriate field size for your application.

Step 2: **Set the Table Properties**

- Point to the **selector box** in the upper-left corner, then click the **right mouse button** and display the Table Properties dialog box as shown in Figure 8.10b. You are viewing the properties of the entire table, rather than the properties of a specific field.

- Click in the **Validation Rule box** and enter **[CampusPhone] Is Not Null Or [PermanentPhone] Is Not Null** to ensure that the user enters one phone number or the other. (The field names should not contain any spaces and are enclosed in square brackets.)

- Press **Enter**, then type, **You must enter either a campus or permanent phone number** (which is the validation text that will be displayed in the event of an error).

- Click the **Save button** to save the table. Click **No** when you see the message asking whether existing data should be tested against the new rules.

- Close the Table Properties dialog box. Close the Students table.

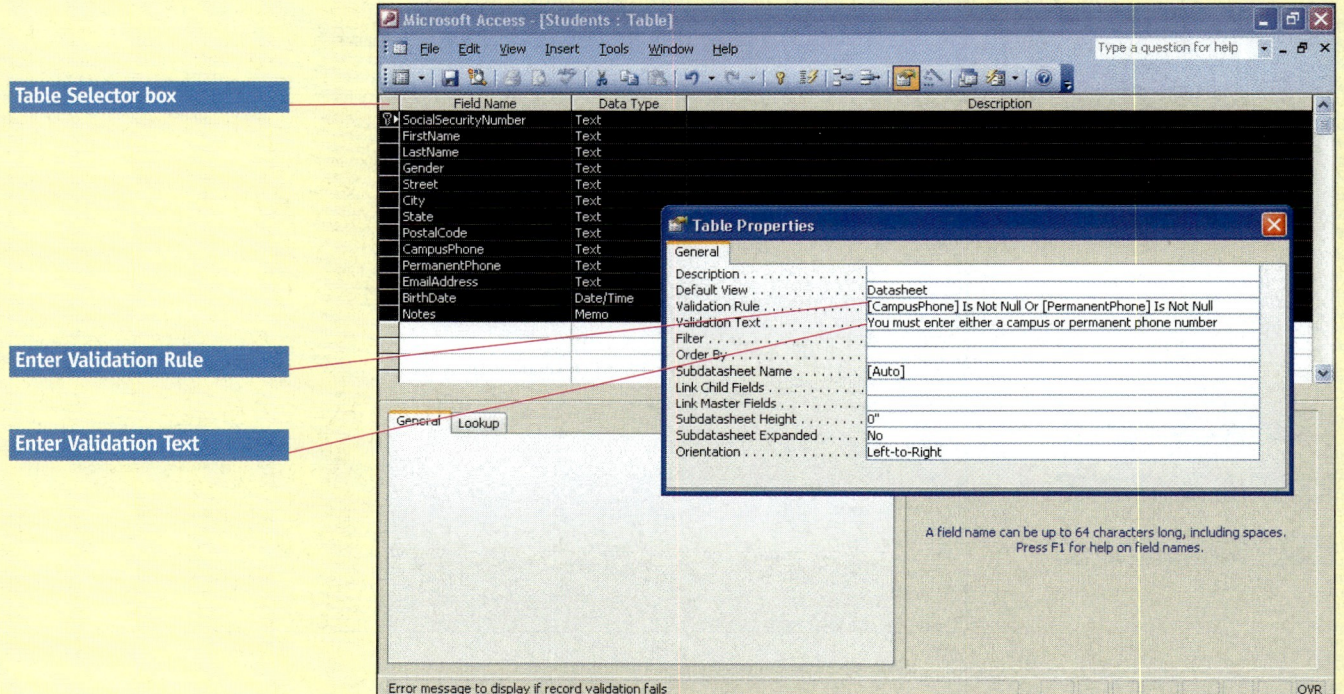

(b) Set the Table Properties (step 2)

FIGURE 8.10 Hands-on Exercise 4 (*continued*)

DAY PHONE OR PERMANENT PHONE

You can set the Required property of a field to force the user to enter data for that field. But what if you wanted the user to enter one of two fields and were indifferent to which field was chosen? Setting the Required property of either or both fields would not accomplish your goal. You can, however, implement this type of validation at the record (rather than the field) level by setting the properties of the table as a whole, rather than the properties of the individual fields. This example forces the user to enter a phone number, but it does not matter which number (campus or permanent) is entered.

Step 3: Test the Validation Rules

- Open the **Completed Student Form** in Form view. If necessary, move to Maryann Jones, the first record in the table.

- Click and drag to select the gender field, then type **X** to replace the gender. Press **Enter**. You will see an error message pertaining to the gender field.

- Press **Esc** (or click **OK**) to close the dialog box. Press **Esc** a second time to restore the original value.

- Click and drag to select the existing CampusPhone number, then press the **Del key** to erase the phone number. Press the **Tab key** to move to the PermanentPhone field. Both phone numbers should be blank.

- Click the ▶ **button** to move to the next record. You should see the error message in Figure 8.10c pertaining to the table properties.

- Press **Esc** (or click **OK**) to close the dialog box. Press **Esc** a second time to restore the original value.

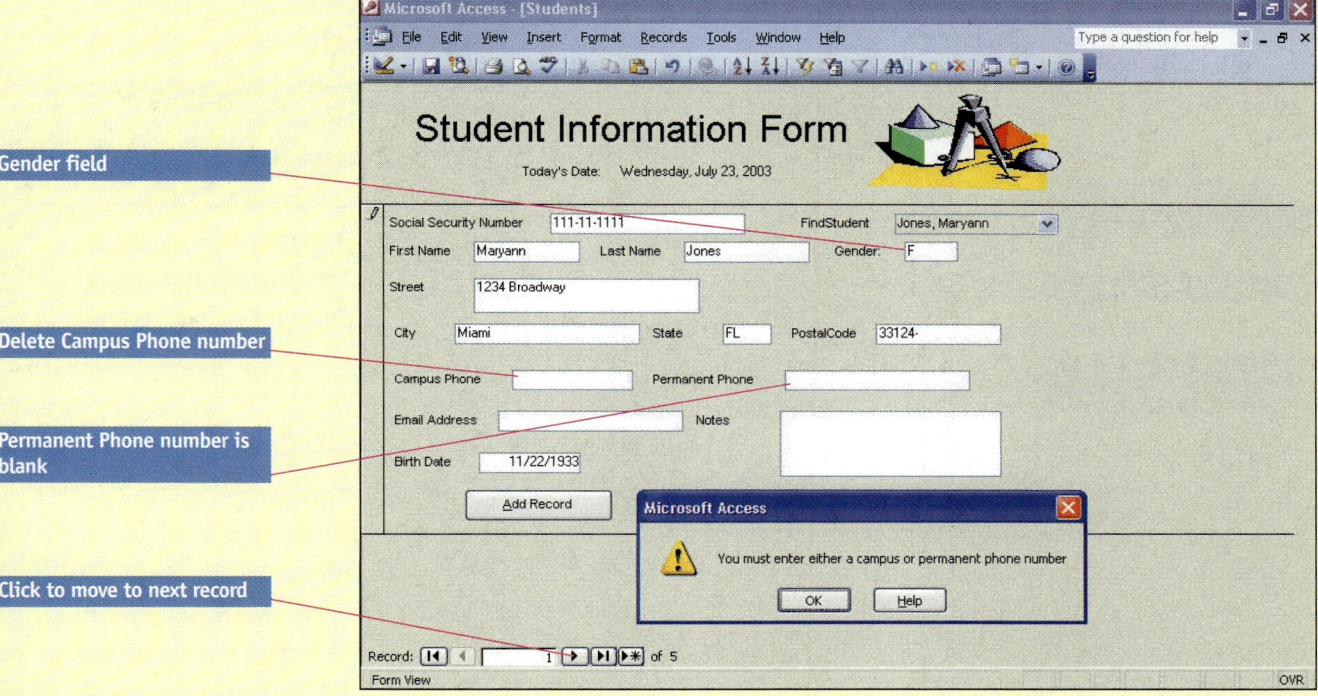

(c) Test the Validation Rules (step 3)

FIGURE 8.10   Hands-on Exercise 4 (*continued*)

VALIDATING AT THE FIELD VERSUS THE RECORD LEVEL

Data validation is performed at the field or record level. If it is done at the field level (e.g., by specifying the Required and Validation Rule properties for a specific field), Access checks the entry immediately as soon as you exit the field. If it is done at the record level, however (e.g., by checking that one of two fields has been entered), Access has to wait until it has processed every field in the record. Thus, it is only on attempting to move to the next record that Access informs you of the error.

Step 4:   **Create the BeforeUpdate Event Procedure**

- Change to the **Form Design view**. Pull down the **View menu** and click **Code** (or click the **Code button**) on the Form Design toolbar. If necessary, click the **Procedure view button** to view one procedure at a time.

- Click the **down arrow** on the Object list box and click **Form**. Click the **down arrow** on the Procedure list box to display the list of events for the form. Click **BeforeUpdate** to create a procedure for this event.

- Press the **Tab key** to indent, then enter the statements exactly as shown in Figure 8.10d. Note that as soon as you enter the period after "EmailAddress," Access displays the methods and properties for the EmailAddress control.

- Type **set** (the first three letters in the SetFocus method), watching the screen as you enter each letter. Access moves through the displayed list automatically, until it arrives at the **SetFocus method**. Press **Enter**.

- Add an **End If** statement to complete the If statement testing the MsgBox function. Press **Enter**, then enter a second **End If** statement to complete the If statement testing the IsNull condition.

- Save the procedure.

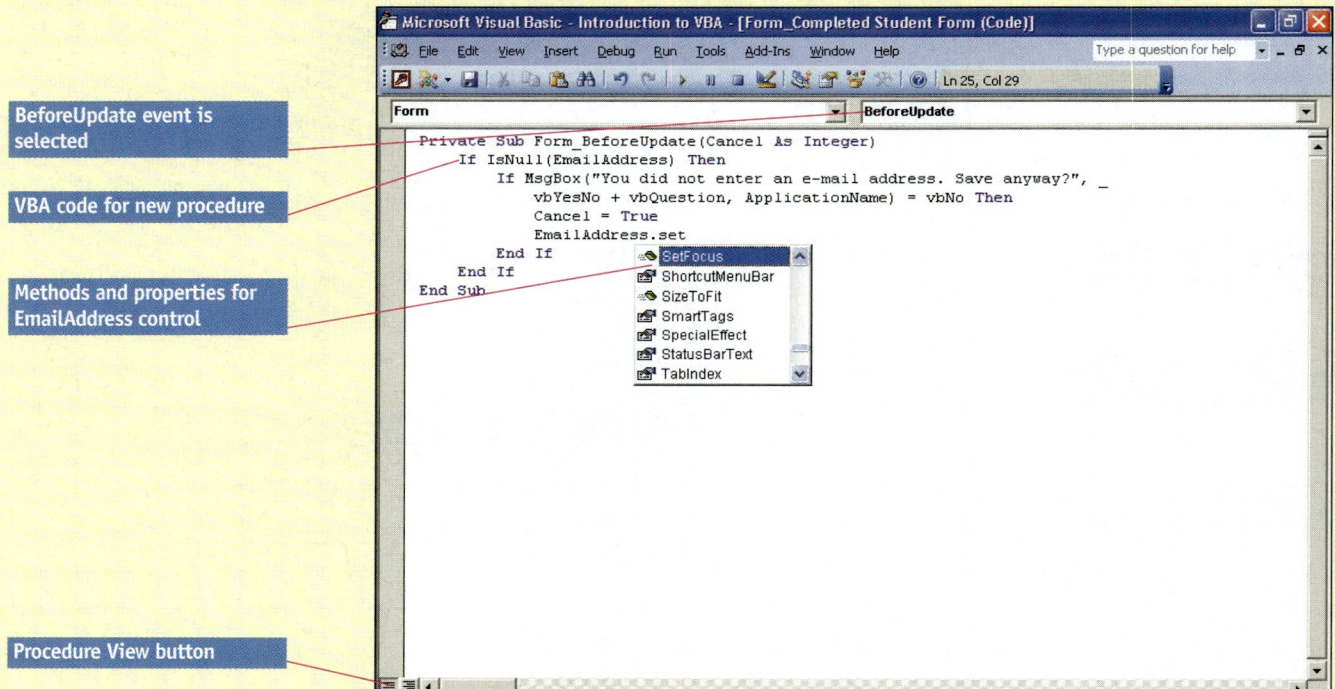

BeforeUpdate event is selected

VBA code for new procedure

Methods and properties for EmailAddress control

Procedure View button

(d) Create the BeforeUpdate Event Procedure (step 4)

FIGURE 8.10   Hands-on Exercise 4 (*continued*)

AUTOLIST MEMBERS—HELP IN WRITING CODE

Access displays the methods and properties for a control as soon as you enter the period after the control name. Type the first several letters to select the method or property. Press the space bar to accept the selected item and remain on the same line, or press the Enter key to accept the item and begin a new line.

Step 5:   **Test the BeforeUpdate Event Procedure**

- Click the taskbar button for the Access form. Change to the **Form view**. Click in the **memo field** and enter the text shown in Figure 8.10e.

- Check the remaining fields, but be sure to leave the Email Address blank. Click the navigation button to (attempt to) move to the next record.

- You should see the error message in Figure 8.10e. Note the entry in the title bar that corresponds to the value of the ApplicationName constant you entered earlier.

- Click **No** to cancel the operation, close the dialog box, and automatically position the insertion point within the text box for the Email Address.

- Enter an e-mail address such as **mjones@anyschool.edu**, then click the navigation button to move to the next record. This time Access does not display the error message and saves the record.

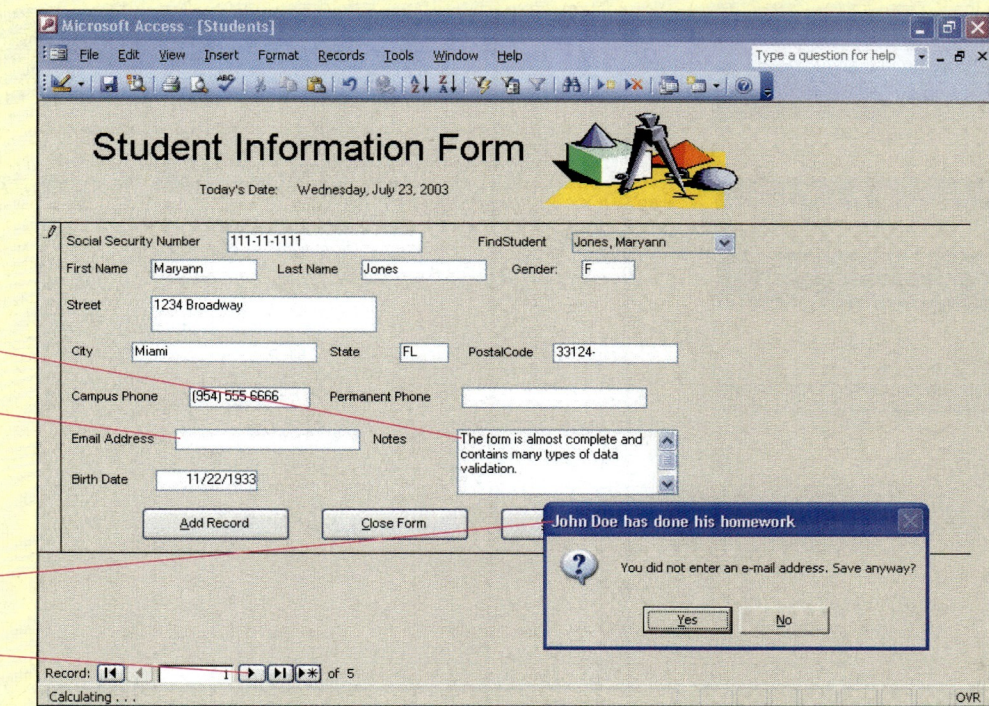

Enter memo field text

Email Address is blank

Customized title bar

Click to move to next record

(e) Test the BeforeUpdate Event Procedure (step 5)

FIGURE 8.10   Hands-on Exercise 4 (*continued*)

MEMO FIELDS VERSUS TEXT FIELDS

A text field can store up to 255 characters. A memo field, however, can store up to 64,000 characters and is used to hold descriptive data that runs for several sentences, paragraphs, or even pages. A vertical scroll bar appears in the Form view when the memo field contains more data than is visible at one time. Note, too, that both text and memo fields store only the characters that have been entered; that is, there is no wasted space if the data does not extend to the maximum field size.

Step 6: Create the CloseForm Event Procedure

- Change to the **Form Design view**, then click the **Code button** on the Form Design toolbar to display the Module window. If necessary, click the **Object box** to select **Form**, then click the **Procedure box** to select the **Close event**.

- You should see the event procedure in Figure 8.10f. Press **Tab** to indent the statement, then enter **MsgBox** followed by a blank space. The Quick Info feature displays the syntax of this statement.

- Complete the message, ending with the closing quotation mark and comma. The AutoList feature displays the list of appropriate arguments. Type **vbc**, at which point you can select the **vbCritical** parameter by typing a **comma**.

- Type a **space** followed by an **underscore** to continue the statement to the next line. Press **Enter** and type **ApplicationName** as the last parameter.

- Save the module.

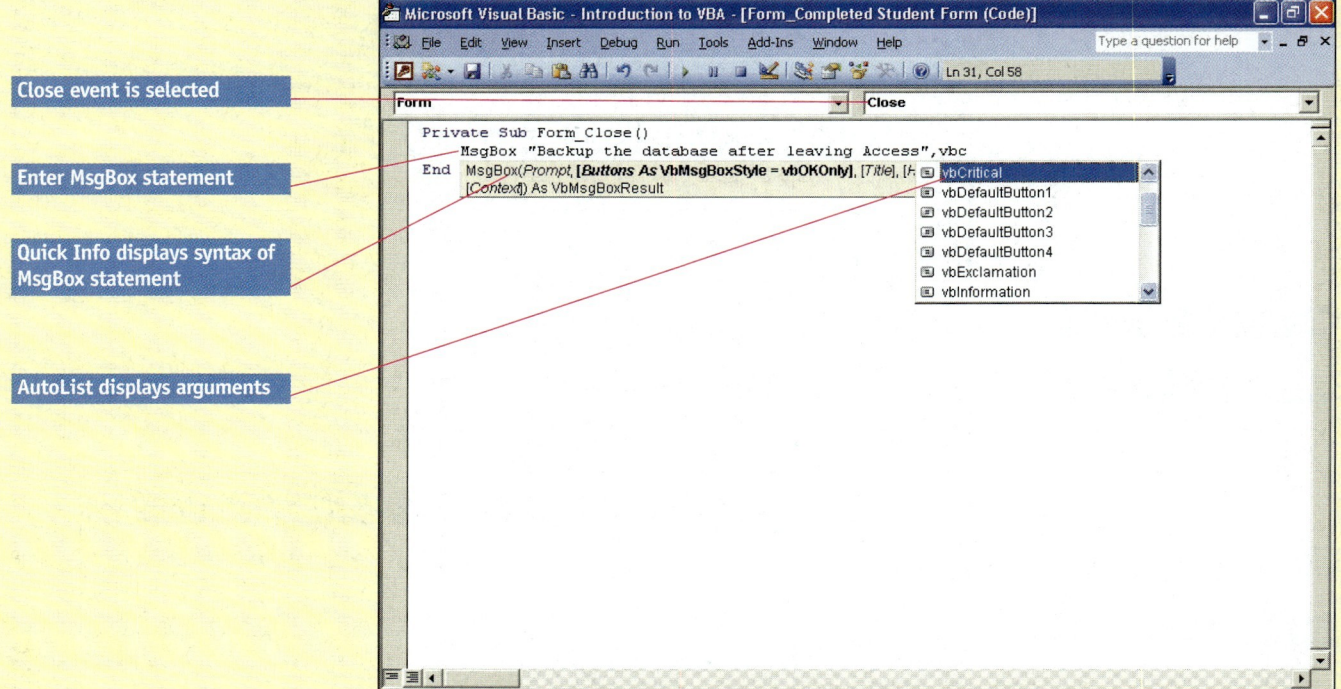

Close event is selected

Enter MsgBox statement

Quick Info displays syntax of MsgBox statement

AutoList displays arguments

(f) Create the CloseForm Event Procedure (step 6)

FIGURE 8.10 Hands-on Exercise 4 (*continued*)

CHOOSE THE RIGHT EVENT

We associated the message prompting the user to back up the database with the Close event for the form. Would it work equally well if the message were associated with the Click event of the Close Form command button? The answer is no, because the user could bypass the command button and close the form by pulling down the File menu and choosing the Close command, and thus never see the message. Choosing the right object and associated event is one of the subtleties in VBA.

Step 7: **Close the Form**

■ Click the **Access form button** on the taskbar. Return to **Form view**. The form looks very similar to the form with which we began, but it has been enhanced in subtle ways:
  ❏ The drop-down list box has been added to locate a specific student.
  ❏ Accelerator keys have been created for the command buttons (e.g., Alt+A to add a record and Alt+C to close the form).
  ❏ The Ctrl+1 and Ctrl+2 keyboard shortcuts have been created. (Click the shortcuts button to display the associated action.)
  ❏ The data validation has been enhanced through custom error messages.
  ❏ The application has been customized through the entry on the title bar.

■ Click the **Close Form button** to display the dialog box in Figure 8.10g. Click **OK** to close the dialog box, which in turn closes the form.

■ Close the database. Exit Access. Congratulations on a job well done.

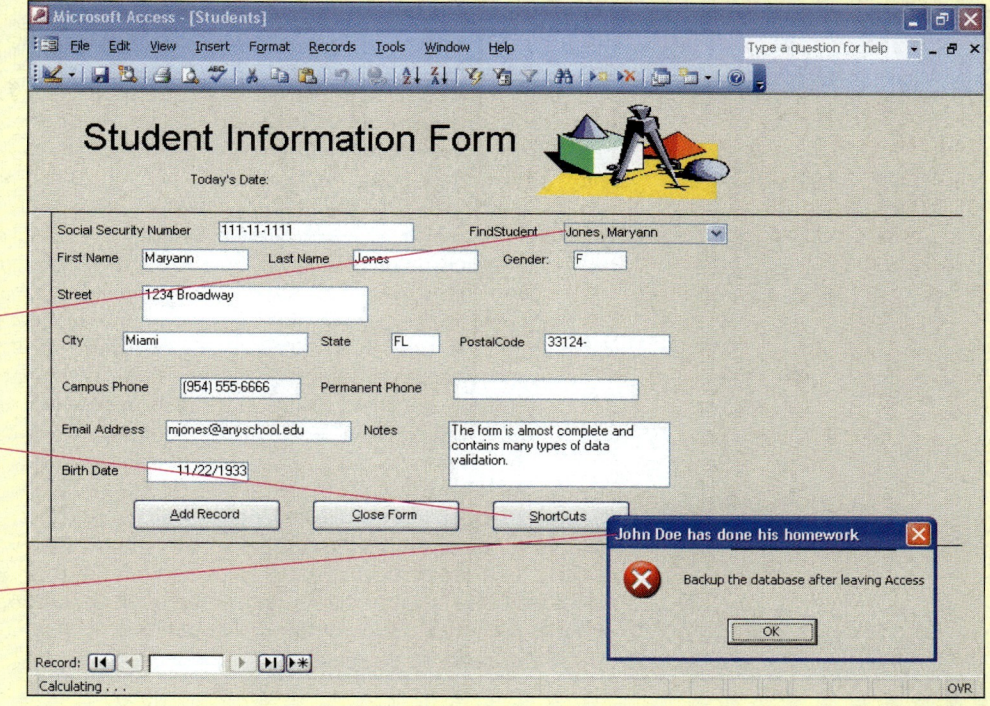

(g) Close the Form (step 7)

FIGURE 8.10   Hands-on Exercise 4 (*continued*)

TAKE IT ON THE ROAD

Multiple copies of the same database can be used by different individuals, in different locations, that are not networked together. Eventually, however, the data in the underlying tables of the different databases must be synchronized. This is accomplished through replication, which enables you to create multiple copies (replicas) of a database, enter or modify data into any one of those copies, then merge (synchronize) the changes back into the original database. See practice exercises 7 and 8 at the end of the chapter.

SUMMARY

Visual Basic for Applications (VBA) is a subset of Visual Basic that is accessible from every application in Microsoft Office. The programming statements (such as If and MsgBox) are identical for every application. The objects on which those statements operate (such as forms and reports in Access) differ from one application to the next. A general introduction to VBA is presented in the "Getting Started with VBA" module that appears at the end of this text.

VBA is different from traditional programming languages in that it is event-driven. An event is any action that is recognized by the application. Thus, to enhance an application through VBA, you decide which events are significant and what is to happen when those events occur. Then you develop the appropriate event procedures—for example, a keyboard shortcut for data entry that occurs when the user presses a particular keystroke combination in filling out a form. The execution of the event procedure depends entirely on the user, because he or she triggers the underlying events through an appropriate action.

Visual Basic code is developed in units called procedures. There are two types of procedures—general procedures and event procedures. Event procedures are the essence of an Access application and run automatically in response to an event such as clicking a button or opening a form. General procedures are called explicitly from within another procedure.

All VBA procedures are stored in modules. Every form in an Access database has its own module that contains the event procedures for that form. All procedures are either public or private. A private procedure is accessible only from within the module in which it is contained. A public procedure is accessible from anywhere. All procedures are displayed and edited in the Module window within Access.

Several event procedures were created in this chapter to illustrate how VBA can be used to enhance an Access application. Hands-on exercise 1 focused on the Current event to synchronize the displayed record in a form with a combo box used to locate a record by last name. Exercise 2 developed a KeyDown event procedure to facilitate data entry. Exercise 3 developed the Error event to substitute application-specific error messages for the default messages provided by Access. Exercise 4 created a BeforeUpdate event procedure to enhance the data validation for the form. Additional procedures can be developed by expanding the existing code through inference and observation.

The MsgBox statement has three arguments—the prompt (or message to the user), a VBA intrinsic constant that specifies the icon to be displayed within the box, and the text that is to appear on the title bar of the box. MsgBox may be used as a statement or a function. The difference between the two is that the MsgBox function displays a prompt to the user, then returns a value (such as which button a user clicked). A MsgBox statement, however, simply displays a message. MsgBox, when used as a function, requires parentheses around the arguments. MsgBox, as a statement, does not use parentheses.

KEY TERMS

Argument 392
BeforeUpdate event 424
Case statement 411
Class module 391
Click event .401
Close Form Event 392
Compile error 404
Complete Word tool 405
Concatenation 396
Continuation 415
Current event 392
Data validation 420
Default property 401
Error trapping 411

Event procedure 391
Event 388
Full Module view 403
General Declarations section 411
General procedure 391
If statement 411
Immediate window 411
Intrinsic constant 392
Key Preview property 406
KeyCode argument 402
KeyDown event 401
Module window 391
MsgBox statement 392
Nested If statement 420

Object box 418
Parameter 392
Private procedure 391
Procedure 388
Procedure box 418
Procedure header 402
Procedure view 403
Public procedure 391
Replica 427
SetFocus method 402
Synchronization 427
Visual Basic for
    Applications (VBA) 388

MULTIPLE CHOICE

1. Which of the following applications can be enhanced through VBA?

   (a) Word and Excel

   (b) Access and PowerPoint

   (c) Outlook

   (d) All of the above

2. Which application enhancements are accomplished using VBA event procedures?

   (a) Improved data validation

   (b) Creation of keyboard shortcuts for data entry

   (c) Substitution of customized error messages for the standard messages provided by Access

   (d) All of the above

3. Which of the following is necessary in order to establish a keyboard shortcut to facilitate data entry on a form?

   (a) Create a procedure for the KeyUp event of the form and set the Key Preview property to No

   (b) Create a procedure for the KeyUp event of the form and set the Key Preview property to Yes

   (c) Create a procedure for the KeyDown event of the form and set the Key Preview property to No

   (d) Create a procedure for the KeyDown event of the form and set the Key Preview property to Yes

4. Which of the following characters continues a VBA statement?

   (a) A hyphen

   (b) An underscore

   (c) A hyphen and an ampersand

   (d) An underscore and an ampersand

5. Which of the following types of data validation requires an event procedure?

   (a) Checking that a required field has been entered

   (b) Checking that one of two fields has been entered

   (c) Prompting the user with a message indicating that an optional field has been omitted, and asking for further instruction

   (d) All of the above

6. Which of the following is *not* used to implement a validation check that requires the user to enter a value of Atlanta or Boston for the City field?

   (a) Set the Required property for the City field to Yes

   (b) Set the Validation Rule property for the City field to either "Atlanta" or "Boston"

   (c) Set the Default property for the City field to either "Atlanta" or "Boston"

   (d) Set the Validation Text property for the City field to display an appropriate error message if the user does not enter either Atlanta or Boston

7. Which of the following would you use to require the user to enter either a home or a business phone?

   (a) Set the Required property of each field to Yes

   (b) Set the Validation Rule property for each field to true

   (c) Set the Validation Rule for the table to [HomePhone] or [BusinessPhone]

   (d) All of the above are equally acceptable

8. Which is a true statement about the Procedure box in the Module window?

   (a) Events that have procedures appear in bold

   (b) Clicking an event that appears in boldface displays the event procedure

   (c) Clicking an event that is not in bold creates a procedure for that event

   (d) All of the above

9. Which event procedure was created in conjunction with the combo box to locate a record on the form?

   (a) An On Current event procedure for the combo box control

   (b) An On Current event procedure for the form

   (c) A KeyDown event procedure for the combo box

   (d) A KeyDown event procedure for the form

10. Which event procedure was created to warn the user that the e-mail address was omitted and asking whether the record is to be saved anyway?

    (a) An On Error event procedure for the e-mail control

    (b) An On Error event procedure for the form

    (c) A BeforeUpdate event procedure for the e-mail control

    (d) A BeforeUpdate event procedure for the form

... continued

multiple choice

11. Which of the following does *not* create an event procedure for a form?

(a) Display the Properties box for the form in Design View, click the Event tab, select the event, then click the Build button

(b) Select the form in the Object box of the Module window, then click the event (displayed in regular, as opposed to boldface) in the Procedure box

(c) Pull down the View menu in the Database window and click the code command or click the Code button on the Database toolbar

(d) All of the above create an event procedure

12. You want to display a message in conjunction with closing a form. Which of the following is the best way to accomplish this?

(a) Write a VBA procedure for the Close Form event

(b) Create a Close command button for the form, then write a VBA procedure for the On Click event of the command button to display the message

(c) Either (a) or (b)

(d) Neither (a) nor (b)

13. Which of the following is not an Access-intrinsic constant?

(a) ApplicationName

(b) vbCritical

(c) acCtrlMask

(d) vbKey1

14. Which of the following would display "Hello" in a message box?

(a) MsgBox "Hello", vbCritical, "Your Name"

(b) MsgBox "Your Name", "Hello", vbCritical

(c) MsgBox vbCritical, "Hello", "Your Name"

(d) MsgBox "Your Name", vbCritical, "Hello"

15. Which of the following statements was used to display the Error Number associated with an error in data entry?

(a) Debug.Print "Error Number = "

(b) Debug.Print "Error Number = ", DataErr

(c) Print "Error Number = "

(d) Print "Error Number = ", DataErr

16. Which of the following is true about indented text in a VBA procedure?

(a) The indented text is always executed first

(b) The indented text is always executed last

(c) The indented text is rendered a comment and is never executed

(d) None of the above

17. Which of the following is likely to be used within an Add Record procedure to position the insertion point?

(a) The SetFocus method

(b) The SetFocus property

(c) The SetFocus event

(d) The SetFocus procedure

18. What advantage, if any, is gained by using VBA to create a keyboard shortcut to enter the city, state, and zip code in an incoming record, as opposed to using the Default Value property in the table definition?

(a) It's easier to use VBA than to specify the Default Value property

(b) The Default Value property cannot be applied to multiple fields for the same record, and thus VBA is the only way to accomplish this task

(c) VBA can be used to create different shortcuts for different sets of values, whereas the Default Value property is restricted to a single value

(d) All of the above

ANSWERS

1. d	**7.** c	**13.** a
2. d	**8.** d	**14.** a
3. d	**9.** b	**15.** b
4. b	**10.** d	**16.** d
5. c	**11.** c	**17.** a
6. c	**12.** a	**18.** c

1. **MsgBox Examples:** VBA is different from Visual Basic in that its procedures must exist within an Office document. Thus, you have to create a new database to contain the procedures in Figure 8.11. (The database need not contain any tables.) Start Access, create a new database, and then click the Modules button from within the Database window. Click the New button to create a general module (called Module1 by default). This opens the VBA editor as shown in Figure 8.11.

   a. Define a constant to hold your name. The constant will be available to all of the procedures within the module and should be referenced as the third parameter in all three MsgBox statements. This will display your name in the title bar of the associated dialog boxes.

   b. Create the first procedure, consisting of three simple MsgBox statements, with one, two, and three parameters, respectively. Click the procedure header, then click the Run button on the VBA toolbar to test the procedure. Do you see the effect of each procedure on the associated dialog boxes?

   c. Create the second procedure that uses the MsgBox function to test the value of the user's response by comparing it to the vbYes intrinsic constant. Change the second argument to vbYesNo+vbQuestion and note the effect in the resulting dialog box.

   d. Add the third procedure, which closes the database and exits Access. The MsgBox statement should remind the user to back up the database.

   e. Pull down the File menu and click the Print command to print the entire module for your instructor.

   f. Use the Switchboard Manager to create a simple switchboard with three buttons—to run MsgBoxStatement procedure, to run the MsgBoxFunction procedure, and to exit the database.

   g. Use the Startup property to display the switchboard automatically when the database is opened. Test the switchboard completely to be sure that it works properly.

   h. Print the Switchboard form and table of Switchboard Items for your instructor. Add a cover sheet to complete the assignment.

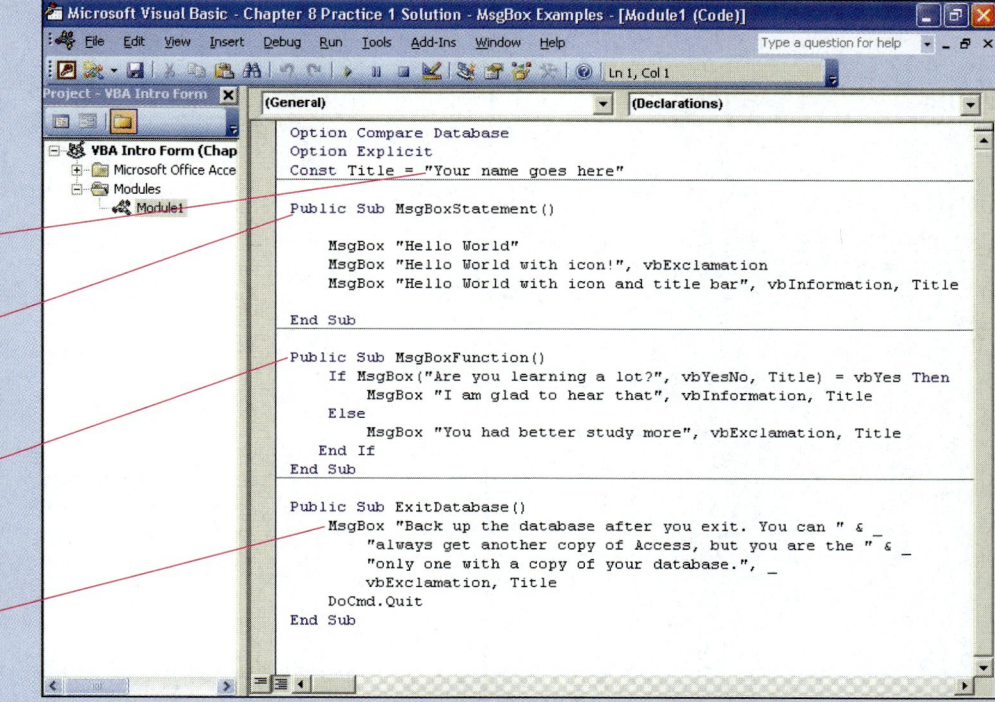

Constant stores your name

Procedure One has three MsgBox statements

Procedure Two uses MsgBox function to determine whether Yes or No button was clicked

Procedure Three displays a message to back up after you exit Access

FIGURE 8.11 MsgBox Examples (exercise 1)

2. **Expanded Student Form:** VBA includes a variety of string processing functions that enable you to test the individual characters within a character string. Two of these functions are illustrated in conjunction with the procedure to validate an e-mail address as shown in Figure 8.12. (Use the VBA Help command to learn more about the Len and InStr functions.) Complete the four hands-on exercises in the chapter, then proceed as follows to modify the Student form:

a. Open the completed Student form in Design view. Right click the Email Address control, click the Properties command to display the property sheet, click the Event tab, then click the Build button for the Before Update property. Click Code Builder and click OK.

b. Click the Procedure View button. Create the procedure in Figure 8.12, which consists of three simple If statements. The first statement uses the Len function to ensure that there are at least ten characters in the e-mail address. The next two statements use the InStr function to start at the first character in the EmailAddress control and search for the @ and period, respectively. Omission of either character will result in an error message during data entry.

c. Modify the BeforeUpdate procedure for the form to test for the student's birth date, and then if the birth date is omitted, to warn the user and give the option to save the record anyway.

d. Add a new keyboard shortcut, Ctrl+3, to the existing KeyDown procedure that will enter New York, NY, and 10010 in the city, state, and postal code controls, respectively.

e. Modify the VBA procedure associated with the Add Record button, so that the insertion point moves automatically to the SocialSecurityNumber control. (See the tip at the end of step 8 in Hands-on Exercise 1 in the chapter for help.)

f. Print the completed VBA module for the Student form for your instructor.

g. Can you think of any other procedures that would further enhance the form? Summarize your thoughts in a short note to your instructor.

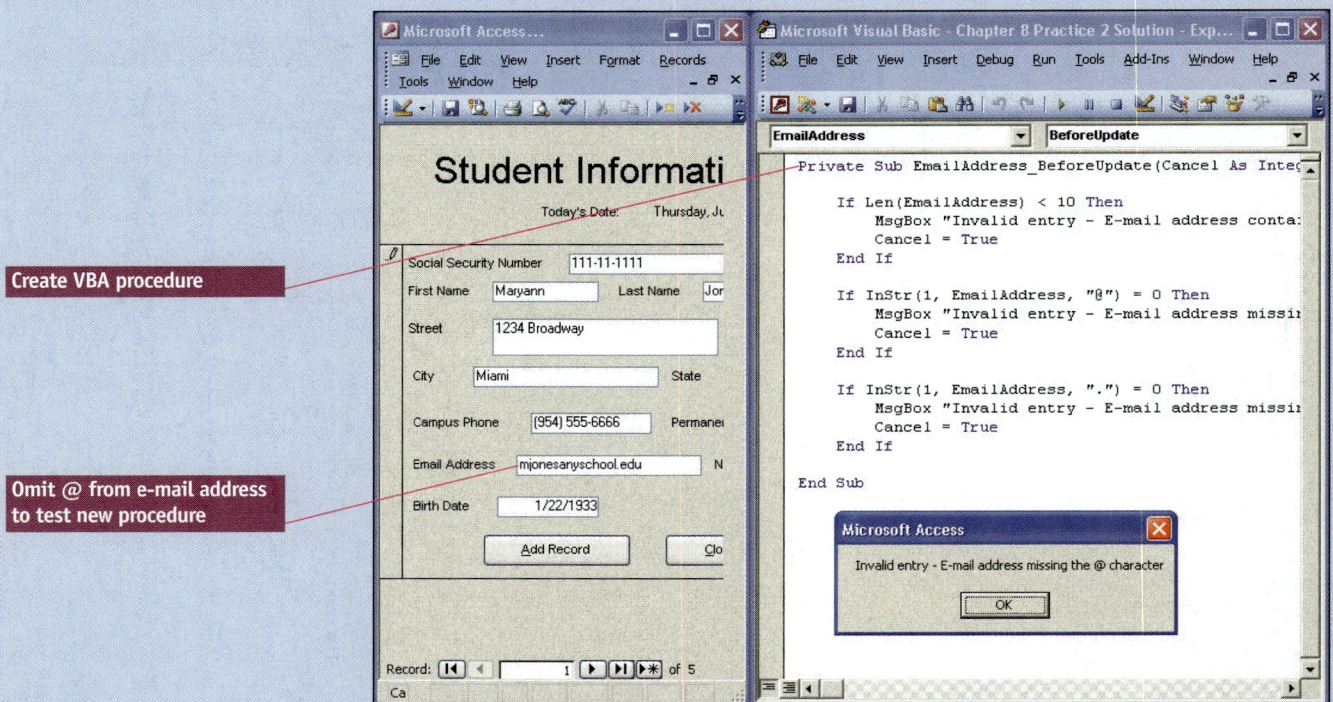

FIGURE 8.12 Expanded Student Form (exercise 2)

3. **Return to Soccer:** Figure 8.13 contains a modified version of the Players form for the *Any Sports League* database. The form does not appear very different from the original form in Chapter 7, but it has been enhanced with several underlying VBA procedures to facilitate data entry. Open your latest version of the *Sports Objects* database from Chapter 7 and proceed as follows:

a.   Add a combo box to the form to locate a player within the Players table. Create the necessary VBA procedure to update the contents of the combo box when the navigation buttons are used to move to a different record.

b.   Add a VBA statement to the On Click event procedure, which is associated with the Add Player button, to position the user in the First Name text box after clicking the Add button. (See the boxed tip at the end of step 8 in Hands-on Exercise 1 in the chapter for help.)

c.   Create a procedure for the BeforeUpdate event for the form that tests if the player's birth date was entered, warns the user if the birth date is omitted, and then gives the user the option to save the record anyway. Display a message in the same procedure that asks the user to try out for an all-city team if a player rating of A (upper- or lowercase) is entered.

d.   Create two shortcuts to simplify data entry. The Ctrl+1 shortcut should enter Miami, FL, and 33124 in the city, state, and zip code fields, respectively. Create a similar shortcut for Ctrl+2 to enter Coral Springs, FL, and 33071. Create a Shortcuts button that will display this information for the user. (Remember to set the Key Preview property to "Yes" so that the shortcuts are operational.)

e.   Print the completed Player's form and associated VBA module for your instructor.

f.   Modify the Coaches form so that it parallels the Players form with respect to the procedures in parts (a), (b), (c), and (d). You may find it convenient to copy procedures, such as those that create and display keyboard shortcuts, from one form to another, as opposed to reentering the code.

g.   Print the completed Coach's form and associated VBA module for your instructor. Do you see how VBA procedures can enhance an application?

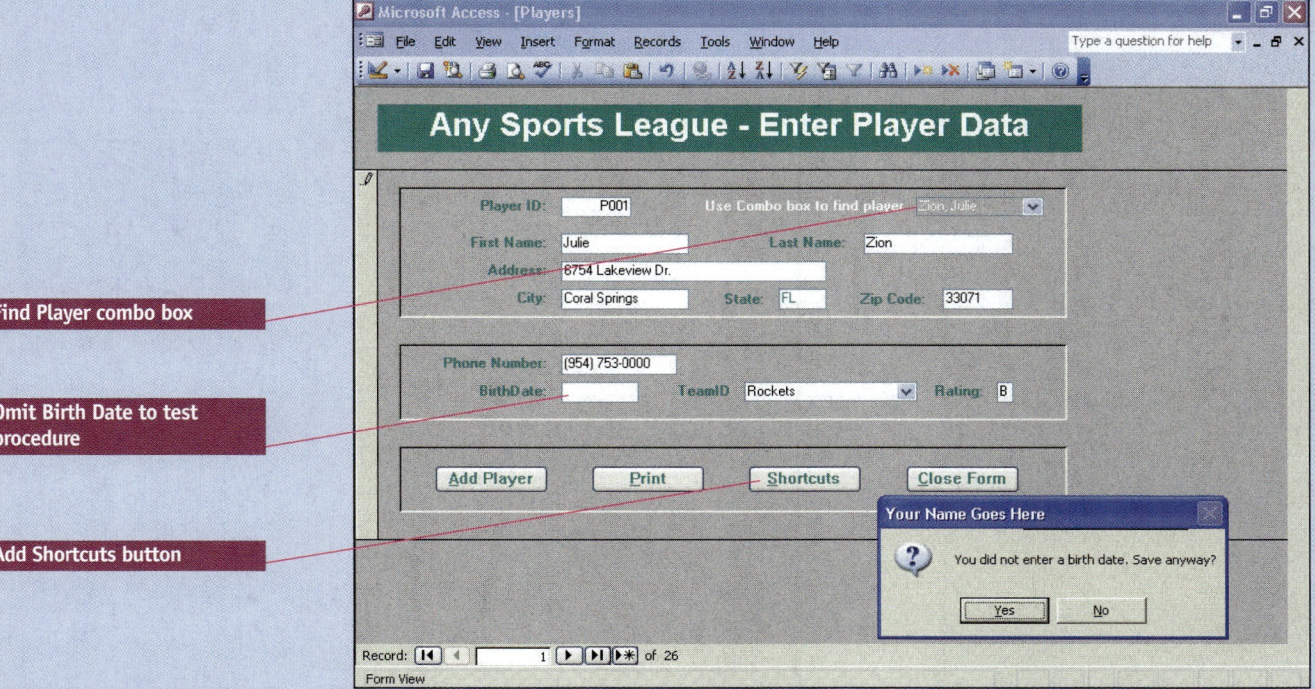

FIGURE 8.13   Return to Soccer (exercise 3)

4. **Enhancing a Report.** The screen in Figure 8.14 is divided in two so that you can view the VBA code and the associated report at the same time. The left portion of the screen displays the VBA editor whereas the right side shows the associated report. Look closely, and you will see that alternating lines in the report are displayed in gray, so that the names on the report are easier to read. This is accomplished by adding the appropriate code to the Print Detail event of the report. Open your latest version of the *Sports Object* database and proceed as follows:

a. Open the Master Coaching List report in Design view. (See *Chapter 7 Practice Exercise 3*). Right click the Detail section, click the Properties command, click the Event tab, and click the On Print event. Click the Build button, select Code Builder, then click OK to open the VBA editor and create the Detail Print event procedure shown in Figure 8.14. Note the following:

   i. VBA defines a series of intrinsic constants such as vbRed, vbWhite, and vbBlue, but additional colors must be defined by the user. This is accomplished most easily in a Const statement within the procedure as shown in Figure 8.14. Thus, conGray is associated with the indicated numeric value, which corresponds to a shade of gray.

   ii. The If statement in Figure 8.14 tests the background color of the current detail line. If the color is gray, then the color is changed to white. If the color is not gray, the Else clause sets it to gray. The effect of the statement is to print every other line in the report in gray.

   iii. Comments are added within the procedure to explain the code.

b. Click the save button to save the procedure. Print the completed procedure for your instructor. Close the VBA window.

c. Return to Access to preview the report, and then print the completed report for your instructor. Experiment with different colors and/or highlighting a different set of records; for example, you could highlight only those coaches who have not been assigned to a team.

d. Add a cover sheet to complete the assignment.

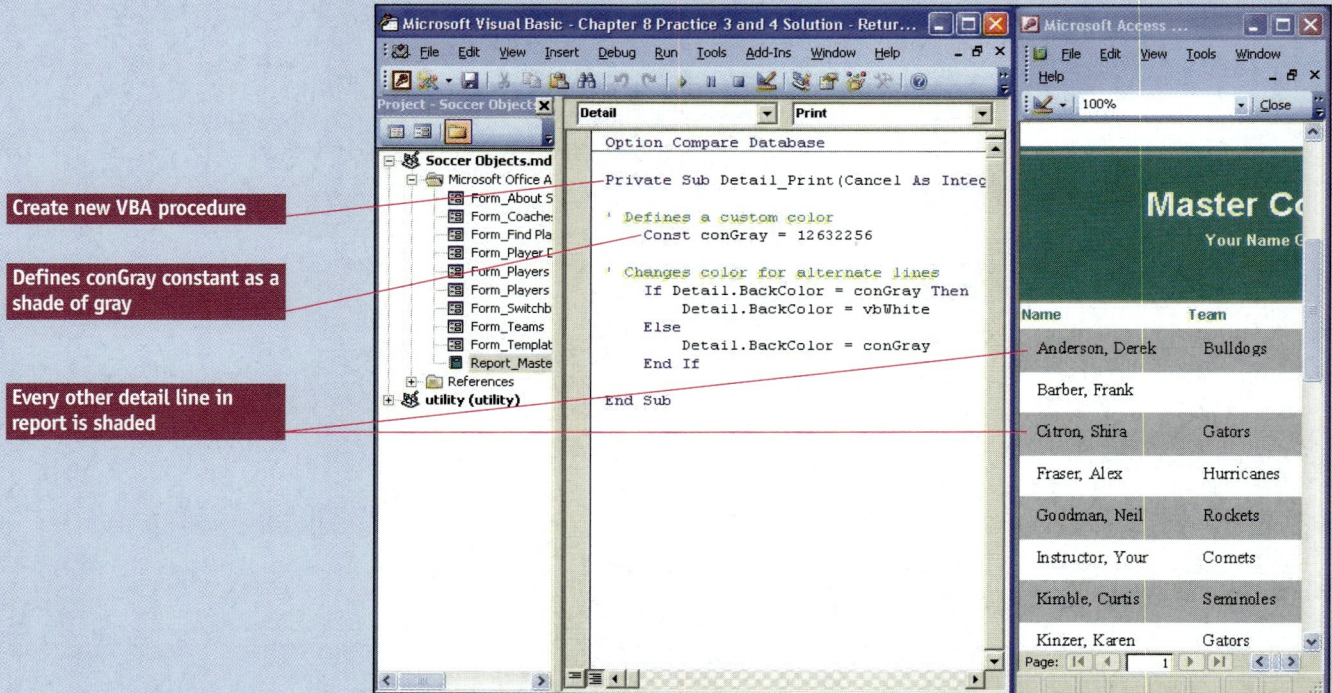

FIGURE 8.14 Enhancing a Report (exercise 4)

5. **Acme Computers:** The *Acme Computers* database in Figure 8.16 provides additional practice with forms and basic VBA procedures. The form itself is unremarkable and similar to virtually all of the forms that have been presented throughout the text. The differences are "under the hood" within the various VBA procedures that you will create in this exercise. Open the *Chapter 8 Practice 5* database in the Exploring Access folder and proceed as follows:

a. Change the properties of the Customers table so that the user must enter either a home or a business phone. (You have to set the required property at the record level rather than the field level.) Close the Customers table.

b. Open the Customers form in Design view. Use the Command Button Wizard to create a button to add a new customer. Add a VBA statement to the procedure to position the user in the FirstName field after clicking the button.

c. Create a BeforeUpdate event procedure that asks the user if the record should be saved if zip code is omitted.

d. Add a combo box to find a customer record. Be sure to change the On Current event so that the value shown in the Find Customer control matches the customer information currently displayed on the form.

e. Create a KeyDown procedure so that Ctrl+1 enters a credit rating of A and a credit limit of $10,000, Ctrl+2 enters a credit rating of B and a credit limit of $5,000, and Ctrl+3 enters a credit rating of C and a credit limit of $1,000. Create a command button to display the shortcuts for the user. Remember to set the KeyPreview property to "Yes" for the shortcuts to be operational.

f. Create a procedure to validate the e-mail address by checking for the presence of the @ sign and a period, and further that the length of the field is at least ten characters (see practice exercise 2).

g. Use the completed form to add a record for yourself as a customer, then print that form for your instructor. Print the VBA module as well.

h. Create a simple switchboard with three menu items—a button to display an About form, a button to display the Customers form, and a button to exit the database. Use the Startup property to display the switchboard automatically when the database is opened.

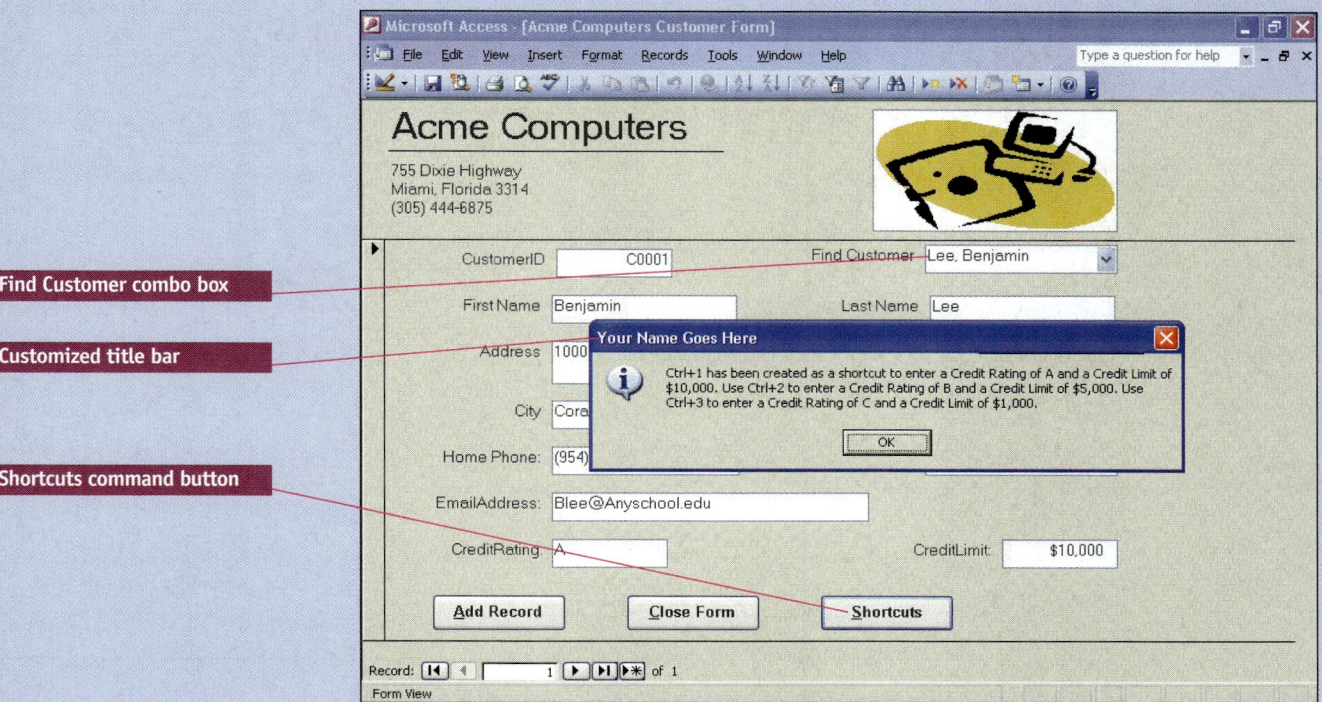

FIGURE 8.15 Acme Computers (exercise 5)

6. **The Documenter:** The IT department is apt to insist on written documentation for all of its systems. Access makes it possible to generate the documentation quickly and easily, but it comes at a price in that it can run hundreds of pages. This exercise gives you an opportunity to examine the process. Open the completed *Chapter 8 Practice 5—Acme Computers* database from the previous exercise and proceed as follows.

a. Pull down the Tools menu, click Analyze, then click Documenter to display the Documenter dialog box. Click the Tables tab and check the box for the Customers table. (Leave the other check box blank.) Click the Options button to display the Print Table Definition dialog box. The box to print Properties for the table should already be checked, and you will need to uncheck the other two check boxes. Click the option buttons to print Names, Data Types, Sizes, and Properties for the Fields, and nothing for the indexes. Click OK to close the Print Table Definition dialog box.

b. Click the Forms tab, check the Customers form (leave the other check boxes blank), then click Options to display the Print Form Definition dialog box. The check boxes to include the properties and code for the form should already be checked. Uncheck the box for Permissions by User and Group. Click the option to include nothing for the Sections and Controls. Click OK to close the Print Form Definition dialog box. Click OK a second time to generate the documentation.

c. The system is busy for a little while, after which it generates the report in Figure 8.16. Use the navigation buttons to skim through the report, which runs nine pages. The documentation for the table appears first, followed by the properties for the form, followed by the VBA code.

d. Click the down arrow on the Office Links button, and then select the option to publish the documentation with Microsoft Word. What advantage is gained by viewing the documentation in Word, as opposed to Access?

e. The documentation for this exercise ran 9 pages and included only partial documentation for one table and one form. The complete documentation for larger databases with multiple objects runs literally hundreds of pages. How useful do you think the documentation is? Summarize your thoughts in a brief note to your instructor.

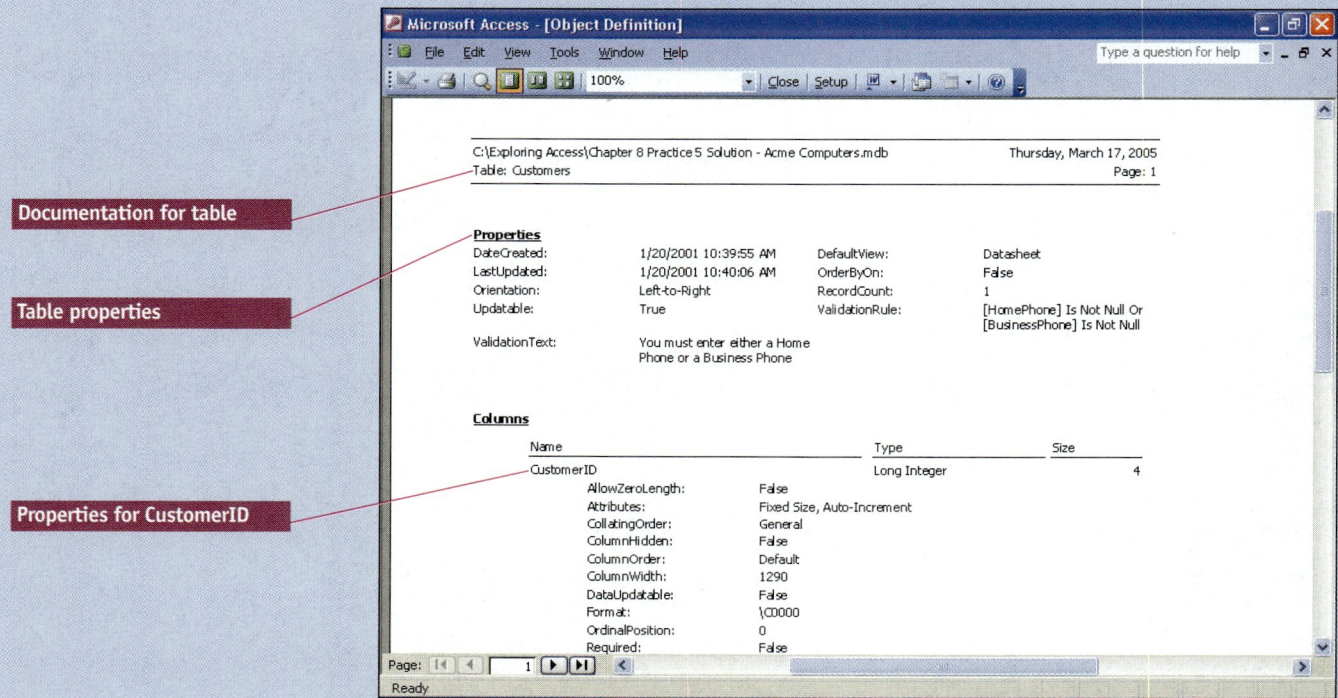

FIGURE 8.16 The Documenter (exercise 6)

7. **Take It on the Road:** Replication enables you to enter data into multiple copies of a database, and then synchronize those databases with one another. In this exercise you create the Design Master and two replicas, then in the next exercise you enter data and synchronize the changes. Proceed as follows:

a. Open the *Introduction to VBA* database that you have been working on throughout the chapter. Click the Tables button in the Database window, and then open the Students table. There should be five records in the table, but it doesn't matter if you have a different number. Close the table, but make sure it remains selected in the Database window.

b. Pull down the Tools menu, click Replication, then click Create Replica. Click Yes when told that the database must be closed in order to create a replica. Access prompts you with a second message suggesting that you create a backup copy before you create the Design Master. Click Yes.

c. The database closes and then the Location of New Replica dialog box appears. The Save in folder is the same folder that contained the original database (e.g., Exploring Access). The file name is already entered as *Replica of Introduction to VBA*. Click OK. The replica is created, the database closes, and then you are prompted to reopen the *Introduction to VBA* database.

d. Access indicates that it has converted the *Introduction to VBA* database to a Design master and that it has created a replica. Data can be entered into either database, but only the Design Master can accept changes to the database structure. Click OK.

e. You are back in the Database window, which has changed in two ways. The words "Design Master" appear next to the database name in the Database window title bar, and the icon next to the Students table indicates a replica has been created.

f. We will now create a second replica. Pull down the Tools menu, click Replication, and then click Create Replica. You see the Location of New Replica dialog box as before, but the file name has changed to *Replica1 of Introduction to VBA*. Click OK. The second replica is created, and you see the message in Figure 8.17. Click Yes.

g. The *Introduction to VBA* database closes, then reopens. Close the database so that you can enter data into the two replicas in our next exercise.

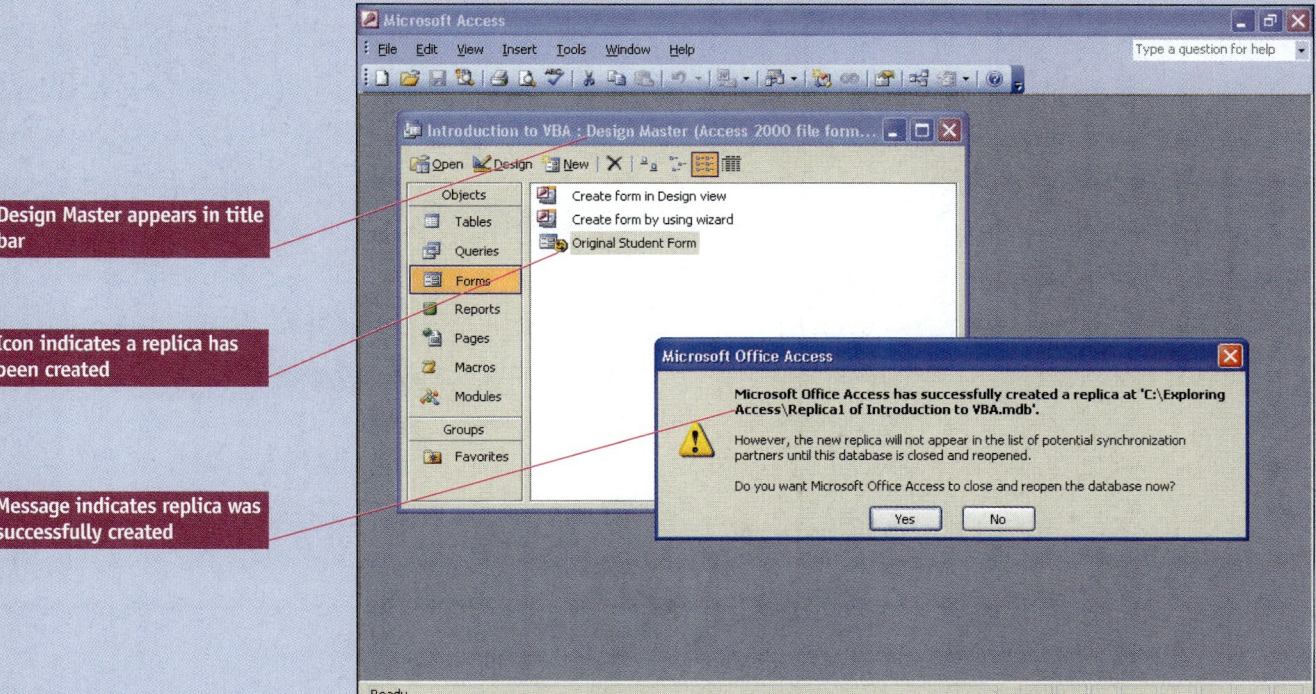

Design Master appears in title bar

Icon indicates a replica has been created

Message indicates replica was successfully created

FIGURE 8.17 Take It on the Road (exercise 7)

8. **Take It on the Road (continued):** This exercise continues the previous exercise by having you enter data into multiple copies (replicas) of a database, and then synchronize those changes. Open the *Replica of Introduction to VBA* database from the previous exercise and proceed as follows:

a. Click the Forms button and open the Completed Student form that was developed in the chapter. Click the Add Record button and enter data for a new student, Brian Street, with Social Security Number 987-65-4321. Close the form and then close the database.

b. Open the second replica, *Replica1 of Introduction to VBA* database. Click the Forms button, then use the Completed Student form to delete the record for Maryann Jones, Social Security Number 111-11-1111. Close the form and then close the database.

c. Open the *Introduction to VBA* database as shown in Figure 8.18. Pull down the Tools menu, click Replication, then click Synchronize Now to display the Synchronize Database dialog box. The first replica is selected. Click OK, then Click Yes when you see the message indicating that the database must be closed prior to synchronization. The database closes, after which you should see a message indicting that the synchronization was completed successfully. Click OK.

d. The database containing the Design Master should reopen automatically. Repeat the process to synchronize the database, but this time specify Replica1. Click Yes in response to the warning message, and once again you should see a message indicating that the synchronization was successful. Click OK and return to the Database window for the Design Master.

e. Click the Tables button and open the Students table. The record for Maryann Jones has been deleted and a new record appears for Brian Street. Print the table for your instructor (two pages are required because of the many fields in the table).

f. Use the Access Help facility to learn more about replication and resolving potential conflicts that may occur. Summarize your thoughts in a brief note to your instructor.

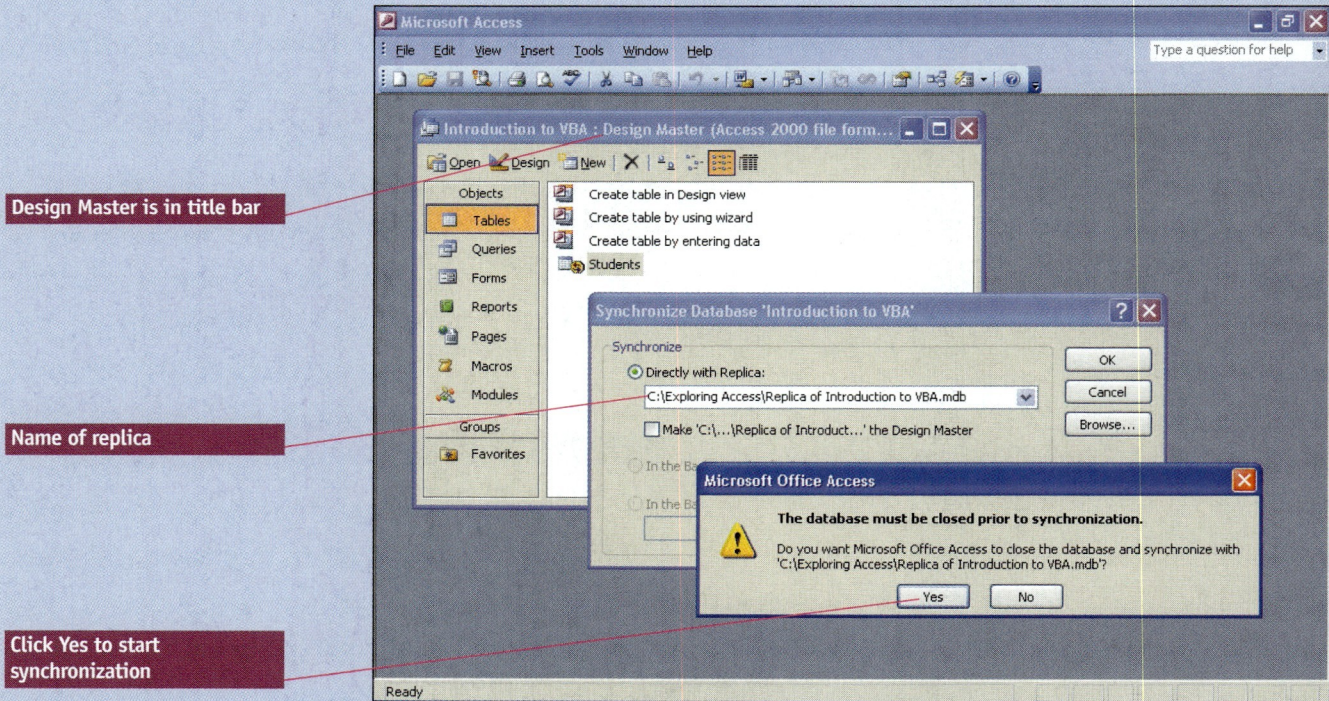

Design Master is in title bar

Name of replica

Click Yes to start synchronization

FIGURE 8.18   Take It on the Road (*continued*) (exercise 8)

Expanding Soccer

The Sports Objects (Soccer) database that was used throughout Chapter 7 contained three tables: a Teams table, a Players table, and a Coaches table. This exercise extends the database to include a Sponsors table that has been created for you in another database. Thus, your first task is to import the Sponsors table and associated form into the Sports Objects database that you have been working on. Open the *Sports Objects* database from Chapter 7. Close the switchboard and return to the Database window. Click the Tables button, pull down the File menu, click the Get External Data command, and then import the Sponsors table from the *Chapter 8 Mini Case—Expanding Soccer* database. Import the Sponsors form from the same database.

For the sake of simplicity, we will import the other tables, as opposed to maintaining the external links. Thus, delete the existing links to the Players, Teams, and Coaches tables, and then import these tables into the database. Your next task is to modify the existing tables to accommodate the one-to-many relationship that exists between sponsors and teams. One sponsor can support many teams, but a specific team has only one sponsor. Open the Teams table in Design view, add the SponsorID as a foreign key, and set the Format property to \S00. Go to Datasheet view and assign sponsor number 1 to teams 1, 3, and 5. Assign sponsor number 2 to teams 2, 4, and 6.

Pull down the Tools menu, click the Relationships command, then modify the Relationships window to include the one-to-many relationship between sponsors and teams. Delete the existing Relationships report, then create a new report that includes the Sponsors table. Modify the Team form to contain the name of the team's sponsor and the associated contact person and phone number. The user should be able to select the sponsor from a drop-down list box; the name of the contact person and the phone number will appear automatically. Modify the main switchboard to include an option to display the Sponsors form. Print the new and/or modified objects for your instructor as proof that you completed this exercise. Do you see how a well-designed database is easily expanded to accommodate an additional table?

The VBA Primer

VBA is a powerful programming language that can be accessed from any application within Microsoft Office. Each application uses the same basic statements such as MsgBox or If/Else to create procedures that are executed from within the application. It helps, therefore, to examine basic VBA statements in depth, which is the purpose of the VBA primer at the end of this text. This is an appropriate time for you to study the primer and to complete the first three hands-on exercises. Use Access as the Office application to host the resulting VBA procedures. Print the completed module for your instructor. How would the exercises differ if you used Excel as the application?

Debugging

The Debug toolbar contains several tools to help you debug a procedure if it does not work as intended. The Step Into command is especially useful as it executes the procedure one statement at a time. Choose any of the procedures you created in this chapter, then investigate the procedure in detail using the Debug toolbar. Summarize your results in a short note to your instructor.

Help for VBA

Review the hands-on exercises in the chapter to review the various ways to obtain help in VBA. In addition, you can click on any Visual Basic key word, then press the F1 key to display a context-sensitive help screen. Summarize this information in a short note to your instructor. It will be an invaluable reference as you continue to explore VBA in Access as well as other applications in Microsoft Office.

Chapter Recap—Back to Natalie's

You have been working at Natalie's Cuppa Joe, the locally famous coffee shop, for almost two years. It has been a rewarding experience, and business has grown steadily during your employment. With so many new customers the data entry has become quite time-consuming, and Natalie has asked you to improve the database. She is leaving the specific changes to your discretion, but Natalie would like you to focus on facilitating data entry. She would also like the reports in the database to be easier to read, and suggests that you shade the alternate lines in the "Cuppa Card" report that is generated daily.

You have become quite proficient in Access, but you will need to take it to the next level and develop VBA code to make the necessary improvements to the database. Thankfully, you are enrolled in a more advanced computer applications course and will soon have the skill required to comply with Natalie's request. This ability will increase your value as an employee and it may even help you earn a promotion!

Your assignment is to review the chapter, paying special attention to the many ways to enhance a database through VBA. You will then open *Chapter 8 Ending Case Study—Back to Natalie's* Access database and add procedures to the existing Customers form, basing your enhancements on the code that was developed in the chapter. Start by modifying the existing Add Record procedure to move directly to the appropriate field on the form, as opposed to having the user click in the text box. You should also include a Find Record combo box to the form to locate a specific customer, as well as shortcuts to enter the city, state, and zip code with a single keystroke combination. And finally, be sure to display a message that reminds the user to back up the system upon closing the database.

Design and Implementation:
A Capstone Chapter

CASE STUDY
THE SD COFFEE COMPANY

Sarah Davis is a good businesswoman who knows how to seize an opportunity when it presents itself. It was only last year that Sarah was working in a large office building when she noticed that her coworkers were continually complaining that there was no more coffee. Or, if there was coffee, there was no sugar, the creamer was gone, there were no cups, and so on. And rarely was there the promised muffin or bagel to go along with the coffee.

Investigating further, Sarah discovered that money was not the problem because her employer was more than happy to supply coffee (and the associated caffeine kick) to his workers. The difficulty was with the department secretary, who did not drink coffee, but who was responsible for purchasing the coffee and associated items from the local supermarket. Unfortunately, she had no incentive other than the goodwill of her coworkers to ensure an adequate supply.

Sarah approached the secretary and asked if she would contract with a company that made deliveries. The secretary could not say "yes" quickly enough and thus the SD Coffee Company was born. The service was an instant success as ten other companies signed on within the first month. Sarah began with a manual ordering and reporting system but is intent on converting to an Access database. You have been hired as a consultant to design and implement the project. ■

Your assignment is to read the chapter and complete the associated hands-on exercises to create the SD Coffee application. You will be asked to follow the suggested milestones in the *Chapter 9 SD Coffee Project Milestones* document, which is found in the Exploring Access folder. Your first task is to open the document and meet with the client (your instructor) to agree on an implementation schedule. It is a complex project and thus you will be working with Bob and Maryann, who will supply some of the objects for you.

The chapter focuses on the development cycle that takes you from the initial concept to the finished application. You will begin by "meeting" with the client (your instructor) to determine the *information requirements*, and then you will design and implement an Access database to satisfy those requirements. This project will require you to utilize everything you have learned thus far, and indeed, much of the detailed material has been presented earlier. The review is beneficial, however; it will reinforce what you already know and it will help you put it all together.

The workload is greater than in previous chapters, and thus you will work in a team environment, which is what you would encounter in the "real world." The team approach enables you to "divide and conquer" and build a sophisticated application that would not be possible if you were working by yourself. Bob and Maryann (the authors of your text) are the other team members, and they will supply various database objects as you work your way through the hands-on exercises.

One last point before we get started is that the success of any application depends on continued communication between the developer and the client. Accordingly, you will "meet" periodically with the client throughout the chapter in accordance with a well-defined set of milestones to measure your progress. Each milestone is associated with a deliverable item, be it a PowerPoint presentation to present your technical design, Version 1.0 of the database to present the visual design, or subsequent versions of the database that reflect the actual forms and reports. Let's begin.

From Output to Input

Every project starts with a "wish list" in which the client describes the information (the output) that he/she wants to obtain from the system. The task of the developer is to ensure that the available data (the input) is sufficient to produce the desired output. In other words, it is the output that drives the input. The client has given you a partial set of reporting requirements, which includes the report in Figure 9.1a. In essence, the database is to provide detailed reporting for every aspect of the sales operation—the total sales of the company for a given period, the total sales for each sales person or each product, the total purchased by each customer, and so on. The database should also create additional reports for the Human Resources Department: the number of men and women that work in the company, the average salary and experience by gender, the average salary increase, and so on.

The client also gives you the paper order form in Figure 9.1b, which is essential to the operation of the company. You can see at a glance that the form displays information about the different entities in the physical system (orders, customers, products, and sales representatives), and indeed, you may already be thinking ahead to the database design, which will require a separate table for each of these objects. Initially, however, you should study the form to see what data is presently collected and whether it is sufficient to produce the requested information. You also need to determine how the various fields in the form relate to one another.

There is, for example, a space on the order form to enter the name of the sales representative who took the order. Does this mean that the same customer always uses the same sales representative? (The answer in this case is yes.) The question may not seem important, but the answer influences the design of the database. You learn that the SD Coffee Company is a wholesale operation in which each sales representative has an exclusive territory. Thus, there is a one-to-many relationship between sales representatives and customers; one sales representative has many customers, but a given customer has only one sales representative.

In any event, you conclude that the order form is very comprehensive and that it contains the necessary data to create many of the requested sales reports. The various employee reports however, require data that is not contained in the order form, but which is most likely present somewhere within the company.

SD Coffee Order Summary
www.SDCoffee.com
(305) 555-5555

Order ID	Date	Customer	Payment Type	Sales Rep	Amount
O0001	1/3/2005	Abel & Young	Check	Barber	$41.50
O0002	1/3/2005	Department of CIS	Cash	Grauer	$168.00
O0003	1/5/2005	Advantage Sales	Check	Barber	$200.50
O0004	1/6/2005	Kinzer & Sons	Credit Card	Barber	$104.88
O0005	1/6/2005	Milgrom Associates	Purchase Order	Grauer	$72.00
O0006	1/6/2005	Abel & Young	Check	Barber	$125.50
O0007	1/7/2005	Advantage Sales	Purchase Order	Barber	$219.00
O0008	1/10/2005	Lugo Computer Sales	Credit Card	Barber	$76.00
O0009	1/10/2005	Bethune Appliance Sales	Check	Barber	$51.63
O0010	1/11/2005	Baker Auto Supply	Purchase Order	Grauer	$114.00
O0011	1/11/2005	Department of CIS	Check	Grauer	$50.13
O0012	1/13/2005	Howard Animal Hospital	Check	Grauer	$92.00
O0013	1/13/2005	Katie's Casual Wear	Check	Barber	$109.75
O0014	1/14/2005	Bethune Appliance Sales	Cash	Barber	$152.50
O0015	1/14/2005	Little, Joiner, & Jones	Purchase Order	Grauer	$130.50

(a) Partial Order Summary

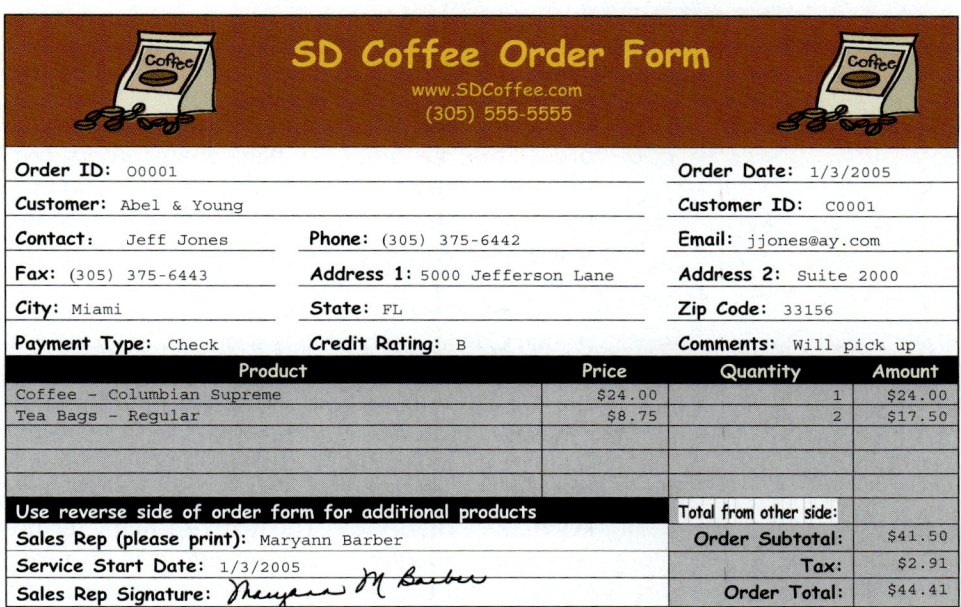

(b) Order Form

FIGURE 9.1   From Output to Input

Database Design

Access is a means to an end; that is, you cannot create a database successfully unless the underlying design is correct. You begin therefore with pencil and paper, away from the computer, to arrive at a design in ***third normal form***, as described in Appendix A. Simply stated, the value of every field in every table must be dependent on the primary key of that table, the entire primary key, and nothing but the primary key. You can create a good design by following the guidelines below:

1. Identify the entities (objects) that exist in the physical system, each of which requires its own table. Create a separate table for each object.

2. Identify and implement the relationships that exist in the physical system. A one-to-many relationship is implemented by including the primary key of the "one" table as a foreign key in the "many" table. A many-to-many relationship requires an additional table where the primary key contains (at least) the primary keys of the individual entities.

3. Complete each table in the database by defining the additional fields that are necessary to produce the information that is required of the database.

4. Study the completed design to ensure that the value of every field in every table is dependent on the primary key of that table, the entire primary key, and nothing but the primary key.

5. Ask "questions" of the finished database to determine the completeness of the design; that is, if you cannot answer a specific question, you will have to add fields to one or more tables and repeat some (all) of the previous steps.

The SD Coffee Database is concerned with customers, products, orders, and sales representatives, each of which requires its own table in the database. There is a one-to-many relationship between sales representatives and customers as explained earlier. There is also a one-to-many relationship between customers and orders; one customer can place many orders, but a given order is associated with only one customer. And finally there is a many-to-many relationship between orders and products; one order can contain many products, and one product can appear in many orders. This gives rise to an Order Details table that contains the OrderID, ProductID, and associated quantity.

These observations take us almost immediately to the design in Figure 9.2a. The primary key of each table is shown in bold; for example, SalesRepID is the primary key in the Sales Reps table. The Order Details table has a composite key consisting of the OrderID and the ProductID. The one-to-many relationship between sales representatives and customers is implemented by including the primary key of the one table (the SalesRepID) as a foreign key in the many (Customers) table. In similar fashion, the primary key of the Customers table (CustomerID) appears as a foreign key in the Orders table. The many-to-many relationship between orders and products is implemented as a pair of one-to-many relationships; between the Orders and Order Details tables, and between the Products and Order Details tables.

Your first attempt at the design should include only the tables and the indicated relationships, defining the primary key in each table and including foreign keys as appropriate. You then expand each table to include the additional fields that are needed to satisfy the information requirements. At that point, it is convenient to create a simple Access database in order to develop the relationships diagram. You can then present your design to your team and/or to the client in the form of a ***PowerPoint presentation*** as shown in Figure 9.2b.

The design of the database is the most important step in the entire development cycle, and any mistakes in the design will come back to haunt you later on. It is important therefore to put your ego aside and to show your work to your colleagues to find any mistakes that may exist. There is no stigma to having your work reviewed, and indeed, every member of the team is expected to do so.

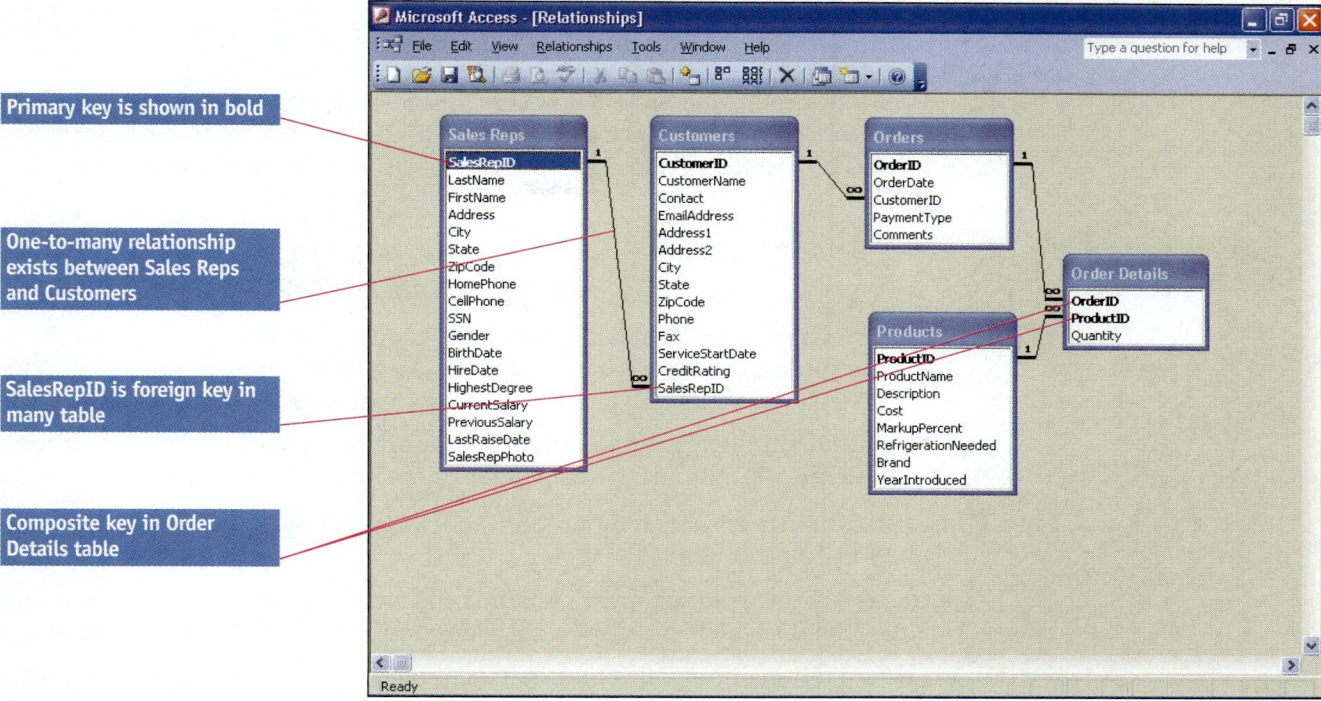

(a) The Relationships Diagram

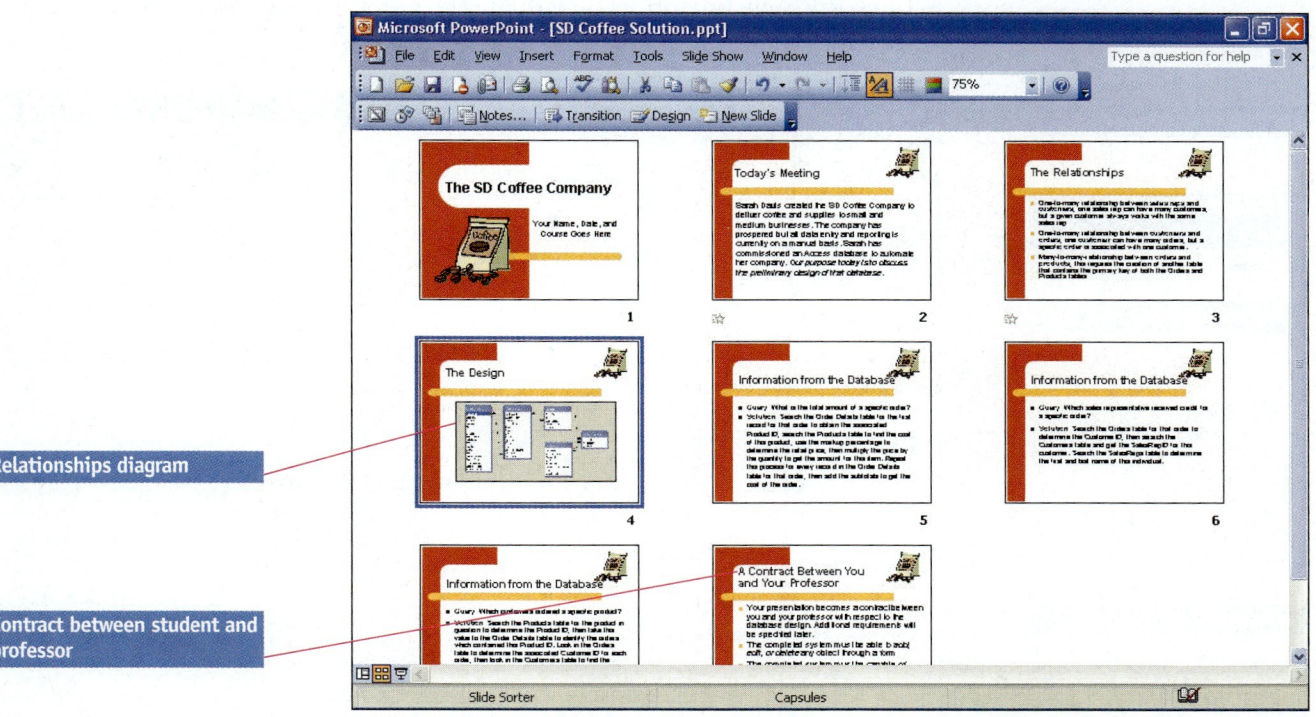

(b) PowerPoint Presentation

FIGURE 9.2 Database Design

1 Database Design

Objective Create the initial design for the SD Coffee database, define the required tables, and create a relationships diagram. Present the completed design in a PowerPoint presentation. Use Figure 9.3 as a guide in the exercise.

Step 1: **Create the Sales Reps Table**

- Start Access. Create a new database, **SD Coffee** in the **Exploring Access folder**.

- Click the **Tables button** in the Database window. Double click the option to **Create table in Design view**. Maximize the window so that you have more room to work.

- Enter **SalesRepID** as the first field (do not leave spaces in the field name). Choose **AutoNumber** as the data type.

- Click the **Primary Key icon** on the Table Design toolbar to establish the primary key for this table.

- Click in the **Format property text box** toward the bottom of the screen and enter **\S0000**, which will display the SalesRepID as S0001, S0002, and so on.

- Enter the remaining fields and indicated field types as shown in Figure 9.3a. Do not be concerned about the other field properties at this time.

- Enter **SalesRepPhoto** as the last field (it is not visible in Figure 9.3a). Choose **OLE object** as the data type.

- Click the **Save button** to save the table, enter **Sales Reps** as the table name, then click **OK**. Close the window.

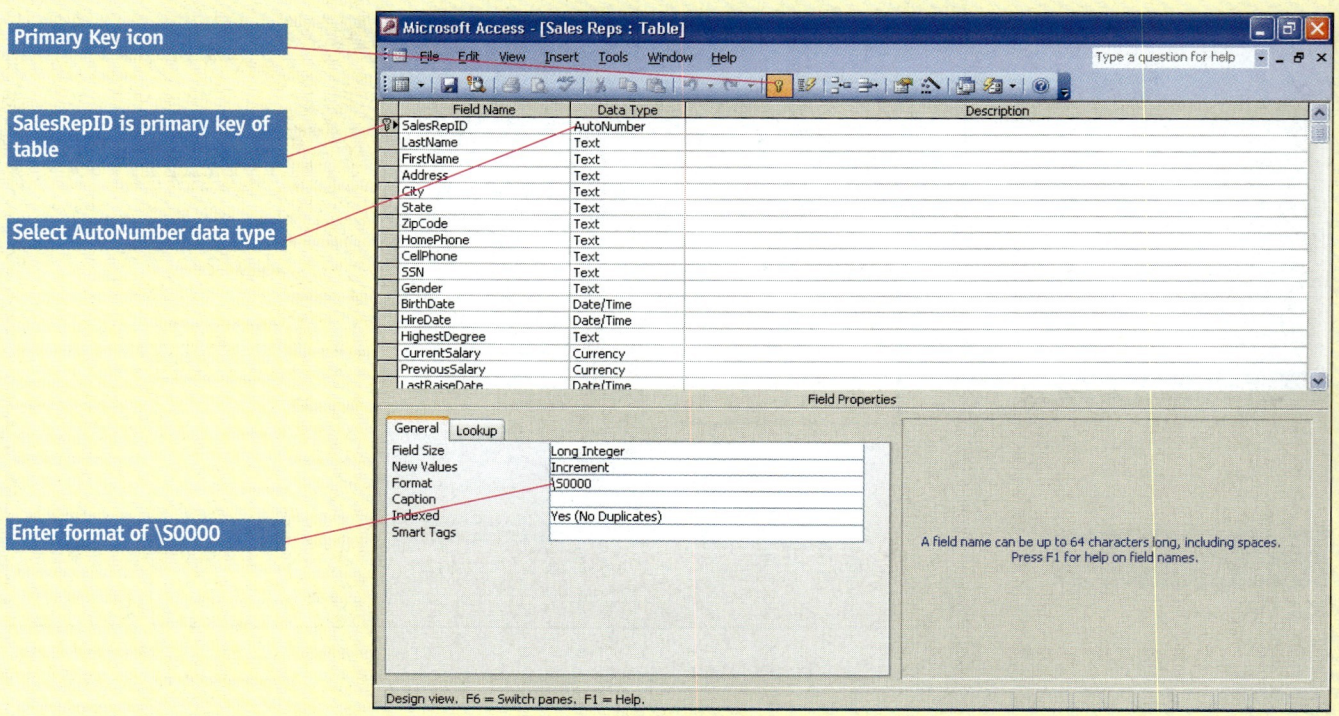

(a) Create the Sales Reps Table (step 1)

FIGURE 9.3 Hands-on Exercise 1

Step 2: **Divide and Conquer**

- The Database window should be visible on your screen with the Tables button selected. Pull down the **File menu**, click **Get External Data**, then click the **Import command**.

- Select the **SD Coffee by Maryann database** in the **Exploring Access folder**. Click the **Import button** to display the Import Objects dialog box as shown in Figure 9.3b.

- Click the **Tables button**. Click the **Select All button**, then click **OK**. The Customers, Order Details, Orders, and Products tables are imported and appear in the Database window.

- Open the various tables in Datasheet view and note that none of the tables contains data at this time; that is, you do not need data in order to create the relationships.

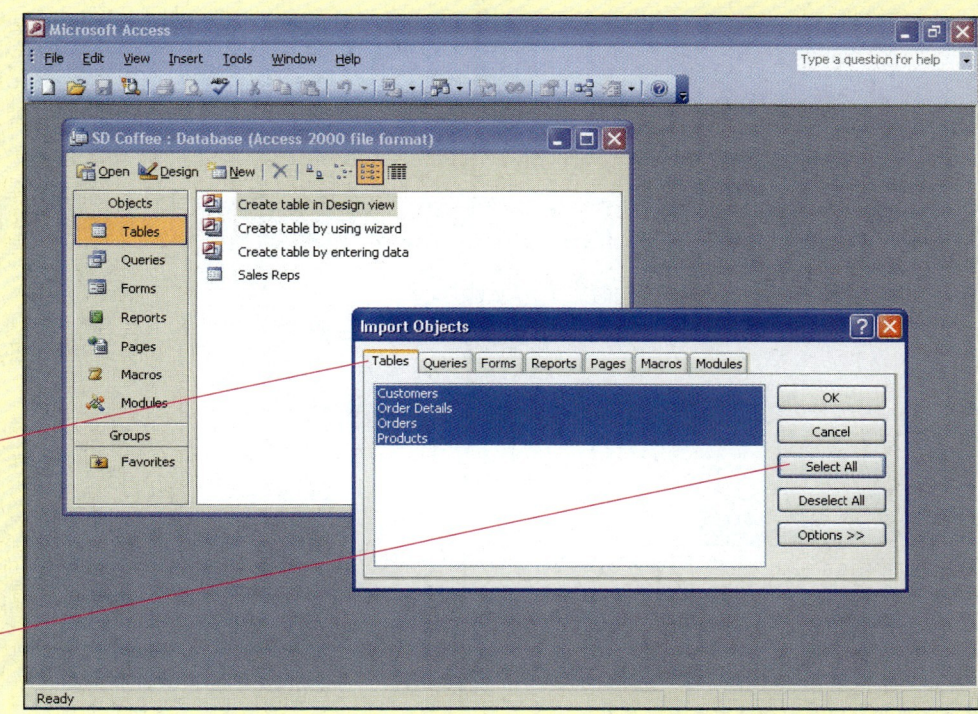

Click Tables button

Click Select All button

(b) Divide and Conquer (step 2)

FIGURE 9.3 Hands-on Exercise 1 (*continued*)

WORKING IN A GROUP

Eventually, you will find yourself in a group environment, either in the workplace or in a group project at school, where you will encounter four people named Everybody, Somebody, Anybody, and Nobody. There was an important job to be done and Everybody was sure that Somebody would do it. Anybody could have done it, but Nobody did it. Somebody got angry because it was Everybody's job. Everybody thought Anybody could do it, but Nobody realized that Everybody wouldn't do it. It ended up that Everybody blamed Somebody when Nobody did what Anybody could have. Don't let this happen to you.

Step 3: **Create the Relationships**

- Pull down the **Tools menu** and click the **Relationships command** to open the Relationships window.

- Pull down the **Relationships menu** and click the **Show Table command** to display the Show Table dialog box. Double click each table to display the table in the Relationships window. Close the dialog box.

- Maximize the Relationships window, then arrange the tables as shown in Figure 9.3c. Click and drag the bottom and/or right border of each table so that you see all of the fields in each table.

- Click and drag the **OrderID field** from the Orders table to the Order Details table, then release the mouse to display the Relationships dialog box.

- Check the box to **Enforce Referential Integrity**. Check the boxes to **Cascade Deleted Records** and **Cascade Update Related Fields**. Click the **Create button**.

- Create the remaining one-to-many relationships (between the Sales Reps and Customers tables, between the Customers and Orders tables, and between the Products and Order Details tables). Be sure to enforce referential integrity in each relationship, but do not check the boxes to Cascade Update Related Fields or Cascade Delete Related Records. Click the **Save button**.

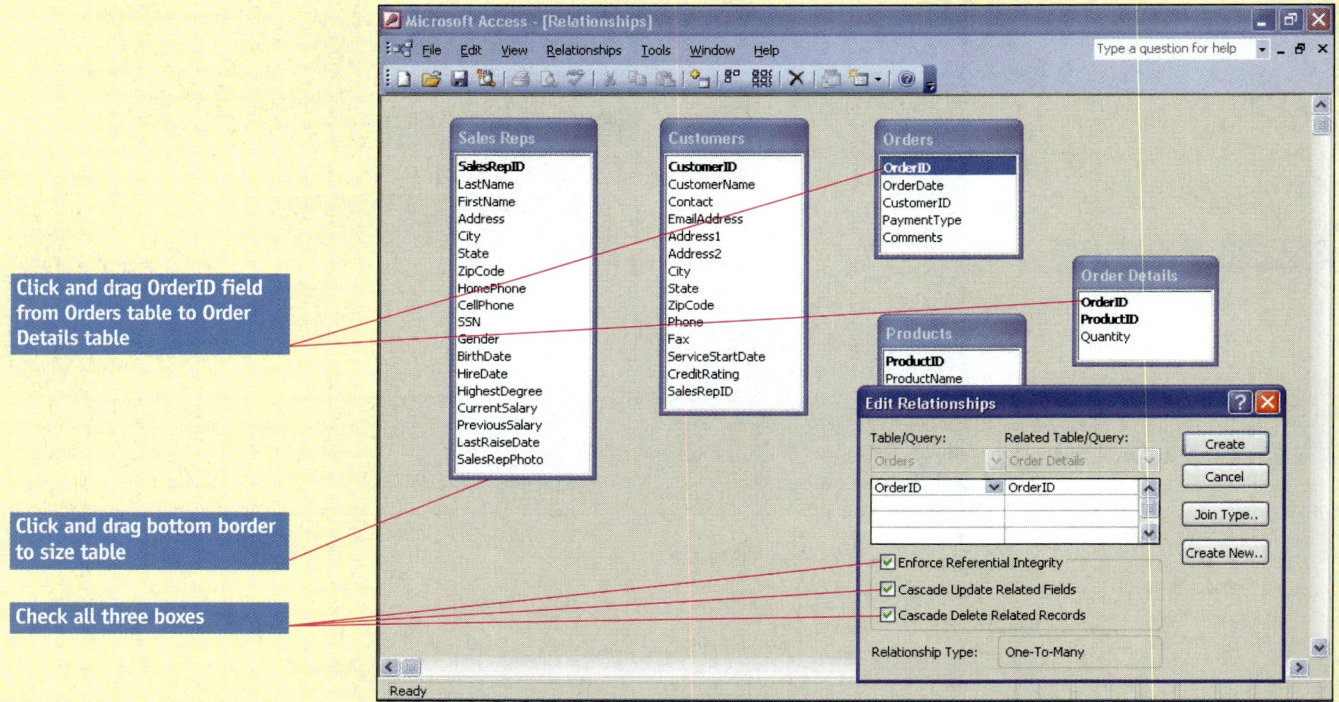

Click and drag OrderID field from Orders table to Order Details table

Click and drag bottom border to size table

Check all three boxes

(c) Create the Relationships (step 3)

FIGURE 9.3 Hands-on Exercise 1 (*continued*)

CASCADE DELETED RECORDS

The enforcement of referential integrity prevents the deletion of a record in the Orders table if there is a corresponding record in the Order Details table; that is, to delete an order, you first have to delete all of the associated order details. This restriction can be relaxed if you modify the relationship to Cascade Deleted Records, in which case the Order Details are deleted automatically with the order.

Step 4: Print the Relationships

- Pull down the **File menu** and click the **Print Relationships command**. You will see the Print Preview screen of a report. Maximize the window.

- Click the **View button** to change to the Design view. Increase the size of the Page Header as shown in Figure 9.3d.

- The width of the report should not extend beyond 7.5 inches, or else it will not fit on one page in portrait mode. (If it does, close this report without saving it, return to the Relationships window, move the tables closer to one another, and then repeat the Print Relationships command.)

- Change the text of the title, increase the size of the font, and then center the title in the report. Move the date under the title.

- Click the **Label tool**, then click and drag to create an unbound control that contains your name.

- Pull down the **File menu**, click the **Page Setup command**, click the **Margins tab,** then change the left and right margins to **.5 inch** each.

- Click the **Save button** to display the Save As dialog box. Change the name of the report to **Relationships Diagram**, then click **OK**. Close the Report window.

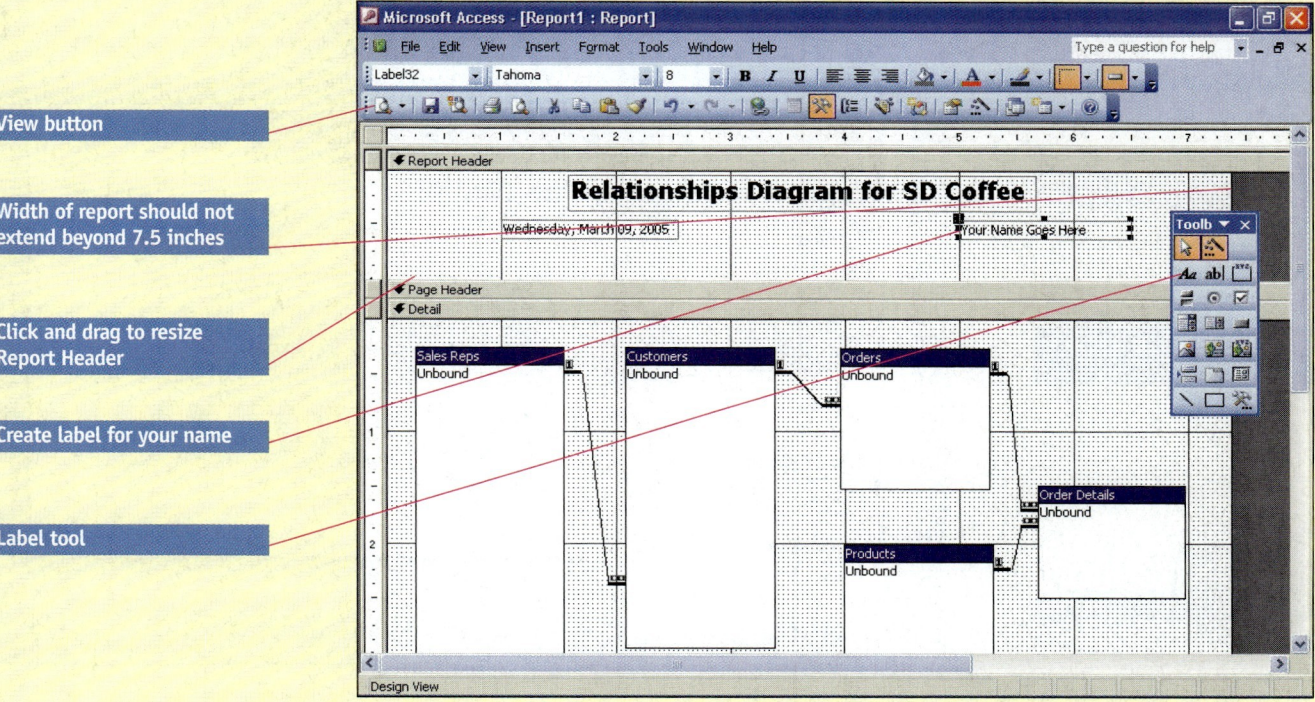

(d) Print the Relationships (step 4)

FIGURE 9.3 Hands-on Exercise 1 (*continued*)

DISPLAY THE CURRENT DATE

A report typically displays one of two dates—the date it was created or the current date. We prefer the latter, which is obtained through the Now() function. Click in the Report header and delete the control containing today's (fixed) date. Click the Text Box tool, click and drag where you want the date to appear, then release the mouse. Click in the text box and enter the function =Now(). Save the report. The next time you open the report, it will display the current date.

Step 5: **Start PowerPoint**

- Start PowerPoint. Open the **SD Coffee presentation** in the **Exploring Access folder**. Save the presentation as **SD Coffee Solution** so that you can retrieve the original presentation if necessary.

- Select the fourth slide, which will contain the Relationships diagram. Click the **Access button** on the Windows taskbar to return to the Relationships window in the SD Coffee database. Press the **Print Screen key** to capture the screen to the Windows clipboard.

- Click the **PowerPoint button** on the Windows taskbar to return to the presentation. Click anywhere on the slide, then press **Ctrl+V** (or click the **Paste button**) to paste the contents of the clipboard (the Relationships window) onto the current slide. Select the picture.

- The Picture toolbar should be displayed automatically. (If not, pull down the **View menu**, click **Toolbars**, and then check the **Picture toolbar**.)

- Click the **Crop tool** on the Picture toolbar, then click and drag a corner or side handle inward to crop the Relationships diagram as shown in Figure 9.3e. Move and size the finished figure. Save the presentation.

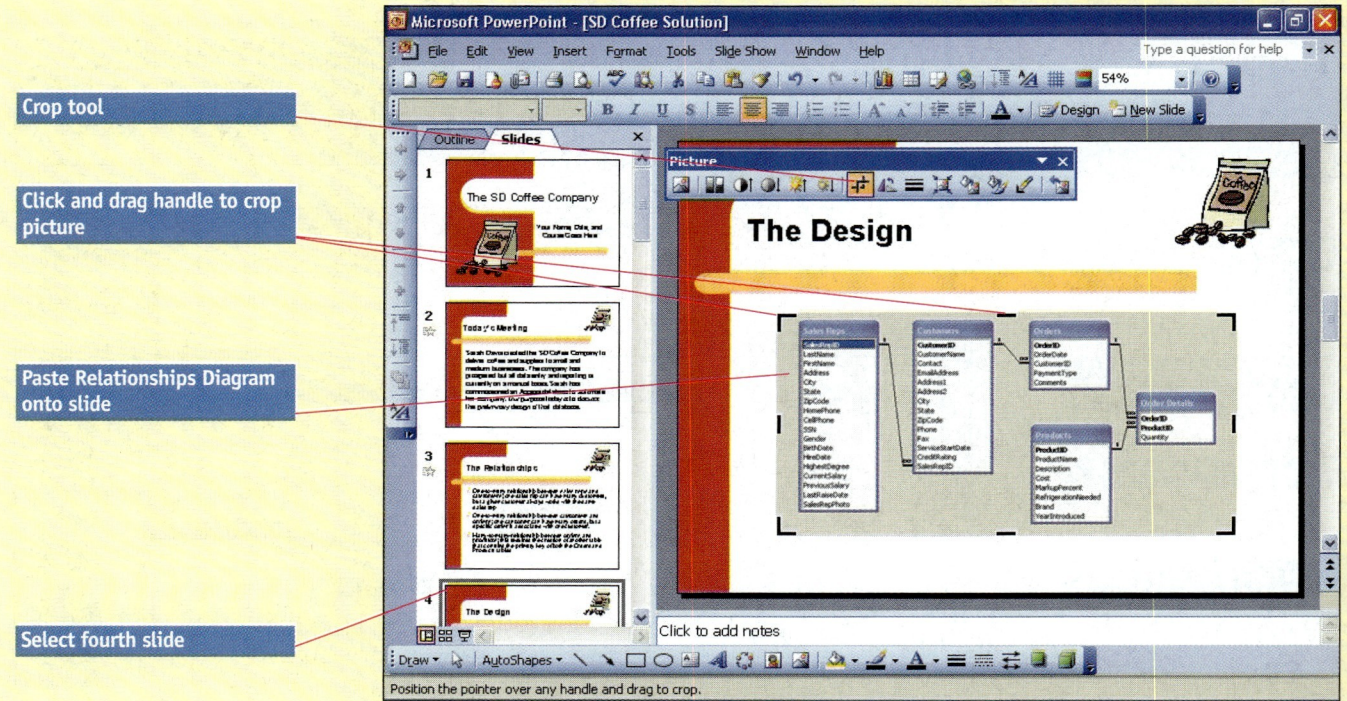

(e) Start PowerPoint (step 5)

FIGURE 9.3 Hands-on Exercise 1 (*continued*)

ALT+TAB STILL WORKS

The taskbar is one way to switch between open applications, but you can also use the Alt+Tab keyboard shortcut that was introduced in the initial release of Windows. Press and hold the Alt key while you press and release the Tab key repeatedly to cycle through the open applications, whose icons are displayed in a small rectangular window in the middle of the screen. Release the Alt key when you have selected the icon for the application you want.

Step 6: Complete the Presentation

- Select the fifth slide, which contains the query, "What is the total amount of a specific order?" Look at the Relationships diagram, and then enter the verbal description shown in Figure 9.3f.

- Select the sixth slide, which contains the query, "Which sales representative received credit for a specific order?" Enter an appropriate answer that describes how to retrieve the information from the database. Complete the third query on slide seven in similar fashion.

- Press **Ctrl+Home** to move to the first slide. Pull down the **View menu** and click **Slide Show** to start the presentation. Press the **PgDn key** to move from one bullet to the next on a given slide, then to move from one slide to the next.

- Rehearse the presentation as though you were delivering it in front of your class. Press **Esc** when you come to the black screen at the end of the show.

- Pull down the **File menu** and click the **Print command**. Click the **down arrow** in the Print What list box, select **Handouts**, and then specify **2 slides per page**. Check the box to **Frame slides**, then click **OK** to print the presentation.

- Save the presentation. Exit PowerPoint. Exit Access.

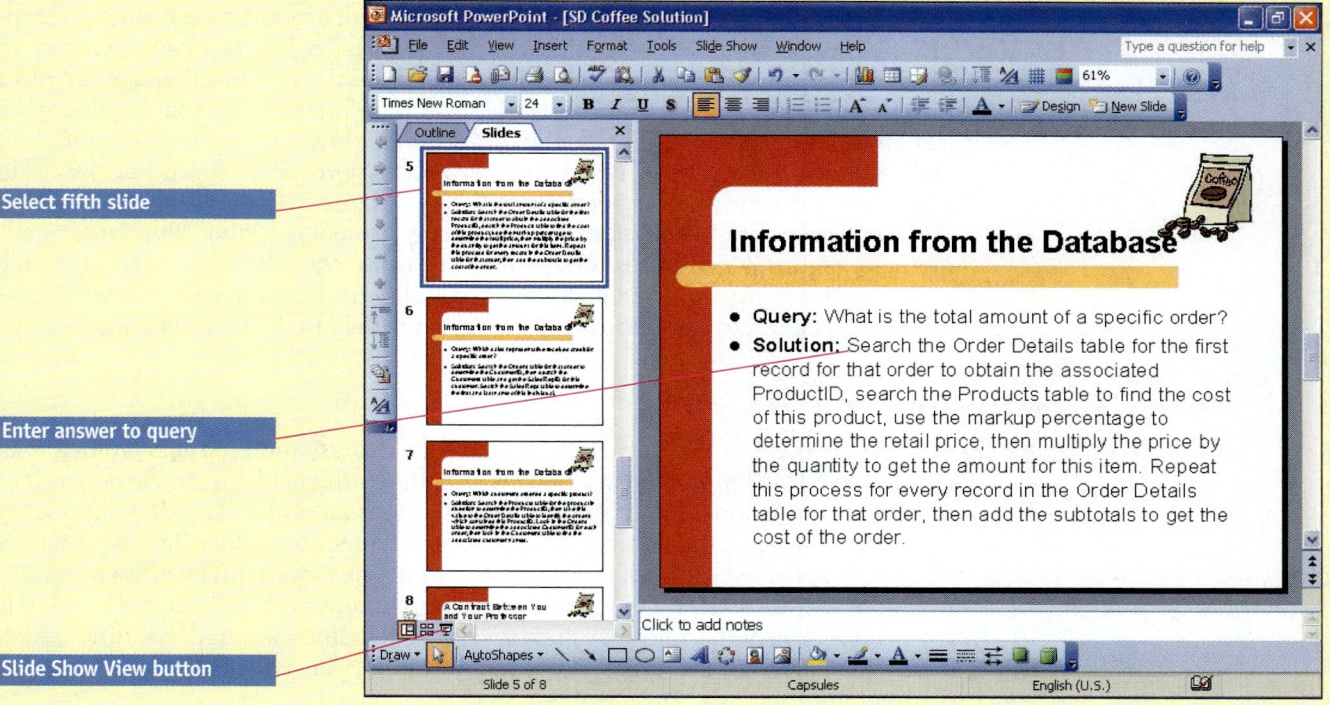

(f) Complete the Presentation (step 6)

FIGURE 9.3 Hands-on Exercise 1 (*continued*)

ANNOTATE A SLIDE

Press Ctrl+P to change the mouse pointer to a point, then click and drag on the slide during a presentation to annotate the slide. Use the PgDn and PgUp keys to move forward and back in the presentation when annotation is in effect. The annotations will disappear when you exit the slide show unless you elect to keep them permanently when prompted at the end of the show. Press Ctrl+A to change the mouse pointer back to an arrow if you tire of the annotations.

The design process is an iterative process in which you present the initial relationships diagram, have it reviewed by the other members of your design team, implement the necessary changes, and then resubmit the design until it is deemed to be correct. You are then ready for the ***detailed design*** where you define the properties for every field in every table.

The field type is perhaps the most important property since it automatically determines the settings of certain other properties. The numeric field type should be restricted to fields on which you perform calculations, such as salary. Accordingly, fields such as Social Security Number, zip code, and telephone number are defined as text fields even though they contain numbers, as opposed to letters. The additional characters that appear within these fields in a form or report are displayed by the input mask and are not counted in the field size. Social Security Number, for example, is displayed as 123-45-6789 but has a field size of 9.

Each field can have as many as twelve properties, so this is, indeed, a detailed step. That said, you can use the default settings for many properties, but you will have to set other properties explicitly, especially those that deal with formatting, data validation, and input masks. The properties that you establish for the fields in a table are automatically propagated to the forms and reports that are based on that table. Properties that deal with ***data validation*** are especially important.

Access will automatically prevent certain types of errors. You cannot, for example, enter a record into a table with a duplicate primary key. Nor can you enter an invalid date (such as February 30) into a date field or enter nonnumeric data into a numeric field. Other types of validation are implemented by the developer, as shown in Figure 9.4. Figure 9.4a illustrates the ***Required property*** in conjunction with the Last Name field. (The ***Allow Zero Length property*** should be set to no whenever the Required property is set to yes.) Figure 9.4b shows the ***Validation Rule*** (and associated ***Validation Text***) ***property*** to ensure a valid value for the gender field. Figure 9.4c imposes the ***Limit to List property*** to force the highest degree to be selected from a specified list. And finally, Figure 9.4d imposes data validation at the record level by comparing the value of one field in the record to another.

AutoNumber and Field Type

The primary keys of the Sales Reps, Customers, Orders, and Products tables are all defined as ***AutoNumber fields***, which in turn affects the field type of the dependent field in each relationship. In general, the join fields on both sides of a relationship must have the same data type. The exception is the AutoNumber field type, which cannot be specified for both fields. For example, the SalesRepID is used to implement the one-to-many relationship between sales reps and customers. This field is the primary key in the Sales Reps table where it is defined as an AutoNumber field; it is a foreign key in the Customers table where it (SalesPersonID) is defined as a Number field, with the Field Size property set to Long Integer.

Referential Integrity and Required fields

Every relationship is defined to enforce ***referential integrity***, which ensures that the data within the related tables is consistent. There is, for example, a one-to-many relationship between Customers and Orders (one customer can place many orders), which is implemented by including the CustomerID as a foreign key in the Orders table. Access will prevent you from assigning an invalid customer to a new order; that is, you cannot assign an order to a customer that does not exist. Access will, however, allow you to add a new Order *without* specifying a customer; that is, you can leave the field blank. To prevent this from happening, the CustomerID should be a required field in the Orders table.

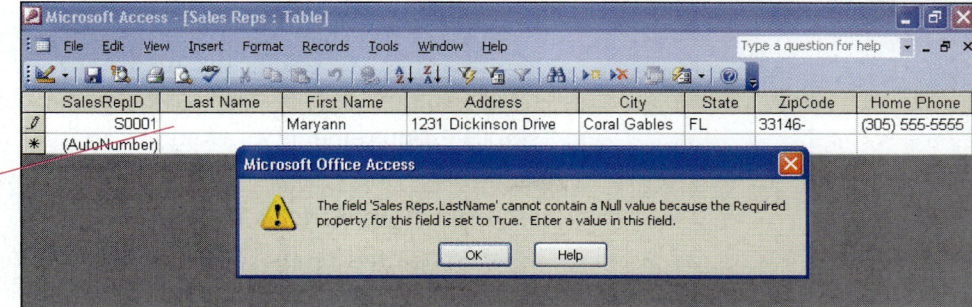

Last Name was left blank

(a) Required Property

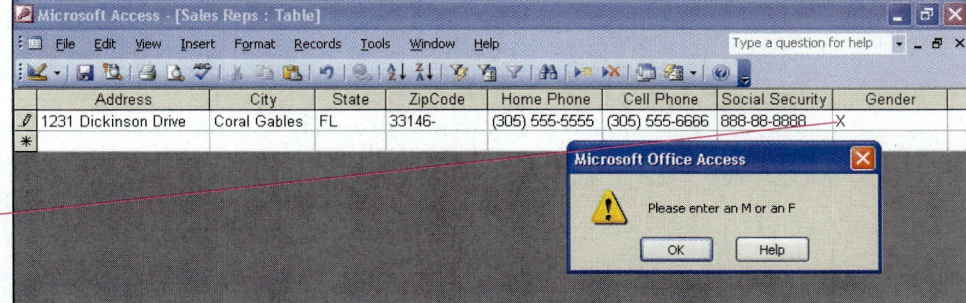

An invalid entry was made for gender

(b) Validation Rule Property

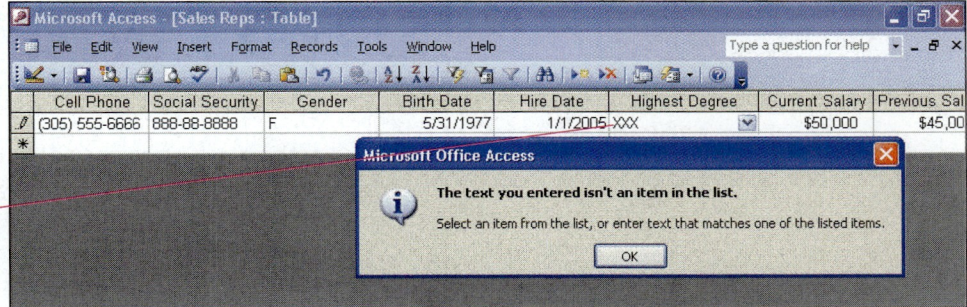

Entry was not selected from drop-down list

(c) Limit to List Property

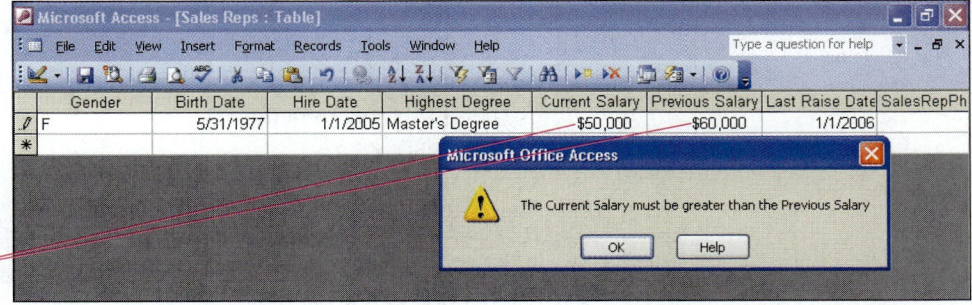

Current Salary must be greater than Previous Salary

(d) Validation at the Record Level

FIGURE 9.4 Data Validation

Objective   Establish the detailed design for the SD Coffee database, set field properties, and establish requirements for data validation. Use Figure 9.5 as a guide.

Step 1:   **The Name and Address Fields**

- Open the **SD Coffee database** from the previous exercise. Click the **Tables button** in the Database window, and then open the Sales Reps table in Design view.

- Click the field selector column for **LastName**, then set the **Field Size**, **Caption**, **Required**, and **Allow Zero Length properties** as shown in Figure 9.5a. The other properties use default settings and do not have to be changed. Set the properties for the **FirstName field** to match the LastName field.

- The **Address**, **City**, **State**, and **ZipCode fields** should be required fields with **field sizes** of **30**, **25**, **2**, and **9**, respectively. Set the **Allow Zero Length** property to **No** for all four fields.

- Set the **Format property** of the State field to a **> sign** and the **Input Mask property** to **LL**. This displays the state in uppercase and requires both characters.

- Create an **input mask** for the ZipCode field of **00000-9999** to require the first five digits, but leave the last four as optional entries. Save the table.

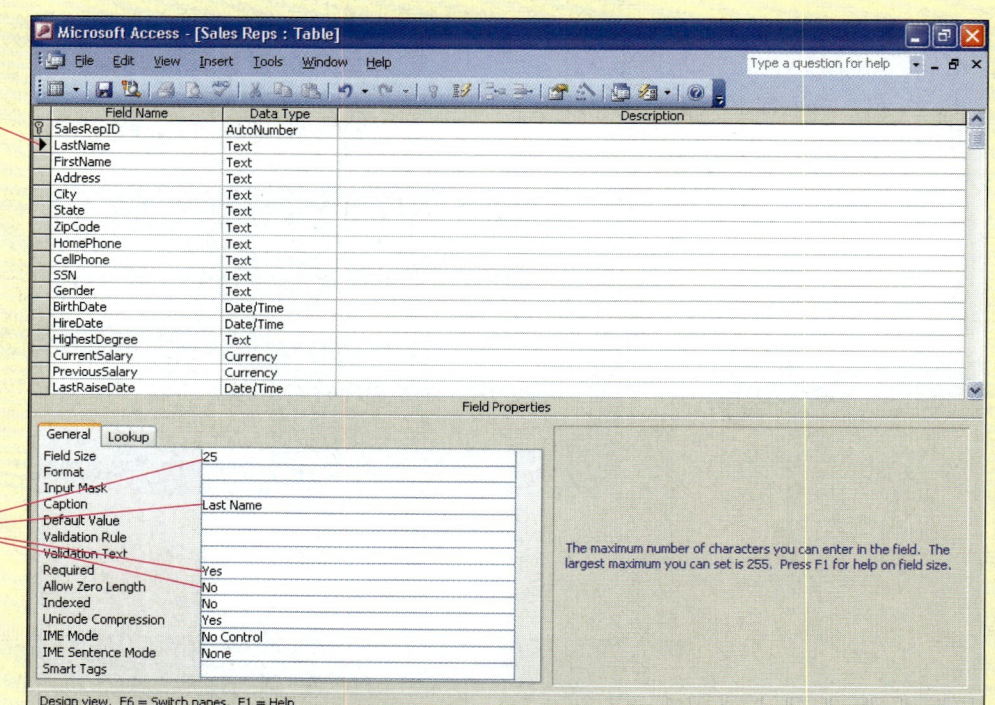

Click field selector column for LastName

Set field properties as shown

(a) The Name and Address Fields (step 1)

FIGURE 9.5   Hands-on Exercise 2

THE CAPTION PROPERTY

The caption property determines the label (unbound control) that appears next to a field in a form or report. The default value of the caption is the same as the field name—for example, "LastName". There is no need to change the property if the field name is acceptable as written; change it only to create a different caption such as "Last Name" to include a space between the words in the label.

Step 2: The Telephone and Social Security Number Fields

- Click the field selector for **HomePhone**. Change the **Field Size property** to **10**. Change the **Caption property** to **Home Phone**.

- Click the **InputMask** box in the Properties area. (The box is currently empty.) Click the **Build button** to display the Input Mask Wizard. Click **Yes** if asked to save the table. The Phone Number is already selected as shown in Figure 9.5b.

- Click the **Try It** text box and enter a telephone number to see how the mask works. If necessary, press the **left arrow key** until you are at the beginning of the text box, then enter a phone number (digits only). Click **Next**.

- The next screen asks if you want to change the input mask. We suggest you delete the exclamation point and change the 9's to zeros; that is, change the mask to **(000) 000-000**. Click **Next**.

- Click the option button to **store the data without the symbols** in the mask. Click the **Finish button** when the wizard has the necessary information.

- Enter appropriate field sizes, masks, and captions for the **CellPhone** and **SSN fields**. Save the table.

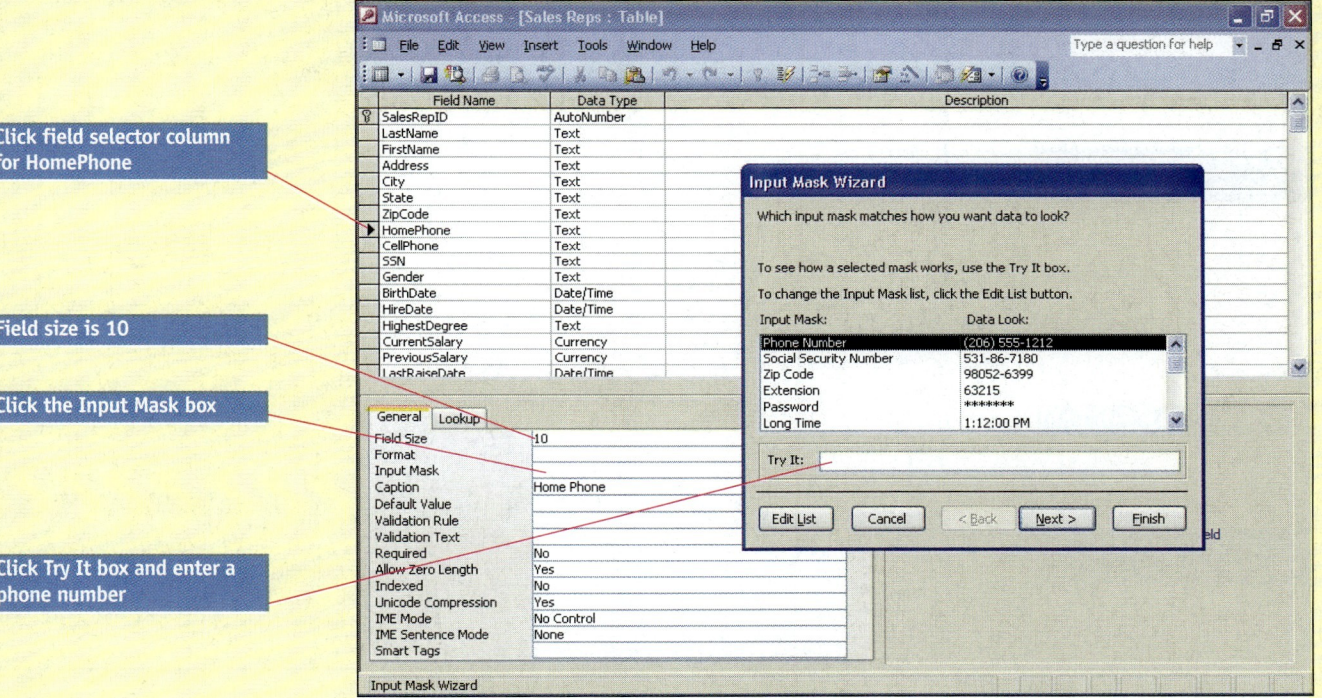

(b) The Telephone and Social Security Number Fields (step 2)

FIGURE 9.5 Hands-on Exercise 2 *(continued)*

UNDERSTANDING THE INPUT MASK

The input mask imposes character-by-character data validation according to the specified characters. A mask of either zero or nine restricts the entry to a numeric value; the difference is that a zero indicates a required character whereas a nine is an optional entry. The mask for zip code of 00000\-9999 requires digits in the first five positions but permits blanks thereafter. The character following the slash (a hyphen) is an insertion character that appears during data entry. The Social Security mask of 000\-00\-0000 requires numeric entries throughout and also displays a hyphen in the appropriate places.

Step 3: The Gender, Birth Date, and Hire Date Fields

- Set the properties for the **Gender field** as shown in Figure 9.5c. The **Field Size property** restricts the input to one character, the **Format property** displays an uppercase letter regardless of what is entered, and the input mask of "L" restricts the input value to a letter.

- The validation rule allows only "M" or "F", but it is not case sensitive; that is, it will accept either "m" or "M". The **Format property**, however, always displays the entry in uppercase. The **Validation Text property** displays a message to the user if the validation rule is violated.

- The **BirthDate** and **HireDate fields** should both specify **Date/Time** as the data type. Set the **Input Mask** and **Format properties** to a **short date**. Modify the **Caption property** to include a space between the words.

- The HireDate field should have its **Validation Rule property** set to restrict the entry to dates **>=1/1/2005**, the date when the company went into business. The **Validation Text property** should display an appropriate error message if the validation rule is violated. Save the table.

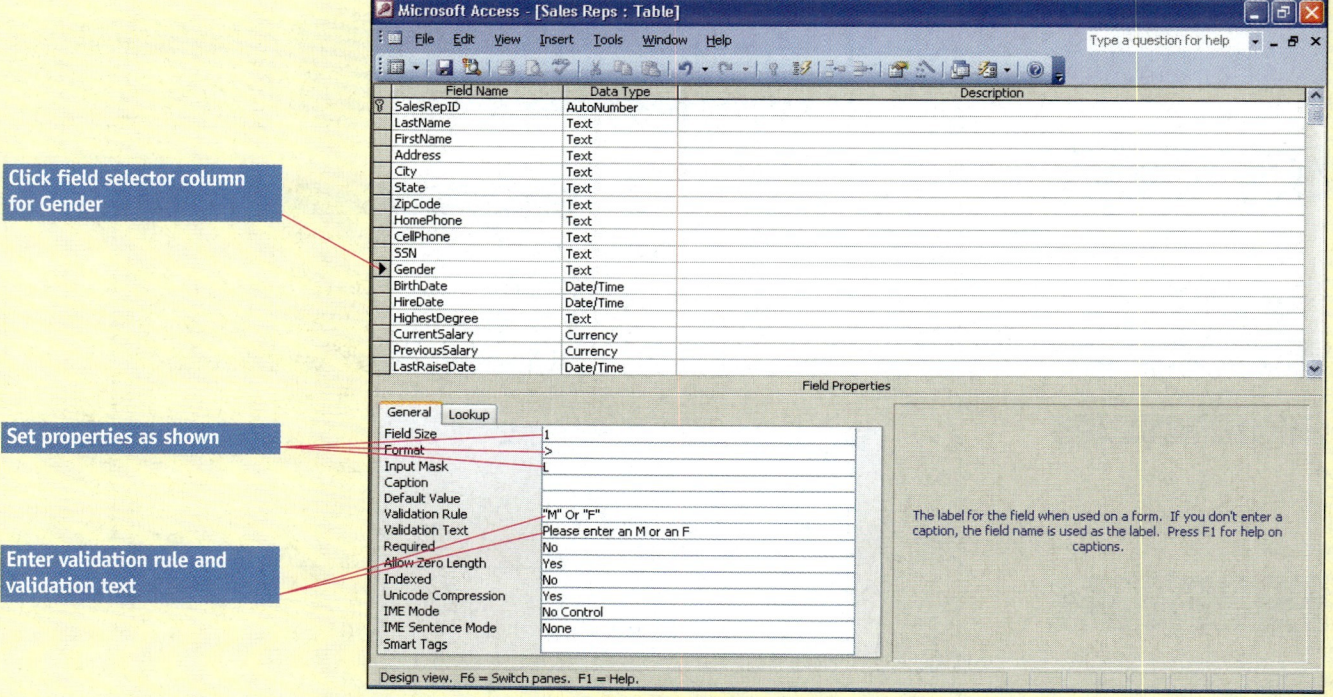

(c) The Gender, Birth Date, and Hire Date Fields (step 3)

FIGURE 9.5 Hands-on Exercise 2 (*continued*)

MORE ABOUT THE INPUT MASK

Use the input mask characters "L" and "A" to limit the input in a text field to letters or letters and/or numbers, respectively. An input mask of LLL, for example, permits only alphabetic characters while requiring you to enter all three characters. A question mark following the L or A indicates an optional entry of that character type; for example, A?? will accept from one to three characters, each of which can be a letter or number. You can also include the > and < formatting characters within the input mask; for example, a mask of >L<????????? is suitable for a first name field and capitalizes the first letter, while allowing up to nine additional characters in lower case.

Step 4: **The Highest Degree Field**

- Click the field selector column for the **Highest Degree field**. Click the **down arrow** in the Data Type list box and click **Lookup Wizard** to start the Lookup Wizard.

- Click the option button that indicates **I will type in the values that I want**. Click **Next**. You should see the dialog box in Figure 9.5d. The number of columns is already entered as one.

- Click the text box to enter the first degree. Type **High School Diploma**. Press **Tab** or the **down arrow key** (but do not press Enter) to enter the next degree.

- Enter **Associate's Degree**. Press the **down arrow key** to move to the next entry, then complete the table as shown in Figure 9.5d. Click **Next**.

- The wizard asks for a label to identify the column. (HighestDegree is already entered.) Click **Finish** to exit the wizard and return to Design view.

- The data type has been set to text, which is consistent with the entries you made. Change the Caption property to **Highest Degree**. Click the **Lookup tab**. Set the **Limit to List property** to **Yes**. Save the table. Click the **General tab** and set the **Field Size** to **19**.

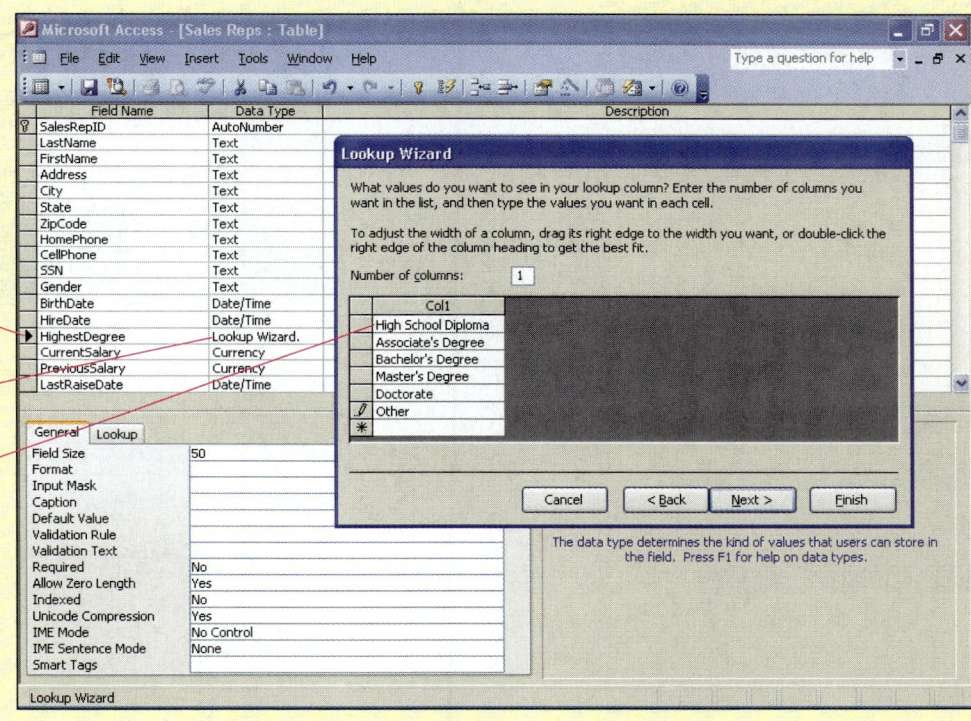

Click field selector column for Highest Degree

Select Lookup Wizard

Enter drop-down list items

(d) The Highest Degree Field (step 4)

FIGURE 9.5 Hands-on Exercise 2 (*continued*)

THE LOOKUP WIZARD

How do you search a database for employees with a master's degree? Do you search on "Master's degree", "M.S.", "Master of Science", "M.A.", or still another entry, all of which imply the same educational status? It would be much easier to search for a single uniform entry. You could enter a numeric education code, but that would require you to explain the codes in forms and reports. It is much easier to use the Lookup Wizard where you enter the potential values directly into a table, then select from a drop-down list during data entry.

Step 5: The Salary Fields

- Click in the field selector column for the Current Salary. Set the **Decimal Places** to **zero**, the **Required property** to **yes**, and the **Caption Property** to **Current Salary**.

- Create a validation rule that requires the current salary to be greater than or equal to $35,000. Enter an appropriate message in the Validation Text box if the data entered does not conform to the specified criteria.

- Set the **Decimal Places, Caption**, and **Validation properties** for the previous salary in similar fashion. (Do not set the Required property to yes.)

- Click the selector box in the upper-left corner, click the **right mouse button**, and then click **Properties** to display the Table Properties box.

- Click in the Validation Rule box and enter **[CurrentSalary]>[PreviousSalary]** to ensure that the current salary is greater than the previous salary. Be sure that the field names do not contain any spaces and that they are enclosed in square brackets.

- Click in the Validation Text box and enter the message shown in Figure 9.5e. Close the Table Properties dialog box.

- Click in the field selector column for the **LastRaiseDate**, then set the **Format, Input Mask**, and **Caption properties** appropriately. Save the table.

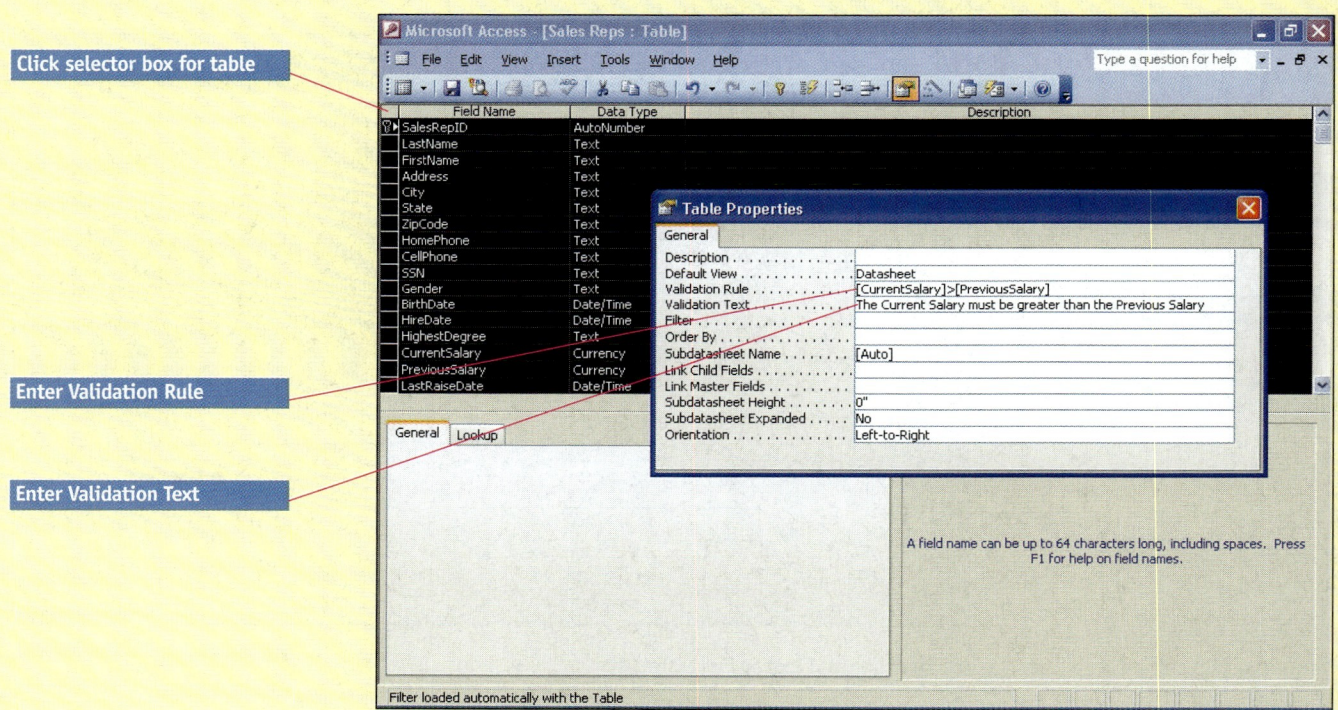

(e) The Salary Fields (step 5)

FIGURE 9.5 Hands-on Exercise 2 (*continued*)

VALIDATING AT THE FIELD VERSUS THE RECORD LEVEL

Data validation is performed at the field or record level. If it is done at the field level (e.g., by specifying the Required and Validation Rule properties for a specific field), Access checks each field independently of every other field. You can also impose validation at the record level to compare one field against another—for example, to ensure the current salary is greater than the previous salary.

Step 6: **Data Entry**

- Change to the Datasheet view. Click in the **Last Name column** and enter your **last name**. Note that as soon as you begin typing, the SalesRepID is entered automatically. The value of this field is 1, but it is displayed as S0001 because of the Format property.

- Press **Tab** to move to the next field and enter your **first name**. Enter data in the remaining fields, experimenting as you go; for example, enter lowercase letters in the State field, then notice how they are displayed in uppercase.

- Continue to enter data, but experiment by deliberately entering invalid data. Omit the zip code to display the error message in Figure 9.5f. (The message appears only after you attempt to move to the next record.)

- Try to enter nonnumeric data into either the Home Phone or Cell Phone fields. (You can't.) Try entering a previous salary that is greater than the current salary. (You can't.) Try entering XXX for the Highest Degree field. (You can't.)

- Experiment further, but end with a valid record for yourself. Do *not* enter your real Social Security Number (use 111-22-3333 instead).

- Close the table. Exit Access if you do not want to continue with the next exercise at this time.

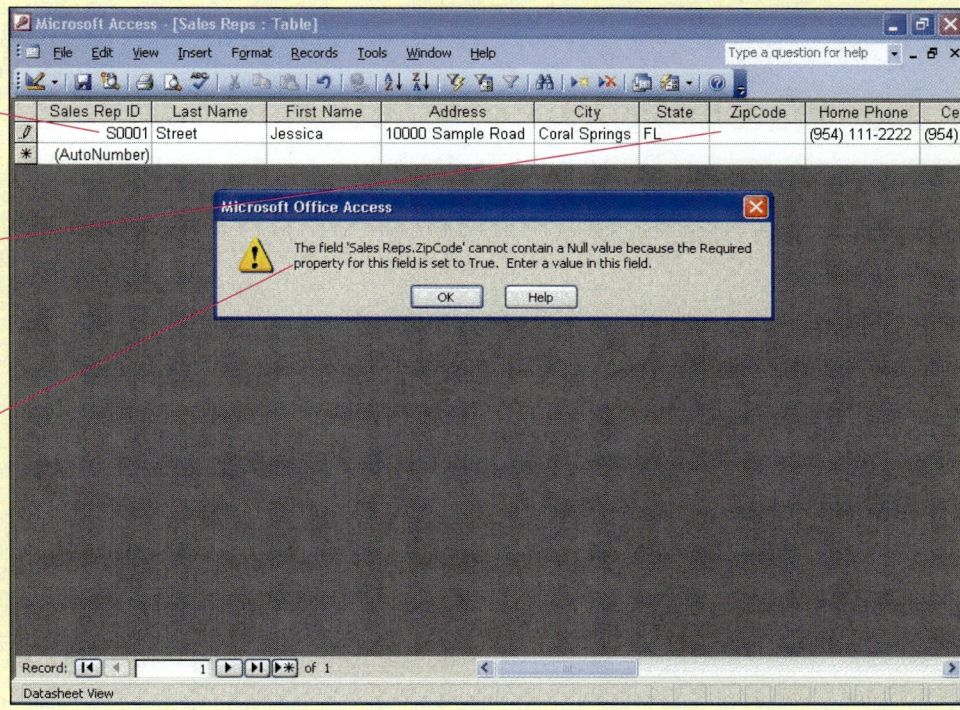

SalesRepID is entered automatically

ZipCode was not entered

Message indicates ZipCode is a required field

(f) Data Entry (step 6)

FIGURE 9.5 Hands-on Exercise 2 (*continued*)

THE AUTONUMBER VALUES REMAIN CONSTANT

The values in an AutoNumber field type are permanent and are not affected by deletions to the table; for example, if there are 10 records initially numbered from 1 to 10, and you delete record 6, the remaining records retain the values 7 to 10. The next record will be given an AutoNumber of 11. If you attempt to add that record and are unsuccessful for any reason, the next sequential number (11 in this example) will not appear in the table.

The *technical design* is complete. You have created the necessary tables, have defined all of the fields and associated properties in each table, and have implemented the appropriate relationships between the tables. The next step is to create a *visual design*, which is every bit as important as the technical design. Indeed, the typical client, especially a nontechnical client, is apt to be much more interested in the appearance of the system than in the details of how it works. Any requested changes should be made immediately. The sooner an error is detected, the easier and less costly it is to correct.

The visual design—consisting of a switchboard, form template, report template, and an "About" form—is presented in Version 1.0 of the database as shown in Figure 9.6. The switchboard is displayed automatically when the database is opened, and the client is told to experiment with the various menu options. He or she clicks the first button (or uses the Alt+A keyboard shortcut) to display the form in Figure 9.6a, which contains licensing information and also indicates the version number. The client closes the form, continues to explore, and in this way is given the first glimpse at the look and feel of the eventual system.

You may take Access for granted, but the initial reaction of a client when he or she first sees the system come to life is very important. Is the color scheme OK? Is the logo appropriate? Is the navigation intuitive? Even when the design is familiar to the client, as in the case of SD Coffee—which presented the design to the developer in the paper form and reports that already existed—the effect is positive. The client sees a fully functional database, and that inspires confidence.

The Templates

The visual design also provides access to the templates that are the basis for every form and report in the completed application. A *template* is a partially completed form or report that contains graphic elements, command buttons in the case of a form, and other formatting specifications. A template does not, however, have an underlying record source.

The form template in Figure 9.6b was created in Design view without benefit of a wizard. The Form Header displays the company logo and identifying information. The template also shows the format for the labels (*unbound controls*) in the body of the form as well as the style of the associated *bound controls*. The bottom of the form contains four command buttons; to add, delete, and print a record, and to close the form. The buttons are of uniform size and appearance. The Close and Print buttons are fully functional in the template; the other buttons become functional as soon as the template is associated with a record source.

To create a new form, you go to the Database window where you copy the form template to create a new form, then you open that form in Design view and associate it with the appropriate table or query. The field list will appear automatically, which enables you to add the required fields to the form. Once the controls have been added, you can use the Format Painter button to copy the format from the "dummy" fields in the template, and then you delete these fields. You follow this procedure to create every form in the database, and in this way you create a uniform look throughout the application.

The report template is accessed via the third menu option in the switchboard, and it functions identically to the form template. The report template contains a uniform *Report Header*, *Page Header*, and *Page Footer*; it also shows the format for the *Detail section*. All subsequent reports are based on this template.

The next hands-on exercise has you create Version 1.0 of the SD Coffee database. You will start by creating the form and report templates. You will then create the switchboard. And finally, you will use the *Startup command* to display the switchboard automatically when the database is opened.

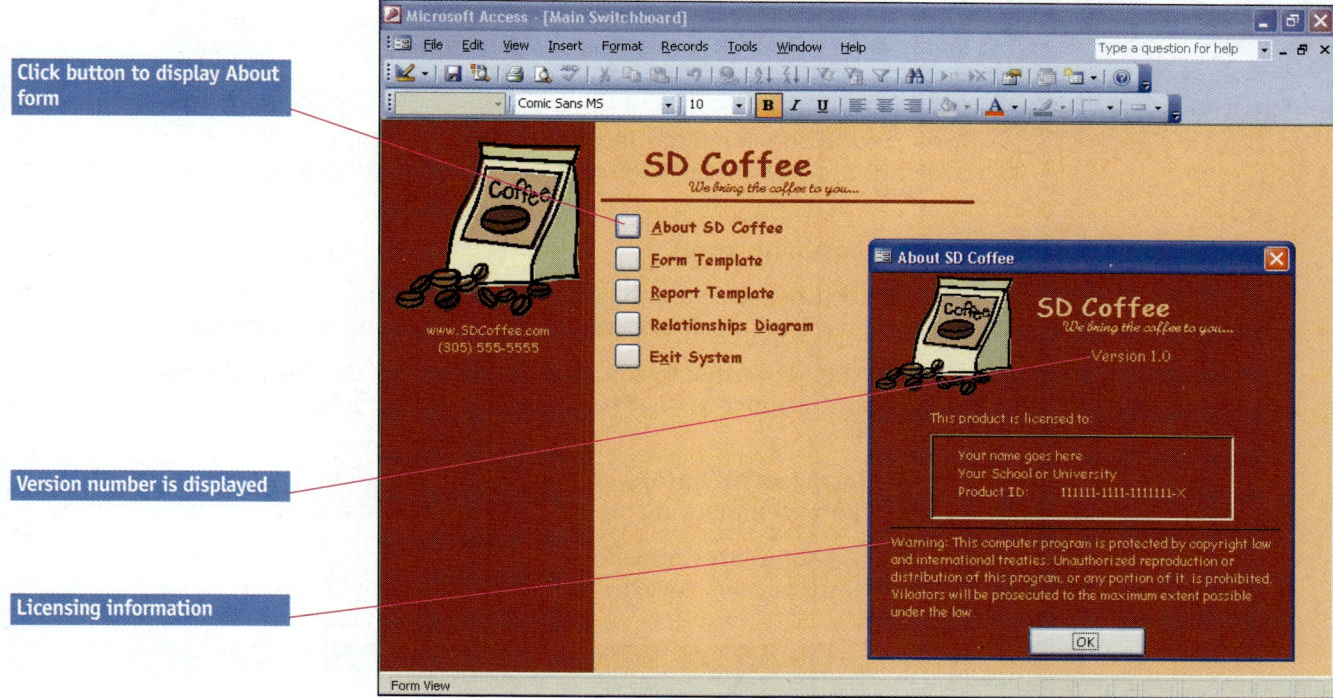

Click button to display About form

Version number is displayed

Licensing information

(a) The Switchboard and About Form

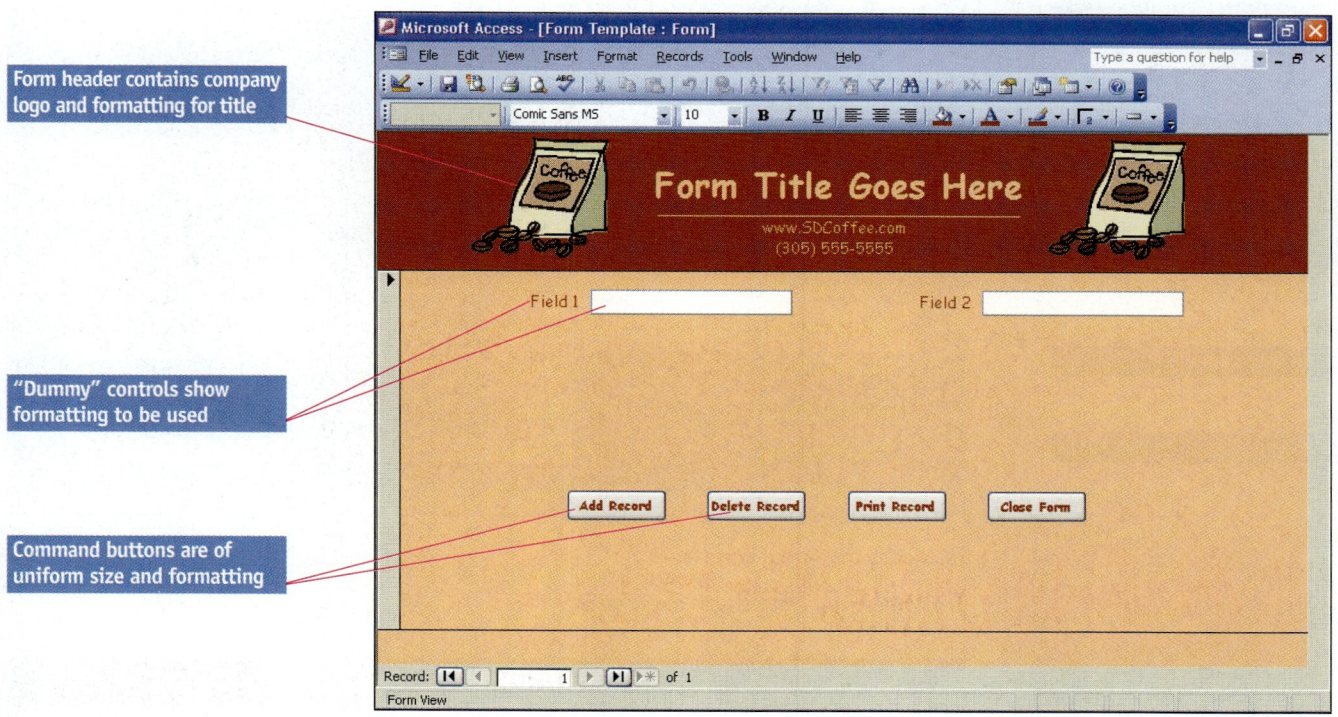

Form header contains company logo and formatting for title

"Dummy" controls show formatting to be used

Command buttons are of uniform size and formatting

(b) The Form Template

FIGURE 9.6   The Visual Design

3   The Visual Design

Objective   Establish a visual design that includes a logo and color scheme, create a form and report template that reflect this design, and then create an initial switchboard to complete Version 1.0 of the database. Use Figure 9.7.

Step 1:   **Modify the About Form**

- Open the **SD Coffee database** from the preceding exercise. Pull down the **File menu**, click **Get External Data**, then click the **Import command**.

- Select the **SD Coffee by Maryann database** in the **Exploring Access folder**, then click **Import** to display the Import Objects dialog box. Click the **Forms button**.

- Click the **Select All button**, then click **OK**. The About Form and partially completed Form Template are brought into the database as shown in Figure 9.7a.

- Open the **About SD Coffee form** in Design view. Add your name and school or university as shown. Save the form. Close the About form.

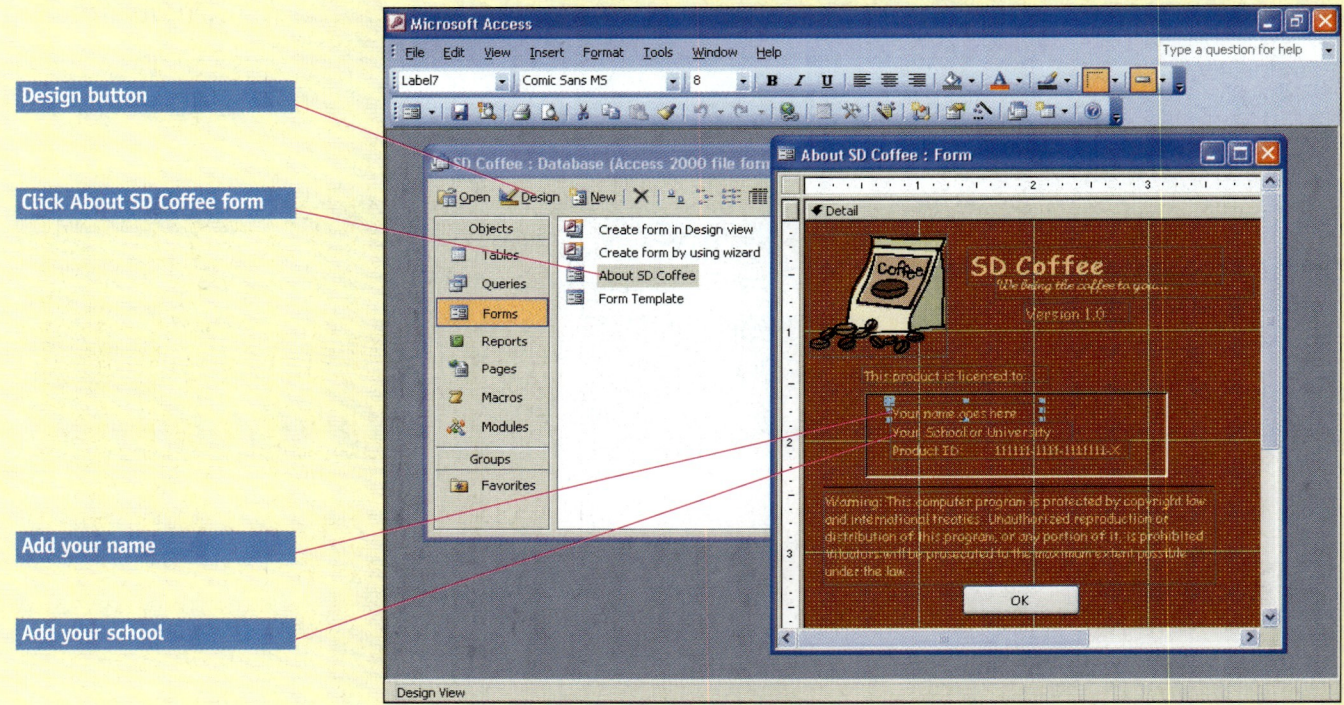

(a) Modify the About Form (step 1)

FIGURE 9.7   Hands-on Exercise 3

THE BACKUP DATABASE COMMAND

It is a good idea to back up your database before you start to make changes. Pull down the Tools menu, click Database Utilities, and then click the Back Up Database command to display the Save Backup as dialog box. Access supplies a default name consisting of the original name of the database followed by today's date. Click Save. Access creates the backup copy in the same folder as the original, then it reopens the original database.

Step 2: **Open the Form Template**

- Open the **Form Template** in Design view as shown in Figure 9.7b. The top portion of the form has been created for you, but it is up to you to add the command buttons.

- Click the **Command button** tool on the Toolbox toolbar. (Click the **Toolbox button** on the Form Design toolbar if the Toolbox toolbar is not visible.)

- Click and drag toward the bottom of the form where you want the button to go, then release the mouse. This draws a button and simultaneously opens the Command Button Wizard as shown in Figure 9.7b.

- Click **Record Operations** in the Categories list box. Choose **Add New Record** as the operation. Click **Next**.

- Click the **Text option button** in the next screen (Add Record appears automatically). Click **Next**.

- Type **AddRecordButton** as the name of the button, then click **Finish**. The completed command button should appear on your screen.

- Repeat these steps to add the remaining buttons that are shown in Figure 9.7c (in step 3). Save the form.

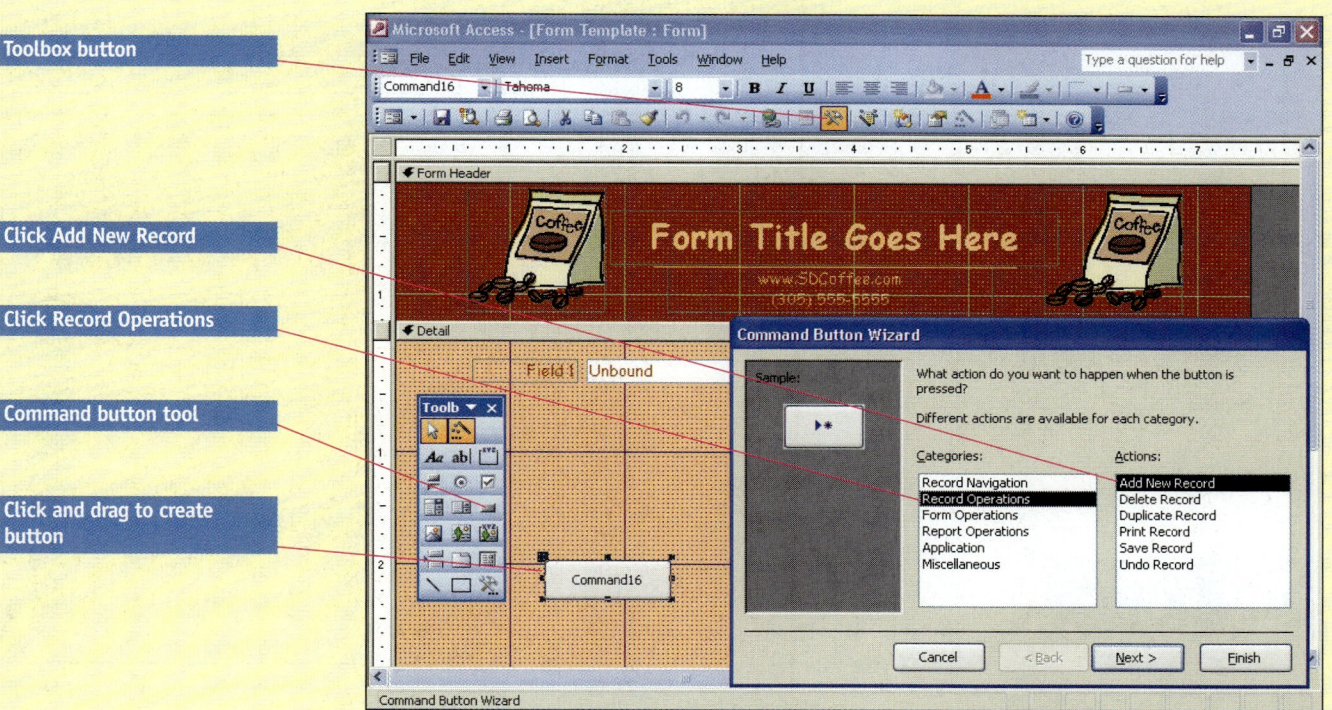

Toolbox button

Click Add New Record

Click Record Operations

Command button tool

Click and drag to create button

(b) Open the Form Template (step 2)

FIGURE 9.7 Hands-on Exercise 3 (*continued*)

WINDOWS THEMES AND ROUNDED COMMAND BUTTONS

It's a subtle difference, but we prefer the sleeker look of rounded command buttons in our forms, as opposed to the rectangular buttons that are created by default. Pull down the Tools menu, click the Options command, click the Forms/Reports tab, and check the box to Use Windows Themed Controls on forms. Click the Apply button, and then close the dialog box. Save the form you are working on, close the form, and then reopen it. You should see rounded buttons.

Step 3: **Size and Align the Command Buttons**

- Press and hold the **Shift key** to select the four command buttons. Release the Shift key when all the buttons are selected. Change the font to **Comic Sans bold.**

- Pull down the **Format menu.** Click **Size** to display the menu shown in Figure 9.7c. Click **To Tallest** to set a uniform height.

- Pull down the **Format menu** a second time, click **Size**, then click **To Widest** to set a uniform width.

- Pull down the **Format menu** again, click **Horizontal Spacing**, then click **Make Equal** so that each button is equidistant from the other buttons. (You can execute the Horizontal Spacing command additional times to increase or decrease the spacing between buttons.)

- Pull down the **Format menu** a final time, click the **Align command**, then click **Bottom** to complete the alignment. Center the buttons horizontally between the margins.

- Save the Form Template, but leave it open.

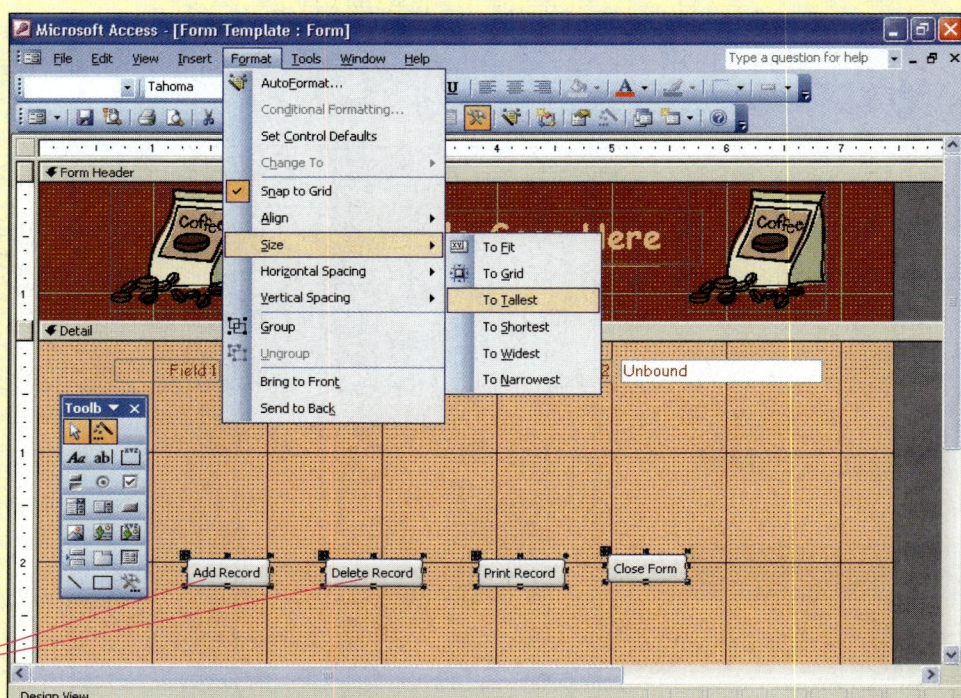

Press and hold Shift key as you select four command buttons

(c) Size and Align the Command Buttons (step 3)

FIGURE 9.7 Hands-on Exercise 3 (*continued*)

SELECTING MULTIPLE CONTROLS

Multiple controls are selected in one of two ways. You can press and hold the Shift key as you click one control after another, or you can simply click and drag to draw a box around the controls you want. You can then use the toolbar and/or the property sheet to change the properties of the selected controls in a single command. It's easy and it ensures identical properties for every control.

Step 4: Create the Report Template

- Press **F11** to return to the Database window, click the **Reports button**, and then double click the icon to **Create report in Design View**.

- Pull down the **View menu**. Click the **Report Header/Footer command** to insert a Report Header.

- Minimize the Database window. Pull down the **Window menu**, and click the **Tile Horizontally command** to tile the windows as shown in Figure 9.7d.

- Press and hold the **Shift key** as you select the clip art, horizontal line, and other objects in the header. Click the **Copy button** on the Standard toolbar.

- Click in the **Report Header section** of the Report Window. Click and drag the bottom border of the **Report Header** down to increase the size of the header.

- Click the **Paste button** to copy the selected objects onto your report. Adjust the width of the report so that it is just under **7.5 inches**.

- Click an empty area in the Report Header, then change the **background color** to match the color in the form template. Change the title to **Report Title Goes Here**.

- Close the Form template. Click **Yes** if prompted whether to save the template.

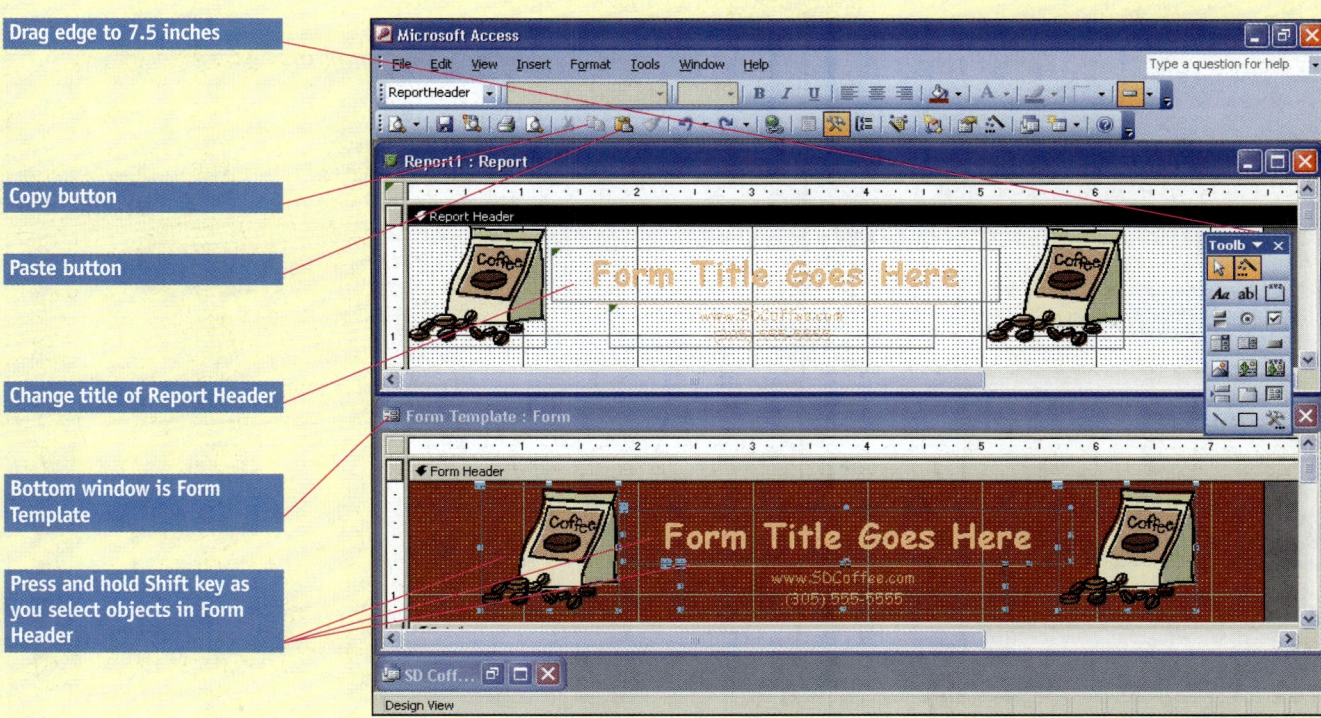

(d) Create the Report Template (step 4)

FIGURE 9.7 Hands-on Exercise 3 (*continued*)

THE REPORT GROUPS

It's easy to remember the seven types of report groups if you think of them in pairs. The Report Header contains the title of the report and appears once at the beginning of the report; the Report Footer appears at the end of the report and may contain a summary total. The Page Header appears at the top of every page; the Page Footer appears at the bottom of every page. The Group Header appears before each new group; the Group Footer appears at the end of a group with summary information. The Detail section is printed once for each record.

Step 5:   **Finish the Report Template**

- Pull down the **File menu**, click the **Page Setup command**, and click the **Margins tab**. Change the left and right margins to **.5 inch** each.

- Increase the size of the Page Header. Click the **Label tool** to create the heading for the first field, enter **Field 1** as the text, and then format the text. (We used **10-point Comic Sans bold** as the font.)

- Create the label to represent the bound control for the first field. Change the font to **10-point Comic Sans** and align it with the corresponding label in the Page Header. Size both labels identically.

- Press and hold the **Shift key** as you select both labels, click the **Copy button**, click in the background area of either section, then click the **Paste button** to create a second field. Move and size the copied labels as necessary. Complete the Page Header and Detail sections as shown in Figure 9.7e.

- Complete the **Page Footer**, which consists of a horizontal line and two text boxes to display the date and page number, respectively. Close the Report Footer. Use Figure 9.7e as a reference.

- Click the **Save button**, enter **Report Template** as the report name, then click **OK** to save the report. Close the Report window.

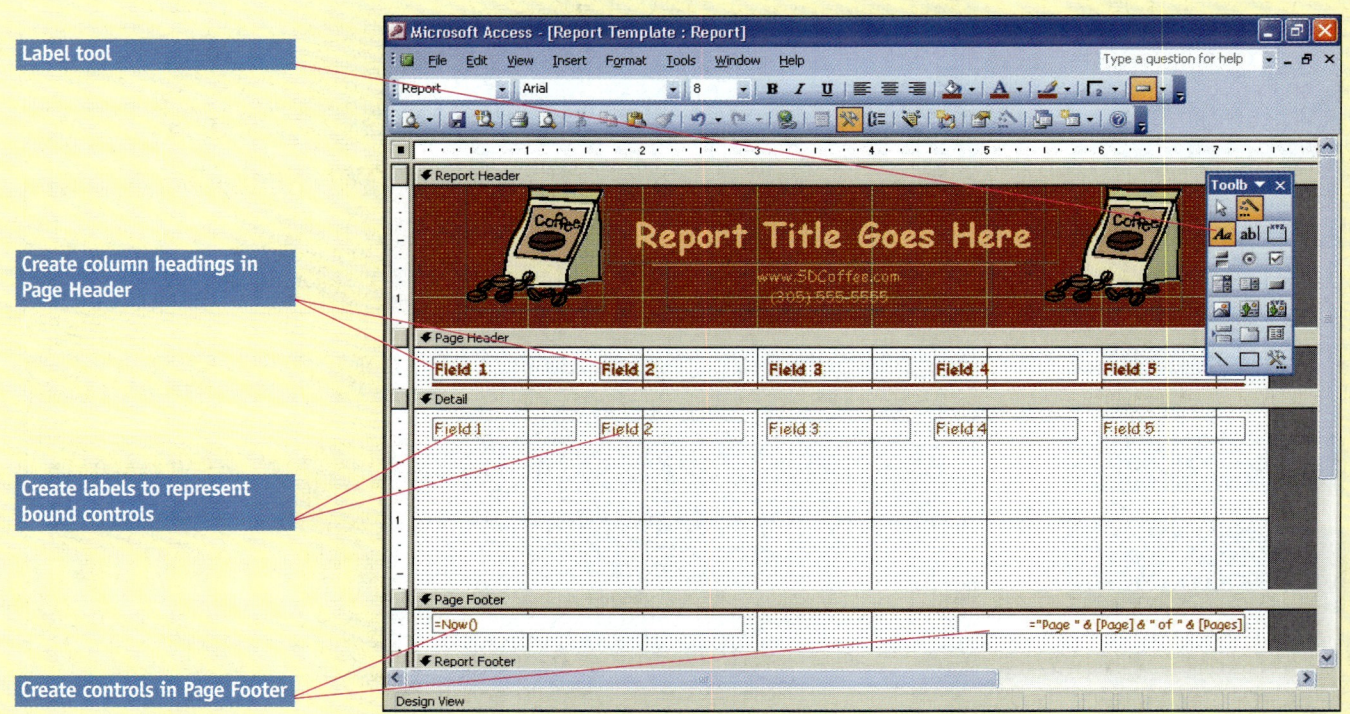

(e) Finish the Report Template (step 5)

FIGURE 9.7   Hands-on Exercise 3 (*continued*)

DRAW A STRAIGHT LINE

Click the line tool on the Toolbox, click in the Page Footer, then press and hold the Shift key as you click and drag to create a horizontal line. Click the down arrow next to the Line/Border Width tool to change the thickness of the line. Use the Line/Border Color tool and/or Special Effect tools to change these properties. To change the length of the line, right click the line, click Properties, click the Format tab, click in the Width text box, and enter the new value.

Step 6: **Start the Switchboard Manager**

- Pull down the **Tools menu**, click the **Database Utilities command**, and choose **Switchboard Manager**. Click **Yes** if you see a message indicating there is no valid switchboard and asking if you want to create one. You should see the Switchboard Manager dialog box.

- Click the **Edit command button** to edit the **Main Switchboard**, which displays the Edit Switchboard Page dialog box. Click the **New command button** to add an item to this page, which in turn displays the Edit Switchboard Item dialog box.

- Click in the Text list box and type **&About SD Coffee**. Click the **drop-down arrow** on the Command list box and choose the command to **Open the form in Edit mode**. Click the **down arrow** in the Form list box and choose **About SD Coffee**. Click **OK** to create the item.

- Add the other items on the switchboard as shown in Figure 9.7f. Click the **Close button** to close the Edit Switchboard Page dialog box after you add the last item.

- Close the Switchboard Manager dialog box.

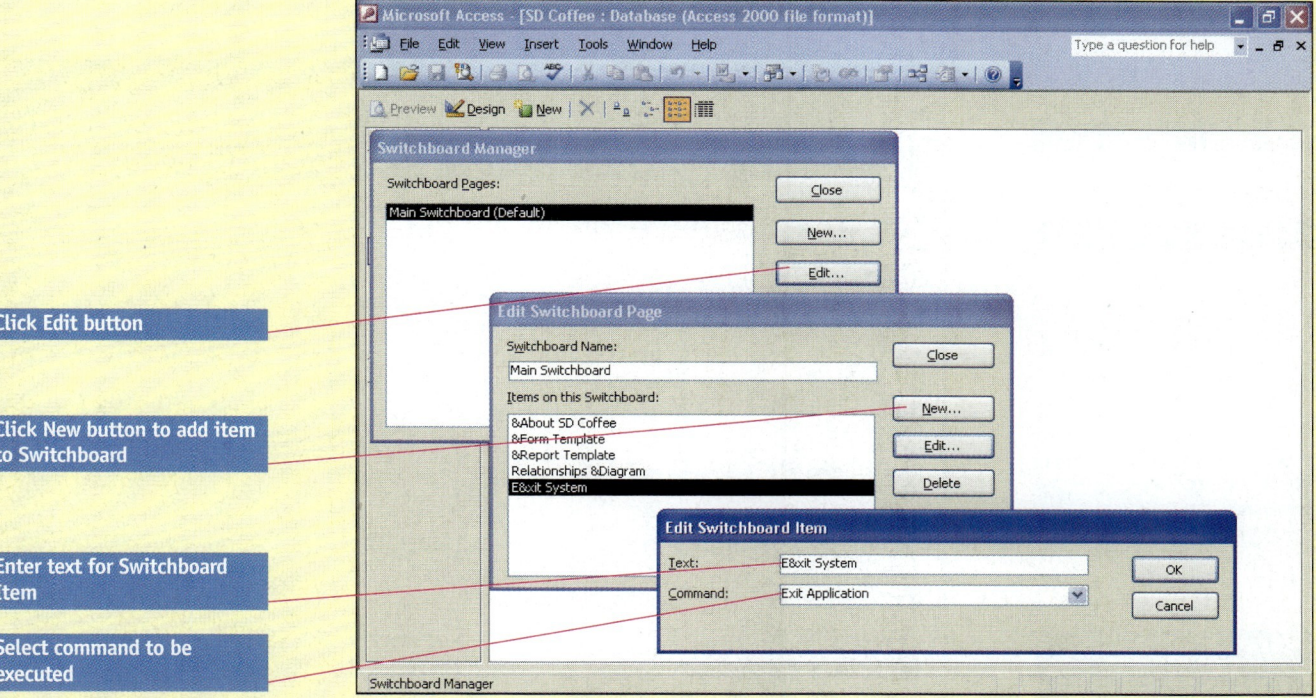

(f) Start the Switchboard Manager (step 6)

FIGURE 9.7 Hands-on Exercise 3 (*continued*)

CREATE A KEYBOARD SHORTCUT

The ampersand (&) has special significance when used within the name of a menu item, because it creates a keyboard shortcut to that command. Enter "&About SD Coffee", for example, and the letter A (the letter immediately after the ampersand) will be underlined and appear as "About SD Coffee" on the switchboard. From there, you can execute the item by clicking its button, or you can use the Alt+A keyboard shortcut (where "A" is the underlined letter in the menu option).

Step 7: **Complete the Switchboard**

- Click the **Forms button** and open the newly created switchboard in Design view. The default switchboard does not conform to the visual design we selected earlier. Delete the green rectangle, the vertical gray line, and the existing title.

- Open the **About SD Coffee** form in Design view, copy the clip art image, then paste that image onto the switchboard form. Copy the title and logo as shown in Figure 9.7g. Close the About form.

- Create a label on the switchboard that contains the Web address and phone. Right click the left side of the switchboard, click the **Fill/Back Color command**, and then choose the appropriate color.

- You also have to format the menu items. Press and hold the **Shift button** as you click each control and its associated button in succession. Be sure to select all eight buttons even if you do not have eight different commands.

- Change the font, color, and size of the text boxes as appropriate. We used a **rust color** and chose **10-point Comic Sans bold** as the font. Complete the design of the switchboard so that it matches Figure 9.7g. Click the **Save button**.

- Go to the Form view to see the switchboard, then return to the Design view to make the final adjustments. Save the form. Close the switchboard.

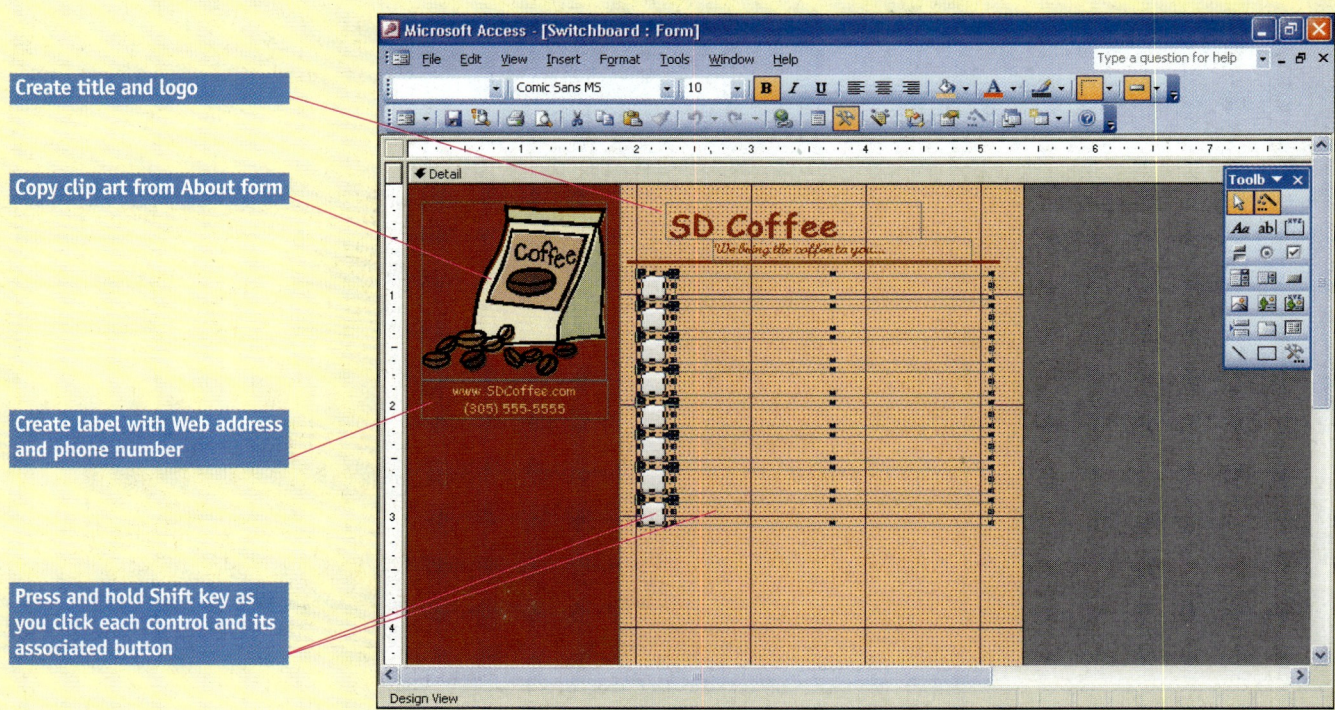

Create title and logo

Copy clip art from About form

Create label with Web address and phone number

Press and hold Shift key as you click each control and its associated button

(g) Complete the Switchboard (step 7)

FIGURE 9.7 Hands-on Exercise 3 (*continued*)

ADD A HYPERLINK

You can enhance the appeal of your switchboard through inclusion of a hyperlink. Open the switchboard form in Design view, then click the Insert Hyperlink button to display the Insert Hyperlink dialog box. Enter the text to be displayed and the Web address, then click OK to close the dialog box. Right click the hyperlink to display a shortcut menu, click the Properties command to display the Properties dialog box, then change the font and/or point size as appropriate.

Step 8: Test the Switchboard

■ Pull down the **Tools menu** and click the **Startup command**. Enter **Switchboard** in the Display Form/Page text box, then click **OK**.

■ Pull down the **Tools menu**, click **Database Utilities**, then click **Compact and Repair Database**. The database will close and then reopen. The switchboard should be displayed automatically. Maximize the window.

■ Click the button next to the About command (or use the **Alt+A** keyboard short-cut) to display the About form in Figure 9.7h. Click **OK** to close the form.

■ Test the buttons and/or the keyboard shortcuts to display the form and report templates. Click the **Exit System button** when you are satisfied that the switchboard works correctly.

■ Congratulations. You have completed Version 1.0 and are ready to demon-strate your working database to the client. This is an important milestone because it presents the client with a working database that inspires confidence and provides a feeling for the eventual system.

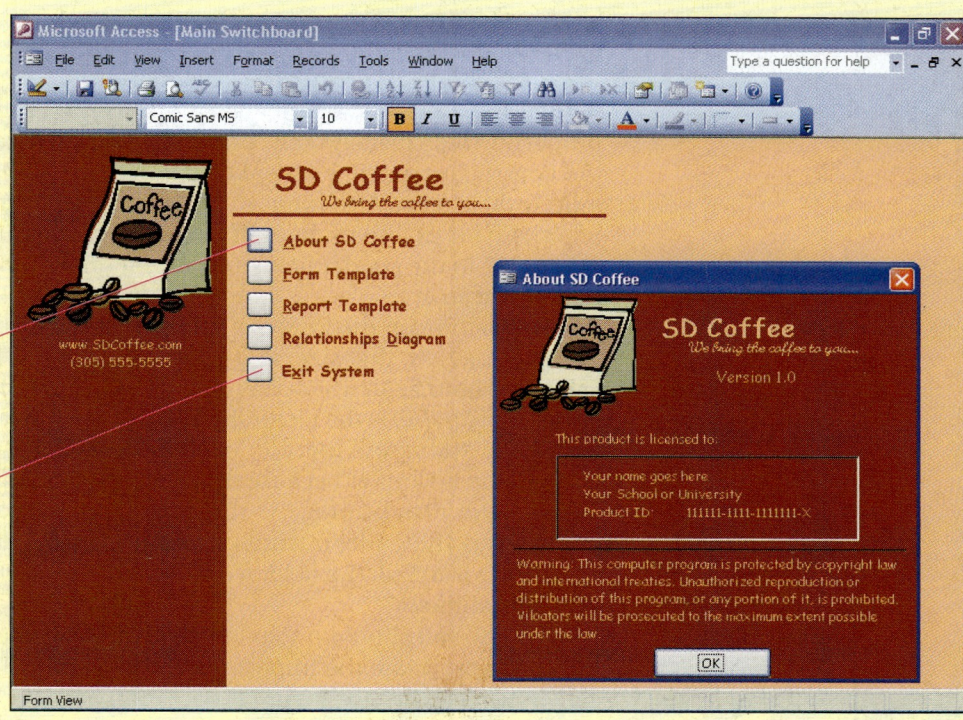

Click button to display About form

Click Exit System button to exit Access

(h) Test the Switchboard (step 8)

FIGURE 9.7 Hands-on Exercise 3 (*continued*)

THE SWITCHBOARD ITEMS TABLE

You can modify an existing switchboard in one of two ways—by using the Switchboard Manager or by making changes directly in the underlying table of switchboard items. Press the F11 key to display the Database window, click the Tables button, then open the Switchboard Items table where you can make changes to the various entries on the switchboard. We encourage you to experi-ment, but start by changing one entry at a time. The ItemText field is a good place to start.

The project is going very well. The customer has approved the visual design and is anxious to see more. Your next task is to use the templates that were developed in the visual design to create the form and report in Figure 9.8. To create a new form or report, you go to the Database window where you copy the appropriate template to create a new form or report. You then open the new object in Design view and associate it with the appropriate table, such as the Sales Reps table. The field list appears automatically, and you follow the normal steps to create and format the form or report, as described in Chapters 2 and 3, respectively. The result is a uniform look throughout the system that adds to its visual appeal.

The Sales Reps form contains all of the fields in the underlying table, which enables you to add a new record and/or to edit or delete an existing record. The various controls are accessed in sequence (left to right, top to bottom) via the Tab key. Note, however, that since the SalesRepID is an AutoNumber field, its value is input automatically as soon as you start to enter the last name. Thus, there is no point tabbing to the SalesRepID control on the form and hence we set its **Tab Stop property** to No. Note, too, that the command buttons at the bottom of the form can be executed by a keyboard shortcut (Alt + the underlined letter), which is consistent with the technique we used for the menu items on the switchboard.

Each bound control on the form inherits its properties from the corresponding field in the underlying table. The State control, for example, inherits the Format property, which displays the entry in uppercase letters; that is, you can enter "fl" in the control and it will be displayed as "FL". The telephone and zip code controls inherit their respective input masks. All of the data validation properties are also inherited; for examples, both first and last names are required; you can enter only "M" or "F" in the gender field; the current salary must be greater than the previous salary; and so on.

The picture on the form is a "nice touch," but it comes with a price: a substantial increase in the size of the database. The picture is inserted into the SalesRepPhoto field, which was defined as an OLE Object field. **Object Linking and Embedding (OLE)** is the technology used to share data within Microsoft Office. The data (e.g., Maryann's picture) can be linked or embedded into an Access table. Embedding is simpler because the image becomes part of the database and travels with it. The disadvantage is that you can embed only bitmapped images (as opposed to JPEG files), which rapidly increases the size of the database. The alternative is to link the field to a JPEG image, but the image is then displayed in a separate window.

By now you should understand the importance of the various properties and thus can appreciate the importance of the detailed design that was implemented earlier. Realize, too, the logical progression in the development of the database. We began with the overall design of the database, after which we created the detailed design to set the properties of the individual fields, and then we created the visual design. *Each step depended on its predecessor and was reviewed and approved before moving on.* Now we are creating a form and a report, and indeed it is possible that as we use the form to enter data and/or when we print the report to view the data, we may discover an error. A property may have been set incorrectly and/or the templates may require adjustment. Either way you have to return to the previous step to make the necessary correction. (The good news is that you can modify the properties of a field in Table Design view and have the new property reflected automatically in a form or report, provided you set the Property Update Options correctly.)

Our next exercise has you create the Sales Reps form in Figure 9.8a, then use it to enter data for Maryann as a sales representative. You will then create the Sales Reps report in Figure 9.8b, which displays two records (the record containing your data from the second hands-on exercise, plus a new record for Maryann).

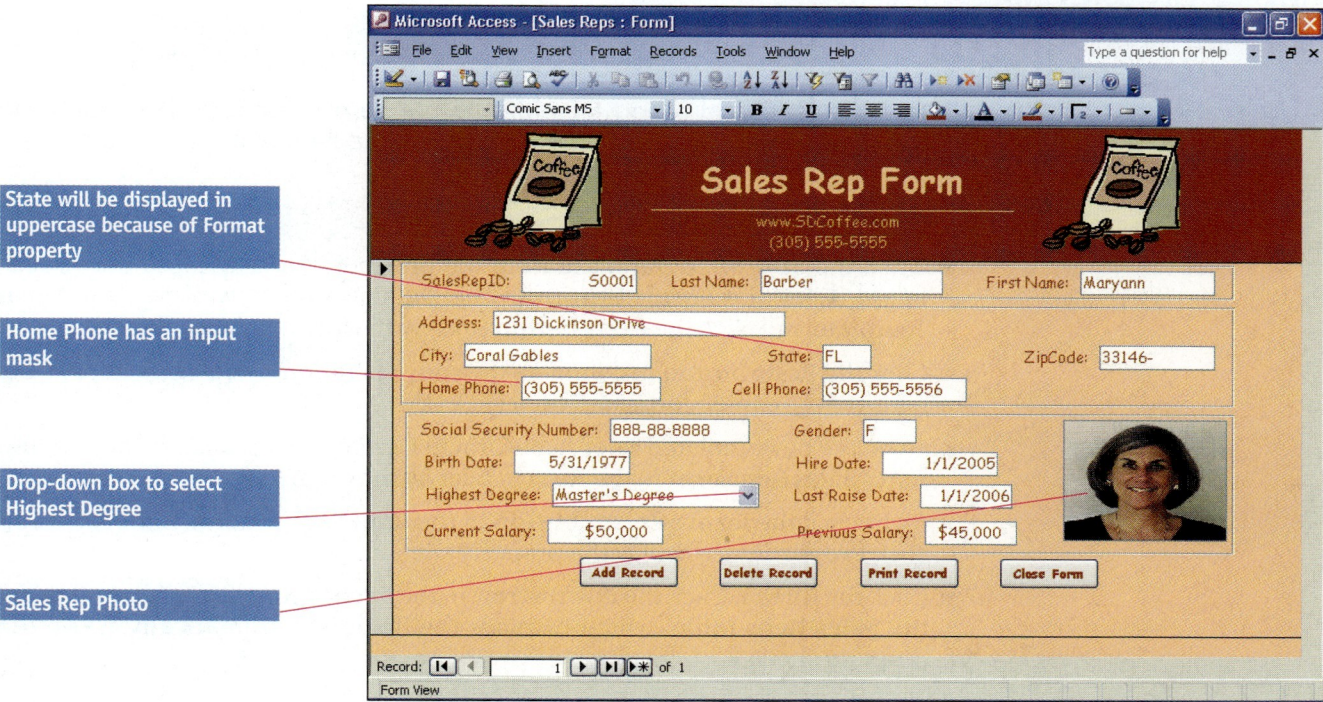

State will be displayed in uppercase because of Format property

Home Phone has an input mask

Drop-down box to select Highest Degree

Sales Rep Photo

(a) The Sales Reps Form

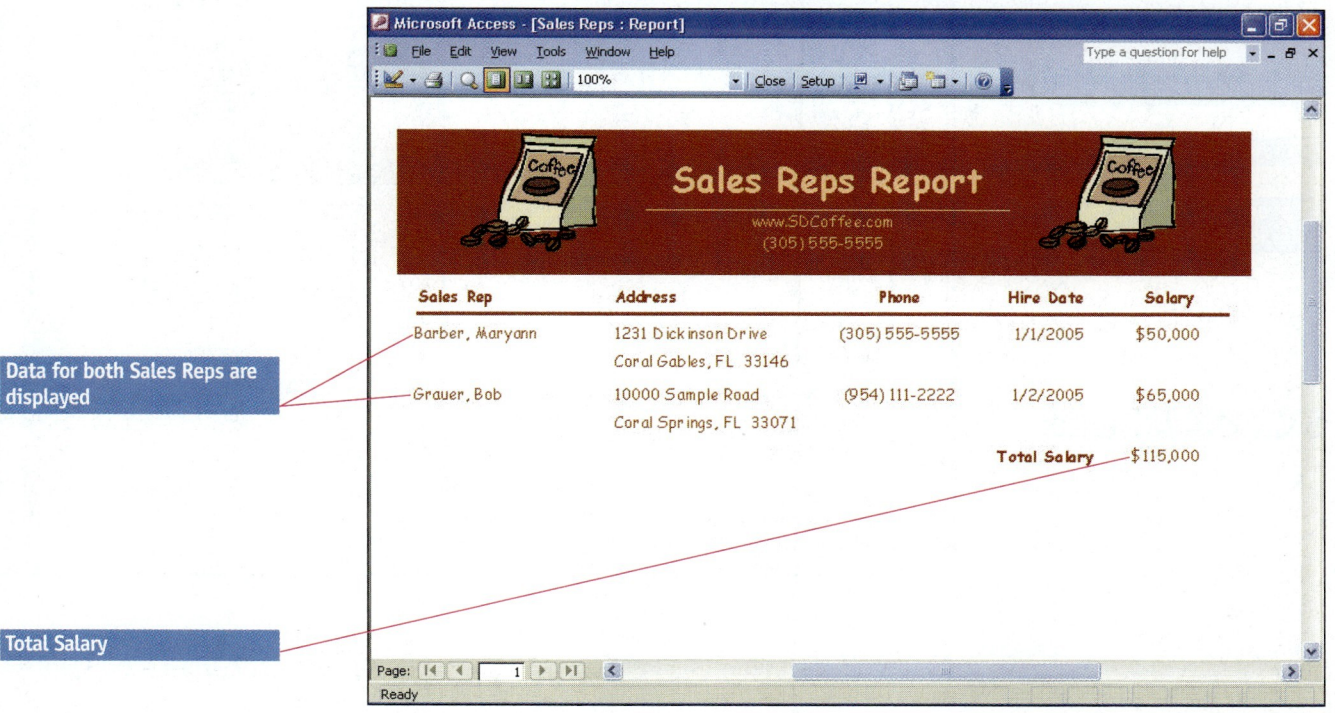

Data for both Sales Reps are displayed

Total Salary

(b) The Sales Reps Report

FIGURE 9.8 A Basic Form and Report

4   A Basic Form and Report

Objective   To use the form and report templates to create a basic form and report; to insert a picture into an OLE field on a form. Use Figure 9.9 as a guide.

Step 1:   Copy the Form Template

- Open the **SD Coffee Database** from the previous exercise. Close the switch-board. Click the **Forms button** in the Database window. Select the **Form Template** and click the **Copy button** to copy the form to the clipboard.

- Click the **Paste button** to complete the copy operation, enter **Sales Reps** as the name of the copied form, and then click **OK**.

- Open the newly created Sales Reps form in Design view. Maximize the window. Enter **Sales Rep Form** in the form header as shown in Figure 9.9a.

- Right click the **form selector button** in the upper-left portion of the form and click **Properties** to display the property sheet.

- Click the **All tab**. Click the **down arrow** in the Record Source text box and select the **Sales Reps table**, which displays the field list automatically. Close the property sheet.

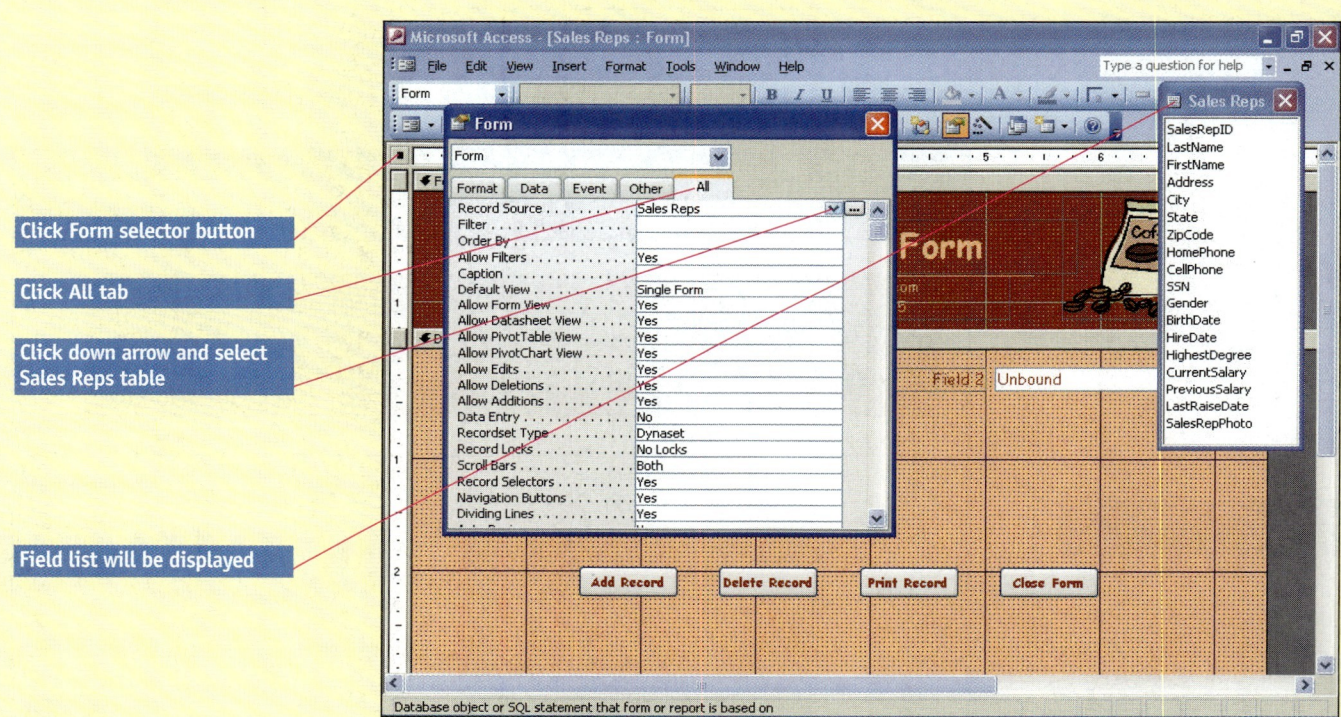

Click Form selector button

Click All tab

Click down arrow and select Sales Reps table

Field list will be displayed

(a) Copy the Form Template (step 1)

FIGURE 9.9   Hands-on Exercise 4

FIND YOUR DATABASE QUICKLY

The My Recent Documents menu in Windows XP contains shortcuts to the last 15 files that were opened. Click the Start button, click (or point to) the My Recent Documents menu, then click the document you wish to open—for example, the SD Coffee database, assuming that it appears on the menu. Windows will start the associated application and then it will open the selected document.

Step 2: **Arrange the Controls**

■ This is a detailed step and it will take time, but there are no shortcuts. Increase the size of the Detail section. Drag the command buttons to the bottom of the form to give yourself more room.

■ Click and drag every field in the field list to its approximate position on the form as shown in Figure 9.9b.

■ Resize the control for the **SalesRepPhoto** to make it smaller (approximately 1.2 inches square). Delete the label next to the photo. Be sure the width of the form is less than 7.5 inches. Close the field list.

■ Press and hold the **Shift key** as you select the multiple controls on each line of the form. Be sure to select both the label and the control. Pull down the **Format menu** and click the **Align command**. Click **Top** to align the forms in a straight line.

■ Use the **Format Size command** to change the height of every control to match the height of Field1 on the template. Use the **Format Painter tool** to copy the formatting of the text box for Field1 to the unbound controls and their associated labels.

■ Delete the **Field1** and **Field2 labels** and the associated text boxes as they are no longer needed.

■ Click in the upper-left portion of the Detail section (outside the first control), then click and drag to draw a "box" around every object in the Detail section, which in turn selects these objects. Drag the selected controls up, so that they take the empty space left by the removal of Field1 and Field2.

■ Save the form.

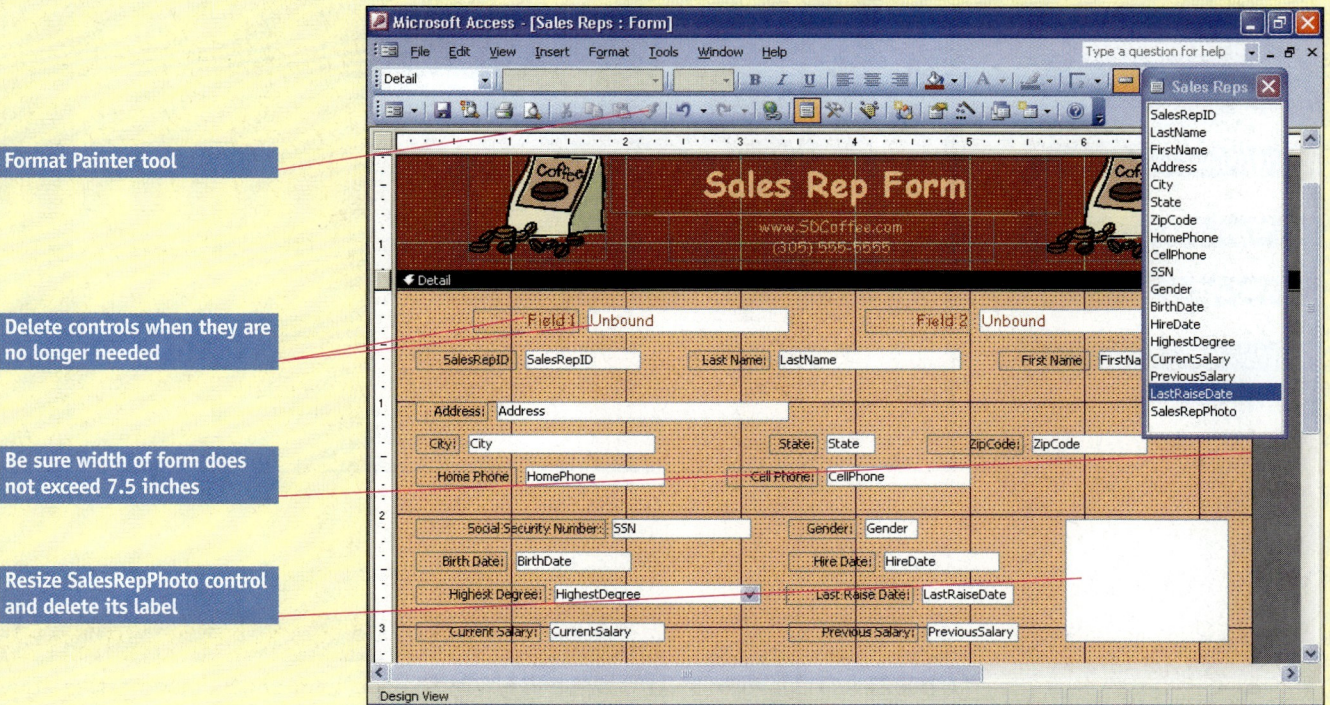

(b) Arrange the Controls (step 2)

FIGURE 9.9 Hands-on Exercise 4

Step 3: Complete the Sales Reps Form

■ Size, move, and format the various controls to match the design in Figure 9.9c.

■ Click the **Rectangle tool** on the Toolbox toolbar, then click and drag to draw a rectangle around the three controls at the top of the Detail section (SalesRepID, LastName, and FirstName).

■ Draw a second rectangle around the address and telephone fields. Draw a third rectangle around the remaining controls as shown in Figure 9.9c.

■ Pull down the **View menu**, click **Tab Order** to display the associated dialog box, click the **AutoOrder button**, then click **OK** to accept the settings.

■ Right click the **SalesRepID control**, click **Properties** to display the associated property sheet, then click the **All tab**. Scroll down to the **Tab Stop property** and set it to **No**. Close the property sheet.

■ Right click the **SalesRepPhoto control**, click **Properties** to display the associated property sheet, then click the **All tab**. Change the **Size Mode property** to **Stretch**. Close the Property sheet.

■ Go to Form view to view the form and test the Tab order, then return to Design view to make any additional changes. Save the form.

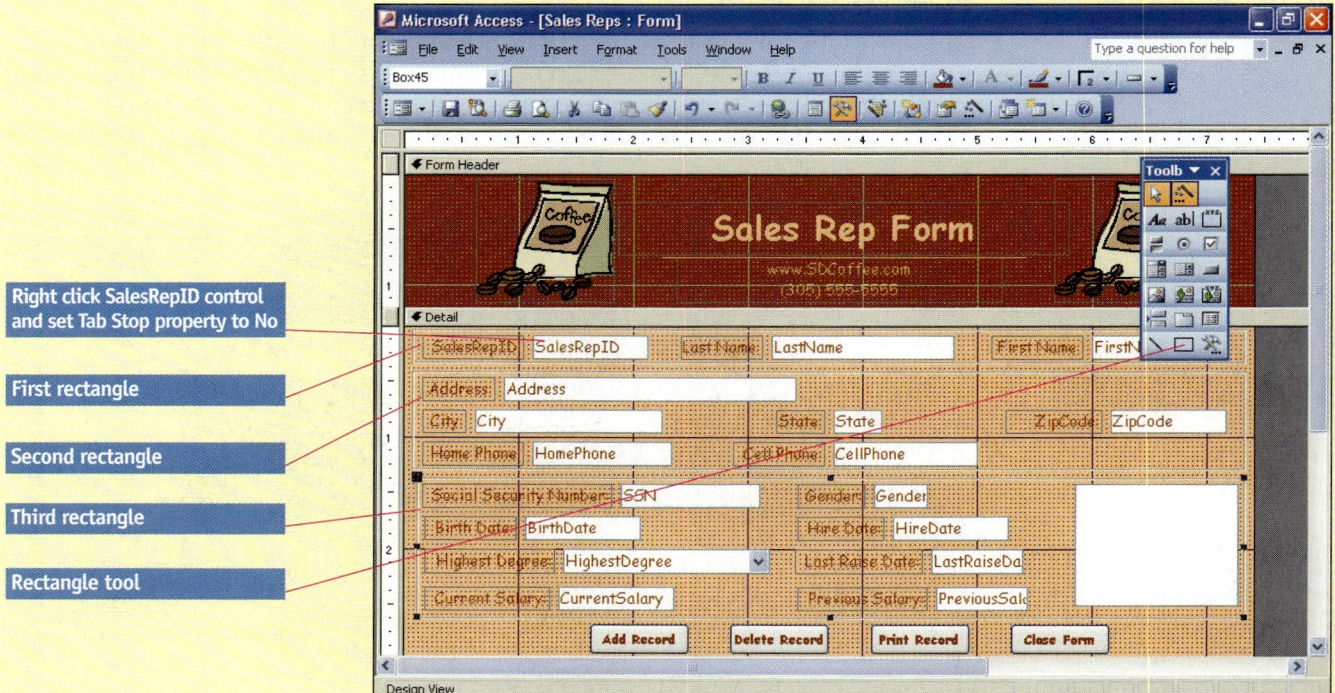

Right click SalesRepID control and set Tab Stop property to No

First rectangle

Second rectangle

Third rectangle

Rectangle tool

(c) Complete the Sales Reps Form (step 3)

FIGURE 9.9 Hands-on Exercise 4 (*continued*)

USE VBA TO SIMPLIFY DATA ENTRY

The Sales Reps form is attractive and fully functional, but it can be made better. You could, for example, modify the Add command button so that clicking it positions you directly in the Last Name field to begin data entry. You can also add shortcuts for data entry—for example, Ctrl+1 to add a specific city, state, and zip code, Ctrl+2 to add a different city, state, and zip code, and so on. Both of these enhancements are accomplished through VBA. See practice exercise 6 at the end of the chapter.

Step 4: **Test the Sales Reps Form**

- Change to Form view. Click the **Add button** (or use the **Alt+A** keyboard short-cut) to add a new record as shown in Figure 9.9d. This should be the second record in the Sales Reps table.

- Click in the **Last Name control** and enter **Barber** as the last name. Note that as soon as you begin typing, the SalesRepID is entered automatically.

- Press **Tab** to move to the next field and enter **Maryann**, then proceed to enter hypothetical data in the remaining fields, experimenting as you go; for example, enter lowercase letters in the State field, then notice how they are displayed in uppercase.

- You can insert Maryann's picture if you like. Click in the control for the picture, pull down the **Insert menu**, and click the **Object command**.

- Click the **Create from File** option button. Click the **Browse button** to locate the picture of **Maryann** in the **Exploring Access folder**. Click **OK** twice to insert the picture.

- Close the form when you have finished entering the data.

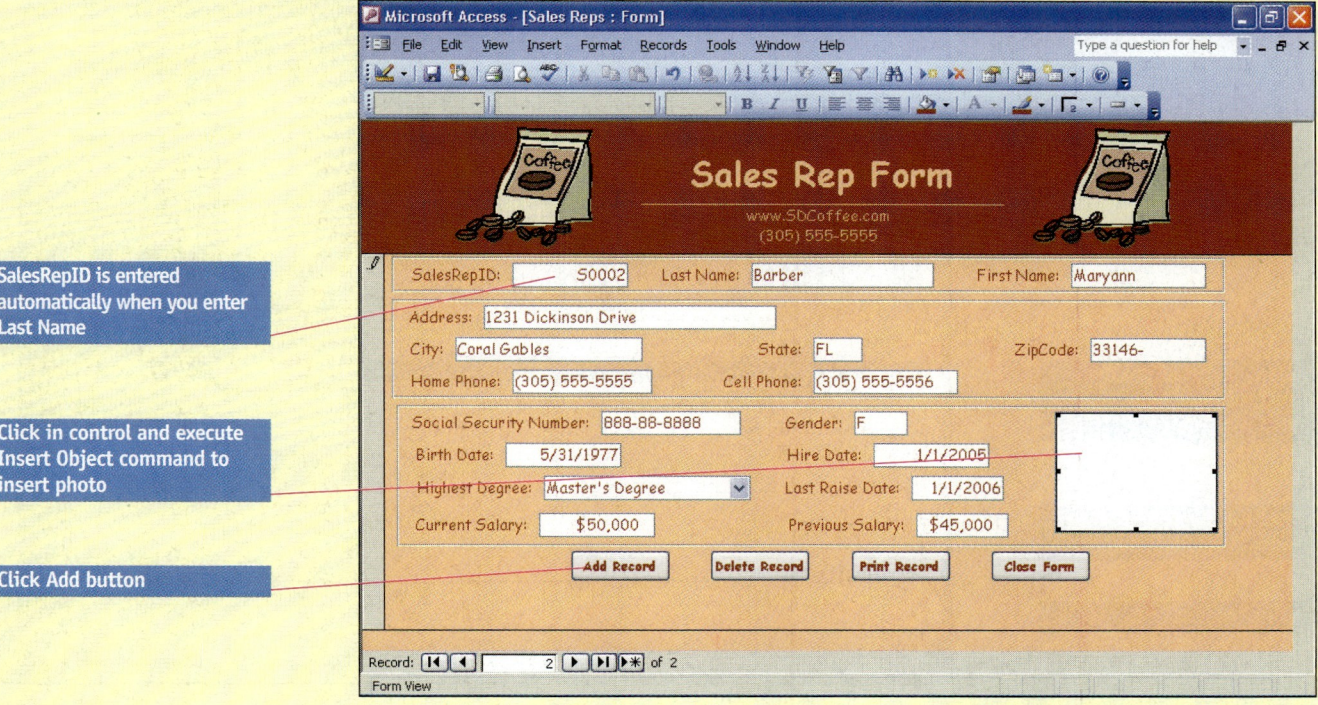

(d) Test the Sales Reps Form (step 4)

FIGURE 9.9 Hands-on Exercise 4 (*continued*)

CHANGING FIELD PROPERTIES

A bound control inherits its properties from the associated field in the underlying table. What if, however, you change the field's properties after you have created the form? Fortunately, you can ensure that those changes are automatically propagated throughout the database. Open the table that contains the field in Design view, change the property, and then press Enter. You will see the Property Update Options button if the property is inherited. Click the button, click the Update command, select the forms and reports that contain the controls that must be updated, then click Yes.

Step 5: **Create the Sales Reps report**

- Click the **Reports button** in the Database window. Select the **Report Template** and click the **Copy button** to copy the report to the clipboard.

- Click the **Paste button** to complete the copy operation, enter **Sales Reps** as the name of the copied report, and then click **OK**.

- Open the newly created **Sales Reps report** in Design view and enter **Sales Reps report** in the Report Header as shown in Figure 9.9e.

- Right click the **Report selector button** in the upper-left portion of the report and click **Properties** to display the property sheet.

- Click the **All tab**. Click the **down arrow** in the Record Source text box and select the **Sales Reps table**, which displays the field list automatically. Close the property sheet.

- Click the **Text box tool** and enter the calculated control to display the rep's name as shown in Figure 9.9e. Delete the associated label.

- Save the form.

Right click Report selector button

Sales Reps field list will be displayed when table is associated with form

Create calculated control to display Sales Rep's name

Text box tool

(e) Create the Sales Reps Report (step 5)

FIGURE 9.9 Hands-on Exercise 4 (*continued*)

CREATE A SINGLE NAME FIELD

An individual's first and last names are typically defined as separate fields, to enable you to sort or select on either field. A report, however, may display both fields as a single entity such as "Grauer, Robert". This is accomplished by the ampersand (or concatenation operator), which joins together the elements on either side of an expression. Note, too, how the expression in the calculated control contains a comma and a space between the last name and the first name.

Step 6: Complete the Sales Reps Report

- Click and drag the **Address**, **HomePhone**, **HireDate**, and **CurrentSalary** from the field list to the indicated positions on the form. Delete the associated labels, then change the field headings to match those in Figure 9.9f. Close the field list.

- Click the **Text box tool** and enter the calculated control for the second line of the address. (The **UCase function** is required to display the state in uppercase letters; that is, the Format property is not reflected in a concatenated field.) Delete the associated label.

- Use the **Format Painter** to copy the formatting for the field headings and corresponding values.

- Delete the controls representing the bound controls in the Detail section as they are no longer needed. Move the controls up to take the empty space left by the removal of these fields.

- Resize the Detail section. Create a control in the Report Footer to display the total salary for all records on the form. Change the format to **Currency** with **zero decimals**. Save the report.

- Click the **Print Preview button** to view the report. Return to Design view and make any necessary changes. Print the completed report.

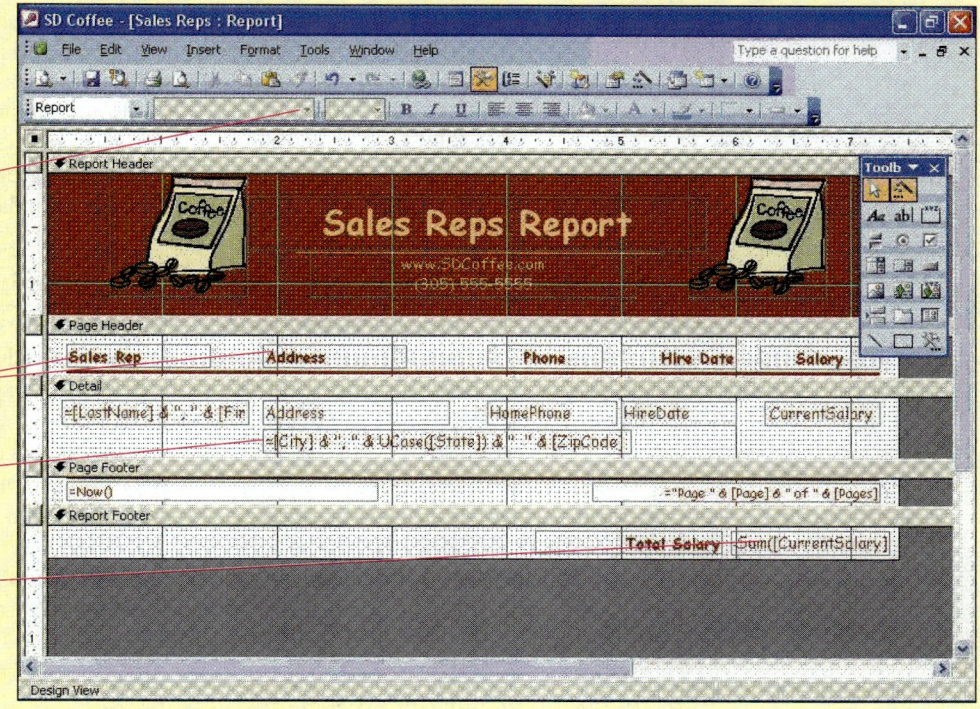

(f) Complete the Sales Reps Report (step 6)

FIGURE 9.9 Hands-on Exercise 4 (*continued*)

COMPACT AND REPAIR THE DATABASE

Access databases tend to grow very quickly, especially as you create and edit new forms and reports, and thus you should always compact a database before you exit. Pull down the Tools menu; click Database Utilities, then click Compact and Repair Database. The database will close and then reopen, after the compacting process has eliminated the fragmentation that occurs as you work on a database.

It's time to "finish" the project. Don't panic! A finished project does not mean that you have to complete every form and report. Instead, you will develop a multiple-level switchboard that lets you step through the various menu items without necessarily completing every individual item. This approach is known as *prototyping* and it is invaluable in testing a system and obtaining user feedback. The main switchboard in Figure 9.10a is an expanded version of the switchboard that was developed earlier in Version 1.0. The buttons to open the Form and Report Templates have been removed and two new buttons have been added in their place, to go to a Data Entry menu and Report menu, respectively. In addition, the Exit System command has been modified to display a reminder to the user to back up the system.

The Report and Data Entry menus are implemented as subsidiary switchboards. (The Report menu provides access to the available reports; it is not shown explicitly.) The Data Entry menu is depicted in Figure 9.10b. The menu options must be carefully thought out; that is, data entry is not arbitrary, and the complete system must enable the user to add, edit, and/or delete records in every table. This will be accomplished through separate forms for Orders, Customers, Products, and Sales Reps. The latter three are based entirely on the respective tables. The Orders form is more complex, and it will parallel the paper form that was presented at the beginning of the chapter.

As indicated, the actual forms and reports do not have to exist in order to create the multilevel switchboard. Indeed, only the Sales Reps form is available at this time (it was developed in the previous exercise). Every other menu option displays the message in Figure 9.10b indicating that the form will be developed in a later version. Even so, the system is complete in the sense that it has all of the menu options of the finished system. The user is able to experiment freely and in this way gains a better appreciation of the finished system. Moreover, the user is able to provide feedback on any potential problems, which can be addressed immediately and thus resolved more easily (and inexpensively) than when the actual objects have been created.

Macros—A Quick Review

The dialog boxes in Figure 9.10 are produced by the *MsgBox action*, which is executed from a macro. Macros were discussed in Chapter 7, but a brief review is in order. A *macro* automates a command sequence; that is, instead of using the mouse or keyboard to execute a series of commands, you store the commands (actions) in a macro and execute the macro. Macros can be created to open a table, query, form, or report, or simply to display an informational message, then beep to call attention to that message. Macros can also move or size a window, or minimize, maximize, or restore a window. In short, you can create a macro to execute any command (or combination of commands) in an Access menu.

The SD Coffee database incorporates three macros—an AutoExec macro, which is executed automatically when the database is opened, an Exit System macro to close the database and remind the user to back up the system, and a Prototype macro to display the message indicating that the menu option will be developed later. The *AutoExec macro* typically opens the main switchboard (or alternatively, the switchboard can be opened by the StartUp command as was done in Version 1.0). In addition, the AutoExec maximizes the current window (something that cannot be done via the StartUp command), so that all subsequent forms and reports take the entire screen. There is no requirement for the AutoExec macro to be present, but it is a nice touch.

To create a macro, select the Macros button in the Database window, then click the New button to display the Macro window where you enter the various commands and associated arguments. You save the macro under its own name and then you test the macro to be sure that it is working. You then execute the macro as appropriate via a switchboard command. We are ready to develop Version 2.0.

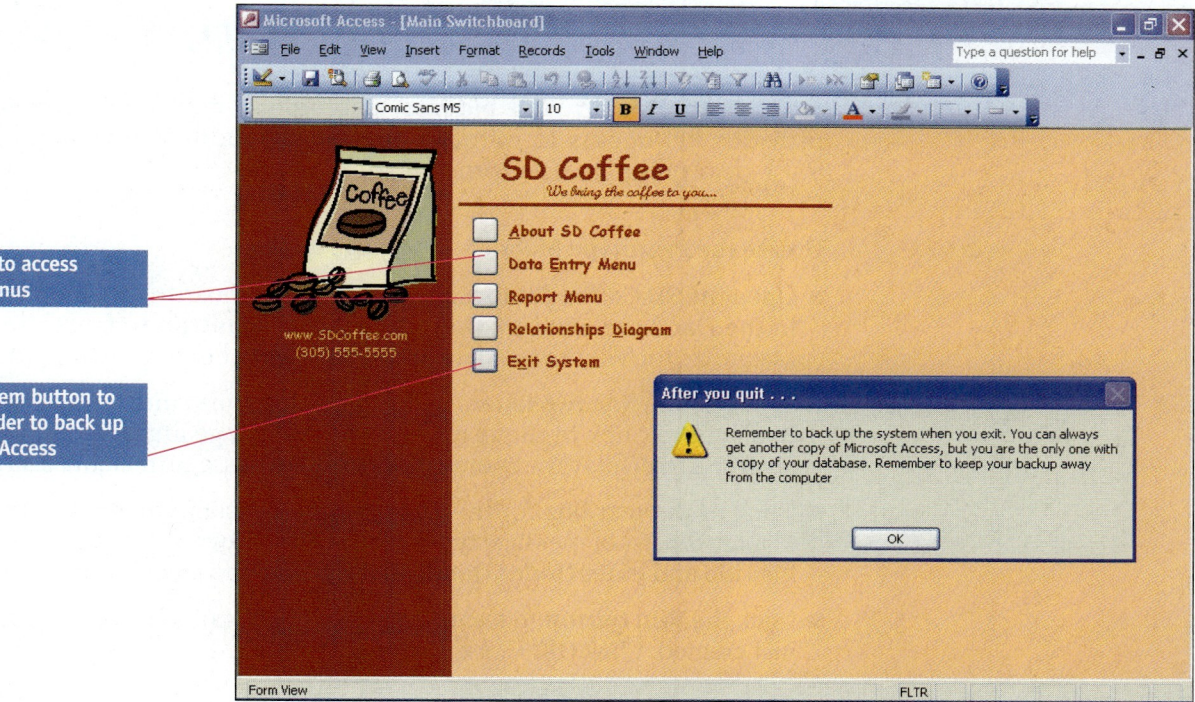

Click buttons to access subsidiary menus

Click Exit System button to display reminder to back up and then exit Access

(a) The Main Switchboard

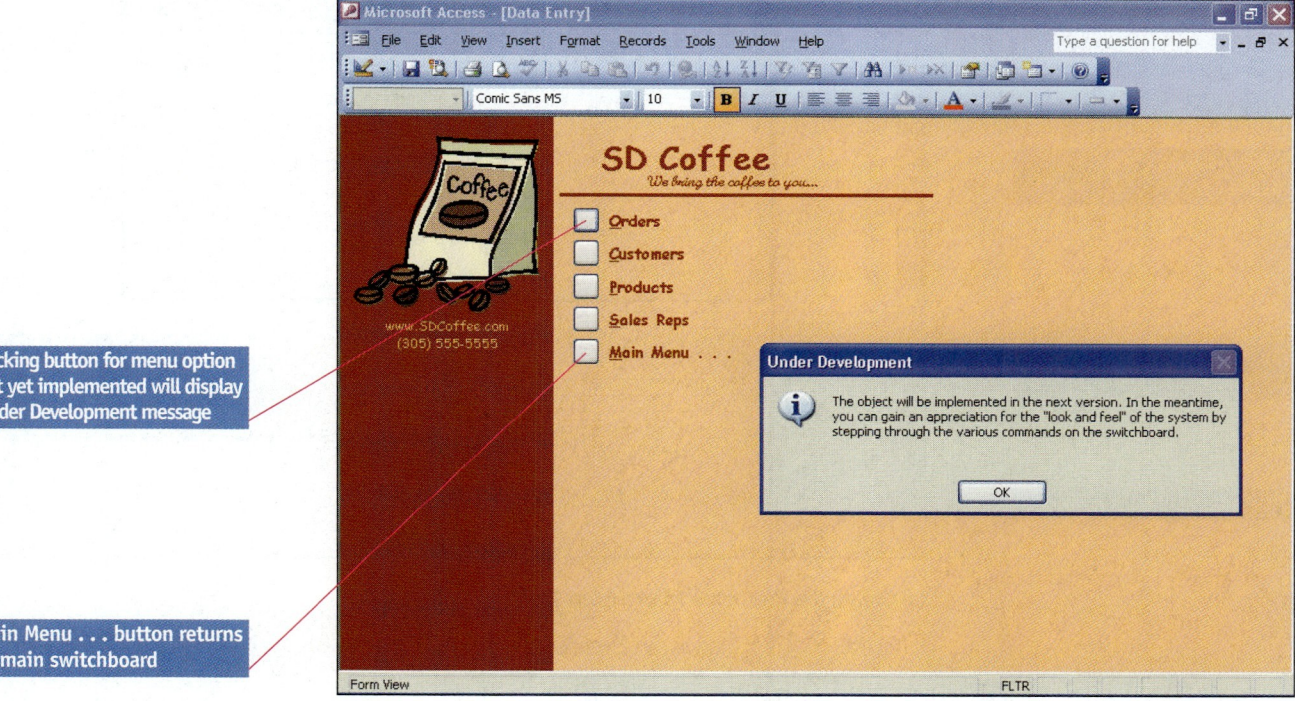

Clicking button for menu option not yet implemented will display Under Development message

Main Menu . . . button returns to main switchboard

(b) The Data Entry Menu

FIGURE 9.10   Prototyping—"Complete the System"

5   Prototyping—Complete the System

Objective   To use prototyping and macros to create a multilevel switchboard that provides full access to all data entry and reporting functions. Use Figure 9.11 as a guide in the exercise.

Step 1:   **Create the Prototype Macro**

- Open the **SD Coffee database**. Close the switchboard. Click the **Macros button** in the Database window, then click the **New button** to create a new macro. Maximize the window so that you have more room in which to work.

- Type **Ms** (the first two letters in the MsgBox action), then press **Enter** to accept this action. Click in the text box for the Message argument, and then press **Shift+F2** to display the zoom box. Enter the message in Figure 9.11a. Click **OK**.

- Click in the text box for the Type argument, click the **drop-down arrow** to display the list of message types, and select **Information**. Click in the text box for Title and enter **Under Development**. Save the macro as **Prototype**.

- Click the **Run button** to test the macro, which should display the message you just created. Click **OK**. Close the macro.

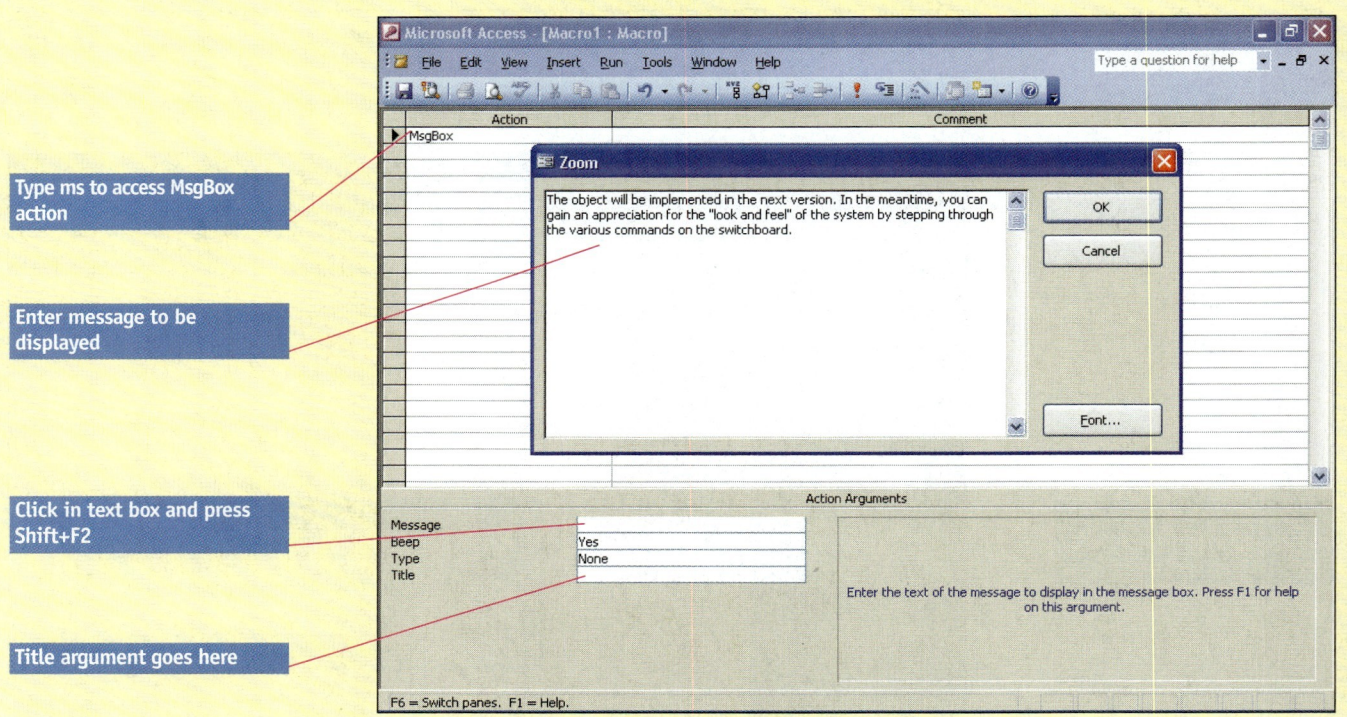

(a) Create the Prototype Macro (step 1)

FIGURE 9.11   Hands-on Exercise 5

USE KEYBOARD SHORTCUTS—F6, F11, AND SHIFT+F2

Use the F6 key to move back and forth between the top and bottom halves of the Macro (or any) window. Press Shift+F2 to display a zoom box that enables you to view long arguments in their entirety. Use the F11 key at any time to display the Database window.

Step 2: Create the AutoExec and Exit System Macros

- Click the **New button** in the Database window to create a new macro. Enter **Maximize** as the only action (no arguments are required), then save the macro as **AutoExec**. Close the macro.

- Click the **New button** a final time to create the **Exit System macro** in Figure 9.11b.

- The argument for the **MsgBox action** should be a message reminding the user to back up the database after exiting Access.

- The **Close action** closes the switchboard; thus, it should specify **Form** as the object type and **Switchboard** as the object name. The **Quit action** closes the database and also closes Microsoft Access.

- Save the macro as **Exit System**, then click the **Run button** to test the macro. You should see the message reminding you to back up the database. Click **OK** to accept the message and close the database.

- Reopen the database. The switchboard should appear automatically (because of the setting in the Startup command) and its window should be maximized. Close the switchboard.

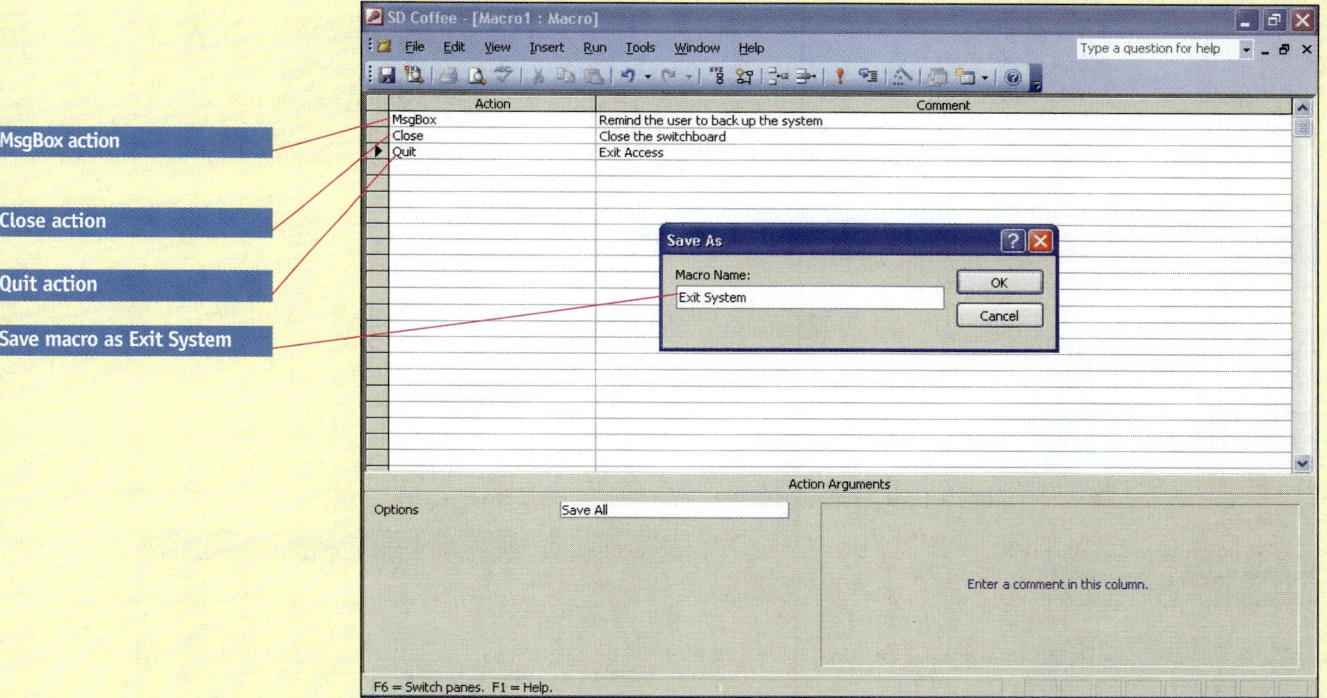

(b) Create the Exit System Macro (step 2)

FIGURE 9.11 Hands-on Exercise 5 (*continued*)

USE QUIT, NOT CLOSE

The Close action (with no arguments) closes the database but leaves Access open, whereas the Quit action closes both the database and Access. A novice may inadvertently use Close rather than Quit, but there is a subtle danger. The Close action will *not* close a database if the Database window was previously hidden, and thus the user may walk away from the computer when he or she sees a "blank screen," when in reality the database is still open. See step 4 in Hands-on Exercise 8 later in the chapter.

Step 3: **Create the Data Entry Switchboard**

- Start the Switchboard Manager. Click the **New button** in the Switchboard Manager dialog box. Enter **Data Entry** as the name of the switchboard page. Click **OK**.

- Select the **Data Entry page** in the Switchboard Manager dialog box, click **Edit** to open the Edit Switchboard Page dialog box, then click **New** to open the Edit Switchboard Item dialog box.

- Click in the Text box and type **&Orders**. Press **Tab** to move to the Command list box. Select the **Run Macro command**, and choose **Prototype** as the macro. Add the next two items, **&Customers** and **&Products**, in similar fashion, both of which should run the **Prototype macro**.

- Add **&Sales Reps** as the fourth menu item, but this time specify **Open Form in Edit mode**. Enter **Sales Reps** as the form name (the form you created in the previous exercise).

- Add the last item as shown in Figure 9.11c to return the user to the main switchboard. Click **OK** to close the Edit Switchboard Item dialog box. Click **Close** to close the Edit Switchboard Page dialog box.

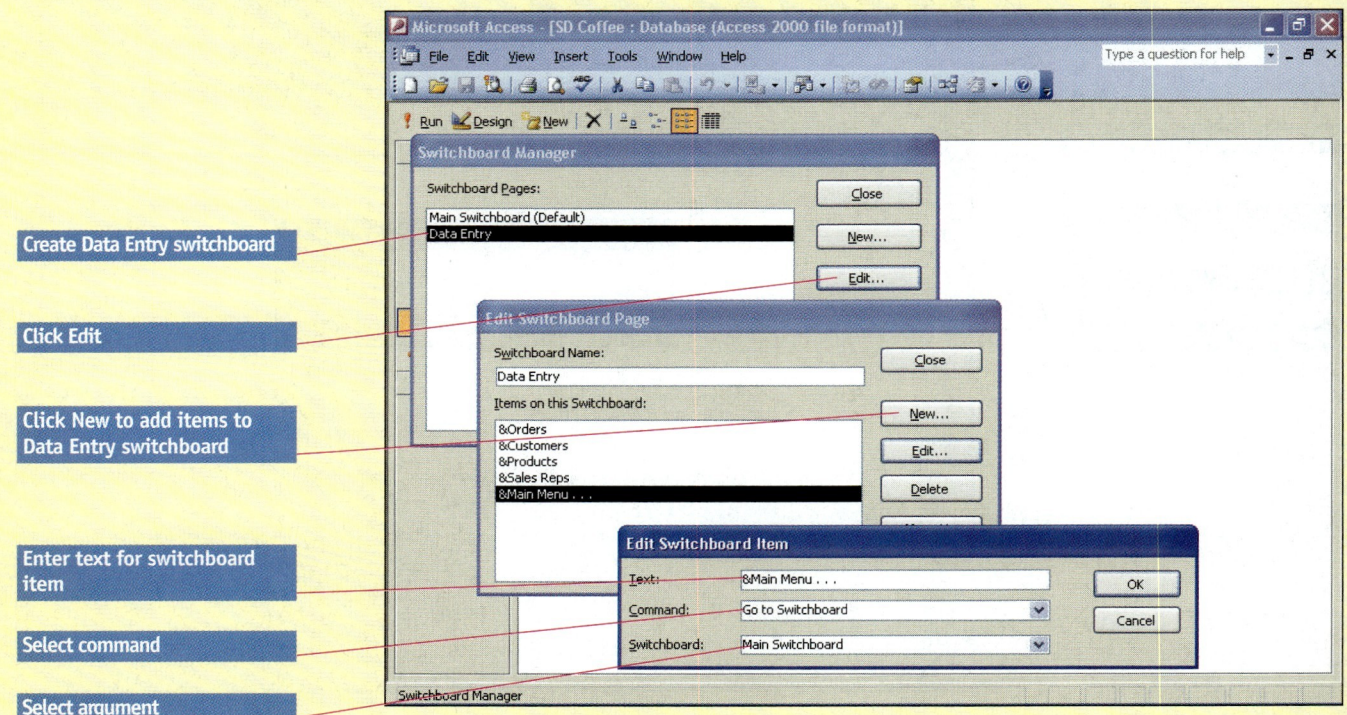

(c) Create the Data Entry Switchboard (step 3)

FIGURE 9.11 Hands-on Exercise 5 (*continued*)

EDIT MODE VERSUS ADD MODE

It's easy to miss the difference between opening a form in the Add mode versus opening it in the Edit mode. The Add mode lets you add new records to a table, but it precludes you from viewing records already in the table; that is, you can add, but you cannot edit. The Edit mode is more general as it lets you do both—add or edit. Select the Add mode only if you want to prevent a user from seeing or modifying existing data. Choose the Edit mode to give the user unrestricted access to the table.

Step 4: **Create the Report Switchboard**

- The Switchboard Manager dialog box should still be open. Click the **New button**, type **Reports** as the name of the switchboard page. Click **OK**.

- Select the **Reports page** in the Switchboard Manager dialog box. Click **Edit** to open the Edit Switchboard Page dialog box, then click **New** to open the Edit Switchboard Item dialog box.

- Click in the Text box and type **&Sales Reps report**. Press **Tab** to move to the Command list box, choose the **Open Report command**, then enter **Sales Reps** as the report name (this is the report you created in the previous exercise).

- Add the next six menu items as shown in Figure 9.11d. The reports are not yet created, and thus each menu option should specify the **Run Macro command** with **Prototype** as the name of the macro.

- Add the last menu item to return the user to the main switchboard. Click **OK** to close the Edit Switchboard Item dialog box. Click **Close** to close the Edit Switchboard Page dialog box.

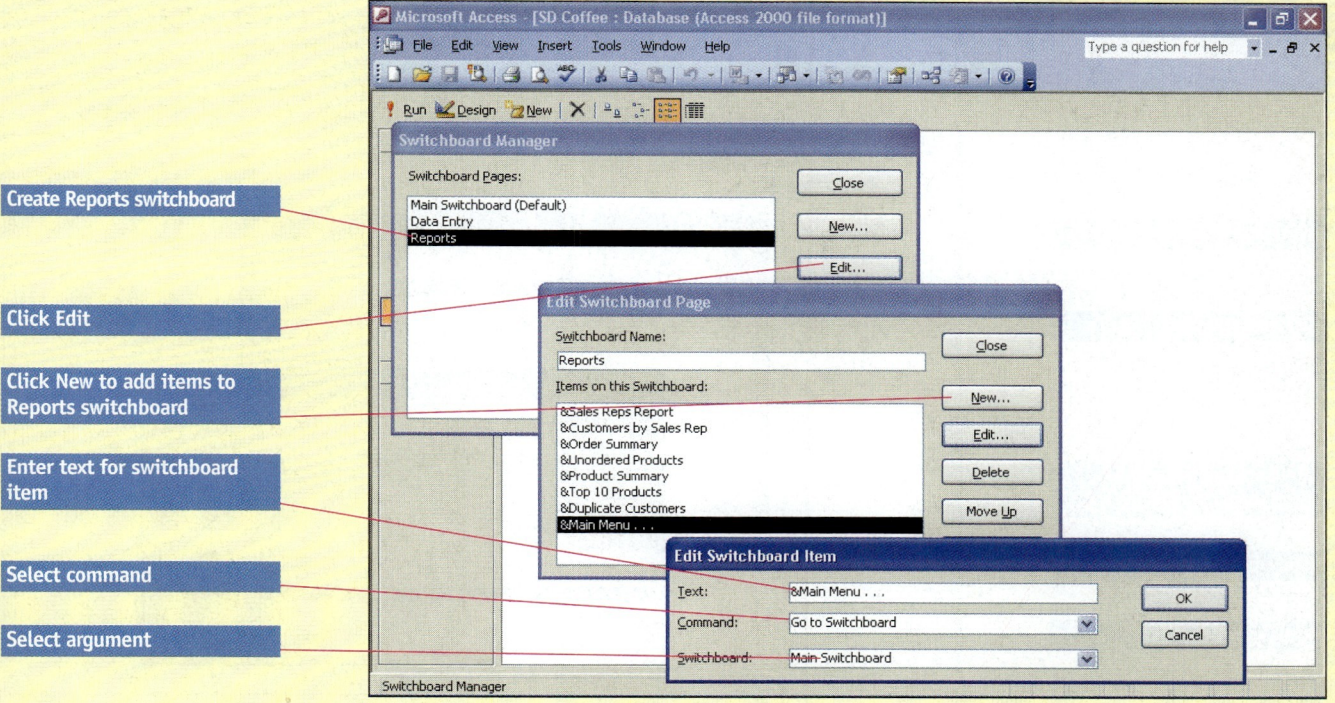

(d) Create the Report Switchboard (step 4)

FIGURE 9.11 Hands-on Exercise 5 (*continued*)

AUTOMATING THE SWITCHBOARD

Enter "&Sales Reps report" as the text of the switchboard item and the letter S (the letter immediately after the ampersand) will be underlined and appear as "Sales Reps report" on the switchboard. From there, you can execute the item by clicking its button, or you can use the Alt+S keyboard shortcut (where "S" is the underlined letter). The ampersands may look confusing when they appear in a list of switchboard commands in the Switchboard Manager, but the underlined letters give the menu a professional appearance on the actual switchboard. (Each menu item on the same switchboard must have a different underlined letter.)

Step 5: **Modify the Main Switchboard**

- Select the **Main Switchboard** in the Switchboard Manager dialog box, click the **Edit button** to open the Edit Switchboard Page dialog box, then click **New** to create a new menu option.

- Add a new switchboard item to open the **Data Entry Menu**. Add a second menu option to open the **Report menu**.

- The main switchboard now has seven items as shown in Figure 9.11e. Select the option for the **Form Template** and click the **Delete button**. Click **Yes** if asked whether to delete the item. Delete the **Report template**.

- Select the **Data Entry Menu** item, then click the **Move Up button** as needed to move this item immediately under the About form. Move up the **Reports Menu** item as well.

- Finally, modify the menu option for **&Exit System** to run the **Exit System** macro you created earlier. Close the Edit Switchboard Page dialog box. Close the Switchboard Manager.

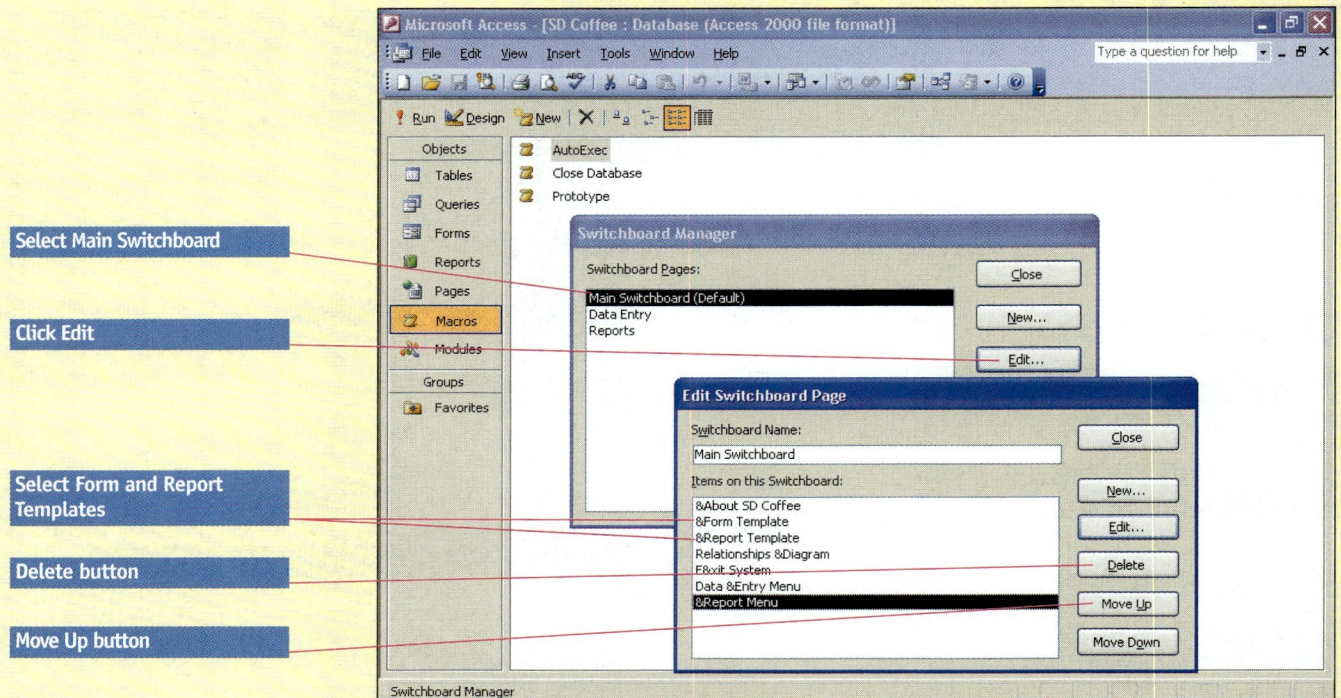

(e) Modify the Main Switchboard (step 5)

FIGURE 9.11 Hands-on Exercise 5 (*continued*)

THE SWITCHBOARD ITEMS TABLE

You can modify an existing switchboard in one of two ways—by using the Switchboard Manager or by making changes directly in the underlying table of switchboard items. Press the F11 key to display the Database window, click the Tables button, then open the Switchboard Items table where you can make changes to the various entries on the switchboard. We encourage you to experiment, but start by changing one entry at a time. The ItemText field is a good place to start.

Step 6: **Test the Main Switchboard**

- Click the **Forms button** in the Database window, then open the **About SD Coffee form** in Design view. Change the **Version number** to **2.0**. Save the form. Close the form.

- Pull down the **Tools menu**, click **Database Utilities**, then click the **Compact and Repair command**. The database closes and then reopens with the switchboard already displayed.

- Go to the **Data Entry menu**. Click the button for **Sales Reps** to open the form, click the **Add Record button**, then enter a new record for your instructor. Close the form.

- Test the other menu options, each of which should display a message that the object is not yet implemented. Return to the **Main Menu** when you have tested every option.

- Go to the **Reports menu**. Click **Sales Reps report** to view the list of existing sales reps. You should see yourself and Maryann from the previous exercises, and your instructor from this exercise. Print this report.

- Test the other menu options that display the not-yet-completed message, and then return to the main menu. Click the button to exit the system, which displays a message to back up the system. Click **OK**.

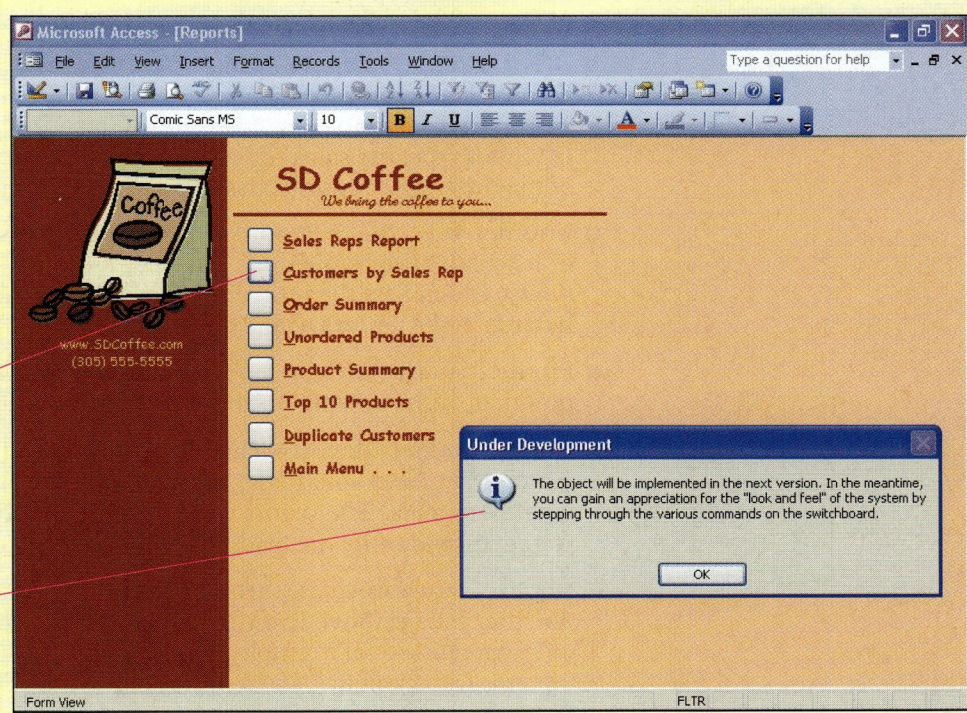

(f) Test the Main Switchboard (step 6)

FIGURE 9.11 Hands-on Exercise 5 (*continued*)

A FULLY FUNCTIONAL SYSTEM

Version 2.0 is the first "complete system" in the sense that it contains all of the eventual menu options. It does not matter that many of the commands display a message indicating the form or report is not yet implemented, because the user is able to execute every command and thus experience the "look and feel" of the eventual system. Subsequent versions add the forms and reports.

The client has just seen Version 2.0 of the SD Coffee database, in which the user was able to step through a complete system that contained both a data entry menu and a report menu. Most of the reports existed only as menu items, with an associated message indicating that the report will be developed later. Even so, the menu options convey the title and content of the various reports, providing the user with a true look and feel of the eventual system.

Every report is based on either a table or a query. The most basic type of query is a select query, but there are also several other types of specialized queries. It is helpful therefore to list the title of each report together with a brief description of its contents and associated data source. One report has already been created, two more will be created in the next hands-on exercise, and the remaining reports will be developed in the end-of-chapter exercises. The reports are:

■ Sales Reps Report—An alphabetical listing of all sales reps; this report was created in the fourth hands-on exercise to illustrate the use of a template in creating a report.

■ Customers by Sales Rep Report—The user enters the name of a sales rep, after which the customers for that representative are displayed in alphabetical order. The user can also decline to enter the name of a specific sales rep, in which case the customers for every sales rep will appear. The report is based on a *parameter query* and it is illustrated in Figure 9.12a.

■ Order Summary Report—This report was requested by the client at the initial meeting and is shown in Figure 9.12b. The report lists every order in sequence by OrderID. It also displays the date of the order, the name of the customer, the payment type, the sales rep who received credit for the order, and the amount of the order. The report is based on a *total query*.

■ Unordered Products Report—This report shows any product that is currently in inventory, but which has not been ordered. It is based on an *unmatched query*, which lists the records in the Products table that do not have matching records in the Order Details table.

■ Product Summary Report—This report displays an alphabetical listing of all products, with information about each product. It is based on the Products table.

■ Top 10 Products Report—This report displays the total amount of each product that has been sold in descending order by amount. (Only the top 10 products are shown.) The report is based on a total query that uses the *Top Values property* to identify the leading products.

■ Duplicate Customers Report—This report identifies duplicate records, a situation that can occur when the same customer is entered twice, each time under a different name—for example, "Department of CIS" and "Computer Information Systems Department." The report is based on a *Find Duplicates query*.

To create a new report, you first create the underlying query, and then you go to the Database window and copy the report template to a new report. You then open the new report in Design view and associate it with the appropriate data source (a query or a table). Next, you drag the required fields from the field list to the report and format each field and its label according to the formatting in the report template. And finally, you have to modify the Switchboard Items table to open the newly created report, as opposed to running the prototype macro.

You must also validate the reports after they have been created to be sure they are working correctly. The *test data* on which the reports are based can be generated in different ways—initially by entering the data directly in the Datasheet view, and then by using the appropriate forms after they have been created.

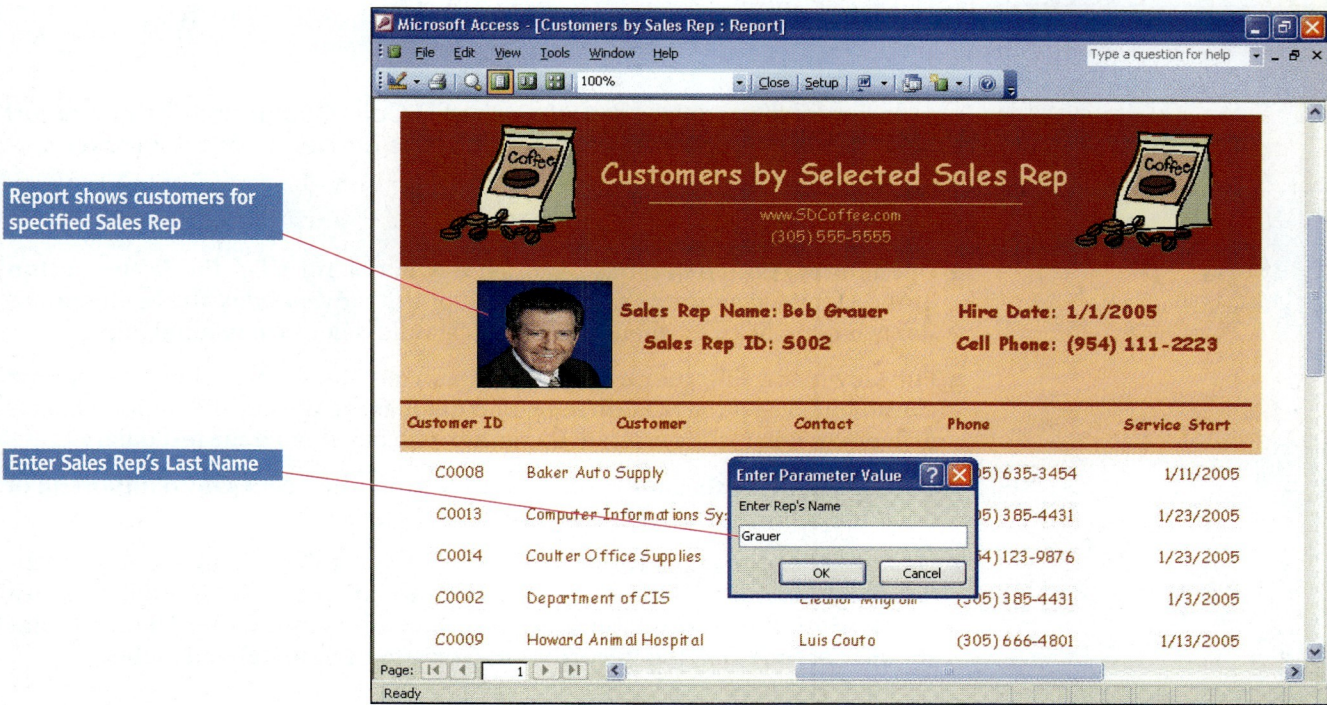

Report shows customers for specified Sales Rep

Enter Sales Rep's Last Name

(a) The Customers by Selected Sales Rep Report (Parameter Query)

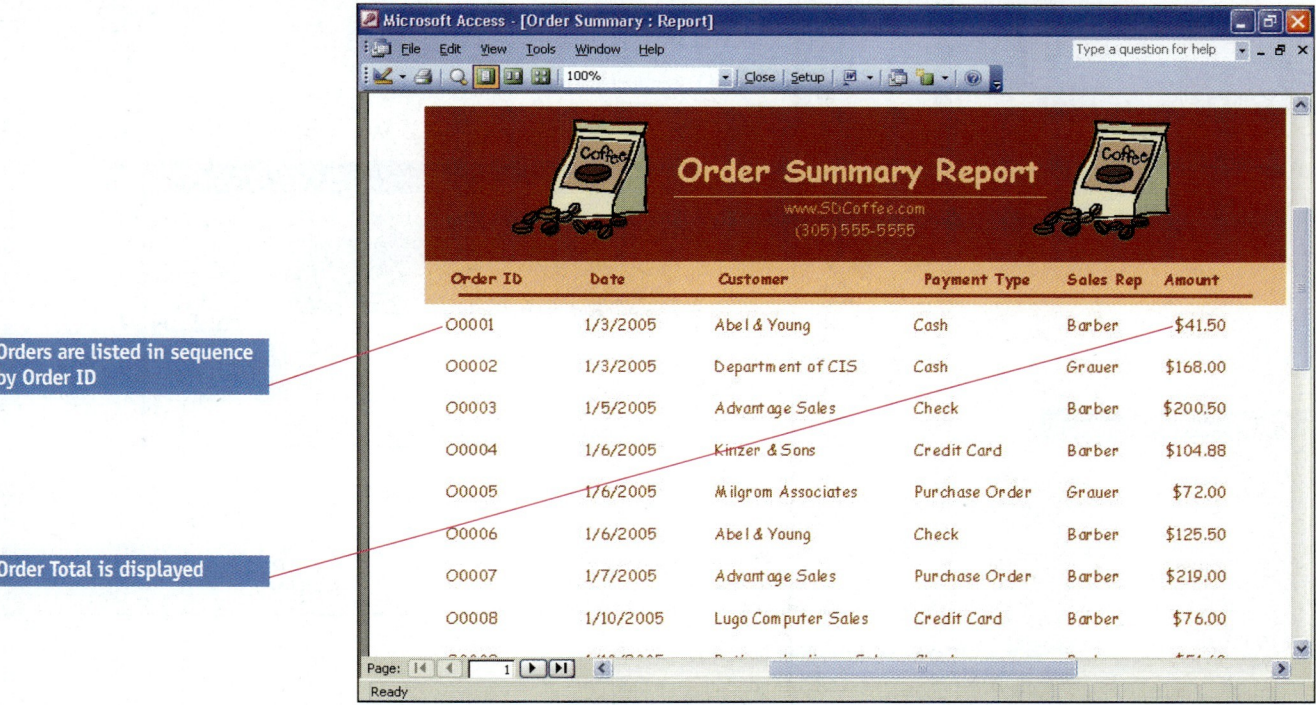

Orders are listed in sequence by Order ID

Order Total is displayed

(b) The Order Summary Report (Total Query)

FIGURE 9.12   Selected Reports

6 Add the Reports

Objective Create two of the required reports in the SD Coffee database; the first report is based on a parameter query; the second is derived from a total query.

Step 1: **Import the Test Data**

■ Open the **SD Coffee Database**. Close the switchboard. Click the **Tables button** in the Database window and delete all of the tables *except* the Switchboard Items table. Click **Yes** when asked if you should delete the relationships.

■ Pull down the **File menu**, click **Get External Data**, then click the **Import command**. Select the **SD Coffee by Bob database** to display the Import Objects dialog box. Bob is the person in our group who has created the test data.

■ Click the **Tables tab**, click the **Select All button**, then click **OK** to import all of the tables into your database as shown in Figure 9.13a.

■ Open the Relationships window, add the missing tables (if any), and reestablish the relationships. Every relationship should enforce referential integrity. In addition, the relationship between the Orders and Order Details tables should **Cascade Deleted Records** and **Cascade Update Related Fields**.

Click Tables tab

Click Select All button

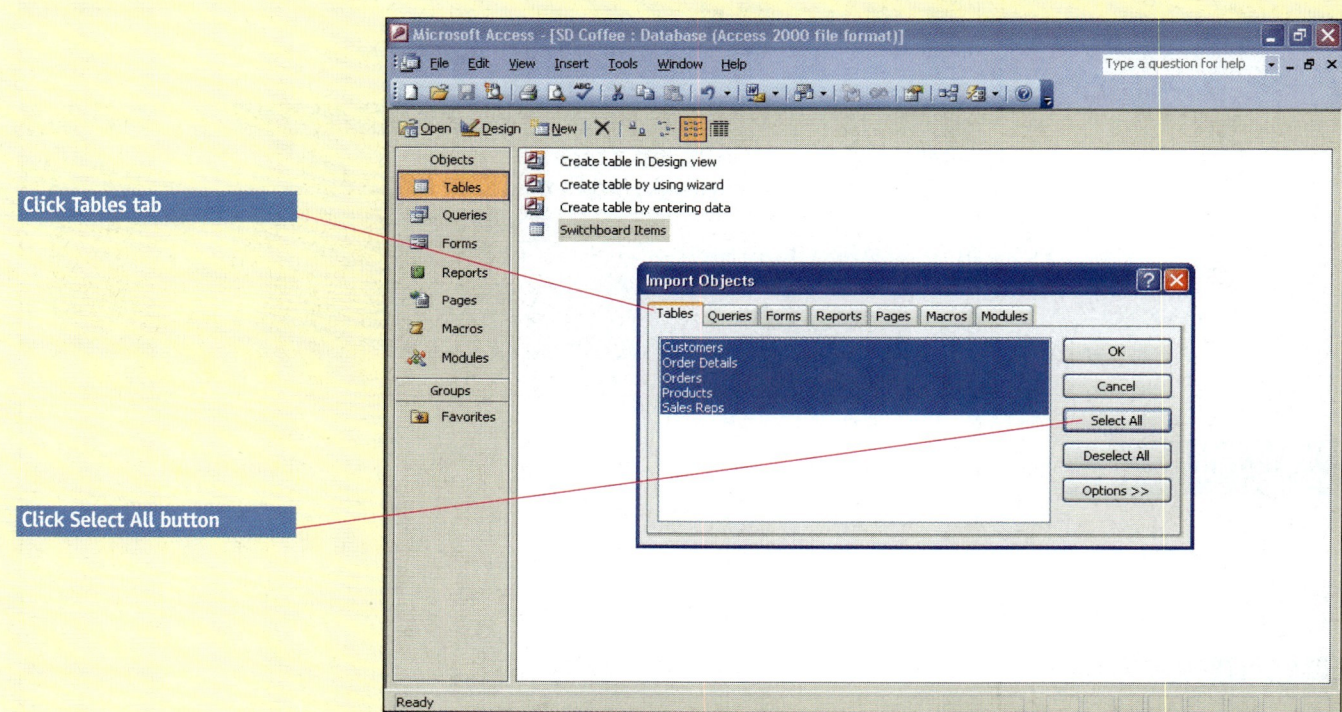

(a) Import the Test Data (step 1)

FIGURE 9.13 Hands-on Exercise 6

THE IMPORTANCE OF TEST DATA

You cannot assume that reports and queries are correct unless they have been adequately tested, which in turn requires the availability of carefully constructed test data. If, for example, you are looking for products that have never been ordered, such products must exist. We cannot overstate the importance of continued testing with a variety of test data.

Step 2: **Create the Customers by Sales Rep Query**

- Create a new query in Design view, then add the **Sales Reps** and **Customers tables** as shown in Figure 9.13b. Double click the **SalesRepID field** from the **Sales Reps table** to add it to the query.

- Click in the second column and enter the expression to concatenate the sales rep's first and last name.

- Add the **LastName field** from the **Sales Reps table** to the query. Click in the **criteria row** for this field and enter the expression **Like [Enter Rep's Last Name] & "*"**.

- Add the **CellPhone**, **HireDate**, and **SalesRepPhoto fields** from the **Sales Reps table** to the query. Complete the query by adding the **CustomerID**, **CustomerName**, **Contact**, **Phone**, and **ServiceStartDate fields** from the **Customers table**.

- Save the query as **Customers by Sales Rep**. Click the **Run button** to test the query, and then enter **Grauer** as the name of the rep. You should see all of Bob's customers.

- Return to Design view to rerun the query, but this time do not enter a sales rep. You should see Bob's customers as well as Maryann's. Close the query.

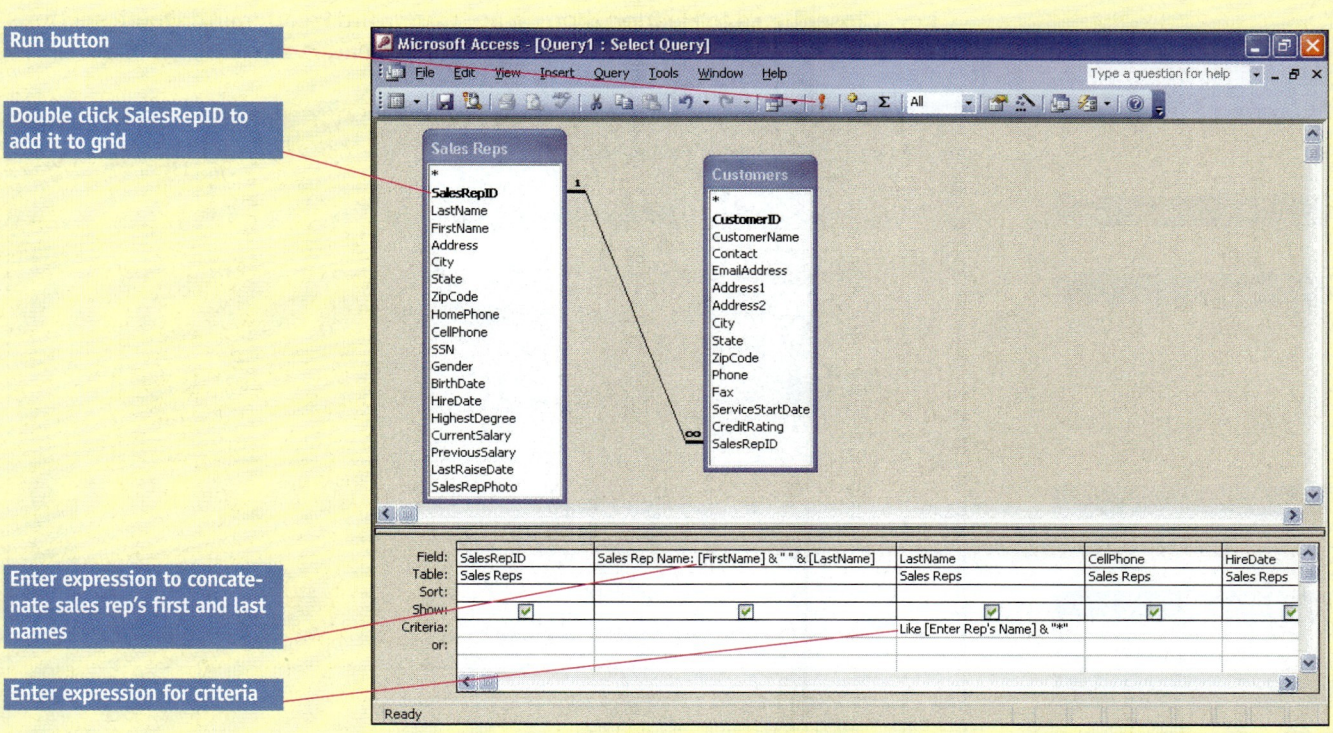

(b) Create the Customers by Sales Rep Query (step 2)

FIGURE 9.13   Hands-on Exercise 6 (*continued*)

PARAMETER QUERIES AND THE LIKE OPERATOR

The square brackets in the criteria row create a parameter query, which prompts you for the criteria (the sales rep's last name in this example) each time you execute the query. What if, however, you wanted every sales rep? You cannot omit the name because you will get zero records. Thus, you have to modify the criteria to include the Like operator concatenated with the asterisk wild card character. Now if you enter "Grauer" you get Like "Grauer*" which returns every rep whose last name begins with Grauer. And if you omit the name, you get Like "*" which returns every record.

Step 3:   **Create the Customers by Sales Rep Report**

- Click the **Reports button** in the Database window. Select the **Report Template**, press **Ctrl+C** to copy it, and then press **Ctrl+V**. Enter **Customers by Sales Rep** as the report name. Open the report in Design view.

- Right click the **Report selector button** in the upper-left portion of the report and click **Properties** to display the property sheet. Click the **All tab**. Click the **down arrow** in the Record Source text box and select the **Customers by Sales Rep query** you just created. Close the property sheet.

- Pull down the **View menu**, click the **Sorting and Grouping command**, and select **LastName** as the field on which to group the report. Enter **CustomerName** as the second field on which to group (sort) the report.

- Select the **LastName field**, then enter **Yes** for both a **Group Header** and a **Group Footer**. Close the Sorting and Grouping dialog box.

- Click the **Page Break tool** on the Toolbox, then click in the Group Footer to force each rep to begin on a new page. Make the Group Footer as small as possible to avoid a blank page at the end of the report.

- Click and drag to select the elements in the page header, then press the **Del key**. Close the Page Header, then create the Group Header and Detail sections in Figure 9.13c. Change the title in the Report Header. Save the report.

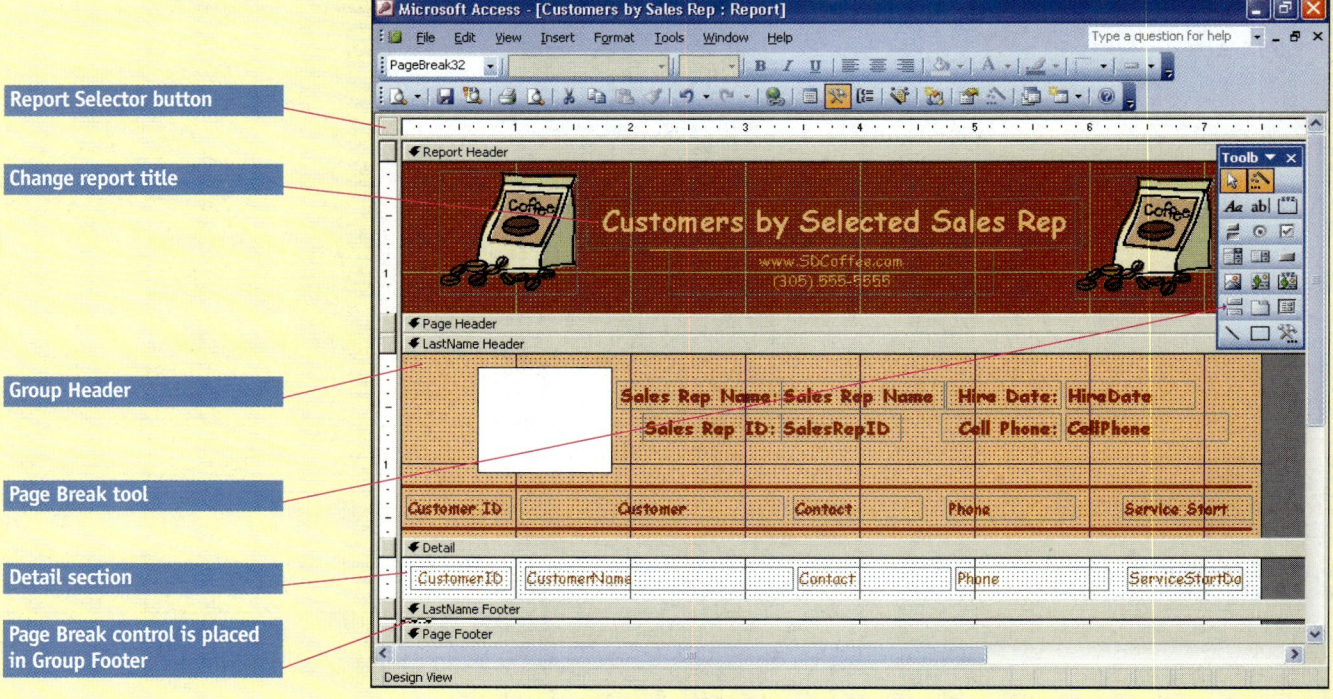

(c) Create the Customers by Sales Rep Report (step 3)

FIGURE 9.13   Hands-on Exercise 6 (*continued*)

CHOOSE THE RIGHT HEADER

You must visualize a report in order to create it correctly. We want a heading prior to each new sales representative and then we want to see all of the customers for that representative. There is different information for each representative and thus we choose a Group Header instead of a Page Header. We then add a page break to the Group Footer to force each representative to start on top of a new page.

Step 4: **View the Report**

- Click the **Print Preview button**. You will see the dialog box that prompts you to enter the last name of the sales representative. Enter **Grauer**.

- Look closely at the report, which displays Bob's customers, then return to Design view to make any adjustments. (The **Size Mode property** of the **SalesRepPhoto control** must be set to **Stretch**.) Save the changes.

- Click the **Print Preview button** a second time, but this time click **OK** without entering a last name to display customers for every sales rep.

- Click the **Two Pages button** on the Print Preview toolbar to display the report as shown in Figure 9.13d. The Report Header appears at the top of the first page, followed by the Group Header for Maryann, followed by Maryann's customers in alphabetical order.

- The page break in the Group Footer forces Bob's header onto the second page. Maryann appears before Bob in the report because her last name (Barber) comes before Bob's last name (Grauer).

- Click the **Close button** to return to Design view. Save, then close the report.

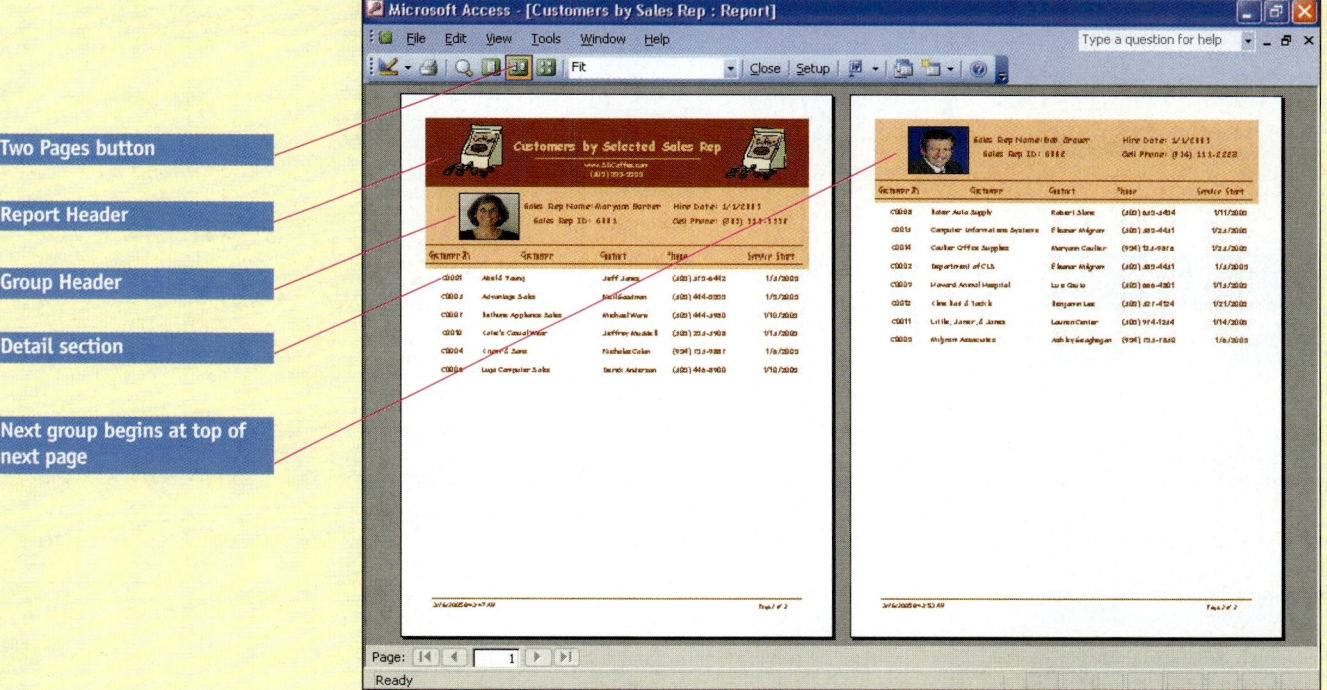

(d) View the Report (step 4)

FIGURE 9.13   Hands-on Exercise 6 (*continued*)

THE FIND DUPLICATES QUERY

Have you entered the same customer twice? "It's not possible," you say, but it's easier than you think; for example, you may enter "Computer Information Systems Department" one day, then "Department of CIS" the next. This is really the same customer (the address, phone, contact information, and so on are identical), but the names are different and thus your database will contain two records for the same customer. The Find Duplicates Query Wizard can eliminate the problem. See practice exercise 5 at the end of the chapter.

Step 5: Create the Order Summary Query

- Click the **Queries button** in the Database window. Double click the icon that says **Create query in Design view**. Add all five tables to the query as shown in Figure 9.13e. Save the query as **Order Summary**.

- Add the **OrderID, LastName, CustomerName, OrderDate,** and **PaymentType fields** from the indicated tables. Specify an **Ascending sort** for the OrderID.

- Click in the first empty column. Type **=Quantity*(Cost+Cost*MarkupPercent)**. Press **Enter**. Click and drag to replace Expr1 with **Amount.**

- Run the query. You will see two amounts for Order O0001 of $17.50 and $24.00; you now have to sum those values to arrive at the total cost for the order. Return to Design view.

- Click the **Totals button** to display the Total row. Type **Sum**, followed by an **opening parenthesis** in front of the expression; put a **closing parenthesis** at the end of the expression. Click in the Total row and select **Expression** as shown in Figure 9.13e.

- Click the **Run button**. You should see the total amount for each order—for example, $41.50 for Order O0001. Save the query. Close the query.

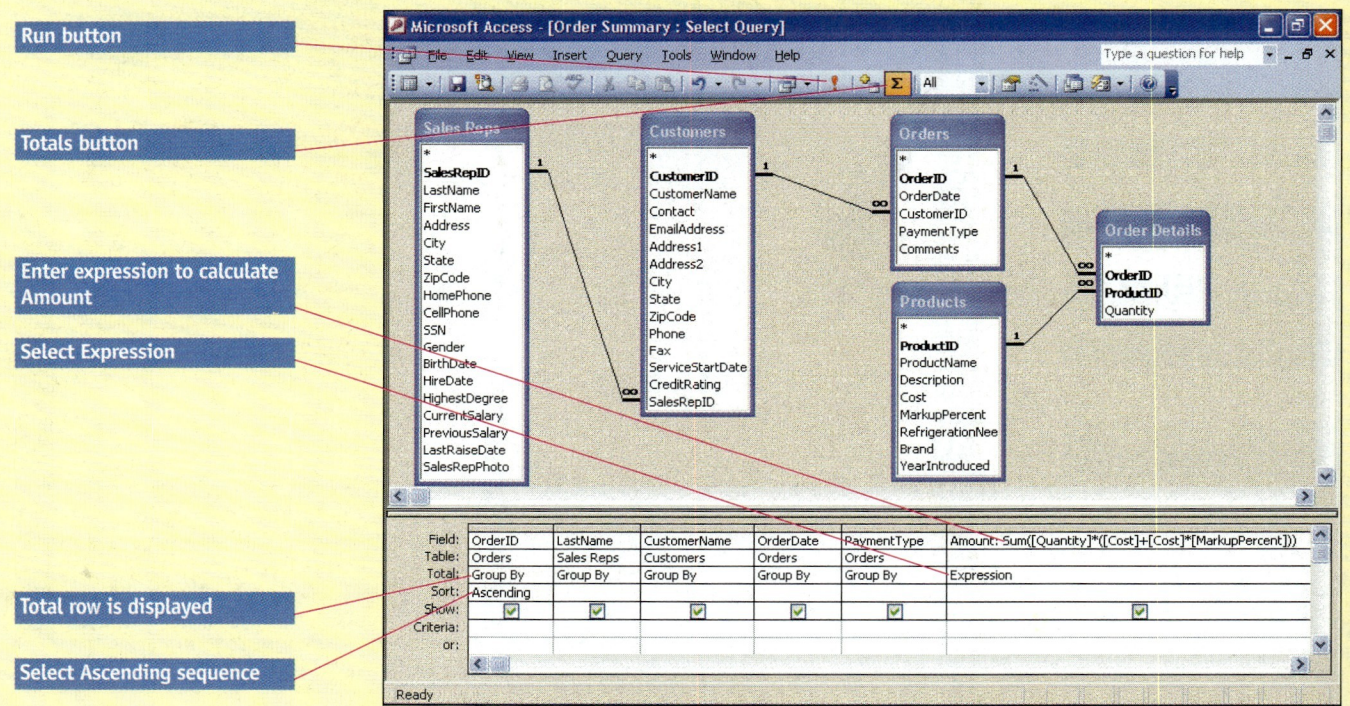

(e) Create the Order Summary Query (step 5)

FIGURE 9.13 Hands-on Exercise 6 *(continued)*

THE TOP VALUES PROPERTY

The Top Values property returns a specified number of records. Open a query in Design view and remove any sort keys that may be present. Click in the column where you want the top (or bottom) values, then choose the appropriate sequence; descending if you want to see the top values or ascending if you want the bottom values. Now click in the Top Values box and enter the desired value as either a number or percent—for example, 5 to list the top 5 records or 5% to list the top five percent. See practice exercise 1 at the end of the chapter.

Step 6: Create the Order Summary Report

- Create the **Order Summary Report** in Figure 9.13f. Your report should be based on the total query you just created and the report template that you have used throughout the chapter.

- Preview the report and make adjustments as necessary. Save the report and then close it. It's time to update the switchboard to reflect the two reports that were created in this exercise.

- Start the Switchboard Manager, select the **Reports page** in the Switchboard Manager dialog box, and click **Edit** to open the Edit Switchboard Page dialog box.

- Select the **Customers by Sales Rep** menu item and click the **Edit button**. Change the existing command, which runs the prototype macro to open the **Customers by Sales Rep report**. Modify the command associated with the **Order Summary** menu item in similar fashion.

- Close the Switchboard Manager, then open the Switchboard form to test the new commands. You are well on your way to finishing the system.

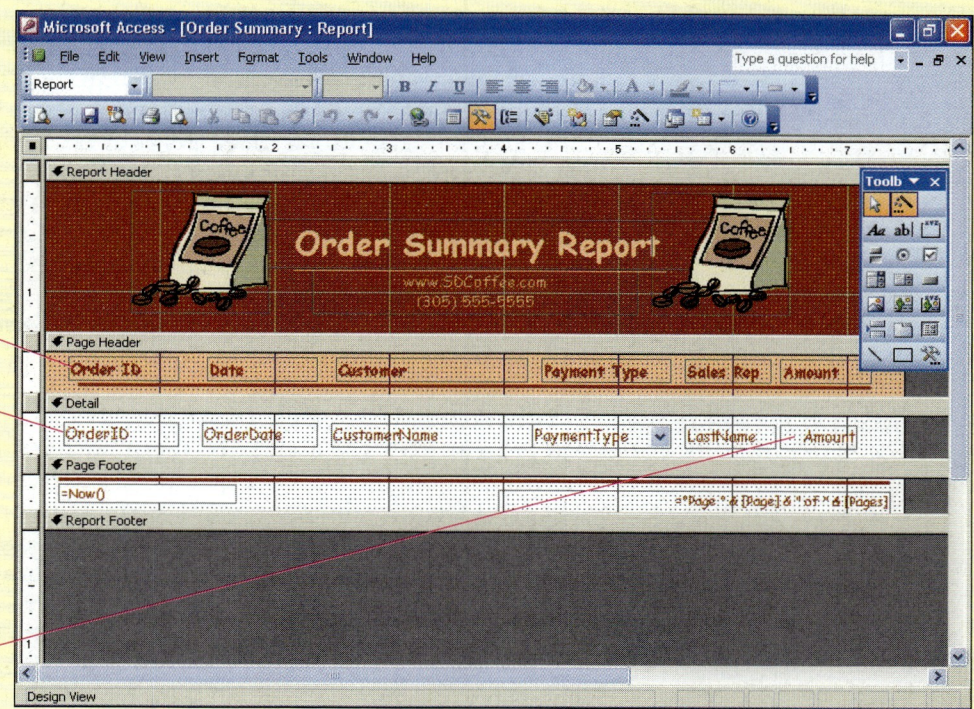

(f) Create the Order Summary Report (step 6)

FIGURE 9.13   Hands-on Exercise 6 *(continued)*

THE UNMATCHED QUERY WIZARD

It's good to know your best-selling products, but what about products that have not done so well; for example, are there any products that have never been ordered? The Unmatched Query Wizard identifies records in one table (the Products table) that do not have matching records in another table (the Order Details table). Click the Queries button in the Database window, click the New button on the Database toolbar, then select the Find Unmatched Query Wizard to create the query. See exercise 2 at the end of the chapter.

THE ORDERS FORM

The orders form for the SD Coffee database is comprised of a main form and a subform that are linked to one another. The main form in Figure 9.14a displays order number O00031; the subform shows the three products that comprise the order as the third product is being entered. The main form is displayed in Form view, whereas the subform is displayed in Datasheet view.

The main form is based on a query that contains fields from the Sales Reps, Customers, and Orders tables. Look at the form and visualize how the data is actually entered. The user clicks the command button to add an order in the bottom-right portion of the form, and then enters the date of the order and the method of payment. Comments are optional. The user then selects the name of the customer from a drop-down list box, which in turn displays all of the customer information.

Some fields on the form are outside the user's control; for example, the CustomerID is associated with the customer name and cannot be changed. Other fields are accessible to the user, but optional; for example, one can modify the customer's address or telephone, and the change will be reflected in the underlying customer table. The nature of an entry (whether it is required, optional, or prohibited) is conveyed to the user by the legend in the lower-left portion of the main form. Different fill colors are used to indicate the required, optional, and prohibited (e.g., calculated) entries. Note, too, that the OrderID is generated automatically (it is an AutoNumber field) and thus is outside the user's control.

The actual data entry is made easier by modifying the action of the Tab key to bypass the optional and prohibited fields. You begin a new order by entering the date of the order. The Tab (or Enter) key takes you to the payment type and then to the name of the customer, but once you select the customer you are taken directly to the subform. This is accomplished by setting the Tab Stop property to No, to skip the optional fields and prohibited fields. (Data entry can be further simplified through limited use of VBA; for example, the **SetFocus method** can be used to automatically position the user in the Order Date field in conjunction with the command button to add an order.)

The subform is based on a second query that takes data from the Product and Order Details tables. The users select the product from a drop-down list box, the price is determined automatically, the quantity is entered, and the amount is computed by multiplying the price times the quantity. The Tab Stop property is used to bypass the Price and Amount fields; that is, the user enters the first product, presses Tab (or Enter) to enter the quantity, then presses Tab to move directly to the next product.

The arithmetic calculations on the main form (the subtotal, the tax, and the order total) are more complex than on the subform. The expression to compute the subtotal *=[Order Details with Product Information].Form!OrderTotal* is only partially visible in Figure 9.14b, but it is explained here in depth. The bracketed entry is the name of the subform. This is followed by the period qualifier, the type of object (a form), and the name of the control on that subform (OrderTotal). In other words, we create the OrderTotal control in the footer of the subform, then we reference that control on the main form. (It sounds more complicated than it is, and you get to practice in the next hands-on exercise.) Once the order subtotal has been computed, the two remaining controls reference the subtotal.

The command buttons at the lower right also merit attention. The buttons to add a new order or to print the current order are straightforward. So, too, is the button to delete an order, but realize that you can delete an order only because the relationship between the Orders and Order Details tables was defined with cascade deleted records in effect. The button to add a new customer opens the Customers form because it is not possible to add a new customer directly from the order form. (The Customers form is displayed in add mode to show only the new record, as opposed to edit mode where every record is visible.) And finally, we enabled keyboard shortcuts to access the command buttons; thus, Alt+C will close the form.

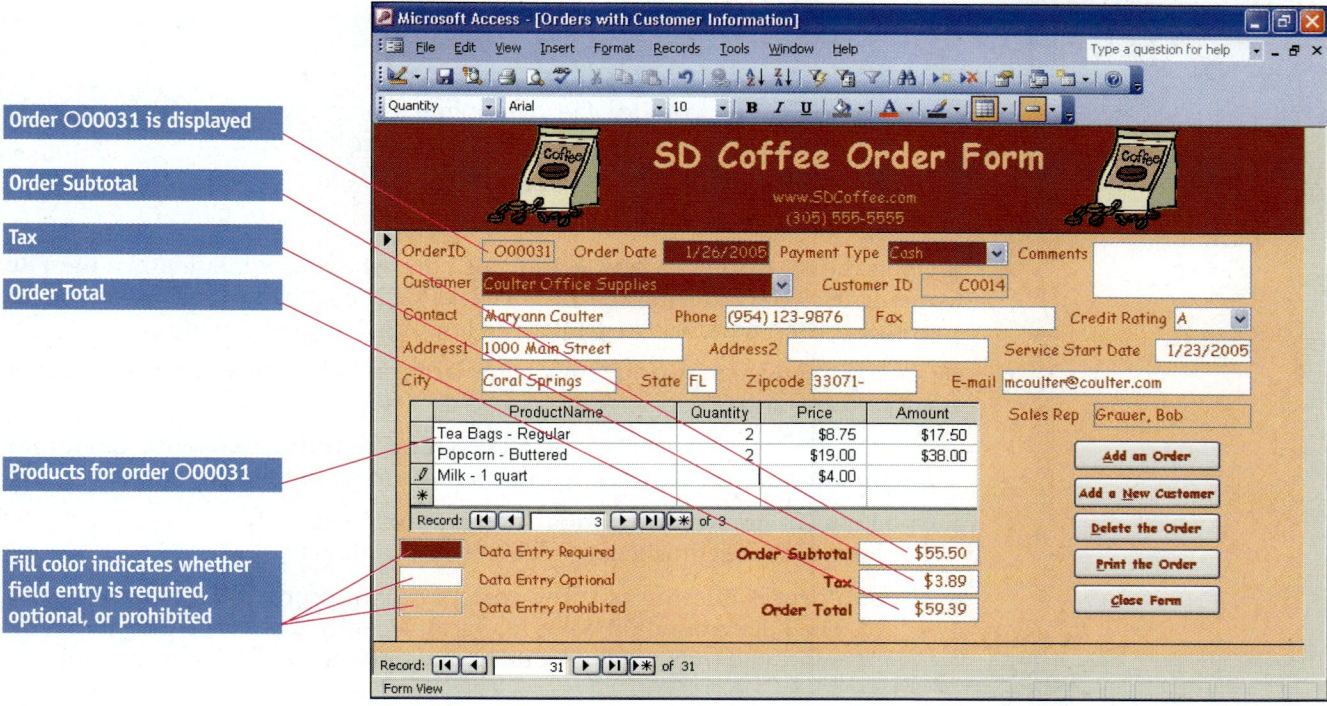

Order O00031 is displayed

Order Subtotal

Tax

Order Total

Products for order O00031

Fill color indicates whether field entry is required, optional, or prohibited

(a) Order Form (Form View)

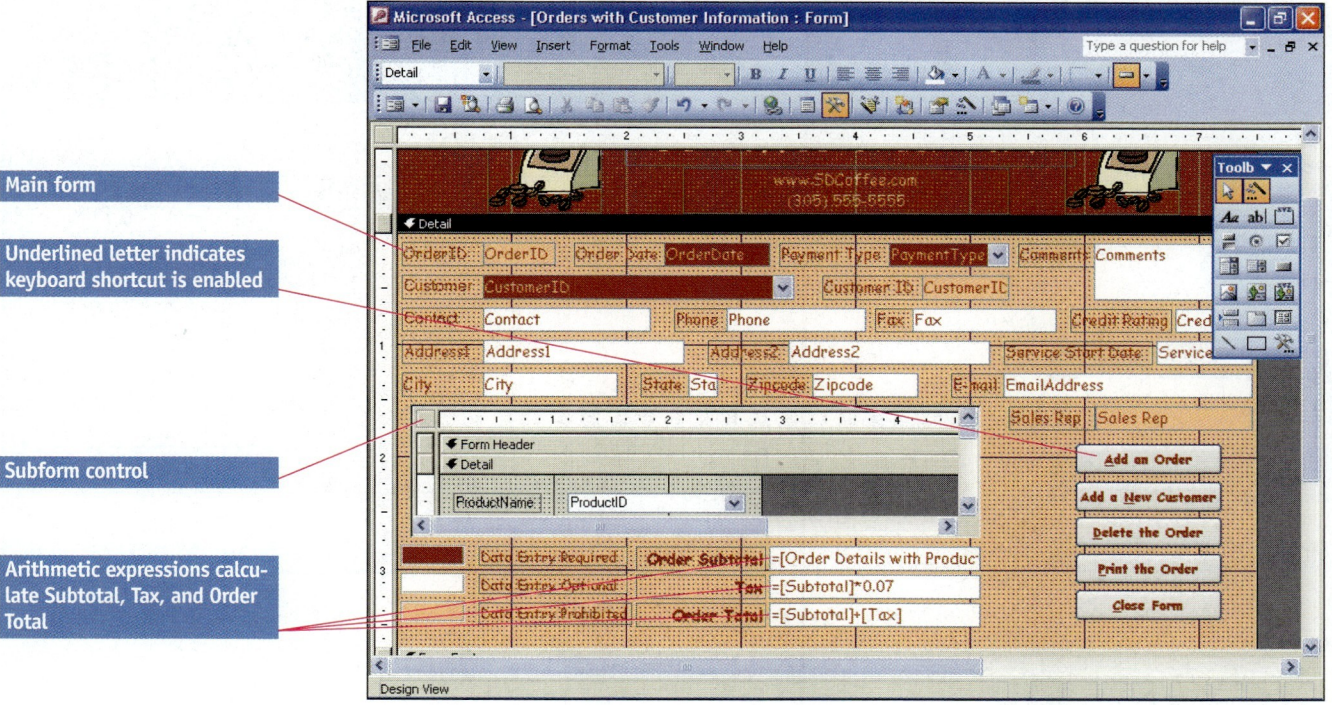

Main form

Underlined letter indicates keyboard shortcut is enabled

Subform control

Arithmetic expressions calculate Subtotal, Tax, and Order Total

(b) Order Form (Design View)

FIGURE 9.14 The SD Coffee Order Form

Objective   To create the order form for the SD Coffee Company; to use multiple-table queries as the basis for a main form and associated subform.

Step 1:   **Import the Main Form and Query**

- Open the **SD Coffee database** and close the switchboard. Pull down the **File menu**, click **Get External Data**, then click the **Import command**. Select the **SD Coffee by Bob database** to display the Import Objects dialog box.

- Click the **Queries button**, select the **Orders with Customer Information** query, then click **OK**.

- Click the **Forms button**. Select the **Customers** and **Orders with Customer Information** forms. Click **OK** to import these forms into the database.

- Open the **Orders with Customer Information form** as shown in Figure 9.15a. The form is almost finished, but there is still work to do.

- The subform is missing as is the command button to add a new customer record. The background fill color for various controls also needs to be set on the main form, to indicate the required and optional fields. Close the form.

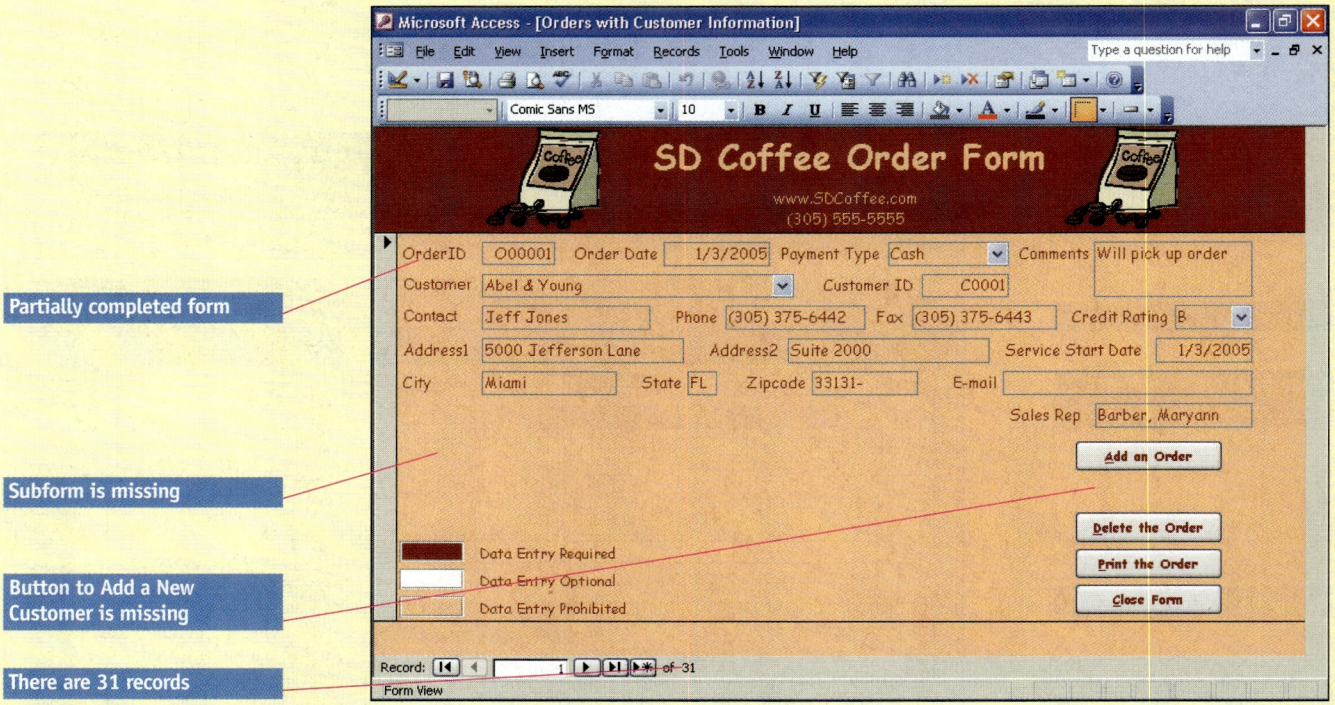

(a) Import the Main Form and Query (step 1)

FIGURE 9.15 Hands-on Exercise 7

FILE MANAGEMENT AT YOUR FINGERTIPS

Use the toolbar in the File New Database and/or Open dialog boxes to perform basic file management within Access. You can select any existing file, and delete it or rename it. You can create a new folder, which is very useful when you begin to work with a large number of documents. You can also use the Views button to change the way the files are listed within the dialog box.

Step 2: **Create the Subform Query**

- Click the **Queries button** in the Database window, then double click **Create query in Design view** to display the Query Design window. The Show Table dialog box appears automatically.

- Double click the **Products** and **Order Details** tables to add them to the query, and then arrange the tables as shown in Figure 9.15b.

- Add the **OrderID**, **ProductID**, **ProductName**, and **Quantity fields**. Be sure to add the fields from the correct table. Sort the query by **OrderID** and then by **ProductID** as shown.

- Click in the first empty column. Enter **=[Cost]+[Cost]*[MarkupPercent]**. Press **Enter**. Click and drag to select **Expr1** (do not select the colon). Type **Price** to create a more meaningful name. (The price is what the customer pays, as opposed to the cost of the item, which is what the company pays.)

- Right click the newly created field and click **Properties** to display the associated dialog box. Set the **Format property** to **Currency**.

- Create and format the **Amount field** in similar fashion. Run the query to be sure that it works. Return to Design view and make changes as necessary.

- Save the query as **Order Details with Product Information**. Close the query.

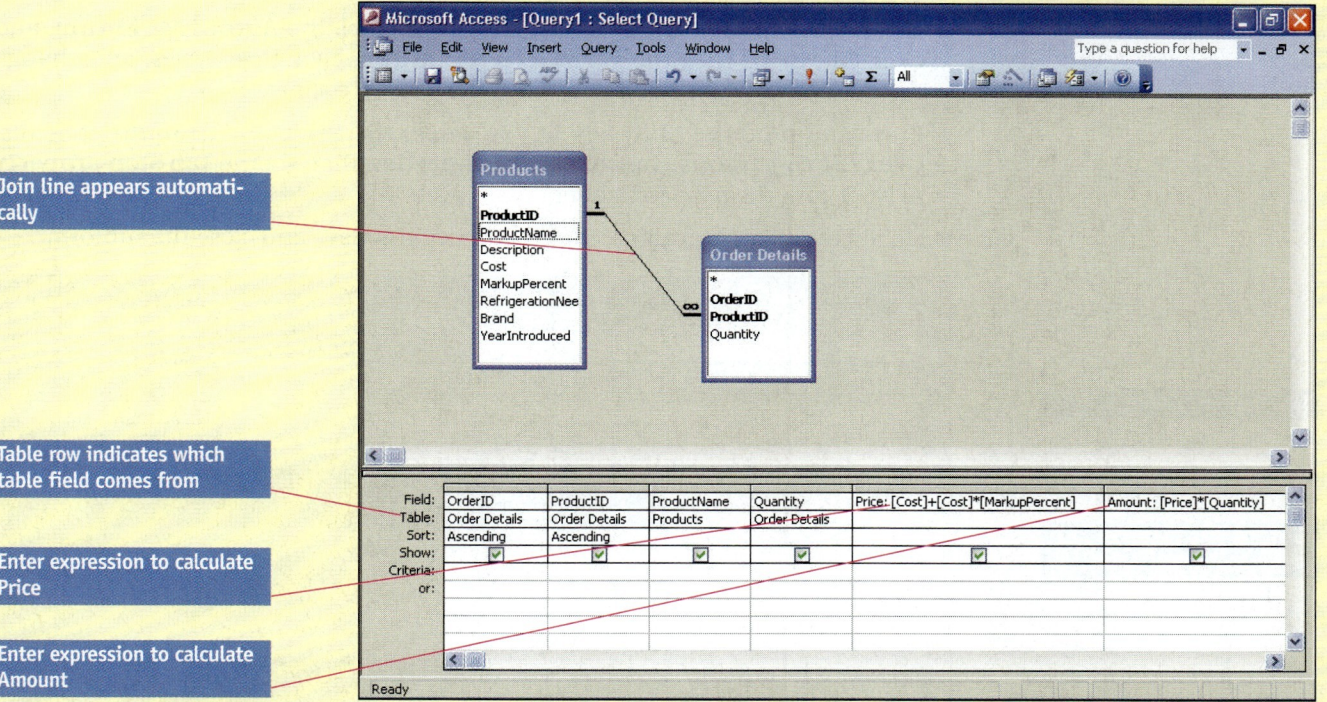

Join line appears automatically

Table row indicates which table field comes from

Enter expression to calculate Price

Enter expression to calculate Amount

(b) Create the Subform Query (step 2)

FIGURE 9.15 Hands-on Exercise 7 (*continued*)

ENTER PARAMETER VALUE—A PUZZLING ERROR

If you see a prompt to enter a parameter value, it is most likely because you misspelled a field name—for example, "Cst" instead of "Cost" in the design grid. Access interprets the misspelling as a parameter query and asks you to enter a value (the erroneous field name is displayed in a dialog box). Press Esc to cancel the query, then return to Design view to correct the error.

Step 3: **Create the Subform**

- Click the **Forms button**, then double click **Create form by using wizard**.

- Select the **Order Details with Product Information** query. Select the **Quantity**, **Price**, and **Amount fields** for use on the form. Use the suggested defaults in the remaining steps, then open the form in Design view.

- Click and drag to create the Form Footer. Click the **Text box control**, click and drag in the Form Footer to create the control, then enter **=Sum(Amount)**. Change the text of the label to **Order Total.**

- Right click the control, click **Properties**, then enter **OrderTotal** as the name of the control. Change the **Format property** to **Currency**. Go to Form view. You should see the order total of $3,435.63 at the bottom of the form.

- Return to Design view. Move the existing controls down in the Detail section. Click the **Combo Box control**, click and drag at the top of the Detail section, then tell the wizard that you want the **combo box to look up values in a table or query**. Specify the **Products table**, then specify the **ProductID** and **ProductName fields**.

- Sort by the **Product Name**. You should see the dialog box in Figure 9.15c.

- Click **Next**, then click the option button to **Store that value in this field**, choose **ProductID**, click **Next**, and select **ProductName** as the name of the combo box. Click **Finish**.

- Pull down the **View menu**, click **Tab Order**, click the **AutoOrder button**, and click **OK**. Right click the **Form selector button**, click **Properties**, and change the default view to **Datasheet**. Close the property sheet.

- Press and hold the **Shift key** as you select **the Price** and **Amount** controls. Click the **right mouse button**, click **Properties**, then set the **Tab Stop property** to **No**. Close the property sheet.

- Go to Form view and adjust the column widths. Save and close the subform.

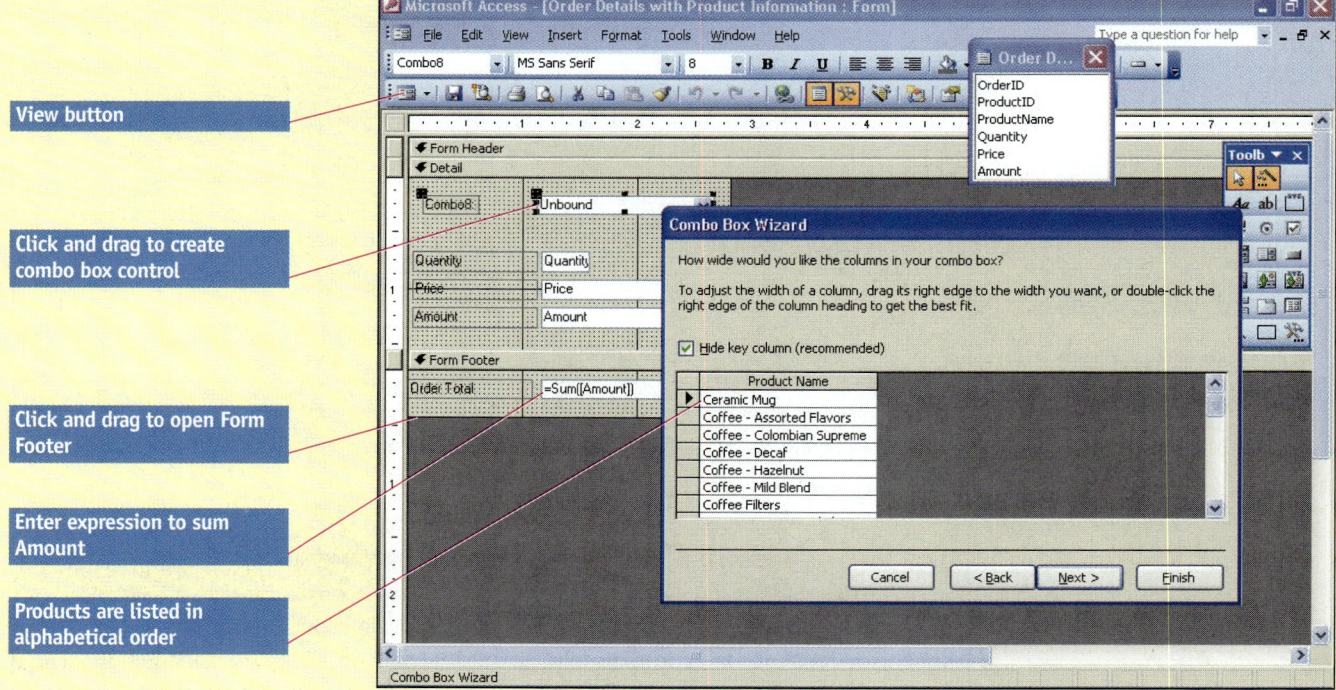

(c) Create the Subform (step 3)

FIGURE 9.15 Hands-on Exercise 7 (*continued*)

Step 4: **Link the Main Form to the Subform**

- Return to Design view for the main form as shown in Figure 9.15d. Click the **Subform/Subreport tool**, then click and drag on the main form where you want the subform to go.

- The Subform Wizard starts automatically. Click the button to **Use an existing form**, select the newly created **Order Details with Product Information**. Click **Next**.

- The **Choose from a list option button** is selected as is the entry beginning with **Show Order Details with Product Information.** Click **Next**.

- **Order Details with Product Information** is chosen as the name of the subform. Click **Finish**. The subform is inserted into the main form.

- Click and drag to change the size and/or position of the subform as necessary. Go to Form view to see the subform in the main form. Adjust column widths as necessary.

- Go back and forth between Design view and Form view until the subform is sized and positioned correctly. Click the label for the subform, then press the **Del key** to delete the label. (Use the Undo command if you accidentally delete the subform with the label.)

- Save the form.

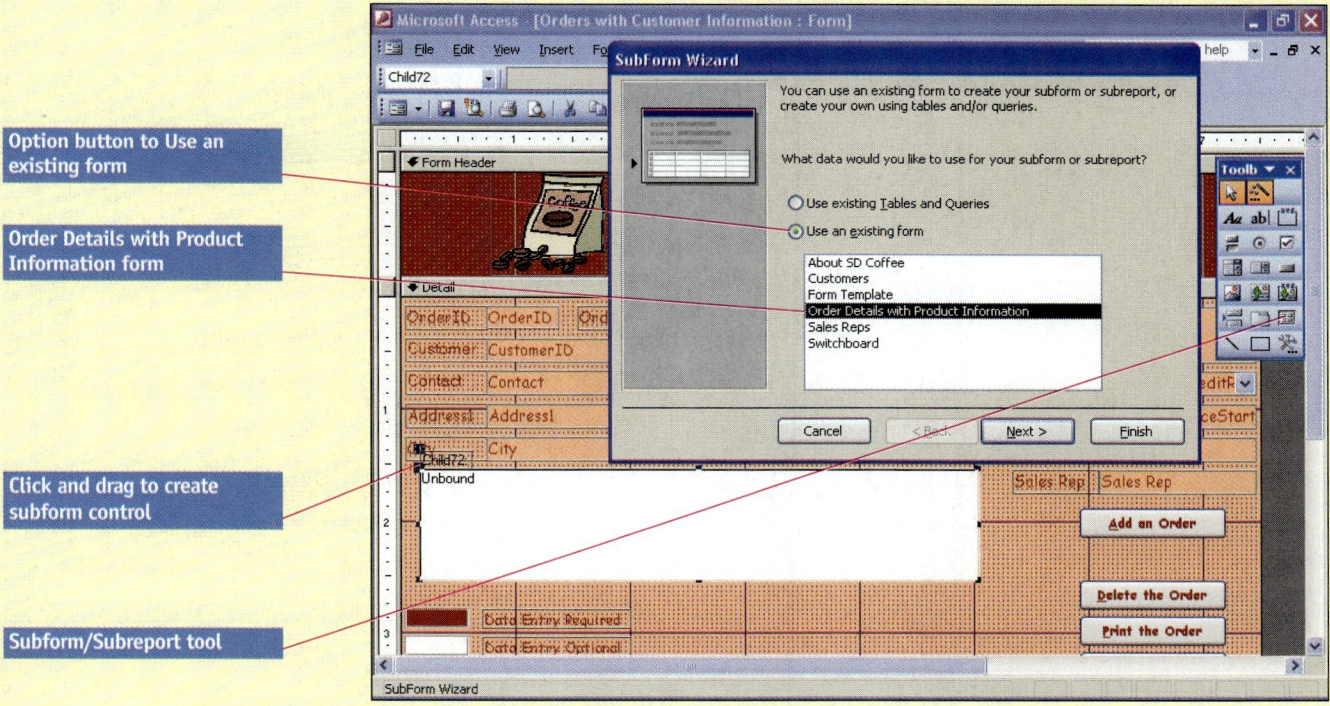

Option button to Use an existing form

Order Details with Product Information form

Click and drag to create subform control

Subform/Subreport tool

(d) Link the Main Form to the Subform (step 4)

FIGURE 9.15 Hands-on Exercise 7 (*continued*)

A FASTER WAY TO LINK

Close every object except the main form and database window. Pull down the Window menu and click the Tile Vertically command so that you can see both windows at the same time. Click the Forms tab in the Database window, then click and drag the Order Details with Product Information subform onto the main form. The result is identical.

Step 5: **Create the Subtotal, Tax, and Total Controls**

- Use the **Text box tool** to create the three calculated controls at the bottom of the main form. The syntax must be entered exactly as shown in Figure 9.15e.

- Right click the first control, click **Properties** to display the Property sheet, click the **All tab**, then enter **Subtotal** as the name of the control. (This name is referenced in the next two expressions.)

- Right click to select the second control, click **Properties**, then change the name to **Tax**. (We are assuming a **7%** sales tax.)

- Change the **Format property** of all three bound controls to **Currency**. Format the labels and calculated controls as shown in Figure 9.15e.

- Go to Form view to be sure that you see numeric values displayed in all three controls and that the calculations are correct. If you see an error in the first control, it is most likely because you did not enter the expression correctly.

- An error in the second control (but not the first) means that you spelled "Subtotal" incorrectly or that you forgot to name the first control. Similar logic pertains to the third control. Save the form.

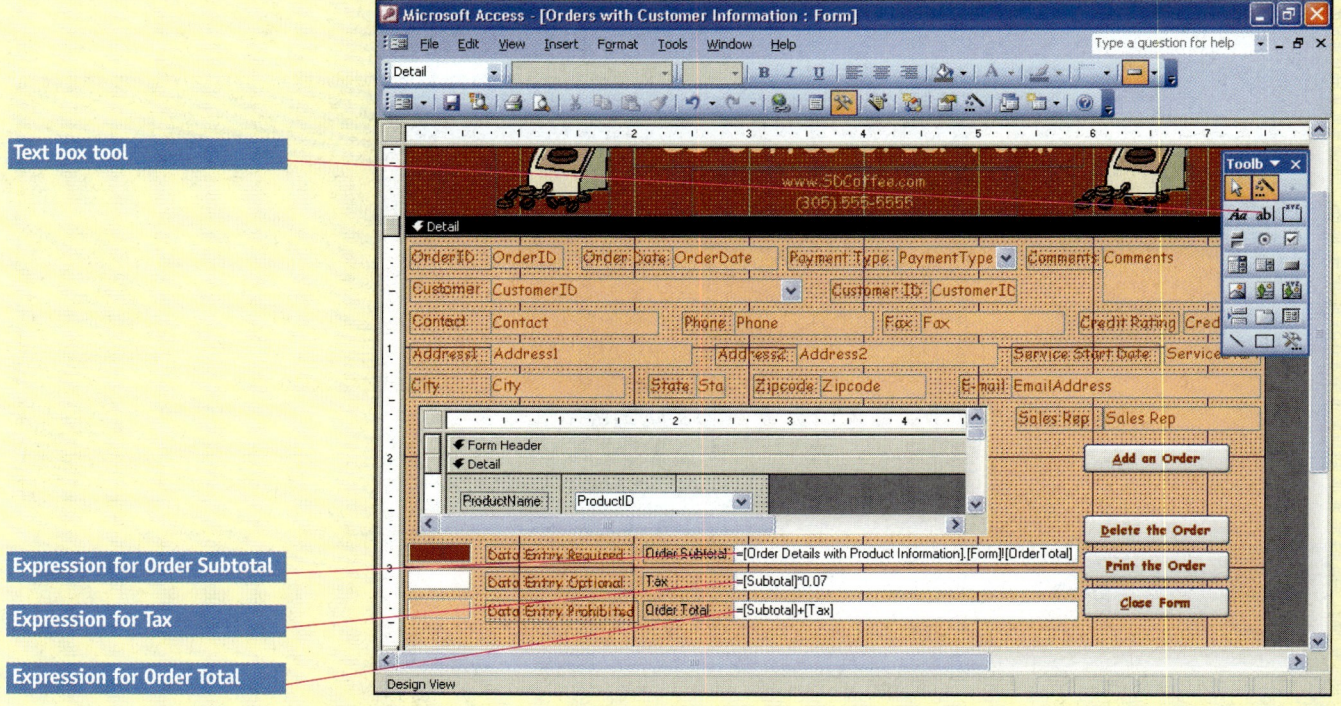

(e) Create the Subtotal, Tax, and Total Controls (step 5)

FIGURE 9.15 Hands-on Exercise 7 (*continued*)

CALCULATING THE ORDER TOTAL

It's easy to compute the total cost of an order when you know how. It starts with the footer of the subform where you create a summary total using the expression =Sum([Amount]). You then create a bound control on the main form that references the total from the subform. The name of the subform is enclosed in square brackets and is followed by a period and the object type (the word "Form" followed by an exclamation point). The last entry OrderTotal is the name of the control as it was defined on the subform.

Step 6: **Create the Add New Customer Button**

- Click the **Command button tool**, then click and drag to create a new command button as shown in Figure 9.15f. The Command Button Wizard opens:
  - ❑ Click **Form Operations** in the Category area and **Open Form** in the Action area. Click **Next**. Select the **Customers** form. Click **Next**.
  - ❑ The option button to **Open the form and show all records** is selected. Click **Next**. Click the Option button for **Text** and enter **Add a &New Customer** in the associated text box. Click **Next**.
  - ❑ Enter **OpenCustomerForm** as the name of the button. Click **Finish**.

- Right click the newly created command button, click **Properties**, click the **Event tab**, then click the **Build button** next to the **On Click property**.

- Click immediately before the statement that says stDocName = "Customers", Type **DoCmd.Close** and press **Enter** to close the Orders form.

- Click at the end of the statement that begins DoCmd.OpenForm. Type a **comma** followed by a **space**, then type **acAdd**. Click the **Save button**. Close the VB editor, then close the property sheet.

- Format, move, and size the button so that it matches the other command buttons. Save the form. Go to Form view to see the Orders form. Click the **Add a New Customer button** to be sure it works properly. Close the form.

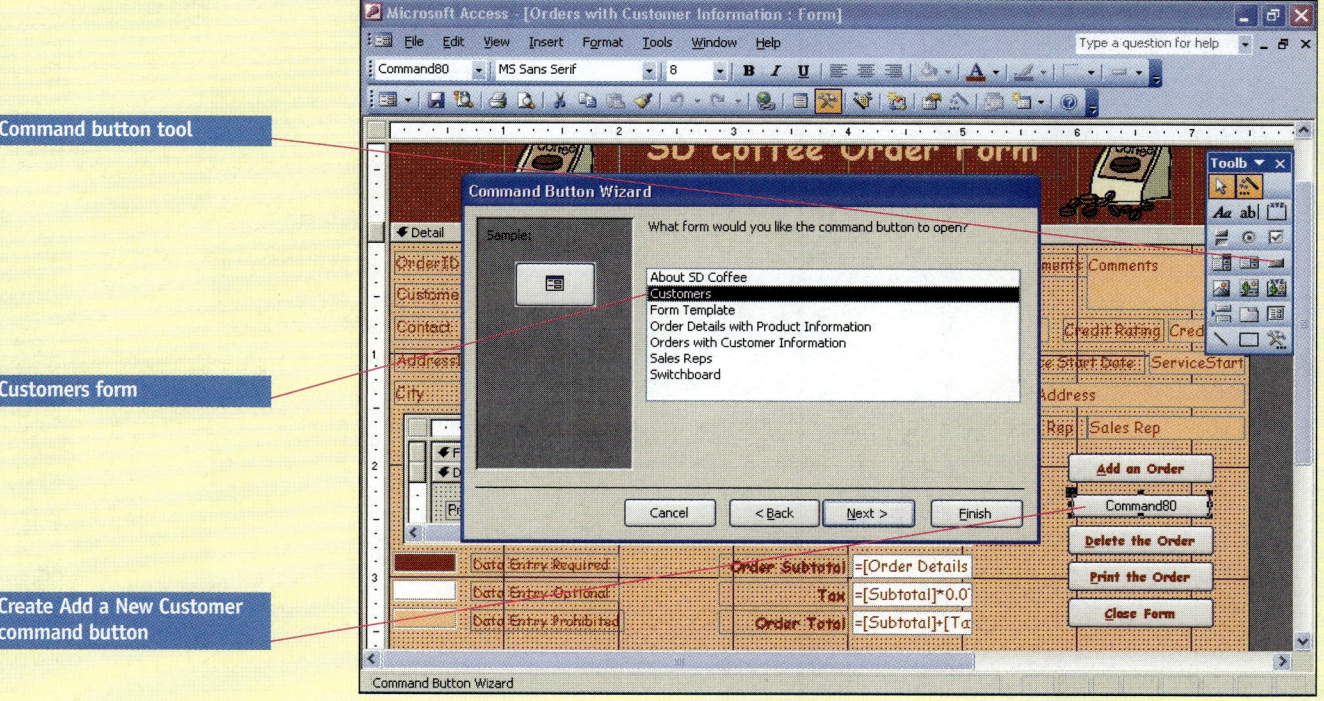

(f) Create the Add New Customer Button (step 6)

FIGURE 9.15 Hands-on Exercise 7 (*continued*)

THE NORTHWIND DATABASE

We wanted to open the Customer form in Add mode (to see only the current customer), as opposed to the Edit mode where you see every customer. We weren't sure how to do it, so we consulted the Northwind database, a sample database created by Microsoft to illustrate a variety of Access techniques. Pull down the Help menu, click Sample Databases, then click Northwind Sample database.

Step 7: The Finishing Touches

- Return to the Design view of the main form. Press and hold the **Shift key** as you select the **Order Date**, **Payment Type**, and **CustomerID** bound controls.

- Click the **drop-down arrow** on the **Fill/Back Color button** and change the color as shown in Figure 9.15g. Change the font color as well.

- Press and hold the **Shift key** as you select the controls containing the optional customer information as in Figure 9.15g. Change the **fill color** to **white**.

- Right click the selected controls, click **Properties**, and click the **All tab**. Click in the **Tab Stop property** and change it to **No**. You can still access these controls, but the **Tab key** will bypass them.

- Pull down the **View menu**, click **Tab Order**, click the **Auto Order button**, then click **OK**. Save, then close the form. Open the Switchboard Manager.

- Select the **Data Entry Switchboard** in the Switchboard Manager dialog box and click the **Edit button** to open the Edit Switchboard Page dialog box. Select the **&Orders menu option** and click the **Edit button**. Change the command to open the **Orders with Customer Information** form in **Edit mode**.

- Change the **&Customers menu option** to open the **Customers form** in Edit mode. Close the Switchboard Manager.

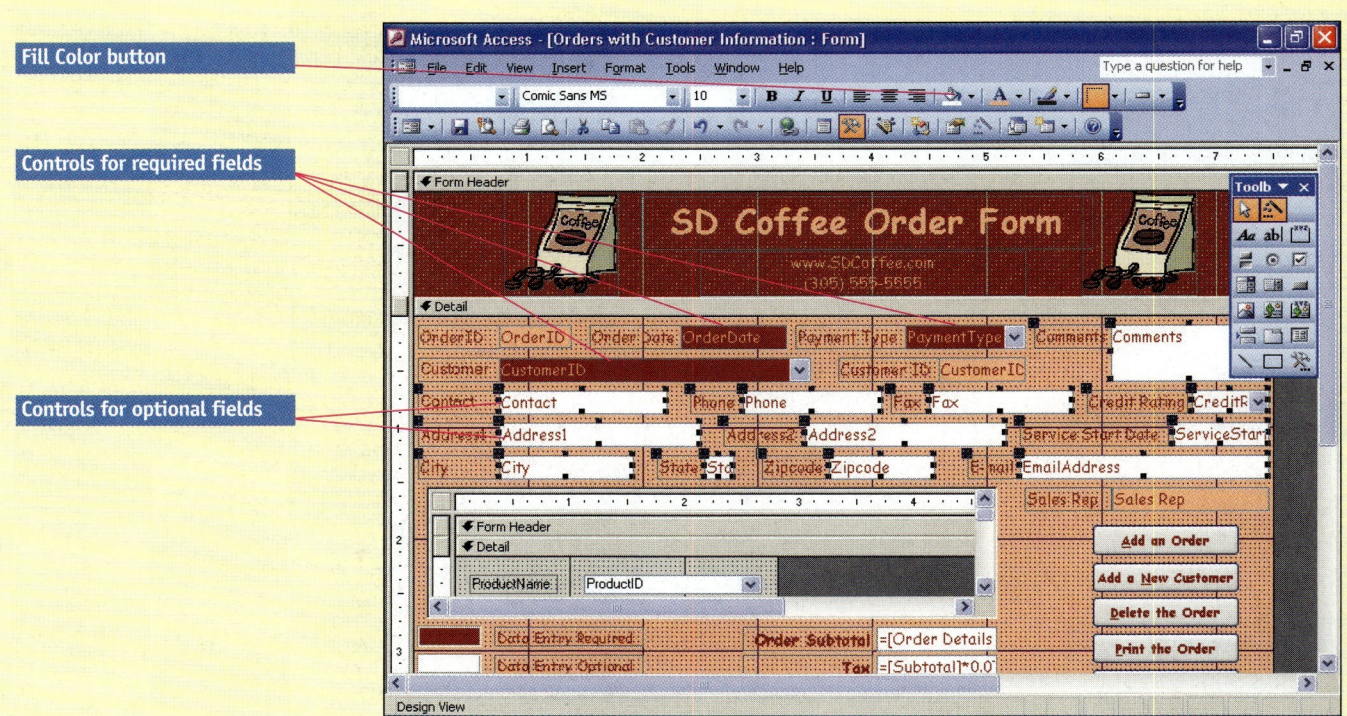

(g) The Finishing Touches (step 7)

FIGURE 9.15 Hands-on Exercise 7 (*continued*)

THE TAB STOP PROPERTY

The Tab key provides a shortcut in the finished form to move from one field to the next. AutoNumber fields, such as the SalesRepID, are not entered explicitly, however, and should be bypassed. Right click the SalesRepID control, click Properties to display the associated property sheet, and then click the All tab to view all of the properties for this control. Scroll down to the Tab Stop property and set it to No.

Step 8: Add an Order

- Open the **Switchboard form**, click the **Data Entry Menu button**, then click **Orders** to display the form you just created. Click the button to **Add a New Customer**.

- Click the **Service Start Date** text box field and enter today's date. Press the **Tab key** to move to the **Sales Rep field**, select **Grauer**, and press **Tab**.

- Enter a company name of your own choosing; then enter **your instructor** as the contact name. Complete the customer information, and then click the **Close Form button**.

- You are back in the Data Entry menu. Click the **Orders button** to open the Order form, then click the **Add an Order button**. Click in the **Order Date** text box and enter **today's date**. Press **Tab**.

- Enter **Cash** and press **Tab** to move to the list box for customer name. Click the **down arrow** to locate the customer you just entered.

- Press **Tab** to move to the subform. (The remaining fields are bypassed because the Tab Stop property was set to no.)

- Select the first product, press **Tab** to enter the quantity, then press **Tab** to enter the second item. The amount is calculated automatically as soon as you complete the first item.

- Complete the order as shown in Figure 9.15h. Print the completed order.

- Close the form to return to the switchboard. Click the button to return to the Main Menu, and then exit the system.

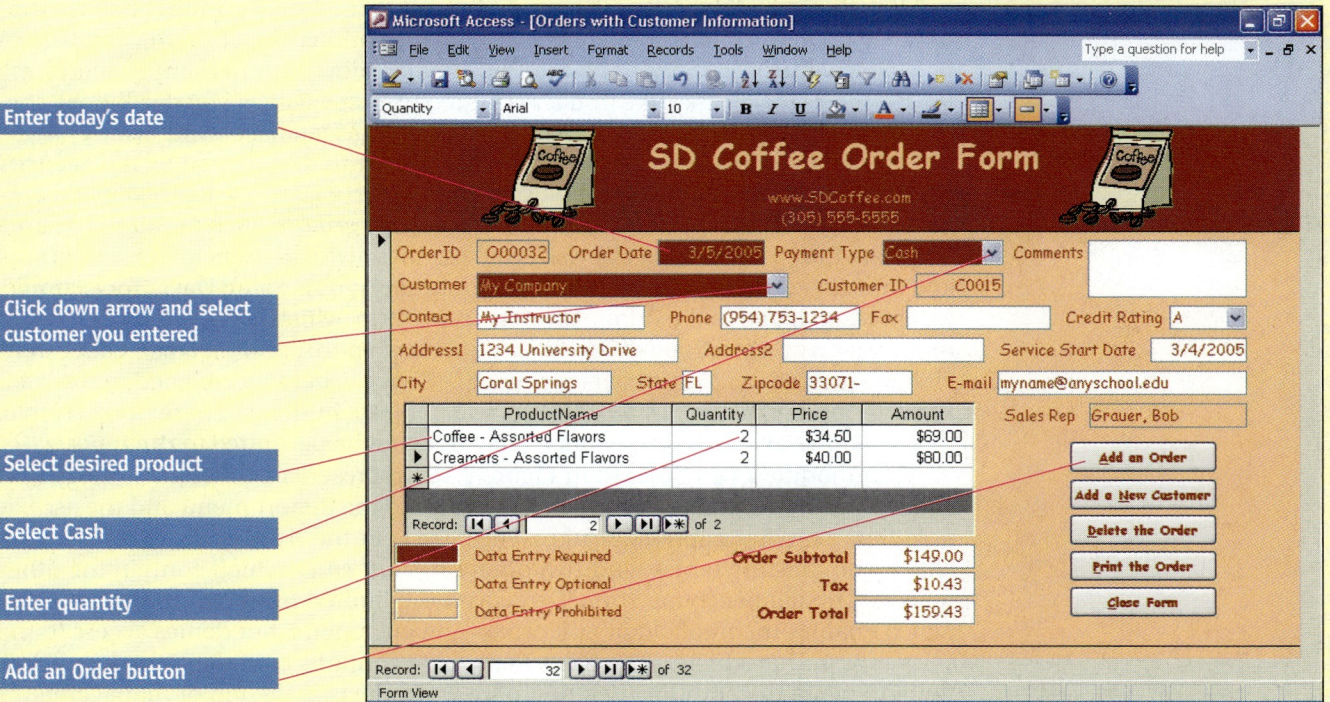

(h) Add an Order (step 8)

FIGURE 9.15 Hands-on Exercise 7 (*continued*)

The SD Coffee Database is complete, but is it secure; that is, is it protected from unauthorized access by individuals from both inside and outside the company? Security is a complex topic and may take several forms. There may be a guard at the front desk to prevent outsiders from entering the building. There may be a firewall installed on the system to prevent hackers from attacking the system and/or an antivirus program to prevent viruses from infecting the system. All of these are valid and necessary measures. Our discussion, however, will focus on security precautions from within Microsoft Access. There are four basic things that you can do, each of which denies (or impedes) access to the database in some way. These are:

1. Require a password to open the database

2. Hide the Database window once a database is open

3. Create an **MDE version** to prevent the modification of forms or reports

4. Establish user-level security to grant different permissions to different users

5. Split the database into multiple front ends that are linked to a common back end; different users have access to different front ends.

The imposition of a **password** is easily done, but it requires that the database be opened with **exclusive access**. This means that you have sole access to the database while you are establishing the password, and that others are prevented from opening or using the database during that time. Once the password is set, you close the database, then reopen it as usual (with shared access), which is what you have been doing throughout the text. The only other time you would open the database under exclusive access is to remove the password.

You can also make a database more difficult to use by hiding the Database window, which in turn makes it harder to access the various objects in the database. A knowledgeable user can unhide the Database window, but this simple action will thwart the casual hacker. We find it very effective, especially if you disable the special access keys (e.g., the F11 key, which displays the Database window).

Figure 9.16a displays the beginning of a report that is created by the **Security Wizard** when you establish **user-level security**. The wizard creates a single **workgroup**, which in turn is comprised of multiple **user groups**, such as Administrators and Data Entry. The wizard also asks you to add individual users to the workgroup, and then assign those users to the appropriate user group. Sarah Davis, for example, would be assigned to the Administrators user group, which is given full permission to access every object (all tables, forms, queries, reports, and macros). Other individuals, such as the clerical personnel at SD Coffee, would be assigned to the Data Entry group and given limited access to the objects in the database; for example, they would be allowed to enter data, but would not be permitted to run reports.

The modified switchboard in Figure 9.16b represents a different strategy as it contains only four items and precludes access to the Report menu and the associated reports. What happened? In essence, we split the database into a **back end**, which contains the tables, and two different **front ends**, which contain the other objects. The data entry personnel are given the limited front end in Figure 9.16b, which enables them to add or edit orders and customers, but denies access to the sales reps and products. (The Sales Reps table contains confidential salary information, while the addition/deletion of new products is the job of management.) Administrators, however, are given a different front end that contains every object in the database. Not only does this help to secure the database but it also facilitates the subsequent delivery of enhanced versions of the database. All the developer has to do is provide a new (enhanced) front end, then link the new front end to the existing back end, which contains the data. The limited data entry and MDE versions are created in end-of-chapter exercises.

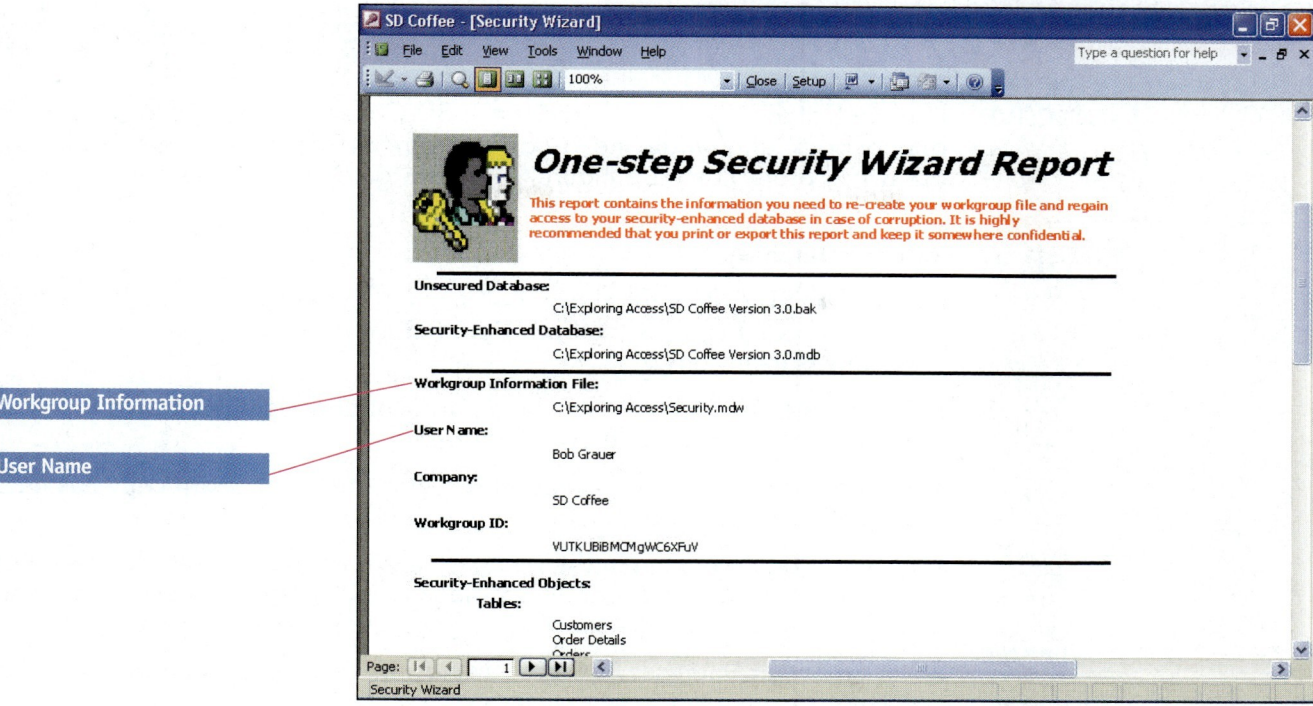

Workgroup Information

User Name

(a) User and Group Permissions

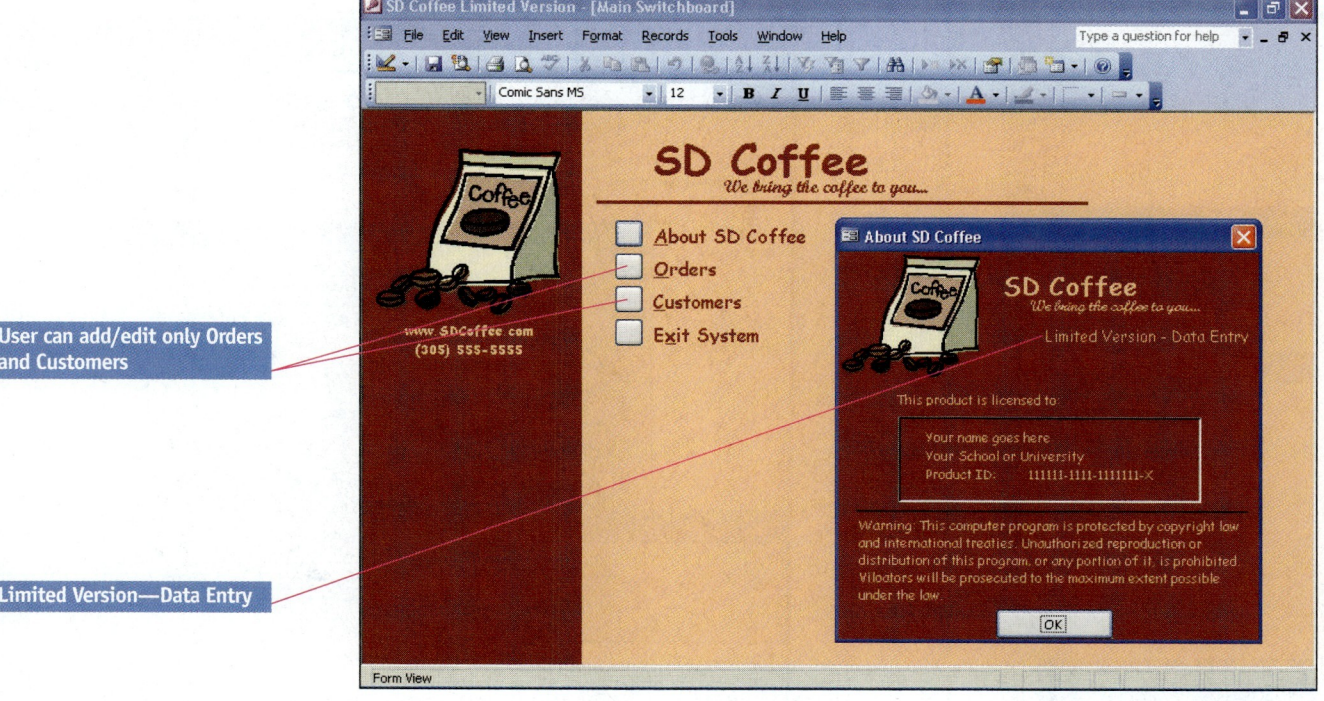

User can add/edit only Orders and Customers

Limited Version—Data Entry

(b) Limited Version for Data Entry

FIGURE 9.16   Security Issues

8   Submission to the Client

Objective   Use the Database splitter to divide the SD Coffee database into a front end and a back end; hide the database window from the user; implement password protection. Use Figure 9.17 as a guide in the exercise.

Step 1:   **Split the Database**

- Open the **SD Coffee database**. Pull down the **Tools menu**, click **Database Utilities**, and then click the **Back Up Database command** to display the Save Backup As dialog box.

- Access supplies a default name consisting of the original name of the database, followed by today's date. Click **Save**.

- The database should reopen automatically after the backup copy has been created. Close the switchboard.

- Click the **Tables button** in the Database window. Pull down the **Tools menu**, click **Database Utilities**, and click **Database Splitter** to start the wizard. (Note the warning to make a backup copy of your database before splitting it.)

- Click the **Split Database button** to display the Create Back-end Database dialog box.

- The file name **SD Coffee_be.mdb** is entered for you. Change to the **Exploring Access folder**, then click the **Split command**.

- You should see a message indicating that the database was successfully split as shown in Figure 9.17a. Click **OK**.

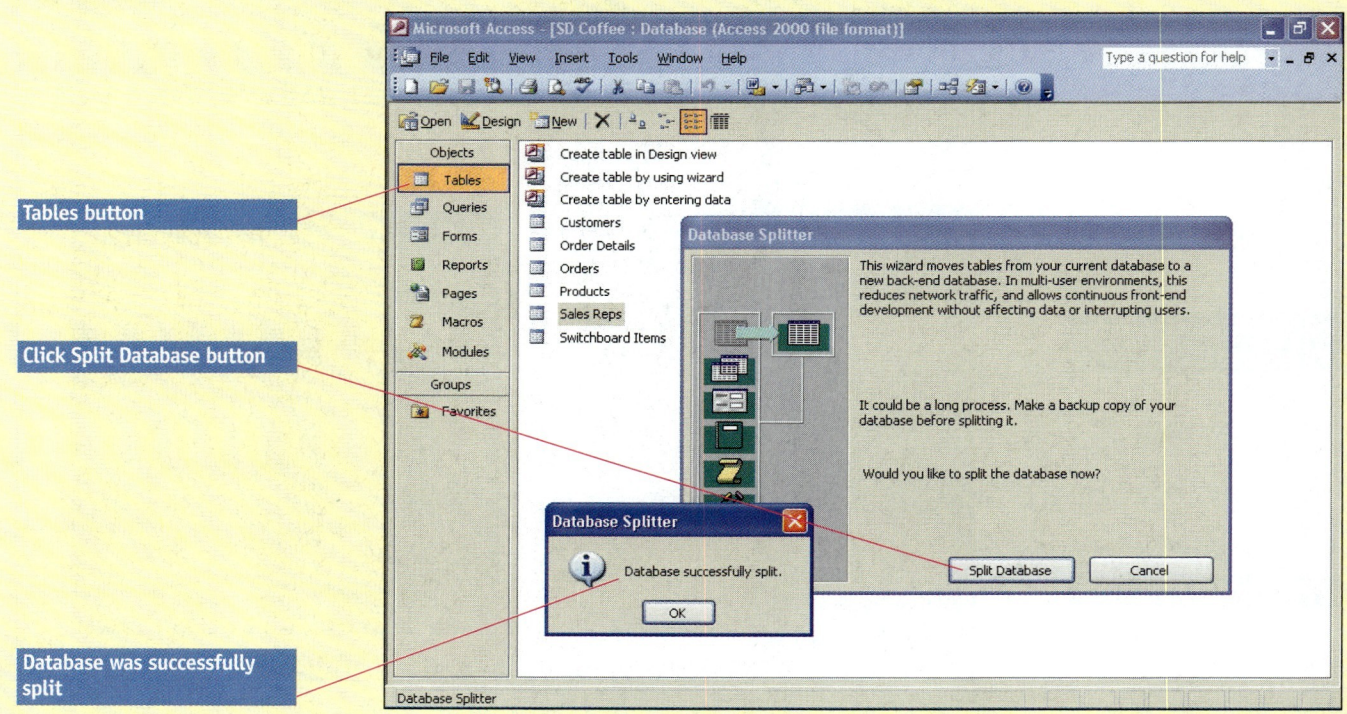

(a) Split the Database (step 1)

FIGURE 9.17   Hands-on Exercise 8

Step 2: **Import the Switchboard Items Table**

- You should see six tables in the Database window, each with an icon that indicates the table is linked to another database. The switchboard, however, should be under the control of the developer and thus the Switchboard Items table should be in this database.

- Select the **Switchboard Items table**. Press the **Del key**, then click **Yes** when asked if you want to remove the link to the table from the database.

- Pull down the **File menu**, click **Get External Data**, then click the **Import command**. Select the **SD Coffee_be database** and click **Import** to display the Import Objects dialog box.

- Click the **Table button**, select the **Switchboard Items table** as shown in Figure 9.17b, then click **OK**.

- The Switchboard Items table is imported into the database and appears in the Database window. Notice how this table has a different icon because the table is physically in the database.

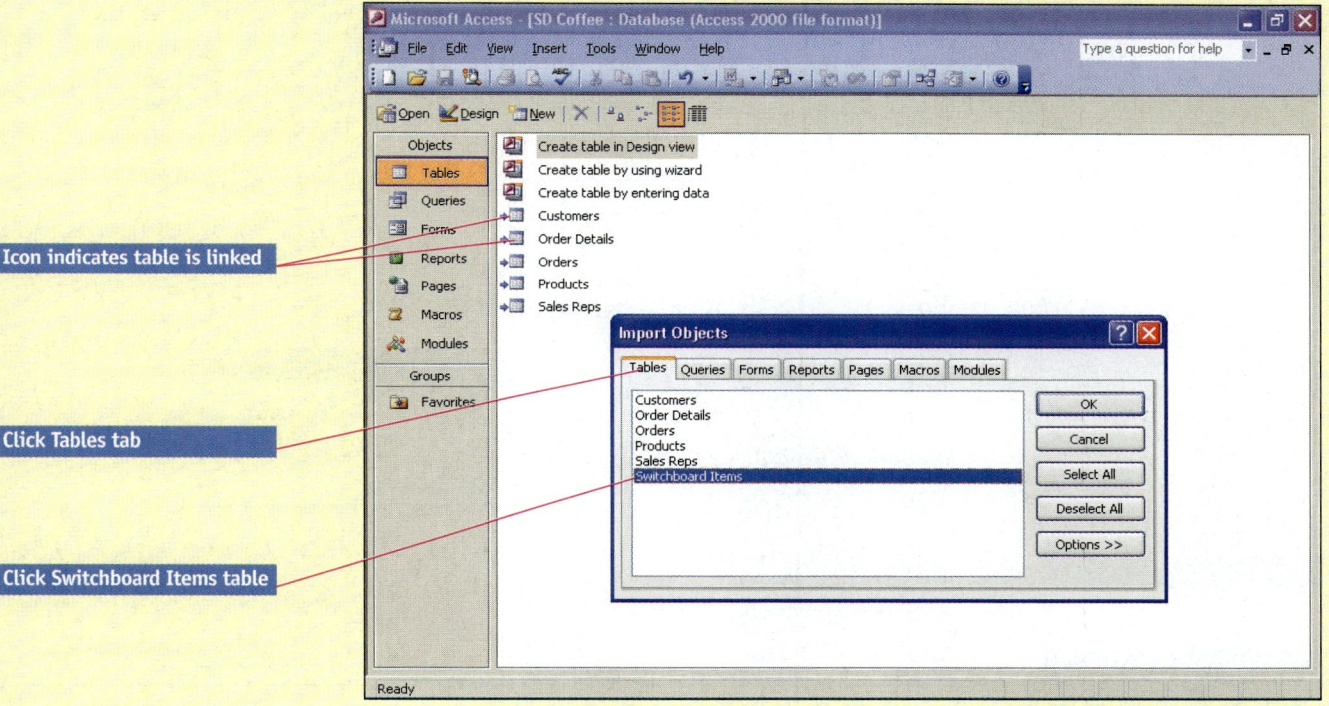

Icon indicates table is linked

Click Tables tab

Click Switchboard Items table

(b) Import the Switchboard Items Table (step 2)

FIGURE 9.17 Hands-on Exercise 8 (*continued*)

IMPORTING VERSUS LINKING

The Get External Data command displays a cascaded menu to import or link tables. Importing a table brings a copy of the table into the database and does not maintain a tie to the original data. Linking, on the other hand, does not bring the table into the database but only a pointer to the data source. Any changes to the data are made in the original source and are reflected automatically in any database that is linked to that source.

Step 3: Set a Password

- Close the database. Pull down the **File menu**, click the **Open command** to display the Open dialog box, go to the **Exploring Access folder**, and select the **SD Coffee database**. Click the **down arrow** on the **Open command button**, choose **Open Exclusive**, and open the database.

- Pull down the **Tools menu**, click **Security**, and click **Set Database Password** to display the dialog box in Figure 9.17c. Enter the password, enter it a second time, then click **OK** to set the password.

- Test the password to be sure that it works. Close the database and then reopen it. Enter the password when prompted, after which the database will open as before.

- Be sure that you remember the password or else you will not be able to reopen the database in the future. You can remove the password by pulling down the **Tools menu**, clicking **Security**, and then clicking **Unset Database Password command**.

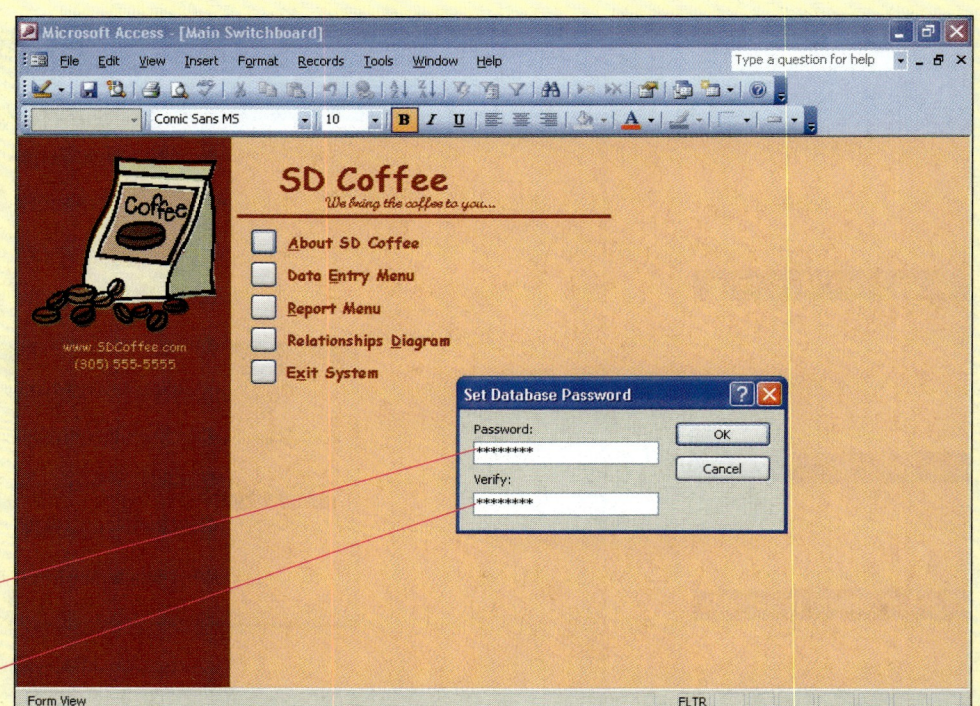

Enter password

Confirm password

(c) Set a Password (step 3)

FIGURE 9.17 Hands-on Exercise 8 (*continued*)

CHOOSE YOUR PASSWORD CAREFULLY

A good password should be easy to remember, but difficult to break. One way of creating such a password is to think of a sentence and use the first letter in each word to create the password; for example, "My wife's birthday is March 23" yields MwbiM23 as the password. It looks like a series of random characters, but it's easy to remember because you created the sentence in the first place. Note, too, the combination of upper- and lowercase letters as well as numbers, making it more difficult to break.

Step 4: **Hide the Database Window**

- Pull down the **Tools menu** and click the **Startup command** to display the Startup dialog box. Click in the **Application Title** text box and enter **SD Coffee** (to display SD Coffee in the title bar, as opposed to Microsoft Access).

- Clear the checkbox to **Display Database window**. This provides an additional measure of security by denying the (casual) user access to the Database window. Click **OK**.

- Pull down the **Tools menu**, click **Database Utilities**, then click the command to **Compact and Repair the Database**. This closes the database, and then reopens it.

- You see the switchboard as before. Close the switchboard, which displays the "empty" screen in Figure 9.17d. Look closely, however, and you see SD Coffee (the name of the open database) in the title bar. The database is still open!

- Pull down the **Window menu**, click the **Unhide command**, then click **OK** when you see the Unhide Window dialog box to restore the Database window. (You can also press the **F11 key**).

Name of open database appears in title bar

Empty screen

(d) Hide the Database Window (step 4)

FIGURE 9.17 Hands-on Exercise 8 (*continued*)

DISABLE SPECIAL KEYS AND MENUS WITH CAUTION

Take the protection one step further by disabling the special keys and full menus. Display the Startup dialog box, and clear the boxes to Allow Full Menus and Use Access Special keys. Click OK. Now close, and then reopen the database. You will not be able to display the Database window or access the full menus. All is not lost. Close, then reopen the database. Enter the password when prompted, but press and continue to hold the Shift key until the database opens to bypass the startup menu options.

Step 5: **Submission to the Client**

■ Open the **About SD Coffee form** in Design view. Change the **version number** to **3.0**. Save the form. Close the form.

■ Pull down the **Tools menu**, click **Database Utilities**, then click **Compact and Repair Database**. The database will close and then reopen. The switchboard should be displayed automatically.

■ Click the button next to the About command (or use the **Alt+A** keyboard shortcut) to display the About form in Figure 9.17e. Click **OK** to close the form. Test the various menu options to be sure that they are working correctly.

■ Your system is "complete" but incomplete. It is complete in the sense that the client can run through every menu option, but incomplete because some of the commands still display the prototype message. The remaining objects are added in the end-of-chapter exercises.

■ Click the menu option to **Exit System**. Click **OK** when you see the reminder to back up the system. Congratulations on a job very well done!

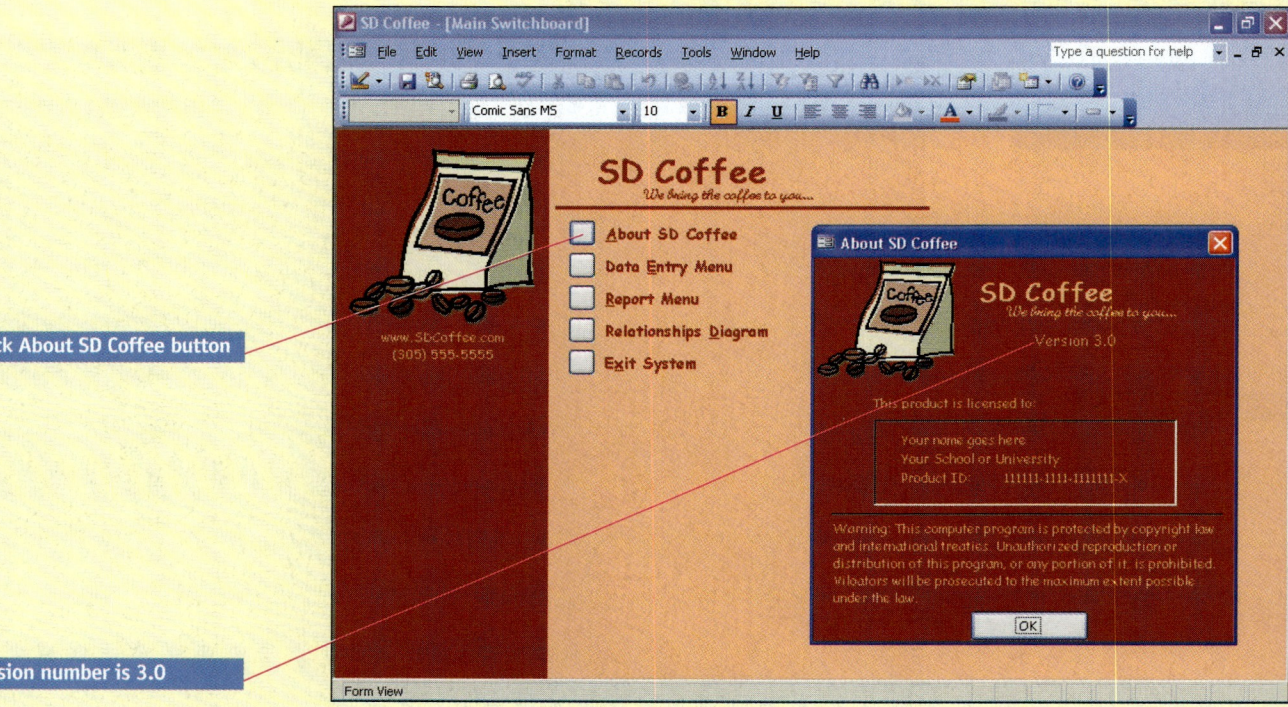

(e) Submission to the Client (step 5)

FIGURE 9.17 Hands-on Exercise 8 (*continued*)

CREATE THE LIMITED DATA ENTRY VERSION

There are two different ways to create the parallel but limited data entry version of the SD Coffee database. You use the Copy command in Windows Explorer to copy the existing Access database to a new database, then open the new database and delete the objects you do not need—that is, the forms, queries and reports that are not used in the limited version. Alternatively, you can create a new database within Access, then import (and link) the objects that you do need. Both techniques require you to modify the switchboard. See practice exercise 7 at the end of the chapter.

SUMMARY

This capstone chapter incorporated material from throughout the text to design and implement the SD Coffee database. Our objective was to pull together information from individual chapters in the context of a disciplined approach to application development. We began by studying the information requirements of a hypothetical client, the SD Coffee Company, and moved steadily through a series of well-defined milestones to arrive at the finished application. Each milestone was associated with a deliverable item, and it was essential that each step be completed in sequence before moving on to the next. (The milestones are described in the *Chapter 9 SD Coffee Project Milestones* document that was referenced in the chapter opening case study. You may want to review that document at this time.)

The first task was to arrive at an overall database design in which we identified the required tables and the relationships between those tables. We then moved on to the detailed design where we defined all of the fields in each table and established the properties for those fields. Next came the visual design, which consisted of a switchboard, an About form with licensing information, a form template, and a report template. The visual design represented Version 1.0 and it gave the client the first glimpse at the look and feel of the eventual system.

Our next task was to use the existing templates to create a working form and report to confirm the visual design. We then used macros to expand the original switchboard into Version 2.0, which was a full prototype of the eventual system that included all menu options for data entry and reporting. The application was now complete in the sense that it contained every menu item, but incomplete because the associated objects (the forms and reports) were not yet created.

The remaining tasks filled in the blanks within the prototype. We created two sample reports and used carefully constructed test data to ensure the validity of those reports and the underlying queries. We added the complex order form that contained data from every table in the database. We also implemented a password to protect the database from unauthorized access. And finally, we split the database into a front end containing the forms and reports and a back end containing the tables. The resulting database constituted Version 3.0. Additional modifications are suggested in the end-of-chapter exercises to arrive at Version 4.0.

KEY WORDS AND CONCEPTS

Allow Zero Length property 452	Limit to List property 452	SetFocus method 494
AutoExec macro 478	Macro 478	Startup command 460
AutoNumber field type 452	MDE version 504	Tab Stop property 470
Back end 504	MsgBox action 478	Technical design 460
Bound control 460	Northwind database 501	Template 460
Calculated control 476	Object linking and embedding	Test data 486
Cascade deleted records 448	(OLE) 470	Third normal form 444
Data validation 452	Page Footer 460	Top Values property 486
Database Splitter 506	Page Header 460	Total query 486
Detail section 460	Parameter query 486	Unbound control 460
Detailed design 452	Password 504	Unmatched query 486
Exclusive access 504	PowerPoint Presentation 444	User groups 504
Find Duplicates query 486	Prototyping 478	User-level security 504
Front End 504	Referential integrity 452	Validation Rule property 452
Group Footer 490	Report Footer 465	Validation Text property 452
Group Header 490	Report Group 465	Visual design 460
Information requirements 442	Report Header 460	Workgroup 504
Input Mask property 454	Required property 452	
Like operator 489	Security Wizard 504	

1. Which command is used to associate tables in one database with objects in another?

    (a) Compact and Repair Database

    (b) Import Tables

    (c) Set Relationships

    (d) Link Tables

2. Which macro is executed automatically when a database is opened?

    (a) Startup

    (b) Switchboard

    (c) AutoExec

    (d) Start Database

3. Is it possible to delete an order in the Orders table without first explicitly deleting the associated records in the Order Details table?

    (a) Yes, under all circumstances

    (b) No, under all circumstances

    (c) Yes, but only by enforcing referential integrity

    (d) Yes, by enforcing referential integrity with the cascaded deletion of related records

4. Which combination of fields serves as the primary key in the Order Details table?

    (a) OrderID, ProductID, and Date

    (b) OrderID and ProductID

    (c) OrderID, ProductID, and Quantity

    (d) OrderID, ProductID, and CustomerID

5. Which of the following is true regarding the one-to-many relationship between customers and orders?

    (a) The OrderID is the primary key in the Customers table

    (b) The CustomerID is the primary key in the Orders table

    (c) The CustomerID is a foreign key in the Orders table

    (d) The OrderID is a foreign key in the Customers table

6. The SD Coffee switchboard contains a main menu, a data entry menu, and a report menu. This requires:

    (a) Three switchboard forms and three Switchboard Items tables

    (b) Three switchboard forms and one Switchboard Items table

    (c) One switchboard form and three Switchboard Items tables

    (d) One switchboard form and one Switchboard Items table

7. Which of the following is an example of validation at the record level?

    (a) Ensuring that a gender field contains either "M" or "F"

    (b) Ensuring that the current salary is greater than the previous salary

    (c) Ensuring that every numeric field in a record contains only numeric data

    (d) Ensuring that the primary key of each new record is unique

8. Which of the following was defined as a numeric field in the Sales Reps table?

    (a) The Social Security number

    (b) The Telephone number

    (c) Both (a) and (b)

    (d) Neither (a) nor (b)

9. Which fields are commonly associated with an input mask?

    (a) Social Security Number, Telephone Number, and Zip Code

    (b) First Name, Last Name, and Middle Initial

    (c) Address, City, and State

    (d) All of the above

10. Which combination of properties is typically used in conjunction with a "State" field within an address?

    (a) Format property is >, Input mask is AA

    (b) Format property is >, Input mask is LL

    (c) Format property is <, Input mask is AA

    (d) Format property is <, Input mask is LL

. . . continued

11. Which of the following is true about a main form and an associated subform?

    (a) The main form may be based on either a table or a query

    (b) The subform may be based on either a table or a query

    (c) Both (a) and (b)

    (d) Neither (a) nor (b)

12. Which of the following is true about a split database?

    (a) The back end of the database contains the tables

    (b) The front end of the database contains forms, queries, reports, and macros

    (c) Multiple front ends may be linked to the same back end

    (d) All of the above

13. Which table should be in the front end of a database?

    (a) The Switchboard Items table

    (b) The Orders and Order Details tables

    (c) The Customers and Products tables

    (d) The Sales Reps table

14. Which of the following is a *false* statement about the use of bitmapped photographs in a database?

    (a) They are defined with the OLE Object field type

    (b) They can be entered into a record from the Datasheet view or Form view

    (c) They can be displayed in either a report or a form

    (d) The storage requirements are modest and do not significantly affect the size of the database

15. Which of the following can be used to identify products that have never been ordered?

    (a) Top Values property

    (b) Parameter query

    (c) Unmatched query

    (d) Find Duplicates query

16. Which of the following enables you to change the criteria when the query is executed?

    (a) Top Values query

    (b) Parameter query

    (c) Unmatched query

    (d) Find Duplicates query

17. Which of the following is used to hide the Database window?

    (a) The Database splitter

    (b) User and Group permissions

    (c) The Startup command

    (d) Password protection

18. The Northwind database is:

    (a) The group project that was developed in this chapter

    (b) A paid service of Microsoft technical support

    (c) Available only from the Grauer/Barber Web site

    (d) None of the above

ANSWERS

1.	d	7.	b	13.	a
2.	c	8.	d	14.	d
3.	d	9.	a	15.	c
4.	b	10.	b	16.	b
5.	c	11.	c	17.	c
6.	d	12.	d	18.	d

PRACTICE WITH ACCESS

1. **The Top Ten Products Report:** The report in Figure 9.18 displays the top 10 products according to the total amount of product that was sold. It is based on a total query that computes the amount for each product, then it sorts those amounts in descending sequence. The Top 10 property is applied to the query to show only the first ten products, as opposed to every product. Proceed as follows:

   a. Create a new query that contains fields from the Products and Order Details tables. Add the ProductID, ProductName, Description, YearIntroduced, and Cost fields from the Products table. Add the Quantity field from the OrderDetails table.

   b. Create a new Amount field in the query that computes the price of the item from its cost. Enter Amount: ([Cost]+[Cost]*[MarkupPercent])*[Quantity] in the field row. Be sure to spell the field names correctly.

   c. Run the query to be sure it is correct thus far (it is not yet finished). If you see a dialog box asking you to enter a parameter value, it is because you misspelled a field name.

   d. Click the Totals button on the Query Design toolbar to display the Total row. Select the Sum function in both the Quantity and Amount fields.

   e. Click in the Sort row under the Amount field and choose Descending. Click in the Top Values list box, delete the existing entry, and enter 10. Run the query. You should see the 10 products with the highest sales. Save the query as Top Ten Products.

   f. Create the Top 10 Products Report in Figure 9.18. Your report should be based on the total query you just created and the report template that you have used throughout the chapter.

   g. Be sure that the width of the report does not extend past 7.5 inches. Preview the report and make adjustments as necessary. Save the report.

   h. Modify the menu item in the Reports switchboard to open this report, as opposed to running the prototype macro. Close the Switchboard Manager.

   i. Open the switchboard, go to the Report Menu, and test the command to view the Top Ten Products Report.

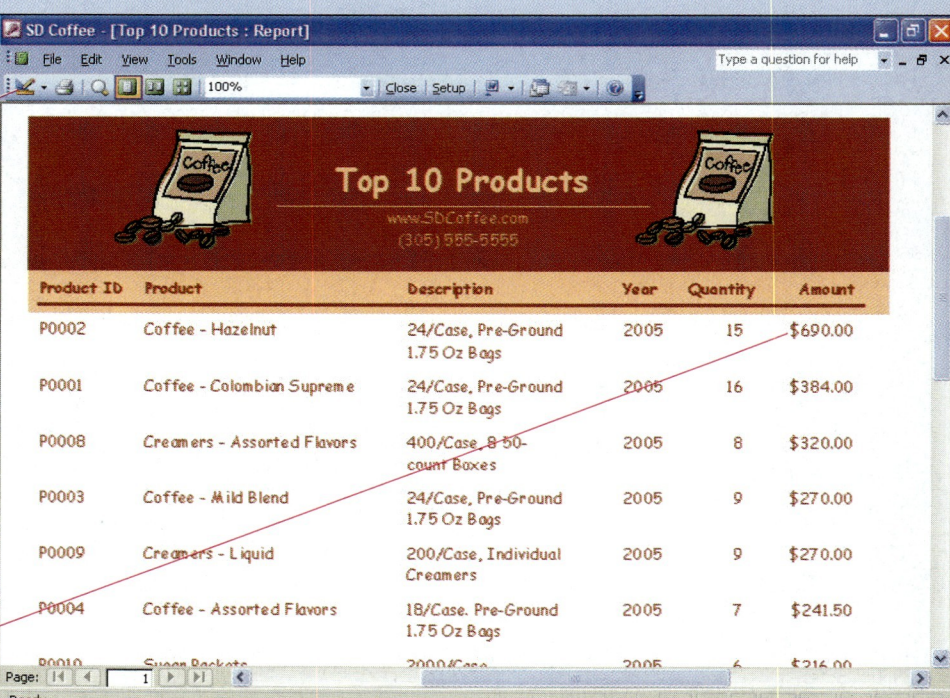

Click to return to Design view to make changes in report design

Products are listed in descending order of Amount

FIGURE 9.18 The Top Ten Products Report (exercise 1)

2. **The Unordered Products Report:** The report in Figure 9.19 is the "opposite" of the Top 10 Products report as it indicates the products that have never been ordered. This type of information is very valuable to management, which can realize significant cost savings by eliminating these products from inventory. The report is based on an unmatched query that takes each record in the Products table and searches for a matching entry in the Order Details table. Any products that do not appear in the latter table are "unmatched entries" and correspond to a product that has never been ordered. Proceed as follows:

   a. Click the Queries button in the Database window. Click the New button, select the Find Unmatched Query Wizard, and click OK. Choose Products as the table whose records you want to see in the query results. Click Next.

   b. Choose Order Details as the table that contains the related records. Click Next.

   c. ProductID is selected automatically as the matching field. Click Next. Select the ProductID, ProductName, Description, Cost, MarkupPercent, and YearIntroduced fields from the Available Fields list. Click Next. Enter Unordered Products as the name of the query.

   d. Click Finish to display a list of the products that have never been purchased. You should see the same data as in Figure 9.19. Close the query.

   e. Click the Reports button in the Database window. Select the Report template, copy it, and then paste it to create the Unordered Products report. Open the new report in Design view, right click the report selector in the upper-left corner, click Properties, then choose the Unordered Products query as the record source.

   f. Complete the report as shown in Figure 9.19. Be sure that the width of the report does not extend past 7.5 inches. Preview the report and make adjustments as necessary. Save the report.

   g. Modify the menu item in the Reports switchboard to open this report, as opposed to running the prototype macro. Close the Switchboard Manager.

   h. Open the switchboard, go to the Report menu, and test the command to view the Unordered Products Report. Compact and Repair the database. Close the switchboard.

Click to return to Design view to make changes in report design

Products that have not been ordered

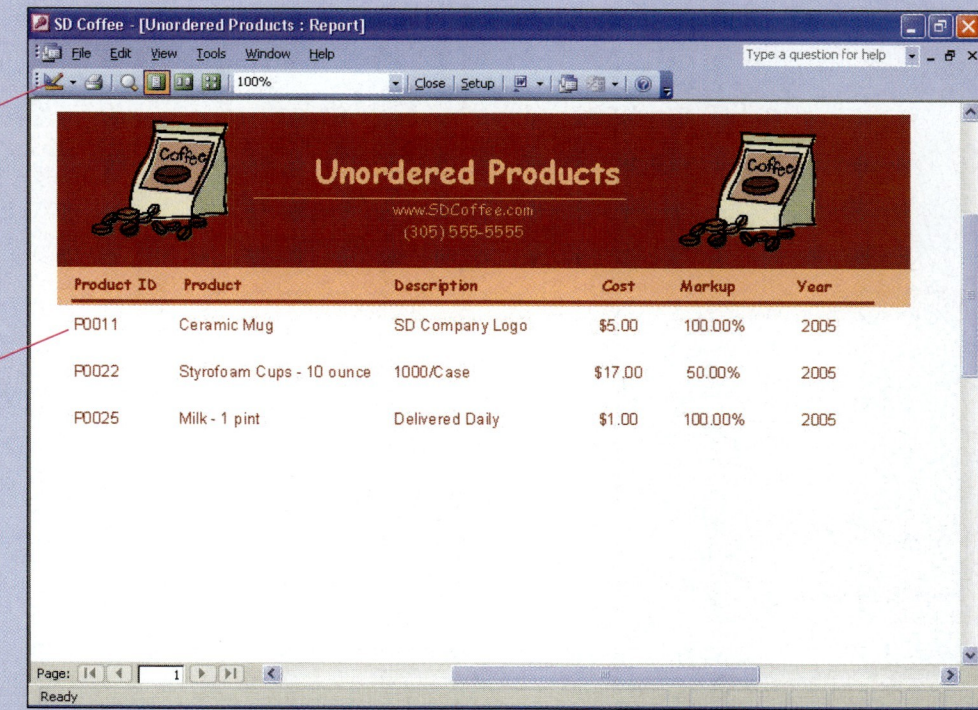

FIGURE 9.19 The Unordered Products Report (exercise 2)

3. **The Product Summary Report:** The report in Figure 9.20 is a "straightforward" product summary that has been enhanced through VBA to shade the alternate lines. The right portion of the screen displays the VBA editor so that you can see the required code. Proceed as follows:

a. Use the Report template to create the Product Summary report, which is based solely on the Products table. The report contains the ProductID, ProductName, Description, MarkupPercent, and Cost fields from the Products table. The query also requires a calculated control for the retail price, which is equal to the cost plus the cost times the markup percentage. The products are listed in sequence by ProductID. Leave the report open in Design view. Be sure that the width of the report is less than 7.5 inches.

b. Right click the Detail section, click the Properties command, click the Event tab, and click the On Format event. Click the Build button, select Code Builder, then click OK to open the VBA editor and create the event procedure shown in Figure 9.20. Note the following:

i. The Project Explorer displays all of the Access objects that contain VBA Code. We closed it, however, to simplify the figure. (Pull down the View menu in the VBA editor and click Project Explorer.)

ii. VBA defines intrinsic constants such as vbWhite, but additional colors must be defined by the user. We defined the custom color, conOrange by looking at the background color property in the Page Header.

iii. The If statement tests the background color of the current detail line. If the color is orange, it is changed to white. If the color is not orange, the Else clause sets it to orange. The effect of the statement is to shade every other line.

iv. Save the procedure, then return to Access and view the report.

c. Modify the menu item in the Reports switchboard to open this report, as opposed to running the prototype macro. Close the Switchboard Manager.

d. Open the switchboard, go to the Report menu, and test the command to view the Summary Report.

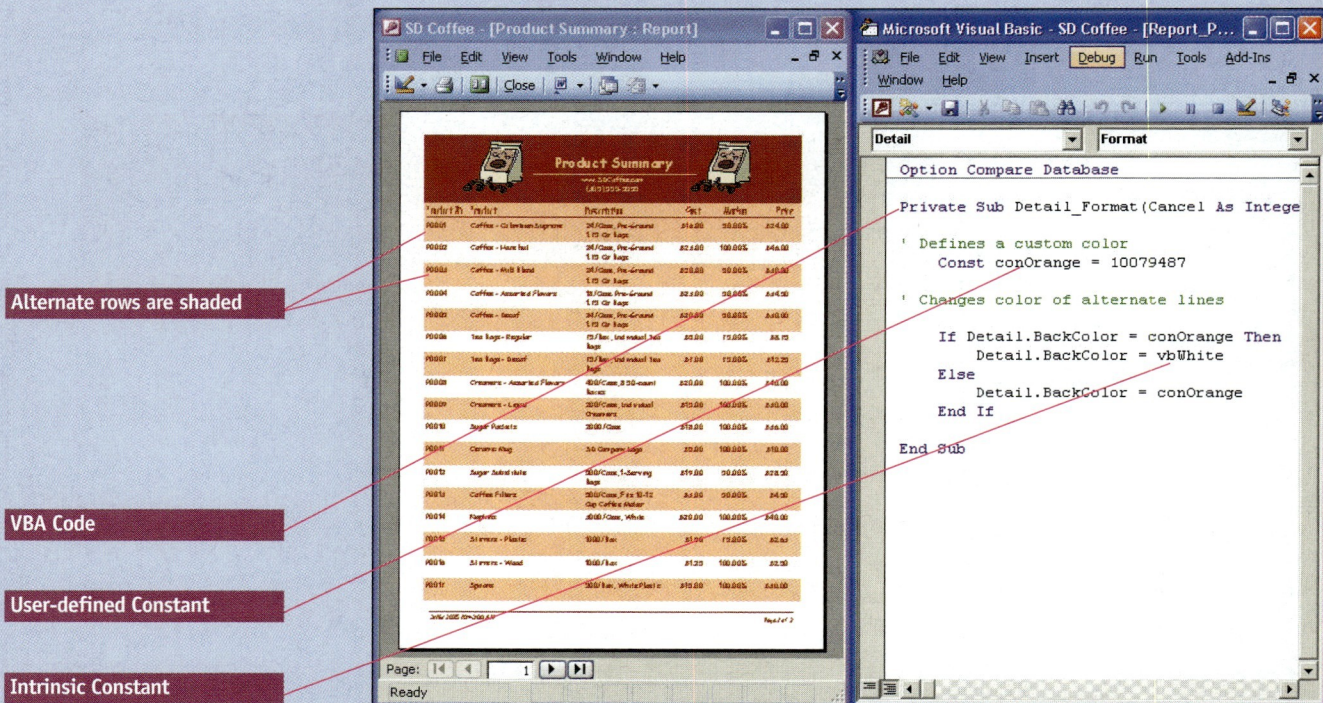

FIGURE 9.20 The Product Summary Report (exercise 3)

4. **The Products Form:** The complete application must be able to add, edit, and/or delete records from every table in the database. This exercise fulfills that requirement by creating the Products form in Figure 9.21, the only form that was not developed in the body of the chapter. Proceed as follows:

a. Click the Forms button in the Database window. Select the Form Template, copy it, and then paste it to create the Products form. Open the new form in Design view, right click the form selector in the upper-left corner, click Properties, then choose the Products table as the record source.

b. Click and drag every field from the field list to its approximate position on the form. Format, move, size, and align the various controls to conform to the standard formatting within the form template. Be sure that the width of the form does not extend past 7.5 inches.

c. Use the Command Button Wizard to create an additional button to view the list of products. Select Report Operations as the category and Preview Report as the action, then choose the Product Summary report that was created in the previous exercise. Enter "&View Products" as text of the button to create the Alt+V keyboard shortcut.

d. Right click the Add Record button and display the Properties dialog box. Click the Event tab, click the On Click property, then click the Build button. Insert the statement ProductName.SetFocus immediately after the DoCmd statement. (This statement will automatically position you in the product name control when you click the Add Record button.) Save the procedure, then close the window.

e. Pull down the View menu, click Tab Order, then click the Auto Order button to set the Tab order. Complete the form as shown in Figure 9.21. Preview the form and make adjustments as necessary. Save the report.

f. Modify the menu item in the Data Entry switchboard to open this form, as opposed to running the prototype macro. Close the Switchboard Manager.

g. Open the switchboard, go to the Data Entry menu, and test the command to open the Products form. Compact and Repair the database. Close the database.

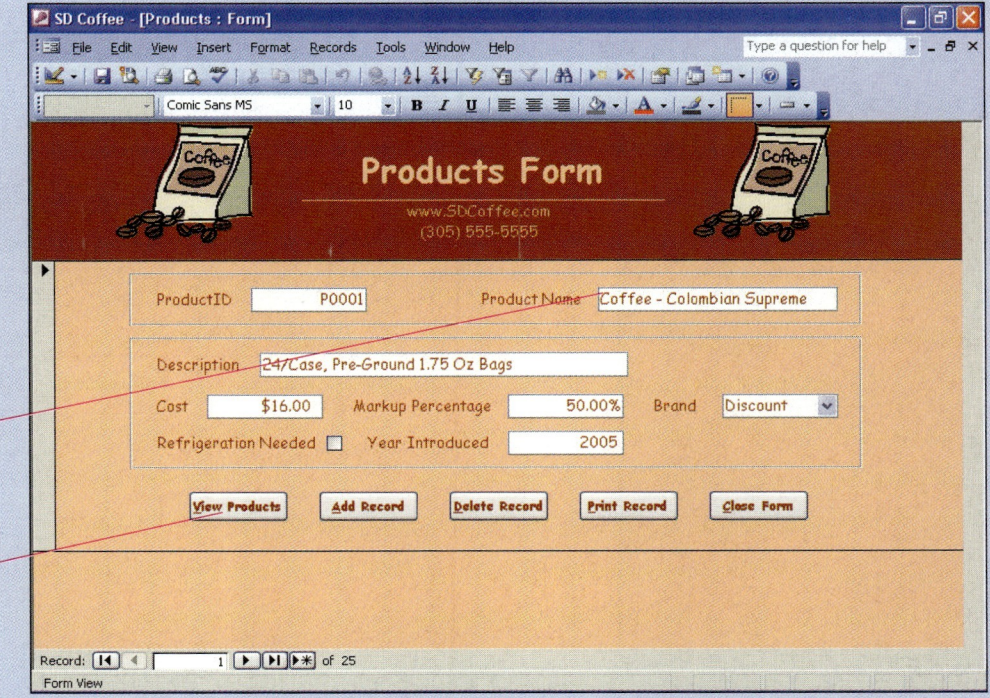

Insertion point will be positioned in Product Name control when you add a record

Create command button to view product list

FIGURE 9.21 The Products Form (exercise 4)

5. **The Duplicate Customers Report:** The report in Figure 9.22 displays duplicate customers, that is, customers with the same contact information but entered under a different customer name. The duplicate records should be eliminated to avoid redundant mailings and/or erroneous reports. Proceed as follows:

   a. Click the Queries button in the Database window. Click the New button, select the Find Duplicates Query Wizard, and click OK. Select Customers as the table you want to search for duplicate records. Click Next.

   b. Select Contact and Phone as the fields that might contain duplicate information. Click Next. Select CustomerID, CustomerName, Address1, and Address2 as the additional fields to show in the query. Click Next.

   c. Enter Duplicate Customers as the name of the query. Click Finish to display the list of duplicate customers. Close the query.

   d. Use the report template and Duplicate Customers query to create the Duplicate Customers report in Figure 9.22. Modify the menu item in the Report switchboard to open this report, as opposed to running the prototype macro. Close the Switchboard Manager.

   e. Open the switchboard, go to the Report Menu, and run the command to view the Duplicate Customers report. Print the report for your instructor.

   f. You should also eliminate one of the duplicate records (e.g., C0013), but first you must assign the orders for that customer (C0013) to the other record (C0002). Open the Orders table in Datasheet view. Click in the CustomerID field, then click the Sort Ascending button to group orders by customer. Only one order (O0020) is associated with customer C0013. Change the customer for this order to C0002. (The Order Details table is updated automatically because Cascade Update Related Fields is in effect.) Close the Orders table.

   g. Open the switchboard. Go to the Data Entry menu and open the Customers form. Delete Customer C0013 (Computer Information Systems). Go to the Report menu and run the Order Summary report. Order 20 has been assigned to the Department of CIS. Rerun the Duplicate Customers report, which should be empty.

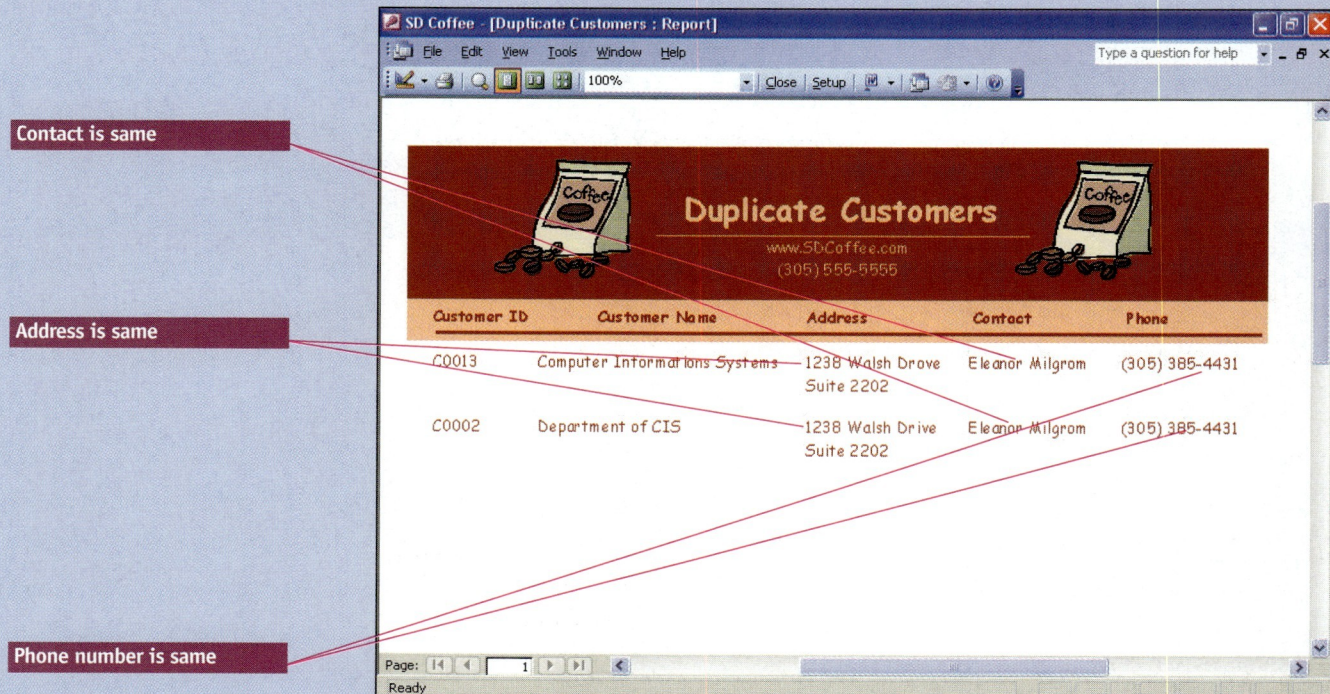

FIGURE 9.22 The Duplicate Customers Report (exercise 5)

6. **An Enhanced Customer Form:** The Customers form in Figure 9.23 is a modified version of the form that was presented in the chapter. (Only a portion of the form is visible.) The differences are subtle and have to do with VBA enhancements that were added to facilitate data entry. (You may want to review Chapter 8 before attempting this assignment.) Proceed as follows:

a. Copy the existing form from within the Database window to create a backup version. It takes only a minute to do, and you will thank us in the unlikely event you edit the current form beyond repair.

b. Add a Set Focus statement to the On Click event for the Add Record button; this statement will position the user in the Service Start Date text box immediately after clicking the button.

c. Create four shortcuts for data entry. Ctrl+1 should enter Miami, FL, and 33131 in the city, state, and zip code fields, respectively. Create similar shortcuts for Ctrl+2 (Coconut Grove, FL, and 33133), Ctrl+3 (Coral Gables, FL, 33124), and Ctrl+4 (Coral Springs, FL, and 33071). Create a Shortcuts button that will display this information for the user. (Remember to set the Key Preview property to "Yes" so that the shortcuts are operational.)

d. Create a Before Update event for the EmailAddress control that tests for a valid e-mail address. The portion of the procedure that is visible in Figure 9.23 tests for the presence of the @ sign. A second If statement should test for the presence of a period.

e. Create a procedure for the Before Update event for the form that tests if the customer's e-mail address was entered, warns the user if the field is omitted, and then gives the user the option to save the record anyway.

f. Go to Form view and test the enhancements, then close the form when you are satisfied that everything works as expected. Delete the backup form you created at the beginning of this exercise.

g. Review the other forms (Sales Reps, Products, and Orders) that are in the database and decide whether to include some or all of the VBA enhancements. Do you think VBA adds significant value to the application?

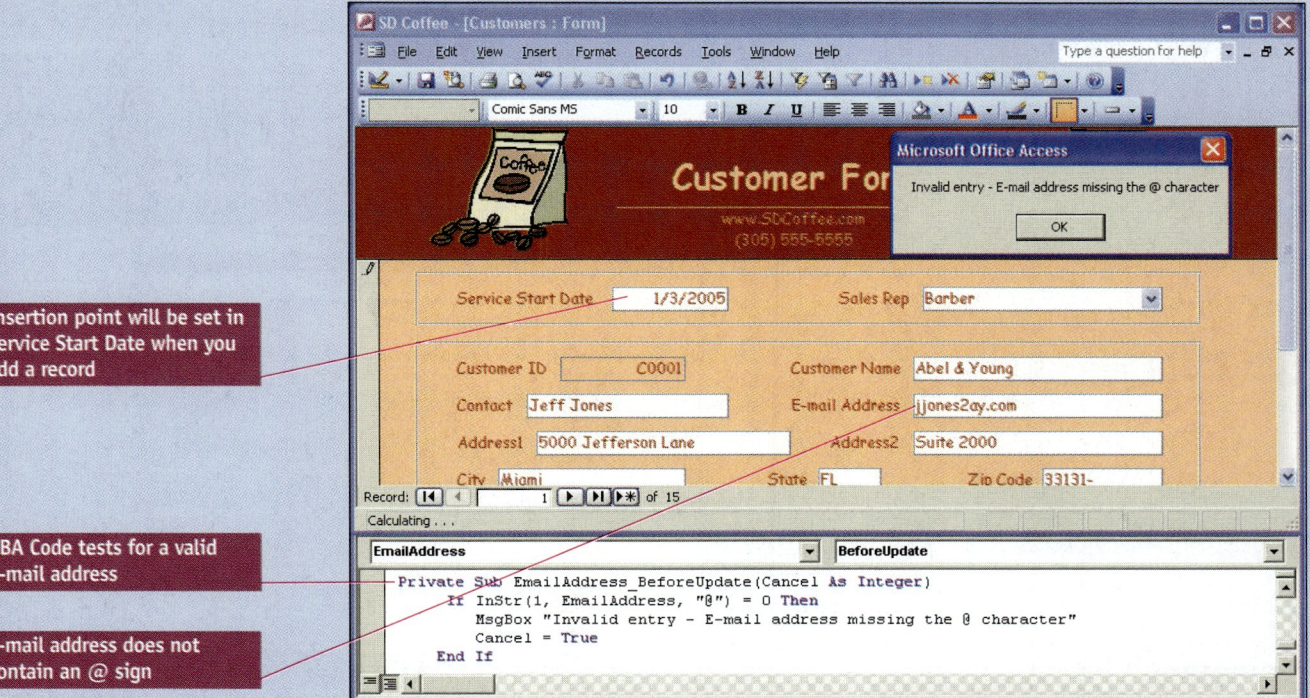

FIGURE 9.23 An Enhanced Customer Form (exercise 6)

7. **The Performance Analyzer:** The database works, but the professional developer is not quite finished as he or she typically analyzes the performance of the database to make it run more efficiently. The results of this analysis are shown in Figure 9.24. Proceed as follows:

   a. Open the SD Coffee Database. Close the switchboard but leave the application open (Click the Close button in the upper-right corner of the switchboard.) Press the F11 key to display the Database window.

   b. Pull down the Tools menu, click the Analyze command, and then click Performance to display the Performance Analyzer dialog box. Click the All Object Types tab, click the Select All button to select every object in the database, and then click OK to display the results in Figure 9.24.

   c. The analyzer displays three types of results: recommendations, suggestions, and ideas. (Our analysis returns only the last category.) Recommendations are typically unequivocal and should (always) be implemented. Suggestions involve a tradeoff, and they should be analyzed individually prior to implementation. Access can perform recommendations and suggestions for you; that is, select the item, then click the Optimize button. The user must implement ideas manually.

   d. Select the first idea, "The application is not saved in a fully compiled state", then read the analysis note at the bottom of the dialog box. Close the Performance Analyzer dialog box. Pull down the Tools menu, click Macro, and then click Visual Basic Editor (or use the Alt+F11 keyboard shortcut) to open the VBA Editor. Pull down the Debug menu and click the Compile command as suggested. Click the Save button.

   e. Close the VBA editor to return to the Database window. Repeat step b to rerun the Performance Analyzer. The first idea has been replaced by an idea to save the Application as an MDE database. (We do this in practice exercise 9).

   f. Look briefly at several of the other ideas. Some have no merit, such as using fewer controls on the Customers form (how else would we enter Customer data?), whereas other ideas are more worthwhile but are best evaluated by the developer. We do not intend to make you a VBA expert, but we did want to acquaint you with the concept of performance analysis.

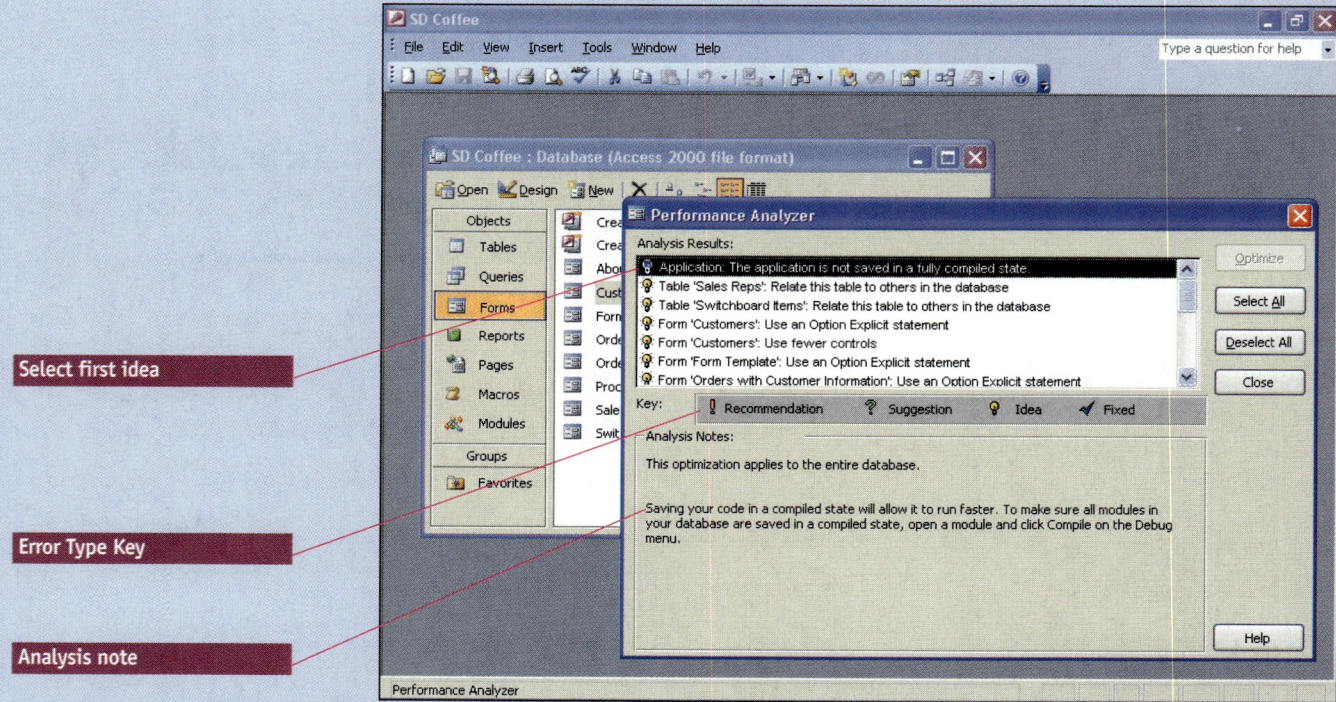

FIGURE 9.24 The Performance Analyzer (exercise 7)

8. **Limited Version for Data Entry:** The SD Coffee database was previously split into a back end containing the various tables (except for the Switchboard Items table) and a front end with the other objects. This exercise creates a second (limited) front end as shown in Figure 9.25. Proceed as follows:

a. Close the SD Coffee Database if it is open and then create a new database named SD Coffee Limited Version.

b. Use the Get External Data/Link Tables command to link the new database to the Customers, Orders, Order Details, Products, and Sales Reps tables in the back end database. The relationships are established automatically although you may want to rearrange the tables in the Relationships window.

c. Import the following objects from the full version of the SD Coffee database into the new database. Select *all* of the objects before clicking OK:
   i. Tables: Switchboard Items
   ii. Forms: About SD Coffee, Customers, Orders with Customer Information, Order Details with Product Information, and Switchboard
   iii. Queries: Orders with Customer Information and Order Details with Product Information
   iv. Macros: AutoExec and Exit System

d. Start the Switchboard Manager. Delete the Data Entry and Report menus, and then modify the main switchboard so that it contains the four menu items in Figure 9.25.

e. Modify the About SD Coffee form to reflect the Limited Version. Set the Startup menu to hide the Database window, to display the switchboard automatically, and to display SD Coffee as the application title.

f. Compact and Repair the database. The database should close, and then reopen. The switchboard should appear automatically. Enter a new customer, *Brian Street Associates,* (use any contact information you like) and a new order for this customer. Click the Exit System button.

g. Open the full version of the database. Click the Report Menu button, then open and print the Order Summary report. You should see the order for Brian Street Associates as the last line of this report.

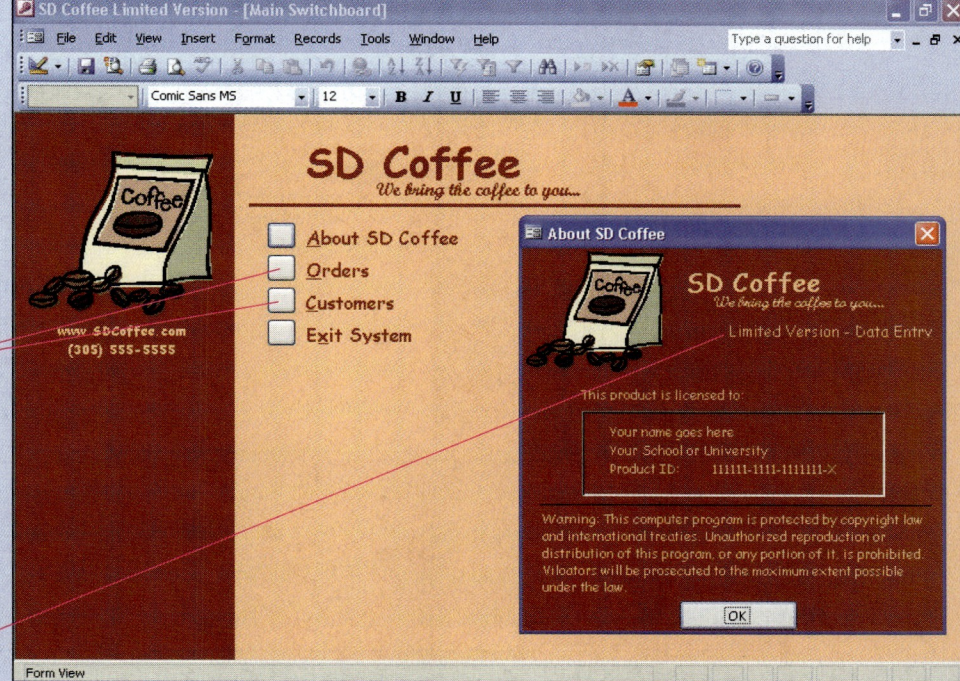

User can add/edit only Orders and Customers

Limited Version is for Data Entry only

FIGURE 9.25 Limited Version for Data Entry (exercise 8)

9. **The MDE Version:** At first glance the Database window in Figure 9.26 looks identical to the various windows we have seen throughout the text. Look closely, however, and you will see that the Design and New buttons are dimmed out (i.e., they are inaccessible) and further, that there is no option to create a form, either in Design view or using the Form Wizard. Look again and you will see that the database is in Access 2002–2003 format, as opposed to the 2000 format we have used throughout the text. All of these changes have occurred because the Limited Version database has been converted to an MDE database, which is a special version of an Access database that runs normally, except you cannot modify forms or reports. This is intended as a security measure. Proceed as follows:

a. Open the SD Coffee Limited Version database from the previous exercise. Close the switchboard. Press the F11 key to view the Database window.

b. Pull down the Tools menu, click Database Utilities, and click the Make MDE File command. You will see a warning message indicating that you cannot create an MDE file from a database saved in 2000 format. Click OK.

c. Pull down the Tools menu, click the Database Utilities menu a second time, click Convert Database, then click the command To Access 2002–2003 File Format to display the Convert Database Into dialog box. Choose a temporary name, perhaps Temp, then click Save. Click OK when you see the message indicating that you will not be able to share the database with Access 2000 or Access 97 users. Close the SD Coffee Limited Version database, which is still open.

d. Open the Temp database that you just created. Pull down the Tools menu, click Database Utilities, and click the Make MDE File command. Enter SD Coffee Limited MDE Version as the name of the database. Click the Save button, then reopen the database when prompted. Close the switchboard, press the F11 key, then close the Temp database. (You can delete this database later from Windows Explorer.)

e. Open the SD Coffee Limited MDE Version database. Close the switchboard, then press the F11 key to display the Database Window in Figure 9.26. Select the Customers form and try to open it in Design view. You can't. Press the Alt+F11 key to open the VBA editor, then try to view the code behind the form. You can't. What do you think of the MDE version?

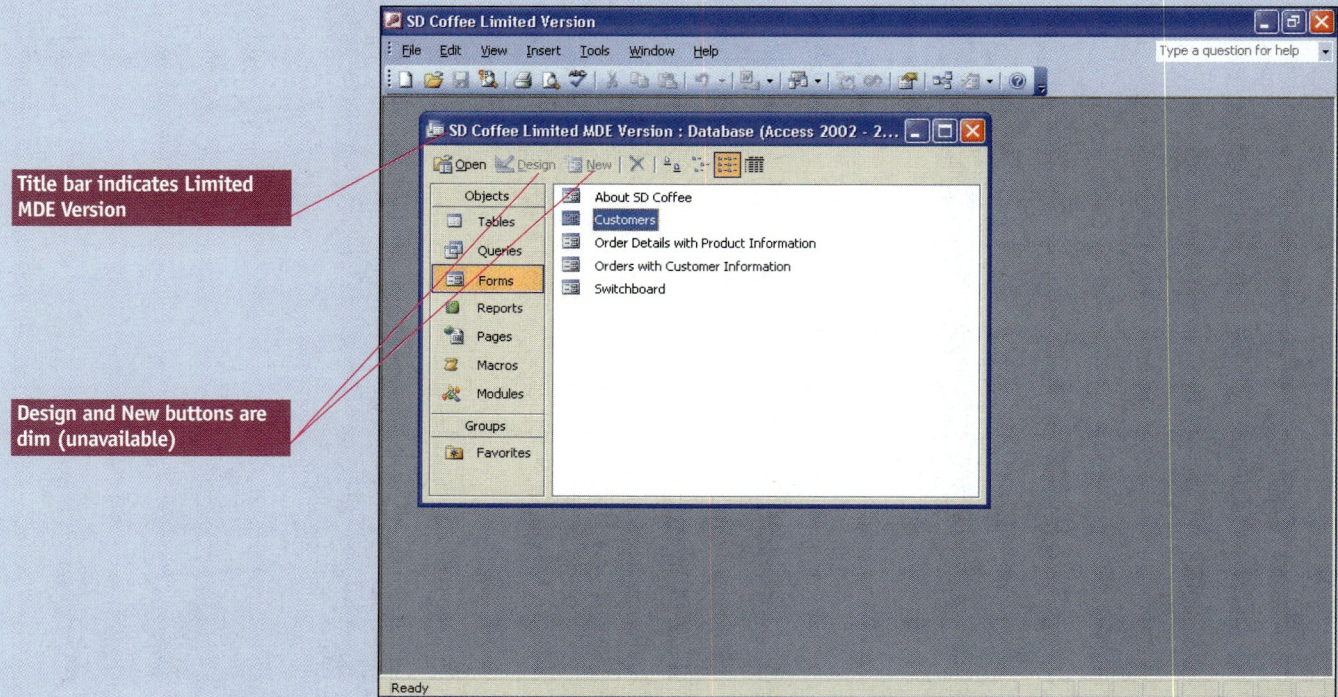

FIGURE 9.26 The MDE Version (exercise 9)

10. **Resubmission to the Client (Version 4.0):** You're finished! You have completed all of the hands-on exercises in the chapter as well as the additional end-of-chapter practice exercises. It is time therefore to submit the final project to the client. You will be expected to demonstrate a working database, and in addition you are to prepare a written report to document the system. Proceed as follows:

   a. Open the complete version of the SD Coffee Database (as opposed to the restricted version from the previous exercise). Be sure that the appropriate security measures are in effect; that is, you should be prompted for a password to open the database.

   b. Close the switchboard. The Database window should be hidden, which means that you have to press the F11 key to display it. Click the Forms button, then change the version number in the About form to Version 4.0. Save the form. Compact and Repair the database.

   c. Open the Switchboard Items table as shown in Figure 9.27. Check the Argument field to be sure that all references to the Prototype macro are gone.

   d. Close the Switchboard Items table and reopen the switchboard. Test the database completely; that is, you should be able to add, edit, and delete records in every table, then run one or more reports to verify that those transactions have taken place.

   e. Prepare a written report that will be an impressive (lengthy) document but one which is easily generated, as much of the material is created directly from the SD Coffee database. You are to include the Switchboard Items table (for both front ends), plus hard copy of every form and report. The objective is for you to have a project of which you will be proud and something that you can demonstrate in the future. The report should include title page and a table (list) of contents. The pages need not be numbered, but there should be loose-leaf dividers for each section.

   f. Copy the completed database to a CD (be sure to include both front ends and the common back end), then submit the CD together with your written report. Congratulations on a job that is truly well done!

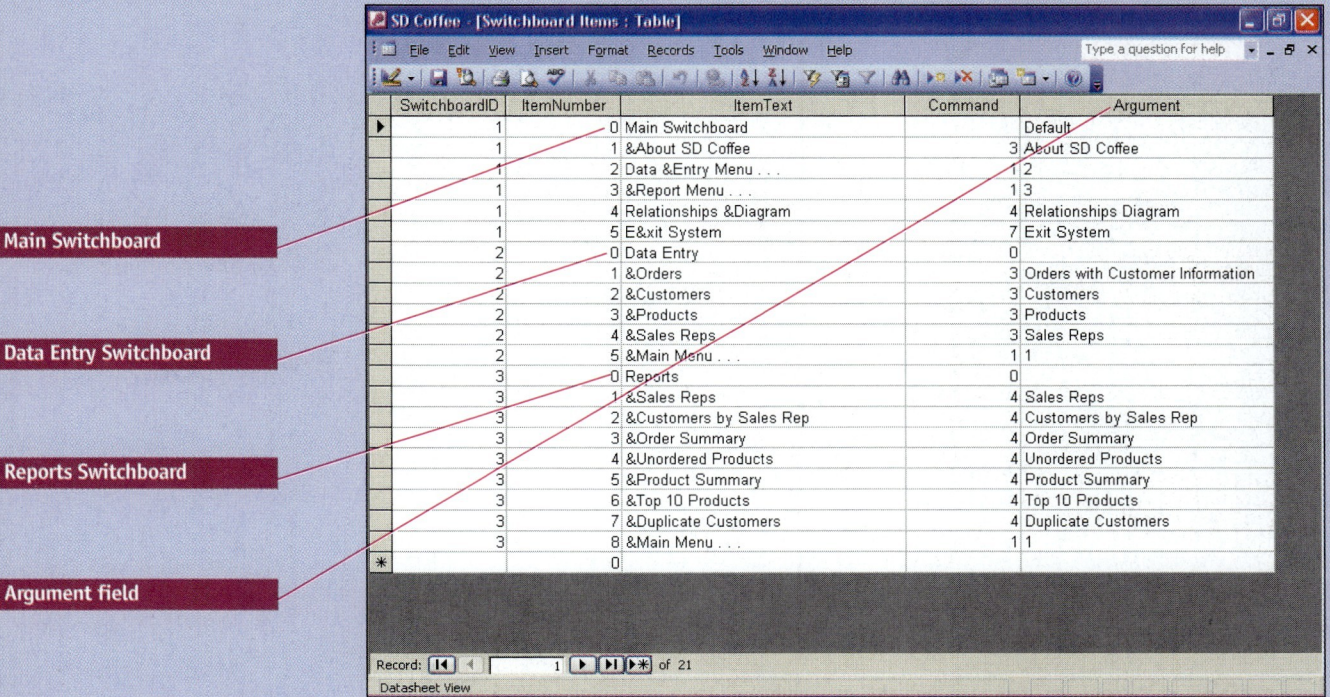

FIGURE 9.27 Resubmission to the Client (exercise 10)

THE GROUP PROJECT

The methodology in the SD Coffee application is easily extended to a capstone project that is implemented in student groups. The group project is typically unstructured, and students are required to develop a database of their own design. The key to a successful project is the disciplined approach—that is, the establishment and adherence to a series of well-defined milestones that were presented in this chapter.

The class is divided into groups of three or four students each, and students work together to submit a collective project. It is critical that the groups are balanced with respect to student abilities, and hence our groups are always formed after the first exam, when we have additional information with which to create the groups. We distribute a questionnaire in which we ask students with whom they want to work and conversely, if there is anyone with whom they would be uncomfortable. We try to honor the former requests, and we always honor the latter, so that the groups work as smoothly as possible.

Once the groups have been formed, we establish a series of milestones such as those that were presented in the chapter opening case study. There is absolutely no requirement for your class to follow our milestones exactly. We have found, however, that providing detailed feedback through a series of sequential assignments is the most effective way to move each group toward its final goal. We also suggest that the groups engage in a continuing presentation to the class as a whole, and we devote the beginning of each class to group presentations of 10 to 15 minutes. (Different groups present on different days.) The group presentations accomplish two goals—they enable students to learn from each other, and they provide valuable practice in presenting one's work to an audience.

Students are required to demonstrate a working system and submit both the Access database and a written document that contains hard copy of every form and report in the application. It is an impressive (lengthy) document but one that is easily generated. The objective is for students to take away a project that they can demonstrate to perspective employers.

The authors' experience with group projects at the University of Miami has been uniformly positive. Students work hard, but they are proud of the end result, and we are continually impressed at the diversity and quality of student projects. The project is what students remember most about our course, and it truly enhances the learning experience.

The Design of a Relational Database

OBJECTIVES

After reading this appendix you will:

1. Distinguish between a primary key and a foreign key.
2. Describe the additional table that is required to implement a many-to-many relationship.
3. Describe three types of anomalies that can occur if data redundancy is present.
4. Define *normalization;* distinguish between the first, second, and third normal forms.
5. Explain the meaning of the phrase, *"the key, the whole key, and nothing but the key, so help me Codd".*
6. Summarize the guidelines for successful database design.

practice in design

Chapter 1: The Look Ahead Database (discussion)

Chapter 4 Case Study: Disc Jockey; **Mini Case:** Attorneys for Athletes

Chapter 5 Case Study: Residential Colleges, Consumer Loans; **Additional Mini Cases:** University Apartments, Automobile Dealership, Evergreen Flying Club

Chapter 6 Case Study: At Your Service, The Computer Super Store; **Additional Mini Cases:** Health Clubs, Morning Paper, College Bookstore, University Placement Center

Chapter 7 Case Study: The Movie Studio, A Recreational Sports League; **Additional Mini Cases:** Computer Repair, Find a Mate Dating Service, Medical Practice, Eco Adventures Cruise Line

OVERVIEW

The goal of any database is to enter data and then retrieve useful information. This is accomplished through mastery of Microsoft Access, but Access is only a means to an end; it is impossible to use Access effectively unless the underlying database is structured properly. Hence the design of a relational database is perhaps the most important topic in the entire text.

Why, then, is database design covered in an appendix, as opposed to a chapter? One reason is that every instructor introduces the topic at a different point in the course, and thus an appendix provides a convenient reference. In addition, database design is discussed in multiple chapters *throughout the text* as different databases are developed. Again, the appendix provides a convenient reference.

Our approach to teaching database design is intuitive rather than theoretical. We begin with two very different case studies and describe the problems (anomalies) that can occur through data redundancy. The first case centers on franchises for fast food restaurants and incorporates the concept of a one-to-many relationship. The second case is a database for student transcripts that incorporates a many-to-many relationship. We then move to a third example that incorporates both types of relationships, but more significantly introduces the concept of normalization to formalize the process of database design. ■

Your assignment is to read this appendix and learn the rudiments of database design. You will then apply that knowledge to multiple databases as directed by your instructor. There are many opportunities for practice as can be seen by the list of chapter opening case studies and end-of-chapter mini cases that are listed on the left. The physical environments of the cases are very different from one another, yet the database designs have many characteristics in common. And as with anything else, the more you practice, the better you become.

CASE STUDY: FAST FOOD FRANCHISES

The case you are about to read is set within the context of a national corporation offering franchises for fast food restaurants. The concept of a franchise operation is a familiar one and exists within many industries. The parent organization develops a model operation, then franchises that concept to qualified individuals (franchisees) seeking to operate their own businesses. The national company teaches the franchisee to run the business, aids the person in site selection and staffing, coordinates national advertising, and so on. The franchisee pays an initial fee to open the business, followed by subsequent royalties and marketing fees that are paid to the parent corporation.

The essence of the case is how to relate the data for the various entities (the restaurants, franchisees, and contracts) to one another. One approach is to develop a single-restaurant table, with each restaurant record containing data about the owner and contract arrangement. As we shall see, that design leads to problems of **redundancy** whenever the same person owns more than one restaurant or when several restaurants have the same contract number. A better approach is to develop a separate table for each object (restaurants, franchisees, and contracts), then relate the tables to one another.

The entities in the case have a definite relationship to one another, which must be reflected in the database design. The corporation encourages individuals to own multiple restaurants, creating a **one-to-many relationship** between franchisees and restaurants. One person can own many restaurants, but a given restaurant is owned by only one person. There is also a one-to-many relationship between contracts and restaurants; that is, the franchisee can select the contract that is best suited to his or her financial situation. Thus, one contract can have many restaurants, but a given restaurant has only one contract.

The company wants to develop a database that can retrieve all data for a given restaurant, such as the annual sales, the contract number in effect, and/or detailed information about the restaurant owner. The company also requires various reports that reflect the location of each restaurant, all restaurants in a given state, and all restaurants managed by a particular contract number. The various contract arrangements are described below:

Contract 1: 99-year term, requiring a one-time fee of $250,000 payable at the time the franchise is awarded. In addition, the franchisee must pay a royalty of 2 percent of the restaurant's gross sales to the parent corporation, and contribute an additional 2 percent of sales to the parent corporation for advertising.

Contract 2: 5-year term (renewable at franchisee's option), requiring an initial payment of $50,000. In addition, the franchisee must pay a royalty of 4 percent of the restaurant's gross sales to the parent corporation, and contribute an additional 3 percent of sales to the parent corporation for advertising.

Contract 3: 10-year term (renewable at franchisee's option), requiring an initial payment of $75,000. In addition, the franchisee must pay a royalty of 3 percent of the restaurant's gross sales to the parent corporation, and contribute an additional 3 percent of sales to the parent corporation for advertising.

Other contracts may be offered in the future. The company currently has 500 restaurants, of which 200 are company owned. Expansion plans call for opening an additional 200 restaurants each year for the next three years, all of which are to be franchised. There is no limit on the number of restaurants an individual may own. Your task is to design the database so that it satisfies the information requirements of the client. We begin with the single-table solution.

Single-table Solution

The single-table solution is shown in Figure A.1. Each record within the table contains data about a particular restaurant, its franchisee (owner), and the contract in effect. There are five restaurants in our example, each with a unique restaurant number. At first glance, Figure A.1 appears satisfactory; yet there are three specific types of problems (**anomalies**) associated with this solution. These are:

1. Difficulties in the modification of data for an existing franchisee or contract number, in that the same change has to be made in multiple places. This is known as an **update** (or modification) **anomaly**.

2. Difficulties in the addition of a new franchisee or contract in that we cannot add this information until we add a restaurant that is associated with the new franchisee or contract. This is known as an **insertion anomaly**.

3. Difficulties in the deletion of a restaurant in that data for a particular franchisee or contract number may be unintentionally removed from the database. This is known as a **deletion anomaly**.

The first problem, modification of data about an existing franchisee or contract, occurs because the same data is stored in multiple places. Thus, any change to a duplicated entry, such as updating the phone number for a franchisee with multiple restaurants (e.g., Grauer, who owns restaurants in Miami and Fort Lauderdale), requires a search through the entire table to find all instances of that data so that the identical modification can be made to each of the records. A similar procedure would have to be followed should data change about a duplicated contract (e.g., a change in the royalty percentage for contract 1, which applies to restaurants R1, R2, and R4). This is, to say the least, a time-consuming and error-prone procedure.

The addition of a new franchisee or contract poses a different type of problem. It is quite logical, for example, that potential franchisees must apply to the corporation and qualify for ownership before having a restaurant assigned to them. It is also likely that the corporation would develop a new contract prior to offering that contract to an existing restaurant. Neither of these events is easily accommodated in the table structure of Figure A.1, which would require the creation of a dummy restaurant record to accommodate the new franchisee or contract.

The deletion of a restaurant creates yet another type of difficulty. What happens, for example, if the company decides to close restaurant R5 because of insufficient sales? The record for this restaurant would disappear as expected, but so would the data for the franchisee (Coulter) and the contract (C3), which is not intended. The corporation might want to award Coulter another restaurant in the future and/or offer this contract to other restaurants. Neither situation would be possible as the relevant data would be lost with the deletion of the restaurant record.

Restaurant Number	Restaurant Data (Address, annual sales . . .)	Franchisee Data (Name, telephone, address . . .)	Contract Data (Number, term, initial fee . . .)
R1	Restaurant data for Miami . . .	Franchisee data (Grauer . . .)	Contract data (Contract 1 . . .)
R2	Restaurant data for Coral Gables . . .	Franchisee data (Moldof . . .)	Contract data (Contract 1 . . .)
R3	Restaurant data for Fort Lauderdale. . .	Franchisee data (Grauer . . .)	Contract data (Contract 2 . . .)
R4	Restaurant data for New York . . .	Franchisee data (Glassman . . .)	Contract data (Contract 1 . . .)
R5	Restaurant data for Coral Springs . . .	Franchisee data (Coulter . . .)	Contract data (Contract 3 . . .)

FIGURE A.1 Fast Food Franchises Single-table Solution

Multiple-table Solution

A much better solution appears in Figure A.2, which uses a separate table for each of the entities (restaurants, franchisees, and contracts) that exist in the system. Every record in the Restaurant table is assigned a unique restaurant number (e.g., R1 or R2), just as every record in the Franchisee table is given a unique franchisee number (e.g., F1 or F2), and every contract record a unique contract number (e.g., C1 or C2).

The tables are linked to one another through the franchisee and/or contract numbers, which also appear in the Restaurant table. Every record in the Restaurant table is associated with its appropriate record in the Franchisee table through the franchisee number common to both tables. In similar fashion, every restaurant is tied to its appropriate contract through the contract number, which appears in the restaurant record. This solution may seem complicated, but it is really quite simple and elegant.

Assume, for example, that we want the name of the franchisee for restaurant R5, and further, that we need the details of the contract for this restaurant. We retrieve the appropriate restaurant record, which contains franchisee and contract numbers of F4 and C3, respectively. We then search through the Franchisee table for franchisee F4 (obtaining all necessary information about Coulter) and search again through the Contract table for contract C3 (obtaining the data for this contract). The process is depicted graphically in Figure A.2.

The multiple-table solution may require slightly more effort to retrieve information, but this is more than offset by the advantages of table maintenance. Consider, for example, a change in data for contract C1, which currently governs restaurants R1, R2, and R4. All that is necessary is to go into the contract table, find record C1, and make the changes. The records in the restaurant table are not affected because the restaurant records do not contain contract data per se, only the number of the corresponding contract record. In other words, the change in data for contract C1 is made in one place (the Contract table), yet that change would be reflected for all affected restaurants. This is in contrast to the single-table solution of Figure A.1, which would require the identical modification in three places.

The addition of new records for franchisees or contracts is done immediately in the appropriate tables of Figure A.2. The corporation simply adds a franchisee or contract record as these events occur, without the necessity of a corresponding restaurant record. This is much easier than the approach of Figure A.1, which required an existing restaurant in order to add one of the other entities. The deletion of a restaurant is also better than with the single-table organization in that you can delete restaurant R5 without losing the associated franchisee and contract data.

Queries to the Database

The ultimate objective of any system is to produce information, and it is in this area that the multiple-table design excels. Look once again at Figure A.2 and note that it includes several fields in each table. Note, too, how the tables are linked to one another through the franchisee and/or contract numbers, which are *color-coded* throughout so that you can see the relationships more clearly.

The multiple-table design is capable of providing complete information about the franchise operation as stated in the original case study. Some queries can be answered with data from a single table; other queries require data from two tables, while more complex queries require data from all three tables. In each instance, however, the solution should be readily apparent although the more complex calculations may take a minute or too. Realize, too, that once the database has been implemented in Access, the answer to all of these queries is available with the click of a mouse.

(a) Restaurant Table

Restaurant Number	Street Address	City	State	Zip Code	Annual Sales	Franchisee Number	Contract Number
R1	1001 Ponce de Leon Blvd	Miami	FL	33361	$600,000	F1	C1
R2	31 West Rivo Alto Road	Coral Gables	FL	33139	$450,000	F2	C1
R3	333 Las Olas Blvd	Fort Lauderdale	FL	33033	$250,000	F1	C2
R4	1700 Broadway	New York	NY	10010	$1,750,000	F3	C1
R5	1300 Sample Road	Coral Springs	FL	33071	$50,000	F4	C3

(a) Restaurant Table

(b) Franchisee Table

Franchisee Number	Franchisee Name	Telephone	Street Address	City	State	Zip Code
F1	Grauer	(305) 755-1000	2133 NW 102 Terrace	Coral Springs	FL	33071
F2	Moldof	(305) 753-4614	1400 Lejeune Blvd	Miami	FL	33365
F3	Glassman	(212) 458-5054	555 Fifth Avenue	New York	NY	10024
F4	Coulter	(305) 755-0910	1000 Federal Highway	Fort Lauderdale	FL	33033

(b) Franchisee Table

(c) Contract Table

Contract Number	Term (years)	Initial Fee	Royalty Pct	Advertising Pct
C1	99	$250,000	2%	2%
C2	5	$50,000	4%	3%
C3	10	$75,000	3%	3%

(c) Contract Table

FIGURE A.2   Fast Food Franchises (Multiple-table Solution)

Questions

1. Who owns restaurant R2? Which contract is in effect for this restaurant?
2. What is the address of restaurant R4?
3. Which restaurant(s) are owned by Mr. Grauer?
4. List all restaurants that are tied to contract C1.
5. Which restaurants in Florida have gross sales over $300,000?
6. How many franchisees are there? What are their names?
7. What are the royalty and advertising percentages for restaurant R3? What are the dollar amounts?

Answers

1. Restaurant R2 is owned by Moldof; contract C1 is in effect.
2. Restaurant R4 is located at 1700 Broadway, New York, NY 10010.
3. Mr. Grauer owns restaurants R1 and R3.
4. R1, R2, and R4 are governed by contract C1.
5. The restaurants in Florida with gross sales over $300,000 are R1 ($600,000) and R2 ($450,000).
6. There are four franchisees: Grauer, Moldof, Glassman, and Coulter.
7. Restaurant R3 is governed by contract C2 with royalty and advertising percentages of 4% and 3%, respectively. The dollar amounts are $10,000 and $7,500, respectively.

THE RELATIONAL MODEL

The concept of a relational database originated with a classic paper by **Edgar Codd** of IBM (*A Relational Model of Data for Large Shared Databanks*, Communications of the ACM, June, 1970, pages 377–387). The idea was simple yet powerful: namely, to store data in separate tables called **relations**, and to establish relationships between these tables. (Codd refers to each row in a relation as a **tuple**, and to each column in a relation as an **attribute**. We will, however, use the more common terms **table**, **record**, and **field** for relation, tuple, and attribute, respectively.) The relational model has since become the industry standard.

The restaurant case study illustrated that a separate table was required for each entity in the physical system (restaurants, franchisees, and contracts). Every occurrence of an entity (a specific restaurant, franchisee, or contract) appears as a record (row) within the appropriate table. The properties of an entity (a restaurant's address, owner, or sales) appear as fields (columns) within the appropriate table.

Every record in a table must differ in some way from every other record in that table. This is accomplished by designating one field (or combination of fields) as a unique identifier called the **primary key**. The restaurant number, for example, is different for every restaurant in the Restaurant table. The franchisee number is unique in the Franchisee table, as is the contract number in the Contract table.

The same field can, however, appear in multiple tables. The franchisee number, for example, appears in both the Franchisee table, where its values are unique, and in the Restaurant table, where they are not. The franchisee number is the primary key in the Franchisee table, but it is a foreign key in the Restaurant table. (A **foreign key** is simply the primary key of another table.)

The inclusion of a foreign key in the Restaurant table enables us to implement the one-to-many relationship between franchisees and restaurants. We enter the franchisee number (the primary key in the Franchisee table) as a column in the Restaurant table, where it (the franchisee number) is a foreign key. In similar fashion, contract number (the primary key in the Contract table) appears as a foreign key in the Restaurant table to implement the one-to-many relationship between contracts and restaurants.

CASE STUDY: STUDENT TRANSCRIPTS

Our second case is set within the context of student transcripts and expands the concept of a relational database to implement a **many-to-many relationship**. The system is intended to track students and the courses they take. The many-to-many relationship occurs because one student takes many courses, while at the same time, one course is taken by many students. The objective of this case is to relate the Student and Course tables to one another to produce the desired information.

The system should be able to display information about a particular student as well as information about a particular course. It should also display information about a student–course combination, such as when a student took the course and what grade he or she received.

The (intuitive and incorrect) solution of Figure A.3 consists of two tables, one for courses and one for students, corresponding to the two entities in the physical system. The Student table contains the student's name, address, major, date of entry into the school, cumulative credits, and cumulative quality points. The Course table contains the unique six-character course identifier, the course title, and the number of credits.

There are no problems of redundancy. The data for a particular course (its description and number of credits) appears only once in the Course table, just as the data for a particular student appears only once in the Student table. New courses will be added directly to the Course table, just as new students will be added to the Student table.

Course Number	Course Description	Credits
ACC101	Introduction to Accounting	3
CHM100	Survey of Chemistry	3
CHM101	Chemistry Lab	1
CIS120	Microcomputer Applications	3
ENG100	Freshman English	3
MTH100	Calculus with Analytic Geometry	4
MUS110	Music Appreciation	2
SPN100	Spanish I	3

(a) Course Table

Student Number	Student Data	Courses Taken with Grade and Semester													
S1	Student data (Adams. . .)	ACC101	SP05	A	CIS120	FA04	A	MU100	FA04	B				
S2	Student data (Fox. . .)	ENG100	SP05	B	MTH100	SP05	B	SPN100	SP05	B	CIS120	FA04	A
S3	Student data (Baker. . .)	ACC101	SP05	C	ENG100	SP05	B	MTH100	FA04	C	CIS120	FA04	B
S4	Student data (Jones. . .)	ENG100	SP05	A	MTH100	SP05	A							
S5	Student data (Smith. . .)	CIS120	SP05	C	ENG100	SP05	B	CIS120	FA04	F				

(b) Student Table

FIGURE A.3 Student Transcripts (repeating groups)

The design of the Student table makes it easy to list all courses for one student. It is more difficult, however, to list all students in one course. Even if this were not the case, the solution is complicated by the irregular shape of the student table. The rows in the table are of variable length, according to the number of courses taken by each student. Not only is this design awkward, but how can we know in advance how much space to allocate for each student?

The problems inherent in Figure A.3 stem from the many-to-many relationship that exists between students and courses. The solution is to eliminate the *repeating groups* (course number, semester, and grade), which occur in each row of the student table in Figure A.3, in favor of the additional table shown in Figure A.4. Each row in the new table is unique because the combination of student number, course number, and semester is unique. Semester must be included since students are allowed to repeat a course. Smith (student number S5), for example, took CIS120 a second time after failing it initially.

The implementation of a many-to-many relationship requires an additional table, with a *composite key* (also called a *combined key* or a *concatenated key*) consisting of (at least) the keys of the individual entities. The many-to-many table may also contain additional columns, which exist as a result of the combination (intersection) of the individual keys. The combination of student S5, course CIS120, and semester SP05 is unique and results in a grade of C.

Note, too, how the design in Figure A.4 facilitates table maintenance as discussed in the previous case. A change in student data is made in only one place (the Student table), regardless of how many courses the student has taken. A new student may be added to the Student table prior to taking any courses. In similar fashion, a new course can be added to the Course table before any students have taken the course.

Course Number	Course Description	Credits
ACC101	Introduction to Accounting	3
CHM100	Survey of Chemistry	3
CHM101	Chemistry Lab	1
CIS120	Microcomputer Applications	3
ENG100	Freshman English	3
MTH100	Calculus with Analytic Geometry	4
MUS110	Music Appreciation	2
SPN100	Spanish I	3

(a) Course Table

Student Number	Student Data
S1	Student data (Adams. . .)
S2	Student data (Fox. . .)
S3	Student data (Baker. . .)
S4	Student data (Jones. . .)
S5	Student data (Smith. . .)

(b) Student Table

Student Number	Course Number	Semester	Grade
S1	ACC101	SP05	A
S1	CIS120	FA04	A
S1	MU100	FA04	B
S2	ENG100	SP05	B
S2	MTH100	SP05	B
S2	SPN100	SP05	B
S2	CIS120	FA04	A
S3	ACC101	SP05	C
S3	ENG100	SP05	B
S3	MTH100	FA04	C
S3	CIS120	FA04	B
S4	ENG100	SP05	A
S4	MTH100	SP05	A
S5	CIS120	SP05	C
S5	ENG100	SP05	B
S5	CIS120	FA04	F

(c) Student–course Table

FIGURE A.4   Student Transcripts (improved design)

Questions

1. How many courses are currently offered?
2. List all three-credit courses.
3. Which courses has Smith taken during his stay at the university?
4. Which students have taken MTH100?
5. Which courses did Adams take during the fall 2004 semester?
6. Which students took Microcomputer Applications in the fall 2004 semester?
7. Which students received an A in Freshman English during the spring 2005 semester?

Answers

1. Eight courses are offered.
2. The three-credit courses are ACC101, CHM100, CIS120, ENG100, and SPN100.
3. Smith has taken CIS120 (twice) and ENG100.
4. Fox, Baker, and Jones have taken MTH100.
5. Adams took CIS120 and MU100 during the fall 2004 semester.
6. Adams, Fox, Baker, and Smith took Microcomputer Applications in the fall 2004 semester.
7. Jones was the only student to receive an A in Freshman English during the spring 2005 semester.

INTRODUCTION TO NORMALIZATION

We "know" that the designs for the restaurant and student databases are "good designs," but knowing something is different from proving it. *Normalization* is a way of organizing a database so that the storage and retrieval of its data is more efficient. It is a multistep process that continually refines the design of a database until all redundant data has been eliminated. This is accomplished by examining the *dependencies* (relationships) between the fields in a table and eliminating the partial and transitive dependencies (both terms are defined shortly) that may exist.

The end result is a design in which every field within a table is *functionally dependent* on the primary key. This is an important concept and, indeed, it is the ultimate goal of the normalization process. A field is said to be functionally dependent on the primary key if a given value of the primary key (e.g., a student number) yields only one value of the dependent field (e.g., the student's name).

This sounds complicated, but the normalization process can be summed up by a single phrase, "*the key, the whole key, and nothing but the key, so help me Codd.*" This simple sentence not only gives credit to Edgar Codd, who first postulated the relational model, but it also states the essence of good database design: namely, that the value of every field in a table is dependent on the primary key, on the entire primary key, and on nothing but the primary key.

CASE STUDY: ORDER ENTRY

Our next example examines the database for a classic order entry system for a retail establishment that focuses on customers, products, and orders. The system maintains the usual customer data (name, address, phone, and so on). It also keeps track of the available products, storing for each product the product number, name, and price. And finally, it maintains data about every order, storing the date of the order, the customer who placed the order, the products that were ordered, and the quantity of each product in that order.

The database should be able to supply information about a specific customer (e.g., his or her phone number and address). It should also be able to supply the name of the customer who placed a particular order and/or retrieve all orders that were placed by a specific customer. The database must be able to list all of the products that are carried by the store and/or compute the cost of a particular order. The potential queries are endless.

You may already see the two distinct relationships that exist within this system. There is a one-to-many relationship between customers and orders; that is, one customer can place many orders, but a given order is associated with only one customer. There is also a many-to-many relationship between orders and products; that is, one order can contain many products, and the same product can appear in many orders. This insight enables you to create the required tables and to bypass some or all of the steps in the normalization process. We think it important, however, to go through normalization at least once so that you will better understand the theoretical foundation of database design.

The Normalization Process

Normalization is a multistep process where you progress from one normal form to the next until the design is acceptable. Figure A.5a shows the raw data with no normalization whatsoever; that is, all of the data exists in a single Orders table. This design contains all of the potential anomalies that were raised in the initial restaurant example, and is further complicated because each record is of variable length, depending on the number of products that appear in a specific order. Hence, the first step in the normalization process is to eliminate the *repeating groups* (the

Orders Table

OrderID	Date	Customer Information	Product Information	Quantity	Product Information	Quantity

(a) Unstructured Data

Repeating group

Order Details Table

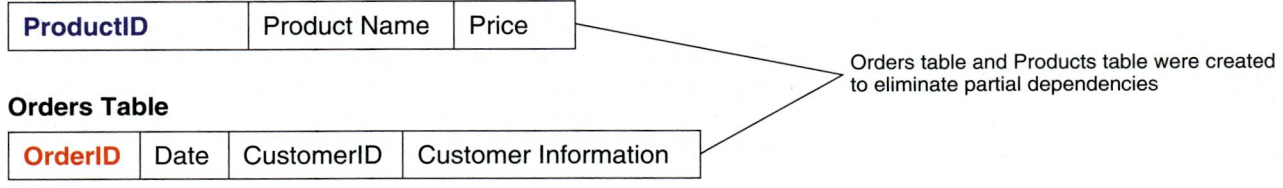

OrderID	ProductID	Product Information	Quantity	Date	CustomerID	Customer Information

(b) First Normal Form (eliminates repeating groups but retains partial dependencies)

Products Table

ProductID	Product Name	Price

Orders Table

OrderID	Date	CustomerID	Customer Information

Orders table and Products table were created to eliminate partial dependencies

Order Details Table

OrderID	ProductID	Quantity

(c) Second Normal Form (eliminates partial dependencies but retains transitive dependencies)

Customers Table

CustomerID	Name	Address	Telephone	Credit Rating

Customers table was created to eliminate transitive dependency

Products Table

ProductID	ProductName	Price

Orders Table

OrderID	Date	CustomerID

Order Details Table

OrderID	ProductID	Quantity

(d) Third Normal Form (eliminates transitive dependencies leaving only functional dependencies)

FIGURE A.5   The Normalization Process

product information and quantity) that occur in each order record. The result is the *first normal form* in Figure A.5b, where the original Orders table has been converted to an Order Details table.

The Order Details table contains a record for each product in each order (as opposed to a single record for each order in the original Orders table). Every record in the new table is the same length as every other record. The primary key of the new table is a composite key consisting of the OrderID and the ProductID. (The remaining fields contain the product information for the selected product, the quantity ordered, the date of the order, the CustomerID, and the associated customer information.) This design is significantly better than the unstructured data, but there is still a significant problem, because the product information depends on only part of the composite primary key (the ProductID, as opposed to the combination of OrderID and ProductID). This is known as a *partial dependency*, and it has to be eliminated.

The second step in the normalization process removes the partial dependencies to create the *second normal form* in Figure A.5c. Two additional tables, a Products table and an Orders table, have been created. The Products table contains three fields, ProductID, ProductName, and Price; the ProductName and Price depend on the ProductID (the primary key), which is the proper design. The partial dependency has been eliminated, but another type of dependency is present in the Orders table. The date of the order and the CustomerID depend on the OrderID, which is as it should be, because the OrderID is the primary key. The problem is that the customer information depends on the CustomerID, as opposed to the OrderID. This is known as a *transitive dependency*, and it has to be eliminated.

The third step in the normalization process removes the transitive dependencies to create the *third normal form* in Figure A.5d. There are now four tables in the database (Customers, Products, Orders, and Order Details). Every field in every table is functionally dependent on the primary key of that table; that is, a given value of the primary key always yields the same value of the dependent field. Think again of our summary phrase, *"the key, the whole key, and nothing but the key"*; that is, every field in every table depends on the value of the primary key, the entire primary key, and nothing but the primary key.

An Easy Way to Third Normal Form

Normalization is essential to the successful implementation of a relational database. As you gain experience, however, normalization becomes intuitive and more of an implicit rather than an explicit process. You can in fact arrive at the third normal form almost immediately if you follow these guidelines:

1. Identify the entities (objects) that exist in the physical system, each of which requires its own table.

2. Create the required tables and identify the primary key in each table. (The additional fields need not be added at this time.)

3. Identify and implement the relationships that exist in the physical system. A one-to-many relationship is implemented by including the primary key of the "one" table as a foreign key in the "many" table. A many-to-many relationship requires an additional table, which contains the primary keys of the individual entities.

4. Complete each table in the database by including any other fields that are necessary to produce the information that is required of the database.

5. Study the completed design to ensure that the value of every field in every table is dependent on the primary key of that table, the entire primary key, and nothing but the primary key.

6. Ask "questions" of the finished database to determine the completeness of the design; if you cannot answer a specific question, you will have to add fields to one or more tables and repeat some (all) of the previous steps.

Let's return to the original description of the order entry database and apply these guidelines to arrive immediately at the third normal form. We recognize three distinct entities in the physical system: customers, orders, and products, each of which requires its own table. We see that there is a one-to-many relationship between customers and orders; that is, one customer can have many orders, but a given order is associated with only one customer. Thus, we take the primary key of the "one" table (the Customers table) and place it as a foreign key in the "many" table (the Orders table).

We also recognize a many-to-many relationship between products and orders, which requires a new Order Details table. The primary key for this table is the combination of ProductID and OrderID. The only additional field in this table is the quantity (of that particular product in that particular order) that was ordered. At this point you are very close to the third normal form that was shown in Figure A.5d. All you have to do to complete the design is to add the remaining fields in each table to satisfy the information requirements of the system.

Queries to the Database

We have completed the design of the order entry system. It is a good design without data duplication that enables us to add, edit, or modify the records for a customer, product, or order. Equally important, the design enables us to retrieve detailed information about any customer, product, or order. Consider, for example, the following queries in conjunction with Figure A.6.

Query: Which customers ordered a gazebo?

Answer: Bob Barker and Jennie Jones are the only two customers who ordered a gazebo.

Method: Search the Products table for "gazebo" to determine the ProductID (P0007), then take this value to the Order Details table to identify the orders that contained this product, orders O0006 and O0009. Now look in the Orders table to determine the associated CustomerID for each order (C0004 and C0007), then look in the Customers table to find the associated customer names, which are Bob Barker and Jennie Jones.

Query: What is the total cost of order O0010? Which products are in the order, and how many units of each product?

Answer: The total cost of order O0010 is $262.00. The order is composed of four orchids that cost $16 each and two three-foot fountains that sell for $99 each.

Method: Search the Order Details table for the first record for order O0010 to determine the associated ProductID (P0017) and quantity, search the Products table to find the name of this product and its price, and then multiply the price ($16) by the quantity (4 units) to get the cost of this item ($64). Repeat this process for every record in the Order Details table for order O0010 (there is only one additional record for two units of product P0018), then add the subtotals to arrive at the total cost of the order.

Remember, too, that once the database has been implemented in Access, the answer to these and other queries is available with the click of a mouse. We think you will be pleased at what you can do with Access, but your success depends on the validity of your design.

(a) Customers Table

CustomerID	Last Name	First Name	Address	City	State	Zip code	Phone Number
C0001	Jones	Sarah	1234 Main Street	Ft. Lauderdale	FL	33120	(305) 555-5678
C0002	Green	Tom	5678 Blackberry Blvd.	Miami	FL	33123	(305) 876-5489
C0003	Chen	Susie	992 Forest Pond Ct.	Coral Gables	FL	33146	(305) 642-5859
C0004	Barker	Bob	642 Second Ave.	Miami	FL	33124	(305) 587-3252
C0005	Smith	Margaret	6485 Third St.	Miami	FL	33214	(305) 876-4598
C0006	Macon	Jason	3858 Bird St.	Miami	FL	33120	(305) 678-7451
C0007	Jones	Jennie	1698 Palmetto Dr.	Coral Gables	FL	32147	(305) 976-4615
C0008	Baker	Sue	2308 Ibis Dr.	Coral Gables	FL	33145	(305) 418-5627

(a) Customers Table

(b) Orders Table

OrderID	CustomerID	Order Date
O0001	C0005	1/1/2005
O0002	C0006	1/1/2005
O0003	C0001	1/2/2005
O0004	C0002	1/2/2005
O0005	C0001	1/3/2005
O0006	C0004	1/3/2005
O0007	C0003	1/3/2005
O0008	C0006	1/4/2005
O0009	C0007	1/5/2005
O0010	C0001	1/5/2005

(b) Orders Table

(c) Products Table

Product ID	Product Name	Price
P0001	6" potted plant	$10.99
P0002	10" potted plant	$14.99
P0003	15" potted plant	$20.99
P0004	50' garden hose	$12.99
P0005	100' garden hose	$19.99
P0006	Garden tools	$29.99
P0007	Gazebo	$499.00
P0008	8" clay pot	$5.99
P0009	12" clay pot	$7.99
P0010	18" clay pot	$12.99
P0011	10 lbs potting soil	$5.00
P0012	25 lbs potting soil	$10.00
P0013	Walking sprinkler	$49.99
P0014	Garden gloves	$4.99
P0015	50 pounds fertilizer	$19.99
P0016	Watering can	$5.99
P0017	Orchid of the week	$16.00
P0018	3' fountain	$99.00

(c) Products Table

(d) Order Details Table

OrderID	ProductID	Quantity
O0001	P0002	2
O0001	P0003	1
O0001	P0005	3
O0001	P0006	2
O0002	P0001	5
O0002	P0002	1
O0003	P0004	2
O0003	P0010	3
O0004	P0003	2
O0004	P0010	2
O0005	P0005	3
O0005	P0011	2
O0005	P0013	5
O0005	P0014	1
O0005	P0018	1
O0006	P0002	1
O0006	P0007	1
O0007	P0001	2
O0007	P0016	3
O0008	P0018	1
O0008	P0005	1
O0009	P0007	1
O0009	P0001	1
O0009	P0016	3
O0010	P0017	4
O0010	P0018	2

(d) Order Details Table

FIGURE A.6 Order Entry Database

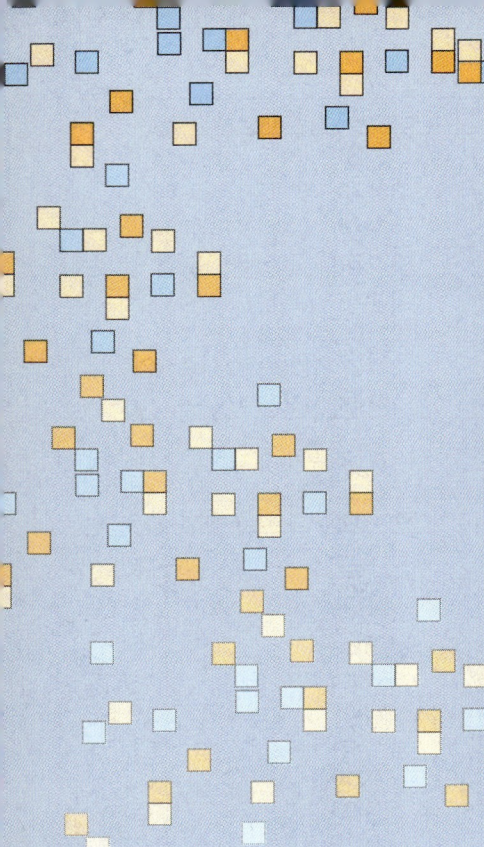

SUMMARY

The concept of a relational database originated with a classic paper by Edgar Codd of IBM. The idea was simple yet powerful: namely, to store data in separate tables called relations, and to establish relationships between these tables. The design of a relational database is crucial if one is to use Access successfully. Good design will eliminate data redundancy, which results in problems (anomalies) during data entry.

This appendix began with two case studies that presented an intuitive approach to database design. The first example was a franchise operation for a restaurant chain and illustrated one-to-many relationships that exist between the various entities in the physical system; for example, one franchisee can own many restaurants, but a given restaurant is owned by only one person. A one-to-many relationship is implemented by including the primary key (the field or combination of fields that makes a record unique) of the "one" table as a foreign key in the "many" table. (A foreign key is the primary key of another table.)

The second example developed a university database that focused on the many-to-many relationship between students and the courses they take. Implementation of a many-to-many relationship requires an additional table, which contains (at least) the primary keys of the individual tables. The completed design contained three tables: a Student table, a Course table, and a Student–Course table mandated by the many-to-many relationship between students and courses.

We then moved to a more formal approach called normalization and applied this technique to a third database that contained both a one-to-many and a many-to-many relationship. We showed that normalization is a multistep process where you progress from one normal form to the next until the design is acceptable. First normal form eliminates repeating groups. Second normal form eliminates partial dependencies where a field is dependent on only part of a primary key. Third normal form (the end result) eliminates transitive dependencies, which occur when a field is dependent on a field other than the primary key.

The theory behind normalization can be summed up by a single phrase, "*the key, the whole key, and nothing but the key, so help me Codd.*" This simple sentence not only gives credit to Edgar Codd, who first postulated the relational model, but it also states the essence of good database design: namely, that the value of every field in a table is dependent on the primary key, on the entire primary key, and on nothing but the primary key. As one gains experience, normalization becomes intuitive and more of an implicit rather than an explicit process. You can in fact arrive at the third normal form almost immediately if you follow basic guidelines. (Identify the entities in the physical system and create a table for each; identify, then implement the relationships that exist between these tables; complete the individual tables by adding the necessary fields to produce the required information; and ensure that every field is dependent on the primary key of the table in which it is found.)

KEY TERMS

Anomaly 527
Attribute 530
Codd, Edgar 530
Combined key 531
Composite key 531
Concatenated key 531
Deletion anomaly 527
Dependencies 533
Field 530
First normal form 535

Foreign key 530
Functional dependence 533
Insertion anomaly 527
Many-to-many relationship 530
Normalization 533
One-to-many relationship 526
Partial dependency 535
Primary key 530
Record 530
Redundancy 526

Relation 530
Relational database 527
Repeating group 531
Second normal form 535
Table 530
Third normal form 535
Transitive dependency 535
Tuple 530
Update anomaly 527

MULTIPLE CHOICE

1. Who is given credit for the relational model?

   (a) Bill Gates
   (b) E. F. Codd
   (c) Charles Babbage
   (d) Grauer and Barber

2. The First Normal Form eliminates:

   (a) Functional dependencies
   (b) Transitive dependencies
   (c) Partial dependencies
   (d) Repeating groups

3. The Second Normal Form eliminates:

   (a) Functional dependencies
   (b) Transitive dependencies
   (c) Partial dependencies
   (d) Repeating groups

4. The Third Normal Form eliminates:

   (a) Functional dependencies
   (b) Transitive dependencies
   (c) Partial dependencies
   (d) Repeating groups

5. The end result of the normalization process is a database in:

   (a) First normal form
   (b) Second normal form
   (c) Third normal form
   (d) Any normal form

6. A partial dependency occurs when:

   (a) The primary key of one table appears as a foreign key in another table
   (b) A field depends on one of two fields in a composite primary key
   (c) A database contains both a one-to-many relationship and a many-to-many relationship
   (d) The database is partially completed

7. A transitive dependency occurs when:

   (a) The database is in transition, that is, during data entry
   (b) Every field in a table is dependent on the primary key
   (c) One field is dependent on another field that is not the primary key
   (d) A database contains both a one-to-many relationship and a many-to-many relationship

8. A database in third normal form should contain several:

   (a) Partial dependencies
   (b) Transitive dependencies
   (c) Functional dependencies
   (d) None of the above

9. Which of the following is true about a sports database that contains a one-to-many relationship between teams and players?

   (a) The PlayerID will appear as the primary key in the Teams table
   (b) The TeamID will appear as the primary key in the Players table
   (c) The PlayerID will appear as a foreign key in the Teams table
   (d) The TeamID will appear as a foreign key in the Players table

10. Which of the following was not a suggested guideline for database design?

   (a) Every entity in the physical system requires its own table in the database
   (b) Every table must have at least one primary key and one foreign key
   (c) A many-to-many relationship requires an additional table where the primary key consists of (at least) the primary keys of the individual entities.
   (d) A one-to-many relationship is implemented by including the primary key of the "one" table as a foreign key in the "many" table

11. A composite key consists of two fields that are:

   (a) Partially dependent on one another
   (b) Transitively dependent on one another
   (c) Functionally dependent on one another
   (d) None of the above

12. Which of the following was selected as the composite key for the Order Entry database?

   (a) OrderID and ProductID
   (b) OrderID, ProductID, and Quantity
   (c) OrderID, ProductID, and Date
   (d) OrderID, ProductID, and CustomerID

ANSWERS

1.	b	5.	c	9.	d
2.	d	6.	b	10.	b
3.	c	7.	c	11.	d
4.	b	8.	c	12.	a

B

Toolbars for Microsoft® Office Access 2003

TOOLBARS

Alignment and Sizing

Database

Filter/Sort

Form Design

Form View

Formatting (Datasheet)

Formatting (Form/Report)

Formatting (Page)

Formatting (PivotTable/PivotChart)

Macro Design

Page Design

Page View

PivotChart

PivotTable

Print Preview

Query Datasheet

Query Design

Relationship

Report Design

Shortcut Menus

Source Code Control

Table Datasheet

Table Design

Toolbox

Utility 1

Utility 2

Web

OVERVIEW

Microsoft Access has 27 predefined toolbars that provide access to commonly used commands. The toolbars are displayed in Figure B.1 and are listed here for convenience: Alignment and Sizing, Database, Filter/Sort, Form Design, Form View, Formatting (Datasheet), Formatting (Form/Report), Formatting (Page), Formatting (PivotTable/PivotChart), Macro Design, Page Design, Page View, PivotChart, PivotTable, Print Preview, Query Datasheet, Query Design, Relationship, Report Design, Shortcut Menus, Source Code Control, Table Datasheet, Table Design, Toolbox, Utility 1, Utility 2, and Web.

The buttons on the toolbars are intended to be indicative of their function. Clicking the Printer button, for example (the fifth button from the left on the Database toolbar), executes the Print command. If you are unsure of the purpose of any toolbar button, point to it, and a ScreenTip will appear that displays its name.

You can display multiple toolbars at one time, move them to new locations on the screen, customize their appearance, or suppress their display.

■ To display or hide a toolbar, pull down the View menu and click the Toolbars command. Select (deselect) the toolbar that you want to display (hide). The selected toolbar will be displayed in the same position as when last displayed. You may also point to any toolbar and click with the right mouse button to bring up a shortcut menu, after which you can select the toolbar to be displayed (hidden). If the toolbar to be displayed is not listed, click the Customize command, click the Toolbars tab, check the box for the toolbar to be displayed, and then click the Close button.

■ To change the size of the buttons, suppress the display of the ScreenTips, or display the associated shortcut key (if available), pull down the View menu, click Toolbars, and click Customize to display the Customize dialog box. If necessary, click the Options tab, then select (deselect) the appropriate check box. Alternatively, you can right click on any toolbar, click the Customize command from the context-sensitive menu, then select (deselect) the appropriate check box from within the Options tab in the Customize dialog box.

■ Toolbars are either docked (along the edge of the window) or floating (in their own window). A toolbar moved to the edge of the window will dock along that edge. A toolbar moved anywhere else in the window will float in its own window. Docked toolbars are one tool wide (high), whereas floating toolbars can be resized by clicking and dragging a border or corner as you would with any other window.

❑ To move a docked toolbar, click anywhere in the background area and drag the toolbar to its new location. You can also click and drag the move handle (the single vertical line) at the left of the toolbar.

❑ To move a floating toolbar, drag its title bar to its new location.

■ To customize one or more toolbars, display the toolbar on the screen. Then pull down the View menu, click Toolbars, and click Customize to display the Customize dialog box. Alternatively, you can click on any toolbar with the right mouse button and select Customize from the shortcut menu.

❑ To move a button, drag the button to its new location on that toolbar or any other displayed toolbar.

❑ To copy a button, press the Ctrl key as you drag the button to its new location on that toolbar or any other displayed toolbar.

❑ To delete a button, drag the button off the toolbar and release the mouse button.

❑ To add a button, click the Commands tab in the Customize dialog box, select the category (from the Categories list box) that contains the button you want to add, then drag the button to the desired location on the toolbar.

❑ To restore a predefined toolbar to its default appearance, pull down the View menu, click Toolbars, click Customize, click the Toolbars tab, select (highlight) the desired toolbar, and click the Reset command button.

■ Buttons can also be moved, copied, or deleted without displaying the Customize dialog box.

❑ To move a button, press the Alt key as you drag the button to the new location.

❑ To copy a button, press the Alt and Ctrl keys as you drag the button to the new location.

❑ To delete a button, press the Alt key as you drag the button off the toolbar.

■ To create your own toolbar, pull down the View menu, click Toolbars, click Customize, click the Toolbars tab, then click the New command button. Alternatively, you can click on any toolbar with the right mouse button, select Customize from the shortcut menu, click the Toolbars tab, and then click the New command button.

❑ Enter a name for the toolbar in the dialog box that follows. The name can be any length and can contain spaces.

❑ The new toolbar will appear on the screen. Initially it will be big enough to hold only one button. Add, move, and delete buttons following the same procedures as outlined above. The toolbar will automatically size itself as new buttons are added and deleted.

❑ To delete a custom toolbar, pull down the View menu, click Toolbars, click Customize, and click the Toolbars tab. *Verify that the custom toolbar to be deleted is the only one selected (highlighted)*. Click the Delete command button. Click Yes to confirm the deletion. (Note that a predefined toolbar cannot be deleted.)

Alignment and Sizing

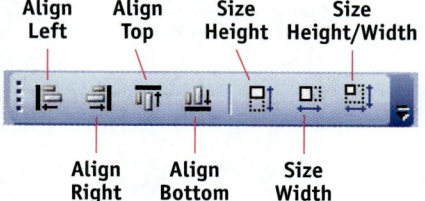

Align Left · Align Top · Size Height · Size Height/Width

Align Right · Align Bottom · Size Width

Database

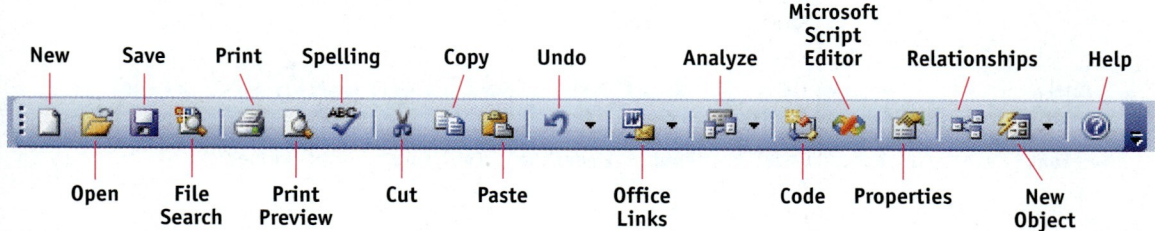

New · Save · Print · Spelling · Copy · Undo · Analyze · Microsoft Script Editor · Relationships · Help

Open · File Search · Print Preview · Cut · Paste · Office Links · Code · Properties · New Object

Filter/Sort

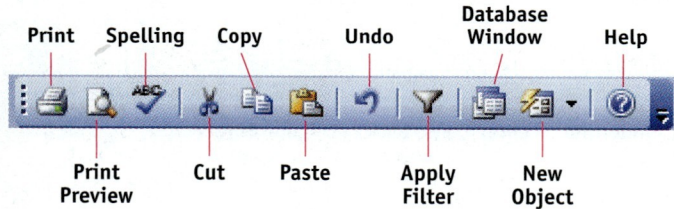

Print · Spelling · Copy · Undo · Database Window · Help

Print Preview · Cut · Paste · Apply Filter · New Object

Form Design

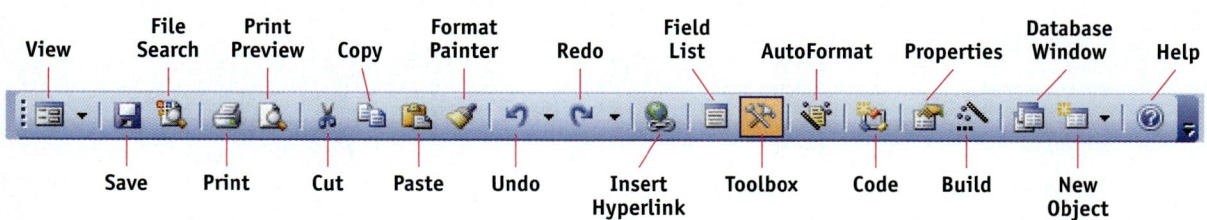

View · File Search · Print Preview · Copy · Format Painter · Redo · Field List · AutoFormat · Properties · Database Window · Help

Save · Print · Cut · Paste · Undo · Insert Hyperlink · Toolbox · Code · Build · New Object

FIGURE B.1   Access Toolbars

Form View

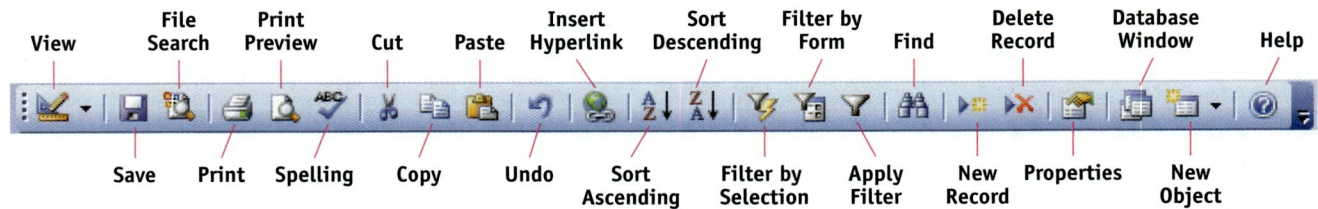

View | File Search | Print Preview | Cut | Paste | Insert Hyperlink | Sort Descending | Filter by Form | Find | Delete Record | Database Window | Help

Save | Print | Spelling | Copy | Undo | Sort Ascending | Filter by Selection | Apply Filter | New Record | Properties | New Object

Formatting (Datasheet)

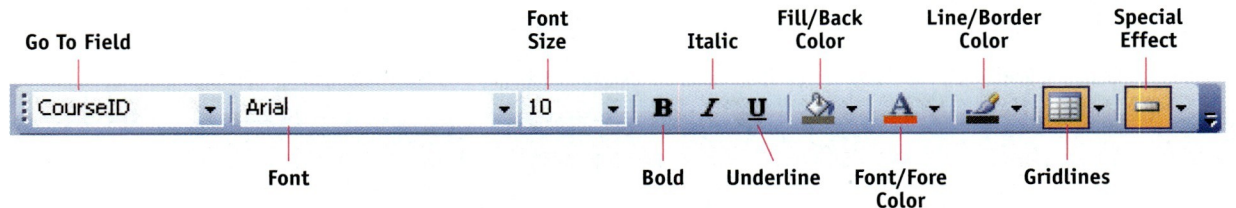

Go To Field | Font Size | Italic | Fill/Back Color | Line/Border Color | Special Effect

CourseID | Arial | 10 | B | I | U

Font | Bold | Underline | Font/Fore Color | Gridlines

Formatting (Form/Report)

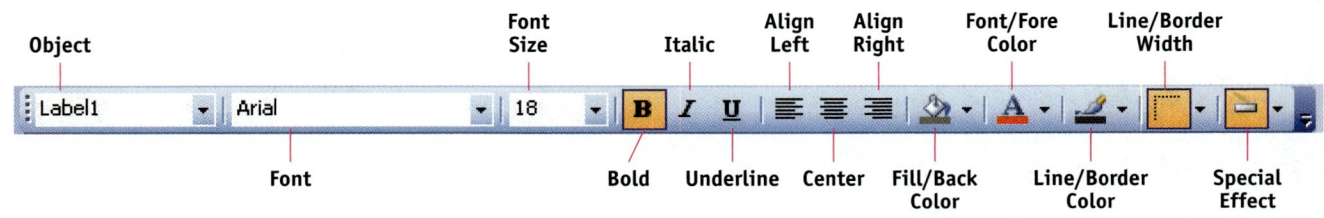

Object | Font Size | Italic | Align Left | Align Right | Font/Fore Color | Line/Border Width

Label1 | Arial | 18 | B | I | U

Font | Bold | Underline | Center | Fill/Back Color | Line/Border Color | Special Effect

Formatting (Page)

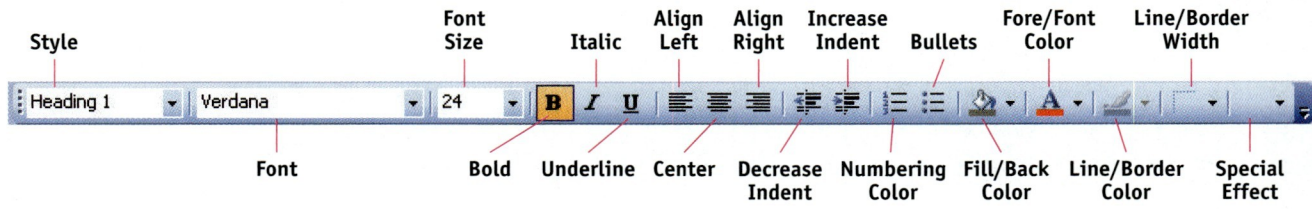

Style | Font Size | Italic | Align Left | Align Right | Increase Indent | Bullets | Fore/Font Color | Line/Border Width

Heading 1 | Verdana | 24 | B | I | U

Font | Bold | Underline | Center | Decrease Indent | Numbering Color | Fill/Back Color | Line/Border Color | Special Effect

Formatting (PivotTable/PivotChart)

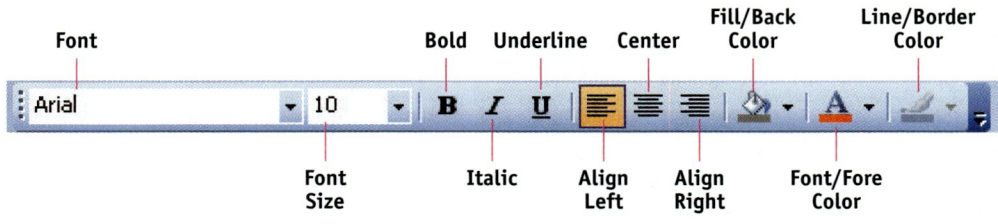

Font | Bold | Underline | Center | Fill/Back Color | Line/Border Color

Arial | 10 | B | I | U

Font Size | Italic | Align Left | Align Right | Font/Fore Color

FIGURE B.1 Access Toolbars (*continued*)

Macro Design

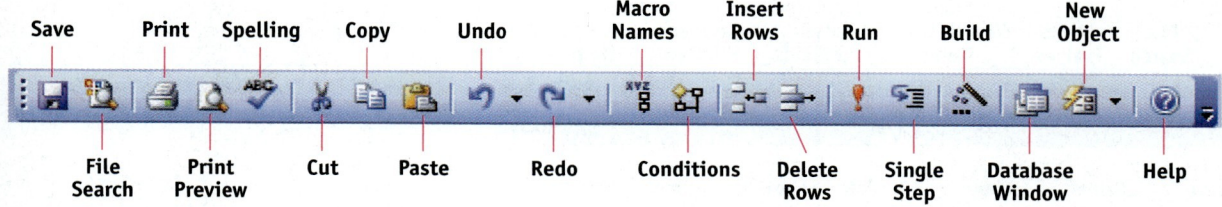

Save   Print   Spelling   Copy   Undo   Macro Names   Insert Rows   Run   Build   New Object

File Search   Print Preview   Cut   Paste   Redo   Conditions   Delete Rows   Single Step   Database Window   Help

Page Design

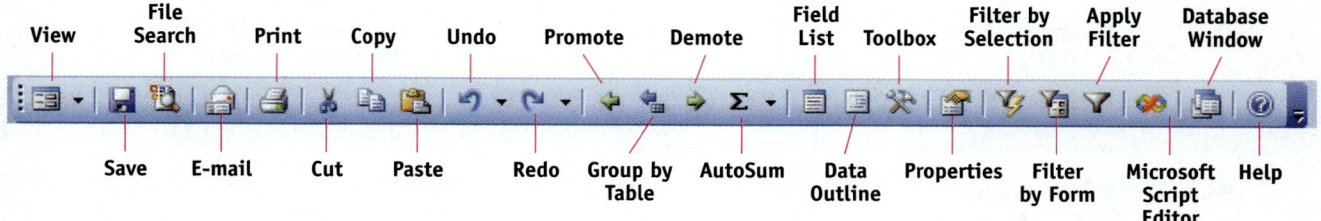

View   File Search   Print   Copy   Undo   Promote   Demote   Field List   Toolbox   Filter by Selection   Apply Filter   Database Window

Save   E-mail   Cut   Paste   Redo   Group by Table   AutoSum   Data Outline   Properties   Filter by Form   Microsoft Script Editor   Help

Page View

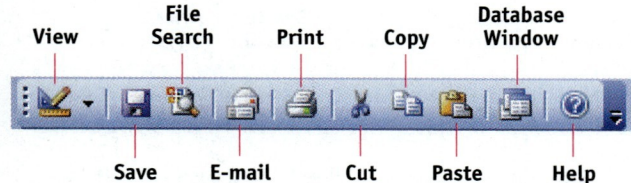

View   File Search   Print   Copy   Database Window

Save   E-mail   Cut   Paste   Help

PivotChart

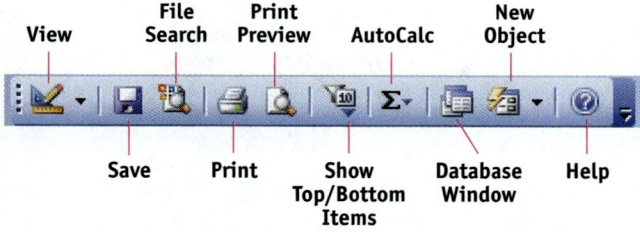

View   File Search   Print Preview   AutoCalc   New Object

Save   Print   Show Top/Bottom Items   Database Window   Help

FIGURE B.1   Access Toolbars (*continued*)

PivotTable

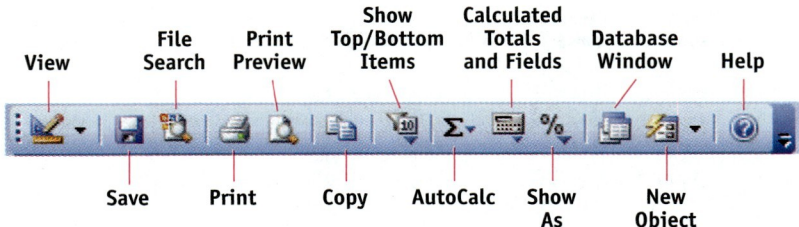

Print Preview

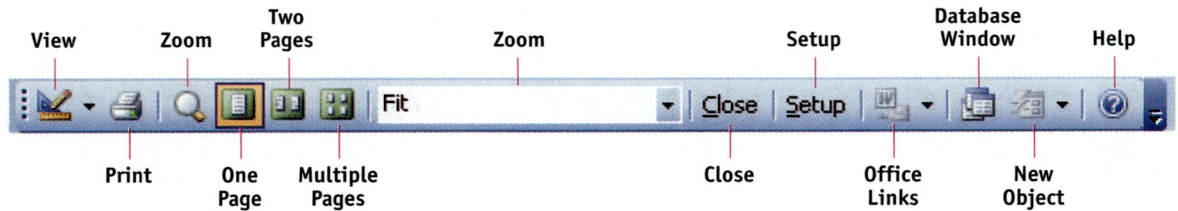

Query Datasheet

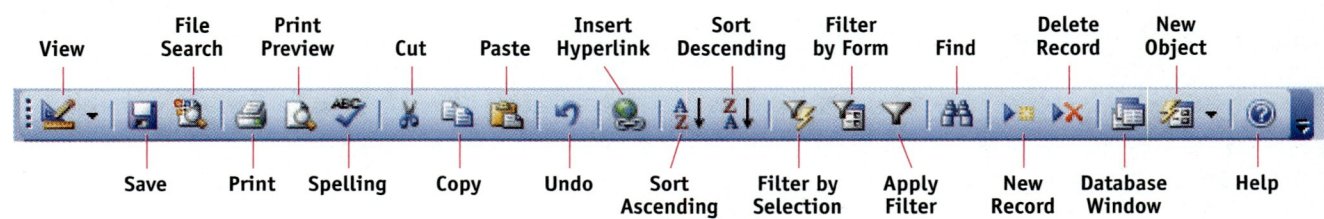

Query Design

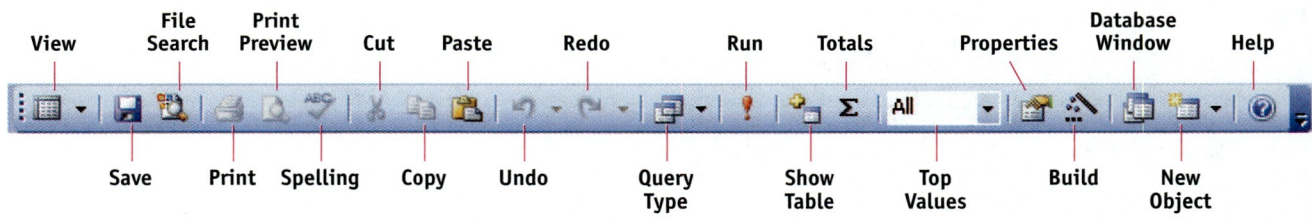

FIGURE B.1   Access Toolbars (*continued*)

Relationship

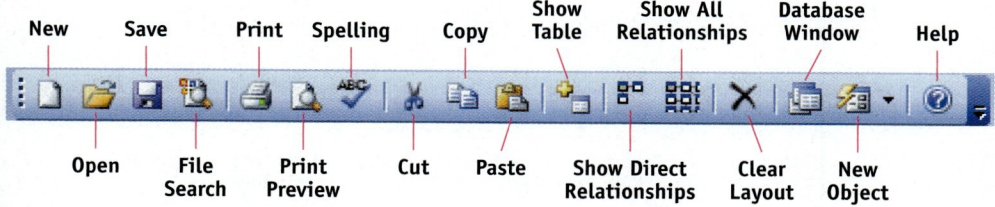

New · Save · Print · Spelling · Copy · Show Table · Show All Relationships · Database Window · Help

Open · File Search · Print Preview · Cut · Paste · Show Direct Relationships · Clear Layout · New Object

Report Design

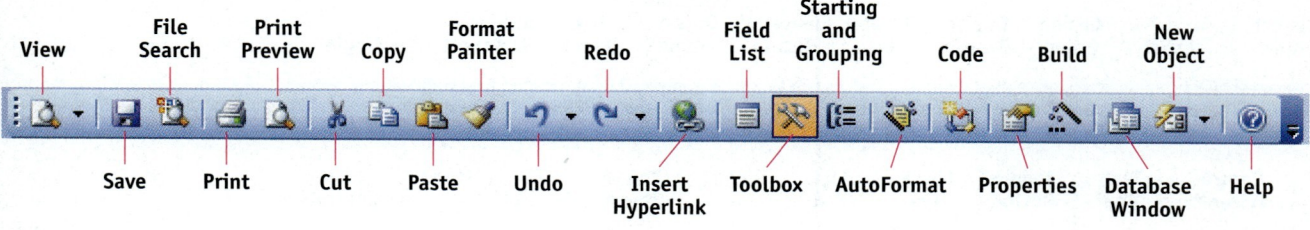

View · File Search · Print Preview · Copy · Format Painter · Redo · Field List · Starting and Grouping · Code · Build · New Object

Save · Print · Cut · Paste · Undo · Insert Hyperlink · Toolbox · AutoFormat · Properties · Database Window · Help

Shortcut Menus

Database ▾ Filter ▾ Form ▾ Index ▾ Macro ▾ Module ▾ Query ▾ Relationship ▾ Report ▾ Table ▾ View Design ▾ Other ▾ Custom ▾

Source Code Control

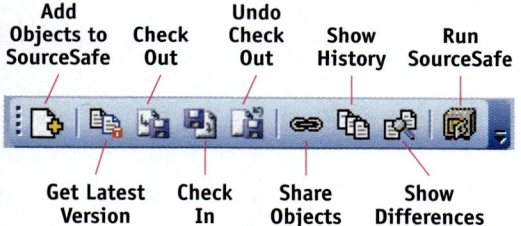

Add Objects to SourceSafe · Check Out · Undo Check Out · Show History · Run SourceSafe

Get Latest Version · Check In · Share Objects · Show Differences

Table Datasheet

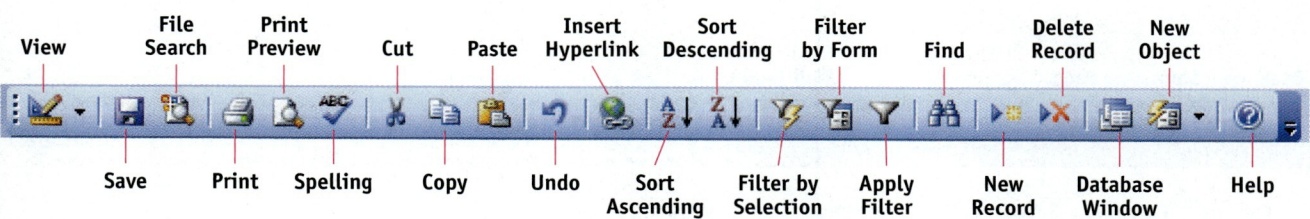

View · File Search · Print Preview · Cut · Paste · Insert Hyperlink · Sort Descending · Filter by Form · Find · Delete Record · New Object

Save · Print · Spelling · Copy · Undo · Sort Ascending · Filter by Selection · Apply Filter · New Record · Database Window · Help

FIGURE B.1 Access Toolbars (*continued*)

Table Design

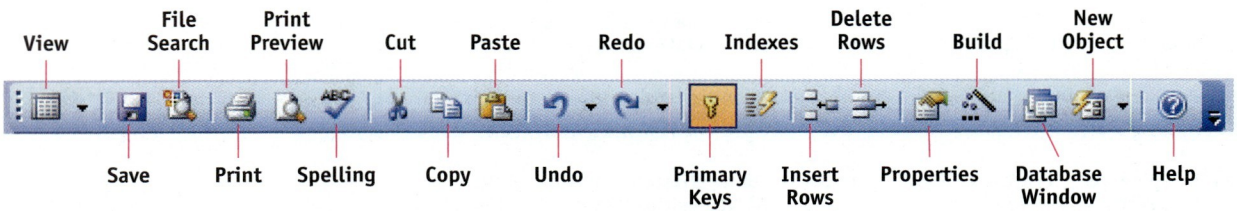

View   File Search   Print Preview   Cut   Paste   Redo   Indexes   Delete Rows   Build   New Object

Save   Print   Spelling   Copy   Undo   Primary Keys   Insert Rows   Properties   Database Window   Help

Toolbox

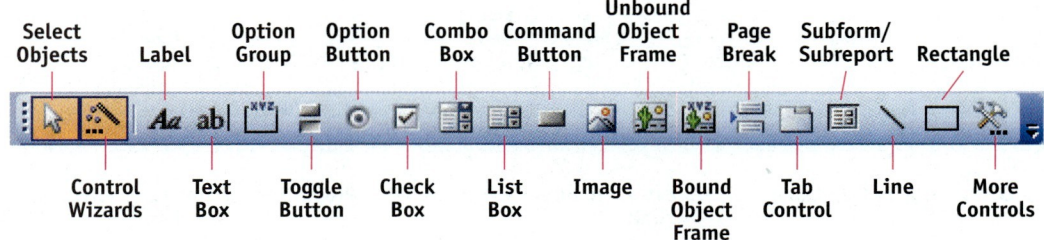

Select Objects   Label   Option Group   Option Button   Combo Box   Command Button   Unbound Object Frame   Page Break   Subform/ Subreport   Rectangle

Control Wizards   Text Box   Toggle Button   Check Box   List Box   Image   Bound Object Frame   Tab Control   Line   More Controls

Utility 1

Add or Remove Buttons

Utility 2

Add or Remove Buttons

Web

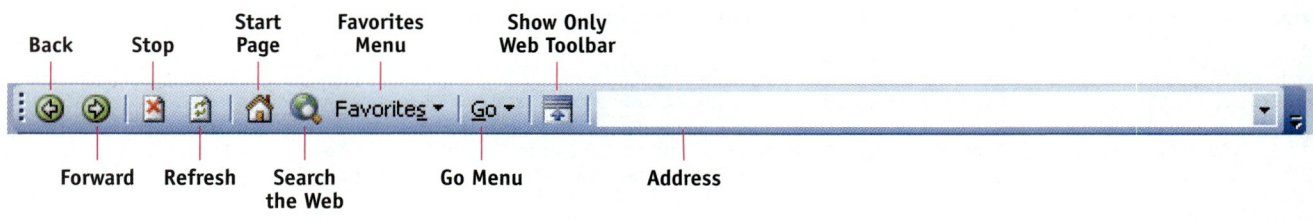

Back   Stop   Start Page   Favorites Menu   Show Only Web Toolbar

Forward   Refresh   Search the Web   Go Menu   Address

FIGURE B.1   Access Toolbars (*continued*)

Mail Merge:
An Access Database and a Word Form Letter

OVERVIEW

One of the greatest benefits of using the Microsoft Office suite is the ability to combine data from one application with another. An excellent example is a *mail merge*, in which data from an Access table or query is input into a Word document to produce a set of individualized form letters. You create the *form letter* using Microsoft Word, then you merge the letter with the *records* in the Access table or query. The merge process creates the individual letters, changing the name, address, and other information as appropriate from letter to letter. The concept is illustrated in Figure C.1, in which John Smith uses a mail merge to seek a job upon graduation. John writes the letter describing his qualifications, then merges that letter with a set of names and addresses to produce the individual letters.

The mail merge process uses two input files (a main document and a data source) and produces a third file as output (the set of form letters). The *main document* (e.g., the cover letter in Figure C.1a) contains standardized text together with one or more *merge fields* that indicate where the variable information is to be inserted in the individual letters. The *data source* (the set of names and addresses in Figure C.1b) contains the data that varies from letter to letter and is a table (or query) within an Access database. (The data source may also be taken from an Excel list, or alternatively, it can be created as a table in Microsoft Word.)

The main document and the data source work in conjunction with one another, with the merge fields in the main document referencing the corresponding fields in the data source. The first line in the address of Figure C.1a, for example, contains three merge fields, each of which is enclosed in angle brackets, <<Title>> <<FirstName>> <<LastName>>. (These entries are not typed explicitly but are entered through special commands as described in the hands-on exercise that follows shortly.) The merge process examines each record in the data source and substitutes the appropriate field values for the corresponding merge fields as it creates the individual form letters. For example, the first three fields in the first record will produce *Mr. Jason Frasher;* the same fields in the second record will produce, *Ms. Lauren Howard,* and so on.

In similar fashion, the second line in the address of the main document contains the <<Job Title>> field. The third line contains the <<Company>> field. The fourth line references the <<Address1>> field, and the last line contains the <<City>>, <<State>>, and <<Postalcode>> fields. The salutation repeats the <<Title>> and <<LastName>> fields. The first sentence in the letter uses the <<Company>> field a second time.

The mail merge prepares the letters one at a time, with one letter created for every record in the data source until the file of names and addresses is exhausted. The individual form letters are shown in Figure C.1c. Each letter begins automatically on a new page.

The same data source can be used to create additional form letters, mailing labels, or envelopes. You could, for example, use a mail merge in a marketing campaign in which you send an initial letter to the entire list, and then send follow-up letters at periodic intervals to the same mailing list. Alternatively, you could filter the original mailing list to include only a subset of names, such as the individuals who responded to the initial letter. You can also sort the data source prior to printing the mailing labels or envelopes to print the documents in zip-code order to take advantage of bulk mail.

A mail merge can be started from either Microsoft Word or Microsoft Access. Either way, two input files are required—the form letter (main document) and the data source. The order in which these files are created depends on how the merge is initiated. When starting in Microsoft Word, you begin with the form letter, then create the data source. The process is reversed in Access—you start with a table or query, then exit to Word to create the form letter. The merge itself, however, is always performed from within Microsoft Word.

John H. Smith

426 Jenny Lake Drive   **Coral Gables, FL 33146**   **(305) 555-5555**

August 8, 2003

«Title» «FirstName» «LastName»
«JobTitle»
«Company»
«Address1»
«City», «State» «PostalCode»

Dear «Title» «LastName»:

I would like to inquire about a position with «Company» as an entry-level programmer. I have just graduated from the University of Miami with a Bachelor's Degree in Computer Information Systems (May 2001) and I am very interested in working for you. I am proficient in all applications in Microsoft Office and also have experience with Visual Basic, C++, and Java. I have had the opportunity to design and implement a few Web applications, both as a part of my educational program, and during my internship with Personalized Computer Designs, Inc.

I am eager to put my skills to work and would like to talk with you at your earliest convenience. I have enclosed a copy of my résumé and will be happy to furnish the names and addresses of my references. You may reach me at the above address and phone number. I look forward to hearing from you.

Sincerely,

John H. Smith

(a) The Form Letter (a Word document)

FIGURE C.1   The Mail Merge

Title	First Name	Last Name	JobTitle	Company	Address1	City	State	Postal Code
Mr.	Jason	Frasher	President	Frasher Systems	100 S. Miami Avenue	Miami	FL	33103-
Ms.	Lauren	Howard	Director of Human Resources	Unique Systems	475 LeJeune Road	Coral Gables	FL	33146-
Ms.	Elizabeth	Scherry	Director of Personnel	Custom Computing	8180 Kendall Drive	Miami	FL	33156-
*								

(b) The Data Source (an Access table or query)

John H. Smith
426 Jenny Lake Drive   Coral Gables, FL 33146   (305) 555-5555

August 8, 2003

Mr. Jason Frasher
Frasher Systems
100 S. Miami Avenue
Miami, FL 33103

Dear Mr. Frasher:

I would like to inquire about a position wi
have just graduated from the University
Information Systems (May 2001) and I am
all applications in Microsoft Office and also
have had the opportunity to design and imp
educational program, and during my interns

I am eager to put my skills to work and wou
I have enclosed a copy of my résumé and
my references. You may reach me at the a
hearing from you.

Sincerely,

John H. Smith

John H. Smith
426 Jenny Lake Drive   Coral Gables, FL 33146   (305) 555-5555

August 8, 2003

Ms. Lauren Howard
Unique Systems
475 LeJeune Road
Coral Gables, FL 33146

Dear Ms. Howard:

I would like to inquire about a position wi
have just graduated from the University
Information Systems (May 2001) and I am
all applications in Microsoft Office and also
have had the opportunity to design and imp
educational program, and during my interns

I am eager to put my skills to work and wou
I have enclosed a copy of my résumé and
my references. You may reach me at the a
hearing from you.

Sincerely,

John H. Smith

John H. Smith
426 Jenny Lake Drive   Coral Gables, FL 33146   (305) 555-5555

August 8, 2003

Ms. Elizabeth Scherry
Custom Computing
8180 Kendall Drive
Miami, FL 33156

Dear Ms. Scherry:

I would like to inquire about a position with Custom Computing as an entry-level programmer. I have just graduated from the University of Miami with a Bachelor's Degree in Computer Information Systems (May 2001) and I am very interested in working for you. I am proficient in all applications in Microsoft Office and also have experience with Visual Basic, C++, and Java. I have had the opportunity to design and implement a few Web applications, both as a part of my educational program, and during my internship with Personalized Computer Designs, Inc.

I am eager to put my skills to work and would like to talk with you at your earliest convenience. I have enclosed a copy of my résumé and will be happy to furnish the names and addresses of my references. You may reach me at the above address and phone number. I look forward to hearing from you.

Sincerely,

John H. Smith

(c) The Printed Letters

FIGURE C.1 The Mail Merge (*continued*)

1   Mail Merge

Objective   To merge data from an Access database with a Word document to create a set of individual form letters. Use Figure C.2 as a guide.

Step 1:   **Open the Names and Addresses Database**

- Start Access. Open the **Names and Addresses database** in the Exploring Access folder. The Tables button is selected. The Contacts table is the only table in the database.

- Click the **down arrow** on the **Office Links button** on the Database toolbar, then click **Merge It with Microsoft Office Word** to display the dialog box in Figure C.2a.

- The form letter has already been created for you. Thus, you can select the option to **Link your data to an existing Word document**. Click **OK**.

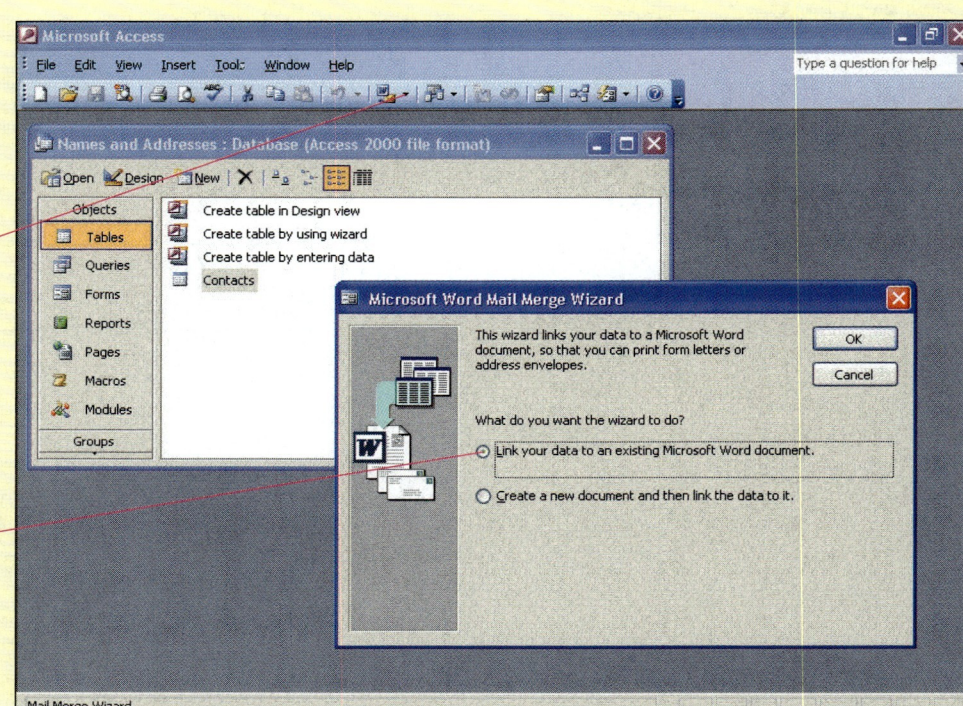

> **Click down arrow on Office Links button**

> **Click option button to Link your data to an existing Microsoft Word document**

(a) Open the Names and Addresses Database (step 1)

FIGURE C.2   Hands-on Exercise 1

START ANYWHERE

A mail merge can be started from Microsoft Word or Microsoft Access. Either way, two input files are required, a form letter and a data source. The order in which these files are created is unimportant, and you can switch back and forth between the two. Eventually, however, the data source will be merged with the form letter to create the individual set of form letters.

Step 2: **Open the Form Letter**

- You should see the Select Microsoft Word Document dialog box as shown in Figure C.2b. Click the **down arrow** in the Look in box and select the **Exploring Access folder**.

- Select the **Form Letter** document and click the **Open button**. This starts Microsoft Word and opens the Form Letter document.

- Click anywhere within the date to select it, then press **Shift+F9** to toggle between the displayed value and the date code, which is set to always display today's date (see boxed tip below).

- The task pane also opens automatically. If necessary, maximize the application window for Word so that you have more room in which to work.

- Pull down the **File menu**, click the **Save As command** to display the Save As dialog box, and enter **Form Letter Solution** as the name of the document. Click **Save**.

- You are ready to begin the mail merge process.

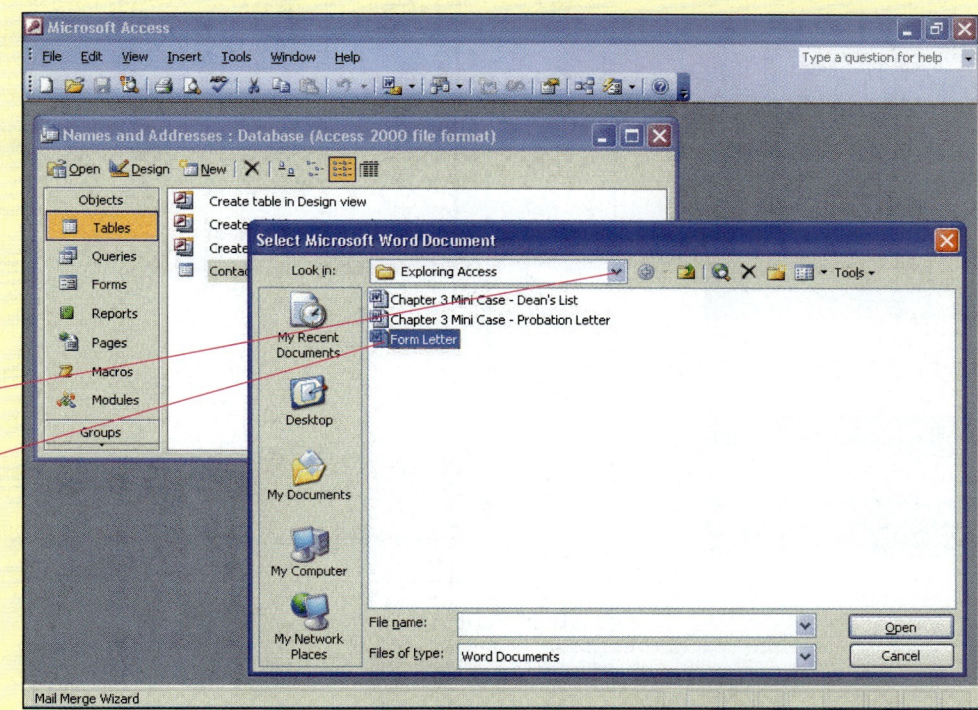

Click down arrow to select drive/folder

Click Form Letter

(b) Open the Form Letter (step 2)

FIGURE C.2   Hands-on Exercise 1 (*continued*)

THE INSERT DATE COMMAND

Pull down the Insert menu and click the Date and Time command to display the associated dialog box, where you choose the desired format for the date and/or time information. You can insert today's date as a fixed date (by clearing the box to Update automatically). Alternatively, you can check the box, in which case the current date will appear whenever the document is opened.

Step 3: Edit the Recipient List

- Click the link to **Edit recipient list** to display the Mail Merge Recipients dialog box, as shown in Figure C.2c. Three names appear, corresponding to the records within the Names and Addresses database that you opened to begin the exercise.

- Clear the check box for Elizabeth Scherry. Click **OK**. The form letter will be sent to the two remaining recipients, Jason Frasher and Lauren Howard.

- Modify the letterhead to reflect your name and address. Select **"Your Name Goes Here"**, then type a new entry to replace the selected text. Enter your address on the second line.

- Save the document. Click the link to **Next: Write your letter** at the bottom of the task pane to continue with the mail merge.

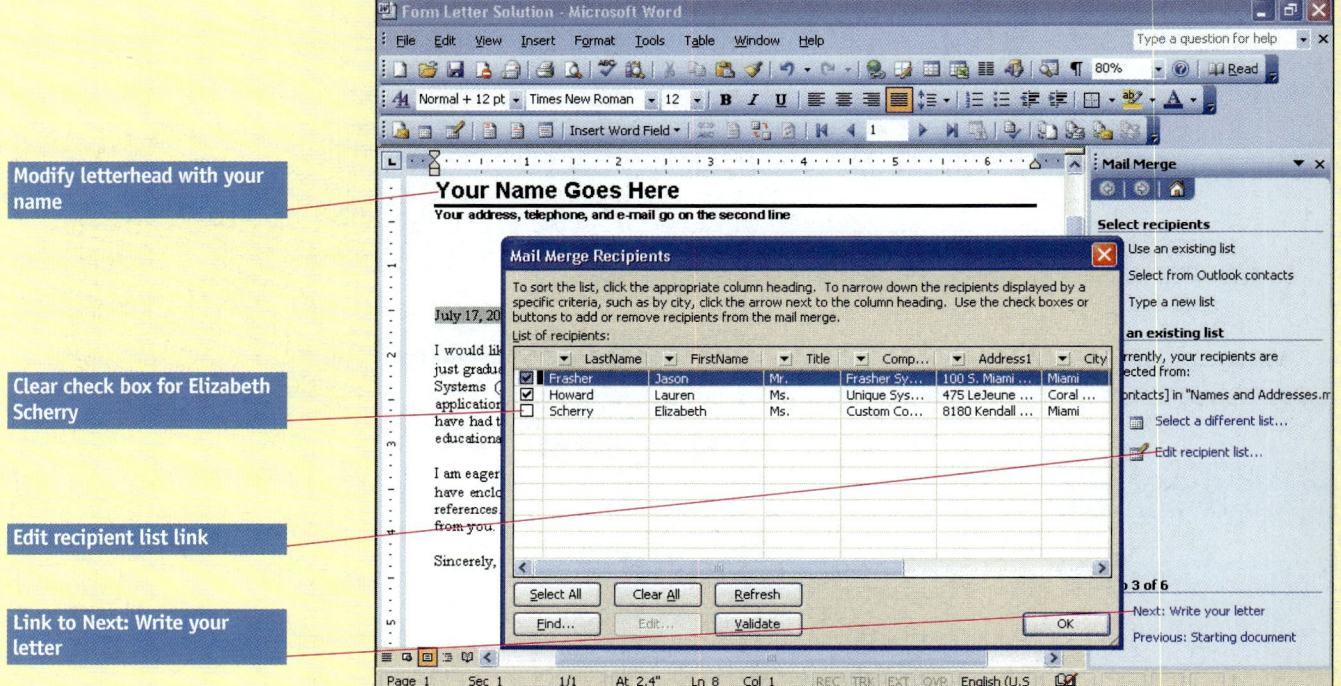

Modify letterhead with your name

Clear check box for Elizabeth Scherry

Edit recipient list link

Link to Next: Write your letter

(c) Edit the Recipient List (step 3)

FIGURE C.2 Hands-on Exercise 1 (*continued*)

THE MAIL MERGE WIZARD

The Mail Merge Wizard simplifies the process of creating form letters and other types of merge documents through step-by-step directions that appear automatically in the task pane. The options for the current step appear in the top portion of the task pane and are self-explanatory. Click the link to the next step at the bottom of the pane to move forward in the process, or click the link to the previous step to return to a previous step to correct any mistakes you might have made.

Step 4: Insert the Fields

- The task pane indicates that you are in step 4 of the merge process. Click immediately after the date. Press the **Enter key** twice to insert a blank line. Click the link to the **Address block** in the task pane to display the dialog box in Figure C.2d.

- Verify that the four check boxes have been selected as shown in Figure C.2d. Click **OK** to insert the AddressBlock field into the document.

- Press the **Enter key** twice to leave a blank line after the address block. Click the link to the **Greeting line** to display the Greeting Line dialog box. Choose the type of greeting you want.

- Change the comma that appears after the greeting to a colon since this is a business letter. Click **OK**. The GreetingLine field is inserted into the document and enclosed in angled brackets.

- Save the document. Click **Next: Preview your letters** to continue.

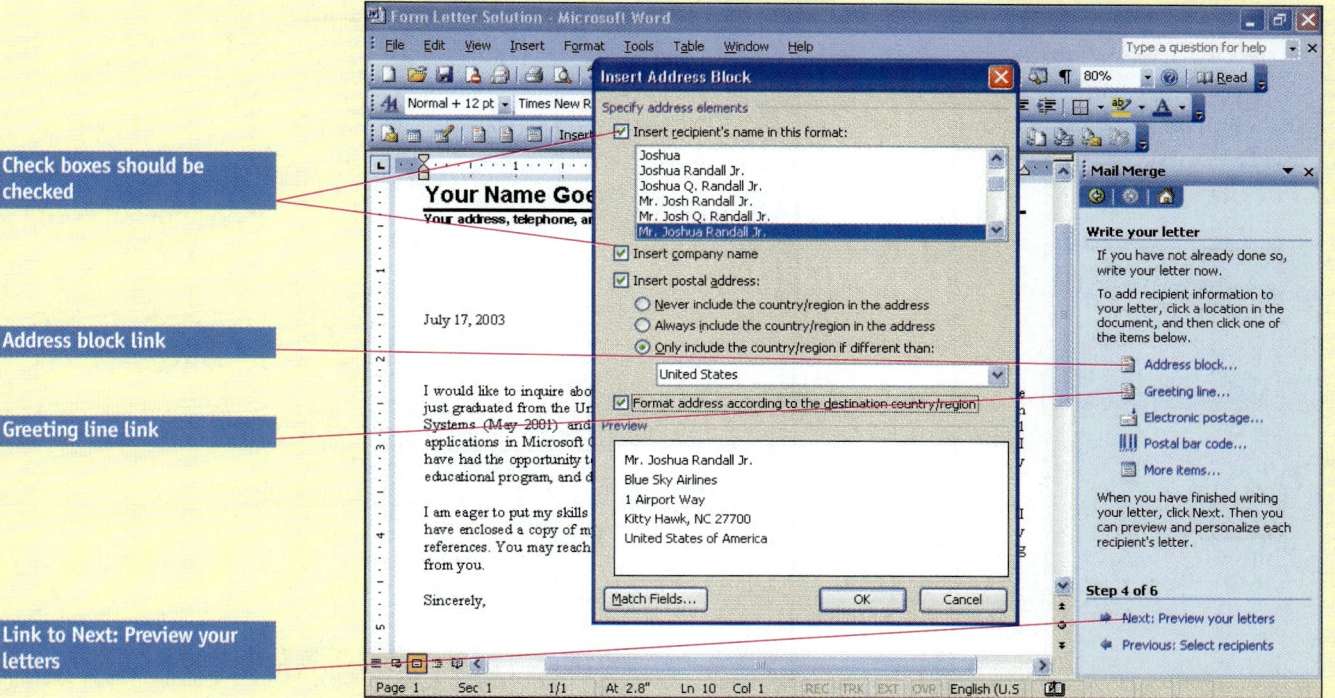

(d) Insert the Fields (step 4)

FIGURE C.2 Hands-on Exercise 1 (*continued*)

BLOCKS VERSUS INDIVIDUAL FIELDS

The Mail Merge Wizard simplifies the process of entering field names into a form letter by supplying two predefined entries, AddressBlock and GreetingLine, which contain multiple fields that are typical of the ways in which an address and salutation appear in a conventional letter. You can still insert individual fields, by clicking in the document where you want the field to go, then clicking the Insert Merge Fields button on the Mail Merge toolbar. The blocks are easier.

Step 5: Preview the Letters

■ You should be in step 5 of the mail merge, where you see the first form letter, as shown in Figure C.2e. (If you see a date code, rather than an actual date, pull down the **Tools menu** and click the **Options command** to display the Options dialog box. Click the **View tab** and clear the check box next to Field Codes.)

■ View the records individually to be sure that the form letter is correct and that the data has been entered correctly. Use the link to the previous step(s) at the bottom of the task pane to make corrections if necessary.

■ Save the letter. Click the link to **Next: Complete the merge** to continue.

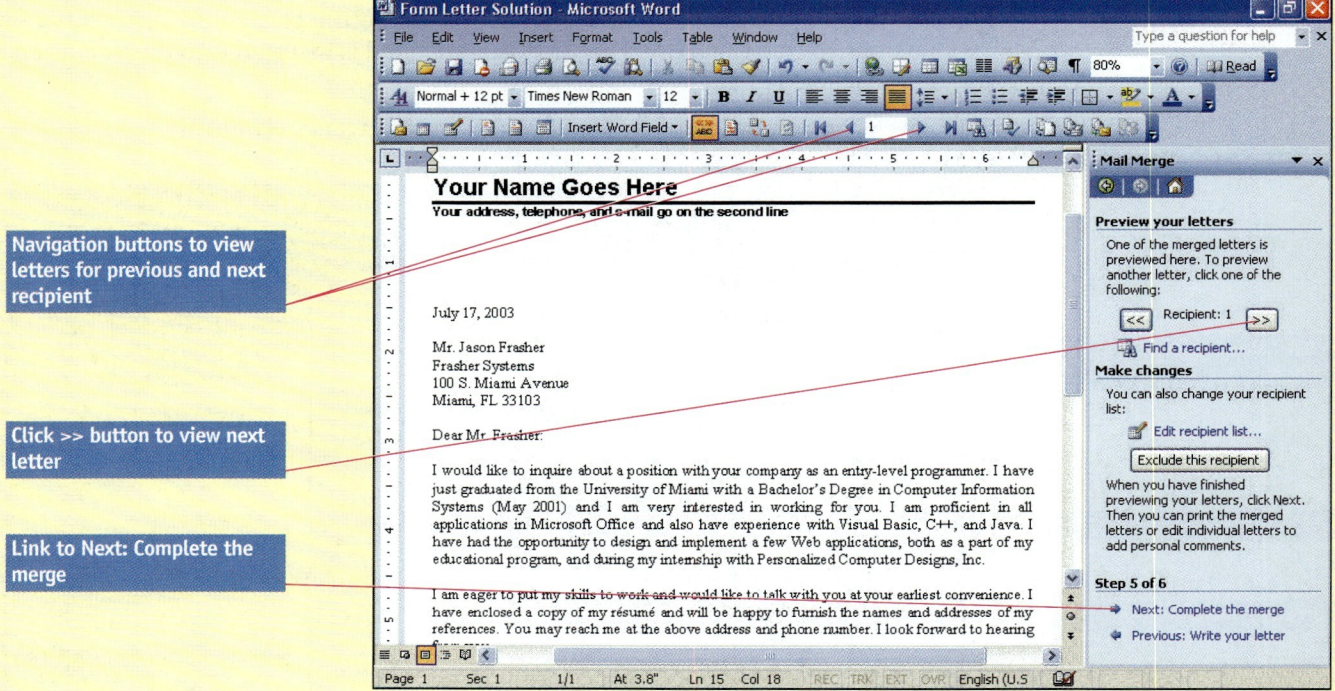

Navigation buttons to view letters for previous and next recipient

Click >> button to view next letter

Link to Next: Complete the merge

(e) Preview the Letters (step 5)

FIGURE C.2   Hands-on Exercise 1 (*continued*)

THE MAIL MERGE TOOLBAR

The Mail Merge toolbar appears throughout the mail merge process and contains various buttons that apply to different steps within the process. Click the <<abc>> button to display field values rather than field codes. Click the button a second time, and you switch back to field codes from field values. Click the <<abc>> button to display the field values, then use the navigation buttons to view the different letters. Click the ▶ button, for example, and you move to the next letter. Click the ▶| button to display the form letter for the last record.

Step 6: **Edit and Print the Individual Letters**

■ You should be in step 6 of the mail merge. Click the link to **Edit individual letters** in the task pane, which displays the Merge to New Document dialog box. The All option is selected. Click **OK** to create a third document (Letters1), consisting of the individual form letters as shown in Figure C.2f.

■ Click the **Next (Previous) Page button** to move forward (backward) within the set of individual letters. (You have the option to personalize any of the individual letters.)

■ Pull down the **File menu** and click the **Print command** to display the Print dialog box. Check the option to print all of the letters. Click **OK**.

■ Close the Letters1 document. Click **No** if prompted to save changes to this document because you can always re-create the individual letters from the form letter and Access database.

■ Close the Form Letter Solution document. Click **Yes** when asked to save changes to this document.

■ Exit Word. Exit Access.

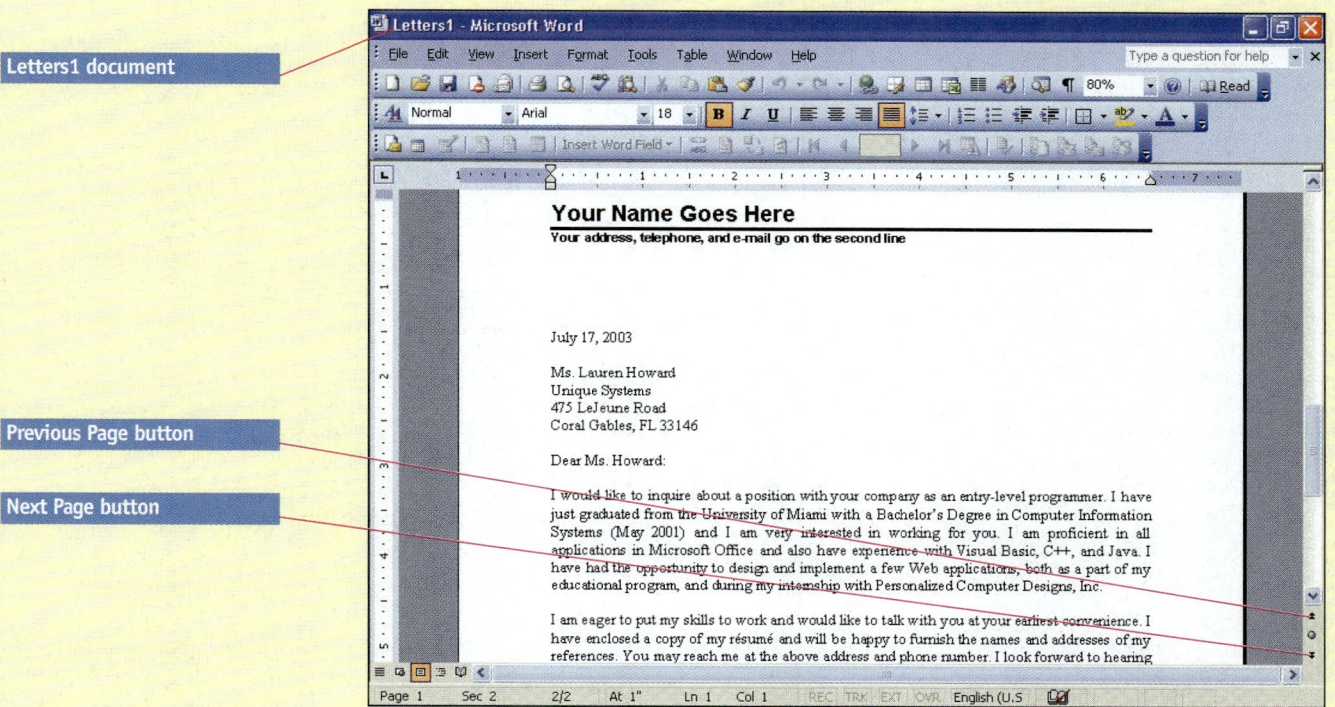

Letters1 document

Previous Page button

Next Page button

(f) Edit and Print the Individual Letters (step 6)

FIGURE C.2 Hands-on Exercise 1 (*continued*)

THREE DIFFERENT FILES

A mail merge works with a minimum of two files. The main document and data source are input to the mail merge, which creates a set of merged letters as output. The latter can be saved as a separate file, but typically that is not done. You can use the same data source (e.g., a set of names and addresses) with different main documents (a form letter and an envelope) and/or use the same main document with multiple data sources. You typically save, but do not print, the main document(s) and the data source(s). As indicated earlier, you print the set of merged letters, but typically do not save them.

SUMMARY

One of the greatest benefits of the Microsoft Office suite is the ability to combine data from one application with that from another. A mail merge is an excellent example, as it combines data from an Access table or query with a Word document. The mail merge creates the same letter many times, changing only the variable data, such as the addressee's name and address, from letter to letter. The merge fields within the main document indicate where the variable information is to be inserted in the individual letters. The same data source can be used with different documents (e.g., to create form letters, envelopes, and/or mailing labels) for a single set of names and addresses. Conversely, the same document (such as a form letter) can be used with different data sources as additional data is obtained.

A mail merge can be started from either Microsoft Word or Microsoft Access, but either way, two input files are required—the form letter and the data source. The order in which the files are created is not important. The main document and data source are saved but typically not printed. The merged file (e.g., the set of form letters) is usually printed, but not saved because you can always recreate the form letters by rerunning the mail merge. The Mail Merge Wizard provides step-by-step instructions.

KEY TERMS

Data source 549
Form letter 549
Insert Date command 553
Mail Merge 549

Mail Merge toolbar 556
Mail Merge Wizard 554
Main document 549

Merge fields 549
Recipient list 554
Records 549

Using XML with Microsoft® Access 2003

OBJECTIVES

After reading this chapter you will be able to:

1. Define XML; describe how XML differs from HTML.

2. Describe the XML syntax; create an XML document using the Notepad accessory.

3. Explain how Internet Explorer is XML-enabled and how Notepad is not.

4. Import XML data into an Access database; export an Access query as an XML file.

5. Modify an XML document to reference a schema and a style sheet.

hands-on exercises

1. INTRODUCTION TO XML
   Input: None
   Output: Apartment (XML)

2. ACCESS AND XML
   Input: Health Insurance database, Employees table (XML), Insurance Claims Style Sheet
   Output: Health Insurance database (modified), Insurance Claims XML, Insurance Claims Schema

OVERVIEW

Today's corporate enterprise runs a variety of applications on different hardware and different operating systems. Individuals within the organization are accessing the same data from different cities or countries, using notebooks, desktops, cell phones, mainframes, and a variety of other hardware. The applications vary greatly, but the one thing in common is the data that moves through the organization. Thus, the various applications and system components have to understand one another so that data can be captured once, and then reused as often as necessary. The solution is to adopt a common standard that describes data in such a way that it can be used by any application.

XML (eXtensible Markup Language) is an industry standard for structuring data across applications, operating systems, and hardware devices. It enables data to be sent and retrieved between disparate and otherwise incompatible systems; in theory, you can start a transaction on a PC at your office, check on the status of that transaction on your way home using a cell phone or PDA, then check further on your PC when you arrive home. XML is but the latest step in the evolution of markup languages. It follows the *Standard Generalized Markup Language (SGML)*, which you may not recognize, and *Hypertext Markup Language (HTML)*, which you should recognize because it made the World Wide Web possible. Despite its success, however, HTML has significant limitations and hence the development of XML. Our intent is not to make you an XML expert, but to provide an overview of its capability and implementation within Microsoft Office 2003. ■

Your assignment is to read the material, paying special attention to the development and characteristics of XML and its use within the organization. You will complete two hands-on exercises that describe how to create a simple XML document, and further how Microsoft Access 2003 supports XML technology.

XML (eXtensible Markup Language) describes the structure of data, but not its appearance or formatting. Its elements are created by the user for each individual application, as opposed to a central authority. But what does this really mean? What is a markup language and what makes it extensible? Why is it so flexible? The text below provides insight into the significance of XML:

2 bedrooms/2 bathrooms – $600 per month – (305) 111-2222

You should recognize the sentence immediately as an advertisement for an apartment that might have been taken from the classified section of a newspaper. It makes sense to you, but not to a computer that cannot discern the individual entries within the text; that is, the computer has no way of interpreting the sentence without additional information. Now look at the same text as it would appear in XML:

<Apartment>

    <Description> 2 bedrooms/2 bathrooms </Description>

    <Rent> $600 per month </Rent>

    <Telephone> (305) 111-2222 </Telephone>

</Apartment>

The data has been "marked up" with various ***tags*** (enclosed in angled brackets) to give it structure. Each piece of data is enclosed in a beginning and ending tag, where the name of the tag was defined by the user. Various tags are nested within one another; for example, the Description, Rent, and Telephone tags are nested within the Apartment tag. The tags seem rather obvious, but no one said that XML was complicated. XML is simply data about data; its tags are defined by the user according to the application, and they can be read by any XML-compliant application and processed accordingly.

Look further and you will see that the XML document does not contain any information about how to display the data; XML describes the data itself rather than the formatting of the data. XML is very different therefore from HTML, which specifies how to display the data, but not the meaning of the data. The distinction is apparent if we examine the apartment listing as it would appear in HTML:

<B><I> 2 bedrooms/2 bathrooms – $600 per month – (305) 111-2222 </I></B>

HTML uses a finite set of predefined tags, such as <B> or <I>, for bold and italics, respectively. XML, however, is much more general because it has an infinite number of tags that are defined as necessary in different applications. In other words, XML is ***extensible***, meaning that it can be expanded as necessary to include additional data. Consider:

<Apartment>

    <Description> 2 bedrooms/2 bathrooms </Description>

    <Availability> Immediate occupancy </Availability>

    <Amenities> Swimming pool; close to campus </Amenities>

    <Telephone> (305)111-2222 </Telephone>

    <Rent> $600 per month </Rent>

    <Security> 1 month </Security>

</Apartment>

The original document has been expanded to include information on availability, amenities, and security deposit for our apartment listing. The syntax is straightforward, but it behooves us to make the following observations:

1. An XML document is divided into **elements**. Each element contains a start tag, an ending tag, and the associated data. The start tag contains the name of the element. The ending tag contains the element's name preceded by a slash.

2. XML tags are case sensitive; for example, <Security> 1 month </security> is *incorrect* because the start and ending tags are not the same case.

3. XML elements can be nested to any depth, but each inner element (or child) must be entirely contained within the outer element (or parent); for example, the Description and Availability elements are nested within the Apartment element.

Figure D.1 displays an XML document that was created in the **Notepad accessory**, a simple text editor that is provided with Windows. The **XML declaration** in line one specifies the XML version and **character encoding** used in the document. Our document uses the Unicode Transformation Format that corresponds to the standard ASCII character scheme, wherein each character is represented by 8 bits. The question mark and angled brackets are part of the declaration. (A declaration is not required, but it is good practice to include it.) The document also contains a comment in line two to identify the author. The indentation throughout the document makes it easier to read and is not required.

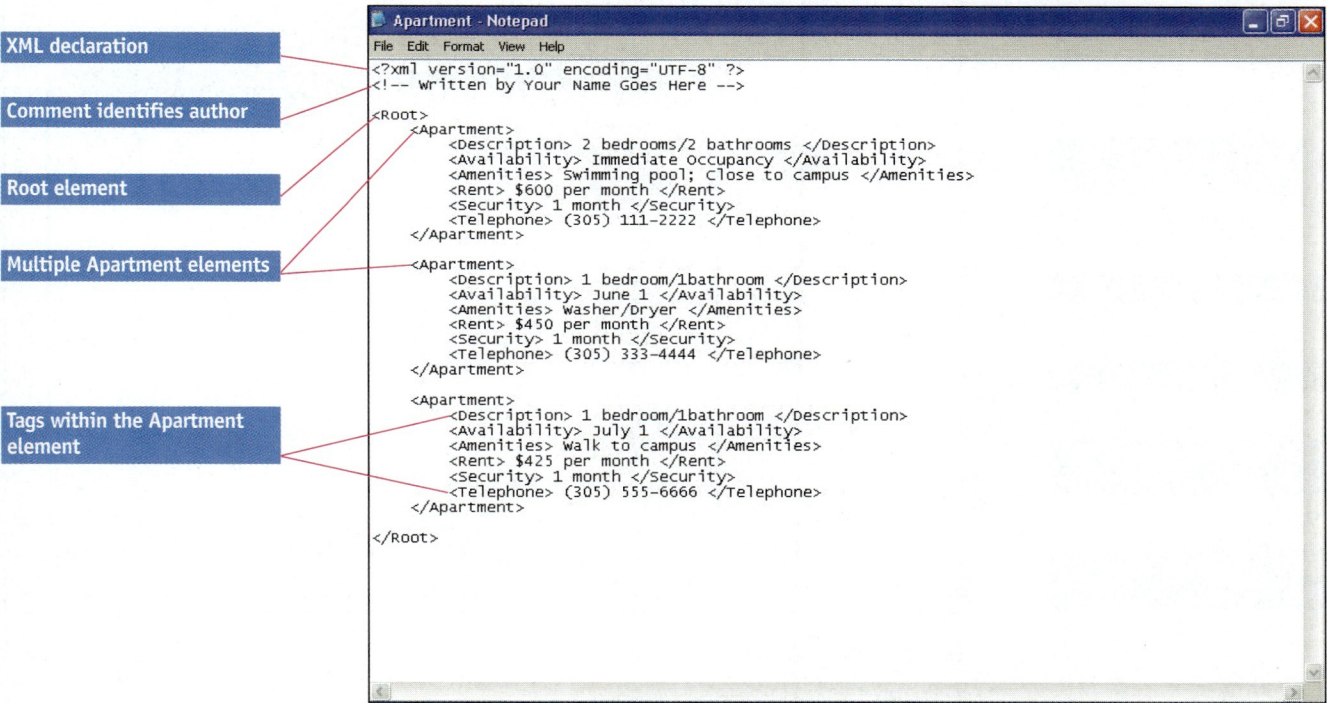

FIGURE D.1 Introduction to XML

Figure D.1 includes a **root element** to permit multiple occurrences of the apartment element within the same XML document; i.e., each apartment element is nested within the root element. The root element may also be given a different name—for example, "Listing" or "ClassifiedListing"—that is more descriptive of the data in the document. The completed document is in essence a "data file" with multiple apartment records that can be used by any XML-compliant application. We continue with a hands-on exercise in which you create the document in Figure D.1.

1   Introduction to XML

Objective   Use the Notepad accessory to create and edit a simple XML document; use Internet Explorer to view the XML document; use Figure D.2 as a guide.

Step 1:   **Create the XML Document**

■ Click the **Start button**, click **All Programs**, click **Accessories**, and then open and maximize the **Notepad accessory**. Enter the text of the document exactly as it appears in Figure D.2a. Note the following:
  ❏ We omitted the starting bracket in front of the Telephone tag deliberately to show you what happens when you make a syntax error.
  ❏ The indentation (four spaces in our example) is not required, but is included to make the document easier to read.

■ Pull down the **File menu**. Click the **Save command** to display the Save As dialog box. Click the **Create New Folder button** to create the **Exploring XML folder**.

■ Enter **Apartment.xml** as the file name, select **Text Documents** as the file type, and **UTF-8** as the encoding type. Click the **Save button**. Close Notepad.

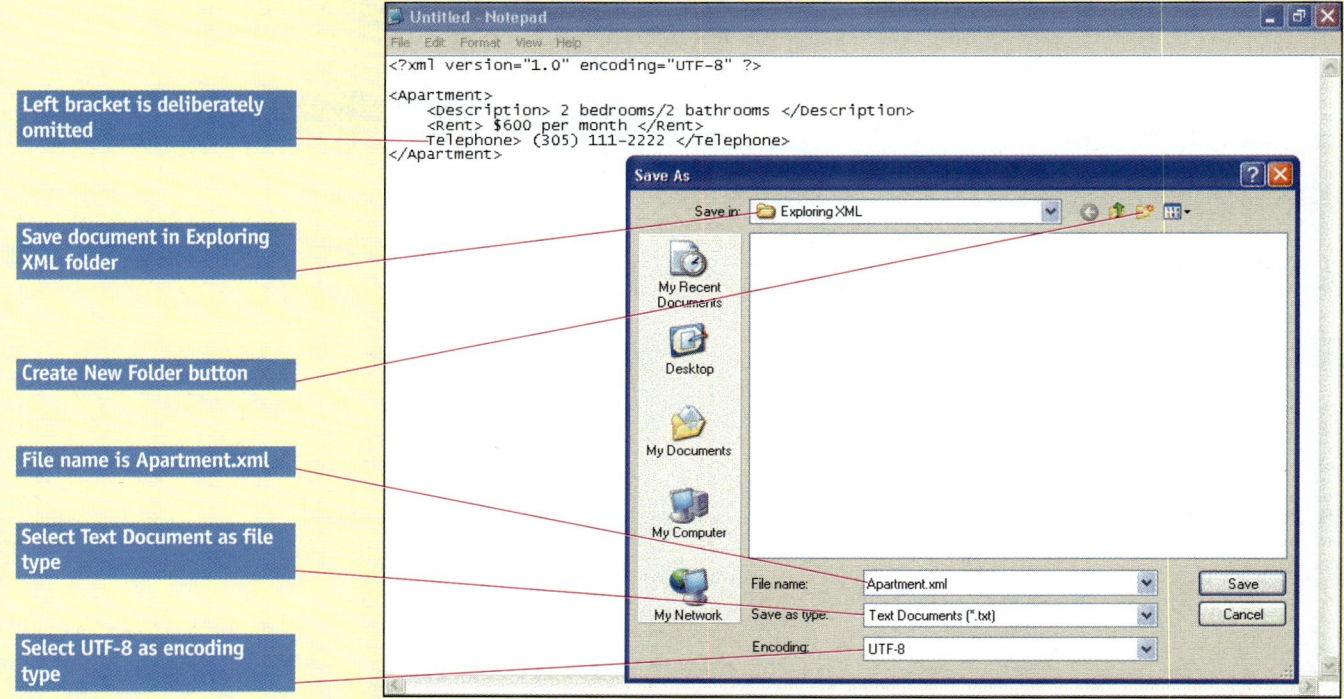

Left bracket is deliberately omitted

Save document in Exploring XML folder

Create New Folder button

File name is Apartment.xml

Select Text Document as file type

Select UTF-8 as encoding type

(a) Create the XML Document (step 1)

FIGURE D.2   Hands-on Exercise 1

CHARACTER ENCODING

Every character (e.g., the letters of the alphabet, punctuation symbols, numbers, and so on) is stored internally (in memory or in auxiliary storage) as a numeric value. The character encoding determines which number represents which character; for example, UTF-8 stands for Unicode Transformation Format and corresponds to the standard ASCII character scheme wherein each character is represented by one byte (8 bits). Other encoding schemes are also possible.

Step 2: **Check for Errors**

■ Start Internet Explorer. Pull down the **File menu**, click the **Open command**, then click the **Browse button** in the Open dialog box. Change to the **Exploring XML folder**.

■ Click the **drop-down arrow** in the Files of type list box and select **All files**, and then (try to) open the **Apartment.xml document** that you just created. The document will not open because of the omitted bracket in front of the Telephone tag (and/or because you made additional errors).

■ You should see an error message similar to the one in Figure D.2b. Click the tool to **Edit with XML editor** on the Standard toolbar in Internet Explorer.

■ The document opens in Notepad. Click in front of the Telephone tag and insert the left bracket (and/or correct any additional errors you may have made).

■ Pull down the **File menu** and click the **Save command**. Click in the **Internet Explorer window**, and then click the **Refresh button** on the Standard toolbar.

■ The XML document will open, provided you have corrected all of the errors.

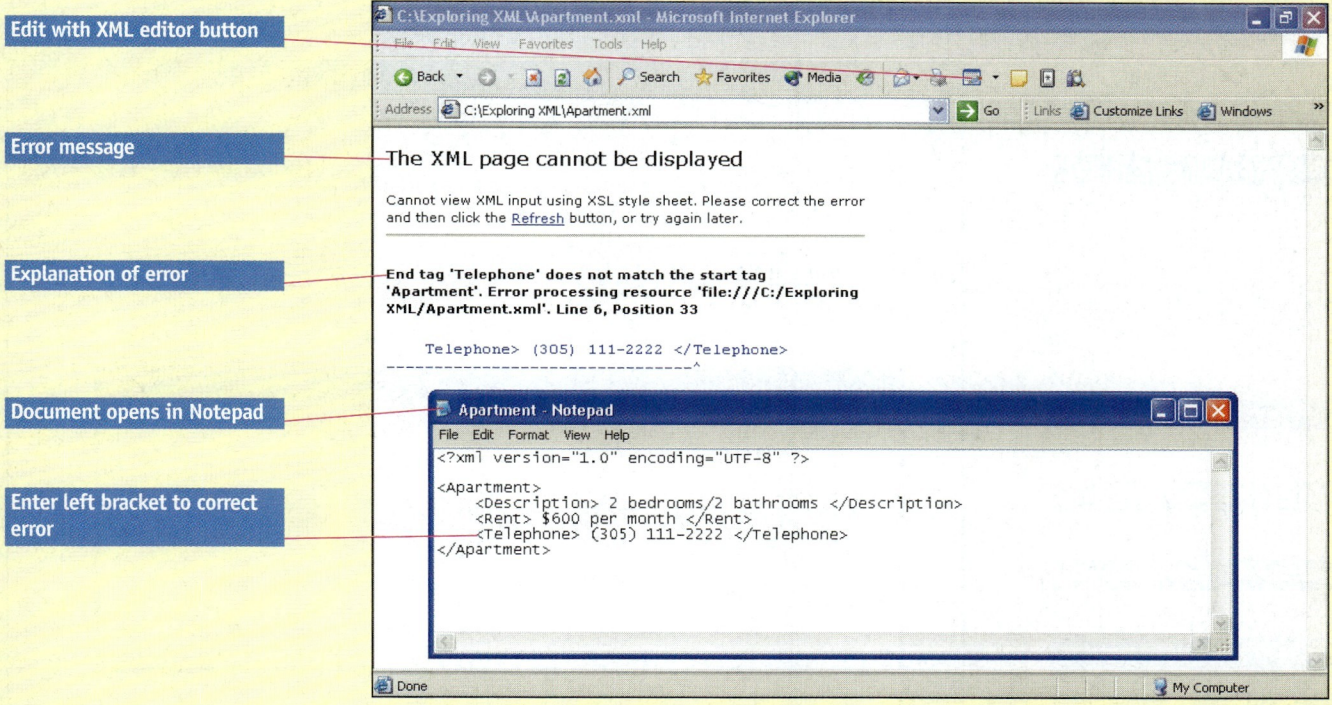

(b) Check for Errors (step 2)

FIGURE D.2 Hands-on Exercise 1 (*continued*)

NOTEPAD VERSUS INTERNET EXPLORER

The creation of an XML document is an iterative process that requires the user to switch back and forth between the Notepad accessory and Internet Explorer. You create the document in Notepad, view it in Internet Explorer, and return to Notepad to make the necessary changes. You must remember to save the document in Notepad and to click the Refresh button in Internet Explorer to see the latest version. The document is displayed differently in each application. Notepad is a simple text editor and does not handle the XML tags differently from other text. Internet Explorer is XML-aware and displays the tags and associated data with different formatting.

Step 3: **Expand the Document**

- You should see the corrected XML document as shown in the Internet Explorer window of Figure D.2c. There are two ways to return to the Notepad accessory:
  - ❏ We recommend that you click the **Notepad button** on the Windows taskbar since the Apartment document is still open.
  - ❏ Alternatively, you can click the **Edit with XML editor button** on the Internet Explorer toolbar, but this opens a second copy of Notepad if the document is already open. Multiple copies are confusing, but will not cause a problem, provided you remember to save all of your editing changes.
- Add the comment as shown in the second line. The syntax is very precise; that is, the comment begins and ends with <!-- and -->, respectively.
- Add the **Availability**, **Amenities**, and **Security elements** to complete the description of the apartment listing. Save the document.
- Click in the **Internet Explorer window**. Click the **Refresh button** on the Internet Explorer toolbar to view the expanded document.
- Correct any errors by returning to Notepad. Save the document after each editing change. Be sure to click the **Refresh button** to see the results of those changes in Internet Explorer.

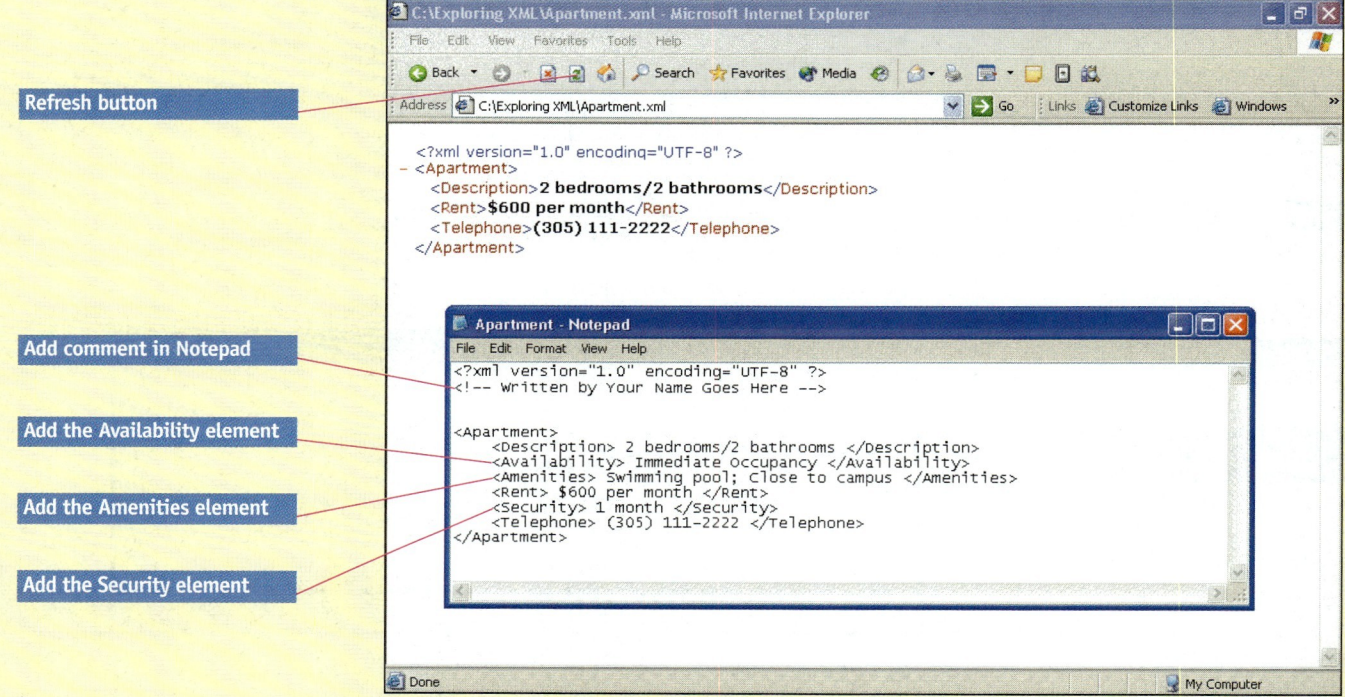

(c) Expand the Document (step 3)

FIGURE D.2 Hands-on Exercise 1 (*continued*)

A QUICK REVIEW OF XML SYNTAX

Each element in an XML document contains a start tag, an ending tag, and the associated data. The start tag contains the name of the element. The ending tag contains the element's name preceded by a slash. The element name can contain letters, numbers, and other characters, but it cannot start with a number or punctuation character, nor can it start with the letters xml. Element names may not contain spaces (an underscore or initial caps are used instead) and are case sensitive.

Step 4: **Add the Root Element**

- Continue the development of the XML document by adding the Root element as shown in the Notepad window in Figure D.2d.
  - ❏ Click at the end of the second line, which contains the comment. Press **Enter** to start a new line.
  - ❏ Type **<Root>** to create the root element.
  - ❏ Press **Ctrl+End** to move to the end of the document. Press **Enter**.
  - ❏ Type **</Root>** to complete the root element. Press **Enter**.
  - ❏ Add indentation (four spaces per line) or not as you see fit. The indentation in our document is not required.

- Add a second Apartment element as shown in Figure D.2d that contains only the Description element. Save the document.

- Click in the **Internet Explorer window**. Click the **Refresh button** on the Internet Explorer toolbar to view the expanded document.

- Correct any errors by returning to Notepad. Save the document after each editing change. Be sure to click the **Refresh button** to see the results of those changes in Internet Explorer.

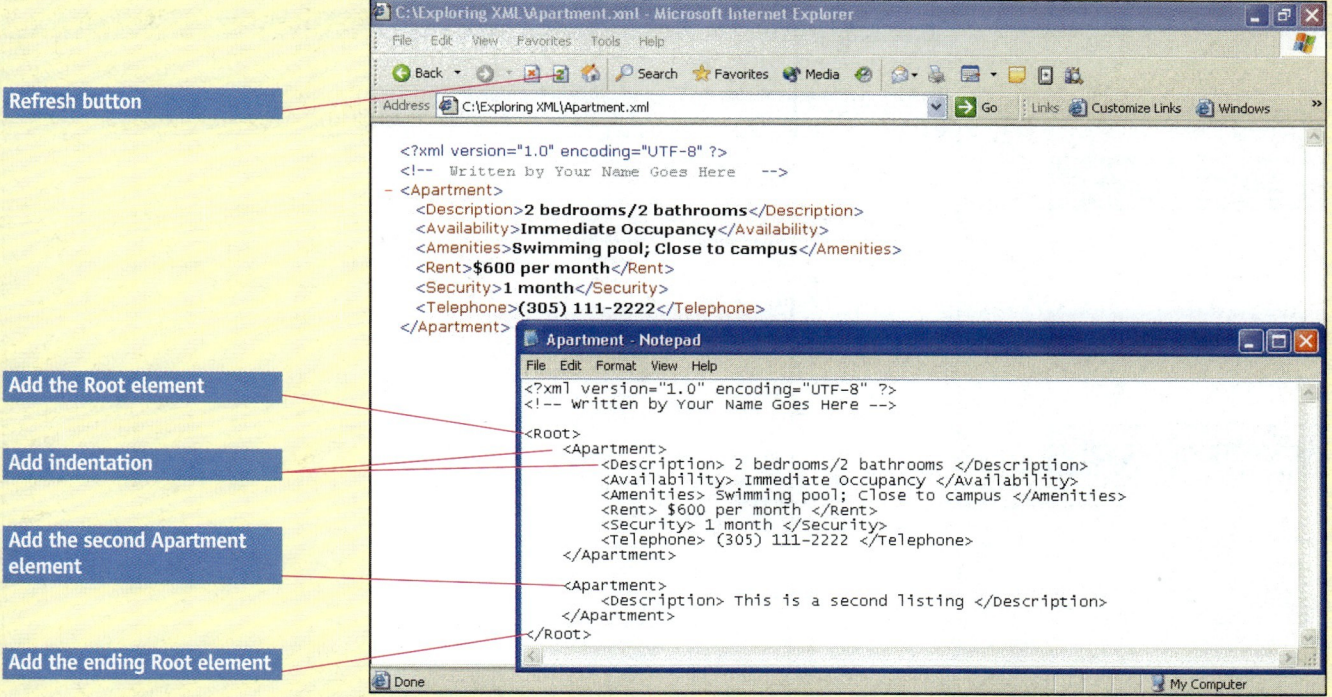

(d) Add the Root Element (step 4)

FIGURE D.2 Hands-on Exercise 1 (*continued*)

USE WHAT YOU KNOW

Notepad is a Windows accessory that follows common conventions and keyboard shortcuts; for example, Ctrl+X, Ctrl+C, and Ctrl+V are keyboard shortcuts to cut, copy, and paste, respectively. Other shortcuts are also available, such as Ctrl+S and Ctrl+P to save and print the document, respectively. (You can also use the Alt key plus an underlined letter to pull down a menu, such as Alt+F to pull down the file menu, and then type the letter S or P to save or print.) And don't forget the Edit menu, which provides access to the Find and Replace commands.

Step 5: **Complete the Document**

- You should be back in Internet Explorer as shown in Figure D.2e. (The third apartment listing for a 1 bedroom/1 bath apartment has not yet been entered.)

- Click the – **sign** that appears next to the second Apartment element. The minus sign changes to a plus sign and the information within the Apartment element is no longer visible.

- Click the – **sign** next to the Root element, which collapses the Root element. Click the + **sign** (that now appears) next to the Root element to expand the element.

- Use Notepad to add a third apartment listing (**1 bedroom/1 bathroom**) as shown in Figure D.2e. Check the document for accuracy, save it, and then print the completed document from Notepad for your instructor.

- Close Notepad. Click **Yes** if you are prompted to save the changes.

- Click in the **Internet Explorer window**, click the **Refresh button**, and then print the XML document from Internet Explorer. How does this document differ from the one printed in Notepad?

- Close Internet Explorer.

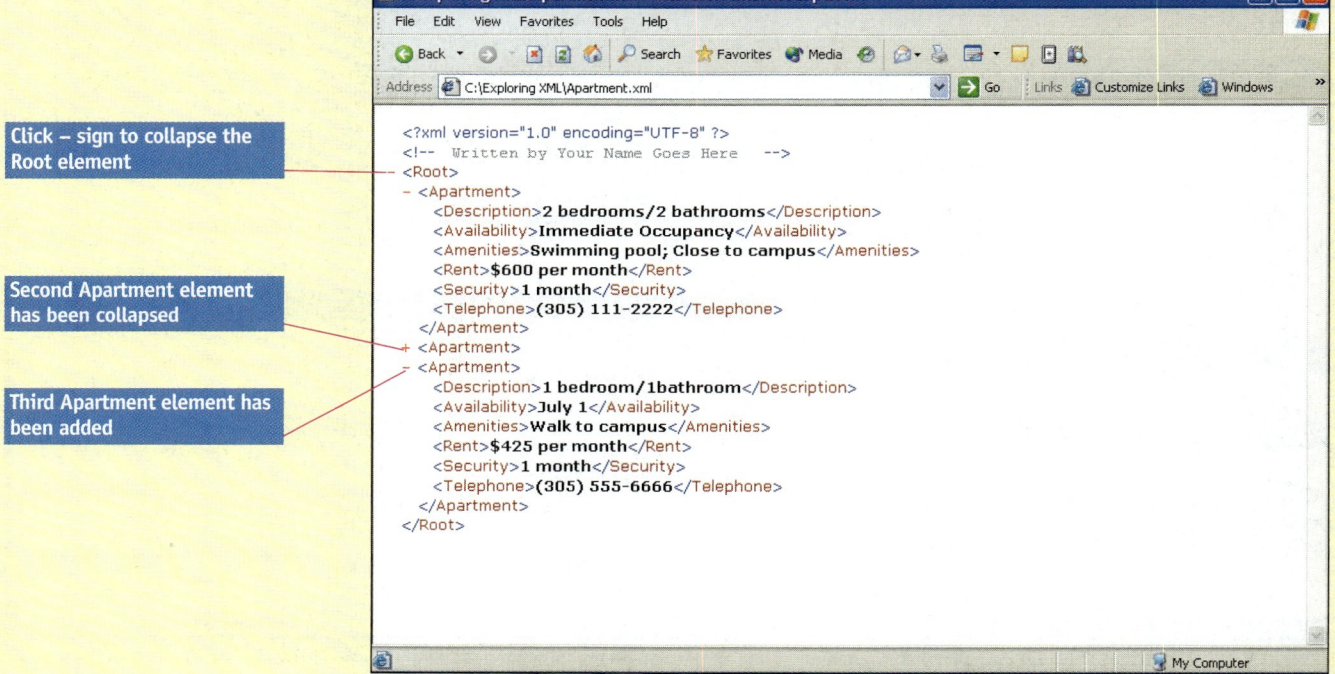

(e) Complete the Document (step 5)

FIGURE D.2 Hands-on Exercise 1 (*continued*)

EXPAND AND COLLAPSE THE DATA

The plus and minus signs that appear next to the elements within an XML document follow the same conventions as the plus and minus signs next to the folders in Windows Explorer. Click a plus sign and the data expands. Click a minus sign and the data collapses. Internet Explorer is XML-aware and prints the document to show only the expanded elements. Notepad, however, is unaware of the XML tags and prints the entire document.

MICROSOFT ACCESS AND XML

Figure D.3 introduces a health insurance database that will illustrate the use of XML in conjunction with an Access database. The database contains two tables, an Employees table in Figure D.3a that is imported from an existing XML document, and a Claims table in Figure D.3b that originates within the Access database. There is a one-to-many relationship between employees and claims; that is, one employee can have many claims, but a specific claim is associated with only one employee. Dottie Balchunas (EmployeeID 22222), for example, has three records in the Claims table.

Each record in the Claims table contains five fields: the ClaimID, which is the primary key; the EmployeeID to associate the claims record with the corresponding employee record; the date the claim was submitted; the amount that was submitted; and the amount that was reimbursed. The total query in Figure D.3c computes the sum of the individual records in the Claims table; for example, Dottie Balchunas submitted three individual claims for $1000, $250, and $100, which total $1,350. Note, too, that the total query contains the employee's first and last names, which are taken from the Employees table, and which are concatenated as a single field.

The Access database creates the total query, then exports the total query as an XML document as shown in Figure D.3d. The XML document references a *schema* (or data model) called InsuranceClaims.xsd, but it does *not* reference a style sheet. Hence, the XML data is displayed with the associated tags clearly visible.

Figure D.3e displays the same XML document as Figure D.3d, except that we have added a reference to a **style sheet** that we provided. The data is the same as in the previous figure, but the formatting is much improved. Remember that XML is intended to describe data, but it does not format the data; the latter is accomplished by **XSL** (**eXtensible Stylesheet Language**). You do not have to be concerned about creating the actual style sheet.

Related records for Dottie Balchunas are in Claims table

	EmployeeID	FirstName	LastName	HireDate	HomeAddress	HomeCity	HomeState	HomeZip
▶	11111	Jim	Antonucci	1/2/1999	8990 SW 71 Avenue	Miami	FL	33176-
	22222	Dottie	Balchunas	12/15/1999	400 Canopy Blvd	Pensacola	FL	32504-
	33333	Steve	Spann	3/23/2002	5900 West Highway	Boca Raton	FL	33427-
	44444	Benjamin	Grauer	1/21/2003	4 Grove Road	Orlando	FL	32801-
	55555	Megan	Miller	11/24/1998	903 SW 1 Street	Vero Beach	FL	32960-
	66666	Jessica	Kinzer	4/15/2001	1239 College Drive	Gainesville	FL	32601-
	77777	Carlos	Portu	3/16/2003	500 Highway East	Miami	FL	33176-
*								

(a) Employees Table (imported from an XML document)

Multiple records (claims) are associated with same employee (Dottie Balchunas)

	ClaimID	EmployeeID	Date	AmountSubmitted	AmountReimbursed
▶	C0001	11111	1/2/2004	$150	$100
	C0002	11111	2/1/2004	$150	$100
	C0003	11111	2/15/2004	$500	$400
	C0008	11111	4/1/2004	$2,500	$2,000
	C0011	11111	5/15/2004	$2,500	$2,000
	C0014	11111	6/15/2004	$100	$0
	C0005	22222	2/25/2004	$1,000	$750
	C0010	22222	4/30/2004	$250	$100
	C0013	22222	6/4/2004	$100	$0
	C0006	33333	3/6/2004	$500	$400
	C0007	33333	3/6/2004	$250	$0
	C0012	33333	5/22/2004	$500	$400

(b) Claims Table (partial set of records)

One summary record for each employee with totals for all claims

	Name	SumOfAmountSubmitted	SumOfAmountReimbursed
▶	Antonucci, Jim	$5,900.00	$4,600.00
	Balchunas, Dottie	$1,350.00	$850.00
	Grauer, Benjamin	$175.00	$175.00
	Kinzer, Jessica	$500.00	$400.00
	Portu, Carlos	$50.00	$0.00
	Spann, Steve	$1,250.00	$800.00

(c) Total Query

FIGURE D.3 Access and XML

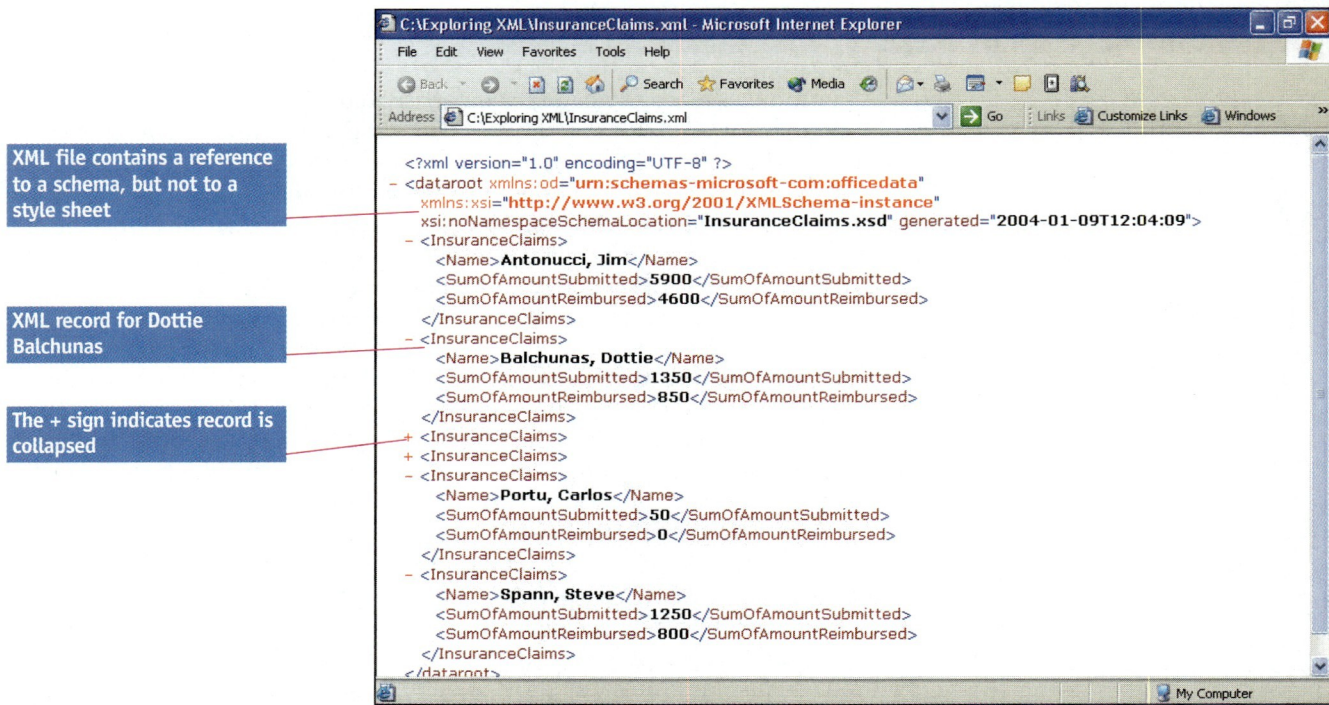

XML file contains a reference to a schema, but not to a style sheet

XML record for Dottie Balchunas

The + sign indicates record is collapsed

(d) XML File without Style Sheet

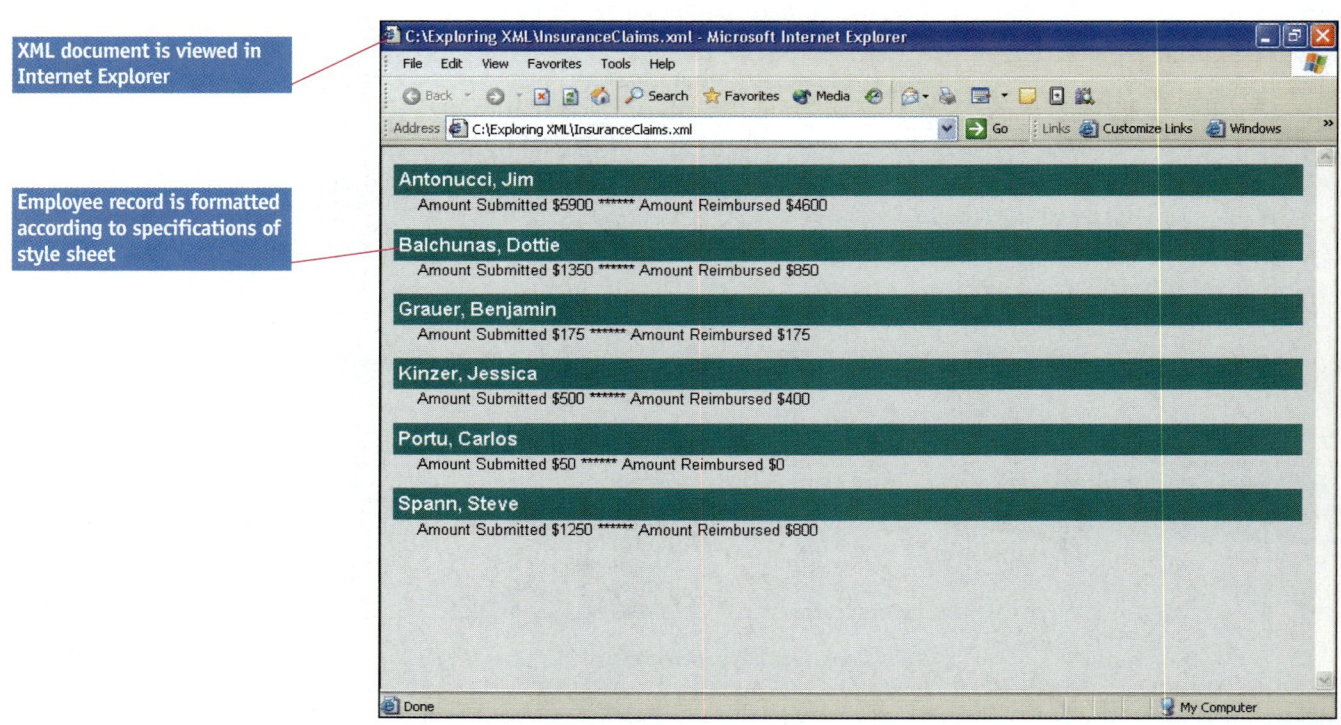

XML document is viewed in Internet Explorer

Employee record is formatted according to specifications of style sheet

(e) XML File with Style Sheet Added

FIGURE D.3 Access and XML (*continued*)

2 Access and XML

Objective Import an XML document into an Access database, create a one-to-many relationship and a query based on that relationship, then export the query as an XML document; apply a style sheet to an XML document.

Step 1: **Import the Employees Table**

- Start Access. Pull down the **File menu** and click the **Open command** to display the Open dialog box. Click the **down arrow** in the Look in box to select the **Exploring XML folder** within the **Exploring Access folder**. Select the **Health Insurance database**.

- Click the **Open button** in the Open dialog box, then click the **Open button** within the Security Warning dialog box if you see a warning message.

- Click the **Tables button**. The database contains both the Claims and Employees tables, but the latter table does not yet contain any data. Pull down the **File menu**, click **Get External data**, and then click the **Import command** to display the Import dialog box.
  - ❏ Click the **down arrow** in the Look in box to select the **Exploring XML folder**.
  - ❏ Click the **down arrow** in the Files of type list box and select **XML** as the file type, select the **Employees document** with the XML file type. (You may find it necessary to click the down arrow on the View button to change to the Detail view to see the file type.)
  - ❏ Click the **Import button** to display the Import XML dialog box in Figure D.4a. Click the **Options button** and then select the option to **Append Data to Existing Table(s)**. Click **OK**.

- You should see the dialog box in Figure 8a indicating that the XML file was imported successfully. Click **OK**.

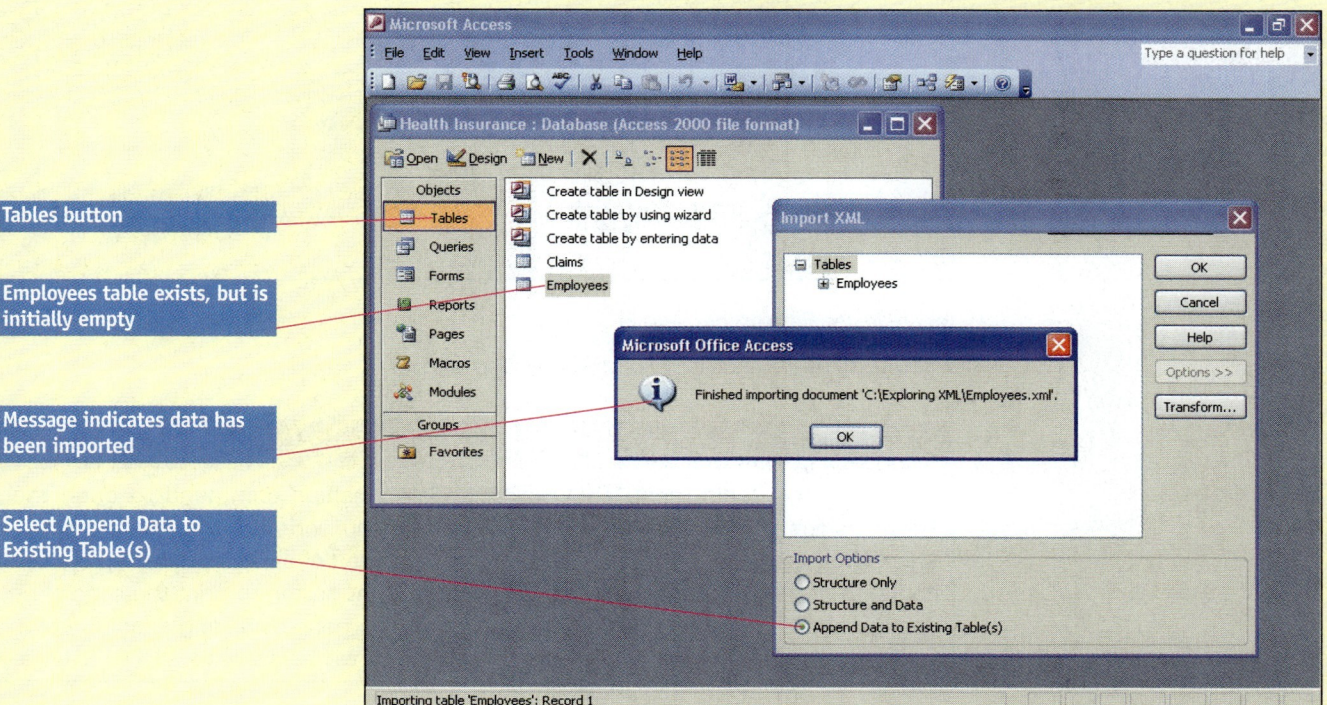

(a) Import the Employees Table (step 1)

FIGURE D.4 Hands-on Exercise 2

Step 2: **Create the Relationship**

- Pull down the **Tools menu**. Click **Relationships** to open the Relationships window as shown in Figure D.4b. (The tables are not yet visible.) Click the **Maximize button**.

- Pull down the **Relationships menu** and click the **Show Table command**. Click the **Tables button** if necessary, and then double click each table to add the table to the Relationships window. Close the Show Table dialog box.

- Move and/or size the tables as shown in Figure D.4b. Click and drag the **EmployeeID field** from the Employees table to the **EmployeeID field** in the Claims table.

- Check the box to **Enforce Referential Integrity**. Click the **Create button** to create the relationship. Click the **Save button** to save the Relationships window.

- Close the Relationships window.

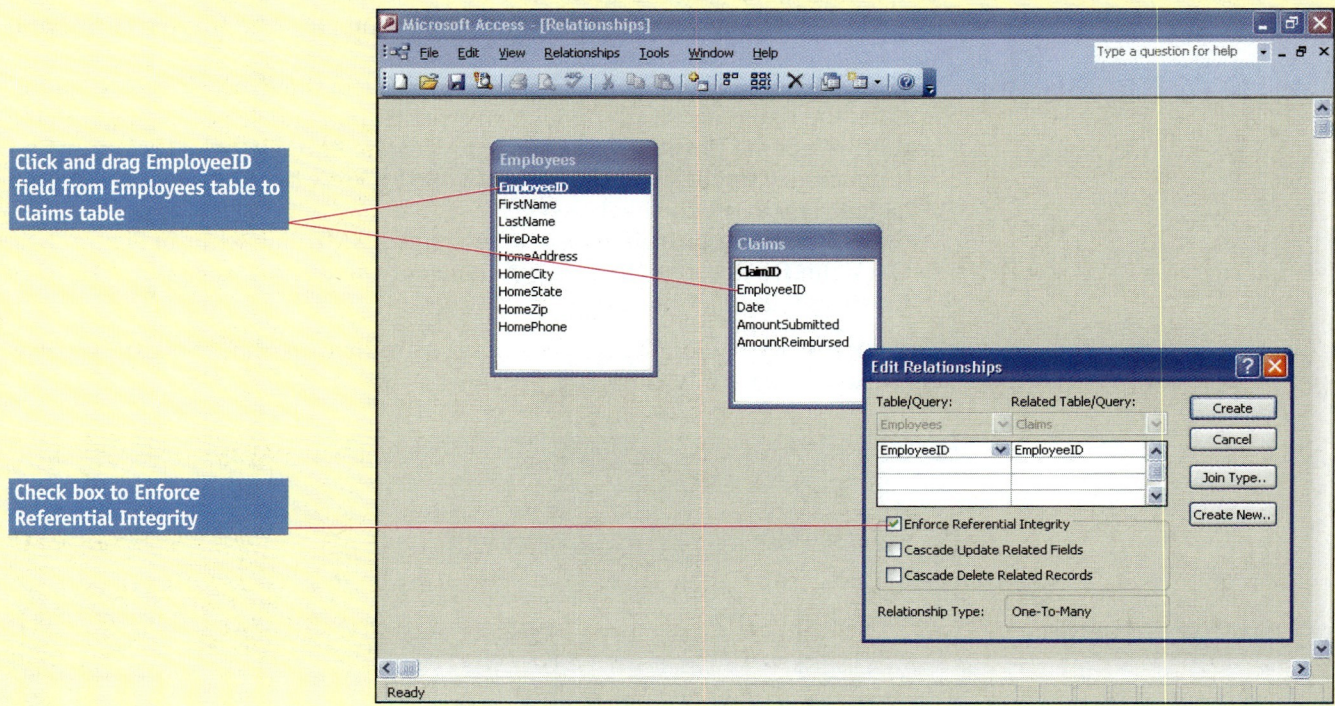

(b) Create the Relationship (step 2)

FIGURE D.4 Hands-on Exercise 2 (*continued*)

PRINT THE RELATIONSHIPS DIAGRAM

Pull down the Tools menu and click the Relationships command to open the Relationships window, then pull down the File menu and click the Print Relationships command. You will see the Print Preview screen of a report that displays the contents of the Relationships window. Click the Print button to print the report, or change to the Design view to modify the report, perhaps by adding a logo and/or your name. Save the report after printing so that it will be available at a later time.

Step 3:   **Create the Total Query**

- Click the **Queries button** in the Database window. Double click **Create query in Design view** to display the Query Design window in Figure D.4c. The Show Table dialog box appears automatically.

- Add the **Employees** and **Claims tables** to the Design grid as shown in Figure D.4c. (The relationship is shown automatically.) Close the Show Table dialog box.

- The insertion point is in the Field row of the first column. Type =[**LastName**] & **", " & [FirstName]** and press **Enter**. Increase the width of the first column so that you have more room in which to work.

- Double click **Expr1**, which is generated automatically as the name of the field, then type **Name** to replace the selected text. Add the other fields to the design grid as shown in Figure D.4c.

- Pull down the **View menu** and click the **Totals command** to display the Total row. Click the **down arrow** in the Total row in the **AmountSubmitted field** and choose **Sum**. Sum the **AmountReimbursed field** in similar fashion.

- Save the Query as **InsuranceClaims**. Click the **Run button**. You should see six summary records (one for each employee) that show the totals for each employee. Close the query.

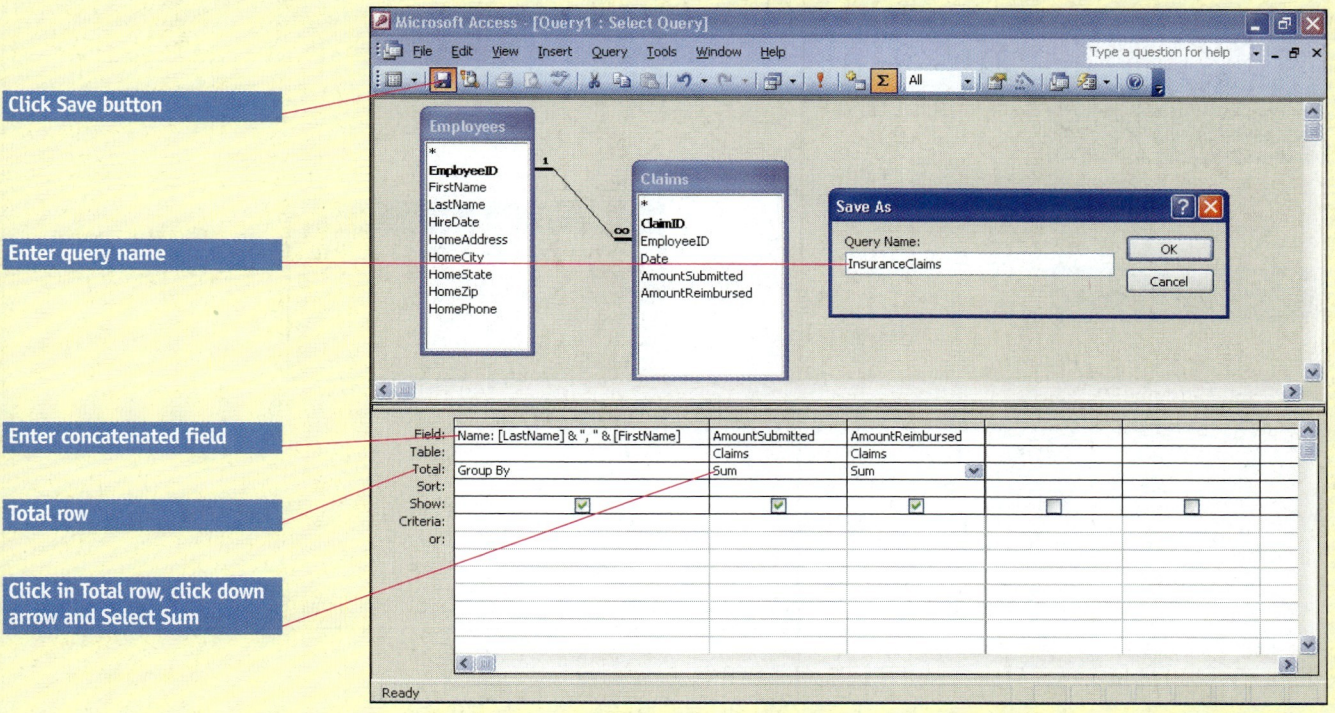

(c) Create the Total Query (step 3)

FIGURE D.4   Hands-on Exercise 2 (*continued*)

CONCATENATING A FIELD

A table stores an individual's last name, first name, and middle initial in separate fields, whereas reports and queries combine the components into a single field, such as "Anderson, John". This is accomplished by the ampersand, which concatenates (strings together) multiple fields.

Step 4: Export the Data

- You should be back in the Database window. Select the **InsuranceClaims query**, pull down the **File menu**, and click the **Export command** to display the Export Query dialog box.

- Click the **down arrow** in the Save In list box to change to the Exploring XML folder. Click the down arrow in the Save As type list box and select **XML**. Click the **Export button** to display the Export XML dialog box in Figure D.4d.

- The Data (XML) and Schema of the data (XSD) boxes should be checked. Click **OK**. The XML and associated schema have been created, but you will have to exit Access to see the files. Close the Health Insurance database.

- Start **Windows Explorer** and change to the **Exploring XML folder**. If necessary, click the **Name column** to sort the files alphabetically.

- You should see three files with the "same" filename (InsuranceClaims) but with different file types; that is, you see the **XML document**, the **XSD schema** that was just created by Access, and the **XSL style sheet** that we provided. Each file has a different purpose.

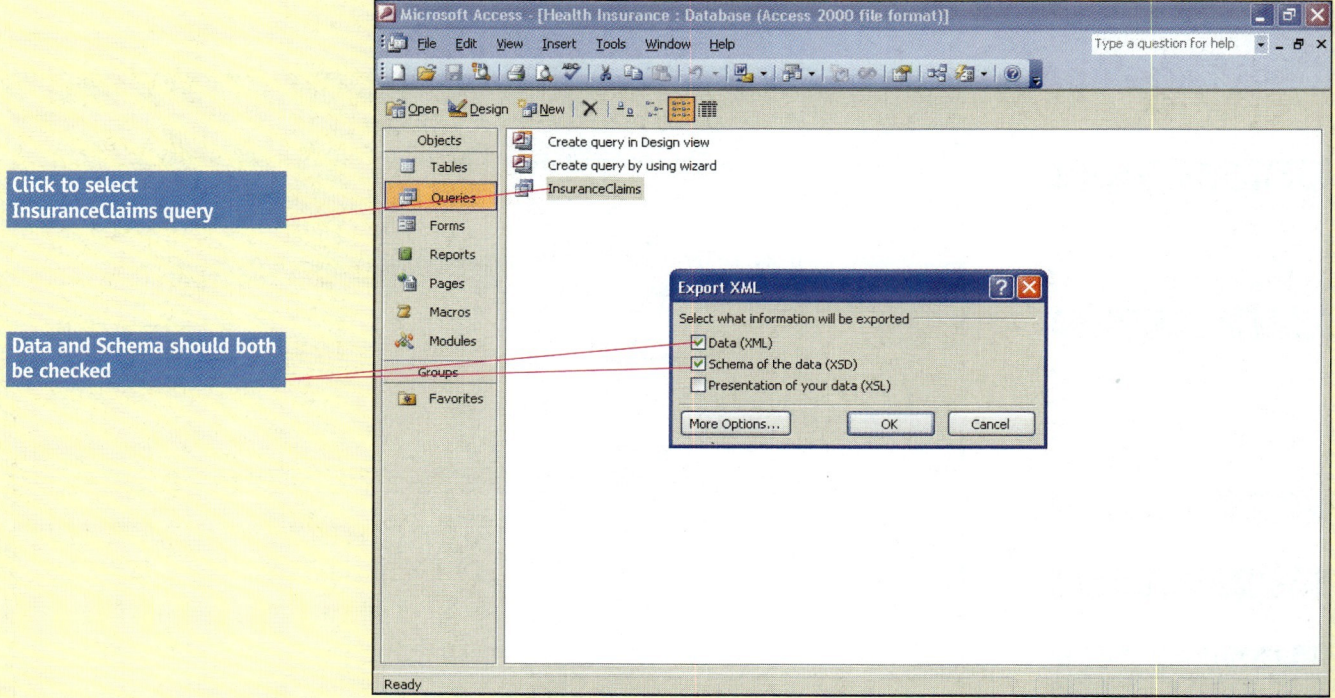

(d) Export the Data (step 4)

FIGURE D.4   Hands-on Exercise 2 (*continued*)

VIEW THE FILE EXTENSIONS IN WINDOWS EXPLORER

Pull down the Tools menu, click the Folder Options command to display the associated dialog box, click the View tab, clear the box to Hide extensions for known file types, and click OK. The display in Windows Explorer changes to show a three-letter extension after each file name—for example, XML, XSD, and XSL for the document, schema, and style sheet, respectively. Each file has a different purpose of which you should be aware.

Step 5: **Add the Style Sheet**

- Double click the **InsuranceClaims XML document** in Windows Explorer to view the data. (Be sure that you open the XML document, as opposed to the XSL style sheet or XSD schema.)
- You should see the results of the Access total query in Internet Explorer as shown in Figure D.4e. The data is displayed without any formatting.
- Click the **down arrow** next to the **Edit button** and select the command to **Edit with the XML editor**. You should open the **Insurance Claims XML document** in Notepad as shown in Figure D.4e.
- Click at the end of the first line, and then press **Enter** to start a new line. Type the entry **<?xml-stylesheet type="text/xsl" href="InsuranceClaims.xsl" ?>**. Pull down the **File menu** and click the **Save command**.
- Click in the **Internet Explorer window**, then click the **Refresh button** on the Standard toolbar. The display of the XML document should change to reflect the associated style sheet; that is, each employee should appear in white letters on a teal background. Go to step 6 if the document does not display correctly.
- Print the formatted XML document. Close Internet Explorer.

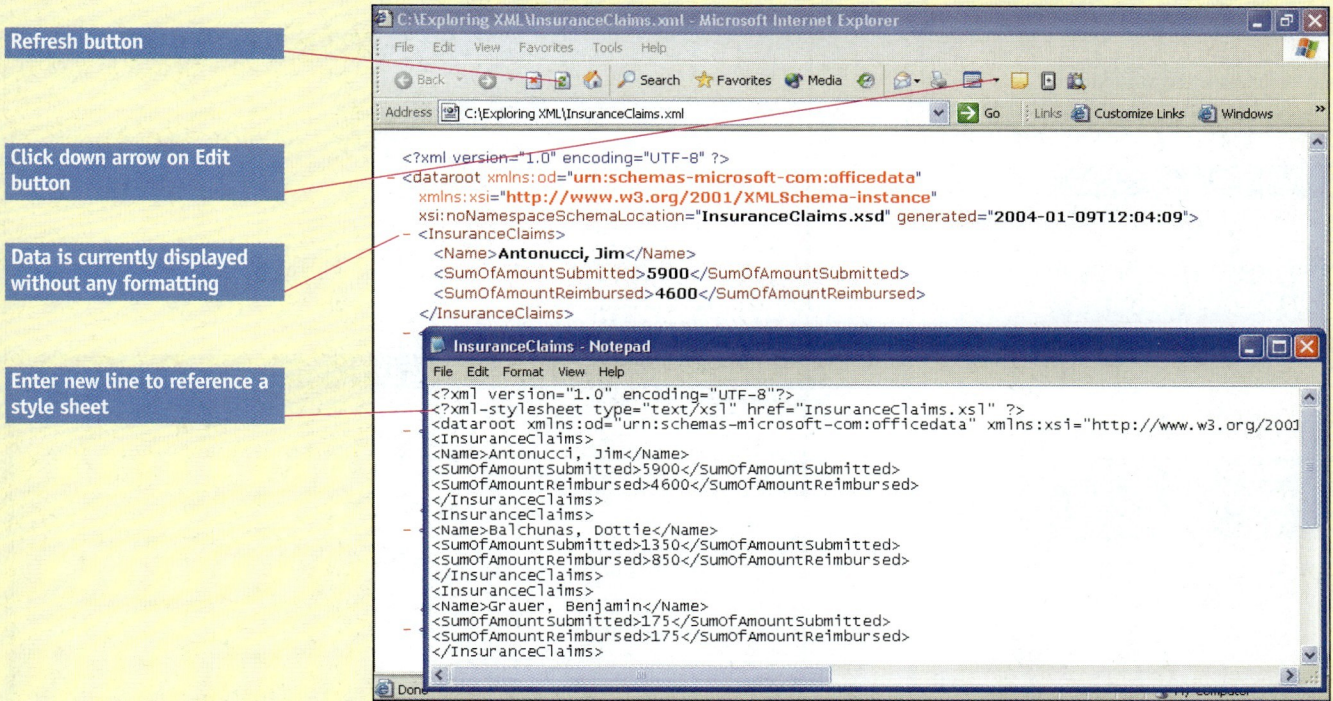

Refresh button

Click down arrow on Edit button

Data is currently displayed without any formatting

Enter new line to reference a style sheet

(e) Add the Style Sheet (step 5)

FIGURE D.4 Hands-on Exercise 2 (*continued*)

EXTENSIBLE STYLESHEET LANGUAGE

A style sheet formats data for display within a Web browser. XSL has its own syntax, which is beyond the scope of this discussion. You can, however, view an XSL file and make inferences about the formatting. Start the Notepad accessory and open the InsuranceClaims style sheet in the Exploring XML folder. Do you know how the font style and size are specified? How would you change the formatting and/or the elements that are displayed? You can experiment freely with the style sheet, but make a backup copy before you begin.

Step 6: **Correct the Error**

- Do this step only if you have an error in the XML file. The XML syntax is rigid and it is easy to make an error, which in turn displays an error message such as the one in Figure D.4f.

- Look closely at the text of the message to determine the nature of the error. In this example, we (deliberately) misspelled the name of the style sheet by including a space where none belongs; that is, the correct entry is **InsuranceClaims.xsl**.

- Click the **down arrow** next to the **Edit button** and select the command to **Edit with XML editor** to open the XML document in Notepad. Correct the error by deleting the space in the name of the style sheet.

- Pull down the **File menu** and click the **Save command**. Close Notepad. Click in the **Internet Explorer window**, then click the **Refresh button**.

- The display of the XML document should change to reflect the associated style sheet; that is, the name of each employee should appear in white letters on a teal background. Print the formatted XML document for your instructor.

- Close Internet Explorer. Congratulations on a job well done.

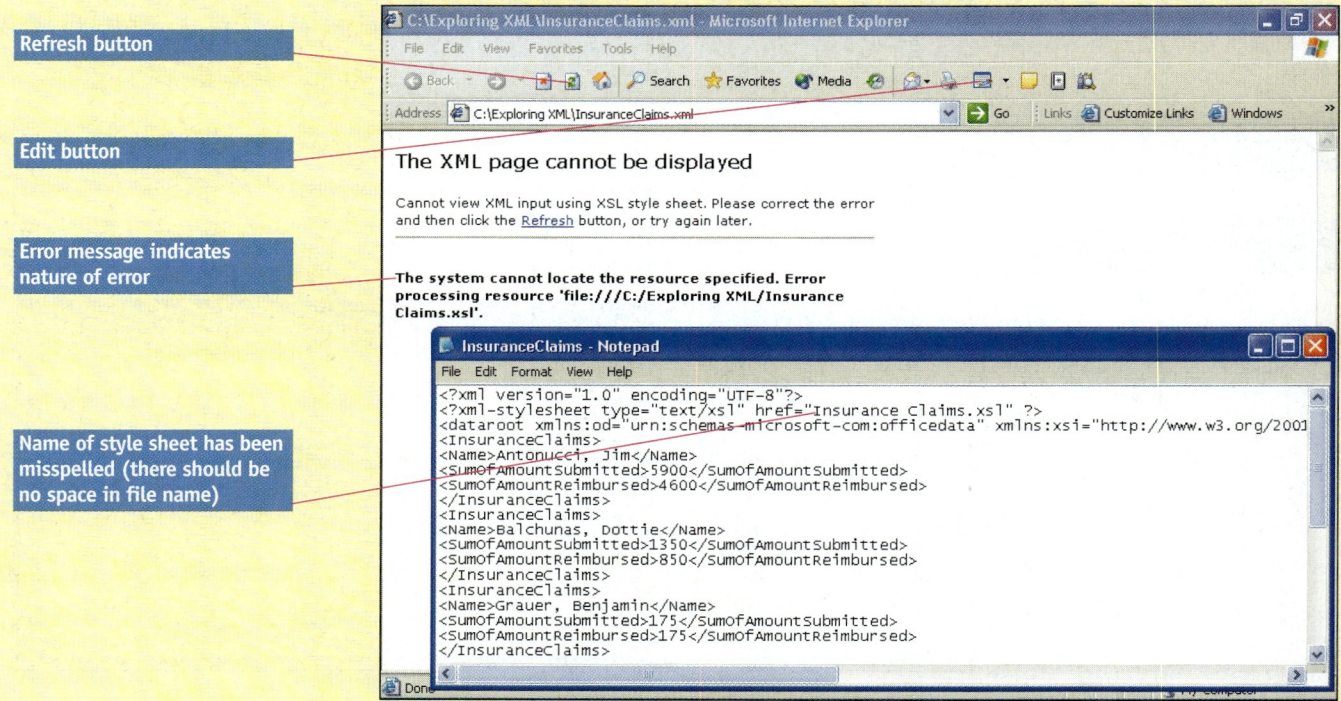

(f) Correct the Error (step 6)

FIGURE D.4 Hands-on Exercise 2 (*continued*)

ERRORS ARE NOT PERMITTED

An XML document must be error free if it is to open in Internet Explorer. The errors are displayed one at a time until every error is corrected, at which point the document will open. Remember, too, the difference between a well-formed XML document and a valid document. A well-formed XML document has correct XML syntax. A valid XML document is well formed, and in addition, conforms to the rules of a Document Type Definition (DTD) or XML schema.

SUMMARY

XML (eXtensible Markup Language) is an industry standard for structuring data across applications, operating systems, and hardware devices. The XML syntax, known officially as the XML recommendation, was developed by the World Wide Web Consortium (commonly known as W3C), a public organization with the sole purpose of creating standards or recommendations for the Internet. (W3C also published the HTML specification. You can learn more about the organization and its standards by visiting their Web site at www.w3.org.)

XML is the latest step in the evolution of markup languages. It is not intended to replace HTML (Hypertext Markup language), which describes the formatting of a document rather than its structure. HTML uses a finite set of tags, such as <B> or <I>, for bold and Italics, respectively. XML is more general because it is extensible (expandable) and thus has an infinite number of tags that are defined as necessary by the developer. XML is "data about data" and it does not contain any information about how to display that data.

An XML document is divided into elements. Each element contains a start tag, an ending tag, and the associated data. The start tag contains the name of the element. The ending tag contains the element's name preceded by a slash. XML tags are case sensitive; that is, the start and ending tags must match. XML elements can be nested to any depth, but each inner element (or child) must be entirely contained within the outer element (or parent). Every XML document has a root element, which is the single element in an XML file that contains all other elements.

The creation of an XML document is an iterative process that requires the user to switch back and forth between an editor (e.g., the Notepad accessory) and Internet Explorer. You create the document in Notepad, view it in Internet Explorer, and return to Notepad to make the necessary changes. It is important to save the document in Notepad after each set of changes, and to click the Refresh button in Internet Explorer to see the latest version. The document is displayed differently in each application. Notepad is a simple text editor and does not handle the XML tags differently from other text. Internet Explorer is XML-aware and displays the tags and associated data with appropriate formatting.

An XML document may contain a reference to a schema and/or a style sheet. The schema (XSD file) contains the rules, such as which fields are required and/or the type of data each field may contain. The style sheet (XSL document) describes the formatting or display of the data. Both documents, the schema and the style sheet, may be viewed and edited with the Notepad accessory.

XML is fully supported throughout Microsoft Office 2003. XML documents may be imported and/or exported into Word, Excel, and Access. Microsoft Office InfoPath 2003 is a new application in the Office suite that simplifies the creation of an XML form.

KEY TERMS

Character encoding 561
Element 561
Extensible .560
HTML (Hypertext
   Markup Language) 559
Internet Explorer 563
Notepad accessory 561

Root element 561
SGML (Standard Generalized
   Markup Language) 559
Tag 560
World Wide Web
   Consortium (W3C) 575

XML (eXtensible
   Markup Language) 559
XML declaration 561

MULTIPLE CHOICE

1. What does XML stand for?

    (a) eXternal Machine Library

    (b) eXtreme Manipulation Language

    (c) eXhaustive Manual Labor

    (d) eXtensible Markup Language

2. The XML recommendation was developed by:

    (a) The Department of Defense

    (b) Microsoft and IBM in a joint effort

    (c) The World Wide Web Consortium (W3C)

    (d) The European Laboratory for Particle Physics (CERN)

3. Which of the following is an *invalid* element name?

    (a) Address

    (b) ADDRESS

    (c) address

    (d) xmladdress

4. Which of the following is an *invalid* element name?

    (a) FirstName

    (b) First Name

    (c) First_Name

    (d) None of the above; they are all valid element names

5. The XML element <Telephone>(111)222-3333 </telephone>

    (a) Is correct as written

    (b) Is invalid because of the editing characters that appear in the phone number

    (c) Is invalid because the start tag is missing a slash

    (d) Is invalid because the start and end tags are not the same case

6. Which program can be used to create and/or edit an XML document?

    (a) Internet Explorer

    (b) The Notepad accessory

    (c) Both (a) and (b)

    (d) Neither (a) nor (b)

7. Which of the following best describes Notepad and Internet Explorer?

    (a) Notepad is XML-aware, Internet Explorer is not

    (b) Internet Explorer ix XML-aware, Notepad is not

    (c) Both applications are XML-aware

    (d) Neither application is XML-aware

8. Which of the following statements is true?

    (a) HTML contains a finite number of tags; XML has an infinite number

    (b) XML contains a finite number of tags; HTML has an infinite number

    (c) XML and HTML both contain a finite number of tags

    (d) XML and HTML both contain an infinite number of tags

9. Which of the following is most likely to occur if you double click an XML document that references *a style sheet and a schema*?

    (a) The document is displayed in Word, Excel, or Access, depending on the application that created it

    (b) The document is displayed in Notepad

    (c) The document is displayed in Internet Explorer and the XML tags are visible

    (d) The document is displayed in Internet Explorer, the data within the document is formatted, and the XML tags are not shown

10. Which of the following is most likely to occur if you double click an XML document that references *a schema but not a style sheet*?

    (a) The document is displayed in Word, Excel, or Access, depending on the application that created it

    (b) The document is displayed in Notepad

    (c) The document is displayed in Internet Explorer and the XML tags are visible

    (d) The document is displayed in Internet Explorer, the data within the document is formatted, and the XML tags are not shown

ANSWERS

1. d	6. b
2. c	7. b
3. d	8. a
4. b	9. d
5. d	10. c

Getting Started with VBA:
Extending Microsoft Office 2003

OBJECTIVES

After reading this chapter you will:

1. Describe the relationship of VBA to Microsoft Office 2003.

2. Explain how to create, edit, and run a VBA procedure.

3. Use the MsgBox statement and InputBox function.

4. Explain how to debug a procedure by stepping through its statements.

5. Use the If. . . Then. . .Else statement to implement a decision.

6. Explain the Case statement.

7. Create a custom toolbar.

8. Describe several statements used to implement a loop.

9. Describe event-driven programming.

hands-on exercises

1. INTRODUCTION TO VBA
Input: None
Output: VBA workbook

2. DECISION MAKING
Input: VBA workbook
Output: VBA workbook

3. LOOPS AND DEBUGGING
Input: VBA workbook
Output: VBA workbook

4. EVENT-DRIVEN PROGRAMMING
Input: VBA workbook;
Financial Consultant
workbook
Output: VBA workbook;
Financial Consultant
workbook

5. EVENT-DRIVEN PROGRAMMING
Input: VBA Switchboard and
Security database
Output: VBA Switchboard and
Security database

CASE STUDY
ON-THE-JOB TRAINING

Your first job is going exceedingly well. The work is very challenging and your new manager, Phyllis Simon, is impressed with the Excel workbooks that you have developed thus far. Phyllis has asked you to take it to the next level by incorporating VBA procedures into future projects. You have some knowledge of Excel macros and have already used the macro recorder to record basic macros. You are able to make inferences about the resulting code, but you will need additional proficiency in VBA to become a true expert in Excel.

The good news is that you work for a company that believes in continuing education and promotes from within. Phyllis has assigned you to a new interdepartmental team responsible for creating high-level Excel applications that will be enhanced through VBA. Moreover, you have been selected to attend a week-long seminar to learn VBA so that you can become a valued member of the team. The seminar will be held in San Diego, California, where there is a strong temptation to study sand and surf rather than VBA. Thus, Phyllis expects you to complete a series of VBA procedures upon your return—just to be sure that you were not tempted to skip class and dip your toes in the water. ■

Your assignment is to read this chapter and focus on the first three hands-on exercises that develop the syntax for basic VBA statements—MsgBox, InputBox, decision making through If/Else and Case statements, and iteration through the For . . . Next and Do Until statements. You will then open the partially completed *VBA Case Study—On-the-Job Training*, start the VBA editor, and then complete the tasks presented in the procedures in Module1. (The requirements for each procedure appear as comments within the procedure.) Add a command button for each macro to the Excel workbook, and then print the worksheet and a copy of the completed module for your instructor. Last, but not least, create a suitable event procedure for closing the workbook.

Visual Basic for Applications (VBA) is a powerful programming language that is accessible from all major applications in Microsoft Office XP. You do not have to know VBA to use Office effectively, but even a basic understanding will help you to create more powerful documents. Indeed, you may already have been exposed to VBA through the creation of simple macros in Word or Excel. A ***macro*** is a set of instructions (i.e., a program) that simplifies the execution of repetitive tasks. It is created through the ***macro recorder*** that captures commands as they are executed, then converts those commands into a VBA program. (The macro recorder is present in Word, Excel, and PowerPoint, but not in Access.) You can create and execute macros without ever looking at the underlying VBA, but you gain an appreciation for the language when you do.

The macro recorder is limited, however, in that it captures only commands, mouse clicks, and/or keystrokes. As you will see, VBA is much more than just recorded keystrokes. It is a language unto itself, and thus, it contains all of the statements you would expect to find in any programming language. This lets you enhance the functionality of any macro by adding extra statements as necessary—for example, an InputBox function to accept data from the user, followed by an If . . . Then . . . Else statement to take different actions based on the information supplied by the user.

This supplement presents the rudiments of VBA and is suitable for use with any Office application. We begin by describing the VBA editor and how to create, edit, and run simple procedures. The examples are completely general and demonstrate the basic capabilities of VBA that are found in any programming language. We illustrate the MsgBox statement to display output to the user and the InputBox function to accept input from the user. We describe the For . . . Next statement to implement a loop and the If . . . Then . . . Else and Case statements for decision making. We also describe several debugging techniques to help you correct the errors that invariably occur. The last two exercises introduce the concept of event-driven programming, in which a procedure is executed in response to an action taken by the user. The material here is application-specific in conjunction with Excel and Access, but it can be easily extended to Word or PowerPoint.

One last point before we begin is that this supplement assumes no previous knowledge on the part of the reader. It is suitable for someone who has never been exposed to a programming language or written an Office macro. If, on the other hand, you have a background in programming or macros, you will readily appreciate the power inherent in VBA. VBA is an incredibly rich language that can be daunting to the novice. Stick with us, however, and we will show you that it is a flexible and powerful tool with consistent rules that can be easily understood and applied. You will be pleased at what you will be able to accomplish.

VBA is a programming language, and like any other programming language its programs (or procedures, as they are called) are made up of individual statements. Each ***statement*** accomplishes a specific task such as displaying a message to the user or accepting input from the user. Statements are grouped into ***procedures***, and procedures, in turn, are grouped into ***modules***. Every VBA procedure is classified as either public or private. A ***private procedure*** is accessible only from within the module in which it is contained. A ***public procedure***, on the other hand, can be accessed from any module.

The statement, however, is the basic unit of the language. Our approach throughout this supplement will be to present individual statements, then to develop simple procedures using those statements in a hands-on exercise. As you read the discussion, you will see that every statement has a precise ***syntax*** that describes how the statement is to be used. The syntax also determines the ***arguments*** (or parameters) associated with that statement, and whether those arguments are required or optional.

THE MSGBOX STATEMENT

The **MsgBox statement** displays information to the user. It is one of the most basic statements in VBA, but we use it to illustrate several concepts in VBA programming. Figure 1a contains a simple procedure called MsgBoxExamples, consisting of four individual MsgBox statements. All procedures begin with a **procedure header** and end with the **End Sub statement**.

The MsgBox statement has one required argument, which is the message (or prompt) that is displayed to the user. All other arguments are optional, but if they are used, they must be entered in a specified sequence. The simplest form of the MsgBox statement is shown in example 1, which specifies a single argument that contains the text (or prompt) to be displayed. The resulting message box is shown in Figure 1b. The message is displayed to the user, who responds accordingly, in this case by clicking the OK button.

Example 2 extends the MsgBox statement to include a second parameter that displays an icon within the resulting dialog box as shown in Figure 1c. The type of icon is determined by a VBA **intrinsic** (or predefined) **constant** such as vbExclamation, which displays an exclamation point in a yellow triangle. VBA has many such constants that enable you to simplify your code, while at the same time achieving some impressive results.

Example 3 uses a different intrinsic constant, vbInformation, to display a different icon. It also extends the MsgBox statement to include a third parameter that is displayed on the title bar of the resulting dialog box. Look closely, for example, at Figures 1c and 1d, whose title bars contain "Microsoft Excel" and "Grauer/Barber", respectively. The first is the default entry (given that we are executing the procedure from within Microsoft Excel). You can, however, give your procedures a customized look by displaying your own text in the title bar.

Procedure header

```
Public Sub MsgBoxExamples()
'This procedure was written by John Doe on 6/10/2003

    MsgBox "Example 1 - VBA is not difficult"
    MsgBox "Example 2 - VBA is not difficult", vbExclamation
    MsgBox "Example 3 - VBA is not difficult", vbInformation, "Grauer/Barber"
    MsgBox "Example 4 - VBA is not difficult", , "Your name goes here"
```

End Sub statement

```
End Sub
```

(a) VBA Code

Message only

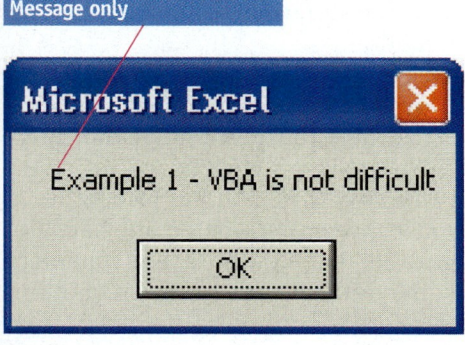

(b) Example 1—One Argument

Icon is displayed

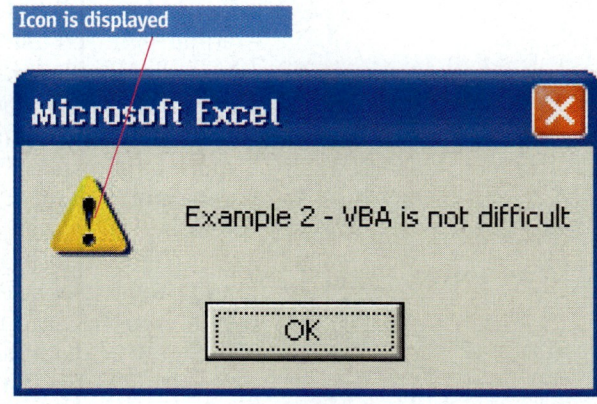

(c) Example 2—Two Arguments

FIGURE 1   The MsgBox Statement

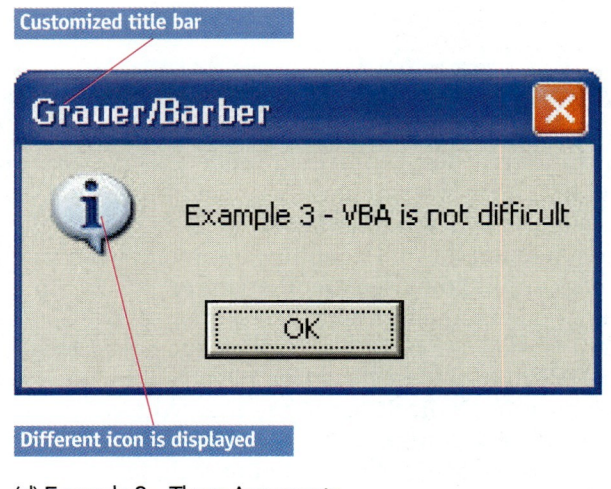

Customized title bar

Grauer/Barber

Example 3 - VBA is not difficult

OK

Different icon is displayed

(d) Example 3—Three Arguments

Customized title bar

Your name goes here

Example 4 - VBA is not difficult

OK

Message only

(e) Example 4—Omitted Parameter

FIGURE 1 The MsgBox Statement (*continued*)

Example 4 omits the second parameter (the icon), but includes the third parameter (the entry for the title bar). The parameters are positional, however, and thus the MsgBox statement contains two commas after the message to indicate that the second parameter has been omitted.

THE INPUTBOX FUNCTION

The MsgBox statement displays a prompt to the user, but what if you want the user to respond to the prompt by entering a value such as his or her name? This is accomplished using the ***InputBox function***. Note the subtle change in terminology in that we refer to the InputBox *function*, but the MsgBox *statement*. That is because a function returns a value, in this case the user's name, which is subsequently used in the procedure. In other words, the InputBox function asks the user for information, then it stores that information (the value returned by the user) for use in the procedure.

Figure 2 displays a procedure that prompts the user for a first and last name, after which it displays the information using the MsgBox statement. (The Dim statement at the beginning of the procedure is explained shortly.) Let's look at the first InputBox function, and the associated dialog box in Figure 2b. The InputBox function displays a prompt on the screen, the user enters a value ("Bob" in this example), and that value is stored in the variable that appears to the left of the equal sign (strFirstName). The concept of a variable is critical to every programming language. Simply stated, a ***variable*** is a named storage location that contains data that can be modified during program execution.

The MsgBox statement then uses the value of strFirstName to greet the user by name as shown in Figure 2c. This statement also introduces the ampersand to ***concatenate*** (join together) two different character strings, the literal "Good morning", followed by the value within the variable strFirstName.

The second InputBox function prompts the user for his or her last name. In addition, it uses a second argument to customize the contents of the title bar (VBA Primer in this example) as can be seen in Figure 2d. Finally, the MsgBox statement in Figure 2e displays both the first and last name through concatenation of multiple strings. This statement also uses the ***underscore*** to continue a statement from one line to the next.

VBA is not difficult, and you can use the MsgBox statement and InputBox function in conjunction with one another as the basis for several meaningful procedures. You will get a chance to practice in the hands-on exercise that follows shortly.

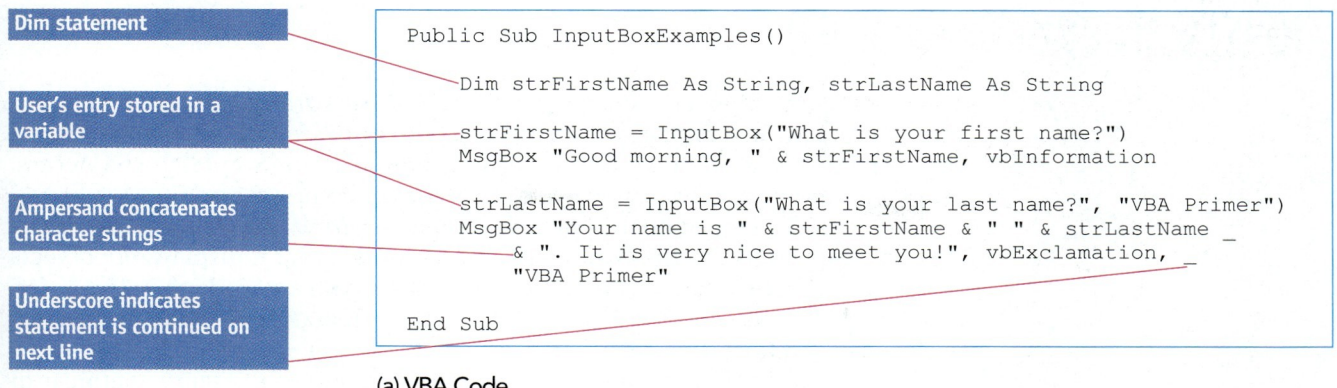

```
Dim statement ————— Public Sub InputBoxExamples()

                      Dim strFirstName As String, strLastName As String

User's entry stored in a   strFirstName = InputBox("What is your first name?")
variable ——————         MsgBox "Good morning, " & strFirstName, vbInformation

Ampersand concatenates   strLastName = InputBox("What is your last name?", "VBA Primer")
character strings ——————  MsgBox "Your name is " & strFirstName & " " & strLastName _
                             & ". It is very nice to meet you!", vbExclamation, _
Underscore indicates          "VBA Primer"
statement is continued on
next line —————————    End Sub
```

(a) VBA Code

(b) InputBox

(c) Concatenation

(d) Input Box Includes Argument for Title Bar

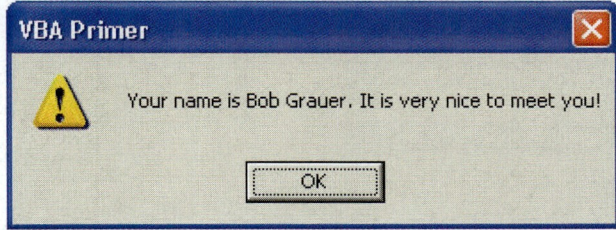

(e) Concatenation and Continuation

FIGURE 2   The InputBox Function

Declaring Variables

Every variable must be declared (defined) before it can be used. This is accomplished through the ***Dim*** (short for Dimension) ***statement*** that appears at the beginning of a procedure. The Dim statement indicates the name of the variable and its type (for example, whether it will hold characters or numbers), which in turn reserves the appropriate amount of memory for that variable.

A variable name must begin with a letter and cannot exceed 255 characters. It can contain letters, numbers, and various special characters such as an underscore, but it cannot contain a space or the special symbols !, @, &, $, or #. Variable names typically begin with a prefix to indicate the type of data that is stored within the variable such as "str" for a character string or "int" for integers. The use of a prefix is optional with respect to the rules of VBA, but it is followed almost universally.

THE VBA EDITOR

All VBA procedures are created using the ***Visual Basic editor*** as shown in Figure 3. You may already be familiar with the editor, perhaps in conjunction with creating and/or editing macros in Word or Excel, or event procedures in Microsoft Access. Let's take a moment, however, to review its essential components.

The left side of the editor displays the ***Project Explorer***, which is similar in concept and appearance to the Windows Explorer, except that it displays the objects associated with the open document. If, for example, you are working in Excel, you will see the various sheets in a workbook, whereas in an Access database you will see forms and reports.

The VBA statements for the selected module (Module1 in Figure 3) appear in the code window in the right pane. The module, in turn, contains declarations and procedures that are separated by horizontal lines. There are two procedures, MsgBoxExamples and InputBoxExamples, each of which was explained previously. A ***comment*** (nonexecutable) statement has been added to each procedure and appears in green. It is the apostrophe at the beginning of the line, rather than the color, that denotes a comment.

The ***Declarations section*** appears at the beginning of the module and contains a single statement, ***Option Explicit***. This option requires every variable in a procedure to be explicitly defined (e.g., in a Dim statement) before it can be used elsewhere in the module. It is an important option and should appear in every module you write.

The remainder of the window should look reasonably familiar in that it is similar to any other Office application. The title bar appears at the top of the window and identifies the application (Microsoft Visual Basic) and the current document (VBA Examples.xls). The right side of the title bar contains the Minimize, Restore, and Close buttons. A menu bar appears under the title bar. Toolbars are displayed under the menu bar. Commands are executed by pulling down the appropriate menu, via buttons on the toolbar, or by keyboard shortcuts.

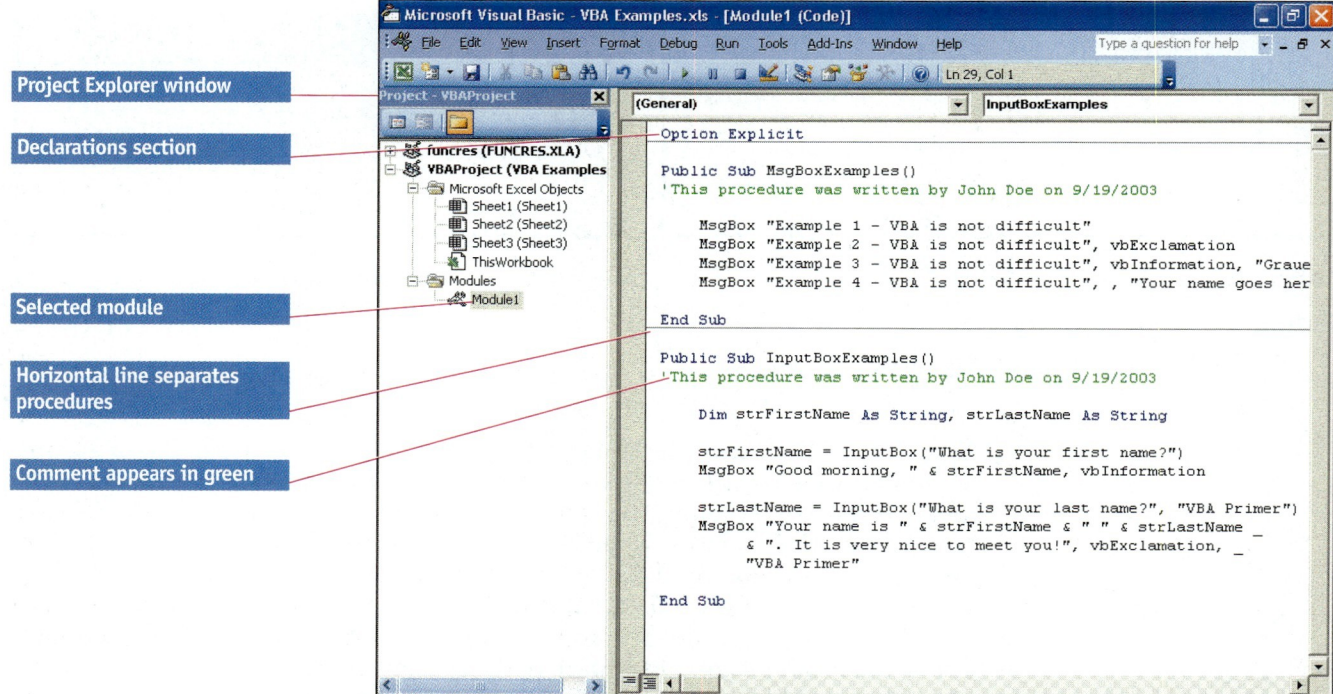

FIGURE 3 The VBA Editor

Introduction to VBA

Objective To create and test VBA procedures using the MsgBox and InputBox statements. Use Figure 4 as a guide in the exercise. You can do the exercise in any Office application.

Step 1a: **Start Microsoft Excel**

■ We suggest you do the exercise in either Excel or Access (although you could use Word or PowerPoint just as easily). Go to step 1b for Access.

■ Start **Microsoft Excel** and open a new workbook. Pull down the **File menu** and click the **Save command** (or click the **Save button** on the Standard toolbar) to display the Save As dialog box. Choose an appropriate drive and folder, then save the workbook as **VBA Examples**.

■ Pull down the **Tools menu**, click the **Macro command**, then click the **Visual Basic Editor command** as shown in Figure 4a. Go to step 2.

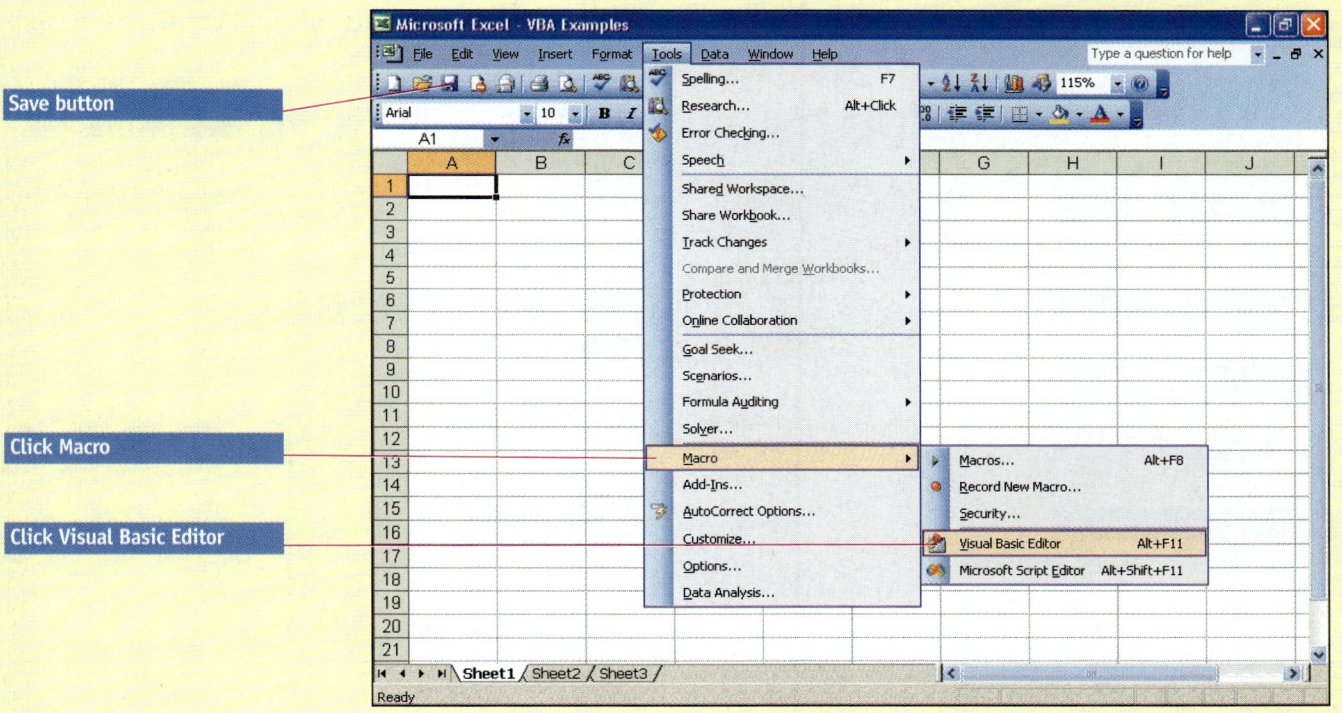

(a) Start Microsoft Excel (step 1a)

FIGURE 4 Hands-on Exercise 1

Step 1b: **Start Microsoft Access**

■ Start **Microsoft Access** and choose the option to create a **Blank Access database**. Save the database as **VBA Examples**.

■ Pull down the **Tools menu**, click the **Macro command**, then click the **Visual Basic Editor command**. (You can also use the **Alt+F11** keyboard shortcut to open the VBA editor without going through the Tools menu.)

Step 2: **Insert a Module**

- You should see a window similar to Figure 4b, but Module1 is not yet visible. Close the Properties window if it appears.

- If necessary, pull down the **View menu** and click **Project Explorer** to display the Project Explorer pane at the left of the window. Our figure shows Excel objects, but you will see the "same" window in Microsoft Access.

- Pull down the **Insert menu** and click **Module** to insert Module1 into the current project. The name of the module, Module1 in this example, appears in the Project Explorer pane.

- The Option Explicit statement may be entered automatically, but if not, click in the code window and type the statement **Option Explicit**.

- Pull down the **Insert menu** a second time, but this time select **Procedure** to display the Add Procedure dialog box in Figure 4b. Click in the **Name** text box and enter **MsgBoxExamples** as the name of the procedure. (Spaces are not allowed in a procedure name.)

- Click the option buttons for a **Sub procedure** and for **Public scope**. Click **OK**. The sub procedure should appear within the module and consist of the Sub and End Sub statements.

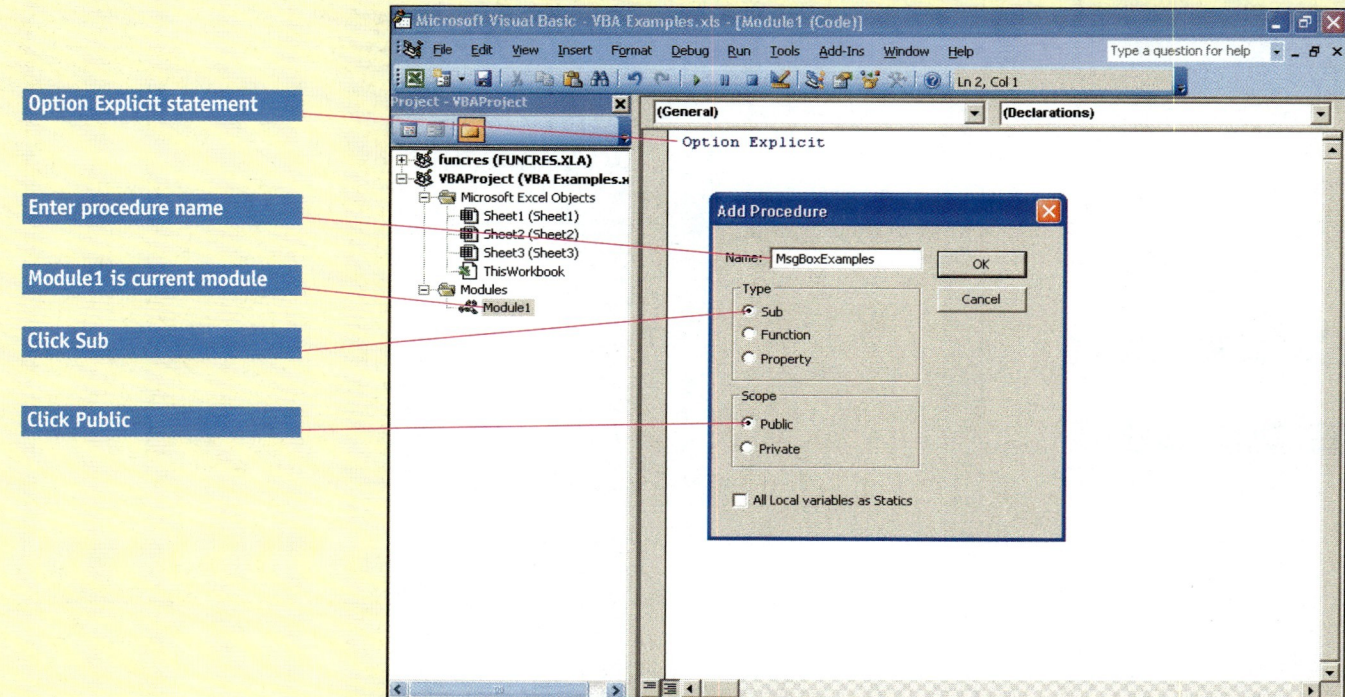

(b) Insert a Module (step 2)

FIGURE 4 Hands-on Exercise 1 (*continued*)

THE OPTION EXPLICIT STATEMENT

The Option Explicit statement is optional, but if it is used it must appear in a module before any procedures. The statement requires that all variables in the module be declared explicitly by the programmer (typically with a Dim, Public, or Private statement), as opposed to VBA making an implicit assumption about the variable. It is good programming practice and it should be used every time.

Step 3: The MsgBox Statement

- The insertion point (the flashing cursor) appears below the first statement. Press the **Tab key** to indent the next statement. (Indentation is not a VBA requirement, but is used to increase the readability of the statement.)

- Type the keyword **MsgBox**, then press the **space bar**. VBA responds with Quick Info that displays the syntax of the statement as shown in Figure 4c.

- Type a **quotation mark** to begin the literal, enter the text of your message, **This is my first VBA procedure**, then type the closing **quotation mark**.

- Click the **Run Sub button** on the Standard toolbar (or pull down the **Run menu** and click the **Run Sub command**) to execute the procedure.

- You should see a dialog box, containing the text you entered, within the Excel workbook (or other Office document) on which you are working.

- After you have read the message, click **OK** to return to the VBA editor.

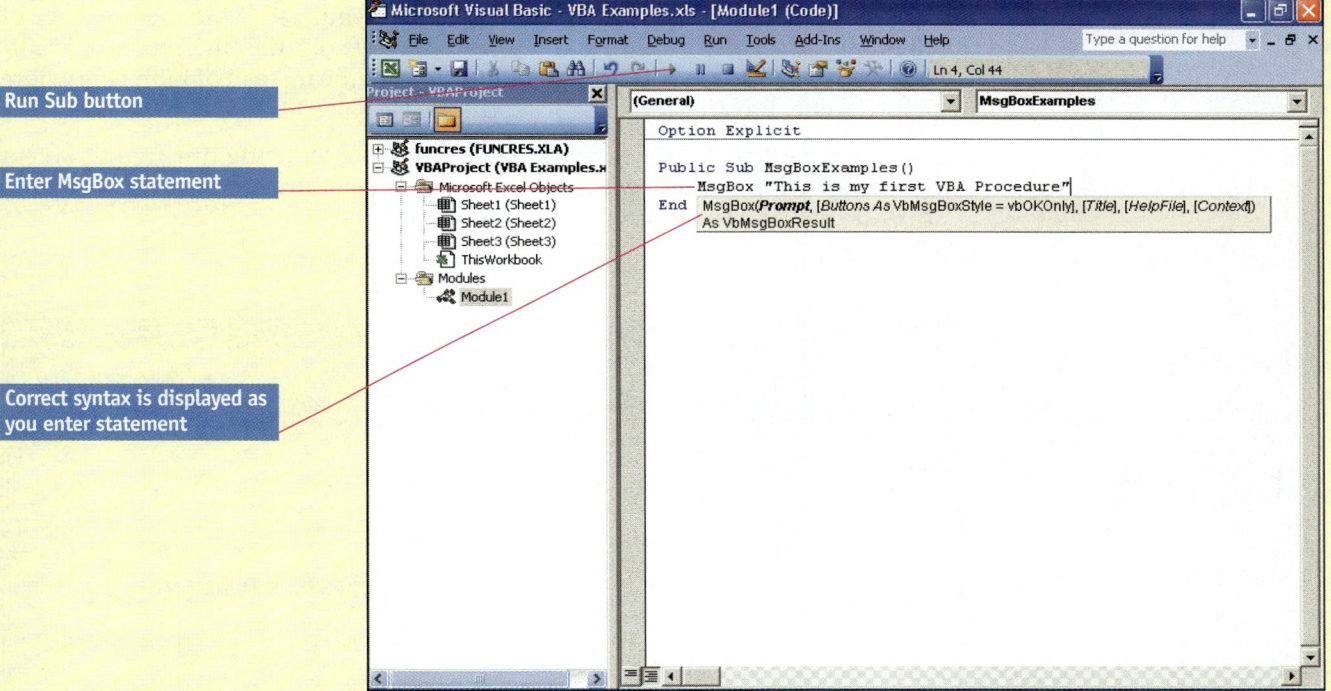

(c) The MsgBox Statement (step 3)

FIGURE 4 Hands-on Exercise 1 (*continued*)

QUICK INFO—HELP WITH VBA SYNTAX

Press the space bar after entering the name of a statement (e.g., MsgBox), and VBA responds with a Quick Info box that displays the syntax of the statement. You see the arguments in the statement and the order in which those arguments appear. Any argument in brackets is optional. If you do not see this information, pull down the Tools menu, click the Options command, then click the Editor tab. Check the box for Auto Quick Info and click OK.

Step 4: Complete the Procedure

- You should be back within the MsgBoxExamples procedure. If necessary, click at the end of the MsgBox statement, then press **Enter** to begin a new line. Type **MsgBox** and press the **space bar** to begin entering the statement.

- The syntax of the MsgBox statement will appear on the screen. Type a **quotation mark** to begin the message, type **Add an icon** as the text of this message, then type the closing **quotation mark**. Type a **comma**, then press the **space bar** to enter the next parameter.

- VBA automatically displays a list of appropriate parameters, in this case a series of intrinsic constants that define the icon or command button that is to appear in the statement.

- You can type the first several letters (e.g., **vbi**, for vbInformation), then press the **space bar**, or you can use the **down arrow** to select **vbInformation** and then press the **space bar**. Either way you should complete the second MsgBox statement as shown in Figure 4d. Press **Enter**.

- Enter the third MsgBox statement as shown in Figure 4d. Note the presence of the two consecutive commas to indicate that we omitted the second parameter within the MsgBox statement. Enter your name instead of John Doe where appropriate. Press **Enter**.

- Enter the fourth (and last) MsgBox statement following our figure. Select **vbExclamation** as the second parameter, type a **comma**, then enter the text of the title bar, as you did for the previous statement.

- Click the **Save button** to save the changes to the module.

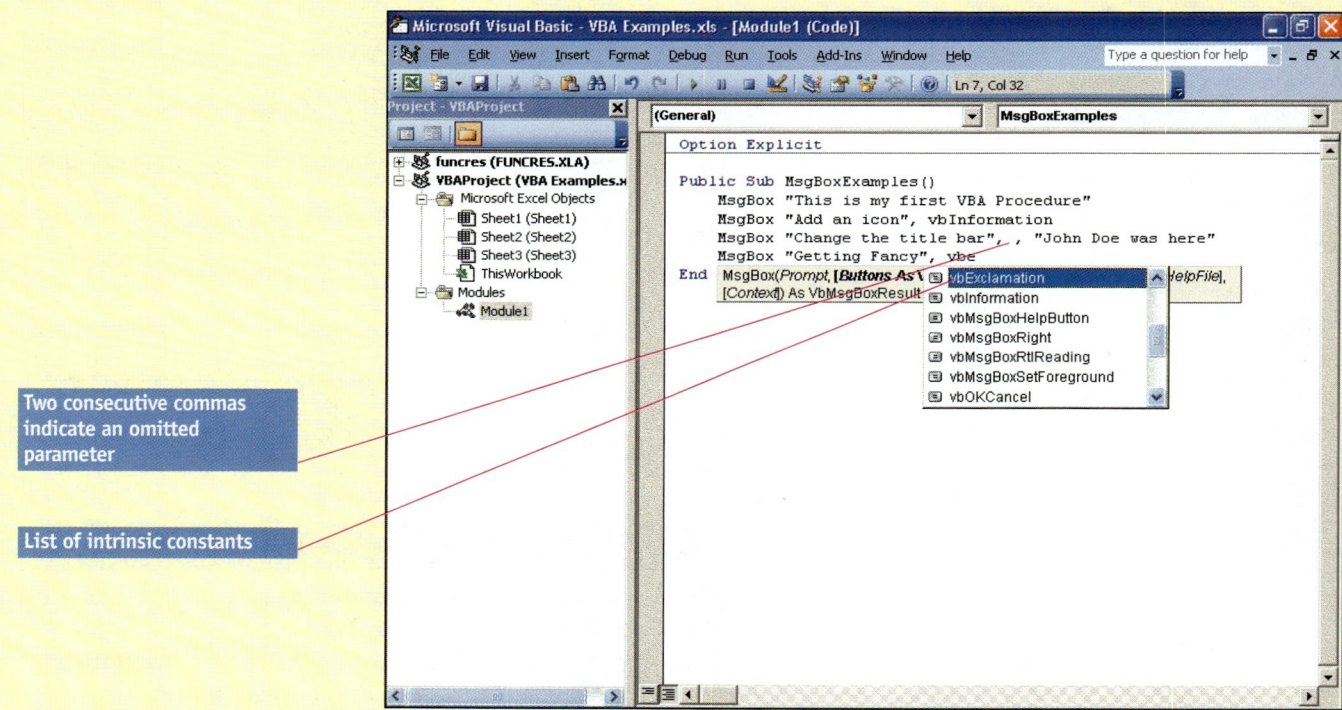

(d) Complete the Procedure (step 4)

FIGURE 4   Hands-on Exercise 1 (*continued*)

Step 5: Test the Procedure

- It's convenient if you can see the statements in the VBA procedure at the same time you see the output of those statements. Thus we suggest that you tile the VBA editor and the associated Office application.

- Minimize all applications except the VBA editor and the Office application (e.g., Excel).

- Right click the taskbar and click **Tile Windows Horizontally** to tile the windows as shown in Figure 4e. (It does not matter which window is on top. If you see more than these two windows, minimize the other open window, then right click the taskbar and retile the windows.)

- Click anywhere in the VBA procedure, then click the **Run Sub button** on the Standard toolbar.

- The four messages will be displayed one after the other. Click **OK** after each message.

- Maximize the VBA window to continue working.

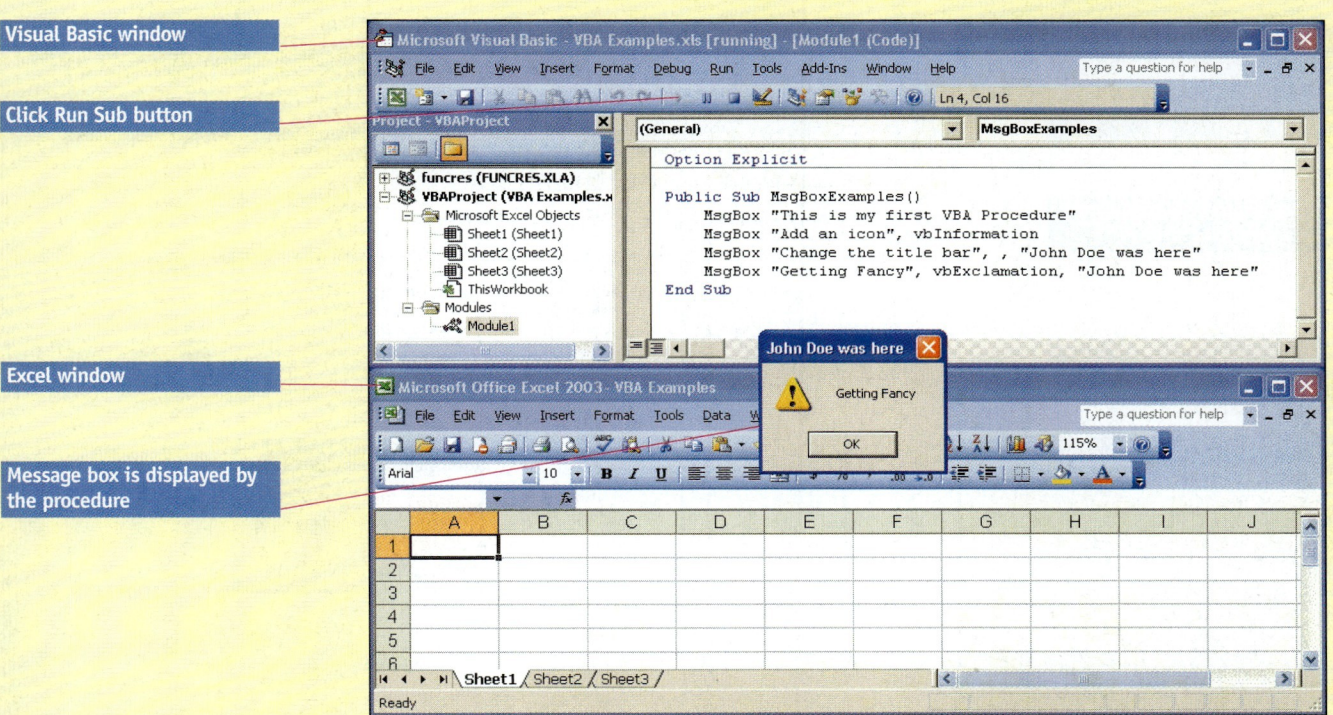

(e) Test the Procedure (step 5)

FIGURE 4 Hands-on Exercise 1 (*continued*)

HIDE THE WINDOWS TASKBAR

You can hide the Windows taskbar to gain additional space on the desktop. Right click any empty area of the taskbar to display a context-sensitive menu, click Properties to display the Taskbar properties dialog box, and if necessary click the Taskbar tab. Check the box to Auto Hide the taskbar, then click OK. The taskbar disappears from the screen but will reappear as you point to the bottom edge of the desktop.

Step 6: Comments and Corrections

■ All VBA procedures should be documented with the author's name, date, and other comments as necessary to explain the procedure. Click after the procedure header. Press the **Enter key** to leave a blank line.

■ Press **Enter** a second time. Type an **apostrophe** to begin the comment, then enter a descriptive statement similar to Figure 4f. Press **Enter** when you have completed the comment. The line turns green to indicate it is a comment.

■ The best time to experiment with debugging is when you know your procedure is correct. Go to the last MsgBox statement and delete the quotation mark in front of your name. Move to the end of the line and press **Enter**.

■ You should see the error message in Figure 4f. Unfortunately, the message is not as explicit as it could be; VBA cannot tell that you left out a quotation mark, but it does detect an error in syntax.

■ Click **OK** in response to the error. Click the **Undo button** twice, to restore the quotation mark, which in turn corrects the statement.

■ Click the **Save button** to save the changes to the module.

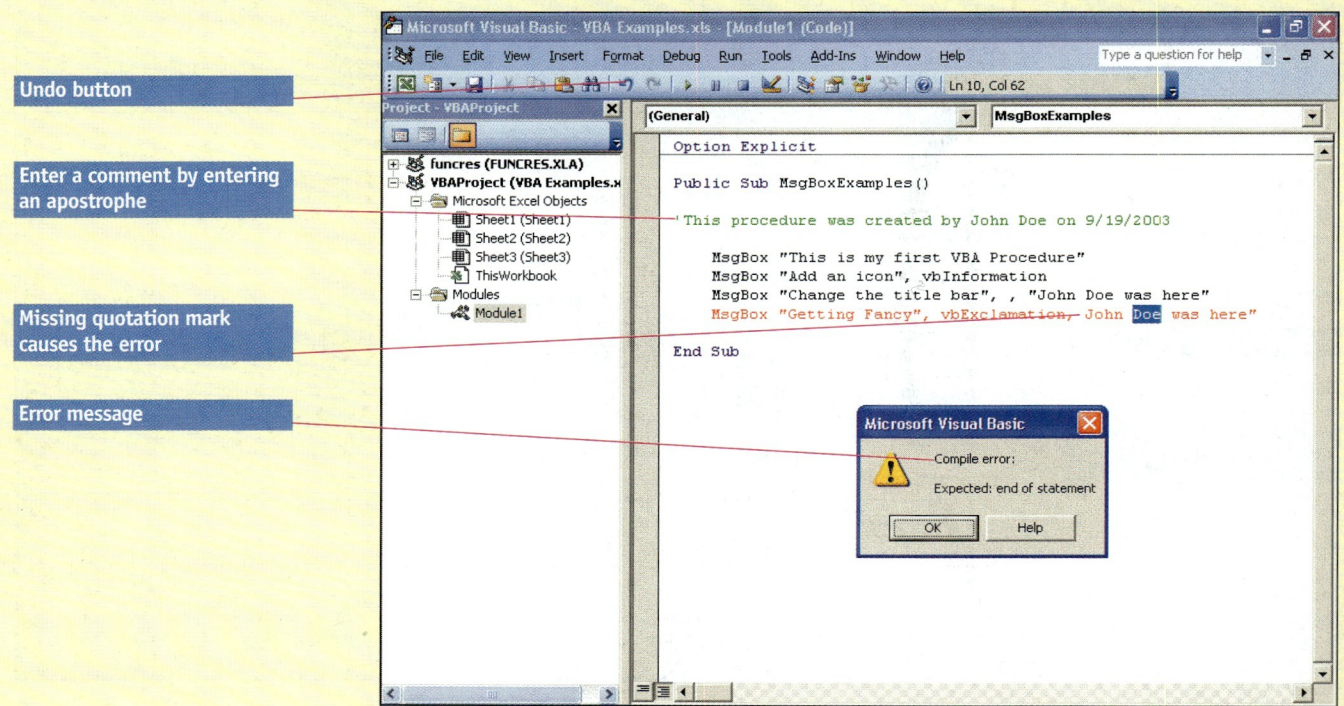

Undo button

Enter a comment by entering an apostrophe

Missing quotation mark causes the error

Error message

(f) Comments and Corrections (step 6)

FIGURE 4 Hands-on Exercise 1 (*continued*)

RED, GREEN, AND BLUE

Visual Basic for Applications uses different colors for different types of statements (or a portion of those statements). Any statement containing a syntax error appears in red. Comments appear in green. Keywords, such as Sub and End Sub, appear in blue.

Step 7: Create a Second Procedure

■ Pull down the **Insert menu** and click **Procedure** to display the Add Procedure dialog box. Enter **InputBoxExamples** as the name of the procedure. (Spaces are not allowed in a procedure name.)

■ Click the option buttons for a **Sub procedure** and for **Public scope**. Click **OK**. The new sub procedure will appear within the existing module below the existing MsgBoxExamples procedure.

■ Enter the statements in the procedure as they appear in Figure 4g. Be sure to type a space between the ampersand and the underscore in the second MsgBox statement. Click the **Save button** to save the procedure before testing it.

■ You can display the output of the procedure directly in the VBA window if you minimize the Excel window. Thus, **right click** the Excel button on the taskbar to display a context-sensitive menu, then click the **Minimize command**. There is no visible change on your monitor.

■ Click the **Run Sub button** to test the procedure. This time you see the Input box displayed on top of the VBA window because the Excel window has been minimized.

■ Enter your first name in response to the initial prompt, then click **OK**. Click **OK** when you see the message box that says "Hello".

■ Enter your last name in response to the second prompt and click **OK**. You should see a message box similar to the one in Figure 4g. Click **OK**.

■ Return to the VBA procedure to correct any mistakes that might occur. Save the module.

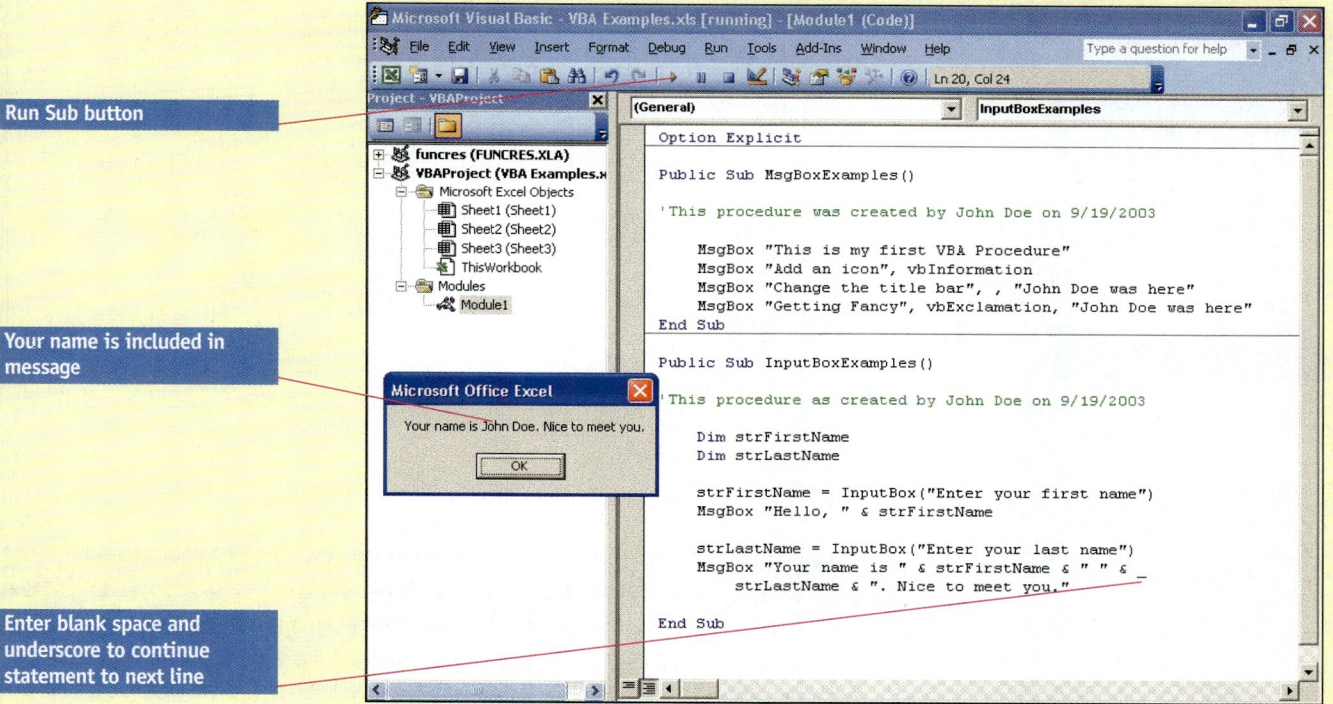

(g) Create a Second Procedure (step 7)

FIGURE 4 Hands-on Exercise 1 (*continued*)

Step 8:   Create a Public Constant

■ Click after the Options Explicit statement and press **Enter** to move to a new line. Type the statement to define the constant, **ApplicationTitle**, as shown in Figure 4h, and press **Enter**.

■ Click anywhere in the MsgBoxExamples procedure, then change the third argument in the last MsgBox statement to ApplicationTitle. Make the four modifications in the InputBoxExamples procedure as shown in Figure 4h.

■ Click anywhere in the InputBoxExamples procedure, then click the **Run Sub button** to test the procedure. The title bar of each dialog box will contain a descriptive title corresponding to the value of the ApplicationTitle constant.

■ Change the value of the ApplicationTitle constant in the General Declarations section, then rerun the InputBoxExamples procedure. The title of every dialog box changes to reflect the new value.

■ Save the procedure. Do you see the advantage of defining a title in the General Declarations section?

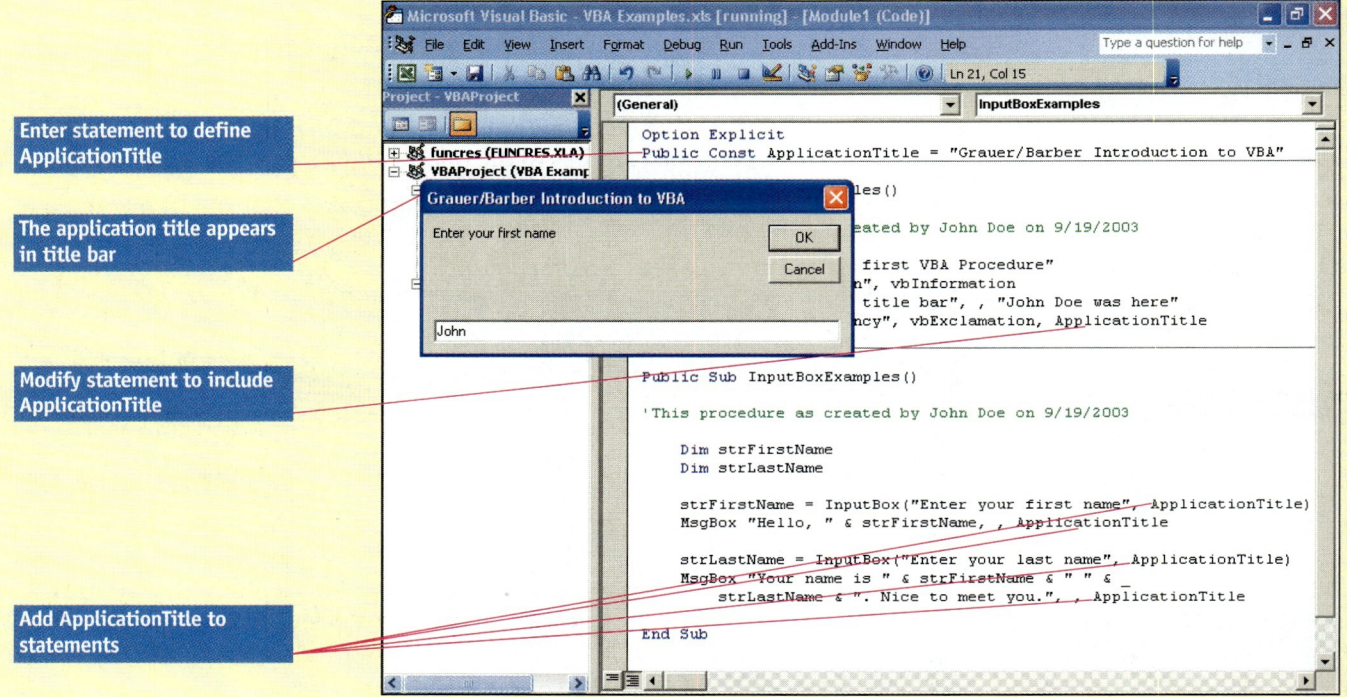

(h) Create a Public Constant (step 8)

FIGURE 4   Hands-on Exercise 1 (*continued*)

CONTINUING A VBA STATEMENT—THE & AND THE UNDERSCORE

A VBA statement can be continued from one line to the next by typing a space at the end of the line to be continued, typing the underscore character, then continuing on the next line. You may not, however, break a line in the middle of a literal (character string). Thus, you need to complete the character string with a closing quotation mark, add an ampersand (as the concatenation operator to display this string with the character string on the next line), then leave a space followed by the underscore to indicate continuation.

Step 9: Help with VBA

- You should be in the VBA editor. Pull down the **Help menu** and click the **Microsoft Visual Basic Help command** to open the Help pane.

- Type **Input Box function** in the Search box, then click the arrow to initiate the search. The results should include a hyperlink to InputBox function. Click the **hyperlink** to display the Help screen in Figure 4i.

- Maximize the Help window, then explore the information on the InputBox function to reinforce your knowledge of this statement.
  - ❏ Click the **Print button** to print this page for your instructor.
  - ❏ Click the link to **Example** within the Help window to see actual code.
  - ❏ Click the link to **See Also**, which displays information about the MsgBox statement.

- Close the Help window, but leave the task pane open. Click the **green** (back) **arrow** within the task pane to display the Table of Contents for Visual Basic Help, then explore the table of contents.
  - ❏ Click any closed book to open the book and "drill down" within the list of topics. The book remains open until you click the icon a second time to close it.
  - ❏ Click any question mark icon to display the associated help topic.

- Close the task pane. Pull down the **File menu** and click the **Close and Return to Microsoft Excel command** (or click the **Close button** on the VBA title bar) to close the VBA window and return to the application. Click **Yes** if asked whether to save the changes to Module1.

- You should be back in the Excel (or Access) application window. Close the application if you do not want to continue with the next exercise at this time.

- Congratulations. You have just completed your first VBA procedure. Remember to use Help any time you have a question.

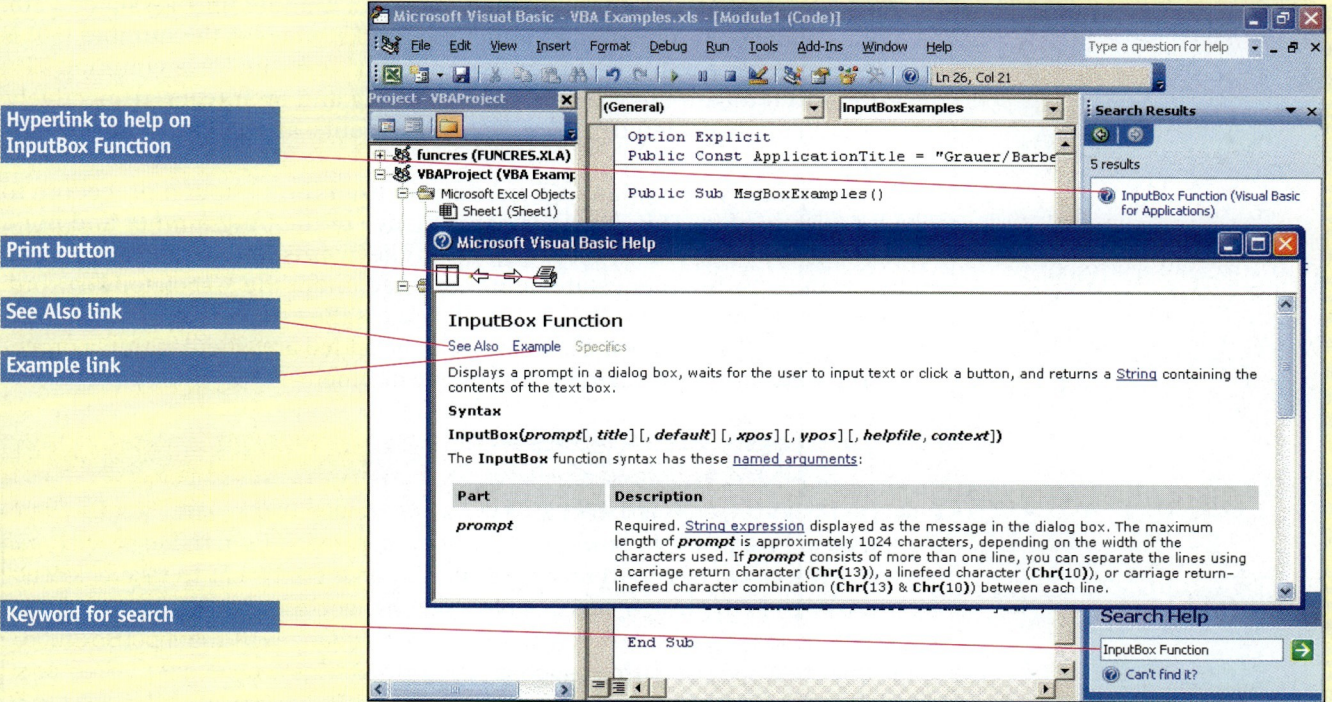

(i) Help with VBA (step 9)

FIGURE 4   Hands-on Exercise 1 (*continued*)

The ability to make decisions within a program, and then execute alternative sets of statements based on the results of those decisions, is crucial to any programming language. This is typically accomplished through an ***If statement***, which evaluates a condition as either true or false, then branches accordingly. The If statement is not used in isolation, however, but is incorporated into a procedure to accomplish a specific task as shown in Figure 5a. This procedure contains two separate If statements, and the results are displayed in the message boxes shown in the remainder of the figure.

The InputBox statement associated with Figure 5b prompts the user for the name of his or her instructor, then it stores the answer in the variable strInstructorName. The subsequent If statement then compares the user's answer to the literal "Grauer". If the condition is true (i.e., Grauer was entered into the input box), then the message in Figure 5c is displayed. If, however, the user entered any other value, then the condition is evaluated as false, the MsgBox is not displayed, and processing continues with the next statement in the procedure.

The second If statement includes an optional ***Else clause***. Again, the user is asked for a value, and the response is compared to the number 50. If the condition is true (i.e., the value of intUserStates equals 50), the message in Figure 5d is displayed to indicate that the response is correct. If, however, the condition is false (i.e., the user entered a number other than 50), the user sees the message in Figure 5e. Either way, true or false, processing continues with the next statement in the procedure. That's it—it's simple and it's powerful, and we will use the statement in the next hands-on exercise.

You can learn a good deal about VBA by looking at existing code and making inferences. Consider, for example, the difference between literals and numbers. ***Literals*** (also known as ***character strings***) are stored differently from numbers, and this is manifested in the way that comparisons are entered into a VBA statement. Look closely at the condition that references a literal (strInstructorName = "Grauer") compared to the condition that includes a number (intUserStates = 50). The literal ("Grauer") is enclosed in quotation marks, whereas the number (50) is not. (The prefix used in front of each variable, "str" and "int", is a common VBA convention to indicate the variable type—a string and an integer, respectively. Both variables are declared in the Dim statements at the beginning of the procedure.)

Note, too, that indentation and spacing are used throughout a procedure to make it easier to read. This is for the convenience of the programmer and not a requirement for VBA. The If, Else, and End If keywords are aligned under one another, with the subsequent statements indented under the associated keyword. We also indent a continued statement, such as a MsgBox statement, which is typically coded over multiple lines. Blank lines can be added anywhere within a procedure to separate blocks of statements from one another.

THE MSGBOX FUNCTION—YES OR NO

A simple MsgBox statement merely displays information to the user. MsgBox can also be used as a function, however, to accept information from the user such as clicking a Yes or No button, then combined with an If statement to take different actions based on the user's input. In essence, you enclose the arguments of the MsgBox function in parentheses (similar to what is done with the InputBox function), then test for the user response using the intrinsic constants vbYes and vbNo. The statement, If MsgBox("Are you having fun?", vbYesNo)=vbYes asks the user a question, displays Yes and No command buttons, then tests to see if the user clicked the Yes button.

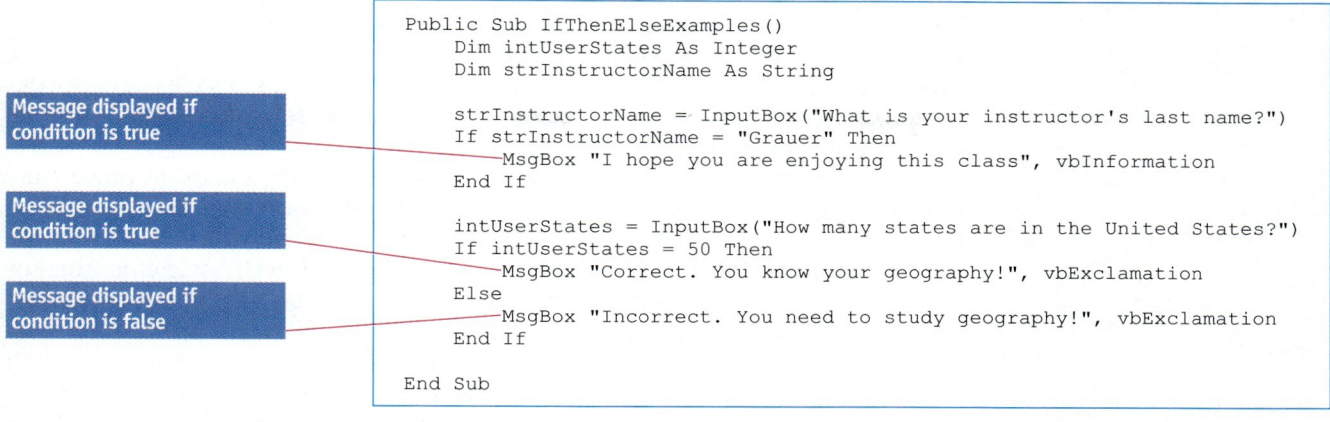

```
Public Sub IfThenElseExamples()
    Dim intUserStates As Integer
    Dim strInstructorName As String

    strInstructorName = InputBox("What is your instructor's last name?")
    If strInstructorName = "Grauer" Then
        MsgBox "I hope you are enjoying this class", vbInformation
    End If

    intUserStates = InputBox("How many states are in the United States?")
    If intUserStates = 50 Then
        MsgBox "Correct. You know your geography!", vbExclamation
    Else
        MsgBox "Incorrect. You need to study geography!", vbExclamation
    End If

End Sub
```

Message displayed if condition is true

Message displayed if condition is true

Message displayed if condition is false

(a) VBA Code

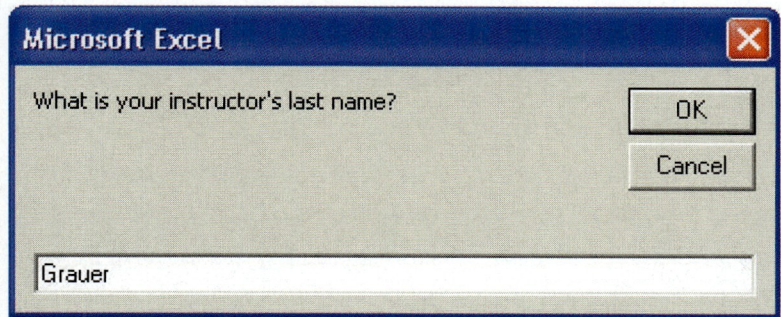

(b) InputBox Prompts for User Response

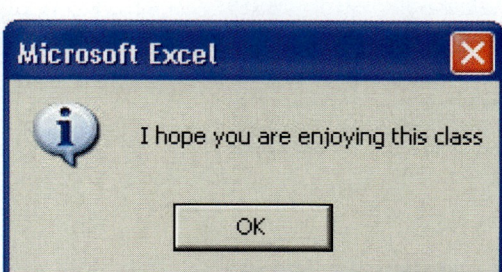

(c) Condition Is True

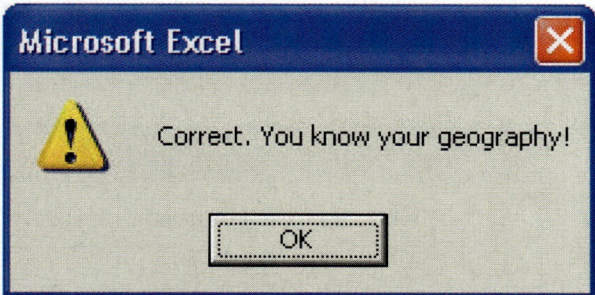

(d) Answer Is Correct (condition is true)

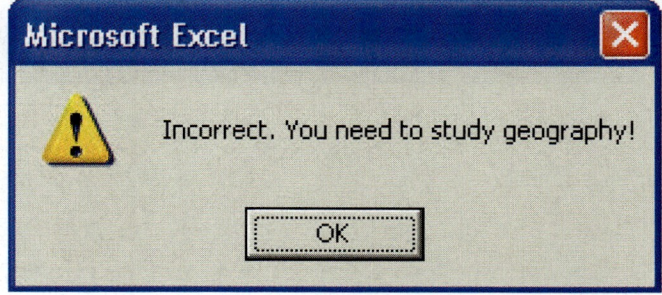

(e) Answer Is Wrong (condition is false)

FIGURE 5 The If Statement

CASE STATEMENT

The If statement is ideal for testing simple conditions and taking one of two actions. Although it can be extended to include additional actions by including one or more ElseIf clauses (If . . . Then . . . ElseIf . . . ElseIf . . .), this type of construction is often difficult to follow. Hence the **Case statement** is used when multiple branches are possible.

The procedure in Figure 6a accepts a student's GPA, then displays one of several messages, depending on the value of the GPA. The individual cases are evaluated in sequence. (The GPAs must be evaluated in descending order if the statement is to work correctly.) Thus, we check first to see if the GPA is greater than or equal to 3.9, then 3.75, then 3.5, and so on. If none of the cases is true, the statement following the Else clause is executed.

Note, too, the format of the comparison in that numbers (such as 3.9 or 3.75) are not enclosed in quotation marks because the associated variable (sngUserGPA) was declared as numeric. If, however, we had been evaluating a string variable (such as, strUserMajor), quotation marks would have been required around the literal values (e.g., Case Is = "Business", Case Is = "Liberal Arts", and so on). The distinction between numeric and character (string) variables is important.

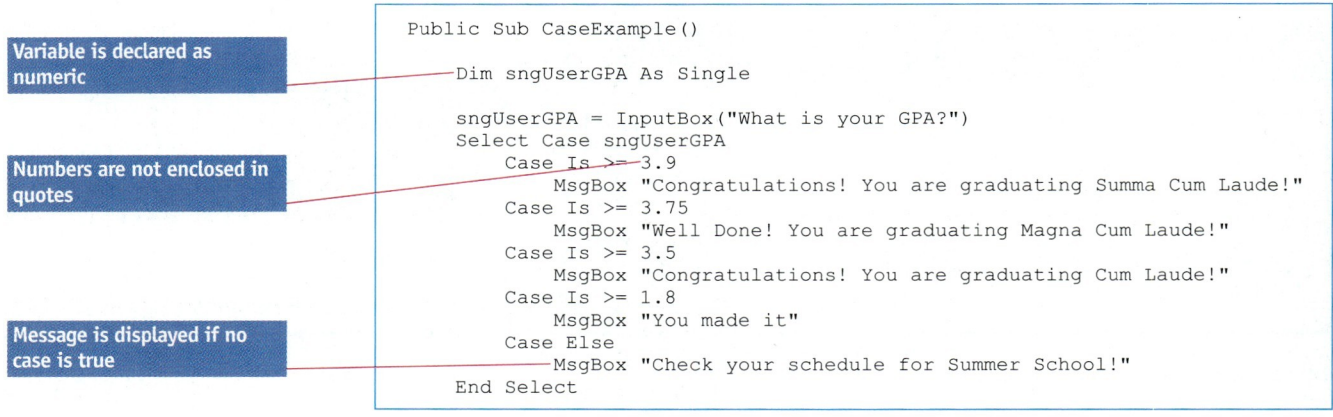

Variable is declared as numeric

Numbers are not enclosed in quotes

Message is displayed if no case is true

```
Public Sub CaseExample()

    Dim sngUserGPA As Single

    sngUserGPA = InputBox("What is your GPA?")
    Select Case sngUserGPA
        Case Is >= 3.9
            MsgBox "Congratulations! You are graduating Summa Cum Laude!"
        Case Is >= 3.75
            MsgBox "Well Done! You are graduating Magna Cum Laude!"
        Case Is >= 3.5
            MsgBox "Congratulations! You are graduating Cum Laude!"
        Case Is >= 1.8
            MsgBox "You made it"
        Case Else
            MsgBox "Check your schedule for Summer School!"
    End Select
```

(a) VBA Code

(b) Enter the GPA

(c) Third Option Is Selected

FIGURE 6 The Case Statement

CUSTOM TOOLBARS

A VBA procedure can be executed in several different ways. It can be run from the Visual Basic editor by pulling down the Run menu and clicking the Run Sub button on the Standard toolbar, or using the F5 function key. It can also be run from within the Office application (Word, Excel, or PowerPoint, but not Access), by pulling down the Tools menu, clicking the Macro command, then choosing the name of the macro that corresponds to the name of the procedure.

Perhaps the best way, however, is to create a ***custom toolbar*** that is displayed within the application as shown in Figure 7. (A custom menu can also be created that contains the same commands as the custom toolbar.) The toolbar has its own name (Bob's Toolbar), yet it functions identically to any other Office toolbar. You have your choice of displaying buttons only, text only, or both buttons and text. Our toolbar provides access to four commands, each corresponding to a procedure that was discussed earlier. Click the Case Example button, for example, and the associated procedure is executed, starting with the InputBox statement asking for the user's GPA.

A custom toolbar is created via the Toolbars command within the View menu. The new toolbar is initially big enough to hold only a single button, but you can add, move, and delete buttons following the same procedure as for any other Office toolbar. You can add any command at all to the toolbar; that is, you can add existing commands from within the Office application, or you can add commands that correspond to VBA procedures that you have created. Remember, too, that you can add more buttons to existing office toolbars.

Once the toolbar has been created, it is displayed or hidden just like any other Office toolbar. It can also be docked along any edge of the application window or left floating as shown in Figure 7. It's fun, it's easy, and as you may have guessed, it's time for the next hands-on exercise.

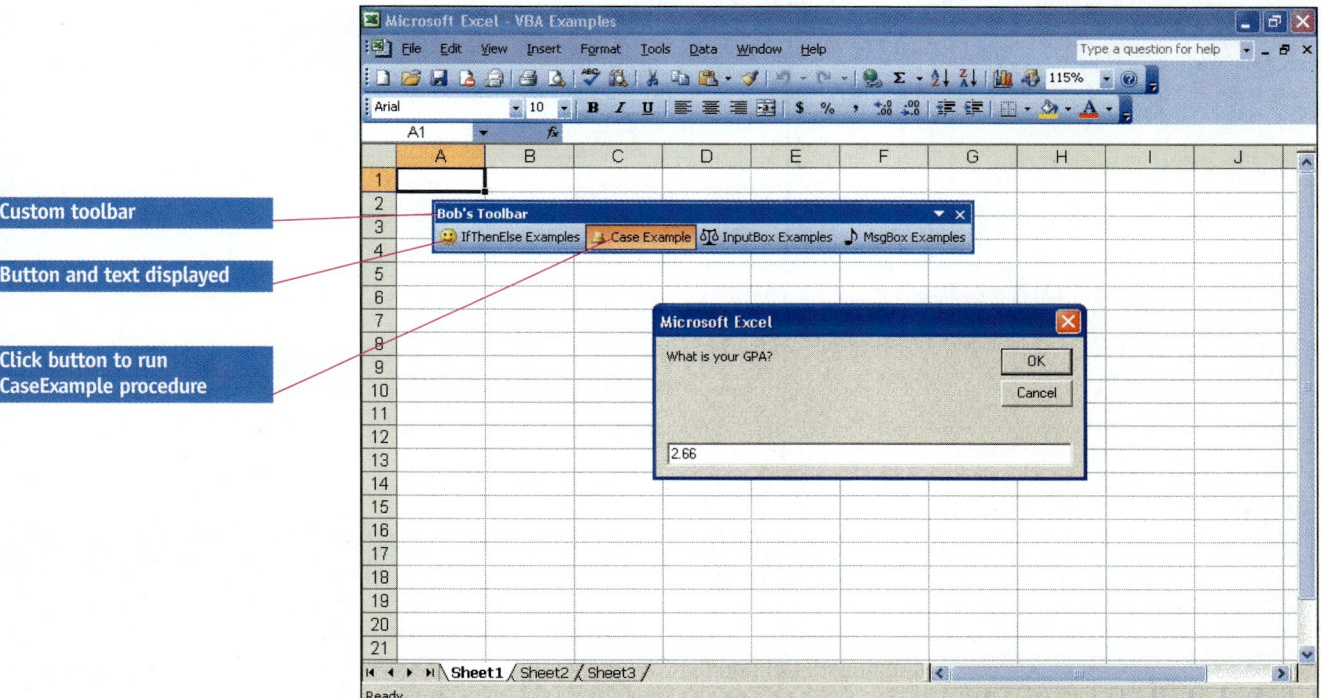

Custom toolbar

Button and text displayed

Click button to run CaseExample procedure

FIGURE 7 Custom Toolbars

Decision Making

Objective To create procedures with If . . . Then . . . Else and Case statements, then create a custom toolbar to execute those procedures. Use Figure 8 as a guide in the exercise.

Step 1: **Open the Office Document**

- Open the **VBA Examples workbook** or Access database from the previous exercise. The procedure differs slightly, depending on whether you are using Access or Excel.
  - ❑ In Access, you simply open the database.
  - ❑ In Excel you will be warned that the workbook contains a macro as shown in Figure 8a. Click the button to **Enable Macros**.

- Pull down the **Tools menu**, click the **Macro command**, then click the **Visual Basic Editor command**. You can also use the **Alt+F11** keyboard shortcut to open the VBA editor without going through the Tools menu.

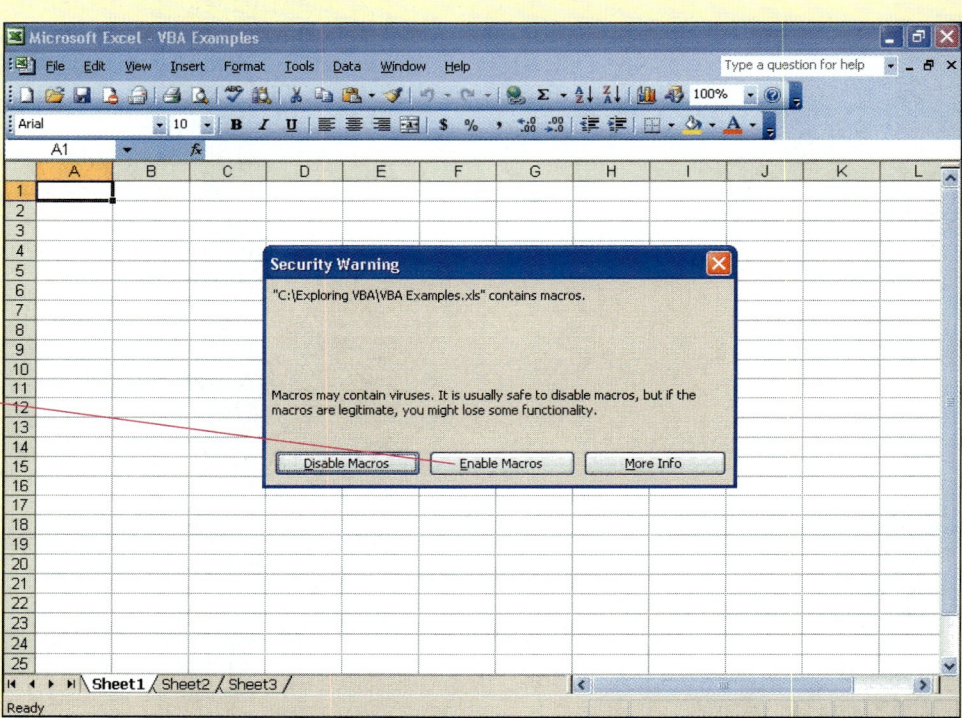

Click Enable Macros

(a) Open the Office Document (step 1)

FIGURE 8 Hands-on Exercise 2

MACRO SECURITY

A computer virus could take the form of an Excel macro; thus, Excel will warn you that a workbook contains a macro, provided the security option is set appropriately. Pull down the Tools menu, click the Options command, click the Security tab, and then set the Macro Security to either High or Medium. High security disables all macros except those from a trusted source. Medium security gives you the option to enable macros. Click the button only if you are sure the macro is from a trusted source.

Step 2:   Insert a New Procedure

- You should be in the Visual Basic editor as shown in Figure 8b. If necessary, double click **Module1** in the Explorer Window to open this module. Pull down the **Insert menu** and click the **Procedure command** to display the Add Procedure dialog box.

- Click in the **Name** text box and enter **IfThenElseExamples** as the name of the procedure. Click the option buttons for a **Sub procedure** and for **Public scope**. Click **OK** to create the procedure.

- The Sub procedure should appear within the module and consist of the Sub and End Sub statements as shown in Figure 8b.

- Click within the newly created procedure, then click the **Procedure View button** at the bottom of the window. The display changes to show just the current procedure.

- Click the **Save button** to save the module with the new procedure.

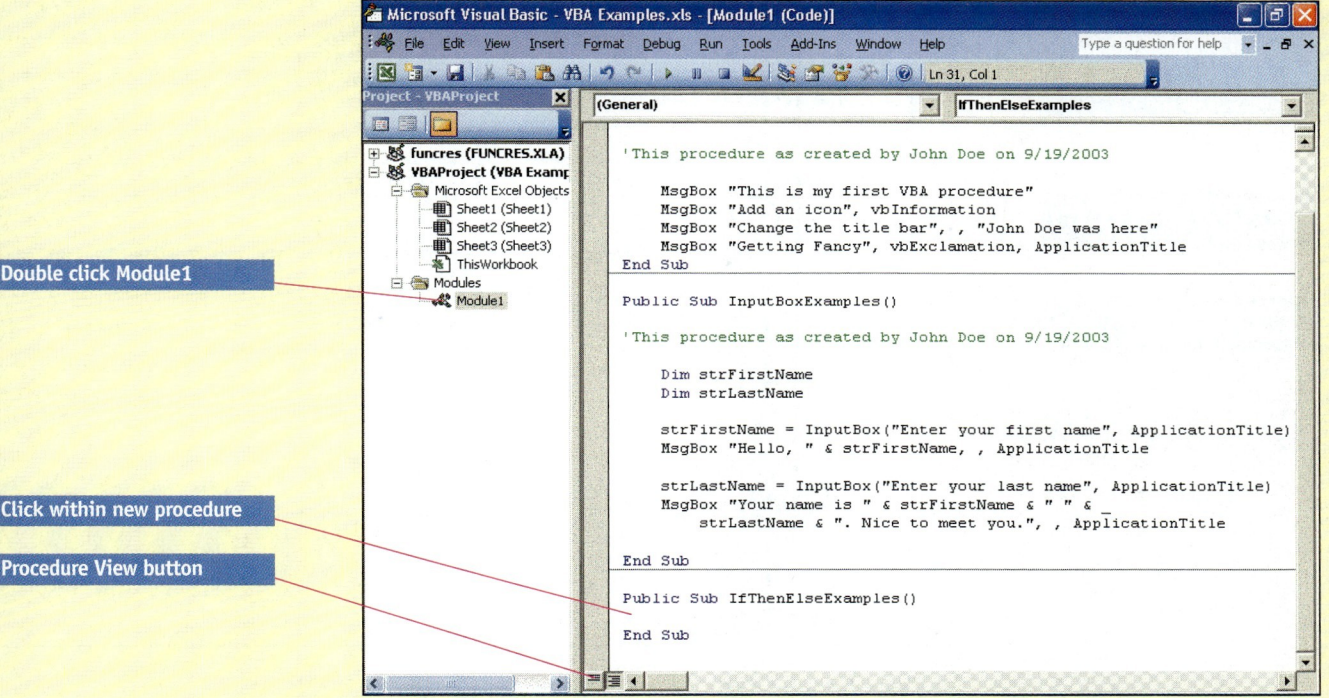

(b) Insert a New Procedure (step 2)

FIGURE 8   Hands-on Exercise 2 (*continued*)

PROCEDURE VIEW VERSUS FULL MODULE VIEW

The procedures within a module can be displayed individually, or alternatively, multiple procedures can be viewed simultaneously. To go from one view to the other, click the Procedure View button at the bottom of the window to display just the procedure you are working on, or click the Full Module View button to display multiple procedures. You can press Ctrl+PgDn and Ctrl+PgUp to move between procedures in either view.

Create the If ... Then ... Else Procedure

- Enter the IfThenElseExamples procedure as it appears in Figure 8c, but use your instructor's name instead of Bob's. Note the following:
  - ❑ The Dim statements at the beginning of the procedure are required to define the two variables that are used elsewhere in the procedure.
  - ❑ The syntax of the comparison is different for string variables versus numeric variables. String variables require quotation marks around the comparison value (e.g., strInstructorName = "Grauer"). Numeric variables (e.g., intUserStates = 50) do not.
  - ❑ Indentation and blank lines are used within a procedure to make the code easier to read, as distinct from a VBA requirement. Press the **Tab key** to indent one level to the right.
  - ❑ Comments can be added to a procedure at any time.
- Save the procedure.

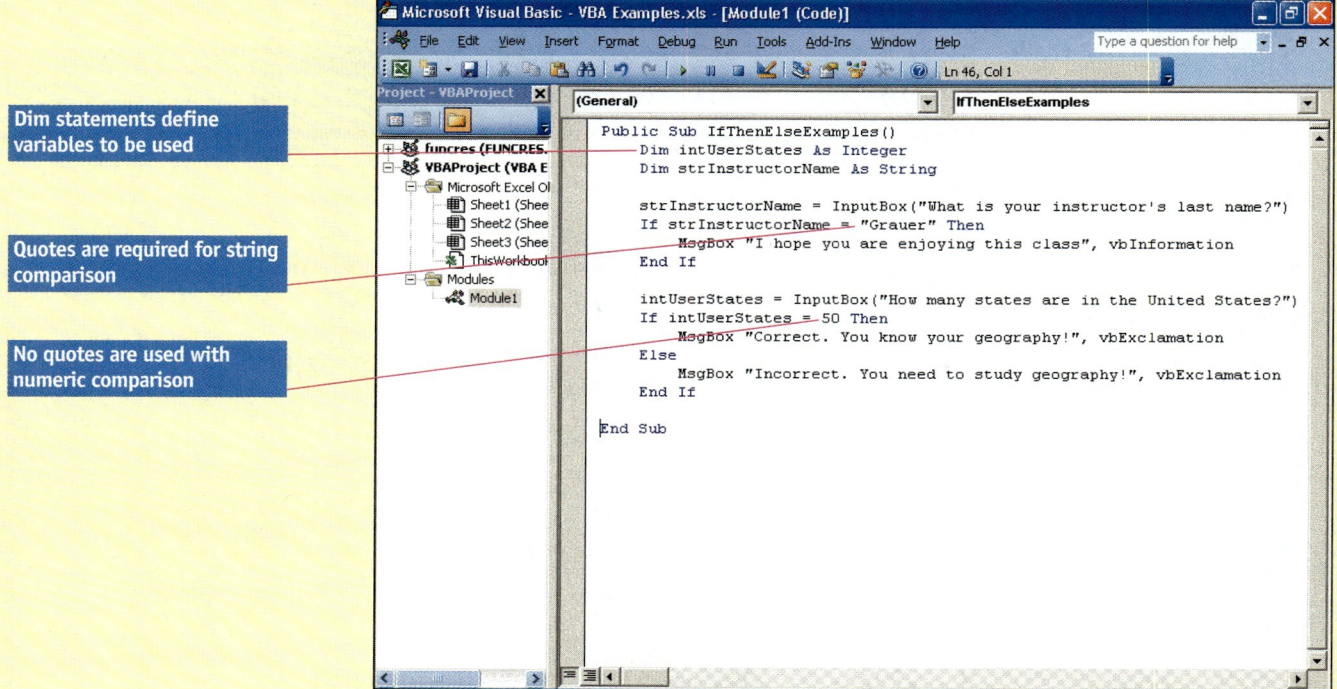

(c) Create the If ... Then ... Else Procedure (step 3)

FIGURE 8 Hands-on Exercise 2 (*continued*)

THE COMPLETE WORD TOOL

It's easy to misspell a variable name within a procedure, which is why the Complete Word tool is so useful. Type the first several characters in a variable name (such as "intU" or "strI" in the current procedure), then press Ctrl+Space. VBA will complete the variable name for you, provided that you have already entered a sufficient number of letters for a unique reference. Alternatively, it will display all of the elements that begin with the letters you have entered. Use the down arrow to scroll through the list until you find the item, then press the space bar to complete the entry.

Step 4: Test the Procedure

- The best way to test a procedure is to display its output directly in the VBA window (without having to switch back and forth between that and the application window). Thus, right click the Excel button on the taskbar to display a context-sensitive menu, then click the **Minimize command**.

- There is no visible change on your monitor. Click anywhere within the procedure, then click the **Run Sub button**. You should see the dialog box in Figure 8d.

- Enter your instructor's name, exactly as it was spelled within the VBA procedure. Click **OK**.

- You should see a second message box that hopes you are enjoying the class. This box will be displayed only if you spell the instructor's name correctly. Click **OK**.

- You should see a second input box that asks how many states are in the United States. Enter **50** and click **OK**. You should see a message indicating that you know your geography. Click **OK** to close the dialog box.

- Click the **Run Sub button** a second time, but enter a different set of values in response to the prompts. Misspell your instructor's name, and you will not see the associated message box.

- Enter any number other than 50, and you will be told to study geography.

- Continue to test the procedure until you are satisfied it works under all conditions. We cannot overemphasize the importance of thorough testing!

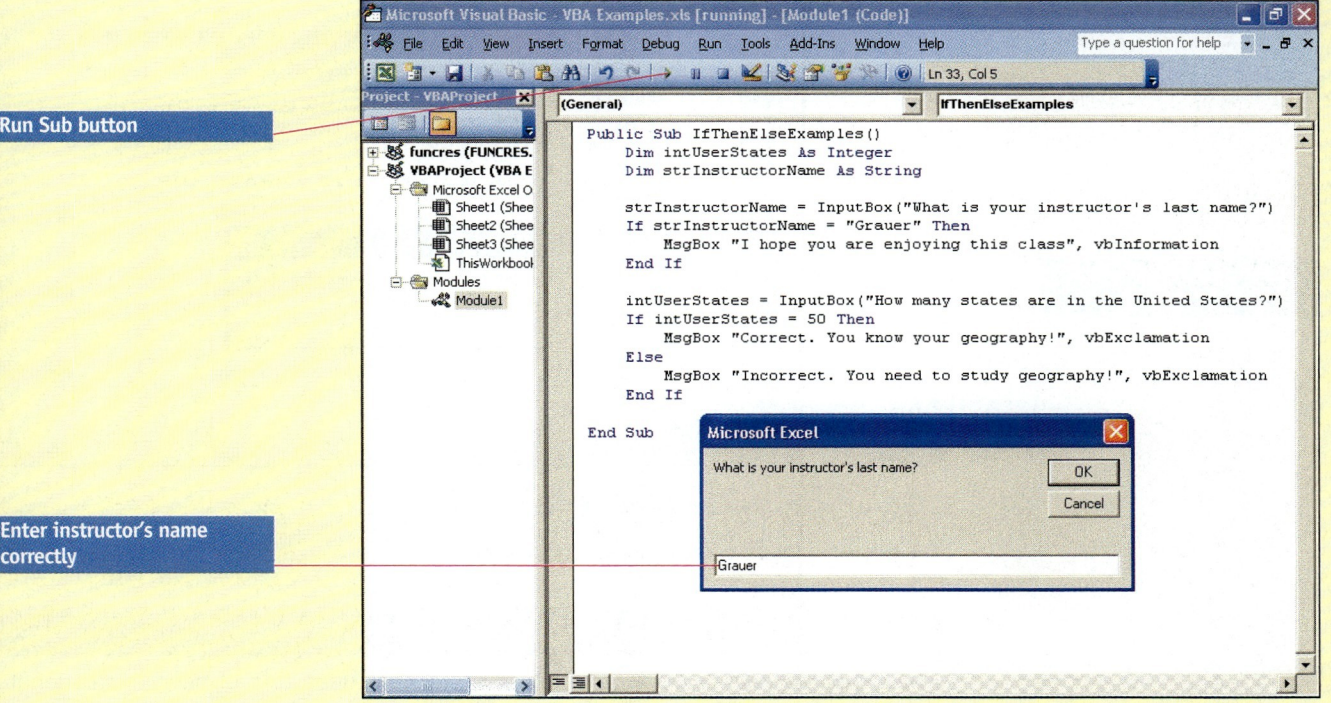

(d) Test the Procedure (step 4)

FIGURE 8   Hands-on Exercise 2 (*continued*)

Step 5: Create and Test the CaseExample Procedure

■ Pull down the **Insert menu** and create a new procedure called **CaseExample**, then enter the statements exactly as they appear in Figure 8e. Note:
  ❏ The variable sngUserGPA is declared to be a single-precision floating-point number (as distinct from the integer type that was used previously). A floating-point number is required in order to maintain a decimal point.
  ❏ The GPA must be tested in descending order if the statement is to work correctly.
  ❏ You may use any editing technique with which you are comfortable. You could, for example, enter the first case, copy it four times in the procedure, then modify the copied text as necessary.
  ❏ The use of indentation and blank lines is for the convenience of the programmer and not a requirement of VBA.

■ Click the **Run Sub button**, then test the procedure. Be sure to test it under all conditions; that is, you need to run it several times and enter a different GPA each time to be sure that all of the cases are working correctly.

■ Save the procedure.

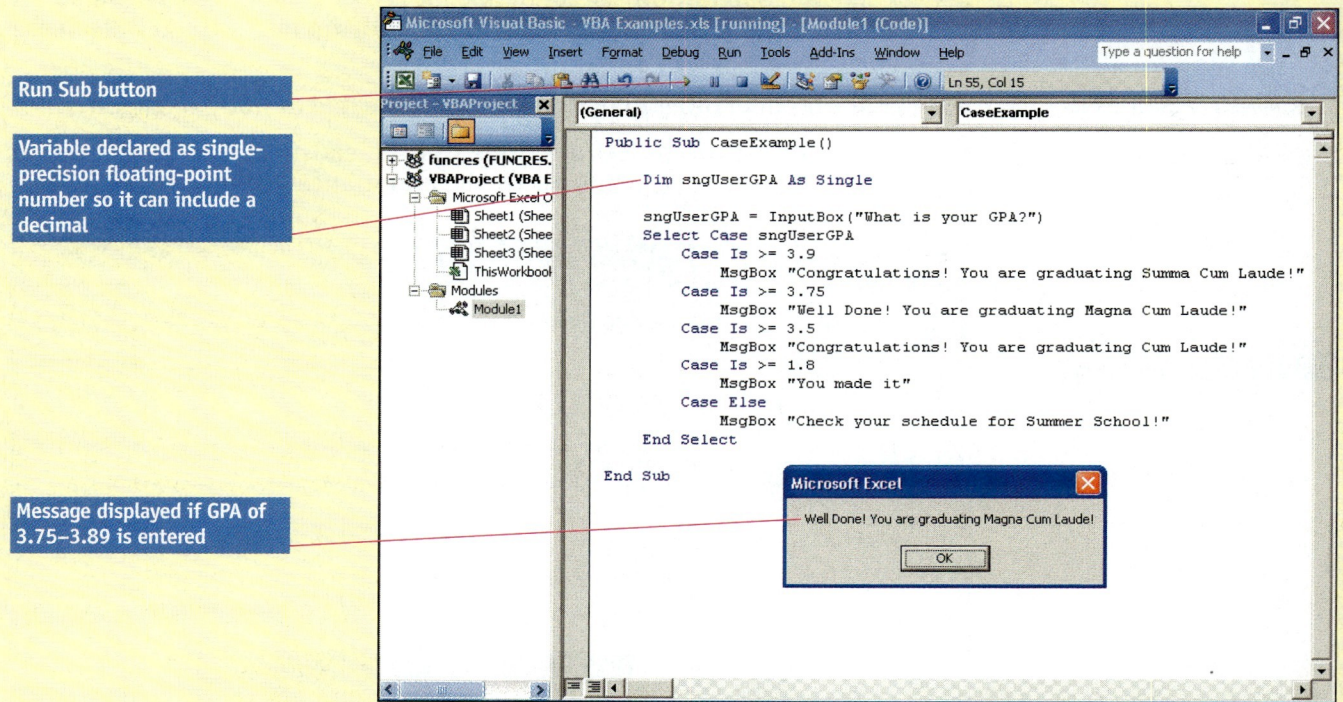

Run Sub button

Variable declared as single-precision floating-point number so it can include a decimal

Message displayed if GPA of 3.75–3.89 is entered

(e) Create and Test the CaseExample Procedure (step 5)

FIGURE 8 Hands-on Exercise 2 (*continued*)

RELATIONAL OPERATORS

The condition portion of an If or Case statement uses one of several relational operators. These include =, <, and > for equal to, less than, or greater than, respectively. You can also use >=, <=, or <> for greater than or equal to, less than or equal to, or not equal. This is basic, but very important, information if you are to code these statements correctly.

Step 6: **Create a Custom Toolbar**

■ Click the **View Microsoft Excel** (or **Access**) **button** to display the associated application window. Pull down the **View menu**, click (or point to) the **Toolbars command**, then click **Customize** to display the Customize dialog box in Figure 8f. (Bob's toolbar is not yet visible.) Click the **Toolbars tab**.

■ Click the **New button** to display the New Toolbar dialog box. Enter the name of your toolbar—e.g., **Bob's toolbar**—then click **OK** to create the toolbar and close the New Toolbar dialog box.

■ Your toolbar should appear on the screen, but it does not yet contain any buttons. If necessary, click and drag the title bar of your toolbar to move the toolbar within the application window.

■ Toggle the check box that appears next to your toolbar within the Customize dialog box on and off to display or hide your toolbar. Leave the box checked to display the toolbar and continue with this exercise.

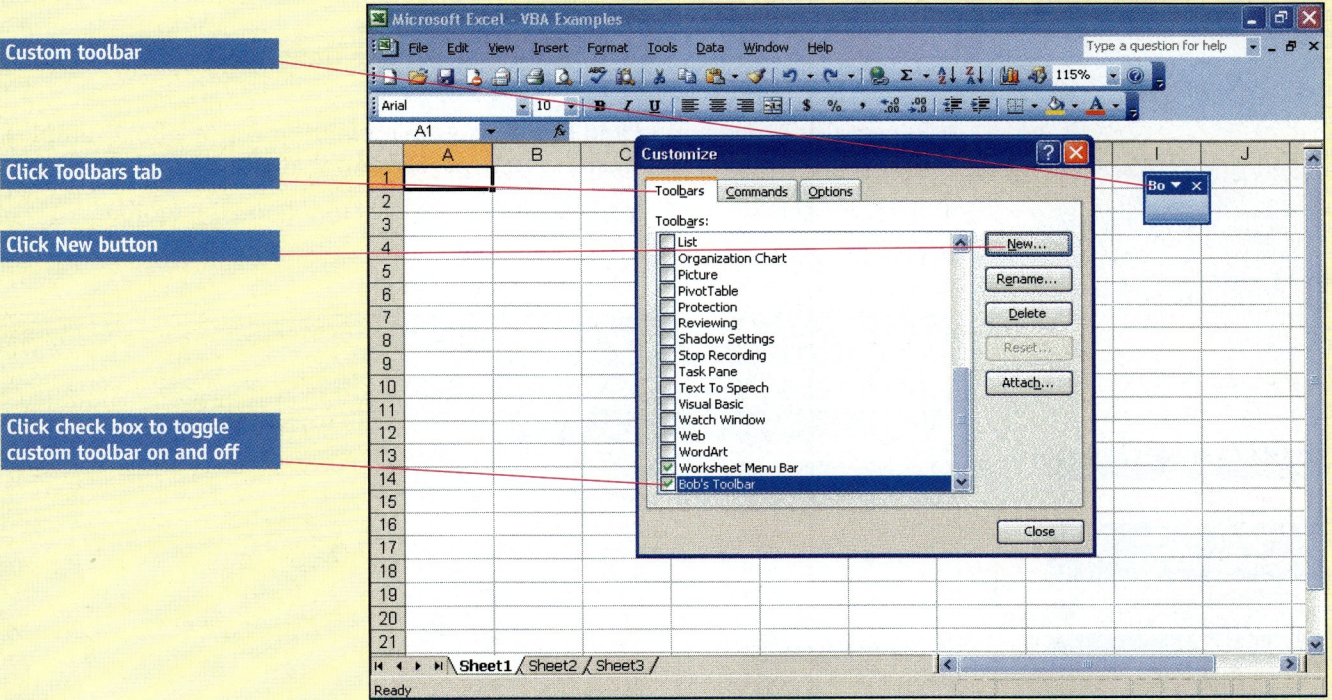

Custom toolbar

Click Toolbars tab

Click New button

Click check box to toggle custom toolbar on and off

(f) Create a Custom Toolbar (step 6)

FIGURE 8 Hands-on Exercise 2 (*continued*)

FIXED VERSUS FLOATING TOOLBARS

A toolbar may be docked (fixed) along the edge of the application window, or it can be displayed as a floating toolbar anywhere within the window. You can switch back and forth by dragging the move handle of a docked toolbar to move the toolbar away from the edge. Conversely, you can drag the title bar of a floating toolbar to the edge of the window to dock the toolbar. You can also click and drag the border of a floating toolbar to change its size.

Step 7: Add Buttons to the Toolbar

- Click the **Commands tab** in the Customize dialog box, click the **down arrow** in the Categories list box, then scroll until you can select the **Macros category**. (If you are using Access and not Excel, you need to select the **File category**, then follow the steps as described in the boxed tip on the next page.)

- Click and drag the **Custom button** to your toolbar and release the mouse. A "happy face" button appears on the toolbar you just created. (You can remove a button from a toolbar by simply dragging the button from the toolbar.)

- Select the newly created button, then click the **Modify Selection command button** (or right click the button to display the context-sensitive menu) in Figure 8g. Change the button's properties as follows:
  - ❏ Click the **Assign Macro command** at the bottom of the menu to display the Assign Macro dialog box, then select the **IfThenElseExamples macro** (procedure) to assign it to the button. Click **OK**.
  - ❏ Click the **Modify Selection button** a second time.
  - ❏ Click in the **Name Textbox** and enter an appropriate name for the button, such as **IfThenElseExamples**.
  - ❏ Click the **Modify Selection button** a third time, then click **Text Only (Always)** to display text rather than an image.

- Repeat this procedure to add buttons to the toolbar for the MsgBoxExamples, InputBoxExamples, and CaseExample procedures that you created earlier.

- Close the Customize dialog box when you have completed the toolbar.

- Save the workbook.

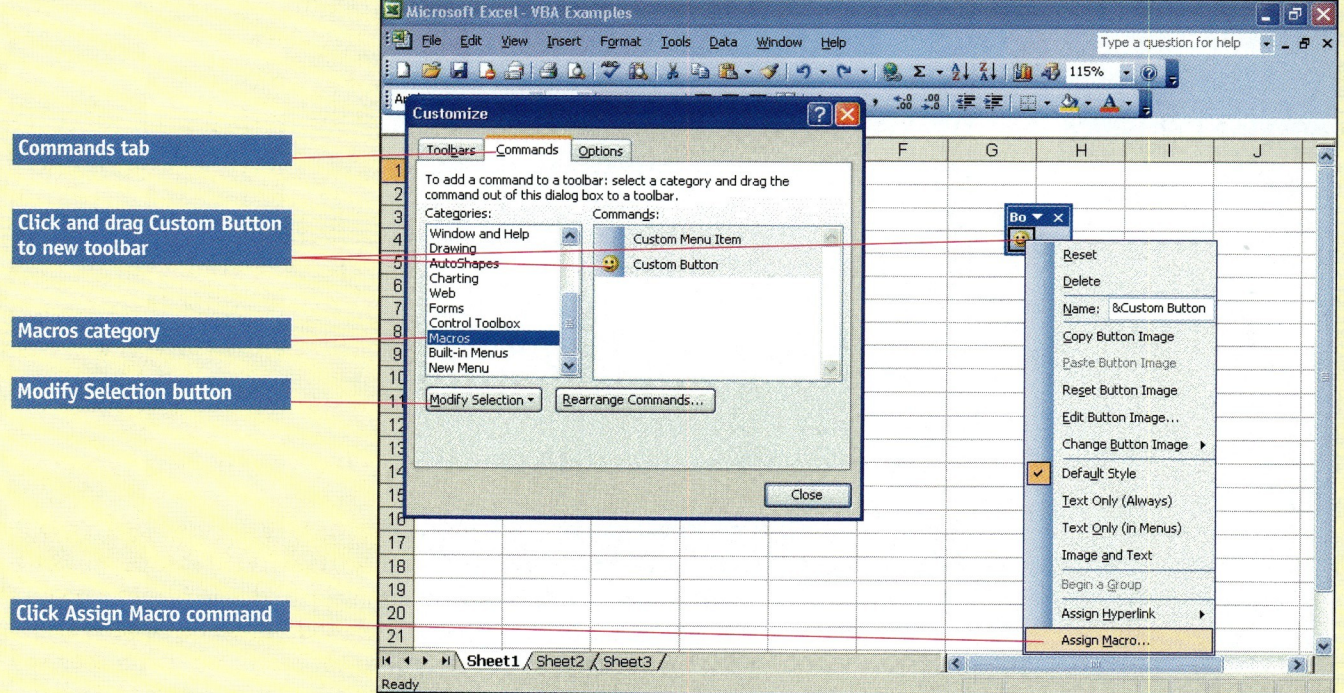

(g) Add Buttons to the Toolbar (step 7)

FIGURE 8   Hands-on Exercise 2 (*continued*)

Step 8:   **Test the Custom Toolbar**

- Click any command on your toolbar as shown in Figure 8h. We clicked the **InputBoxExamples button**, which in turn executed the InputBoxExamples procedure that was created in the first exercise.

- Enter the appropriate information in any input boxes that are displayed. Click **OK**. Close your toolbar when you have completed testing it.

- If this is not your own machine, you should delete your toolbar as a courtesy to the next student. Pull down the **View menu**, click the **Toolbars command**, click **Customize** to display the Customize dialog box, then click the **Toolbars tab**. Select (highlight) the toolbar, then click the **Delete button** in the Customize dialog box. Click **OK** to delete the button. Close the dialog box.

- Exit Office if you do not want to continue with the next exercise.

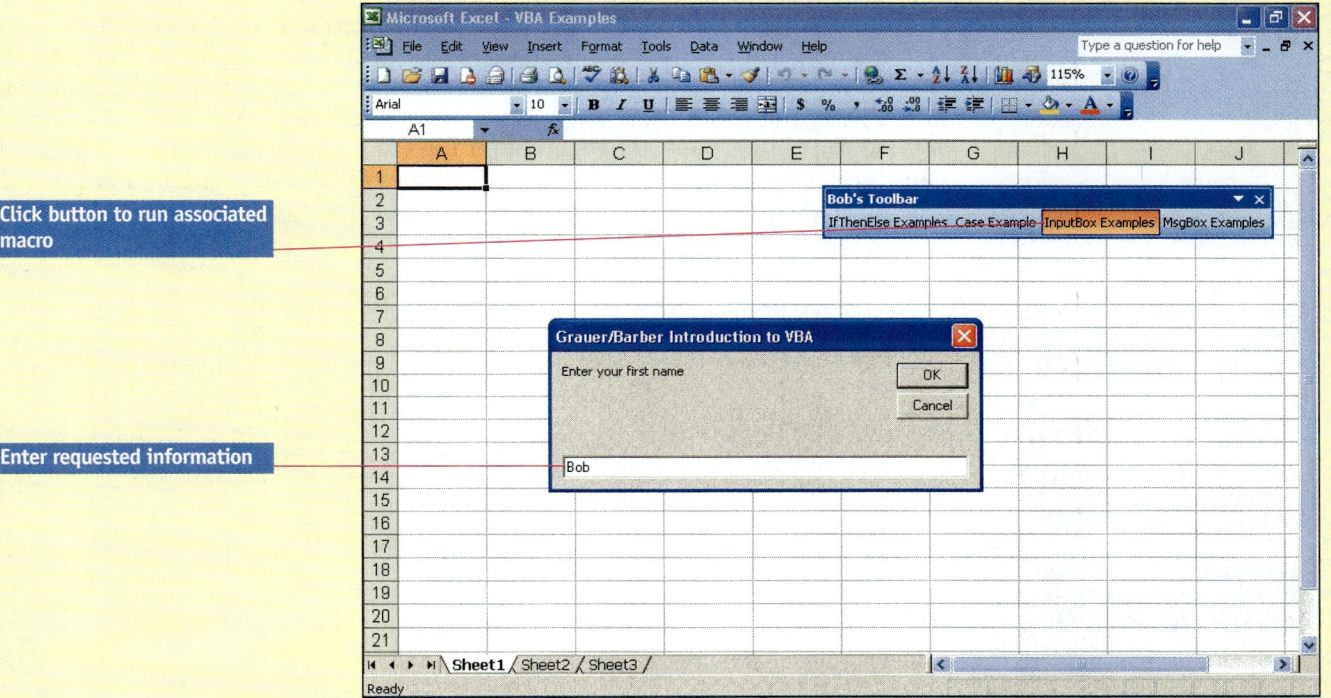

Click button to run associated macro

Enter requested information

(h) Test the Custom Toolbar (step 8)

FIGURE 8   Hands-on Exercise 2 (*continued*)

ACCESS IS DIFFERENT

The procedure to add buttons to a custom toolbar in Access is different from the procedure in Excel. Pull down the View menu, click the Toolbars command, then click the Customize command. Select the File category within the Customize dialog box, then click and drag the Custom command to the newly created toolbar. Select the command on the toolbar, then click the Modify Selection command button in the dialog box. Click Properties, click the On Action text box, then type the name of the procedure you want to run in the format, =procedurename(). Close the dialog boxes, then press Alt+F11 to return to the VBA editor. Change the keyword "Sub" that identifies the procedure to "Function". Return to the database window, then test the newly created toolbar.

FOR . . . NEXT STATEMENT

The **_For . . . Next statement_** executes all statements between the words For and Next a specified number of times, using a counter to keep track of the number of times the statements are executed. The statement, For intCounter = 1 to N, executes the statements within the loop N times.

The procedure in Figure 9 contains two For . . . Next statements that sum the numbers from 1 to 10, counting by 1 and 2, respectively. The Dim statements at the beginning of the procedure declare two variables, intSumofNumbers to hold the sum and intCounter to hold the value of the counter. The sum is initialized to zero immediately before the first loop. The statements in the loop are then executed 10 times, each time incrementing the sum by the value of the counter. The result (the sum of the numbers from 1 to 10) is displayed after the loop in Figure 9b.

The second For . . . Next statement increments the counter by 2 rather than by 1. (The increment or step is assumed to be 1 unless a different value is specified.) The sum of the numbers is reset to zero prior to entering the second loop, the loop is entered, and the counter is initialized to the starting value of 1. Each subsequent time through the loop, however, the counter is incremented by 2. Each time the value of the counter is compared to the ending value, until it (the counter) exceeds the ending value, at which point the For . . . Next statement is complete. Thus the second loop will be executed for values of 1, 3, 5, 7, and 9. After the fifth time through the loop, the counter is incremented to 11, which is greater than the ending value of 10, and the loop is terminated.

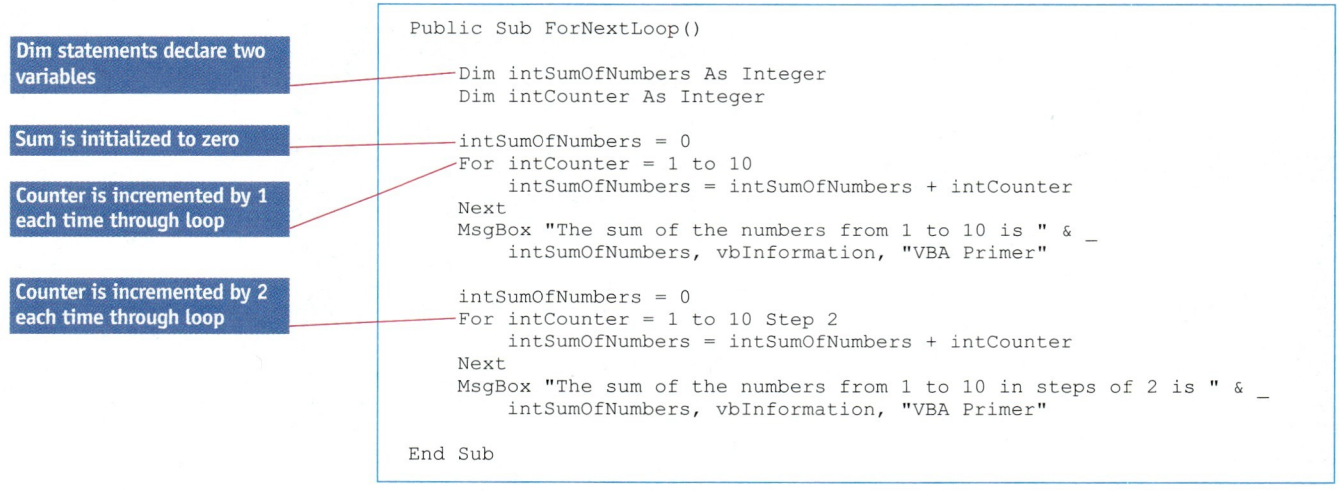

```
Public Sub ForNextLoop()

    Dim intSumOfNumbers As Integer
    Dim intCounter As Integer

    intSumOfNumbers = 0
    For intCounter = 1 to 10
        intSumOfNumbers = intSumOfNumbers + intCounter
    Next
    MsgBox "The sum of the numbers from 1 to 10 is " & _
        intSumOfNumbers, vbInformation, "VBA Primer"

    intSumOfNumbers = 0
    For intCounter = 1 to 10 Step 2
        intSumOfNumbers = intSumOfNumbers + intCounter
    Next
    MsgBox "The sum of the numbers from 1 to 10 in steps of 2 is " & _
        intSumOfNumbers, vbInformation, "VBA Primer"

End Sub
```

Dim statements declare two variables

Sum is initialized to zero

Counter is incremented by 1 each time through loop

Counter is incremented by 2 each time through loop

(a) VBA Code

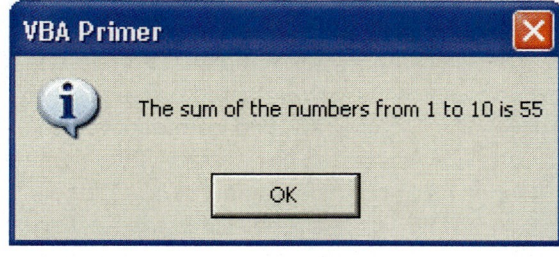

(b) In Increments of 1

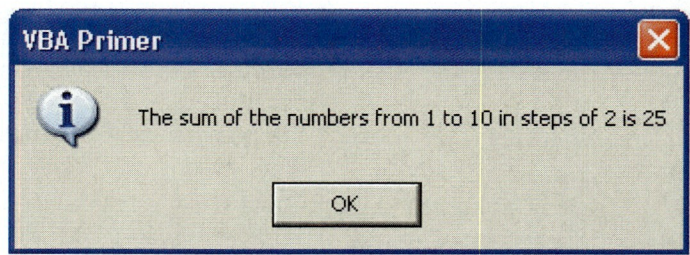

(c) In Increments of 2

FIGURE 9   For . . . Next Loops

DO LOOPS

The For . . . Next statement is ideal when you know in advance how many times you want to go through a loop. There are many instances, however, when the number of times through the loop is indeterminate. You could, for example, give a user multiple chances to enter a password or answer a question. This type of logic is implemented through a Do loop. You can repeat the loop as long as a condition is true (Do While), or until a condition becomes true (Do Until). The choice depends on how you want to state the condition.

Regardless of which keyword you choose, Do While or Do Until, two formats are available. The difference is subtle and depends on whether the keyword (While or Until) appears at the beginning or end of the loop. Our discussion will use the Do Until statement, but the Do While statement works in similar fashion.

Look closely at the procedure in Figure 10a, which contains two different loops. In the first example the Until condition appears at the end of the loop, which means the statements in the loop are executed, and then the condition is tested. This ensures that the statements in the loop will be executed at least once. The second loop, however, places the Until condition at the beginning of the loop, so that it (the condition) is tested prior to the loop being executed. Thus, if the condition is satisfied initially, the second loop will never be executed. In other words, there are two distinct statements ***Do . . . Loop Until*** and ***Do Until . . . Loop***. The first statement executes the loop, then tests the condition. The second statement tests the condition, then enters the loop.

```vba
Public Sub DoUntilLoop()

    Dim strCorrectAnswer As String, strUserAnswer As String

    strCorrectAnswer = "Earth"

    Do
        strUserAnswer = InputBox("What is the third planet from the sun?")
    Loop Until strUserAnswer = strCorrectAnswer
    MsgBox "You are correct, earthling!", vbExclamation

    strUserAnswer = InputBox("What is the third planet from the sun?")
    Do Until strUserAnswer = strCorrectAnswer
        strUserAnswer = InputBox("Your answer is incorrect. Try again.")
    Loop
    MsgBox "You are correct, earthling!", vbExclamation

End Sub
```

Until appears at end of loop

Until appears at beginning of loop

(a) VBA Code

(b) Input the Answer

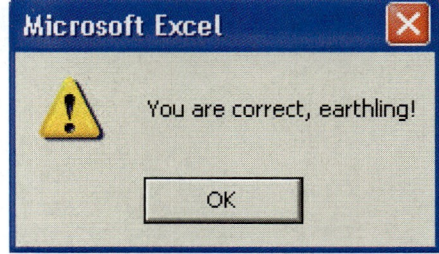

(c) Correct Response

FIGURE 10 Do Until Loops

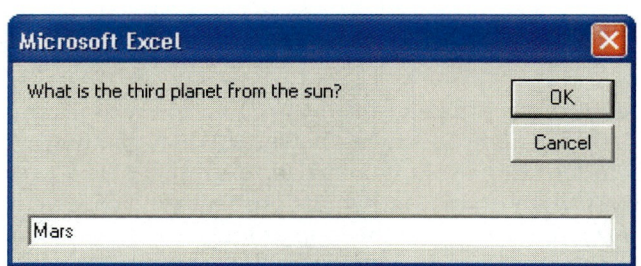

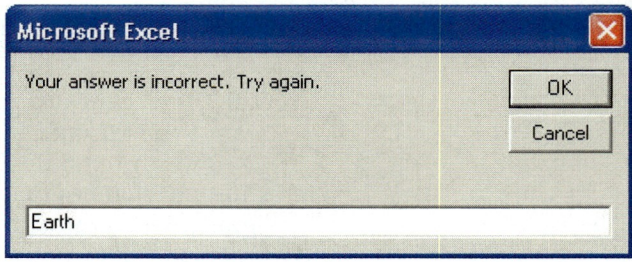

(d) Wrong Answer Initially   (e) Second Chance

FIGURE 10 Do Until Loops (*continued*)

It's tricky, but stay with us. In the first example the user is asked the question within the loop, and the loop is executed repeatedly until the user gives the correct answer. In the second example the user is asked the question outside of the loop, and the loop is bypassed if the user answers it correctly. The latter is the preferred logic because it enables us to phrase the question differently, before and during the loop. Look carefully at the difference between the InputBox statements and see how the question changes within the second loop.

DEBUGGING

As you learn more about VBA and develop more powerful procedures, you are more likely to make mistakes. The process of finding and correcting errors within a procedure is known as *debugging* and it is an integral part of programming. Do not be discouraged if you make mistakes. Everyone does. The important thing is how quickly you are able to find and correct the errors that invariably occur. We begin our discussion of debugging by describing two types of errors, *compilation errors* and *execution* (or *run-time*) *errors*.

A compilation error is simply an error in VBA syntax. (Compilation is the process of translating a VBA procedure into machine language, and thus a compilation error occurs when the VBA editor is unable to convert a statement to machine language.) Compilation errors occur for many reasons, such as misspelling a keyword, omitting a comma, and so on. VBA recognizes the error before the procedure is run and displays the invalid statement in red together with an associated error message. The programmer corrects the error and then reruns the procedure.

Execution errors are caused by errors in logic and are more difficult to detect because they occur without any error message. VBA, or for that matter any other programming language, does what you tell it to do, which is not necessarily what you want it to do. If, for example, you were to compute the sales tax of an item by multiplying the price by 60% rather than 6%, VBA will perform the calculation and simply display the wrong answer. It is up to you to realize that the results of the procedure are incorrect, and you will need to examine its statements and correct the mistake.

So how do you detect an execution error? In essence, you must decide what the expected output of your procedure should be, then you compare the actual result of the procedure to the intended result. If the results are different, an error has occurred, and you have to examine the logic in the procedure to find the error. You may see the mistake immediately (e.g., using 60% rather than 6% in the previous example), or you may have to examine the code more closely. And as you might expect, VBA has a variety of tools to help you in the debugging process. These tools are accessed from the *Debug toolbar* or the *Debug menu* as shown in Figure 11 on the next page.

The procedure in Figure 11 is a simple For . . . Next loop to sum the integers from 1 to 10. The procedure is correct as written, but we have introduced several debugging techniques into the figure. The most basic technique is to step through the statements in the procedure one at a time to see the sequence in which the statements are executed. Click the **Step Into button** on the Debug toolbar to enter (step into) the procedure, then continue to click the button to move through the procedure. Each time you click the button, the statement that is about to be executed is highlighted.

Another useful technique is to display the values of selected variables as they change during execution. This is accomplished through the **Debug.Print statement** that displays the values in the **Immediate window**. The Debug.Print statement is placed within the For . . . Next loop so that you can see how the counter and the associated sum change during execution.

As the figure now stands, we have gone through the loop nine times, and the sum of the numbers from 1 to 9 is 45. The Step Into button is in effect so that the statement to be executed next is highlighted. You can see that we are back at the top of the loop, where the counter has been incremented to 10, and further, that we are about to increment the sum.

The **Locals window** is similar in concept except that it displays only the current values of all the variables within the procedure. Unlike the Immediate window, which requires the insertion of Debug.Print statements into a procedure to have meaning, the Locals window displays its values automatically, without any effort on the part of the programmer, other than opening the window. All three techniques can be used individually, or in conjunction with one another, as the situation demands.

We believe that the best time to practice debugging is when you know there are no errors in your procedure. As you may have guessed, it's time for the next hands-on exercise.

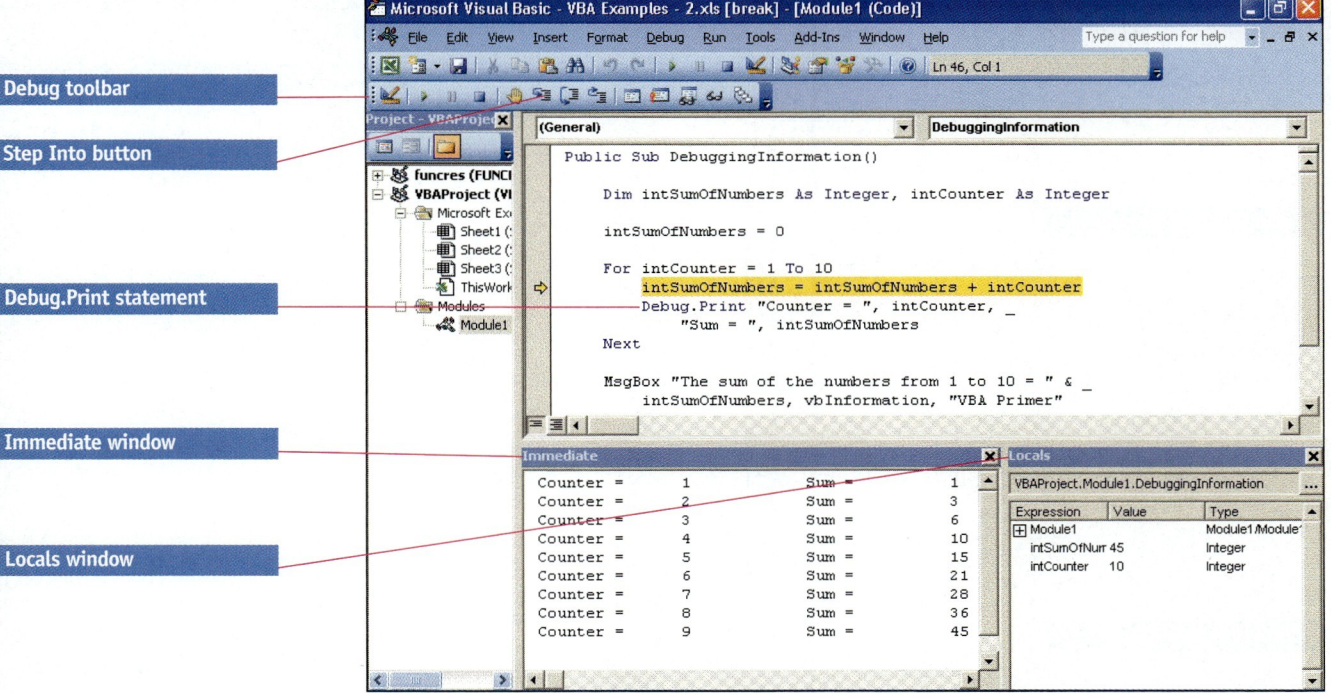

FIGURE 11 Debugging

3 Loops and Debugging

Objective To create a loop using the For . . . Next and Do Until statements; to open the Locals and Immediate windows and illustrate different techniques for debugging. Use Figure 12 as a guide in the exercise.

Step 1: **Insert a New Procedure**

- Open the **VBA Examples workbook** or the Access database from the previous exercise. Either way, pull down the **Tools menu**, click the **Macro command**, then click **Visual Basic editor** (or use the **Alt+F11** keyboard shortcut) to start the VBA editor.

- If necessary, double click **Module1** within the Project Explorer window to open this module. Pull down the **Insert menu** and click the **Procedure command** to display the Add Procedure dialog box.

- Click in the **Name** text box and enter **ForNextLoop** as the name of the procedure. Click the option buttons for a **Sub procedure** and for **Public scope**. Click **OK** to create the procedure.

- The Sub procedure should appear within the module and consist of the Sub and End Sub statements as shown in Figure 12a.

- Click the **Procedure View button** at the bottom of the window as shown in Figure 12a. The display changes to show just the current procedure, giving you more room in which to work.

- Save the module.

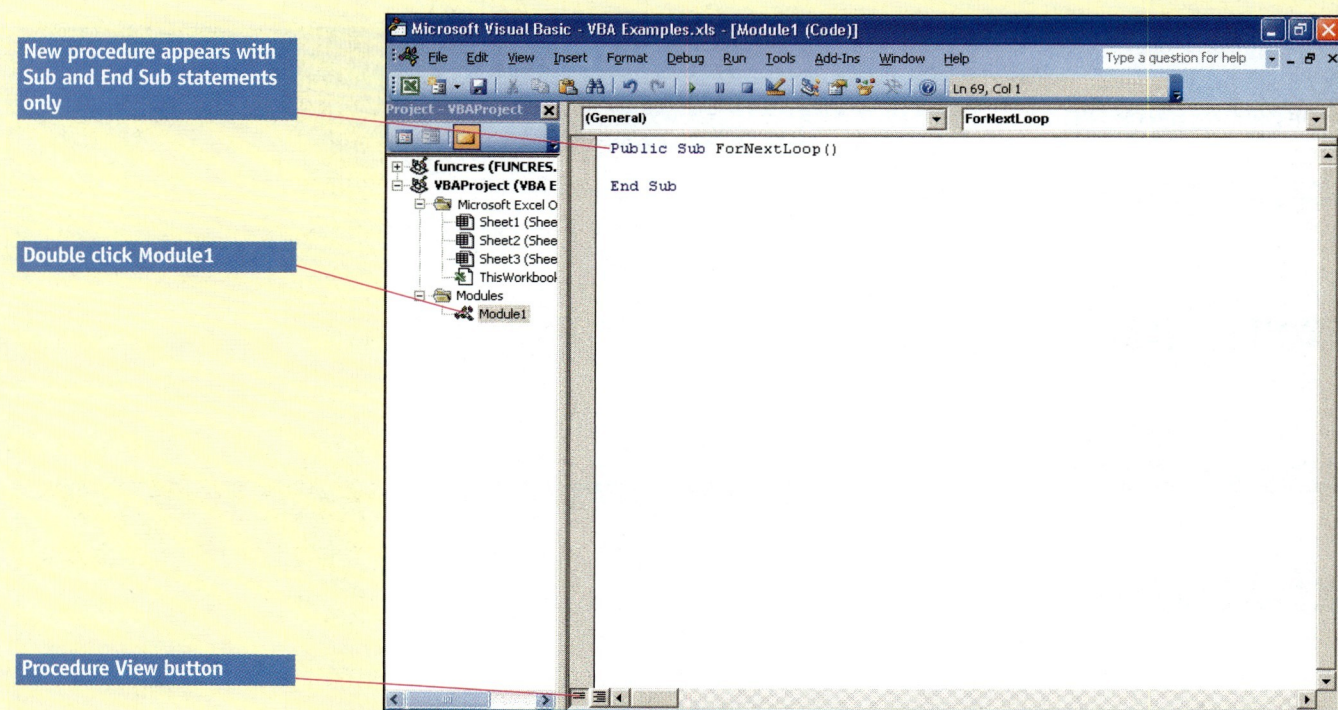

New procedure appears with Sub and End Sub statements only

Double click Module1

Procedure View button

(a) Insert a New Procedure (step 1)

FIGURE 12 Hands-on Exercise 3

Step 2: **Test the For . . . Next Procedure**

■ Enter the procedure exactly as it appears in Figure 12b. Note the following:
   ❑ A comment is added at the beginning of the procedure to identify the author and the date.
   ❑ Two variables are declared at the beginning of the procedure, one to hold the sum of the numbers and the other to serve as a counter.
   ❑ The sum of the numbers is initialized to zero. The For . . . Next loop varies the counter from 1 to 10.
   ❑ The statement within the For . . . Next loop increments the sum of the numbers by the current value of the counter. The equal sign is really a replacement operator; that is, replace the variable on the left (the sum of the numbers) by the expression on the right (the sum of the numbers plus the value of the counter.
   ❑ Indentation and spacing within a procedure are for the convenience of the programmer and not a requirement of VBA. We align the For and Next statements at the beginning and end of a loop, then indent all statements within a loop.
   ❑ The MsgBox statement displays the result and is continued over two lines as per the underscore at the end of the first line.
   ❑ The ampersand concatenates (joins together) the text and the number within the message box.

■ Click the **Save button** to save the module. Right click the **Excel button** on the Windows taskbar to display a context-sensitive menu, then click the **Minimize command**.

■ Click the **Run Sub button** to test the procedure, which should display the MsgBox statement in Figure 12b. Correct any errors that may occur.

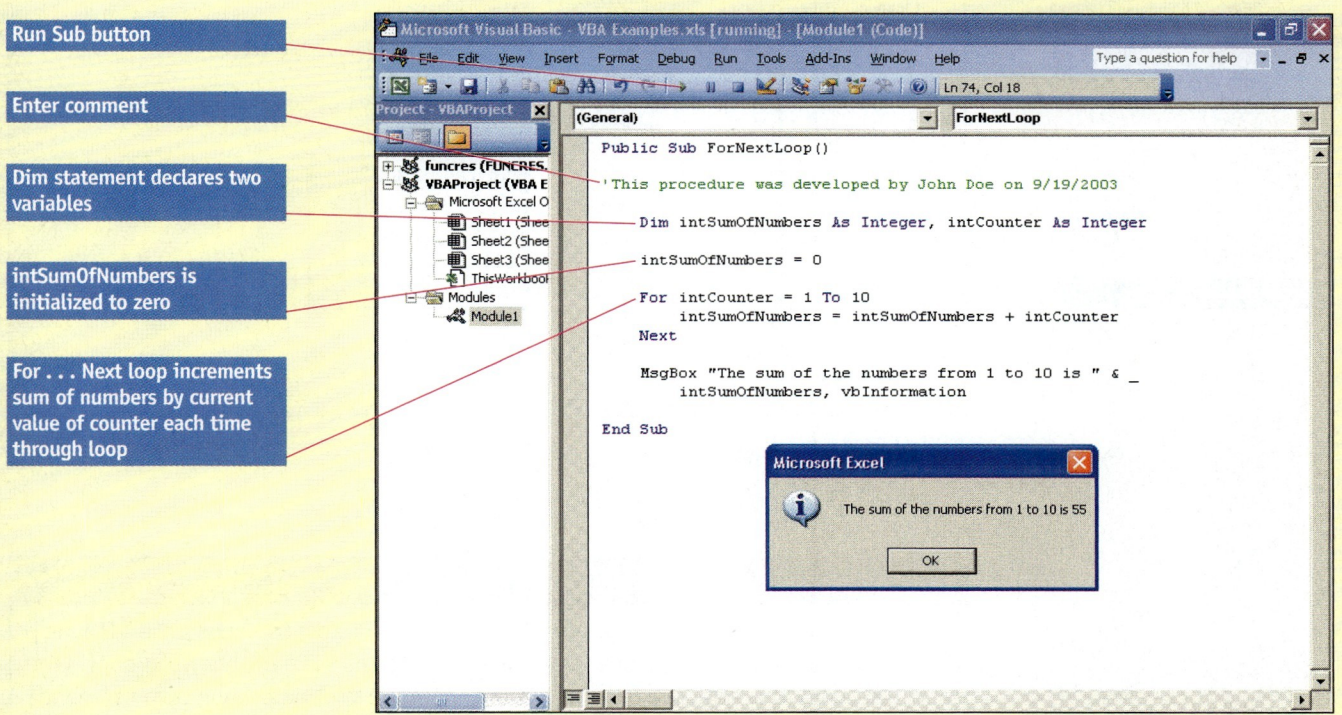

(b) Test the For . . . Next Procedure (step 2)

FIGURE 12 Hands-on Exercise 3 (*continued*)

Step 3:   **Compilation Errors**

- The best time to practice debugging is when you know that the procedure is working properly. Accordingly, we will make some deliberate errors in our procedure to illustrate different debugging techniques.

- Pull down the **View menu**, click the **Toolbars command**, and (if necessary) toggle the Debug toolbar on, then dock it under the Standard toolbar.

- Click on the statement that initializes intSumOfNumbers to zero and delete the "s" at the end of the variable name. Click the **Run Sub button**.

- You will see the message in Figure 12c. Click **OK** to acknowledge the error, then click the **Undo button** to correct the error.

- The procedure header is highlighted, indicating that execution is temporarily suspended and that additional action is required from you to continue testing. Click the **Run Sub button** to retest the procedure.

- This time the procedure executes correctly and you see the MsgBox statement indicating that the sum of the numbers from 1 to 10 is 55. Click **OK**.

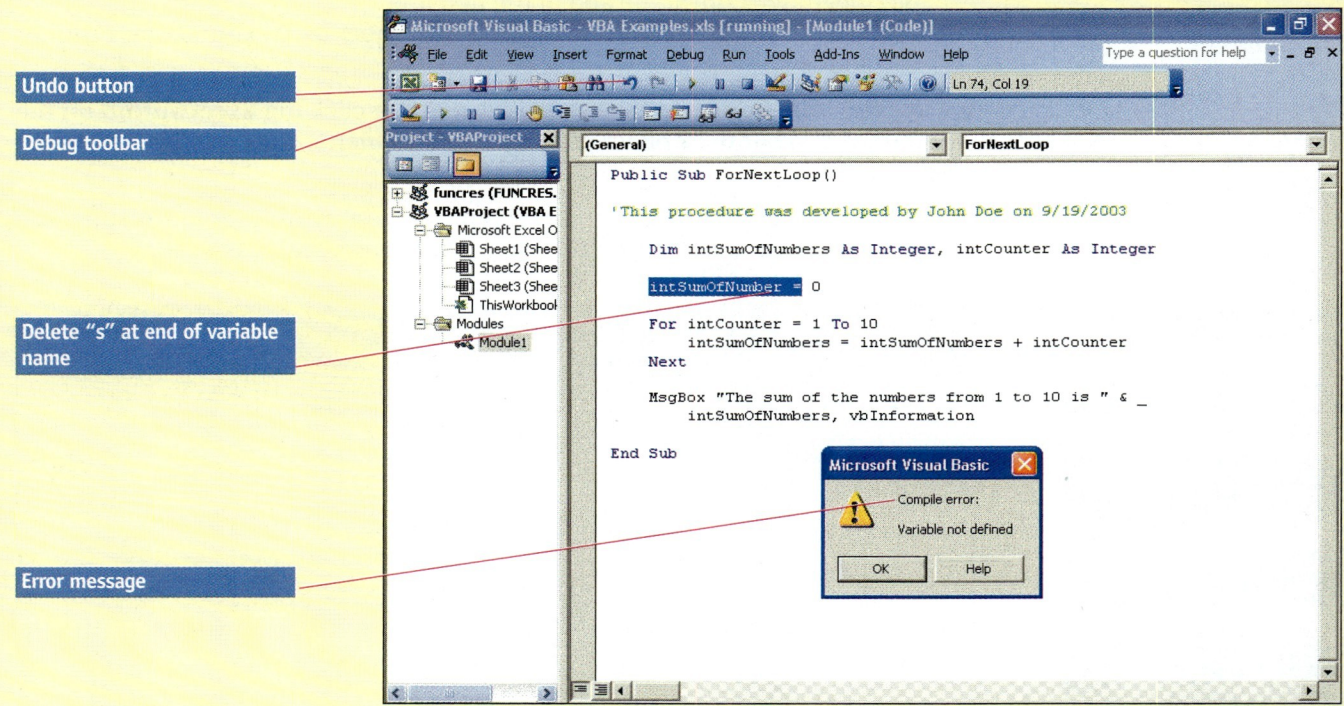

(c) Compilation Error (step 3)

FIGURE 12   Hands-on Exercise 3 (*continued*)

USE HELP AS NECESSARY

Pull down the Help menu at any time (or press the F1 key) to access the VBA Help facility to explore at your leisure. Use the Print command to create hard copy. (You can also copy the help text into a Word document to create your own reference manual.) The answers to virtually all of your questions are readily available if only you take the time to look.

Step 4: Step through a Procedure

- Pull down the **View menu** a second time and click the **Locals Window command** (or click the **Locals Window button** on the Debug toolbar).

- If necessary, click and drag the top border of the Locals window to size the window appropriately as shown in Figure 12d.

- Click anywhere within the procedure. Pull down the **Debug menu** and click the **Step Into command** (or click the **Step Into button** on the Debug toolbar). The first statement (the procedure header) is highlighted, indicating that you are about to enter the procedure.

- Click the **Step Into button** (or use the **F8** keyboard shortcut) to step into the procedure and advance to the next executable statement. The statement that initializes intSumOfNumbers to zero is highlighted, indicating that this statement is about to be executed.

- Continue to press the **F8 key** to step through the procedure. Each time you execute a statement, you can see the values of intSumOfNumbers and intCounter change within the Locals window. (You can click the **Step Out button** at any time to end the procedure.)

- Correct errors as they occur. Click the **Reset button** on the Standard or Debug toolbars at any time to begin executing the procedure from the beginning.

- Eventually you exit from the loop, and the sum of the numbers (from 1 to 10) is displayed within a message box.

- Click **OK** to close the message box. Press the **F8 key** a final time, then close the Locals window.

- Do you see how stepping through a procedure helps you to understand how it works?

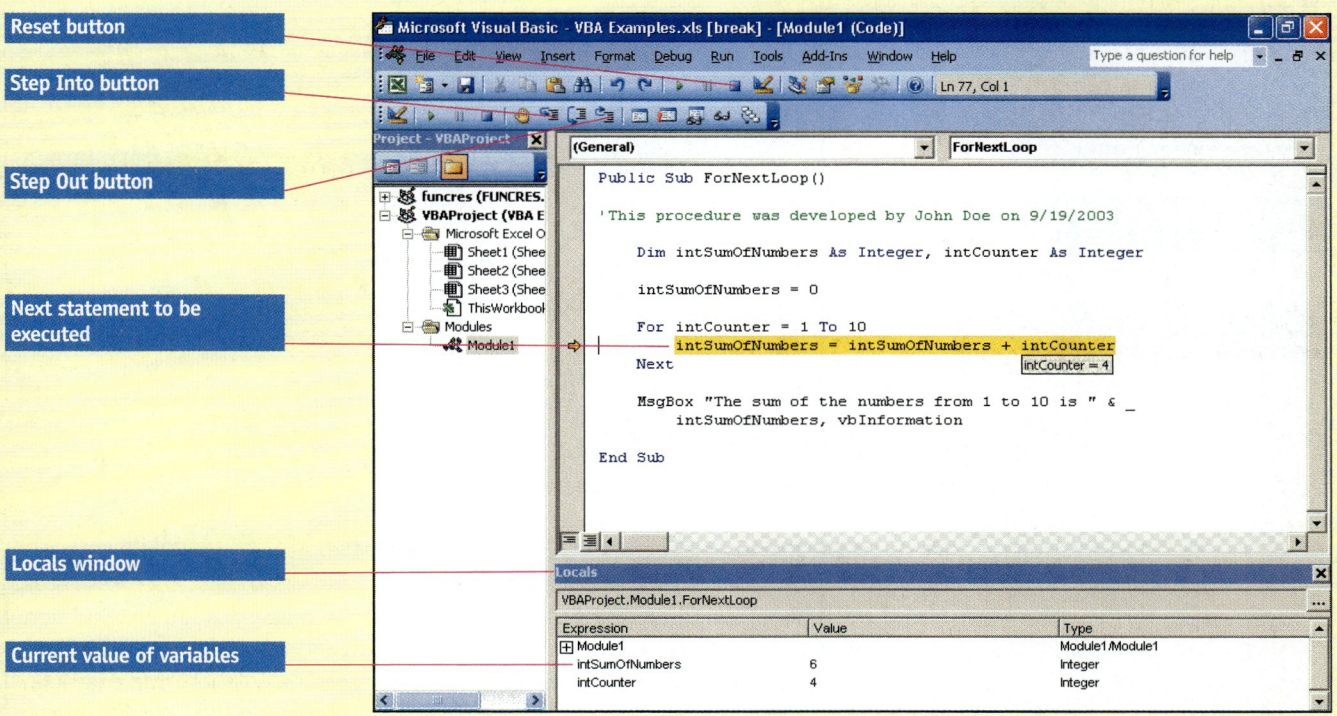

(d) Step through a Procedure (step 4)

FIGURE 12 Hands-on Exercise 3 (*continued*)

Step 5: The Immediate Window

■ You should be back in the VBA window. Click immediately to the left of the Next statement and press **Enter** to insert a blank line. Type the **Debug.Print** statement exactly as shown in Figure 12e. (Click **OK** if you see a message indicating that the procedure will be reset.)

■ Pull down the **View menu** and click the **Immediate Window command** (or click the **Immediate Window button** on the Debug toolbar). The Immediate window should be empty, but if not, you can click and drag to select the contents, then press the **Del key** to clear the window.

■ Click anywhere within the For . . . Next procedure, then click the **Run Sub button** to execute the procedure. You will see the familiar message box indicating that the sum of the numbers is 55. Click **OK**.

■ You should see 10 lines within the Immediate window as shown in Figure 12e, corresponding to the values displayed by the Debug.Print statement as it was executed within the loop.

■ Close the Immediate window. Do you see how displaying the intermediate results of a procedure helps you to understand how it works?

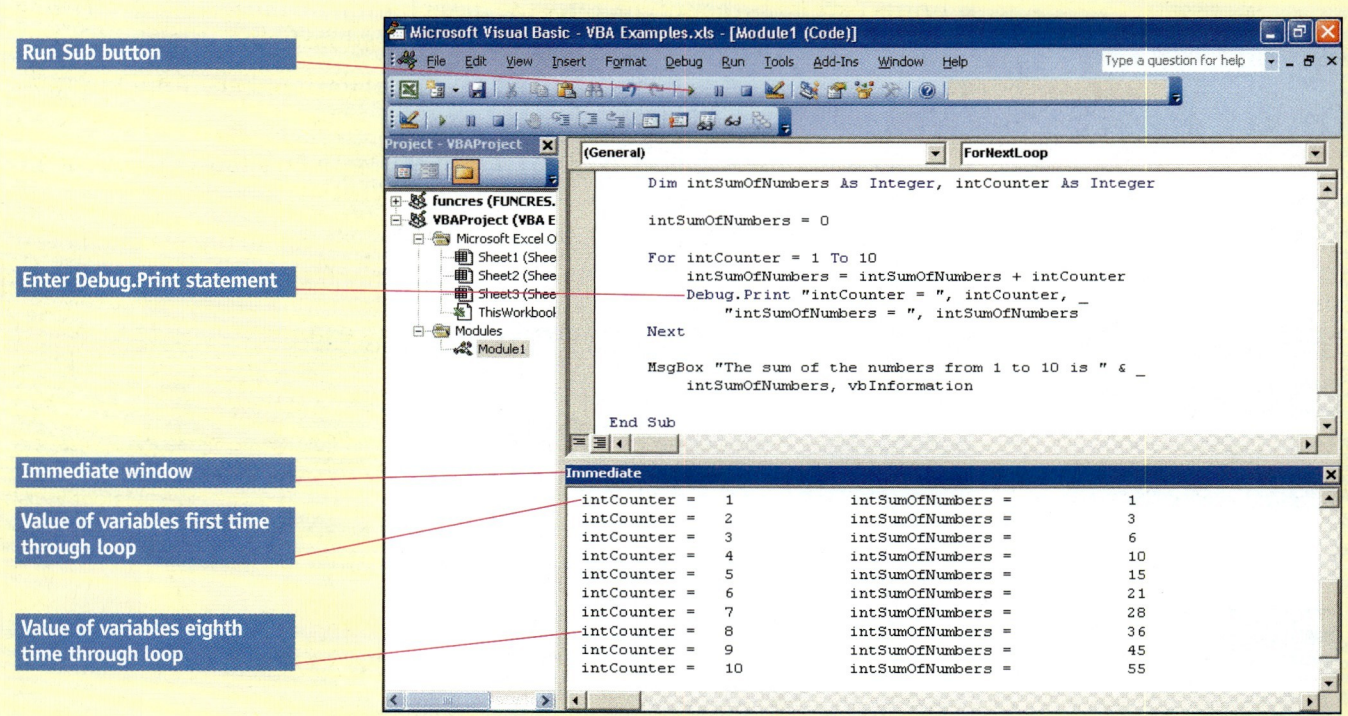

(e) The Immediate Window (step 5)

FIGURE 12 Hands-on Exercise 3 *(continued)*

INSTANT CALCULATOR

Use the Print method (action) in the Immediate window to use VBA as a calculator. Press Ctrl+G at any time to display the Immediate window. Click in the window, then type the statement Debug.Print, followed by your calculation, for example, Debug.Print 2+2, and press Enter. The answer is displayed on the next line in the Immediate window.

Step 6: A More General Procedure

- Modify the existing procedure to make it more general—for example, to sum the values from any starting value to any ending value:
  - ❏ Click at the end of the existing Dim statement to position the insertion point, press **Enter** to create a new line, then add the second **Dim statement** as shown in Figure 12f.
  - ❏ Click before the For statement, press **Enter** to create a blank line, press **Enter** a second time, then enter the two **InputBox statements** to ask the user for the beginning and ending values.
  - ❏ Modify the For statement to execute from **intStart** to **intEnd** rather than from 1 to 10.
  - ❏ Change the MsgBox statement to reflect the values of intStart and intEnd, and a customized title bar. Note the use of the ampersand and the underscore, to indicate concatenation and continuation, respectively.

- Click the **Save button** to save the module.

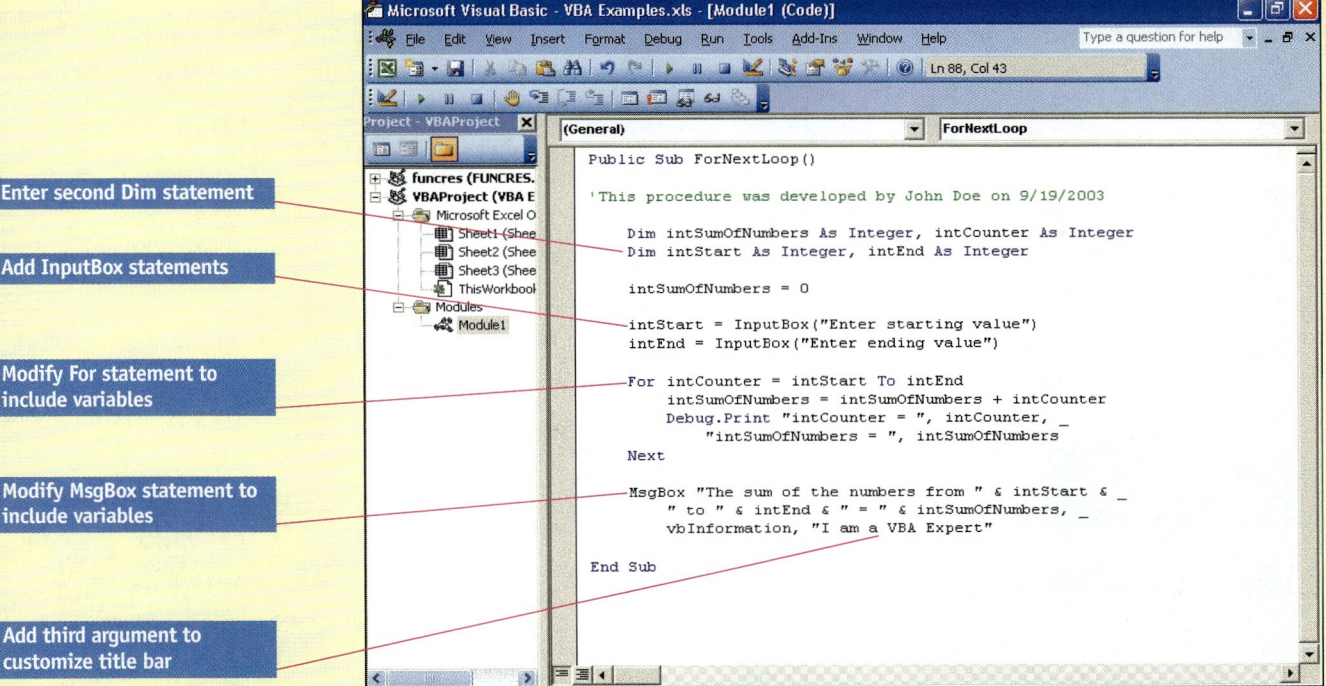

(f) A More General Procedure (step 6)

FIGURE 12 Hands-on Exercise 3 (*continued*)

USE WHAT YOU KNOW

Use the techniques acquired from other applications such as Microsoft Word to facilitate editing within the VBA window. Press the Ins key to toggle between the insert and overtype modes as you modify the statements within a VBA procedure. You can also cut, copy, and paste statements (or parts of statements) within a procedure and from one procedure to another. The Find and Replace commands are also useful.

Step 7: Test the Procedure

- Click the **Run Sub button** to test the procedure. You should be prompted for a beginning and an ending value. Enter any numbers you like, such as 10 and 20, respectively, to match the result in Figure 12g.

- The value displayed in the MsgBox statement should reflect the numbers you entered. For example, you will see a sum of 165 if you entered 10 and 20 as the starting and ending values.

- Look carefully at the message box that is displayed in Figure 12g. Its title bar displays the literal "I am a VBA expert", corresponding to the last argument in the MsgBox statement.

- Note, too, the spacing that appears within the message box, which includes spaces before and after each number. Look at your results and, if necessary, modify the MsgBox statement so that you have the same output. Click **OK**.

- Save the procedure.

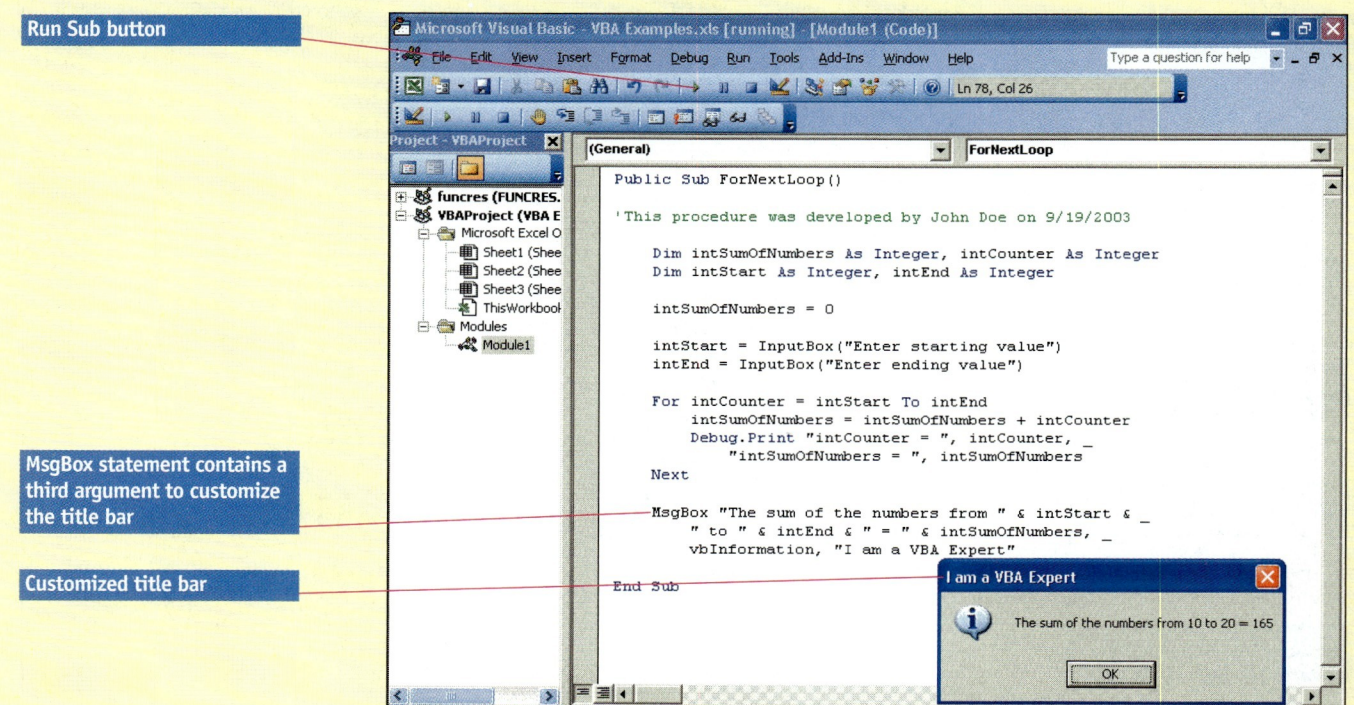

Run Sub button

MsgBox statement contains a third argument to customize the title bar

Customized title bar

(g) Test the Procedure (step 7)

FIGURE 12 Hands-on Exercise 3 *(continued)*

CHANGE THE INCREMENT

The For . . . Next statement can be made more general by supplying an increment within the For statement. Try For intCount = 1 To 10 Step 2, or more generally, For intCount = intStart to intEnd Step intStepValue. "Step" is a Visual Basic keyword and must be entered that way. intCount, intEnd, and intStepValue are user-defined variables. The variables must be defined at the beginning of a procedure and can be initialized by requesting values from the user through the InputBox statement.

Step 8:   Create a Do Until Loop

- Pull down the **Insert menu** and click the **Procedure command** to insert a new procedure called **DoUntilLoop**. Enter the procedure as it appears in Figure 12h. Note the following:
  - ❑ Two string variables are declared to hold the correct answer and the user's response, respectively.
  - ❑ The variable strCorrectAnswer is set to "Earth", which is the correct answer for our question.
  - ❑ The initial InputBox function prompts the user to enter his/her response to the question. A second InputBox function appears in the loop that is executed if and only if the user enters the wrong answer.
  - ❑ The Until condition appears at the beginning of the loop, so that the loop is entered only if the user answers incorrectly. The loop executes repeatedly until the correct answer is supplied.
  - ❑ A message to the user is displayed at the end of the procedure after the correct answer has been entered.

- Click the **Run Sub button** to test the procedure. Enter the correct answer on your first attempt, and you will see that the loop is never entered.

- Rerun the procedure, answer incorrectly, then note that a second input box appears, telling you that your answer was incorrect. Click **OK**.

- Once again you are prompted for the answer. Enter **Earth**. Click **OK**. The procedure ends.

- Save the procedure.

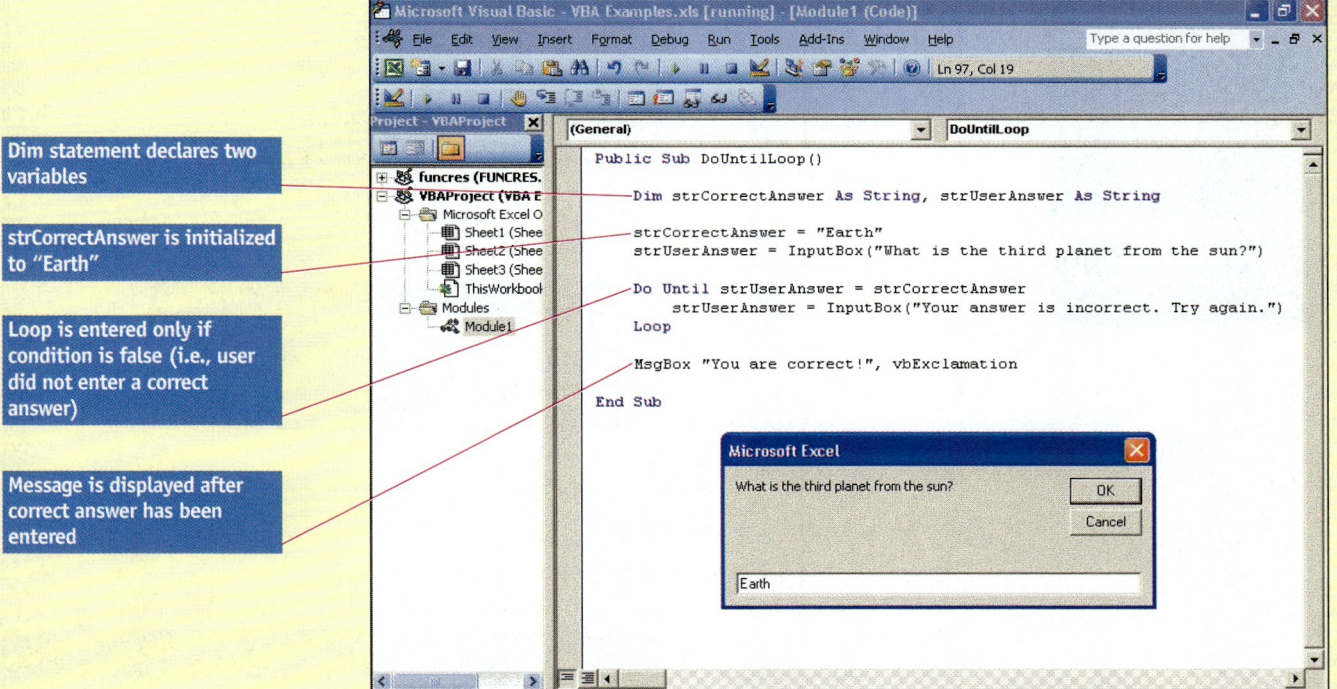

Dim statement declares two variables

strCorrectAnswer is initialized to "Earth"

Loop is entered only if condition is false (i.e., user did not enter a correct answer)

Message is displayed after correct answer has been entered

(h) Create a Do Until Loop (step 8)

FIGURE 12   Hands-on Exercise 3 (*continued*)

Step 9: A More Powerful Procedure

- Modify the procedure as shown in Figure 12i to include the statements to count and print the number of times the user takes to get the correct answer.
  - ❑ The variable intNumberOfAttempts is declared as an integer and is initialized to 1 after the user inputs his/her initial answer.
  - ❑ The Do loop is expanded to increment intNumberOfAttempts by 1 each time the loop is executed.
  - ❑ The MsgBox statement after the loop is expanded prints the number of attempts the user took to answer the question.

- Save the module, then click the **Run Sub button** to test the module. You should see a dialog box similar to the one in Figure 12i. Click **OK**. Do you see how this procedure improves on its predecessor?

- Pull down the **File menu** and click the **Print command** to display the Print dialog box. Click the option button to print the current module for your instructor. Click **OK**.

- Close the Debug toolbar. Exit Office if you do not want to continue with the next hands-on exercise at this time.

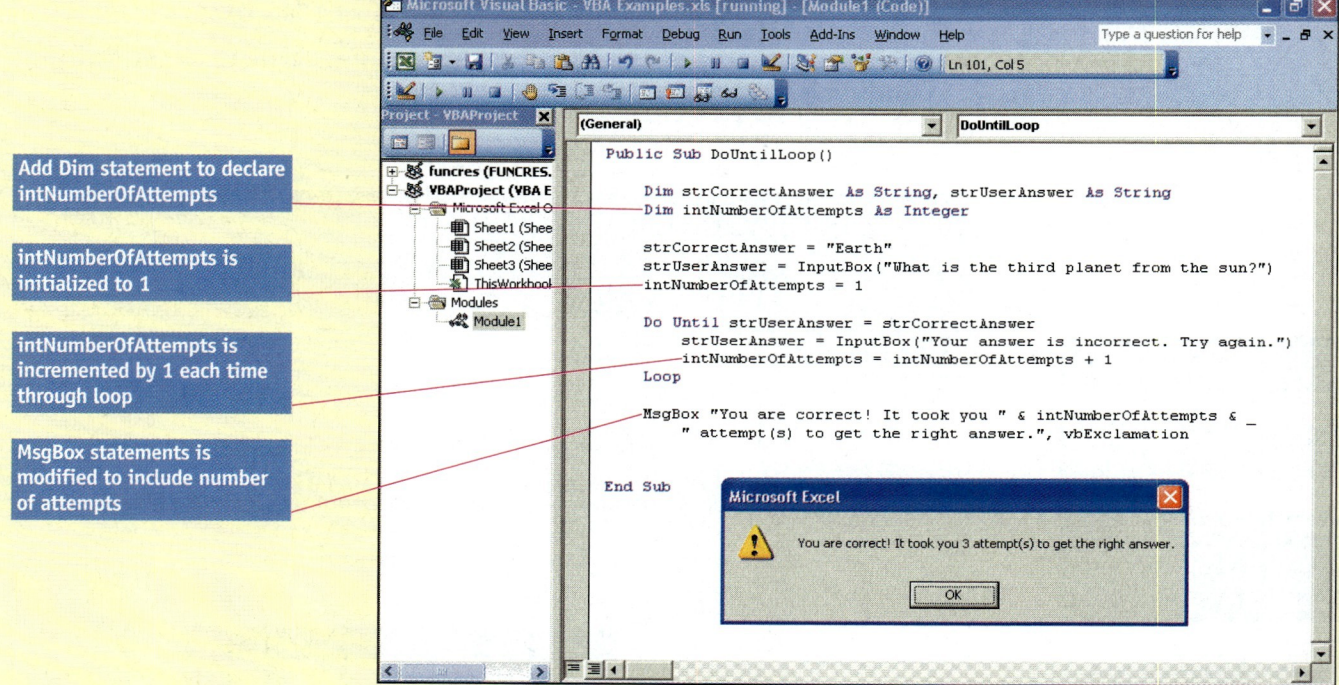

Add Dim statement to declare intNumberOfAttempts

intNumberOfAttempts is initialized to 1

intNumberOfAttempts is incremented by 1 each time through loop

MsgBox statements is modified to include number of attempts

(i) A More Powerful Procedure (step 9)

FIGURE 12 Hands-on Exercise 3 (*continued*)

IT'S NOT EQUAL, BUT REPLACE

All programming languages use statements of the form N = N + 1, in which the equal sign does not mean equal in the literal sense; that is, N cannot equal N + 1. The equal sign is really a replacement operator. Thus, the expression on the right of the equal sign is evaluated, and that result replaces the value of the variable on the left. In other words, the statement N = N + 1 increments the value of N by 1.

Our approach thus far has focused on VBA as an independent entity that can be run without specific reference to the applications in Microsoft Office. We have covered several individual statements, explained how to use the VBA editor to create and run procedures, and how to debug those procedures, if necessary. We hope you have found the material to be interesting, but you may be asking yourself, "What does this have to do with Microsoft Office?" In other words, how can you use your knowledge of VBA to enhance your ability in Microsoft Excel or Access? The answer is to create *event procedures* that run automatically in response to events within an Office application.

VBA is different from traditional programming languages in that it is event-driven. An *event* is defined as any action that is recognized by an application such as Excel or Access. Opening or closing an Excel workbook or an Access database is an event. Selecting a worksheet within a workbook is also an event, as is clicking on a command button on an Access form. To use VBA within Microsoft Office, you decide which events are significant, and what is to happen when those events occur. Then you develop the appropriate event procedures.

Consider, for example, Figure 13, which displays the results of two event procedures in conjunction with opening and closing an Excel workbook. (If you are using Microsoft Access instead of Excel, you can skip this discussion and the associated exercise, and move to the parallel material for Access that appears after the next hands-on exercise.) The procedure associated with Figure 13a displays a message that appears automatically after the user executes the command to close the associated workbook. The procedure is almost trivial to write, and consists of a single MsgBox statement. The effect of the procedure is quite significant, however, as it reminds the user to back up his or her work after closing the workbook. Nor does it matter how the user closes the workbook—whether by pulling down the menu or using a keyboard shortcut—because the procedure runs automatically in response to the Close Workbook event, regardless of how that event occurs.

The dialog box in Figure 13b prompts the user for a password and appears automatically when the user opens the workbook. The logic here is more sophisticated in that the underlying procedure contains an InputBox statement to request the password, a Do Until loop that is executed until the user enters the correct password or exceeds the allotted number of attempts, then additional logic to display the worksheet or terminate the application if the user fails to enter the proper password. The procedure is not difficult, however, and it builds on the VBA statements that were covered earlier.

The next hands-on exercise has you create the two event procedures that are associated with Figure 13. As you do the exercise, you will gain additional experience with VBA and an appreciation for the potential event procedures within Microsoft Office.

HIDING AND UNHIDING A WORKSHEET

Look carefully at the workbooks in Figures 13a and 13b. Both figures reference the identical workbook, Financial Consultant, as can be seen from the title bar. Look at the worksheet tabs, however, and note that two worksheets are visible in Figure 13a, whereas the Calculations worksheet is hidden in Figure 13b. This was accomplished in the Open workbook procedure and was implemented to hide the calculations from the user until the correct password was entered.

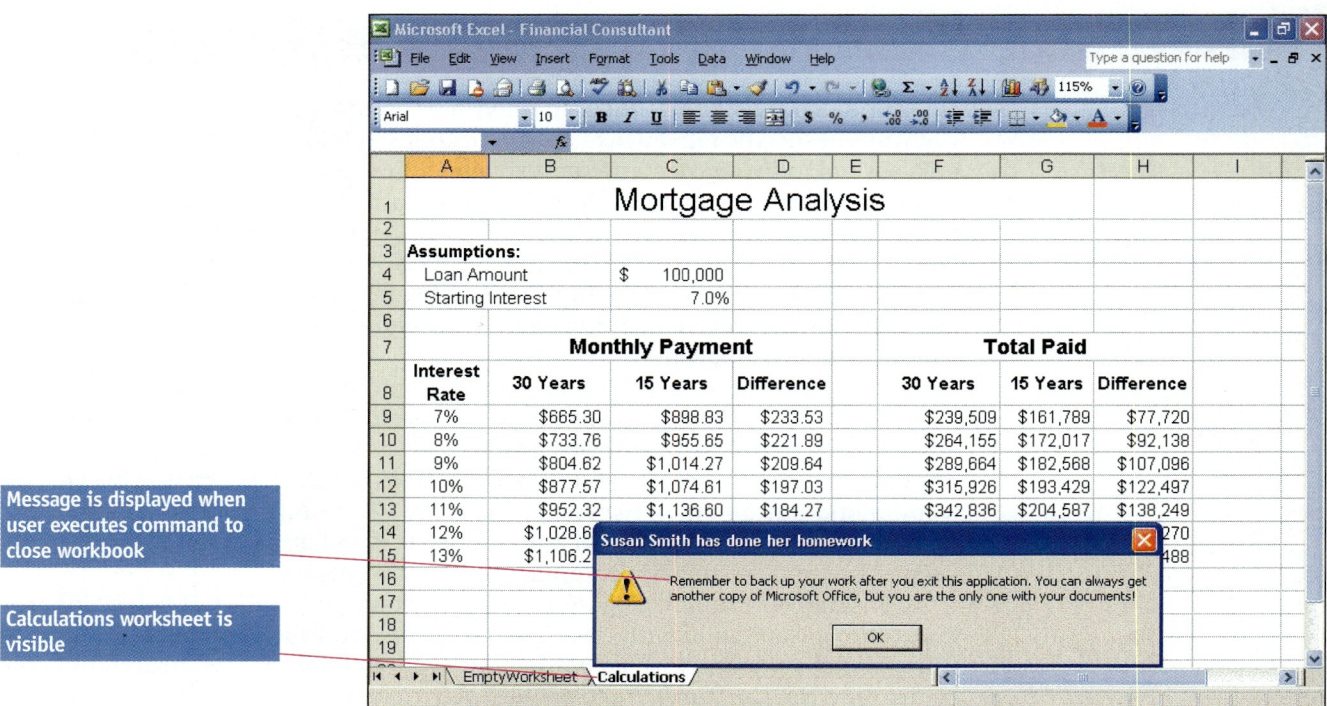

Message is displayed when user executes command to close workbook

Calculations worksheet is visible

(a) Message to the User (Close Workbook event)

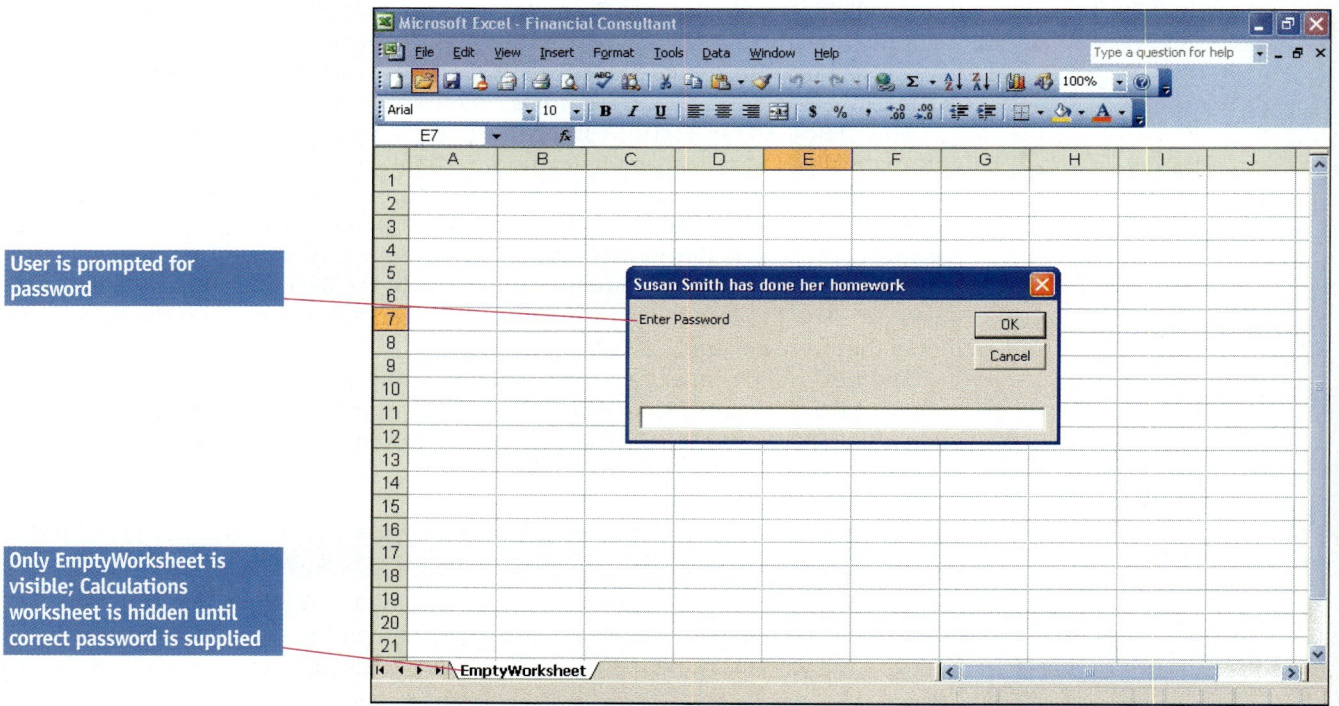

User is prompted for password

Only EmptyWorksheet is visible; Calculations worksheet is hidden until correct password is supplied

(b) Password Protection (Open Workbook event)

FIGURE 13   Event-Driven Programming

4   Event-Driven Programming (Microsoft Excel)

Objective   To create an event procedure to implement password protection that is associated with opening an Excel workbook; to create a second event procedure that displays a message to the user upon closing the workbook. Use Figure 14 as a guide in the exercise.

Step 1:   **Create the Close Workbook Procedure**

- Open the **VBA Examples workbook** you have used for the previous exercises and enable the macros. If you have been using Access rather than Excel, start Excel, open a new workbook, then save the workbook as **VBA Examples**.

- Pull down the **Tools menu**, click the **Macro command**, then click the **Visual Basic Editor command** (or use the **Alt+F11** keyboard shortcut).

- You should see the Project Explorer pane as shown in Figure 14a, but if not, pull down the **View menu** and click the **Project Explorer**. Double click **ThisWorkbook** to create a module for the workbook as a whole.

- Enter the **Option Explicit statement** if it is not there already, then press **Enter** to create a new line. Type the statement to declare the variable, **ApplicationTitle**, using your name instead of Susan Smith.

- Click the **down arrow** in the Object list box and select **Workbook**, then click the **down arrow** in the Procedure list box and select the **BeforeClose event** to create the associated procedure. (If you choose a different event by mistake, click and drag to select the associated statements, then press the **Del key** to delete the procedure.)

- Enter the comment and MsgBox statement as it appears in Figure 14a.

- Save the procedure.

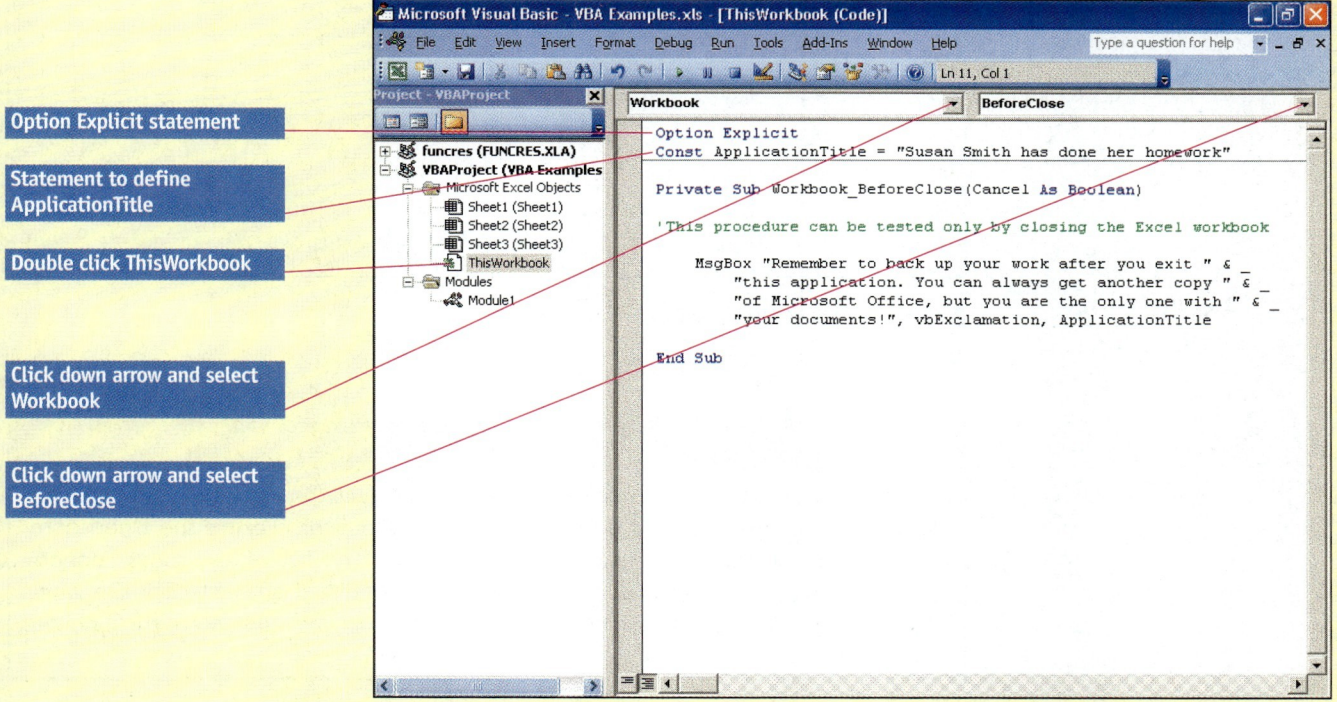

(a) Create the Close Workbook Procedure (step 1)

FIGURE 14   Hands-on Exercise 4

Step 2: **Test the Close Workbook Procedure**

- Click the **View Microsoft Excel button** on the Standard toolbar or on the Windows taskbar to view the Excel workbook. The workbook is not empty; that is, it does not contain any cell entries, but it does contain multiple VBA procedures.

- Pull down the **File menu** and click the **Close command**, which runs the procedure you just created and displays the dialog box in Figure 14b. Click **OK** after you have read the message, then click **Yes** if asked to save the workbook.

- Pull down the **File menu** and reopen the **VBA Examples workbook**, enabling the macros. Press **Alt+F11** to return to the VBA window to create an additional procedure.

- Double click **ThisWorkbook** from within the Project Explorer pane to return to the BeforeClose procedure and make the necessary corrections, if any.

- Save the procedure.

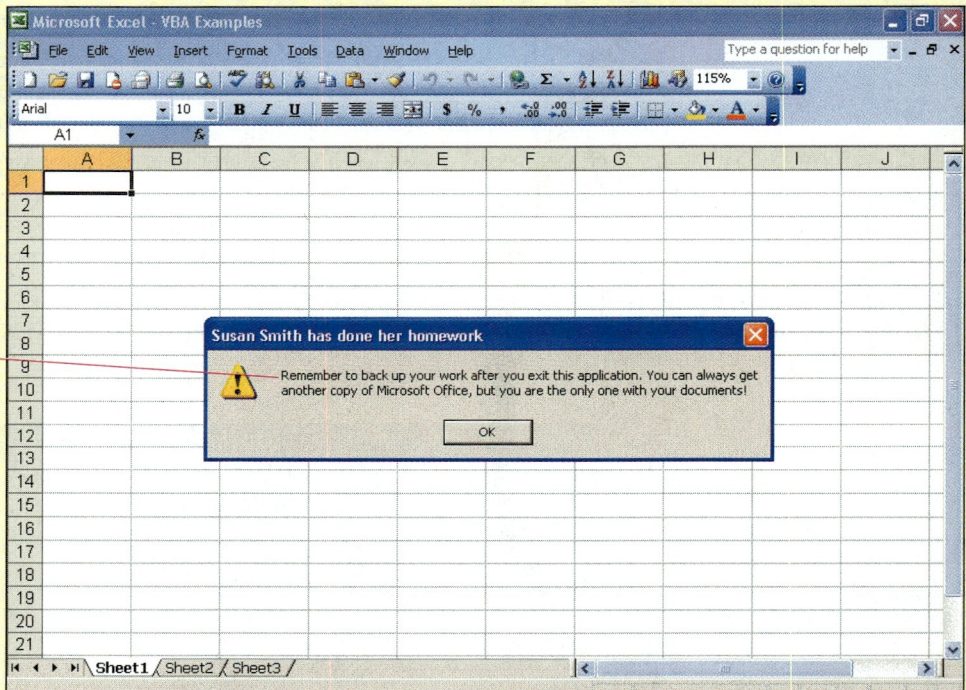

Message is displayed when you execute the Close command

(b) Test the Close Workbook Procedure (step 2)

FIGURE 14   Hands-on Exercise 4 (*continued*)

THE MOST RECENTLY OPENED FILE LIST

One way to open a recently used workbook is to select the workbook directly from the File menu. Pull down the File menu, but instead of clicking the Open command, check to see if the workbook appears on the list of the most recently opened workbooks located at the bottom of the menu. If so, just click the workbook name, rather than having to make the appropriate selections through the Open dialog box.

Step 3: **Start the Open Workbook Event Procedure**

- Click within the Before Close procedure, then click the **Procedure View button** at the bottom of the Code window. Click the **down arrow** in the Procedure list box and select the **Open event** to create an event procedure.

- Enter the VBA statements as shown in Figure 14c. Note the following:
  - ❑ Three variables are required for this procedure—the correct password, the password entered by the user, and the number of attempts.
  - ❑ The user is prompted for the password, and the number of attempts is set to 1. The user is given two additional attempts, if necessary, to get the password correct. The loop is bypassed, however, if the user supplies the correct password on the first attempt.

- Minimize Excel. Save the procedure, then click the **Run Sub button** to test it. Try different combinations in your testing; that is, enter the correct password on the first, second, and third attempts. The password is case-sensitive.

- Correct errors as they occur. Click the **Reset button** at any time to begin executing the procedure from the beginning. Save the procedure.

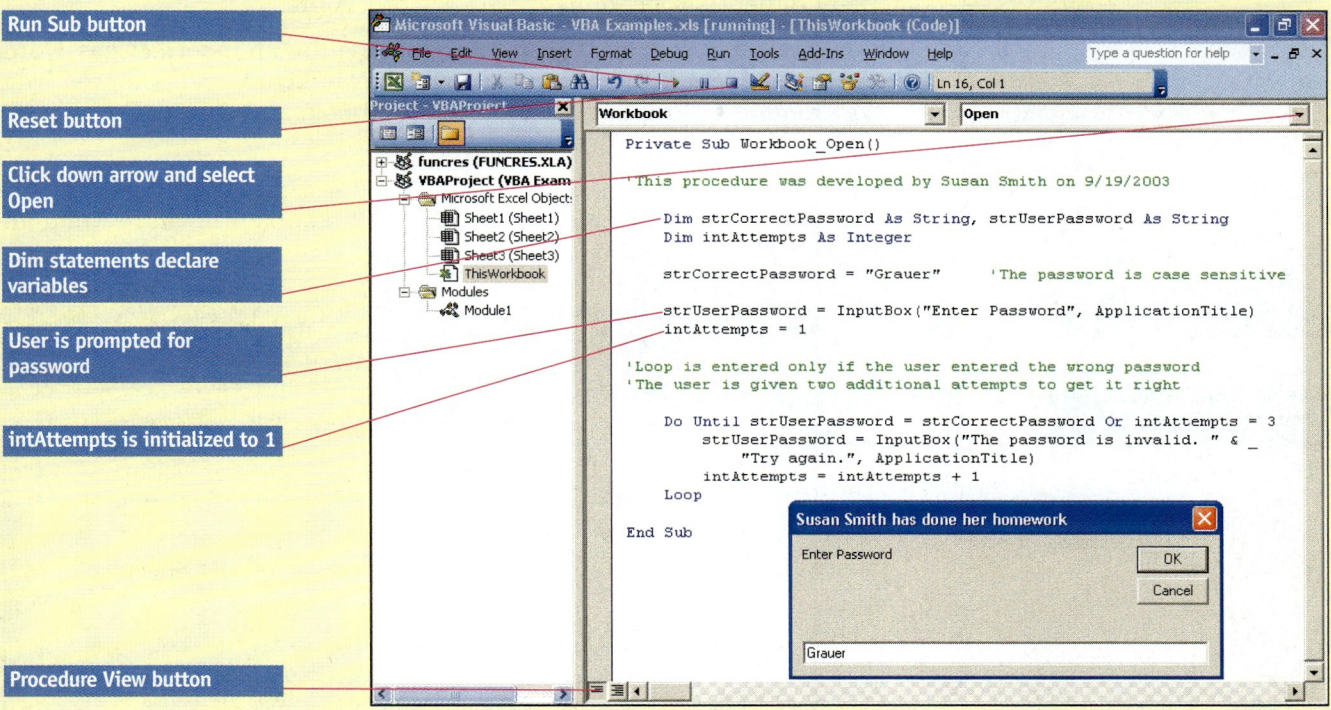

(c) Start the Open Workbook Event Procedure (step 3)

FIGURE 14   Hands-on Exercise 4 (*continued*)

THE OBJECT AND PROCEDURE BOXES

The Object box at the top of the code window displays the selected object such as an Excel workbook, whereas the Procedure box displays the name of the events appropriate to that object. Events that already have procedures appear in bold. Clicking an event that is not bold creates the procedure header and End Sub statements for that event.

Step 4: **Complete the Open Workbook Event Procedure**

- Enter the remaining statements in the procedure as shown in Figure 14d. Note the following:
  - ❏ The If statement determines whether the user has entered the correct password and, if so, displays the appropriate message.
  - ❏ If, however, the user fails to supply the correct password, a different message is displayed, and the workbook will close due to the **Workbooks.Close statement** within the procedure.
  - ❏ As a precaution, put an apostrophe in front of the Workbooks.Close statement so that it is a comment, and thus it is not executed. Once you are sure that you can enter the correct password, you can remove the apostrophe and implement the password protection.

- Save the procedure, then click the **Run Sub button** to test it. Be sure that you can enter the correct password (**Grauer**), and that you realize the password is case-sensitive.

- Delete the apostrophe in front of the Workbooks.Close statement. The text of the statement changes from green to black to indicate that it is an executable statement rather than a comment. Save the procedure.

- Click the **Run Sub button** a second time, then enter an incorrect password three times in a row. You will see the dialog box in Figure 14d, followed by a message reminding you to back up your workbook, and then the workbook will close.

- The first message makes sense, the second does not make sense in this context. Thus, we need to modify the Close Workbook procedure when an incorrect password is entered.

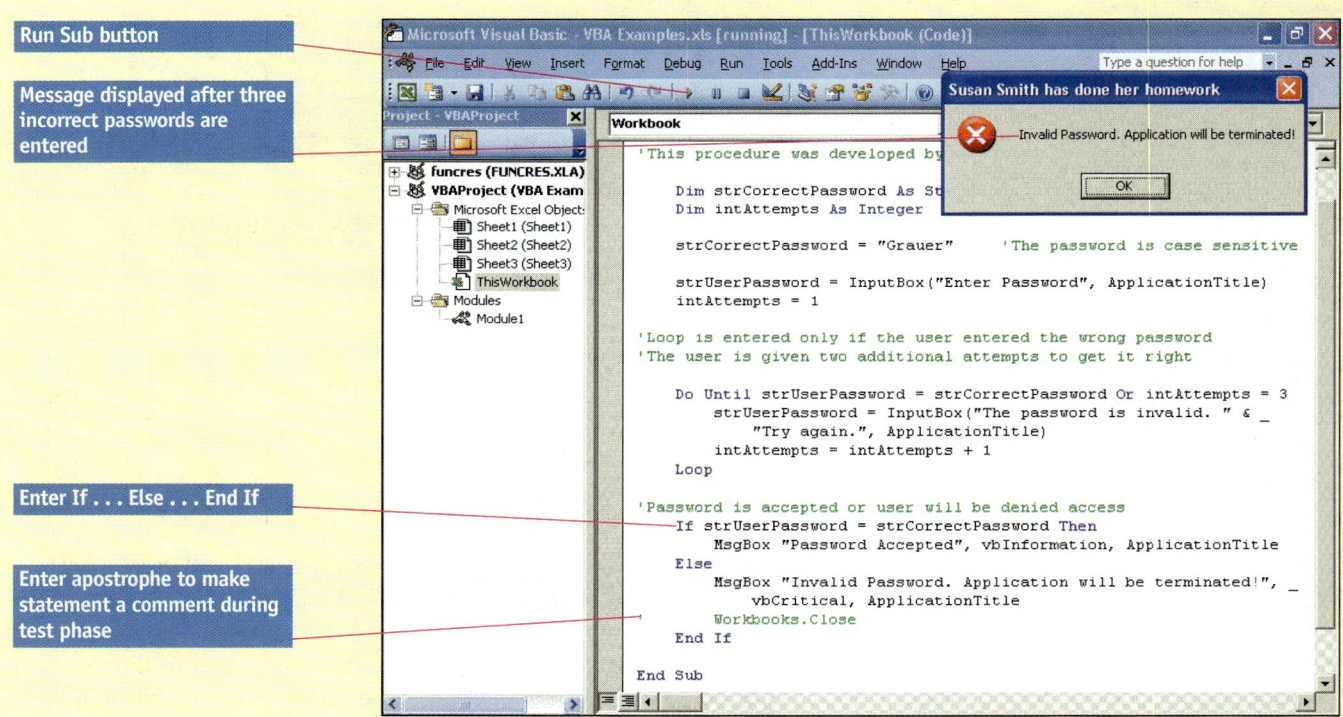

(d) Complete the Open Workbook Event Procedure (step 4)

FIGURE 14 Hands-on Exercise 4 (*continued*)

Step 5: Modify the Before Close Event Procedure

■ Reopen the **VBA Examples workbook**. Click the button to **Enable Macros**.

■ Enter the password, **Grauer** (the password is case-sensitive), press **Enter**, then click **OK** when the password has been accepted.

■ Press **Alt+F11** to reopen the VBA editor, and (if necessary) double click **ThisWorkbook** within the list of Microsoft Excel objects.

■ Click at the end of the line defining the ApplicationTitle constant, press **Enter**, then enter the statement to define the **binNormalExit** variable as shown in Figure 14e. (The statement appears initially below the line ending the General Declarations section, but moves above the line when you press Enter.)

■ Modify the BeforeClose event procedure to include an If statement that tests the value of the binNormalExit variable as shown in Figure 14e. You must, however, set the value of this variable in the Open Workbook event procedure as described in step 6.

■ Save the procedure.

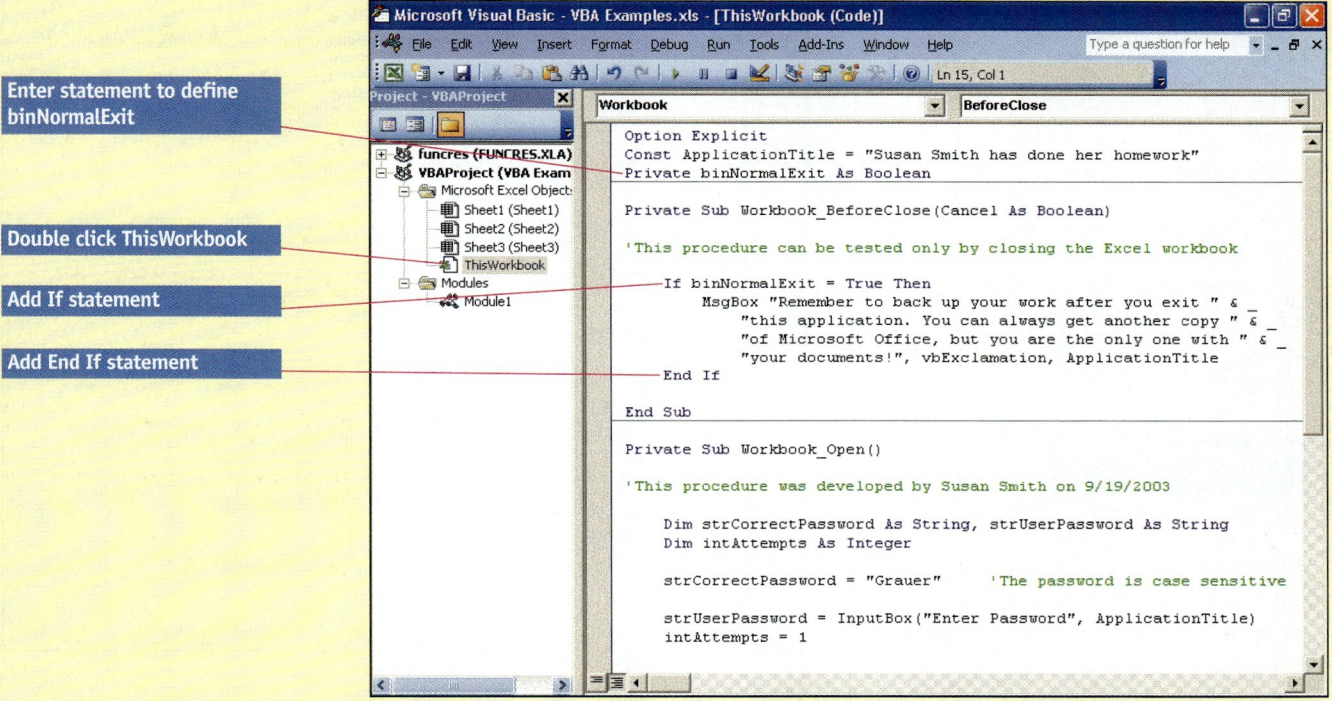

Enter statement to define binNormalExit

Double click ThisWorkbook

Add If statement

Add End If statement

(e) Modify the Before Close Event Procedure (step 5)

FIGURE 14 Hands-on Exercise 4 (*continued*)

SETTING A SWITCH

The use of a switch (binNormalExit, in this example) to control an action within a procedure is a common programming technique. The switch is set to one of two values according to events that occur within the system, then the switch is subsequently tested and the appropriate action is taken. Here, the switch is set when the workbook is opened to indicate either a valid or invalid user. The switch is then tested prior to closing the workbook to determine whether to print the closing message.

Modify the Open Workbook Event Procedure

- Scroll down to the Open Workbook event procedure, then modify the If statement to set the value of binNormalExit as shown in Figure 14f:
  - ❑ Take advantage of the Complete Word tool to enter the variable name. Type the first few letters, "**binN**", then press **Ctrl+Space**, and VBA will complete the variable name.
  - ❑ The indentation within the statement is not a requirement of VBA per se, but is used to make the code easier to read. Blank lines are also added for this purpose.
  - ❑ Comments appear throughout the procedure to explain its logic.
  - ❑ Save the modified procedure.

- Click the **Run Sub button**, then enter an incorrect password three times in a row. Once again, you will see the dialog box indicating an invalid password.

- Click **OK**. This time you will not see the message reminding you to back up your workbook. The workbook closes as before.

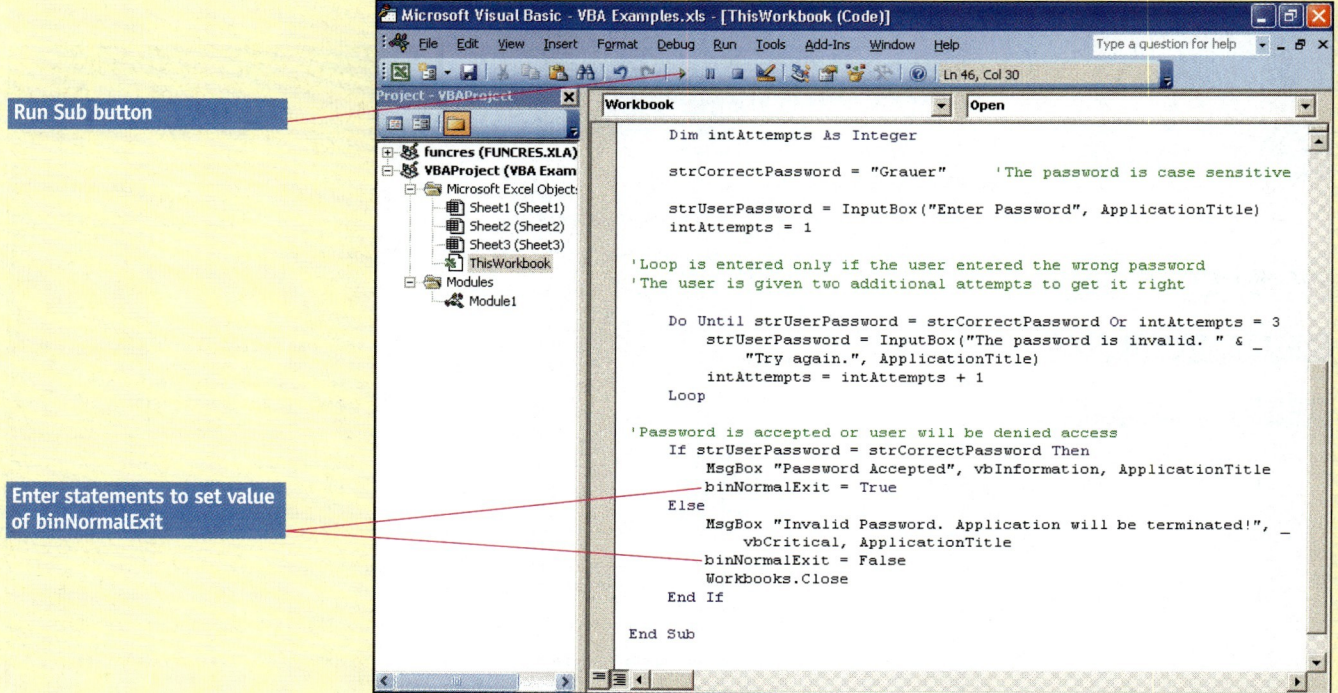

(f) Modify the Open Workbook Event Procedure (step 6)

FIGURE 14   Hands-on Exercise 4 (*continued*)

TEST UNDER ALL CONDITIONS

We cannot overemphasize the importance of thoroughly testing a procedure, and further, testing it under all conditions. VBA statements are powerful, but they are also complex, and a misplaced or omitted character can have dramatic consequences. Test every procedure completely at the time it is created, while the logic of the procedure is fresh in your mind.

Step 7: **Open a Second Workbook**

- Reopen the **VBA Examples workbook**. Click the button to **Enable Macros**.

- Enter the password, **Grauer**, then press **Enter**. Click **OK** when you see the second dialog box telling you that the password has been accepted.

- Pull down the **File menu** and click the **Open command** (or click the **Open button** on the Standard toolbar) and open a second workbook. We opened a workbook called **Financial Consultant**, but it does not matter which workbook you open.

- Pull down the **Window menu**, click the **Arrange command**, click the **Horizontal option button**, and click **OK** to tile the workbooks as shown in Figure 14g. The title bars show the names of the open workbooks.

- Pull down the **Tools menu**, click **Macro**, then click **Visual Basic editor**.

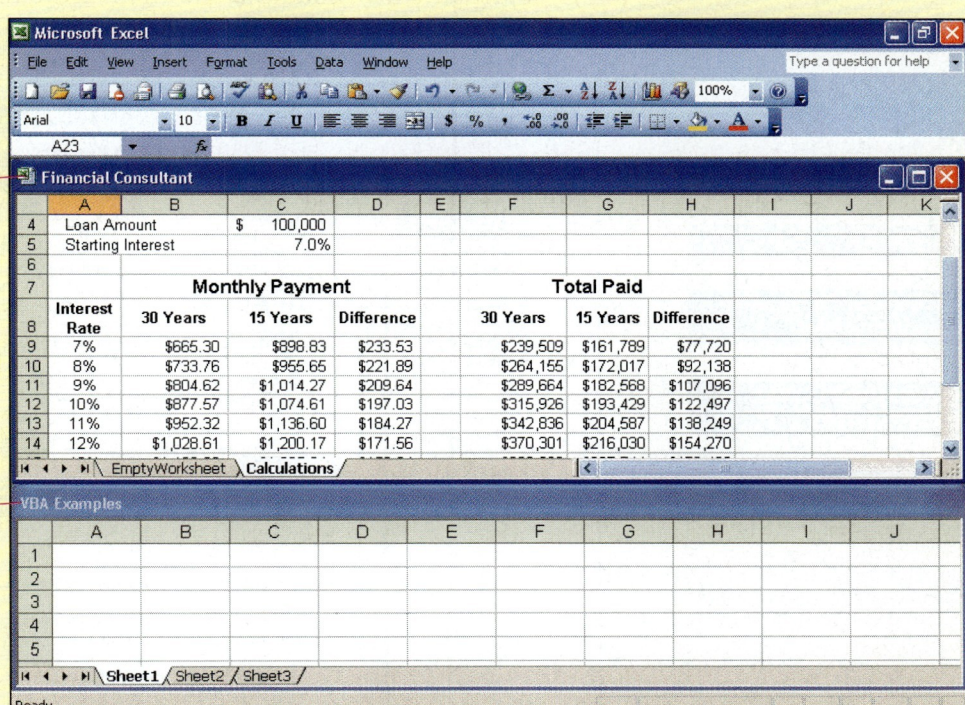

(g) Open a Second Workbook (step 7)

FIGURE 14 Hands-on Exercise 4 (*continued*)

THE COMPARISON IS CASE-SENSITIVE

Any literal comparison (e.g., strInstructorName = "Grauer") is case-sensitive, so that the user has to enter the correct name and case for the condition to be true. A response of "GRAUER" or "grauer", while containing the correct name, will be evaluated as false because the case does not match. You can, however, use the UCase (uppercase) function to convert the user's response to uppercase, and test accordingly. In other words, UCase(strInstructorName) = "GRAUER" will be evaluated as true if the user enters "Grauer" in any combination of upper- or lowercase letters.

Step 8: **Copy the Procedure**

- You should be back in the Visual Basic editor as shown in Figure 14h. Copy the procedures associated with the Open and Close Workbook events from the VBA Examples workbook to the other workbook, Financial Consultant.
  - ❏ Double click **ThisWorkbook** within the list of Microsoft Excel objects under the VBA Examples workbook.
  - ❏ Click and drag to select the definition of the ApplicationTitle constant in the General Declarations section, the binNormalExit definition, plus the two procedures (to open and close the workbook) in their entirety.
  - ❏ Click the **Copy button** on the Standard toolbar.
  - ❏ If necessary, expand the Financial Consultant VBA Project, then double click **ThisWorkbook** with the list of Excel objects under the Financial Consultant workbook. Click underneath the **Option Explicit command**.
  - ❏ Click the **Paste button** on the Standard toolbar. The VBA code should be copied into this module as shown in Figure 14h.
- Click the **Save button** to save the module.

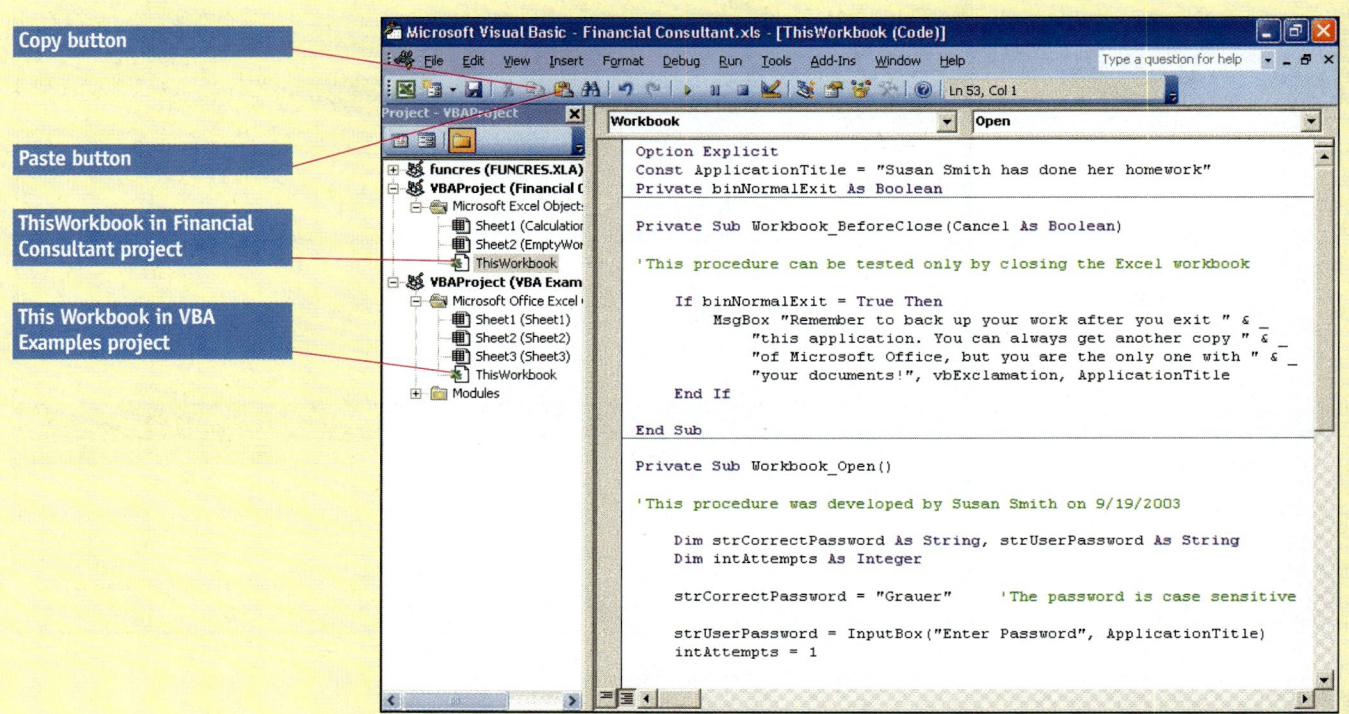

(h) Copy the Procedure (step 8)

FIGURE 14 Hands-on Exercise 4 (*continued*)

THE VISIBLE PROPERTY

The Calculations worksheet should be hidden until the user enters the correct password. This is accomplished by setting the Visible property of the worksheet to false at the beginning of the Open Workbook event procedure, then setting it to true after the correct password has been entered. Click in the Open Workbook event procedure after the last Dim statement, press Enter, then enter the statement Sheet1.Visible = False to hide the Calculations worksheet. Scroll down in the procedure (below the MsgBox statement within the If statement that tests for the correct password), then enter the statement Sheet1.Visible = True followed by the statement Sheet1.Activate to select the worksheet.

Step 9: **Test the Procedure**

- Click the **View Microsoft Excel button** on the Standard toolbar within the VBA window (or click the **Excel button** on the Windows taskbar) to view the Excel workbook. Click in the window containing the Financial Consultant workbook (or whichever workbook you are using), then click the **Maximize button**.

- Pull down the **File menu** and click the **Close command**. (The dialog box in Figure 14i does not appear initially because the value of binNormalExit is not yet set; you have to open the workbook to set the switch.) Click **Yes** if asked whether to save the changes to the workbook.

- Pull down the **File menu** and reopen the workbook. Click the button to **Enable Macros**, then enter **Grauer** when prompted for the password. Click **OK** when the password has been accepted.

- Close this workbook, close the **VBA Examples workbook**, then pull down the **File menu** and click the **Exit command** to quit Excel.

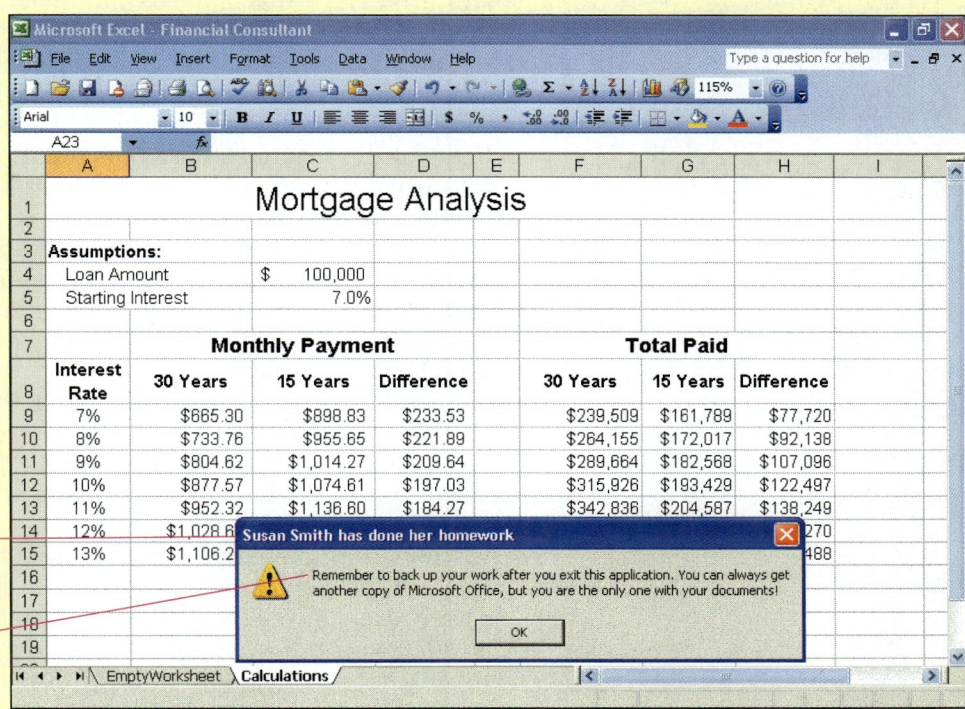

Customized title bar

Message is displayed when you execute command to close workbook

(i) Test the Procedure (step 9)

FIGURE 14 Hands-on Exercise 4 (*continued*)

SCREEN CAPTURE

Prove to your instructor that you have completed the hands-on exercise correctly by capturing a screen, then pasting the screen into a Word document. Do the exercise until you come to the screen that you want to capture, then press the PrintScreen key at the top of the keyboard. Click the Start button, start Word, and open a Word document, then pull down the Edit menu and click the Paste command to bring the captured screen into the Word document. Right click the screen within the Word document, click the Format Picture command, click the Layout tab, and select the Square layout. Click OK to close the dialog box. You can now move and size the screen within the document.

The same VBA procedure can be run from multiple applications in Microsoft Office, despite the fact that the applications are very different. The real power of VBA, however, is its ability to detect events that are unique to a specific application and to respond accordingly. An event is defined as any action that is recognized by an application. Opening or closing an Excel workbook or an Access database is an event. Selecting a worksheet within a workbook is also an event, as is clicking on a command button on an Access form. To use VBA within Microsoft Office, you decide which events are significant, and what is to happen when those events occur. Then you develop the appropriate *event procedures* that execute automatically when the event occurs.

Consider, for example, Figure 15, which displays the results of two event procedures in conjunction with opening and closing an Access database. (These are procedures similar to those we created in the preceding pages in conjunction with opening and closing an Excel workbook.) The procedure associated with Figure 15a displays a message that appears automatically after the user clicks the Switchboard button to exit the database. The procedure is almost trivial to write, and consists of a single MsgBox statement. The effect of the procedure is quite significant, however, as it reminds the user to back up his or her work. Indeed, you can never overemphasize the importance of adequate backup.

The dialog box in Figure 15b prompts the user for a password and appears automatically when the user opens the database. The logic here is more sophisticated in that the underlying procedure contains an InputBox statement to request the password, a Do Until loop that is executed until the user enters the correct password or exceeds the allotted number of attempts, then additional logic to display the switchboard or terminate the application if the user fails to enter the proper password. The procedure is not difficult, however, and it builds on the VBA statements that were covered earlier.

The next hands-on exercise has you create the event procedures that are associated with the database in Figure 15. The exercise references a switchboard, or user interface, that is created as a form within the database. The switchboard displays a menu that enables a nontechnical person to move easily from one object in the database (e.g., a form or report) to another.

The switchboard is created through a utility called the Switchboard Manager that prompts you for each item you want to add to the switchboard, and which action you want taken in conjunction with that menu item. You could do the exercise with any database, but we suggest you use the database we provide to access the switchboard that we created for you. The exercise begins, therefore, by having you download a data disk from our Web site.

EVENT-DRIVEN VERSUS TRADITIONAL PROGRAMMING

A traditional program is executed sequentially, beginning with the first line of code and continuing in order through the remainder of the program. It is the program, not the user, that determines the order in which the statements are executed. VBA, on the other hand, is event-driven, meaning that the order in which the procedures are executed depends on the events that occur. It is the user, rather than the program, that determines which events occur, and consequently which procedures are executed. Each application in Microsoft Office has a different set of objects and associated events that comprise the application's object model.

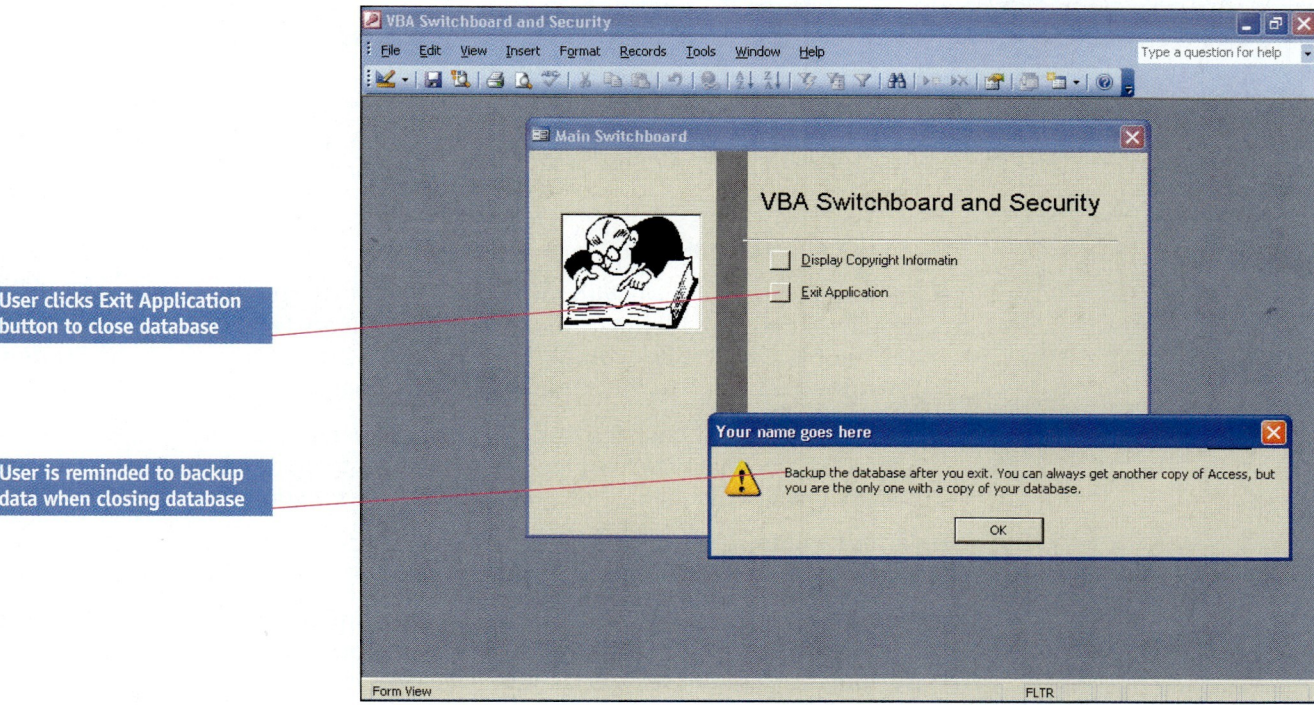

User clicks Exit Application button to close database

User is reminded to backup data when closing database

(a) Reminder to the User (Exit Application event)

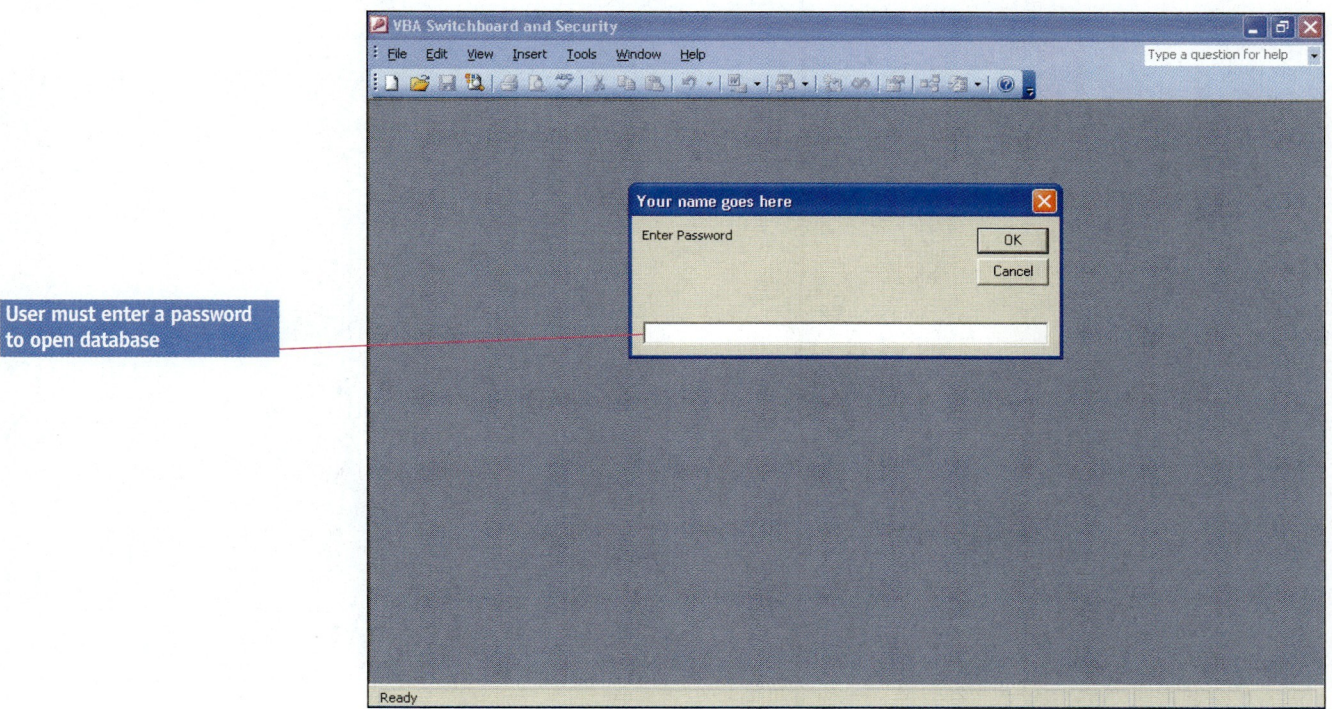

User must enter a password to open database

(b) Password Protection (Open Form event)

FIGURE 15 Event-Driven Programming (Microsoft Access)

5 Event-Driven Programming (Microsoft Access)

Objective To implement password protection for an Access database; to create a second event procedure that displays a message to the user upon closing the database. Use Figure 16 as a guide in the exercise.

Step 1: Open the Access Database

- You can do this exercise with any database, but we suggest you use the database we have provided. Go to **www.prenhall.com/grauer**, click the **Office 2003 book**, which takes you to the Office 2003 home page. Click the **Student Download tab** to go to the Student Download page.

- Scroll until you can click the link for **Getting Started with VBA**. You will see the File Download dialog box asking what you want to do. Click the **Save button** to display the Save As dialog box, then save the file on your desktop.

- Double click the file after it has been downloaded and follow the onscreen instructions to expand the self-extracting file that contains the database.

- Go to the newly created **Exploring VBA folder** and open the **VBA Switchboard and Security database**. Click the **Open button** when you see the security warning. You should see the Database window in Figure 16a.

- Pull down the **Tools menu**, click the **Macro command**, then click the **Visual Basic Editor command**. Maximize the VBA editor window.

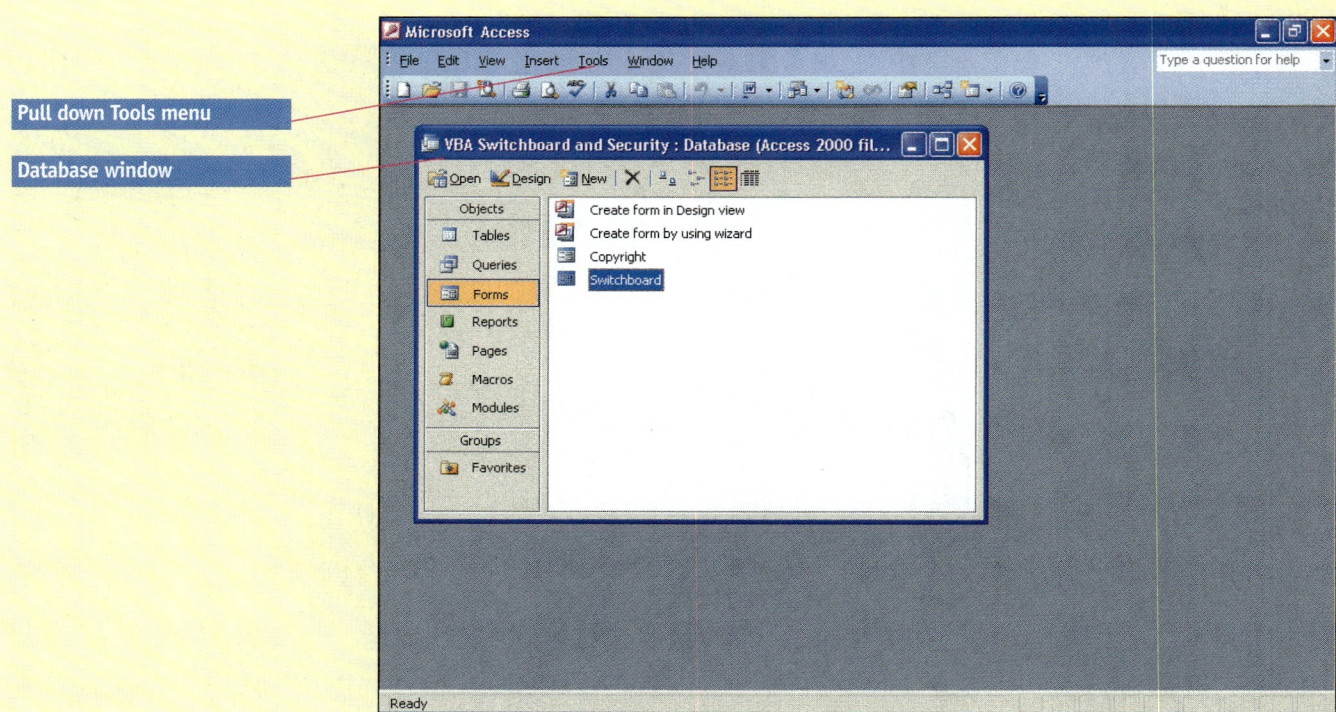

(a) Open the Access Database (step 1)

FIGURE 16 Hands-on Exercise 5

Step 2: **Create the ExitDatabase Procedure**

- Pull down the **Insert menu** and click **Module** to insert Module1. Complete the **General Declarations section** by adding the Option Explicit statement (if necessary) and the definition of the ApplicationTitle constant as shown in Figure 16b.

- Pull down the **Insert menu** and click **Procedure** to insert a new procedure called **ExitDatabase**. Click the option buttons for a **Sub procedure** and for **Public scope**. Click **OK**.

- Complete the ExitDatabase procedure by entering the **MsgBox** and **DoCmd.Quit** statements. The DoCmd.Quit statement will close Access, but it is entered initially as a comment by beginning the line with an apostrophe.

- Click anywhere in the procedure, then click the **Run Sub button** to test the procedure. Correct any errors that occur, then when the MsgBox displays correctly, **delete the apostrophe** in front of the DoCmd.Quit statement.

- Save the module. The next time you execute the procedure, you should see the message box you just created, and then Access will be terminated.

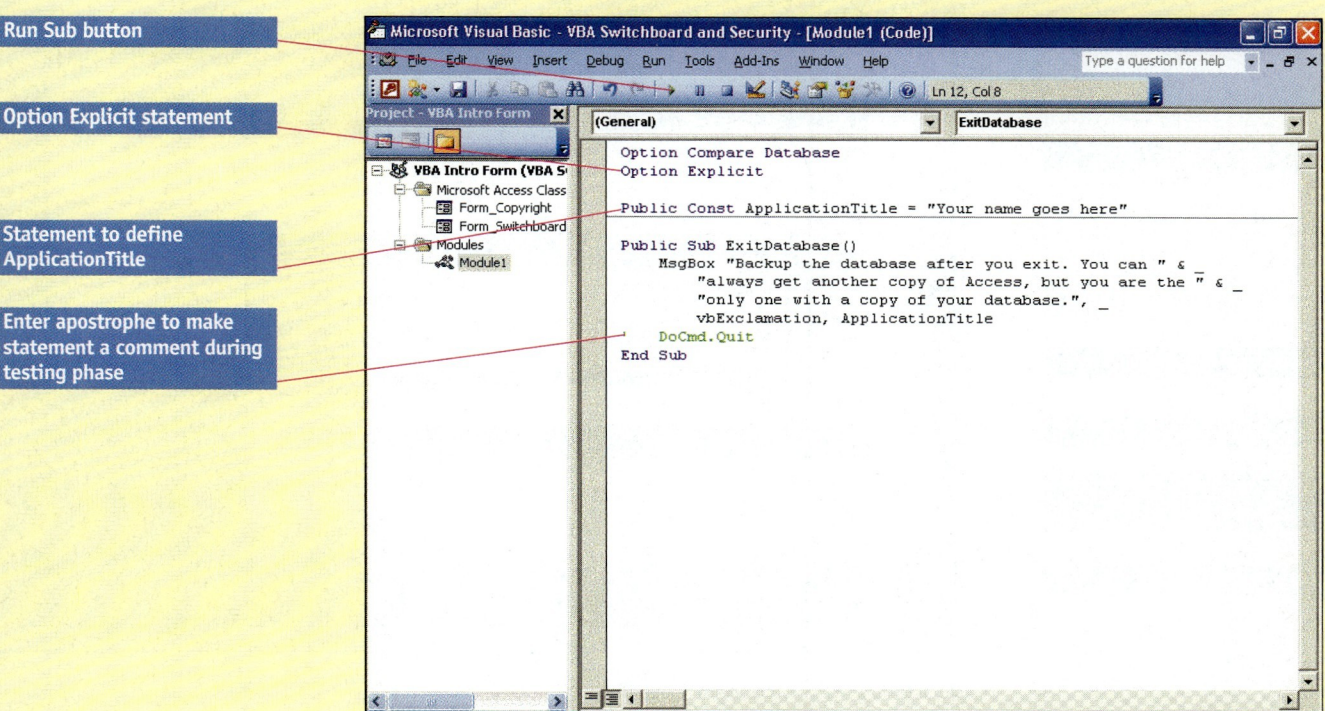

Run Sub button

Option Explicit statement

Statement to define ApplicationTitle

Enter apostrophe to make statement a comment during testing phase

(b) Create the ExitDatabase Procedure (step 2)

FIGURE 16 Hands-on Exercise 5 (*continued*)

CREATE A PUBLIC CONSTANT

Give your application a customized look by adding your name or other identifying message to the title bar of the message and/or input boxes that you use. You can add the information individually to each statement, but it is easier to declare a public constant from within a general module. That way, you can change the value of the constant in one place and have the change reflected automatically throughout your application.

Step 3: **Modify the Switchboard**

■ Click the **View Microsoft Access button** on the Standard toolbar within the VBA window to switch to the Database window (or use the **F11** keyboard shortcut).

■ Pull down the **Tools menu**, click the **Database Utilities command**, then choose **Switchboard Manager** to display the Switchboard Manager dialog box in Figure 16c.

■ Click the **Edit button** to edit the Main Switchboard and display the Edit Switchboard Page dialog box. Select the **&Exit Application command** and click its **Edit button** to display the Edit Switchboard Item dialog box.

■ Change the command to **Run Code**. Enter **ExitDatabase** in the Function Name text box. Click **OK**, then close the two other dialog boxes.

■ The switchboard has been modified so that clicking the Exit button will run the VBA procedure you just created.

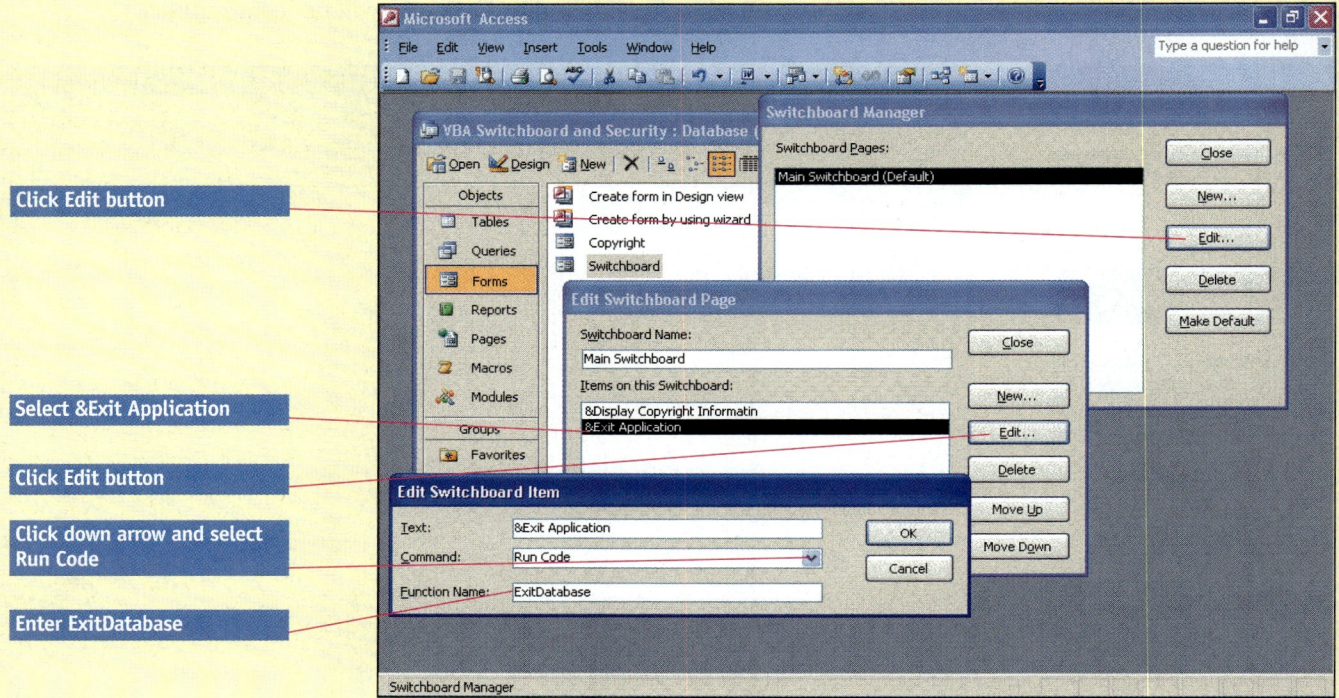

(c) Modify the Switchboard (step 3)

FIGURE 16 Hands-on Exercise 5 (*continued*)

CREATE A KEYBOARD SHORTCUT

The & has special significance when used within the name of an Access object because it creates a keyboard shortcut to that object. Enter "&Exit Application", for example, and the letter E (the letter immediately after the ampersand) will be underlined and appear as "Exit Application" on the switchboard. From there, you can execute the item by clicking its button, or you can use the Alt+E keyboard shortcut (where "E" is the underlined letter in the menu option).

Step 4: **Test the Switchboard**

- If necessary, click the **Forms button** in the Database window. Double click the **Switchboard form** to open the switchboard as shown in Figure 16d. The switchboard contains two commands.

- Click the **Display Copyright Information command** to display a form that we use with all our databases. (You can open this form in Design view and modify the text to include your name, rather than ours. If you do, be sure to save the modified form, then close it.)

- Click the **Exit Application command** (or use the **Alt+E** keyboard shortcut). You should see the dialog box in Figure 16d, corresponding to the MsgBox statement you created earlier. Click **OK** to close the dialog box.

- Access itself will terminate because of the DoCmd.Quit statement within the ExitDatabase procedure. (If this does not happen, return to the VBA editor and remove the apostrophe in front of the DoCmd statement.)

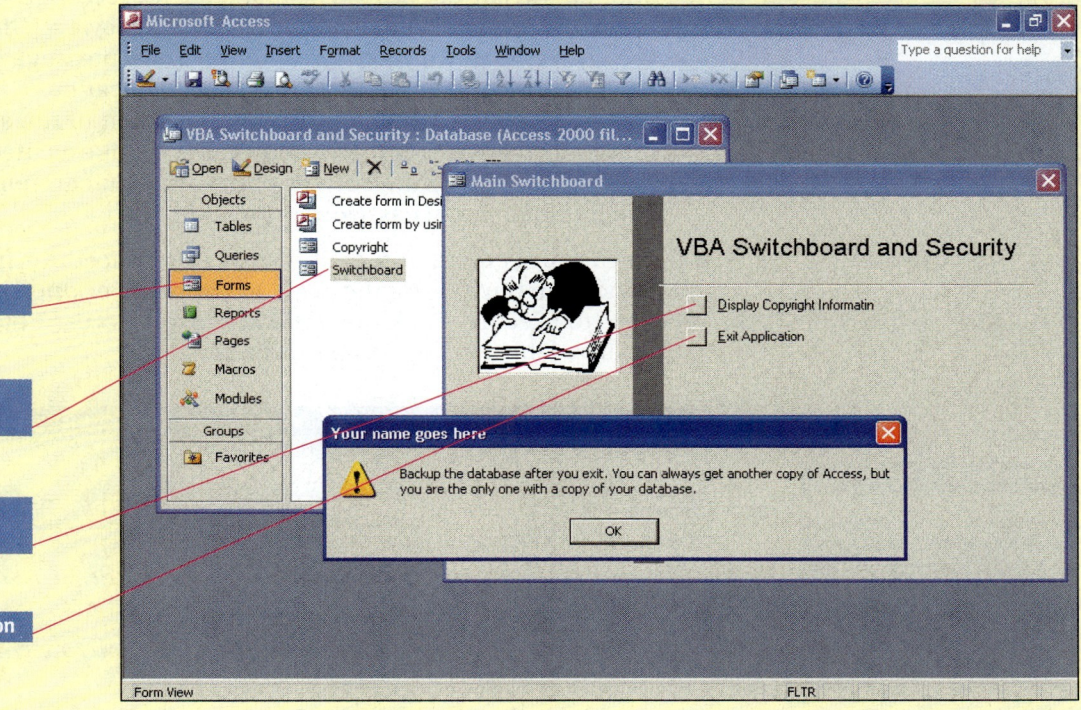

(d) Test the Switchboard (step 4)

FIGURE 16   Hands-on Exercise 5 (*continued*)

BACK UP IMPORTANT FILES

It's not a question of *if* it will happen, but *when*—hard disks die, files are lost, or viruses may infect a system. It has happened to us, and it will happen to you, but you can prepare for the inevitable by creating adequate backup before the problem occurs. The essence of a backup strategy is to decide which files to back up (your data), how often to do the backup (whenever it changes), and where to keep the backup (away from your computer). Do it!

Step 5: **Complete the Open Form Event Procedure**

- Start Access and reopen the **VBA Switchboard and Security database**. Press **Alt+F11** to start the VBA editor.

- Click the **plus sign** next to Microsoft Office Access Class objects, double click the module called **Form_Switchboard**, then look for the partially completed **Form_Open procedure** as shown in Figure 16e.

- The procedure was created automatically by the Switchboard Manager. You must, however, expand this procedure to include password protection. Note the following:
  - ❑ Three variables are required—the correct password, the password entered by the user, and the number of attempts.
  - ❑ The user is prompted for the password, and the number of attempts is set to 1. The user is given two additional attempts, if necessary, to get the correct password.
  - ❑ The If statement at the end of the loop determines whether the user has entered the correct password, and if so, it executes the original commands that are associated with the switchboard. If, however, the user fails to supply the correct password, an invalid password message is displayed and the **DoCmd.Quit** statement terminates the application.
  - ❑ We suggest you place an **apostrophe** in front of the statement initially so that it becomes a comment, and thus it is not executed. Once you are sure that you can enter the correct password, you can remove the apostrophe and implement the password protection.

- Save the procedure. You cannot test this procedure from within the VBA window; you must cause the event to happen (i.e., open the form) for the procedure to execute. Click the **View Microsoft Access button** on the Standard toolbar to return to the Database window.

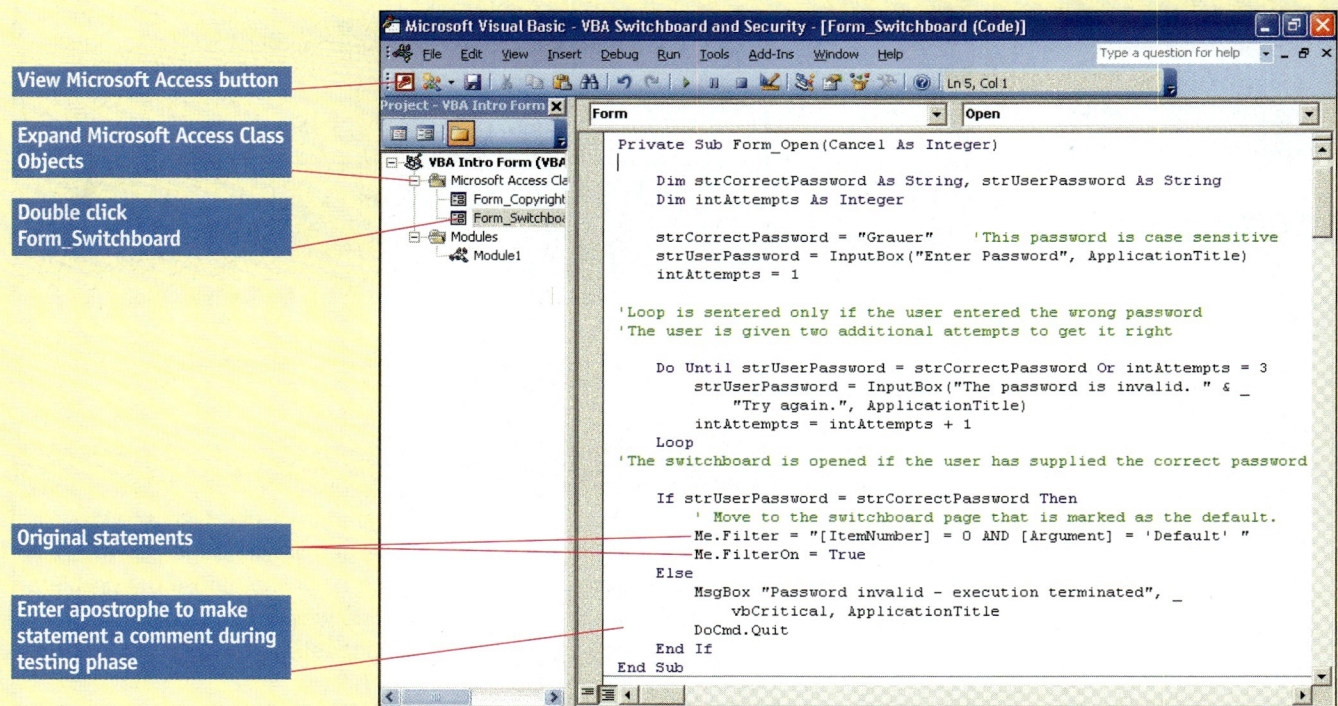

(e) Complete the Open Form Event Procedure (step 5)

FIGURE 16 Hands-on Exercise 5 (*continued*)

Step 6:   **Test the Procedure**

- Close all open windows within the Access database except for the Database window. Click the **Forms button**, then double click the **Switchboard form**.

- You should be prompted for the password as shown in Figure 16f. The password (in our procedure) is **Grauer**.

- Test the procedure repeatedly to include all possibilities. Enter the correct password on the first, second, and third attempts to be sure that the procedure works as intended. Each time you enter the correct password, you will have to close the switchboard, then reopen it.

- Test the procedure one final time, by failing to enter the correct password. You will see a message box indicating that the password is invalid and that execution will be terminated. Termination will not take place, however, because the DoCmd.Quit statement is currently entered as a comment.

- Press **Alt+F11** to reopen the VBA editor. Open the **Microsoft Access Class Objects folder** and double click on **Form_Switchboard**. Delete the apostrophe in front of the DoCmd.Quit statement. The text of the statement changes from green to black to indicate that it is an executable statement. Save the procedure.

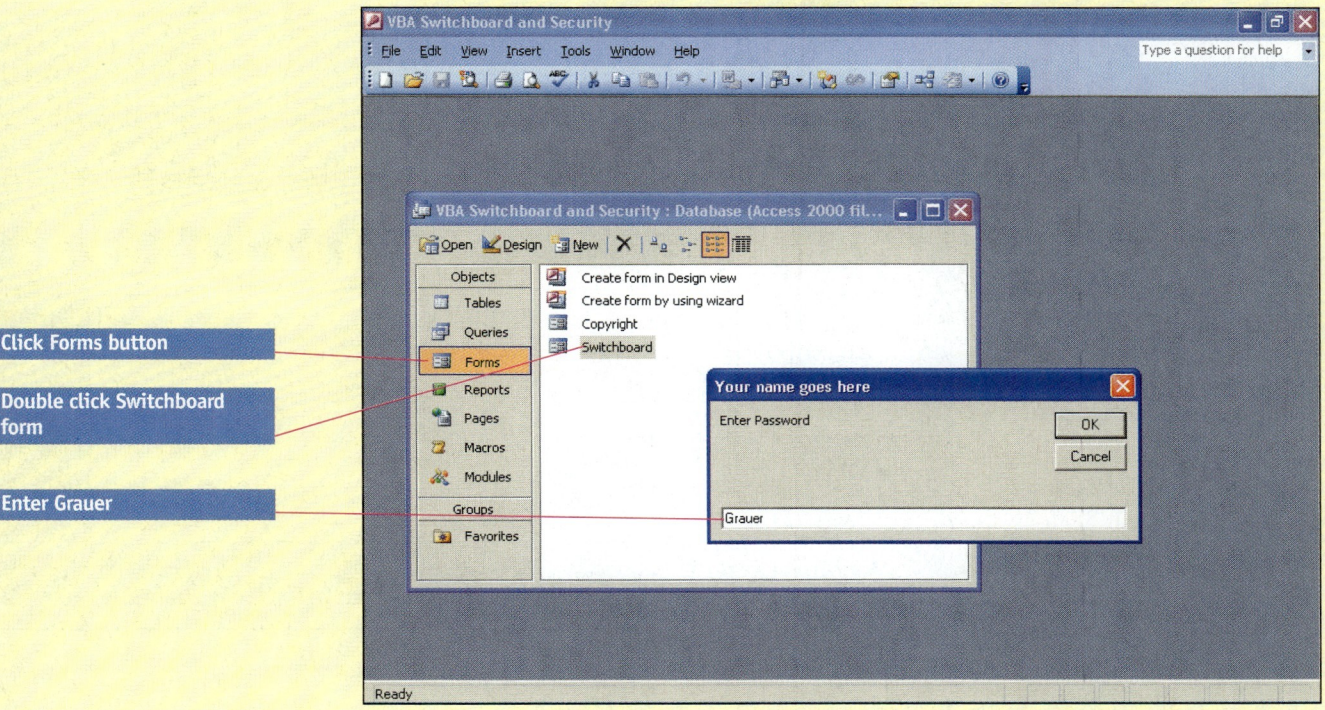

(f) Test the Procedure (step 6)

FIGURE 16   Hands-on Exercise 5 (*continued*)

TOGGLE COMMENTS ON AND OFF

Comments are used primarily to explain the purpose of VBA statements, but they can also be used to "comment out" code as distinct from deleting the statement altogether. Thus, you can add or remove the apostrophe in front of the statement, to toggle the comment on or off.

Step 7:   Change the Startup Properties

■ Click the **View Microsoft Access button** on the VBA Standard toolbar to return to the Database window.

■ Close all open windows except the Database window. Pull down the **Tools menu** and click **Startup** to display the Startup dialog box as shown in Figure 16g.

■ Click in the **Application Title** text box and enter the title of the application, **VBA Switchboard and Security** in this example.

■ Click the **drop-down arrow** in the Display Form/Page list box and select the **Switchboard form** as the form that will open automatically in conjunction with opening the database.

■ Clear the check box to display the Database window. Click **OK** to accept the settings and close the dialog box.

■ The next time you open the database, the switchboard should open automatically, which in turn triggers the Open Form event procedure that will prompt the user to enter a password.

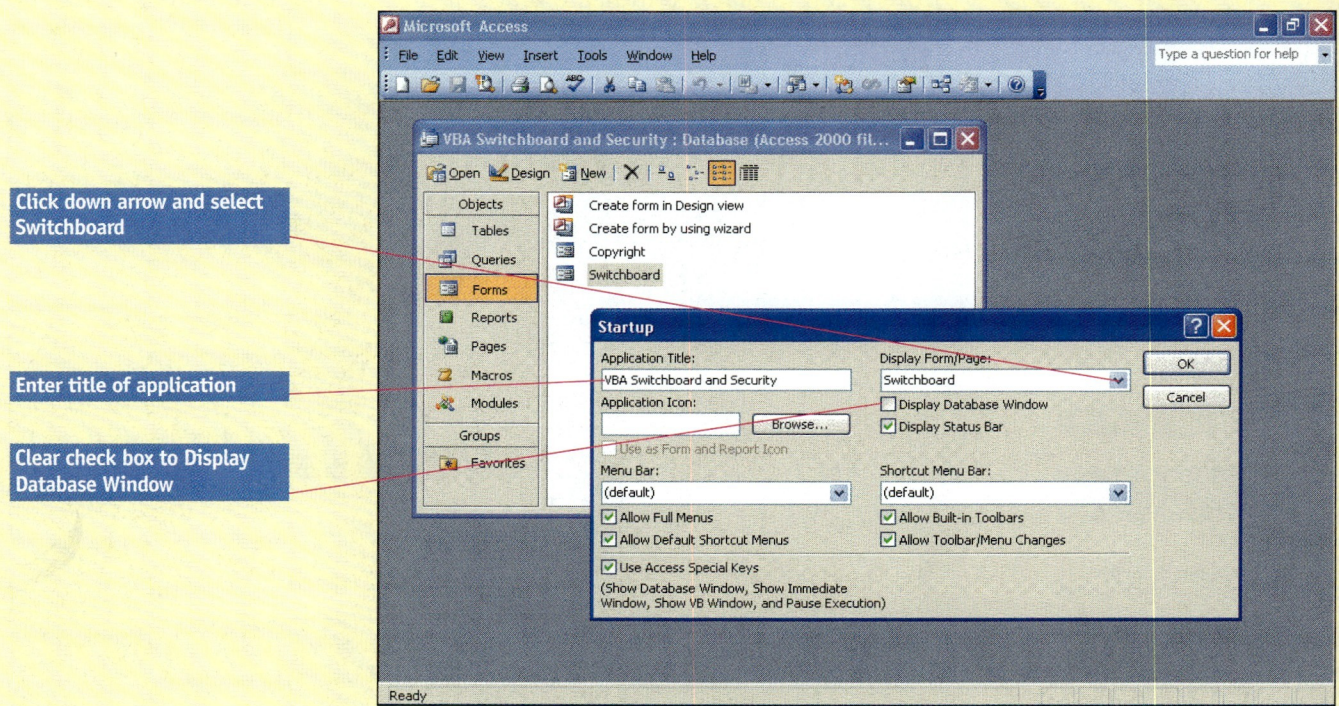

(g) Change the Startup Properties (step 7)

FIGURE 16   Hands-on Exercise 5 (*continued*)

HIDE THE DATABASE WINDOW

Use the Startup property to hide the Database window from the novice user. You avoid confusion and you may prevent the novice from accidentally deleting objects in the database. Of course, anyone with some knowledge of Access can restore the Database window by pulling down the Window menu, clicking the Unhide command, then selecting the Database window from the associated dialog box. Nevertheless, hiding the Database window is a good beginning.

Step 8: **Test the Database**

- Close the database, then reopen the database to test the procedures we have created in this exercise. The sequence of events is as follows:
  - ❏ The database is loaded and the switchboard is opened but is not yet visible. The Open Form procedure for the switchboard is executed, and you are prompted for the password as shown in Figure 16h.
  - ❏ The password is entered correctly and the switchboard is displayed. The Database window is hidden, however, because the Startup Properties have been modified.

- Click the **Exit Application command** (or use the **Alt+E** keyboard shortcut). You will see the message box reminding you to back up the system, after which the database is closed and Access is terminated.

- Reopen the database. This time, however, you are to enter the wrong password three times in a row. You should see a message indicating that the execution was terminated due to an invalid password.

- Testing is complete and you can go on to add the other objects to your Access database. Congratulations on a job well done.

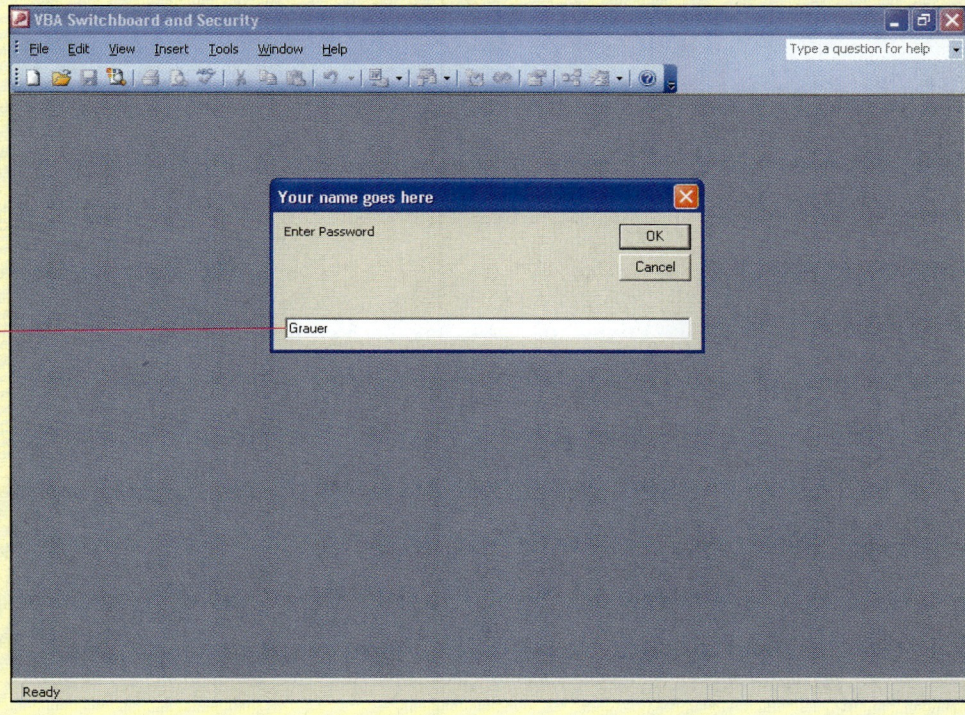

Enter password

(h) Test the Database (step 8)

FIGURE 16 Hands-on Exercise 5 (*continued*)

RESTORING HIDDEN MENUS AND TOOLBARS

You can use the Startup property to hide menus and/or toolbars from the user by clearing the respective check boxes. A word of caution, however—once the menus are hidden, it is difficult to get them back. Start Access, pull down the File menu, and click Open to display the Open dialog box, select the database to open, then press and hold the Shift key when you click the Open button. This powerful technique is not widely known.

SUMMARY

Visual Basic for Applications (VBA) is a powerful programming language that is accessible from all major applications in Microsoft Office XP. A VBA statement accomplishes a specific task such as displaying a message to the user or accepting input from the user. Statements are grouped into procedures, and procedures in turn are grouped into modules. Every procedure is classified as either private or public.

The MsgBox statement displays information to the user. It has one required argument, which is the message (or prompt) that is displayed to the user. The other two arguments—the icon that is to be displayed in the dialog box and the text of the title bar—are optional. The InputBox function displays a prompt to the user requesting information, then it stores that information (the value returned by the user) for use later in the procedure.

Every variable must be declared (defined) before it can be used. This is accomplished through the Dim (short for Dimension) statement that appears at the beginning of a procedure. The Dim statement indicates the name of the variable and its type (for example, whether it will hold a character string or an integer number), which in turn reserves the appropriate amount of memory for that variable.

The ability to make decisions within a procedure, then branch to alternative sets of statements is implemented through the If . . . Then . . . Else or Case statements. The Else clause is optional, but may be repeated multiple times within an If statement. The Case statement is preferable to an If statement with multiple Else clauses.

The For . . . Next statement (or For . . . Next loop as it is also called) executes all statements between the words For and Next a specified number of times, using a counter to keep track of the number of times the loop is executed. The Do . . . Loop Until and/or Do Until . . . Loop statements are used when the number of times through the loop is not known in advance.

VBA is different from traditional programming languages in that it is event-driven. An event is defined as any action that is recognized by an application, such as Excel or Access. Opening or closing an Excel workbook or an Access database is an event. Selecting a worksheet within a workbook is also an event, as is clicking on a command button on an Access form. To use VBA within Microsoft Office, you decide which events are significant, and what is to happen when those events occur. Then you develop the appropriate event procedures.

KEY TERMS

Argument 578
Case statement 594
Character string 592
Comment 582
Compilation error 606
Complete Word tool 598
Concatenate 580
Custom toolbar 595
Debug menu 606
Debug toolbar 606
Debug.Print statement 607
Debugging 606
Declarations section 582
Dim statement 581
Do Loops 605
Else clause 592
End Sub statement 579

Event 617
Event procedure (Access) 628
Event procedure (Excel) 617
Execution error 606
For . . . Next Statement 604
Full Module view 597
If statement 592
Immediate window 607
InputBox function 580
Intrinsic constant 579
Literal 592
Locals window 607
Macro 578
Macro recorder 578
Module 578
MsgBox statement 579
Option Explicit 582

Private procedure 578
Procedure 578
Procedure header 579
Project Explorer 582
Public procedure 578
Run-time error 606
Statement 578
Step Into button 607
Syntax 578
Underscore 580
Variable 580
VBA 578
Visible property 626
Visual Basic editor 582
Visual Basic for Applications . . . 578

MULTIPLE CHOICE

1. Which of the following applications in Office XP has access to VBA?

   (a) Word

   (b) Excel

   (c) Access

   (d) All of the above

2. Which of the following is a valid name for a VBA variable?

   (a) Public

   (b) Private

   (c) strUserFirstName

   (d) int Count Of Attempts

3. Which of the following is true about an If statement?

   (a) It evaluates a condition as either true or false, then executes the statement(s) following the keyword "Then" if the condition is true

   (b) It must contain the keyword Else

   (c) It must contain one or more ElseIf statements

   (d) All of the above

4. Which of the following lists the items from smallest to largest?

   (a) Module, procedure, statement

   (b) Statement, module, procedure

   (c) Statement, procedure, module

   (d) Procedure, module, statement

5. Given the statement, MsgBox "Welcome to VBA", "Bob was here", which of the following is true?

   (a) "Welcome to VBA" will be displayed within the resulting message box

   (b) "Welcome to VBA" will appear on the title bar of the displayed dialog box

   (c) The two adjacent commas will cause a compilation error

   (d) An informational icon will be displayed with the message

6. Where are the VBA procedures associated with an Office document stored?

   (a) In the same folder, but in a separate file

   (b) In the Office document itself

   (c) In a special VBA folder on drive C

   (d) In a special VBA folder on the local area network

7. The Debug.Print statement is associated with the:

   (a) Locals window

   (b) Immediate window

   (c) Project Explorer

   (d) Debug toolbar

8. Which of the following is the proper sequence of arguments for the MsgBox statement?

   (a) Text for the title bar, prompt, button

   (b) Prompt, button, text for the title bar

   (c) Prompt, text for the title bar, button

   (d) Button, prompt, text for the title bar

9. Which of the following is a true statement about Do loops?

   (a) Placing the Until clause at the beginning of the loop tests the condition prior to executing any statements in the loop

   (b) Placing the Until clause at the end of the loop executes the statements in the loop, then it tests the condition

   (c) Both (a) and (b)

   (d) Neither (a) nor (b)

10. Given the statement, For intCount = 1 to 10 Step 3, how many times will the statements in the loop be executed (assuming that there are no statements in the loop to terminate the execution)?

    (a) 10

    (b) 4

    (c) 3

    (d) Impossible to determine

... continued

11. Which of the following is a *false* statement?

    (a) A dash at the end of a line indicates continuation

    (b) An ampersand indicates concatenation

    (c) An apostrophe at the beginning of a line signifies a comment

    (d) A pair of quotation marks denotes a character string

12. What is the effect of deleting the apostrophe that appears at the beginning of a VBA statement?

    (a) A compilation error will occur

    (b) The statement is converted to a comment

    (c) The color of the statement will change from black to green

    (d) The statement is made executable

13. Which of the following If statements will display the indicated message if the user enters a response other than "Grauer" (assuming that "Grauer" is the correct password)?

    (a) If strUserResponse <> "Grauer" Then MsgBox "Wrong password"

    (b) If strUserResponse = "Grauer" Then MsgBox "Wrong password"

    (c) If strUserResponse > "Grauer" Then MsgBox "Wrong password"

    (d) If strUserResponse < "Grauer" Then MsgBox "Wrong password"

14. Which of the following will execute the statements in the loop at least once?

    (a) Do . . . Loop Until

    (b) Do Until ….. Loop

    (c) Both (a) and (b)

    (d) Neither (a) nor (b)

15. The copy and paste commands can be used to:

    (a) Copy statements within a procedure

    (b) Copy statements from a procedure in one module to a procedure in another module within the same document

    (c) Copy statements from a module in an Excel workbook to a module in an Access database

    (d) All of the above

16. Which of the following is true about indented text in a VBA procedure?

    (a) The indented text is always executed first

    (b) The indented text is always executed last

    (c) The indented text is rendered a comment and is never executed

    (d) None of the above

17. Which statement will prompt the user to enter his or her name and store the result in a variable called strUser?

    (a) InputBox.strUser

    (b) strUser = MsgBox("Enter your name")

    (c) strUser = InputBox("Enter your name")

    (d) InputBox("Enter strUser")

18. Given that strUser is currently set to "George", the expression "Good morning, strName" will return:

    (a) Good morning, George

    (b) Good morning, strName

    (c) Good morning George

    (d) Good morning strName

ANSWERS

1. d	7. b	13. a
2. c	8. b	14. a
3. a	9. c	15. d
4. c	10. b	16. d
5. a	11. a	17. c
6. b	12. d	18. b

Getting Started with Microsoft® Windows® XP

OBJECTIVES

After reading this chapter you will:

1. Describe the Windows desktop.
2. Use the Help and Support Center to obtain information.
3. Describe the My Computer and My Documents folders.
4. Differentiate between a program file and a data file.
5. Download a file from the Exploring Office Web site.
6. Copy and/or move a file from one folder to another.
7. Delete a file, and then recover it from the Recycle Bin.
8. Create and arrange shortcuts on the desktop.
9. Use the Search Companion.
10. Use the My Pictures and My Music folders.
11. Use Windows Messenger for instant messaging.

hands-on exercises

1. WELCOME TO WINDOWS XP
   Input: None
   Output: None

2. DOWNLOAD PRACTICE FILES
   Input: Data files from the Web
   Output: Welcome to Windows XP (a Word document)

3. WINDOWS EXPLORER
   Input: Data files from exercise 2
   Output: Screen Capture within a Word document

4. INCREASING PRODUCTIVITY
   Input: Data files from exercise 3
   Output: None

5. FUN WITH WINDOWS XP
   Input: None
   Output: None

CASE STUDY
UNFORESEEN CIRCUMSTANCES

Steve and his wife Shelly have poured their life savings into the dream of owning their own business, a "nanny" service agency. They have spent the last two years building their business and have created a sophisticated database with numerous entries for both families and nannies. The database is the key to their operation. Now that it is up and running, Steve and Shelly are finally at a point where they could hire someone to manage the operation on a part-time basis so that they could take some time off together.

Unfortunately, their process for selecting a person they could trust with their business was not as thorough as it should have been. Nancy, their new employee, assured them that all was well, and the couple left for an extended weekend. The place was in shambles on their return. Nancy could not handle the responsibility, and when Steve gave her two weeks' notice, neither he nor his wife thought that the unimaginable would happen. On her last day in the office Nancy "lost" all of the names in the database—the data was completely gone!

Nancy claimed that a "virus" knocked out the database, but after spending nearly $1,500 with a computer consultant, Steve was told that it had been cleverly deleted from the hard drive and could not be recovered. Of course, the consultant asked Steve and Shelly about their backup strategy, which they sheepishly admitted did not exist. They had never experienced any problems in the past, and simply assumed that their data was safe. Fortunately, they do have hard copy of the data in the form of various reports that were printed throughout the time they were in business. They have no choice but to manually reenter the data. ■

Your assignment is to read the chapter, paying special attention to the information on file management. Think about how Steve and Shelly could have avoided the disaster if a backup strategy had been in place, then summarize your thoughts in a brief note to your instructor. Describe the elements of a basic backup strategy. Give several other examples of unforeseen circumstances that can cause data to be lost.

Windows® XP is the newest and most powerful version of the Windows operating system. It has a slightly different look than earlier versions, but it maintains the conventions of its various predecessors. You have seen the Windows interface many times, but do you really understand it? Can you move and copy files with confidence? Do you know how to back up the Excel spreadsheets, Access databases, and other documents that you work so hard to create? If not, now is the time to learn.

We begin with an introduction to the desktop, the graphical user interface that lets you work in intuitive fashion by pointing at icons and clicking the mouse. We identify the basic components of a window and describe how to execute commands and supply information through different elements in a dialog box. We stress the importance of disk and file management, but begin with basic definitions of a file and a folder. We also introduce Windows Explorer and show you how to move or copy a file from one folder to another. We discuss other basic operations, such as renaming and deleting a file. We also describe how to recover a deleted file (if necessary) from the Recycle Bin.

Windows XP is available in different versions. Windows ***XP Home Edition*** is intended for entertainment and home use. It includes a media player, new support for digital photography, and an instant messenger. Windows ***XP Professional Edition*** has all of the features of the Home Edition plus additional security to encrypt files and protect data. It includes support for high-performance multiprocessor systems. It also lets you connect to your computer from a remote station.

The login screen in Figure 1 is displayed when the computer is turned on initially and/or when you are switching from one user account to another. Several individuals can share the same computer. Each user, however, retains his or her individual desktop settings, individual lists of favorite and recently visited Web sites, as well as other customized Windows settings. Multiple users can be logged on simultaneously, each with his or her programs in memory, through a feature known as ***fast user switching***.

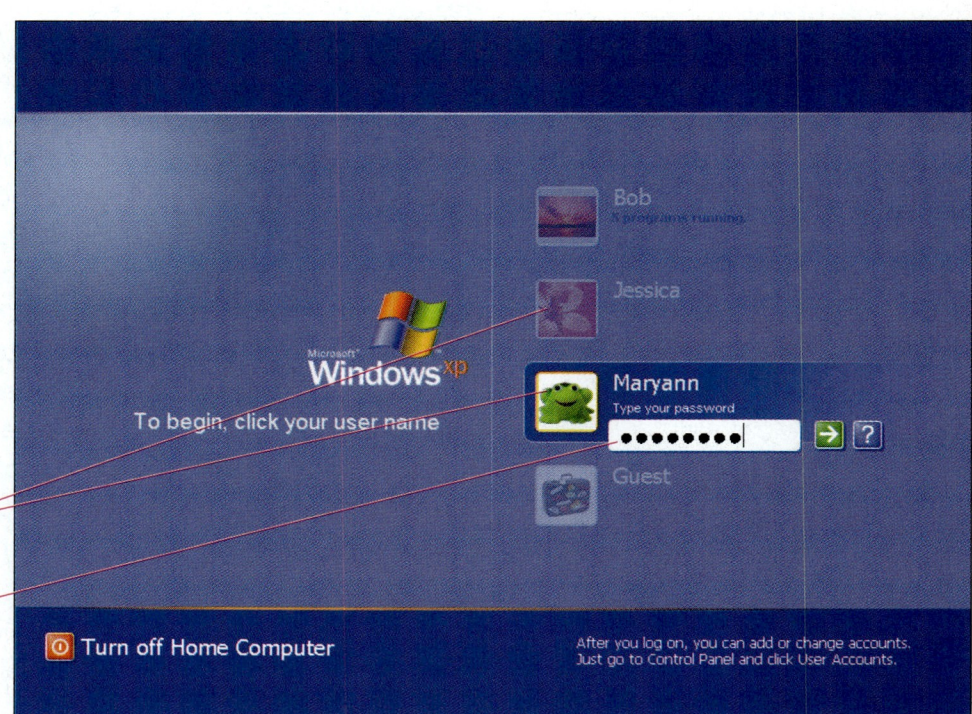

Multiple users can be logged on

Accounts can be password-protected

FIGURE 1 Windows XP Login

Windows XP, as well as all previous versions of Windows, creates a working environment for your computer that parallels the working environment at home or in an office. You work at a desk. Windows operations take place on the *desktop*. There are physical objects on a desk such as folders, a dictionary, a calculator, or a phone. The computer equivalents of those objects appear as icons (pictorial symbols) on the desktop. Each object on a real desk has attributes (properties) such as size, weight, and color. In similar fashion, Windows assigns properties to every object on its desktop. And just as you can move the objects on a real desk, you can rearrange the objects on the Windows desktop.

Windows XP has a new interface, but you can retain the look and feel of earlier versions as shown in Figure 2. The desktop in Figure 2a uses the default *Windows XP theme* (the wallpaper has been suppressed), whereas Figure 2b displays the "same" desktop using the *Windows Classic theme*. The icons on either desktop are used to access specific programs or other functions.

The *Start button*, as its name suggests, is where you begin; it works identically on both desktops. Click the Start button to see a menu of programs and other functions. The Windows XP *Start menu* in Figure 2a is divided into two columns. The column on the left displays the most recently used programs for easy access, whereas the column on the right contains a standard set of entries. It also shows the name of the individual who is logged into the computer. The *Classic Start menu* in Figure 2b contains only a single column. (Note the indication of the Windows XP Professional operating system that appears at the left of the menu.)

Do not be concerned if your desktop is different from ours. Your real desk is arranged differently from those of your friends, just as your Windows desktop will also be different. Moreover, you are likely to work on different systems—at school, at work, or at home; what is important is that you recognize the common functionality that is present on all desktops.

Look now at Figure 2c, which displays an entirely different desktop, one with four open windows that is similar to a desk in the middle of a working day. Each window in Figure 2c displays a program or a folder that is currently in use. The ability to run several programs at the same time is known as *multitasking*, and it is a major benefit of the Windows environment. Multitasking enables you to run a word processor in one window, create a spreadsheet in a second window, surf the Internet in a third window, play a game in a fourth window, and so on. You can work in a program as long as you want, then change to a different program by clicking its window.

The *taskbar* at the bottom of the desktop contains a button for each open window, and it enables you to switch back and forth between the open windows by clicking the appropriate button. A *notification area* appears at the right end of the taskbar. It displays the time and other shortcuts. It may also provide information on the status of such ongoing activities as a printer or Internet connection.

The desktop in Figure 2d is identical to the desktop in Figure 2c except that it is displayed in the Windows Classic theme. The open windows are the same, as are the contents of the taskbar and notification area. The choice between the XP theme or Windows Classic (or other) theme is one of personal preference.

Moving and Sizing a Window

A window can be sized or moved on the desktop through appropriate actions with the mouse. To *size a window*, point to any border (the mouse pointer changes to a double arrow), then drag the border in the direction you want to go—inward to shrink the window or outward to enlarge it. You can also drag a corner (instead of a border) to change both dimensions at the same time. To *move a window* while retaining its current size, click and drag the title bar to a new position on the desktop.

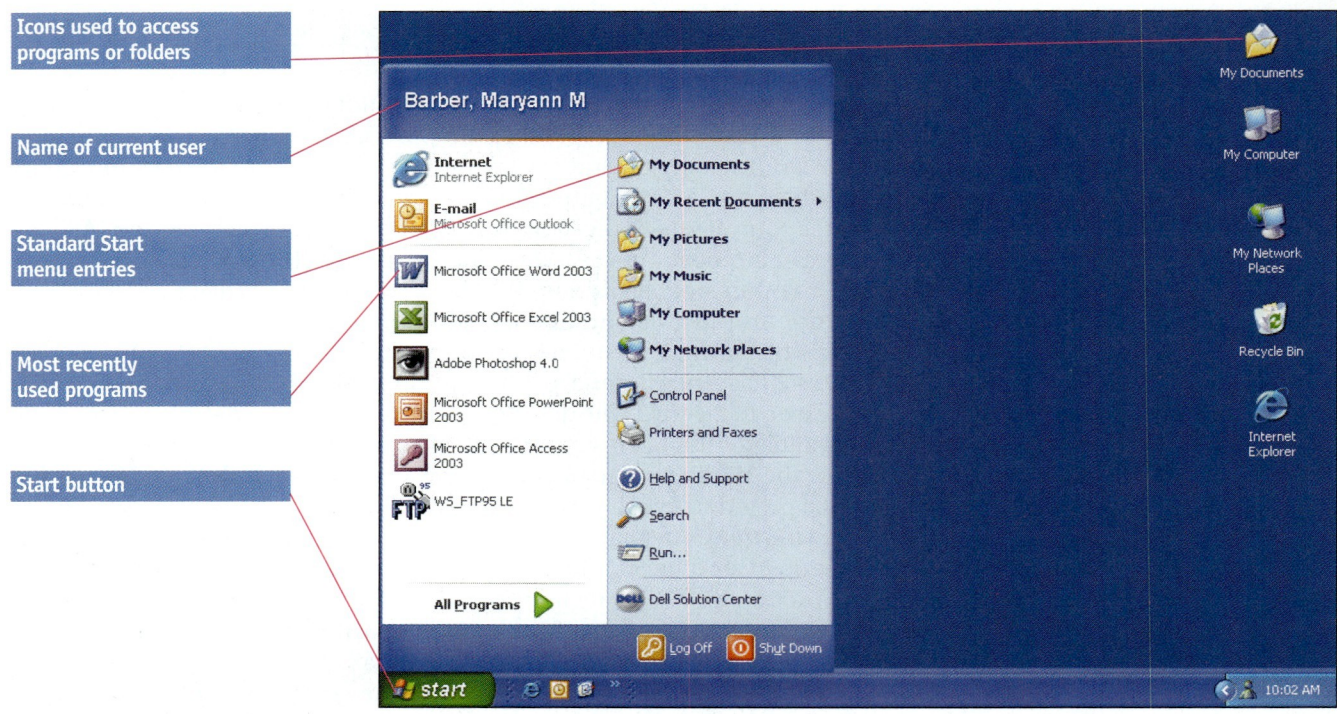

Icons used to access programs or folders

Name of current user

Standard Start menu entries

Most recently used programs

Start button

(a) Windows XP Theme and Start Menu

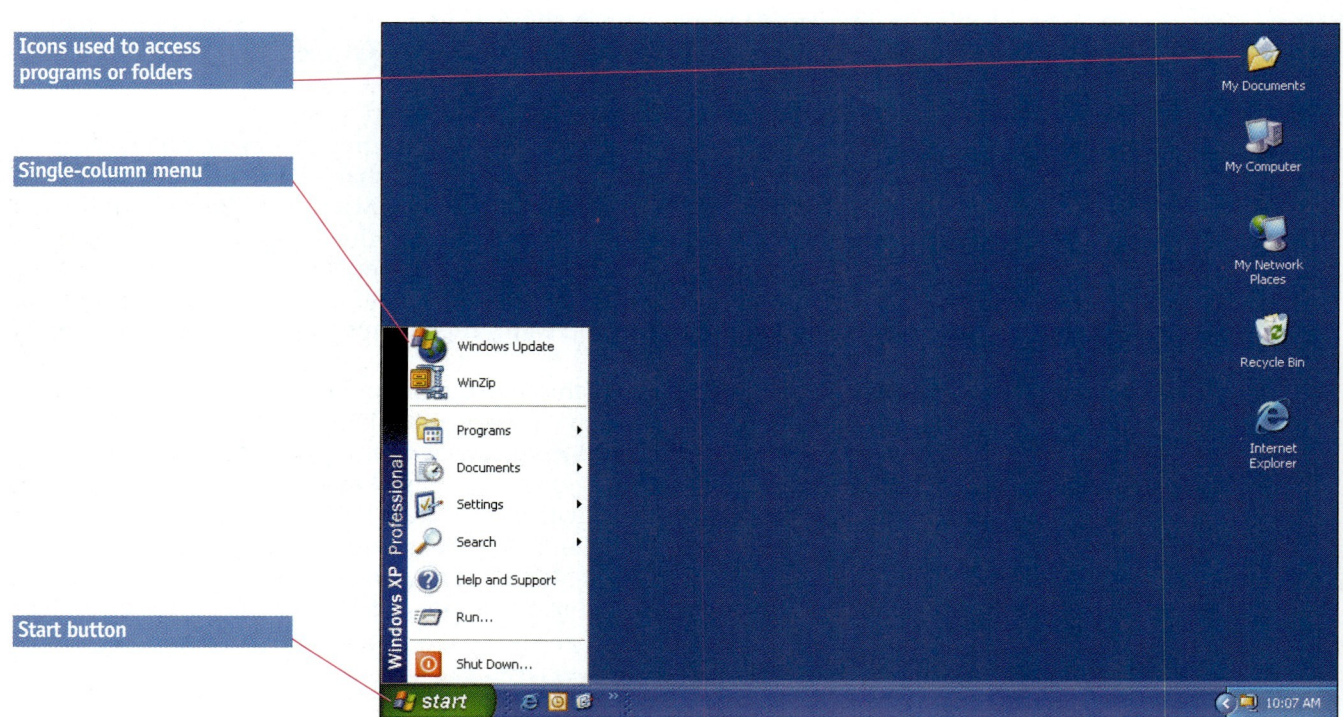

Icons used to access programs or folders

Single-column menu

Start button

(b) Windows Classic Theme and Start Menu

FIGURE 2 The Desktop and Start Menu

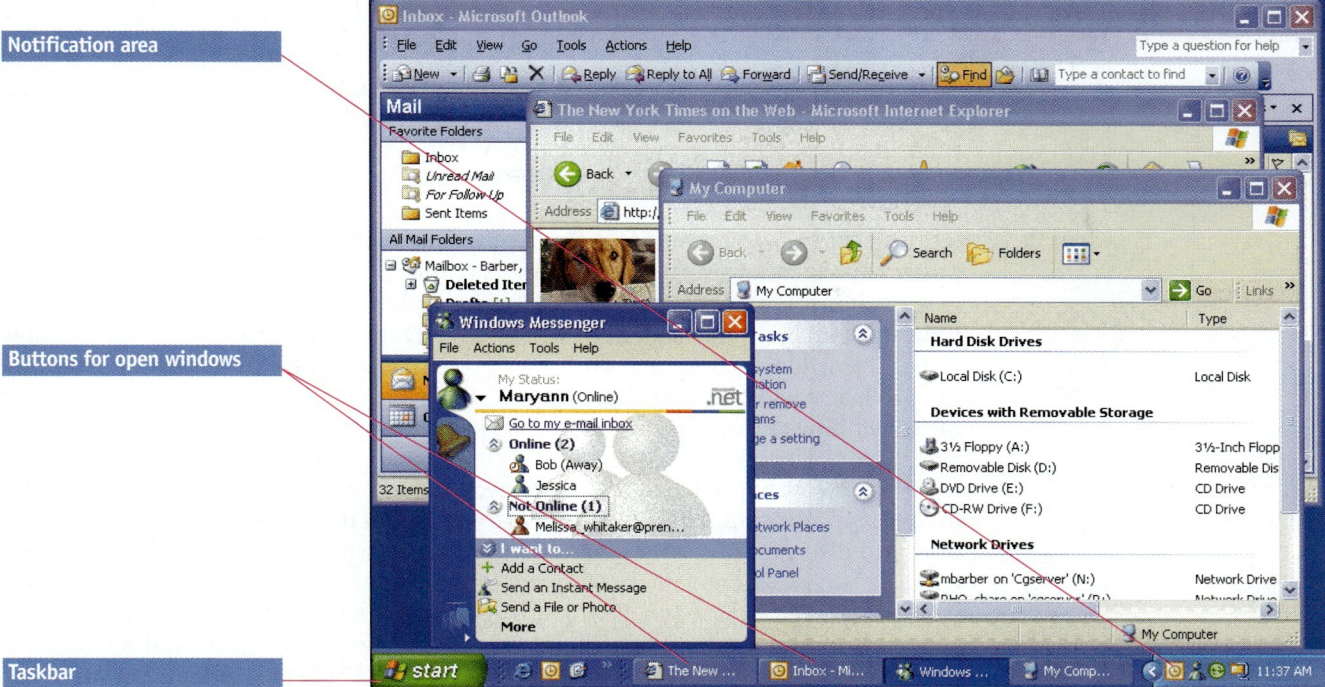

Notification area

Buttons for open windows

Taskbar

(c) Windows XP Theme

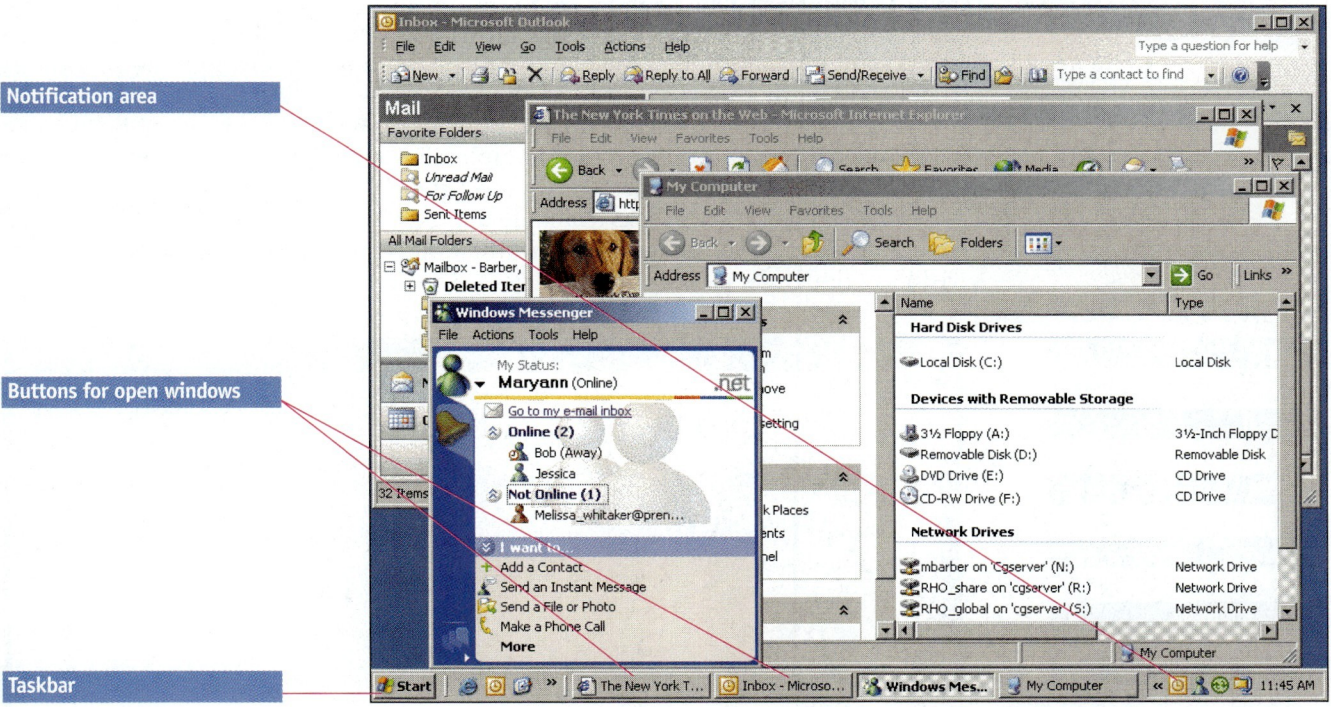

Notification area

Buttons for open windows

Taskbar

(d) Windows Classic Theme

FIGURE 2 The Desktop and Start Menu (*continued*)

All Windows applications share a common user interface and possess a consistent command structure. This means that every Windows application works essentially the same way, which provides a sense of familiarity from one application to the next. In other words, once you learn the basic concepts and techniques in one application, you can apply that knowledge to every other application.

The **My Computer folder** in Figure 3 is used to illustrate basic technology. This folder is present on every system, and its contents depend on the hardware of the specific computer. Our system, for example, has one local disk, a floppy drive, a removable disk (an Iomega Zip® drive), a DVD drive, and a CD-RW (recordable) drive. Our intent at this time, however, is to focus on the elements that are common to every window. A **task pane** (also called a task panel) is displayed at the left of the window to provide easy access to various commands that you might want to access from this folder.

The **title bar** appears at the top of every window and displays the name of the folder or application. The icon at the extreme left of the title bar identifies the window and also provides access to a control menu with operations relevant to the window, such as moving it or sizing it. Three buttons appear at the right of the title bar. The **Minimize button** shrinks the window to a button on the taskbar, but leaves the window in memory. The **Maximize button** enlarges the window so that it takes up the entire desktop. The **Restore button** (not shown in Figure 3) appears instead of the Maximize button after a window has been maximized, and restores the window to its previous size. The **Close button** closes the window and removes it from memory and the desktop.

The **menu bar** appears immediately below the title bar and provides access to pull-down menus. One or more **toolbars** appear below the menu bar and let you execute a command by clicking a button, as opposed to pulling down a menu. The **status bar** at the bottom of the window displays information about the window as a whole or about a selected object within a window.

A vertical (or horizontal) **scroll bar** appears at the right (or bottom) border of a window when its contents are not completely visible and provides access to the unseen areas. The vertical scroll bar at the right of the task panel in Figure 3 implies that there are additional tasks available that are not currently visible. A horizontal scroll bar does not appear since all of the objects in the My Computer folder are visible at one time.

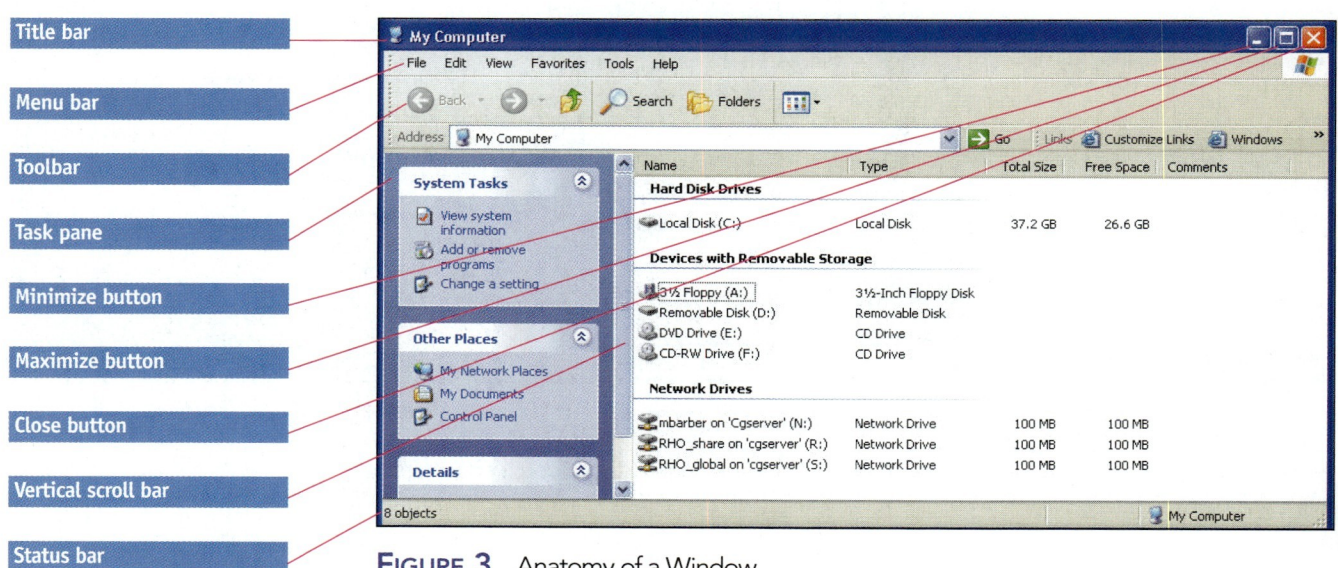

FIGURE 3   Anatomy of a Window

Pull-down Menus

The menu bar provides access to ***pull-down menus*** that enable you to execute commands within an application (program). A pull-down menu is accessed by clicking the menu name or by pressing the Alt key plus the underlined letter in the menu name; for example, press Alt+V to pull down the View menu. (You may have to press the Alt key to see the underlines.) Figure 4 displays three pull-down menus that are associated with the My Computer folder.

Commands within a menu are executed by clicking the command or by typing the underlined letter. Alternatively, you can bypass the menu entirely if you know the equivalent shortcuts shown to the right of the command in the menu (e.g., Ctrl+X, Ctrl+C, or Ctrl+V to cut, copy, or paste as shown within the Edit menu). A dimmed command (e.g., the Paste command in the Edit menu) means the command is not currently executable, and that some additional action has to be taken for the command to become available.

An ellipsis (. . .) following a command indicates that additional information is required to execute the command; for example, selection of the Format command in the File menu requires the user to specify additional information about the formatting process. This information is entered into a dialog box (discussed in the next section), which appears immediately after the command has been selected.

A check next to a command indicates a toggle switch, whereby the command is either on or off. There is a check next to the Status Bar command in the View menu of Figure 4, which means the command is in effect (and thus the status bar will be displayed). Click the Status Bar command and the check disappears, which suppresses the display of the status bar. Click the command a second time and the check reappears, as does the status bar in the associated window.

A bullet next to an item, such as Icons in the View menu, indicates a selection from a set of mutually exclusive choices. Click a different option within the group—such as Thumbnails—and the bullet will move from the previous selection (Icons) to the new selection (Thumbnails).

An arrowhead after a command (e.g., the Arrange Icons by command in the View menu) indicates that a submenu (also known as a cascaded menu) will be displayed with additional menu options.

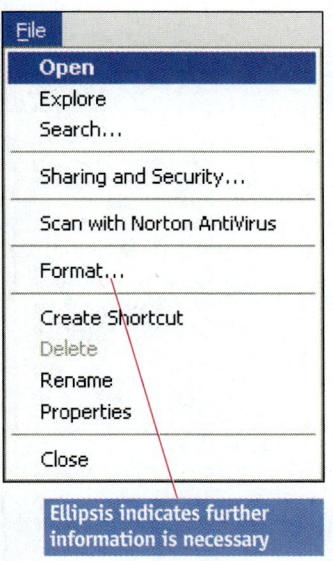

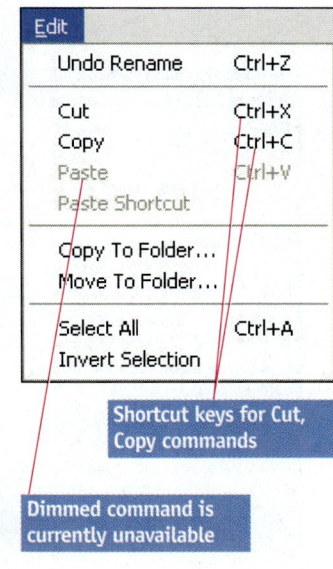

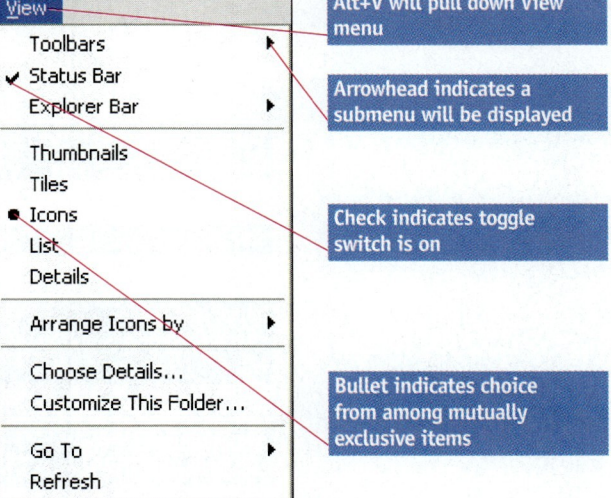

FIGURE 4   Pull-down Menus

Dialog Boxes

A *dialog box* appears when additional information is necessary to execute a command. Click the Print command in Internet Explorer, for example, and you are presented with the Print dialog box in Figure 5, requesting information about precisely what to print and how. The information is entered into the dialog box in different ways, depending on the type of information that is required. The tabs at the top of the dialog box provide access to different sets of options. The General tab is selected in Figure 5.

Option (radio) buttons indicate mutually exclusive choices, one of which *must* be chosen, such as the page range. In this example you can print all pages, the selection (if it is available), the current page (if there are multiple pages), or a specific set of pages (such as pages 1–4), but you can choose *one and only one* option. Any time you select (click) an option, the previous option is automatically deselected.

A *text box* enters specific information such as the pages that will be printed in conjunction with selecting the radio button for pages. A *spin button* is another way to enter specific information such as the number of copies. Click the up or down arrow to increase or decrease the number of pages, respectively. You can also enter the information explicitly by typing it into a spin box, just as you would a text box.

Check boxes are used instead of option buttons if the choices are not mutually exclusive or if an option is not required. The Collate check box is checked, whereas the Print to file box is not checked. Individual options are selected and cleared by clicking the appropriate check box, which toggles the box on and off. A *list box* (not shown in Figure 5) displays some or all of the available choices, any one of which is selected by clicking the desired item.

The *Help button* (a question mark at the right end of the title bar) provides help for any item in the dialog box. Click the button, then click the item in the dialog box for which you want additional information. The Close button (the X at the extreme right of the title bar) closes the dialog box without executing the command.

All dialog boxes also contain one or more *command buttons*, the function of which is generally apparent from the button's name. The Print button in Figure 5, for example, initiates the printing process. The Cancel button does just the opposite and ignores (cancels) any changes made to the settings, then closes the dialog box without further action.

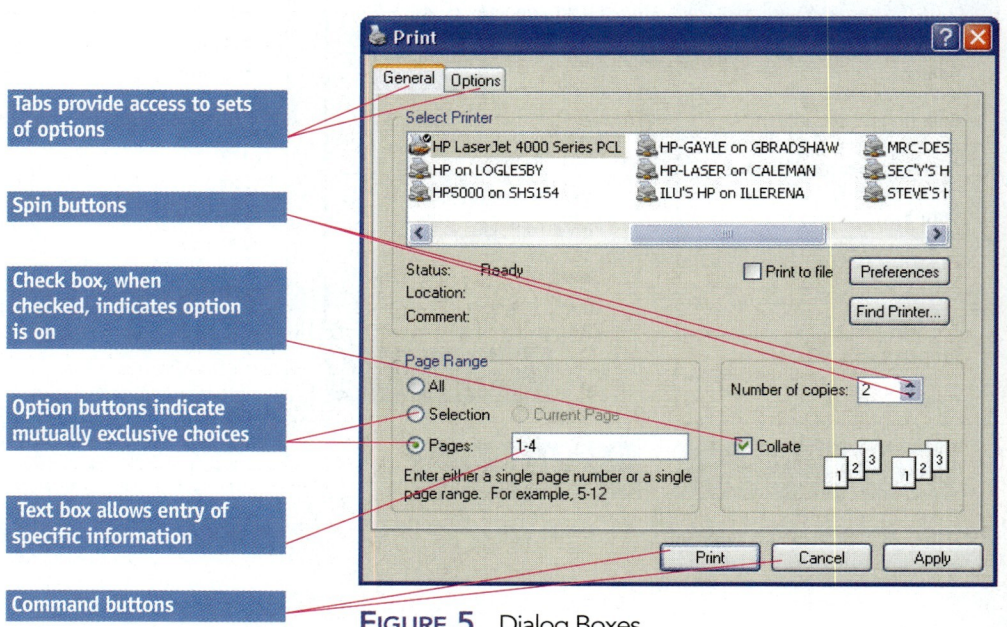

FIGURE 5 Dialog Boxes

The **Help and Support Center** combines such traditional features as a search function and an index of help topics. It also lets you request remote help from other Windows XP users, and/or you can access the Microsoft Knowledge base on the Microsoft Web site. Click the Index button, type the keyword you are searching for, then double click the subtopic to display the associated information in the right pane. The mouse is essential to Windows, and you are undoubtedly familiar with its basic operations such as pointing, clicking, and double clicking. Look closely, however, at the list of subtopics in Figure 6 and you might be surprised at the amount of available information. Suffice it to say, therefore, that you will find the answer to almost every conceivable question if only you will take the trouble to look.

The toolbar at the top of the window contains several buttons that are also found in **Internet Explorer 6.0**, the Web browser that is built into Windows XP. The Back and Forward buttons enable you to navigate through the various pages that were viewed in the current session. The Favorites button displays a list of previously saved (favorite) help topics from previous sessions. The History button shows all pages that were visited in this session.

The Support button provides access to remote sources for assistance. Click the Support button, then click the link to ask a friend to help, which in turn displays a Remote Assistance screen. You will be asked to sign in to the Messenger service (Windows Messenger is discussed in more detail in a later section). Your friend has to be running Windows XP for this feature to work, but once you are connected, he or she will be able to view your computer screen. You can then chat in real time about the problem and proposed solution. And, if you give permission, your friend can use his or her mouse and keyboard to work on your computer. Be careful! It is one thing to let your friend see your screen. It is quite a leap of faith, however, to give him or her control of your machine.

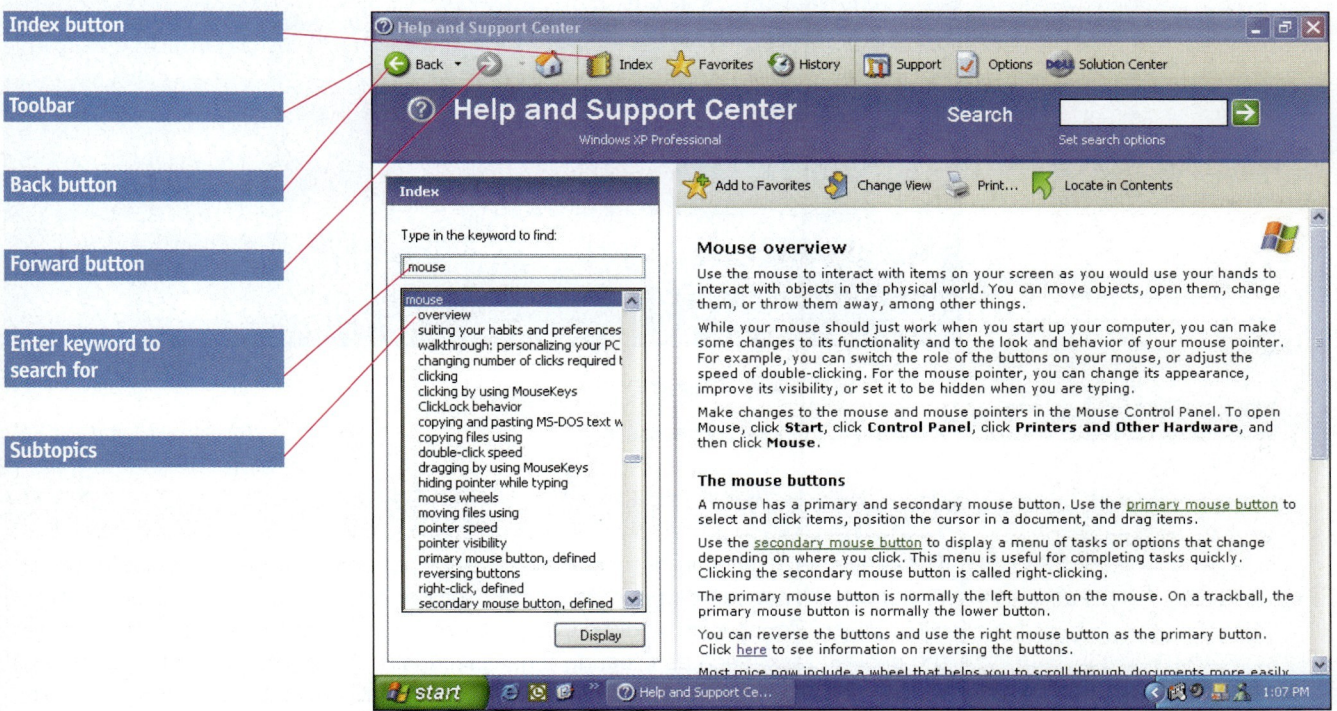

FIGURE 6   Help and Support Center

1   Welcome to Windows XP

Objective   To log on to Windows XP and customize the desktop; to open the My Computer folder; to move and size a window; to format a floppy disk and access the Help and Support Center. Use Figure 7 as a guide.

Step 1:   **Log On to Windows XP**

- Turn on the computer and all of the peripheral devices. The floppy drive should be empty prior to starting your machine.

- Windows XP will load automatically, and you should see a login screen similar to Figure 7a. (It does not matter which version of Windows XP you are using.) The number and names of the potential users and their associated icons will be different on your system.

- Click the icon for the user account you want to access. You may be prompted for a password, depending on the security options in effect.

Click icon for user account to be accessed

(a) Log On to Windows XP (step 1)

FIGURE 7   Hands-on Exercise 1

USER ACCOUNTS

The available user names are created automatically during the installation of Windows XP, but you can add or delete users at any time. Click the Start button, click Control Panel, switch to the Category view, and select User Accounts. Choose the desired task, such as creating a new account or changing an existing account, then supply the necessary information. Do not expect, however, to be able to modify user accounts in a school setting.

Step 2: Choose the Theme and Start Menu

■ Check with your instructor to see if you are able to modify the desktop and other settings at your school or university. If your network administrator has disabled these commands, skip this step and go to step 3.

■ Point to a blank area on the desktop, click the **right mouse button** to display a context-sensitive menu, then click the **Properties command** to open the Display Properties dialog box. Click the **Themes tab** and select the **Windows XP theme** if it is not already selected. Click **OK**.

■ We prefer to work without any wallpaper (background picture) on the desktop. **Right click** the desktop, click **Properties**, then click the **Desktop tab** in the Display Properties dialog box. Click **None** as shown in Figure 7b, then click **OK**. The background disappears.

■ The Start menu is modified independently of the theme. **Right click** a blank area of the taskbar, click the **Properties command** to display the Taskbar and Start Menu Properties dialog box, then click the **Start Menu tab**.

■ Click the **Start Menu option button**. Click **OK**.

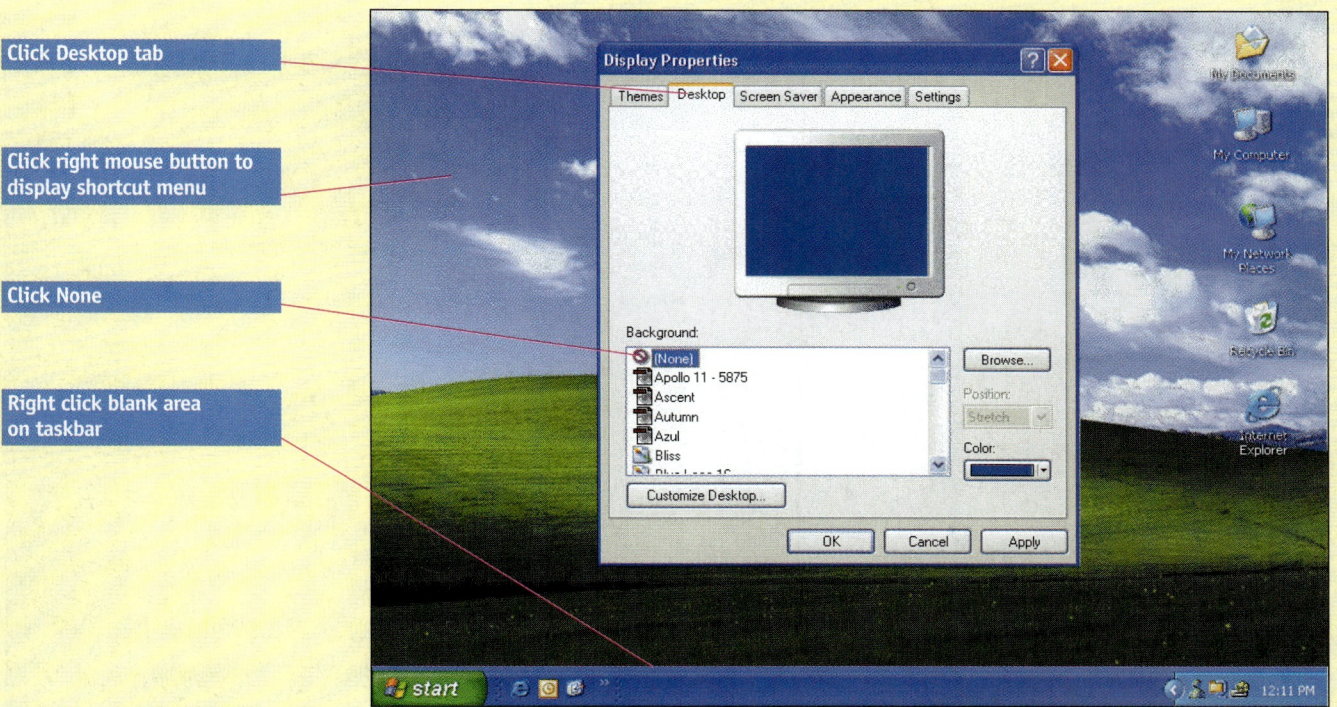

Click Desktop tab

Click right mouse button to display shortcut menu

Click None

Right click blank area on taskbar

(b) Choose the Theme and Start Menu (step 2)

FIGURE 7 Hands-on Exercise 1 (*continued*)

IMPLEMENT A SCREEN SAVER

A screen saver is a delightful way to personalize your computer and a good way to practice with basic commands in Windows XP. Right click a blank area of the desktop, click the Properties command to open the Display Properties dialog box, then click the Screen Saver tab. Click the down arrow in the Screen Saver list box, choose the desired screen saver, then set the option to wait an appropriate amount of time before the screen saver appears. Click OK to accept the settings and close the dialog box.

Step 3: **Open the My Computer Folder**

■ Click the **Start button** to display a two-column Start menu that is characteristic of Windows XP. Click **My Computer** to open the My Computer folder. The contents of your window and/or its size and position on the desktop will be different from ours.

■ Pull down the **View menu** as shown in Figure 7c to make or verify the following selections. (You have to pull down the View menu each time you make an additional change.)
   ❏ The **Status Bar command** should be checked. The Status Bar command functions as a toggle switch. Click the command and the status bar is displayed; click the command a second time and the status bar disappears.
   ❏ Click the **Tiles command** to change to this view. Selecting the Tiles view automatically deselects the previous view.

■ Pull down the **View menu**, then click (or point to) the **Toolbars command** to display a cascaded menu. If necessary, check the commands for the **Standard Buttons** and **Address Bar**, and clear the other commands.

■ Click the **Folders button** on the Standard Buttons toolbar to toggle the task panel on or off. End with the task panel displayed as shown in Figure 7c.

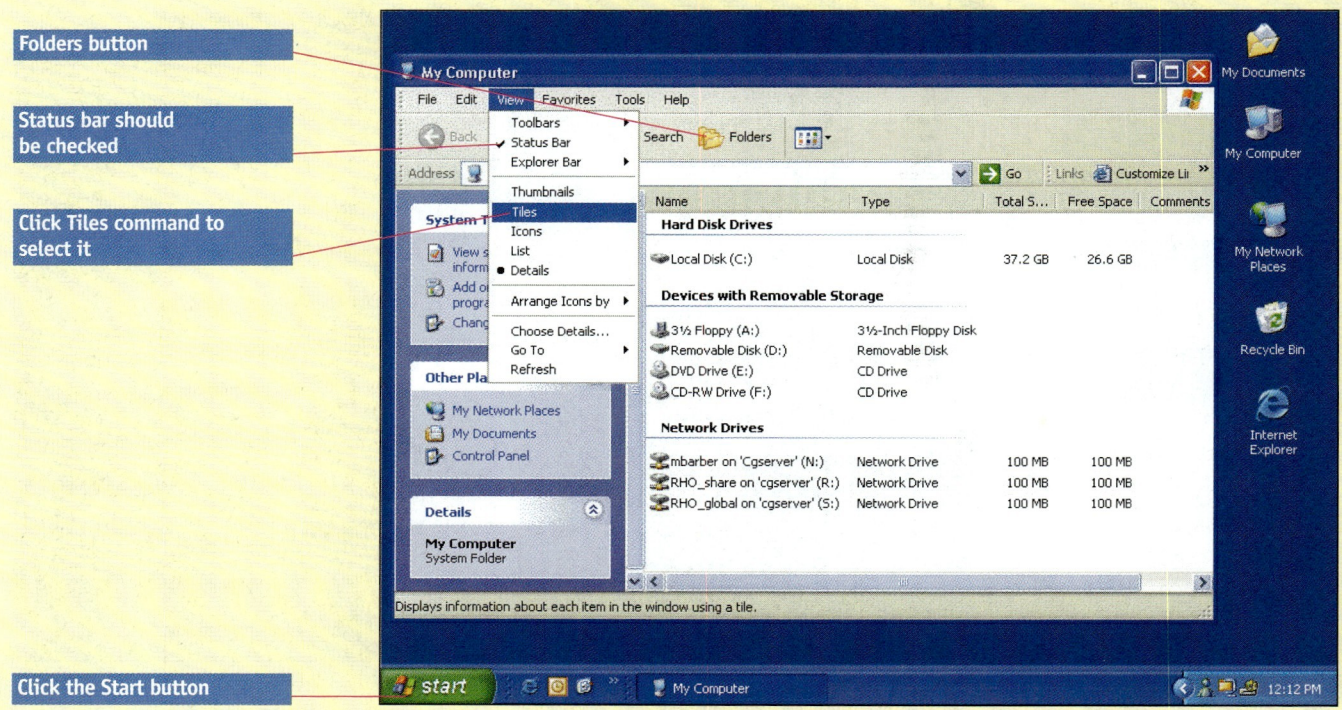

(c) Open the My Computer Folder (step 3)

FIGURE 7 Hands-on Exercise 1 (*continued*)

DESIGNATING THE DEVICES ON A SYSTEM

The first (usually only) floppy drive is always designated as drive A. (A second floppy drive, if it were present, would be drive B.) The first hard (local) disk on a system is always drive C, whether or not there are one or two floppy drives. Additional local drives, if any, such as a zip (removable storage) drive, a network drive, a CD and/or a DVD, are labeled from D on.

Step 4: Move and Size a Window

- Move and size the My Computer window on your desktop to match the display in Figure 7d.
  - ❏ To change the width or height of the window, click and drag a border (the mouse pointer changes to a double arrow) in the direction you want to go; drag the border inward to shrink the window or outward to enlarge it.
  - ❏ To change the width and height at the same time, click and drag a corner rather than a border.
  - ❏ To change the position of the window, click and drag the title bar.

- Click the **Minimize button** to shrink the My Computer window to a button on the taskbar. My Computer is still active in memory although its window is no longer visible. Click the **My Computer button** on the taskbar to reopen the window.

- Click the **Maximize button** so that the My Computer window expands to fill the entire screen. Click the **Restore button** (which replaces the Maximize button and is not shown in Figure 7d) to return the window to its previous size.

- Practice these operations until you can move and size a window with confidence.

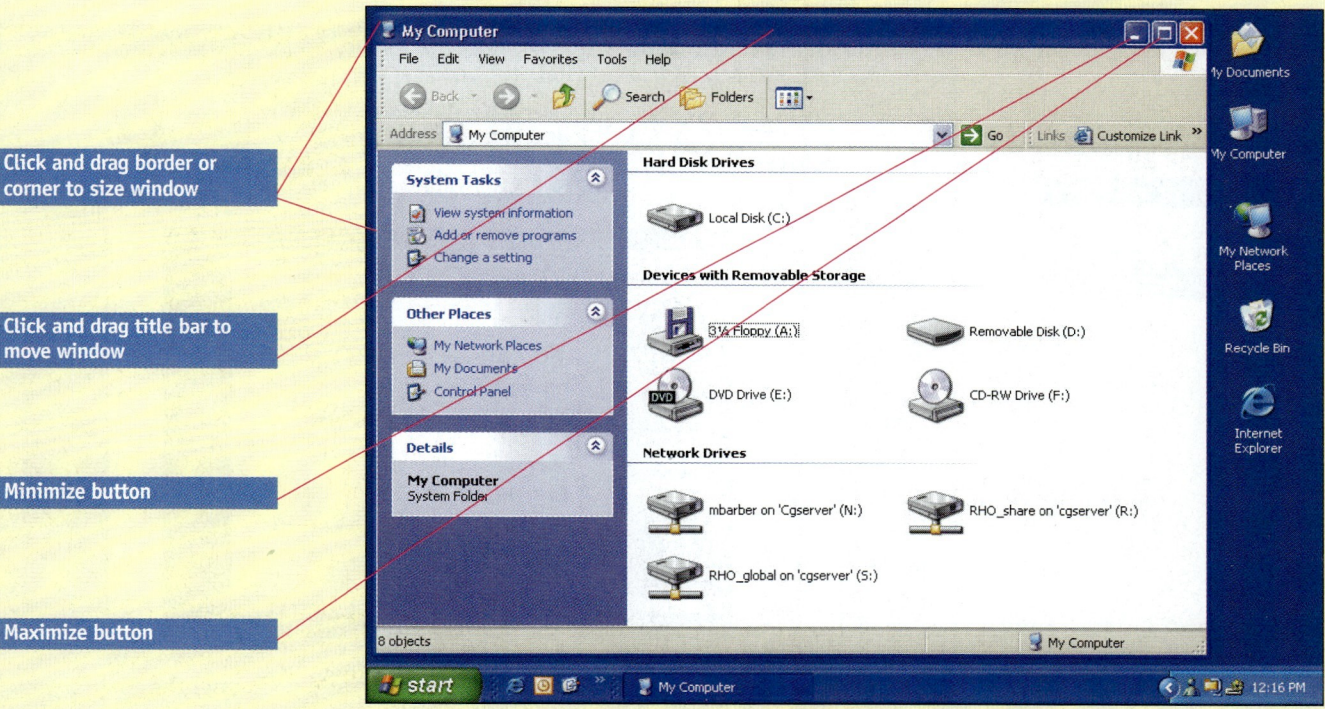

(d) Move and Size a Window (step 4)

FIGURE 7 Hands-on Exercise 1 (*continued*)

MINIMIZING VERSUS CLOSING AN APPLICATION

Minimizing a folder or an application leaves the object open in memory and available at the click of the appropriate button on the taskbar. Closing it, however, removes the object from memory, which also causes it to disappear from the taskbar. The advantage of minimizing an application or folder is that you can return to it immediately with the click of the mouse. The disadvantage is that too many open applications will eventually degrade the performance of a system.

Step 5: Capture a Screen

■ Prove to your instructor that you have sized the window correctly by capturing the desktop that currently appears on your monitor. Press the **Print Screen key** to copy the current screen display to the **clipboard**, an area of memory that is available to every application.

■ Nothing appears to have happened, but the screen has in fact been copied to the clipboard and can be pasted into a Word document. Click the **Start button**, click the **All Programs command**, then start **Microsoft Word** and begin a new document.

■ Enter the title of your document (I Did My Homework) followed by your name as shown in Figure 7e. Press the **Enter key** two or three times to leave blank lines after your name.

■ Pull down the **Edit menu** and click the **Paste command** (or click the **Paste button** on the Standard toolbar) to copy the contents of the clipboard into the Word document.

■ Print this document for your instructor. There is no need to save this document. Exit Word.

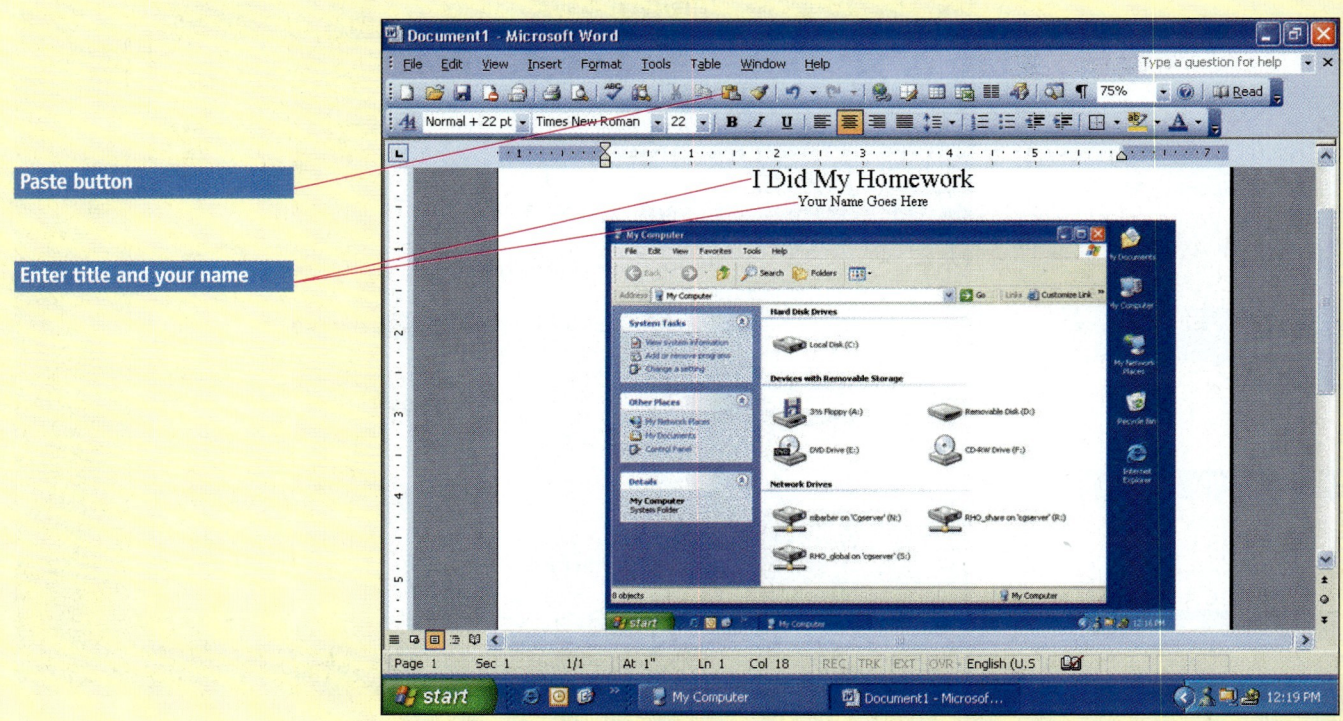

(e) Capture a Screen (step 5)

FIGURE 7 Hands-on Exercise 1 (*continued*)

THE FORMAT PICTURE COMMAND

Use the Format Picture command to facilitate moving and/or sizing an object within a Word document. Right click the picture to display a context-sensitive menu, then click the Format Picture command to display the associated dialog box. Click the Layout tab, choose any layout other than Inline with text, and click OK. You can now click and drag the picture to position it elsewhere within the document.

Step 6: Format a Floppy Disk

- Place a floppy disk into drive A. Select (click) **drive A** in the My Computer window, then pull down the **File menu** and click the **Format command** to display the Format dialog box in Figure 7f.
  - ❏ Set the **Capacity** to match the floppy disk you purchased (1.44MB for a high-density disk and 720KB for a double-density disk. The easiest way to determine the type of disk is to look for the label HD or DD, respectively.).
  - ❏ Click the **Volume label text box** if it's empty, or click and drag over the existing label if there is an entry. Enter a new label (containing up to 11 characters), such as **Bob's Disk**.
  - ❏ You can check the **Quick Format box** if the disk has been previously formatted, as a convenient way to erase the contents of the disk.

- Click the **Start button,** then click **OK**—after you have read the warning message—to begin the formatting operation. The formatting process erases anything that is on the disk, so be sure that you do not need anything on the disk.

- Click **OK** after the formatting is complete. Close the dialog box, then save the formatted disk for the next exercise. Close the My Computer window.

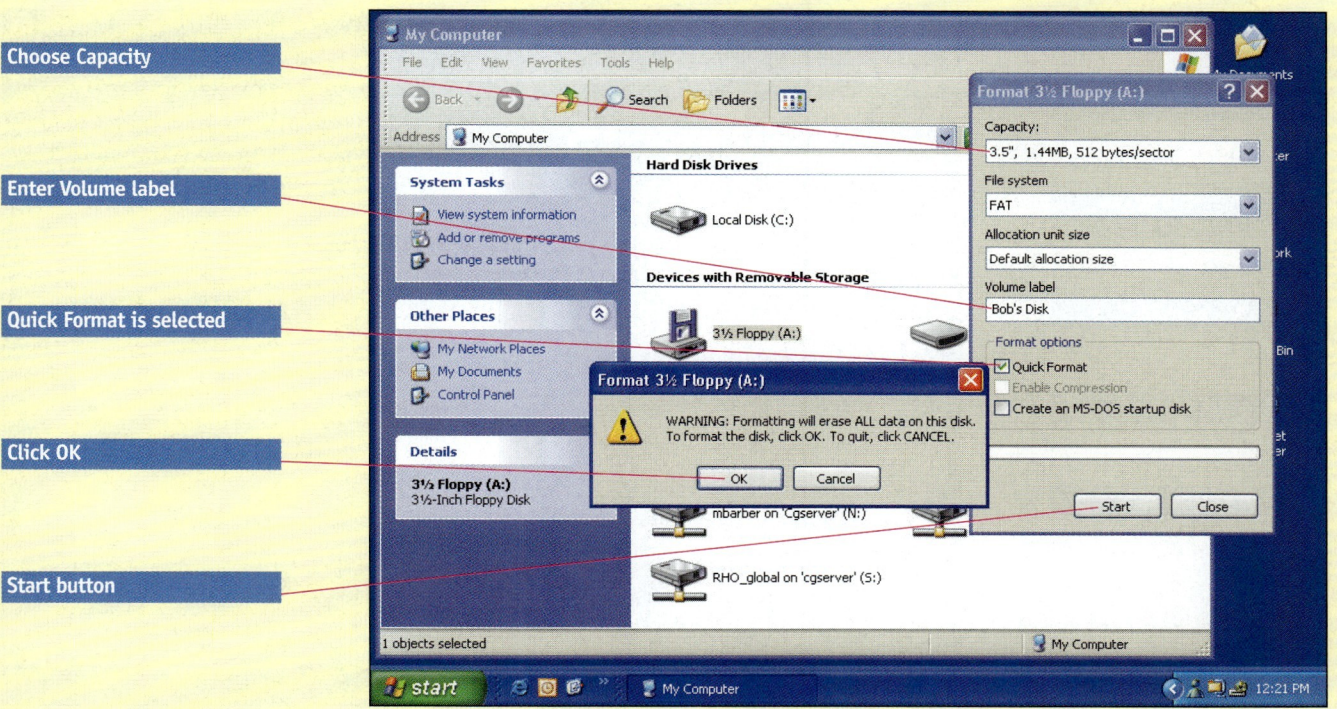

(f) Format a Floppy Disk (step 6)

FIGURE 7 Hands-on Exercise 1 (*continued*)

THE DEMISE OF THE FLOPPY DISK

You may be surprised to discover that your system no longer has a floppy disk drive, but it is only the latest victim in the march of technology. Long-playing records have come and gone. So too have 8-track tapes and the laser disk. The 3½-inch floppy disk has had a long and successful run, but it, too, is slated for obsolescence with Dell's recent announcement that it will no longer include a floppy drive as a standard component in desktop systems. Still, the floppy disk will "live forever" in the Save button that has the floppy disk as its icon.

Step 7: **The Help and Support Center**

- Click the **Start button**, then click the **Help and Support command** to open the Help and Support Center. Click the **Index button** to open the index pane. The insertion point moves automatically to the text box where you enter the search topic.

- Type **help**, which automatically moves you to the available topics within the index. Double click **central location for Help** to display the information in the right pane as shown in Figure 7g.

- Toggle the display of the subtopics on and off by clicking the plus and minus sign, respectively. Click the **plus sign** next to Remote Assistance, for example, and the topic opens. Click the **minus sign** next to Tours and articles, and the topic closes.

- Right click anywhere within the right pane to display the context-sensitive menu shown in Figure 7g. Click the **Print command** to print this information for your instructor.

- Close the Help and Support window.

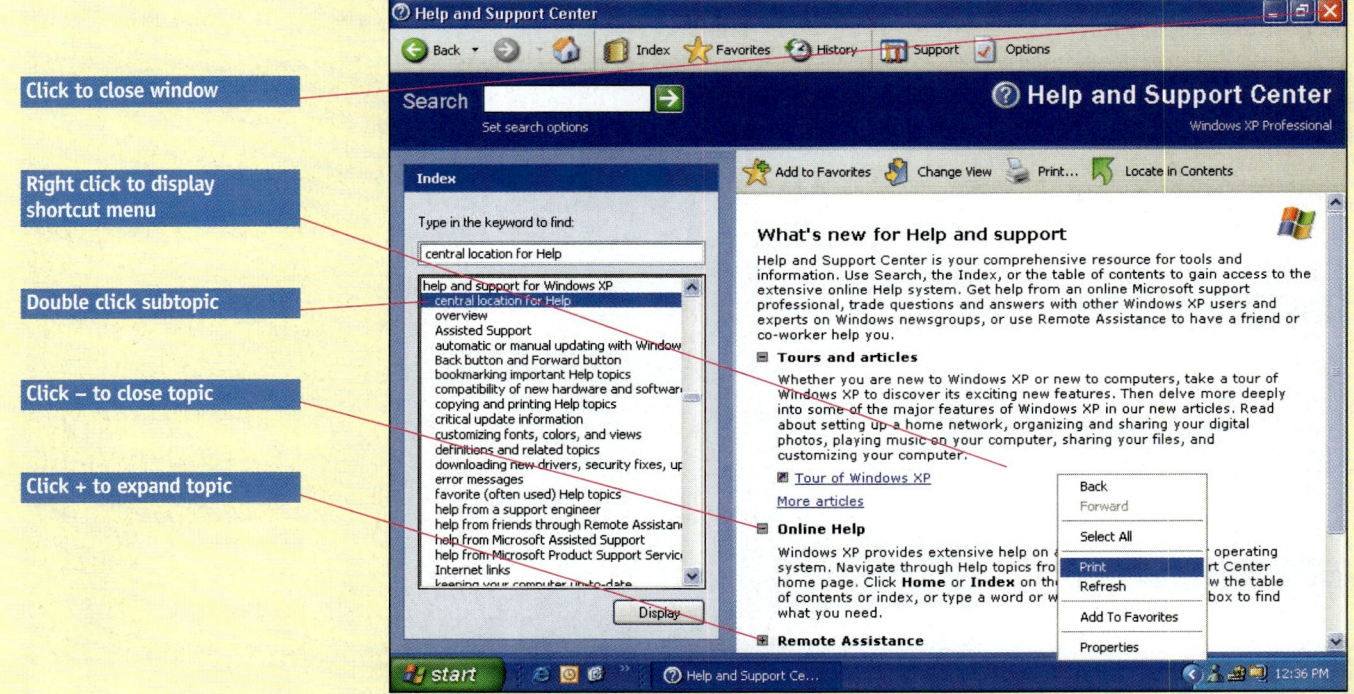

(g) The Help and Support Center (step 7)

FIGURE 7 Hands-on Exercise 1 (*continued*)

THE FAVORITES BUTTON

Do you find yourself continually searching for the same information? If so, you can make life a little easier by adding the page to a list of favorite help topics. Start the Help and Support Center, use the Index button to display the desired information in the right pane, and then click the Add to Favorites button to add the topic to your list of favorites. You can return to the topic at any time by clicking the Favorites button at the top of the Help and Support window, then double clicking the bookmark.

Step 8: **Log (or Turn) Off the Computer**

- It is very important that you log off properly, as opposed to just turning off the power. This enables Windows to close all of its system files and to save any changes that were made during the session.

- Click the **Start button** to display the Start menu in Figure 7h, then click the **Log Off button** at the bottom of the menu. You will see a dialog box asking whether you want to log off or switch users.
  - ❑ Switching users leaves your session active. All of your applications remain open, but control of the computer is given to another user. You can subsequently log back on (after the new user logs off) and take up exactly where you left off.
  - ❑ Logging off ends your session, but leaves the computer running at full power. This is the typical option you would select in a laboratory setting at school.

- To turn the computer off, you have to log off as just described, then select the **Turn Computer Off command** from the login screen. Welcome to Windows XP!

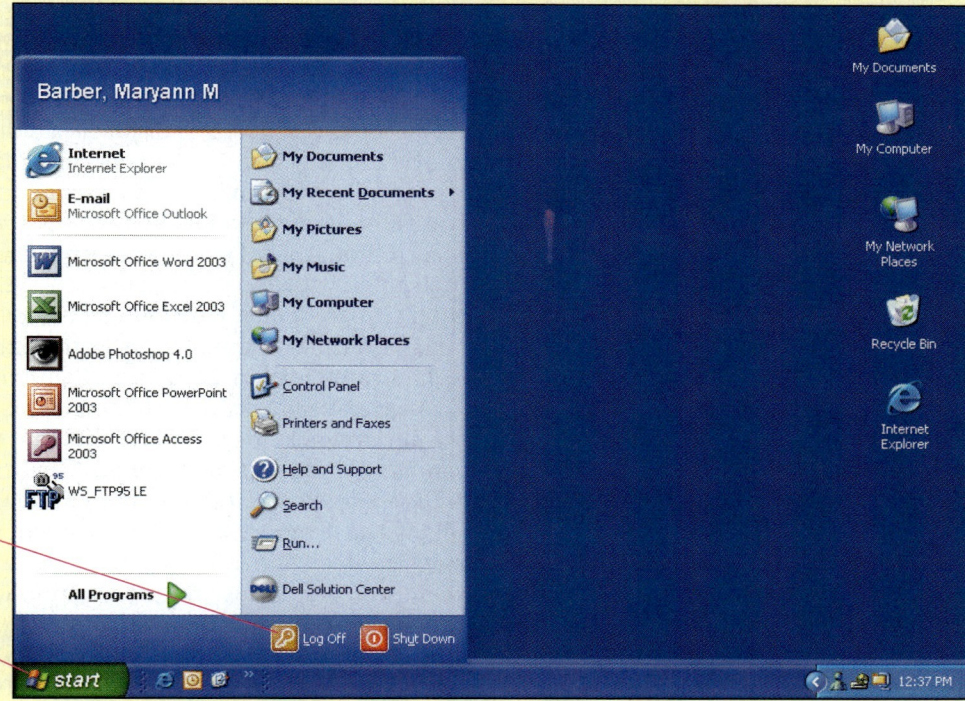

Click Log Off

Click Start button

(h) Log (or Turn) Off Computer (step 8)

FIGURE 7 Hands-on Exercise 1 (*continued*)

THE TASK MANAGER

The Start button is the normal way to exit Windows. Occasionally, however, an application may "hang"—in which case you want to close the problem application but continue with your session. Press Ctrl+Alt+Del to display the Windows Task Manager dialog box, then click the Applications tab. Select the problem application (it will most likely say "not responding"), and click the End Task button. This capability is often disabled in a school setting.

A *file* is a set of instructions or data that has been given a name and stored on disk. There are two basic types of files, *program files* and *data files*. Microsoft Word and Microsoft Excel are examples of program files. The documents and workbooks that are created by these programs are data files. A program file is executable because it contains instructions that tell the computer what to do. A data file is not executable and can be used only in conjunction with a specific program. In other words, you execute program files to create and/or edit the associated data files.

Every file has a *filename* that identifies it to the operating system. The filename can contain up to 255 characters and may include spaces and other punctuation. (Filenames cannot contain the following characters: \, /, :, *, ?, ", <, >, and |.) We find it easier, however, to restrict the characters in a filename to letters, numbers, and spaces, as opposed to having to remember the special characters that are not permitted.

Files are kept in *folders* to better organize the thousands of files on a typical system. A Windows folder is similar to an ordinary manila folder that holds one or more documents. To continue the analogy, an office worker stores his or her documents in manila folders within a filing cabinet. Windows stores its files in electronic folders that are located on a disk, CD-ROM, or other device.

Many folders are created automatically by Windows XP, such as the My Computer or My Documents folders that are present on every system. Other folders are created whenever new software is installed. Additional folders are created by the user to hold the documents he or she creates. You might, for example, create a folder for your word processing documents and a second folder for your spreadsheets. You could also create a folder to hold all of your work for a specific class, which in turn might contain a combination of word processing documents and spreadsheets. The choice is entirely up to you, and you can use any system that makes sense to you. A folder can contain program files, data files, or even other folders.

Figure 8 displays the contents of a hypothetical folder with nine documents. Figure 8a displays the folder in *Tiles view*. Figure 8b displays the same folder in *Details view*, which also shows the date the file was created or last modified. Both views display a file icon next to each file to indicate the *file type* or application that was used to create the file. *Introduction to E-mail*, for example, is a PowerPoint presentation. *Basic Financial Functions* is an Excel workbook.

The two figures have more similarities than differences, such as the name of the folder (*Homework*), which appears in the title bar next to the icon of an open folder. The Minimize, Restore, and Close buttons are found at the right of the title bar. A menu bar with six pull-down menus appears below the title bar. The Standard Buttons toolbar is below the menu, and the Address bar (indicating the drive and folder) appears below the toolbar. Both folders also contain a task pane that provides easy access to common tasks for the folder or selected object.

Look closely and you will see that the task panes are significantly different. This is because there are no documents selected in Figure 8a, whereas the *Milestones in Communications* document is selected (highlighted) in Figure 8b. Thus, the File and Folder Tasks area in Figure 8a pertains to folders in general, whereas the available tasks in Figure 8b are pertinent to the selected document. The Details areas in the two task panes are also consistent with the selected objects and display information about the Homework folder and selected document, respectively. A status bar appears at the bottom of both windows and displays the contents of the selected object.

The last difference between the task panes reflects the user's preference to open or close the Other Places area. Click the upward chevron in Figure 8a to suppress the display and gain space in the task pane, or click the downward chevron in Figure 8b to display the specific links to other places. The task pane is new to Windows XP and did not appear in previous versions of Windows.

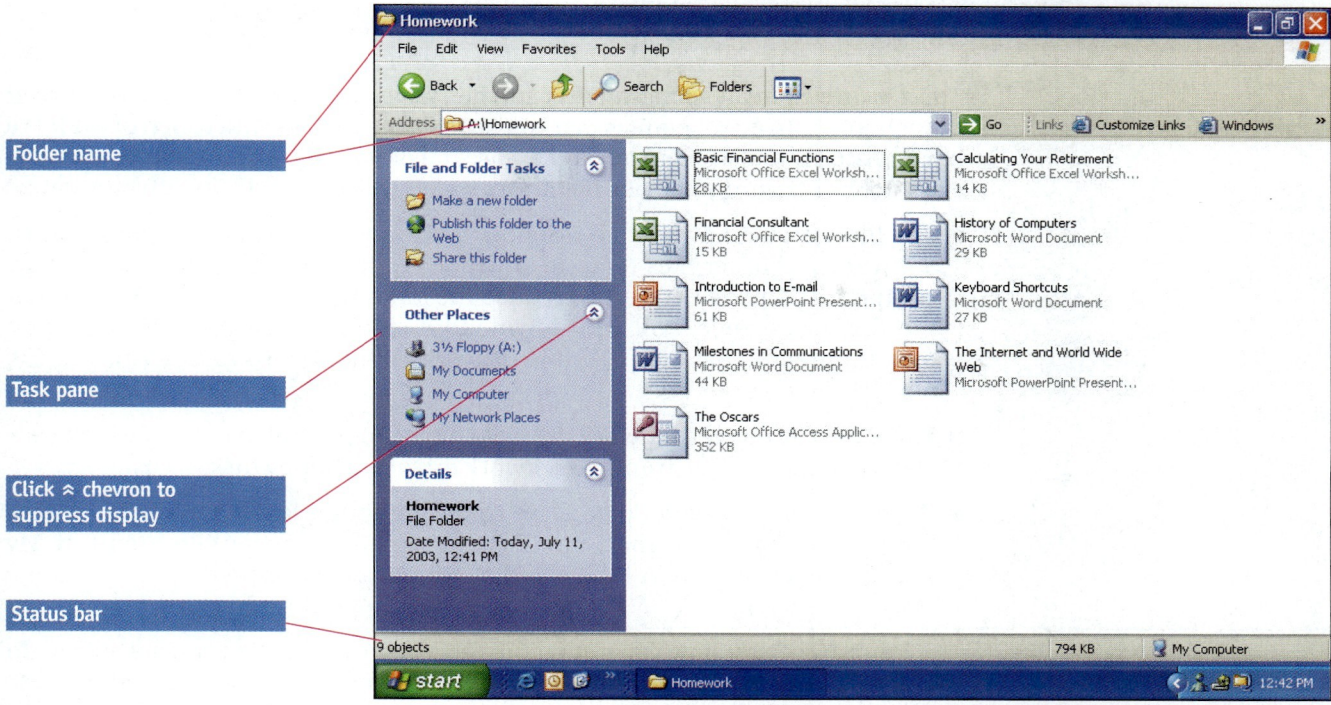

(a) Tiles View

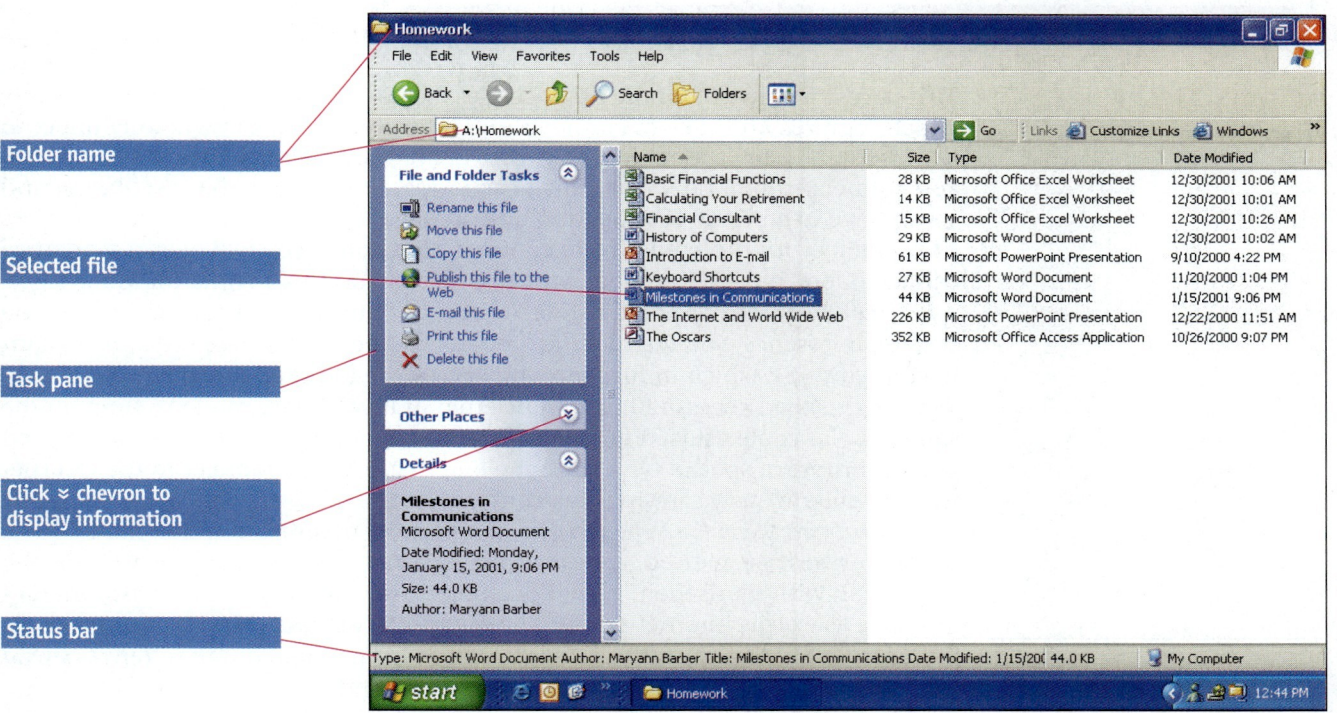

(b) Details View

FIGURE 8 Files and Folders

THE EXPLORING OFFICE PRACTICE FILES

There is only one way to master disk and file management and that is to practice at the computer. To do so requires that you have a series of files with which to work. We have created these files for you, and we use the files in the next two hands-on exercises. Your instructor will make the practice files available to you in different ways:

■ The files can be downloaded from our Web site at www.prenhall.com/grauer. Software and other files that are downloaded from the Internet are typically compressed (made smaller) to reduce the amount of time it takes to transmit the file. In essence, you will download a single *compressed file* and then uncompress the file into multiple files onto a local drive as described in the next hands-on exercise.

■ The files may be on a network drive at your school or university, in which case you can copy the files from the network drive to a floppy disk.

■ There may be an actual "data disk" in the computer lab. Go to the lab with a floppy disk, then use the Copy Disk command (on the File menu of My Computer when drive A is selected) to duplicate the data disk and create a copy for yourself.

It doesn't matter how you obtain the practice files, only that you are able to do so. Indeed, you may want to try different techniques to gain additional practice with Windows XP. Note, too, that Windows XP provides a *firewall* to protect your computer from unauthorized access while it is connected to the Internet. (See exercise 2 at the end of the chapter.)

CONNECTING TO THE INTERNET

The easiest way to obtain the practice files is to download the files from the Web, which requires an Internet connection. There are two basic ways to connect to the Internet—from a local area network (LAN) or by dialing in. It's much easier if you connect from a LAN (typically at school or work) since the installation and setup have been done for you, and all you have to do is follow the instructions provided by your professor. If you connect from home, you will need a modem, a cable modem, or a DSL modem, and an Internet Service Provider (or ISP).

A *modem* is the hardware interface between your computer and the telephone system. In essence, you instruct the modem, via the appropriate software, to connect to your ISP, which in turn lets you access the Internet. A cable modem provides high-speed access (20 to 30 times that of an ordinary modem) through the same type of cable as used for cable TV. A DSL modem also provides high-speed access through a special type of phone line that lets you connect to the Internet while simultaneously carrying on a conversation.

An *Internet Service Provider* is a company or organization that maintains a computer with permanent access to the Internet. America Online (AOL) is the largest ISP with more than 30 million subscribers, and it provides a proprietary interface as well as Internet access. The Microsoft Network (MSN) is a direct competitor to AOL. Alternatively, you can choose from a host of other vendors who provide Internet access without the proprietary interface of AOL or MSN.

Regardless of which vendor you choose as an ISP, be sure you understand the fee structure. The monthly fee may entitle you to a set number of hours per month (after which you pay an additional fee), or it may give you unlimited access. The terms vary widely, and you should shop around for the best possible deal. Price is not the only consideration, however. Reliability of service is also important. Be sure that the equipment of your provider is adequate so that you can obtain access whenever you want.

2 Download the Practice Files

Objective To download a file from the Web and practice basic file commands. The exercise requires a formatted floppy disk and access to the Internet. Use Figure 9 as a guide.

Step 1: **Start Internet Explorer**

■ Click the **Start button**, click the **All Programs command**, and then click **Internet Explorer** to start the program. If necessary, click the **Maximize button** so that Internet Explorer takes the entire desktop.

■ Click anywhere within the **Address bar**, which automatically selects the current address (so that whatever you type replaces the current address). Enter **www.prenhall.com/grauer** (the http:// is assumed). Press **Enter**.

■ You should see the Exploring Office Series home page as shown in Figure 9a. Click the book for **Office 2003**, which takes you to the Office 2003 home page.

■ Click the **Student Downloads tab** (at the top of the window) to go to the Student Download page.

Enter www.prenhall.com/grauer in Address bar

Click book for Office 2003

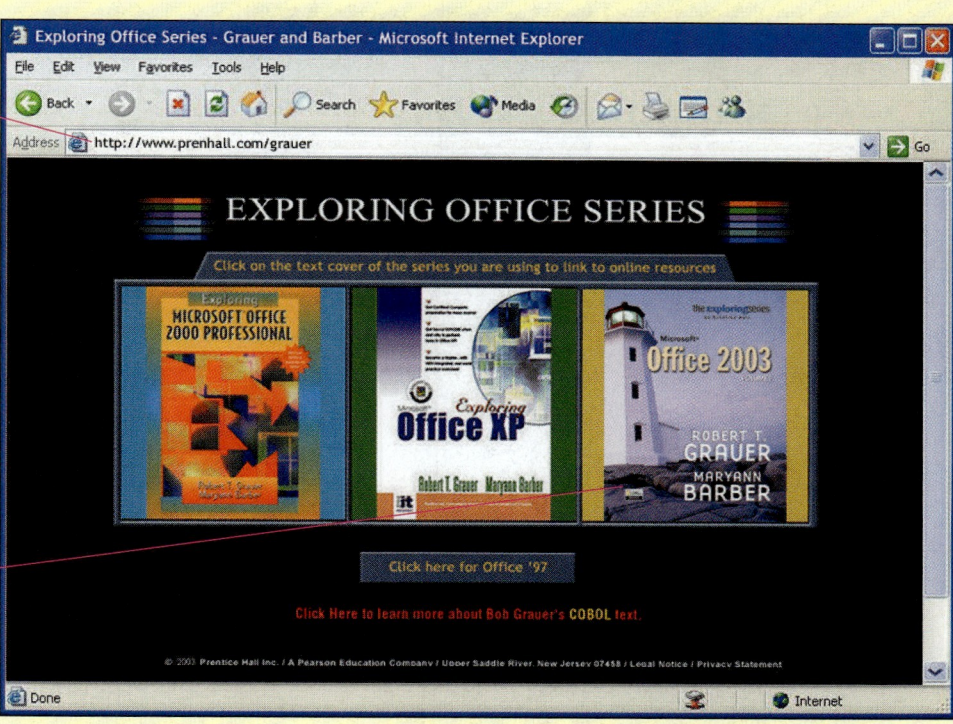

(a) Start Internet Explorer (step 1)

FIGURE 9 Hands-on Exercise 2

A NEW INTERNET EXPLORER

The installation of Windows XP automatically installs a new version of Internet Explorer. Pull down the Help menu and click the About Internet Explorer command to display the current release (version 6.0). Click OK to close the About Internet Explorer window.

Step 2:   **Download the Practice Files**

- You should see the Student Download page in Figure 9b. Place the formatted floppy disk from the first exercise in drive A. Be sure there are no files on this disk.

- Scroll down the page until you see the link to the student data disk for **Windows XP**. Click the link to download the practice files.

- You will see the File Download dialog box, asking what you want to do. Click the **Save button** to display the Save As dialog box. Click the **drop-down arrow** on the Save in list box, and select (click) **drive A**.

- Click **Save** to download the file. The File Download window may reappear and show you the status of the downloading operation as it takes place.

- If necessary, click **Close** when you see the dialog box indicating that the download is complete. Minimize Internet Explorer.

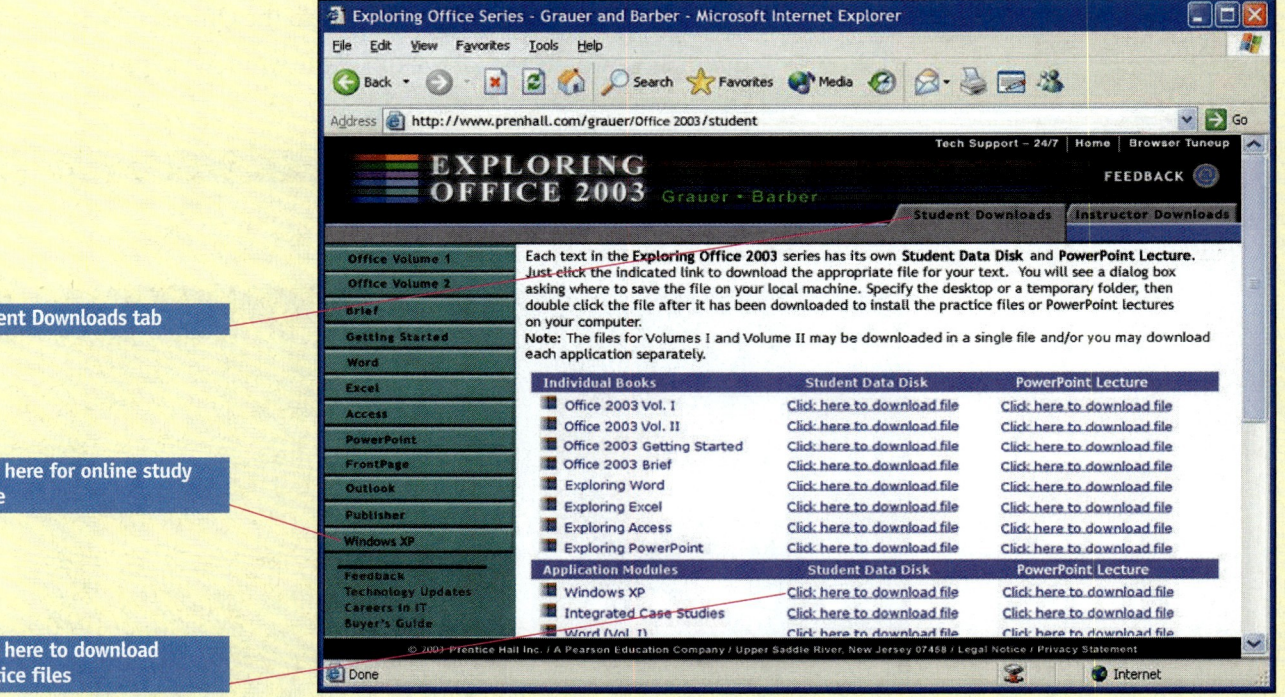

(b) Download the Practice Files (step 2)

FIGURE 9   Hands-on Exercise 2 (*continued*)

EXPLORE OUR WEB SITE

The Exploring Office Series Web site offers an online study guide (multiple-choice, true/false, and matching questions) for each individual textbook to help you review the material in each chapter. You can take practice quizzes by yourself and/or e-mail the results to your instructor. These online study guides are available via the tabs in the left navigation bar. You can return to the Student Download page at any time by clicking the tab toward the top of the window and/or you can click the link to Home to return to the home page for the Office 2003 Series. And finally, you can click the Feedback button at the top of the screen to send a message directly to Bob Grauer.

Step 3: **Install the Practice Files**

■ Click the **Start button**, then click the **My Computer command** on the menu to open the My Computer folder. If necessary, click the Maximize button so that the My Computer window takes up the entire desktop. Change to the **Details view**.

■ Click the icon for **drive A** to select it. The description of drive A appears at the left of the window. Double click the icon for **drive A** to open this drive. The contents of the My Computer window are replaced by the contents of drive A as shown in Figure 9c.

■ Double click the **XPData file** to install the practice files, which displays the dialog box in Figure 9c. When you have finished reading, click **OK** to continue the installation and display the WinZip Self-Extractor dialog box.

■ Check that the Unzip To Folder text box specifies **A:** to extract the files to the floppy disk. Click the **Unzip button** to extract (uncompress) the practice files and copy them onto the designated drive.

■ Click **OK** after you see the message indicating that the files have been unzipped successfully. Close the WinZip dialog box.

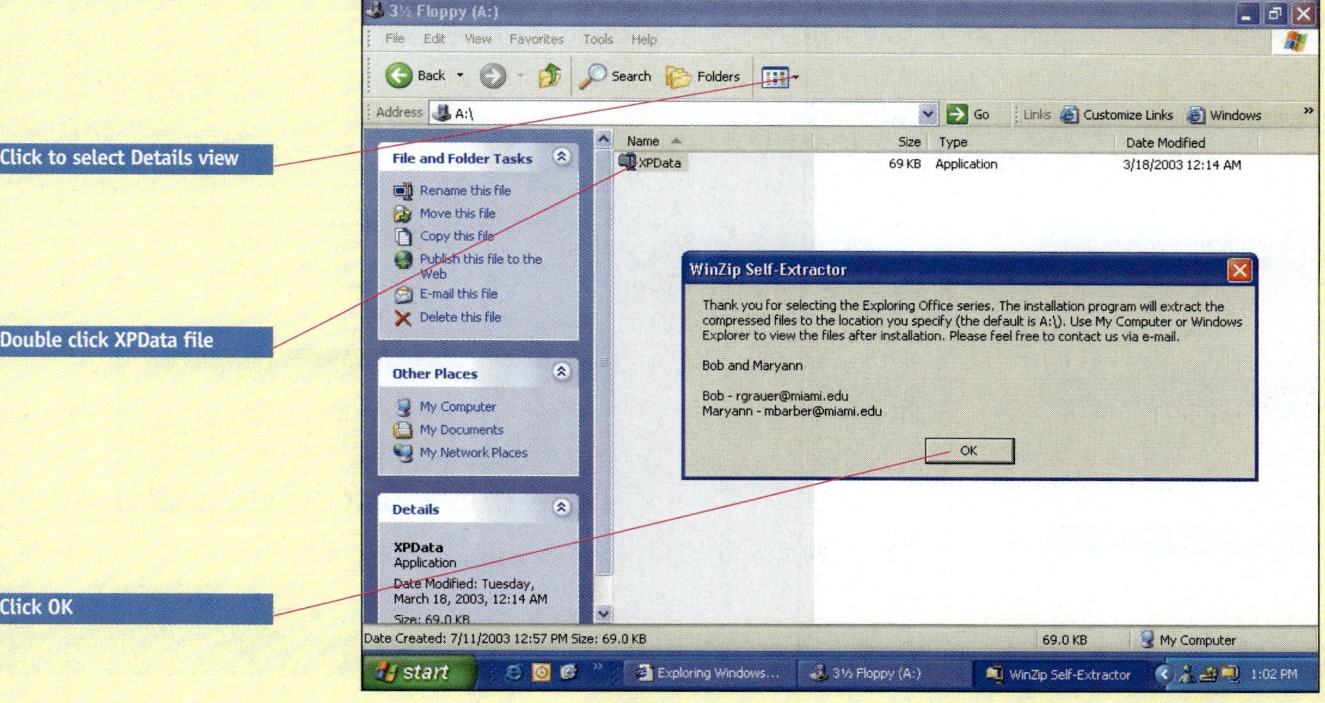

(c) Install the Practice Files (step 3)

FIGURE 9 Hands-on Exercise 2 (*continued*)

DOWNLOADING A FILE

Software and other files are typically compressed (made smaller) to reduce the amount of storage space the files require on disk and/or the time it takes to download the files. In essence, you download a compressed file (which may contain multiple individual files), then you uncompress (expand) the file on your local drive to access the individual files. After the file has been expanded, it is no longer needed and can be deleted.

Step 4: **Delete the Compressed File**

- The practice files have been extracted to drive A and should appear in the Drive A window. If you do not see the files, pull down the **View menu** and click the **Refresh command**.

- If necessary, pull down the **View menu** and click **Details** to change to the Details view in Figure 9e. You should see a total of eight files in the drive A window. Seven of these are the practice files on the data disk. The eighth file is the original file that you downloaded earlier. This file is no longer necessary, since it has been already been expanded.

- Select (click) the **XPData file**. Click the **Delete this file command** in the task pane (or simply press the **Del key**). Pause for a moment to be sure you want to delete this file, then click **Yes** when asked to confirm the deletion as shown in Figure 9d.

- The XPData file is permanently deleted from drive A. (Items deleted from a floppy disk or network drive are not sent to the Recycle bin, and cannot be recovered.)

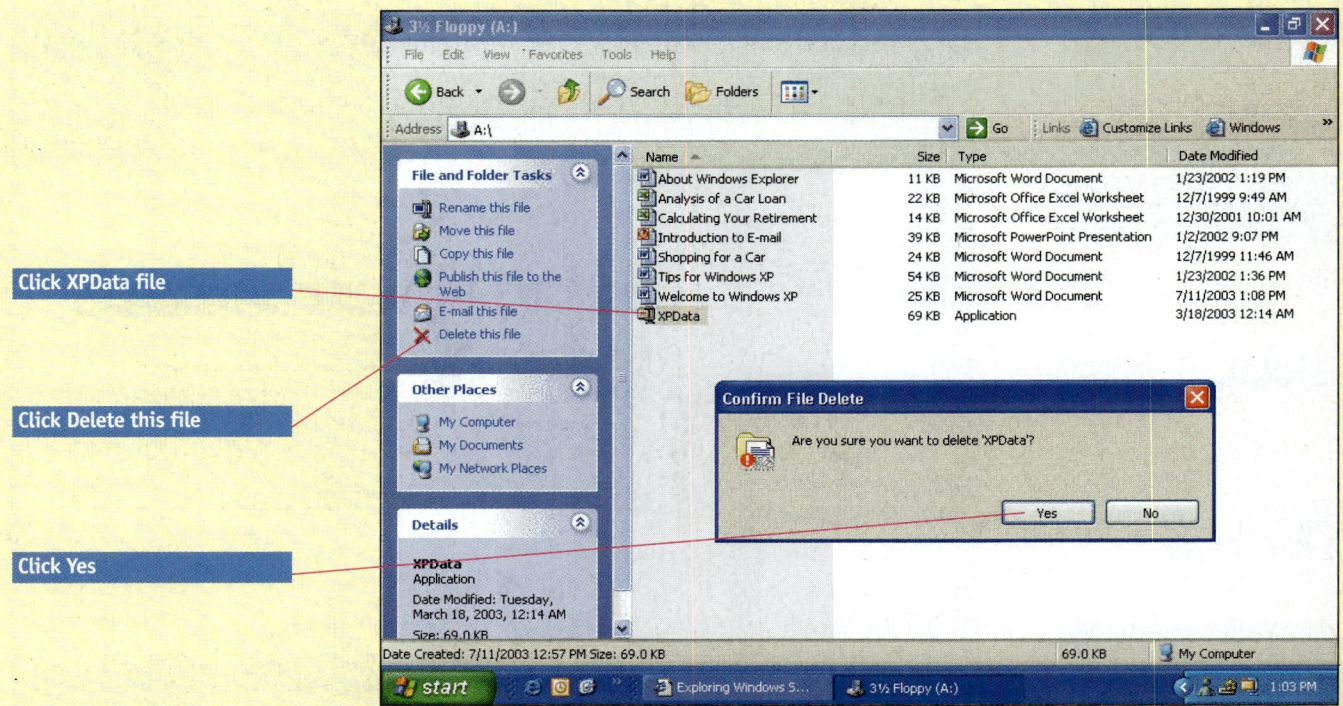

(d) Delete the Compressed File (step 4)

FIGURE 9 Hands-on Exercise 2 (*continued*)

SORT BY NAME, DATE, FILE TYPE, OR SIZE

The files in a folder can be displayed in ascending or descending sequence, by name, date modified, file type, or size, by clicking the appropriate column heading. Click Size, for example, to display files in the order of their size. Click the column heading a second time to reverse the sequence; that is, to switch from ascending to descending, and vice versa. Click a different column heading to display the files in a different sequence.

Step 5: **Modify a Document**

- Double click the **Welcome to Windows XP** document from within My Computer to open the document as shown in Figure 9e. (The document will open in the WordPad accessory if Microsoft Word is not installed on your machine.)

- Maximize the window for Microsoft Word. Read the document, and then press **Ctrl+End** to move to the end of the document. Do not be concerned if your screen does not match ours exactly.

- Add the sentence shown in Figure 9e, press the **Enter key** twice, then type your name. Click the **Save button** on the Standard toolbar to save the document.

- Pull down the **File menu**, click the **Print command**, and click **OK** (or click the **Print button** on the Standard toolbar) to print the document and prove to your instructor that you did the exercise.

- Pull down the **File menu** and click **Exit** to close Microsoft Word. You should be back in the My Computer folder.

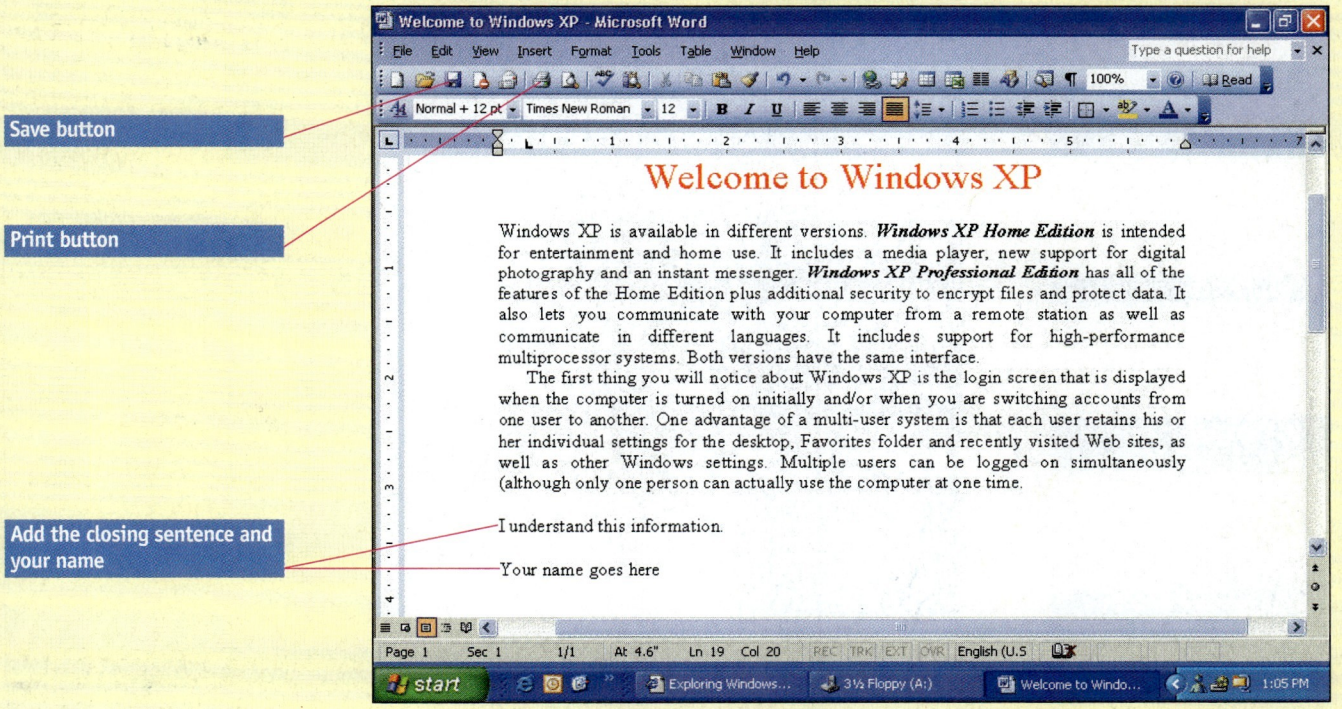

Save button

Print button

Add the closing sentence and your name

(e) Modify a Document (step 5)

FIGURE 9   Hands-on Exercise 2 (*continued*)

THE DOCUMENT, NOT THE APPLICATION

The Windows operating system is document oriented, which means that you are able to think in terms of the document rather than the application that created it. You can still open a document in traditional fashion, by starting the application that created the document, then using the File Open command in that program to retrieve the document. It's often easier, however, to open the document from within a folder by double clicking its icon. Windows will start the associated application and then open the document for you.

Step 6: **Create a New Folder**

- Look closely at the date and time that are displayed next to the Welcome to Windows XP document in Figure 9f. It should show today's date and the current time (give or take a minute) because that is when the document was last modified. Your date will be different from ours.

- Look closely and see that Figure 9f also contains an eighth document, called "Backup of Welcome to Windows XP". This is a backup copy of the original document that will be created automatically by Microsoft Word if the appropriate options are in effect. (See the boxed tip below.)

- Click **a blank area** in the right pane to deselect the Welcome to Windows XP document. The commands in the File and Folder Tasks area change to basic folder operations.

- Click the command to **Make a New folder**, which creates a new folder with the default name "New Folder". Enter **New Car** as the new name. You will move files into this folder in step 7.

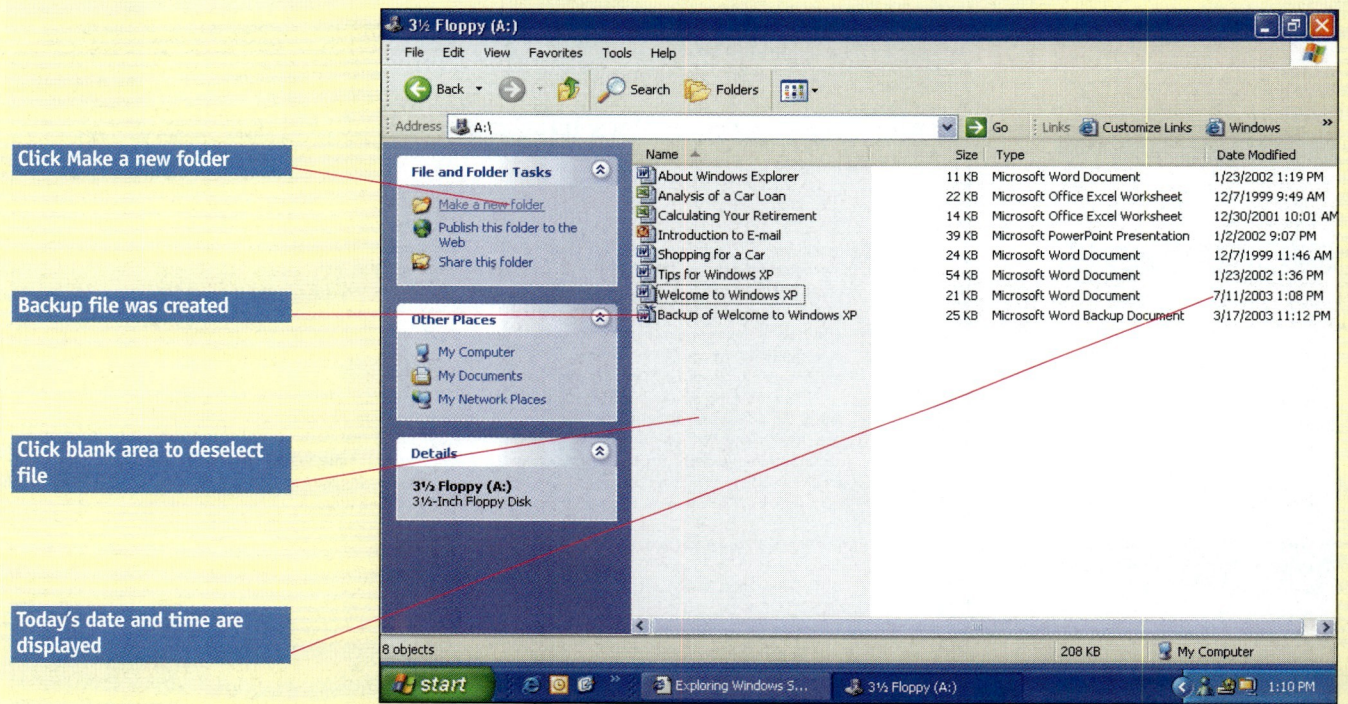

Click Make a new folder

Backup file was created

Click blank area to deselect file

Today's date and time are displayed

(f) Create a New Folder (step 6)

FIGURE 9 Hands-on Exercise 2 (*continued*)

USE WORD TO CREATE A BACKUP COPY

Microsoft Word enables you to automatically keep the previous version of a document as a backup copy. The next time you are in Microsoft Word, pull down the Tools menu, click the Options command, click the Save tab, then check the box to Always create backup copy. Every time you save a file from this point on, the previously saved version is renamed "Backup of document", and the document in memory is saved as the current version. The disk will contain the two most recent versions of the document, enabling you to retrieve the previous version if necessary.

Step 7: **Move the Files**

- There are different ways to move a file from one folder to another. The most basic technique is to
  - ❏ Select (click) the **Analysis of a Car Loan** workbook to highlight the file, then click the **Move this file command** in the task pane.
  - ❏ You will see the Move Items dialog box in Figure 9g. Click the plus sign (if it appears) next to the 3½ floppy disk to expand the disk and view its folders. Click the **New Car folder**, then click the **Move button**.
  - ❏ The selected file is moved to the New Car folder and the dialog box closes. The Analysis of a Car Loan document no longer appears in the right pane of Figure 9g because it has been moved to a new folder.

- If the source and destination folders are both on the same drive, as in this example, you can simply click and drag the file to its new destination. Thus, click and drag the **Shopping for a Car** Word document to the New Car folder. Release the mouse when the file is directly over the folder to complete the move.

- Double click the **New Car folder** to view the contents of this folder, which should contain both documents. The Address bar now says A:\New Car.

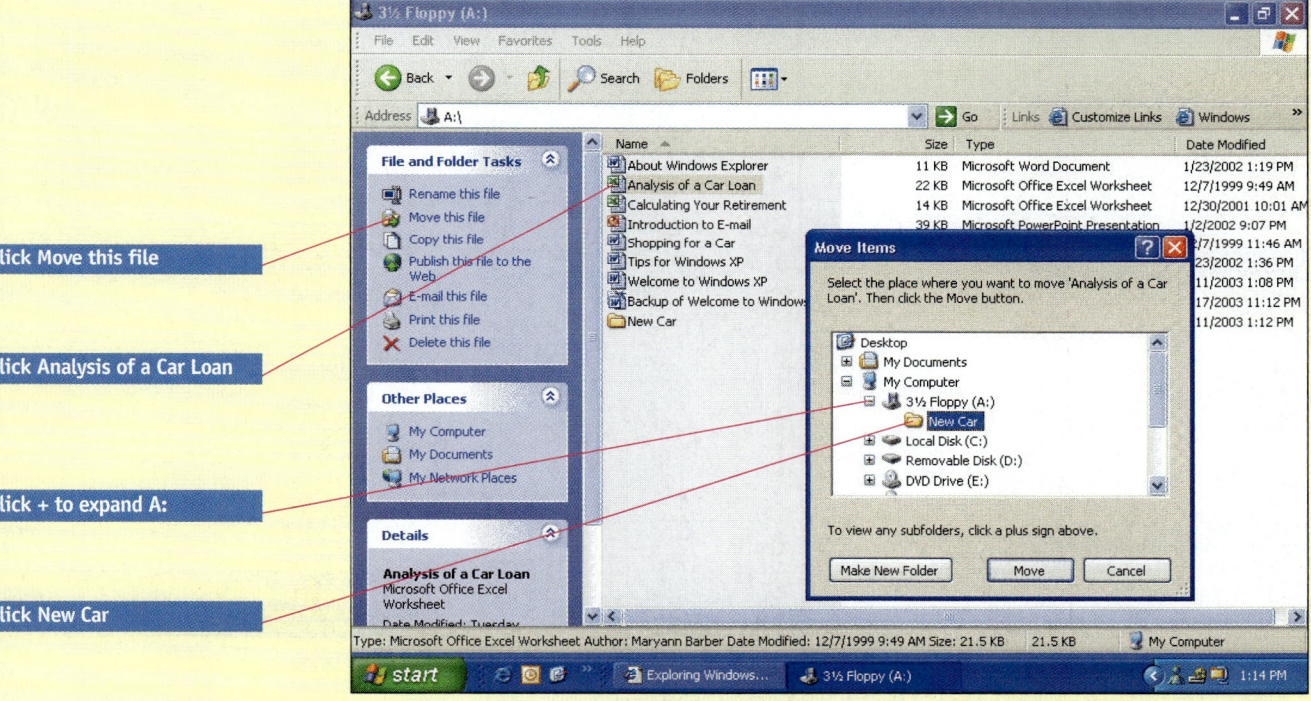

(g) Move the Files (step 7)

FIGURE 9 Hands-on Exercise 2 (*continued*)

THE PLUS AND MINUS SIGNS

Any drive, be it local or on the network, may be expanded or collapsed to display or hide its folders. A minus sign indicates that the drive has been expanded and that its folders are visible. A plus sign indicates the reverse; that is, the device is collapsed and its folders are not visible. Click either sign to toggle to the other. Clicking a plus sign, for example, expands the drive, then displays a minus sign next to the drive to indicate that the folders are visible. Clicking a minus sign has the reverse effect.

Step 8:   **A Look Ahead**

■ Click the **Folders button** to display a hierarchical view of the devices on your computer as shown in Figure 9h. This is the same screen that is displayed through Windows Explorer, a program that we will study after the exercise.

■ The Folders button functions as a toggle switch; click the button a second time and the task pane (also called task panel) returns. Click the **Folders button** to return to the hierarchical view.

■ The New Car folder is selected (highlighted) in the left pane because this is the folder you were working in at the previous step. The contents of this folder are displayed in the right pane.

■ Click the icon for the **3½ floppy drive** to display the contents of drive A. The right pane displays the files on drive A as well as the New Car folder.

■ Close the My Computer folder. Close Internet Explorer. Log off if you do not want to continue with the next exercise at this time.

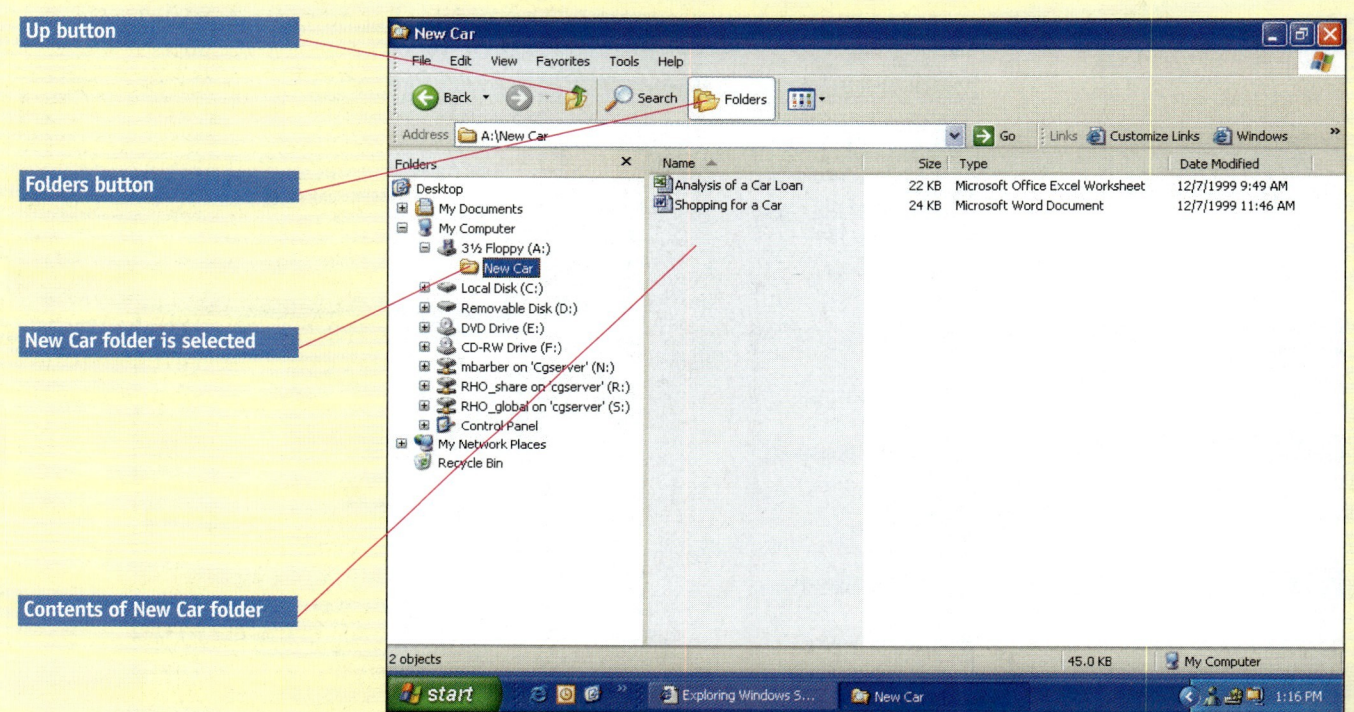

(h) A Look Ahead (step 8)

FIGURE 9   Hands-on Exercise 2 (*continued*)

NAVIGATING THE HIERARCHY

Click the Up button on the Standard Buttons toolbar to move up one level in the hierarchy in the left pane and display the associated contents in the right pane. Click the Up button when you are viewing the New Car folder, for example, and you are returned to drive A. Click the Up button a second time and you will see the contents of My Computer. Note, too, how the contents of the Address bar change each time you view a different folder in the right pane.

WINDOWS EXPLORER

Windows Explorer is a program that displays a hierarchical (tree) structure of the devices on your system. Consider, for example, Figure 10a, which displays the contents of a hypothetical Homework folder as it exists on our computer. The hierarchy is displayed in the left pane, and the contents of the selected object (the Homework folder) are shown in the right pane. The advantage of viewing the folder in this way (as opposed to displaying the task pane) is that you see the location of the folder on the system; that is; the Homework folder is physically stored on drive A.

Let's explore the hierarchy in the left pane. There is a minus sign next to the icon for drive A to indicate that this drive has been expanded and thus you can see its folders. Drive C, however, has a plus sign to indicate that the drive is collapsed and that its contents are not visible. Look closely and you see that both drive A and drive C are indented under My Computer, which in turn is indented under the desktop. In other words, the desktop is at the top of the hierarchy and it contains the My Computer folder, which in turn contains drive A and drive C. The desktop also contains a My Documents folder, but the plus sign next to the My Documents folder indicates the folder is collapsed. My Computer, on the other hand, has a minus sign and you can see its contents, which consist of the drives on your system as well as other special folders (Control Panel and Shared Documents).

Look carefully at the icon next to the Homework folder in the left pane of the figure. The icon is an open folder, and it indicates that the (Homework) folder is the active folder. The folder's name is also shaded, and it appears in the title bar. Only one folder can be active at one time, and its contents are displayed in the right pane. The Milestones in Communications document is highlighted (selected) in the right pane, which means that subsequent commands will affect this document, as opposed to the entire folder. If you wanted to work with a different document in the Homework folder, you would select that document. To see the contents of a different folder, such as Financial Documents, you would select (click) the icon for that folder in the left pane (which automatically closes the Homework folder). The contents of the Financial Documents folder would then appear in the right pane.

You can create folders at any time just like the Homework and Financial Documents folders that we created on drive A. You can also create folders within folders; for example, a correspondence folder may contain two folders of its own, one for business correspondence and one for personal letters.

Personal Folders

Windows automatically creates a set of personal folders for every user. These include the *My Documents folder* and the *My Pictures folder* and *My Music folder* within the My Documents folder. The My Documents folder is collapsed in Figure 10a, but it is expanded in Figure 10b, and thus its contents are visible. The My Music folder is active, and its contents are visible in the right pane.

Every user has a unique set of personal folders, and thus Windows has to differentiate between the multiple "My Documents" folders that may exist. It does so by creating additional folders to hold the documents and settings for each user. Look closely at the Address bar in Figure 10b. Each back slash indicates a new folder, and you can read the complete path from right to left. Thus, the My Music folder that we are viewing is contained in My Documents folder within Maryann's folder, which in turn is stored in a Documents and Settings folder on drive C.

Fortunately, however, Windows does the housekeeping for you. All you have to do is locate the desired folder—for example, My Music or My Pictures—in the left pane, and Windows does the rest. *Personal folders* are just what the name implies—"personal," meaning that only one person has access to their content. Windows also provides a *Shared Documents folder* for files that Maryann may want to share with others.

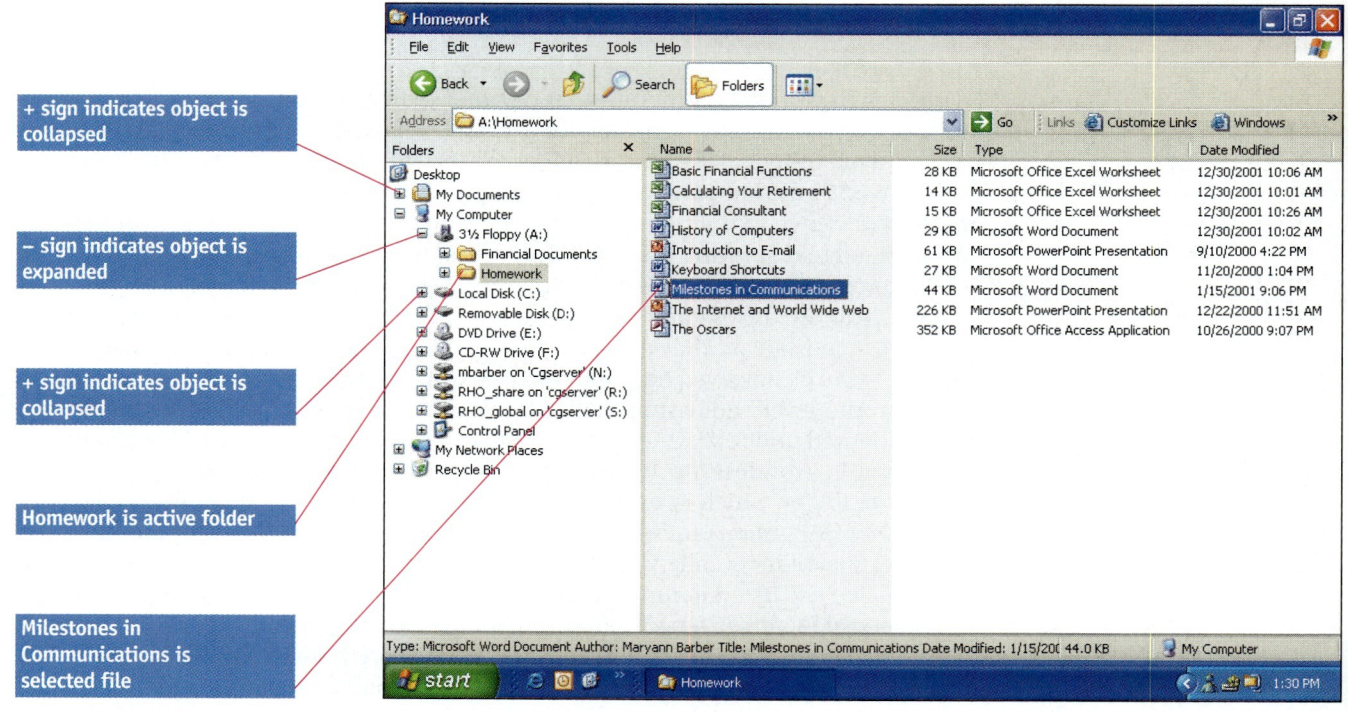

+ sign indicates object is collapsed

– sign indicates object is expanded

+ sign indicates object is collapsed

Homework is active folder

Milestones in Communications is selected file

(a) Homework Folder

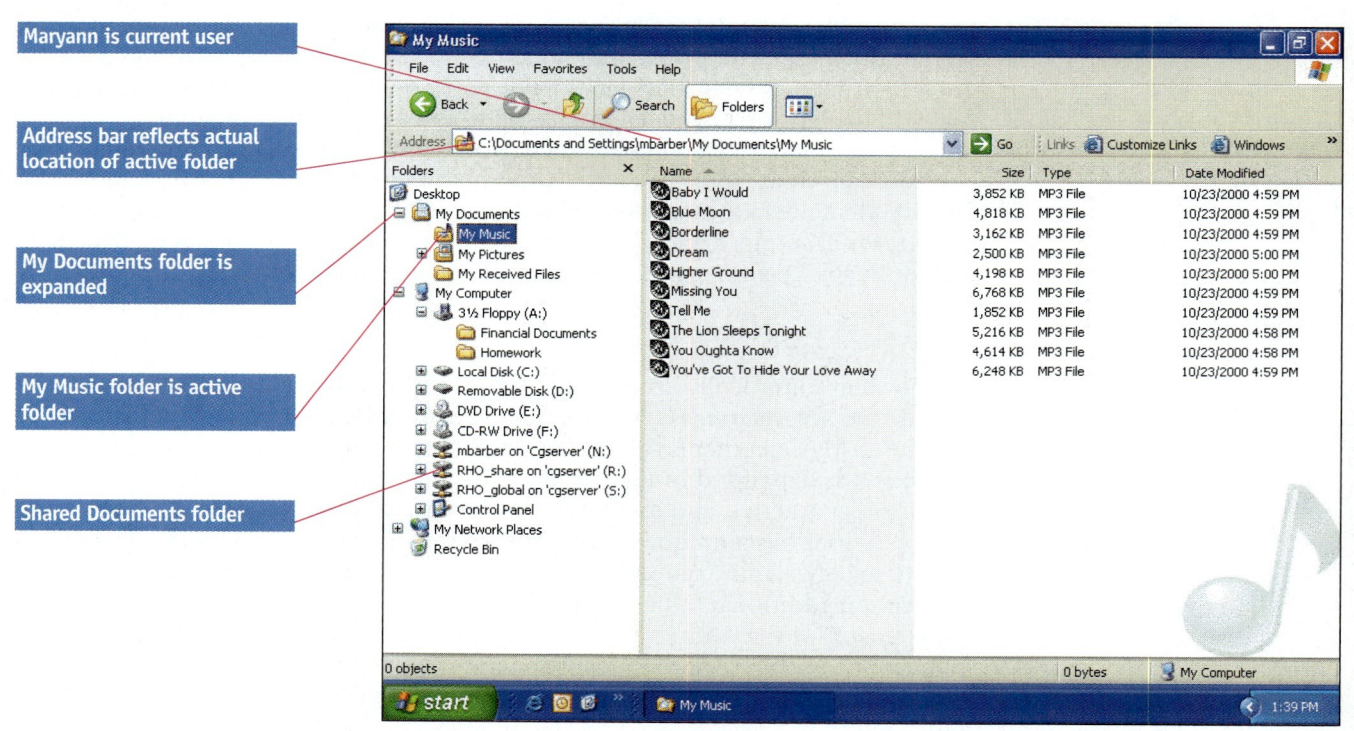

Maryann is current user

Address bar reflects actual location of active folder

My Documents folder is expanded

My Music folder is active folder

Shared Documents folder

(b) My Music Folder

FIGURE 10 Windows Explorer

Moving and Copying a File

The essence of file management is to **move** and **copy a file** or folder from one location to another. This can be done in different ways. The easiest is to click and drag the file icon from the source drive or folder to the destination drive or folder, within Windows Explorer. There is one subtlety, however, in that the result of dragging a file (i.e., whether the file is moved or copied) depends on whether the source and destination are on the same or different drives. Dragging a file from one folder to another folder on the same drive moves the file. Dragging a file to a folder on a different drive copies the file. The same rules apply to dragging a folder, where the folder and every file in it are moved or copied, as per the rules for an individual file.

This process is not as arbitrary as it may seem. Windows assumes that if you drag an object (a file or folder) to a different drive (e.g., from drive C to drive A), you want the object to appear in both places. Hence, the default action when you click and drag an object to a different drive is to copy the object. You can, however, override the default and move the object by pressing and holding the Shift key as you drag.

Windows also assumes that you do not want two copies of an object on the same drive, as that would result in wasted disk space. Thus, the default action when you click and drag an object to a different folder on the same drive is to move the object. You can override the default and copy the object by pressing and holding the Ctrl key as you drag. It's not as complicated as it sounds, and you get a chance to practice in the hands-on exercise, which follows shortly.

Deleting a File

The **Delete command** deletes (erases) a file from a disk. The command can be executed in different ways, most easily by selecting a file, then pressing the Del key. It's also comforting to know that you can usually recover a deleted file, because the file is not (initially) removed from the disk, but moved instead to the Recycle Bin, from where it can be restored to its original location. Unfortunately, files deleted from a floppy disk are not put into the Recycle Bin and hence cannot be recovered.

The **Recycle Bin** is a special folder that contains all files that were previously deleted from any hard disk on your system. Think of the Recycle Bin as similar to the wastebasket in your room. You throw out (delete) a report by tossing it into a wastebasket. The report is gone (deleted) from your desk, but you can still get it back by taking it out of the wastebasket as long as the basket wasn't emptied. The Recycle Bin works the same way. Files are not deleted from the hard disk per se, but moved instead to the Recycle Bin from where they can be restored to their original location. (The protection afforded by the Recycle Bin does not extend to files deleted from a floppy disk.)

Backup

It's not a question of *if* it will happen, but *when*—hard disks die, files are lost, or viruses may infect a system. It has happened to us and it will happen to you, but you can prepare for the inevitable by creating adequate backup *before* the problem occurs. The essence of a **backup strategy** is to decide which files to back up, how often to do the backup, and where to keep the backup.

Our strategy is very simple—back up what you can't afford to lose, do so on a daily basis, and store the backup away from your computer. You need not copy every file, every day. Instead, copy just the files that changed during the current session. Realize, too, that it is much more important to back up your data files than your program files. You can always reinstall the application from the original disks or CD, or if necessary, go to the vendor for another copy of an application. You, however, are the only one who has a copy of the term paper that is due tomorrow. Once you decide on a strategy, follow it, and follow it faithfully!

3   Windows Explorer

Objective   Use Windows Explorer to move, copy, and delete a file; recover a deleted file from the Recycle Bin. Use Figure 11 as a guide.

Step 1: **Create a New Folder**

- Place the floppy disk from the previous exercise into drive A. Click the **Start Button**, click the **All Programs command**, click **Accessories**, then click **Windows Explorer**. Click the **Maximize button**.

- Expand or collapse the various devices on your system so that My Computer is expanded, but all of the devices are collapsed.

- Click (select) **drive A** in the left pane to display the contents of the floppy disk. You should see the New Car folder that was created in the previous exercise.

- Point to a blank area anywhere in the **right pane**, click the **right mouse button**, click the **New command**, then click **Folder** as the type of object to create.

- The icon for a new folder will appear with the name of the folder (New Folder) highlighted. Type **Windows Information** to change the name. Press **Enter**.

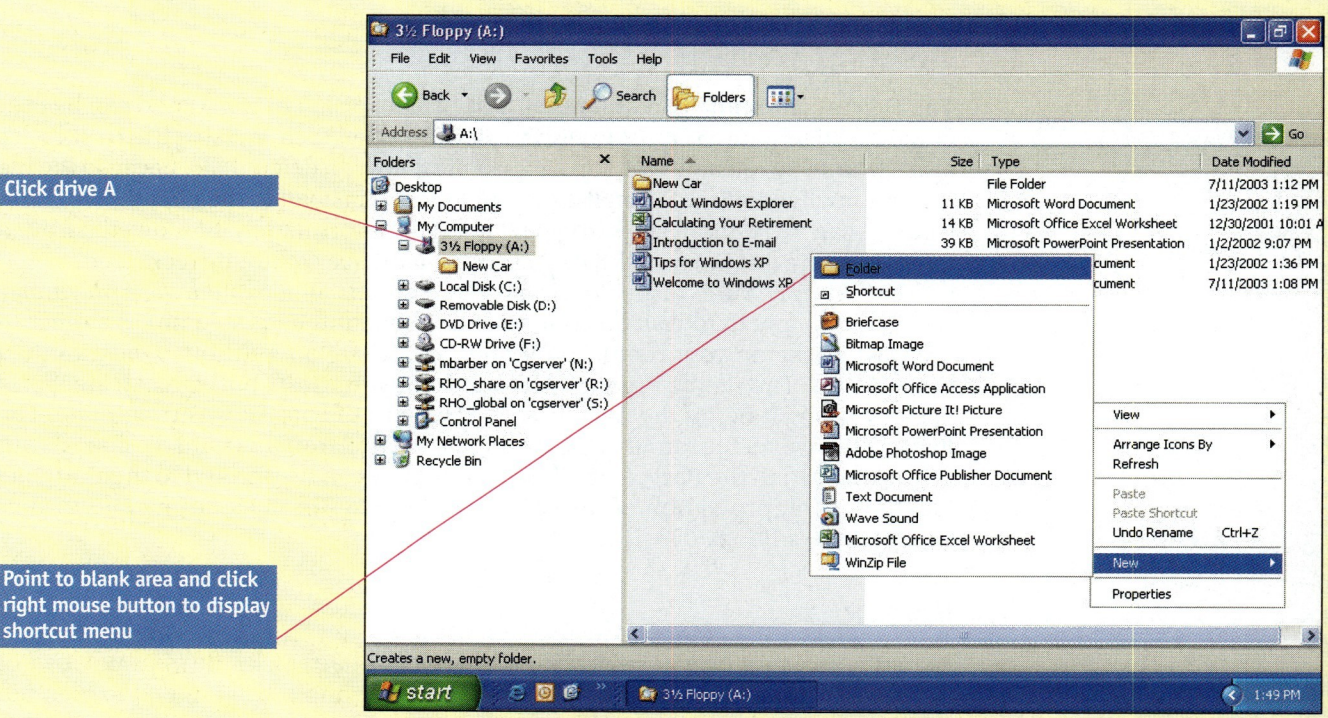

(a) Create a New Folder (step 1)

FIGURE 11   Hands-on Exercise 3 (*continued*)

THE RENAME COMMAND

Right click the file or a folder whose name you want to change to display a context-sensitive menu, and then click the Rename command. The name of the folder will be highlighted with the insertion point at the end of the name. Enter (or edit) the new (existing) name and press Enter.

Step 2: **Move the Files**

■ If necessary, change to the **Details view** and click the **plus sign** next to drive A to expand the drive as shown in Figure 11b. Note the following:
  ❏ The left pane shows that drive A is selected. The right pane displays the contents of drive A (the selected object in the left pane). The folders are shown first and appear in alphabetical order. If not, press the **F5 (Refresh) key** to refresh the screen.
  ❏ There is a minus sign next to the icon for drive A in the left pane, indicating that it has been expanded and that its folders are visible. Thus, the folder names also appear under drive A in the left pane.

■ Click and drag the **About Windows Explorer** document in the right pane to the **Windows Information folder** in the left pane, to move the file into that folder.

■ Click and drag the **Tips for Windows XP** and the **Welcome to Windows XP** documents to move these documents to the **Windows Information folder**.

■ Click the **Windows Information folder** in the left pane to select the folder and display its contents in the right pane. You should see the three files that were just moved.

■ Click the **Up button** to return to drive A.

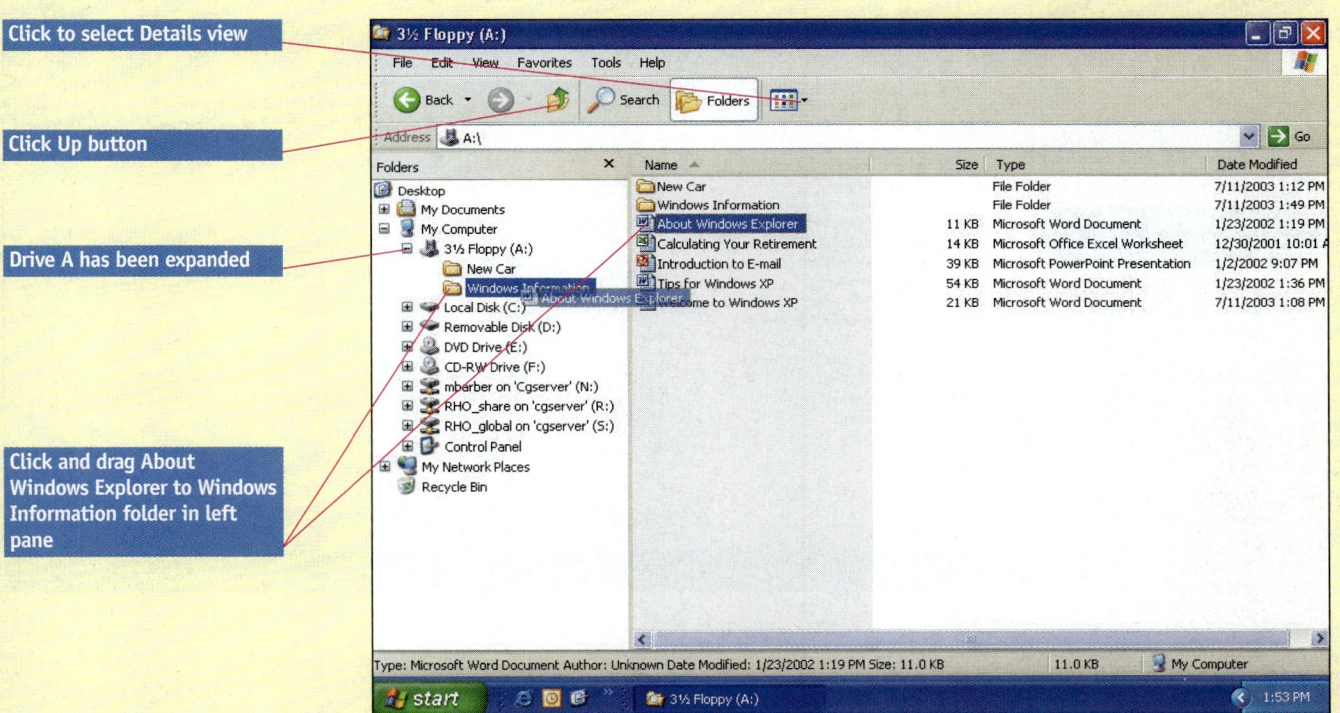

Click to select Details view

Click Up button

Drive A has been expanded

Click and drag About Windows Explorer to Windows Information folder in left pane

(b) Move the Files (step 2)

FIGURE 11 Hands-on Exercise 3 (*continued*)

SELECT MULTIPLE FILES

Selecting (clicking) one file automatically deselects the previously selected file. You can, however, select multiple files by clicking the first file, then pressing and holding the Ctrl key as you click each additional file. Use the Shift key to select multiple files that are adjacent to one another by clicking the icon of the first file, then pressing and holding the Shift key as you click the icon of the last file.

Step 3: **Copy a Folder**

- Point to the **Windows Information folder** in the right pane, then **right click and drag** this folder to the **My Documents folder** (on drive C) in the left pane. Release the mouse to display a context-sensitive menu.

- Click the **Copy Here command** as shown in Figure 11c.
  - ❏ You may see a Copy files message box as the individual files within the Windows Information folder are copied to the My Documents folder.
  - ❏ If you see the Confirm Folder Replace dialog box, it means that you (or another student) already copied these files to the My Documents folder. Click the **Yes to All button** so that your files replace the previous versions in the My Documents folder.

- Click the **My Documents folder** in the left pane. Pull down the **View menu** and click the **Refresh command** (or press the **F5 key**) so that the hierarchy shows the newly copied folder. (Please remember to delete the Windows Information folder from drive C at the end of the exercise.)

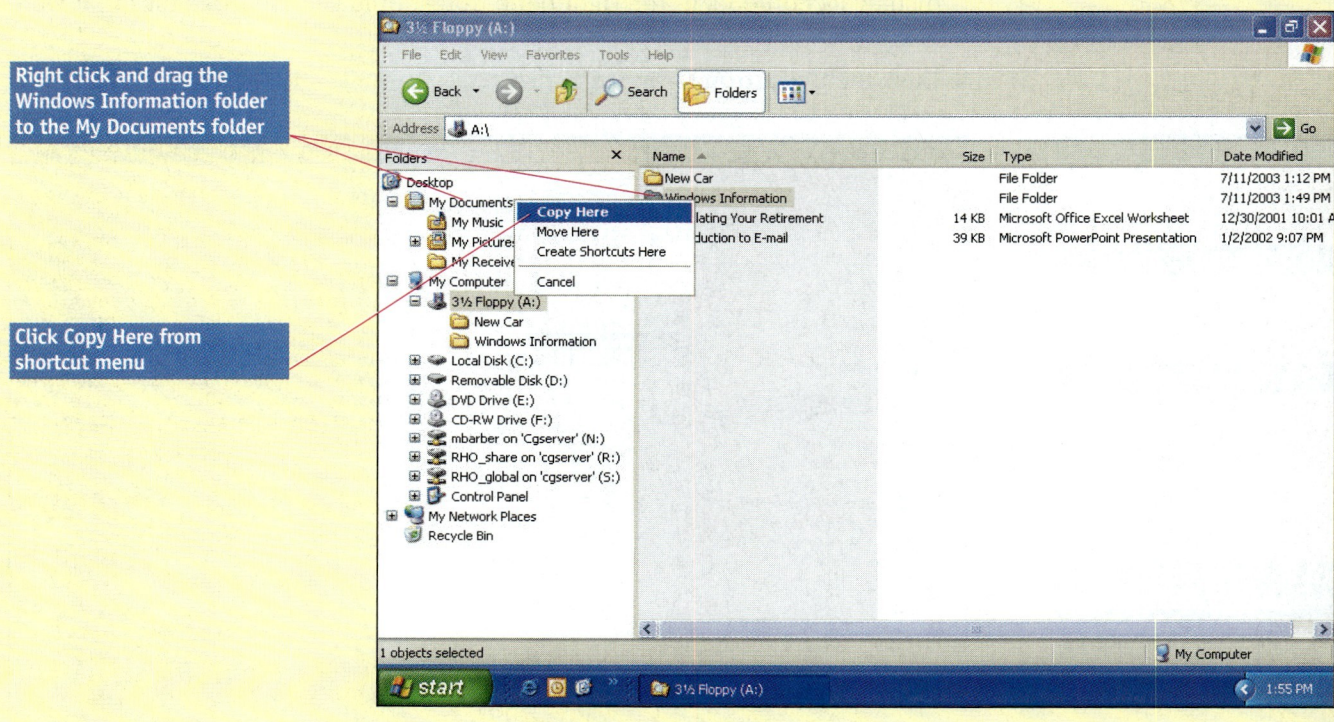

Right click and drag the Windows Information folder to the My Documents folder

Click Copy Here from shortcut menu

(c) Copy a Folder (step 3)

FIGURE 11 Hands-on Exercise 3 (*continued*)

RIGHT CLICK AND DRAG

The result of dragging a file with the left mouse button depends on whether the source and destination folders are on the same or different drives. Dragging a file to a folder on a different drive copies the file, whereas dragging the file to a folder on the same drive moves the file. If you find this hard to remember, and most people do, click and drag with the right mouse button to display a context-sensitive menu asking whether you want to copy or move the file. This simple tip can save you from making a careless (and potentially serious) error. Use it!

Step 4: Modify a Document

- Click the **Windows Information folder** within the My Documents folder to make it the active folder and to display its contents in the right pane. Change to the **Details view**.

- Double click the **About Windows Explorer** document to start Word and open the document. Do not be concerned if the size and/or position of the Microsoft Word window are different from ours. Read the document.

- If necessary, click inside the document window, then press **Ctrl+End** to move to the end of the document. Add the text shown in Figure 11d.

- Pull down the **File menu** and click **Save** to save the modified file (or click the **Save button** on the Standard toolbar). Pull down the **File menu** and click **Exit** to exit from Microsoft Word.

- Pull down the **View menu** and click the **Refresh command** (or press the **F5 key**) to update the contents of the right pane. The date and time associated with the About Windows Explorer document (on drive C) have been changed to indicate that the file has been modified.

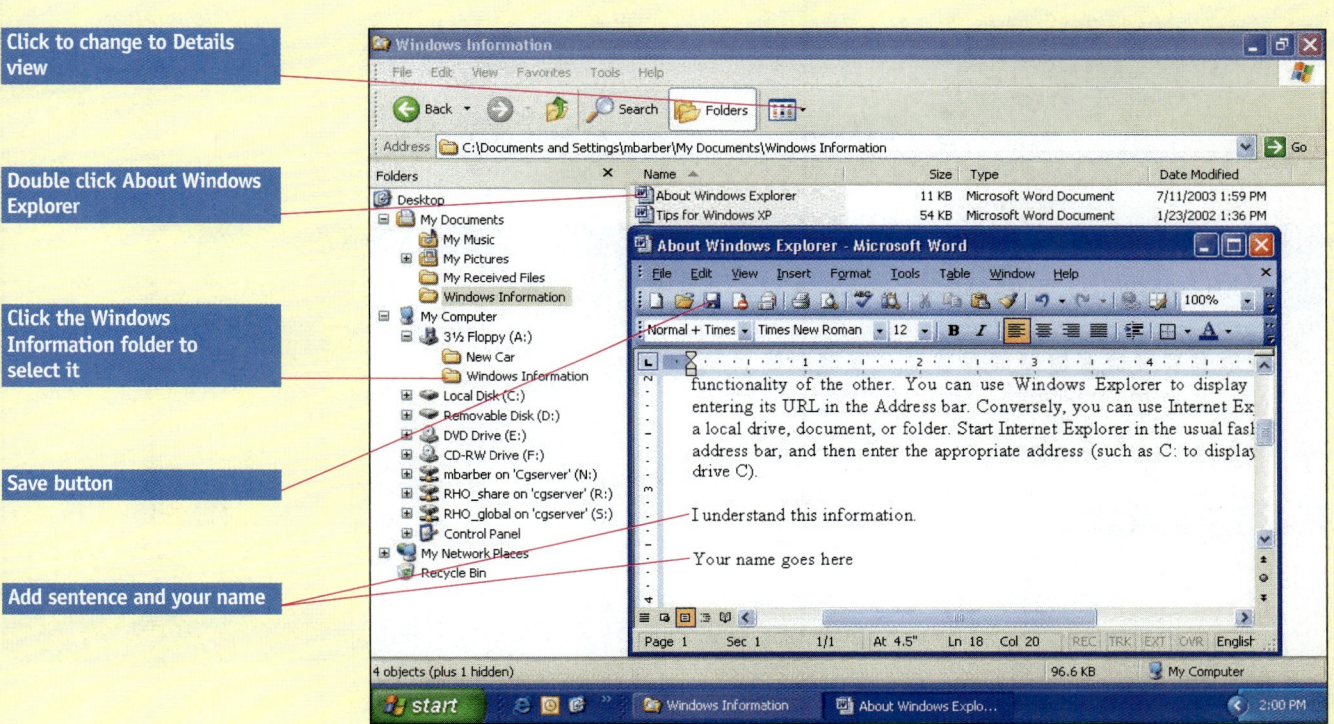

Click to change to Details view

Double click About Windows Explorer

Click the Windows Information folder to select it

Save button

Add sentence and your name

(d) Modify a Document (step 4)

FIGURE 11 Hands-on Exercise 3 (*continued*)

KEYBOARD SHORTCUTS

Most people begin with the mouse, but add keyboard shortcuts as they become more proficient. Ctrl+B, Ctrl+I, and Ctrl+U are shortcuts to boldface, italicize, and underline, respectively. Ctrl+X (the X is supposed to remind you of a pair of scissors), Ctrl+C, and Ctrl+V correspond to Cut, Copy, and Paste, respectively. Ctrl+Home and Ctrl+End move to the beginning or end of a document. These shortcuts are not unique to Microsoft Word, but are recognized in virtually every Windows application.

Step 5: **Copy (Back Up) a File**

- Verify that the **Windows Information folder** (on drive C) is the active folder, as denoted by the open folder icon. Click and drag the icon for the **About Windows Explorer** document from the right pane to the **Windows Information folder** on **drive A** in the left pane.

- You will see the message in Figure 11e, indicating that the folder (on drive A) already contains a file called About Windows Explorer and asking whether you want to replace the existing file.

- Click **Yes** because you want to replace the previous version of the file on drive A with the updated version from the My Documents folder.

- You have just backed up a file by copying the About Windows Explorer document from a folder on drive C to the disk in drive A. In other words, you can use the floppy disk to restore the file to drive C should anything happen to it.

- Keep the floppy disk in a safe place, away from the computer.

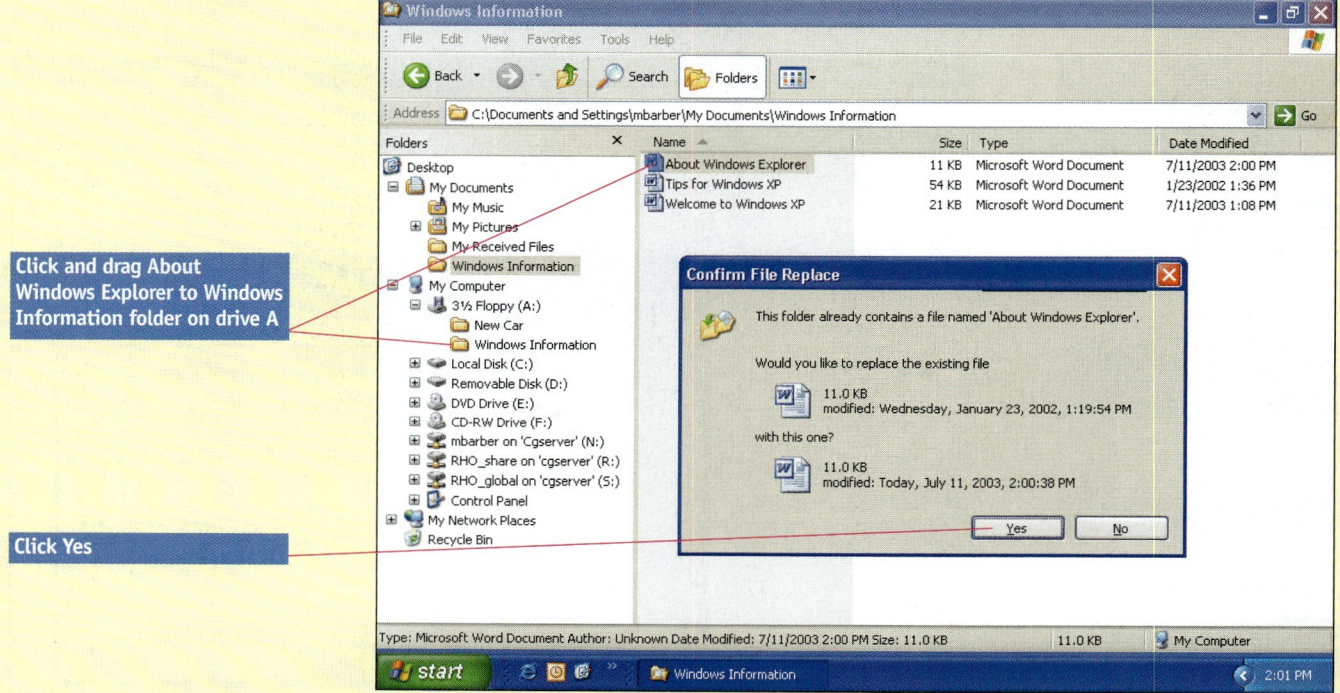

Click and drag About Windows Explorer to Windows Information folder on drive A

Click Yes

(e) Copy (Back Up) a File (step 5)

FIGURE 11 Hands-on Exercise 3 (*continued*)

THE MY DOCUMENTS FOLDER

The My Documents folder is created by default with the installation of Windows XP. There is no requirement that you store your documents in this folder, but it is convenient, especially for beginners who may lack the confidence to create their own folders. The My Documents folder is also helpful in a laboratory environment where the network administrator may prevent you from modifying the desktop and/or from creating your own folders on drive C, in which case you will have to use the My Documents folder.

Step 6: **Delete a Folder**

■ Select (click) **Windows Information folder** within the My Documents folder in the left pane. Pull down the **File menu** and click **Delete** (or press the **Del key**).

■ You will see the dialog box in Figure 11f, asking whether you are sure you want to delete the folder and send its contents to the Recycle Bin, which enables you to restore the folder at a later date.

■ Click **Yes** to delete the folder. The folder disappears from drive C. Note that you have deleted the folder and its contents.

■ Now pretend that you do not want to delete the folder. Pull down the **Edit menu**. Click **Undo Delete**.

■ The deletion is cancelled and the Windows Information folder reappears in the left pane. If you do not see the folder, pull down the **View menu** and click the **Refresh command** (or press the **F5 key**).

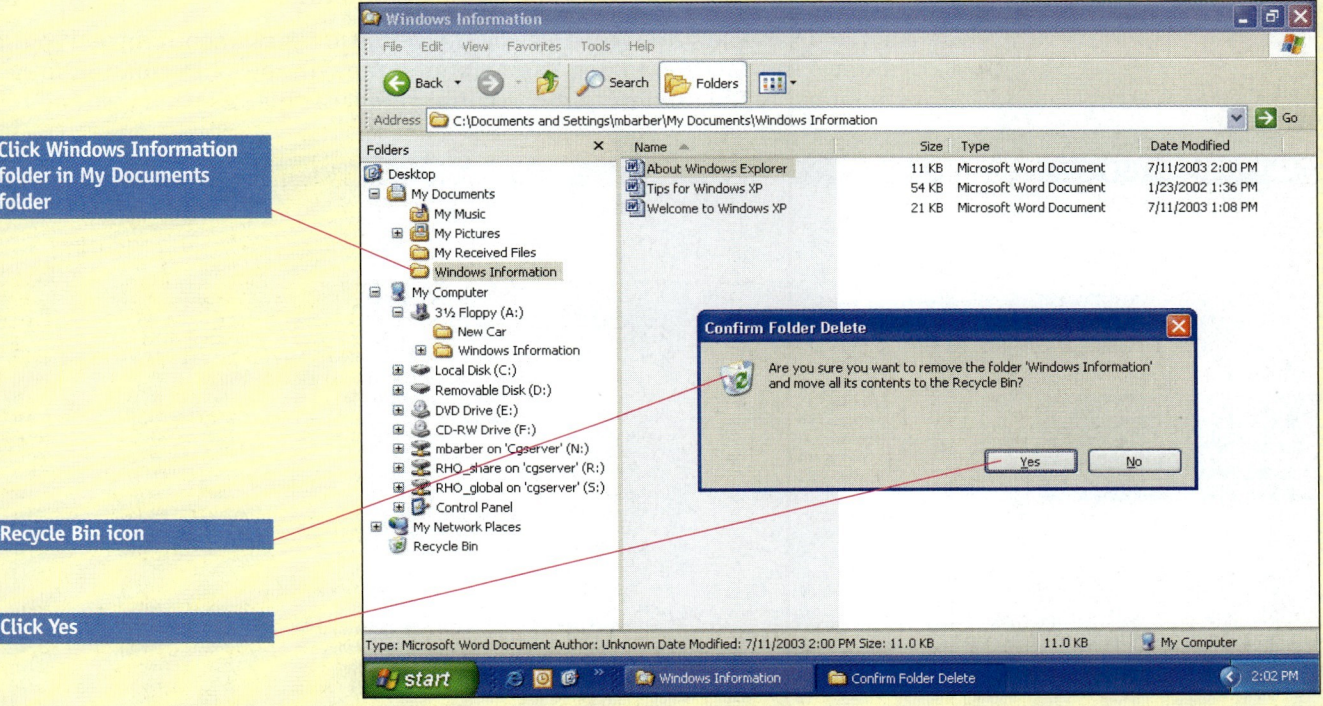

(f) Delete a Folder (step 6)

FIGURE 11 Hands-on Exercise 3 (*continued*)

CUSTOMIZE WINDOWS EXPLORER

Increase or decrease the size of the left pane within Windows Explorer by dragging the vertical line separating the left and right panes in the appropriate direction. You can also drag the right border of the various column headings (Name, Size, Type, and Modified) in the right pane to increase or decrease the width of the column and see more or less information in that column. And best of all, you can click any column heading to display the contents of the selected folder in sequence by that column. Click the heading a second time and the sequence changes from ascending to descending and vice versa.

Step 7: The Recycle Bin

- If necessary, select the **Windows Information folder** within the My Documents folder in the left pane. Select (click) the **About Windows Explorer** file in the right pane. Press the **Del key**, then click **Yes** when asked to delete the file.

- Click the **down arrow** in the vertical scroll bar in the left pane until you can click the icon for the **Recycle Bin**.

- The Recycle Bin contains all files that have been previously deleted from the local (hard) disks, and hence you will see a different number of files than those displayed in Figure 11g.

- Change to the **Details view**. Pull down the **View menu**, click (or point to) **Arrange Icons by**, then click **Date Deleted** to display the files in this sequence. Execute this command a second time (if necessary) so that the most recently deleted file appears at the top of the window.

- Right click the **About Windows Explorer** file to display the context-sensitive menu in Figure 11g, then click the **Restore command**.

- The file disappears from the Recycle bin because it has been returned to the Windows Information folder. You can open the Windows Information folder within the My Documents folder to confirm that the file has been restored.

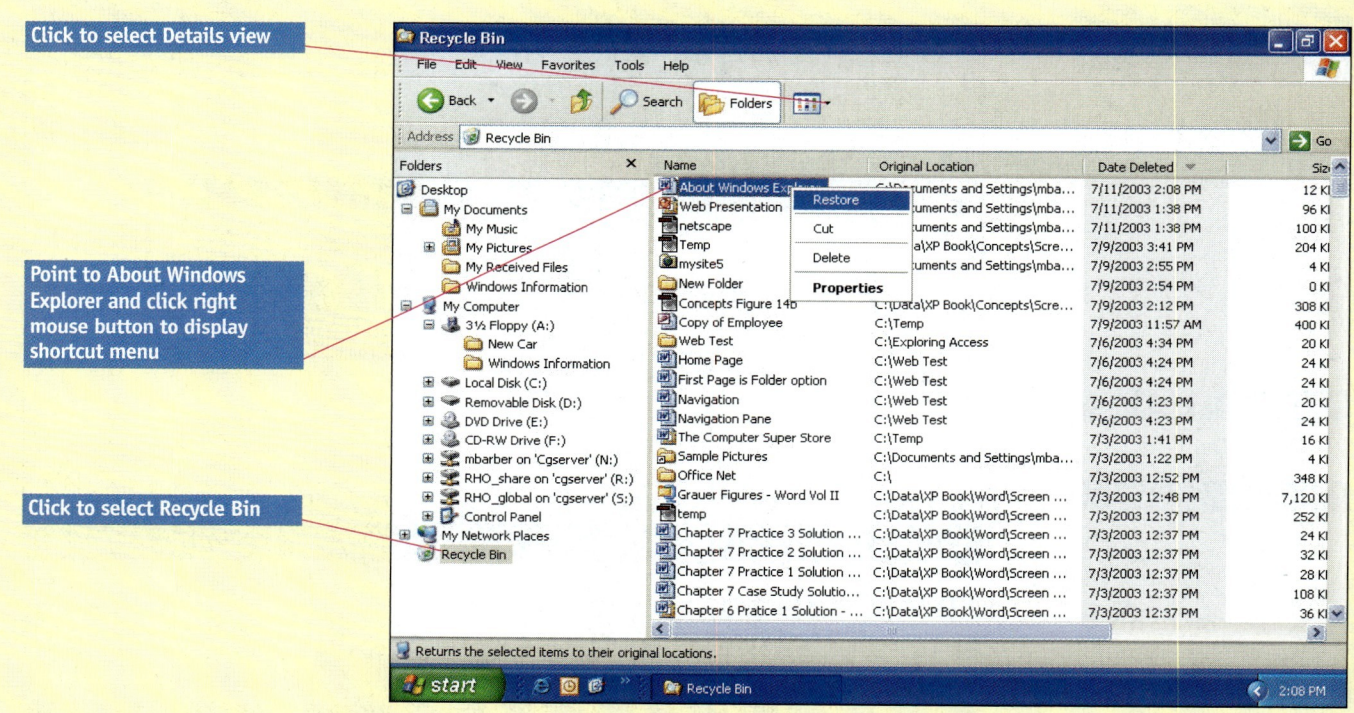

Click to select Details view

Point to About Windows Explorer and click right mouse button to display shortcut menu

Click to select Recycle Bin

(g) The Recycle Bin (step 7)

FIGURE 11   Hands-on Exercise 3 (*continued*)

TWO WAYS TO RECOVER A FILE

The Undo command is present in Windows Explorer. Thus, you do not need to resort to the Recycle Bin to recover a deleted file provided you execute the Undo command immediately (within a few commands) after the Delete command was issued. Some operations cannot be undone (in which case the Undo command will be dimmed), but Undo is always worth a try.

Step 8: **The Group By Command**

- Select (click) the **Windows Information folder** on drive A. You should see the contents of this folder (three Word documents) in the right pane.

- Pull down the **View menu**, (click or) point to the **Arrange Icons by command**, then click the **Show in Groups command** from the cascaded menu.

- You see the same three files as previously, but they are displayed in groups according to the first letter in the filename. Click the **Date Modified** column, and the files are grouped according to the date they were last modified.

- The Show in Groups command functions as a toggle switch. Execute the command and the files are displayed in groups; execute the command a second time and the groups disappear.

- Select (click) the icon for **drive A** in the left pane to display the contents of drive A. You should see two folders and two files. Pull down the **View menu**, (click or) point to the **Arrange Icons by command**, and then click the **Show in Groups command** from the cascaded menu.

- Change to the **Details view**. Click the **Type column** to group the objects by folder and file type.

Click Date Modified column heading

Files are displayed in groups by date

Click Windows Information folder on drive A

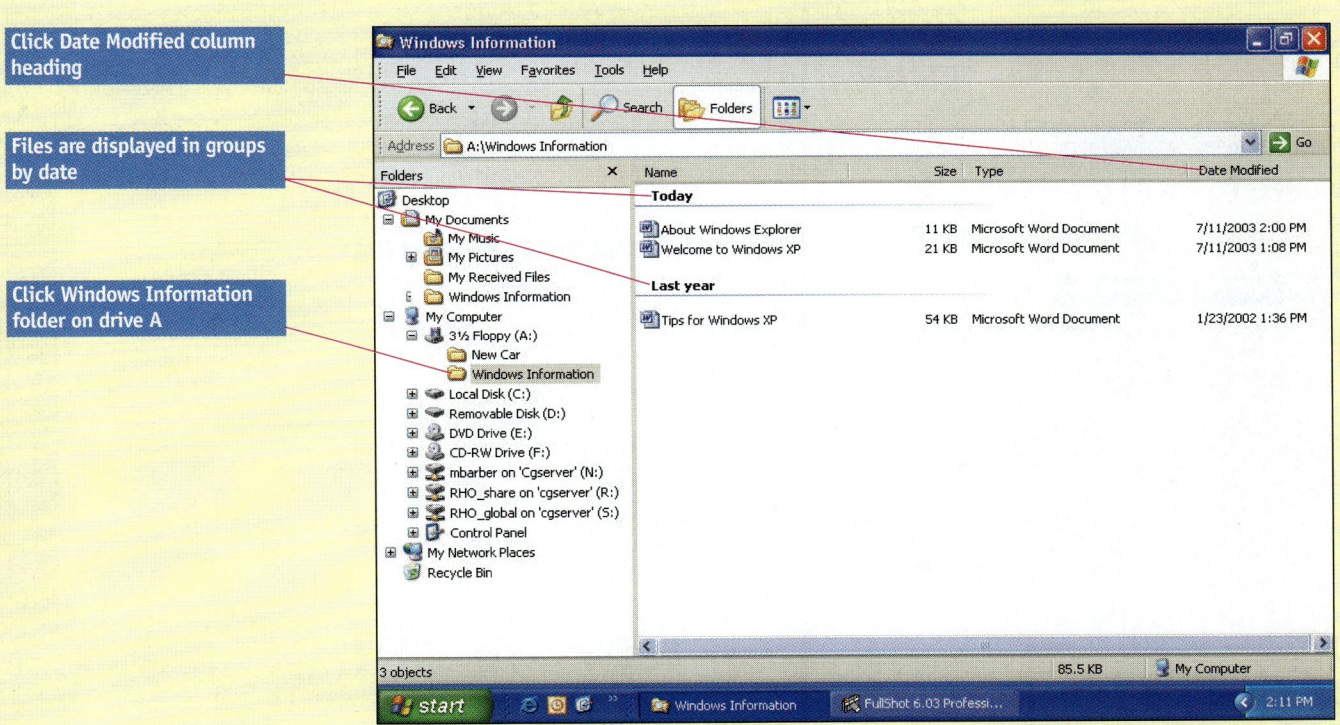

(h) The Group By Command (step 8)

FIGURE 11 Hands-on Exercise 3 (*continued*)

KEEP THE VIEW

Once you set the desired view in a folder, you may want to display every other folder according to those parameters. Pull down the Tools menu, click the Folder Options command, and click the View tab. Click the button to Apply to All folders, then click Yes when prompted to confirm. Click OK to close the Folder Options dialog box. The next time you open another folder, it will appear in the same view as the current folder.

Step 9: Complete the Exercise

- Prove to your instructor that you have completed the exercise correctly by capturing the screen on your monitor. Press the **Print Screen key**. Nothing appears to have happened, but the screen has been copied to the clipboard.

- Click the **Start button**, click the **All Programs command**, then start Microsoft Word and begin a new document. Enter the title of your document, followed by your name as shown in Figure 11i. Press the **Enter key** two or three times.

- Pull down the **Edit menu** and click the **Paste command** (or click the **Paste button** on the Standard toolbar) to copy the contents of the clipboard into the Word document.

- Print this document for your instructor. There is no need to save this document. Exit Word.

- Delete the **Windows Information folder** from the My Documents folder as a courtesy to the next student. Close Windows Explorer.

- Log off if you do not want to continue the next exercise at this time. (Click the **Start button**, click **Log Off**, then click **Log Off** a second time to end your session.)

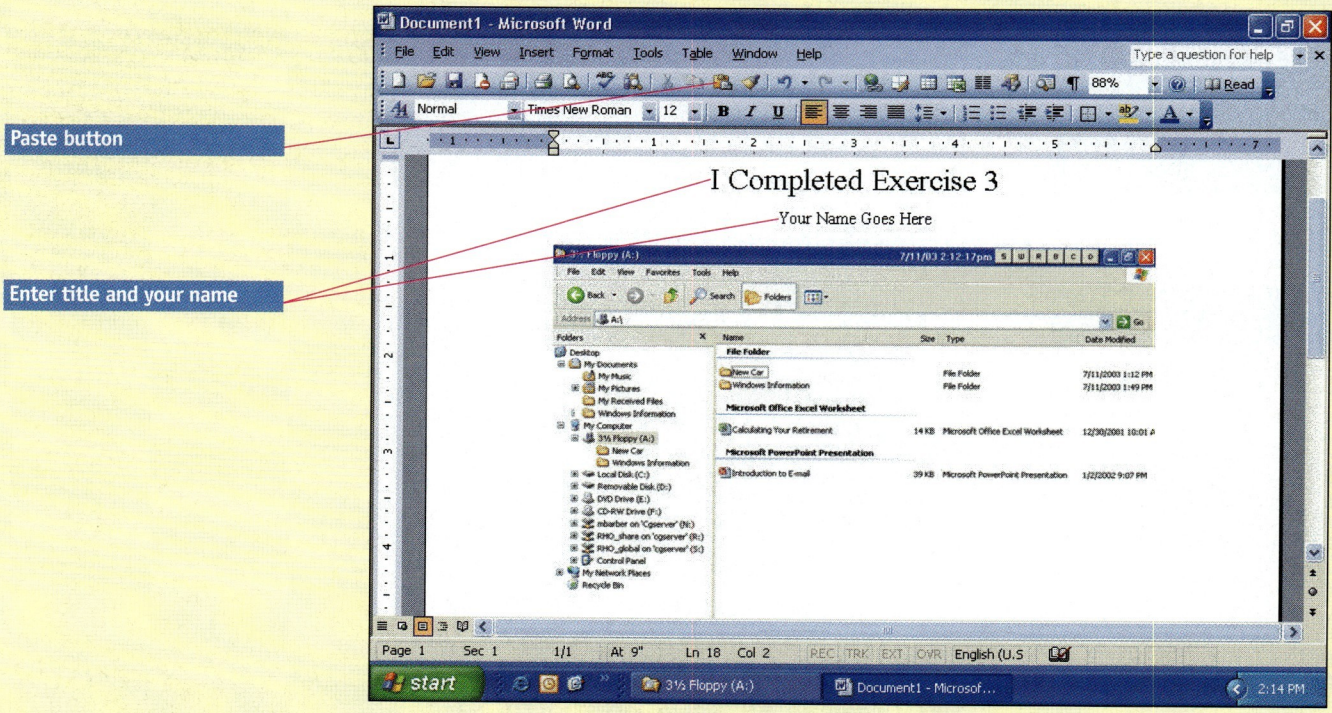

(i) Complete the Exercise (step 9)

FIGURE 11   Hands-on Exercise 3 (*continued*)

SWITCHING USERS VERSUS LOGGING OFF

Windows XP gives you the choice of switching users or logging off. Switching users leaves all of your applications open, but it relinquishes control of the computer to another user. This lets you subsequently log back on (after the new user logs off) and take up exactly where you were. Logging off, on the other hand, closes all of your applications and ends the session, but it leaves the computer running at full power and available for someone else to log on.

You have learned the basic concepts of disk and file management, but there is so much more. Windows XP has something for everyone. It is easy and intuitive for the novice, but it also contains sophisticated tools for the more knowledgeable user. This section describes three powerful features to increase your productivity. Some or all of these features may be disabled in a school environment, but the information will stand you in good stead on your own computer.

The Control Panel

The **Control Panel** affects every aspect of your system. It determines the appearance of your desktop, and it controls the performance of your hardware. You can, for example, change the way your mouse behaves by switching the function of the left and right mouse buttons and/or by replacing the standard mouse pointers with animated icons that move across the screen. You will not have access to the Control Panel in a lab environment, but you will need it at home whenever you install new hardware or software. You should be careful about making changes, and you should understand the nature of the new settings before you accept any of the changes.

The Control Panel in Windows XP organizes its tools by category as shown in Figure 12. Point to any category and you see a Screen Tip that describes the specific tasks within that category. The Appearance and Themes category, for example, lets you select a screen saver or customize the Start menu and taskbar. You can also switch to the Classic view that displays every tool in a single screen, which is consistent with all previous versions of Windows.

The task pane provides access to the **Windows Update** function, which connects you to a Web site where you can download new device drivers and other updates to Windows XP. You can also configure your system to install these updates automatically as they become available. Some updates, especially those having to do with Internet security, are absolutely critical.

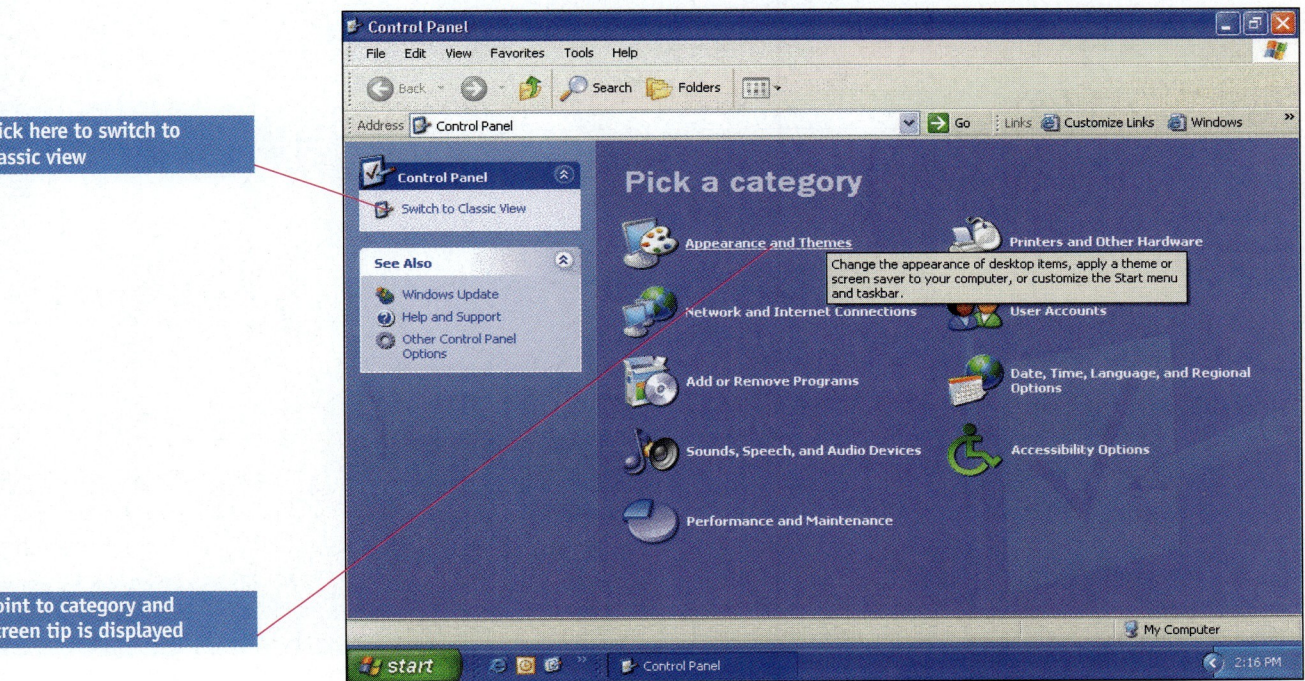

FIGURE 12   The Control Panel

Shortcuts

A **shortcut** is a link to any object on your computer, such as a program, file, folder, disk drive, or Web page. Shortcuts can appear anywhere, but are most often placed on the desktop or on the Start menu. The desktop in Figure 13 contains a variety of shortcuts, each of which contains a jump arrow to indicate a shortcut icon. Double click the shortcut to Election of Officers, for example, and you start Word and open this document. In similar fashion, you can double click the shortcut for a Web page (Exploring Windows Series), folder, or disk drive (drive A) to open the object and display its contents.

Creating a shortcut is a two-step process. First, you use Windows Explorer to locate the object such as a file, folder, or disk drive. Then you select the object, use the right mouse button to drag the object to the desktop, and then click the Create Shortcut command from the context-sensitive menu. A shortcut icon will appear on the desktop with the phrase "shortcut to" as part of the name. You can create as many shortcuts as you like, and you can place them anywhere on the desktop or in individual folders. You can also right click a shortcut icon after it has been created to change its name. Deleting the icon deletes the shortcut and not the object.

Windows XP also provides a set of predefined shortcuts through a series of desktop icons that are shown at the left border of the desktop in Figure 13. Double click the My Computer icon, for example, and you open the My Computer folder. These desktop icons were displayed by default in earlier versions of Windows, but not in Windows XP. They were added through the Control Panel as you will see in our next exercise.

Additional shortcuts are found in the **Quick Launch toolbar** that appears to the right of the Start button. Click any icon and you open the indicated program. And finally, Windows XP will automatically add to the Start menu shortcuts to your most frequently used programs. Desktop shortcuts are a powerful technique that will increase your productivity by taking you directly to a specified document or other object.

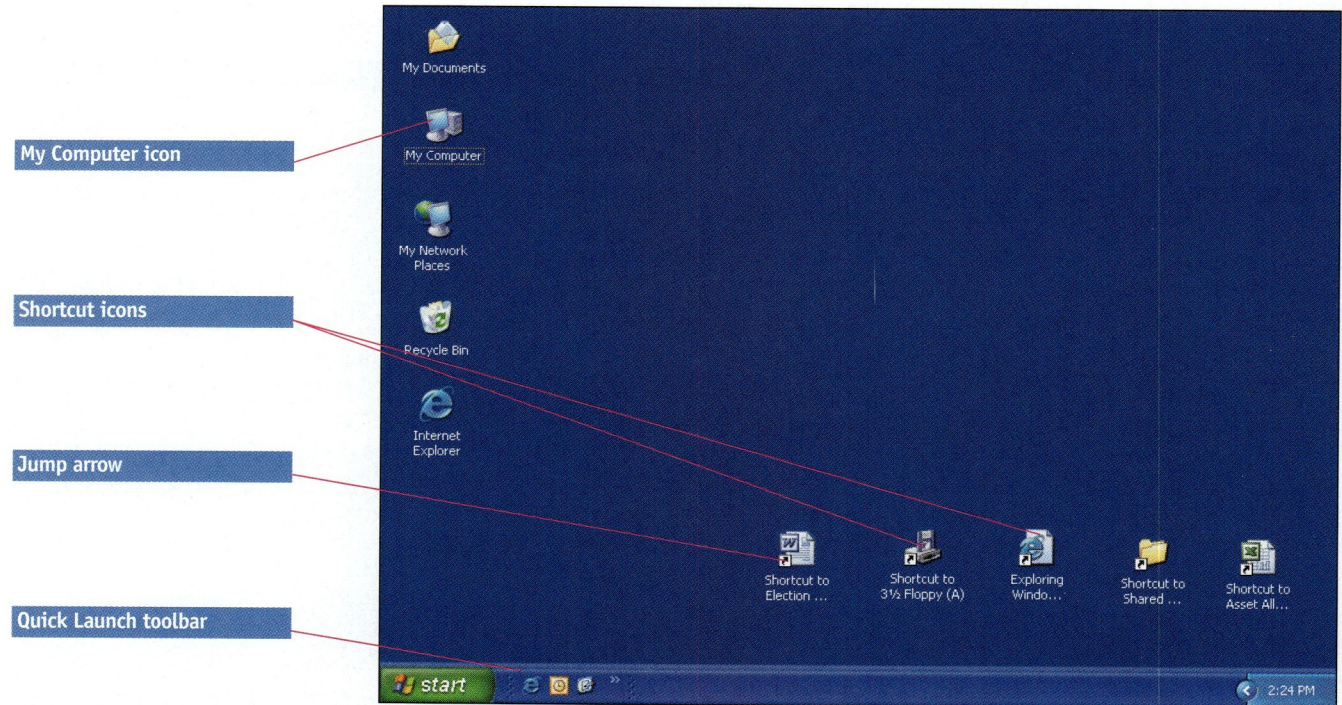

FIGURE 13 Desktop with Shortcuts

The Search Companion

Sooner or later you will create a file, and then forget where (in which folder) you saved it. Or you may create a document and forget its name, but remember a key word or phrase in the document. Or you may want to locate all files of a certain file type—for example, all of the sound files on your system. The ***Search Companion*** can help you to solve each of these problems and is illustrated in Figure 14.

The Search Companion is accessed from within any folder by clicking the Search button on the Standard Buttons toolbar to open the search pane at the left of the folder. You are presented with an initial search menu (not shown in Figure 14) that asks what you want to search for. You can search your local machine for media files (pictures, music, or video), documents (such as spreadsheets or Word documents), or any file or folder. You can also search the Help and Support Center or the Internet.

Once you choose the type of information, you are presented with a secondary search pane as shown in Figure 14. You can search according to a variety of criteria, each of which will help to narrow the search. In this example we are looking for any document on drive C that has "Windows" as part of its filename and further, contains the name "Maryann" somewhere within the document. The search is case sensitive. This example illustrates two important capabilities, namely that you can search on the document name (or part of its name) and/or its content.

Additional criteria can be entered by expanding the chevrons for date and size. You can, for example, restrict your search to all documents that were modified within the last week, the past month, or the last year. You can also restrict your search to documents of a certain size. Click the Search button after all of the criteria have been specified to initiate the search. The results of the search (the documents that satisfy the search criteria) are displayed in the right pane. You can refine the search if it is unsuccessful and/or you can open any document in which you are interested. The Search Companion also has an indexing service to make subsequent searches faster.

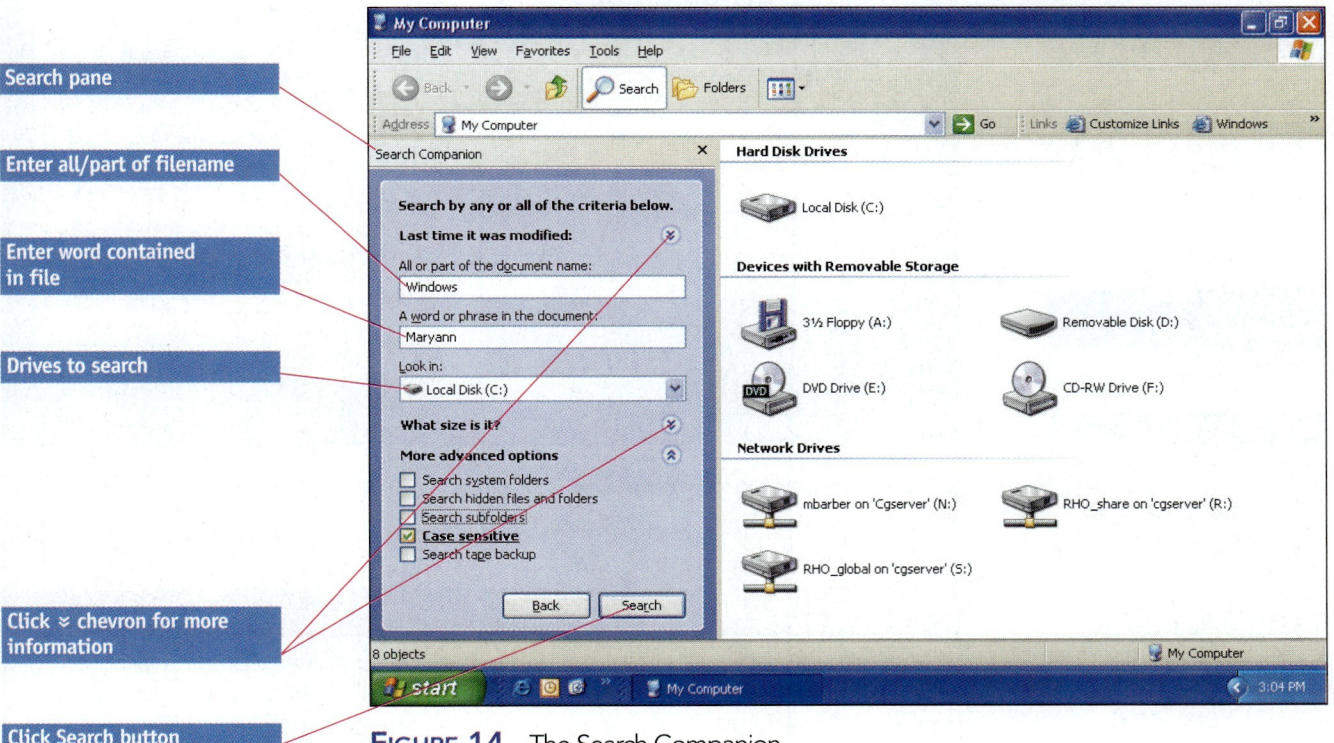

FIGURE 14 The Search Companion

Increasing Productivity

Objective To create and use shortcuts; to locate documents using the Search Companion; to customize your system using the Control Panel; to obtain a passport account. The exercise requires an Internet connection. Use Figure 15 as a guide.

Step 1: **Display the Desktop Icons**

- Log on to Windows XP. Point to a blank area on the desktop, click the **right mouse button** to display a context-sensitive menu, then click the **Properties command** to open the Display Properties dialog box in Figure 15a.

- Click the **Desktop tab** and then click the **Customize Desktop button** to display the Desktop Items dialog box.

- Check the boxes to display all four desktop icons. Click **OK** to accept these settings and close the dialog box, then click **OK** a second time to close the Display Properties dialog box.

- The desktop icons should appear on the left side of your desktop. Double click any icon to execute the indicated program or open the associated folder.

Click Desktop tab

Right click blank area of desktop to display shortcut menu

Click Customize Desktop button

Check boxes for all four desktop icons

Quick Launch toolbar

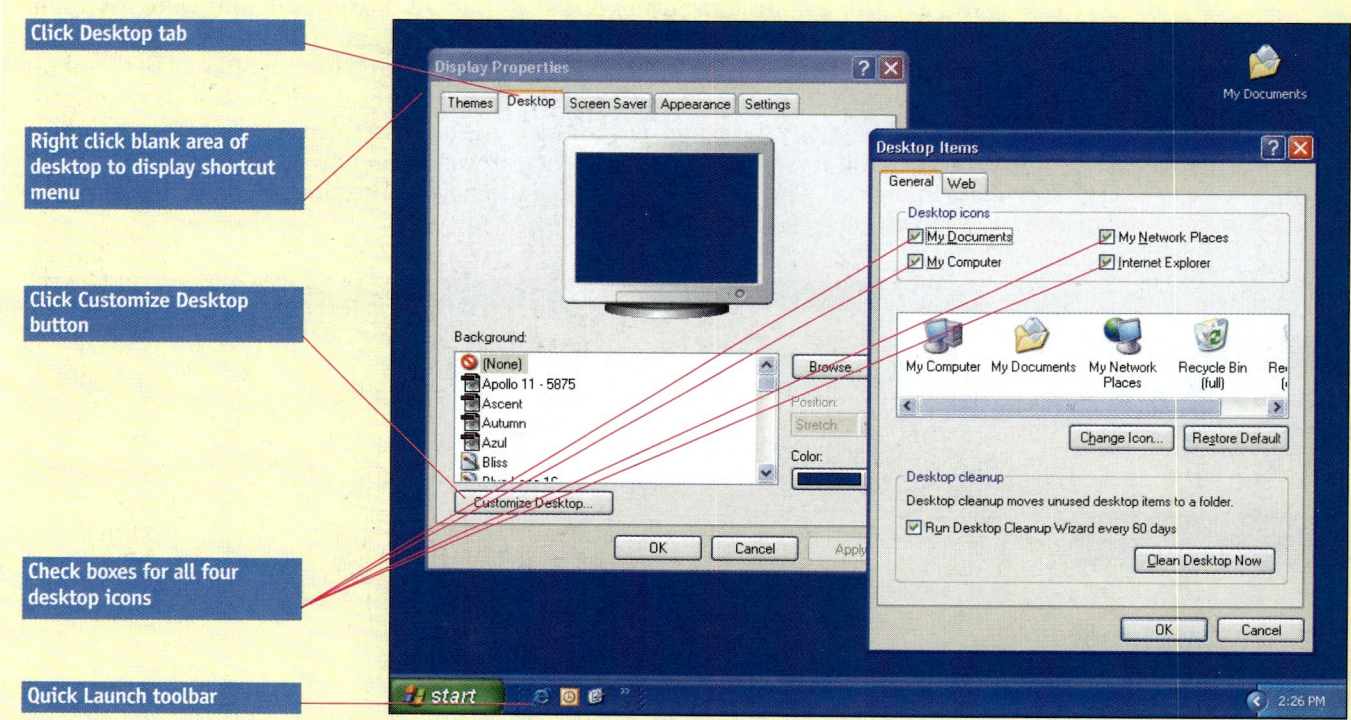

(a) Display the Desktop Icons (step 1)

FIGURE 15 Hands-on Exercise 4

THE QUICK LAUNCH TOOLBAR

The Quick Launch toolbar is a customizable toolbar that executes a program or displays the desktop with a single click. Right click a blank area of the taskbar, point to (or click) the Toolbars command, then check the Quick Launch toolbar to toggle its display on or off.

Step 2: Create a Web Shortcut

- Start Internet Explorer. You can double click the newly created icon at the left of the desktop, or you can single click its icon in the Quick Launch toolbar. Click the **Restore button** so that Internet Explorer is not maximized, that is, so that you can see a portion of the desktop.

- Click in the Address bar and enter the address **www.microsoft.com/windowsxp** to display the home page of Windows XP. Now that you see the page, you can create a shortcut to that page.

- Click the **Internet Explorer icon** in the Address bar to select the entire address, point to the Internet Explorer icon, then click and drag the icon to the desktop (you will see a jump arrow as you drag the text). Release the mouse to create the shortcut in Figure 15b.

- Prove to yourself that the shortcut works. Close Internet Explorer, and then double click the shortcut you created. Internet Explorer will open, and you should see the desired Web page. Close (or minimize) Internet Explorer since you do not need it for the remainder of the exercise.

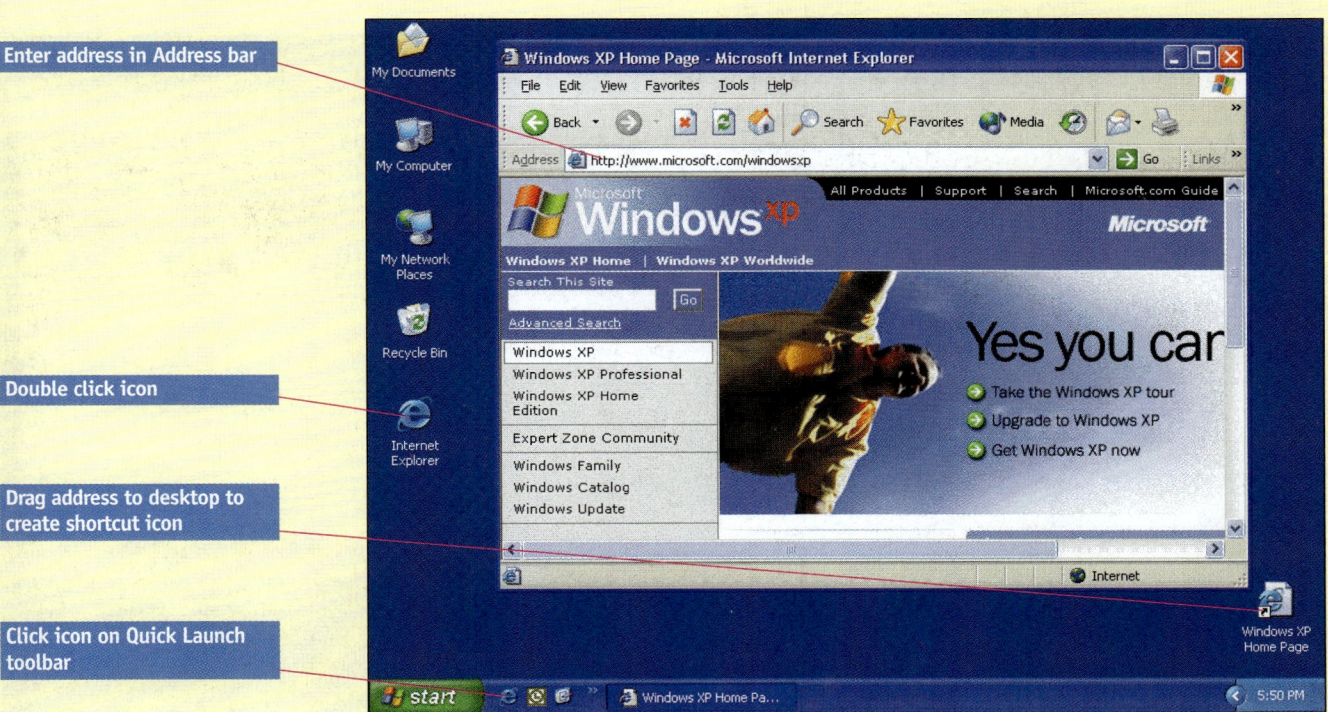

Enter address in Address bar

Double click icon

Drag address to desktop to create shortcut icon

Click icon on Quick Launch toolbar

(b) Create a Web Shortcut (step 2)

FIGURE 15 Hands-on Exercise 4 (*continued*)

WORKING WITH SHORTCUTS

You can work with a shortcut icon just as you can with any other icon. To move a shortcut, drag its icon to a different location on the desktop. To rename a shortcut, right click its icon, click the Rename command, type the new name, then press the enter key. To delete a shortcut, right click its icon, click the Delete command, and click Yes in response to the confirming prompt. Deleting a shortcut deletes just the shortcut and not the object to which the shortcut refers.

Step 3: Create Additional Shortcuts

- Double click the **My Computer icon** to open this folder. Place the floppy disk from hands-on exercise 3 into the floppy drive. Double click the icon for **drive A** to display the contents of the floppy disk as shown in Figure 15c.

- The contents of the Address bar have changed to A:\ to indicate the contents of the floppy disk. You should see two folders and two files.

- Move and size the window so that you see a portion of the desktop. Right click and drag the icon for the **Windows Information folder** to the desktop, then release the mouse. Click the **Create Shortcuts Here command** to create the shortcut.

- Look for the jump arrow to be sure you have created a shortcut (as opposed to moving or copying the folder). If you made a mistake, right click a blank area of the desktop, then click the **Undo command** to reverse the unintended move or copy operation.

- Right click and drag the icon for the **PowerPoint presentation** to the desktop, release the mouse, and then click the **Create Shortcuts Here command**.

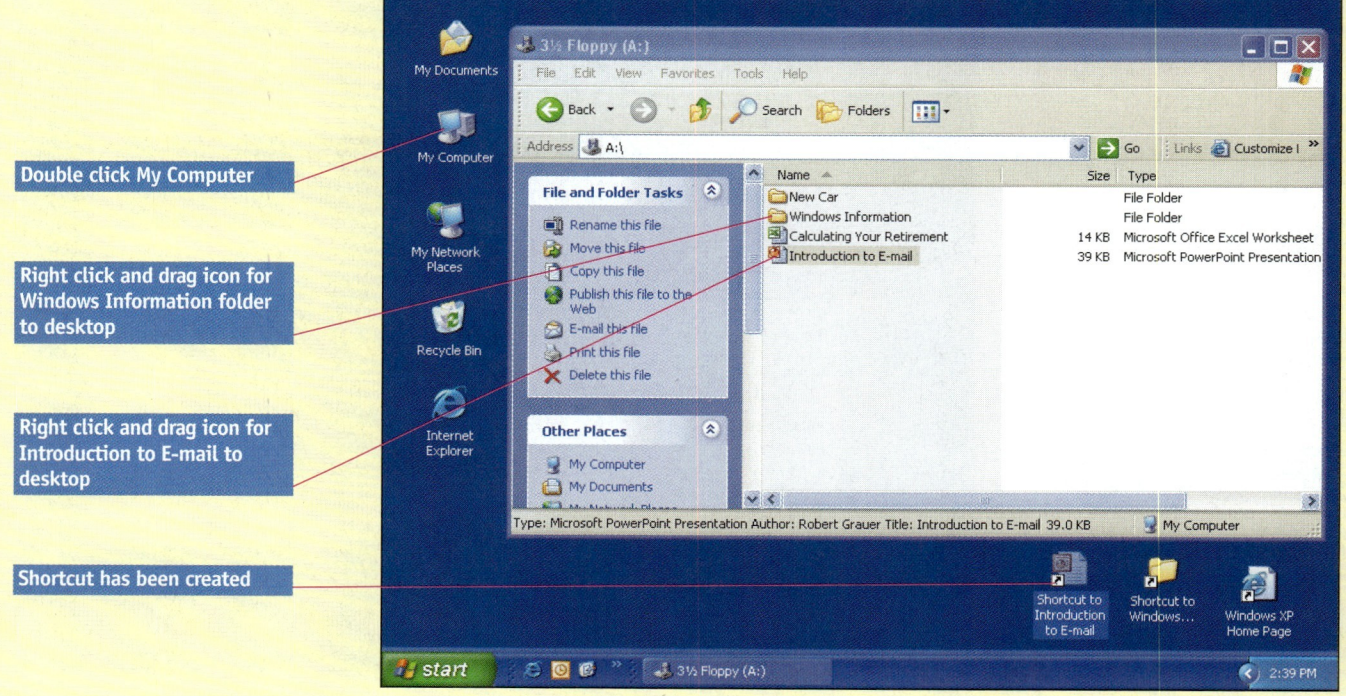

(c) Create Additional Shortcuts (step 3)

FIGURE 15   Hands-on Exercise 4 (*continued*)

THE ARRANGE ICONS COMMAND

The most basic way to arrange the icons on your desktop is to click and drag an icon from one place to another. It may be convenient, however, to have Windows arrange the icons for you. Right click a blank area of the desktop, click (or point to) the Arrange Icons by command, then click Auto Arrange. All existing shortcuts, as well as any new shortcuts, will be automatically aligned along the left edge of the desktop. Execute the Auto Arrange command a second time to cancel the command, and enable yourself to manually arrange the icons.

Step 4: **Search for a Document**

■ Maximize the My Computer window. Click the **Search button** on the Standard Buttons toolbar to display the Search pane. The button functions as a toggle switch. Click the button and the Search pane appears. Click the button a second time and the task pane replaces the Search Companion.

■ The initial screen (not shown in Figure 15d) in the Search Companion asks what you are searching for. Click **Documents (word processing, spreadsheet, etc.)**.

■ You may be prompted to enter when the document was last modified. Click the option button that says **Don't Remember**, then click **Use advanced search options**. You should see the screen in Figure 15d.

■ Enter the indicated search criteria. You do not know the document name and thus you leave this text box blank. The other criteria indicate that you are looking for any document that contains "interest rate" that is located on drive A, or in any subfolder on drive A.

■ Click the **Search button** to initiate the search. You will see a Search dialog box to indicate the progress of the search, after which you will see the relevant documents.

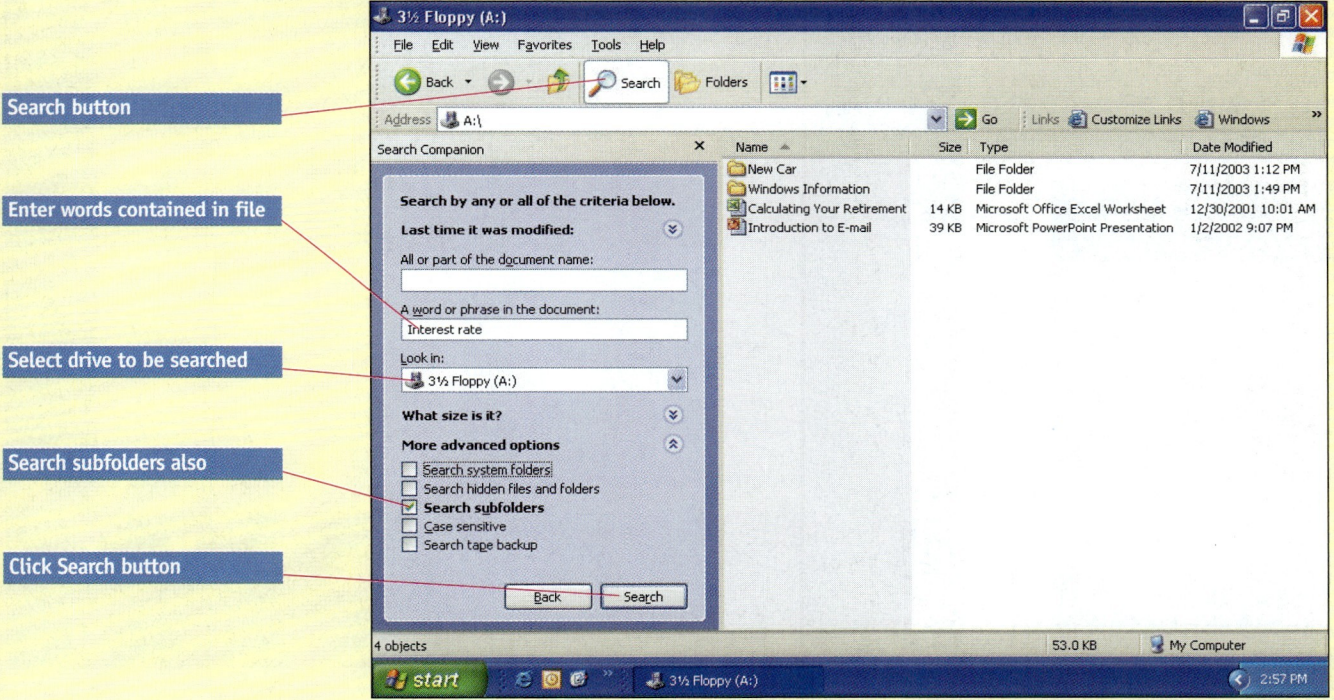

(d) Search for a Document (step 4)

FIGURE 15 Hands-on Exercise 4 (*continued*)

YOU DON'T NEED THE COMPLETE FILENAME

You can enter only a portion of the filename, and the Search Companion will still find the file(s). If, for example, you're searching for the file "Marketing Homework", you can enter the first several letters such as "Marketing" and Windows will return all files whose name begins with the letters you've entered—for example, "Marketing Homework" and "Marketing Term Paper".

Step 5: **Search Results**

- The search should return two files that satisfy the search criteria as shown in Figure 15e. Click the **Views button** and select **Tiles view** if you want to match our figure. If you do not see the same files, it is for one of two reasons:
  - ❏ You did not specify the correct search criteria. Click the **Back button** and reenter the search parameters as described in step 4. Repeat the search.
  - ❏ Your floppy disk is different from ours. Be sure to use the floppy disk as it existed at the end of the previous hands-on exercise.

- Click the **Restore button** so that you again see a portion of the desktop. Right click and drag the **Calculating Your Retirement** workbook to the desktop to create a shortcut on the desktop.

- Close the Search Results window, close the My Documents window, then double click the newly created shortcut to open the workbook.

- Retirement is a long way off, but you may want to experiment with our worksheet. It is never too early to start saving.

- Exit Excel when you are finished.

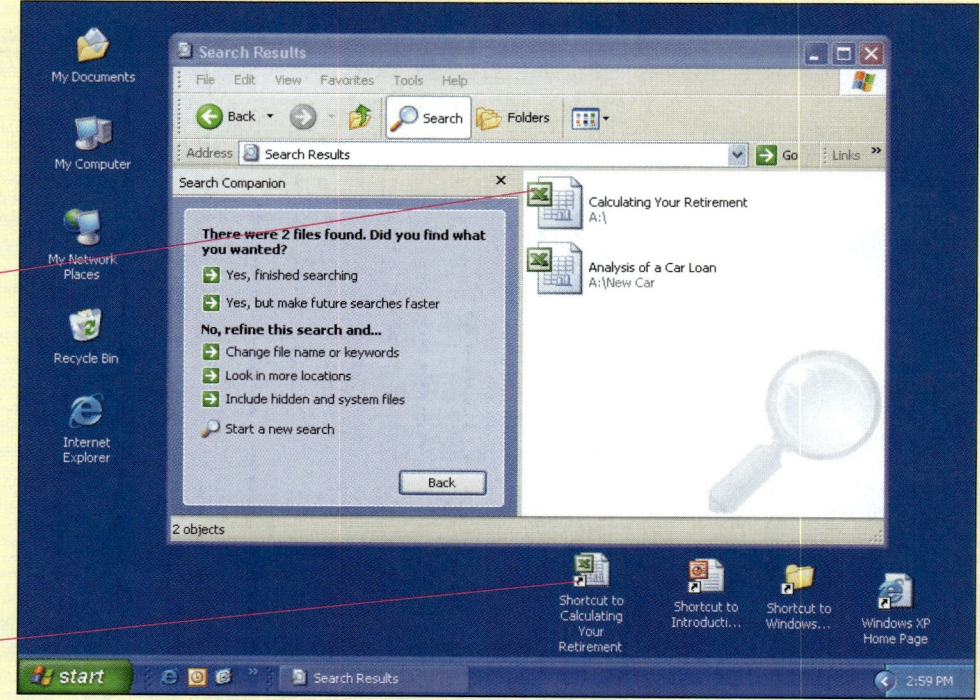

Right click and drag Calculating Your Retirement to desktop

Double click the shortcut to open the workbook

(e) Search Results (step 5)

FIGURE 15   Hands-on Exercise 4 (*continued*)

SHORTCUT WIZARD

Shortcuts can be created in many ways, including the use of a wizard. Right click a blank area of the desktop, click (or point) to the New command, then choose Shortcut to start the wizard. Enter the Web address in the indicated text box (or click the Browse button to locate a local file). Click Next, then enter the name for the shortcut as it is to appear on the desktop. Click the Finish button to exit the wizard. The new shortcut should appear on the desktop.

Step 6: Open the Control Panel Folder

- Click the **Start button**, then click **Control Panel** to open the Control Panel folder. Click the command to **Switch to Classic View** that appears in the task pane to display the individual icons as shown in Figure 15f. Maximize the window.

- Double click the **Taskbar and Start Menu icon** to display the associated dialog box. Click the **Taskbar tab**, then check the box to **Auto-hide the taskbar.** Your other settings should match those in Figure 15f. Click **OK** to accept the settings and close the dialog box.

- The taskbar (temporarily) disappears from your desktop. Now point to the bottom edge of the desktop, and the taskbar reappears. The advantage of hiding the taskbar in this way is that you have the maximum amount of room in which to work; that is, you see the taskbar only when you want to.

- Double click the **Fonts folder** to open this folder and display the fonts that are installed on your computer. Change to the **Details view**.

- Double click the icon of any font other than the standard fonts (Arial, Times New Roman, and Courier New) to open a new window that displays the font. Click the **Print button**. Close the Font window.

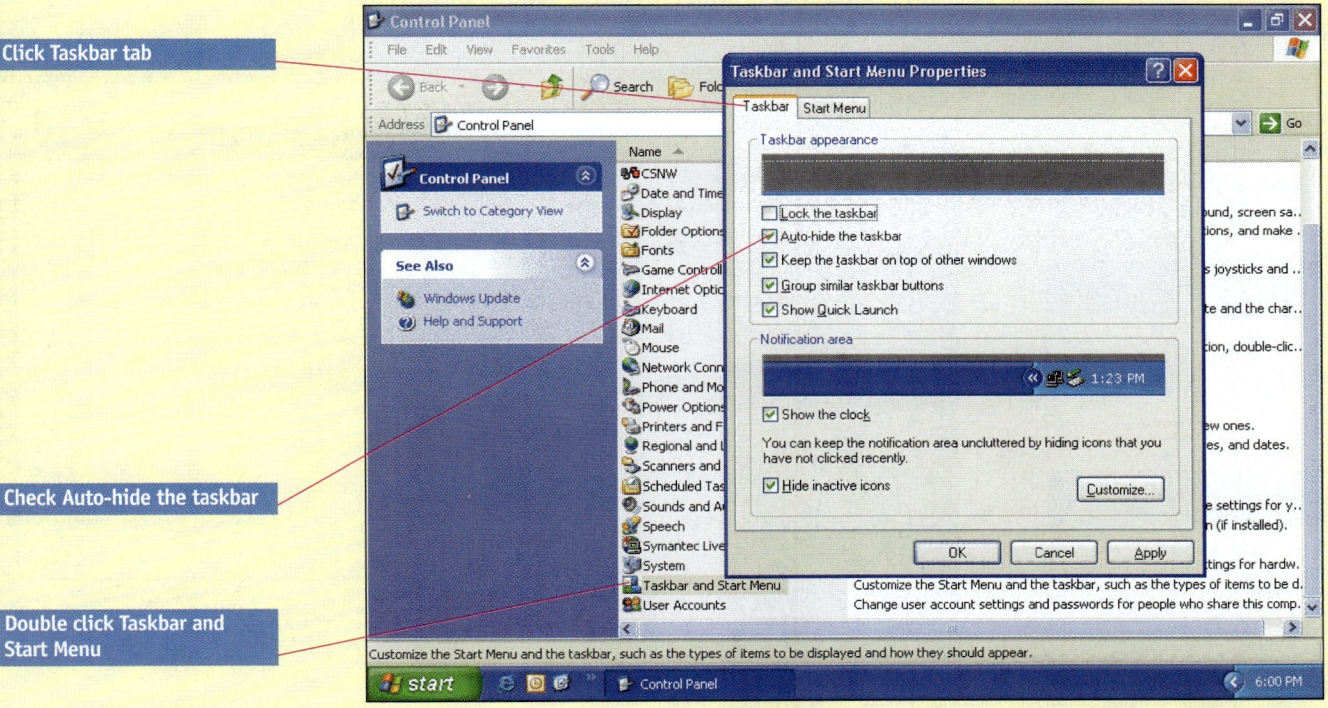

Click Taskbar tab

Check Auto-hide the taskbar

Double click Taskbar and Start Menu

(f) Open the Control Panel Folder (step 6)

FIGURE 15 Hands-on Exercise 4 (*continued*)

MODIFY THE START MENU

Click and drag a shortcut icon to the Start button to place the shortcut on the Start menu. It does not appear that anything has happened, but the shortcut will appear at the top of the Start menu. Click the Start button to display the Start menu, then press the Esc key to exit the menu without executing a command. You can delete any item from the menu by right clicking the item and clicking the Unpin from the Start menu command.

Step 7: **Obtain a .NET Passport**

- Click the **Back button** to return to the Control Panel, then double click the **User Accounts icon** in the Control Panel folder. Maximize the User Accounts window so that it takes the entire desktop.

- Click the icon corresponding to the account that is currently logged to display a screen similar to Figure 15g. Click the command to **Set up my account to use a .NET passport**. You will see the first step in the Passport Wizard.

- Click the link to **View the privacy statement**. This starts Internet Explorer and goes to the .NET Passport site on the Web. Print the privacy agreement. It runs nine pages, but it contains a lot of useful information.

- Close Internet Explorer after you have printed the agreement. You are back in the Passport Wizard. Click **Next** to continue.

- Follow the instructions on the next several screens. You will be asked to enter your e-mail address and to supply a password. Click **Finish** when you have reached the last screen.

- You will receive an e-mail message after you have registered successfully. You will need your passport in our next exercise when we explore Windows Messenger and the associated instant messaging service.

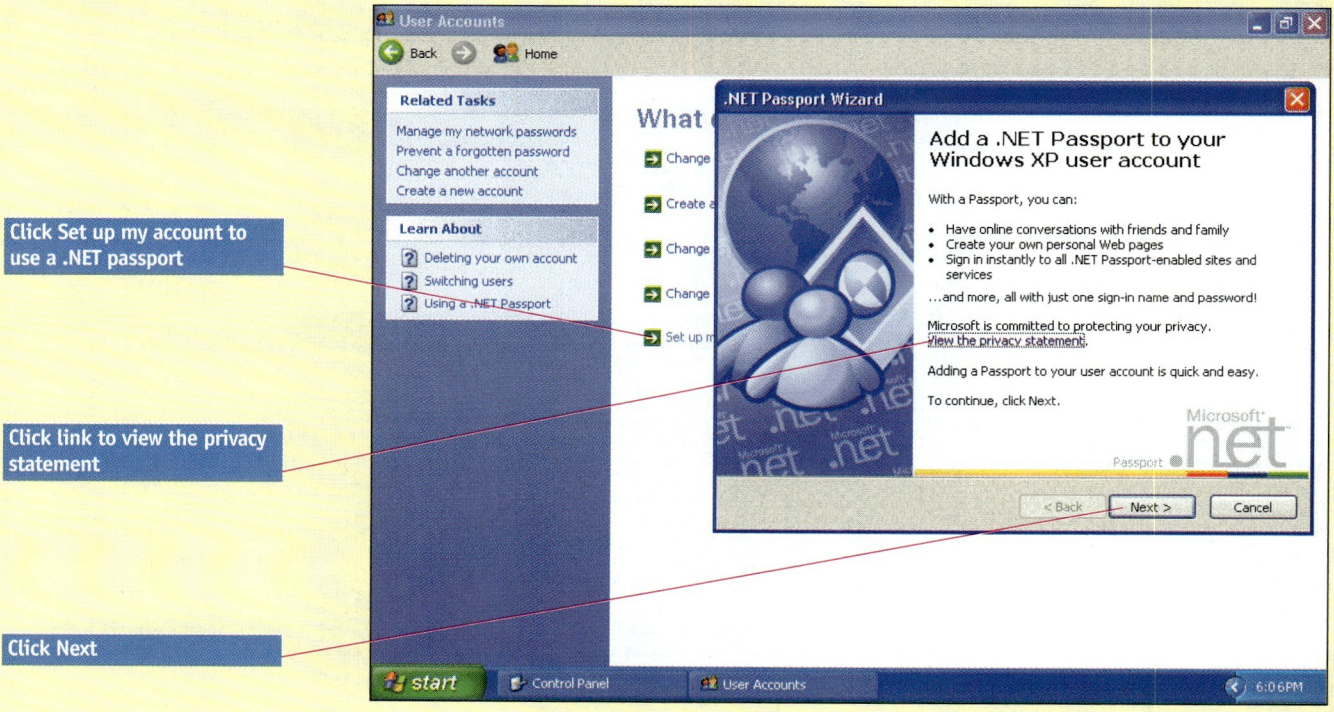

Click Set up my account to use a .NET passport

Click link to view the privacy statement

Click Next

(g) Obtain a .NET Passport (step 7)

FIGURE 15   Hands-on Exercise 4 (*continued*)

UPDATING YOUR PASSPORT

You can modify the information in your passport profile at any time. Open the Control Panel, click User Accounts, select your account, then click the command to Change Your .NET passport. You can change your password, change the question that will remind you about your password should you forget it, and/or change the information that you authorize the passport service to share with others.

Step 8: **Windows Update**

- Close the User Accounts window to return to the Control Panel folder. Click the link to **Windows Update** to display a screen similar to Figure 15h.

- Click the command to **Scan for updates**. (This command is not visible in our figure.) This command will take several seconds as Windows determines which (if any) updates it recommends. Our system indicates that there are no critical updates but that additional updates are available.

- Click the link(s) to review the available updates. You do not have to install the vast majority of available updates. It is essential, however, that you install any updates deemed critical. One critical update appeared shortly after the release of Windows XP and closed a hole in the operating system that enabled hackers to break into some XP machines.

- Click the link to **View installation history** to see which updates were previously installed. Print this page for your instructor.

- Close the Update window. Log off the computer if you do not want to continue with the next exercise at this time.

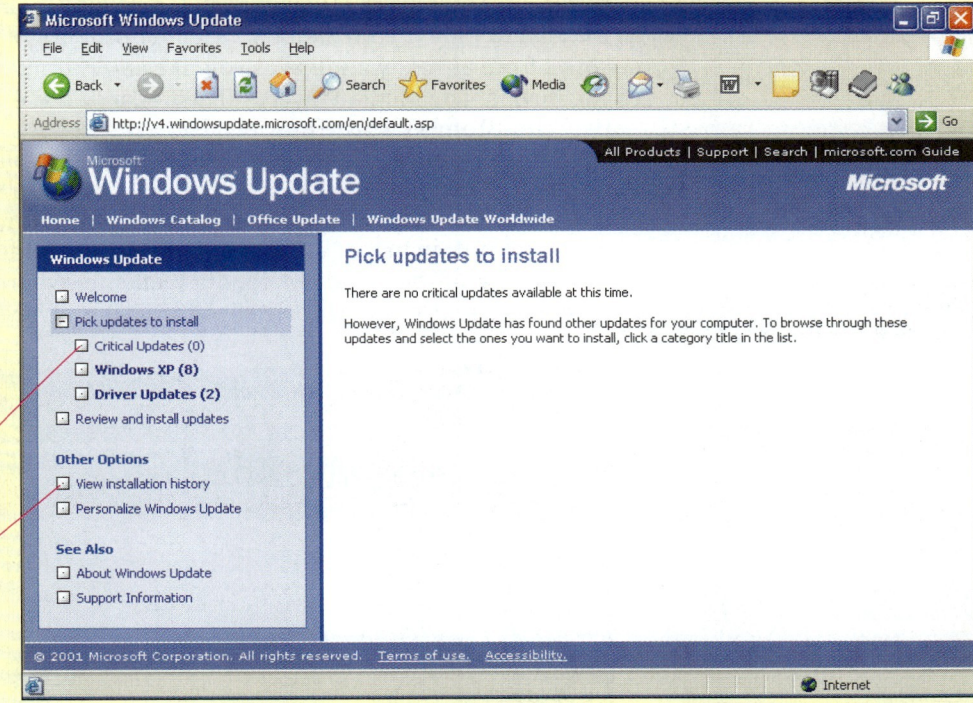

(h) Windows Update (step 8)

FIGURE 15 Hands-on Exercise 4 (*continued*)

THE SHOW DESKTOP BUTTON

The Show Desktop button or command minimizes every open window and returns you immediately to the desktop. You can get to this command in different ways, most easily by clicking the Show Desktop icon on the Quick Launch toolbar. The button functions as a toggle switch. Click it once and all windows are minimized. Click it a second time and the open windows are restored to their position on the desktop.

The "XP" in Windows XP is for the experience that Microsoft promises individuals who adopt its operating system. Windows XP makes it easy to enjoy music and video, work with **digital photographs**, and chat with your friends. This section describes these capabilities and then moves to a hands-on exercise in which you practice at the computer. All of the features are available on your own machine, but some may be disabled in a laboratory setting. It's not that your professor does not want you to have fun, but listening to music or engaging in instant messaging with your friends is not practical in a school environment. Nevertheless, the hands-on exercise that follows enables you to practice your skills in disk and file management as you work with multiple files and folders.

Windows Media Player

The **Windows Media Player** combines the functions of a radio, a CD, or DVD player, and an information database into a single program. It lets you listen to radio stations anywhere in the world, play a CD, or watch a DVD movie (provided you have the necessary hardware). You can copy selections from a CD to your computer, organize your music by artist and album, and then create a customized **playlist** to play the music in a specified order. The playlist may include as many songs from as many albums as you like and is limited only by the size of your storage device. The Media Player will also search the Web for audio or video files and play clips from a favorite movie.

The buttons at the left of the Media Player enable you to switch from one function to the next. The Radio Tuner button is active in Figure 16, and the BBC station is selected. Think of that—you are able to listen to radio stations from around the world with the click of a button. The Media Guide button connects you to the home page of the Windows Media Web site, where you can search the Web for media files and/or play movie clips from your favorite movies.

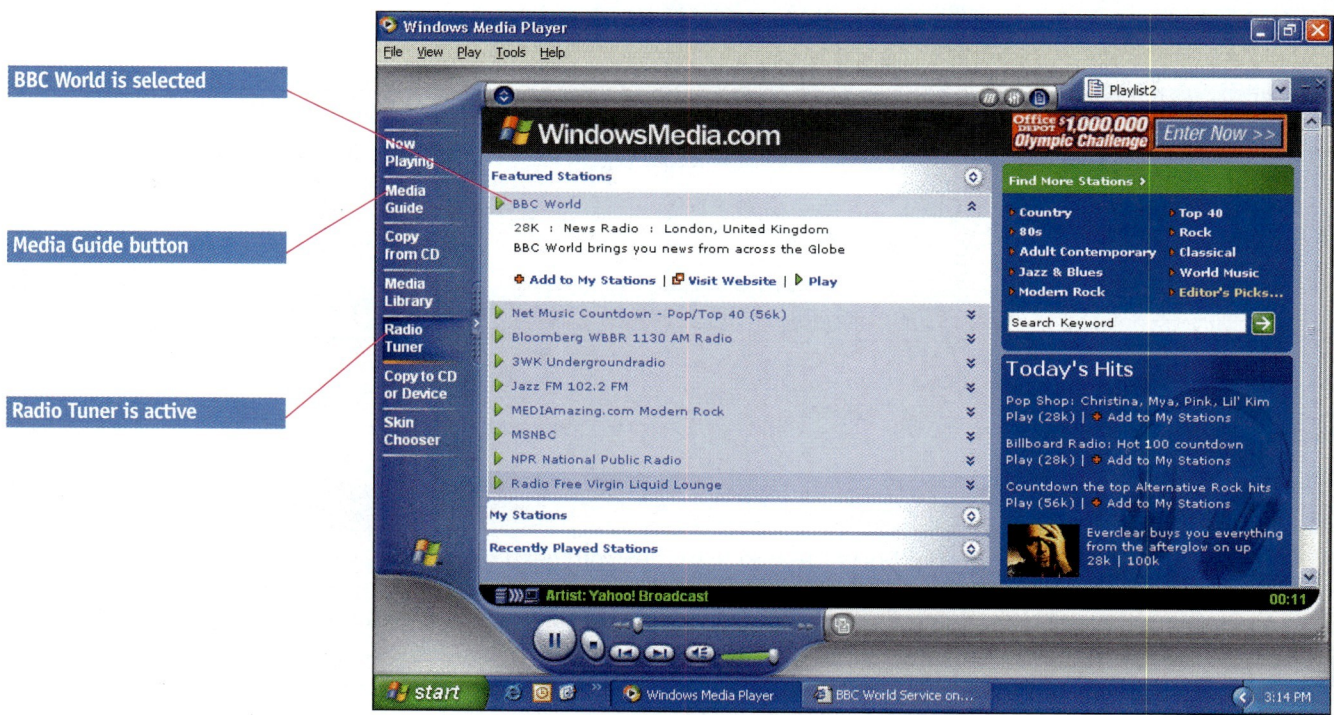

FIGURE 16 Windows Media Player

Digital Photography

Windows XP helps you to organize your pictures and share them with others. The best place to store photographs is in the My Pictures folder or in a subfolder within this folder as shown in Figure 17. The complete path to the folder appears in the Address bar and is best read from right to left. Thus, you are looking at pictures in the Romance Folder, which is in the My Pictures folder, which in turn is stored in a My Documents folder. Remember that each user has his or her unique My Documents folder, so the path must be further qualified. Hence, you are looking at the My Documents folder, within a folder for Jessica (one of several users), within the Documents and Settings folder on drive C. The latter folder maintains the settings for all of the users that are registered on this system.

The pictures in Figure 17 are shown in the **Thumbnails view**, which displays a miniature image of each picture in the right pane. (Other views are also available and are accessed from the View menu or Views button.) The Picture Tasks area in the upper right lists the functions that are unique to photographs. You can view the pictures as a slide show, which is the equivalent of a PowerPoint presentation without having to create the presentation. You can print any picture, use it as the background on your desktop, or copy multiple pictures to a CD, provided you have the necessary hardware. You can also order prints online. You choose the company; select print sizes and quantities, supply the billing and shipping information, and your photographs are sent to you.

One photo is selected (BenWendy) in Figure 17, and the associated details are shown in the Details area of the task pane. The picture is stored as a JPG file, a common format for photographs. It was created on January 21, 2002.

The File and Folder Tasks area is collapsed in our figure, but you can expand the area to gain access to the normal file operations (move, copy, and delete). You can also e-mail the photograph from this panel. Remember, too, that you can click the Folders button on the Standard Buttons toolbar to switch to the hierarchical view of your system, which is better suited to disk and file management.

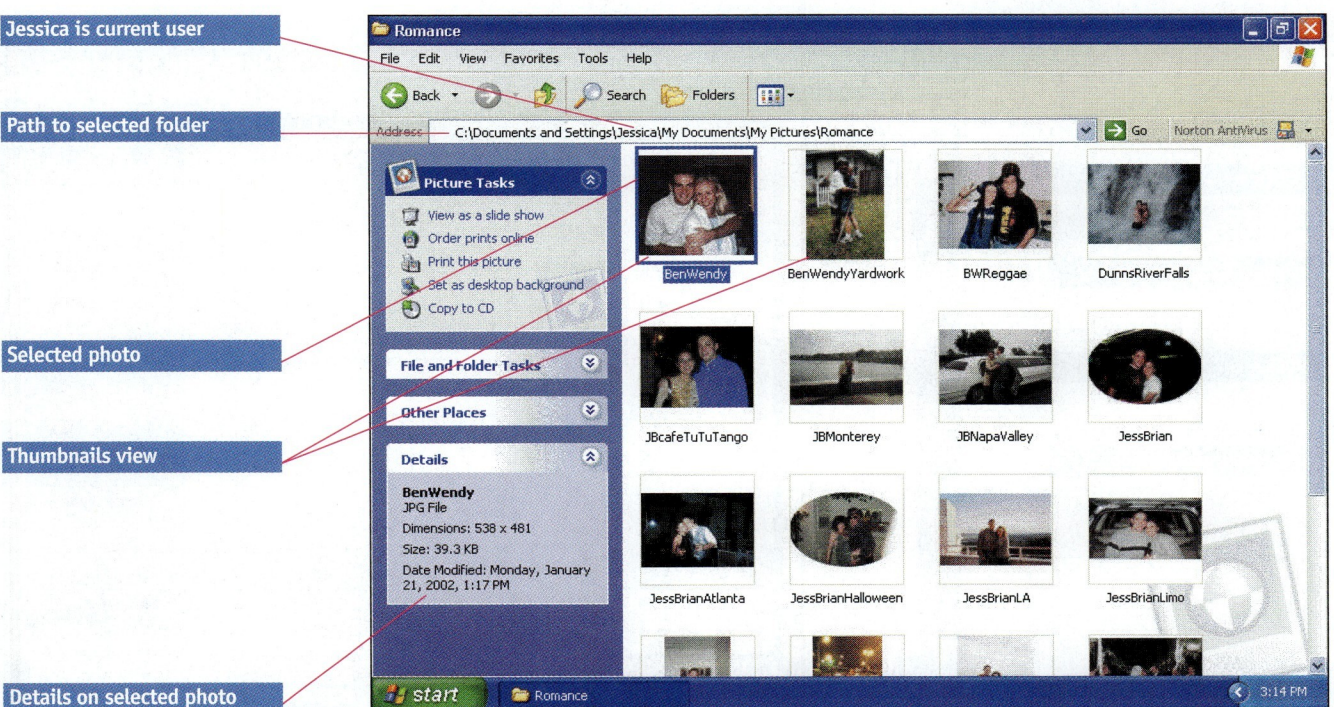

FIGURE 17 Working with Pictures

Windows Messenger

Windows Messenger is an instant messaging system in which you chat with friends and colleagues over the Internet. (It is based on the same technology as the "buddies list" that was made popular by America Online.) You need an Internet connection, a list of contacts, and a **Microsoft passport** that is based on your e-mail address. The passport is a free Microsoft service that enables you to access any passport-enabled Internet site with a single user name and associated password. (Step 7 in the previous hands-on exercise described how to obtain a passport.)

You can initiate a conversation at any time by monitoring the contacts list to see who is online and starting a chat session. Up to four people can participate in the same conversation. It is easy, fun, and addictive. You know the instant someone signs on, and you can begin chatting immediately. The bad news, however, is that it is all too easy to chat incessantly when you have real work to do. Hence you may want to change your status to indicate that you are busy and unable to participate in a conversation.

Figure 18 displays a conversation between Maryann and Bob. The session began when Maryann viewed her contact list, noticed that Bob was online, and started a conversation. Each person enters his or her message at the bottom of the conversation window, and then clicks the Send button. Additional messages can be sent without waiting for a response. Emoticons can be added to any message for effect. Note, too, the references to the file transfer that appear within the conversation, which are the result of Maryann clicking the command to send a file or photo, then attaching the desired file.

Windows Messenger is more than just a vehicle for chatting. If you have speakers and a microphone, you can place phone calls from your computer without paying a long distance charge. The most intriguing feature, however, is the ability to ask for remote assistance, whereby you can invite one of your contacts to view your desktop as you are working in order to ask for help. It is as if your friend were in the room looking over your shoulder. He or she will see everything that you do and can respond immediately with suggestions.

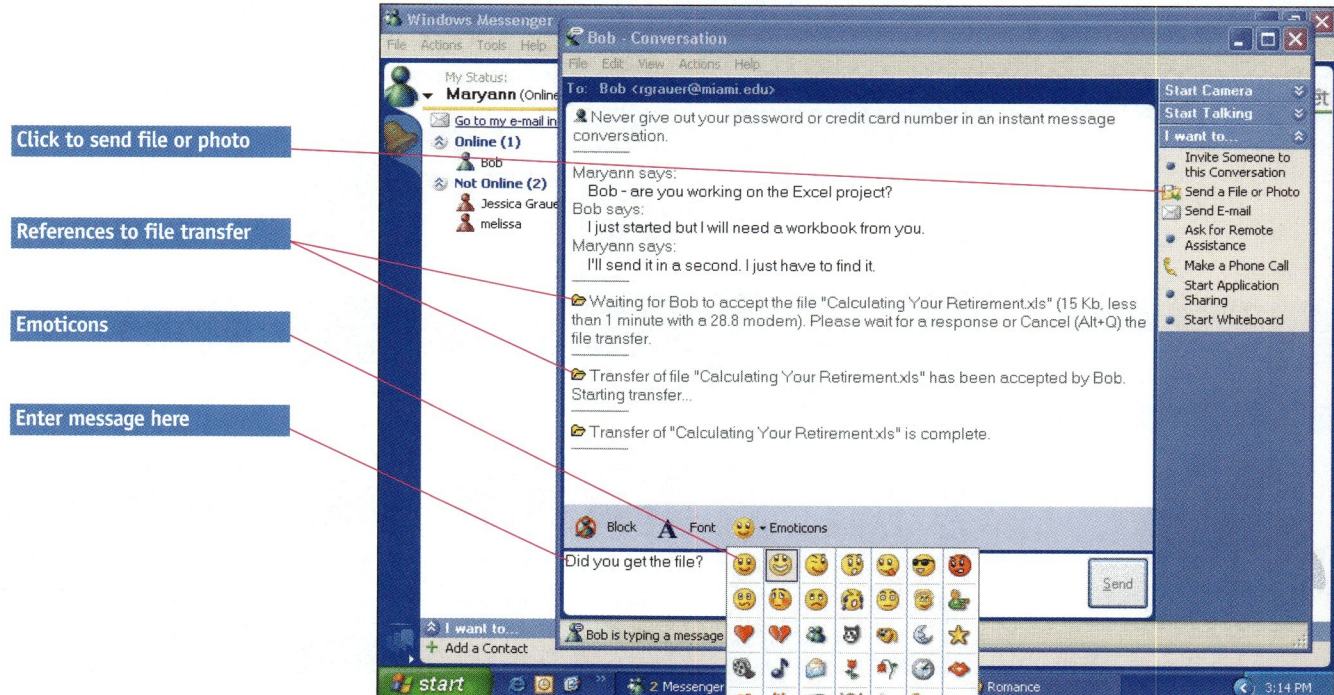

FIGURE 18 Windows Messenger

5 Fun with Windows XP

Objective To use Windows Media Player, work with photographs, and experiment with Windows Messenger. Check with your professor regarding the availability of the resources required for this exercise. Use Figure 19.

Step 1: **Open the Shared Music Folder**

■ Start Windows Explorer. Click the **Folders button** to display the tree structure. You need to locate some music to demonstrate the Media Player.

■ The typical XP installation includes some files within the Shared Documents folder. Expand the My Computer folder to show the **Shared Documents folder**, expand the **Shared Music folder**, and then open the **Sample Music folder** as shown in Figure 19a.

■ Point to any file (it does not matter if you have a different selection of music) to display the ScreenTip describing the music. Double click the file to start the Media Player and play the selected music.

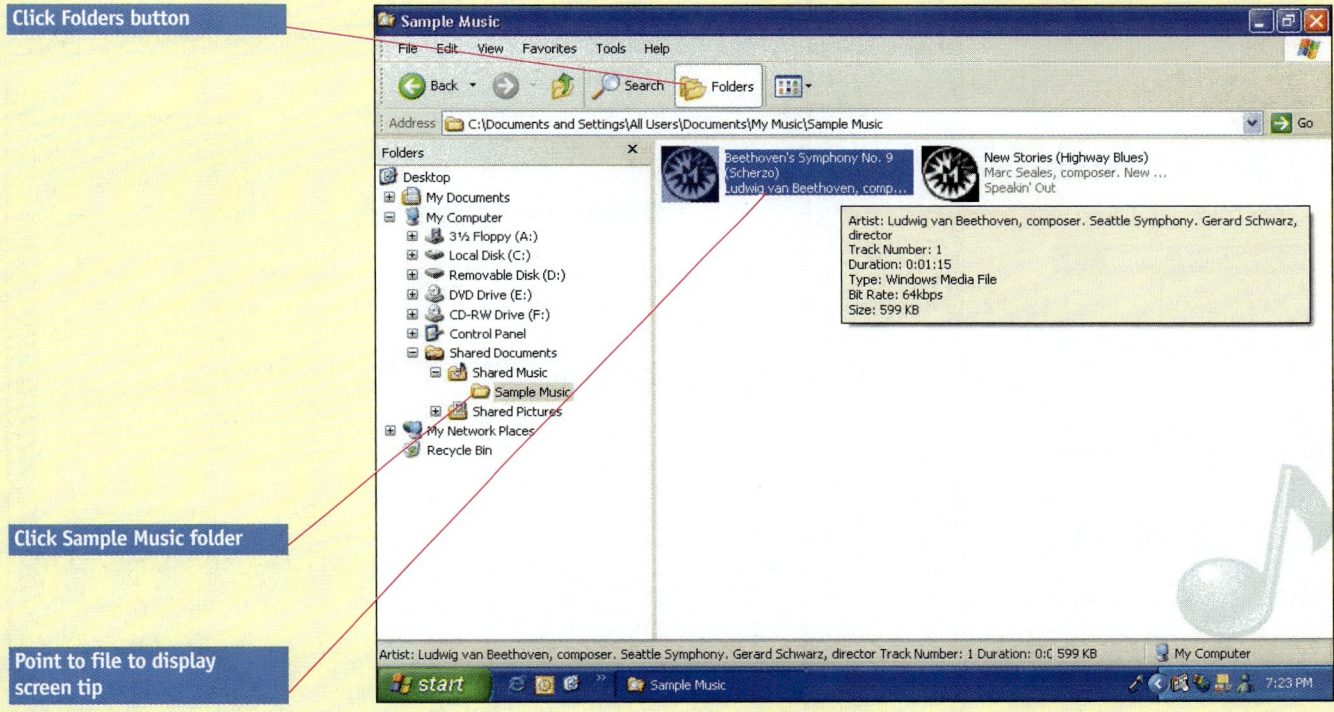

(a) Open the Shared Music Folder (step 1)

FIGURE 19 Hands-on Exercise 5

SHARED FOLDERS VERSUS PERSONAL FOLDERS

Windows XP automatically creates a unique My Documents folder for every user, which in turn contains a unique My Pictures folder and My Music folder within the My Documents folder. These folders are private and cannot be accessed by other users. Windows also provides a Shared Documents folder that is accessible to every user on a system.

Step 2: **Listen to the Music**

■ You should hear the music when the Windows Media Player opens in its own window as shown in Figure 19b. The controls at the bottom of the window are similar to those on any CD player.

    ❑ You can click the **Pause button**, then click the **Play button** to restart the music at that point.

    ❑ You can click the **Stop button** to stop playing altogether.

    ❑ You can also drag the slider to begin playing at a different place.

■ You can also adjust the volume as shown in Figure 19b. Double click the **Volume Control icon** in the notification area at the right of the taskbar to display the Volume Control dialog box. Close this window.

■ Click the **Radio Tuner button** at the side of the Media Player window. The system pauses as it tunes into the available radio stations.

■ Select a radio station (e.g., **BBC World**) when you see the list of available stations, then click the **Play button** after you choose a station.

■ You will see a message at the bottom of the window indicating that your computer is connecting to the media, after which you will hear the radio station.

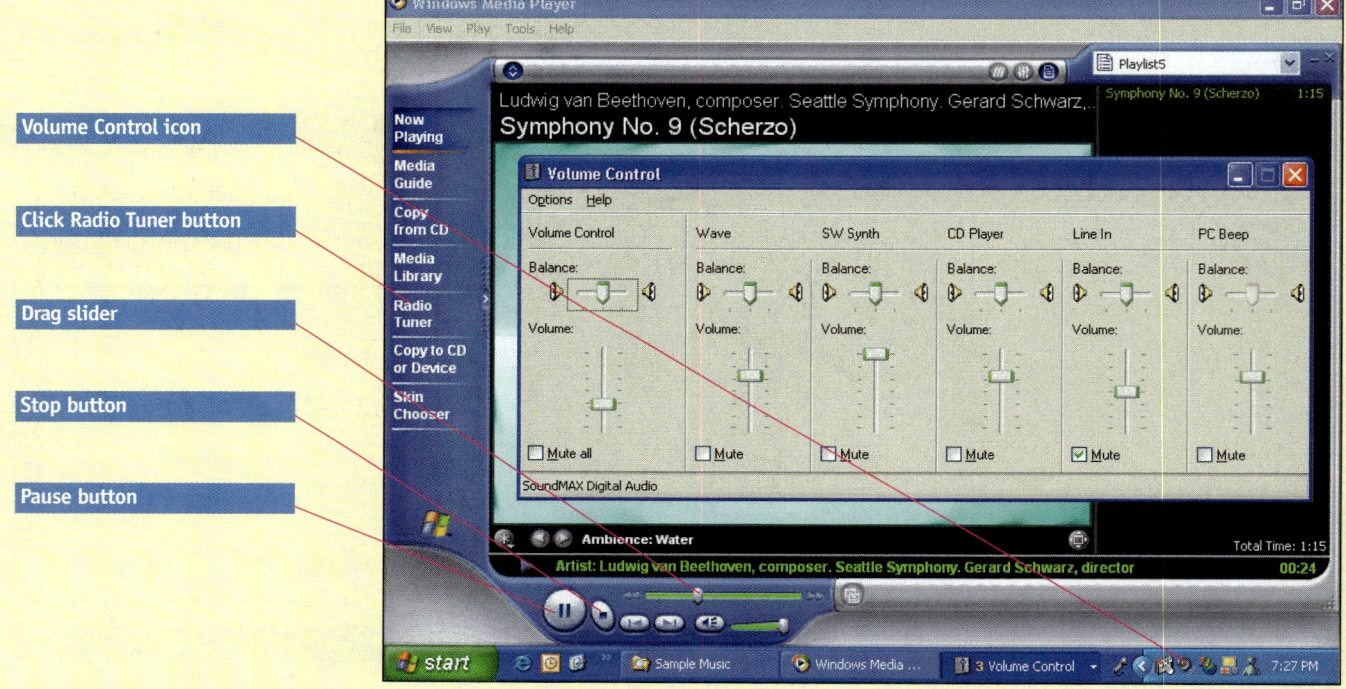

(b) Listen to the Music (step 2)

FIGURE 19 Hands-on Exercise 5 (*continued*)

OTHER MEDIA PLAYERS

If you double click a music (MP3) file, and a program other than Windows Media starts to play, it is because your system has another media player as its default program. You can still use the Windows Media Player, but you will have to start the program explicitly from the Start menu. Once the Media Player is open, pull down the File menu and click the Open command, then select the music file you want to play.

Step 3: Create a Playlist

- Click the **Media Library button** at the side of the Media player to display the media files that are currently on your computer.
  - ❏ The left pane displays a tree structure of your media library. Thus, you click the plus or minus sign to collapse or expand the indicated folder.
  - ❏ The right pane displays the contents of the selected object (the My Music playlist) in Figure 19c.

- Do not be concerned if your media library is different from ours. Click the **New playlist button**, enter **My Music** as the name of the new list, and click **OK**.

- Click the newly created playlist in the left pane to display its contents in the left pane. The playlist is currently empty.

- Start **Windows Explorer**. Open the **My Music Folder** within the My Documents folder. If necessary, click the **Restore button** to move and size Windows Explorer so that you can copy documents to the Media library.

- Click and drag one or more selections from the My Music folder to the right pane of the Media library to create the playlist. Close Windows Explorer.

- Click the **down arrow** in the list box at the upper right of the Media Gallery and select the My Music playlist to play the songs you have selected.

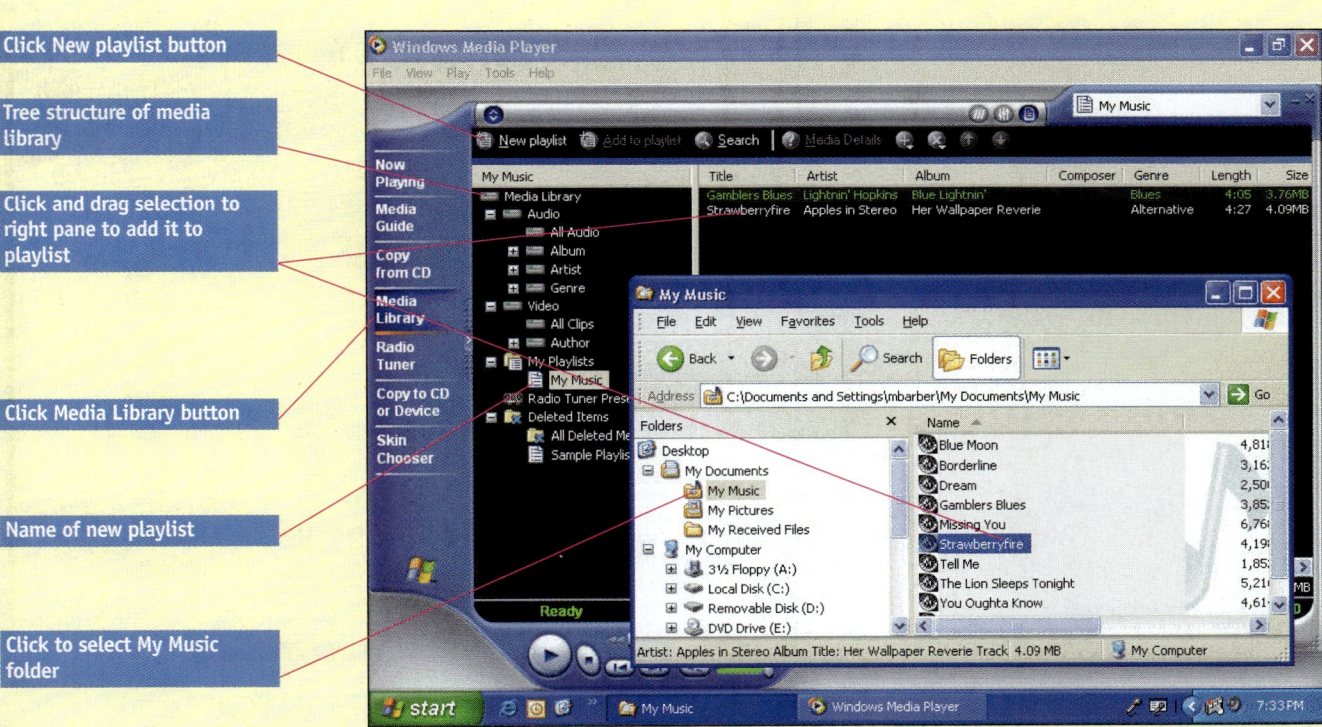

(c) Create a Playlist (step 3)

FIGURE 19 Hands-on Exercise 5 *(continued)*

THE MEDIA GUIDE

Click the Media Guide button at the left of the Media Player to display the home page of the Windows Media Site. You can also get there by starting Internet Explorer and entering windowsmedia.com in the Address bar. Either way, you will be connected to the Internet and can search the Web for media files and/or play clips from your favorite movie.

Step 4: **Create a Pictures Folder**

■ You can use your own pictures, or if you don't have any, you can use the sample pictures provided with Windows XP. Start (or maximize) Windows Explorer. Open the **My Pictures folder** within the **My Documents folder**.

■ Do not be concerned if the content of your folder is different from ours. Our folder already contains various subfolders with different types of pictures in each folder.

■ Click the **Views button** and change to the **Thumbnails view**. This view is especially useful when viewing folders that contain photographs because (up to four) images are displayed on the folder icon.

■ Right click anywhere in the right pane to display a context-sensitive menu as shown in Figure 19d. Click **New**, and then click **Folder** as the type of object to create.

■ The icon for a new folder will appear with the name of the folder (New Folder) highlighted. Enter a more appropriate name (we chose **Romance** because our pictures are those of a happy couple), and press **Enter**.

■ Copy your pictures from another folder, a CD, or floppy disk to the newly created folder.

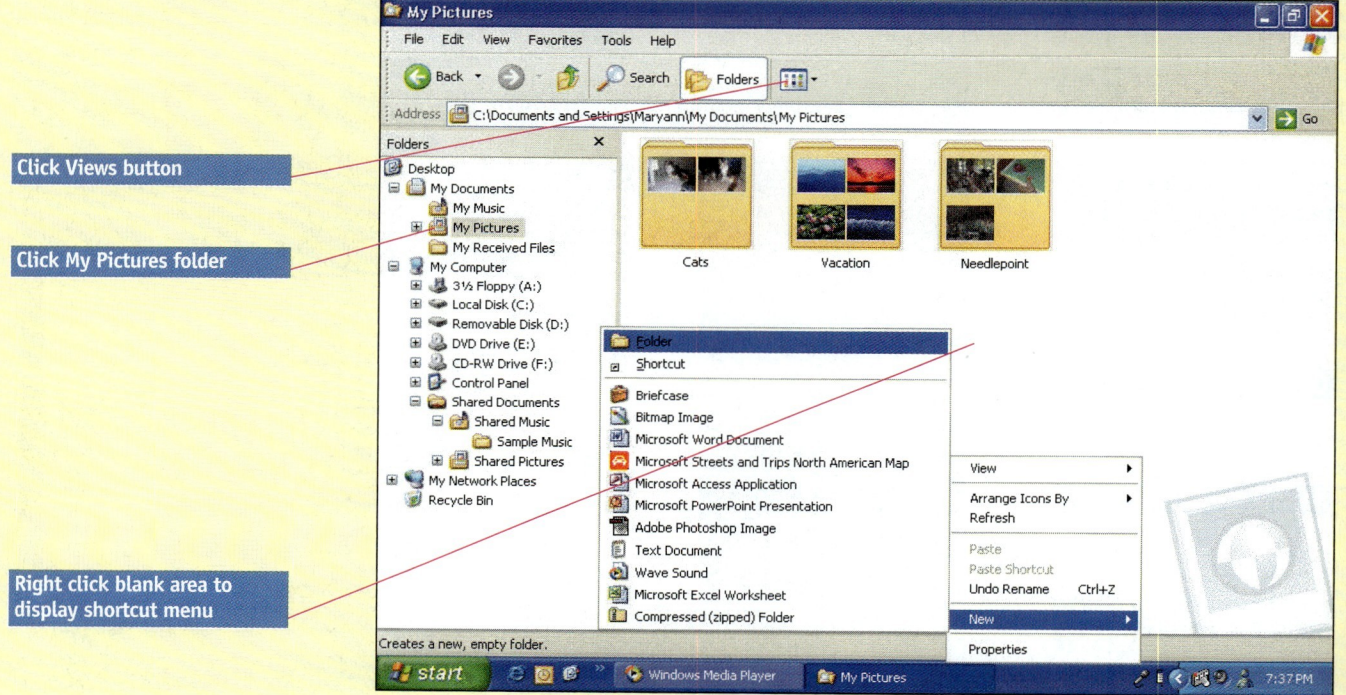

(d) Create a Pictures Folder (step 4)

FIGURE 19   Hands-on Exercise 5 *(continued)*

DESIGN GALLERY LIVE

The Microsoft Design Gallery is an excellent source of photographs and other media. Start Internet Explorer and go to the Design Gallery at dgl.microsoft.com. Enter the desired topic in the Search for text box, indicate that you want to search everywhere, and specify that the results should be photos. Download one or more of the photos that are returned by the search and use those pictures to complete this exercise.

Step 5: **Display Your Pictures**

- Double click the newly created folder to display its contents. Click the **Folders button** to display the Windows Explorer task pane, as opposed to the hierarchy structure. Click the **Views button** and change to the **Filmstrip view** as shown in Figure 19e.

- Click the **Next Image** or (**Previous Image**) **button** to move from one picture to the next within the folder. If necessary, click the buttons to rotate pictures clockwise or counterclockwise so that the pictures are displayed properly within the window.

- Click the command to **View as a slide show**, then display your pictures one at a time on your monitor. This is a very easy way to enjoy your photographs. Press the **Esc key** to stop.

- Choose any picture, then click the command to **Print this picture** that appears in the left pane. Submit this picture to your instructor.

- Choose a different picture and then click the command to **Set as desktop background**. Minimize Windows Explorer.

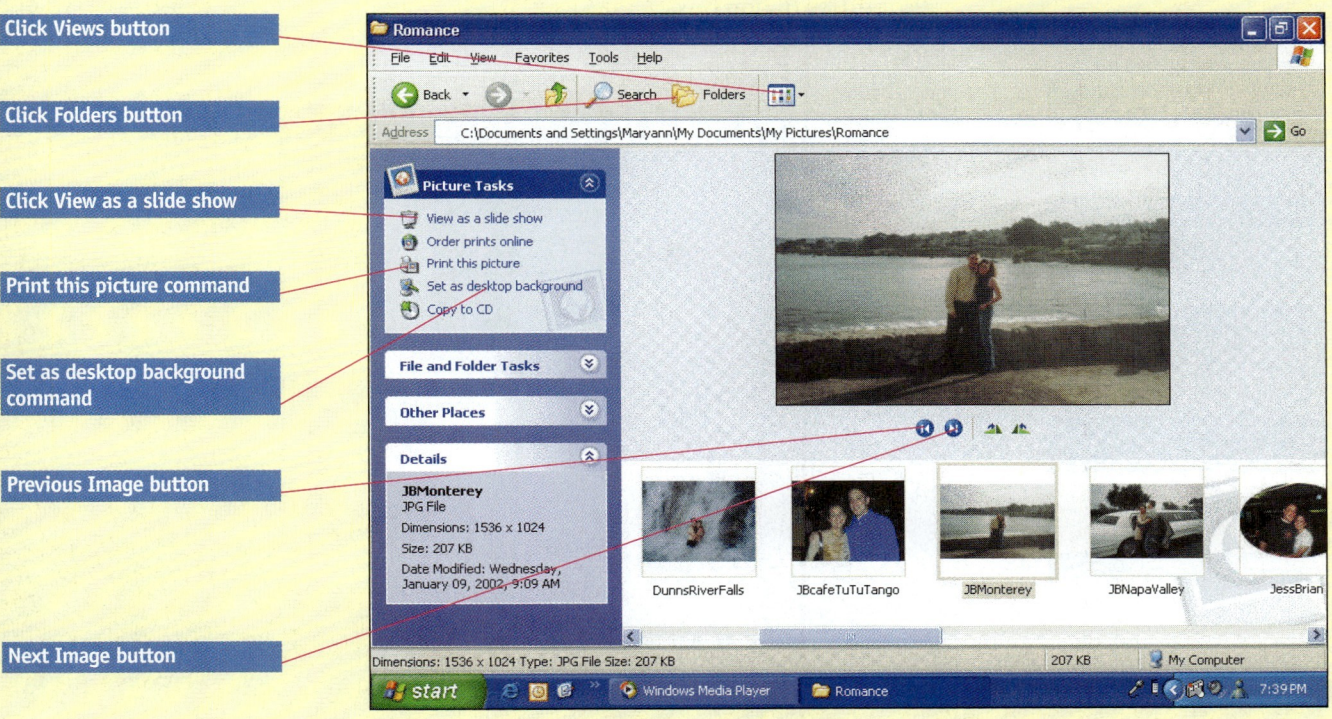

(e) Display Your Pictures (step 5)

FIGURE 19 Hands-on Exercise 5 (*continued*)

CHANGE THE VIEW

Click the down arrow next to the Views button on the Standard toolbar to change the way files are displayed within a folder. The Details view provides the most information and includes the filename, file type, file size, and the date that the file was created or last modified. (Additional attributes are also possible.) Other views are more visual. The Thumbnails view displays a miniature image of the file and is best used with clip art, photographs, or presentations. The Filmstrip view is used with photographs only.

Step 6: **Customize the Desktop**

- Your desktop should once again be visible, depending on which (if any) applications are open. If you do not see the desktop, right click a blank area of the taskbar, then click the **Show Desktop command**.

- You should see the picture you selected earlier as the background for your desktop. The picture is attractive (you chose it), but it may be distracting.

- To remove the picture, **right click** the background of the desktop and click the **Properties command** to display the Display Properties dialog box in Figure 19f.

- Click the **Desktop tab**, then click **None** in the Background list box. Click **OK** to accept this setting and close the dialog box. The picture disappears.

- Regardless of whether you keep the background, you can use your pictures as a screen saver. Redisplay the Display Properties dialog box. Click the **Screen Saver tab** in the Display Properties box, then choose **My Picture Slideshow** from the screen saver list box.

- Wait a few seconds and the picture within the dialog box will change, just as it will on your desktop. Click **OK** to accept the screen saver and close the Display Properties dialog box.

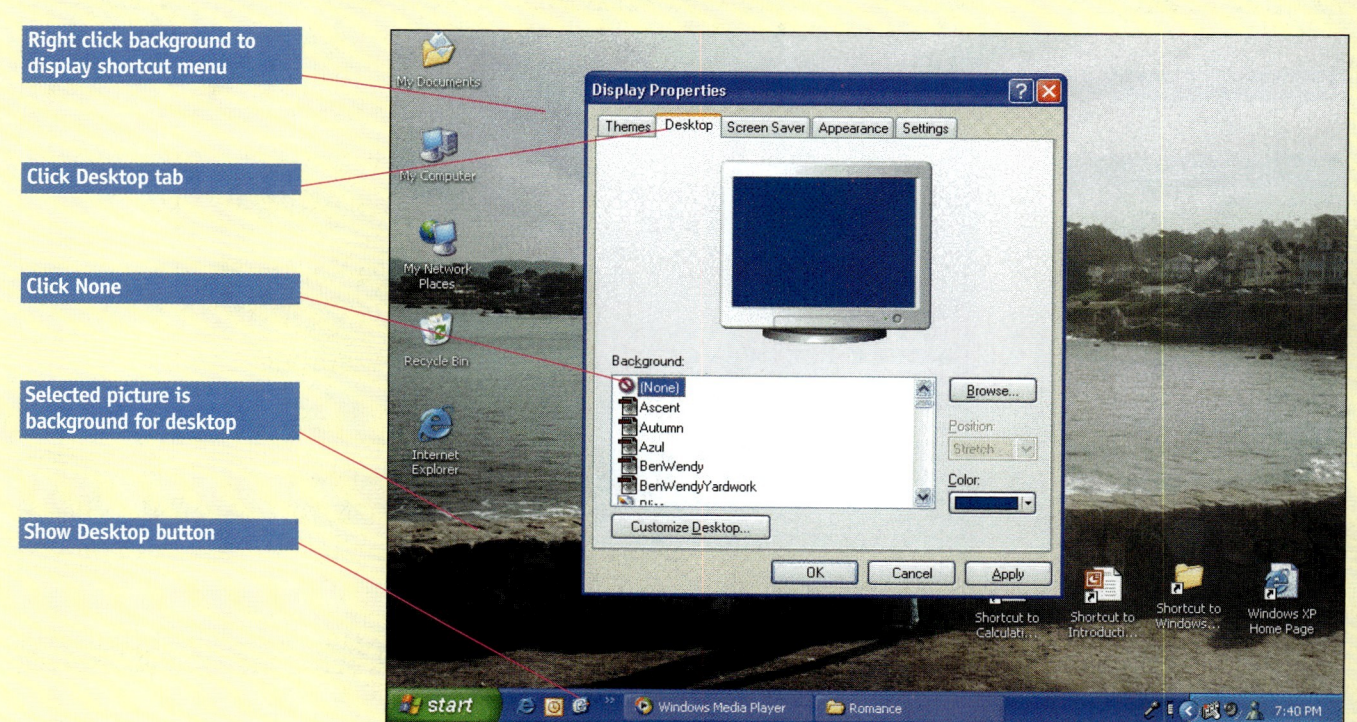

Right click background to display shortcut menu

Click Desktop tab

Click None

Selected picture is background for desktop

Show Desktop button

(f) Customize the Desktop (step 6)

FIGURE 19 Hands-on Exercise 5 *(continued)*

CHANGE THE RESOLUTION

The resolution of a monitor refers to the number of pixels (picture elements or dots) that are displayed at one time. The higher the resolution, the more pixels are displayed, and hence you see more of a document at one time. You can change the resolution at any time. Right click the desktop, click the Properties command to show the Display Properties dialog box, then click the Settings tab. Drag the slider bar to the new resolution, then click OK.

Step 7: **Start Windows Messenger**

- You need a passport to use Windows Messenger. Double click the **Windows Messenger icon** in the notification area of the taskbar to sign in.

- Maximize the Messenger window. You will see a list of your existing contacts with an indication of whether they are online.

- Add one or more contacts. Pull down the **Tools menu**, click the command to **Add a Contact**, then follow the onscreen instructions. (The contact does not have to have Windows XP to use instant messaging.)

- Double click any contact that is online to initiate a conversation and open a conversation window as shown in Figure 19g.

- Type a message at the bottom of the conversation window, then click the **Send button** to send the message. The text of your message will appear immediately on your contact's screen. Your friend's messages will appear on your screen.

- Continue the conversation by entering additional text. You can press the **Enter key** (instead of clicking the **Send button**) to send the message. You can also use **Shift + enter** to create a line break in your text.

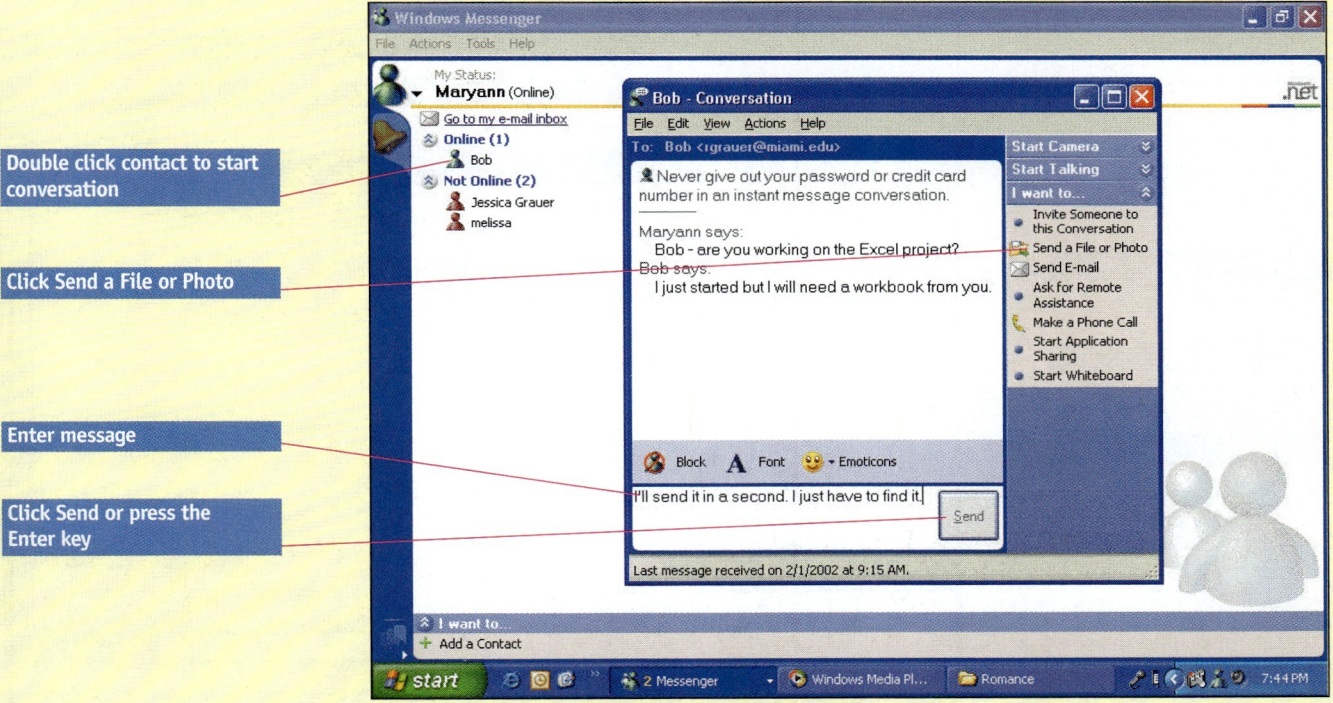

(g) Start Windows Messenger (step 7)

FIGURE 19 Hands-on Exercise 5 *(continued)*

CHANGE YOUR STATUS

Anyone on your contact list knows immediately when you log on; thus, the larger your contact list, the more likely you are to be engaged in idle chitchat when you have real work to do. You can avoid unwanted conversations without being rude by changing your status. Click the down arrow next to your name in the Messenger window and choose a different icon. You can appear offline or simply indicate that you are busy. Either way you will be more likely to get your work done.

Step 8: Attach a File

- Click the command to **Send a File or Photo**, which displays the Send a File dialog box in Figure 19h. It does not matter which file you choose, since the purpose of this step is to demonstrate the file transfer capability.

- A series of three file transfer messages will appear on your screen. Windows Messenger waits for your friend to accept the file transfer, then it indicates the transfer has begun, and finally, that the transfer was successful.

- Click the command to **Invite someone to this conversation** if you have another contact online. You will see a second dialog box in which you select the contact.

- There are now three people in the conversation. (Up to four people can participate in one conversation.) Your friends' responses will appear on your screen as soon as they are entered.

- Send your goodbye to end the conversation, then close the conversation window to end the chat session. You are still online and can participate in future conversations.

- Close Windows Messenger. You will be notified if anyone wants to contact you.

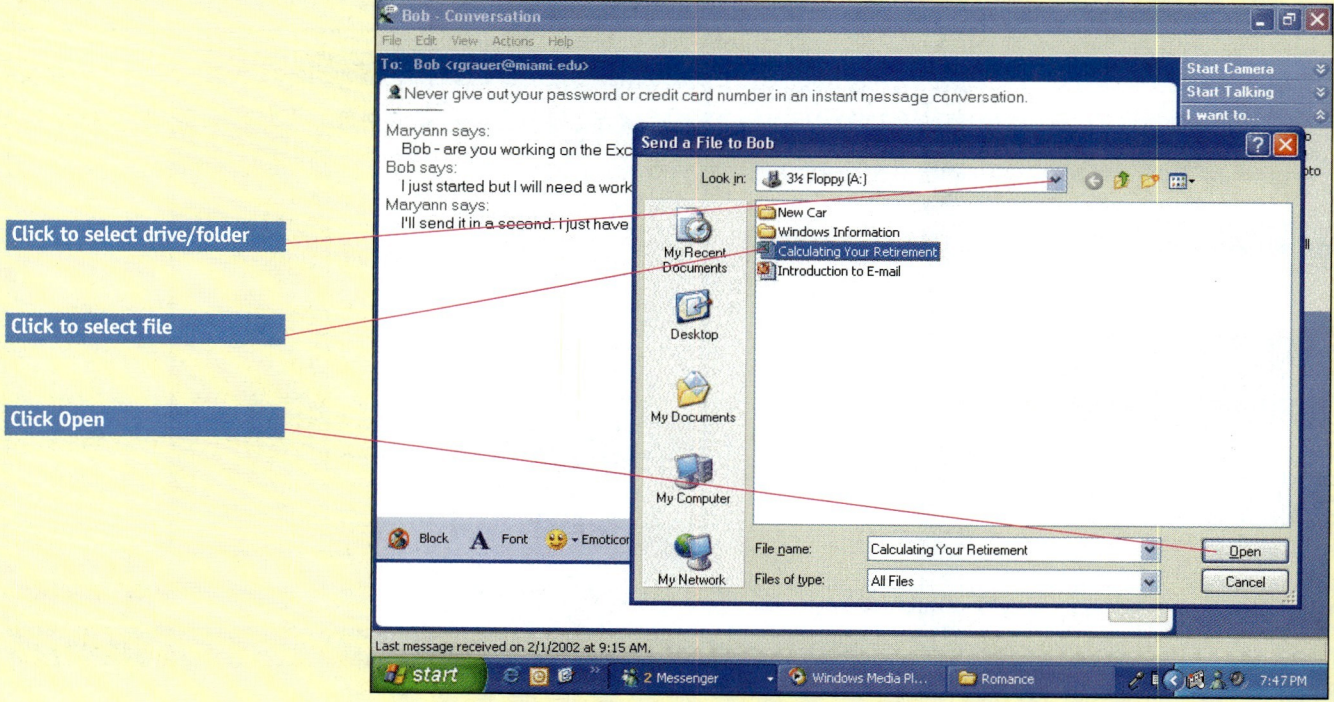

(h) Attach a File (step 8)

FIGURE 19 Hands-on Exercise 5 (*continued*)

E-MAIL VERSUS INSTANT MESSAGING

E-mail and instant messaging are both Internet communication services, but there are significant differences. E-mail does not require both participants to be online at the same time. E-mail messages are also permanent and do not disappear when you exit your e-mail program. Instant messaging, however, requires both participants to be online. Its conversations are not permanent and disappear when you end the session.

Step 9: **Ask for Assistance**

- Your contacts do not require Windows XP to converse with you using Windows Messenger. Windows XP is required, however, to use the remote assistance feature.

- Click the **Start button**, then click the **Help and Support command** to display the home page of the Help and Support Center. Click the **Support button**, then click the command to **Ask a friend to help**.

- A Remote Assistance screen will open in the right pane. Click the command to **Invite someone to help**, which will display your contact list as shown in Figure 19i. You can choose any contact who is online, or you can enter the e-mail address of someone else.

- You will see a dialog box indicating that an invitation has been sent. Once your friend accepts the invitation, he or she will be able to see your screen. A chat window will open up in which you can discuss the problem you are having. Close the session when you are finished.

- Pull down the **File menu** and click the command to **Sign out**. The Windows Messenger icon in the notification will indicate that you have signed out.

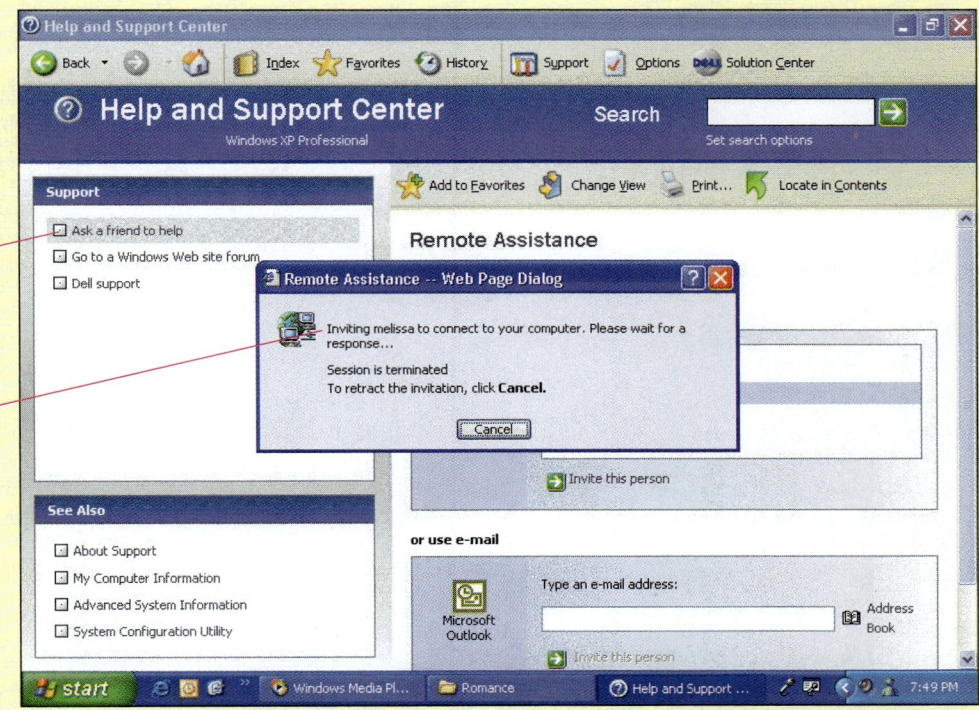

(i) Ask for Assistance (step 9)

FIGURE 19 Hands-on Exercise 5 (*continued*)

SUPPORT ONLINE

Microsoft provides extensive online support in a variety of formats. Start at the Windows XP home page (www.microsoft.com/windowsxp), then click the Support button to see what is available. You will be able to search the Microsoft Knowledge Base for detailed information on virtually any subject. You can also post questions and participate in threaded discussions in various newsgroups. Support is available for every Microsoft product.

SUMMARY

Windows XP is the newest and most powerful version of the Windows operating system. It has a slightly different look than earlier versions, but it maintains the conventions of its predecessors. All Windows operations take place on the desktop. Every window contains the same basic elements, which include a title bar, a Minimize button, a Maximize or Restore button, and a Close button. All windows may be moved and sized. The taskbar contains a button for each open program and enables you to switch back and forth between those programs by clicking the appropriate button. You can obtain information about every aspect of Windows through the Help and Support Center.

A file is a set of data or set of instructions that has been given a name and stored on disk. There are two basic types of files, program files and data files. A program file is an executable file, whereas a data file can be used only in conjunction with a specific program. Every file has a filename and a file type.

Files are stored in folders to better organize the hundreds (or thousands) of files on a disk. A folder may contain program files, data files, and/or other folders. Windows automatically creates a set of personal folders for every user. These include the My Documents folder and the My Pictures folder and My Music folder within the My Documents folder. Windows also provides a Shared Documents folder that can be accessed by every user. The My Computer folder is accessible by all users and displays the devices on a system.

Windows Explorer facilitates every aspect of disk and file management. It presents a hierarchical view of your system that displays all devices and, optionally, the folders on each device. Any device may be expanded or collapsed to display or hide its folders.

Windows XP contains several tools to help you enjoy your system. The Windows Media Player combines the functions of a radio, CD player, DVD player, and an information database into a single program. Windows Messenger is an instant messaging system in which you chat with friends and colleagues over the Internet.

The Control Panel affects every aspect of your system. It determines the appearance of your desktop and it controls the performance of your hardware. A shortcut is a link to any object on your computer, such as a program, file, folder, disk drive, or Web page. The Search Companion enables you to search for a file according to several different criteria.

KEY TERMS

Backup strategy 671
Check box 648
Classic Start menu 643
Close button 646
Command button 648
Compressed file 660
Control Panel 681
Copy a file 671
Data file 658
Delete command 671
Desktop 643
Details view 658
Dialog box 648
Digital photographs 692
Fast user switching 642
File 658
File type 658
Filename 658
Filmstrip view 699
Firewall 660
Folder 658
Help and Support Center 649
Help button 648
Internet Explorer 6.0 649
Internet Service Provider 660

List box 648
Maximize button 646
Menu bar 646
Microsoft passport 694
Minimize button 646
Modem 660
Move a file 671
Move a window 643
Multitasking 643
My Computer folder 646
My Documents folder 669
My Music folder 669
My Pictures folder 669
Notification area 643
Option button 648
Personal folders 669
Playlist 692
Program file 658
Pull-down menu 647
Quick Launch toolbar 682
Radio button 648
Recycle Bin 671
Rename command 672
Restore button 646
Scroll bar 646

Search Companion 683
Shared Documents folder 669
Shortcut 682
Size a window 643
Spin button 648
Start button 643
Start menu 643
Status bar 646
Task pane 646
Taskbar 643
Text box 648
Thumbnails view 693
Tiles view 658
Title bar 646
Toolbar 646
Windows Classic theme 643
Windows Explorer 669
Windows Media Player 692
Windows Messenger 694
Windows Update 681
Windows® XP 642
Windows XP theme 643
XP Home Edition 642
XP Professional Edition 642

MULTIPLE CHOICE

1. Which of the following is true regarding a dialog box?

   (a) Option buttons indicate mutually exclusive choices
   (b) Check boxes imply that multiple options may be selected
   (c) Both (a) and (b)
   (d) Neither (a) nor (b)

2. Which of the following is the first step in sizing a window?

   (a) Point to the title bar
   (b) Pull down the View menu to display the toolbar
   (c) Point to any corner or border
   (d) Pull down the View menu and change to large icons

3. Which of the following is the first step in moving a window?

   (a) Point to the title bar
   (b) Pull down the View menu to display the toolbar
   (c) Point to any corner or border
   (d) Pull down the View menu and change to large icons

4. Which button appears immediately after a window has been maximized?

   (a) The Close button
   (b) The Minimize button
   (c) The Maximize button
   (d) The Restore button

5. What happens to a window that has been minimized?

   (a) The window is still visible but it no longer has a Minimize button
   (b) The window shrinks to a button on the taskbar
   (c) The window is closed and the application is removed from memory
   (d) The window is still open but the application has been removed from memory

6. What is the significance of a faded (dimmed) command in a pull-down menu?

   (a) The command is not currently accessible
   (b) A dialog box appears if the command is selected
   (c) A Help window appears if the command is selected
   (d) There are no equivalent keystrokes for the particular command

7. The Recycle Bin enables you to restore a file that was deleted from

   (a) Drive A
   (b) Drive C
   (c) Both (a) and (b)
   (d) Neither (a) nor (b)

8. Which of the following was suggested as essential to a backup strategy?

   (a) Back up all program files at the end of every session
   (b) Store backup files at another location
   (c) Both (a) and (b)
   (d) Neither (a) nor (b)

9. A shortcut may be created for

   (a) An application or a document
   (b) A folder or a drive
   (c) Both (a) and (b)
   (d) Neither (a) nor (b)

10. What happens if you click the Folders button (on the Standard Buttons toolbar in the My Computer folder) twice in a row?

    (a) The left pane displays a task pane with commands for the selected object
    (b) The left pane displays a hierarchical view of the devices on your system
    (c) The left pane displays either a task pane or the hierarchical view depending on what was displayed prior to clicking the button initially
    (d) The left pane displays both the task pane and a hierarchical view

... continued

11. The Search Companion can

   (a) Locate all files containing a specified phrase

   (b) Restrict its search to a specified set of folders

   (c) Both (a) and (b)

   (d) Neither (a) nor (b)

12. Which views display miniature images of photographs within a folder?

   (a) Tiles view and Icons view

   (b) Thumbnails view and Filmstrip view

   (c) Details view and List view

   (d) All views display a miniature image

13. Which of the following statements is true?

   (a) A plus sign next to a folder indicates that its contents are hidden

   (b) A minus sign next to a folder indicates that its contents are hidden

   (c) A plus sign appears next to any folder that has been expanded

   (d) A minus sign appears next to any folder that has been collapsed

14. Ben and Jessica are both registered users on a Windows XP computer. Which of the following is a *false statement* regarding their personal folders?

   (a) Ben and Jessica each have a My Documents folder

   (b) Ben and Jessica each have a My Pictures folder that is stored within their respective My Documents folders

   (c) Ben can access files in Jessica's My Documents folder

   (d) Jessica cannot access files in Ben's My Documents folder

15. When is a file permanently deleted?

   (a) When you delete the file from Windows Explorer

   (b) When you empty the Recycle Bin

   (c) When you turn the computer off

   (d) All of the above

16. What happens if you (left) click and drag a file to another folder on the same drive?

   (a) The file is copied

   (b) The file is moved

   (c) The file is deleted

   (d) A shortcut menu is displayed

17. How do you shut down the computer?

   (a) Click the Start button, then click the Turn Off Computer command

   (b) Right click the Start button, then click the Turn Off Computer command

   (c) Click the End button, then click the Turn Off Computer command

   (d) Right click the End button, then click the Turn Off Computer command

18. Which of the following can be accomplished with Windows Messenger?

   (a) You can chat with up to three other people in the conversation window

   (b) You can place telephone calls (if you have a microphone and speaker) without paying long-distance charges

   (c) You can ask for remote assistance, which enables your contact to view your screen as you are working

   (d) All of the above

ANSWERS

1. c	**7.** b	**13.** a
2. c	**8.** b	**14.** c
3. a	**9.** c	**15.** b
4. d	**10.** c	**16.** b
5. b	**11.** c	**17.** a
6. a	**12.** b	**18.** d

PRACTICE WITH WINDOWS XP

1. **Two Different Views:** The document in Figure 20 is an effective way to show your instructor that you understand the My Computer folder, the various views available, the task pane, and the hierarchy structure. It also demonstrates that you can capture a screen for inclusion in a Word document. Proceed as follows:

   a. Open the My Computer folder, click the Views button, and switch to the Tiles view. Click the Folders button to display the task pane. Size the window as necessary so that you will be able to fit two folders onto a one-page document as shown in Figure 20.

   b. Press and hold the Alt key as you press the Print Screen key to copy the My Computer window to the Windows clipboard. (The Print Screen key captures the entire screen. Using the Alt key, however, copies just the current window.) Click the Start menu, click Programs, and then click Microsoft Word to start the program. Maximize the window.

   c. Enter the title of the document, press Enter, and type your name. Press the Enter key twice in a row to leave a blank line.

   d. Pull down the Edit menu. Click the Paste command to copy the contents of the clipboard to the document. Press the Enter key to add a figure caption, then press the Enter key two additional times.

   e. Click the taskbar to return to the My Computer folder. Change to the Details view. Click the Folders button to display the hierarchy structure, as opposed to the task pane. Expand My Computer in the left pane, but collapse all of the individual devices. Press Alt+Print Screen to capture the My Computer folder in this configuration.

   f. Click the taskbar to return to your Word document. Press Ctrl+V to paste the contents of the clipboard into your document. Enter an appropriate caption below the figure. Save the completed document and print it for your instructor.

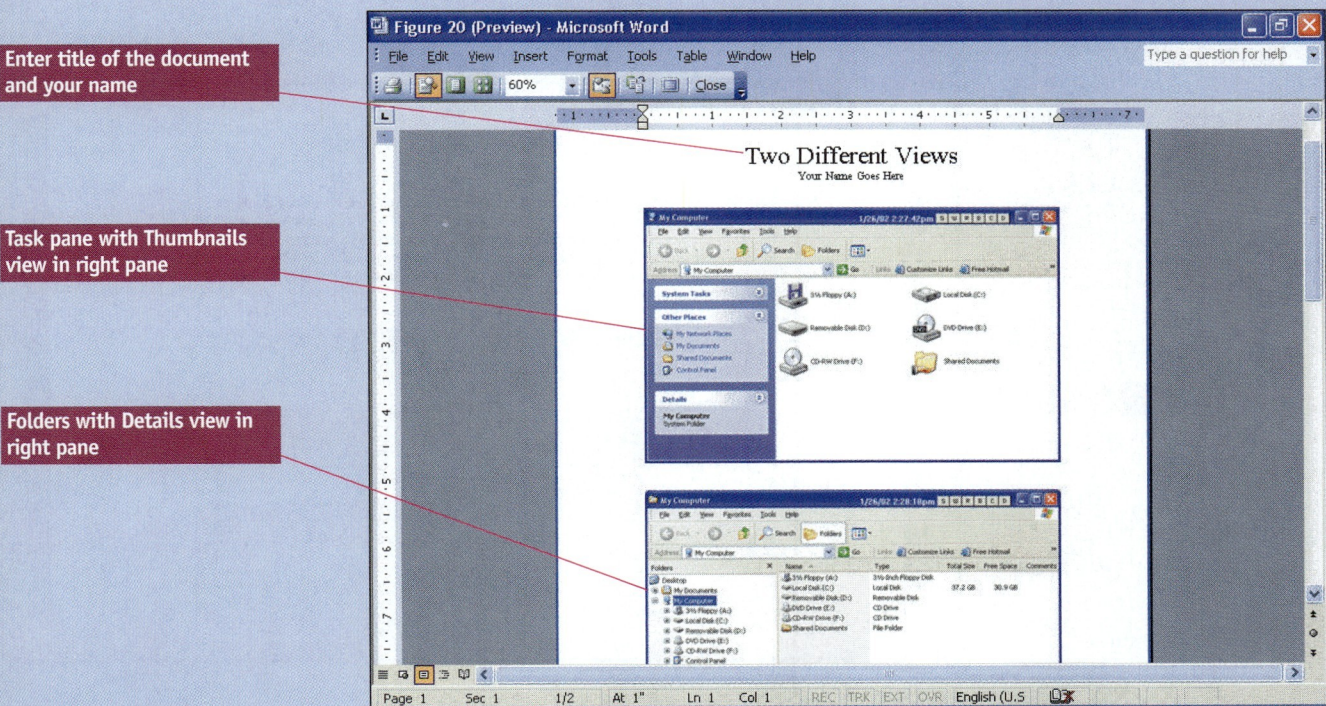

Enter title of the document and your name

Task pane with Thumbnails view in right pane

Folders with Details view in right pane

FIGURE 20 Two Different Views (exercise 1)

2. **Network Connections:** The document in Figure 21 displays the network connections on our system as well as the status of one of those connections. Your assignment is to create the equivalent document for your computer. Proceed as follows:

a. Open the Control Panel, switch to the Classic view, then double click the Network Connections icon to display the Network Connections folder. (You can also get to this folder from My Computer, by clicking the link to My Network Places, and then clicking Network Connections from within the Network Tasks area.)

b. Maximize the Network Connections folder so that it takes the entire desktop. Change to the Tiles view. Click the Folders button to display the task pane. Select (click) a connection, then click the link to View status of the connection, to display the associated dialog box.

c. Press the Print Screen key to print this screen. Start Microsoft Word and open a new document. Press the Enter key several times, then click the Paste button to copy the contents of the clipboard into your document.

d. Press Ctrl+Home to return to the beginning of the Word document, where you can enter the title of the document and your name. Compose a paragraph similar to the one in our figure that describes the network connections on your computer. Print this document for your instructor.

e. Experiment with the first two network tasks that are displayed in the task pane. How difficult is it to set up a new connection? How do you set a firewall to protect your system from unauthorized access when connected to the Internet? How do you establish a home or small office network?

f. Use the Help and Support Center to obtain additional information. Print one or two Help screens for your instructor.

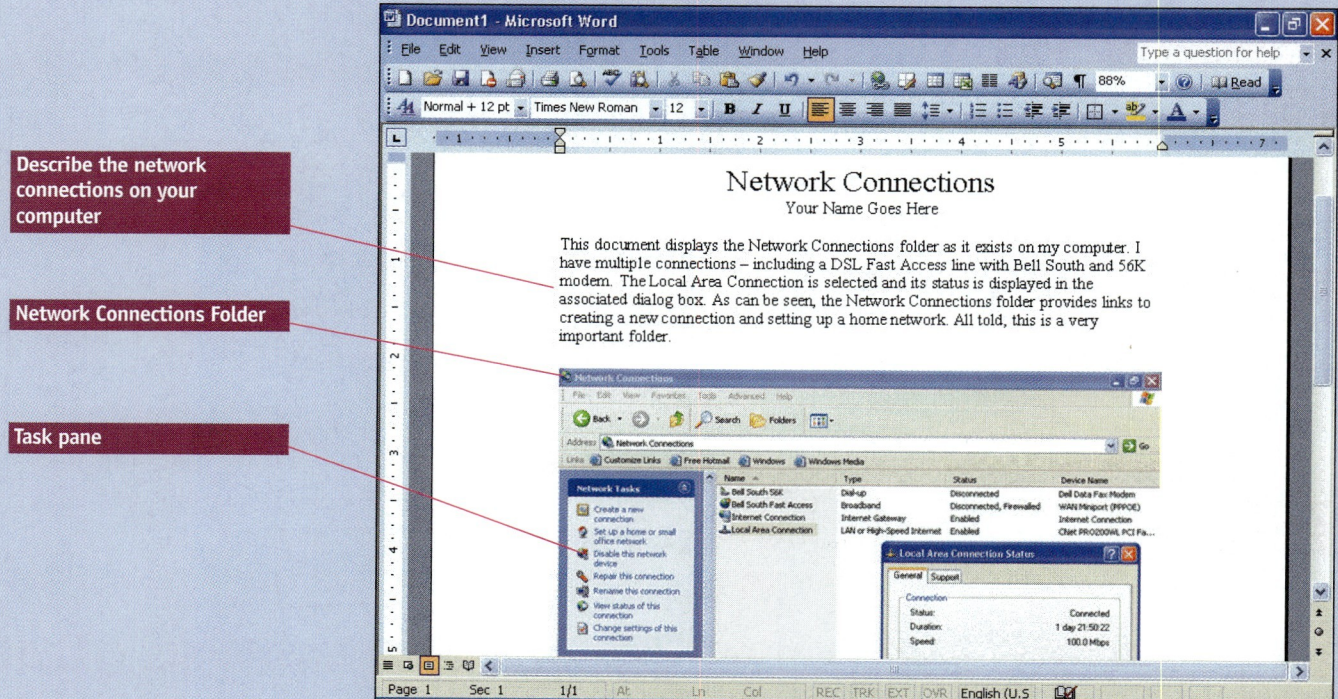

FIGURE 21   Network Connections (exercise 2)

3. **Create Your Own Folders:** Folders are the key to the Windows storage system. Folders can be created at any time and in any way that makes sense to you. The My Courses folder in Figure 22, for example, contains five folders, one folder for each class you are taking. In similar fashion, the Correspondence folder in this figure contains two additional folders according to the type of correspondence. Proceed as follows:

a. Place the floppy disk from hands-on exercise 3 into drive A. Start Windows Explorer. Click the Folders button to display the hierarchy structure in the left pane. Change to the Details view.

b. Create a Correspondence folder on drive A. Create a Business folder and a Personal folder within the Correspondence folder.

c. Create a My Courses folder on drive A. Create a separate folder for each course you are taking within the My Courses folder. The names of your folders will be different from ours.

d. Pull down the View menu, click the Arrange Icons by command, and click the command to Show in Groups. Click the Date Modified column header to group the files and folders by date. The dates you see will be different from the dates in our figure.

e. The Show in Groups command functions as a toggle switch. Execute the command, and the files are displayed in groups; execute the command a second time, and the groups disappear. (You can change the grouping by clicking the desired column heading.)

f. Use the technique described in problems 1 and 2 to capture the screen in Figure 22 and incorporate it into a document. Add a short paragraph that describes the folders you have created, then submit the document to your instructor.

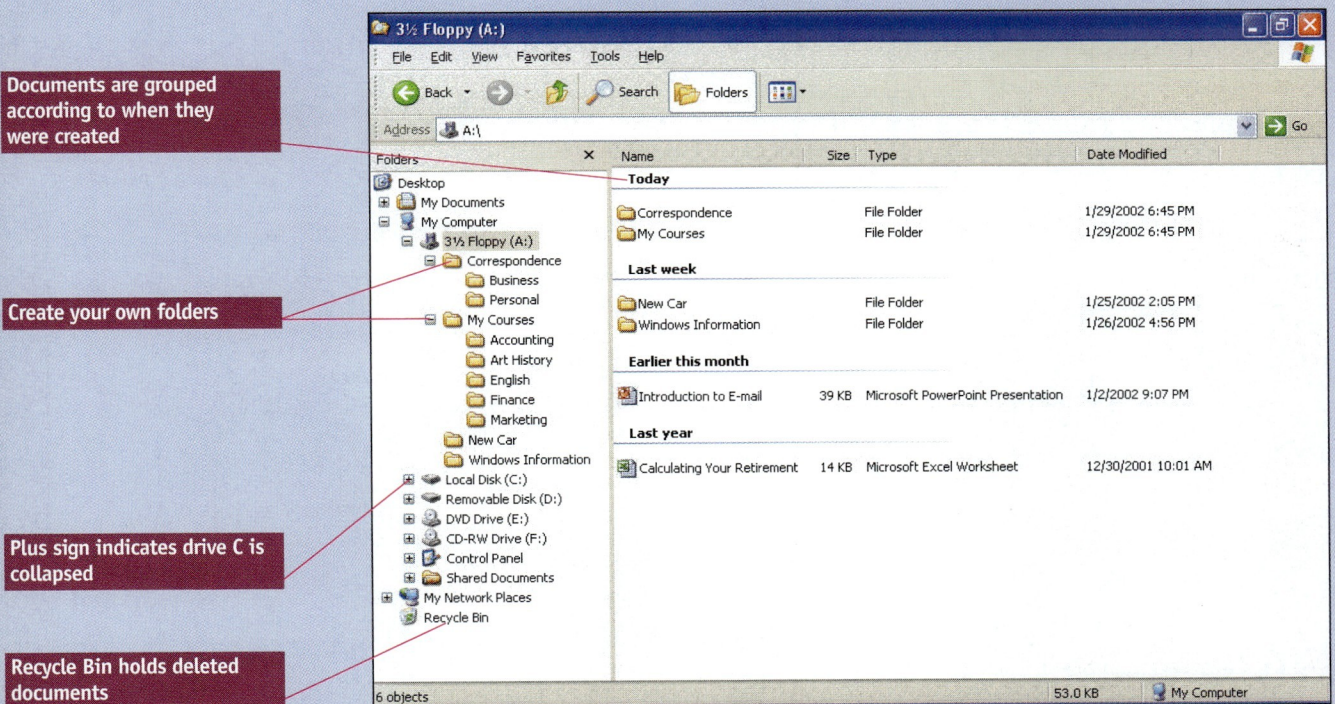

Documents are grouped according to when they were created

Create your own folders

Plus sign indicates drive C is collapsed

Recycle Bin holds deleted documents

FIGURE 22   Create Your Own Folders (exercise 3)

4. **What's New in Windows XP:** Anyone, whether an experienced user or a computer novice, can benefit from a quick overview of new features in Windows XP. Click the Start button, click Help and Support, and then click the link to What's New in Windows XP. Click the second link in the task pane (taking a tour or tutorial), select the Windows XP tour, and choose the desired format. We chose the animated tour with animation, music, and voice narration.

a. Relax and enjoy the show as shown in Figure 23. The task bar at the bottom of the figure contains three buttons to restart the show, exit, or toggle the music on and off. Exit the tutorial when you are finished. You are back in the Help and Support window, where you can take a tour of the Windows Media Player. Try it. Click the Close button at the upper right of any screen or press Escape to exit the tour. Write a short note to your instructor with comments about either tour.

b. Return to the Help and Support Center and find the topic, "What's New in Home Networking". Print two or three subtopics that describe how to create a home network. Does the task seem less intimidating after you have read the information?

c. Locate one or more topics on new features in digital media such as burning a CD or Windows Movie Maker. Print this information for your instructor.

d. Return once again to the Help and Support Center to explore some of the other resources that describe new features in Windows XP. Locate the link to Windows News Groups, and then visit one of these newsgroups online. Locate a topic of interest and print several messages within a threaded discussion. Do you think newsgroups will be useful to you in the future?

e. You can also download a PowerPoint presentation by the authors that describes new features in Windows XP. Go to www.prenhall.com/grauer, click the text for Office XP, then click the link to What's New in Windows XP, from where you can download the presentation.

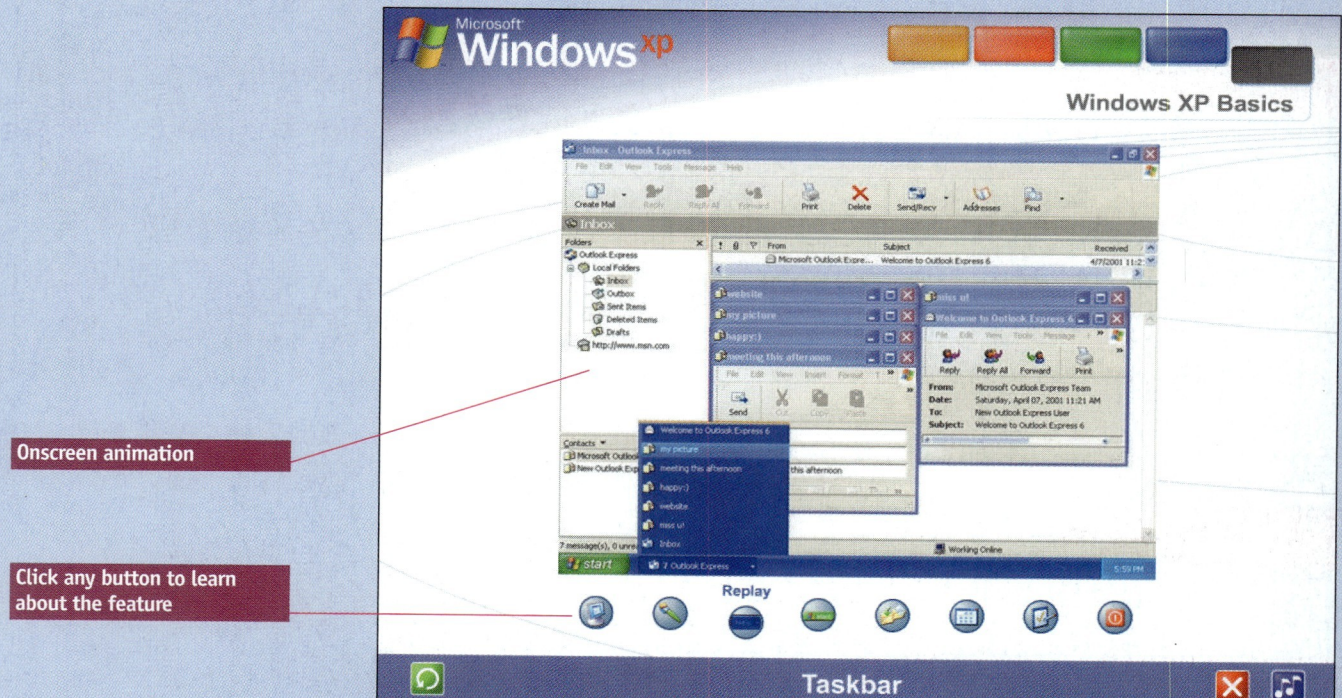

FIGURE 23   What's New in Windows XP (exercise 4)

5. **Keyboard Shortcuts:** Almost every command in Windows can be executed in different ways, using either the mouse or the keyboard. Most people start with the mouse and add keyboard shortcuts as they become more proficient. There is no right or wrong technique, just different techniques, and the one you choose depends entirely on personal preference. If, for example, your hands are already on the keyboard, it is faster to use the keyboard equivalent if you know it.

There is absolutely no need to memorize these shortcuts, nor should you even try. A few, however, have special appeal and everyone has favorites. You are probably familiar with general Windows shortcuts such as Ctrl+X, Ctrl+C, and Ctrl+V to cut, copy, and paste, respectively. (The X is supposed to remind you of a pair of scissors.) Ctrl+Z is less well known and corresponds to the Undo command. You can find additional shortcuts through the Help command.

a. Use the Help and Support Center to display the information in Figure 24, which shows the available shortcuts within a dialog box. Two of these, Tab and Shift+Tab, move forward and backward, respectively, from one option to the next within the dialog box. The next time you are in a physician's office or a dentist's office, watch the assistant as he or she labors over the keyboard to enter information. That person will typically type information into a text box, then switch to the mouse to select the next entry, return to the keyboard, and so on. Tell that person about Tab and Shift+Tab; he or she will be forever grateful.

b. The Help and Support Center organizes the shortcuts by category. Select the Natural keyboard category (not visible in Figure 24), then note what you can do with the ⊞ key. Press the ⊞ key at any time, and you display the Start menu. Press ⊞+M and you minimize all open windows. There are several other, equally good shortcuts in this category.

c. Select your five favorite shortcuts in any category, and submit them to your instructor. Compare your selections to those of your classmates. Do you prefer the mouse or your newly discovered shortcuts?

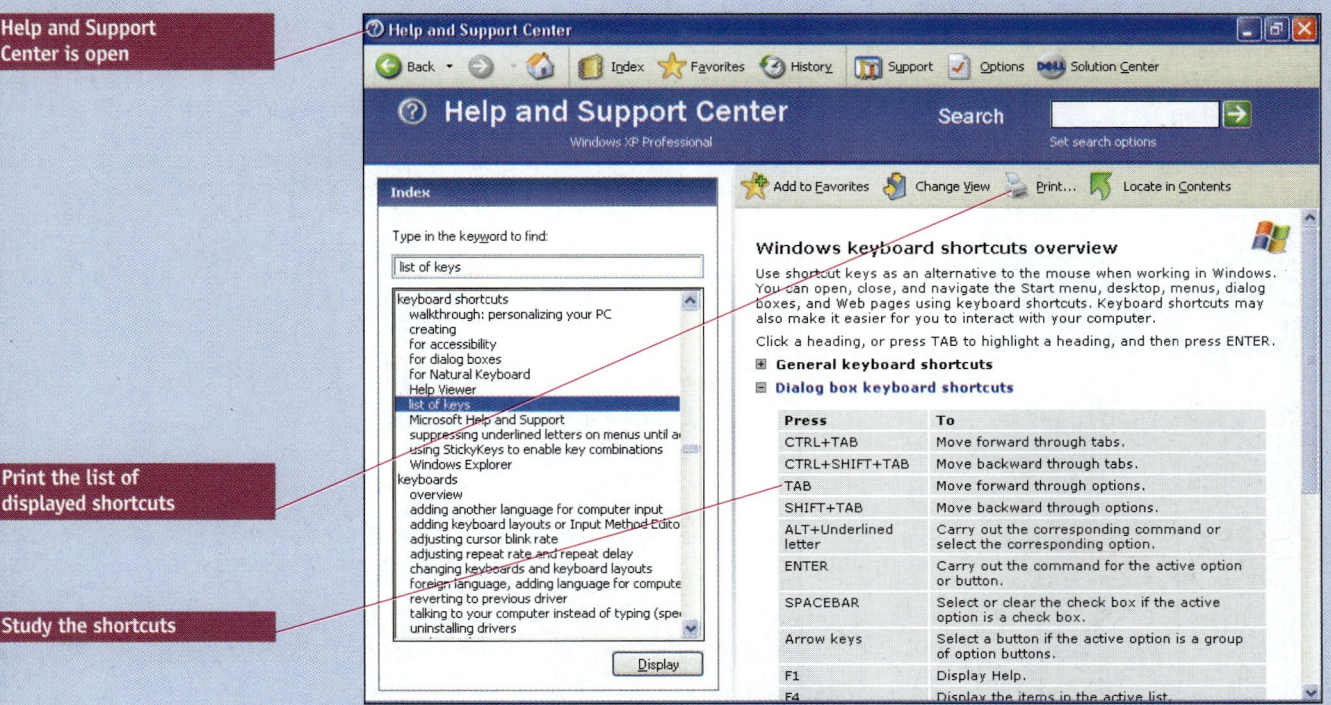

FIGURE 24 Keyboard Shortcuts (exercise 5)

MINI CASES

Planning for Disaster

Do you have a backup strategy? Do you even know what a backup strategy is? You had better learn, because sooner or later you will wish you had one. You will erase a file, be unable to read from a floppy disk, or worse yet, suffer a hardware failure in which you are unable to access the hard drive. The problem always seems to occur the night before an assignment is due. The ultimate disaster is the disappearance of your computer, by theft or natural disaster. Describe, in 250 words or less, the backup strategy you plan to implement in conjunction with your work in this class.

Tips for Windows XP

Print the *Tips for Windows XP* document that was downloaded as one of the practice files in the hands-on exercises. This document contains many of the boxed tips that appeared throughout the chapter. Read the document as a review and select five of your favorite tips. Create a new document for your instructor consisting of the five tips you selected. Add a cover page titled, "My Favorite Tips". Include your name, your professor's name, and a reference to the Grauer/Barber text from where the tips were taken.

File Compression

You've learned your lesson and have come to appreciate the importance of backing up all of your data files. The problem is that you work with large documents that exceed the 1.44MB capacity of a floppy disk. Accordingly, you might want to consider the acquisition of a file compression program to facilitate copying large documents to a floppy disk in order to transport your documents to and from school, home, or work. You can download an evaluation copy of the popular WinZip program at www.winzip.com. Investigate the subject of file compression and submit a summary of your findings to your instructor.

The Threat of Virus Infection

A computer virus is an actively infectious program that attaches itself to other programs and alters the way a computer works. Some viruses do nothing more than display an annoying message at an inopportune time. Most, however, are more harmful, and in the worst case, erase all files on the disk. Use your favorite search engine to research the subject of computer viruses to answer the following questions. When is a computer subject to infection by a virus? What precautions does your school or university take against the threat of virus infection in its computer lab? What precautions, if any, do you take at home? Can you feel confident that your machine will not be infected if you faithfully use a state-of-the-art anti-virus program that was purchased in June 2002?

Your First Consultant's Job

Go to a real installation such as a doctor's or attorney's office, the company where you work, or the computer lab at school. Determine the backup procedures that are in effect, then write a one-page report indicating whether the policy is adequate and, if necessary, offering suggestions for improvement. Your report should be addressed to the individual in charge of the business, and it should cover all aspects of the backup strategy; that is, which files are backed up and how often, and what software is used for the backup operation. Use appropriate emphasis (for example, bold italics) to identify any potential problems. This is a professional document (it is your first consultant's job), and its appearance should be perfect in every way.

Index

#Error, 77, 236
#Name, 77

A

Action, 348
Action query, 143–150, 162
Add button (modification of), 400
Add mode (versus Edit mode), 342, 482
Aggregate functions, 180
Allow Zero Length property, 55, 452, 454
Alt+Tab (keyboard shortcut), 450
Ampersand
   as concatenation operator, 396,
     476, 590
   in keyboard shortcut, 197
AND operator, 121
Anomaly, 527
Append query, 143, 148
Argument, 348, 392, 578
Arrange Icons command, 686
Ascending sort, 19, 24, 118
Attribute, 530
AutoCorrect, 11
AutoExec macro, 349, 352, 478, 481
AutoForm, 68
AutoLookup, 284
AutoNumber field, 53, 221, 225, 452, 459
   in relationship, 224, 310
Avg function, 131

B

Back end, 504
Backup, 392, 633, 671
Back Up Database command, 195, 202,
    462, 506
BeforeClose event procedure,
    619–620
BeforeUpdate event, 424
Between operator, 122
Block fields (in mail merge), 555
Bound control, 65, 110, 460

C

Calculated control, 65, 73, 110,
    134, 476
Calculated field, 52
Caption property, 55, 408, 454
Cascade deleted records, 227, 278,
    282–283, 448
Cascaded update related records, 278
Case statement, 411–412, 594, 600
Character encoding, 561
Character string, 592

Chart Wizard, 180, 182, 187–188
Check box, 78, 648
Class module, 391
Classic Start menu, 643
Click event, 401, 409
Clip art, 86, 141, 199, 346
Clip Organizer, 141
Close action, 481
Close button, 646
Close Form Event, 392
Codd, Edgar, 530
Code builder, 398
Columnar report, 106
Combined key, 276, 531
Combo box, 359
Combo Box Wizard, 314, 394
Command button (rounded), 463
Command button, 78, 648
   adding to a form, 83–84
   rounded, 83
Comment, 582, 588
   toggle on or off, 635
Compact and Repair Database
    command, 195, 202, 247, 369
Compilation error, 404, 606, 610
Complete Word tool, 405, 598
Composite key, 531
Compressed file, 660
Concatenate, 130, 134, 580
Concatenated key, 531
Concatenation, 396, 476, 590
Conditional formatting, 131, 141
Continuation (of VBA statement),
    415, 590
Control, 65
   alignment of, 75
   moving and sizing, 68, 72
   selection of, 84, 139, 464
Control Panel, 681, 689
Convert Database command, 195
Copy command (shortcut for), 393
Count function, 131, 180
Criteria row, 118, 121–122, 124, 126
Crosstab query, 143, 151, 162
Currency field, 53
Current event, 392, 399
Current record, 4
Custom toolbar, 595, 601–603
Cut command (shortcut for), 393

D

Data (versus information), 26, 106
Data disk (downloading of), 8
Data entry (facilitation of), 401–410
Data file, 658
Data source, 549
Data type mismatch, 244

Data type, 53
Data validation, 15, 420–427, 452–453
   field versus record level, 423, 458
Database, 2
   expansion of, 248–249, 305–306
Database design, 223, 444, 525–539
   PowerPoint presentation for, 261,
     444–445, 450–451
Database properties, 150, 316, 339
Database splitter, 340, 506
Database window, 3
   hiding of, 504, 509, 636
Database Wizard, 212
Datasheet (formatting of), 16, 42
Datasheet view, 4, 54, 228
Date/Time field, 53
Debug menu, 606
Debug toolbar, 606
Debug.Print statement, 607
Debugging, 349, 416, 606
Declarations section, 582
Default folder, 55
Default Value property, 55, 401
Default View property, 253
Delete command, 671
Delete query, 143, 146–147
Deletion anomaly, 527
Dependencies, 533
Descending sort, 19, 24, 118
Description property, 302
Design grid, 120
Design master, 437–438
Design view, 4, 54
Desktop, 643
   customization of, 700
Detail section, 108, 460
Detailed design, 452
Details view, 658
Dialog box, 648
Digital photography, 693
Dim statement, 581
Display When property, 345
Do Loops, 605, 615–616
Documenter, 419, 436
Documents submenu, 309
Drop-down list box, 78
Dynaset, 118, 125

E

Edit mode (versus Add mode), 342, 482
Else clause, 592, 598
End Sub statement, 579
Error (green triangle), 128
Event, 337, 388, 617
Event procedure, 344, 391, 617, 628
   creation of, 398
Event-driven programming, 413

Exclusive access, 504
Execution error, 606
Export command, 171, 179
Expression, 65
Expression Builder, 235
Extensible, 560
Extensible Markup Language, 559

F

Fast user switching, 642
Favorites button, 656
Field, 2, 530
Field list (in pivot table), 183–184
Field name, 53
Field row, 118
Field Size property, 55, 62
Field width, 64
File, 658
   attaching, 702
   copying, 671
   moving, 671
   selection of, 673
File format, 9, 56
File type, 658
Filename, 658
Filmstrip view, 699
Filter by form, 19–20, 23
Filter by selection, 19
Filter excluding selection, 22
Filter, 19–20
   with form, 32, 47, 129
   removal of, 25
Find command, 12
Find Duplicates query, 486, 491, 518
Firewall, 660
First normal form, 535
Fixed toolbar, 601
Floating toolbar, 71, 601
Floppy disk
   demise of, 655
   formatting of, 655
Folder, 658
   copying of, 674
   creation of, 666, 672
   deletion of, 677
Fonts folder, 689
For . . . Next Statement, 604, 609, 613–614
Foreign key, 169, 221, 530
Form, 5, 15, 65–69
   with picture, 102
   removing background, 87
   tab control, 101
Form header, 76
Form letter, 549
Form view, 65, 228
Form Wizard, 68–69, 71
   with subform, 230–232, 289
Format property, 55, 221, 277, 454
FormOpen event procedure, 634
Front end, 504
Full Module view, 403, 597
Functional dependence, 533

G

General Declarations section, 411
General procedure, 391
Get External Data command, 171, 309, 340
GIGO (garbage in, garbage out), 2, 48
Group By command, 180, 293
Group Footer, 108, 116, 140, 490
Group Header, 108, 116, 490
Grouping records, 246

H

Help, 591
Help and Support Center, 649, 656, 703, 711
Help button, 648
Help menu, 18
Hopper, Grace, 416
HTML, 559
Hyperlink, 176
   insertion of, 468
Hyperlink field, 53
Hypertext Markup Language (See HTML)

I

If statement, 411, 592, 598
IME Mode property, 55
IME Sentence Mode property, 55
Immediate IF function, 130, 136, 236, 376
Immediate window, 411, 414, 607, 612
Import Spreadsheet Wizard, 171
Import Text Wizard, 173
Indexed property, 55
Information requirements, 442
Inheritance, 81
Input Mask property, 55, 61, 455–456
InputBox function, 580, 589
Insert Date command, 553
Insert Hyperlink command, 357
Insertion anomaly, 527
Internet Explorer 6.0, 649
Internet Service Provider, 660
Intrinsic constant, 392, 579
Is Null criterion, 362

J

Join line, 177, 239
Join properties, 376

K

Keep Together property, 139, 299
Key Preview property, 406
Keyboard shortcut, 197, 675, 711
   function keys in Access, 354, 480
   on switchboard, 341, 467

KeyCode argument, 402
KeyDown event, 401, 403–405

L

Like operator, 122, 489
   with parameter query, 489
Limit to List property, 452, 457
Link Tables command, 338, 340
Linked subforms, 251–257
Linked Table Manager, 337–338
Linked Tables command, 521
List box, 648
Literal, 592
Locals window, 607
Log off, 657, 680
Log on, 650
Lookup Wizard, 80, 457

M

Macro, 348–350, 478, 578
   assign to command button, 368
Macro group, 360, 365
Macro recorder, 578
Macro security, 596
Macro toolbar, 349
Macro window, 348
Mail merge, 165, 549–558
Mail Merge toolbar, 556
Mail Merge Wizard, 554
Main document, 549
Main form, 228, 284
Make-Table query, 143, 144–145
Many-to-many relationship, 276, 530
Max function, 131
Maximize button, 646
MDE Version, 504, 522
Media Guide, 697
Memo field, 53, 425
Menu bar, 646
Merge fields, 549
Microsoft Excel
   exporting to, 179
   importing from, 171–173, 213
Microsoft Graph, 180
Microsoft passport, 690, 694
Min function, 131
Minimize button, 646, 653
Modem, 660
Module, 578
Module window, 391
MsgBox action, 349, 478
MsgBox Function, 592
MsgBox statement, 392, 409, 417, 579, 585–596
Multiple-table query, 169–170, 177–178, 239–240, 284–288, 297
Multitasking, 643
My Computer folder, 646, 652
My Documents folder, 669, 676
My Music folder, 669
My Pictures folder, 669, 698

N

Navigation buttons
   with subform, 250, 257
   suppression of, 367
Nested If statement, 136, 420
Network Connections folder, 708
Normalization, 533–535
Northwind database, 501
NOT operator, 122
Notepad accessory, 561
Notification area, 643
Now() function, 175, 449
Number field, 53
   size of, 421

O

Object box, 418
Object dependencies, 201, 316
Object linking and embedding
   (OLE), 470
Office Assistant, 18
Office Links button, 117, 552
OLE Object field, 53, 102
On Click property, 360
One-to-many relationship, 28, 169,
   219–220, 274, 526
Option button, 648
Option Explicit, 582, 584
Option group, 78, 82
OR operator, 121

P

Page Footer, 108
Page Header, 108, 460
Parameter, 392
Parameter query, 293–294, 364, 486
   with Like operator, 489
Partial dependency, 535
Password, 508
Password protection, 370
Paste command (shortcut for), 393
Performance Analyzer, 520
Personal folders, 669
Pivot chart, 183–184, 192
Pivot table, 183–184, 191
PivotChart view, 4, 54
PivotTable view, 4, 54
Play list, 692, 697
PMT function, 228–229, 235
PowerPoint presentation, 444,
   450–451
Practice files (downloading of), 8,
   661–663
Primary key, 4, 53, 169, 221, 274, 530
   changing of, 60
Print Preview, 14, 113, 142
Private procedure, 391, 578
Procedure, 388, 578
Procedure box, 418
Procedure header, 402, 579

Procedure view, 403, 597
Program file, 658
Project Explorer, 582
Prompt, 293
Property, 55
Property sheet, 55, 74
Prototype, 350, 353, 478
Public constant, 590, 631
Public procedure, 391, 578
Pull-down menu, 647

Q

Query, 5, 16, 118
   copying of, 185
   with a filter, 129
   multiple table, 169–170, 177–178,
     284–188, 297
   updating of, 303
Query window, 124
Quick Launch toolbar, 682, 684
Quit action, 481

R

Radio button, 648
Record, 2, 530
   adding of, 11
   deleting of, 13
   editing of, 12
   printing of, 14
Record selector (suppression of), 367
Recycle Bin, 671, 678
Redundancy, 526
Referential integrity, 30–31, 170, 174,
   221, 224, 227, 278, 280, 448, 452
Relation, 530
Relational database, 27–35, 527
Relational operator, 122, 600
Relationship
   editing of, 282
   printing of, 175, 312, 449
Relationship line, 221, 277
Relationships window, 221, 223–224,
   251, 277, 280, 312
Remove filter, 19
Rename command, 146, 672
Repeating group, 531, 534
Replace command, 12
Replica, 427, 437–438
Report, 5, 17, 106
   error in, 128
   with picture, 164
   printing of, 26
   removing background, 87
Report Footer, 108, 466
Report group, 465
Report Header, 108, 460
Report properties, 245
Report switchboard, 355, 000
Report Wizard, 106, 108–110, 112, 114,
   127, 246, 298
Requery command, 365

Required property, 55, 452
Resolution (changing of), 700
Restore button, 646
Right click, 674
Root element, 561
Run-time error, 606

S

Screen capture, 627, 654
Screen saver, 651
Scroll bar, 646
Search Companion, 683, 687–688
Second normal form, 535
Security, 504–505
Security Wizard, 504
Select query, 118
SetFocus method, 400, 402, 494
SGML, 559
Shared Documents folder,
   669, 695
Shortcut, 682, 685–686
Shortcut Wizard, 688
Show Desktop button, 691, 700
Show row, 118
Simple Query Wizard, 118, 123
Size Mode property, 128
Sort, 19, 24
   on multiple fields, 25, 178
Sort row, 118, 133
Sorting and Grouping command, 116,
   139, 299, 375
Spin button, 648
Standard format, 242
Standard Generalized Markup
   Language (See SGML)
Start button, 643
Start menu, 643
   modification of, 689
Startup command, 200, 255, 460
Statement, 578
Status bar, 646
Step Into button, 607, 611
Structured Query Language (SQL),
   239–240
Subdatasheet, 190, 221–222, 226
Subform, 228, 231–238, 250–257, 284,
   286–292
   totals in, 323, 494, 500
Subreport, 292, 324
Sum function, 131, 180, 293
Switch, 623
Switchboard, 193, 334–337,
   339–343
Switchboard form, 337
Switchboard Items table, 195, 198, 337,
   343, 469
   importing of, 507
Switchboard Manager, 195–201, 337,
   341–342
   shortcuts with, 467
Switching users, 680
Synchronization, 427, 438
Syntax, 578

T

Tab control (on a form), 101
Tab order, 85, 407
Tab Stop property, 85, 470, 502
Table
   creation of, 446
   properties of, 422
Table row, 170, 239
Table Wizard, 53, 57–58
Table, 2, 4
   design of, 50–55, 79
Tabular report, 106
Task Manager, 657
Task pane, 141, 646
Taskbar, 643
   hiding of, 311
Template, 350, 366, 460–461
Test data, 486–487
Text box, 648
Text field, 53, 59
Third normal form, 444, 535
Thumbnails view, 693
Tiles view, 658
Tip of the day, 17
Title bar, 646
Toolbar
   customization of, 541–542
   displaying of, 115
   floating, 71
   list of, 543–548
Top Values property, 134, 157, 304, 486,
   492, 514
Total query, 180–181, 186, 293, 295, 486
Total row, 180–181, 293
Transitive dependency, 535
Tuple, 530

U

Ucase function, 625
Unbound control, 65, 110, 115, 460
Underscore, 580, 590
Undo command 13
Unicode Compression property, 55
Unmatched Query Wizard, 186, 301,
   321, 359, 361, 486, 493, 515
Up button, 673
Update anomaly, 527
Update query, 143, 149
User accounts, 650
User groups, 504
User level security, 504

V

Validation Rule property, 55, 63, 456
   record level, 422
Validation Text property, 55, 63, 456
Variable, 580
VBA, 388, 578
VBA statement (continuation of), 415
VBA syntax, 585
View menu, 679
Visible property, 626
Visual Basic editor, 582
Visual Basic for Applications (*See* VBA)
Visual design, 460–461

W

W3C, 575
Web page, 93

Wild card (in a query), 120
Windows Classic theme, 643
Windows Explorer, 669, 672–680
   customization of, 677
Windows Media Player, 692
Windows Messenger, 694, 701–702
Windows taskbar (hiding of), 587
Windows themed controls, 83
Windows Update, 681, 691
Windows XP, 7, 642
   log off, 657
   log on, 650
   new features, 710
Windows XP theme, 643
WorkbookOpen event procedure,
   621–622, 624
Workgroup, 504
Worksheet (hiding of), 617
World Wide Web Consortium
   (*See* W3C)

X

XP Home Edition, 642
XP Professional Edition, 642
XML, 559–574
XML declaration, 561

Y

Yes/No field, 53